ECONOMICS

D. C. HEATH AND COMPANY
Lexington, Massachusetts Toronto London

ECONOMICS

Daniel R. Fusfeld
University of Michigan

For
I. S. F.

Cover and title page illustration: *Loom* (1965).
Sculpture in nickel silver on Monel metal by Seymour Lipton.

International Standard Book Number: 0-669-75218-5

Library of Congress Catalog Card Number: 71-162642

PREFACE

This is a time of turmoil in the social sciences. Contemporary events are forcing a reconsideration of approaches and emphases that until very recently have been taken for granted by all but a minority of social scientists. Many of the old moorings have been cut, and old truths are adrift in an ocean of doubt.

We are only dimly aware of the reasons: the march of technology, the brutality of power politics, the burgeoning numbers of the human family, the conflict between races, the persistence of poverty, the clash of values, the rapid pace of change. In the face of these realities, the old confidence that we can resolve our conflicts and solve our problems as mankind moves toward a better world has eroded. Instead, we wonder if the path has not been backward toward a less benign condition of man, with the appearance of progress only a mirage.

In times like these we inevitably turn toward reconsideration and reevaluation of the knowledge derived from the past. We seek to apply it to our present condition and to derive new approaches and new meanings. That is the purpose of this book.

Such a task implies the broadest of approaches and the broadest of questions. We inquire into the directions our economic activity is moving us and the directions we ourselves impart to it. We examine the way in which our economic system functions, as objectively and scientifically as we can, based on the reality that our empirical methods discern for us. We evaluate the desirability of the results of our economic activity and policy, the goals that they imply, and the values they embody. The approach taken in this book is an amalgam of theoretical analysis based on an empirical and descriptive reality that is directed toward large questions of policy and social goals. Out of it should come a better understanding of the economic aspects of our lives and our social order, acquaintance with a highly useful method of analysis, and a more sophisticated appreciation of the dilemmas of values, goals, and policy in our time.

Based on the post-Keynesian macroeconomics and the revised neoclassical microeconomics of the quarter century that followed the Second World War, this book looks forward in an attempt to achieve a new synthesis. It brings the process of economic growth into a central position, equal in importance to the processes that determine level of economic activity and allocation of scarce resources among competing uses. It gives extended discussion to the distribution of income and alternative types of economic organization. These topics require more extensive treatment of the institutional arrangements within which economic activity is carried on. Rigorous theoretical analysis is not slighted, but in cutting loose from its assumptions of an individualistic market economy the argument gives greater attention to the nature of economic organization as a determinant of the results the economy achieves.

Finally, this book has a strong normative aspect. It is biased in favor of using the social sciences to improve the condition of man and promote the development of a more humane social order. Indeed, this may well be the key element in the new synthesis this book seeks to achieve—or moves toward, at least. A great deal of contemporary economics has been oriented toward solving immediate problems—which is, in itself, quite useful. But in the process some of the concern we should have toward fundamental goals and human values seems to have been lost. One aim of this book is to bring those concerns once more into the heart of economics.

Ann Arbor, Michigan
March 21, 1971

CONTENTS

ECONOMICS

BASIC CONCEPTS

I

The first five chapters of this book introduce the fundamental ideas on which the rest is built. They are intended to be read relatively quickly rather than studied in detail, in order to provide an overview of the subject matter as a whole. All of the ideas in them will be developed in greater detail later on, yet it is important to know ahead of time the pattern into which the details fit. The purpose of these first chapters is to provide that pattern.

Chapter 1 introduces economics as a field of inquiry. It emphasizes three points: the present dilemma of contemporary economics occasioned by the breakup of the post-World War II synthesis of theory and policy; the scientific approach to economics that has sought to avoid value judgments; and the three divisions into which present-day economics can be divided. The chapter closes with a statement of the book's goals: to move toward a new synthesis of theory and policy as objectively and scientifically as possible and to explain how and why the economic system functions as it does.

Chapter 2 presents the fundamental idea of economic analysis: choices have to be made. People have preferences about what they want to consume. As individuals, they seek to maximize benefits to be derived from the choices they make Their choices are constrained by the income at their disposal. Social choices also have to be made about matters that affect people as part of the social order. Both of these areas of choice are constrained by the amount of things available to satisfy individual and social wants. In the end, every social system must decide three things: how rapidly that amount is to be expanded, the extent to which its productive capacity will be used, and the things that capacity will be used for.

Chapter 3 discusses the first of those three choices, the process of economic growth. The modern industrial nations have moved toward affluence and opulence. In the process they have overcome problems of growing populations, diminishing returns, and limited natural resources. Although these limitations have been overcome in the past, they present problems for the present and issues for the future that are forcing economists as well as citizens in general to reexamine what has been an almost single-minded emphasis on economic growth. Chapter 3 provides a basis for Chapters 6 and 7, in which measures of economic performance are examined, and Chapters 8 through 10, which carry the analysis of economic growth still further.

Chapter 4 deals with the level of economic activity by developing the concept of the flow of spending. It shows why the decisions made in the private sector about spending, saving, and investment can lead to economic instability; the role played by the monetary system; and how governmental policies can promote greater stability. We shall deal with all of these issues in detail in Chapters 11 through 20, again using the empirical foundations of Chapters 6 and 7.

Chapter 5 moves into decisions about what is to be produced and how it is to be divided, matters based on and limited by the production potential discussed in Chapter 3 and the extent to which the production potential is used as explained in Chapter 4. The focus of attention is on the market economy and how it causes production to respond to the wants of consumers. The concepts of demand, supply, and the self-adjusting market that are developed in this chapter are vital to an understanding of the entire second half of this book, from Chapter 21 onward.

The overriding purpose of these five chapters is to provide a conceptual framework within which each of the later sections of the book can be placed. Read them with that in mind.

Modern economics has entered a period of crisis. The "post-Keynesian synthesis" [1] —the term used to describe the theoretical consensus on which economic policy has been based for the last quarter century or more—has failed to explain satisfactorily or resolve a series of important economic problems. The result has been a rising tide of criticism and a search for new and better approaches. It is a wonderful time to begin the study of economics, for a period of open-ended inquiry has begun in which no one takes the received wisdom of the past as final.

THE POST-KEYNESIAN SYNTHESIS

As recently as 1965, most non-Marxist economists felt that the answers to the important economic problems of modern society were available. The Keynesian economics that rose to dominance in the great depression of 1929–39 seemed to have solved the problem of maintaining full employment. The policies derived from it in the areas of monetary management, taxation, and government spending were highly successful in Europe after World War II, providing jobs for all and sustaining rapid rates of economic growth. In the United States they were not wholeheartedly applied until 1960, but they had the same results here when they were used.

The success of economics and economic policy in handling the large aggregative variables in the economy—total spending and output, consumption, investment, savings—gave greater significance to the older economics of the individualistic market economy. The proposition that a private enterprise economy tends to maximize individual welfare was given a new lease on life.

Adam Smith was the first to build a comprehensive theoretical analysis around that conclusion, in his *Nature and Causes of the Wealth of Nations* (1776). The idea was reconfirmed by the so-called neoclassical economists of the 1890–1920 period and has been a major tenet of modern economics ever since. In simple terms, the argument runs as follows:

> Consumers spend their incomes in a fashion designed to maximize their welfare.

Modern Economics: Crisis and Continuity

1

---

[1] *Keynesian* refers to John Maynard Keynes (1883–1946), the great English economist whose work on problems of full employment revolutionized economics in the 1930s. His name is pronounced like *canes* (rhymes with *pains*); hence *Keynesian* is "canes-ian."

Consumer decisions provide signals to producers about what to produce.

The producers who are most alert to those signals make the most profit, survive, and expand. Others fail. The result is a pattern of production that tends to match consumer preferences, achieved "as if by an invisible hand," to use Smith's felicitous phrase.

Consumer incomes depend on the value of their productive effort, thereby achieving a rough economic justice.

The whole argument rests heavily on the presence of competition and the absence of concentrated control over markets. But if we add strong antitrust legislation to preserve competition, and vigorous regulation of "natural" monopolies, the whole system begins to make sense, particularly if the threat of major depressions can be countered by proper government action.

Under such circumstances, economic growth would provide a steadily rising standard of living to meet the growing aspirations of the working man. Full-employment policies would assure prosperity and draw even the poor and disadvantaged into the tide of growing affluence. And growth would provide the means with which aid to underdeveloped countries could get them started on the same upward drive to well-being.

This, then, was the synthesis of theory and policy during the quarter century following World War II. Government's role was to assure full employment by the proper mix of spending, taxation, and monetary policy. The private sector would be free to pursue its goals of individual gain, to bring about a production pattern matching consumer wants, and to assure the economic growth inherent in a success-oriented society. The beneficence of the system was assured by government policies of preserving competition and regulating monopolies and of helping to solve other problems as they might arise.

In a sense, the post-Keynesian synthesis was the liberal economist's unintended contribution to the strategy of containment in the cold war that dominated national policies in Western Europe and North America after World War II. The threat to the Western social and economic system posed by communism was to be met by political containment while the economic superiority of the Western, market-oriented economies enabled them to outdistance and outperform the less efficient, planned economies of the Soviet system. One reason for the great vitality of the neoclassical synthesis was its consistency with the political needs of the time. More important, however, was the fact that its policy prescriptions seemed to work, for prosperity and economic growth were, in fact, achieved.

THE BREAKDOWN OF THE
POST-KEYNESIAN SYNTHESIS

By the mid-1960s the combination of Keynesian economics and the theory of the competitive market economy began to show some serious deficiencies. One of the first to show up was the problem of the underdeveloped countries. The growth of the advanced economies was supposed to generate capital resources that could be channeled into the less developed economies, getting them started on the path to self-sustaining economic growth. They were then supposed to be able to continue to grow without outside assistance. It didn't work out that way. Economic growth was spotty, and in many areas there was a reverse drain of capital and skilled manpower out of the underdeveloped areas and into the advanced countries. Meanwhile, the medical and public health technology of the advanced countries that had been imported into the backward nations triggered a decline in the death rate and rapid population expansion that literally ate up the bulk of the gains from economic growth. The gap between the rich and the poor nations tended to widen rather than narrow.

A second problem was inability to control inflation within the advanced countries. Policies designed to achieve full employment seemed to generate rising prices as unemployment fell. A school of critics who emphasized the importance of the money supply and its relationship to the price level began to question the validity of the Keynesian theories on which national policy was based.

A third problem was the appearance of deficiencies in the international monetary system. With each individual nation pursuing its own interests, no one was looking out for the welfare of the world economy as a whole. The result was a bewildering succession of devaluations and revaluations of national currencies, a continuing problem of the value of the British pound, and successive annual deficits in the U.S. balance of payments. No one of these problems was itself crucial, but the unsettling problem continued: how to reconcile the national economic policies of individual countries with the needs of the international economic system as a whole.

These issues of underdeveloped nations, inflation, and the international financial system resulted from gaps or deficiencies in the economic theory and policy of the post-Keynesian synthesis. But they were of more interest to specialists than to the general public, and did not go to the heart of the system of economic analysis itself or to its implicit goals. In the second half of the 1960s and early 1970s, a series of issues that did just that came to the fore, however. These were the issues of economic growth, the environment, the racial problem, and militarism. All raised, in one form or another, the question of whether the government-managed private enterprise economy was benign or malignant. It wasn't that the economic analysis itself was called into question, but rather the social and economic institutions it sought to explain and the policy goals it implied.

The goal of economic growth was the first to be criticized. An economy dominated by private decisions about consumption and production is likely to starve its public sector. This is especially true when motivations center on individual gains in income and wealth. Private expenditures on luxuries and entertainment may expand while the foundations of the future such as education and basic science are slighted. In the years after World War II, this feature of the advanced industrial economies was subject to increasing attention from social critics.

Within the public sector, the increase in military spending and military-related programs in the fields of space exploration and atomic energy became more evident as the 1950s gave way to the 1960s. The greatest industrial nation in the world, the United States, was using between 10 and 15 percent of its huge and increasing output for military and military-related purposes. The obvious question arose: What is the advantage of economic growth if a large portion of the gain is used for wasteful or destructive purposes? But underlying that was an even more basic question: What is it about the economic system that drives it (or allows it to be driven) to such ends? Had military expenditures created such strong vested interests in the "military-industrial complex" that there was no going back to a humane economy? If these issues generated breezes of doubt before 1965, after the war in Southeast Asia escalated to high levels they brought storms of dissent.

An equally fundamental issue arose as many people became aware of the potential environmental crisis the industrial nations seemed to be heading for. A growing economy produces increasing amounts of waste, and one in which "consumerism" is a chief feature contributes even more. Modern industrial technology, furthermore, was not developed with compatibility with the natural environment in mind. Would continued economic growth destroy the ecological base of not only the economy but human life as well? The economics of the neoclassical synthesis had no answer to that question and the ameliorative measures suggested were only partial responses to a huge problem.

Finally, the persistence of poverty and the emergence of the urban-racial crisis in the United States in the late 1960s emphasized another deficiency. A large portion of the American people were not participating adequately in the affluence achieved by many. A devastating social and economic conflict emerged. Yet the theory of the market was supposed to show how conflicts are resolved. In a market-oriented economy, if A wants something that B has, he gets it by giving up something else that B wants in exchange. Both are better off and hence satisfied. Marxists had long argued that this schema ignored the conflicts created by the class structure of an industrial society. But the ability of modern nations to keep labor-management relations peaceful (if sometimes acrimonious) seemed to answer the Marxist critique. The emergence of the seemingly insoluble problem of racial conflict in the midst of what should have been a society with reduced conflict, by reason of growing affluence, was a shock. It became clear that the benefits of affluence were *not* being so widely diffused as to strengthen the social fabric. Instead, after a quarter century of growing affluence there were more social tensions than ever before.

One aspect of the social conflict had been perceived by a number of economists for some time: the economy had come to be dominated by a relatively small number of giant corporations that were able to manage markets to their own advantage. The theory of the competitive market was not working out in practice, in this view, nor was antitrust and other regulatory legislation keeping the growth of big business in check. This critique from within the economics profession had not interfered seriously with acceptance of the neo-classical synthesis, but in the environment of criticism that appeared in recent years it received growing attention.

The youth movement of the last few years brought all of these issues to a head. One of its themes is that modern society is empty. Modern society is held to lack meaningful human relationships; to emphasize material goals and economic affluence at the expense of human values; to be destructive of the environment and of people; and to be oriented toward the achievement and use of power. These ideas are in sharp contrast to the value judgments implicit in the post-Keynesian synthesis, that economic growth and material welfare are desirable goals for modern society.

THE SCIENTIFIC ECONOMIST RESPONDS

If economics is approached as a science, many of these issues of values and goals can be shunted aside. Every society, however it may be organized or whatever its goals or values may be, has a limited amount of resources. If they are to be used for a purpose, whether maximization of individual welfare, governmental power, glorification of a deity, or any other goals singly or in combination, there are a variety of ways of doing so. Some of those ways are better than others, in the sense that the net benefits are greater. Choices have to be made. If the goals can be defined, an analysis of the resources available and the constraints on their use imposed by the social order can lead to a judgment concerning the "best" alternative.

For example, suppose we want to maximize individual welfare by providing the maximum amount of satisfactions over and above the cost of producing them. Is a system of free competitive markets better for that task than one dominated by a few large producers who have a large degree of control over markets? Is a planned economy more effective in achieving that goal?

Now change the goal to that of achieving a high and sustained rate of economic growth. Which of the three alternative ways of organizing the economy can do the job most effectively?

The goals need not be as big and complicated as the ones just postulated. Let's be more modest. What is the best method for delivering medical care to a large and diverse population: the present largely individual enterprise approach, the larger-scale group practice system, or a socialized system in which medical practitioners are employed by a publicly owned enterprise? There are alternative paths to achievement of the goal, with a limited amount of resources and constraints on their use created by technology, attitudes, and customs. The economic problem is how to make the most effective choice.

The scientific economist views his subject as concerning:

1. The use of scarce resources
2. ... subject to constraints ...
3. To achieve given ends.

The formal approach to economics as the study of choices among alternatives in a situation of scarcity can be applied to a variety of problems. A general who seeks to defeat an enemy with a minimum of losses to his own army has a similar problem; so does a chess player trying to win a game, a politician seeking election, or a lover attempting to win the affections of his mistress. All have a goal in view, limited resources for achieving it, a choice of actions, and limitations within which the goal must be attained.

But economics is not the study of military strategy, chess, politics, or amours. Rather, it deals with the production and distribution of material things. People need food, clothing, and shelter. They want ease and leisure and a variety of experiences. They have social needs arising from group action: recognition,

SOME DEFINITIONS OF ECONOMICS

As a social science:
"Economics is a study of mankind in the ordinary business of life; it examines that part of individual and social action which is most closely connected with the attainment and with the use of the material requisites of well-being." (Alfred Marshall, Principles of Economics, 8th ed., New York: Macmillan, 1920, p. 1.)

As a formal theoretical science:
"Economics is the science which studies human behavior as a relationship between ends and scarce means which have alternative uses." (Lionel Robbins, An Essay on the Nature and Significance of Economic Science, 2nd ed., New York: St. Martin's, 1935, p. 16.)

As an objective science:
"Positive economics . . . deals with 'what is,' not with 'what ought to be.' Its task is to provide a system of generalizations that can be used to make correct predictions about the consequences of any change in circumstances. Its performance is to be judged by the precision, scope, and conformity with experience of the predictions it yields." (Milton Friedman, Essays in Positive Economics. Chicago: University of Chicago Press, 1953, p. 4.)

As a normative science:
"The task of economics is to study economic organization, to appraise its efficiency and equity, and to suggest ways and means whereby its imperfections can be lessened or eliminated." (Tibor Scitovsky, Welfare and Competition: The Economics of a Fully Employed Economy. Stanford: Stanford University Press, 1951, p. 4.)

status, interaction with others, a feeling of worthiness. Material things and the ways in which they are obtained can help provide all of those things. That is the specific subject matter of economics to which the economist seeks to apply the analysis of choices among alternatives.

If that point of view is taken, economics becomes an operational or instrumental science. Once the goals are specified, an economic analysis can identify alternatives for achieving them and the benefits and costs attached to each. The economist may assist in discussing and choosing the goals, but the scientific economist would consider such discussions as value-laden and unscientific. He would consider them as falling into the realms of philosophy or theology or politics. He sees his role as the social engineer, designing practical solutions to definable problems whose dimensions can be specified.

THREE DIVISIONS OF ECONOMICS

Whatever the approach to economics, the subject as a whole deals with three major topics or divisions. The first topic is the growth process. Every economic system follows a path through time, during which its capacity to produce changes. The rate of growth may be positive, creating an expanding economy that can lead to higher living standards and greater welfare for the participants. Or the economy's growth rate may be negative, with the economy regressing toward lower levels, as in some parts of Asia and Africa in recent decades. Some economies may stagnate, moving neither upward nor downward on the scale of prosperity as time passes. But whatever the pattern, the growth path (Figure 1-1) is determined by basic relationships in the way the economy's resources are used.

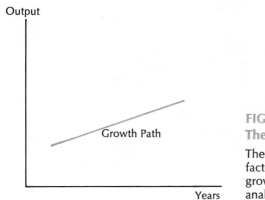

FIGURE 1-1

The Conceptual Framework: I

The Path of Economic Growth. The factors determining the rate of economic growth are one major topic of economic analysis.

Secondly, at any point in time, the economy will generate a particular level of output and incomes (Figure 1-2). This level may be high, pressing against the economy's capacity to produce. Or it may be low, with human and material

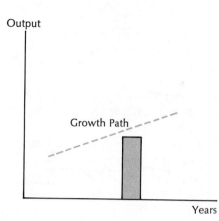

FIGURE 1-2
The Conceptual Framework: II
The Level of Output. Within the existing growth path, the level of output at any time is determined by another, but related, set of economic relationships.

resources unused and making possible the potentiality for substantial increases in output and incomes by a fuller use of those resources.

Finally, any level of output consists of a particular mix of products: so many swords, so much butter, so many plowshares, and so on. Resources in the form of labor, capital, and land must be combined in order to produce that output. And the products must be divided among potential users. This allocation of resources, as illustrated in Figure 1-3, involves three questions:

What is to be produced?
How should the various resources be combined?
Who is to get the product?

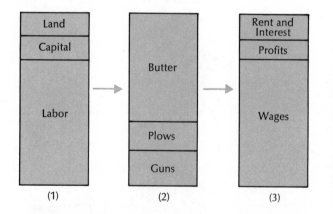

FIGURE 1-3
The Conceptual Framework: III

Allocation of Resources. Available resources (1) must be combined to produce a pattern of output (2), with the incomes generated in production being distrib-uted back to the owners of the resources (3) in order to keep the process going.

There are many points of contact between these three subdivisions of economics. For example, the efficiency with which resources are combined influences the level of output. And the level of output in any year will affect the ability of the economy to grow. Growth, in turn, will influence both the quality and quantity of the resources available to the economy for allocation to particular uses. Although conceptually separable, the three topics overlap.

ECONOMIC INSTITUTIONS

All societies must make decisions about economic growth, the level of output, and the allocative questions of what? how? and who? Those decisions can be left partially or wholly to the operation of impersonal and undirected economic forces. Or they can be partially or largely controlled through planning or regulation of various sorts. Whatever the pattern, those decisions emerge out of a framework of economic institutions that influences the outcome of events.

In the present-day world a variety of institutional frameworks compete for the loyalties of men. In the Soviet Union, a system based on public ownership of the chief means of production and central economic planning dominates economic life. In the United States, the form is private ownership and reliance on the forces of a market economy, coupled with considerable conscious management by big government, big business, and big labor. The nations of eastern and western Europe generally fall between the types exemplified by the U.S. and the USSR, while the "third world" of underdeveloped countries seeks to emulate the material advances made in Europe and North America through a wide variety of methods.

Economic institutions are made by men. They are the product of the conscious and unconscious development of social organization. They change over time. Their operation is subject to the influence of economic policy—the efforts of government to channel and direct economic forces and processes. Any study of economics must therefore include the institutional framework of economic life and the economic policies that seek to guide it. Economics is as much a study of types of economic systems and economic policy as it is a study of economic forces and processes. This aspect of economics has developed special importance in recent years, as the post-Keynesian synthesis has disintegrated. When an economic system has questioned raised about its beneficence, the way it organizes economic activity becomes a subject for analysis, and alternative methods of organization provide a useful topic for inquiry.

TOWARD A NEW SYNTHESIS

An unresolved tension exists between these varied aspects of economics. Revising the theory and policy synthesis implies concern about goals and values that the scientific economist would exclude from the discussion. It also implies a questioning attitude about economic institutions that the operational, problem-solving economist tends to take for granted. Yet any sophisticated inquiry into the proper goals of economic activity requires an objective and scientific understanding of how economic processes unfold. The process of economic growth and its limitations, the flow of spending, the market mechanism and its possible alternatives must all be understood if informed conclusions are to be drawn about man's condition and the effect on it of production and distribution of material things.

Economics must cast a wide net. At one extreme it is a moral inquiry into the nature of the good life and how it can be achieved. At the other extreme it is a science that seeks the optimal adjustment of means to ends. Yet it must seek these goals in the context of a specific time and place, within the constraints of what it is possible to accomplish at the present stage of human history and social development.

Contemporary economics is moving toward a new synthesis of theory and policy that takes all of these matters into consideration. The economic ideas developed in the past are part of that synthesis: analysis of the process of economic growth, the determinants of the level of output, the ways in which resources are directed toward meeting individual and social needs, the distribution of benefits among people, and international economic relationships. The methodology that stresses a scientific, objective approach based on facts has become the favored method, and a new synthesis must pass its tests. Orientation toward public policy is retained as well, but its concerns are broader than in recent years. Economics is beginning to go beyond the present pattern of institutions and arrangements to question whether institutions themselves are not in need of fundamental change. In so doing it is bringing to the fore issues of human welfare, social goals and economic organization that the post-Keynesian synthesis tended to set aside or take for granted. New approaches are needed, using the accumulated knowledge of the past and applying it to the future. This is an undertaking of great magnitude, and if the author of this book does not fully succeed perhaps the reader will. Indeed, that is the ultimate goal of this book—to help the reader find his way through the puzzling labyrinth of the economic issues of our time to achieve his own understanding, not only of how the modern economy functions, but also of the path to a humane society.

Summary

The synthesis of theory and policy that has dominated economic thinking in the last quarter century has broken up in the face of a series of new and unresolved problems. Serious questions are now being raised about whether the affluent society for which post-Keynesian economics was able to provide prosperity and growth is as beneficent as its advocates claim. Problems of values and goals that the scientific economist tends to shunt aside are raised in searching for practical solutions to economic problems. Yet economists generally agree on the basic conceptual framework of their discipline. It deals with economic growth, the level of economic activity, and the allocation of resources (including distribution of the product). These topics are analyzed within the framework of economic institutions whose significance as an object of study is increasing at a time when values and goals are being questioned. Contemporary economics is starting to move toward a new synthesis. Using the analytical concepts and methods of economic science, and based on our knowledge of the fundamentals of economics as it now stands, inquiry is directed toward the issues of values, goals, and economic organization in a troubled social order.

Any economic system that hopes to maximize the welfare of individuals must provide a decision-making mechanism responsive to those individuals' wants and needs. Unless an economy produces the things people want, it will waste part of its effort and resources. On the other hand, an economy whose pattern of production matches the pattern of individual wants will have satisfied the most basic criterion of welfare maximization: it will be producing the things people want to use.

SOME BASIC PRINCIPLES

Even if it were possible to have all that anyone wanted, choices would still have to be made. Individual preferences differ, and the choices that bring bliss to one may be another's misery. I like mushrooms, you may enjoy turnips. I prefer fried chicken, while you would rather have a steak. I'd rather hear folk music than rock, while you may prefer baroque chamber music. Choices, furthermore, will change with the passage of time. The person who likes hamburgers this year may detest them the next, for no apparent reason. Tastes can also be learned: Acquaintance with modern art may bring an appreciation of abstraction that displaces a former preference for realism. Variety also seems to be a characteristic of individual preferences. A steak every night for dinner may pale, while steak one night, lobster the next, pheasant the following, may be preferable. Finally, our preferences are strongly culture-bound. Patterns of food consumption differ widely in different parts of the world. Jews and Moslems eat no pork, devout Hindus eat no meat at all, and many Catholics eat fish on Fridays even though the religious sanction has been removed. Clothing styles can change quite drastically from one era to the next. Traditions and value systems can change from one generation to the next.

Whatever the sources of preferences, and however stable or unstable they may be, they lead to choices among the available alternatives. We can presume that the choices made are the "best" that the individual can make at the time. That is, with a given income, and within the framework of knowledge and experience available to him, each person tries to obtain the highest level of satisfaction that he can, juggling all of the possible courses of action until he finds the one that suits him best.

The Logic of Choice

2

CHOICES AND COSTS

All choices among alternatives involve costs. Eating a steak means that a lobster can't be eaten, because the consumption capacity to do both just isn't there. A date with Mary means that you can't go out with Jane or Alice, because of time constraints. If you buy a car, you may have to pass up a trip to the Bahamas, because your income won't permit both. In each of these instances alternative courses of action had to be given up because of the choice that was made.

The benefits from the foregone alternatives are the real costs of the action taken. Economists have given a special name to this concept: *opportunity costs*.

> **OPPORTUNITY COSTS.** *The real costs of anything are the benefits from alternative choices that have to be given up in order to obtain the benefits of the actual choice.*

Alternatives are always available, no matter what the situation may be, and there are usually more than two. A multiplicity of choices is the common situation, although most people tend to reduce the matter to either-or, or bad guys versus good, as part of the process by which rational analysis narrows the choices to ones that can be simply comprehended. In the end, the expected benefits from various courses of action are compared and the final choice represents the action from which the greatest benefits are expected.

It is in this sense that the term *rational economic man* should be understood. It means that people make decisions designed to give them the greatest satisfaction, within the framework of existing constraints that limit the alternatives that can be selected. It does not mean that everyone is continually seeking the largest possible monetary gain, or that only material gains are sought. It does mean, however, that we can accept individual choices as the ones that people think will maximize their welfare.

PREFERENCES, FREEDOM, AND CONSTRAINTS

Behind the choices that people make lie their patterns of preferences. It is impossible to tell from looking at someone just what he likes and dislikes. It is sometimes difficult to tell even by asking him, for people sometimes do not make decisions consciously but from habit or custom or from motives deep within their psyches. The only way that preferences become known is through the process of choice itself. The choices made reveal the preferences.

The larger the number of choices the greater are the opportunities for welfare maximization. For example, a college with a wide variety of courses and a system of free selection is more likely to provide educational opportunities that fit the needs of each individual than one with a prescribed curriculum and limited choice. Likewise, in a poor and backward country where the only choice among foods is rice or more rice, there are fewer opportunities for choices and the satisfaction of individual preferences than in a rich country with a wide variety of alternatives open to each person.

Finally, the larger one's income, the greater the level of satisfaction that can be achieved. This is true of nations as well as individuals. Sometimes, however, larger incomes are created by postponing current consumption in favor of capital creation to make possible greater incomes in the future. One of the fundamental choices, then, involves the premium put on the present as against the future. Like the grasshopper in the fable, we can take maximum enjoyment now and leave the future to take care of itself. Or like the ant, we can devote current effort to preparing for the future. As each individual makes this choice for himself, he affects the possibilities for economic growth of the economy as a whole.

The logic of choice is complex. Individuals can be expected to seek maximization of their own welfare, as they see it, within the constraints established by their incomes and the norms of the society in which they live. To the extent that the economic system can respond to these choices by producing the things people want, it will contribute to a maximization of welfare. In the long run, however, it must do more than that: it must provide for the maximum freedom of choice, for a wide variety of choices, and for growth of income.

EQUITY

These basic propositions about preferences, choices, and welfare must be qualified by considerations of equity. An economy that responds to individual choices will develop one pattern of production if income is distributed equally among consumers, and quite a different pattern if a highly unequal income distribution prevails. In each case it would be responding to individual preferences. In each case welfare could be maximized, *within the constraint of the existing income pattern*. Yet one situation would provide for a largely equalitarian distribution of the fruits of the economy, while the other would have great extremes of wealth for a few and poverty for many.

Taking income from the rich to provide more to the poor may well increase the welfare and satisfactions of the poor more than it reduces that of the rich. In this way a more equalitarian distribution of income may increase the total welfare of the population as a whole and move the economy toward a more effective use of its resources. On the other hand, such a policy might increase consumption more than savings, and reduce the rate at which the economy grows. Present welfare may be increased at the expense of future income for the economy as a whole. These economic considerations may well be measurable (or able to be estimated) in order to indicate the results that a particular policy might have.

It is impossible to avoid decisions on these matters. Every society has standards of equity and justice. These standards may change; conditions accepted a hundred years ago would be considered intolerable today. Indeed, there are many who feel that today's patterns of income distribution are outrageous and unjust. Social choices must be made on these matters, and they will affect both economic growth and the pattern of production.

INDIVIDUAL CHOICES AND SOCIAL CHOICES

Some of the things desired by consumers can be readily provided only by a public agency that acts on behalf of everyone. For example, a lighthouse on a rocky shore will benefit shipowners and travelers directly by increasing their safety, and the entire economy indirectly by reducing the cost of shipping. Furthermore, no one can be excluded from the benefits of the beacon; anyone can see it and use it. Since no one can be excluded from the benefits, no individual can be forced to pay for it, and it is impossible for a private, profit-making enterprise to provide the services. It is a *public good,* and if it is to be produced at all it will have to be done through a public agency.

Although opinions differ widely over the question of what should be produced or consumed socially rather than individually, even diehard individualists usually agree that governments must be responsible for such things as national defense, police protection, and the administration of justice. Others would add some minimum level of education to the list. Then there are public improvements such as roads, ports, reclamation of land, sanitation systems, and similar types of capital investments, which have benefit for all but which would not be constructed or maintained privately. Other additions might be made to the category of social consumption or production, depending on the importance one places on individual preferences as against social preferences. Here again, in the making of economic decisions and in determining the pattern of production in the economy, value judgments must be made about the role of the individual and that of the group.

THREE TYPES OF CHOICES

Choices among alternatives have to be translated into decisions about production. These decisions can be divided into three types:

1. If the economy has unused productive capacity and unemployed labor, more of most things can be produced without giving up some quantity of anything else. This means that there is no economic cost associated with increased output. The unemployed resources can be put to work increasing total output, making more products and services available to everyone. There may be a money cost involved, but "real" costs are zero, because the alternative is to let the unused resources remain idle.

2. If the economy does not have unused productive resources and is operating at its existing capacity, more of one product can be obtained only at the cost

of giving up something else. Additional resources can be found to produce more food only by taking resources away from producing other things. In this case there is a "real" cost involved in making choices. We cannot have more of anything without giving up something else.

3. The choices we make between consumption and saving will determine how rapidly the economy's output capacity can be increased. Savings release resources from the production of consumers' goods and make them available for investment that will increase output in the future. Higher living standards in the present mean a slower pace of growth, while keeping current standards of living a little lower than they might otherwise be means achieving a higher growth rate.

THE TRANSFORMATION CURVE

The three types of choices open to any economy can be illustrated in a little economic model called the transformation curve. It pictures a hypothetical production frontier based on the rates at which one product or service can be transformed into another by shifting productive resources from one to the other. In Figure 2-1 we have taken consumers' goods and investment goods as an example.

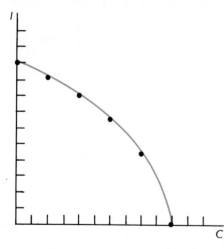

Production Possibilities	
C	I
0	100
20	92
40	81
60	67
80	44
100	0

FIGURE 2-1
The Transformation Curve: Consumption and Investment

As we increase production of consumers' goods C, we have to give up increasing amounts of investment goods I. And vice versa. That is the reason for the concave shape of the transformation curve, and is the result of the well-known law of diminishing returns. The first resources shifted away from production of investment goods provide a large increase in output of con-

sumption goods. The next shift brings a smaller increase, and so on. We will
have more to say about diminishing returns in the next chapter, but this illustration helps to introduce the concept.

Now let us look at the three types of choices available to an economic system
in relation to the transformation curve. In the first case (Figure 2-2) we have
unemployed resources and are producing some combination of $C+I$ that lies
within the transformation curve. Once full employment is reached, consumption
can be increased only by giving up some investment, and vice versa (Figure 2-3).

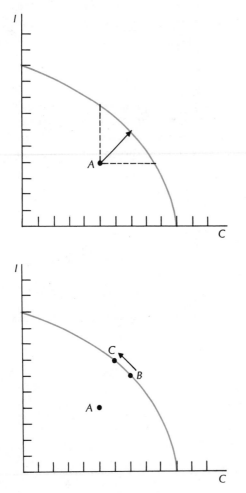

FIGURE 2-2
Situation I: Unused Resources

At point A the economy produces $5C$ and
$4I$. It could put its unemployed resources
to use and increase output out to the
limits of the transformation curve (say $7C$
and $6I$) and have more of both.

FIGURE 2-3
Situation II: Full Employment

When the economy is operating at its full
capacity we can get more I only by giving
up some C. Increasing I from 6 to 7
means reducing C from 7 to 6 (at that section of the transformation curve).

Finally, the rate of growth of the economy will depend on the combination of
C and I chosen by the economy when it is fully employed (Figure 2-4).

These propositions are, of course, great simplifications. We do not choose
only between consumption and investment, but include public expenditures
also among our alternatives. This creates a third dimension for our diagram and

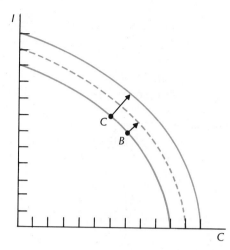

FIGURE 2-4
Situation III: Growth

More investment and less consumption (choosing C instead of B) pushes the transformation curve outward more rapidly.

makes the transformation curve into a transformation surface. Even that is only a beginning, however. Within each of the three different categories we can choose between an almost infinite variety of consumers' goods, types of investment, and patterns of public expenditure. The number of alternatives is staggering and cannot possibly be visualized in a geometric model, as we have done in this simplified version. The transformation surface develops an almost infinite number of dimensions.

Nevertheless, any economy has a series of fundamental choices to be made. One concerns the level of economic activity: whether it will push its employment of men and resources to the outer limits of the existing production possibilities. One concerns the combination of outputs that it finds most desirable: that is, where it wishes to be on the transformation surface. The third concerns the rate of economic growth: how fast the transformation surface is to be pushed outward. The next three chapters deal with these three choices. First, economic growth; second, the level of economic activity; and third, the market economy as a means of making allocative decisions.

Summary

If we wish to maximize welfare, the economy must be responsive to the choices made by individuals. We assume that those choices are based on individual preferences and are directed toward achieving the most satisfaction possible, given the alternatives available, the costs attached to each one, and the constraints on choice that may be present. It is in that context that the economist uses the terms *rational action* and *economic man*.

The distribution of income is one of the most important constraints. The logic of choice assumes the existing distribution as an initial position, yet the question of whether a more equalitarian distribution will promote greater welfare must ultimately be considered. Social choices are also important. They concern things that would not ordinarily be produced in a purely individualistic, market-oriented economy, and provide a role for government in any economy that seeks to maximize welfare.

When choices among alternatives are translated into production, three areas of choice are opened up, which can be illustrated by use of the transformation curve. If the economy is operating at less than its full potential (within the transformation curve), total production can be increased at no real cost simply by using unemployed resources. When the economy is producing at capacity (on the transformation curve), output of one good can be increased only if output of other goods is reduced. If investment goods are produced, the economy's output capacity can be increased (the transformation curve is pushed outward), making it possible to produce more of all goods.

Key Concepts

Economic man.   The behavior pattern in people that causes them to seek to maximize their satisfactions, making choices based on preferences, within the constraints imposed by incomes, social norms, and the availability of freedom to choose.

Opportunity cost.   The cost of anything is the benefit or satisfaction that could have been obtained by choosing something else. Often referred to as *real cost* (to emphasize the contrast to money costs or prices) and sometimes as *alternative cost*.

Rational action.   Behavior that results from a conscious or unconscious weighing of benefits against costs.

Transformation curve.   A hypothetical curve representing the amounts of two different goods that can be obtained by shifting resources from production of one to production of the other.

Public good.   A product or service not normally produced in socially desirable amounts by private enterprise. It is usually characterized by having indirect benefits to persons other than the direct user, or by inability to exclude non-paying individuals from using it, or by both conditions.

Individual choices.   Choices made by individuals on the basis of their preferences. Contrasted with *social choices* made by a social system through formal political systems and informal social mechanisms. One of the most important areas of social choice involves *equity,* or the consensus about the economic and social position of individuals within the social order.

When the first men climbed down out of the trees—or up out of the slime, depending on the theory of evolution you adhere to—the struggle of man to improve his condition began. Few things are produced in nature in the form most useful to man. Most must be transformed into the food, clothing, shelter, and other things that are required for human existence, comfort, and ease. Human beings have found many ways to do this. Tools have been devised to assist in the task. Supplies have been stored today to meet tomorrow's needs. New uses have been devised for old products and new resources found to meet greater demands. But through it all a single main thread has run: man's struggle with an often niggardly and recalcitrant nature to produce the things human beings need and want.

This struggle of man against nature has been a quest for abundance and ease, against poverty and want. Some societies have moved a long way from the poor life of a primitive hunting and gathering tribe. Ours has perhaps been the most successful. Even in our society, however, the quest for abundance has not been completed. Many Americans are poor by our standard or any other, and the quest for the good life goes on.

No one would argue that material goals are the only ones that men seek. But they are among the chief goals, and they have helped to determine the way people live and act and the type of social organization they use to carry on their lives.

The Progress of Wealth

3

WEALTH AND INCOME

We should not confuse wealth with income. Wealth consists of all those things that satisfy human wants. It includes material things that can be directly used by people, such as food, clothing, and shelter. It includes the means of production that produce them, such as machinery, factories, and agricultural land. A wealthy nation produces large quantities of products and services each year, because its productive resources are large. Most of this *income* is consumed, and does not add to wealth or to productive capacity. But some of it is saved, and that portion does add to society's stock of wealth.

Wealth is a stock of useful and productive things; income is a flow of products. Yet the two are related. A large stock of wealth leads to a large flow of income, part of which (savings) can then be used to increase the stock of wealth so as to produce an even larger income the following year. Any society able to do this on a large scale will be well on its way toward increasing its wealth.

REAL WEALTH AND MONEY WEALTH

Money is not wealth. Wealth is useful products and services. We may be able to buy useful things with money, and we may measure wealth in monetary terms. But no matter how much money we have, real wealth comprises only those products and services that have usefulness to people. For example, businessmen may increase their borrowings from banks to buy common stocks or speculate in commodities. As we shall see later, this action increases the money supply. Prices of stocks or commodities may go up as a result, making some individuals "richer" because their assets are now worth more. But no new wealth has been produced, no additional goods and services were produced, and no more people are employed. The nation's wealth has not increased.

But suppose the businessmen use their loans to buy materials, increase their employment and turn out more products and services. This action will increase the nation's income, for it makes more products available to satisfy the wants of consumers. Everyone can have more. To the extent that portions of that income are saved, the goods produced can be used to increase the productive capacity and the wealth of the economy.

WEALTH AND ILLTH

There are complications. We produce many things that do not add to the satisfactions that people get, but that remove dissatisfactions brought about by other things we do. For example, part of the wealth produced in the United States each year consists of cigarettes consumed by millions of smokers. We include the value of those cigarettes in measuring our annual production. Yet one by-product of cigarette smoking is lung cancer and other illnesses, which require medical treatment, hospital facilities, funerals, and other services. Production of those things is also included in our measurement of the annual production. Yet, in fact, they are required because of the illth that results from smoking cigarettes.

There are many similar examples: automobiles and automobile accidents; steel furnaces and air pollution; chemical plants and water pollution; and many others. It is not enough to simple-mindedly add up the value of annual production to derive a measure of production. Nor is it enough to add up our stocks of goods to determine our accumulated wealth. We can hardly consider our stocks of nuclear weapons and nerve gas to be wealth in the same sense as houses or steel mills.

WEALTH AND POVERTY

We like to think of the United States as a wealthy society, and in many ways it is. In normal times, most Americans can be assured of an adequate and varied diet;

most are reasonably healthy and normally have access to the medical care and services necessary to maintain their health; housing is comfortable and adequate; clothing is warm; and a wide variety of choice is available to consumers. The average American can expect to live better as he grows older, to achieve a higher level of living than his parents, to start his children out in life with more advantages than he had, and to live a comfortable old age. These are the marks of a wealthy society.

Indeed, the relative ease and comfort of a wealthy society makes existence seem dull and uninteresting to many. For some there are no more worlds to conquer, and like Alexander, they despair at the absence of further challenges.

Although the great majority of Americans may share in the benefits of an abundant society, there are many who remain poor, whose food, clothing, shelter, and health are substandard, who lack the opportunity to rise in the world and create a better life for themselves and their children. Their condition is one of illth rather than wealth, of poverty rather than abundance.

A nation with a growing economy can make significant progress in reducing poverty. In the United States, for example, the number of persons living in family units with income *less* than the "minimum subsistence" level was reduced from about 33 million in 1929 to about 20 million in 1960.[1] This represents a decline from 27 percent to 12 percent of the total population. This dramatic decline, while heartening, should not lead to complacency; during the same period most of the nations of northwestern Europe have succeeded in almost completely eliminating incomes below the minimum subsistence level. Furthermore, the decline in poverty in the United States has been less spectacular for families above the minimum subsistence level but below the levels of "minimum adequacy" or "minimum comfort."

Figure 3-1 shows the progress made by the United States in reducing poverty between 1929 and 1960, according to the best available study of the problem. Note the large increase in poverty due to the Great Depression of the 1930s, and the difficulties in reducing the *number* of poor even though the percentage has fallen significantly since World War II.

Wealth and poverty are, of course, relative concepts. Conditions of affluence differ widely among the nations of the world. Some, like the nations of North America and Western Europe, have a history of economic growth that has led to high incomes and standards of living. Others, like many parts of Asia, Africa, or Latin America, have not been able to sustain a continuing pattern of economic growth, and they remain poor. Figure 3-2 shows some of the wide disparities that now exist between rich and poor nations, as measured by the value of output per person.

---

[1] These figures are based on a minimum subsistence income for a family of four, based on contemporary standards of living and needs, as computed by the Poverty Study Staff of the New School for Social Research, New York.

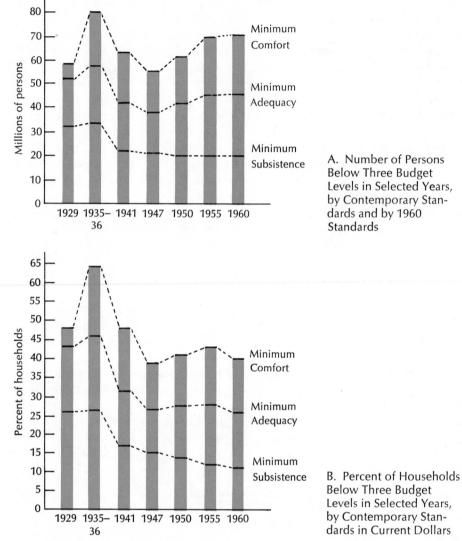

A. Number of Persons Below Three Budget Levels in Selected Years, by Contemporary Standards and by 1960 Standards

B. Percent of Households Below Three Budget Levels in Selected Years, by Contemporary Standards in Current Dollars

FIGURE 3-1
Poverty in the United States, 1929–60
(Source: Oscar Ornati, Poverty and Affluence, *New York, the Twentieth Century Fund, 1966, pp. 28, 30, 158.)*

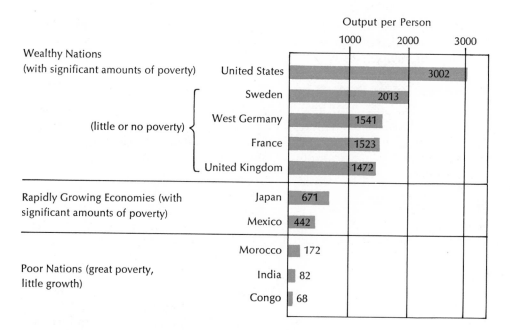

FIGURE 3-2
Value of Output per Person, 1964, Selected Countries
(In Dollars)
(Source: United Nations, Yearbook of National Accounts Statistics, *1965.)*

THE GROWTH OF WEALTH

The fundamental building blocks of wealthy societies have everywhere been the same: *land, labor, and capital.* Economists call them the *factors of production.* The first two are present in varying amounts everywhere, but capital is itself the product of economic activity. It is created by using effort and resources in the present to produce the means of production for the future. A sacrifice (or cost) is involved: Effort and resources that could be used to produce for present consumption are used instead to increase the economy's capacity to produce at some future time. This process of capital accumulation is the key to economic growth. The more rapidly a society accumulates capital and the more willing it is to forego consumption now for consumption in the future, the greater its economic growth will be and the more rapidly it will raise the standards of living of its people.

Capital consists of two essentially dissimilar elements. One is the actual physical things that man has devised to help him in using natural resources, ranging all the way from such simple tools as hoes and hammers to complex ones like petroleum refineries, electrical generating plants and steel mills. The second form of capital is knowledge stored up in the minds of individuals that tells them how to build and use capital equipment. The latter form of capital is by far the most important: equipment may wear out or be destroyed, but the knowledge of how to make and run it can be used to rebuild, replace, and even improve what has been lost.[2]

BARRIERS TO GROWTH

Capital accumulation and its accompanying increase in output is the basic source of increased wealth. But while necessary for growth, it is not sufficient. There are four barriers that must be overcome: the population trap, diminishing returns, exhaustion of resources, and failure to use existing productive resources fully.

The Population Trap

Improved living standards can be achieved only by increasing output faster than the population increases. Man's breeding knows no seasons. The long-run trend in human history has been for the population of the world to grow, despite wars, famines, and other disasters. As a result, the fundamental economic problem becomes one not only of increasing output but of achieving a rate of growth above that of population. Maintaining existing levels of output while population grows means that mankind will fall behind in its efforts to improve its material conditions of life. Raising output only at a rate that matches population growth means stagnation. There are only three possibilities:

1. Where the rate of increase of output is less than the rate of increase of population, the economy moves toward misery.

2. Where the rate of increase of output equals the rate of increase of population, living standards neither rise nor fall.

3. Where the rate of increase of output exceeds the rate of increase of population, the economy can move toward bliss.

Clearly then, the relationship between output and population growth determines whether or not economic welfare will be increased by capital accumulation and economic growth.

The population trap appears when increases in output *cause* population to grow by providing the means by which death rates can be reduced. This is

---

[2] The definition of *capital* is one of the most disputed points in all of economics. The term is used here in a *real* rather than a *monetary* sense. That is, we do not mean "the money value of asset," which is the usual businessman's definition. Instead, the term includes *capital goods* (products used to produce other outputs) and *knowledge* about how to organize and run the system of production. More formally, capital is defined as *the tangible and intangible tools of production that the economy has accumulated as a result of its past productive efforts.* It excludes labor (but not labor's knowledge of how to produce). It excludes land and other natural resources (but not certain types of improvements, such as irrigation systems, that have increased the productive capacity of land). The problem of careful definition arises because in the course of economic growth capital becomes so intricately joined with other factors of production that, in many instances, it cannot be separated.

particularly true of underdeveloped countries, where birth rates tend to be high and population growth is held in check by high death rates. An increase in output may enable living standards to rise temporarily in such a situation, but this in turn may cause a decline in death rates, an increase in population, and a reversion of living standards to their old level.

This sequence of events is at the heart of the Malthusian theory of population, developed by the English economist Thomas R. Malthus (1766–1834) in 1798. Incorporation of this analysis into the body of economic theory of that period led English essayist Thomas Carlyle (1795–1881) to call economics "the dismal science," a verdict that many students concur in, but for somewhat different reasons. Even today, however, the population trap is an important reason why some billions of people in much of the world live at very low subsistence levels.

Where the trap has been avoided, it has been done through reductions in the birth rate that paralleled the declining death rate. Unless birth and death rates can be brought down together, accumulation of capital and increases in output may have little or no effect on standards of living.

The more advanced nations of the world are more fortunate. For a variety of reasons that are not very well understood, they have arrived at the situation in which both birth rates and death rates are relatively low. Under these conditions an increase in living standards will have little impact on death rates, population will not be induced to rise significantly, and real advances in welfare can more readily be achieved. For much of the rest of the world, however, the population trap is a major problem.

Diminishing Returns

The second barrier that the processes of economic expansion must overcome is embodied in the principle of diminishing returns. Wherever the amount of one factor of production is fixed and cannot be increased, and other factors of production are added to it in the production process, output will be increased as the other factors are added, but after a certain point the increases will gradually decline in size. For example, if one unit of fertilizer is added to unfertilized agricultural land, a relatively large increase in the size of the crop can be expected. Alternatively, two units of fertilizer may increase the crop by more than twice the increase from one unit. At some point, however, the crop increases will stop accelerating and start slowing down, until further increases in fertilizer use will bring little or no increase in output.

> **THE PRINCIPLE OF DIMINISHING RETURNS.** *As units of a variable factor of production are added to a fixed factor of production, at some point the resulting increases in output will begin to diminish in size.*

Experimental studies demonstrating the principle of diminishing returns are most readily found in agriculture, where the acreage of a farm or size of a herd of cattle can be held constant. For example, one study of dairying concerned the effects of varying amounts of feed inputs on the milk output of a large number of cows over a three-year period. The results are shown in Table 3–1 and Figure 3-3 below.

TABLE 3–1
Feed Input and Milk Output Per Cow Per Year For 392 Cows Fed at Six Levels

Number of Cows in Each Group	Average Total Digestible Nutrients Consumed (lb per yr)	Average 4% Fat Corrected Milk Produced (lb per yr)	Increase in Milk Output per lb of Increase in Feed Input (lb)
65	5,654	7,626	
60	6,117	8,184	1.20
66	6,575	8,824	1.62
55	7,132	9,400	1.03
52	7,531	9,780	0.95
94	7,899	9,965	0.50

Source: Einar Jensen, John W. Klein, Emil Rauchenstein, T. E. Woodward, and Ray Smith, "Input-Output Relationships in Milk Production," *U.S. Department of Agriculture Technical Bulletin No. 815,* May 1942.

Note: "Total digestible nutrients" includes all types of feed (grain, hay, etc.) expressed as pounds of carbohydrate feed (dry weight) according to feed value. A correction was applied to express all milk production as of a uniform butterfat content.

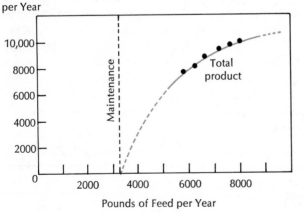

FIGURE 3-3
Feed Input and Milk
Output Per Cow
Per Year
(Source: Jensen et al.,
"Input-Output in Milk
Production," p. 39.)

Diminishing returns are clearly indicated by Column 4 in the table. Note also the somewhat erratic nature of the data: they do not fit the trend line perfectly, nor is this study a perfect example of the general principle. This is always true of illustrations drawn from actual experience.

The principle of diminishing returns is a basic proposition that applies to any production situation, and it will be met with time and again in this book. Here, however, it is significant in helping to define the basic economic problems faced by any society. It indicates that *by itself, capital accumulation is not enough for sustained economic growth*. If the type and amount of natural resources are fixed, and if the work force does not grow, diminishing returns from increased capital accumulation will eventually appear. As returns to capital decline, they will ultimately no longer be large enough to induce consumers to forego present consumption in order to add to the stock of capital.

This proposition of the trend toward a "stationary state" is associated with the name of David Ricardo (1772–1823), a contemporary and friend of Malthus. It became an important building block of the "classical" economics of the nineteenth century, but is given little stress today. The reason for its fall from grace is that the factors of production have proven to be much more flexible and variable than the earlier economists thought, and the presence of a fixed factor, invariable in amount, has not arisen. Population has grown, new areas of the world have been opened for development, increased specialization in production has cut costs, and most important, advances in science and engineering have made possible considerable restructuring of the relationships between factors of production in the production process. These developments have prevented the huge growth of capital that has occurred over the last two hundred years from being limited by diminishing returns. Indeed, there is some evidence that the industrial nations of the world, in spite of their high degree of development, are still in the stage of increasing returns to capital.

Nevertheless, the principal of diminishing returns is important. With a fixed economic base provided by the world's natural resources, capital accumulation *alone* will not be able continually to generate rates of economic growth large enough to overcome the effects of a rising world population. An additional ingredient is needed: the type of scientific and technological change that raises productivity enough to enable the economy to overcome the long-run tendency toward diminishing returns.

Exhaustible Resources

Many natural resources are not only limited, they are exhaustible. Except for a relatively small supply of hydroelectric power, the bulk of the energy resources used today are derived from fossil fuels (coal, petroleum, natural gas) whose supplies are limited by the amounts of organic material preserved in fossilized form within the earth's surface. Other minerals have limitations on their ultimate supply as well, including the iron, copper, and other metals on which modern civilization is largely based.

All exhaustible resources have one characteristic in common. Production becomes gradually more costly as the deposits easiest to work and cheapest to draw from are used up. Greater amounts of labor and capital are needed to obtain and transport coal or ores as the mines become deeper, as the richer deposits are exhausted, and as sources further from the market must be utilized. New mines may be opened as old ones peter out, but the very fact that the new ones were not in operation is a good indication that their costs of production are probably higher than those of the old operations.

The fact that exhaustible resources lead to rising costs of production can have significant consequences for economic growth. For example, in the nineteenth century, much of England's predominance in manufacturing rested upon large supplies of rich, easily mined coal. As the mines became deeper and as the richer veins were used up, other coal-producing regions in Germany and France could compete with England more effectively, until by the mid-twentieth century English industry had poorer supplies of coal that could be mined only at relatively high costs in comparison with other industrial areas. This exhaustion of cheap coal resources has not been the only reason for England's economic difficulties in the twentieth century, but it is a fundamental one.

The iron ore of the Lake Superior region in the United States may turn out to be a somewhat similar case. Much of the economic strength of the United States has been based on cheaper iron ore than most other industrial regions of the world have. Now that this advantage has been eliminated by exhaustion of the richest Lake Superior mines, the American economy's international position has been reshaping itself, although again there are many other elements in the situation.

The problem is that costs of production rise wherever economic activity is based on an exhaustible resource, unless technological changes can overcome the tendency for costs to increase. New materials, new production techniques, and better organization *can* bring costs down faster than exhaustion of resources pushes them up. On the other hand, they might not, as the case of the British economy in the last fifty years can show.

Fortunately, much of the technological change of the last fifty years has been moving toward reducing the economy's dependence on exhaustible resources. Atomic energy reactors that breed more fuel than they use, the conversion of solar energy into electric power, the synthesis of hydrocarbons from air and water and similar recent scientific breakthroughs supplement the revolution in plastics and synthetics of a generation or two ago. They promise reduced reliance on exhaustible resources and less dependence on materials and sources of power subject to increasing costs of production.

In the long run, however, even greater changes will have to be achieved. The present industrial technology is based on a continuing flow of natural resource inputs that are transformed into outputs at the end of the production process. New inputs are continually required in order to keep the system functioning. In the future we shall have to move much more fully toward a closed system in which the outputs themselves become inputs. Among other things, all waste products would be recycled into the production system as raw material inputs in such a system. Both the technology and the economics of that stage of development have yet to be worked out.

Full Use of Resources

Economic growth can also be hampered by failure to use the productive capacity of the economy fully. During the Great Depression of the 1930s in the United States, for example, the existence of large numbers of unemployed workers and unused industrial plants kept production well below the capacity of the economy. Resources that could have been used to produce both consumers' goods and investments were lying idle. Incomes and purchasing power fell, new investment was postponed, and the productive capacity of the economy stagnated.

In the late 1950s a somewhat different situation prevailed. The economy grew, but purchasing power did not increase as rapidly as the potential output capacity of the economy. The result was unemployment and unused plant capacity at a time when the economy was expanding. But the expansion was slow and inadequate, and gradually the unused labor and plant capacity came to hang like a cloud over the economy, creating a widening gap between the actual and the potential performance of the economy.

Still a third type of break can occur in the pattern of economic growth. Relatively brief interruptions in economic growth or short downturns in economic activity can occur, creating for a year or more a situation in which resources are not fully used.

All three of these situations—long and serious depressions, stagnation, and brief recession—are related to the same fundamental cause. Purchasing power either does not keep pace with the potential growth of the economy or actually declines, creating a gap between the level of spending that will bring full use of resources and the level that actually exists. These conditions hamper economic growth in two ways. First, incomes are reduced, and the savings that finance investment fall below the levels they might attain. Second, the existence of unused productive capacity acts as a barrier to investment expenditure. Expansion is not needed until existing productive capacity is fully or nearly fully used. Under these conditions neither the resources for growth (savings) nor the incentive (need to increase output) is adequate.

Another requirement for economic growth, therefore, is a level of purchasing power that pushes output up to the capacity of the economy and generates substantial amounts of savings.

BARRIERS TO THE GROWTH OF WEALTH

These, then, are the barriers to increased wealth:

1. The population trap. Improvement in living standards can literally be eaten up by population increases.
2. The principle of diminishing returns. When one resource, such as land, is

fixed in amount, the increased output from added units of other resources tends to fall. Where this is the case, capital must be accumulated at an increasing rate just to keep the economy where it was before. The economy will have to run faster just to stay where it is.

3. Exhaustible resources. Some resources vary in quality even though they may not be completely "fixed" in amount. Where this is the case, costs of production will rise in the long run as the resources are used up, irrespective of the rate at which capital is accumulated.

4. Unemployed resources. The economy can fail to use its full potential, leaving capital and labor unemployed.

The growth of the world economy over the last several hundred years indicates that none of these problems are insurmountable. Four conditions are necessary for economic progress, however:

1. The economic system must generate a high rate of capital accumulation. People must be able and willing to devote a substantial portion of their production to building capital rather than to present consumption.

2. A balance between birth and death rates must be established that is largely independent of standards of living so that the population trap may be avoided.

3. The social and economic system must generate a high rate of scientific discovery and technological change in order to avoid the effects of diminishing returns and exhaustible resources.

4. The economy must operate at its potential capacity or very close to it.

Some nations of the world have been able to achieve the four conditions of economic growth consistently over the last several hundred years. They are the ones that are moving toward opulence. Others have not been so fortunate. Even the fortunate ones face a series of problems created by economic growth itself. The scientific discoveries and technological changes that are a major feature of a modern economy's growth can pollute the environment as they already have done, so that the very continuance of the human race has been cast in doubt. The whole growth process will have to come under greater control if it is not to destroy the ecological system. A second long-run problem remains. The failure of underdeveloped nations to develop growth processes of their own, together with rapid population growth, is rapidly dividing the world into nations of haves and nations of have-nots. The political instabilities created by these economic disparities may also threaten the viability of the economic system itself. Third, the affluent society has failed to distribute the benefits of growth to everyone. Progress has not eliminated poverty.

Finally, affluence itself is bringing second thoughts. Material gains are not enough, particularly if they bring an economic organization composed of large bureaucratic units run from the top. Men seek to control their own fates.

Happiness is seldom found through following rules, staying within relatively narrow limits and obeying directives from above. A growing economy will have to organize itself in ways that resolve this inherent conflict between the individual and the organization. A humane world becomes possible if affluence is achieved, but it isn't inevitable.

The "growth machine" of the advanced economies, therefore, faces some significant challenges. It must adapt itself to the natural environment more effectively. It must distribute its fruits more widely, both internally and internationally. And it will have to provide more scope for the fulfillment of broader human values. While these may not seem to be economic problems in a narrow definition, they are problems created by an economic system and their solution may require some fundamental economic changes.

Summary

Man's drive to achieve abundance and eliminate want is perhaps as old as humanity itself. Even the affluent nations of the present have not succeeded in eliminating poverty, however, and many poor nations are a long way from affluence. The fundamental economic process required for growing abundance involves saving and capital accumulation. A nation must abstain from current consumption in order to allocate a significant amount of its resources for expansion of production.

Sustained economic growth requires more than capital accumulation, however. A balance between births and deaths must be achieved so that output can rise more rapidly than population. An advancing technology is required to overcome diminishing returns and exhaustible resources. And full use of the economy's production potential is necessary if substantial capital accumulation is to take place. When all of that is accomplished, a nation will grow economically and produce more for everyone. It will then face issues related to the use of wealth: preservation of the environment, distribution of the fruits of growing abundance, and the development of a more humane world.

Key Concepts

Wealth.   The stock of useful products and services at any point in time.

Income.   The flow of useful products and services over a period of time.

Illth.   The decrease in welfare created by harmful aspects of wealth and income and the processes by which they are produced.

Economic growth.   Expansion of an economy's capacity to produce. Economic growth permits an increase in human welfare if it is faster than the increase of population.

Factors of production.   Inputs into the production process, usually designated as *land, labor,* and *capital.*

Capital.   Tangible and intangible tools of production that the economy has accumulated as a result of its past productive efforts. Includes *capital goods* (instruments of production) as well as *knowledge.*

Population trap.   As output rises, a nation's ability to sustain a larger population also increases. Unless population is held in check, output per person will fall back to its original level.

Diminishing returns.   As long as one or more factors of production are limited in amount, increased use of a variable factor will bring a diminishing rate of increase in output.

Exhaustible resources.   Resources whose quantity is reduced when they are used as a means of production.

In an economy like that of the United States the level of economic activity is determined by the flow of spending. The economy's capacity to produce is one limit beyond which production cannot go, but within that limit the level of output depends on the flow of spending between consumers and business firms, the flow of savings and investment through the money markets, the creation of credit by banks, and the fiscal activities of governments.

THE FLOW OF SPENDING: CONSUMERS AND BUSINESS FIRMS

A description of the flow of spending may begin at almost any point. It is such a closely interconnected web of relationships that moving from any starting point will bring the analysis through all of the parts and back again to the beginning. As shown in Figure 4-1, we can begin with the payment of income from business firms to consumers in exchange for productive services and resources. Owners and employees of business firms supply labor services, land, and capital to productive enterprises in exchange for wages and salaries, rent, interest, and profits. This exchange establishes one of the basic flows of income in the economy.

Business firms transform the resources supplied to them into products and services of other kinds, and, of course, sell them back to consumers. Consumers, in turn, use their incomes to buy products and services from business firms. As we see in Figure 4-2, this exchange represents a second basic flow of income in the economy.

In the process of production, however, some of the capital equipment used by business firms wears out. This is known as *depreciation*. Capital stock has to be replaced if production is to be continued without interruption. A part of the business community's output, therefore, will be used to restock its capital equipment rather than being sold to consumers. Productive services and resources are used in producing this part of the nation's output and incomes are paid to consumers for use of their services and resources, even though the output is retained by business firms for their own use. Since this is a cost of doing business, the prices charged for products and services sold to consumers must include a charge to cover the cost of depreciation. Both the incomes earned by consumers and the costs of the products they buy will

The Flow
of Spending

4

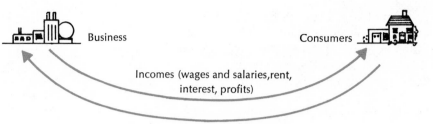

FIGURE 4-1
The Flow of Spending: I

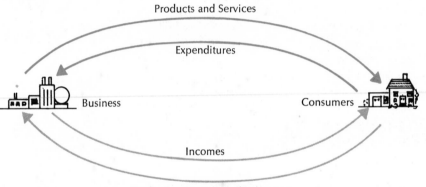

FIGURE 4-2
The Flow of Spending: II

include the value of the capital used up in production as well as the inputs of new quantities of labor, land and capital. The basic diagram of the flow of spending then appears as illustrated in Figure 4-3.

The flow of spending described here is highly simplified. There are, however, several important aspects of the flow of spending that we should note carefully before proceeding further.

1. The flow of monetary payments is balanced by a flow of real products, services, and resources in the opposite direction. Money payments (the inner ring in the diagram) are the counterpart of resources and products flowing in the opposite direction.

2. These flows of money payments and real products offer two alternative ways of measuring the size of the flow of spending. The flow can be measured by calculating the incomes earned by consumers in the form of wages and salaries, interest, rent, and profits. Or alternatively, it can be

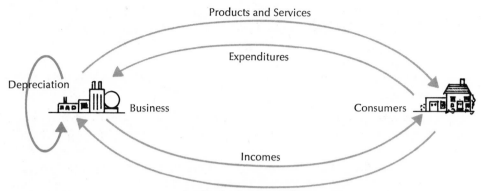

FIGURE 4-3
The Flow of Spending: III

measured by calculating the money value of the final products and services sold to consumers (or added to the inventories of producers).

3. The prices of products and services, and the prices of the factors of production, are determined by the markets in which producers and consumers interact with each other. Producers buy services and resources from consumers, who in turn buy products and services from producers. In these markets the prices of products and resources are determined and decisions are made by consumers and producers about what will be bought and produced. These markets, which will be described in the following chapter, are shown on the flow-of-spending diagram in Figure 4-4.

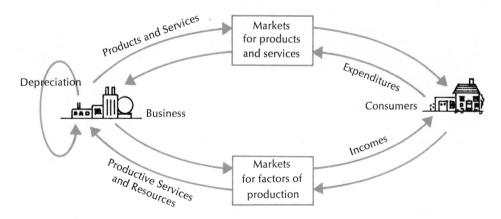

FIGURE 4-4
The Flow of Spending: IV

4. The flow of spending, as it has been described to this point, will neither increase nor decrease in size. Funds flow without interruption between consumers and producers, and between producers and owners of resources. There are no *leakages* that might cause instability in the flow of spending or in employment and output. The reason for this stability is worth noting.

If consumers spend all of their incomes they will return to producers an amount equal to the sums business firms paid out for the use of productive resources. Since the sums paid out include a normal profit to the owners of the enterprises, they should be happy to continue producing. Output will be sustained at existing levels and incomes will continue to be paid to consumers in payment for their labor and productive resources. The level of production and the level of employment will not change.

If, however, consumers were to spend less than the incomes they receive, they would not buy back from business firms all of the output produced, unsold products would pile up, profits would be inadequate, and business firms would cut back on their employment and output.

Conversely, if consumers spend *more* than the incomes they are currently earning (perhaps by drawing on past savings or by borrowing), the enlarged purchasing power would encourage expansion of output and increased employment by business firms.[1]

Here is one of the first great principles to be learned from the flow of spending: *the level of employment and output depends on the total amount spent* by the economic units that make up the economy. If total spending, or *aggregate demand* according to the economists' lexicon, rises, employment and output will increase and prosperity will bless the land. If aggregate demand falls, employment and output will decline, and factories will be idle and the economy depressed.

SAVING, INVESTMENT, AND CHANGES IN AGGREGATE DEMAND

In the real world, consumers and business firms do not spend all of their incomes. Part is saved. Savings from both sources flow into financial institutions such as banks, insurance companies, savings and loan associations, and credit unions, where they represent a pool of liquid assets that can be borrowed by others and used to finance all kinds of purchases. Financial institutions serve as middlemen in the money markets, gathering the savings of the economy and lending them to borrowers. They also hold funds until their owners withdraw them. They charge for their loans, and the money markets establish the interest rates at which money is made available.

---

[1] The alert reader will immediately note the related proposition that changes in total spending will also affect price levels and price relationships within the markets for products and services and for factors of production.

The diagram of the flow of spending can readily be expanded to include the financial sector, as shown in Figure 4-5. This portion of the flow of spending, involving saving and investment, is the part that is responsible both for economic fluctuations (depressions and inflation) and for economic growth. When savings are withdrawn from the flow of spending, the level of aggregate demand is reduced. Some of the incomes that consumers might spend on products and services is not spent. The incomes of business firms are correspondingly reduced, and they hire less labor and other productive services. This, in turn, reduces the incomes of consumers and their purchasing power still further. The same is true of business savings: every dollar set aside in reserves by business firms is a dollar that is not used to hire workers or buy materials for production. It is a *leakage* from the flow of spending and reduces aggregate demand.

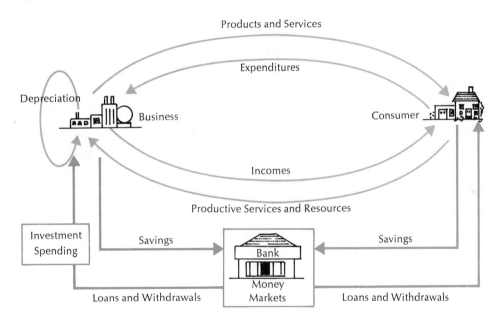

FIGURE 4-5
The Flow of Spending: V

Total spending and employment can be sustained at high levels only if the economy's savings are offset by a counterbalancing flow back into the hands of consumers and business firms. The most important offsets to savings in the private sector of the economy are:

1. Loans to consumers for the financing of purchases of houses, automobiles, and other durable goods, and for other purposes.
2. Loans to business firms

a. to finance current operations, and

b. for *investment* in new plants, equipment, and inventories.

3. Withdrawal of funds by consumers and business firms (rather than loans) for the purposes listed above.

In any case, unless the leakage of savings is offset by loans and withdrawals from financial institutions, the flow of spending will shrink and the level of output and employment will fall.

The other side of the coin is also important. Borrowing by consumers and businessmen can add more purchasing power to the flow of spending than is leaking out in savings. When that happens aggregate demand will rise. Output and employment will increase. But prices may also go up, particularly if the economy is at or near its productive capacity. The flow of spending is potentially unstable both upward and downward.

SAY'S LAW OF MARKETS

Prior to the great depression of the 1930s, most economic theorists felt that there was no tendency for the relationships between savings and investment to produce anything but full employment. As the French economist Jean-Baptiste Say (1767–1832) pointed out, the incomes paid out in the process of production create enough purchasing power to buy back the output and sustain the level of production. Most economists argued that any tendency for savings to pile up unused in the money markets would result in a fall in the rate of interest. This would encourage more investment spending because the price paid for money would be lower. At the same time the tendency to save would be diminished because of a lower rate of interest. These changes, it was held, would continue until the flow of investment increased enough to fully offset the flow of savings. Savings and investments would be equated with each other, and full employment would be maintained.

Indeed, there were some who argued that savings would always equal investment, and that the only observable changes would be rising and falling rates of interest. Others argued that even if savings and investment were unequal for short periods of time, rapid adjustments in prices would enable the economy to snap back to full employment quickly. For example, they argued that unemployment would be quickly cured by a drop in wage rates. But the key to the argument is that the rate of interest was thought to act as a stabilizing agent, causing savings to equal investment without any significant changes in the level of employment and output.

These older economists recognized that depressions did occur, but attributed their causes either to noneconomic factors or to a malfunctioning of the monetary system.

THE KEYNESIAN REVOLUTION

This view of the matter was drastically changed during the Great Depression of the 1930s. Waiting for changes in interest rates and prices to bring back full employment seemed to be just too costly under the circumstances that prevailed. Largely through the influence of English economist John Maynard Keynes a new analysis was developed.

Keynes pointed out that the motives for saving differed quite substantially from the motives for investment. Savings, he observed, were regular and steady, and often contractual in nature, such as monthly payments on insurance policies and mortgages or regular deposits in savings banks. Keynes noted a strong tendency for the flow of savings to depend on the incomes that people earned: the larger the flow of spending, the higher the income of consumers and business firms, and the greater the flow of savings. The opposite was also true: if incomes fell, savings would be reduced. Investment, on the other hand, was far more volatile, rising or falling sharply with the expectations businessmen had about the future and depending heavily on their state of optimism or pessimism. The *desire* to save, Keynes argued, could readily differ from the *desire* to invest.

When this happens, he argued, the rate of interest doesn't bring the two magnitudes into equality. When businessmen are pessimistic, for example, they don't want to borrow—nor do pessimistic bankers care to lend, either. At such a time business firms and banks both want to increase their liquid assets (money) rather than invest or lend. This changed attitude toward money that accompanies pessimistic expectations prevents any decline in interest rates from increasing the amount of investment. Even if interest rates were to fall, Keynes argued, businessmen would still want to increase their liquid assets rather than their production capacity. At the same time, the contractual nature of much of the economy's savings prevents lower interest rates from having a significant effect on the desire to save. The result is a downward spiral in economic activity.

The downward spiral will continue until desired savings is equal to desired investment. For example, postulate a great reduction in the desire to invest on the part of businessmen, perhaps because of a large decline in the prices of securities, and examine its consequences for the flow of spending. Savings are still drawn off, and part of the economy's output piles up in unsold inventories held by business firms. This *undesired* investment in larger inventories causes business firms to reduce their output, thereby reducing the incomes of consumers and causing the flow of spending to shrink in size. Lower incomes will mean lower levels of savings, so at the next trip around the circular flow of spending, less will be saved. This process of a decline in aggregate demand will continue until the flow of savings is brought down to a level just equal to the flow of *desired* investment spending.

Throughout the process the total amount of savings always equals the total of desired investment plus undesired investment. But total spending continues to shrink until a low enough level of income is reached so that savings just equals the amount of investment businessmen are *willing* to make.

Just the opposite effects occur when businessmen become optimistic and increase their expenditures for investment. They add to the flow of spending by hiring more workers and other productive resources, the flow of spending increases, and at the higher levels of income, consumers will save larger amounts. The expansion continues until the amounts consumers save out of their higher incomes just balance the investments businessmen wish to make. When that happens the leakages from the flow of spending will balance the flow of investments and aggregate demand will be stabilized. As long as there are unused resources and unemployed labor available the expansion can be a smooth one. But as the economy approaches full employment it is quite likely that the rising aggregate demand will start pushing prices up.

These relationships can be summarized in a few brief statements that contain the essence of the Keynesian theories:

1. Total savings and total investment will *always* be equal.
2. When investment incentives deteriorate, and desired savings is greater than desired investment, total spending will decline. The decline will continue until the inducement to invest is brought into line with the desire to save.
3. When businessmen want to increase investment expenditures, and desired investment exceeds desired savings at existing levels of total spending, aggregate demand will rise. The increase will continue until rising incomes generate savings equal to the amounts businessmen wish to invest.

Note carefully, however, that these results occur under the limiting condition, or assumption, that there is a stable relationship between aggregate demand and total savings. If that relationship is erratic, there is no way to tell which way total spending would move when the inducement to invest changes.

One key concept of the new economics is the *multiplier.* Any increase in either consumer spending or investment spending will have a multiplied effect on total spending. This is the case because money flows from consumer to producer and back again almost indefinitely, financing purchases and employment each time it is spent and respent. A part of any new income is saved, however, so less is respent each time. Ultimately it will all leak out into savings. In the meantime, however, many circuits will have been made and total spending will have increased by an amount substantially greater than the original increase. Decreased spending will also have a multiplied effect. Aggregate demand will fall by more than the amount of a reduction in business investment, for example.[2]

---

[2] The size of the multiplier depends on the saving and spending behavior of consumers and business firms. The speed with which it operates depends on how rapidly people respend their incomes. Knowledge of these factors enables economists to estimate the size of the multiplier and hence the impact on total spending of any change in its component parts. In recent years in the United States, the annual multiplier has been about 2. That is, if business investment spending were to rise by $1 billion from one year to the next, the gross national product would increase by about $2 billion during that year. Neat, isn't it? The theory of the multiplier and its estimation will be covered in detail in Chapter 12 of Part IV. At this stage all that is necessary is to know

The Keynesian reformulation of the relationship between savings and investment involved a new equilibrating factor. It substituted changes in the level of total spending for changes in the rate of interest as the factor that brings the economy back to stability.

This stable level of aggregate demand may or may not be at the full-employment level. It may leave resources unused and workers idle. Or it may be so great as to push prices up in an inflationary spiral. Only by accident, and then probably only very temporarily, is it likely to be at exactly the level that produces full employment without inflation.

CREATION OF CREDIT AND CHANGES IN AGGREGATE DEMAND

Up to this point we have discussed changes in the flow of spending caused by the actions of consumers and business firms. There is another source of change in the flow of spending: the money markets themselves. One of the economy's financial institutions, the commercial bank, can create purchasing power through its loans to consumers and business firms. This creation of credit is independent of the incomes earned by consumers or business firms (although they have to be credit-worthy in order to obtain a loan), and can add to the effective demand for products and services. It adds a further source of instability to the flow of spending.

When a shoe retailer borrows from a bank in order to buy his inventories, the bank creates a deposit in the retailer's name that the retailer can then write checks against. The retailer writes a check to a shoe manufacturer to pay for his shoe inventory, the manufacturer presents the check for payment through his bank, and the bank that originally made the loan is obligated to pay. In the meantime, however, the manufacturer gets payments for the shoes he has produced and is able to continue producing more. Purchasing power that did not exist before was created and starts its journey through the flow of spending.

There are limitations on the process. If one bank were to make loans and thereby increase its deposits faster than other banks, it would soon find that checks were coming in for payment very rapidly and that its payments were exceeding its receipts. It would be forced to reduce its loans to keep its incoming deposits and its outgoing payments in balance. But when all banks expand loans together it is easy for a single bank to make new loans because its incoming deposits will be rising also. As a result, during periods of prosperity, when bankers and businessmen are optimistic and eager to make higher profits, it is easy for purchasing power to be expanded rapidly by creation of bank credit. In these situations, aggregate demand can rise more rapidly than the economy's capacity to produce and a classic inflationary situation can be created.

---

that once a change starts it will ultimately end and a new level of aggregate demand will be reached unless other changes occur in the meantime.

Under these *easy money* conditions, the creation of credit can readily supplement the earnings of consumers and business firms and add to total purchasing power. On the other hand, when hard-to-obtain loans and relatively high rates of interest exist, these *tight money* conditions dampen down the flow of funds back into the stream of spending and hold back increases in aggregate demand.

The potential instability inherent in the banking system has led every advanced industrial nation to devise means by which the creation of credit can be controlled. In the United States, a central bank, the Federal Reserve System, has that responsibility. It has authority to specify the reserve a bank must keep behind its deposits, it controls the total amount of reserves available to the banking system as a whole, and it attempts to influence the availability of credit and rates of interest. In short, it seeks to manage the monetary system in order to promote stability in the flow of spending.[3]

THE FLOW OF SPENDING:
THE ROLE OF GOVERNMENT

Consumers, business firms, and financial institutions are not the only actors in the drama of the flow of spending. Governments are also involved. When governments spend money they add to the flow of spending. When they collect taxes they reduce the flow of spending. These flows can be shown diagrammatically much as the flows of savings and investment are shown (see Figure 4-6).

Taxes, like savings, are a leakage out of the main flow of spending. Like savings, they reduce purchasing power and reduce the total output of the economy. Government expenditures, like loans and investments, offset the leakage of taxes and raise purchasing power. In the process, governments use their receipts to finance their many and varied programs: public services such as law enforcement and defense, social security and social insurance programs, education, construction of highways and other public facilities, and production of commodities for sale (such as electric power or water supplies in many communities). In some of these programs governments merely transfer purchasing power from one person to the other, as from taxpayers to those who receive veterans' pensions, and these *transfer payments* do not add to the total output of products and services. In other cases, governments directly employ people who provide services to the public. Or governments may purchase the output of private firms, such as military supplies, or produce goods in their own factories and shipyards. In these instances, government expenditures increase the total output of the economy and the incomes earned by consumers and business firms. They swell aggregate demand to higher levels by providing productive employment. Government spending,

[3] A more detailed analysis of credit creation and money management that gets into the details of the system and the effectiveness of monetary policy is given in Part IV, Chapters 16 and 17.

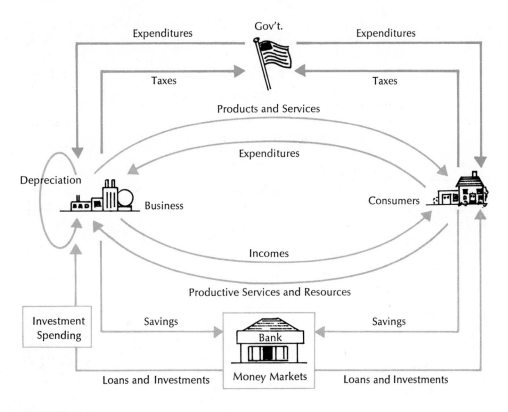

FIGURE 4-6
The Flow of Spending: VI

then, can add substantially to aggregate demand and increase both the output of the economy and the incomes of consumers and producers.

The place of government in the flow of spending goes beyond the fact that government expenditures can add to output and incomes. Control over the flow of taxes and the level of expenditures can be used to stabilize the flow of spending at full-employment levels. If the private sector of the economy does not generate full employment, government expenditures can be increased until full employment is reached. These expenditures can be of several sorts. Transfer payments such as unemployment insurance benefits can be increased, public works projects such as highway construction can be expanded, or purchases from business firms can be increased. In practice, all three types of spending are likely to be expanded simultaneously. Conversely, taxes might be reduced while expenditure levels are maintained. This will have the effect of sustaining the government's contribution to total income and employment while consumers' purchasing power is increased and business taxes are reduced.

In any case, whether government expenditures are increased, or taxes are reduced, or both policies are followed, the object is to create a deficit in the public finances in which expenditures exceed tax revenues. The deficit will have to be financed by borrowing, in a sale of government bonds, which will draw funds out of the money markets and into the flow of spending. In this way, another offset to savings is created to supplement loans and investments from financial institutions to consumers and business firms. This pattern can be shown on the diagram of the flow of spending (Figure 4-7).

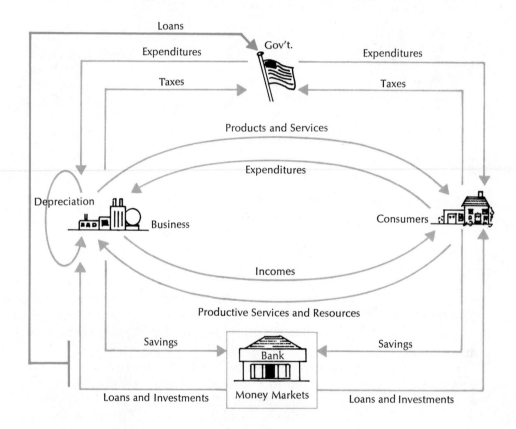

FIGURE 4-7
The Flow of Spending: VII

Conversely, if total spending is too great and inflationary price increases are occurring, government fiscal policy can operate in the opposite direction. A government *surplus* can be created, in which taxes exceed expenditures. This will draw out of the economy more purchasing power than is brought into it, total spending will fall, and the upward pressure on prices will be alleviated.

Government fiscal affairs, then, have three different kinds of effects on the flow of spending:

1. *Transfer payments* shift purchasing power from taxpayers to other persons, presumably in order to achieve social goals not achieved by the pattern of income levels and distribution that would otherwise prevail.

2. *Government expenditures* provide a variety of products and services through government agencies, and add to total incomes, employment, and output.

3. Fiscal *surpluses* and *deficits* can be used to promote economic stability. If properly managed, they can reduce—some hope eliminate—the depressions and inflations that would otherwise be generated in the private sector of the economy.[4] This stabilizing function of government expenditure and tax policy is usually coordinated with the policies of the monetary authorities that control the flow of credit. Monetary policy and fiscal policy can be used jointly in an effort to achieve economic stability.

INFLATIONS AND DEPRESSIONS

The flow of spending is continually changing. Although the relationship between income and saving may be a relatively stable one, both the creation of credit and the investment decisions of business firms can vary widely from one year to the next.

When optimism and the expectation of increased business and rising profits are prevalent, the flow of spending can expand readily as investment expenditures and credit creation increase. The resultant increases in aggregate demand, under the impact of the multiplier, can increase optimism still further and induce more expansion. Under these conditions the economy can push forward rapidly and reach levels of full employment. There is nothing that will necessarily stop expansion of aggregate demand beyond full-employment levels. Yet when full employment is reached, output can grow only very slowly. If purchasing power continues to rise rapidly something must give, and that something is the level of prices. Inflation begins, and will continue so long as aggregate demand continues to grow more rapidly than output.

---

[4] It should be noted here that a balanced government budget can also be used to help stabilize the economy by raising or lowering its total. If expenditures and taxes are increased together, and the expenditures are used to increase employment rather than for transfer payments, aggregate demand and total output will be increased. Incomes of consumers and business firms will be left at the same total as before, because the increased expenditures give them back what the taxes took away. But in the meantime government has used the money to employ people, pay them incomes, and produce (or buy) products and services. An increased but balanced budget acts as a stimulant to the economy, and a decreased but balanced budget as a depressant. Deficits or surpluses substantially increase the impact, however, because the change in expenditures is not balanced by an offsetting change in tax receipts. The multiplied effect is greater. There is more on these matters in Part IV, especially Chapters 14 and 20.

It will be shown in Part IV that an inflation of this sort tends to bring itself to an end but usually continues its momentum for a time even after aggregate demand is no longer growing faster than output. Indeed, inflation can start even before full employment is reached. This is one of the most serious problems that the makers of economic policy have had to face in recent years; it is discussed more fully in Chapter 19.

The traditional policy prescription for inflation caused by excessive spending is to tighten the money supply in order to make loans harder to get and push interest rates up, hold back on government expenditures, and, if possible, run a government budgetary surplus. The policy problem is a difficult one, however, since too vigorous an anti-inflationary policy can start a recession, while too timid a one may not be strong enough to eliminate the excessive demand that is pushing prices up. The economic policy maker's lot is not a happy one.

Inflation is not the only problem. Just the opposite conditions of recession and depression can prevail. Then the problem is one of supplementing the existing flow of spending and of using monetary policies to encourage creation of more credit. Here the problem is simpler, since the unlimited credit of a national government allows it to borrow and spend whatever is necessary to raise aggregate demand to full-employment levels. This may entail an increase in the national debt, but as will be shown in Part IV, the economic burdens created by such a debt are insignificant when compared with the benefits derived from high levels of output and employment. Indeed we are fortunate, in the mid-twentieth century, to have governments that spend and tax in large amounts: they provide a strong base for high levels of aggregate demand, and relatively small changes in their total budgets can have a large multiplied effect on the flow of spending. This was not true of national governments fifty years ago or more, when they accounted for a much smaller proportion of total spending.

The fact that aggregate demand in the private sector of the economy is either rising or falling at all times is one of the unpleasant characteristics of the modern economy. This condition in itself creates the changing expectations that in turn spur further changes in the level of aggregate demand and the levels of employment and output. This characteristic of the private sector creates a significant role for government: promotion of greater economic stability. The government sector of the economy can be used to counterbalance the instability of the private sector. When the flow of spending tends to shrink, government policies can move in the opposite direction. When expansion seems to be too great, government action can dampen the exuberance. Successful policies of this sort are admittedly difficult to manage. However, not only can they promote greater economic stability, but in doing so they can also reduce the volatile changes in expectations that underlie the instability of the private sector. Just as instability feeds on itself, so stability can create conditions favorable to its continuation.

THE FLOW OF SPENDING
AND ECONOMIC GROWTH

One of the keys to high levels of employment and output is the maintenance of high levels of business investment. The reason is simple. When aggregate demand is large, savings are also large. Without large investment expenditures to offset large savings, aggregate demand would fall and output and employment would shrink unless countered by government spending. One role played by business investment, then, is to bring savings back into the flow of spending and sustain the level of economic activity.

Investment has a second role. It results in an expanded *capacity* to produce. Construction of new factories, addition of new and improved equipment, and improvements in efficiency enable the economy to produce more than it was able to do before the investment expenditures were made.

The fact of expansion creates another problem. Growth of capacity requires a larger aggregate demand in order to dispose of the enlarged output. Unless total spending is sustained at higher levels than before, the expanded capacity will lie idle and the incentive to continue high levels of investment into the future will be diminished. But higher total spending will require still higher levels of investment to offset the increased savings that will be made. Investment expenditures must *increase* from year to year if the newly created output capacity is to be fully utilized.

A simple numerical example will make the problem clear. Let us start out with an economy at full employment, with a gross national product of $800 billion, and a simplified relationship between income and spending such that 80 percent of all income is spent for consumption. Leave government out of the picture. The initial position will be:

Gross national product	$800 billion
Consumption	640 billion
Savings	160 billion
Investment	160 billion

The new investment in this year will make possible an expansion of output to, let us say, $880 billion.[5] For that new capacity to be utilized, GNP will have to rise to $880 billion in the following year. Since 20 percent of GNP will appear as savings, the higher level of GNP would generate $176 billion in new savings. These new savings would have to be offset in the next year by investment spending equal to $176 billion. In the second year the economy would have to move to the following position:

---

[5] That is, two dollars of new capital investment brings an annual increase of one dollar in potential output (in this hypothetical example).

Gross national product	$880 billion
Consumption (80% of GNP)	704 billion
Savings (20% of GNP)	176 billion
Investment (= savings)	176 billion

What would happen if investment did not rise to $176 billion? Clearly, the GNP would not rise to $880 billion, excess production capacity would appear, and the inducement to invest and expand further would be weakened. Under these conditions it would become difficult to avoid a decline in investment spending and a consequent multiplied decline in GNP.

The proposition should be clear. In order to sustain a stable and growing economy, investment must *grow* from year to year. It is not enough merely to maintain high levels. The amount of required growth in investment, furthermore, depends on two relationships:

1. The relationship between investment and output, that is, the expansion of output brought about by an increase in capital. This relationship determines the increase in aggregate demand needed in order that the new capacity may be fully utilized.

2. The relationship between consumption and income, that is, the increase in consumption brought about by expansion of income. This ratio determines the amount of investment necessary to bring about the increase in aggregate demand determined above.

Economic growth creates a host of additional policy problems. Investment must grow continually in order that high levels of economic activity can be maintained. If it fails to sustain the required rate of growth, the conditions of economic stagnation can quickly appear: excess capacity, inadequate aggregate demand, and unemployed labor. A pause in the growth of the economy creates conditions that make it increasingly difficult to maintain existing levels of output and employment. Unless growth begins again, a downturn is almost inevitable. The economy must either move forward to higher levels of production and employment or fall back to lower ones.

Summary

The level of economic activity is determined by the flow of spending from households to business firms and back. Leakages in the form of savings and taxes are offset by investment and government spending. When they are not fully offset, the flow of spending falls and the level of economic activity declines. The monetary sector is able to supplement the flow of spending by credit created by the banking system, leading to a need for government to manage the money supply. Government budgets can act as a stabilizing element through adjustment of taxes and government expenditures to compensate for the fluctuations inherent in the private sector.

Prior to the 1930s the accepted doctrine among economists was that savings would always be offset by investment because of changes in the rate of interest. Keynes changed that belief, pointing out that savings and investment were done by different people and for different reasons. Fluctuations in the level of total spending resulted:

1. Investment spending, based on the expectations and attitudes of businessmen, tends to be relatively unstable.
2. Savings, based on consumer incomes, tends to be a relatively stable proportion of income.
3. Disparities between the desire to save and the desire to invest can lead to significant changes in the levels of output and income.
4. These fluctuations can be magnified by changes in the flow of credit created by the banking system.

The inherent instability of the private sector of the economy can be countered by government tax and spending policies, and can be dampened by controls over credit creation by banks. Fiscal and monetary policies developed by modern governments are designed to achieve those goals. Stability, however, is not enough: the levels of aggregate demand, investment and consumer spending needed to achieve full employment one year will be inadequate the next. Unless those elements of aggregate demand grow at just the right amounts, the economy can develop symptoms of stagnation (if they grow too slowly) or inflation (if they grow too rapidly). Public economic policies must therefore be activist in nature, but they are continually forced to move along the knife-edge that divides too little from too much.

Key Concepts

Flow of spending. The stream of purchasing power that flows from business firms to households in the form of income payments, and back again through buying of products and services by households.

Leakages. Funds leaving the flow of spending, chiefly through savings and taxes.

Aggregate demand. The level of total spending in the economy.

Offsets to savings.   Types of spending that replace savings and maintain the flow of spending and the level of aggregate demand. Examples: business investment, bank loans to customers, government spending.

Say's law of markets.   The money paid out to the factors of production creates enough purchasing power to buy back the output of the production process. This law, which implies that aggregate demand is always large enough to maintain full employment, was a primary theoretical principle in orthodox economics until it was demolished by the experience of the Great Depression and Keynesian economic analysis.

The multiplier.   Any change in spending, such as business investment, will have a multiplied effect on the level of aggregate demand.

Easy money and **tight money.**   Conditions of the money markets. Money is said to be easy when interest rates are low and loans easy to get. Money is tight when interest rates are high and it is difficult to borrow.

Transfer payments.   Payments to an individual that are not in return for productive effort. Example: social security benefits.

Government deficits and surpluses.   A deficit occurs when expenditures exceed receipts. A surplus is the opposite. In the old days, economists thought government deficits would cause grass to grow in the streets. Now they are used to keep the economy humming.

Most people think of an economy like that of the United States as a "private enterprise" or "capitalist" economy. Such phrases stress the legal basis of the economy and the fact that the means of production are privately owned. These phrases also stress the contrast between capitalism[1] and other economic systems, such as socialism.

When we look at the way in which the American economy *functions,* however, a different emphasis emerges. The economy appears as a gigantic system of interrelated markets within which vast quantities of commodities and services are exchanged. Joe Stack, for example, goes to work every day at an automobile assembly plant in Detroit. He earns wages that he and his family spend on purchases of all the things they use. At the factory he works on an assembly line that is fed with parts and components purchased from other companies or produced in the plant from materials and parts bought elsewhere. The finished automobile is then sold to a retailer, who in turn sells it to a customer. The customer probably pays for the automobile with money he has borrowed from a bank and will repay out of earnings from his own job. He may be Joe Stack's next-door neighbor, or he may live thousands of miles away. But the wages paid to Joe Stack ultimately come from the buyer by way of the interrelated market transactions of the economy, and the automobile finds its way to the buyer by the same route.

Every unit in the economic system, whether it is a business firm or an individual, is continually engaged in buying and selling. Markets are the structural framework within which economic activity is carried on.

A market for a commodity or service is defined by the price that prevails in it. Perhaps the best definition was given as early as 1838 by the French mathematician and economist Augustin Cournot (1801–1877). He defined a market as "the whole of any region in which buyers and sellers are in such free intercourse with one another that the prices of the same goods tend to equality easily and quickly." Some markets have a central location and are easily identified, such as the stock exchanges in New York or London or the wheat pit and corn exchange in Chicago. Others, such as the market for iron ore mined in the Great

The Market Economy

5

---

[1] Karl Marx (1818–1883) was apparently the first to use the word *capitalism* to describe the modern economy, stressing his point that the system was controlled by a narrow group of capitalists.

Lakes region, have no central location. That market is defined by the boundaries of the area in which the iron ore is bought and sold at the price established by the large producers and published annually in Cleveland.

Markets may be wide or narrow. A standardized product that is in wide demand and is easily described and transported, such as a particular type and grade of wheat, will have a market that extends over a large area. Other markets of this sort are those for stock exchange securities and precious metals. In these markets, buyers and sellers from all parts of the world compete with each other. At the other extreme are secluded local markets in which competition from outside is absent, although even there the effect of competition from outside may be felt indirectly. Between these extremes lie most of the markets with which the average person is familiar.

The modern market is a *price-making market*. Its essential element is the interaction between buyers and sellers. This interaction establishes a price, and results in the exchange at that price of a unique quantity of the commodity or service being traded. Prices are determined by the interaction of the forces of demand and supply. A strong demand for a relatively scarce item will bring about a relatively high price, while weak demand for a plentiful commodity will keep the price low. Market prices reflect the relative strength or weakness of demand and supply conditions.

This price-making function of the modern market can, of course, be modified by governments, as we see in the examples of public utility regulation or war-time price controls. It can also be modified by large corporations able to use their economic power to influence or control the prices of what they sell. Even these controlled or administered markets are influenced by the market forces of demand and supply, however, especially over long periods of time. Monopolies are continually threatened by potential competitors. And efforts of governments to hold prices at levels significantly different from the normal market price have seldom succeeded for any length of time.

The price-making function of markets is an integral part of their *allocative function*. Buyers have many alternatives in spending their incomes, and one of the factors they consider is the relative prices attached to the alternatives. Producers, in turn, are influenced by the prices they must pay for labor and materials, as well as by the prices of what they sell. Resources are allocated to their various alternative uses as a result of these interactions of consumers, producers, and market prices.

When consumers and producers operate within the framework of a system of price-making, allocative markets, they tend to orient their thinking and their decisions toward maximizing their gains. Consumers will try to maximize the benefits they derive from their expenditures to the extent that they are able to do so. Sellers and producers, in turn, tend to maximize the difference between their revenues and their costs. Relative prices in the market provide an easily measured standard for these decisions. The result is that the motive of economic gain becomes the driving force behind the operation of markets.

Without trying to push the concept of "economic man" too far, or to apply it to anything but economic decisions, we can say that as *consumers and producers in a market environment,* most individuals try to maximize their economic gains. Sometimes past experiences are the best guide, and habit seems to rule. Sometimes differences between alternatives are so small that chance seems to be the guide. Sometimes lack of knowledge of better alternatives leaves one less well off than might be. But by and large, the motive of gain guides market behavior.

THE ADJUSTMENT MECHANISM: GENERAL EQUILIBRIUM

In a market economy unfettered by private or public control over prices or production, there is a strong and continuing tendency for prices and quantities of output to adjust automatically to two powerful forces: consumers' preferences and producers' costs. The continual effort on the part of rational consumers to maximize their satisfactions creates the demand on which profits are based. Producers, meanwhile, trying to maximize their profits, have to supply the things consumers want. A seller who does so will prosper, while one who does not will fail. At the same time, the returns to producers must cover their costs and make a profit if production is to continue. The profit itself is limited by competition among sellers. The result is a pattern of prices and output that enables consumers to maximize their welfare, limited by the constraint that producers must maximize their gains. A highly complex set of relationships is involved, in which an equilibrium between these contrary forces is continually being automatically sought, much as water seeks to find its level. When the equilibrium is broken, the market system will try to find another that is consistent with the new situation. This process of self-adjustment is continually at work, and an understanding of it is fundamental to the science of economics.

Let us take, as an example, an economy that produces just two commodities, milk and whiskey. Consumers spend all of their incomes on either or both of these products, and all workers and other productive resources are employed in either dairies or distilleries or their related industries. It is a competitive economy: no producer or seller is large enough to influence prices in the markets in which his product is sold or in which his resources are bought. Let us assume further that the two industries have arrived at a long-run equilibrium condition: profits are at a level just large enough to support the existing producers, and profits on the last investments made in each industry are equal. This last point is important, for as we shall see, profits are a key to the adjustments a market economy makes. We want to start our hypothetical case from a situation in which producers have incentives to continue their present operations unchanged, without expanding, contracting, or shifting to production of something else.

There are two basic conditions that define the economic equilibrium in which this economy finds itself. First, output has been adjusted to the demands of buyers in such a way that consumption of one more bottle of whiskey, and one less bottle of milk, would move someone to a lower level of satisfactions and welfare. Consumers are maximizing their welfare at the existing ratio between the consumption of milk and the consumption of whiskey. Second, owners of productive resources are maximizing their incomes. No unit of labor, capital, or land could earn more by shifting to any other use or employment.

These two conditions of equilibrium are, of course, just as hypothetical as the simplified two-commodity economy. But note this: Where consumers and producers act rationally there should be a constant tendency for a market economy to approach those conditions. When something occurs that shifts the economy away from this equilibrium, a process of readjustment will be set in motion that starts the economy back toward it. It is this process of self-adjustment that is the key to understanding how a market economy functions.

> **EQUILIBRIUM.** *Economists use the term equilibrium in the same sense that it is used in other sciences. An equilibrium is a situation in which there is no tendency to change. A stable equilibrium is one that tends to move back to its original position if it is disturbed. An unstable equilibrium will tend to move further away from the original position if it is disturbed, but will stay where it is unless disturbed. Most economic analysis at the introductory level is concerned with stable equilibria.*

At any rate, into our economic Eden of full employment, adequate profits, and firms producing just what consumers want, we shall introduce a change in consumer tastes, and see what happens. Let us assume that there is a substantial shift in preferences toward drinking more whiskey and less milk. We don't have to know why the change occurs, or whether or not it is desirable. But we do know that the pattern of production will change to match it, and that the process of change is an intricate one.

The first effects will be felt by the sellers of milk and whiskey. Milk producers will find that their sales have fallen and the price of milk will start to decline. Supplies of milk coming into the market initially will continue at the same level, because no one knows yet that consumer preferences have changed; but demand for milk has been reduced. The reduced sales will cause prices to sag and will bring down the profits of milk producers. They will start to reduce their output. Much of this will happen almost simultaneously, particularly if the markets reflect changes quickly. Whiskey sellers, on the other hand, will notice an increase in demand, will have difficulties in maintaining their inventories at the desired level, and will take advantage of the growing shortage of alcoholic beverages to raise their prices. The wholesale price of whiskey will rise, and so will the profits of the producers, who will then increase their output to take advantage of the favorable conditions in the market.

These, then, are the first effects of the shift in demand. The price and output of milk will fall along with the profits of dairies, while the price and output of whiskey will rise, along with the profits of distilleries. Already the pattern of production has begun to change to match the new pattern of demand.

But more is yet to come. Profits in the two industries are no longer equal. Some of the more astute dairy farmers will quickly see that they can increase their incomes by shifting their efforts from dairying to whiskey manufacturing. Enterprising new businessmen will enter the whiskey business and leave milk production and distribution alone. The resources of the economy will begin a slow shift from milk to whiskey production with the following results:

1. Workers laid off in dairying will find jobs opening up in distilleries.

2. Corn will be fed into stills rather than cows.

3. The least productive cows will be sent to the glue factory (for glue to paste labels on whiskey bottles).

4. Banks will be eager to lend money to profitable distilleries, replacing their former loans to now struggling dairies.

All of these changes will begin to affect the markets for whiskey and milk, this time from the supply side. As resources shift out of dairying, the supply of milk regularly coming into the market will fall. This, in turn, will cause prices to stop declining and start rising back toward their former levels. As this happens, the incentive of producers to shift out of dairying will gradually decrease and the industry will begin to approach stability once more. Just the opposite pattern will occur in the whiskey business. As more resources are devoted to whiskey production, the supply of whiskey coming into the market will increase. This, in turn, will bring prices and profits down from their former high levels. As profits start falling, the incentive to expand whiskey output will diminish and this industry, too, will begin to approach stability.

These trends in the two industries can be expected to continue until profits in the two are equalized. At that point the economy will be back in equilibrium, for then there will no longer be any incentive to shift productive resources out of one and into the other. But notice what has happened in the meantime: Output of whiskey has expanded to new high levels and is sustained there, and a larger proportion of the economy's resources are used in whiskey production. Conversely, output of milk is lower and requires a smaller proportion of the economy's resources. This is exactly the change the economy needed to make in order to accommodate to the shift in consumer preferences from milk to whiskey.

A simultaneous adjustment process has been going on with respect to other factors of production besides capital. As the whiskey industry expanded and the dairy industry contracted, opportunities for profitable employment of land and capital began to differ in the two industries, becoming better in whiskey than in milk. With the owners of resources presumably seeking the most profitable use for their assets—whether the labor time of the worker, the land of the farmer, or the money of the investor—resources shifted from milk to whiskey production. The growing whiskey industry bid them away from the dairy industry until at the final equilibrium position the amounts paid to the factors of production were equalized from one industry to the next. This does not mean that unskilled labor is paid the same amount as skilled labor. But it does mean that skilled labor employed in dairying earns the same amount as labor of comparable quality in the whiskey industry. The same conditions prevail for all types and grades of labor, land, and managerial skills, as well as capital.

The economy will be back in equilibrium once more. Throughout the adjustment process, consumers have allocated their expenditures so as to maximize their welfare. Indeed, it was a shift in consumer preferences that started the whole process of adjustment originally. The adjustment began on the demand side of the market and shifted to the supply side, and ultimately the interactions between the two brought about a new equilibrium in which no producer or owner of a factor of production could better his position. The result was a pattern of production and consumption in which consumers maximized their satisfactions and welfare, subject to the constraint of paying incomes to the factors of production just necessary to draw forth their use in the patterns and proportions established by consumer preferences.

THE ADJUSTMENT MECHANISM IN INDIVIDUAL MARKETS: DEMAND, SUPPLY, AND PRICE

A better understanding of how the system of markets adjusts itself will be provided by a close look at the adjustment mechanism in individual markets. There are two basic principles involved, the so-called "laws" of demand and supply:

The law of demand: Everything else remaining the same, consumers will buy more of a product when its price is low and less when its price is high.

The law of supply: Everything else remaining the same, sellers will be willing to sell more of a product when its price is high, less when its price is low.

There are exceptions to these laws, and in real life everything seldom remains the same. But as generalizations, these laws are two of the fundamental facts of life in a market economy.[2] The interaction of the two laws determines the equilibrium price in any specific market. For example, as the price of one commodity rises, while other prices remain the same, consumers will buy less

---

[2] The two laws and exceptions to them will be examined in detail in Chapters 22 through 25.

of the commodity while sellers would be willing to sell more. At some point the willingness of consumers to buy and of sellers to sell will exactly match each other, and *at that price* the market will be in equilibrium. That is, there will be no unsatisfied buyers or sellers at the existing price, and there will be no tendency for the price either to rise or to fall from that amount. To view this market equilibrium, we can go back to our hypothetical whiskey-milk economy and examine the demand for whiskey and the supply and how these factors interact.

The Demand Schedule and the Demand Curve
A hypothetical schedule of the demand for whiskey might look like Table 5–1.

TABLE 5–1
Hypothetical Schedule of Demand for Whiskey

Price per Quart	Quarts Purchased
$3.00	130,000
2.90	140,000
2.80	150,000
2.70	160,000
2.60	170,000
2.50	180,000
2.40	190,000
2.30	200,000

According to this demand schedule, we find that consumers will buy larger quantities of whiskey at lower prices than they will at higher prices, assuming that all other influences on consumer choices except the price of whiskey are held constant. This *demand schedule* can be readily transferred to a graph, providing a visual representation of the *demand curve* (Figure 5-1).

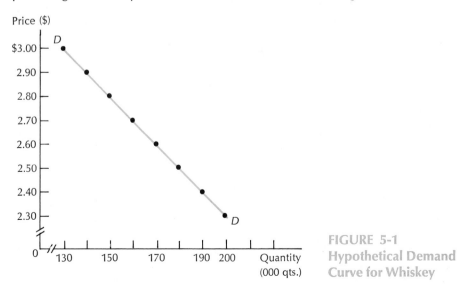

FIGURE 5-1
Hypothetical Demand
Curve for Whiskey

In real life, of course, the numbers are never rounded off, the demand curve is never smooth, and the observed data are scattered around the curve (which is a trend line or average) rather than falling on it. But since we are dealing with a hypothetical case to illustrate a general principle, estimates can be made so that everything comes out exactly right. The essential point is that the demand curve slopes downward to the right.

The Supply Schedule and the Supply Curve

Similarly, the amounts of whiskey that sellers would be willing to sell can be illustrated through a hypothetical supply schedule and supply curve (Table 5–2, Figure 5-2).

TABLE 5–2
Hypothetical Schedule of Supply of Whiskey

Price per Quart	Quantity Sellers Will Supply (Qts.)
$3.00	200,000
2.90	190,000
2.80	180,000
2.70	170,000
2.60	160,000
2.50	150,000
2.40	140,000
2.30	130,000

In the case of the supply curve the trend is just the opposite of the demand curve. The higher the price, the larger the quantity that sellers will be willing to sell. The supply curve slopes upward to the right.

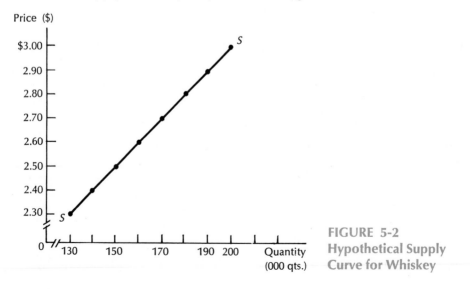

FIGURE 5-2
Hypothetical Supply
Curve for Whiskey

Determination of Price

Prices in the market will be determined by the interaction of the forces of demand and supply. In the case of our hypothetical whiskey market, putting the demand and supply curves on the same diagram will indicate the price that will prevail under market equilibrium (Figure 5-3). Under the assumed demand and supply conditions, the normal price of whiskey would be $2.65 per gallon and 165,000 gallons would be exchanged between sellers and buyers. At that point the amount that buyers wish to buy will be just equal to the amount sellers wish to sell, and there will be no unsatisfied buyers at the existing price. The market will be cleared.

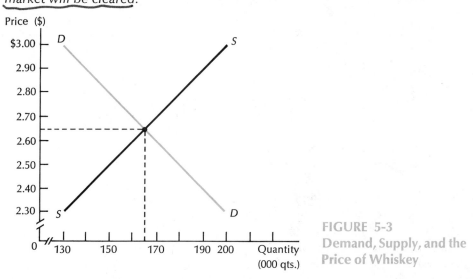

FIGURE 5-3
Demand, Supply, and the Price of Whiskey

No other price could long prevail under the existing market conditions. Suppose, for example, the price were $2.70 per quart. At that price, according to the demand schedule and curve, buyers would take only 160,000 quarts while sellers would like to sell 170,000. Competition among sellers for the limited number of customers would quickly start the price moving down toward $2.65, and it would continue moving down as long as the amount demanded remained less than the amount sellers wanted to sell. Only when the price reached $2.65 per quart and the amount demanded equaled the amount supplied would the price stop falling. Conversely, if the price were to fall below the equilibrium level, say to $2.50 per quart, the amount of whiskey demanded would exceed the quantity sellers were willing to supply at that price, sellers would raise their prices to take advantage of the favorable market conditions, and the price would rise toward $2.65, stopping only when the amounts demanded and supplied were equal.

Under conditions of perfect competition, the market mechanism is a wonderful device. It automatically adjusts prices and quantities to the market conditions created by buyers and sellers. If at any time the existing price leaves some

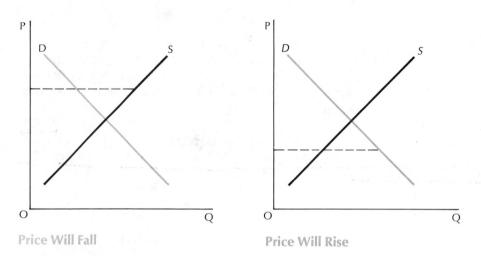

Price Will Fall   Price Will Rise

buyers unsatisfied, the price will tend to rise as they bid for the amounts they want. If, on the other hand, some sellers would like to sell more at the existing price but cannot find buyers, the price will tend to fall. When the desire to buy and sell is satisfied for everyone in the market at the existing price, then only will the normal or equilibrium price prevail.

Changes in Demand and Supply

In our hypothetical whiskey-milk economy, the market adjustment process began with a change in demand: an increase in the demand for whiskey and a decline in the demand for milk. Let's see how that will work out in the market for whiskey (Figures 5-4 and 5-5).

Demand Schedule

	Quarts Purchased	
Price per Quart	Before (D_1)	After (D_2)
$3.00	130,000	145,000
2.90	140,000	155,000
2.80	150,000	165,000
2.70	160,000	175,000
2.60	170,000	185,000
2.50	180,000	195,000
2.40	190,000	205,000
2.30	200,000	215,000

Demand Curve

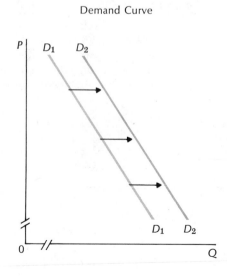

FIGURE 5-4
Increase in the Demand for Whiskey

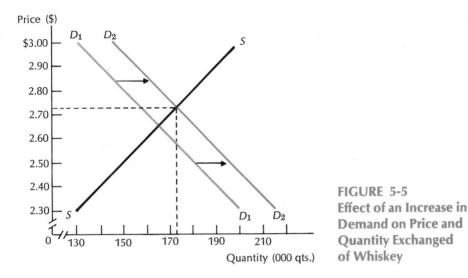

FIGURE 5-5
Effect of an Increase in
Demand on Price and
Quantity Exchanged
of Whiskey

An increase in demand means that, at all prices, the amount that consumers will buy is larger than before. Quantities in the demand schedule will be greater all down the line, and on the diagram the demand curve will shift to the right. An increase in demand means an increase in the whole demand schedule and a shift to the right in the demand curve. The effect of an increase in demand on the market will be to increase both the market price and the amount exchanged. In the case of our hypothetical whiskey market, the price will rise to $2.70, and 180,000 quarts of whiskey will be sold after the increase in demand has occurred.

Just the opposite effects will occur when demand decreases. The price of the commodity will fall and the amount sold will decline (see Figure 5-6). This is just what happened in our whiskey-milk economy at the initial stages of the adjustment when consumer tastes shifted against milk.

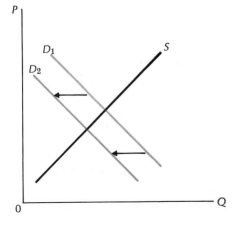

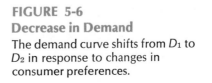

FIGURE 5-6
Decrease in Demand
The demand curve shifts from D_1 to
D_2 in response to changes in
consumer preferences.

In the market adjustment process the changes seldom stop with a single market. As we saw in our hypothetical whiskey-milk economy, the increase in demand for whiskey and the decrease in demand for milk changed the relationship between the market prices of the two commodities. This, in turn, changed the prospects for profits in two industries, including a shift in resource use that resulted in changes in the supply schedules. The supply of whiskey coming into the market was increased, and the supply of milk declined.

These shifts in the supply schedules and supply curves can also be shown graphically (see Figures 5-7 and 5-8) in much the same way that changes in demand are shown.

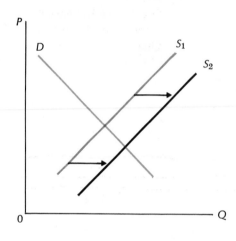

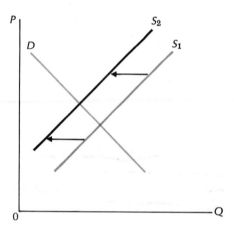

FIGURE 5-7
Increase in Supply
An increase in supply means that at all prices the amounts sellers wish to sell will be greater. The supply curve shifts to the right.

FIGURE 5-8
Decrease in Supply
A decrease in supply means that at all prices the amounts sellers wish to sell will be less. The supply curve shifts to the left.

At this point you should be well equipped to go through the simple analysis of the market adjustment process, starting with changes on either the demand or supply side of the market, and following through with the many-sided reactions that a change at one point in the system induces in the other parts. For example, in the whiskey-milk economy, the increase in demand for whiskey pulled its price up. This, in turn, triggered an increase in supplies brought to the market, which resulted in a decline in prices and profits back toward their former levels. This sequence of events is readily illustrated in Figures 5-9, 5-10, and 5-11 by use of demand and supply curves.

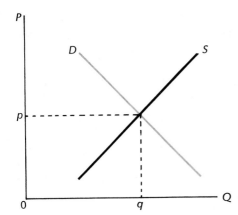

FIGURE 5-9
Stage 1: The Original Equilibrium

The market for whiskey is cleared and a normal price established by the interaction of market demand and supply.

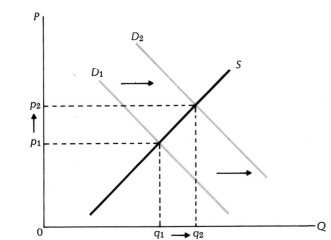

FIGURE 5-10
Stage 2:

An increase in demand for whiskey causes the price and quantity purchased to rise.

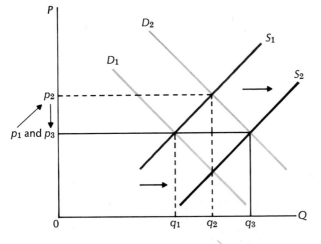

FIGURE 5-11
Stage 3: The Final Equilibrium

The increase in price and quantity sold increases profits of suppliers. New firms are attracted to the industry, production of whiskey is increased, and the increase in supply brings prices down again while the amount sold increases further.

At the final equilibrium in Stage 3, we have shown the new equilibrium price as identical with the price in the original equilibrium. Such would be the case if there were no changes in the cost of production, that is, if the resources moving into this expanding industry could be hired away from their former employment at the same costs as before. If the new resources had to be paid more to get them to move, or if diminishing returns or exhaustible resources were involved, production costs would rise from the first to the third stage in the adjustment, and p_3 would be greater than p_1. On the other hand, an expanded industry might have lower costs than one with a smaller output, and in this case p_3 would be lower than p_1. But whatever the situation, whether it be one of increasing costs, constant costs, or decreasing costs, a new equilibrium price would be established at which profits in the industry would be equated to those in other sectors of the economy.

While these adjustments have been going on in the whiskey industry, just the opposite has been happening in milk production. Work out the three steps for yourself, with diagrams showing the original equilibrium, the initial effects of the *decrease* in demand, and the final equilibrium after the *decrease* in supply.

THE SIGNIFICANCE OF THE
MARKET-ADJUSTMENT PROCESS

The self-adjusting system of markets is able to create order out of the apparent chaos of an individualistic society in which each person seeks his own goals, and does so without the imposition of political authority. It results in welfare-maximizing positions for both producer and consumer, based on the existing distribution of income and property ownership. Producers and consumers have to be satisfied with the result or else the adjustment process will continue until they are. The beauties of the system have led social philosophers from Adam Smith to mid-twentieth century libertarians like Ayn Rand to eulogize the market economy as the economic foundation of individual freedom.

The market mechanism is indeed a powerful instrument for achieving individual goals. Every alternative open to the individual as a consumer or as a producer has a price or a payoff that is stated in terms of money and can be compared with every alternative open to him. The choice is up to the individual and the outcome is the result of his own decision. It is in this kind of economic environment that a poet[3] could write,

> I am the master of my fate;
> I am the captain of my soul.

It is an environment in which individualism can flourish.

Yet the interests of others are not ignored. The individual is driven by his own self-interest to produce the things others want. If he wants to eat, if he

---

[3] W. E. Henley, *Echoes IV: In Memoriam R. T. Hamilton Bruce* ["*Invictus*"].

wants "success," he must sell either his efforts or his products in the market. This means that he must produce what others are willing to buy. He must produce the things that will enable others to maximize their own economic positions. In this sense, the welfare of one is tied inextricably to the welfare of all in a general system of relationships in which each serves the ends of everyone else while he is pursuing his own goals.

Ideally, it is a marvelous scheme for resolving the conflicts inherent in the meeting of buyer and seller in an exchange situation. Each tries to make the best bargain for himself that he can, but each has the opportunity to buy or sell only at the going market price. Businessman and customer, worker and employer, borrower or lender must all submit their differences to the arbitration of the market price.

Individualism and freedom within a context of welfare maximization for all and a resolution of economic conflicts—that is the great promise inherent in the market mechanism. It is hardly surprising that once the mechanism was understood, a whole series of social philosophers hailed it as one of the great social inventions in the history of mankind.

LIMITATIONS OF THE SELF-ADJUSTING MARKET

Nevertheless, the market economy has several very serious limitations that have prevented modern nations from relying fully upon it in making economic decisions.

Full Employment

Historically, the most serious limitation of the free market has been its inability consistently to maintain full employment. In the previous chapter we took a close look at the flow of spending and showed in broad outline why instability seems to be one of the inherent characteristics of an uncontrolled market economy. At this point it is sufficient to note such instability and point out that the theory of welfare maximization through the free market *assumes* that the adjustments take place under conditions of full employment. Indeed, the maintenance of full employment may be taken as a necessary precondition for the effective operation of the market-adjustment process we have described.

Competition and Monopoly

Many of the advantages of the self-adjusting market system depend on the maintenance of competition. Monopoly interferes with the adjustment process and prevents the achievement of a welfare-maximizing equilibrium. For example, a monopolist may be able to prevent or seriously delay the entry of new firms into an expanding industry, thereby keeping prices high and retaining monopolistic profits for himself. The monopolist makes large profits, but the far more serious difficulty is that output does not expand adequately and fails to adjust properly to consumer demand. A broadly pervasive pattern of competition is a second precondition for the effective operation of the market mechanism.

Equity in Income Distribution

The market economy pays incomes to the factors of production in amounts large enough to obtain their services in production. That is, workers, land, and capital are paid only for their usable productive effort. If a man does not work he will not eat, and when he works he will earn an amount equal only to his contribution to total output. His employers have no reason to pay him more.

There are three important drawbacks to these principles of income distribution as they work in practice. First, not all income is earned; some comes from inherited wealth and favored positions. Second, the uncertainties and luck that prevail in a world in which the future is not revealed can create inequities that have nothing to do with ability or productivity. Third and most important, payments according to productive effort can run counter to the ethical standards of a civilization that values an individual because he is a human being, not solely because he is a producer. Even if there were no unearned income and luck were eliminated, the equity of income distribution in a market economy is a special kind of *economic* equity that does not necessarily coincide with other standards of justice.

For example, suppose that in our whiskey-milk economy, the whiskey industry uses large amounts of capital relative to labor per dollar of output, while the dairy industry is more labor-intensive. As resources shift from milk to whiskey production, some of the labor used in the economy will become unnecessary at the existing level of wages. The unused supply of labor will tend to bring wages down, while the level of profits in the final equilibrium may rise because more of the economy's scarce capital will be demanded by an expanding capital-intensive industry. The new pattern of income distribution will then tend to benefit the owners of capital while the economic position of the workers is worsened. Whether desirable or not, the market mechanism will make the adjustment, and will make no moral judgments about it. But many people, from social philosophers to revolutionaries, may object on grounds of justice and equity.

Disagreements about economic justice have led to some of the most difficult problems of modern society. Socialists have argued for years that profits should go to producers rather than owners, and have advocated social rather than private ownership of the means of production. Even when private ownership is accepted as the institutional base of the economy, workers contest with management over "fair" wages and managerial "prerogatives." Problems of conflict between wage earner and employer, between workers and owners, have never been fully resolved by the market mechanism.

Conservation of Resources

The fact that property is privately owned and subject to the profit-maximizing decisions of its owner has led to wasteful use of resources. Where forests have been wastefully cut, land exhausted from overuse, and rivers polluted, the reason has usually been that short-run gains can be made by the owner while some of the long-run costs can be shifted to others. It may be quite profitable for a coal-mining company to leave behind exhausted mines from which all the usable coal has been taken, along with crippled and silicosis-ridden miners who become wards of the public rather than of the mine companies. At times, it is almost impossible to levy the full cost of resource use, both natural and human, on the producer of the final product. The user of the resource can thus waste with profit for himself, but not for society as a whole.

In three areas of concern, society has stepped in to protect itself against potential destructive effects on the resource base through the free market. The first has been in natural resources conservation. Every industrial nation has developed methods to protect land, water, and forests, and sometimes other resources from completely free exploitation. But as we all know, much remains to be done. The second has been in monetary policy. This sensitive area, in which the value of assets and the supply of money are determined, is controlled in a variety of ways by modern governments in order to avoid the recurrent monetary crises that have plagued the economy in past years and have played havoc with the accumulation of capital. Finally, human resources have been protected from the risks of the marketplace by a variety of social insurance and welfare programs that seek to preserve human values in an uncertain economic environment. Although land, capital, and labor are essential elements of the market economy, no modern nation leaves their disposition solely to market forces.

Individual and Social Goals

The emphasis on individualism that prevails in the market economy can lead to an undue emphasis on expenditures that benefit the individual, and a slighting of those that benefit the total community. Success may come with acquisition of wealth, but status and prestige come only if others are aware of one's success. In the impersonality of modern life, the display of wealth through spending has therefore become an important part of the market way of life—conspicuous consumption, it was called by the economists John Rae and Thorstein Veblen— in an effort to validate one's claim to recognition from friends and neighbors. This continuing pressure to spend helps to sustain high levels of economic activity, but it also tends to starve public agencies. People don't like to pay taxes, even though the purposes may be highly important for economic growth and well-being. Education, for example, which is largely carried out through public agencies in the United States and is essential for both individual improve- ment and economic development, is continually hampered for lack of funds, while the American consumer gratifies his desires for a second automobile, color television, and similar luxuries. This pattern of expenditures may well maximize satisfactions according to the existing pattern of consumer prefer- ences. But the preferences themselves are not independent of the cultural environment of the consumer and the marketing programs of producers.

Preferences are in part determined by the social and economic environment within which choices are made. The fact that the market economy tends to maximize benefits does not resolve the problem of whether those benefits are socially desirable or not.

Value Judgments

Social goals and patterns of individual behavior are closely related to value judgments. The market does not decide whether a particular pattern of production is good or bad. It merely adjusts to consumer preferences and to production costs. For example, moral judgments may consider a shift from milk to whiskey consumption to be bad for the individual and for society. But the market makes no judgments of this sort; it only reflects the economic realities that lie behind the demand and supply curves.

The market economy puts a premium on self-centered competitive behavior, on acquisition of material wealth, and on concern with monetary values. It is part of a pecuniary society with materialistic values. Esteem and approval go to those who are successful in market activity, those who accumulate wealth and earn large incomes.

This pattern of attitudes and motivations is one of the chief reasons for the growing wealth of our society. It drives people to acquire more; and doing it through the mechanism of the market means that the whole system becomes more productive. The same motives that lead to the welfare-maximizing equilibrium of the market economy push it ahead to greater output and increased wealth. Nevertheless, a price is paid in terms of a materialistic value system. Where beauty conflicts with profits, profits tend to win out, and billboards line the highways. Where it is cheaper to flush sewage into streams instead of treating it, streams and lakes are polluted. When children have finished their educations, parents begin to take a dim view of school taxes. A mediocre painting becomes a primary tourist attraction when bought by a famous gallery of art for $5,000,000. The market economy answers the great philosophical question, What has value? with the assertion that "if you can sell it, it has value"—and leaves modern man in the Faustian dilemma of wondering whether it isn't his soul that has been sold.

THE ROLE OF GOVERNMENT

Once the implications of a society based on a system of self-adjusting markets are understood, it is easy to understand why government has come to play a substantial role in economic affairs. It is not enough merely to establish the legal framework for the market economy—private property, freedom of contract, inheritance—and to support private economic activity through police protection and enforcement of laws. Those functions, plus national defense, have always been considered essential government activities even by the most convinced libertarians. Taxes are necessary if those governmental activities are to be supported, and that represents one form of interference with private economic activity.

But there is more. The system cannot operate effectively without reasonably full employment; yet it cannot be expected to generate this condition by itself. Competition is necessary for effective operation, yet there are strong incentives for private business firms to reduce or eliminate it in their own interests. Resources, capital, and people must often be protected against the ravages of the competitive market. Standards of equity must be applied. Certain products and services must be produced, yet private interest will not do so. And there is always the problem of the ultimate goals that individuals and the social system *ought* to seek. All of these considerations have led to a significant intervention of government into economic affairs. In the United States a kind of mixed economy has developed, in which a large degree of government influence and direction supplements the workings of the system of self-adjusting markets. In other countries such as the Soviet Union and China, efforts have been made largely to eliminate the market mechanism or reduce its significance. The question of how much a nation should rely on the market economy, and for what, has become one of the fundamental issues of modern times.

Summary

The United States has a market economy in which the bulk of economic activity is carried on in a system of interrelated markets. Markets determine the prices at which goods can be exchanged and allocate resources among their alternative uses. Welfare-maximizing consumers and profit-maximizing producers are brought together by the system of self-adjusting markets in such a way that the pattern of production tends to match the pattern of consumer preferences, while resources are drawn into those uses where they receive the highest compensation.

The self-adjusting market economy has limitations, however. There is no guarantee that full employment will prevail. It requires a pervasive competition in order that its best results may prevail. It may or may not distribute its output according to society's standards of equity. It may not adequately preserve natural resources. It may slight social goals in favor of individual preferences. It tends toward a strongly materialistic value system.

Yet with all of its limitations, the market-adjustment process brings order to the potential chaos of an individualistic society, and a high degree of freedom, and tends toward results that maximize individual welfare.

Key Concepts

Market economy. An economic system in which decisions about what is produced, how it is produced, and who gets it, are made within the framework of a system of self-adjusting, price-making markets.

General equilibrium. A situation in which no buyer or seller can improve his position by making a change. The *conditions* of *equilibrium* are: (1) Consumer welfare cannot be increased by altering the pattern of production or the allocation of resources; (2) No unit of any factor of production can earn more in any alternative use.

Demand schedule. The quantities that buyers would be willing to purchase at alternative prices. Shown graphically as a *demand curve*. *Quantity demanded* is the amount buyers would buy at a given price.

Supply schedule. The quantities that sellers would be willing to sell at alternative prices. Shown graphically as a *supply curve*. *Quantity supplied* is the amount sellers would supply at a given price.

Change in demand or **change in supply.** A shift in the entire demand or supply schedule. It shows graphically as a movement of the demand or supply curve. Must be distinguished from a shift along the curve.

Law of demand. At higher prices the quantity demanded is less than at lower prices.

Law of supply. At higher prices the quantity supplied is greater than at lower prices.

Clearing the market. At the existing price the amount supplied equals the amount demanded. The price at which the market is cleared is often called the *equilibrium price*.

MEASURING ECONOMIC PERFORMANCE

II

For more than a quarter of a century public policy has given heavy emphasis to maintaining high levels of economic activity and strong economic growth. Successive national administrations have held that both the domestic well-being and the national security of the United States demand high priority for those goals. Emphasis on these aspects of the economy requires a quantitative means for enabling policy makers to determine where they stand in relationship to their goals. The next two chapters explain the measuring devices that have been developed.

Chapter 6 shows how the national product and national income are measured, and discusses related concepts. It also discusses some limitations of these tools, in an effort to warn against improper use. The Appendix to Chapter 6 discusses index numbers and the way economists correct data for changes in price levels.

Chapter 7 uses the concepts of Chapter 6 in an evaluation of the recent performance of the American economy. The purpose of this chapter is to show how empirical data can be used to draw conclusions based on facts.

Concepts of measurement in the social sciences are not developed out of thin air. They have a purpose. The things that are measured and the way in which they are measured are related to the purposes for which the statistics are used. Measurements of the national product and income were originally developed to measure the level of prosperity and depression, that is, the amount of productive activity going on at any time. They were closely related to the problem of unemployment and economic slack. When policy concerns shifted to economic growth, the same measures turned out to be highly useful, but not quite so well adapted to that purpose. It is difficult to use a measurement made this year to make comparisons with a time, say fifty years back, when the economy has changed significantly in the meantime. Index numbers are used to meet that problem but are not fully satisfactory as a solution.

In recent years, policy concerns have shifted to the uses we make of our output and productive capacity and to the impact of economic growth on the environment and human welfare. Our measurements have severe limitations when used for those purposes and have to be interpreted with great care.

In spite of these difficulties, an objective social science cannot function without measurements. We must know the dimensions and magnitude of the phenomena we deal with, and we have to continually check our analysis against the real world. Conclusions about policy require an empirical base for theoretical analysis if they are to be meaningful. In Parts III and IV the present-day theories about economic growth and the level of economic activity will be developed, and policy issues in those areas will be discussed. The analysis will have an empirical dimension whose foundation is developed in Chapters 6 and 7, which make up Part II of this book. Modern economics is an amalgam of empirical studies, theory, and policy. The next two chapters help lead into that style of inquiry.

Objective evaluation of the performance of an economic system starts with measurements that enable the economist and policy maker to determine the level of economic activity and the direction and speed of its movement. Other quantitative measures can then be used to indicate the way in which the economy's output is used and how it is distributed. The most important measures of economic performance are national product and income accounts. In this chapter, we define those measures, briefly describe how they are computed, and explain some of their limitations.

THE NATIONAL PRODUCT

The most widely used yardstick of economic performance is the nation's *gross national product*, usually abbreviated as GNP. It is a statistical invention that sums up, in one neat little figure, the nation's total production for any one year. We can watch it grow over long periods of time. We can observe its fluctuations from one year to the next. Corrected for changes in the price level, it can tell us how the "real" economic conditions have been changing over time. Divided by the nation's population, it can provide a measure of output per person. Its rate of change can be computed, to show the speed of economic growth. Comparisons of the level of GNP with estimates of potential output can tell us if our economic performance is all that it might be.

Comparisons between nations with widely differing types of economic systems can be made. For example, the GNP of the U.S. is substantially greater than that of the USSR: In 1963 the figures were $584 billion for the U.S. and $265 billion for the USSR. The disparity was even greater for GNP per person: $3,084 for the U.S. and $1,178 for the USSR. Nevertheless, the Soviet Union continues to gain: In 1960–64 the average annual rate of growth in GNP was 4.6 percent for the USSR (an abnormally slow rate of growth for them) and 4.0 percent for the U.S. (an abnormally high growth rate for us).[1] More

The National Product and Income

6

---

[1] These data are taken from official U.S. sources: Joint Economic Committee, *Current Economic Indicators for the USSR* (Washington, D.C.: U.S. Government Printing Office, 1965). Russia authorities dispute the accuracy of the figures for the USSR. Because of difficulties in comparing the GNPs of nations as disparate as the U.S. and the USSR, these figures should be taken as approximations only.

recently (up to 1969), Soviet growth seems to have speeded up a little to a growth rate of about 5 percent annually, while U.S. growth has slowed a little under the impact of war and inflation. Comparisons like these have important consequences for national policy, and the gross national product is the basis for all of them.

Gross National Product Defined

A nation's gross national product is *the money value of all final products newly produced in a year*, in current prices. It measures the value of a year's production that is purchased by consumers, business firms and government, plus the difference between exports and imports. All of this adds up to a measure of how much productive effort took place.

GNP as an Estimate

Calculation of the GNP is not exact. It is essentially an estimate rather than an actual counting-up of objects. Although a wide variety of data gathered by the Department of Commerce from all sectors of the economy is the basis for the GNP, all of the necessary data are never available, and the figures are continually being revised. Sometimes the revisions continue for as much as ten years after the first announcement.

Reasonable accuracy is, of course, maintained. More important, the same techniques of calculation are used from one year to the next, so that annual changes are quite accurately measured. If the inexactness of one year parallels that of another, most of the errors of estimation will be washed out by the fact that the methods of estimation were the same.

Why Money Value is Used

To calculate the gross national product, economists use actual prices prevailing during the year. The many products and services of an economy have to be reduced to some common denominator in order to be added together. That common denominator is their money value, measured by the prices at which they were sold (or if they were not sold but held in inventories, at the value assigned to them by accountants). This provides a value expressed in current prices for all of the component parts of the GNP.

Final Products: Avoiding Double Counting

Only finished products and services that have been bought by their ultimate users are included in the GNP. Take this textbook, for example. It was bought at the bookstore by the consumer who uses it, and its value is included in the GNP at its final sale price. Intermediate stages of production are *not* included in the GNP. In the case of this book, a wide variety of intermediate products were used: trees cut and sold to a paper mill; paper, ink, and cloth sold to the printing and manufacturing plant, and so forth. If each intermediate transaction were included, some parts of the book would be included in

GNP two, three, four or even more times. Yet only one book is produced, with a value of only a few dollars. Including the intermediate stages would only artificially inflate the ultimate figure for GNP.

The method used by statisticians to eliminate double counting of intermediate products is to calculate the *value added* at each stage of the production process. For example, the value added at the paper-mill stage is calculated by subtracting the cost of pulpwood and other raw materials from the selling price of the paper. The difference will equal the wages and salaries, rent, interest, and profits paid to the factors of production for their productive effort: the value they have added to the value of the raw materials to give the final product its market value. When the value added at each stage is added up, the sum will equal the final selling price of the book.

Even inventories and goods in process of production pose no problem, though they are not yet in the hands of final consumers. The value added by all the productive effort that has gone into them is included in GNP, and their "final" user is considered to be the business firm that owns them as of December 31.

Goods Must be Newly Produced

In order to be included in the GNP for any year, goods must have been produced in that year. For example, if you bought this book secondhand, the transaction is not part of GNP because nothing new has been produced, no new income has been created or paid out, and no addition has been made to the total stock of goods, except for the services of the clerk and the profits of the bookstore. They are included in GNP because they were useful services newly performed and paid for during the year. But the wholesale cost of the book is excluded because the book was produced in an earlier year and was included in the GNP for that year.

This principle is widely applied. The value of a used house that is sold and bought is not included in GNP, but the agent's commission is. Sales of securities are not included, but brokers' commissions are. The old house, the securities, and any already existing asset are not newly produced goods, but the commissions are payments for productive services performed during the year.

THE COMPONENT PARTS OF GNP

The GNP has three basic component parts: consumption, investment, and government purchases of goods and services. A fourth, minor one is usually added: "net exports" of goods and services. These four categories are distinguished from each other, in part, by the different economic units that do the buying. More important, they differ because of the factors that influence the level of spending in each category. Distinction between them is useful in analyzing what happens in the circular flow of spending and why the level of GNP rises or falls from year to year.

Consumption

Personal consumption expenditures are by far the largest component of GNP, amounting to about 63 percent of GNP in the United States in recent years. Some of the important types of purchases included in this category are:

Durable goods, such as automobiles, furniture, and household equipment.

Nondurable goods, such as food and clothing.

Services, such as housing, transportation, and household operation.

Some idea of the relative size of these expenditures can be obtained from the national product accounts for 1970 (Table 6–1).

TABLE 6–1
Consumption Expenditures, 1970
(Billions of Dollars)

Gross national product	976.8
Personal consumption	616.8
Durable goods	89.4
Nondurable goods	264.7
Services	262.7

Investment

Investment, which is called gross private domestic investment in the national product accounts, is a particularly crucial part of the GNP because it is the main offset to savings. It also replaces the capital used up in production and increases the economy's capacity to produce. High levels of investment are essential for the maintenance of high levels of output and for the expansion of the economy's capacity to produce. Gross private domestic investment includes several components:

New plants and equipment built or installed by business firms and farmers.

New houses and other residential units.

Changes in business inventories. This component may be positive if business inventories have increased during the year, or negative if they have declined.

In 1970 the national product accounts showed the largest amounts in our history in all of these categories except residential structures (Table 6–2).

TABLE 6–2
Gross Private Domestic Investment, 1970
(Billions of Dollars)

Gross national product	976.8
Gross private domestic investment	135.8
New plants and equipment	102.6
Residential structures	29.7
Change in business inventories	3.6

Net and Gross Investment

One of the functions of investment is the replacement of capital used up in the process of production. The share of investment expenditures used for that purpose helps create employment and income, but it really represents a cost of production and does not add to the economy's capacity to produce. It merely replaces what was already there. In that sense it can be thought of as an intermediate product and should not be counted toward the value of newly produced product during the year. This leads to a new concept, the *net national product,* or NNP.

The net national product is the gross national product minus depreciation charges:[2]

$$GNP - depreciation = NNP.$$

The national product accounts for 1970 showed this calculation as follows, in billions of dollars:

$$976.8 - 84.3 = 892.4.$$

This tells us that $84.3 billion of the GNP in 1970 was investment that replaced capital used up during the year, so that the net product was only $892.4 billion of goods and services.

Note this relationship: Depreciation in recent years has been about 1/11 GNP, and NNP is about 10/11 GNP.

Government Expenditures on Goods and Services

Governments at all levels are among the largest spenders in the country. Rather than try to allocate these expenditures to either consumption or investment, the national product accounts lump together all government expenditures on goods and services into a single category. The reason is essentially a practical one: it is the easiest way to do it. Furthermore, as we have already seen, government expenditures can be used as one of the chief instruments for achieving a stable economy. Putting them in a separate category helps economists analyze their influence.

Government budgets are complex documents. Some of the expenditures included in them are for direct purchases of goods and services. These enter into the national product accounts because they are payments for newly produced goods and services. This includes payments of wages and salaries to government employees—on the assumption that government services are useful and productive,[3] and are worth the cost of producing them.

---

[2] In order to confuse noneconomists, depreciation charges are called "capital consumption allowances" in the national product accounts.

[3] That assumption is not made in the Soviet Union, for example, which does not include the wages and salaries of government employees in its calculation of GNP.

But not all expenditures in government budgets are payments for newly produced goods and services. In particular, *transfer payments* are not included in the GNP, even though they make up a substantial portion of most government budgets. A transfer payment merely transfers purchasing power from one person to another without an accompanying production of new goods and services. Typical examples are veterans' pensions, interest payments on the national debt, welfare payments, and social security benefits.

The government component of GNP is large. In 1970 it was as in Table 6-3. Note that state and local governments spent more on goods and services than the federal government, and that national defense accounted for the great bulk of federal expenditures.

TABLE 6-3
Government Purchases of Goods and Services, 1970
(Billions of Dollars)

Gross national product	976.8
Government purchases of goods and services	220.5
Federal government	99.7
National defense	76.6
Other	23.1
State and local governments	120.8

Net Exports of Goods and Services

When American businessmen sell products and services to foreigners (exports), the production takes place in the United States and income is paid to American workers and businessmen. The exports represent newly produced goods and services and should be included in the U.S. GNP even though they may be consumed by foreigners. Conversely, when Americans buy goods and services produced in foreign countries (imports), the production is part of other nations' GNPs. The goods may be sold in the U.S., but they were not produced here and should not be included in our GNP.

The two sets of transactions come close to canceling each other. The difference between the two (exports minus imports) is called "net exports" and is included in the GNP. Thus if exports exceed imports, our international trade position has brought about a net increase in our output and income, and a positive contribution is made to GNP. If exports are less than imports, net exports will be negative and GNP will be reduced. Whatever the results, the impact on GNP is usually quite small. In 1970 the relevant data in the national product accounts were as in Table 6-4.

TABLE 6-4
Net Exports of Goods and Services, 1970
(Billions of Dollars)

Gross national product	976 8
Net exports (X)	3.6
Total exports (E)	62.3
Total imports (M)	58.7

Summary: Putting the Component Parts Together

We can now put together the component parts of the gross national product:

$$GNP = C + I_g + G + X.$$

These symbols stand for the four chief components of gross national product. Together with their amounts in 1970, they add up as in Table 6-5.

TABLE 6-5
Chief Components of GNP, 1970
(Billions of Dollars)

C	(personal consumption expenditures)	616.8
I_g	(gross private domestic investment)	135.8
G	(government purchases of goods and services)	220.5
X	(net exports of goods and services)	3.6
GNP	(gross national product)	976.8

Subtracting depreciation, or capital consumption allowances, will give an alternative measure, the net national product NNP. It doesn't matter where the subtraction is made. Depreciation can be subtracted from gross investment I_g to give net investment I_n, and then everything added up to give NNP. Or it can be subtracted from GNP itself, and this is the way the calculation is usually made:

GNP	(gross national product)	976.8
less:	capital consumption allowances	84.3
NNP	(net national product)	892.5

THE NATIONAL INCOME

Up to this point we have been discussing the national product and measuring the productive effort of the economy. An alternative approach is to calculate the national income NI as a measure of how much is *earned* from productive effort.

You will recall from the earlier description of the flow of spending (Chapter 4; Figure 6-1) that the flow of products in one direction is accompanied by a flow of payments in the other. The national product is derived from the upper loop; it measures final products at the prices at which they were actually bought. The national income is derived from the lower loop. It measures the incomes earned by the factors of production that have been used to turn out the national product of the upper loop.[4]

---

[4] This has been simplified to get at the essence of the national income; remember that government purchases and business investment must be included, with their products and income payments.

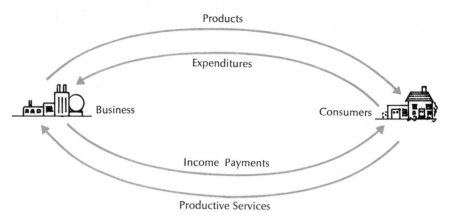

FIGURE 6-1
The Flow of Spending: Money Payments and Real Flows

Payments to the factors of production for the use of their labor, land, and capital include:

Wages, salaries and other payments made to employees (payments for social insurance, health and welfare funds, and other minor items).

Interest paid on loans.

Rental income of individuals.

Business profits, which are usually divided into—
corporate profits;
income of unincorporated enterprises.

Don't become confused by the fact that these payments are both incomes to the people who receive them and costs to the firms that pay them. This dual nature of the payments is inherent in the fact that they are part of the circular flow of spending, and that we are now measuring the national *income* in terms of the earnings of the factors of production.

Not all corporate profits become actual income for individuals. Only part is normally paid out as dividends. A substantial portion is usually retained for spending by the firm itself and another large portion is paid to the government in taxes. Nevertheless, all profits are included as part of the incomes earned in production, just as all wages and salaries are. The reason is simple: Profits are considered to be income of the owners of an enterprise whether they are paid out to the owners or not. An idea of what happens to corporate profits can be provided by the figures for 1970 (Table 6-6).

There is one additional component of the costs of producing the national product that is not part of the incomes earned by the factors or production. Certain types of business taxes are included in production costs and are embodied in the selling prices of goods and services. These are items such as local

TABLE 6-6
Corporate Profits, 1970
(Billions of Dollars)

Corporate profits before taxes (adjusted)	77.4
Dividend payments	25.2
Undistributed profits	19.2
Corporate tax liability	37.9
Inventory valuation adjustment	4.9 *
Corporate profits after taxes	44.4

* Prices change during the year, and the value of inventories will consequently move up or down. The change has to be applied to the total of corporate profits. This is the "adjustment" made in corporate profits before taxes that explains why the three component parts differ from the amount of the adjusted total.

property taxes, franchise taxes for public utilities, and similar tax obligations that do not vary with the level of output or earnings of the firm. Accounting procedures normally include these *indirect business taxes* in the costs of production for the individual firm and they are passed on to the buyer through higher prices. Since the national product is valued at current prices, these indirect business taxes are blanketed into the national product accounts, but should not be included in the national income because they are not earned by any of the factors of production. In 1970 indirect business taxes totaled $92.0 billion and made up the bulk of the difference between national income and the net national product.

TABLE 6-7
National Income, 1970
(Billions of Dollars)

Wages and salaries with supplements		599.8
Net interest payments		33.5
Rental income of individuals		22.7
Business profits		145.0
(adjusted)	77.4	
Income of unincorporated enterprises		
Corporate profits (adjusted)	67.6	
NATIONAL INCOME		801.0

THE RELATIONSHIP BETWEEN NATIONAL INCOME AND NATIONAL PRODUCT

The national income and the national product add up to different amounts. The national income does not include indirect business taxes or depreciation charges. The gross national product does, while the net national product includes indirect business taxes but not depreciation charges. All this may seem confusing, but reference to Table 6-8 will help straighten it out.

TABLE 6-8
NI, NNP, and GNP, 1970
(Billions of Dollars)

National Income	801.0
Indirect business taxes	92.0
Minor adjustment items	−0.6
Net National Product	892.4
Capital consumption allowances (depreciation)	84.3
Gross National Product	976.8

Remember that there is a reason for having the three concepts. Gross national product (GNP) is a measure of total product. Net national product (NNP) is a measure of total product minus the capital used up in production. And national income (NI) measures incomes earned. They tell us different things about the flow of spending and each has its own meaning and use. Figure 6-2 shows the relationship graphically.

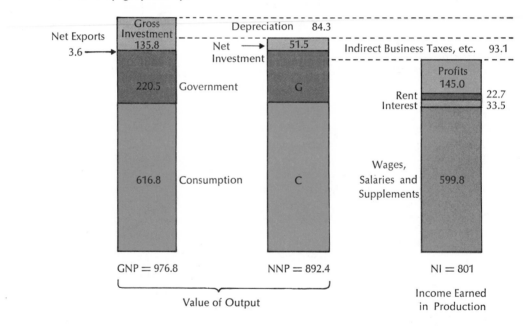

FIGURE 6-2
Relationships Between National Product and National Income Concepts
(Figures are for 1970 and are in billions of dollars.)

DISPOSABLE INCOME AND CONSUMER SAVINGS

The three concepts of gross national product, net national product, and national income are the basic measures of a nation's economic performance. They are related to each other in a systematic way, and all measure the flow of income and the value of output in slightly different ways.

A fourth concept, *disposable income,* is also useful. It measures the incomes of consumers available for spending. It is important to businessmen because it can be used to forecast how much consumers are likely to spend. It is also important to makers of economic policy and to economists because part of disposable income is normally saved. In recent years, some 5–7 percent of disposable income has been saved and about 93–95 percent spent. These savings by consumers plus the retained earnings of business firms are the chief leakages from the flow of spending that are offset by net investment as the level of output and income rises and falls.

Disposable income is derived from the national income. Subtract from the income earned in producing the national product all those portions that consumers do not receive directly or do not have available for spending. This will include such items as income taxes paid by individuals and corporations, deductions from wages and salaries for social insurance, and undistributed corporate profits. Then add income received by individuals that was not earned in production. This includes government transfer payments and payment of interest on the national debt to individuals. In addition there are a few minor items to be accounted for on both sides, and in practice the calculation is carried out somewhat differently. Table 6-9 shows how the essential computations looked in 1970.

TABLE 6-9

Relation of National Income and Disposal Income, 1970

(Billions of Dollars)

National Income		801.0
Less:	corporate profits (adjusted)	77.4
	contributions for social insurance	57.1
		666.5
Plus:	interest paid to consumers, and other items	35.4
	government transfer payments	73.9
	dividends	25.2
Personal Income		801.0
Less:	personal income taxes	116.4
Disposable Personal Income		684.7

CORRECTING FOR CHANGES IN THE PRICE LEVEL

All of the measures of national income and product use prices that prevail in the year for which the calculation is made. If comparisons are made between different years, a distortion will appear because of changes in price levels. For example, the increase in U.S. gross national product from $208.5 billion in

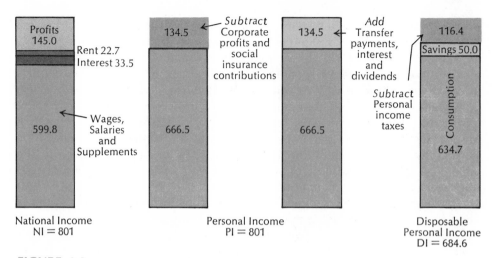

FIGURE 6-3

The Relationship Between National Income and Disposable Income

(Figures are for 1970 and are in billions of dollars.)

In 1970 the national income—the earnings of the factors of production to producing the national product—was $801 billion. Of that amount, some $685 billion was available for spending (disposable income). Most of the disposable income was spent for consumption, but about 7.3 percent ($50 billion) was saved. National income and personal income were equal, an accidental congruence that never occurred before and which probably will change when the estimates are revised.

1946 to $976.8 billion in 1970 reflects both a large increase in output *and* the inflation of prices that took place between those years. An accurate comparison requires elimination of the price increase as a factor in the calculation.

Removal of price trends from national income and product accounts is a time-consuming matter. The first step is the construction of *index numbers* of prices for the various component parts of the national product. This is an intricate process involving the following steps:

1. Selection of a "base period" from which changes are to be calculated. As this is written the year 1958 is the base period for calculation of the national product "deflators," as they are called.

2. Prices in the base period are arbitrarily given an index number value of 100, or 100 percent.

3. Prices in other years are then expressed as percentages of the base year prices.[5] For example, in 1970 consumers' durable goods stood at an index of 109.0, while nondurables were 127.3. This means that there was a 9 percent increase in prices of consumers' durable goods between 1958 and 1970, while nondurables rose in price by 27.3 percent.

---

[5] This is where the calculations become intricate. To learn how these percentages are calculated, see the appendix to this chapter.

The second step in eliminating price trends is to apply the index numbers, or deflators as they are called, to the data for national product. There will be no change in the calculations for 1958, since that is the base year and all prices have an index number of 100. But there will be changes in other years. For example, the 1970 calculation of consumers' durable goods will have to be decreased by 9 percent, that for nondurables decreased by 27.3 percent, and so on for all of the component parts of the national product for each year. When this has been done, the GNP will have been calculated on the basis of prices as they existed in 1958, and distortions due to price changes will have been eliminated.

Fortunately, all of this work has been done for the hard-working economist by government statisticians, at least for GNP. Data are available for GNP calculated in both current and 1958 prices, as shown in Figure 6-4.

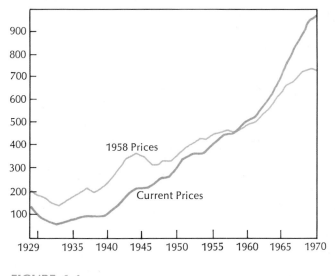

FIGURE 6-4
U.S. Gross National Product, 1929–70 in Current Prices
and 1958 Prices
(Billions of Dollars)

Correcting the GNP for changes in the price level may seem to be a neat, clean little adjustment. But there are pitfalls in using and interpreting the corrected data. The most important arise from the so-called "index number problem." When an index number is constructed for a base year, it is weighted according to the economic importance of the various products and services included. For example, very few television sets were produced in 1946, so they would not be a significant part of the GNP computations for that year. If 1946 were the base year for the price index, television sets would be given very low weights in computing the index. By 1958, however, the base year for the national prod-uct deflators, television sets were an important part of the market basket of products bought by consumers. They would be weighted heavily in computing the price index. This means that rather different results will be obtained, depending on the base year chosen, because of changes in the economy that have occurred. If the GNP is corrected on the basis of 1958 prices and weights, the data for 1946 will be distorted. Conversely, if the GNP in 1958 is corrected using 1946 prices and weights, the data for 1958 will be distorted.

The index number problem is an insoluble one. The greater the economic changes that have taken place over the period for which comparisons are being made, the greater the distortion in the results. Furthermore, comparisons over a time period will be less accurate if the base period of the index number is close to one of the terminal dates of the comparison than if the base period is in the middle. Deflators based on 1958 prices and weights give a better picture of the economy of 1959 than they do of the economy of 1929. If those two years are to be compared with the least inaccuracies, the national product deflators would have to be computed on the basis of prices in 1947 (a midpoint) rather than prices in 1958.

The same problem applies to comparisons between nations. The pattern of consumption in the United States differs from that of the Soviet Union. We consume much beer and little vodka. In Russia it is just the opposite. We use leather shoes and few made of felt. In the USSR much greater use is made of felt shoes. The GNPs of the two countries will be based on differing market baskets of goods and services and will not measure the same things. When comparisons are made, it will be like comparing apples with oranges. They are both fruits, but there the similarities stop.

The essential point is that the comparisons involve dissimilar things. The use of a common measuring rod inevitably introduces distortions whose extent cannot be accurately estimated. As a result any comparisons of national product or income are only close approximations, whether those comparisons are made within one country over time or between countries in the same year.

WHAT DOES THE NATIONAL PRODUCT MEASURE?

It is important to go beyond the definitions of national income and product, and a description of how they are calculated, to consider exactly what is being measured. Even a quick look at the concepts indicates several important limitations.

First, some output of new goods and services is not included. Work done at home for consumption by the family is left out, because it does not enter markets and is not bought and sold. This includes the services of the housewife in cooking, cleaning, and doing other household chores, and also the products of the home workshop operated by her husband. Note the anomaly of this: If the housewife were to take a job outside the home and hire someone to do housework for her, the earnings of *both* would be included in GNP. Unpaid housework done by the wife is not included. Yet an exception is made for farm production consumed on the farm. This is estimated and included in GNP.

Question: By how much is the long-term growth of U.S. GNP overstated because of the shift of women into the labor market that has taken place over the last 60 to 70 years?

Question: By how much is it understated because of the growth of home workshop production?

Answer: No one knows, and the national income accounts won't tell us.

To make the picture more complicated, some items that *do* enter markets and *are* bought and sold are not included in GNP. The most important of these are goods and services illegally traded: the services of the numbers racketeer or gambling-house operator (except where gambling is legal!), bootleg whiskey, narcotics, the services of prostitutes, and so on. Even some income that is legally earned but not reported never gets into the national income accounts at all, such as part of the cash income of some professional people who try to evade income taxes. How important are these items of the "underworld" national income and product? Would you believe 10 percent of GNP? No one knows.

There is a second limitation inherent in the national income and product accounts. The accounts include a wide variety of products and services that merely preserve the existing economy as a functioning entity, or reconstruct parts of it that have been damaged or depleted. We have already seen that one of these items, depreciation of capital, is properly deducted from gross national product to derive a net product available for consumption or investment. But what about expenditures for control of air pollution, garbage removal, sewage treatment, and so forth? Should we include in GNP the services of doctors and hospitals in treating the victims of automobile accidents or cigarette smokers with cancer of the lung? All of these items, and many more, serve to reconstruct or preserve the economy or the individual as a functioning unit. They make the system whole again rather than adding to the net product. If the national product accounts were to be used as a measure of production available for increasing the national welfare, a large number of additional deductions would have to be made.

These limitations of the national product and income accounts should be borne in mind whenever the accounts are used. The national product measures the value of current output, but not all output is included. The national income measures the incomes earned in producing the national product, but not all income is included. From the viewpoint of national welfare, too much is included.

But with all of these limitations, the national product and income accounts are reasonably useful measures of the level of economic activity and the flow of spending. They are especially useful in showing changes that take place from year to year. They are an essential tool in analyzing the way in which the economy functions and in the determination of economic policies for the present and the immediate future. Like one's wife or husband, they may not be perfect but they're all you've got.

Summary

The gross national product is the most widely used measure of a nation's economic performance. It measures the money value (at current prices) of all newly produced products and services during a year. Corrected for changes in price levels, it can be used to make comparisons over time. Divided by population, it provides a measure of output per person. Percentage changes from one year to the next can be computed to determine rates of growth. It permits rough international comparisons to be made.

The national product is a measure of total consumption, investment, government purchases of products and services, and net exports. The national income is the sum of all incomes earned in producing the national product, including wages and salaries (with fringe benefits), rent, interest and profit. When calculated accurately they should equal each other, since each is designed to measure the same flow of spending in different ways.

Key Concepts

Gross national product. Annual output of newly produced final products valued at current prices. Its components are consumption goods and services, investment goods, government purchases of goods and services and the difference between exports and imports.

$$GNP = C + I + G + X.$$

Net national product. Gross national product less capital used up in production.

$$GNP - depreciation = NNP.$$

National income.   Incomes earned by the factors of production in producing the national product. Differs from net national product by the amount of indirect business taxes and some minor adjustments.

$$\text{NNP} - \text{indirect business taxes}, \ldots = \text{NI}.$$

$$\text{NI} = \text{wages and salaries} + \text{rent} + \text{interest} + \text{profits}.$$

Disposable income.   National income plus income received but not earned minus income earned but not received. This is the amount actually available to households either to spend or to save.

Appendix 6

MEASUREMENT OF CHANGES
IN THE GENERAL LEVEL OF PRICES

It is easy enough to measure price changes over a period of time for single goods. It is much more difficult to get a measurement of the overall change in prices. Prices of goods do not change at the same rate, and prices of some goods may be falling even when the general level (average) of prices is rising, or vice versa. Say, for example, that we are interested in comparing the price level of 1964 with that of 1960. If bread were the only commodity produced in the economy, our task would be simple. Knowing the average price for bread in the two years, we could compute the ratio of these prices (called a *price relative*):

$$\frac{\text{Average price of bread in 1964}}{\text{Average price of bread in 1960}} = \frac{\$0.16}{\$0.14} = 1.143, \quad \text{or} \quad 114.3\%.$$

This tells us that the price of bread in 1964 was 114.3 percent of the price of bread in 1960, or that the price of bread was 14.3 percent greater in 1964 than in 1960.

But one commodity will not do. We are interested in measuring the average price change for a large number of commodities, for example, of consumer retail purchases (as measured by the Consumer Price Index), where prices of different commodities change by different percentage amounts.

To see how such an index is obtained, assume for the sake of simplicity that bread, shirts, and coal are the only commodities that consumers buy, and that the quantities purchased in 1964 are of the same quality and type but differing in amount. (In reality, several hundred goods and services are included in the Consumer Price Index.) The data for our example are given in Table 6A-1.

TABLE 6A-1
Data for Computing Simple Price Index

	1960		1964		Price Relatives (1964 Price ÷ 1960 Price)
	Price	Quantity	Price	Quantity	
Bread	$0.14/loaf	2,000	$0.16/loaf	2,200	$1.143
Shirts	$4.00/shirt	25	$3.50/shirt	30	$0.875
Coal	$12.00/ton	20	$15.00/ton	15	$1.250

If we wanted to keep our efforts simple, we could just add the prices in each year and compare the totals. The total for 1960 is $16.14, while the total for 1964 is $18.66.

Prices appear to have risen, but by how much? We might calculate a simple ratio to get the level in 1964 as compared with 1960:

$$\frac{18.66}{16.14} = 1.156, \quad \text{or } 115.6\%.$$

We can get an answer that way, but it's not very satisfactory. The method requires adding loaves, shirts, and tons, and this procedure is meaningless.

Let's try again. The price relatives show the increase in individual prices from 1960 to 1964. We could add them together and then get a simple arithmetic mean:

$$\frac{1.143 + 0.875 + 1.250}{3} = 1.089, \quad \text{or } 108.9\%.$$

This is a little better; but not much, because it assigns equal importance to each of the three commodities in consumers' budgets.

We are obviously on the wrong track. The trouble is that we have been single-mindedly focusing on prices and ignoring the fact that consumers buy a market basket of different goods that will have a total cost to them. The average price level is associated with that market basket, and not with just the individual prices.

Let's try that approach. We calculate the cost of the consumers' market basket in 1964, compare it with a similar figure for 1960, and compute the percentage increase:

$$\frac{0.16(2200) + 3.50(30) + 15.00(15)}{0.14(2000) + 4.00(25) + 12.00(20)} = \frac{682.0}{620.0} = 1.100, \quad \text{or } 110.0\%.$$

The trouble with this procedure is that there are two variables, prices *and* quantities. We are interested in measuring the change in only one, prices. The other will have to be held constant so that it does not affect the results.

That's easy to do. We'll pick 1960 as the base, and use the market basket for that year. We can get the value of that market basket in both 1964 and 1960 prices, and calculate the percentage change:

$$\frac{0.16(2000) + 3.50(25) + 15.00(20)}{0.14(2000) + 4.00(25) + 12.00(20)} = \frac{707.5}{620.0} = 1.141, \quad \text{or } 114.1\%.$$

This tells us how much it would cost in 1964 compared with 1960 to buy the same amounts of these goods that were purchased in 1960. The year 1960 is the *base year,* with which the level of prices in 1964 is compared. Therefore 1960 = 100. This is a very simplified version of the method used in computing the Consumer Price Index.

We can now say that since prices in 1964 were, on the average, 114.1 percent of 1960 prices, the value of the dollar in 1964 was 87.5 percent of its value in 1960:

$$\frac{100.0}{114.1} \times 100 = 87.5.$$

THE "INDEX NUMBER PROBLEM"

The method we have just worked through is good, but it has some flaws. The index number for any year is expressed as a percentage of the base year. But if the pattern of consumer purchases changes significantly, the comparison will not be very meaningful. That's why a comparison of prices in 1964 as compared with 1864 is only a very rough one. Who buys a buggy today? Or who bought a television set then?

Different market baskets of goods can make a big difference in the results. Suppose, for instance, we were to shift the base year from 1960 to 1964 in the example used above. Between those two years, consumer purchases of bread rose by 10 percent and of shirts by 20 percent, but purchases of coal fell by 25 percent. A rather different pattern of consumer buying has appeared. How much difference will this make in the price index? Here are the calculations:

$$\frac{0.14(2200) + 4.00(30) + 12.00(15)}{0.16(2200) + 3.50(30) + 15.00(15)} = \frac{608.0}{682.0} = 0.891, \quad \text{or } 89.1\%.$$

When 1964 is the base year, then, prices in 1960 were 89.1 percent of 1964 prices. The increase between 1960 and 1964 was 12.2 percent,

$$\frac{100}{89.1} \times 100 = 112.2,$$

instead of the 14.1 percent increase calculated from the 1960 base. Which answer is correct? Did prices in our hypothetical economy increase between 1960 and 1964 by 12.2 percent or 14.1 percent? Actually, *both* answers are correct, depending on which base year is chosen!

Statisticians have devised several ways to minimize this "index number problem." But more calculations only take the final result further from reality without entirely solving the problem. The government statisticians who compute our most widely used price indices have wisely decided to use the simple methods of computation explained here and let those who use the indices worry about how far their conclusions can be pushed.

CHANGES WITHIN THE INDEX

Index numbers are a composite made up of many parts. They measure an average, or consensus, of elements whose behavior may differ widely from the group as a whole. Indeed, it would be very surprising if the component parts of a price index moved similarly. The reason we need an index is *because* they do not. No one price can be used as a proxy for the others, so we have to construct an index that we can use. For example, in Figure 6-5 look at the way some major component parts of the Consumer Price Index have changed in the years since 1946.

While the average level of prices paid by consumers rose by some 66 percent in the twenty years from 1946 to 1966, food prices rose by 71 percent, nonfood items by 43 percent, and services by 95 percent. These differences are quite large, and are another illustration of the fact that averages can conceal large disparities.

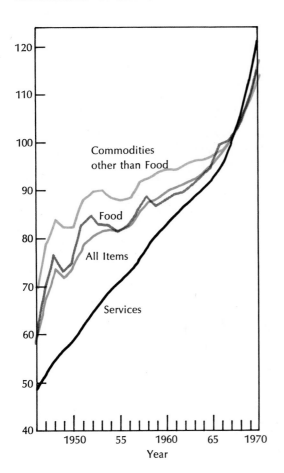

FIGURE 6-5
Consumer Price Index and
Major Components, 1946–70
(1967 = 100)
(Note: 1970 data are based on an
eleven-month average. Source:
Economic Report of the President,
1971.)

Using the Data: An Evaluation of the U.S. Economy

7

The national accounts are the starting point for most evaluations of economic performance. Although they are only a simple yardstick they can be used to develop measures of economic growth, the uses to which production is put, and the amount of unused potential production, or economic slack. A full picture requires other data as well, particularly regarding such things as employment and unemployment, and movement of price levels, and patterns of income distribution. Comparisons over time and between countries in these and other areas enable economists to arrive at conclusions about how well the economy has been performing its task of producing and distributing material things. This chapter will focus on the facts about the performance of the American economy and try to identify some principal areas in which that performance might be improved.

MEASURING ECONOMIC GROWTH

Measurement of national product and income opens up ways of measuring overall economic growth. The rate of change in GNP from one year to the next can be readily calculated. For example:

$$\frac{\text{GNP in 1966}}{\text{GNP in 1965}} = \frac{647.7}{614.4} = 1.055.$$

The figures are in billions of dollars, corrected for changes in the price level (using 1958 prices). The computation shows that GNP in constant dollars was 5.5 percent higher in 1966 than in 1965. When periods longer than one year are used, an average annual increase can be computed by use of the standard compound interest formula.[1] Or better yet, a simple percentage change between any two years can be computed as above and converted into an average annual change by using tables that have already been calculated by hard-working digital computers.[2]

---

[1] This formula is written

$$X_2 = X_1(1 + r)^n,$$

where X_2 = quantity at end of period;
$\quad X_1$ = quantity at beginning of period;
$\quad r$ = relative increase or decrease, expressed as a decimal;
$\quad n$ = number of years.

[2] The most readily available source is U.S. Department of Commerce, *Long Term Economic Growth*, Washington, 1966, Appendix 1.

The long-term trend of economic growth in the United States has been impressive but not spectacular. One set of estimates made by Raymond Goldsmith of New York University goes all the way back to the early years of industrialization in the U.S., even though the data on GNP before 1870 is weak. Goldsmith's estimates showed an average annual rate of growth of GNP of 3.66 percent over the 120 years from 1839 to 1959, in constant prices. Since population grew at almost 2 percent annually over this period, the growth of GNP per capita was just 1.64 percent.[3] Goldsmith's estimates showed a gradual slowing of the GNP growth rate when the whole period was divided into 40-year subperiods, but not in the growth of GNP per capita (Table 7–1).

TABLE 7–1
Rate of Growth of GNP and GNP per Capita,
1839–1959, Goldsmith Study
(Average Annual Percent Increase)

	Entire Period 1839–1959	40–Year Subperiods		
		1839–79	1879–1919	1919–59
GNP	3.66	4.31	3.72	2.97
GNP/capita	1.64	1.55	1.76	1.64

Source: *Employment, Growth and Price Levels,* Hearings Before the Joint Economic Committee, Congress of the United States, Washington, 1959, Part 2, p. 271.

Goldsmith's findings have been corroborated by similar work done by the U.S. Department of Commerce, which calculated growth rates for the period since 1870, eliminating the early years for which the data are less reliable. Those findings are shown in Table 7–2.

TABLE 7–2
Rate of Growth of GNP and GNP per Capita,
1870–1965, U.S. Dept. of Commerce Data
(Average Annual Percent Increase)

	Entire Period 1870–1965	Subperiods		
		1870–1913	1913–29	1929–65
GNP	3.6	4.5	2.8	3.1
GNP/capita	1.9	2.2	1.3	1.8

Source: U.S. Dept. of Commerce, *Long Term Economic Growth,* Washington, 1966, p. 101.

These estimates provide some guidelines for evaluating the recent performance of the American economy. The growth rate for the recent decades since

[3] A reasonably accurate measure of the growth rate of GNP per capita can be obtained by subtracting the population growth rate from the GNP growth rate for the same period. There are more exact ways of doing it, but since population figures are not very accurate anyway and figures for GNP are estimates, there isn't much point in elaborate calculations.

World War II of 3.9 percent per year (1946–1969) is better than the presumably declining long-run trend would have led us to expect. However, the very slow growth of GNP in 1953–60 of less than 2.5 percent annually, and of GNP per capita of about 0.5 percent in those years, is clearly below the level of performance we have come to expect in the past. The rapid growth in GNP in 1960–69, about 4.5 percent per year, is clearly above the long-term trend and can be explained in part as the result of eliminating the slack that developed during the previous period (1953–60).

The growth of GNP per capita is a particularly important piece of data. It is probably the best single indicator of growth in living standards, since it takes into account the rise in population. For example, if a nation has a GNP growth rate of 5 percent annually, but population growth averages 6 percent per year, living standards will be falling and poverty increasing. Growth in welfare requires a positive rate of growth in GNP per person.

In the United States, an average annual increase in GNP per person of 1.6–2 percent has been an acceptable one in the past. It has been sufficient to satisfy, at least minimally and perhaps more, Americans' desires for rising living standards, success, and growth of welfare. It can be used as a benchmark to aim for as a minimum goal in the future. It can also be used as a warning signal if growth of GNP per person should rise more slowly, as it did during 1953–1960. When that happens, the average increase in living standards to which Americans have become accustomed is not being achieved, and we can expect frustration, resentment, and rising social tensions.

Some argue that economic growth must slow down as an economy matures. We noted earlier that both the Goldsmith and Department of Commerce data indicated a slowing down in the growth rate for GNP as a long-term trend. This is only a historical trend, however; it shows what happened in the past, but does not *necessarily* indicate what may be expected in the future. In Chapter 8, when we analyze the potential rate of economic growth in the immediate future, it will become evident that a GNP growth rate of 4 and perhaps 4.5 percent annually is quite feasible. This is well above the long-term trend, whether measured from 1839 or 1870, and is about equal to the growth rate of the earlier years, when the American economy was in its full youthful vigor. Contrary to popular impression, an economy does not necessarily generate slower growth rates as it reaches maturity.

International comparisons provide another way of viewing a nation's economic growth. When the U.S. is compared with other countries, three important conclusions emerge:

1. For the entire period since 1870, U.S. economic growth has been as rapid as that of any other major industrial nation and faster than most.

2. Between 1913 and 1950, most of the major industrial nations performed about equally poorly, so far as growth rates are concerned, but the U.S. did not do quite so badly as most.

3. Since 1950, a number of large industrial nations have grown much more rapidly than the U.S. Our growth performance has lagged, not in relation to the long-term trend in the U.S., but in relation to the recent speedup in growth elsewhere.

The data in Table 7-3 show these relationships:

TABLE 7-3
Rate of Growth of GNP for Selected Industrial Nations, 1870–1964
(Average Annual Percent Increase)

	Entire Period	Subperiods			
	1870–1964	1870–1913	1913–29	1929–50	1950–64
United States	3.6	4.5	2.8	2.7	3.6
Japan	3.8	3.3	3.9	0.6	9.9
Germany	2.8	2.8	0.4	1.9	7.0
United Kingdom	1.9	2.1	0.8	1.6	3.0
France	1.7	1.6	1.7	0.0	4.8
Italy	2.0	1.4	1.8	1.0	5.8
Canada	3.5	3.8	2.4	3.2	4.3

Source: U.S. Dept. of Commerce, *Long Term Economic Growth,* Washington, 1966, p. 101.

THE END USES OF GNP: U.S. AND WORLD MILITARY EXPENDITURES

Growth is not an end in itself. An economic system functions to serve people and to meet their needs. An economy that is growing relatively rapidly devotes a substantial portion of its GNP to capital investment of a growth-producing sort. A less rapidly growing economy will devote a larger share of its annual output to other uses. It may put heavy stress on production for consumers—or it may build pyramids, maintain a large bureaucracy, fight wars, or shoot at the moon. Whatever may be the value of these other activities, there is a significant trade-off between growth-producing investment and all other uses for current output.

The Soviet Union is a good illustration. Soviet economic policy has consistently emphasized economic growth at the expense of increases in living standards. Resources and savings have been channeled into investments designed to expand the capacity to produce, and Soviet planning until recent years has almost single-mindedly stressed expansion of output. The results have been spectacular, with increases in industrial production consistently falling in the range of 6–10 percent per year, even when measured by suspicious Western economists. Agricultural production has not matched industrial production, which pulls the economy's growth rate to levels below that of industry. But the reason for the backwardness of agriculture has been the planners' heavy emphasis on industrial production and their relative lack of concern for living standards.

The Soviet economy maintains high growth rates *because* its living standards are kept low. The Soviet economy, in comparison with the American economy, simply allocates a larger proportion of its GNP to investment. As long as that keeps up, their GNP will grow more rapidly than ours, assuming that the same technology is available in both countries, that neither one has a major advantage in its resource base, and that the investment funds and resources are used rationally.

Estimates are available for the final uses to which national product is put in the United States and the Soviet Union. The most recent is for the year 1955, and is shown in Figure 7-1. Even though the Soviet GNP in 1955 was somewhat less than half that of the United States, the Soviet planners were able to invest a larger proportion of their final output than the American economy did. The resources came primarily from keeping consumption standards down.

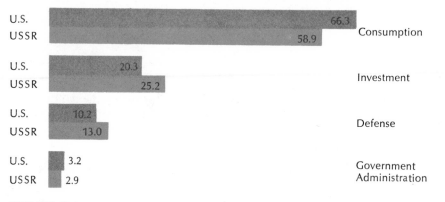

FIGURE 7-1
GNP by End Use in the USSR and the United States, 1955
(Percent of Total)
(Source: Morris Bornstein, "A Comparison of Soviet and United States National Product," U.S. Congress, Joint Economic Committee, Comparisons of the United States and Soviet Economies, *Washington, 1959, Part II, pp. 377–95.)*

Some might take comfort from the fact that although the rate of investment was lower in the U.S., total investment was higher. This was true because our GNP was more than twice that of the Soviet Union. After all, 20 percent of 100 is larger than 25 percent of 50. But this still will not prevent the USSR from eventually catching up, as long as their rate of growth is more rapid. In a race of infinite duration between two participants, the faster runner will always win.[4]

---

[4] Remember Zeno's Paradox from your first course in geometry? Achilles runs twice as fast as the hare, which has a 10-yard start. By the time Achilles covers the 10 yards the hare is 5 yards further on. When he covers those 5 yards, the hare is still 2½ yards ahead. Zeno couldn't prove that Achilles ever caught the hare, but we can, with the aid of analytical geometry and semi-logarithmic charts. A modern version of this paradox might be called the "Richard Nixon fallacy." The Republican presidential candidate in 1960 tried to show that the Soviet economy would never catch up to ours, in spite of a faster growth rate, because the U.S. had such a large lead.

The trade-off between consumption and investment should be clear enough. Aesop understood it: A nation of live-it-up-now grasshoppers can have a higher standard of living than a nation of store-it-up-now ants. But this may mean serious problems for the next generation of grasshoppers of a kind that future generations of ants will not have to face.

A similar trade-off exists between military production and other uses of output. The more a nation spends for armaments, the less it can spend either for current consumption or for expansion of output. If we are justified in assuming that modern economic policies can keep a nation's output at or very close to its capacity, *any* expenditures for armaments must result in a loss of either consumption or investment, and probably both. In terms of economic welfare, peace is preferable to war and disarmament preferable to arms races. A respectable rate of economic growth will make more output available for all uses, including consumption, investment, and armaments. But the share going to armaments could instead be used to increase both the rate of economic growth and the current standard of living even more.

A recent study of world expenditures on armaments, by Emile Benoit of Columbia University, indicates the magnitude of the sacrifices that are made by the United States and the Soviet Union in their contest for world power. Benoit estimated that some $154 billion was spent on armaments by all countries in 1966. The U.S. and the USSR accounted for two-thirds of the total (about $100 billion), with the U.S. spending about 60 percent of that. In armaments expenditure per capita, the United States was far ahead of everyone else, as shown by Figure 7-2.

The trend of U.S. military expenditures has been upward in this century, both in amount and as a percentage of GNP. The fluctuations caused by wars has been very great, but the trend can be shown by looking at military spending during relatively peaceful times.[5] Table 7–4 shows the data for each census year since 1900 (1913 is used instead of 1910 because data for 1910 are not available). The large expenditures for 1920 reflect incomplete demobilization after World War I. Note that a fivefold increase in military expenditures from 1900 to 1930 represented no increase in the proportion of GNP, and that the years after World War II were the ones that showed a significant shift in the proportion of GNP going into military and military-related uses.

Some idea of the magnitude of U.S. military and military-related expenditures can be obtained by making a few comparisons. The total of $63.5 billion in 1960 was:

1. About 50 percent greater than the total GNP of India, which had a population of about 400 million persons.
2. Equal to 85 percent of U.S. gross private domestic investment in 1960.
3. Equal to 20 percent of consumption expenditures in 1960.

---

[5] The U.S. has been either actively at war or has had military forces overseas and in occupation of other countries in every year since 1898 except 1904, 1908–9, and 1935–40.

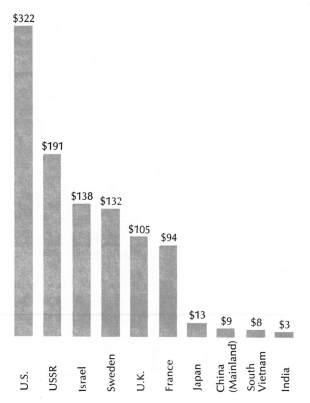

FIGURE 7-2
Estimated Military Expenditures per Person,
for Selected Countries, 1966
(In Dollars)
Estimates were made in terms of each nation's
currency. The currency was converted to dollars, and
then the figures adjusted to account for differences
in purchasing power.

The point should be clear: Military expenditures are one use to which the resources of an affluent nation can be put. But even an affluent nation must give up significant amounts of current consumption and economic growth if it wishes world power.

MEASURING ECONOMIC SLACK

Even a growing economy may fail to utilize fully its human resources and its capital. Unemployed resources, both human and physical, can be present in an economy whose output increases from year to year, whose productive capacity grows, and whose work force increases in efficiency and effectiveness. Growth can take place with varying degrees of tautness and slack.

TABLE 7–4
U.S. Military and Military-Related Expenditures, Selected Years, 1900–1960

Year	Amount (billions of dollars)	Percentage of GNP
1900	0.4	2.1
1913	0.5	1.3
1920	5.8	6.5
1930	2.0	2.2
1940	3.2	3.2
1950	29.3	10.3
1960	63.5	12.6

Source: (Data on military and military-related expenditures): Solomon Fabricant, *The Trend of Government Activity in the United States Since 1900* (New York: National Bureau of Economic Research, 1952, pp. 240–241, for 1900, 1913, and 1920; *Budget of the United States Government,* 1932, 1942, 1952, and 1962, for the period from 1930 onward. The U.S. Government had no official budget before 1921.

Note: The definition of military-related expenditures is a tricky one. Amounts in the table included the following budget items for 1960: Department of Defense, Veterans' Administration, Atomic Energy Commission, Mutual Security Funds, National Security Council, Civil and Defense Mobilization, Central Intelligence Agency, National Aeronautics and Space Administration, U.S. Information Agency, Selective Service System, Defense Materials Activities of the General Services Administration, Department of State, and Interest on the Public Debt. The reasons for including the last two in their entirety are (1) the great bulk of the national debt has been incurred during wars, and (2) a substantial portion of Department of State activities are concerned with supporting the overseas military activities and commitments of the federal government. The over inclusion that occurs because of those two items is balanced, in part at least, by not including military-related activities in several other departments.

For earlier years a similar group of expenditures was included, although the specific titles of the budget items may have differed somewhat.

The amounts have not been corrected for changes in the price level, but this does not affect the percentage of GNP column.

Employment and Unemployment

Employment and unemployment offer the best indicator of slack in the economy and of underutilization of resources. Large numbers of people willing and able to work but unable to find jobs, as in the 1930s, are a sure indication of sub-par performance, while an economy that keeps unemployment to a bare minimum shows that it is producing at or near its capacity.

The American economy has had mixed success in maintaining full employment. The record since 1929 shows that total employment has expanded very substantially. Nevertheless, there have been periods of very high unemployment, periods of great tightness in the labor markets, and periods of significant slack. Figure 7-3 tells the story.

There are several types of unemployment. One is *frictional unemployment*. This type is due to the changes that are continually taking place in a relatively free economy and it is present at all times. A worker may move from one job to

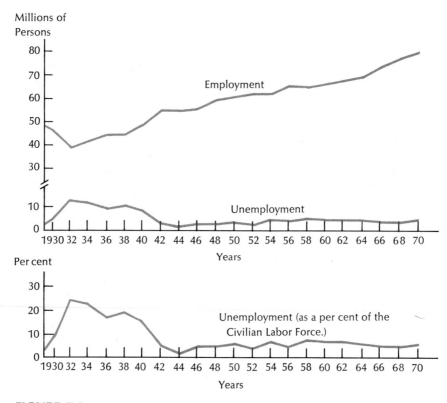

FIGURE 7-3
Employment and Unemployment in the United States, 1929–70
(*Sources:* Economic Report of the President, 1971 *and U.S. Department of Labor,*
Bureau of Labor Statistics, Employment and Earnings, May 1962.)

another and be unemployed for a short time while in transition. A young
person seeking his first job is very likely to be unemployed, sometimes for
weeks or months, before he can find one. Some older workers may also be
entering or leaving the work force and temporarily unemployed as they do so.
Unemployment also occurs because some industries have seasonal peaks, during
which employment is increased temporarily. *Seasonal unemployment* is
sometimes defined as a separate type, but it is included here in the more general
"frictional" category. Frictional unemployment is almost always of short duration but in a large, varied, and flexible economy it can be quite substantial.
Estimates made by economists indicate that frictional unemployment usually
amounts to about 1.5 to 2.5 percent of the labor force in the United States.

A second type of unemployment is *structural unemployment*. It is caused by
the economic changes that eliminate jobs in a situation where workers do not
have the flexibility necessary to find other jobs. For example, mechanization
of coal mines in Appalachia threw hundreds of thousands of miners out of work.

Some were able to adapt by moving to other areas or by finding other jobs in the region. But many were unable to adapt because they lacked the skill or education required in other jobs, because they were middle-aged or partially disabled, or because family responsibilities made a geographical move very difficult. Any kind of economic change can create structural unemployment. Rapid technological change can make skills obsolete, industrial plants may move or fail altogether, and natural resources may become exhausted. Some workers will find it hard to adapt to these changes because of their skill and educational deficiencies, location, age, health, or race. Conditions beyond their control throw them on the labor scrap heap.

No one knows the extent of structural unemployment, although a vigorous debate has been going on among U.S. economists in recent years over whether the number of structurally unemployed has been increasing. Estimates of the total vary. A rough, informal guess would place the present number at about 1–2 percent of the U.S. labor force. That would make a total of some 750,000 to 1,500,000 persons who are economically obsolete.

A third type of unemployment is due to inadequate levels of economic activity, most commonly called *cyclical unemployment*.[6] Whenever the flow of spending is inadequate, as Chapter 4 pointed out, business firms will retrench and reduce their work forces. The situation will not improve until total spending is increased enough to absorb the unemployed. The basic problem in this case is inadequate total demand.

All of these types of unemployment involve workers who are willing to work. Indeed, the official definition of unemployment in the United States includes the requirement that an unemployed individual must be "actively seeking work" to be included in the count. The data shown in Figure 7-3 and the official unemployment rates reflect this stipulation. When a worker becomes discouraged because of long-term unemployment and is no longer actively seeking work he is not included in the count of the work force and is not classed as unemployed. Many of the "structurally unemployed" fall in this group. However, if economic conditions change and more jobs become available, many of these "hidden" unemployed will gravitate back into the labor market and seek work once more. This adds a fourth type, *hidden unemployment,* involving those workers who are not actively in the labor market but who would seek work if the economy were operating at higher levels.[7]

---

[6] This is a bad name, stemming from the days when business cycles were thought to be the chief cause of departures from full employment. We now know that it is possible for a modern economy to stagnate well below full employment and still have business cycles whose *peaks* leave millions unemployed because of inadequate demand. This was one of the lessons of the 1930s.

[7] Hidden unemployment is placed in a separate category only because it is not officially measured as part of the unemployment statistics. Its causes are the same as any of the other types, but it is not regularly reported and its extent can only be estimated.

A period of generally high unemployment can create a large pool of hidden unemployed. This seems to have occurred during the second half of the 1950s in the United States when slowed economic growth caused unemployment rates to rise. By the early 1960s, according to various official and unofficial estimates, hidden unemployment totaled some 1.5 to 2.5 million persons—in addition to the measured unemployment of almost 4 million in 1960. When the turnabout in economic performance came in the early 1960s and the growth of GNP speeded up, official unemployment rates remained high for several years as many of the hidden unemployed moved back into the labor market.

What then is "full employment"? In this book we shall use an unemployment rate of 2.5–3 percent based on the unemployment measurements as a reasonable full-employment level. This definition includes frictional unemployment, since this type is necessary and often useful in a flexible economy. It also includes some structural unemployment—the portion that training and relocation programs cannot effectively eliminate. Presumably, the incomes of most of the workers in these categories could be kept at decent levels by proper unemployment insurance and other income maintenance programs. But it does not include any cyclical unemployment. As for hidden unemployment, maintenance of GNP at levels that kept official unemployment rates in the range of 2.5–3 percent for a long period of time would probably eliminate a substantial amount of hidden unemployment by drawing those affected slowly back into the labor market.

Utilization of Production Capacity

Another way to determine whether the economy is using its resources fully is to measure the extent to which production facilities are being used. Levels of actual production can be compared with estimates of what could be produced if the existing capacity were fully utilized. Statistics in these comparisons are available for the manufacturing sector of the U.S. economy, and are the basis for Figure 7-4.

The index of capacity utilization is especially useful in identifying periods of inadequate aggregate demand. Recessions show up very clearly; note the drops in the index for 1949, 1954, and 1958. The excess production capacity that built up between 1953 and 1960 is also very clearly shown, as well as the long economic expansion after 1960. Finally, the unwholesome accumulation of excess capacity after 1966 and the 1970 recession can be seen.

Don't assume that "full capacity" is 100 percent, however. Most manufacturing firms like to operate with a little slack, both because emergencies may need to be taken care of if they should arise and because costs of production start rising near the upper limit of capacity. For these reasons, "full capacity" is reached when the index rises to around the 92–94 percent range. Even with that qualification, the U.S. economy rarely operates its manufacturing plants at full capacity.

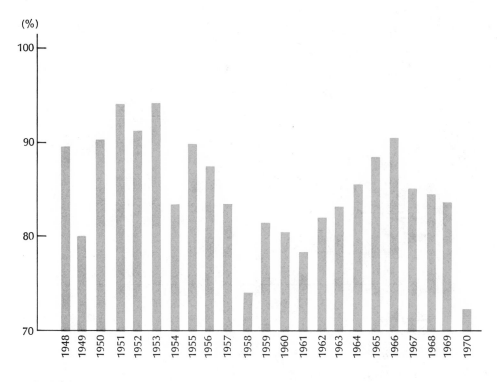

FIGURE 7-4
Utilization of Manufacturing Capacity, 1948–70
(Annual Average, in Percent)

Lost Output

It is possible to estimate the losses in output that occur because of unemployment and excess plant capacity. Rough estimates can be made by calculating
the level of GNP under the assumption of a fixed level of minimal unemployment, such as 3 percent of the work force. Alternatively, an estimate can assume
a steady rate of growth in GNP, such as 4.5 percent annually, starting from a
base year like 1946. Even more complicated methods can be developed to
estimate the potential level of GNP if labor and productive capacity were fully
utilized. These estimates of what might have been can then be compared with
the level of GNP actually realized to determine the amount of "lost" GNP due
to failure to use labor and plant capacity fully.

These comparisons can be shocking. For example, if the American economy
could have kept unemployment rates consistently at a level of 3 percent for the
twenty-four years from 1946 through 1970, the total GNP for the entire period
would have been about $650 billion more than it was. This is about the same as
the total GNP for the entire year of 1966. Figure 7-5 shows that only in 1951–53
did the economy eliminate its slack, and that from 1954 through 1966 production
was significantly below the growth trend of potential GNP.

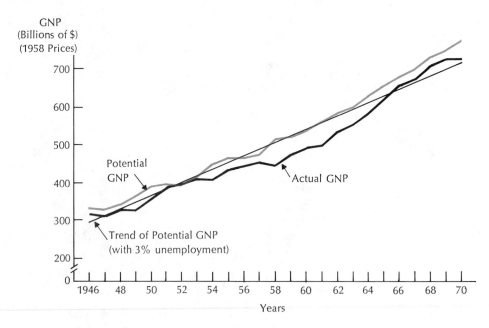

FIGURE 7-5
Economic Slack in the U.S. Economy, 1946–70

Potential GNP at 3% unemployment was derived by applying Okun's formula to actual GNP in constant prices (1958 = 100):

$$P = A [1 + .032 (U - 3)], \text{ for 3\% unemployment.}$$

Where P stands for potential GNP in year t,
        A stands for actual GNP in year t, and
        U stands for the unemployment rate in year t.

The trend line drawn in for potential GNP was derived by applying a least squares regression to the potential GNP data. No adjustment was made for hidden unemployment. *(On Okun's formula see Arthur M. Okun, "Potential GNP: Its Measurement and Significance," American Statistical Association, Proceedings: Business Economics Statistical Section, 1962, pp. 98–104.)*

The lost output is only the beginning, however. An economy operating consistently without slack would have generated higher levels of investment that were actually achieved, and economic growth would have been more rapid. In other words, the trend of growth of potential GNP would have been steeper. Even if this feedback effect is ignored, the loss to the economy was great. It was equal to almost 6 percent of the actual output over the 20-year period.

PRICES

Stability of prices is considered by many to be an important goal. Rising prices can eliminate much of the gains from economic growth. They can also damage the economic position of a nation in the international economy if the prices of its exports rise relative to prices of similar goods produced elsewhere. Rising prices also eat away the value of savings and force people on fixed incomes to reduce their level of living. Economic life would clearly be much simpler if prices did not rise and inflation were not a threat. For these reasons and others, many people feel that an economy is not functioning well unless it can maintain a "reasonable" degree of price stability.

But there are other considerations. Prices today are higher than they have been at some times in the past, yet we are much better off now than we were then. The growth of the American economy to affluence and potential abundance has not been hindered by rising or even by erratic prices. Indeed, a favorite bon mot among economists is to define inflation as "your money won't buy as much as it would have during the Depression, when you didn't have any."

Nevertheless, rising prices have eaten up a substantial portion of the increase in GNP that has occurred in recent years. Between 1946 and 1970, the GNP measured in current dollars rose by $768 billion. But rising prices represent about 46 percent of the gain. The increase measured in constant dollars (1958 prices) was only $412 billion. The difference, $356 billion, was the result of rising prices rather than increased output.

The rate at which prices rose was not overly rapid. Wholesale prices rose at an average annual rate of 1.7 percent and retail prices 2.0 percent. A large portion of these increases came in the first few years after World War II, when the economy was adjusting to peacetime conditions, and during the war period after 1966. If we measure the increase in prices from 1948 through 1966 instead of 1946 through 1970, the average annual rate of increase is only 1.0 percent for wholesale prices and 1.6 percent for retail prices.

Furthermore, part of the postwar price increases were more statistical than real. The price indices make no adjustment for changes in the quality of products. For example, if a product is improved but sells for the same price as before, its "real" value has gone up, but its money value has remained the same and will cause no change in the price index. A substantial amount of product improvement in the 1946–66 period was not reflected in price increases. As a result, part of the rise in prices (no one knows how much) has been offset because consumers are getting more for their money now than they were earlier.

It should be clear by now that price increases of the sort that have occurred in the U.S. economy since World War II are not of primary significance. An even better perspective can be obtained by looking at how they fit into the long-range historical trend. We already know, from the discussion of price indices, that these historical comparisons can be unreliable, but they can at least give a general picture of trends. Keeping that in mind, let's look at an index of wholesale prices for the years since 1800. This includes basic materials as a substantial component and is therefore less subject to distortion than a retail price index would be.

The most striking fact about Figure 7-6 is not the long-term increase in prices, but the wide fluctuations that have occurred. Every large war has brought a

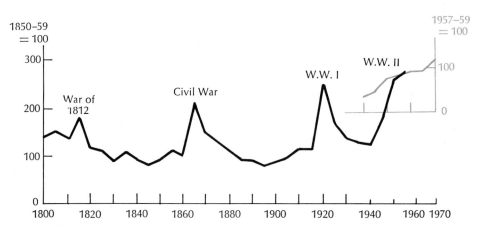

FIGURE 7-6

Wholesale Prices, in the United States, 1800–1970

The wholesale price index used for the 1940–70 period is more comprehensive than the earlier one. This fact probably accounts for its greater stability. A portion of the wide fluctuations in the earlier series is due to the fact that the data are from only five large cities and include a large component of foodstuffs.

(Sources: 1800–1958: Employment, Growth and Price Levels, Hearings Before the Joint Economic Committee, Congress of the United States, *Washington, 1959, Part 2, pp. 395–397. 1958–1971:* Economic Report of the President, 1971.)

period of rapid inflation, followed by a period of large price decline when the war ended—except World War II, and we shall have more to say about that shortly. A second fact is that the long-range trend has only a slight upward tilt. From peak to peak—1814 to 1864 to 1919 to 1970—the average annual increase is negligible and could easily be caused by statistical error. The same is true when the trend is measured from trough to trough—1830 to 1849 to 1897. Even if we try the most unfavorable comparison possible, from the low point of 1897 to the high prices of 1970, the average annual increase is only about 1 to 1.5 percent.

And remember that throughout this whole period a continent was being settled and developed, a great industrial and population expansion occurred, and standards of living rose to new heights. Whatever the effect on individuals may have been, neither rising prices nor falling prices, nor wide fluctuations nor relative price stability seem to have had a significant impact on the growth performance of the economy.

In several respects, however, the movement of prices in the last two decades has been different from what we have previously experienced. First, part of the wartime inflation during World War II was postponed until after the war by price controls, rationing, and other measures during the war. Second, the typical postwar deflation, which was usually accompanied by hard times for both business and labor, has not occurred. Third, prices have been remarkably stable since the late 1940s, moving upward significantly only after escalation of the Viet Nam war in the late 1960s. The price increases that cause so much comment in the press and in the political arena seem little more than blips when compared with the fluctuations of the past.

Nevertheless, the debate over inflation in recent years is important. Significant economic changes may have occurred with respect to the movement of prices and the forces affecting them. Some argue that prices now tend to go up but not down. Others are concerned about the role of labor unions and collective bargaining in imparting an upward push to wages and costs of production. Still others point to the full-employment policies of government as a source of upward stimulus to prices. Some worry that easy money policies stimulate price increases.

One point on which most economists agree is that there is a trade-off between unemployment and price stability in a modern economy. At some point well before full employment is reached prices start to rise as labor markets tighten up and employers compete more sharply for the limited number of persons available for hiring. Where that point is and what determines its location are unresolved issues, but the fact remains that most economists recognize a serious conflict between the elimination of slack and the maintenance of stable prices.

There are sticky economic problems involved in the problem of inflation. They will be discussed at length later in this book. At this stage, however, we can leave the issue temporarily unresolved, noting only that, whatever those difficulties may be, prices in the United States have been relatively stable for the last two decades.

THE GROWTH OF AFFLUENCE

A rising gross national product, together with a growing GNP per person, means growing affluence. At least with respect to material things, Americans now are better off than those of a generation ago, who were in turn richer than their parents. We can roughly approximate a measure of the growth of affluence by using the data on family income gathered by the Bureau of the Census.

In 1947, the median family income in the United States was just under $5,000, measured in dollars of 1969 purchasing power. That is, half of all U.S. families had incomes under about $5,000 (the exact figure was $4,972), and half had incomes over that amount. By 1969, the median family income had risen to over $9,400 ($9,433, to be exact). The great bulk of that increase must represent an increase in real income, since the pattern of income distribution did not change significantly, there was not a large increase in the proportion of family income going for taxes, and the measurement is in terms of dollars with constant purchasing power.

The drive to affluence is sometimes halted by failure of the economy to maintain a full-employment level of output. In the years since World War II, the forward direction has been temporarily broken by recessions in 1949, 1954,

1958, and 1970. But as Figure 7-7 shows, the growth of median family income indicates a strong trend toward increased riches.

In a later chapter we shall examine the distribution of income and make the point that an important part of the U.S. population does not share in the growth of affluence. Poverty persists. Nor is economic growth, by itself, an adequate remedy for poverty even in the long run. There are aspects of our economic system that generate poverty as well as affluence. But in an overall view of the entire economy, it is clear that for most Americans the economic system pays off with greater wealth.

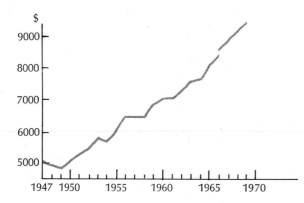

FIGURE 7-7
The Growth of Affluence:
Median Family Income
in the United States,
1947–69

A revised method of calculation started in 1966 is shown by a break in the line.

THE PERFORMANCE OF THE U.S. ECONOMY:
SOME PRELIMINARY CONCLUSIONS

This chapter has been devoted to some important ways in which the performance of an economy can be evaluated using objective economic data. It has looked at macroeconomic performance rather than microeconomic. That is, it has dealt with total production and its growth, the major categories among which the GNP is divided, the extent to which productive capacity is not fully utilized, and the relative stability or instability of prices. All of these topics are closely related to the basic economic health of a nation and to the increase of welfare by way of rising output. Little has been said, however, of the allocation of resources to production of individual goods, the division between private and public products and services, the efficiency of the market mechanism, the role of large and small business, the impact of labor unions, patterns of income distribution, and other aspects of the allocative efficiency of the economic system. These come later. Nevertheless, some important conclusions can be drawn:

1. The United States has had a respectable rate of economic growth, both in total output and in output per person.

2. Since World War II the U.S. has shifted from a nation that has led the

growth parade to an also-ran. This shift has been caused less by a slowing down of U.S. growth than by a speedup in the growth of other nations.

3. The Soviet Union has been able to maintain consistently higher growth rates than the U.S., and if it continues to do so, it will eventually catch up in total output. Whether this is good or bad depends upon one's political preconceptions.

4. The U.S. economy is strongly consumer-oriented, but the growth of military and military-related expenditures, both in total and in proportion to GNP, indicates a development away from the growth and consumer orientation that has the largest economic payoff in the long run.

5. The U.S. economy has tended to use its production potential less than fully. A considerable degree of slack generally exists. This slack is reflected in significant amounts of redundant labor and plant capacity.

6. The record on prices is mixed. In the past there has been considerable variation in the general price level but the historical record does not show any significant trend either upward or downward.

7. The major fluctuations in prices have been associated with wars.

8. Price levels *may* have moved up permanently to a new and higher base level as a result of World War II. Whether this presages an era of consistently rising prices is doubtful, but the trend of price behavior in the future remains to be seen.

9. There has been a significant trend toward higher living standards and greater affluence, however, and this trend should continue into the future.

Many other topics could have been included in this evaluative survey. The nature, extent, and significance of poverty was not discussed directly, for example, even though it is an important problem. It will be examined in detail in a later chapter. Superpatriots or left-wing radicals would probably have chosen different topics and made different comparisons, and perhaps would have drawn some different conclusions. Indeed, the reader may find that some things he thought were true are not borne out by the facts.

And *that* is the point. Some opinions are better than others. The better ones are supported by both analysis and data: they are objective rather than subjective, rational rather than irrational. Objectivity does not mean that normative conclusions are avoided, but that they are arrived at in a reasoned way that uses as much of the available data as possible.

Conclusions, however, have the unfortunate habit of turning into questions, and this is particularly true of economics. The conclusions drawn from the data presented in this chapter suggest a great host of other questions. What are the sources of economic growth? How can economic slack be reduced or eliminated? What are the relationships between growth, employment and price levels? And more. These are some of the fundamental problems of economics to which the remainder of this book will be devoted.

Summary

Aggregative economic data based on national product concepts can be used to provide an objective evaluation of some important aspects of a nation's economic performance. The U.S. economy, for example, has shown a long-term growth rate of a little over 3.5 percent annually, and a growth of GNP per person of a little over 1.5 percent annually. In a comparison including other countries, these growth rates are good but not spectacular. Our economy devotes a large portion of its output to consumption, and (in the last quarter century) a significant amount to military and military-related uses. We seem consistently to maintain a goodly amount of economic slack, which shows up in unemployment and unused plant capacity. Aside from wartime inflation, price levels have been much more stable in the last quarter century than they were in earlier periods. And the growth of affluence has continued, as shown by rising family incomes. Whatever may be the problems of the future, in terms of total output, the data show strong growth in the past.

Key Concepts

Growth rate.   Average annual percentage increase in GNP corrected for changes in the price level.

Full employment.   The definition of full employment depends on whether your political party is in or out of power. The author defines full employment as an unemployment rate of 2.5 to 3 percent, regardless of who is in the White House. Here are some related concepts:

> **Unemployment rate.**   The percent of the civilian labor force out of work, as measured by the U.S. Bureau of Labor Statistics.
>
> **Frictional unemployment.**   Unemployment due to labor mobility. May vary between 1.5 and 2.5 percent of the civilian labor force.
>
> **Structural unemployment.**   Unemployment caused by changes in the economy that workers have been unable fully to adjust to.
>
> **Cyclical unemployment.**   Unemployment due to inadequate aggregate demand.
>
> **Hidden unemployment.**   Unemployment not measured by the unemployment rate, primarily workers who are not considered part of the labor force because they are not actively seeking employment.

Economic slack.   Output lost because of failure of the economy to utilize its manpower resources fully, measured in this chapter from the base of a 3 percent unemployment rate.

ECONOMIC
GROWTH
III

Many of our contemporary social, economic, and political problems are related to the issue of economic growth. Individually and in conjunction with one another, they exist in a highly advanced and complex economy in which all the parts are interdependent. Health, education, discrimination, poverty, military spending, inflation, and unemployment are some of the immediate problems. Some other fundamental issues such as population expansion and the viability of man's natural environment bear directly on the topic of economic growth. Inadequate growth, unbalanced growth, and misdirected growth can have the most serious consequences.

In the heyday of the post-Keynesian synthesis, most economists and policy makers took for granted that proposition that economic growth was good. Indeed, the unspoken assumption that an economy based on private decision making could use the affluence created by growth wisely and properly was usually lurking in the background. This easy assumption is no longer widely accepted. To the post-Keynesian concern about inadequate growth has now been added a larger concern for unbalanced or misdirected or destructive growth.

We start with fundamental propositions. *Chapter 8* examines the potential growth of the American economy. In the short run, the growth of the economy depends on the growth of the work force and the increase in output per man-hour. The latter factor, in turn, is influenced by investment in production capacity, technological change, and investment in human capital. Contrary to popular impression, availability of capital or natural resources does not limit economic growth in the short run.

Chapter 9 discusses recent economic growth in the United States. It emphasizes the proposition that inadequate economic growth leaves people unemployed and substantial amounts of goods unproduced. The human costs of inadequate growth are large.

Chapter 10 investigates the longer-run sources of economic growth and finds them in the attitudes toward wealth and success characteristic of a society holding materialistic standards of value. Even scientific advances and improved technology are seen to have their roots in a pervasive materialism.

These chapters raise the most troubling and difficult issues in contemporary economics. Economic growth has never been steady and even, and has always been interrupted or slowed from time to time. We wish to avoid the wastes and costs generated by inadequate growth, and the Keynesian theories of income determination show us how to do so in the short run. Whether these theories can avoid in the future the interruptions to growth characteristic of the past remains to be seen. But having the goal of sustained economic growth perhaps within our grasp raises the larger issue of the purposes of economic growth. Militarism and national power? Piling up material things to satisfy individual strivings for status? Surely the growth potential that has been built into the fabric and functioning of modern industrial societies can be used for humane purposes if we put our minds to it. Yet, as we shall see in the second half of this book, a market-oriented society does with its wealth what the values of its individual members dictate. And if those values emphasize material wealth and power . . . ?

Two factors determine the rate at which any economy can grow. An increase in the size of the effective labor force can make more man-hours available for productive use. An increase in output per man-hour can increase the output obtained from the available labor. These variables can be measured with fair accuracy. In the short run, from one year to the next, they limit the increased production obtainable from a nation's economy.

For example, output can be increased if unemployed workers can be put to work, or if more women can be drawn into the labor force, or if the retirement age of workers is moved back, or if young people enter the labor market at an earlier age. These are all ways in which the quantity of labor inputs can be increased. The quality of productive effort can also be increased. Use of increased amounts of capital per worker, improved organization of the work effort, a better-educated work force, and improved health of workers increase the productivity of the individual worker.

We are speaking here, of course, about aggregate growth and not growth per capita. That is something else again: An increase in the number of workers can raise the economy's production potential, but unless it is supplemented by productivity gains that push total output up faster than the growth of population, living standards (as measured by GNP per capita) could remain the same or even fall.

GROWTH OF THE LABOR FORCE

In recent decades in the United States, the growth of the labor force has been remarkably steady at about 1.3 percent per year. That is, for every 1,000 workers this year there will be 1,013 next year, on the average. From this source alone, it should be possible to increase the GNP by 1.3 percent annually, simply by putting these additional workers into productive jobs.

This long-term trend was significantly broken only during World War II, when large numbers of women, youngsters, and older persons were drawn temporarily into the work force. Normally, however, growth of the work force depends on long-term trends in population growth, the length of schooling for young men and women, the trend of retirement age, and the labor force participation of women. The most important factor is the trend of popula-

The Potential Growth of the American Economy

8

tion growth. The post-World War II "baby boom" brought the average annual growth of the labor force up to about 1.5 percent for the 1965–75 years, while the slowdown in population growth in the mid-1950s and after will bring it down to about 1.2 percent after 1975.[1]

Political events may also influence labor force trends. The war in Vietnam, for example, pulled young people into the armed forces and caused others to stay in school longer in order to obtain draft deferments. At the same time new manpower-training programs kept still others out of the labor market. Over 500,000 persons who otherwise would have been seeking work were pulled out of the labor market in 1966–67, and the labor force grew much more slowly than it otherwise would have done. The result was an abnormal drop in unemployment rates and an intensification of inflationary pressures.

The long-term trends in the labor force create a need for economic growth. The economy must create additional jobs each year to provide employment for the additional workers. Unless it does, unemployment will increase and bring with it the economic waste and personal tragedy that is involved. A *minimum* requirement is 1.5 new jobs for every 100 old ones in the years until 1975.

GROWTH OF PRODUCTIVITY

The productive efficiency of the labor force also increases from year to year, just as the size of the work force grows. This is the second factor that determines the potential rate of economic growth. The best measure of the productivity of the economy is output per man-hour employed. This output is calculated by dividing the gross national product (value of total output) by an estimate of the number of man-hours required to produce the GNP. Simply:

$$\frac{GNP}{\text{man-hours employed}} = \text{output per man-hour.}$$

This measure of productivity is usually referred to as "simple labor productivity," because it disregards all other factors that might influence the growth

---

[1] Growth of the labor force is determined primarily by the entry of young workers into the labor market. This in turn is the result of births 14 to 20 years earlier. At the same time, some older workers enter the labor market and others leave. For example, women leave the labor market to get married or have children, or both, while others reenter after their families are grown. Some workers die, others retire. Such trends as the lengthening years of schooling, the growing labor force participation of women, improved health and reductions in the death rate, and the gradual lowering of the age for retirement all influence the changes taking place in the number of workers.

The trend toward reduced hours of work and longer vacations also influences the effective working time or potential labor input of the work forces.

All of these factors have been accounted for in the estimates of labor force growth presented here. They are really estimates of the growth of physical labor inputs rather than just the number of new workers, although the latter is by far the most important factor. It would be more accurate to use the label "growth of the labor force adjusted for changes in man-hours worked per year," with no change assumed for the unemployment rate.

of GNP, and there are many. Simple labor productivity is a very convenient measure to use, however, because it sums up all of the elements that affect the efficiency with which GNP is produced.

It is not difficult to list some of the important influences on labor productivity. They include:

Capital investment in plant and equipment.

Technological advances.

Substitution of capital for labor.

Increased use of mechanical forms of power, such as steam, electricity, atomic energy, etc.

Increased organizational efficiency.

Higher educational levels for workers.

Improved health (and hence efficiency) of workers.

And so on, almost ad infinitum.

Add to the list yourself, but they all add up to greater output for each worker employed. Make a note, then, that use of the term "labor productivity" does not imply that increases in output are caused solely by labor. Rather, the increases are due to many factors, but whatever the cause they show up statistically in increased output per man-hour.[2]

Output per man-hour has been rising steadily in this industrial age. Since 1909, which is the initial date for the best statistical series, output per man-hour in the U.S. economy has been rising at a rate of about 2.3 percent annually. That is, the output that requires the labor of 1,000 workers this year could be turned out by only 977 workers next year, on the average.

The trend of labor productivity is much less stable than the growth of the labor force, however, and a close look must be taken at the data. The change from year to year fluctuates greatly. Large productivity gains occur in years of rapid increases in output and employment as economic slack is eliminated. During recession years, however, output per man-hour increases much more slowly and may even decline. This instability in the growth of productivity is shown by the data in Figure 8-1 for the years since World War II.

Note how the growth of productivity slowed down in the recession of 1949, only to spurt ahead rapidly in the recovery of 1950, and how similar declines followed by spurts occurred in the recessions of 1956 and 1960. Note also that in the sustained expansion of the economy after 1960, the growth of productivity first speeded up and then began to slow down as the economy approached closer to full employment and full use of output capacity in 1965. Both of these patterns are typical, and must be borne in mind when trying to estimate the short-term growth potential of the economy.

---

[2] Be careful, too, to use the term "productivity" to mean "output per man-hour" and not "total output." GNP (total output) can fall while productivity (output per man-hour) is rising. The two are quite different.

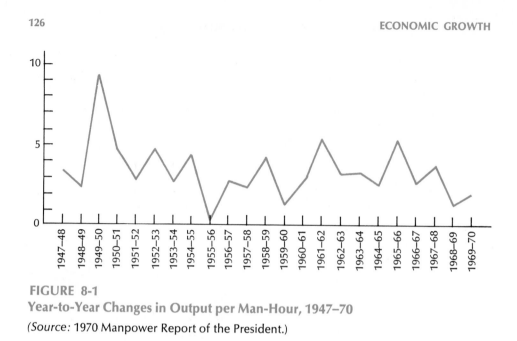

FIGURE 8-1
Year-to-Year Changes in Output per Man-Hour, 1947–70
(*Source:* 1970 Manpower Report of the President.)

Short-term fluctuations in productivity gains are less important for economic growth than the long-term trend, however. An economy with an average annual increase in output per man-hour of 4.5 percent will be able to grow almost twice as fast as one with an average increase of only 2.5 percent, no matter how large the annual fluctuations around those figures might be. But there are pitfalls in determining just what the long-term trend is, particularly since the annual fluctuations can be large.

For example, in the United States in 1960–65, output per man-hour rose at an annual rate of 3.5 percent, compared with the average annual increase in the 1909–1965 period of only 2.3 percent. In the thirty years before World War II (1909–1940), the figure was only 1.7 percent per year, while in the succeeding quarter century (1940–1965) it was 3.1 percent. If you had to estimate the future growth potential of the U.S. economy, which figure would you use? Why?

The data, which for convenience are shown in Figure 8-2, would indicate that productivity gains in the modern American economy have been accelerating. Yet it is hard to be sure: shifts in the trend of productivity growth can occur without warning, and the large year-to-year fluctuations make it difficult to identify a change in the trend until well after it has taken place.

THE CASE FOR HIGH RATES
OF PRODUCTIVITY GAIN

There are good reasons for believing that in the long run the American economy can sustain average rates of increase in output per man-hour at or very near the levels that were reached in the period from 1960 to 1965. First, there

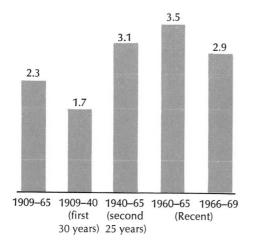

1909–65   1909–40   1940–65   1960–65   1966–69
(first   (second   (Recent)
30 years) 25 years)

FIGURE 8-2
Average Annual Percent Increase of Output per Man-Hour, Selected Periods, 1909–69

(Sources: Computed from the Bureau of Labor Statistics index number series on output per man-hour, U.S. Dept. of Commerce, Long-Term Economic Growth (Washington, D.C.: U.S. Government Printing Office, 1966), pp. 188–189. Data for 1966–69 are from the 1970 Manpower Report of the President.)

has been a very large increase in research and development expenditures by both private firms and the U.S. government. From only $3.4 billion in 1950, total R&D spending rose to $20.5 billion in 1965. This represented an increase from 1.2 percent of GNP to 3.0 percent. The increase in private R&D expenditures alone was from $1.6 billion to $8.0 billion. Spending on research and development is something new that did not exist before. It has been increasing in size and in relation to total spending. Although much of it has been related to military needs and interplanetary exploration, where the payoff for the normal activities of the economy is problematical, much has been directed toward improved production, distribution and organization in the economy. This is particularly true of private R&D expenditures.

An increasing payoff can be expected in both greater efficiency and new products in the years immediately ahead. The results of R&D expenditures, by their very nature, are not felt immediately. One year's project may not lead to applications for a number of years. Even after practical applications are developed it may take years before they are widely used in industry. This means that the rising R&D expenditures of the last fifteen years should generate a rising payoff in the next fifteen years. Even after the growth of R&D expenditures as a percent of GNP begins to level off, as it eventually must, consequent acceleration in output per man-hour will continue for a considerable time.

Secondly, in recent years the commitment of national economic policy to high rates of employment and economic growth has created an economic environment conducive to high business profits and high levels of investment. Under conditions of sustained prosperity, business firms have every inducement to spend for expansion. When they do, they apply the latest and most efficient capital equipment, thereby bringing about substantial increases in output per man-hour. Furthermore, sustained prosperity enables business firms to accumulate or borrow the capital they need for expansion, and for maintaining or increasing their R&D programs. There is a vital feedback from the prosperity of rapid economic growth, through capital investment and rapid productivity gains, back to high rates of economic growth. When this situation is combined with the recent rapid growth of R&D expenditures, a powerful mechanism for the creation of economic gains is present.

Finally, the expansion of education in the years since World War II has greatly improved the nation's skills. The median level of educational achievement for persons over 24 years of age rose from Grade 9 to Grade 12 between 1947 and 1966. There has been a dramatic increase in the proportion of high school and college graduates. In 1946 only 21 percent of persons over 24 years of age had completed high school, as compared with 31 percent in 1966. The proportion that had completed college rose from 5 percent to 10 percent. Advances were even more dramatic at the graduate level. In 1945–46 the nation's universities granted 1,966 Ph.D. degrees; by 1964–65 the number had risen to 16,467 in one year. These increases in educational achievement represent an improvement in the knowledge and problem-solving ability of the productive work force that will make it very unlikely that the economy will fall back to the pre-World War II increases in output per man-hour.

These three structural changes in the economy suggest high rates of productivity gains in the immediate future. Productivity gains averaging 3.5 percent per year seem well within the potential of the economy, and a 3 percent average annual increase highly possible.

THE CASE FOR CAUTION

There are dangers in jumping to conclusions on these matters, especially when economic policy decisions are involved. If policy makers overestimate the growth potential of the economy, they may adopt policies that will push the GNP to levels higher than consistent with the existing level of prices. A small overestimate of long-term productivity gains can lead to a large amount of short-term inflation. Caution may be desirable.

Caution is also suggested by the fact that even five years does not form a long-term trend where productivity gains are concerned, particularly since the whole five-year period (1960–65) was one of economic expansion. Furthermore, there is some doubt about whether a full-employment economy can continue to maintain such high levels of productivity gain. As the economy moves toward full utilization of labor and plant capacity, a number of things happen: cost awareness by plant managers diminishes, plant discipline loosens, inexperienced workers are hired, less efficient machinery is brought back into production, and bottlenecks and lags in deliveries cause production delays. Although there is little experience to rely on, these factors suggest that productivity gains at full employment may fall below the average of the 1960s.

Perhaps for these reasons the President's Council of Economic Advisors bases its estimates of potential economic growth on average annual productivity gains of 3 percent per year. This is very close to the average for the post-World War II years, but below the gains of 1960 through 1965. In the discussions that follow in this book, however, 3 percent will be used as a low estimate and 3.5 percent as an upper limit for potential average annual productivity increases in the American economy.

A METHODOLOGICAL DIGRESSION. *A student might wonder why he has been asked to read this complex discussion of rates of productivity gain. The answer is important: Scientific economics must be rooted in facts about the world as it exists. Facts are derived from the past, and in order that they may be usefully applied to the future, they must be tempered by reason and analysis. This discussion was designed to show how data can be interpreted in order to arrive at meaningful conclusions, and how the results may well be a range of possibilities rather than a definite figure.*

THE POTENTIAL RATE OF GROWTH

Growth of the labor force and the increase in output per man-hour taken together permit us to calculate the potential growth rate of GNP in the American economy in the years immediately ahead. The work force will grow at a rate of about 1.5 percent annually, while productivity can be expected to increase by about 3 to 3.5 percent per year. Putting the two growth rates together gives a potential growth of GNP of about 4.5 to 5 percent per year.[3]

Of course, as the two component parts of the aggregate growth rate change, the estimates of potential growth will also shift. As the growth of the labor

---

[3] The actual calculation should be done as follows:

1. Work force increasing by 1.5 percent per year and output per man-hour increasing by 3.0 percent per year:

$$\frac{101.5 \times 103.0}{100} = 4.545.$$

2. Work force increasing by 1.5 percent per year and output per man-hour increasing by 3.5 percent per year:

$$\frac{101.5 \times 103.5}{100} = 5.0525.$$

We do not just add the two separate rates of growth. This is because the increase in output per man-hour must be applied to both the old work force and the increase. The result is a compound growth rate a little higher than the sum of the two components.

force slows down, as it will after 1975, so will the economy's growth potential. If long-term trends in output per man-hour should shift significantly, the potential growth rate will also change. But for the immediate future the American economy should be able to grow at a rate of about 4.5 to 5 percent annually.

These projections may seem a little optimistic, but not to too great an extent. A recent study made by the Joint Economic Committee of the U.S. Congress projects a potential growth rate of 4 to 4.5 percent. Another study sponsored by the National Planning Association projects a 4 percent growth rate, and so does the President's Council of Economic Advisors.

The differences in the estimated growth rates are not large, but because they are differences in *speed* of growth they can add up to a lot in the long run. And they are well above the actual performance of the economy of only a few years ago, when in the period from 1953 through 1960 the growth rate was *under* 2.5 percent annually. Just as an illustration of payoff from high growth rates, Table 8-1 shows how long it would take for the GNP to double and triple in amount, at varying rates of growth. The comparisons are striking. There is a tremendous payoff from raising the growth rate of GNP from a substandard 2.5 percent per year to the feasible levels of 4 to 5 percent.

TABLE 8-1
Growth Rates and the Increase in GNP

| | Number of Years Required | |
Average Annual Rate of Growth	To Double	To Triple
2.5	28	45
4	18	28
4.5	16	25
5	14	23

A growth of GNP at 4.5 percent annually would make possible a growth rate for GNP per capita of about 2.8 percent annually. This estimate assumes a growth of population of 1.7 percent per year, which is approximately the present level. This growth rate for GNP per capita is well above the historical trend of 1.65–2 percent that was noted in Chapter 7. All indications are that the well-being of Americans can increase more rapidly in the future than it has in the past.

ECONOMIC GROWTH AND CAPITAL FORMATION

This estimate of the potential rate of growth of GNP has *assumed* that there is no barrier to economic growth created by lack of capital. We have taken for granted the proposition that the growth of the economy will draw forth the necessary capital investment. Several studies of capital formation have directly asked whether the American economy will be able to generate the capital necessary to provide for its prospective growth needs. Each one has reached the same conclusion: We shall save enough from current consumption to provide not only resources for our own expansion but also some additional amounts for use in other parts of the world. We don't have to fear a shortage of capital.

The American economy provides a self-generating flow of savings into investment. Three factors contribute to this outcome:

1. An acquisitive, success-oriented population. Americans know that today's savings, invested now, can raise their future incomes and improve their economic position.
2. Open, largely competitive capital markets. Business firms requiring capital bid for it in the capital markets, with the ones having the best profit possibilities being the winners.
3. Growth itself creates both the savings of consumers and the desire to invest. Higher incomes bring larger amounts of savings, along with incentives for business to expand.

There is a vitally important principle here: Normally, *a private economy will generate the capital it needs for economic growth.* Although this self-supporting feedback mechanism is present, it does not guarantee economic growth. A stagnant economy will generate little incentive for expansion, and may remain in the doldrums indefinitely. But a growing economy will generate both opportunities for gain and the rising incomes needed to sustain higher levels of savings. Capital formation promotes economic growth, and economic growth promotes capital formation. This does not mean that economic growth is inevitable and will proceed without interruption to bring the economy to higher and higher levels of affluence. Growth has never been smooth and trouble-free. It has always proceeded irregularly and has been interrupted from time to time. But it does mean that once an economy like ours starts moving forward, the processes of saving and investment tend to keep it moving, and do not create a limit that holds back further progress.

INVESTMENT AND THE PUBLIC SECTOR

It would be nice to add that everything we have just said about private capital formation applies as well to public capital formation. Unfortunately, it doesn't. In the case of public investment, rates of return are often difficult to measure, the people who provide the funds, the taxpayers, sometimes get little direct benefit from the investment, and political factors often influence decisions heavily.

Take public expenditures for education as an example. Three barriers stand in the way of adequate investment in education. One is the prevalent attitude about private wants and public needs. Money spent by an individual on his own private consumption satisfies both his physical and his psychological needs. A new car, a better home, fashionable clothes, and expensive vacations tend to give individual satisfactions and enable one to claim a high status among one's fellows. Taxes paid to support a school system, however, provide a generalized social benefit that is not attributable to any one person, and they do not enable the individual to satisfy his desire for recognition and status. In an individualistic society we can expect resentment and resistance to payment of taxes, which requires that people forego spending on their own personal wants in favor of social needs.

Compounding the problem is the fact that the taxpayer pays the cost of education while the direct benefits are received primarily by nontaxpayers; the young go to school while people who already have their education pay the bills. It can be argued that everyone benefits from a more educated population, and that is undoubtedly true. Education has been one of America's best investments when the full social and economic benefits are calculated. But it is nevertheless true that one group pays while another group obtains the bulk of the immediate and direct benefits. As long as this condition prevails, along with individualistic attitudes, educational institutions will lack financing.

The third barrier to the financing of education lies in the ways in which capital investments are made. Compare education's access to capital with that of business enterprise. The business firm must only pass the test of the market and show that the potential returns, with risks taken into consideration, are greater than the rate of interest. It can then go into money markets, borrow the capital, and pay back the loan out of the profits from the enterprise. The action is simple, impersonal, and readily accomplished. This is not true of education. In the first place, the potential gains are not easily measured. Secondly, those who benefit are not expected to repay directly the costs of their education. And finally, educational funds are obtained by a complex political process in which extraneous issues often impinge on a decision made in the emotional heat of politics. Development of education is thus hampered by institutions that make capital investment difficult and erratic in contrast to the free access to capital enjoyed by a business enterprise.

The difficulties attending public expenditure for education are similar to those faced in other areas equally important for economic growth. Basic scientific research is in an even worse position, because its direct benefits are even more highly restricted than those of education. It is very difficult for governments at all levels to obtain funds for abatement of air and water pollution. The spread of urban blight is another example of a problem that goes unsolved in part because its solution is not a direct benefit to individual taxpayers.

A second principle about capital formation emerges: *An acquisitive society tends to starve its public sector.* Where investment through government is vital to economic growth, in such areas as education, scientific research, urban development, and much of transportation and medical care, there is a tendency for expenditures to be inadequate. The causes are varied, but the most important are:

1. An individualistic success standard that emphasizes private consumption.
2. Difficulties in measuring the benefits and costs associated with public investment.
3. Differences between groups receiving benefits and those paying costs.
4. Ideological and political considerations that influence decisions about the nature and extent of public investment.

Long-sustained economic growth requires substantial investment in the public sector of the economy to create and preserve the framework within which rapid economic growth can continue. Yet the difficulties associated with public capital formation in a private economy can create substantial obstacles to adequate investment in the public sector.

ECONOMIC GROWTH AND NATURAL RESOURCES

Our estimate of the potential rate of growth of GNP also implies an assumption about the availability of natural resources. We assume that there will be no resource shortages that might hinder economic growth. This assumption is a reasonable one. Recent expert studies[4] assure us that

> The American people *can* obtain the natural resources and resource products they will need between now and the year 2000. Whether or not they *will* depends on how hard and how well they work at it.

According to the most authoritative recent study, a growing U.S. economy will require three times as much energy and metals in 2000 as in 1960, a doubling of agricultural production, and at least a doubling of the use of fresh water. Yet resources are not expected to run out. Lower grades of raw materials, substitution of more plentiful for less plentiful ones, more efficiency in use, imports, and development of synthetics and substitutes promise a guarantee against across-the-board shortages.

There may be particular shortages in particular segments of the economy from time to time. This type of shortage, however, is quickly overcome in a market-oriented economy. The resource in short supply rises in price, and two accommodating forces are thereby set in motion:

1. Users economize on its use and substitute other things for it.
2. Research seeks to find cost-reducing methods of production, new sources of supply, or substitute materials.

Forest resources are a good example. Up to about 1920, cutting of the most accessible stands of trees, often in an inefficient and wasteful way, led to

---

[4] Hans H. Lansberg, *Natural Resources for U.S. Growth* (Baltimore, Md.: Johns Hopkins Press, 1964), p. 13. This book is a summary report of a much larger study supported by Resources for the Future, Inc., entitled *Resources in America's Future: Patterns of Requirements and Availabilities, 1960–2000.*

gradually rising prices for lumber. The rising costs led to at least three major changes in the industry: cost-reducing innovations in production and distribution, use of wood wastes to manufacture salable by-products, and a significant shift to such wood substitutes as steel, aluminum, plastics, and cement. These developments tended to economize on the use of forest products or to bring down their price. In addition, both public agencies and producers of forest products began to put forest lands on a continuous-yield basis.

The market-adjustment process and the adaptations it sets in motion are only part of the story. The other part involves technological change: innovation can make new resources available that did not exist before. The search for cost-cutting or new supplies, set in motion by the rising price of a particular resource whose use is increasing, can result in discovery of new technologies with vast and far-reaching effects. The case of rubber is perhaps the classic example. Inadequate supplies of natural rubber led to the development of synthetics, which are not only now cheaper but also better for most uses than the natural product. Advances in basic science have demonstrated the fundamental uniformity of energy and matter, making possible physical transformations undreamed of only one or two generations ago. In theory, the entire earth's crust and all of the energy coming near the earth from the sun are potentially usable productive resources.

Science and technological change as a guarantee against resource shortages bring us back, however, to the process of capital formation. The economy must continually feed back some of the gains from economic growth into the research that will maintain or expand the resource base. Some of the funds can come from private sources. But basic research, and even some product and process development, is also a function of government and nonprofit organizations. And as we have seen, channeling of resources into those areas is not always easy.

Problems of quality are also important. The relationship of people to resources is only partially a market phenomenon and can be taken care of only partially by market adjustments. Polluted streams may sometimes not embody an economic cost, but they can be very unpleasant. Billboards along the highway may represent the best economic use of the space, but they can also be esthetic abominations. These examples emphasize the fact that simply having enough land, water, metals, energy, food, and fiber is not enough. A satisfactory life for most people requires more than that.

One of the costs of economic growth has been a growing pollution of the environment, particularly water and air. In some cities from time to time the pollution has been hazardous to life, as in Donora, Pennsylvania, in 1948, New York in 1963, and London in 1952. Many rivers and lakes that were important recreational resources now can no longer be used for those purposes because of pollution. Economic growth changes the conditions of life, but not always beneficently.

CONSUMER GOODS WASTES*

A large fraction of all consumer goods end up as urban solid waste, though significant amounts are salvaged and recycled back to industry.

Scrap iron and steel are generated at a rate of 12 to 15 million tons a year, of which about a third consists of derelict automobiles. The fraction recovered for use has declined substantially. Recovery of other scrap metals in 1963 included at least 974,000 tons of copper, 493,000 tons of lead, and 268,000 tons of zinc.

From 25 to 30 million tons of paper products produced annually, about 10 million tons of waste paper were salvaged in 1964 and used to make new paper. In 1962, about 263,000 long tons of reclaimed rubber were used in the United States, about 15 percent of all rubber. The same year about 10 percent of the 8 billion pounds of plastics produced was recovered and reconverted.

Each year we must dispose of 48 billion cans (250 per person), 26 billion bottles and jars (135 per person), 65 billion metal and plastic caps and crowns (338 per person), plus more than half a billion dollars worth of miscellaneous packaging material.

Only a small part of our solid wastes is salvaged and processed for reuse, even though the industries engaged in reprocessing waste materials operate at a level of 5 to 7 billion dollars a year. The unsalvaged remainder represents a vast potential for litter and pollution.

The pollution and waste issue raises a broader question about the resource base that is of far greater significance than merely whether there will be enough inputs available for production. Economic growth changes the natural environment that makes life possible. As population grows and cities expand, as industry spreads and technology changes, demands on the natural environment increase. A 1968 *New York Times* editorial described the problem:

The earth's supply of available oxygen is being depleted both by the diminution of plant life on land and sea and by the increasing amounts of oxygen in newly created carbon compounds. Large bodies of water are steadily being fouled by

---

* From "Restoring The Quality of Our Environment," a report of the Environmental Pollution Panel of the President's Science Committee, 1965.

huge quantities of sewage, industrial wastes and the insecticide and fertilizer run-offs from agricultural lands, with disastrous consequences for the animal and plant life in those waters. In innumerable other ways the precarious balance of nature is being disturbed on a scale without precedent or presently foreseeable end.

With increased pressure on the ecological base, a larger share of the gains from economic growth will have to be diverted to the task of reconstituting the natural environment. Methods will have to be developed to rebuild the resources of air, water, and land that are now being contaminated. This, in itself, can be expected to slow down the process of economic growth. But unless it is done, the accumulation of unmet needs will probably result in an even more drastic slowdown in the end.

THE GOAL OF ECONOMIC GROWTH

The benefits to be derived from high rates of economic growth are important. Growth provides additional resources that can be used to raise living standards, to end poverty as we know it, to rebuild our cities, to provide still better education and health for everyone, to make possible more leisure time, to assist the poor nations in their efforts to raise their standards of living. Whatever one's definition of the good life may be, more material resources will enable more people to achieve it.

The post-Keynesian economics of the last quarter century showed the path to strong economic growth, as we shall see in later chapters. But it generally left determination of the uses to which that growth should be put to the private sector and the political process. As part of the liberal creed, this policy lent support to programs to reduce poverty and assist underdeveloped countries. But by assuming that people and governments would make good use of the dividends from growth, it left open the path to pollution and militarism. When the uses of affluence turned out to be less than benign and humane, the present impasse in social policy appeared. Many people began asking, "Why growth?" This is one of the reasons for the breakup of the post-Keynesian synthesis and why economics is moving rapidly into new fields of inquiry and a new concern with economic institutions and economic systems.

Summary

An economy's growth potential is determined by two factors, both of which can be measured. One is the increase in the labor force available for production. The other is the increase in productivity, or output per man-hour.

Productivity increases are, in turn, brought about by a wide variety of factors, of which the most important are investment in physical capital and investment in human capital. Short-run savings in productivity gains are hard to predict, but long-run trends are more stable, averaging a little less than 2.5 percent annually over the last sixty years. There has been a tendency for the increase in output per man-hour to rise in recent decades, however, and estimates of future annual increases in the range of 3 to 3.5 percent annually are within reason. Together with annual increases in the work force of 1.5 percent (a little less after 1975), this would bring the economy's potential growth rate in the immediate future to a range of 4.5 percent as an upper estimate. A more conservative estimate would put it at 4 to 4.5 percent.

These estimates assume no shortages of capital or natural resources. In the short run, those assumptions are valid. But in the long run there may be important problems in both areas because of the tendency of an individualistic society to starve its public sector and to damage its ecological base. The single-minded pursuit of short-run growth has to be modified in order to preserve the economy's long-run growth potential.

Key Concepts

Growth of the labor force.   The increase in man-hours per year available for productive work.

Productivity.   Output per man-hour. Measured by dividing total output by man-hours employed. Increases in productivity are measured by the percent change in productivity from one year to the next.

Do not confuse productivity (measured by output per man-hour) with production (measured by gross national product or related concepts).

Potential growth.   The growth of output made possible by growth of the work force and increases in productivity.

Recent Economic Growth in the United States

9

The American economy has passed through three distinct phases in the years since World War II. From 1946 through 1953 economic growth was relatively rapid. Then came a period almost of stagnation that started in 1953 and lasted into 1960–61. There was no dramatic break such as that of 1929–33, but the economy gradually fell further and further behind its potential output. A turnabout came in 1961, however, and the economy started on the longest single period of uninterrupted expansion in its history, to be capped by the Vietnam war inflation of 1967–70, and the combined recession cum inflation of 1970–71. The differences among these three periods were striking, and an examination of the reasons for the variation in economic performance can tell us much about the process of economic growth.

RAPID EXPANSION, 1946–1953

The first seven years after World War II saw the American economy grow rapidly. The GNP rose at a rate of 4.0 percent annually, considerably above the long-term historical trend of about 3 percent. By 1953 unemployment was down to the lowest level the American economy has had during times of peace. But it was also a period of inflation, and price levels rose by a little more than 37 percent.

The Employment Act of 1946

The American economy emerged from World War II primed for prosperity, even though most economists at that time were pessimistic about the future. As federal government purchases of goods and services fell from $89 billion in 1944 and $74.2 billion in 1945 all the way down to $12.5 billion in 1947, there was considerable fear that hard times might occur. Much was made of the fact that large wars in the past had usually been followed by a depression, and in 1946 memories of the thirties were still fresh. The result was one of the most important pieces of economic legislation in U.S. history, the Employment Act of 1946. It committed the federal government to:

1. "Creating and maintaining . . . conditions under which there will be afforded useful employment opportunities . . . for those able, willing and seeking to work"; and

2. "To promote maximum employment, production and purchasing power."

The act also established a Council of Economic Advisors to report to the President on the condition of the national economy and to recommend policies directed toward maintaining high levels of employment.

By this piece of legislation the federal government formally took on the responsibility of maintaining full-employment prosperity. Although the wording of the act was not specific, and some key terms such as "maximum employment" were not defined, the meaning of the legislation was clear. It marked the end of laissez-faire in one of the most important areas of economic policy.

Postwar Economic Growth

In spite of the fears, there was tremendous resilience in the private sector of the economy in the late forties. Consumers as a whole had accumulated tremendous amounts of war bonds and savings accounts during the war, to the extent of about $80 billion *more* than normal. Full employment and high wages during the war filled their pockets, and they were literally unable to spend their money because the war had reduced the availability of consumer goods; price control and rationing were in effect; and patriotic appeals kept people from patronizing black markets. The result was a large increase in liquid assets held by consumers. Matching this available purchasing power was a huge backlog of unsatisfied wants, partly because products were not available during the war, partly because of the deprived years of the depressed thirties, and partly because returning servicemen were in a buying mood. Consumers wanted to buy, and they had the money to do it. Figure 9-1 shows what happened to the economy, and illustrates the discussion that follows.

The resulting burst of consumer spending had an immediate impact on businessmen. Corporate profits after taxes rose by 50 percent in two years, from $13.4 billion in 1946 to $20.5 billion in 1948. And as profits rose, business expanded to take advantage of the opportunity: total private domestic investment jumped from $28.1 billion in 1946 to $43.1 billion in 1948, an increase of more than 50 percent. Those early postwar years were a classic example of the dynamism of a private economy when a substantial stimulus to expansion is applied. In this case, the upsurge had its source in a huge outpouring of consumer spending, financed in large part by wartime savings and supplemented by some expansion of credit. The increased consumer spending triggered large business investment expenditures. Together, these two factors were more than able to offset a huge decline in government spending.

A pause came in 1949. A large part of the excess wartime savings had been spent. Inventory accumulation by businessmen had become excessive, and private investment was cut back. It looked as if the first surge of the postwar boom was nearing its end. At this point the American economy received an unexpected stimulus: war in Korea. When hostilities began in 1950, both consumers and businessmen engaged in a spree of scare buying that started another jump upward in GNP. This temporary stimulus was supplemented by a larger and steadier expansion in government spending, primarily for the war effort, that kept the economy moving ahead through 1953.

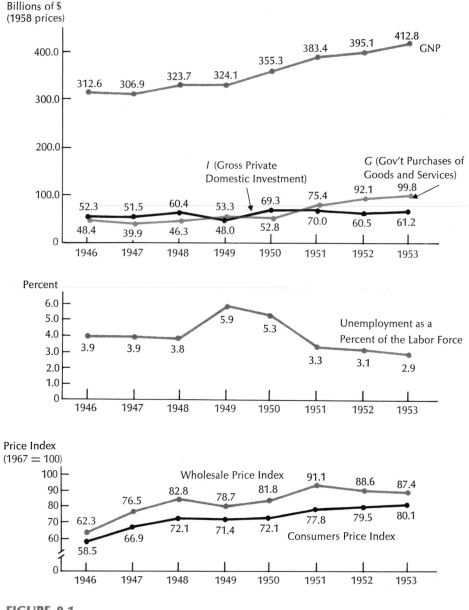

FIGURE 9-1
Economic Growth After World War II, 1946–53

The dependence of the economy upon expansion of government spending in these years is shown vividly by data from the national product accounts. Gross national product rose from $324.1 billion in 1949 to $412.8 billion in 1953.

A DIGRESSION ON WAR AND PROSPERITY

American prosperity and economic growth after World War II was partly due to the economic effects of wars. The liquid assets built up by consumers during World War II, the backlog of unmet wants in the late 1940s, and the stimulus given by the wars in Korea and Vietnam were all factors of significance in promoting rapid economic growth. Unpalatable as it may be to admit it, the prosperity of the years since 1946 have owed much to war.

The wars triggered a private enterprise economy into action. The private sector of the economy responded to spending, not war itself. The wars happened to be the reasons for the spending, unfortunately.

The lesson to be learned is not that American prosperity and economic growth depend on military expenditures, but rather that high levels of spending, whether the source is consumers, business investment, government or all three, are essential to prosperity and economic growth. The reason for the spending need not be wars. It can be higher standards of living, or greater profits, or expansion of government services and enlarged public programs. Seen in this light, the problem is essentially a political one. America can maintain a dynamic economy without wars or huge military expenditures. Whether it will do so is another question entirely.

But where did the stimulus come from? Initially, there was a large jump in business investment, mostly for inventory accumulation, from $48.0 billion in 1949 to $69.3 billion in 1950, but by 1953 it had leveled off at about $60–$61 billion annually. Government purchases of goods and services, however, rose from about $53 billion in both 1949 and 1950 all the way up to $99.8 billion in 1953.[1] One wonders what low level private investment and the GNP might have reached had not government wartime spending pushed the economy to new heights.

---

[1] Although government purchases in 1950 were about the same as in 1949, the economic impact of *orders* for military goods was already being felt in 1950, and goods were in the pipelines. This is a large reason for the upward leap in private inventory investment during 1950: finished goods are counted as business inventories until payment is made, at which time they become government purchases. Note the basic principle: The GNP feels the impact of increased government military spending well before the spending actually takes place.

At any rate, by the end of 1953 unemployment as measured officially by the Bureau of Labor Statistics had fallen to the lowest peacetime levels since the Bureau had started making its estimates. Only 1,870,000 were unemployed, representing just 2.9 percent of the labor force. This level is very close to the minimal "frictional" unemployment that must be expected in a large economy with free choice of occupation and a highly mobile work force.

Full employment had been accompanied by a rapid rate of economic growth. In spite of the readjustment pause of 1946 and the recession of 1949, the economy by 1953 could look back on seven years in which the GNP had risen by an average annual rate of 4 percent, and GNP per capita by 2.6 percent. These rates of growth were higher than for any previous seven-year period since the Civil War. Few economists were talking of "stagnation" or a "mature economy" the way they had in the depressed 1930s.

The one tender spot in the economy was the level of prices. Prices had been kept remarkably steady during World War II. A large part of the excess purchasing power created by the combination of war spending and shortages of consumer goods had been siphoned off into purchases of war bonds and enlarged bank accounts. Rationing and price control limited the ability of consumers to spend, and buying through illegal channels was unpatriotic. The result was that the government's index of consumer prices rose by only about 25 percent from 1940 through 1945. Most of the increase was concentrated in 1940–42 before price controls really caught hold.

Once the war was over, however, price controls and rationing were quickly dropped, the consumer spending boom began, and prices started rising. By 1948 the consumer price index rose by more than it had during the entire war, to a level about one-third above that of 1945. There was a pause in the upsurge during and immediately after the 1949 recession, but the Korean War saw a second round of inflation and prices rose by over 10 percent in 1950–53.

Contributing to both the economic expansion and the inflation of the postwar years was a policy of "easy money," under which the banking system was able to obtain funds to increase its loans to business and consumers, and interest rates were held to relatively low levels. During the war, banks had accumulated large holdings of government bonds, and as the peacetime economy boomed they began to sell these securities in order to get funds for loans to their customers. This continuing sale of government bonds would normally have depressed their prices, making the Treasury's job of managing the public debt increasingly difficult. To prevent this from happening the Federal Reserve Banks stepped in to buy government bonds and keep their price up. Since the sellers of the bonds were banks, this was equivalent to pumping new funds into the credit system and making it easy for borrowers to get loans.

Supporting the price of government bonds also tended to keep interest rates low, partly because of the continual inflow of new funds into the money market from the Federal Reserve Banks. In addition, maintaining the price of government bonds kept their yield, or effective interest rate, from rising. If a $1,000 bond has an annual interest payment of $25, the yield is 2.5 percent. But if the same bond can be bought for $900 the yield will be 2.77 percent. With the Federal Reserve buying bonds to keep their price up, the effective interest rate was held down. Since the rate of return on government bonds is one of the most important interest rates in the economy, "pegging" the price of government bonds tended to keep all other interest rates down as well.

These policies were followed primarily in order to ease the Treasury's problems in managing the national debt. But they had the effect of immobilizing monetary policy as an instrument for holding back price increases at the very time when other inflationary pressures were strong. This use of the instruments of monetary policy did not end until 1951, when the Treasury and the Federal Reserve Board reached a famous "accord" that freed the Fed from responsibility for the prices of government securities. From that time on the monetary authorities were able to use their powers to restrain credit expansion more effectively, and a primary step was taken toward development of a coordinated economic policy whose chief goals were economic growth and stability.

Some important lessons can be learned from the growth record of the 1946–1953 years. First, the good performance of the economy was by no means automatic or self-generating. The two great stimuli came from sources outside the current flow of spending. One was the large amount of liquid assets held by consumers at the start of the period. The second was the increase in government spending after the Korean War began. Other more basic factors were creating an environment favorable to economic growth, such as a growing population, a high rate of family formation, and an advancing technology. But the immediate stimuli to rapid economic growth between 1946 and 1953 were related to war rather than peace and were not generated out of normal economic activity.

The second lesson is related to the first: Government economic policies can be very important influences on the nation's economic performance. Although the purpose of the increase in government spending of 1950–53 was to fight a war, the effect was stimulation of the economy. The federal government gave the economy a shot in the arm while pursuing other policies, indicating what might be accomplished if a conscious effort to stimulate economic growth were made. The experience also showed that spending policy and monetary policy had to be coordinated if the best results were to be obtained.

The third lesson concerns the relationship between full employment and inflation. It became clear that a high-pressure economy performing at or very near its full potential could generate inflationary price increases well before full use of resources was reached. Economists, policy makers and the general public began to wonder whether the two goals of full-employment prosperity and stable prices were compatible. The experience of 1950–53 was the first of several that indicate that there may be a trade-off between those two goals: the more we have of one the less we can have of the other. Unfortunately, the lesson may have been learned too well, for it was fear of inflation that underlay the policy decisions of the next seven years and was an important reason for the poor economic growth that followed 1953.

YEARS OF INADEQUATE GROWTH, 1953–1960

Following the peak year of 1953, the economy entered the doldrums. The average annual growth of GNP over the next seven years was only 2.4 percent. Unemployment rates rose, even when measured only at prosperity peaks within the period: 2.9 percent of the labor force in 1953, 4.2 percent in 1956, and 5.6 percent in 1960. Recessions were more frequent and closer together, until at the end of the period they occurred in both 1958 and 1959.

One important implication of this performance was little understood at the time: it meant practically no increase in living standards. Gross national product per person rose at a rate of only 0.4 percent per year, a rate so low that it may have been only a statistical illusion. No significant progress was made in moving toward greater wealth, in reducing poverty, or in increasing the amount of public services in education, health, and similar areas of need.

Two other developments aggravated the problem. Automation and the scientific revolution in agriculture created added uncertainties for industrial workers and blacks. Both of these developments are long-term trends that were present before 1953 and are still with us. But in the 1950s they took some special turns. Automation of industrial manufacturing processes was applied on a large scale in some of our most important manufacturing industries. For example, production of automobiles and trucks increased from 7,428,040 units in 1953 to 7,869,271 units in 1960. But employment of production workers *fell* by 176,100 from 739,400 to 563,300. This was by no means the whole story of automation in this period, but the fact that it was intensively applied in a number of principal industries created serious employment problems that were not offset by economic growth.

The scientific revolution in agriculture also had a special impact as many farm families and workers left the farm for the cities. The South felt the effect of these changes with particular severity: between 1950 and 1959 the number of farm workers in 14 Southern states fell from 4,550,000 to 3,146,000, a decline of over 30 percent. This pool of unused labor was composed largely of blacks from rural areas with little education and few skills. In large part barred from industrial employment in the South by the racial attitudes of white workers and employers, as well as by their own deficiencies in education and skill, many of them migrated to the urban centers of the Northeastern states and California. There they found few jobs and poor housing as well as employers whose hiring standards were often so high as to exclude them from jobs. Complicating the problem was the fact that most new factories were being built in the suburban fringes of the large cities, blacks were barred from homes in the nearby white suburbs, and public transportation from the central cities to the fringe factories

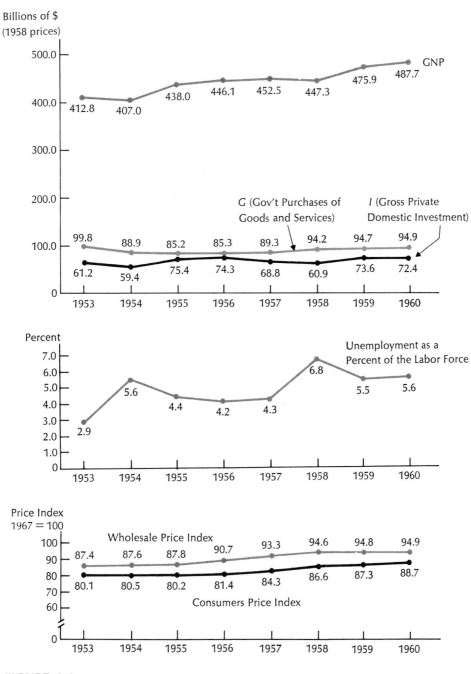

FIGURE 9-2
Years of Inadequate Growth, 1953–60

was largely nonexistent. The migrating blacks might not have been able to get jobs in the suburban factories, but they were not given the chance for the most part. Instead, when they could get jobs, they were funneled into the low-wage industries and service employment of the central cities. Since a large number of the new arrivals were young men and women, the birth rate was high and a population explosion hit the urban ghettos.

Migration of blacks to northern cities was not new. Some 1,500,000 had moved north in the thirty years prior to World War II, and even more during the war. But the wartime migrants had found jobs in a booming economy. Many of the 1,500,000 who followed in the fifties couldn't find employment. Slowed economic growth and automation, together with the old problems of discrimination in employment and housing, saw to that. Then, when the babies of the early 1950s began to enter the labor market in the late 1960s as young men and women and couldn't get jobs, the stage was set for the great urban and racial crisis of our time. Failure to sustain adequate economic growth and to compensate for changes in the structure of the economy were at the root of the problem.

The reasons for the relatively weak economic performance of the period are not hard to find. First, and most important, was the absence of the special kinds of economic stimuli that made the period before 1953 so dynamic. Both the unsatisfied backlogs of consumer demand and the overly large consumer savings of 1946–47 were largely gone. The end of hostilities in Korea caused federal government expenditures to level off. The usual long-run trends that stimulate economic growth continued, of course: rising population, technological change, new products and services, expansion of state and local government expenditures, and similar factors. But while long-term trends can create a favorable environment for economic growth, they do not guarantee growth from year to year to match the economy's potential.

Second, the economic policies of the period inhibited economic growth. In retrospect, this was probably the most important single reason for the economy's poor performance.

A new administration had come into office in 1953, dedicated to a policy of strengthening private enterprise and reducing the economic role of government. It felt that continued inflation was the most important single barrier to the continued health and dynamism of a private economy, arguing that inflation penalized saving and tended to pull investment funds into speculative rather than expansion-creating channels. Stable prices became a primary goal of economic policy, although the administration still held to the policy of promoting full employment. Economic policies had three goals in this period: encouragement of the private sector of the economy, stable prices, and high levels of economic activity. The potential conflict between these goals was not fully appreciated.

To promote the first goal of encouraging private enterprise, the administration cut back federal government expenditures. The reduction between 1953 and 1954 was almost $10 billion, concentrated in the national defense area.[2] Although state and local government spending continued to rise, the result was a substantial reduction in the government contribution to GNP.

To compensate for the decline in government spending, the administration sought to stimulate the private sector of the economy, particularly by cutting taxes. It was felt that releasing business enterprise from the inhibiting effects of taxes would create the dynamism that seemed to have gone out of the private sector; investment expenditures would increase; the multiplied effect on total spending would push GNP to a level that justified the higher levels of investment; and further increases in investment would be promoted. If, at the same time, anti-inflationary policies could hold prices in check, it was expected that there would be a healthy, growing economy that could sustain full employment without inflation. Reduced to its simplest form, the policy was one of "pump priming" through tax reductions rather than federal government expenditures.

The policy got off to a good start. Tax reductions in 1953 and 1954 amounted to about $7.4 billion, with some three-fourths of the total coming out of business tax liabilities. The increased after-tax profits of business firms led to a large jump in private investment, from $59.4 billion in 1954 to $75.4 billion in 1955. The administration's timing was a little off, however: the reduction in government spending was concentrated in 1953, before the stimulus to private investment could take hold. The result was the recession of 1953–54, the second recession of the postwar years, in which unemployment rates rose to 5.6 percent of the labor force and there was a small decline in GNP. Then the tax-stimulated investment boom of 1955–56 took over and the GNP moved up to new and higher levels. It seemed as if the policy of replacing some federal spending with increased business investment was going to work.

The prosperity of those years brought the third arm of the administration's economic policy strategy into play. Prices began to creep upward as unemployment rates fell below 4.5 percent of the labor force, and policy makers turned their attention to the inflation they feared so much. Efforts were made to reduce the federal deficit and bring the budget into balance. In 1956 and 1957 a budget surplus was achieved for the first time since 1948. In addition, the Federal Reserve System began to restrain the ability of the banks to lend, and the Treasury marketed new issues of government securities at higher interest rates. These policies of fiscal and monetary restraint were all designed to dampen down total spending, hold the creation of credit in check and prevent the boom from pushing prices up. Unfortunately, things did not work out that way.

---

[2] This aspect of domestic economic policy had a far-reaching impact on foreign policy. It led to the policies of "massive retaliation" and foreign alliances: U.S. security was to be maintained by creating a threat system based on nuclear weapons, while allies (NATO, SEATO, etc.) took on the task of maintaining the ground forces necessary to contain local problems and ground attacks. This would enable the U.S. to reduce its conventional military forces (army and navy) and thereby reduce federal government expenditures at home.

First of all, the investment boom began to create excess production capacity. The tax reductions of 1953–54 had largely benefited business rather than consumers, and when the lid was clamped on government spending the capacity of the economy to produce began to outrun purchasing power. This development is dramatically shown by the data on utilization of capacity in manufacturing industries (Table 9-1). These figures show essentially "full" utilization of

TABLE 9-1
Utilization of Manufacturing Capacity, 1953–1960
(Percent)

1953	94.2
1954	83.5
1955	90.0
1956	87.7
1957	83.6
1958	74.0
1959	81.5
1960	80.6

Source: *Federal Reserve Bulletin,* July 1967, p. 1098.

plant capacity in 1953. But by 1957–60, use of plant capacity had fallen to and below that of the recession year of 1954. This situation immediately began to feed back on investment decisions, and spending for new plant and equipment leveled off in the late 1950s. Without a corresponding increase in purchasing power, the investment boom of the mid-1950s brought itself to an end and created a serious problem of excess capacity that continued to hang over the economy like an ominous cloud.

Contributing to the failure of purchasing power to grow adequately was the phenomenon of "fiscal drag." Very briefly, it worked like this:

> The progressive nature of the federal tax structure means that tax payments rise faster than incomes as people move up into higher tax brackets. When GNP rises and carries individual incomes upward with it, disposable income (after taxes) rises more slowly than GNP. This "drag" becomes stronger as GNP continues to rise, making it *increasingly* difficult to achieve further increases in GNP.
>
> Indeed, with the tax structure of the late 1950s, the increase of federal revenues brought about by a rising GNP would have resulted in a federal budget surplus well before full employment levels of GNP could have been achieved (assuming the existing level of federal expenditures).

The remedy for "fiscal drag" was either tax reductions for consumers or increased federal spending. Either would have promoted the growth in purchasing power that the economy needed so badly. But neither was consistent with the anti-inflationary policies pursued by the policy makers, for both would result in increased spending.

Finally, prices continued to rise. An upward creep in the index of consumer prices that amounted to about 1.5 percent annually began in 1955 and persisted in the face of both fiscal restraint and tight money. Particularly shocking was an increase of 2.7 percent in consumer prices during the *recession* year of 1958, when GNP fell and unemployment rose to its highest level since early in World War II over 17 years before.

The continuing rise in prices during a period of surplus labor and excess capacity was hard to explain. Many economists at that time accepted the view that prices rose only when excessive demand pulled unemployment up, and that the way to halt price increases was to eliminate the excessive demand. But in the late 1950s the world seemed to stand on its head: excessive demand had been eliminated by fiscal restraint and tight money, yet prices seemed to rise as fast as ever.

By 1960 the policies of the preceding eight years were a shambles. The nation's economic growth had slowed down significantly, and standards of living had almost ceased to rise. Unemployment rates were consistently high. Production levels were well below the economy's capabilities. Prices continued to rise. Like the ancient medical practice of "bleeding," tight money and fiscal restraint had succeeded only in reducing the vitality of the patient. Even the Washington policy makers came partially to recognize their failure, and during the 1958 recession the federal government incurred the largest peacetime budget deficit in its history. But such was the fear of deficits and inflation that by 1960 a budget surplus was achieved once more and the economy was again in the doldrums.

THE "NEW" ECONOMICS, 1960–1966

The period of stagnation for the American economy continued into 1961. Although the GNP rose in both 1960 and 1961, the growth was meager and marred by another recession in late 1960 and early 1961 (see Figure 9-3). Then, beginning in the spring of 1961, a long and steady advance began that ultimately became the longest sustained period of economic expansion in the nation's history. The chief feature of the years from 1960 through 1966 was an average annual increase in GNP of almost 5 percent, accompanied by reduction in official unemployment rates to under 4 percent of the labor force, a steady increase in utilization of manufacturing capacity to over 90 percent, and a surprising degree of price stability that lasted into 1965.

Most economists attribute this remarkable turnabout in economic performance to a dramatic shift in national economic policy from restraint to stimulation. An equally large share of the credit must go to the dynamism of the American economy as a whole, which showed that it could still generate rapid growth if properly encouraged. Encouragement came primarily through increased government expenditures and tax reductions, supplemented by relatively easy credit policies. Increased federal expenditures came first. The previous administration had kept the budget in 1960 to a level slightly above that in 1953, but since transfer payments (such as social security benefits) had risen, the purchase of goods and services, that is, those government expenditures

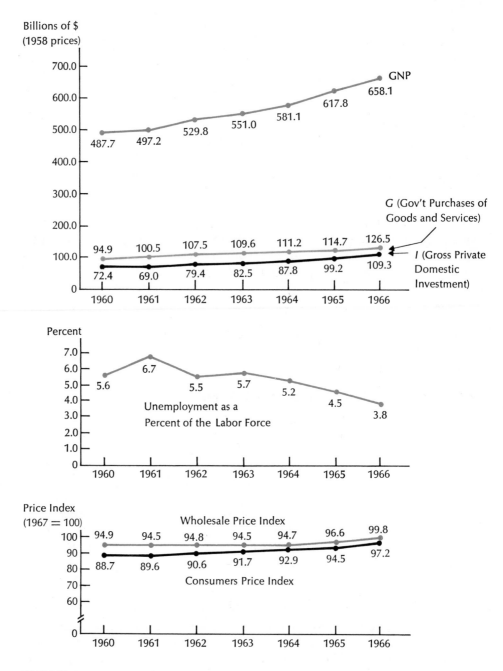

FIGURE 9-3
Economic Growth Under the "New Economics," 1960–66

that contribute to GNP, were almost 10 percent below the 1953 level. The new administration changed that policy. Federal budget expenditures were quickly raised, and along with them purchases of goods and services. The rapidity and size of these changes can be shown by comparing 1953 with 1960 and 1964, as in Figure 9-4.

FIGURE 9-4
Changes in Federal Budget
Expenditures and Federal Purchases
of Goods and Services, 1953–64

Larger federal expenditures were supplemented by substantial increases in spending by state and local governments. Between 1953 and 1960, state and local governments increased their purchase of goods and services by about 50 percent, from $24.6 billion to $46.1 billion. After 1960, they accelerated their spending, and by 1966 it had increased once more by well over 50 percent to $76.2 billion. One reason for the acceleration was the fact that tax revenues were rising more rapidly than in the 1950s because of the rapid economic expansion.

Tax reduction to stimulate the private sector of the economy was the second, and perhaps more important, arm of economic policy in the 1960s. In 1962 two measures were taken to encourage business investment. First, the Treasury liberalized the rules under which business firms could charge depreciation expenses. By enlarging the amounts allowed and reducing the time period over which assets could be depreciated, the government allowed business firms to recapture investment costs more rapidly and reduced business tax liabilities in the short run. In effect, business firms were able to retain larger amounts of cash and had to pay less in taxes while they were depreciating their equipment.

Second, a "tax credit" was permitted on investment expenditures: business tax liabilities were reduced by an amount equal to 7 percent of new investment in plant and equipment. Together, the tax credit and new depreciation rules brought a reduction in business taxes of about $2 billion annually. The new rules were specifically designed to encourage economic growth by stimulating private investment.

The most important tax reductions came in 1964, however. Individual income tax liabilities were cut by a total of $9.1 billion, largely in 1964 but partly in 1965. Corporate tax liabilities were reduced by an additional $2.4 billion, also spread over two years. Other changes in the tax laws provided benefits to low-income families and the aged, and the investment tax credit was broadened. In these years, however, the main tax benefits went to consumers rather than business, reversing the pattern of a decade before.

There was much debate at the time over the effect of tax reductions and increased expenditures on the national budget as a whole. It might appear as if a massive federal budget deficit would result from increased spending and reduced taxes. But those who made that argument overlooked the fact that economic expansion would raise incomes and automatically lead to higher revenues, even with tax rates at lower levels. This indeed was the case: the federal budget deficit rose to over $8.2 billion in 1964 but fell to $4.7 billion in 1965 as the effects of the tax rate reductions began to be felt in higher GNP and higher tax revenues. As far as the budget deficit was concerned, through 1965 and even into 1966 a large deficit was considered to be desirable because of its stimulating effect on aggregate demand. Only in 1965 did it fall below $5 billion, and the total federal deficit for 1961 through 1966 was $40.4 billion.

Monetary policy was relegated to a secondary role in economic policy during the boom of the 1960s. The money supply (currency in circulation plus checking accounts in banks) was allowed to expand somewhat more rapidly than business activity from 1961 through 1965. These relatively easy money market conditions were designed to facilitate expansion to full-employment levels of GNP, and were continued as long as prices remained relatively stable.[3]

These government policies provided a sturdy base for expansion in the private sector of the economy. Business investment in plant and equipment roared ahead at a rate of 9.7 percent annually between 1962 and 1966, a pace almost double that of the growth in GNP. But rising aggregate demand justified the rapid growth of investment, and the utilization of plant capacity gradually rose to over the 90 percent level in 1966.

A second driving force in the private sector of the economy was consumer demand, particularly for automobiles, electrical equipment, and housing. A substantial portion of the increased purchasing power of consumers came from

---

[3] Two qualifications should be made here. First, in the early 1960s "Operation Twist" attempted with some limited success to keep interest rates on long-term borrowing relatively low while short-term interest rates were allowed to rise somewhat. The idea was to facilitate long-run investment expenditures while limiting short-term movements of capital from the United States to foreign countries, in an effort to reduce the deficit in the U.S. balance of payments. Second, starting in late 1965, monetary policy began to be used to fight inflation, as we shall shortly see.

higher incomes, as GNP rose and unemployment fell. Some, however, came from expansion of credit. Consumer credit outstanding reached a level equal to 19 percent of disposable income in 1966, up from 16 percent in 1961. A goodly amount of cash was also raised by refinancing of mortgages, which channeled a large (but unmeasured) chunk of funds from investment in houses to current spending. A subnormal rate of saving prevailed in 1961–66, as a result of these and other factors. Savings as a proportion of disposable income averaged only 5.4 percent in those years, as compared with 6.3 percent in 1953–60.

This then, was the anatomy of the great upswing in prosperity of the first half of the 1960s. Government spending plus tax incentives stimulated more than normal increases in business investment and consumer spending, and monetary policy facilitated the expansion by making adequate credit available. The result was a doubling of the rate of growth of GNP as compared with the previous seven years, a large increase in the economy's productive power, elimination of the gap between actual and potential output, and reduction of unemployment rates to relatively tolerable levels. Yet price levels were remarkably steady until the latter part of 1965. It was a superb economic performance, and showed that the existing concepts of economic policy could push the economy to high levels of economic activity.

The one disquieting development was the persistence of what came to be called "hard-core unemployment," which even very high levels of economic performance could not reduce significantly. Hard-core unemployment was considered a myth by most economists in the early sixties. The term itself refers to persons who lack the qualifications for existing jobs and who are passed over even though the growth of aggregate demand may create enough new jobs to employ them. Many of the hard-core unemployed are not counted in the official unemployment statistics because they no longer try to find employment and are usually classified as "hidden unemployed." Estimates of their number in the mid-1960s varied from about 1,500,000 to over twice that number. The reasons for their difficulty in finding employment are varied, and for many of them more than one reason applies:

Poor education and/or lack of usable skills.

Racial discrimination.

Social stigmas: police or prison records, history of mental illness, poor or erratic employment records, etc.

Age: unemployed workers over 45 have *great* difficulty in getting placed.

Discouragement, because of a history of rejection or failure.

In addition, the logistics of the job market now require a high degree of mobility in order merely to get to the suburban location of many new plants. Poverty reduces that mobility and closes off many opportunities to otherwise qualified persons.

The seriousness of the problem can be shown by looking at the apparent success of the economy in reducing officially measured unemployment to an average level of 3.8 percent in 1966. This was accomplished only through unusual reductions in the size of the labor force by over 1 million persons, most of them young people who would have been entering the labor market for the first time. The reductions were the result of the following factors:

Increased size of the armed forces due to escalation of the war in Viet Nam in 1964–66: about 600,000 persons.

Abnormal increases in college enrollments due to draft avoidance: perhaps as many as 400,000 persons.

Manpower training and development programs: about 20,000 persons.

Not all of these persons would have been unemployed if they had been in the labor market. Nevertheless, probably half of them or more would have been added to the number of unemployed in 1966 under normal conditions. If that were the case, the unemployment rate would still have been close to 5 percent instead of 3.8 percent. A serious problem of unemployment remained in spite of strong growth.

WAR, INFLATION, AND RECESSION, 1966–1970

The drive of the economy toward full employment was capped in the late 1960s by a confused period in which economic policy was subordinated to the needs of a wartime economy. Government expenditures were the chief driving force for expansion and the economy pushed forward to levels that began to move prices upward. Monetary restraint was used in an effort to hold back the expansionary forces, along with an increase in income taxes, but without real success. Not until 1970 did the increase in economic activity slow down, but by then it was too late to halt the continued spread of inflationary pressures through the economy. We witnessed the worst possible combination of events, recession with inflation. Figure 9-5 shows how the chief variables moved.

The chief cause of inflation in the late 1960s was increased government spending associated with the war in Vietnam, culminating in a federal budget deficit of over $25 billion in 1968, on top of an $8.7 billion deficit in 1967. With unemployment rates at 3.8 percent of the work force and manufacturing output capacity utilized at close to 90 percent, there was very little slack to absorb such massive increases in spending. Under the circumstances, there was no way for the economy to avoid a 15 to 25 percent increase in the general price level without moving to price controls.

This point cannot be stressed too much. As we shall see in Chapter 19, which discusses inflation, an inflation caused by excessive demand works its way through the economy in an inflationary spiral that takes some time before its force wears out and prices stop rising. Once the process starts, little can be done about it. The first policy mistake of the late 1960s was to get such a process going.

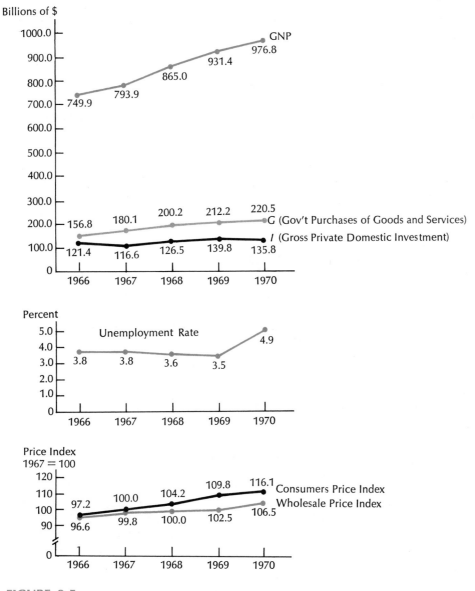

FIGURE 9-5
Inflation and Recession During the Vietnam War, 1966–70

Even before those huge deficits, the difficulties presented by trying to hold an expanding economy in check had been shown by the "credit crunch" of 1966. The Federal Reserve System held back the expansion of the credit system in the face of growing aggregate demand. The result was a shortage of credit in the fall of 1966 so severe that interest rates rose to levels that had last been seen at the close of the Civil War a hundred years before. A credit panic and stock market crash was averted only by a general easing of the tight money policy in late 1966 and early 1967. In retrospect, it is easy to see what happened. The forces pushing the economy forward were stronger than ever, and when monetary brakes were applied the economy threatened to go into a spin. The brakes should have come in the form of reduced government spending and/or tax increases (some minor tax increases were enacted in 1966) in order to get at the source of the problem, but for political reasons those solutions were not feasible.

An unsuccessful effort was also made to establish "guideposts" for wages and prices designed to hold inflation in check. This aspect of anti-inflation policy will be discussed further in Chapter 19. At this point all we need do is note that asking big business and big labor to hold back price and wage increases in the face of continued inflationary pressures from government spending was equivalent to King Canute's edict to halt the movement of the tide. A grand gesture, it was doomed from the start.

An increase in personal income taxes in 1968, in the form of a 10 percent surcharge (in which the tax payment is increased by 10 percent), also failed to halt the growth of demand. Consumers merely reduced their savings and spending increased just about as much as it would have without the tax increase.

Underneath the issues of economic policy in these years lurked the political problem of an unpopular war. The administration was trying to increase its military effort substantially when there was little economic slack, without asking the general public to make any significant sacrifices. The result was another war-born inflation.

A new administration came into office in 1969, determined to halt the inflation. The increase in government spending was slowed to half the pace of the previous few years. A federal budget surplus of over $3 billion was achieved in 1969. This was a dramatic shift from the huge deficit of the previous year, adding up to a net reduction of $28 billion in the federal contribution to aggregate demand and having a depressing effect of double that amount on total spending. In addition, the Federal Reserve System reinstituted its tight money policy in a steadier and less intense form than in 1966. The result of this combination of depressive fiscal and monetary policies was just about as expected. Business investment declined, GNP (in constant dollars) fell, and unemployment rose as the economy went into its planned recession.

But prices kept rising! A 2.5 percent increase in wholesale prices in 1969 was followed by a 4 percent increase in 1970, while consumer prices rose by about 5 percent in each of those years. Concurrently, the unemployment rate rose from 3.5 percent in 1969 to 4.9 percent in 1970 and to over 6 percent in 1971. To the Johnson inflation was added the Nixon recession.

The inherent policy error was the easy assumption that today's economic slack can eliminate yesterday's inflationary pressures. By 1969 there was little to be done about the inflation generated by the federal deficits of 1967–68. A higher price level was inevitable. A recession of the scope generated by the economic policies of 1969–70 might hold it down a bit: perhaps a 15 percent price increase over a three-year period instead of a 25 percent increase over five years. But once the inflationary deficits were eliminated, we could normally expect prices to rise to a new and higher level and level off there. The reasons why an inflation does not feed on itself and keep cumulating are explained in Chapter 19 where the 1971 price and wage freeze is also discussed. These considerations imply that the 1970–71 recession was a needless price to pay for results that would have occurred anyway.

SOME CONCLUSIONS AND SOME ISSUES

The growth of the American economy from the time of World War II provides some interesting lessons. One of the most important is that a large and mature economy can achieve the growth it needs. The growth of the American economy since 1946, uninterrupted by any serious depressions, has been steadier than any other period in the nation's history. It has also been more rapid: at no other time in the past 100 years has the American economy sustained an average annual growth rate of 3.9 percent for a period as long as 25 years. And this was done in spite of the unnecessary slowdown of 1953–60.

A second lesson is that proper public policies are essential if a high level of performance is to be achieved. The potential may be there, but achievement can fall well below possibilities unless economic growth and high levels of performance are conscious goals with high priority.

A third lesson is less satisfying. A high rate of economic growth will not automatically solve all of the nation's economic problems and may bring new ones in its train. Hard-core unemployment and a good deal of the poverty still found in America require more than just general increases in GNP, although that will certainly help. As for new problems, it is now clear that rapid growth can bring significant inflationary pressures. There are other undesirable results of economic growth: everything speeds up, including air and water pollution, urban congestion, and other concomitants of a growing economy. Rapid change is itself one by-product of rapid economic growth, and change is always unsettling. One reason for the unrest of the late 1960s was the way economic change and inflation threatened the status and goals of some Americans.

Growth can be unbalanced, leaving behind some important segments of the population, such as many of the poor and racial minorities like blacks and Latins. It can cause deterioration in areas that are bypassed, such as Appalachia or the central cities of our metropolitan areas. It may focus on consumers' goods like television sets and automobiles, while public facilities such as parks and schools are slighted.

Growth can be misdirected into armaments or moon shots or supersonic aircraft at a time when housing and urban problems and racial conflict and deterioration of the railway system cry for a large allocation of resources.

Growth can be destructive when adequate provision is not made for preservation of the natural environment. Demand for power can bring destructive strip mining for coal or heat pollution of water by atomic power plants. Growth of production and population can bring greater air and water pollution. Use of chemicals in agriculture to increase output can poison the whole food chain.

The very success we have had in sustaining a high growth rate over the last quarter century raises the most fundamental issues for our economic and social order. Growth may well be desirable, although some say it is not. At the very least, it will have to be managed more effectively in the future than it has been in the past. But how? Will greater regulations have to be imposed on the private sector? Can tax and other monetary incentives be relied on? Will private ownership and control of resources have to be modified, and if so, to what extent and in what ways? These issues all relate to the allocation of resources among various uses, and raise serious questions about the extent to which a modern, growing industrial society can rely on the self-adjusting market economy as the mechanism through which these decisions can be made.

Summary

Between the end of World War II and 1970 the U.S. economy was marked by periods of both rapid growth and relative stagnation. Though long-run stimuli to growth were always present in the form of rising population, technological innovation, new products and services, and the expansion of state and local governmental services, the pattern of growth during this period reflected the increasing impact of government policy on economic performance.

Rapid growth in 1946–53 was partly the result of a dynamic private sector that still felt the impact of wartime spending, and partly the result of rising governmental spending due to the war in Korea. This was followed by a period of slow growth and relative stagnation in 1953–60 as the federal government followed policies designed primarily to keep prices from rising, but which had the effect of creating a growing gap between the economy's capacity and its actual performance. The "new economics" of 1960–66 got the economy out of the doldrums and moving back toward full employment, very largely through a policy of planned government deficits and monetary ease. In 1966–70, however, the inflationary effects of wartime spending again began to appear and the trade-off between full employment and price increases became clear. Problems of this period were considerably increased by poorly conceived efforts to halt inflation, which had the effect, primarily, of bringing a recession in 1970–71 instead of stopping the rise of prices.

The very success of the economy in 1960–66 brought to the fore the issue of the goals of economic growth, however, and whether it was not misdirected, unbalanced, and destructive unless it were guided properly.

Key Concepts

Employment Act of 1946. The legislation that formally ended the policy of laissez-faire with respect to the level of output and employment. Henceforth, the federal government was responsible for maintenance of high levels of employment.

Fiscal drag. The tendency of tax payments to rise more rapidly than GNP, thereby acting to hold back continuing economic expansion.

Tax credit. Provision for reduced tax payments designed to encourage some form of economic behavior such as greater investment. It is the opposite of a *tax surcharge,* which is an increase in tax payments aimed at reducing some type of economic activity. Both are based on the same tax rate and represent a change in the amount paid.

Sources and Patterns of Economic Growth

10

Our discussion of economic growth has concentrated on the immediate future. The chapters on potential growth of the American economy and its recent growth performance emphasized the short-run factors that will influence growth over the next ten years. The analysis assumed, however, that there will be no large changes in the underlying forces that produce economic growth. This chapter will look at those underlying forces.

First, a word of warning: There is very little agreement among economists on the issues this chapter discusses. Almost all economists would agree that economic growth depends on investment. The more an economy can divert from current use and set aside for expansion, the greater its ability to expand production will be. Investment requires saving, and together the two are essential to economic growth.

But that is where agreement ends. Why do people save? What are the factors that stimulate investment? What kinds of investment spending will give the greatest payoff in economic growth? Should more be invested in the public sector or in the private sector? Can economic growth proceed smoothly, or is it an erratic and unstable process? In the long run will economic growth slow down in a mature industrial economy? Does economic growth itself so change the social and economic environment that the lessons of the past become less and less applicable to the future? These are some of the very difficult questions on which there is little or no agreement among economists.

Yet they are questions of great importance. They must be considered when policies to influence either the rate or the direction of economic growth in the short run are being designed. If such policies are inconsistent with the longer-run reality of the economy, they may be ineffective or have harmful results, or bring the economy into an entirely unexpected position.

This chapter will range widely. It starts with a discussion of attitudes toward work and wealth. It then moves to education and knowledge as sources of growth and tries to assess their significance as against physical inputs of labor, capital and land. Then comes a discussion of the role of innovation, technological change, and the innovating businessman, or entrepreneur. These topics lead inevitably into discussions of the unevenness of economic growth, the mature-economy question, and changes brought about by growth itself. The conclusion is qualified optimism: the American economy has a strong drive toward economic growth, but there are difficulties along the way that may bring about very much less than ideal results.

ATTITUDES TOWARD WORK AND WEALTH

When Edmund Hillary was asked why he wanted to climb Mt. Everest he responded, "Because it is there." His statement typifies an attitude widely prevalent in our civilization: a desire to excel, to accomplish things that have never been done before, to exceed the achievements of the past. This *achievement motive* is found perhaps in its purest form in sports. Records of all conceivable kinds are kept, and the highest distinction goes not only to those who win, but to those whose performance exceeds that of past competitors. Why should a man try to run a mile in 3 minutes and 50 seconds, jump higher than 6½ feet, or hit 62 home runs? Because no one else has ever done it before? That is indeed the reason, and a silly one at that, when you stop to think about it.

Yet this type of motivation may be an important source of economic growth, perhaps the most fundamental of all. Oswald Spengler, the German philosopher, pointed to the "Faustian soul" of Western man, whom he pictures as striving for an ideal of perfection that is impossible to reach. Even the religious ideal of salvation is similar, something to be striven for but never attainable in this life. All of Western civilization has been influenced by this way of thinking, Spengler argued. Even the architecture of Gothic cathedrals, he said, showed in its arches and buttresses an upward-striving goal, reaching toward an unattainable infinite. Gordon Childe, the English archaeologist, stated the same concept in a different way. He argued that the earliest development of prehistoric European peoples showed a frontier spirit that gladly accepted the challenge of the unknown and sought to move out into the new and the untried. Werner Sombart, the German economic historian, wrote of a capitalist "spirit" of rivalry and competition to excel over others, which motivated the market economy.

In recent years, David McClelland, an American psychologist, has stressed the achievement motive as the key to economic growth. Among the psychological needs of the individual, he argues, is a need for achievement, *n*-achievement, in his terminology. People are not born with it, but acquire it in their early training and upbringing when they are taught to do well, to excel, to exceed others, to compete against a standard of excellence. A high *n*-achievement is acquired through the socialization process early in life. McClelland argues that a "society with a generally high level of *n*-achievement will produce more energetic entrepreneurs who, in turn, produce more rapid economic development."

A high motivation to excel, widely dispersed through the social system, may well be part of the attitudinal base of economic development. But why not excel in warfare, or religion, or sport, or the arts? None of these efforts leads to *economic* growth. It is not a generalized achievement motive that leads to economic growth, but achievement motives aimed specifically at material goals such as wealth and leisure. The values of the social system must place acquisition of wealth at a very high level, and those who are wealthy must be given high status because of their wealth, in order that the achievement motive may pay off in economic development.

There are two connecting links in our society between wealth, status, and economic motives. One is by way of the economic institutions of the market. Thorstein Veblen (1857–1929), the American economist, pointed out that the value system of a market economy must necessarily be highly materialistic. It puts great stress on the acquisition of wealth and tends to consider those things valuable that have a high market value. The reason is not hard to find. The means of subsistence, namely food, clothing, and shelter, are obtained by purchase and sale on markets. The worker sells his labor for a wage, and uses the money he obtains to buy what he needs. Without the wage he and his family would starve, or subsist at the very low and degraded level of private charity or public welfare. Success in the marketplace becomes necessary for subsistence, for life itself. It is only to be expected in such a society, argued Veblen, that achievement and success will be measured in monetary terms.

An analogy will make the point clear. In a society based on hunting, the successful hunter has high status because he produces the things necessary for survival. Similarly, in a market economy success in moneymaking brings recognition and approval. The fundamental achievement criteria become pecuniary.[1]

Veblen argued in *The Theory of the Leisure Class* that pecuniary standards of success lead to waste. The wealthy, in order to claim the status their wealth entitles them to, have to prove their affluence by spending conspicuously. Fine houses, many servants, expensive entertainment, or anything that requires large expenditures will do, so long as it is highly visible. This *conspicuous consumption* causes *pecuniary emulation* on the part of others. For example, the jet set lolls on the beaches of Acapulco or the Riviera, so the college

---

[1] This point should not be pushed too far. An affluent society can afford a multiplicity of values. Recognition of achievement in the arts and sciences does not always bring great monetary gains. But even in those fields the "successful" writer, artist, or scientist earns a good income. If he doesn't, he is not considered successful by more than a small group of aficionados. Veblen himself was "unsuccessful." He never rose above the rank of assistant professor and late in life was able to continue lecturing at the New School for Social Research in New York only because former students were willing to help pay his salary. He was one of America's greatest economists and probably its foremost social scientist by today's judgment, yet he was unable to achieve success in the usually accepted terms of his own time. Late in life he received professional recognition by being elected president of the American Economic Association, but he contemptuously turned down this highest honor that his colleagues could bestow upon him.

sophomore emulates them by going to Fort Lauderdale during spring vacation. The result is a pattern of consumption that emphasizes display and expense at all levels in the social system. Veblen called it wasteful, and in terms of biological needs, it is. But these patterns of consumption gratify fundamental human needs for recognition and status in a market-oriented society with a market-oriented value system. They are part of the fundamental structure of the system.

CONSPICUOUS CONSUMPTION. *Expenditures designed to show possession of wealth.*

PECUNIARY EMULATION. *Imitation of the expenditure patterns of the very wealthy by persons of lesser wealth.*

This materialistic value system is closely tied to the process of economic growth. First, success is defined largely in terms of wealth and income. Amassing of wealth is done in a market economy by producing more of what other people are willing to pay for. This leads to a built-in drive to increase output, sales, and profits. Second, patterns of consumption and emulation emphasize spending. There is a built-in drive to increase consumption. On both the supply and demand sides of the market, in both investment and consumption, people seek to produce more and to spend more.

The second connecting link between wealth, status and economic motives, which reinforces the influence of the market economy, is to be found in ethical and religious values. Max Weber, a German sociologist, and Richard H. Tawney, an English historian, have argued that the Protestant Reformation in the sixteenth century, together with related changes in Catholic countries, resulted in the rise of an economic "ethic," which greatly stimulated economic growth and promoted the rise of capitalism. During the Middle Ages, they argued, the *approved* motive for economic activity was the preservation of a society within which the individual could prepare for salvation. Acquisition of wealth was frowned upon by the Church because it distracted men from salvation and directed their attention to material things. Wealth itself was not evil, but its pursuit was the wrong path to take.

The Reformation changed all that, according to Weber and Tawney. Martin Luther's concept of the "calling," or the idea that each individual is "called" to that task God wills for him on earth, placed all earthly activities, whether those of businessman or priest, on an equal level. The highest morality lay in fulfilling one's duties in worldly affairs, whatever one's calling. To this was added the Calvinist doctrine of the "elect," the idea that salvation was pre-destined rather than earned; that the individual had no control over his fate and God, in his inscrutable ways, had already decided whether one would be damned or saved. This harsh Calvinist doctrine of predestination created serious theological and ethical problems for the individual. Although one's fate was determined, the individual had no way of knowing what it was. How, then, should he behave? Should he throw all caution to the winds and act in any way he liked, irrespective of the moral laws of the Bible and the Word of God? Or should he behave according to the religious laws of morality?

The divines had an answer. Anyone destined to be a saint would lead a saint's life on earth. Transgressions of the moral law were a sure sign of damnation. Even doubts about one's salvation might be a sign that one was not destined to live among the angels in the hereafter. The only way to avoid doubt about one's own destiny was to live a pure and moral life, avoiding all temptation. Work hard in one's calling, which after all was the task assigned one by God, and avoid idleness and luxury, and God's favor would be shown by worldly success. Hard work would leave no time for moral doubts, and wealth obtained by hard work in one's calling was a sign of divine favor. A *Protestant ethic* emerged, which stressed the virtues of saving and work, those traits required for success in a market economy. Material gain was given its ethical letters of credit.

In the years following the Reformation, according to the Weber-Tawney thesis, the Protestant ethic lost its religious basis and became thoroughly secularized. Hard work, saving, and avoidance of luxury came to be valued because they were useful in accumulating wealth, not because they had religious meaning. Wealth and the respect it brought became ends in themselves. By the mid-eighteenth century the business ethic had become pragmatic and utilitarian, and was the approved pattern of behavior.

The Weber-Tawney thesis has been much criticized. It does not provide an explanation for the rise of capitalism. It does not explain the origins of the acquisitive motive or why Western society puts heavy stress on the need for achievement. It is essentially qualitative rather than quantitative in its analysis and for that reason is somewhat old-fashioned from the modern scientific point of view. But it does help explain some of the fundamental attitudes toward work and leisure widely found in our society. As we inquire into the attitudes that lead a nation's economy into the path of self-sustaining economic growth, the concept of the Protestant ethic adds to our understanding of why the achievement motive is directed toward material gains.

At first glance it might appear that Veblen's conspicuous consumption and the Protestant ethic as described by Weber and Tawney are contradictory. One theory emphasizes spending and leisure as central to the motivational pattern of the modern economy. The other stresses hard work, saving, and avoidance of idleness and luxury. They hardly seem consistent with each other.

But in the area of ideologies and motivations, consistency need not necessarily be present. The findings of modern dynamic psychology, from Freud onward, have stressed that individual motivations often conflict and are only poorly understood by the individuals themselves. It is quite possible for an individual to work hard and save, to rationally compute each little addition to profit, to hoard his capital and use it for maximum advantage *in his role as a producer*. The same individual may spend ostentatiously to display his wealth and status to his neighbors and acquaintances *in his role as a consumer*. Both patterns of behavior may be quite rational within the scope of modern social and economic institutions.

The important point here is that both behavior patterns contribute to economic growth (see Figure 10-1). Parsimony in a producer causes him to expand the potential output of his enterprise. Prodigality in a consumer expands demand and keeps pulling the whole economy toward higher levels. They are both part of our growing economy, one on the supply side of the market and the other on the demand side.

A NOTE ON THE BOUNDARIES OF ECONOMICS

This inquiry into the attitudes conducive to economic growth has led us far afield from the areas usually associated with the study of economics. We have drawn on the work of a philosopher, an archaeologist, two historians, a psychologist, an economist, and a sociologist (several were trained in more than one field, however). We are pursuing a topic, the sources of economic growth, that requires a broad net. And in their fundamental roots, all of the social sciences are related. Many aspects of one social science will require material from another. The sources of economic growth is only one example. The important thing for the social scientist to remember is that he is dealing with problems, not a particular branch of social science, and that the search for solutions may lead him far outside his own specialty.

SCIENCE AND TECHNOLOGICAL CHANGE

Motivations and attitudes oriented toward economic growth are essential for a long-range pattern of expansion in output and welfare. Increase of knowledge is also essential. The practical and theoretical sciences and their application to the processes of production and distribution are a second key to economic growth.

The Growth of Knowledge and Skill

The skills stored in human minds are probably the most important part of the productive wealth of mankind. Factories and machinery may be destroyed,

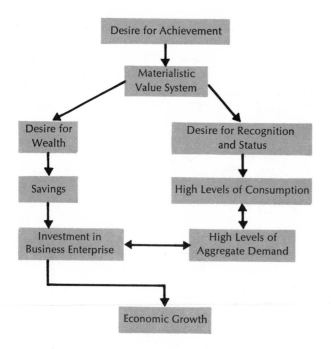

FIGURE 10-1
Economic Growth and
the Value System of the
Market Economy

but they can be quickly replaced so long as knowledge of how to build and operate them remains. Even the terrible destruction of modern wars has been only a temporary setback to the productive capacity of modern nations whose people have the knowledge of modern science and engineering.

Knowledge is cumulative as it passes from generation to generation. Prior to the development of writing the passage of information was by word of mouth, and the accretion of new skills was slow. But with improved methods for the storage of information and for its retrieval and communication, by the agency of books and computers, for example, the development of knowledge has been greatly speeded up. Increased specialization of skills has been possible as knowledge has grown in complexity and sophistication, making possible a truly accelerated growth of technology. This cumulative growth of knowledge and skills means that economic growth will continue, if only because more effective and efficient ways of doing things are continually devised.

It is possible to conceive of an economy that grows only through the accumulation of more resources in the form of more capital, more land, or more manpower. It is also possible to have economic growth even if there is no increase in resources, if knowledge and skills expand and bring improvements in the productivity of existing resources. When the two sources of growth are combined, expansion is even more rapid.

The Role of Science
Growth of knowledge and advancement of skills can take place in two ways. First, existing technology and organization can be improved. Improving the

efficiency of a coal-fired electric generator is one example. That path leads to a changing technology, but one that moves forward step by step from crude to more sophisticated skills and techniques. Dramatic new developments, leaping to completely different technologies, do not appear in that fashion.

The second method is through basic scientific discovery. The classic example is the development of nuclear power out of theoretical physics. Scientific research produced a basic principle, $E = mc^2$, which states the relationship between energy and mass. The principle was supported by the technology of the atom-smasher, a research instrument that had been used in the process of discovering the principle. During World War II, the principle was applied to a production process that was able to turn out the first atomic weapons and later, after World War II, the first nuclear electric power. Even the intermediate stage of pilot plants was eliminated. It was a dramatic instance of the use of a scientific principle to develop a new technology that in a break with the past created a completely new source of energy. No amount of improvement in coal-fired electric generators would have brought such results.

The great leaps in technological change have come precisely because of the application of basic science to technology. The tradition of scientific inquiry that has developed over the last five hundred years is one fundamental reason for the rapidly advancing industrial technology of the modern world. The industrial revolution seems to have started as the result of the application of problem-solving skills directly to production technology, but it has continued and accumulated through the application of problem-solving skills to the discovery of fundamental scientific principles, and the subsequent application of basic science to the solution of technological problems. Without modern science and its interplay with production techniques, the process of technological change would have been limited to the much slower path of step-by-step improvement.

The Ideological Basis of Modern Science

Modern science was itself a product of the learning process by which human society has developed the knowledge and skills for human progress. It was also the product of a scientific and intellectual revolution in western Europe in early modern times. In the period of the Renaissance, from about 1400 to 1600, a new view of the relationship between man and his natural environment appeared, and became the fountainhead of the explosion of scientific knowledge during the last four hundred years. The development of modern science rests on two beliefs about the nature of the physical world and man's relation to it. These beliefs are:

1. It is possible to understand the nature of the physical world.
2. Knowledge of the physical world can be used to predict and control natural phenomena.

There are only a few fundamental attitudes one can take toward the relationship between man and his environment. One is that everything is in the hand of an inscrutable fate, and that the individual has no real control over his own destiny. Another is that man's destiny is controlled by a god or gods whose intent is unfathomable. Or one can believe that chance or caprice rules the world, and that man's destiny is at the mercy of unforeseen circumstance. These beliefs lead to religion, philosophy, or magic as means of bettering the condition of man. They do not lead to an activist effort to change man's environment or to a scientific effort to understand it.

There is a fourth possibility: belief in the ability of men to understand and control nature through systematic observation and reason. This is the basis of the scientific point of view. It is founded on the proposition that logical analysis of facts can lead to knowledge of natural laws, which can then be put to worthwhile uses. This viewpoint rejects fate, chance, and divine intervention as significant influences upon the world. It embodies the assumption that there are natural laws governing natural phenomena, and that understanding those laws can lead to improvements in the condition of man. The scientific point of view is purposive, interventionist, and utilitarian.

This utilitarian emphasis in modern science has focused intellectual effort on the foundations of technology. A fuller understanding of the natural world has brought a series of pathbreaking changes in production techniques: electric power, chemical fertilizers, synthetic fibers and plastics, internal combustion engines, nuclear energy, air transportation, interplanetary rockets—the list could go on almost indefinitely. And the process continues. Yesterday's scientific discoveries led to today's technology, while tomorrow's technological change is being generated in the research laboratories of today. Scientific inquiry has become as much a part of the modern economy as production of housing, food, and clothing. It has brought a continuing process of change and growth as an integral part of modern life.

KNOWLEDGE, PRODUCTIVITY, AND ECONOMIC GROWTH

Economists have given a good deal of attention recently to estimating the relative importance of knowledge, technological change, and related "intangible" factors in economic growth, as compared with the "tangible" inputs of labor, capital, and other resources. In Chapter 7, where we estimated the potential economic growth of the United States in the short-run future, the rate was seen to depend on the growth of the labor force and the growth of productivity (output per man-hour). Since those two variables are readily measurable they were convenient to use. But, as we pointed out at the time, growth in productivity is merely a convenient term under which we can subsume all those factors, *except* labor inputs, that cause economic growth.

Productivity can be increased in several ways. It can be increased by giving workers more capital equipment to work with. A man can dig a ditch with his hands. Give him a shovel and he can do it much faster. Let him use a mechanical ditcher, which is essentially many shovels powered by a machine, and he will be able to do a great deal more in the same amount of time. An increase in the *amount* of capital can raise output per man-hour.

The rate of technological change will also affect the growth of productivity. A mechanical ditching machine represents a change in methods as well as an increase in capital per worker. If this machine is introduced slowly, the rate of growth of productivity in ditchdigging will also rise slowly. A faster rate of application of technological change will raise output per man-hour more rapidly.

Productivity may also be increased by increasing the scale of production. As an economy expands, and as markets widen and enlarge, it becomes possible for firms to specialize more intensively. In doing so, they can improve the efficiency of their operations and increase their output faster than their inputs rise. For example, if a ditchdigging machine can stay in one place digging many ditches it will not have any downtime caused by moving about. The more big jobs it has, the more work it can do over any span of time. This will show up in more output per man-hour for the machine operator.

Finally, productivity can be increased through improvement of skills, of knowledge, and of organization. Better-educated workers will be able to use complex equipment more effectively. Greater knowledge on the part of workers and management will enable production to be carried on more efficiently. More effective organization of work can eliminate inefficiency and can cut down on productive effort.

These, then, are the four chief ways in which productivity can be increased:

1. More physical capital.
2. More rapid technological change.
3. Economies of increased scale of operations.
4. Greater knowledge and skill.

Several estimates have been made of the relative importance of these factors in promoting economic growth. The most important were made by Edward F. Denison for the period 1929–1957.[2] Over that period the GNP of the United States rose at an average annual rate of 2.93 percent. Denison then estimated the sources of that growth rate as shown in Table 10-1.

According to Denison, increased amounts of the factors of production accounted for just 46 percent of U.S. economic growth between 1929 and 1957. Widening of the market, which made possible greater economies of large-scale production, accounted for 11 percent of the growth. The remaining 43 percent was due to qualitative changes brought about by better education and increased knowledge. Most significantly, *investment in human capital through education was more important than the increase in physical capital* (plant, equipment, and inventories).

---

[2] Edward F. Denison, *The Sources of Economic Growth in the United States and the Alternatives Before Us* (New York: Committee for Economic Development, 1962).

TABLE 10–1
Sources of Economic Growth in the United States, 1929–1957

Source of Growth	Percent of Growth Rate
Increase in Inputs	
Labor (adjusted for decreased hours of work, increased use of women workers, etc.)	31
Capital (physical capital only)	15
Land	0
Increase in Productivity (output per unit of input)	
Economies of large scale production from growth of the market	11
Improved education of labor	23
Advance of knowledge	20

Denison's study also showed that capital accumulation is becoming less important as a source of economic growth, and education more important. In 1912–29, capital investment was responsible for 23 percent of economic expansion, as against 15 percent in 1929–57. Education, on the other hand, was the source of 11 percent of economic growth in the earlier period and 23 percent in the later period. This finding is of great importance, for capital investment is primarily found in the private sector of the economy while education is largely a function of the public sector.

Denison's study has some weak spots. He attributes no part of the economic growth to such public investments as highways, public housing, port development, and related expenditures. This is because the national income accounts do not recognize these expenditures as capital formation—a purely arbitrary decision. Yet these expenditures can and do lead to greater efficiency in the private sector of the economy. On other points Denison is reduced to some informed guesses because of inadequate data. For example, the growth resulting from economies of large-scale production is a pure guess. In the area of education, Denison had to make a guess about how much of the differences in income that are associated with differences in education are the result of differences in ability and how much are due to education itself.

Even if these arbitrary decisions were to be made otherwise, the basic thrust of Denison's study would remain. Growth of labor and capital is important for economic growth, but not much more important than better education, improved technology, and more effective organization. Indeed, with slightly different and quite reasonable guesses about the importance of economies of large-scale production and the role of education in bringing higher incomes, education and knowledge could be shown to be more important than the increase in physical inputs.[3]

---

[3] Other efforts have been made to assess the relative importance to economic growth of physical capital and the intangibles of education and knowledge, but with little success. Using methods

INNOVATION AND ECONOMIC GROWTH

Growth and change go together, particularly in economic affairs. A growing economy continually opens up new opportunities, creates new horizons, and stimulates new ideas. Changes in customary relationships create the opportunities for profit that draw resources into new and different efforts. In theory, it would perhaps be possible to conceive of an economy that would grow so evenly in all of its parts that no changes in relationships between the parts could occur. But such balanced growth can hardly take place in the real world. In practice, growth is always uneven, faster in one sector of the economy than in another. This pattern means that economic relationships change as an economy grows. As the changes occur, the economy must adapt, and innovations that bridge the gap between old and new appear.

The reverse is also true. An innovation that develops on its own must be first applied in a limited sector of the economy. The very fact that it is applied means that it is better than something else, and that resources can be used more effectively in a new way. Space for growth is created. Price and profit relationships with other sectors change, imbalances appear, and the use of resources shifts. Change leads to growth and growth leads to change.

Entrepreneurship and Innovation

Change and growth bring to the fore a key figure in the process of economic growth, the entrepreneur. His function is twofold. He is a man who sees the opportunity to make a profit from a new product, a new process, or an unexploited raw material. He then takes the risk of organizing an enterprise to promote the opportunity, bringing together raw materials, manpower, and capital to do it. Innovation is his specialty. An entrepreneur is not usually an inventor. His skills are organizational rather than scientific. He is a manager, but he goes far beyond the work of a salaried manager whose job it is to operate a going concern. He may contribute capital to the enterprise, but usually he obtains the bulk of his capital elsewhere. Chiefly an innovator, he may also be part inventor, part manager, part capitalist.

Joseph Schumpeter, an Austrian economist who taught for many years at Harvard University, attributed the growth process in a private enterprise economy to innovation and to the entrepreneurs who were responsible for innovations. The market equilibrium (see Chapter 5) and the equilibrium in the flow of spending (see Chapter 4) that tend to develop in a private enterprise economy would normally be stable and stationary, according to Schumpeter. It is only when a disturbance changes the circular flow or the market equilibrium that economic growth and development will occur.

---

quite different from Denison's, Professors Robert Solow of MIT, L. C. Thurow of Harvard, and L. D. Taylor of Michigan have shown that increases in physical capital were responsible for somewhere between 20 and 80 percent of American economic growth! They are inclined to consider a figure around 80 percent the most reasonable, but that is just their own estimate and is not demonstrated by the studies they made.

The disturbance comes in the form of an innovation. Its first impact is to require new capital investment by rendering old equipment obsolete, by raising the expected profits to be derived from the innovation, or by arousing consumer demand for a new product. New firms appear, taking advantage of the innovation, and "new men" rise to positions of business leadership. These developments affect the old firms in many industries. Old equipment must be replaced, old products have to be dropped and new ones added as firms adapt to new conditions, and old methods of organization have to be revised. As the new firms and new men rise to prominence, the old ones have to adapt in order to survive.

Although innovation is creative, it is also destructive of old ways and old products. According to Schumpeter, the destructive side of innovation leads to efforts by existing firms to control and slow it down. Business firms threatened by innovation try to protect their positions by patent control, by control over raw materials, and by other devices designed to keep out newcomers. They may establish great research laboratories themselves, in order to gain control over the development of innovation in their own fields, feeding the newly developed products and processes into the market in ways that do not threaten their own positions. Yet in protecting themselves they narrow the field available to the independent entrepreneur and thereby weaken the whole structure of the economic system.

Schumpeter argued in his provocative book *Capitalism, Socialism and Democracy*[4] that capitalism was doomed because it was gradually doing away with the entrepreneur. Big organization, with its carefully calculated, committee method of operation and its long-range planning, eliminates the entrepreneur from within the enterprise, while monopolistic practices reduce the scope of his activities outside the firm. A second reason projected was government controls and regulation, which also reduce the scope of entrepreneurship. Together these two developments were held to destroy the entrepreneur, thereby reducing the growth potential of private enterprise and weakening the whole capitalist system.

Schumpeter may have been right about the individualistic entrepreneur, but he was wrong about entrepreneurship. He did not foresee the institutionalization of innovation in the research laboratory, the emergence of growth-minded and innovation-oriented business firms, or the innovative effects of government research and spending programs. The individual entrepreneur *may* be a vanishing social type but the functions he performed in a largely individualistic society seem to have been taken over by large organizations in a more bureaucratic world.

Several recent studies of innovation in the industrial development of Europe and the United States suggest some further qualifications of Schumpeter's theory that economic growth depends on the daring, individualistic

---

[4] Joseph A. Schumpeter, *Capitalism, Socialism and Democracy*, 3rd ed. (New York: Harper & Row, 1950).

risk-taker. Professor W. Paul Strassmann of Michigan State University has shown that the typical pattern followed even by innovating businessmen in the United States during the nineteenth century was to wait until success was pretty much assured. They did not take large risks. Paul M. Hohenberg's study of the chemical industry of Western Europe prior to 1914 pointed out that Germany's rise to dominance resulted largely from investment in knowledge. Research laboratories and training of scientists gave Germany her favored position in that industry, and the flow of knowledge and skills to other industries stimulated them also.[5] These studies take some of the gloss off of Schumpeter's entrepreneur, but they do not change the fundamental proposition: innovation and the entrepreneurial function, however they may be carried out and by whom, are vitally important to a growing economy.

The Interrelated Nature of Technology and the Clustering of Technological Change

Modern technology is a web of interrelationships in which one process or product feeds into another, which in turn is related to still others. A change in one part of the system will set in motion changes in other parts, often unforeseen and unanticipated. Once new methods or new products appear a series of related innovations is sure to be set in motion.[6]

There are many examples from the history of technology to illustrate the close relationship between techniques in one industry and those in another. Here is one "chain reaction." In the early industrial revolution in England, during the eighteenth century, the mining of coal pushed mines deeper and deeper. Water seepage increased and more powerful pumps were needed than those run by hand or wind. Steam power was applied, in the development first of the simple atmospheric steam engine, and then of the more sophisticated reciprocating type pioneered by Boulton and Watt. The development did not end here. The new steam engines required new types of iron, because their large boilers had to withstand greatly increased steam pressure. The system of valves used in the new engines required closer machining and narrower tolerances than had been customary up to that time. As a result, producers of iron and steel developed new and larger iron and steel furnaces to produce stronger metals that could be machined more closely. Manufacturers developed tools that could do the finer machining, and instruments were developed to make the finer measurements needed in manufacture of the valves. All of these technological innovations had important applications in other industries. The improved metals and metal-working techniques

---

[5] See W. Paul Strassmann, *Risk and Technological Innovation: American Manufacturing Methods During the Nineteenth Century* (Ithaca, New York: Cornell University Press, 1959), and Paul M. Hohenberg, *Chemicals in Western Europe, 1850–1914: An Economic Study of Technical Change* (Chicago: Rand McNally, 1967).

[6] A teacher once asked her first grade class what the world would be like if the electric-light bulb had never been invented. One child replied, "We'd have to watch television by candlelight."

enabled other inventors to develop practical machinery for textile manufacturing. The earliest spinning machines and the later mechanical weaving machines were made possible by the innovations in metallurgy and metal-working developed for the early steam engines. Then, when the steam engine was combined for the first time with the new textile machinery in 1776 (a revolutionary year indeed), the first modern factory was born.

The interrelationships did not end there. Power-driven textile machinery required still further advances in metallurgy and metal-working to compensate for the increased stress on metal parts and to supply the basis for more complex machinery. The next step was the innovation of interchangeable parts, made of sturdy metals so carefully cut and shaped that machines could be disassembled, and the parts mixed, and then the machines reassembled in working order. This improvement was made possible by the better metals, improved metal-working equipment, and better instruments that had already been developed for other purposes. This development did not come first in textile machinery, but in the manufacture of rifles. The innovator was Eli Whitney, most famous for the cotton gin, but whose greatest invention was interchangeable mechanical parts.

The interrelatedness of technology causes a clustering of technological change and innovation. When the output of one production unit becomes the input of another, the two technologies develop a mutual relationship in which one change induces another. An innovation that significantly reduces costs of production for electric power will widen the market for electrical equipment, stimulating an economic expansion there that may require new methods of production if demand is to be met, or new methods of marketing if the product is to be sold. Once a series of changes of this sort is set in motion it can have unforeseen effects through the whole economy.

The clustering of technological changes brings bursts of investment expenditures in a whole series of related industries. The automobile is a good example. Appearance of an inexpensive, mass-produced automobile about 1910 provided a great stimulus to a variety of other industries. They, in turn, had to devise ways to greatly enlarge their output and develop new products. Industries affected in this way included rubber, petroleum production and refining, highway construction, construction equipment, automobile servicing, and even consumer financing. The economy was stimulated to grow not only by the investment required for automobile production, but also by the investment needed in all of the other sectors of the economy affected by widespread use of motor transportation. One of the chief reasons for the prosperity of the 1920s in the United States was the large investment expenditures that clustered around the automobile and its development as an item of mass consumption.

"LONG WAVES" OF ECONOMIC GROWTH?

The interrelatedness of technology and the clustering of innovations is one reason why the pattern of economic growth has been irregular. A number of scholars have argued that the upward growth trend has been marked by "long waves" lasting some 40 to 60 years and comprising alternating eras of good and bad times. The upswings of the long waves have lasted some 25 to 30 years. They were periods in which economic growth was relatively rapid and the depressions that occurred were short and shallow. These good times were followed by equally long periods of relatively poor times, when economic growth slowed down, unemployment rates were high, and depressions tended to be relatively long and deep. The successive periods of good and poor times, together with the pattern of depression and recovery, make the long-term growth pattern a relatively uneven one.

The stimulus at the beginning of a period of good times seems to be a major innovation that spreads widely to other sectors of the economy, triggering large investment expenditures and creating wide new economic opportunities. Expansion and growth are stimulated as long as the investment growth continues. Eventually, however, the new industries are built up, a new economic pattern emerges, and the investment stimulus diminishes. When that happens the growth of the economy will tend to slow down until another cluster of innovations appears.

The economist usually credited with identifying the pattern of long waves was Nikolai Kondratieff, a Russian who disappeared in the political purges of the 1930s. Although statistical data going all the way back to the late eighteenth century are scarce, he found evidence of the long waves in prices, interest rates, wages, patterns of foreign trade, and production of basic commodities such as coal, pig iron, and lead. The precise turning points were hard to identify, but he suggested that up to the time of his work (1926) there had been two and a half long waves:

First long wave: upswing from the late 1780s to about 1810–17;
                     downswing from about 1810–17 to about 1844–51.

Second long wave: upswing from 1844–51 to 1870–75;
                     downswing from 1870–75 to 1890–96.

Third long wave: upswing from 1890–96 to about 1914–20.

To this we could add the second half of the third long wave, a downswing from about 1914–20 to about 1935–40, and the first part of the fourth long wave, an upswing from 1935–40 to the present.

Figure 10-2 is a schematic picture of the pattern of long waves, with approximate dates, and will help clarify the concept.

The best evidence for long waves in the growth pattern is to be found in indices of wholesale prices. Presumably they reflect basic factors underlying economic activity. Rising wholesale prices indicate generally tight markets in which businessmen are bidding up the prices of the things they buy. This would indicate expectations of profits to be derived from things they sell. Together these factors are associated with prosperity and high rates of growth in total output. Just the opposite would be true of times in which wholesale prices are falling.

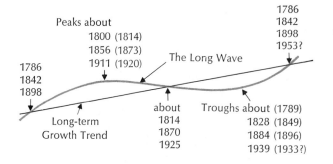

FIGURE 10-2
Generalized Schema of the Long Waves in Economic Growth

Peaks and troughs in wholesale prices, according to Kondratieff, are in brackets. The other dates represent Schumpeter's estimates.

The study of economic growth and long waves has led to identification of another pattern. Economists like Simon Kuznets of Harvard, Moses Abramovitz of Stanford, and Richard Easterlin of the University of Pennsylvania have found, instead of waves of 50 years' duration, swings in economic activity ranging from 15 to 25 years' duration from peak to peak or trough to trough. These "Kuznets cycles," as they have come to be called, are cycles in *rates of economic growth*. Gross national product will rise at a rapid pace for 8 to 15 years and then at a much slower rate for the next 8 to 15 years. One illustration is the rapid increase in U.S. GNP between 1946 and 1953, followed by a much slower growth rate in 1953–61, with another period of rapid growth in 1961–70. Our analysis in Chapter 9 of recent U.S. growth experience gives general empirical support to the concept of long swings, or "Kuznets cycles."

Population and Economic Growth

One of the key elements in these long swings seems to be the growth in population. A rising population leads to increased need for housing space, stimulating the construction and household equipment sectors of the economy. It also stimulates government spending and investment in public utilities, as well as the consumers' goods industries in general. Growth in those sectors triggers larger business investment. These secondary effects of population growth mean that cumulative effects are set in motion that keep the economy growing even after rates of population growth start to taper off and even decline.

Fluctuations in population growth have been associated with some of the irregularities in the economic growth of the United States. Growth of population was severely reduced during the depressed decade of the 1930s, but was high both before and after, as shown by the data in Table 10–2 from the Bureau of the Census. There is considerable disagreement over the relationship between population growth and prosperity. Were the thirties depressed partly because population grew so slowly, or did population grow slowly because the thirties were depressed? Whatever the relationship, relatively slow population growth helps to explain why the outlook for capital formation

TABLE 10–2
Increase in U.S. Population, by Decades, 1900 to 1970

Decade	Increase	Percent Increase
1900–10	16,138,000	21.4
1910–20	14,923,000	15.3
1920–30	15,901,000	15.6
1930–40	9,218,000	7.3
1940–50	19,204,000	15.3
1950–60	27,997,000	18.7
1960–70	26,200,000	14.6

was poor, while the large increases in population of the period since 1940 help to explain the good record of economic growth in recent years.

The outlook for the future is less favorable than that of the immediate past. For reasons not clearly understood, there has been a sharp decline in the birth rate in the United States in recent years, comparable in scope to a similar decline in the 1920s and early 1930s. Birth rates in the United States are now at their lowest in history, with a trend as shown in Figure 10-3.

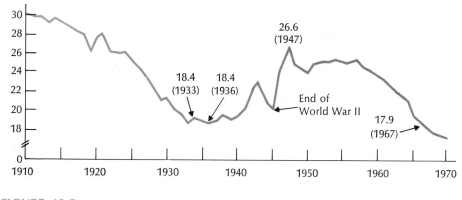

FIGURE 10-3
U.S. Birth Rate, 1910–70

Population experts see the lower birth rates of the present as the normal situation, and look upon the bulge of 1940–65 as abnormal, a by-product of World War II and a temporary shift in attitudes toward large families brought about largely by the war. The return to lower birth rates is seen as a response to the difficulties, problems, and expense of raising a large family in the complex modern world. Incidentally, the recent drop in the birth rate is usually *not* interpreted as the result of "the pill" and "the loop," since other effective methods of birth control were available during the bulge in birth rates of 1940 through 1965. At any rate, logic and the facts about population growth both suggest a connecting link between rates of economic growth and rates of population increase. The strong growth performance of the U.S. economy after World War II was associated with a large increase in population. It is reasonable to expect a less dynamic pattern of economic growth as population growth slows down.

Is Growth Unstable?

At this point we should clearly distinguish between two propositions. One, there exists a *regular, wavelike pattern* in economic growth, in which periods of good times *must* be followed by approximately equal periods of poor times. Weak statistical evidence suggests that this concept of a regularly pulsating growth pattern is not valid. The historical record does show that long periods of good times occur, in which the basic economic conditions that determine the level of investment and economic activity are highly favorable. In the past, these eras have been followed by depressions or periods of stagnation in which basic economic conditions are much less conducive to expansion and growth. The big question is whether periods of the latter type can be avoided in the future.

The second and closely related proposition is: Even during a long wave of prosperity, such as during the period 1945–70, the rate of economic growth speeds up and slows down, perhaps in relation to swings in the rate of population increase.

The beginnings of the long periods of good times have coincided with important innovations that changed the entire structure of economic life. The use of machinery in textile manufacturing (late eighteenth century), the railroad and steamship (1840s), and electricity, chemicals, and the "second industrial revolution" (1890s) are all examples. In the most recent period of good times a prime stimulus has come from the automobile and consumer durables like television and other electrical equipment, to which we may add the airplane, computers, and automation.

Other explanations for the long eras of good times have been suggested but have not found favor with the majority of economists. Some economists have argued that the principal gold discoveries (1849, late 1890s) have triggered the good times by promoting monetary expansion. More recently, some have argued that monetary expansion through the banking system has been a main cause of the good times since 1940. Another explanation sometimes heard is that major wars have occurred during the periods of good times: the Napoleonic wars in the first period; the Crimean War, the American Civil War and the Prussian wars against Denmark, Austria, and France in the second period; World War I and its preliminary armaments race in the third; and World War II, the "cold war" armaments and space races, Korea, and Vietnam most recently.

Perhaps the wisest course would be to grant some degree of validity to all of these explanations. The eras of good times have been characterized by wide new investment opportunities, which have had a pervasive expansionist effect on many sectors of the economy. Monetary expansion has been a feature of the prosperity engendered by growth. And the prosperous periods have had big wars, which stimulated large public expenditures on armaments.

One important fact about the periods of bad times is that they each had a significant depression or period of stagnation that lasted about ten years. Great depressions came every 40 to 50 years in the 1840s, the 1890s, and the 1930s and affected the entire world economy. These periodic interruptions in the pattern of economic growth may create a statistical illusion of "waves" in growth. But the fact that they have interrupted the growth trend cannot be denied.

A MATURE ECONOMY?

Closely related to the problem of long waves is the question of whether economic growth rates have a tendency to slow down as the economy becomes more highly developed. Although the experience of Western Europe and the United States since 1945 seems to show that a mature economy can sustain economic growth rates equal to those prevailing when the economy was much less highly industrialized, the long-range pattern may still be one of deceleration in the growth rate or even economic stagnation.

Keynes on Economic Stagnation

John Maynard Keynes was concerned about economic stagnation in a mature economy. He argued that as incomes rise, the proportion of income spent for consumption will decline, and the proportion saved will be correspondingly larger. A poor family, for example, may spend all of its income or more just to exist. At higher income levels a family will find its essential needs are being satisfied and will tend to save some of its income for future use. Families with much wealth, however, will tend to save a great deal of their current income: their immediate need for more products and services will not be intense because they already have so much. Keynes also pointed out that saving out of *increases* in income may be quite large. For example, a family with an annual income of $8,000 may save only $400 (5 percent), but if it obtains an additional $1,000 of income it may save an additional $250 (25 percent of the increment). These two characteristics of the *propensity to consume* (which will be discussed more fully in Chapter 11) meant, according to Keynes, that (1) A rich society tends to save a larger proportion of its income than it did when it was not so rich; (2) Large increases in the national income may in a rich society bring only relatively small increases in total spending, making it difficult to sustain further increases in output and income. The result of these two characteristics of mature economies, in Keynes's view, was slow growth and possible stagnation. A mature economy will tend to oversave and underspend. This will require high levels of investment to sustain any given rate of economic growth. But these levels of investment will be increasingly difficult to obtain because spending by consumers will fail to rise adequately. In other words, aggregate demand will not grow sufficiently.

Keynes concluded that "the growth of wealth, so far from being dependent on the abstinence of the rich, as is commonly supposed, is more likely to be impeded by it." He therefore advocated policies designed to promote greater equality of income distribution and elimination of the great hereditary fortunes that generate very large savings. He also wanted a monetary policy that would keep interest rates low in order to stimulate investment spending, pointing out that high interest rates would not be needed to encourage savings because of the tendency to oversave anyway.

The fears that Keynes had about the failure of consumption to grow adequately have not been borne out by the recent experience of the United States. Savings as a proportion of disposable income have not tended to rise during the years since World War II, but have consistently fallen within the range of 6 to 10 percent of the income available for spending. This has been true even though disposable income has risen very substantially. The data shown in Figure 10-4 indicate this relationship very clearly. Except for the abnormal years of the Great Depression and World War II, consumption expenditures and disposable income have risen together and the gap between the two has not widened.

This issue is so important, however, that we should take a closer look at the arguments and the facts. Keynes and other economists who took his side have pointed to several phenomena that support their case:

1. People with higher incomes save a larger proportion of their incomes than people with lower incomes. Budget studies of family spending patterns show this fact very clearly. These studies, however, deal with incomes at a single point in time, and not with the behavior patterns of families over time as their incomes rise. It is easy to *assume* that as people move to higher income levels they will take on the savings patterns of the bracket into which they move, as shown by the budget studies. *If* that happened, as time passed and incomes rose, a larger proportion of families would be in the higher savings group and the national figures would show a rise in the proportion of savings out of disposable income.

Unfortunately, the national data do not bear out this hypothesis, as Figure 10-4 shows. Whatever the reason, *we cannot generalize about national saving patterns over time from budget studies of individual families at the same point in time.* The probable reason for this unexpected pattern of consumer behavior is that wealth does not blunt the desire for greater abundance. Quite the opposite appears to be true: higher living standards seem to set the stage for still higher aspirations. Consumer psychology in our affluent society does not show the satiation of wants that would lead to a declining desire to consume as incomes rise. Philosophers may question the value of this undoubtedly

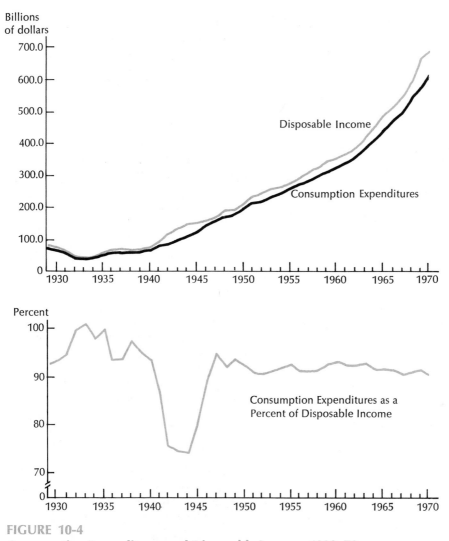

FIGURE 10-4
Consumption Expenditures and Disposable Income, 1929–70

materialistic pattern of behavior, but consumers persist in acting that way.[7] The evidence is against any theory of satiation of demand, at least for the type of society that exists in twentieth-century America.

[7] These counterhypotheses about consumer behavior are derived from the detailed studies of consumer psychology conducted by George Katona and his fellow researchers at the Institute for Social Research of the University of Michigan. For a popular presentation of some of the main findings see George Katona, *The Mass Consumption Society* (New York: McGraw-Hill Book Co., 1964).

2. A second phenomenon that seemingly supports the belief that the proportion of income saved rises as incomes go up may well be a statistical illusion. The reliable national income data available for analysis go back only to 1929. For about 15 years after that date special conditions prevailed, first the depression years and then World War II. Neither of these two periods are good indicators of long-term trends. Yet if one were to have looked at the relationship between savings and income in, say, 1946, the data would have shown a rather rapidly increasing ratio of savings to disposable income as incomes rose. When averaged in with the more normal period since 1946, the earlier data impart a similar increase to the data for the period as a whole.

These problems have led a number of economists to examine the data more carefully. Studies by James Duesenberry (Harvard), Franco Modigliani (MIT), and Milton Friedman (Chicago) have shown that *the proportion of spending out of income that is expected to be permanent is rather constant.* As a family moves from a low income level to a higher one, savings may well increase temporarily, but once the family adjusts to its new and higher income level the proportion of its income spent and saved will return to about the same level as before. A family with a permanent income of $15,000, for example, will save about the same fraction of its income as a family with a permanent income of $7,500.

When these findings about spending out of permanent income are combined with the work on consumer psychology and satiation of demand, there is not much left of the Keynesian argument that economic maturity brings oversaving and inadequate consumption levels. These fears have been laid to rest, at least for the present economy. If the desire for economic growth diminishes, it will be for other reasons.

The Powerful Consumer

One of the great changes that has occurred in the United States in the twentieth century has been the rise of a consumer-oriented economy. Investment in productive plant and equipment remains important, but the key industries that now determine the nation's economic health are automobiles, housing, and other durable consumer goods. In contrast, about 1900 the most important industries were steel, railroads, and other heavy industries, which produced primarily for other business firms rather than directly for consumers. Mass consumption has become the distinguishing feature of the modern economy. Growth of consumer spending is one of its chief supports.

Three aspects of consumer spending have become especially significant. One is large amounts of *discretionary income.* Another is rising *consumer investment* in durable goods. Together, they have led to a large expansion of *consumer credit.* All three of these developments rest on the growing affluence of a large proportion of the families and individuals who make up the body of consumers.

As more families move into moderately affluent income brackets, a smaller proportion of consumer income is used for basic living costs, taxes, and other essential purposes. A large proportion becomes *discretionary income* that can be used with great flexibility by the consumer and his family. It is available, in particular, for improved housing, automobiles, durable goods like television and stereo sets or air-conditioners, and for recreation and leisure-time activities. Estimates made by the National Industrial Conference Board regarding the amount of discretionary income show that it increased from about $69 billion in 1946 (one-third of total consumer purchasing power) to about $220 billion (41 percent of total consumer purchasing power) in 1966. Flexibility and choices have been widening.

The growing affluence of consumers and the appearance of large amounts of discretionary income have increased the importance of *consumer investment*. There are three forms capital formation can take. One is the physical facilities that produce products and services, and includes business plant, equipment, and inventories as well as public facilities such as schools, post offices, and highways. The second is human capital, the skills, knowledge, and health of people. The third is consumer investment, the housing, automobiles, and other durable goods that provide a continuing flow of useful services to their owners.

Consumer investment has been growing both in amount and as a proportion of GNP. As a type of capital formation it is now more important than business investment. This is shown in Figure 10-5, where data for each decade since 1930 are compared (in order to reduce the effect of year-to-year shifts). The importance of consumer investment in the economy as a whole is clearly indicated, even when allowances are made for the depressed 1930s and the lack of availability of consumers' durable goods during World War II.

Consumer credit is the third element that has helped create a consumer-oriented economy. The continued benefits derived from durable goods make

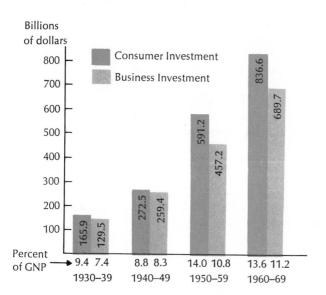

FIGURE 10-5
Consumer Investment
and Business Investment,
1930–69
(1958 Prices)

it desirable to borrow and buy now, with the increased benefits worth more to a family than the cost of borrowing. And installment buying is easier to handle when a family's income rises above the level necessary to meet basic needs.

The growth of consumer credit has been phenomenal, particularly in the years since World War II. From a total of only $8.4 billion (4 percent of GNP) in 1946, total consumer credit outstanding rose to $126 billion at the end of 1970 (12.9 percent of GNP). Mortgage debt, excluding farms, multiple family units, and commercial property, has also jumped upward spectacularly, from $23 billion in 1946 to $280 billion in 1970.

The growing consumer orientation of the American economy has provided a strong stimulus to economic growth. The whole structure of the economy is changing in response to growing affluence, discretionary income, consumer investment, and consumer credit. These changes began to emerge clearly in the 1920s in the United States. In Western Europe similar changes are occurring, but the mass consumption economy[8] has not yet been fully realized. Even the Soviet Union has begun to shift its emphasis in economic development toward the consumer in recent years. Consumer demand is emerging as a continuing source of economic growth.

Private Business Investment

The rise of the consumer as a main source of economic expansion and growth has been paralleled by a decline in the importance of U.S. private business investment since the early years of the twentieth century. This is surprising, because the great bulk of economic activity in the United States takes place in privately owned business firms, the new products that appeal to affluent consumers are produced by business firms, and large corporations are the characteristic economic unit of an advanced economy.

The basic reason for this trend is the fact that the United States has so much capital that the great bulk of new private business investment must be used for replacement rather than for expansion. Although gross business investment in plant and equipment has remained at approximately 10 percent of gross national product since 1900, net business investment in plant and equipment (the total minus depreciation) has fallen from about 7 percent of GNP to about 2 percent.[9] In other words, in 1900 about two-thirds of all business plant and equipment expenditures were for expansion and only about one-third were for replacement. As the capital stock grew, and as technological change reduced its

---

[8] Two economists are responsible for originating the term "mass consumption economy" to characterize contemporary society. W. W. Rostow in *The Stages of Economic Growth* (New York: Columbia University Press and London: Cambridge University Press, 1960) and George Katona, *The Mass Consumption Society* (New York: McGraw-Hill Book Co., 1964). The discussion in this section follows Katona closely.

[9] According to Harvard's Simon Kuznets. Other estimates give different figures but show comparable declines.

usable life, a larger and larger share of new plant and equipment was needed to replace depreciation. By the time we reached the 1960s, the proportions were more than reversed. Now about 80 percent of all business spending for plant and equipment replaces old capital and only 20 percent is a net addition to the stock of capital. During the entire period, however, the total amount of business investment in plant and equipment grew at about the same pace as GNP so that its proportionate share remained the same.

Business investment can be divided into two parts, inventories and productive plant and equipment. The plant and equipment category can, in turn, be subdivided into replacement and expansion. It is the last activity that brings about economic growth (with one exception, to be explained a little later). The division between these categories in 1966 is shown in Figure 10-6.

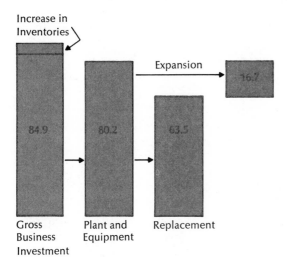

FIGURE 10-6
Business Investment, 1966
(Billions of Dollars)

Two qualifications should be noted at this point. First, we have assumed that depreciation charges are equal to the capital actually used up in production. This probably is not accurate. Our tax laws encourage businessmen to overstate depreciation charges, while the Treasury tries to keep them within reasonable bounds. As a result the actual amount of capital investment used for expansion is probably a little larger than it appears to be.

Second, we come to the exception noted a moment ago. When capital is replaced the new equipment is almost always more efficient, even if it doesn't cost any more than the old. Its output per dollar of investment is greater, because new equipment embodies new technology. So even if all business plant and investment were for replacement only, there would still be some expansion of output capacity. How much? The few studies available indicate that GNP would rise by about 1.5–2.0 percent annually under those circumstances.

These two factors mean that the effect on economic growth of private investment in plant and equipment is probably greater than the raw figures would imply. But the correction would come nowhere near reversing the long-term historical trend. A relatively small and declining portion of U.S. economic growth has its source in the expansion of business plant and equipment.

GOVERNMENT AND ECONOMIC GROWTH

National governments have always taken a strong interest in promotion of economic growth. They have traditionally sought to strengthen the economic base of national power by promoting economic activity, and they have sought political support by aiding various economic interest groups. Government action of this type has been characteristic of American economic policy.

The federal and state governments have been active in developing transportation facilities: roads, canals, railroads, river and harbor improvements, airports, and expressways. Some of the major projects, such as the first transcontinental railroad, the Panama Canal, and the St. Lawrence Seaway, have had primary strategic as well as economic importance. Subsidies for overseas shipping and restriction of coastal shipping to American vessels are similar programs.

Development of natural resource industries has been important to the federal government, which explores for minerals and publishes the results, carries out research on extraction of minerals, and has maintained strategic stockpiles that add to demand and stabilize the market. One principal resource industry, petroleum production, benefits from a complex system of federal and state controls, import restrictions, and tax policies that diminish competition, stabilize prices and promote profits. Another of these industries, agriculture, is stimulated by means of research, county agents, and price supports at the same time that output is limited by means of a variety of controls for important crops.

Industry, in general, is supported and promoted by a system of tariffs, but American policy in this area has shifted dramatically since the 1930s. Prior to that period tariffs were one of the chief instruments by which the federal government sought to promote industrial growth. But with U.S. industry leading the world, this support was not required, and in recent decades the U.S. has led the major nations of the world toward lower tariff barriers.

Government and the Structure of Economic Institutions

Even a laissez-faire policy rather than one of promotion of economic interests is thought of by its advocates as a means of promoting economic growth. Adam Smith (1723–1790), whose *Inquiry Into the Nature and Causes of the Wealth of Nations* (1776) is the greatest statement of laissez-faire economics, argued that government had vital functions to perform in order to promote optimal economic growth, namely, the protection of private property, the even and unprejudiced enforcement of the law, and defense of the nation against foreign attack. To do these things tax revenues were needed, and

Smith argued that taxes should be levied in those ways least likely to interfere with or distort the normal pattern of economic activity. Only one thing more was needed, a sound and stable monetary system maintained but not manipulated by the government. Adam Smith felt that within this framework individuals would be able to save and invest with security and confidence, that this accumulation and use of capital would bring economic growth, and it would all be the result of the free, individualistic effort of ordinary people.

The governmental functions that were simple in Smith's day expanded as the economy became more complex. Economic growth requires a stable financial system to facilitate the flow of savings into channels of investment. This need has brought government into the money mrakets to manage the monetary system as a whole, guarantee bank deposits, and develop special governmental and quasi-governmental agencies to promote agricultural credit and funds for the housing industry.

Government has also concerned itself with the supply of labor for economic growth. Immigration policy prior to World War I assured the economy of a rapidly growing supply of labor, mostly unskilled, to support an expanding agriculture and industry. When the flow of new immigrants was cut back, largely at the insistence of those who came earlier, the focus of government interest in the labor market gradually shifted to resolving labor-management conflict. This was accomplished by national labor legislation designed to diminish substantially the turmoil that periodically leads to strikes and other work stoppages. Such legislation stabilizes the labor market much as federal action stabilizes the money markets.

We have already noted the governmental role in promoting transportation and resource development, and in protecting domestic industry from foreign competition. All of these actions on the part of government help to create an environment conducive to economic growth in which private efforts can be devoted more fully to expansion.

Government's Role in Education and Research

In addition to measures designed directly to promote growth, and others that maintain a growth-oriented structure of economic institutions, governments have taken on two additional tasks that promote economic expansion: (1) Financing of basic scientific research; and (2) Training of manpower able to manage our highly complex technology. It is hard to tell which is the more important. The first is devoted to pushing forward the technological base of the economy and generating increases in productivity. The second makes it possible for private business firms to use the newer techniques. The fact that modern governments have become the primary sources of funds for these two activities means that they have become one of the prime movers of economic expansion. The uses to which new technology and improved skills will be put may be determined by the final buyer of products, but their sources are largely in the government funds made available for these purposes.

Military Expenditures and Economic Growth

In Chapter 6 we showed that a significant and perhaps growing proportion of U.S. gross national product was used for military and military-related purposes. Even in a relatively normal year (1960) about one-eighth of our gross output went into those uses. In a year of heightened conflict (1968) the proportion was about one-seventh, or about 15 percent of GNP. A wealthy nation can "afford" these large expenditures, but a significant cost is nevertheless involved. The resources could be used for consumption: lower military expenditures would make possible tax reductions that would allow consumers to buy more.

Alternatively, lower military expenditures would permit enlarged government expenditures on the sorts of things that promote economic growth. Increased funds for education, health, and other investments in people could be provided. Basic scientific research could be expanded. Investments could be made in such important parts of the economic infrastructure as transportation, housing, and protection of the natural environment. All of these things would benefit future generations, and their lack is the cost paid by our unborn children for today's military programs. The same points can be made about space exploration, which in many ways is similar to military programs.

Private capital formation is a third use for the resources now being devoted to the military. Greater consumption and increased public capital formation could afford opportunities for expansion of private enterprise into areas now neglected. Capital now being invested in capacity for military output would be diverted to civilian uses. In all probability there would be no change in the *amount* of private capital formation, but its *direction* would change, providing production facilities either for more consumers' goods or for the redirected nonmilitary government spending.

A high level of aggregate demand sustained by large government expenditures on the military will initially bring high growth rates, but in the direction of military production. The impact on growth is felt only in the longer run, through smaller government investments in human capital and the economic infrastructure. A shift away from military spending would therefore affect growth in two ways. Initially, the direction of growth would shift toward the consumption sector. Secondarily, as government spending shifted to more useful activities the long-range growth prospects of the economy would improve.

PROSPERITY AS A PRECONDITION
FOR GROWTH

There is little need for expansion of productive capacity if existing resources are not fully used. In a private economy, furthermore, there will be little incentive to expand under those conditions. The first requisite for sustained economic growth, then, is sustained prosperity.

Prosperity encourages economic growth in a variety of ways. It brings high incomes to consumers, thereby stimulating both high levels of spending and substantial savings that can be channeled into investment. It brings profits to business firms, thus giving them incentives to expand, and helps provide the capital as well. Lenders like to lend to prosperous borrowers, for they are likely to be able to repay the loan. All of these conditions make consumers and businessmen optimistic, which in turn serves to extend the prosperity. If the economy is booming, it is easy for expansion to occur.

Stable, full-employment levels of economic activity contribute to economic growth by promoting long-range planning by business firms. For example, if a large corporation can rely on the proposition that the economy will be at full employment levels of GNP ten years from now, it can estimate with some accuracy the potential size of the market for its products. On the basis of these estimates it can plan its capital investment program, introduction of new products and processes, and its entire growth program.

In Part IV we will discuss in some detail the fiscal and monetary policies that could sustain stable prosperity in the U.S. economy, along with some of the difficulties involved. At this point we need only note that the Employment Act of 1946 made the federal government responsible for the maintenance of full employment prosperity and that function is now accepted as one of the chief responsibilities of modern national governments.

U.S. ECONOMIC GROWTH IN PERSPECTIVE

We can conclude from this discussion of the sources of economic growth that a strong drive toward expansion is inherent in the American economy, but there are obstacles.

The United States has a social and economic organization and patterns of thought and behavior that are strongly oriented toward increased affluence, including:

1. A materialistic value system that emphasizes acquisition of wealth as a highly desirable goal.
2. An individualistic, success-oriented attitude toward life, which is deeply ingrained in the social and economic system.
3. Strong emphasis on education and the advance of scientific knowledge, together with strong economic support for them.
4. Well-developed patterns of entrepreneurship and innovation built into the economic system.
5. A consumer-oriented economy based on high and rising incomes that provide a strong base for economic expansion.
6. Commitment of the federal government to maintenance of full employment prosperity and economic expansion.

These factors reach into the foundations of American social organization and embody some of the most important attitudes and beliefs characteristic of twentieth-century America. They forecast a continuing drive toward greater affluence by a society committed to the proposition that greater material wealth is a good thing.

Some other factors suggest difficulties ahead:

1. Growth has been erratic in the past and will probably continue to show an irregular and interrupted pattern.
2. Some signs of economic maturity are present, particularly a slowing down of population growth and a decline in the importance of business capital investment as a source of expansion.
3. The United States has shown a tendency to divert substantial amounts of resources into economically wasteful military uses.

These less favorable factors do not mean that economic growth will be halted. But they do imply that things may not be quite so pleasant in the future as they have been in the very recent past. The years from 1945 to 1970, with all of their difficulties and problems, may yet turn out to be something of a golden age when viewed in terms of economic growth.

Finally, the issue of the uses to which economic growth will be put remains unresolved. Of all the economic (and political) issues of our time it is undoubtedly the most important. It is the dilemma of a society that has committed itself to the material values of growing ease and comfort and in doing so has developed an economic system that cannot help but expand. Concentration on expansion, however, has slighted concern over whether the results are really what is wanted. Having built a growth machine, we now have the task of directing it properly.

Summary

Economic growth is inherent in the economic and social environment of modern industrial society. No one characteristic can be singled out. An entire network of interrelated factors is responsible.

Attitudes toward work and wealth cause men as producers to seek greater wealth and as consumers to consume more, driven by desire for achievement, recognition, and status. The growth of knowledge and science, which have their roots in the same materialistic value system, leads to technological change. Technological change leads, in turn, to the clustering of innovation and bursts of investment activity that impart a wavelike motion to the growth process. Population growth patterns seem also to lead to shorter waves in the rate of economic growth.

Fears of economic stagnation do not appear to be warranted. Although private business investment is no longer as important as it used to be, economic expansion is becoming more closely related to consumer spending and government economic policy, and investment in education and research. Even though growth has been erratic in the past and some signs of economic maturity have appeared in the private sector, the underlying conditions that have pushed our economy toward greater affluence are still strong.

Key Concepts

Achievement motive.   The desire to reach goals not yet attained and to excel over others.

Conspicuous consumption.   Expenditures whose purpose is to show possession of wealth.

Pecuniary emulation.   Imitation of the expenditure patterns of the very wealthy by persons of lesser wealth.

Protestant ethic.   Hard work and savings are desirable goals. Originally based on religious doctrine, the Protestant ethic became secularized as the approved path to economic success.

Human capital.   The knowledge, skills, and health of people. Investment in human capital is now more important than investment in physical capital as a source of economic growth.

Entrepreneur.   The businessman who recognizes and implements new opportunities for making a profit.

Clustering of technological changes.   The tendency of a change in techniques of production to lead to others, thereby opening up numerous opportunities for innovation, bringing a corresponding burst of capital investment. It is the basic cause of long waves in economic activity.

Long waves in economic activity.   A 40–60-year wavelike movement in economic activity about equally divided between good times and bad. Sometimes called *Kondratieff cycles.*

Kuznets cycle.   A 15–25-year wavelike movement in rates of economic growth that appears to be associated with changes in population growth.

Stagnation thesis.   The hypothesis that economic growth will slow down as incomes rise because (1) savings will increase as a proportion of total income, while (2) investment opportunities diminish.

Permanent-income hypothesis.   Savings are related to the level of income that is expected to be permanent, rather than the level of income itself.

Borne out by studies that show that the proportion of income saved tends to be constant above income levels of $7,500 per year.

Discretionary income. Income not required for basic consumer needs such as food, clothing, and shelter.

Consumer investment. Consumer spending on durable goods.

Net business investment. Business investment for expansion of output rather than replacement of capital. Has been falling as a proportion of total investment and as a proportion of GNP.

THE
NATIONAL
INCOME
IV

Prior to the development of Keynesian economics the advanced industrial economies were plagued by periodic depressions that brought unemployment, business failures and all of their accompanying personal tragedies. Economic analysis of the determinants of the level of national output and income, associated closely with the work of John Maynard Keynes, has largely freed the economy from fear of serious depressions. That advance in human knowledge must surely be one of the great scientific discoveries of the twentieth century. It has not solved all of our economic problems, but it has laid to rest one of the most troublesome. Part IV of this book lays out that analysis and the public policies that have been derived from it.

Chapters 11 and 12 present the essential elements of the theory of national income determination, first in terms of the forces that lead to an equilibrium, and then in terms of the dynamic elements that keep the system in flux. Both are always at work, and an understanding of how the system functions requires that both the equilibrium and dynamic forces be kept in mind.

Chapter 13 deals with the relationship between the level of income and the rate of economic growth, tieing national income theory into the analysis of growth in Part III. It is something of a digression from the main line of argument and can be skipped if the reader wants to pursue the simple theory of national income determination.

Chapter 14 brings government into the analysis, the earlier chapters having dealt solely with the private sector. The fundamental point developed is that properly conceived public policies can eliminate the instability inherent in the private sector.

Chapters 15, 16, and 17 bring the monetary sector into the analysis. They deal with the functions of the monetary and credit system, the creation of credit by the privately owned commercial banks, and management of money and credit by the Federal Reserve System. All modern nations manage their monetary system in order to promote economic stability and growth. These chapters explain why and how that is done.

Chapter 18 shows how the monetary equilibrium discussed in Chapters 15 through 17 is related to the "real" equilibrium analyzed in Chapters 11 through 14. The analysis is not complete, for economists have not fully solved the problem. The appendix to this chapter summarizes how far they have gotten.

Chapter 19 discusses inflation, which is the great unsolved problem of contemporary macroeconomic policy. We know more about inflation than recent political controversies imply, and even though the issue has probably been blown up beyond its inherent importance, it remains a knotty problem.

Chapter 20 closes the discussion of national income determination by sketching the broad outlines of the public policies that can assure any modern nation of full employment and strong economic growth. There is no excuse for substantial unemployment and unused productive resources. In terms of the basic choices available to any society, no nation need operate inside its transformation curve for any length of time.

A prosperous economy requires levels of spending high enough to employ the work force fully. If businessmen do not receive enough from sales of their product to cover costs plus an adequate profit, they will reduce output, lay off workers, and buy fewer inputs. The reduction in output and employment will continue until the flow of payments out of business firms is matched by an inflow large enough to induce them to maintain their level of output. At that level, however, there may be large numbers of unemployed and large amounts of unused capacity. On the other hand, total sales may be so large that business firms seek to expand their output beyond the economy's capacity to produce, bringing inflation. Clearly, the relationship between aggregate demand and the economy's output capacity is crucial to maintenance of economic stability. We have already shown how the economy's capacity to produce is determined. Now we shall analyze the determinants of the level of aggregate demand.

The analytical framework is a private economy within which the crucial decisions to save and invest are made. The heart of the theory is the relationship between aggregate demand and aggregate supply. The supply side is discussed first, then aggregate demand. The latter is broken down into its two component parts, the propensity to consume (with its reciprocal, the propensity to save) and the level of investment. Aggregate demand and supply are then put together to determine the equilibrium level of income. This equilibrium level implies a special relationship between investment and the propensity to save, which is the final building block of the analysis at this stage. The whole can be summarized in three fundamental propositions.

Income, Savings, and Investment

11

THE FRAMEWORK OF THE ANALYSIS

We have already examined the flow of spending in summary form and noted the principal factors that influence the level of aggregate demand. To recapitulate, they were

Consumer spending (C)
Business investment (I)
Government spending (G)

When we looked at the national income accounts, a fourth factor was added:

net exports (X).

Putting all these together, we arrived at a statement of the determinants of aggregate demand Y:

$$Y = C + I + G + X.$$

This formulation can be thought of in gross terms, where $Y = $ GNP and I stands for gross investment (I_g). Or it can be thought of in net terms, where $Y = $ NNP and I stands for gross investment less depreciation (I_n). Or it can be thought of in terms of national income, where Y is the total net income of the factors of production earned from current production and the other elements in the equation have appropriate deductions made to bring the accounts into balance. But whether conceived in gross, net, or national income terms, aggregate demand is composed of four sources of spending: consumption, investment, government, and net exports. A change in any component of aggregate demand, we have seen, will have a multiplied effect on the total. Also, the relationship between savings and investment is the key to understanding why aggregate demand rises and falls.

In examining these relationships in some detail, we shall construct a theory that explains the process by which the level of aggregate demand is determined. Some simplifying assumptions, which will be dropped later, one by one, are:

1. The economy consists solely of the private sector. There is no government sector; G is thereby eliminated from the basic formulation. This assumption may seem highly unrealistic (and it is) but is made in order to lay out the essential relationships found in the private sector.
2. The economy is closed. There are no imports or exports. This eliminates X from the basic equation. Alternatively, we could assume that the net foreign balance is zero. This will also eliminate the X term.
3. The price level is constant. Although this assumption will be dropped later, we shall retain it in the basic theory in order to emphasize the "real" aspects of the analysis.

The effect of these assumptions is to limit the analysis initially to a closed, private economy with no government contribution to GNP, and with stable prices. Our basic formulation, in terms of output, becomes

$$Y = C + I. \tag{1}$$

That is, the total output of the economy equals the output used for consumption and the output used for investment.

This basic identity can be stated in terms of monetary flows as well. The total income of the factors of production either can be used to purchase consumption goods or can be saved:

$$Y = C + S. \tag{2}$$

These two identities are quite similar. The value of total output of the economy (Y in Identity (1)) is equal to the incomes paid out in the process of production (Y in Identity (2)). Likewise, the value of the consumption goods turned out (C in Identity (1)) is equal to the amount spent on consumption (C in Identity (2)). Consequently, the value of I in Identity (1) must equal the amount of saving S in Identity 2:

$$S = I. \tag{3}$$

This relationship is a fundamental building block of the theory of national income. Insofar as the private sector of the economy is concerned, the amount saved must equal the amount spent for investment. The equality must hold for any level of income and output.

SOME DEFINITIONS

Saving.   *Income not spent for consumption.*

Investment.   *An increase in the economy's real capital. Investment may take the form of buildings, equipment, or inventories.*

Gross investment includes replacement of worn-out capital. Net investment includes only the increase in real capital over and above the amount used up in production.

The theory of national income that we deal with in this section of the book does not include as investment the intangible capital embodied in knowledge, physical health, or education. Although vitally important for economic growth, these types of investment are classified as consumption in national income theory, partly because of measurement problems and partly for convenience. The justification for this procedure is that in the short run they do not have any special impact on the level of income or employment in any way different from the impact of consumption spending in general.

In these theoretical chapters we shall use the term investment *to mean net real capital formation: plant and equipment used in production, less depreciation, valued in constant prices.*

THE DECISIONS TO SAVE AND INVEST

Investing and saving are usually done by different people for different reasons.

Most capital formation takes place in business firms. An enterprise will try to take advantage of possibilities for profit making by building and equipping production plants. Inventories are also needed— raw materials, partly finished products, and final output in the "pipelines" that end in sales to consumers. All of this is part of the real capital required for production.

The capital formation undertaken by a business firm can be paid for out of several sources:

Earnings retained from current operations.
Reserves accumulated in the past.
Borrowing from financial institutions.
Sale of securities to investors.

Of these sources only the first represents current business savings, and a direct use of savings for real capital formation. The second source, the accumulated reserves, may also have been motivated by a foreseen need for investment at some time in the future, but it may also have been motivated by other considerations. Whatever the source of funds, the actual decision to expand a firm's capital is motivated by such business-oriented desires as additions to profit, maintenance of the firm's position in the industry, the forestalling of competition, growth of the company, or some other aspect of business operations.

By contrast, most saving is done by individuals and families. The reasons for saving can be highly varied: to take care of emergencies, to provide for the future, to make a large expenditure in the future, or just because. An important type of savings is contractual in nature, and is done consistently and regularly. Some examples of contractual savings are periodic payments on many types of insurance policies, mortgage payments on a house, installment payments on a car, and monthly payroll deductions for purchase of savings bonds. These payments go into financial institutions and represent a significant portion of the flow of savings.

Whatever the reason, and whether the savings are contractual or discretionary, it is clear that the motivation for saving is quite different from the motivation for capital formation, and that for the most part, different economic units do the saving and the investing.

These differences beween the processes of saving and investment are of crucial importance. Savings must be brought back into the stream of spending if incomes, output, and employment are to be maintained and grow. In a private economy, only business investment can do that job. Yet there is no automatic mechanism to assure that the flow of investment spending will be at just that level required for high levels of output and employment. There is no assurance that the savings generated by full-employment levels of income will just match the amount of investment businessmen desire to make.

AGGREGATE SUPPLY

Business decisions are based on expectations that the output can be sold at prices that will recover the costs of production and also allow for a normal profit at least. In terms of the flow of spending, this means that the income payments to the factors of production, namely, wages and salaries, profits, rent, and interest payments, must come back to business firms in the form of revenue from sales. That is why savings must be offset by investment spending. Unless unspent income is returned to the stream of spending, total business revenue will fall below total costs (including a normal profit in total costs), businessmen will be unwilling to continue the existing level of production, and output will fall.

Conversely, if income from sales is larger than current costs of production, profits will rise above normal and there will be strong incentives to increase output as well as the enlarged income to do so.[1]

These relationships lead to the concept of the *aggregate supply schedule*. If the level of output is to remain stable, without rising or falling, businessmen must expect to receive revenue from sales equal to the value of their output, as measured by their payments to the factors of production. Expected proceeds must equal the full costs of production (including a normal profit). This relationship must be true at all levels of production. The resulting schedule, assuming no change in prices, is shown in Figure 11-1.

The aggregate supply schedule shows the conditions under which any level of production will continue unchanged. That will be true only if expected proceeds (measured on the vertical axis in Figure 11-1) are equal to the value

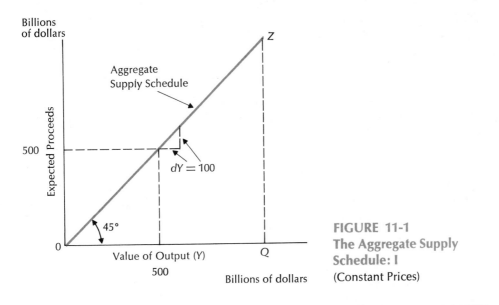

FIGURE 11-1
The Aggregate Supply Schedule: I
(Constant Prices)

---

[1] The formal definition of normal profits is contained within this explanation. Normal profits are those just large enough to get a business firm to continue its existing level of output. Less-than-normal profits bring cutbacks and more-than-normal profits cause expansion.

of output (measured on the horizontal axis). For example, if $500 billion is paid out to the factors of production, the same amount must be received by producers in order that that level of output may continue. If producers are to increase their output, say from $500 billion to $600 billion, as shown by dY in Figure 11-1, they will have to expect an additional $100 billion in sales, and to sustain such an increase they will actually have to receive the additional amount. As a result, the aggregate supply schedule, when measured in constant prices, will be a line that bisects the origin of Figure 11-1 and makes an angle of 45 degrees with each axis. Any point on the aggregate supply schedule is equidistant from the two axes.

Figure 11-1 also shows that the output of the economy is limited by the availability of manpower and productive capacity. The vertical line QZ indicates the limit beyond which production cannot be pushed, and may be thought of as indicating the economy's full-employment level of output. In practice, this is really a zone rather than a line, because hours of work can be extended, people can be induced to enter the work force, and in other ways a certain amount of flexibility can be introduced. But for analytical purposes a line will be used.

Introduction of a full-employment limit to production brings a complication. As the economy approaches full employment, prices can be expected to rise. As resources become scarce, businessmen bid more for their use, and their prices rise. In addition, costs of production will increase. Less efficient machines are brought into use, less efficient workers are hired, and cost problems arise as capacity output is approached. As a result, the proceeds expected by businessmen must rise more rapidly than output. The closer the economy gets to full employment, the greater the disparity will be between increases in the physical volume of output and the expected proceeds of business firms. Once capacity output is reached, a continued expansion can bring only price increases without any increase in output. These *inflationary* conditions can be shown in a modified diagram of the aggregate supply schedule (Figure 11-2).

AGGREGATE DEMAND

The aggregate supply schedule is half of the picture. Aggregate demand makes up the other half. Just as the aggregate supply schedule shows the expected proceeds needed to sustain any single level of output and employment, so an *aggregate demand schedule* will show, for each level of income, how much the various spending units in the economy can be expected to spend.

Those spending units are, of course, consumers and business firms. (We have temporarily excluded from the analysis both government and the net foreign balance.) So we know that the total of aggregate demand comprises expenditures for consumption and business investment, or $Y = C + I$. We turn first to the consumption part of aggregate demand.

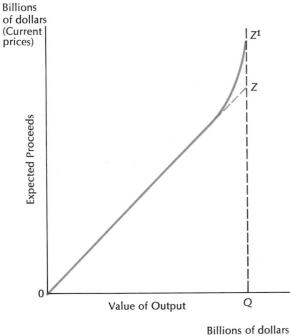

Billions
of dollars
(Current
prices)

Expected Proceeds

0

Value of Output

Q

Billions of dollars
(Constant prices)

FIGURE 11-2
The Aggregate Supply Schedule: II

The value of output (horizontal axis) is still measured in constant prices in order
to show real increases in output. Expected proceeds are measured in current
prices, however, to show how the upper tail of the aggregate supply schedule can
be distorted from the original 45° line by rising costs as the economy approaches
its capacity. Line Z represents the aggregate supply schedule in constant prices,
while line Z^1 is the modified aggregate supply schedule that takes into account the
tightening of markets and rising costs that appear as the economy approaches
and reaches full employment.

The Propensity to Consume

There is a relatively stable relationship between disposable personal income
and the level of consumer spending. This relationship was shown in Chapters
5 and 10, and can be briefly reviewed:

> At very low levels of income, as in the early 1930s, consumers will temporarily
> spend more than they earn as they draw on past savings to tide them over the
> bad times, living off their fat, so to speak, until it is exhausted. At higher levels of
> income, positive amounts of savings begin to appear, as in the years since World
> War II, and consumption spending appears as some fraction of disposable per-
> sonal income.

The national income accounts show the relationships between GNP, NNP, and disposable personal income. The proportions between them vary within relatively narrow limits except for years when special conditions prevail, such as during World War II. This means that there will also be a fairly stable relationship between consumer spending and such larger variables as GNP and NNP, at least in the short run.

The relationship between income and consumption is one of the most important building blocks of the theory of income determination. Called the *propensity to consume,* it is shown in Figure 11-3.

The propensity-to-consume schedule is sometimes called the *consumption function* in modern economic theory. It has been given that name because *there is a systematic relationship between the value of total output and consumption expenditures at any and all levels of output.* In algebraic terms,

$$C = f(Y).$$

This formulation summarizes the fact that consumption is systematically related to income. Figure 11-3 merely pictures that relationship for purposes of analysis, and the algebraic statement is a convenient way of stating it conceptually.

Underlying these geometric and algebraic formulations is a basic economic truth. The level of consumption spending depends on the amount of income received by consumers, which in turn depends on the level of economic activity through the economy as a whole. The path of cause and effect is primarily

$$\text{Income} \longrightarrow \text{Consumption.}$$

That is, changes in the level of consumer spending are the result of changes in the level of income and economic activity. We seldom find changes in the level of income and employment *caused* by changes in consumer spending. It can occur, but when it does, the whole relationship between consumption and income will have shifted. In this case, the propensity-to-consume schedule in Figure 11-3 will shift its location upward or downward. By stating that $C = f(Y)$ we fix the location of the propensity-to-consume schedule in Figure 11-3 and postulate a specific direction for cause-and-effect relationships between Y and C.

A moment's reflection will indicate that this implication of the analysis is correct. The two great determinants of consumer spending are tastes and incomes. Although tastes may change, they influence primarily the allocation of spending rather than its amount. Consumers may decide to shift their purchases from whiskey to milk, from automobiles to Caribbean cruises, for example, but the division between spending and saving tends to be quite stable. When incomes change, however, the level of spending will rise or fall in response. This is particularly true if consumers expect the change in incomes to be permanent or reasonably persistent. Temporary changes in incomes, like windfall gains or losses on securities markets, tend to influence consumer spending much less than changes in the regular flow of income. In other

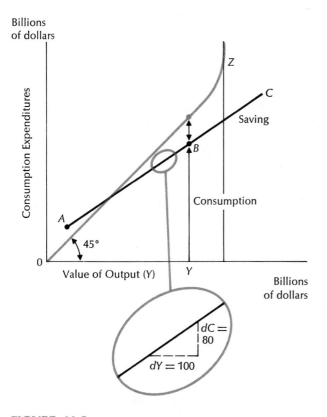

FIGURE 11-3

The Propensity to Consume

Figure 11-3 is constructed with a line drawn through the origin at an angle of 45°. This line, which is identical to that of the aggregate supply schedule Z, is placed there so that the total value of output can be measured either along the horizontal axis or vertically to the 45° line.

The propensity to consume C shows the amount that consumers will want to spend (measured vertically) out of any value of output (measured horizontally). The distance between the schedule of the propensity to consume and the 45° line will equal consumer savings. At point A, total consumer spending is greater than consumer incomes as past savings are drawn down. At point B, consumer spending is less than consumer incomes, and a positive amount of savings occurs.

The enlarged portion of Figure 11-3 shows the slope of the propensity-to-consume schedule, which is not as steep as the 45° line, or the aggregate supply schedule. The basic rule is that consumer spending rises as consumer incomes rise, but not so rapidly, or

$$\frac{dC}{dY} < 1.$$

This relationship is illustrated by assuming that, in the area of the diagram shown, consumers will spend about 80 percent of any increase in income, or

$$\frac{dC}{dY} = \frac{80}{100} = .8.$$

words, shifts along the propensity-to-consume schedule generated by changes in incomes are much more frequent than shifts in the schedule itself caused by changes in the saving habits of consumers.

The Propensity to Save

A propensity-to-save schedule can be readily derived from the propensity to consume. It is the difference between consumption spending and disposable personal income, or, in our simplified analysis, between consumption and the value of output. In Figure 11-3, it is the vertical distance between the propensity-to-consume schedule C and the 45° line Z.

The propensity to save is shown graphically in Figure 11-4. It depicts the relationship between incomes and the amount consumers *do not* spend at each level of income. Net savings are measured vertically, and the value of output Y paid to the factors of production is shown on the horizontal axis. The propensity-to-save schedule shows how much consumers save at each level of income. It is the mirror image of the propensity-to-consume schedule, with the 45° line as the horizontal axis. Points A and B correspond exactly to the same points in Figure 11-3: A is a depression level of income, in which net savings are negative (spending is greater than current income), and B is the more normal situation, in which positive net saving occurs.

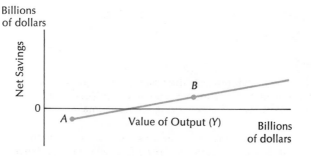

FIGURE 11-4
The Propensity to Save

The Level of Investment

Consumer spending is part of aggregate demand. Business investment makes up the rest in the model of a private, closed economy. In the case of business investment, however, there is no functional relationship between investment and total output. Investment spending rises and falls as the expectations of businessmen change. Optimism about increased sales and the structure of costs will lead toward substantial business investment. Pessimism can be expected to have the opposite effect. And plans for investment can be modified on a moment's notice if business sentiment should change.

An illustration will make the point clear. Suppose total spending last year was $800 billion, and business investment $80 billion. Will those levels persist this year? Not necessarily. If last year's $800 billion was an increase over the year before of, say, $40 billion, *and the increase is expected to continue this year,* businessmen may increase their investment to $100 billion or $110 billion this year. It all depends on how optimistic they are. However, if last year's spending of $800 billion was a decrease from the year before and much unused capacity exists, businessmen may cut their investment spending drastically, even though total spending this year is maintained at levels close to $800 billion.

We cannot draw a propensity-to-invest schedule like that of the propensity to consume. This difficulty in our analysis is overcome by assuming a specific level of investment that business firms desire to make. Adding this amount to the schedule of the propensity to consume will then give us a schedule of aggregate demand, as shown in Figure 11-5.

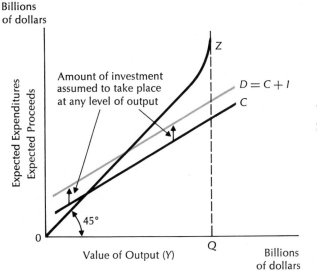

FIGURE 11-5
The Aggregate Demand Schedule

The aggregate demand schedule D is the sum of consumption and investment spending $C + I$ that would occur at each level of output. It is derived from the schedule of the propensity to consume plus an assumed level of investment spending.

THE EQUILIBRIUM LEVEL OF INCOME

We now have all the equipment needed for an analysis of the equilibrium level of economic activity. In brief, the value of output will move to that level at which aggregate demand is equal to aggregate supply. The sum of the amounts consumers are willing to spend and businessmen are willing to invest (aggregate demand) must be just equal to the amount required by businessmen to continue the existing level of economic activity (aggregate supply).

If aggregate demand should be above the amount needed by businessmen to maintain existing output, the additional demand will encourage businessmen to expand production, and the level of economic activity will rise. Should aggregate demand fall below the level required to sustain the existing level of output, business revenues will not cover full costs (including a normal profit), output will be cut back, and economic activity will decline. Only when spending decisions just equal the amount necessary to validate production decisions, in the aggregate, will the level of economic activity remain where it is.

These relationships are shown graphically in Figure 11-6. The level of output

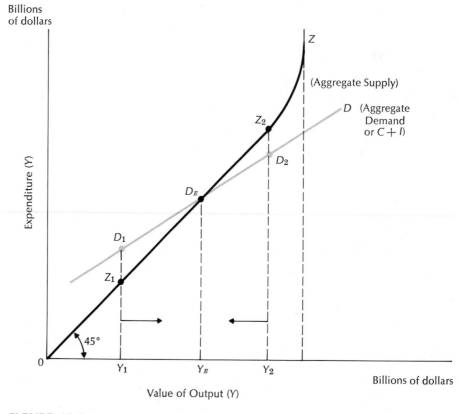

FIGURE 11-6
The Equilibrium Level of Income

Figure 11-6 is simply a combination of Figure 11-1 (the aggregate supply schedule) and Figure 11-5 (the aggregate demand schedule). The value of output Y on the horizontal axis is also the total income of the factors of production. Expenditure Y shown on the vertical axis is also the income received by business firms that produce the output. The level of economic activity will move to an equilibrium at which the two are equal, which is the point at which the aggregate supply schedule intersects the aggregate demand schedule. At that point the amounts spent by buyers will equal the receipts required to keep sellers producing at the existing level of output.

designated as Y_E is the equilibrium level, assuming the patterns of consumer spending and level of investment embodied in the aggregate demand schedule as shown. The reason for this conclusion can best be understood if we assume the continuation of the existing pattern of aggregate demand, but with some other level of output such as Y_1 or Y_2.

At output level Y_1, total spending will be greater than the amounts required to sustain that level of output. At that point the aggregate demand schedule lies above the aggregate supply schedule. Expenditures exceed the value of current output by an amount equal to Z_1D_1. When this happens, inventories are drawn down, markets start to tighten up, and producers will increase their output, moving in the direction of Y_E.

As long as aggregate demand exceeds aggregate supply at existing levels of output, economic activity will increase.

Just the opposite occurs at output level Y_2. Aggregate demand is less than aggregate supply, unwanted inventories start to pile up unsold, and producers cut back on their output in order to correct the situation. The value of output will fall toward Y_E.

As long as aggregate demand is less than aggregate supply at existing levels of output, economic activity will decline.

Only at level Y_E will total expenditures just equal the value of output, providing no incentive for producers to change the level of production. Investment decisions are realized and just balance the savings consumers wish to make. It is this level of economic activity toward which the economy will gravitate.

The Equilibrium of Savings and Investment

The equilibrium level of income requires an equilibrium between decisions to save and invest. We already know that savings and investment remain equal as the level of income rises and falls. But equilibrium requires more than that. For example, if businessmen overestimate the level of consumer spending and produce more than can be sold, they will accumulate unwanted investment in the form of inventories piling up on their shelves. Decisions to reduce output will follow and the level of economic activity will fall. Yet throughout the process savings and investment will equal each other.

A simple numerical example can make this clear (Table 11–1). Suppose that businessmen expect the following flow of spending to prevail during the coming year (first column), but in fact a different flow actually occurs (second column).

TABLE 11–1
Expected and Actual Flow of Spending

Business Expectations	Actual Results
$Y = 1{,}000$	$Y = 1{,}000$
$C = 900$	$C = 880$
$I = S = 100$	$I = S = 120$

In this situation businessmen will find that they have invested $20 billion more than they had expected or planned. The investment came in the form of unwanted inventories of that amount, since they had expected to sell $900 billion of consumers goods but in fact managed to sell only $880 billion. Even though saving and investment remained equal, and the level of investment offset the flow of savings, the situation is not stable. In an effort to eliminate the unwanted inventories, the businessmen can be expected to reduce output. Incomes will decline and the level of economic activity will fall.

An equilibrium in the flow of spending requires not only that savings and investment be equal, but also that both savers and investors be satisfied with the amounts of saving and investment they are able to achieve. Two conditions must be satisfied, which in turn imply a third:

1. The savings actually made by consumers must equal the savings they desire to make at existing levels of income:

$$\text{Desired savings } (S_D) = \text{Realized savings } (S_R).$$

2. The investment actually made by businessmen must equal the investment they wish to make at existing levels of income:

$$\text{Desired investment } (I_D) = \text{Realized investment } (I_R).$$

3. Since realized savings must always equal realized investment, it follows that an equilibrium level of economic activity requires that

$$\text{Desired savings } (S_D) = \text{Desired investment } (I_D).$$

In other words, economic activity will move toward the level at which desired and realized savings are equal, desired and realized investment are equal, and desired savings equals desired investment. Algebraically:

$$S_R = S_D = I_D = I_R.$$

Figure 11-7 illustrates the adjustment process at work. At output level Y_2, the amount of savings withdrawn from the flow of spending is greater than the

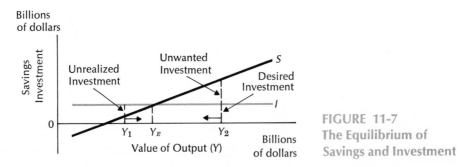

FIGURE 11-7
The Equilibrium of
Savings and Investment

amount businessmen are willing to invest. As long as output continues at that level, unwanted inventories will pile up unsold. This, of course, represents investment businessmen do not want to make. Output will be cut back and the level of output will fall toward Y_E. The decline in output will continue as long as savings are greater than desired investment and unwanted inventories are thereby increased. Only at Y_E will this disparity be eliminated and the decline in output halted.

Conversely, at output level Y_1 the economy's savings are below the level of investment desired by businessmen. If the desired level of investment in plant and equipment is achieved, then inventories must shrink below the desired level. If inventories are maintained, there will not be enough resources to sustain the desired expansion of plant and equipment. In either case, output will rise as business firms seek to achieve their investment goals. The level of output will rise toward Y_E and will continue to do so until the disparity between realized and desired investment is eliminated.

THE HEART OF THE THEORY

At this point, we can recapitulate the central ideas of the theory of income determination. Using the theoretical framework of a purely private, closed economy, three propositions have emerged:

1. The level of economic activity is determined by the amount of total spending, or aggregate demand:

$$Y = C + I.$$

2. The *equilibrium* level of economic activity is the one at which the amount businessmen receive from the sale of their output is just equal to the costs of producing it, including a normal profit. This condition prevails when aggregate demand equals aggregate supply:

$$D = Z.$$

3. Aggregate demand will equal aggregate supply when the savings consumers wish to make equal the investment expenditures desired by businessmen:

$$S_D = I_D.$$

These three propositions embody in summary form the elementary theory of income determination. They tell us that four factors determine the level of economic activity and employment. One is the level of total spending. A second is business costs of production. The third is the propensity to save and spend. The fourth is business investment decisions. Changes in any one of the four will bring changes in the level of economic activity as the economy adjusts to the new conditions. The process of adjustment will continue until a new equilibrium position is reached, at which aggregate demand and aggregate supply are once more equal and desired investment equals desired savings.

We can readily determine the direction of change by postulating a shift in any one of the four schedules involved, assuming no change in the other three. For example, if aggregate demand should increase for any reason, the level of economic activity will rise, as shown in Figure 11-8. Or if investment spending declines, economic activity will fall, as shown in Figure 11-9. The reader can work out other possible changes for himself.[2]

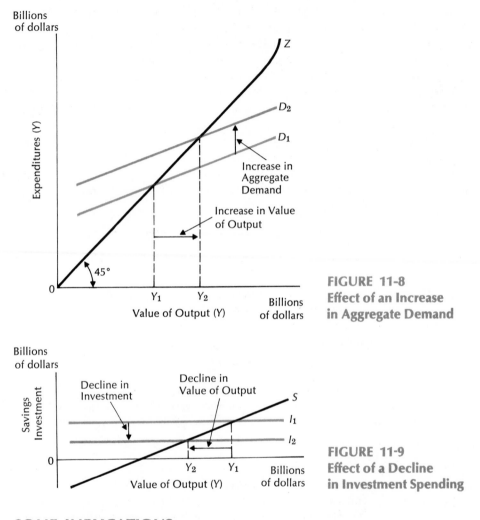

FIGURE 11-8
Effect of an Increase in Aggregate Demand

FIGURE 11-9
Effect of a Decline in Investment Spending

SOME IMPLICATIONS OF THE THEORY

The most important single conclusion to be drawn from the simple theory of income determination is that a private economy requires a guiding hand. Will

[2] Don't try shifting the aggregate supply schedule Z, however. Doing so involves changes in the price level, which we deal with in Chapter 19.

the equilibrium level of income settle at full employment; or at a substantially lower level, bringing unemployment and unused plant capacity; or at levels above full employment, bringing inflation? The answer given by the theory is simple: There is no way to tell. The equilibrium level could fall anywhere and stay there indefinitely, depending on what happens to the four variables that determine it. A level consistent with full employment is only one of many possible levels, and would be achieved in a purely private economy only by chance. Even if full employment were achieved, there is no assurance that it could be maintained. Changes in any one of the four variables could set in motion a chain of events leading to a new equilibrium at either inflationary or depressed levels.

A second conclusion is that the instability of a private economy is inherently difficult to predict. It is hard to tell in advance just what the reaction of consumers, businessmen, borrowers, and lenders is likely to be when changes occur in the economic environment. This lack of predictability makes difficult any kind of policy designed to counter the pattern of instability. Nevertheless, men are optimistic and one of the roles of science in the modern world is to bring intractable natural forces under control. Even if the nature of the economic beast is unpredictable instability, efforts can be made to ameliorate the problems created by its behavior. Those efforts have led in three directions:

1. Development of "automatic stabilizers" designed to reduce the instability of the economy. These measures will be described in Chapter 20 as part of the discussion of government policies and the national income.

2. Use of the government sector of the economy to counterbalance the instability of the private sector. Several instruments of policy are available: taxation and spending (fiscal policy), and management of the monetary sector (monetary policy). These matters will be given considerable attention in the next half-dozen chapters.

3. Forecasting to determine what the economy is likely to do in the near future. Effective forecasting is essential for success in applying economic policies.

There is a still broader and more fundamental implication of the theory of income determination. A private economy will not manage itself, at least with respect to the level of economic activity. The lack of a built-in guidance mechanism that could bring about and sustain economic stability reasonably close to full employment makes government intervention almost inevitable. Whatever may be the merits of a philosophy of laissez-faire, one hard fact remains: A democratic society will hardly tolerate the wastes of an unmanaged economy when its economic theorists can explain why the waste occurs and are able to devise ameliorative policies.

Summary

In the simplified theory of income determination we start with a closed private economy with stable prices, eliminating from consideration the monetary system, the government sector and the effect of the international economy. In this simple model, savings must equal investment. But since saving and investment are undertaken by different economic units for different reasons, there is no reason to believe that the amount consumers wish to save at full-employment levels of national income will be just matched by the amount of investment businessmen wish to make. If desired savings at full employment is greater than desired investment, total spending will fall. The decline in total spending will bring smaller incomes to households and their savings will fall. This process will continue until savings have fallen to the level at which they are equal to desired investment.

Income determination can also be thought of as an equality of aggregate demand with aggregate supply. If total spending is not large enough to compensate business units for the amount they have expended on production, either unwanted inventories will accumulate or prices will be cut in order to dispose of them. In either case, profits will be inadequate to motivate continuation of existing levels of production and economic activity will decline. Just the opposite effects will be felt if aggregate demand should push above aggregate supply. Desired investment levels will not be achieved and business firms will expand their production in order to reach them.

Key Concepts

Aggregate supply. The income businessmen require in order that they may produce a given level of output.

Aggregate demand. Total spending; the amount businessmen actually receive, in the simple income determination model.

Propensity to consume. The proportion of income spent for consumption. The propensity-to-consume schedule, or *consumption function,* shows the systematic relationship between total income and consumption expenditures at all levels of income.

Propensity to save. The proportion of income not spent for consumption. Can also be shown as a propensity-to-save schedule.

Investment. That portion of total output retained by producers, either to increase output or as inventories.

Equilibrium level of income.   That level of income at which aggregate demand is equal to aggregate supply and at which desired savings is equal to desired investment.

Important Diagrams

The student should be able to draw, label properly, and explain how each of the following diagrams illustrates the determination of the equilibrium level of income.

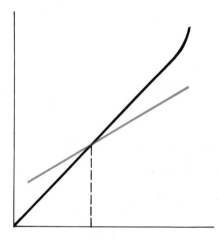

1. **Aggregate Demand Equals Aggregate Supply**

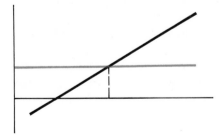

2. **Desired Savings Equals Desired Investment**

The Simple Dynamics of Income Determination

12

Two different kinds of changes can occur in the level of the national product. One is adjustment toward an equilibrium, based on the existing schedules of consumption and investment. This type was analyzed in the last chapter. The second occurs when one or both of those schedules shift. This chapter will analyze the second type of change.

First we shall show that when the aggregate demand schedule shifts, the level of national product will change by an amount greater than the shift in aggregate demand. Secondly, we shall develop the concept of the multiplier, which relates the size of the change in the national product to the amount of the shift in aggregate demand. Third, we shall discuss the tendency for a change in aggregate demand to set up a cumulative movement in the direction established by the original change, through induced investment. We shall emphasize the case in which a change in demand sets in motion accelerated changes in investment spending (the acceleration principle). These three concepts, the multiplier, induced investment, and the acceleration principle, help explain why substantial swings in the level of national product are just as pervasive as the tendency to move toward an equilibrium.

THE MULTIPLIED EFFECT OF INCREASED SPENDING

The multiplier principle is the starting point for an analysis of the dynamics of income determination. It can be stated simply: Any change in the aggregate demand schedule will result in a change in the value of output greater than the initial shift in aggregate demand. This principle is illustrated in Figure 12-1.

The reason for the larger increase in the value of output is to be found in the operation of the circular flow of spending. An initial increase in aggregate demand, coming perhaps from an increase in investment spending, will bring added incomes to the initial group of business firms that sell the goods. They, in turn, pay out incomes to workers and owners of other factors of production to produce the goods or replace inventories. The consumers who receive this income will then spend a part of it and save some. The amount they spend will become a second round of spending that results in added income for a second group of business firms. This, in turn, leads to a

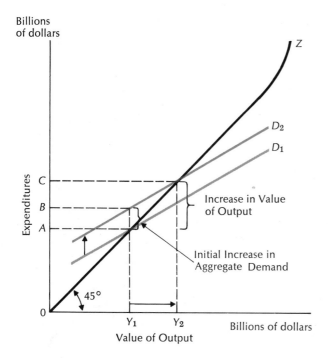

FIGURE 12-1
The Multiplier

An increase in aggregate demand from D_1 to D_2 (equal to AB on the vertical axis) will move the value of output from Y_1 to Y_2 (equal to AC on the vertical axis). The increase in the value of output is more than double the increase in aggregate demand in this illustration of the principle.

third round of spending, somewhat smaller than the second but nevertheless a further increase in the total. Additional income and output are generated at each round.

Each round of spending is less than the previous one because some income leaks out into savings each time. Income and output keep rising by smaller amounts each round, until at some point the increase is so small it has no noticeable effect on the total. Technically, the tiny increments of the late rounds of respending will continue until all of the original increase in aggregate demand has shifted into savings and there is no more left to continue around the economy. At that point the increase in output will stop.

A Numerical Example

This basic principle can be readily illustrated through a numerical example. Assume an increase in new investment, over and above the existing level, of $1 billion. Assume also that consumers will respend half of any increase in income they receive, and that consumer savings are the only "leakage" out of the flow of spending.[1] Figure 12-2 illustrates what happens.

---

[1] In the real world there are other important leakages. Business firms save, too, but we can lump these savings with those of consumers for the sake of convenience. Other leakages occur because of governments: taxes, social security, and other deductions, etc. An open economy with foreign trade will have some further leakages from the flow of spending. In our example the leakages due to government and foreign trade are excluded, because at this stage we are sticking with our simplified private, closed economy.

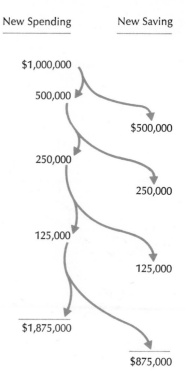

New Spending	New Saving

The original increase in investment causes
an increase in output and income of . . . $1,000,000
The consumers who receive this income
spend half . . .   500,000

. . . and save half. $500,000
Out of this second round of spending, half
is spent by those who receive it . . .   250,000

. . . and half is saved.   250,000
A fourth round of spending increases
output and incomes by half the amount of
the third . . .   125,000

. . . and savings by the same amount.   125,000
At this stage, after four rounds of
spending and respending, the total
increase in output and incomes is
already . . . $1,875,000

And the leakage into savings totals . . . $875,000

FIGURE 12-2
A Numerical Example of the Multiplier Principle

As the rounds of spending continue, the increase at each round become smaller, but continue adding to the total. In this example, the upper limit toward which total spending is moving is $2,000,000. At that point the leakage into savings will equal $1,000,000, and the amount of the original increase in spending will have gone into savings so that there will no longer be any impulse for further expansion. But that is only what the analysis of national income equilibrium in the last chapter would lead us to expect: The value of output will move to a level at which desired savings and desired investment are equal.

The important point in this example, however, is that the increase in total output and incomes was a multiple of the original change in the level of investment. In this case the multiple was 2. Of the total increase in aggregate demand ($2,000,000), half was the original increase in investment ($1,000,000) and half was the result of repeated rounds of respending ($1,000,000).

THE MULTIPLIER

The multiplier is the factor that relates any change in aggregate demand to the resulting change in the value of output. In the last example, the multiplier was 2: an increase of $1 million in aggregate demand led ultimately to an increase of $2 million in the value of output. The general relationship can be written as follows:

$$dY = k(dD),$$

where Y = value of output,

D = aggregate demand,

k = the multiplier.

If the multiplier were 3, for example, and aggregate demand increased initially by $2 billion, the value of output would rise by $6 billion. The multiplier also works in the other direction: if aggregate demand were to *fall* by $2 billion, and the multiplier were 3, the value of output would fall by $6 billion.

The change in aggregate demand can come from any source. It may result from a change in investment spending stimulated by a shift in business expectations. It may come from a shift upward or downward in the propensity-to-consume schedule, resulting from a change in consumer preferences between spending and saving.

In the real world, in contrast to our hypothetical example, aggregate demand can be changed by governments. Any change in government spending will change the level of aggregate demand, while changes in tax schedules can shift consumer spending and business investment patterns. But whatever the source, the original change will have a multiplied effect on the economy as a whole as the system moves toward a new equilibrium.

The Size of the Multiplier

The size of the multiplier depends on the amount of leakages out of the flow of spending. The smaller the leakages, the larger the amount respent and the larger the multiplier. The larger the leakages, the smaller the amount respent and the smaller the multiplier.

The amount respent out of increases in income is so important that economists have a special name for it, the *marginal propensity to consume*.
For example, suppose consumers receive an increase in income of $3 billion and spend $2 billion of it. The marginal propensity to consume will equal 2/3.

> **MARGINAL PROPENSITY TO CONSUME**
>
> *The proportion of additional income that is spent on consumption.*

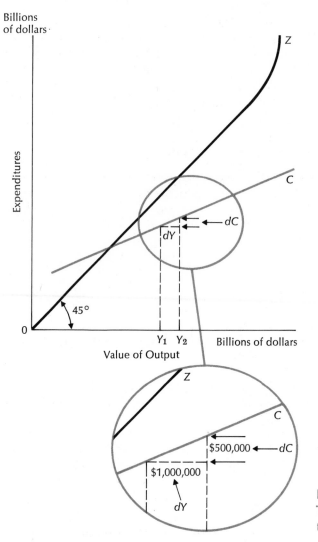

FIGURE 12-3
The Marginal Propensity
to Consume

Therefore,

$$MPC = \frac{dC}{dY},$$

where MPC = marginal propensity to consume,

C = consumption,

Y = value of output (total income).

Now go back to our numerical example of the multiplied effect of a change in aggregate demand, in which consumers spent just half of the increase in income they received. What was the marginal propensity to consume in that example?[2]

In graphical terms, the marginal propensity to consume is the *slope* of the propensity-to-consume schedule. It tells us how steeply the propensity-to-consume schedule rises as incomes increase. Figure 12-3 illustrates this relationship. In Figure 12-3, the propensity-to-consume schedule is drawn so that consumption rises by $500,000 for each $1,000,000 increase in income, to illustrate an *MPC* of 1/2. A higher *MPC*, of 3 for example, would impart a steeper slope to the propensity-to-consume schedule (see Figures 12-4A and 12-4B).

The marginal propensity to consume is the key to the size of the multiplier. It determines the amount spent at each round of respending, in an endless but diminishing progression that approaches a limit. The algebra of such infinite geometric progressions gives us the following formula for the multiplier:

$$k = \frac{1}{1 - MPC}.$$

Where the marginal propensity to consume is 1/2, the multiplier will be 2:

$$k = \frac{1}{1 - \frac{1}{2}} = \frac{1}{\frac{1}{2}} = 2.$$

Where the marginal propensity to consume is 2/3, the multiplier will be 3:

$$k = \frac{1}{1 - \frac{2}{3}} = \frac{1}{\frac{1}{3}} = 3.$$

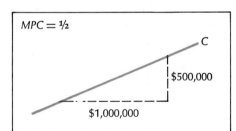

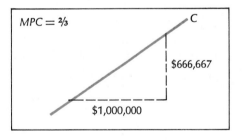

FIGURE 12-4

A. **Consumers spend half of each additional dollar of income**

B. **Consumers spend two-thirds of each additional dollar of income**

---

[2] You're right! 1/2, or 0.5. Figure it out like this:

$$MPC = \frac{dC}{dY} = \frac{500,000}{1,000,000} = \frac{1}{2}.$$

The Multiplier Over Time

Although the size of the multiplier can be readily estimated from the marginal propensity to consume, it is well to remember that the multiplier is part of an economic process that gradually unfolds over a period of time. A change in aggregate demand is felt quickly, but the full effect is spread out over a considerable interval.

Under normal conditions, it takes about three months for an increase in income to be respent. An *income-generation period*, as economists call it, of that length means that there will be four rounds of spending in one year. That number of rounds is enough to include about 80–90 percent of the multiplied effect of an increase in aggregate demand, when the full multiplier lies between 2 and 3. The bulk of the effect is felt within twelve months.

In actual practice the multiplier is usually found within a range of 2 and 2.5, over a year's time. A change in the aggregate demand schedule will bring about a change in GNP some 2 to 2.5 times as large, in about twelve months. This is a very convenient figure to remember in estimating the probable effects of policies that influence the level of aggregate demand. Of course, the chain of respending does not suddenly stop after twelve months, but continues onward in continually decreasing amounts that are usually too small to make much difference when policy decisions are at issue. For the purpose of this book we shall generally assume a twelve-month multiplier of 2, as an approximation close enough for ordinary use.

Of course, if the income-generation period should speed up, the multiplied effect of a change in aggregate demand would be felt more quickly. And if the period should lengthen, the multiplier process would work itself out more slowly.

The time pattern of the multiplier is important for another reason. The effect of an initial increase in aggregate demand quickly diminishes, because each round of respending is smaller than the previous one. This will cause the value of output to fall back to its original level unless the original increase in aggregate demand either

1. is sustained at the new level.
2. induces other changes that will provide a comparable increase in aggregate demand.

The diminishing effect of the multiplier is shown in Figure 12-5. It pictures the effect of a single and noncontinuing increase in aggregate demand: A large impact is soon felt, but the value of output quickly falls back to its original level once the effect of the original change wears off.

The value of output will move to a new and higher level, and stay there, only if the change in aggregate demand is continuously sustained through each income-generation period. This pattern is shown in Figure 12-6, where the same assumptions are made as in Figure 12-5 except that the new investment spending is repeated in each income-generation period. In this case, the value of output rises to approach a limit of $2 million above the starting level.

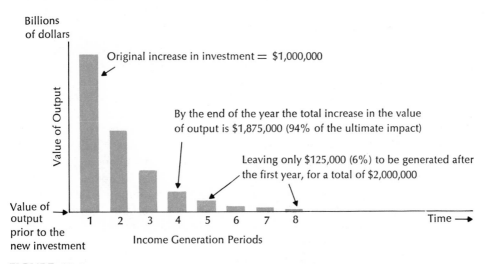

FIGURE 12-5

The Multiplier: Impact of a Single Increment in Aggregate Demand (Assume a single new investment expenditure of $1 million and an *MPC* of 1/2.)

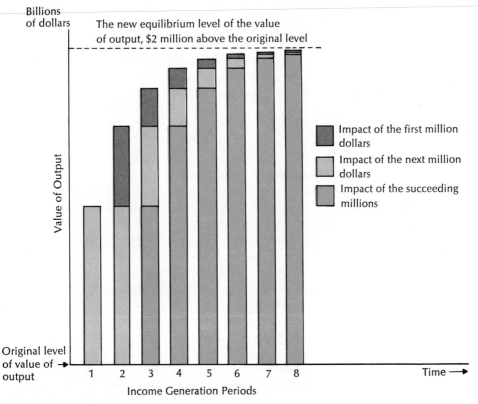

FIGURE 12-6

The Multiplier: Impact of a Continuing Increment in Aggregate Demand (Assume a new investment of $1 million in each income generation period and an *MPC* of 1/2.)

The Importance of the Multiplier

The multiplier is one of the most important concepts in the theory of the national income. It offers a means of quantifying the impact of changes in aggregate demand and any of its component parts. For example, surveys of business plans may show that next year businessmen expect to increase their investment spending above this year's level by some $5 billion. With a twelve-month multiplier of 2, this change would bring a $10 million rise in the value of output in the coming year. Policy makers in both business and government can use this information to analyze the effects of the change, forecast its impact on other sectors of the economy, and take steps to adapt to the new conditions that will prevail. Both private and public planning will be facilitated.

There is a second way in which the multiplier is important. Since the effect of any change is magnified, it is possible to achieve large results from relatively small beginnings. For example, suppose that the economy is currently operating well below its full employment potential by some $20 billion, and the federal government wants to increase aggregate demand so as to move the GNP upward by that amount. Additional spending will have to be generated by government directly or by stimulating consumer spending or business investment. Whatever the path taken, the amount of new spending required to push the GNP upward by $20 million is only half that amount when the twelve-month multiplier is 2.

The multiplier, then, is a key concept in both economic forecasting and economic policy making, at least for relatively short time horizons. For longer periods its usefulness is limited, because of the uncertainties of induced investment.

INDUCED INVESTMENT

Reflect for a moment on the larger meaning of the multiplier: Any change in the flow of spending is magnified. In the modern economy, where all the parts are interrelated, this enlarged effect of an original change *must* have an impact on other events, on other parts of the economic system. Any change in aggregate demand, therefore, cannot be understood as an isolated event. It is inconceivable that the effects of a single increase in investment, for example, should peter out over a few income-generation periods to leave the level of output just as it was before. The very fact that an increase in income has been temporarily generated will induce other changes, for it will have changed the economic environment.

We should expect any change to have cumulative effects. A shift upward in the aggregate demand schedule, even a temporary one, will increase incomes and spending. In the process, businessmen will be induced to add to their inventories or expand their production capacity. Secondary effects will be felt that will add further to an upward swing in economic activity. This induced investment will, in turn, have a multiplied impact on the level of economic activity, continuing still further the process of cumulative change.

It would be tempting to argue that such a continuing economic expansion, once started, would continue until the economy reached full employment, at which point it would level off. This, indeed, was the idea behind the "pump-priming" theory of the 1930s. It was hoped that a relatively small increase in government spending would raise incomes and stimulate greater consumer spending, which in turn would induce additional business investment, and so on until prosperity was restored. And the higher levels of economic activity were expected to generate additional tax revenues to pay for the original increase in government spending.

Unfortunately, the cumulative expansion to full-employment prosperity is not always certain. No one knows in advance whether it will or will not occur, since so much depends on businessmen's expectations and the climate of opinion in the business community. At some times, such as during most of the years since World War II, the process of cumulative expansion has operated to keep the economy at or close to full-employment prosperity most of the time, although government policies have been very important in providing the proper stimulus. At other times, such as during the Great Depression of the 1930s, a number of advances proved to be abortive, failing to generate the induced investment that would lead to a cumulative expansion toward full employment. Perhaps the pessimism of that era was so great, coupled with the serious economic dislocations of the depression, that a complete change in the economic environment was necessary. Perhaps the stimulus provided by government efforts to prime the pump just weren't large enough. Whatever the reason, World War II brought great changes in both of these areas. Government spending was vastly increased, and a huge new market for war industries suddenly appeared. There was no question, at that time, about a cumulative movement toward high levels of economic activity. Since businessmen knew that huge new amounts of purchasing power were going to be pumped into the economy, they increased their own investment spending and the wartime boom was on.

There is, then, a relationship between increases in aggregate demand and the investment component of aggregate demand. An autonomous increase in aggregate demand (that is, independent of the existing flow of spending and level of output) can induce additional investment, to set in motion a cumulative expansion of the economy. Just how much additional investment will be induced, and how long the cumulative advance will last, is uncertain, however.

All that we have said about cumulative expansion of economic activity is equally true of contractions. An initial decline in aggregate demand will reduce incomes and purchasing power by a multiplied amount. This reduction does not occur in an isolated situation, but in an economy of closely interrelated parts. It can easily cause expectations of a further decline and stimulate cutbacks in business investment. A self-reinforcing decline in economic activity will have started.

THE ACCELERATION PRINCIPLE

One aspect of induced investment is particularly important. Called the acceleration principle, it embodies two relationships between demand and investment spending.

1. An increase in demand can cause a proportionately much larger, accelerated increase in investment spending. For example, a 10 percent increase in demand may trigger perhaps a 100 percent increase in investment spending as business firms increase their production capacity to meet the increased demand.

2. When an increase in aggregate demand slows its upward pace and begins to level off, a decline in investment spending can occur.

These two relationships, shown in Figure 12-7, can set in motion a whole series of chain reactions. The accelerated investment induced by an increase in demand will have a multiplied effect on total spending, contributing to a

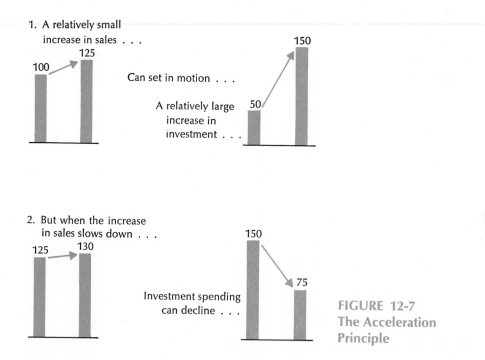

FIGURE 12-7
The Acceleration
Principle

cumulative upswing in economic activity. Yet as economic expansion begins to slow down as the economy begins to reach a peak, the second effect can show up: As aggregate demand starts to level off, investment spending can start to decline. The multiplied effect of an investment drop can then start to pull economic activity downward.

A feedback mechanism in the economic system is at work here. A change in aggregate demand induces changes in investment decisions, which in turn have a multiplied effect on aggregate demand. Under some circumstances a cumulative upswing can result. Under other circumstances the conditions which end an expansion and create a downturn can appear.[3] These relationships develop whenever the level of investment spending is tied closely to the level of consumer demand, as in the case of inventories and some other types of investment. Wherever that is the case, the amount of investment spending will depend on the rate of change in the level of aggregate demand.

An Example of the Acceleration Principle

The acceleration principle can best be understood by use of a simple example. Let us assume, to start with, a business firm that owns ten machines, each of which can turn out 100 units of product each time period. One machine must be replaced each time period, and will last for 10 periods before it must be replaced. The firm starts out with sales of 1,000 units in the first time period, requiring full use of its 10 machines and purchase of one new machine to replace one old one:

Period	Sales	No. of Machines Needed	No. of Machines Purchased		
			Replacement	New	Total
1	1,000	10	1	0	1

In the second period, there is a 100-unit increase in sales, which requires adding another machine to the plant in addition to replacing an old one. This addition increases investment spending by 100 percent to accommodate a 10 percent increase in sales:

Period	Sales	No. of Machines Needed	No. of Machines Purchased		
			Replacement	New	Total
2	1,100	11	1	1	2

Now let us postulate an even faster increase in sales, from 100 units to 200 units in the third time period. This will illustrate the proposition that in this

---

[3] Some economists have combined the multiplier and the acceleration principle to develop theoretical models of the business cycle. We do not go that far here, although it is clear that two aspects of economic fluctuations can be "explained" in this way, namely, the continuation and cumulation of prosperity, and the upper turning point at which a recession starts. Business fluctuations are more complicated than these simple models, however. If you are interested in the "models" approach to multiplier-accelerator relationships, see Paul A. Samuelson, "Interactions Between the Multiplier Analysis and the Principle of Acceleration," in *Readings in Business Cycle Theory* (Blakiston, 1944), pp. 261–69, reprinted from *The Review of Economic Statistics*, Vol. XXI, No. 2 (May, 1939), pp. 75–78.

situation growth in investment spending requires an increase in the rate of growth in final demand. Two new machines must be added, and total machines purchased rises from two in the previous period to three in this period:

Period	Sales	No. of Machines Needed	No. of Machines Purchased		
			Replacement	New	Total
3	1,300	13	1	2	3

Just to clinch the point, suppose sales rise in the fourth period by the same amount as in the third. In this case there is no increase in investment even though final demand continues to rise:

Period	Sales	No. of Machines Needed	No. of Machines Purchased		
			Replacement	New	Total
4	1,500	15	1	2	3

Now what happens when demand for the product continues to rise, but not so fast as before? Let us assume for Period 5 an increase in sales of 100 units. In this case the amount of investment decreases even though output rises:

Period	Sales	No. of Machines Needed	No. of Machines Purchased		
			Replacement	New	Total
5	1,600	16	1	1	2

Finally, examine the results of a decline in demand for the final product, when sales fall by 100 units in the next period, back to the level of Period 4. Even though sales are 50 percent above those of the initial period, new investment falls to nothing. This happens because the decline in sales makes it unnecessary even to replace the machine that wears out:

Period	Sales	No. of Machines Needed	No. of Machines Purchased		
			Replacement	New	Total
6	1,500	15	0	0	0

This example of the acceleration principle is shown graphically in Figure 12-8. At their peak, sales were only 60 percent greater than the initial period. Yet the peak in investment was three times the level of the initial period. Furthermore, the investment peak came before sales topped out, and investment had already started downward while sales were still rising.

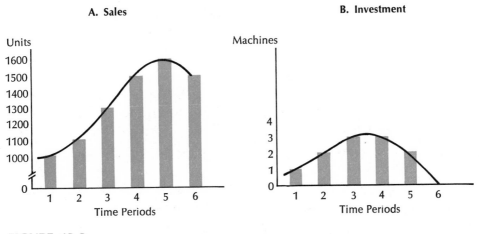

FIGURE 12-8
The Acceleration Principle

The Principle Restated

The acceleration principle is based on the relationship between the *level* of investment and the *rate of growth* in final demand. Whenever investment spending is derived directly and closely from the demand for final products:

1. Investment rises when the rate of growth of sales is increasing.
2. Investment is constant when the rate of growth of sales is constant.
3. Investment falls when the rate of growth of sales is falling.

To this should be added the concept of acceleration: A change in the level of final sales is reflected in a proportionately much larger change in the level of investment spending.

Some Qualifications

The acceleration principle is easier to illustrate in a hypothetical example than in the real world. Few business firms maintain a fixed relationship between sales and investment spending. Long-range planning of capital expenditures in most large firms is seldom based on short-run swings in sales. Nevertheless, some types of investment depend to a substantial degree on sales, including much inventory accumulation and a significant amount of investment by railroads and public utilities.

A more important qualification is that the principle doesn't apply when there is a significant amount of excess capacity. In those circumstances, a large increase in sales may have little impact on investment as old equipment is brought back into use before new investment is made.

The principle must also be modified by the way in which expectations influence decisions. Businessmen don't wait until they have reached capacity operations before they start adding to their production capabilities. They anticipate needs and plan for them in advance whenever they can.

As a result of these three factors, the swings in investment spending that might be expected to result from the operation of the acceleration principle tend to be smoothed out.

Significance of the Acceleration Principle

In spite of these qualifications, the acceleration principle is important. It doesn't apply to all investment spending, but where it does apply, it creates significant economic problems.

> First, investment spending will fluctuate more widely than demand for final products.
>
> Second, investment spending can start to decline while sales are still rising.

These two phenomena help to explain why a private enterprise economy is inherently unstable. When an industry is at or near capacity levels of production, a continued rise in aggregate demand will bring about an accelerated increase in investment spending. Even before capacity output levels are reached, the anticipation of that condition can set the principle in motion. The enlarged investment spending then feeds back a further increase in aggregate demand into the economy.

Once a rise in aggregate demand begins to slacken off, however, the operation of the acceleration principle can cause investment spending to decline. The feedback effect of this decline in investment will slow down the growth of aggregate demand still further and can set the stage for a general downturn in business activity. Timing of these effects, however, is uncertain. When anticipations enter the picture, the downturn in investment spending can come even sooner. If time is required to make investment decisions effective, or to change them, the decline in investment spending may lag behind the original changes in aggregate demand.[4] But whatever the case, an unstable economy is the result.

The Acceleration Principle and Economic Growth

The acceleration principle is also important in the process of economic growth. Almost any important industry illustrates the principle at work. Take railroads as an example. The American railway system was built, for the most part, between 1850 and 1914. Investment in rail lines, bridges and stations, and rolling stock was considerably greater in the 50 years before 1914 than in the 50 years after. In the earlier years investment was for expansion as well as replacement, while in the latter years there was little expansion. Investment in railroads after 1914 was limited primarily to replacement (and to new types of equipment resulting from technological change). As a result, before 1914 the expansion of railroads and the investment spending that went along with it

---

[4] Most empirical studies of the acceleration principle show that it is felt with a time lag, usually three to six months, rather than instantaneously.

was a major stimulant to American economic growth. After 1914, economic growth came from other sources.

The automobile industry showed a similar pattern, but with two important differences. Once the productive capacity of the industry had been built up by the late 1920s, investment in expanded facilities was sharply curtailed, until demand for cars started moving up once more in the years after World War II. Investment by automobile companies for purposes of expansion slowed considerably after the late twenties. But investment of another sort appeared, in jigs, dies, and tools needed for the annual model changes. The built-in obsolescence of annual models helped to sustain investment spending. So did technological change, which brought larger and faster cars. The roads built in the 1920s and 1930s had to be replaced by the expressways of the 1950s and 1960s. A burst of public investment spending was required because of improved automobiles, which would have been necessary even if total sales of cars and trucks had not risen.

The long-run relationship between investment and aggregate demand may well be the most important aspect of the acceleration principle. Roughly speaking, *stability of investment spending requires continual expansion in the rest of the economy.* If expansion slows down in the rest of the economy, a decline can be expected in investment spending. Such a decline will, in turn, serve to reduce expansion in the rest of the economy and contribute to a general economic stagnation.

This relationship is, of course, not exact and precise. Technological change can promote investment. So can changes in consumer tastes. And businessmen's expectations will influence the level of investment spending. In addition, a growing economy will require larger replacement of capital equipment from year to year. These factors may offset or modify the long-run effects of the acceleration principle. Underneath it all, however, stands the fundamental relationship embodied in the feedback mechanisms of the acceleration principle: a sustained level of investment spending requires a sustained rate of growth in the economy as a whole.

EXPECTATIONS AND ANTICIPATIONS

Some of the economic mechanisms that relate changes in investment spending to the level of aggregate demand and vice versa are now apparent. The multiplier shows how an increase in investment spending (or any other type of spending) will push total spending up by more than the original increase. Induced investment introduces a feedback mechanism through which an increase in total spending promotes further increases in investment. This feedback occurs because a change in aggregate demand affects expectations and anticipations. This cause-and-effect relationship is a general one, however: No one can tell *how much* new investment will be induced by a specific increase in total spending, even though we know that under such circumstances there would be a *tendency* for investment spending to increase.

The acceleration principle, a special case of induced investment that depends on maintenance of a fixed proportion between sales and capital investment, can also be influenced by expectations. The wide swings in investment spending that it implies are, in actual practice, strongly modified by forward planning. When expenditures on new plant and equipment are based on expected trends in future sales rather than on this year's sales, a company's investment program will be more stable than the pattern suggested by the acceleration principle.[5]

Expectations and Investment

Forward planning in business reduces expectations to actual quantities of projected sales and revenues, and from them derives production, personnel, and financial plans. In the process, investment decisions emerge from the comparison of expected rates of return on capital investment with the rate of interest that the company would have to pay on borrowed capital.

A hypothetical example will show how these factors influence a firm's decision. An electronics manufacturing firm contemplating construction of a new plant to manufacture transistor radios must decide on the size of the plant it wishes to build. The management can borrow the capital at an interest rate of

TABLE 12–1
Electronics Manufacturing Co. Proposed Transistor Radio Division

(1) Additional Capital Investment (Millions of Dollars)	(2) Cost of Capital (6%)	(3) Expected Average Annual Return on Operations	(4) Expected Increase in Return Due to Additional Investment	(5) Profits
1	$ 60,000	$ 90,000		$ 30,000
2	120,000	175,000	$85,000	55,000
3	180,000	255,000	80,000	75,000
4	240,000	330,000	75,000	90,000
5	300,000	400,000	70,000	100,000
6	360,000	465,000	65,000	105,000
7	420,000	525,000	60,000	105,000
8	480,000	580,000	55,000	100,000
9	540,000	630,000	50,000	90,000
10	600,000	675,000	45,000	75,000

[5] The determinants of business investment decisions have been an important subject of economic research in recent years. One can understand why: Investment is a crucial variable in the theory of income determination. The acceleration principle has been one of the important factors identified by this research. A group of financial factors has also been identified, including rates of profit, dividend yields, the net financial position of companies, and rates of interest.

6 percent, and has no control over this cost of capital.[6] Putting its analysts to work, it develops the projections listed in Table 12-1. Pretend that you are a member of the board of directors responsible for making the investment decision, and that profit maximization is the major criterion applicable in this case. You would also like the firm to obtain as large a share of the market as it can get without compromising the profit maximization goal. How much should the firm invest in its new plant?

The investment decision emerges almost intuitively. Profits will be maximized with an investment of either $6 million or $7 million. An operation of the larger size is slightly preferable, however, since it will provide for higher output and a larger share of the market. This solution has a very special characteristic: The increase in expected returns due to raising the capital investment from $6 million to $7 million is $60,000 (see Column 4), which is exactly equal to the cost of borrowing the additional $1 million. A general rule is involved here: *A profit-maximizing firm will increase its investment up to the point at which the expected rate of return on additional new investment is just equal to the rate of interest.* The principle is illustrated in Figure 12-9.

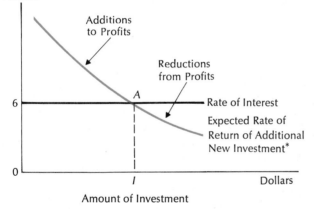

FIGURE 12-9
The Level of Investment Spending
As investment is increased toward *I*, each additional amount of new investment adds to profit. Profits are maximized at *I*, and any further amounts of new investment start bringing total profits down.
* John Maynard Keynes christened this concept "the marginal efficiency of capital." The standard terminology used by contemporary economists is "the marginal efficiency of investment," a term used in later chapters of this book.

[6] Even if the firm made the investment out of retained earnings and paid no interest charge on the capital, the cost would be the same. Presumably, the firm would be able to lend the money to someone else at the market rate of interest and earn the interest charge on the loan. The cost of using the capital in its own business is the amount the firm would have to give up by not lending the money to someone else.

Only one of these two factors is an objective, measurable one. The rate of interest is determined in the money markets and any firm can determine its investment costs quite accurately. The expected rate of return on new investment, however, is the result of the planning process itself. It is an expectation, and may or may not materialize. Like all expectations, it is intangible and ephemeral. It may be based on projections of recent costs and sales, and on highly sophisticated forecasts of the future. But recent trends need not necessarily continue and forecasts are often wrong. As new information is received, the forecasts will be revised and the expectations based on them will change. As a result, the decision to invest may be changed or scaled downward or upward, or its timing changed.

In other words, the schedule of the expected rate of return on additional new investment (called the marginal efficiency of investment) can shift upward or downward, leading to changes in the level of investment. That, in turn, will bring multiplied changes in the level of aggregate demand, which may induce still further changes in investment spending, including some of the type illustrated by the acceleration principle and others that result from further changes in expectations. Clearly, the schedule of investment spending, which looks so stable when we draw it in our diagrams, can move rather substantially if economic conditions are right.

Expectations and Consumer Spending

The schedule of the propensity to consume can also shift in response to consumers' expectations. There is a tendency among economists to assume that it remains stable, that with a given level of GNP we can predict the level of consumer spending rather closely. Much of the time that is true: the propensity to consume does not fluctuate widely in response to economic conditions but is tied closely to income. Once in a while, however, it does shift, creating repercussions that are very difficult to anticipate.

One recent instance occurred in 1968. A 10 percent income tax surcharge was passed by Congress early in the year;[1] it was designed to reduce consumer spending and diminish the inflationary pressures created by high levels of military spending for the Vietnam war. Most economists, including the author, expected the surtax to have that effect. Disposable income would be reduced by about 10 percent and a multiplied decline in GNP was expected to occur, reducing the pressure on prices to rise. But consumers were too smart for the economists. They also knew that military spending was pushing prices up, and that their money would buy less the longer they held it. They reacted by maintaining their levels of spending, in spite of higher taxes. Savings fell from about 7.5 percent of disposable income to about 6.25 percent. This upward shift in the propensity to consume was financed in part by borrowing, in part by reduced savings, and in part by higher wages and salaries brought

---

[1] A 10 percent *surtax* means an increase of 10 percent in the consumer's tax payment. For example, a tax of $100 would be increased to $110. It does not mean that an additional 10 percent of total income would be paid in taxes.

by inflation. The effects of the tax surcharge were cancelled by the effects of a change in consumer expectations and a shift upward in the propensity to consume.

Consumer behavior is becoming less stable over the years, largely because of the increased amounts of discretionary income in consumer hands. Consumers are becoming wealthier, are better educated, have accumulated substantial savings, and have huge credit facilities at their service. Years ago they may have purchased to fill their needs, but now they buy to satisfy their tastes as well. Consumers can borrow or use savings to buy now, or they can postpone their purchases until later. Spending depends not only on ability to buy, but on willingness as well. In addition, consumer spending has become a much more important factor in the economy as incomes have risen. All of these developments have contributed to an increase in the importance of consumer anticipations and expectations.

THE MOVING ECONOMY

We can now summarize the results of our analysis of income determination. The economy is continually moving toward an equilibrium level of income and output. The movement toward that equilibrium can set in motion changes in both the investment and consumption schedules. These changes mean that the equilibrium position is itself changing, even though the tendency to move toward it remains. We are brought to the realization that the level of economic activity is continually moving, never settling down at a single point. A dynamic pattern is always found.

In addition, there is the problem of growth. Since any economy moves along a growth path, another dimension must be added to the dynamics of income determination. The factors crucial to growth, such as accumulation of capital, changes in technology, education, and science, and the process of innovation, interact with the determinants of the level of aggregate demand to produce a continually changing economy. Actual achievement of the equilibrium described in Chapter 12 is well-nigh impossible.

Yet that equilibrium is of major importance. We would like to maintain full-employment levels of aggregate demand. Doing so implies maintenance of the national income equilibrium as the economy moves along a full-employment growth path. That is no easy task, for we now know that any one equilibrium position is a very fragile thing, at least insofar as the private sector of the economy is concerned.

Summary

The movement of the level of income to an equilibrium depends on the existing schedules of consumption and investment. If one of these schedules changes, there will be a move to a new level of income. In the simple theory of income determination, we usually assume that the propensity to consume does not change, and that changes in the investment schedule are the dynamic element.

A change in investment spending has a multiplied effect because of the respending that takes place in the circular flow of spending. The size of the multiplied effect depends on the leakage of savings out of the circular flow. Hence, the size of the multiplier depends upon the marginal propensity to consume:

$$k = \frac{1}{1 - MPC}.$$

A multiplied change in aggregate demand can change business expectations, inducing further changes in the level of investment.

A particularly important form of induced investment is that affected by the acceleration principle. Where invested expenditures are directly tired to the level of sales, a relatively small change in sales can bring a relatively large change in investment. The key to the acceleration principle is that the amount of investment depends on the rate of change in final sales.

These three concepts impart a dynamism to the level of economic activity that continually keeps it in flux in spite of the forces at work that tend to create an equilibrium. At the same time, the forces of equilibrium keep the system from expanding or contracting without limit. A change in one direction tends to generate more change, yet the equilibrium forces tend to bring the system to rest.

None of this assures full employment, which could be achieved but only by chance. Government action is necessary if that goal is to be consistently achieved.

Key Concepts

The multiplier.   The factor that relates a change in spending to the resulting change in the level of economic activity.

Marginal propensity to consume.   The proportion of an addition to income which is spent on consumption. It determines the size of the multiplier in the formula

$$k = \frac{1}{1 - MPC}.$$

Induced investment.   Investment stimulated by an initial increase in aggregate demand.

Acceleration principle.   The amount of certain types of investment is related to the rate of change in demand for the final product.

Investment plays a dual role in determination of the level of national output and income. On one hand, it helps to determine the level of aggregate demand. On the other hand, it affects the capacity of the economy to produce. This dual nature of investment affects the growth path of the economy, for unless aggregate demand and capacity to produce advance at the same rate, economic growth will become unbalanced. As we saw in Chapter 9 when we examined recent U.S. growth, the chief imbalance in recent years has been the inability of aggregate demand to keep pace with the capacity to produce.

We can examine the problem further, now that the determination of aggregate demand in the private sector is understood. Let's phrase the issue in this fashion: Can private investment create additional purchasing power at the same rate at which it raises output capacity? If it can, the private sector may be able to develop a growth path for the economy that can be sustained indefinitely without significant government intervention. But if investment causes capacity to grow faster than purchasing power, the growth of capital cannot be sustained—because some will lie idle—and the economy will find itself facing a downturn. Or if purchasing power rises faster than capacity, prices will eventually start rising and bring the economic dislocations associated with inflation. In either case, economic policy makers will face the choice of instability or intervention.

Capital Investment and the Growth Rate of the Economy

13

INVESTMENT AND ECONOMIC GROWTH

Capital investment increases the economy's capacity to produce in two ways. First, additional facilities create more physical capacity: more cracking units in petroleum refineries, more rolling mills to turn out steel sheets, an additional highway lane to handle more traffic, and so on. Investment can also increase productivity: new and improved techniques enable new facilities to produce more than old facilities, even without any increase in total investment. Better education enables people to produce more. Expanded health facilities enable people to work more effectively. Investment in both physical and human capital can increase output per man-hour.

At the same time, investment increases purchasing power. Money spent on new and expanded plant and equipment comes into the hands of those who produce it, in the form of wages and salaries, profits, and rent. These effects are felt throughout the economy by way of the multiplier. These two relationships enable us to analyze the effects of investment on the growth of both capacity and purchasing power, and determine the conditions under which the two effects are equal.

We can start with the effect of investment on the economy's capacity to produce. The impact is felt through the *capital/output ratio,* which we can designate by the Greek letter sigma (σ). The capital/output ratio shows the effect of capital investment on output capacity. For example, in recent decades some \$3 of capital investment has been required for every \$1 of GNP. This has been true for the total stock of capital relative to total output, as well as for increases in capital relative to increases in output. Thus

$$\sigma = \frac{K}{Y} \tag{1}$$

and

$$\sigma = \frac{dK}{dY} \tag{2}$$

$$\text{where } K = \text{ stock of capital,}$$

$$Y = \text{ output capacity.}$$

Using this formula, we find that $\sigma = 3$ in recent decades.

We note in Equation (2), that the term dK (the change in the stock of capital) is nothing but net investment ($dK = I$). We can multiply both sides of Equation (2) by dY and come up with the following relationship:

$$dK = I = \sigma(dY), \tag{3}$$

which tells us how much investment would be needed to obtain a given increase in capacity. We could also solve for dY by dividing both sides of Equation (3) by σ,

$$dY = I\frac{1}{\sigma} \tag{4}$$

which tells us how much output capacity would be increased by a given amount of investment.

Now we can turn to the demand side of the problem. The multiplier principle tells us that the annual increase in income due to investment is

$$dY = k(dI). \tag{5}$$

Since $k = \dfrac{1}{1 - MPC}$ or $\dfrac{1}{MPS}$, we can rewrite Equation (5) as

$$dY = \frac{1}{a}(dI), \tag{6}$$

where $a = $ the marginal propensity to save.

Equation (6) defines the demand side of the problem, telling us how much of an increase in purchasing power will be produced by a given amount of investment.

If the growth of the economy is to be stable, then the increase in capacity dY in Equation (4) will have to equal the increase in purchasing power dY in Equation (6). That is,

$$dY = I\frac{1}{\sigma} = \frac{1}{a}(dI). \tag{7}$$

We can now solve Equation (7) for the growth rate of investment which will be consistent with stable growth. To do that, we multiply both sides of Equation (7) by a and divide both sides by I. The result is

$$\frac{dI}{I} = a\left(\frac{1}{\sigma}\right). \tag{8}$$

The left-hand term is simply the growth rate of investment. The right-hand term tells us how much it will have to be to achieve stable growth. This equation defines the equilibrium growth rates for investment.

Here is a numerical example. Let the marginal propensity to save equal 15 percent of income ($a = 0.15$). Let the capital/output ratio equal 3. Then

$$\frac{dI}{I} = 0.15\left(\frac{1}{3}\right) = 0.05.$$

Under those conditions investment would have to grow at 5 percent annually for the economy to follow a stable growth path.

We pause for review. Two factors define the growth rate for investment required for stable growth of GNP. One is the proportion of income saved out of increases in income, that is, the marginal propensity to save, a. The second is the increase in output capacity created by investment, expressed in form of the capital/output ratio, σ. Unless investment grows at a rate defined in Equation (8), which is based on those two factors, the growth of the economy will be unstable.

Here are some examples of instability. First, rates of investment that leave a growing gap between capacity and purchasing power. Let $\sigma = 3$ and $a = 0.15$, as in the example above. But instead of a growth rate for investment of 5 percent annually, assume a 4 percent rate. In Year 1, net investment equals 100 and in Year 2 it increases to 104. From Equation (4), capacity will grow by $34\frac{2}{3}$:

$$dY = I\frac{1}{\sigma} \tag{4}$$

$$= 104\left(\frac{1}{3}\right) = 34\frac{2}{3}.$$

Purchasing power, figured from Equation (6), will grow by only 26⅔, however:

$$dY = \frac{1}{a}\,(dI) \tag{6}$$

$$= \frac{1}{0.15}\,(4) = 26\tfrac{2}{3}.$$

With purchasing power growing more slowly than capacity, the unused capacity installed in Year 2 can be expected to discourage investors. They are likely to cut total investment below 104 in Year 3, thereby triggering a decline in aggregate demand and a recession.

Now we can look at the other side: too rapid a growth of investment. Let $\sigma = 3$ and $a = 0.15$ again. But let net investment grow from 100 to 106 between Year 1 and Year 2, a 6 percent increase. Output capacity will grow by 35⅓:

$$dY = I\frac{1}{\sigma} \tag{4}$$

$$= 106\left(\frac{1}{3}\right) = 35\tfrac{1}{3}.$$

But purchasing power will grow by 50:

$$dY = \frac{1}{a}\,(dI) \tag{6}$$

$$= \frac{1}{0.15}\,(6) = 40.$$

If the economy had started from a full-employment–no-excess-capacity position, the extra growth of purchasing power would start prices rising. If the economy had not yet reached its output capacity by the end of Year 2, the extra growth of purchasing power and decline in excess capacity would bring added incentives to invest. Investment in Year 3 would be very likely to increase by even more than 6 percent, perhaps by as much as 8 or 10 percent. Yet once capacity to produce has been reached, the growth of net investment will have to continue at a rate of only 5 percent annually if stability is to be maintained. What will bring it down from 8–10 percent to 5 percent? There is no equilibrating mechanism in the private sector of the economy to assure that it will fall by that amount. Investment decisions rest very heavily upon business expectations of the future, which are based in part on recent experience. We should expect businessmen to continue to be optimistic, pressing for more expansion as the economy approaches full use of capacity rather than thinking of cutting back on their investment and the growth rate of their enterprises.

We emerge from this analysis somewhat chastened. We can show that it is quite possible for the economy to follow a growth path in which the capacity to produce and the capacity to consume move together. Stable growth is feasible. But there is no guarantee that it will be achieved, or even that there is a pervasive tendency in that direction. Rather than a path, we have defined a knife-edge. Once the economy falls off the edge there is no assurance that it will get back.

SOME QUALIFICATIONS

The model we have developed is a simplified one. In particular, it makes two assumptions that qualify the conclusions substantially. First, it assumes a constant capital/output ratio. That assumption may or may not be correct. Recent estimates show a fairly constant ratio for the U.S. in recent decades, but those estimates have not allowed for a rather large amount of capital (about $45 billion worth) owned by the federal government but used by private firms in the defense and space industries. If that capital were included in the estimates, the capital/output ratio would show a somewhat rising trend since World War II.

A stable capital/output ratio means that capital does not face diminishing returns. When the ratio increases, returns to capital diminish in the long run, since it will take increasing amounts of capital to produce a given increase in output. When the ratio decreases (as it seems to have done between 1900 and 1940), returns to capital are increasing. In any case, the growth of output capacity will be affected, and so will the stable growth level of investment.

For example, suppose we have a stable growth path requiring a 5 percent growth of investment each year, based on a capital/output ratio of 3 and an *MPS* of 0.15, as in the last example. Now let the capital/output ratio rise because of diminishing returns to capital. A 5 percent growth of investment will now be too much for stable growth, for it will cause purchasing power to rise faster than capacity to produce. The rate of growth of investment will have to fall in order to preserve a stable growth path.[1]

A second assumption is that the marginal propensity to save remains constant. In the long run it may be highly stable, but in the short run it may shift significantly from year to year. Its instability makes it difficult to rely confidently on even estimating, much less achieving, a year-to-year growth rate for investment that guarantees a stable growth path for the economy.

These qualifications mean that the model developed in this chapter is not highly useful for quantitative estimates and has very limited usefulness as a direct guide to policy. But its purpose was to show whether stable growth is

---

[1] Here are the calculations it the capital/output ratio were to rise from 3 to 4:

$$\frac{dI}{I} = a\left(\frac{1}{4}\right) \tag{8}$$

$$= 0.15 \ (\tfrac{1}{4}) = 3.75.$$

With the rise in capital/output ratio the equilibrium growth rate for investment will fall from 5 to 3.75.

possible. The answer here is *Yes*. A second purpose was to indicate the conditions under which stable growth might be achieved. Results here indicate that the conditions are very fragile and not likely to be achieved or sustained in the private sector alone. There is, then, a substantial role for government in influencing both the level of aggregate demand and the rate of growth of investment.

Summary

Investment adds both to purchasing power and to the capacity to produce. Stable growth with full employment requires that the two effects of investment balance each other. If the capacity to produce grows more rapidly than purchasing power, some of the new capacity will become redundant. If purchasing power grows more rapidly than the capacity to produce, an increasing imbalance will create inflation.

It is possible for a balance to be achieved, but there is no mechanism in the private sector alone that will assure such a balance. Furthermore, once the balance is lost there is no mechanism that brings the economy back to it. Again we find a substantial role for government to play.

Key Concepts

Capital/Output ratio. The ratio between the stock of capital and the output capacity of the economy.

Stable growth. The increase in purchasing power created by investment is equal to the increase in output capacity created by that investment.

Unstable growth. The increase in purchasing power created by investment is different from the increase in output capacity created by that investment.

Conditions for stable growth. $\dfrac{dI}{I} = a\left(\dfrac{1}{\sigma}\right),$

where $\dfrac{dI}{I}$ = rate of growth of investment,

a = the marginal propensity to save,

σ = the capital/output ratio.

The student should be able to explain this formula and show how it can be used.

Our analysis of national income determination has concentrated up to this point on the private sector of the economy. Chapter 11 looked at the tendency for an equilibrium level of national income to emerge from the interaction of consumption, savings, and investment. Chapter 12 examined some of the simple dynamics of the system—the multiplier, induced investment, the acceleration principle, and the effect of expectations and uncertainty. The picture that emerges is one of a fluctuating economy in which the forces continually pushing toward an equilibrium are themselves changing in such a way that economic stability seems impossible to achieve. Relationships within the private sector of the economy lead to instability rather than stability.

This conclusion is of the utmost importance. It means that a policy of laissez-faire would have to be paid for in unemployment, business failures, insecurity, and lost production. The personal costs to individuals and the economic loss to society would be high. The problem lies in relationships between large, impersonal economic variables over which individuals have little control. No matter how hard an individual works or how good a business manager he may be, the instability of a private enterprise economy could wipe out the savings of a lifetime or a business enterprise in a few short months. In a success-oriented society, the most poignant fact of all is that luck rather than effort can determine one's economic destiny.

Modern nations have turned to governments to promote greater economic stability, as the only significant alternative to the costs imposed by a laissez-faire policy. In the absence of mechanisms in the private sector that might keep an economy stable at full-employment levels of activity, governments have stepped in to do the job.

Achievement of a stable, full-employment economy is not easy. The economy itself is not static, for its capacity to produce increases continually. The policies that bring full employment this year may be inadequate next year. Furthermore, the goal of full employment may not be fully consistent with the goal of stability in prices. Difficult compromises may have to be made between unemployment levels and price changes.[1]

Government and the National Income

14

---

[1] The trade-off between unemployment and price levels is one of the chief topics discussed in Chapter 19, which deals with inflation.

One way in which government can intervene in economic affairs to promote full employment and economic stability is through its powers to tax and spend, which compose what is commonly called *fiscal policy*. The government budget can be manipulated so as to increase or decrease aggregate demand and thereby influence the level of employment and output as well as the incomes received by producers. The basic concepts underlying fiscal policy have

---

FISCAL POLICY

The word fiscal *is from the Latin* fiscus, *meaning treasure chest, originally applied to the private purse of the Emperor, and then to the Imperial treasury, from which was derived the meaning of pertaining to revenues through which the government was financed. Fiscal policy, therefore, refers to government taxation and spending, and the budget in which they are embodied.*

Fiscal policy should be clearly distinguished from monetary policy, *which deals with management of the monetary system and is discussed in Chapter 17.*

---

already been outlined in Chapter 4, and need only be restated here in summary form:

1. Taxes reduce aggregate demand by taking purchasing power away from economic units that would otherwise spend a large portion of it.
2. Government expenditures on products and services add to aggregate demand by channeling purchasing power back into the flow of spending.

It follows from these two principles that economic activity can be slowed down by raising taxes and/or reducing government expenditures. These actions reduce the flow of spending. They are appropriate when the economy is becoming "overheated," to use the jargon of the financial community, and price increases are the chief threat to stability. Conversely, economic activity can be increased by tax reductions and/or larger government expenditures, which have the effect of increasing the flow of spending and enlarging aggregate demand. These measures are appropriate when unemployment threatens to increase and the economy needs a boost.

These basic propositions are only the beginning, however. They must be integrated into the general analysis of national income determination, which has been outlined in the two previous chapters. In addition, there are several important qualifications and additions that today's sophisticated knowledge of fiscal policy requires. Finally, the general strategy of fiscal policy needs further elaboration.

GOVERNMENT SPENDING AND THE DETERMINATION OF THE NATIONAL INCOME AND PRODUCT

When government spending is added to our hypothetical economy, which heretofore has been purely private, a new factor is added to the determinants of aggregate demand. Government purchases of goods and services, in addition to consumption and investment spending, now determine the level of national product and income. The basic equation becomes:

$$Y = C + I + G,$$

where G = government purchases of goods and services.

Correspondingly, the uses to which income is put must be expanded. People not only spend and save, they also pay taxes. The equation for the uses of the national income becomes:

$$Y = C + S + T,$$

where T = taxes paid to government.

The identity between savings and investment that prevailed in the private economy is also changed when government enters the picture. Withdrawals from the flow of spending still equal additions to the flow, but now there are two items on each side. The total of savings plus tax payments must equal the total of business investment plus government purchases of goods and services; or

$$S + T = I + G.$$

This does *not* mean that considered separately, savings equal investment and taxes equal government purchases. Those equalities may prevail, but they need not necessarily do so. The essential identity is between withdrawals from and additions to the flow of spending, no matter how the two sides of the equation are constituted.

Finally, the conditions for national income equilibrium are changed. Expectations and plans are still important, but more factors have entered the picture. The national income will move toward that level at which desired savings plus taxes equals desired investment plus government spending. That is,

$$S_D + T = I_D + G.$$

This last point is very important. It tells us that desired savings do not have to equal desired investment in order for a given level of national income to be sustained. Government spending and taxes are just as important as the plans and expectations of the private sector. The national income can be maintained at a level at which desired savings substantially exceed desired investment, as long as government spending is larger than tax revenues by an equal amount.

For example, suppose we have a situation in which desired savings equal $75 billion, but desired investment equals only $60 billion. We would normally expect aggregate demand to fall until the two were brought into equality. But the decline need not necessarily occur: if government expenditures equal $100 billion and tax revenues only $85 billion the gap would be filled and a sustainable level of national income achieved. In terms of the equation that defines the national income equilibrium, we have

$$S_D + T = I_D + G$$
$$75 + 85 = 60 + 100$$
$$160 = 160.$$

Since withdrawals from the flow of spending (the left side of the equation) are equal to increments to the flow of spending (the right side of the equation), *and the desires of both savers and investors are realized,* a sustainable level of national income is achieved.

Remember that this is only a hypothetical example, and that achieving these relationships in the world outside of textbooks is quite complicated; but it does illustrate the basic point: government fiscal policy can be used to achieve and sustain a level of national income consistent with full employment.

GOVERNMENT EXPENDITURES AND THE LEVEL OF AGGREGATE DEMAND

Although aggregate demand is increased by government spending and reduced by tax revenues, the effects are not symmetrical. Common sense might tell us that if government purchases of goods and services are increased by, say, $10 billion, and taxes are raised simultaneously by an equal amount, there will be no net change in the national income and product. In this case, however, common sense is wrong, and knowing the reason helps us to understand the economic effects of fiscal policy more fully.

The fundamental difference is that government expenditures affect aggregate demand directly, while taxes do not. A government purchase of military equipment, for example, enables a business firm to produce and to employ resources in the production process. Output and incomes are directly increased by the amount of the government purchases, and that amount then has the usual multiplied effect on aggregate demand.[2] Taxation, however, exerts a

---

[2] Not all government expenditures add to output and employment. Some merely transfer incomes to consumers from taxpayers. These *transfer payments* (see Chapter 4) include such items as social security payments, veterans' benefits, unemployment insurance benefits, and similar payments, which are not made in payment for products or services. In this chapter we will use the term government expenditures to mean only government purchases of products and services.

direct influence on the schedule of the propensity to consume rather than on aggregate demand as a whole. As a result, the multiplied effects on aggregate demand are of a different magnitude.

Let's look first at the direct effects of government expenditures on aggregate demand. With government in our model of the economy, the national product comprises three components:

$$Y = \text{consumption expenditure} + \text{private investment} + \text{government purchases}$$
$$= C + I + G.$$

This can be shown on the standard diagram of income determination by adding to the schedule of the propensity to consume C, both private investment I and government purchases of goods and services G. This gives us a schedule for aggregate demand, and the level of national product is determined by the intersection of that schedule with the aggregate supply schedule. In Figure 14-1, that intersection is shown at E.

Figure 14-1 shows that the effect of government expenditures on aggregate demand is quite similar to that of private investment. The multiplied effect is felt, and its size is determined by the marginal propensity to consume. To check on your knowledge of these matters, assume a $15 billion increase in

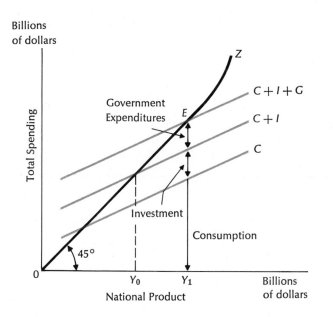

FIGURE 14-1

The Effect of Government Expenditures on the National Product and Income
Adding G to $C + I$ brings the national product from Y_0 to Y_1. Notice how the multiplied effect of G is similar to that of I, both depending on the slope of C (which is, as we know, the marginal propensity to consume).

government expenditures, no change in taxes, and a marginal propensity to consume of ⅔. By how much would the national product be increased?

The answer: by $45 billion. An *MPC* of ⅔ means a multiplier of 3,[3] and 15 billion times 3 equals $45 billion.

The process also works in the other direction. A cut of $15 billion in government expenditures, with no change in taxes and a multiplier of 3, would bring a decline in aggregate demand of $45 billion.

Taxation and the Propensity-to-Consume Schedule

Taxes, on the other hand, do not directly affect aggregate demand and the level of economic activity. Their initial effect is on disposable income. The changes in disposable income then lead to changes in aggregate demand. If the federal government were to maintain the existing level of expenditures and raise its tax revenues, the disposable income available to the public would be reduced and we could expect total spending to fall. Conversely, if taxes were reduced, disposable income would rise and total spending would move upward.[4]

Since tax changes operate through changes in the schedule of the propensity to consume, and not directly on aggregate demand, their effect differs from that of changes in government expenditures. An illustration should make the point clear. Assume that consumption expenditures are $400 billion annually, savings equal $100 billion, and the marginal propensity to consume is ⅔, giving us a multiplier of 3. In this situation, the federal government reduces taxes by $15 billion. How much will the national product rise?

If your answer was $45 billion ($15 billion x 3), you're wrong. The correct answer is $30 billion. Why?

First, a tax reduction of $15 billion adds that amount to disposable income, but an *MPC* of ⅔ means that only $10 billion will be spent and $5 billion will be saved. Second, applying a multiplier of 3 to an increase in spending of $10 billion gives us a total increase in aggregate demand of $30 billion. This $30 billion increase in aggregate demand, coming from a $15 billion decrease in

---

[3] To review: $k = \dfrac{1}{1 - MPC} = \dfrac{1}{1 - 2/3} = \dfrac{1}{1/3} = 3.$

[4] It makes a difference if the tax changes are expected well in advance and if consumers expect them to be permanent or temporary. Anticipated tax changes can trigger consumer responses well in advance of the actual change in consumer incomes. Expectation of a permanent change will have a larger impact on spending than expectation of a temporary change. In the latter case, consumers tend to maintain an even level of spending while adjusting their savings patterns. In any case, discretionary spending seems to be influenced more than spending on necessities, at least in the short run, according to studies of consumer behavior made under the auspices of the University of Michigan's Survey Research Center. We note these differences in order to emphasize the point that the effect of tax changes can only be estimated approximately, and the seemingly exact changes described in the following paragraphs are only approximated in the real world.

taxes, compares with the $45 billion increase that would result from increased government spending of $15 billion. *The indirect impact of tax changes means that they have a smaller quantitative effect on aggregate demand than government expenditures.* The shift in the propensity-to-consume schedule set in motion by a tax *increase* is shown graphically in Figure 14-2.

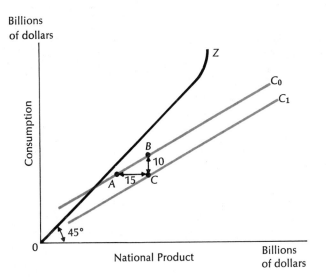

Billions
of dollars

FIGURE 14-2
Effect of Taxes on the Propensity to Consume
A tax increase of $15 billion *AC* moves the propensity-to-consume schedule downward from C_0 to C_1. The decline in consumption spending is $10 billion *BC*, and is determined by the slope of the consumption schedule.

The Balanced-Budget Multiplier

We can now return to the paradox stated earlier in this chapter: an increase in government spending accompanied by an equal increase in tax revenues is not neutral. It serves to increase aggregate demand by an amount equal to the original increase in government spending. Just the opposite is true of a balanced-budget decrease in government spending (expenditures and tax revenues cut by an equal amount). Aggregate demand will fall by an amount equal to the cut in government spending.

This relationship is known among economists as the *balanced-budget multiplier,* and is equal to one. As an example, we can use the assumptions and calculations made in the two preceding sections of this chapter. Assuming an *MPC* of ⅔ ($k = 3$), we showed that an increase in government spending of $15 billion would raise the national product by $45 billion. A simultaneous increase in tax revenues of $15 billion would bring a decline of only $30 billion in the national product. The net increase of $15 billion is just equal to the original increase in government expenditures.[5] The same results can be shown graphically, as in Figure 14-3.

FIGURE 14-3
The Balanced Budget Multiplier at Work

The balanced budget multiplier works through two simultaneous but distinct steps. Taxes decrease consumption by an amount less than the tax. Spending increases aggregate demand by an amount equal to the spending. When changes in taxes and spending are equal the result is an increase in national product.

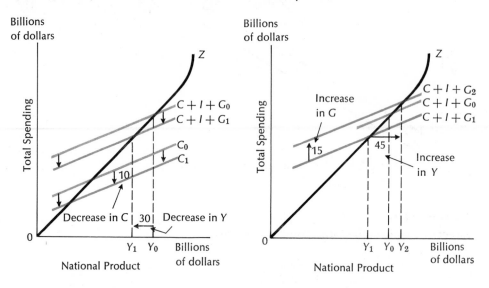

I. The Impact of Increased Taxes

An increase in taxes of $15 billion brings C down by $10 billion (when $MPC=2/3$). Y_0 is reduced to Y_1, a decline of $30 billion ($k=3$).

II. The Impact of Increased Spending

When the government spends the $15 billion it raised from increased taxes, G increases by $15 billion, setting in motion a $45 billion increase from Y_1 to Y_2.

Perhaps the easiest way to understand the balanced-budget multiplier is to think of it in terms of the flow of spending. Taxes take money from the private sector and expenditures put it back in equal amounts. The net result is no change in the money flows that originate in the private sector. But in the meantime government has used the funds to purchase products and services, causing output, employment, and incomes to increase by an amount

---

[5] As these things work out in the real world the results would only approximate those given here. A correct statement would be: In practice, the balanced budget multiplier is approximately one.

equal to the government purchases. As a result, the total flow of spending is just that much larger. The flow of spending originating in the combined private and public sectors is increased.

ECONOMIC GROWTH AND FISCAL DRAG

Up to this point we have been concerned primarily with the effects on aggregate demand of government expenditures and tax receipts. We have not examined some of the reverse effects of changes in aggregate demand on tax receipts and the adjustments in fiscal policy that they might require. These dynamic aspects of fiscal policy are especially important in a growing economy, where the level of GNP changes from year to year. Government must adjust itself to these changes and the impact they have on its fiscal position.

A change in GNP, either upward or downward, changes the amount of incomes received by consumers in the form of salaries, wages, and other payments. Since much of the revenues of the federal government are obtained from taxes on incomes, a change in the level of incomes will be reflected in a change in tax revenues. A change in government revenues, in turn, affects the budget position of the federal government: higher tax receipts can produce a budget surplus, or move a deficit budget into balance, or increase an already existing budget surplus. And we already know that shifts of these sorts in the federal budget affect the level of GNP and the pace of economic growth. Any government that uses its financial operations to seek full employment and satisfactory rates of economic growth must take these feedback effects into consideration when it establishes its budget and determines its economic policies.

These dynamic relationships became matters of general public interest in the United States in the mid-1960s. The situation was this: recovery toward full-employment levels of GNP from the recessions of 1960–61 and the relatively stagnant economy of the 1950s was proceeding well. But as GNP rose, the tax receipts of the federal government rose even more rapidly. This was caused by the fact that the federal income tax is progressive; and as people moved into higher income brackets their income tax rates rose and they paid a higher proportion of their income to the federal government. As a result, federal budget deficits were smaller and the spur given to continued economic expansion was diminished. Estimates made by government economists showed that the federal budget would come into balance well before full-employment levels of GNP were achieved, if expenditures did not increase and the growth of revenues continued. Under those conditions there would be a substantial budget surplus if the economy were able to reach full employment.

There is nothing wrong with a budget surplus, taken by itself. But the policy dilemma was that the surplus would start appearing well before full-employment levels of GNP were reached. Its multiplied effect on aggregate demand would act as a brake on further increases and make it even more difficult for the economy to reach full employment. Instead of stimulating the economy, the federal budget would act as a drag, slowing down the desired expansion. The difficulty is illustrated in Figure 14-4.

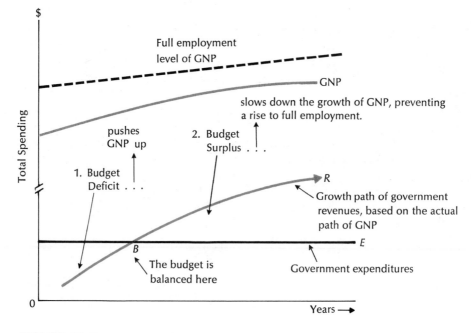

FIGURE 14-4
The Problem of Fiscal Drag

With a given level of government expenditures, the growth of GNP causes government revenue to rise, assisted by initial budget deficits. As the budget moves toward balance (at *B*) the push toward full employment from the public sector diminishes in strength. When budget surpluses appear the growth of GNP is slowed down, causing a halt in the growth of GNP before full employment is reached.

In order to avoid this fiscal drag, as it was called, three alternative policies were available. First, government expenditures could be raised from year to year in order to match the increases in revenue and retain the budget deficit that was providing much of the stimulus for expansion. Second, tax rates could be reduced in order to slow down the increase in revenues. Finally, tax reductions and expenditure increases could be used together to achieve the same results. Indeed, if the proper tax rate structure and expenditure level were selected, it would be possible for the budget deficits to continue, but diminish each year, until the budget was balanced at full-employment levels of GNP. Some economists thought that this would be the ideal situation; diminishing deficits would bring the economy to full employment, followed by growing surpluses if GNP moved beyond that level into an inflationary situation. Figure 14-5 illustrates these relationships.

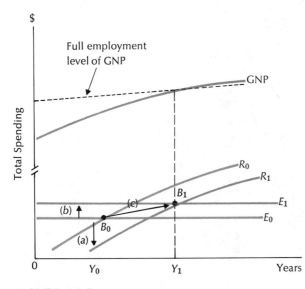

FIGURE 14-5
Solving the Problem of Fiscal Drag

One way to solve the problem of fiscal drag: In year Y_0 reduce taxes (a) from R_0 to R_1 and raise expenditures (b) from E_0 to E_1. This action increases the deficit in the budget, but it stimulates a stronger growth of GNP by (c) moving the balanced budget position from B_0 to B_1. By year Y_1 the economy has been moved to full employment with a balanced budget.

A qualification: If you want to reach full employment before year Y_1, larger tax reductions and spending increases will be necessary, but they will have to be partially rescinded as the economy approaches full employment in order to eliminate inflationary pressures originating in fiscal policy.

The policy actually selected in 1964–65 was a combination of a substantial tax reduction together with a small increase in expenditures. The result was continuation of the drive to higher levels of GNP, which brought with it an increase in tax receipts even though the tax rates were reduced. The budget deficit turned to a surplus. Many people, including a number of prominent congressmen and senators, didn't believe it would actually happen. After all, they asked, how could reduced tax rates and increased spending cause a surplus to appear? It all seemed quite paradoxical to those who were unfamiliar with the dynamics of fiscal policy. They did not realize that both tax reductions and increased spending would push GNP to higher levels, which would then generate greater tax revenues than those lost by reducing tax rates.

That is exactly what happened. Tax rates were reduced in 1964, primarily on personal incomes, by amounts that would have resulted in a revenue loss of about $13 billion if the GNP had remained at the same levels as before. Instead, GNP jumped by over $51 billion between 1964 and 1965, and caused tax revenue to rise by about $5 billion. Table 14–1 shows what happened.

TABLE 14–1
Reduction of Fiscal Drag, 1964–65
(in Billions of Dollars)

| | | Federal Government Budget | | |
	GNP	Receipts	Expenditures	Deficit (−) or Surplus
1964	632.4	115.5	116.9	−1.4
1965	683.9	120.6	118.3	2.3

AN ACTIVE FISCAL POLICY

We can now summarize some of the basic principles of fiscal policy. Perhaps the most important point is that it is impossible for government fiscal action to be neutral with respect to the level of economic activity. As long as a government performs services or buys products, it affects aggregate demand. The only truly neutral government is a nonexistent one.[6]

Since government fiscal activity cannot be neutral, a fiscal policy must be developed. Even a policy of not directing taxation and spending toward achievement of macroeconomic goals implies a policy judgment that those goals are secondary to others. For example, the tax system might be thought of solely as a source of revenue for essential government programs, and the effects on employment and growth ignored. In this case, the policy judgment is that fiscal policy ought not to be used to achieve macroeconomic policy goals.

Contemporary opinion takes the other track. Fiscal policy is seen as an instrument to aid in the achievement of greater economic stability and more rapid economic growth. It can help develop an environment within which individuals and business firms can function more effectively. Specifically, the economy is freed from the restrictions imposed on it by the tendency of a purely private economy to seek a unique equilibrium level of total output that may be well below full employment and thus undesirable. Fiscal policy enables society to choose, within limits, the level of aggregate demand it wants.

This is the second great implication of policy. Properly used, government expenditures and tax receipts provide controlled levers for the management of aggregate demand. In practice, the use of fiscal policy is complex. The simple propositions are easy to understand: Taxes reduce aggregate demand and expenditures increase it, both by a multiplied amount, although the re-

---

[6] Fiscal action can also shift the use of resources from private to public purposes: high government budgets mean that more resources will be used for public purposes than when government spending is less. Fiscal policy can also shift the pattern of income distribution if taxes are paid largely by one group and the benefits from expenditures are received by others. Neutrality in these respects is very difficult to achieve, if not impossible. These matters will be discussed at greater length in Part IX of this book.

sults are not symmetrical. Even a balanced budget has a multiplier of approximately one. But in the context of a growing economy, the growth of tax receipts can act as a drag on continued growth. As a result, policy with respect to levels of expenditure and tax rates must be continually reassessed and revised. This year's tax rates may be quite inappropriate to the needs of next year's economy. The same is true of expenditure levels. The final lesson to be learned is that fiscal policy must be an active one, continually revised in the light of economic events, the direction in which the economy is moving, the level of employment and prices, and all of the other indicators of the state of the economy's health.

Summary

We know that government action is necessary to maintain full employment and stable growth. The primary tools for that purpose are taxation and government purchases of products and services. When they are added to the analytical model, the level of aggregate demand becomes

$$Y = C + I + G.$$

The conditions for equilibrium become

$$S_D + T = I_D + G.$$

Taxation and government spending do not have a symmetrical effect on the level of aggregate demand. Taxes change the propensity-to-consume schedule, which means that a portion of any tax reduction will go into savings and not affect aggregate demand. Conversely, a tax increase will reduce both spending and savings. Government expenditures affect aggregate demand directly, however. The result is a balanced budget multiplier equal to 1. That is, a change in government spending accompanied by an equal change in tax receipts to keep the budget balanced will change aggregate demand by the amount of the change in government expenditures.

In a growing economy tax revenues rise more rapidly than GNP, thereby acting as a drag on continued growth. This fiscal drag can cause economic activity to level off below full employment. As a result, the federal budget must be continually revised from year to year in order effectively to promote full employment and stable growth.

Key Concepts

Fiscal policy.   Taxation and spending on the part of government. Developed in the budget, whose size and balance or imbalance indicates how the government is trying to move the level of aggregate demand.

Balanced-budget multiplier.   A change in the size of a balanced budget affects aggregate demand in an approximately equal amount.

Budget deficit.   The chief instrument of fiscal policy for increasing aggregate demand.

Budget surplus.   The chief instrument for decreasing aggregate demand.

Fiscal drag.   The tendency for tax receipts to rise more rapidly than aggregate demand, thereby holding back further growth.

Money plays a vital part in the modern economy. Its chief function is to facilitate the exchange of goods and services and the organization of production and distribution. A businessman must be able to buy the inputs he requires for his operations as simply and as readily as possible. In our economy he can enter the market, pay the price, and get what he needs. But to get what he needs he must give up something the seller wants. And the seller will want something that he can also use to make purchases. That something is money: an object that is generally acceptable in making payments, in the ordinary exchanges of commercial life.

Money

15

The role of money in the modern economy can be illustrated by contrast. Imagine a Robinson Crusoe economy made up of only one individual. He has no one else with whom he can exchange things, so he has no need for money. Even a small group of people, living in isolation, could exchange goods and services by barter. But a highly complex economy based on voluntary buying and selling in a system of interrelated markets would find a barter system cumbersome and inconvenient. It may be difficult for an individual who has a commodity to exchange for other things to find someone else who has what he wants and wants what he has. Finding him would take time and effort that could be used more productively doing other things. The use of money avoids this drawback of a barter system. With money in use, the goods could be sold for money to anyone, and purchases made from anyone else. As far as the individual is concerned, the person who wants what he has can be different from the person who has what he wants. Any economy based on market exchange would have to invest money if it did not already have it.

THE SPECIFIC FUNCTIONS OF MONEY

The chief function of money, to facilitate exchange, can be divided into four specific tasks that money performs in a modern market economy. Money functions as (1) a means of payment, (2) a unit of value, (3) a standard of deferred payments, and (4) a store of value.

Money As a Means of Payment

The process of exchange creates an obligation on the part of the buyer to make a payment to the seller. Money paid

A DIGRESSION ON THE EVOLUTION OF MONEY

Many writers on money, and most economics textbooks, make the mistake of assuming that the actual historical development of money followed the functional pattern explained in the preceding paragraph. That is, from an economy without exchange, to a barter economy, to a money economy. Nothing could be further from the truth. Historical development was vastly more complicated than that. For example, we know of no cases of human beings living outside a social unit, except for rare accidental cases. Furthermore, we know of no social units without exchange or a system of payments. Yet many human societies existed without the use of money as we know it. Some rather complex civilizations have developed very sophisticated systems of exchange, based on reciprocity and redistribution (see Karl Polanyi, The Great Transformation: The Political and Economic Origins of Our Time *[Boston: Beacon Press, 1957], Chapter 4) which do not require the use of money. Societies using these principles as the framework for their economic systems can develop very high degrees of specialization, cover wide areas, and encompass many people. The period of the Old Empire in ancient Egypt and the Aztec culture of Mexico are two well-known examples.*

The use of money as part of the economic system is closely associated with market exchange. Money is needed to facilitate buying and selling. Its evolution is closely tied to the development of markets and market exchange (a subject beyond the scope of this book) and does not depend on the degree of complexity of the economic system.

There is a lesson here: do not confuse an analytical device used to clarify a concept, like the no-exchange–barter–money schema, with events in the real world. The two may or may not coincide.

to the seller discharges that obligation. The buyer could, of course, pay in something else, as when one professional baseball team trades a pitcher for an outfielder and a shortstop. But in most transactions a payment in the form of something generally acceptable in making payments is preferred.

The general acceptability of money is vital, for it maximizes the freedom of choice of the person who receives payment. For example, the baseball team may strengthen its playing ability by a trade, but it must have cash to operate its stadium or pay its traveling expenses. Selling the pitcher's contract to another team instead of trading him would enable the team to do that. Money enables people to buy what they want, when they want it, in the quantities desired.

In the modern economy people and business firms must continually buy things and make payments. Money is always being paid out: "Like water, away it flows." Yet income is irregular. Some people get paid weekly, others twice a month, others once a month. Business income depends on sales. The income stream for any single economic unit usually does not exactly coincide with the outgo stream. As a result, most people and business firms maintain some holdings of cash to meet their day-to-day needs and carry on the normal transactions of the economy. Economists call this the *transactions demand* for money.

Money As a Unit of Value

The monetary unit acts as a measuring rod that measures the value of any kind of commodity or service. An automobile is worth, say, $3,000, or a certain house $25,000. These values are expressed in dollars, which is the monetary unit, as the most convenient way of stating the value. This function of money results from its general acceptability as a means of payment. Since transactions are completed by making money payments, the automobile or house is valued at the number of dollars for which it can be exchanged. Common stocks, for example, are normally valued at the price paid for them in the last transaction.

The usefulness of money as a unit of value cannot be overestimated. Accountants know only too well that the condition of a business firm depends on the value attributed to widely different assets, such as cash, accounts receivable, real estate, machinery and "good will." Assets can't be added up and a net worth determined for the firm until all are expressed in a common unit. The monetary unit is used for that purpose.

In order for money to perform its function as a unit of measurement, its value (or purchasing power) should remain relatively stable. A yardstick that grows or shrinks is of limited usefulness. Yet the value of money depends on what it will buy, that is, on the average level of prices, and does rise and fall as price levels change. One reason for concern about inflation is the difficulty it creates when businessmen must make decisions in the face of a changing unit of value. Although fluctuations in the value of money are inevitable, money has the advantage of relative stability of value. The value of any single commodity, such as wheat or corn, fluctuates more widely than prices in general. *Relative to other prices* (in markets where prices are not controlled) the purchasing power of money shows a high degree of stability under normal conditions. Nevertheless, the existence of a unit of value that itself fluctuates in value creates problems for the economy.

Money As a Standard of Deferred Payments

Any measure of value and means of payment will become the unit in which future payments are expressed. The modern economy has a huge amount of contracts for payments at some time in the future, or debts; in the United States in 1967, for example, debts amounted to some $1,430 billion. In addition, there are such things as long-term salary contracts, leases on property, and contracts for sale of mineral products for long periods of time.

Deferred payments require stability in the value of the monetary unit. Rising prices hurt people who receive future income and benefit those who make future payments. If you borrow today and repay the money after ten years, and prices have gone up in the meantime, you will be repaying money that has less purchasing power than the money you borrowed. The lender, on the other hand, will have lost on the transaction. This is the chief reason why so many bankers (who lend money for a living) insist on maintaining "sound" money that does not decline in value over the years. Just the opposite situation prevails if prices fall over a period of years and the value of the monetary unit rises. Borrowers lose and lenders gain.

These effects of a changing value of money assume greater importance as the economy grows. More people become borrowers and lenders, or acquire ownership interests in financial institutions. Deferred payments assume greater importance in the everyday lives of more and more people. As this trend develops, the issues of equity and economic self-interest associated with changes in the purchasing power of money become more important, stimulate political interest, and lead to a growing concern on the part of government with prices, price levels, and management of the monetary system.

Money As a Store of Value

Since money can be used to make purchases at any time, it is the most convenient form in which to hold assets. Its instant convertibility into other things makes it a highly desirable way to hold wealth. Money, however, is sterile. It does not earn an income. Coins and paper money in your pocket are valuable enough. They give you power to buy things as you need them, to meet emergencies, and even to take advantage of good buys if they should come along. But they do not earn anything for you as long as you hold them. The same is true of a checking account: banks pay no interest on them.

Money, however, can be transformed into other assets simply by buying them. And those assets can pay an income to the holder. For example, you can deposit cash in a savings account. The bank will make interest payments to you to encourage you to leave your money there while the bank lends it to a borrower at a somewhat higher interest rate. Or, alternatively, you can buy government securities, which will earn a little more income and involve slightly more risk (their price may fall while you hold them). In each case you have given up a highly liquid asset (cash) in order to obtain a somewhat less liquid asset that earns some income. The income you earn is a payment for giving up liquidity and for assuming some risk.

In this sense, money is just like any other asset. It combines liquidity, risk, and earning power. In the case of money, the liquidity is almost perfect while the risk and earning power is nil. Other assets will have less liquidity but more earning power and more risk.

LIQUIDITY

Liquidity is a difficult concept to define. It refers to that quality of an asset that enables it to be used in exchange. Money, for example, can always be used to make a purchase or pay a debt. Other things can be used to make payments only after they have been converted into money. The time and effort required to make that conversion determines the liquidity of an asset. The greater the time and effort, the less the liquidity. For example, a checking account is a more liquid asset than a savings account. You can write a check for a payment at any time of day or night. But money from a savings account can be obtained only during banking hours and only by making a visit to the bank office (except when withdrawals are made by mail, which may take two or more days).

The flexibility achieved through liquidity is maintained at the cost of earning power and (sometimes) safety. The more highly liquid checking account earns no income, but the less liquid savings account does. Cash, which is more liquid than a checking account, earns nothing, and is less safe—it is a prime target for a thief. Crooks like liquidity, too, in their victims.

Owners of assets always have the option of holding their wealth in a variety of forms. Most investors will hold some money at all times, and will distribute their other wealth among a wide variety of other assets with differing combinations of liquidity, safety, and earning power: savings accounts, government bonds, corporate or municipal bonds, common stocks, real estate, precious metals, or jewelry, and many other forms. The various porportions of each in an investor's "portfolio" will depend on his expectations about the future. If he expects prices of assets to rise, he will use some of his cash to buy those he expects to rise in price the most. Expectations of increased value from holding other assets will reduce his desire to hold cash. On the other hand, if he expects prices of assets to fall he will sell some of his assets and shift to greater liquidity all down the line. But he probably won't liquidate entirely and hold all his wealth in cash, since his expectations might be wrong.

Following their own self-interest in this fashion, investors, speculators, and managers of assets influence not only the money markets but the markets for financial assets of all kinds. As their expectations change, their desire for liquidity versus income will shift, and there will be repercussions on the level of output and income as well as on the money and securities markets. Money is an asset, and, like any asset, the demand for it can change as the expectations of consumers, businessmen, and speculators change. This *demand for money as an asset* [1] will shift with changing business conditions and the expectations of businessmen, and in doing so will have an impact on the level of employment and output.

"NEAR MONEY"

Some assets can be so readily converted into money with so little risk of loss that many people look upon them as almost the same thing as money. For example, a college student at the University of Michigan typically uses a savings rather than a checking account for temporarily holding his funds. Even though he is allowed only three withdrawals per month without charge, he manages to avoid the service charges applied to small checking accounts. He deposits his cash monthly and carries with him the amounts he needs in between his thrice-monthly withdrawals. He tends to hold larger amounts of cash this way, but in other respects there is no appreciable influence on his spending behavior.

People or business firms with larger amounts of cash at their disposal will use short-term government securities or large-denomination certificates of deposit in a similar way. For example, a corporation may have cash totaling several hundred thousand dollars that is not needed right away. The money can be invested in 30-day or 90-day Treasury "bills" (short-term promissory notes of the federal government) to earn a little income until the money is needed and the bills are sold.

These types of assets are sometimes called "near money." They are almost as liquid as money itself and, used in this way, earn very little. For some purposes it can be useful to treat them as money, particularly if "total liquid assets" are the subjects of analysis. But in this book they will be treated as nonmonetary assets, albeit the ones next to money itself on the liquidity-of-assets continuum.

---

[1] The demand for money as an asset is sometimes divided into two parts, a *precautionary demand* and a *speculative demand*. For our purposes these distinctions are not necessary.

ARE CREDIT CARDS "NEAR MONEY"?

New financial instruments and arrangements are continually developing, as consumers and businessmen seek better ways to facilitate exchange. Credit cards are an example. They enable a buyer to obtain products and services now, and to pay later. In essence, the buyer obtains a loan from the seller when he makes a credit card purchase, and the credit card serves the function of establishing the buyer's credit.

The credit card facilitates exchange. For some types of transactions it is more readily negotiable than a personal check and equally good as cash. The transaction is completed when the customer is billed for his credit card purchases and pays by check. Like a charge account, a credit card is not money or near money, but a way in which the existing stock of money is used more efficiently.

A DEFINITION OF MONEY

Money is an asset that is generally acceptable in making payments, in the uses to which it is ordinarily put. This definition is both broad and narrow at the same time. It includes coin and paper money because they are customarily used for a wide variety of small retail transactions. But even those forms of money are not acceptable for some payments. Try paying a New York taxicab driver with a $20 bill, for example. This definition also includes checking accounts in banks, because checks are used in making payments in a wide variety of purchases. But not in all. You can't buy a newspaper with a check, where a coin will do; and there are many types of retail transactions in which checks are not accepted.

The inclusion of checking accounts in the money supply is important. By far the largest volume of transactions is carried out by using checks to make payment amounting to upwards of 95 percent of all transactions in the United States. Furthermore, most checking accounts are created out of the economic activity of business firms, and the amount of checking accounts in existence at any time is closely related to the level of economic activity. This form of money is not created by government but by the private sector of the economy. As we shall see in the following chapter, checking accounts are created by banks in their efforts to make a profit for their stockholders. Governments impose constraints on this private creation of a portion of the money supply, but checking accounts remain a private obligation and not a public one.

A savings account is not included in the money supply partly because it is not transferable and partly because technically it is not payable on demand.

However, a savings account is highly liquid in that it can readily be turned into either cash or a check through a simple withdrawal process.

THE MONEY SUPPLY OF THE UNITED STATES

At the present time, the money supply of the United States is about $220 billion. This is in an economy with a GNP of about $800 billion. By far the most important part of the money supply is in checking accounts [2] in commercial banks ($170 billion, or 77 percent). Currency in circulation, mostly Federal Reserve notes, makes up the rest ($50 billion). Table 15–1 shows the figures for December 1970, along with time deposits, which some economists would include in the money supply.

TABLE 15–1
Money Supply of the United States
(In Billions of Dollars, as of December, 1970)

Demand deposits (checking accounts)	171.1
Currency in circulation	50.0
Total money supply	221.1
Time and savings deposits	228.7
Total supply of money and time deposits	449.8

THE VALUE OF MONEY

One of the most widespread of economic fallacies is the belief that money derives its value from some kind of "backing" or "security" that guarantees its value. Gold is the asset usually nominated as the source of the value of money by the makers of this myth. The belief dies hard, but like the unicorn, it is pure mythology.

It is true that coins are made from metal, which has a market value as pure metal. But their market value is usually considerably less than the face value of the coin. If it were not, the coin would be melted down for the value of the metal; which is why silver dollars don't circulate any more.

It is also true that paper money is a government obligation, a government promise to pay. But the promise is empty. For example, a $20 bill used to have, printed on its face, the following inscription:

The United States of America
will pay to the bearer on demand
Twenty Dollars

If you had wanted to collect your $20 from Uncle Sam you could have taken the bill to the U.S. Treasury and asked for payment. You probably would

---

[2] Checking accounts are called "demand deposits" by economists, partly because they are payable on demand and partly to confuse the uninitiated.

have gotten two $10 bills, both bearing the same inscription. If you had demanded payment for *them*, you probably would have gotten back another twenty. So there you are: your $20 bill was a promise to pay, and not much else. Furthermore, your $20 bill was a Federal Reserve note. It wasn't even issued by the federal government, but by the Federal Reserve System. The System's Board of Governors is appointed by the President, but the Federal Reserve Banks are owned by private banks who are members of the System, not by the federal government. In short, the federal government promised to pay, but it had no direct control over how many promises were issued. Nowadays even the promise printed on the bill is gone. The paper money that now circulates says only:

The United States of America
Twenty Dollars

But surely, you might respond, our paper money is "backed" or "secured" by something, like gold. Indeed it is, but not by gold. The Federal Reserve Banks must hold a "reserve" of either government securities or promissory notes from private business firms equal to the value of Federal Reserve notes in circulation. But hold on a moment—a government bond is just a promise to pay a certain amount of money at some future time. And the money in which it is paid is nothing but our friend the Federal Reserve note. We have come full circle. Your $20 bill is a government promise to pay, which is secured by another promise to pay, which in turn is payable in the first promise to pay.

As for gold, its use is restricted to the settlement of international balances. It is buried underground in Fort Knox, Kentucky, or in the vaults of the Federal Reserve Bank of New York (after having been dug up, refined, and transported at great expense, primarily from South Africa or the USSR). Individuals are not allowed to own gold, except for industrial purposes or as jewelry or decorative objects. Paper money is not redeemable in gold.

If money does not derive its value from any intrinsic qualities or from its backing or security, where does its value come from? One clue can be obtained from the functions of money described earlier in this chapter. Money is generally acceptable in making payments. It derives this acceptability in part because the government will take it in payment of taxes. More fundamentally, it is limited in quantity. Money doesn't grow on trees. It cannot be obtained for the asking. It cannot be plucked out of the air. In order to obtain money, something else must be exchanged for it. People work for it, thereby exchanging services for money. Other people sell things in order to get money. As a result, money is worth what it will bring in exchange, just like any other asset. The value of money is determined by the value of the commodities it will buy. If prices rise the value of the dollar falls, because it will buy less. The *purchasing power* of the monetary unit determines its value.

THE QUANTITY THEORY OF MONEY

In a simple economy like that of preindustrial Europe, in which the creation of money was independent of the level of production, a simple relationship between the quantity of money and the level of prices could be observed. If a government increased the quantity of coins or paper money faster than production grew, prices tended to rise. The reason was simple. The amount of goods available for sale was being bid for by an increased purchasing power, and the market adjustment process tended to produce higher prices. Conversely, if the quantity of money remained the same while output fell, perhaps because of war or crop failure, a similar imbalance occurred and prices rose.

These observed relationships led to the famous *quantity theory of money*. It held that changes in the quantity of money caused changes in the level of prices, and that in the long run the value of money depends upon the quantity in circulation. This proposition had considerable validity a century or more ago, but the complexity of a modern economic system made such simplifications quite outmoded. Efforts were made to modernize the theory by arguing that the price level depended on the relationship between total spending and the total value of all monetary transactions, and in this form the theory still survives, known as the *equation of exchange*.

The equation of exchange is a statement of the truism that the total amount spent in an economy equals the value of all goods purchased. It is usually written in the following form:

$$MV = PT,$$

where M = the quantity of money,
V = the velocity of circulation of money,
P = the general level of prices,
T = the number of monetary transactions.

Solving for P yields

$$P = \frac{MV}{T},$$

or in words, the general level of prices is determined by the quantity of money, the velocity of its circulation and the level of economic activity. If the latter two factors remain constant or if the changes in one offset changes in the other, then changes in the quantity of money will cause changes in the level of prices.

Many variations on this theme could be developed. For example, it has been argued that the velocity of circulation of money tends to change very slowly in the long run, although it may fluctuate considerably over short periods of time. If that is true, and a growing economy causes a steadily increasing volume of transactions, it follows that price stability over the long run could be achieved if the quantity of money grew at about the same rate as economic activity as a whole. A slower growth of the money supply would bring lower price levels, while a more rapid growth would cause higher prices. This argument has been put forward by a number of economists who have opposed the use of easy money as a means of stimulating economic activity, on the ground that in the long run that policy is inflationary.

Other economists have argued exactly the opposite. They hold that if M is increased, with no change in V, then PT (the volume of transactions) must rise. If there are substantial unused resources the increased spending will result in expanded economic activity (an increase in T), with little or no change in prices. Only when there is little slack in the economy will prices P start to rise, but that is a signal to the policy makers to stop increasing the quantity of money, taking the pressure off and preventing any significant increase in prices. In this version, easy money policies would be used to promote prosperity.

For good or ill then, the quantity theory of money has been used to support the arguments of those who would use short-run easy money policies to keep the economy at high levels of activity, and by those who would argue against easy money policies in order to achieve stable prices in the long run.

The difficulty with the quantity theory of money is that it assumes a causative role for money that it does not have. As we shall shortly see, money is created in the process of producing and distributing goods and services. The quantity of money is closely associated with the level of economic activity, which in turn influences the level of prices. The chain of cause and effect is not the simple one of

$$\text{Money} \longrightarrow \text{Price level,}$$

but rather

$$\text{Money} \longrightarrow \text{Economic activity} \longrightarrow \text{Price level.}$$

The quantity of money influences the level of economic activity, and in turn is influenced by it, while the general level of prices is determined primarily by the level of economic activity in relation to the amount of unused productive resources. Prices will normally rise if total spending continues to increase after the economy has reached a high level of use of its manpower and productive capacity. Prices need not rise if there is substantial unemployment and unused capacity. If the slack is great enough and lasts long enough, price levels may even fall.

MONEY AND THE LEVEL OF ECONOMIC ACTIVITY

The quantity of money can influence the level of economic activity in two ways. First, the creation of credit by the banking system can make purchasing power available to business firms and consumers. Demand deposits, a part of the money supply, are created through loans made by banks. Money obtained in this way is spent on products and services and increases the flow of spending. In doing so, it stimulates economic activity.

Secondly, the rate of interest is determined, in part, by the quantity of money available. In turn, the rate of interest will influence the amount of investment made by business firms. Other things remaining the same, a higher rate of interest will discourage investment and a lower rate encourage it. Investment expenditures, in turn, will influence the level of aggregate demand. Larger investment spending will increase the GNP, and smaller investment spending will bring it down, other things remaining the same.

These relationships between money and economic activity are crucial ones. Money *is* important. In particular, the lending power of banks and the way that power is controlled are of major significance. The two chapters that follow deal with those aspects of the monetary system.

Summary

Money is an essential part of a market economy organized around exchange. It functions as a means of payment, a unit of value, as a standard for future payments, and as a store of value. These aspects of money are related to its use in an economic system based on exchange in markets.

Money also is an asset that has liquidity, just like other assets that also have varying degrees of liquidity. It is these aspects of money that relate it to the level of economic activity.

The money supply of the United States is dominated by demand deposits (checking accounts), which are supplemented by paper money and coins. Only the coins (and a small part of the paper money) are issued by the federal government. Most of our paper money is issued by the Federal Reserve System and checking accounts are created by privately owned banks.

The value of money is determined by its purchasing power and not by any intrinsic value or backing (see the Appendix to Chapter 15 for the monetary functions of gold). Economists used to think that the quantity of money determined price levels (some still do), but most agree now that the relationship is indirect. The quantity of money affects the level of economic activity by way of credit creation and its influence on the rate of interest, and price levels are influenced by the level of economic activity.

Key Concepts

Functions of money. Money facilitates the process of exchange as a means of payment, unit of value, standard of deferred payments, and store of value.

Liquidity. The quality of an asset that enables it to be used in exchange. Money is the most highly liquid asset of all in most normal uses.

Near money. Other highly liquid assets that can be readily exchanged for money. Savings accounts or government securities are an example of near money.

Demand deposits. Checking accounts. The most important form of money in a modern economy, they are created by banks when they lend to business firms or individuals.

Value of money. Money is worth what it will buy, which means that its value diminishes when price levels go up, and rises when price levels fall.

Quantity theory of money. The older theory that price levels were directly related to the quantity of money. Sometimes stated in the form of the equation of exchange $MV = PT$, which relates the quantity of money M and its velocity of circulation V to the level of economic activity PT.

Supply of money. Defined here as demand deposits plus currency and coin in circulation. Many economists would also include savings accounts, with good reason, but that is not done here.

Appendix 15

THE MONETARY FUNCTIONS OF GOLD

Gold and silver have been monetary metals since ancient times. Coins minted from those metals have circulated widely. Gold and silver have been the basis for defining the monetary units of the major commercial nations of the world, and until World War I most paper currencies were normally redeemable in gold or silver coins.

In the twentieth century, however, the precious metals have been gradually giving up their central positions in the monetary systems of the world. In particular the amount of money and credit within an individual nation is no longer tied to reserves of monetary gold. Gold is still used as an important part of the international monetary system, but even here its importance has been greatly reduced by changes that have occurred over the last fifty years.

THE "GOLD STANDARD"

Contrary to general belief, the so-called "gold standard" is not much older than the nineteenth century. Its heyday was the period between the Napoleonic wars and World War I, an era of economic growth, industrialization, relatively stable international political conditions, and British hegemony in the world economy. The era of the gold standard may be said to have begun with passage of the Coinage Act of 1816 by the English Parliament. Its demise came with World War I and the suspension of gold payments by the Bank of England in 1914, although that measure was thought to be only a temporary wartime expedient. Efforts were made after the war to put Humpty-Dumpty back together, but he was never the same again.

The gold standard of 1816–1914 embodied several key provisions in a nation's monetary system:

1. The monetary unit was defined in gold. For example, the Gold Standard Act of 1900 in the United States defined the gold dollar as equal to 25.8 grains of gold nine-tenths fine (fineness is a measure of purity). This tied the "value" of the monetary unit to the price of gold.

2. The government undertook to coin at the official standard, subtracting something (seignorage) to cover the costs of the mint. That is, anyone could take gold bars to the Treasury and exchange them for the equivalent amount of gold coins. This provision tied the amount of gold coins in circulation to the amount of gold available.

3. Paper money was redeemable in gold. Any legal tender, whether issued by the government itself or by private banks, could be exchanged for gold coins. In this country that meant currency issued by national banks as well as that of the

federal government. This provision tied the amount of paper money to the nation's gold reserve. A government might issue more paper money than its gold reserve, but not much more: it always had to face the possibility that people would try to redeem paper money and get gold. Any government wishing to maintain monetary stability would be careful to avoid the risk of a "run" on its paper money by limiting the amount issued to a sum close to its gold reserve. In practice most countries issued paper money only up to the limit of the gold reserve.

Many countries made exceptions to these rules. For example, the United States Treasury issued silver certificates redeemable in coined silver dollars, but they were a minor part of the money supply. Other exceptions prevailed in other countries, but the basic concept was the same everywhere: Gold was the ultimate reserve for a nation's monetary system.

The gold standard had two important effects. First, it placed a limit on the amount of money available. This was done in two ways. Gold coin and paper money were directly limited by the requirements of the gold standard. Bank credit was indirectly limited. We shall subsequently see that creation of credit by the banking system is limited by the amount of currency in circulation (in the absence of any legal limits). Since the amount of currency under the gold standard was limited by the gold reserve, a limit was also placed on the amount of credit that banks could extend.

Second, the gold standard created fixed relationships between the moneys of the various nations of the world. Each monetary unit—dollar, pound, franc, mark, yen, and other—was defined in specific amounts of gold. These fixed relationships created monetary equivalents for every currency in terms of every other currency. For example, in 1968 (the world's moneys are still defined in terms of gold) the value in dollars of some of the world's leading currencies, based on their definition in gold, were as shown in Table 15–2.

TABLE 15–2
Value of Important Currencies in Dollars, 1968

Country	Currency	Par Value in Dollars
England	Pound	$2.40
France	Franc	.203
Germany	Mark	.250
Italy	Lira	.002
Japan	Yen	.003

That is, the par value of the Italian lira is 2/10 of a cent, the German mark 25 cents, the English pound $2.40, and so on.

General adoption of the gold standard by the major nations of the world created an international monetary system that was vitally important in promoting trade and movement of capital across national boundaries. We shall discuss this aspect of the gold standard later, as part of the treatment of the international economy. Today, gold still plays a role in the world monetary system, but it is not as important as it was before 1914.

GOLD IN THE U.S. MONETARY SYSTEM

The experience of the United States with the gold standard is both interesting and instructive. Our first effort to establish a sound monetary system used a bimetallic standard based on both gold and silver. The Coinage Act of 1792 defined the dollar in terms of gold (24.75 grains) and silver (371.25 grains). This was a ratio of 15 to 1, that is, $24.75 \times 15 = 371.25$. The ratio was very close to the relationship between the prices of gold and silver in commercial markets and seemed reasonable at the time. But the price of silver soon fell (relative to gold) until the market ratio was close to 15½ to 1. As a result, gold disappeared from circulation and the country was, in fact, on a silver standard.

The reason was that silver could be brought to the mint and exchanged for gold at the ratio of one ounce of gold for 15 ounces of silver. The gold could then be exchanged on world markets for 15½ ounces of silver. A profit of one-half ounce of silver could be made on each set of transactions. As long as this differential was greater than the costs of the transactions plus shipping costs, silver would be imported into the United States, exchanged for gold at the Treasury and the gold exported for sale abroad. The result was that the country's gold reserve disappeared and was replaced by silver. It was an illustration of Gresham's law that the cheaper metal circulates and the more expensive one disappears, or "bad money drives out good." [3]

The disappearance of gold from circulation did not make much difference to the nation's economy and caused no problems for anyone until gold was discovered in North Carolina and Georgia. Then it became politically expedient to "keep the gold at home." The result was passage of the Coinage Acts of 1834 and 1837, which revised the ratio of gold to silver to almost 16 to 1. The dollar was revalued to 23.22 grains of gold, but left at 371.25 grains of silver, for a ratio of 15.988 to 1. Since the market ratio was only about 15.73 to 1 at the time, gold was worth more at the mint than in the open market and the flow of metals was reversed. Gold was imported into the United States and exchanged at the Treasury for silver until all the silver was gone and the country's monetary reserve consisted of gold. Gold coins circulated instead of silver, except for subsidiary coinage in which the silver content was so far below the face value of the coin it was not worth while to melt them down.

The United States was now, in effect, on the gold standard while paying lip service to bimetallism. The Coinage Act of 1853 reduced the use of silver to subsidiary coinage (less than $1 face value). After the Civil War, a sop was thrown to silver mining interests by requiring the Treasury to coin silver dollars as "backing" for silver certificates, which circulated as paper money. Then, after the bitter political campaign of 1896 in which the monetary system was the chief issue, the victors passed the Gold Standard Act of 1900 to put the nation firmly on a gold-based standard of value. Except for the Civil War years and their aftermath (1861–1879), when gold payments were suspended, the United States was on a gold standard from 1834 to 1934.

In those years the nation's monetary system changed radically. Prior to the Civil War a wide variety of paper money appeared and circulated. Most of the nation's

---

[3] Gresham's law was named after Thomas Gresham (1519–1579), one of Queen Elizabeth's advisors on monetary affairs, who neither originated nor stated the idea. He was famous for other aspects of monetary policy. The rule that the least valuable money would circulate instead of the most valuable is found in early writings on the precious metals that date from the fifth century B.C. It was probably known but not written down long before then.

monetary gold came to rest in the vaults of the Treasury rather than circulating as gold coin. The development of fractional reserve banking made possible a large expansion of bank loans based on relatively limited reserves, to parallel the vast economic growth of the nation. This made possible a large expansion of the money supply based on relatively small reserves of gold.

In theory, the gold standard should have brought stability to the monetary system. Reserves of gold would permit issuance of a limited amount of paper money, which in turn would permit creation of a limited amount of bank credit. As long as banks lent for legitimate business purposes such as financing investment or harvesting crops, the loans would be sound and excessive expansion of credit could be avoided. The money supply would adjust itself to the needs of the economy. This was the theory behind the National Banking System, which prevailed from 1864 to 1914. National banks, which did the bulk of the banking business, were required to keep their reserves in cash—gold coins, gold certificates, or silver certificates. This meant that once the gold standard was restored in 1879, bank reserves were ultimately redeemable in gold and the amount of bank credit was limited by the size of the nation's monetary gold supply.

But this system did not bring stability. For example, when the Treasury bought gold—and this was an erratic rather than a steady flow—it issued new gold certificates to pay for the purchase. This expanded the money supply. When the new currency was deposited in banks, the reserves of the banking system were increased, to act as a base for further expansion of bank credit. This expansion took place because of Treasury gold purchases, whether the economy needed a larger money supply or not.

Instability could also occur because of the public's desire to hold currency. When cash was needed at Christmas, Easter, or harvest time, it would be withdrawn from banks, reserves would dwindle, bank loans would be cut, and shortages of credit would appear just when the economy needed expansion. Far from bringing stability, the gold standard promoted wide swings in economic activity through large fluctuations in the credit structure.

Nor was inflation prevented by convertibility of paper money into gold. The United States in 1897–1914 experienced its most severe and prolonged peacetime inflation.[4] Prices rose by almost 50 percent in a little over 15 years. Gold discoveries in Alaska, Colorado, and Australia, plus improved methods of obtaining gold from ores, increased gold production substantially. Most of the new gold moved into monetary reserves. The fractional reserve banking system multiplied the effect of the new gold on the monetary system. "Easy money" pushed the expansion of purchasing power upward faster than output expanded and prices rose persistently, not only in the United States but in other nations as well.

An important change in the system came in 1913, with passage of the Federal Reserve Act, and the present era of managed money began. Under the new system the supply of money was adjusted to promote the stability the old system could not achieve. The amount of money came to be limited by men rather than by the gold reserve. Nevertheless, the fiction of a gold base for the monetary system was retained, largely for psychological reasons. Some people feared that the new system might

---

[4] Most of the inflation after World War II was the result of postponing the inflationary pressures of the war to the immediate postwar years. Only the inflation after 1965 matched the earlier period, and it was a wartime inflation.

lead to an unlimited inflationary expansion of the money supply and demanded provisions that put a lid on the potential expansion of credit. Consequently, the act required the Federal Reserve banks to keep a gold reserve against their liabilities: 40 percent against Federal Reserve notes and 35 percent against deposits. But in order to prevent interference with the real purposes of the act, the Board of Governors was empowered to set aside the gold reserve requirement if the need arose.

The Fed, as the Federal Reserve Board is commonly called, has never allowed its management of the monetary system to be influenced by the gold reserve requirement. The money supply has been managed solely with respect to the need for money and credit, and the reserves of member banks have been increased or decreased by the Fed in response to general business conditions rather than the stock of monetary gold. Whenever monetary expansion has caught up with the gold supply, the gold reserve requirement has been reduced by act of Congress. The first occasion was during World War II, when monetary expansion was required to help finance the nation's military effort. In 1945, Congress reduced the gold reserve requirement for both Federal Reserve notes and deposits to 25 percent. The second occasion was in 1965, during the period of serious imbalance in the U.S. balance of payments, when the gold reserve behind deposits in the Federal Reserve banks was eliminated completely. The requirement of a 25 percent gold reserve against Federal Reserve notes was all that remained, and that was removed in 1968. These actions merely formalized what had already become a fact: the supply of money was completely freed from any relationship to gold.

In the meantime, most of the other requirements of the gold standard had been eliminated in 1934. The Great Depression brought both financial collapse and much greater intervention into economic affairs by the federal government. One of the major reforms was in the monetary system, and the gold standard was one of the first things to be changed. Convertibility of paper money into gold was ended. Gold was available from the Treasury only for settlement of international accounts through central banks. American citizens were allowed to own gold only for manufacturing purposes and in jewelry or decorative objects. Gold, for all practical purposes, was no longer a monetary metal in the United States.

GOLD AND THE INTERNATIONAL ECONOMY

Even after the United States formally abandoned the gold standard with regard to domestic monetary affairs, it continued to define the dollar in terms of gold in order to maintain orderly international monetary relationships. Most other countries did the same, and the gold standard as it had existed prior to 1914 virtually ceased to exist. What remained was the so-called "gold exchange standard," in which the world's currencies were defined in gold, and gold could be used to settle balances between central banks.

The dollar was part of this system at 13 5/7 grains of gold, a figure established in 1934 in a reduction from the level of 23.22 grains that had lasted for almost exactly one hundred years. This was the famous "devaluation" of the dollar, which fixed the price at which the Treasury would buy gold at $35 per ounce. The devaluation had little effect on the domestic economy, but the new U.S. price for gold soon became one of the important cornerstones of the international monetary system. The next major change came in 1971, when the Treasury stopped buying gold and let the dollar "float" on the international money markets. This action was taken in an effort to solve some of the problems created by inflation, and will be discussed later in this book.

Gold still remains important in the international economy, and we shall subsequently discuss it further. Until then we can drop the subject. Only to the extent that gold affects the policies adopted to manage the nation's international economic affairs and to the extent that those policies affect the domestic economy, can gold be said to have any influence at all on the domestic monetary system.

The Banking System and the Creation of Credit

16

Bank lends money to borrower, who pledges car as security

↓

Borrower pays for car

↓

Seller deposits check

↓

Banks perform a crucial function in a modern, private enterprise economy. They lend money to consumers and business firms, a procedure that creates both debt and purchasing power. At the same time, bank loans *create* the checking accounts, or demand deposits, which constitute the most important part of a nation's money supply. The lending power of banks has built-in constraints, however, that limit the ability to create credit. This chapter will discuss the lending functions of banks, the relationship of debt to economic activity, the mechanisms through which the banking system creates checking accounts, and the constraints that limit credit creation.

BANKS AND THE MONEY SUPPLY

Loans from banks are essential to a modern economy. They enable business firms to finance production and distribution, and they enable consumers to finance many kinds of important purchases.

Consider the simple purchase of an automobile by a consumer. Relatively few pay cash. Most people use their old car as part or all of the down payment and borrow the rest. They might borrow directly from a bank, or they might borrow through the dealer's finance company. It makes little difference, however, because the finance company gets its funds from a bank loan anyway. Let's follow one of these loan-financed transactions and see what happens.

The buyer of the automobile goes to his bank to borrow enough money to buy the car. He signs a promissory note that specifies the amount borrowed and the terms of repayment, and that pledges the car as security in case he can't repay in cash. In return, the bank creates a checking account in the name of the borrower equal to the amount borrowed.

In order to complete the transaction, a check equal to the amount borrowed is made out to the automobile dealer and signed by the borrower, who gets delivery of the car in exchange for the check.

The automobile dealer, of course, deposits the check in his bank. His account is credited, and he can now write more checks against it to carry on his business activities. His bank, then, sends the check to the borrower's bank for collection, and the funds are transferred from

276

the borrower's bank to the dealer's bank at a clearing-house. Ultimately, the check gets back to the borrower's bank and the amount of the check is deducted from the borrower's bank account. At this point all of the settlements have been made and the funds have been transferred to the account of the automobile dealer.

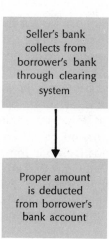

The transaction is not really as intricate as it seems. The complications arise because no actual cash ever changes hands. All of the payments and transfers are made by notations on the books of the banks, triggered by the check as it moves from hand to hand or from bank to bank. Even the transfer of funds between banks is done by charging the accounts and not by an actual payment of cash.

Here is a simple diagram of what happens, as it has just been described:

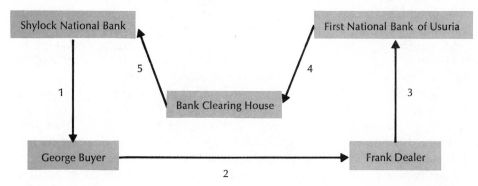

1. Shylock National Bank lends $1,000 to George Buyer, receiving a promissory note secured by Dealer's car.
2. Check for $1,000 is written by Buyer and paid to Frank Dealer in exchange for the car.
3. Dealer deposits the check in the First National Bank of Usuria, which credits his account.
4. First National sends the check to the bank clearing house. Its account at the clearing house is credited, while the account of Shylock National is debited.
5. The clearing house sends the check to Shylock National Bank, which debits the account of George Buyer.

Note carefully just exactly what happened: the borrower's bank has acquired an asset (the promissory note), and created a liability (the demand deposit against which the borrower can write checks which the bank must honor). As for the borrower, he got a new asset (the checking account which he exchanged for a car) and a new liability (the promissory note). The seller merely exchanged one asset (a car) for another (an increase in his bank account). The total of assets and liabilities has been increased, and new purchasing power for the borrower was created that did not exist before. All this was done by a series of paper transactions that created both a loan and a new demand deposit. The ultimate security for the loan and the "backing" for the newly created money is the automobile pledged as security for the loan. More important from the point of view of the economy, however, is the fact that an important transaction was financed and the sale of an automobile occurred. Everyone gained. The buyer got his car, the dealer made a sale and the buyer's bank acquired an income-earning asset. It was all made possible by an addition to the economy's stock of money.

DEBT AND ECONOMIC ACTIVITY

The creation of debt is an essential part of economic activity. Production and distribution could not be carried on unless buyers could borrow to finance their purchases, unless sellers could borrow to buy their inventories, and unless producers could borrow to buy their inputs. It isn't fashionable to praise debt, particularly in a society that has always given high approval to the individual who is debt-free, but the American economy could not function, much less grow, without this form of private "deficit spending."

Take the automobile sale we have just examined, for example. The buyer borrowed to obtain the money for his purchase, creating a debt in order to make the transaction possible. But what about the automobile dealer? He had probably borrowed from a finance company in order to buy the car from the manufacturer. The finance company had probably borrowed its operating funds from a bank, in order to lend to the dealer so he could build up this inventory. And the manufacturer? Like any large firm it had probably borrowed substantial sums to buy its materials and pay its work force. All down the line, wherever there was a transaction it was probably accompanied by creation of a debt.

Indeed, any transaction will result in debt. Even when you buy a newspaper at the corner newsstand, a debt is created, although in that case it is extinguished almost immediately by payment in cash. In most cases, however, debt is not immediately paid and the transaction results in a deferred payment (debt) of some kind. The important point to remember is that economic activity gives rise to deferred payments. The presence of these debts is an indication of economic activity. The less economic activity, the fewer will be the number of transactions and the lower will be the level of debt. Just the opposite is also true: the more economic activity the greater the total amount of debt.

If the level of debt is reduced, the flow of spending will decline and employment and production will fall.

If the level of debt is increased, purchasing power will rise and employment and production will grow.

To illustrate the proposition that economic activity and increased debt go together, Table 16–1 shows some figures for the United States in the 1946 to 1966 period.

TABLE 16–1
Economic Activity and Increased Debt, 1946–1966

Item	Percentage Increase
GNP	255
Total private debt	544
Total public debt	244
Federal	20
State and local	643
Mortgage debt	731
Consumer credit	1031

The level of economic activity rose by 2.5 times in those twenty years. Most types of debt rose faster, with the one exception of public debt, as the private sector of the economy financed itself in large part by borrowing.

In sustaining or increasing purchasing power, it makes little difference where the borrowed funds come from or who does the borrowing. Public debt will stimulate the growth of purchasing power just as well as private debt. Private borrowers spend the money they borrow, and so do governments. In both cases the money enters the stream of spending and adds to aggregate demand. Government spending financed by borrowing will stimulate economic activity in the same way as private spending financed by borrowing.

The relationship of debt to economic activity puts the availability of loanable funds and the terms on which they can be borrowed in a key position. If funds are hard to get and interest rates are high, borrowing will be discouraged. *Tight money* conditions of this sort tend to dampen economic activity. On the other hand, if loans are readily available and interest rates are low, borrowing will be encouraged and economic activity stimulated. *Easy money* conditions can stimulate production, employment and economic growth.

The lending powers of the banking system are of critical importance in the system of money, debt, and credit. Bank loans create both debt and purchasing power. Let's turn now to the conditions that limit their ability to make loans, starting with the process by which checks are cleared and then moving on to the process by which loans are increased.

CLEARING OF CHECKS

When a check is deposited in the same bank on which it is drawn, the process of keeping the accounts is very simple: the bank merely credits one account and debits the other.

When more than one bank is involved, the process is a little more complicated, since funds must be shifted between banks as well as between accounts. To simplify the process and avoid shipment of cash from one bank to another, the banking system makes use of the *clearinghouse*, where all the banks in a city or larger area have accounts. Any one bank will send checks drawn on other banks to the clearinghouse, instead of directly to the other banks, and will receive payment by having its account at the clearinghouse credited. At the same time, checks drawn against it are sent to the clearinghouse by other banks, and its account there is debited. At the end of a business day the bank will have a net change in its account entered on the books. In this way checks are "cleared" without any cash changing hands.

Here is a highly simplified example of how the process works, using three banks and a single clearinghouse:

Bank A sends in checks totaling $100,000 drawn against Bank B.
Bank A sends in checks totaling $60,000 drawn against Bank C.
Bank B sends in checks totaling $120,000 drawn against Bank A.
Bank B sends in checks totaling $90,000 drawn against Bank C.
Bank C sends in checks totaling $70,000 drawn against Bank A.
Bank C sends in checks totaling $110,000 drawn against Bank B.

The balance of the various banks at the clearinghouse are shown in Table 16–2.

TABLE 16–2
Balances of Banks A, B, and C at the Clearing House

Bank		Credits	Debits	Difference
A		$160,000	$190,000	−$30,000
B		210,000	210,000	0
C		180,000	150,000	+30,000
	Totals	550,000	550,000	0

In this case, Bank A's account would be reduced by $30,000 while C's would be increased by $30,000. No change would occur in B's account.

One or two days like this at the clearinghouse would make little difference to any of the banks involved. But if the situation were repeated day after day, A's clearinghouse account would have to be replenished by either a cash deposit or a loan from the clearinghouse. Long before that, however, Bank A would take action to eliminate its negative clearinghouse balances by reducing its loans to its customers so that they would not write so many checks.

Bank C is in just the opposite situation. Its account at the clearinghouse is increasing. If this situation continues indefinitely, Bank C will have a substantial amount of idle assets on which it could be earning some income. It will have strong incentives to increase the volume of loans it makes to its customers. As it does so, its positive clearinghouse balances will gradually be reduced until its account there no longer is increasing.

Bank B, unlike the other two, has achieved perhaps the ideal situation from the banker's point of view. It has not increased its loans so much that its clearinghouse balance is declining, yet it has lent enough to keep all its assets at work earning an income.

An important principle is at work here. Bank A has expanded its loans more rapidly than the system as a whole, and Bank C more slowly. This has caused a drain on A's assets while C has accumulated unused assets. Both will ultimately act to bring their loan policies into conformity with those of the entire banking system.

It should be clear that a single bank cannot indiscriminately increase its loans and thereby increase the amount of demand deposits in the economy. If it does, it will get into trouble at the clearinghouse and have to reduce its excessively expansionist policy. But if all banks act together the banking system as a whole can increase loans, and the money supply, without much hindrance. For then any one bank's credits at the clearing house will increase as fast as its debits. Negative balances will not develop so long as the bank does not expand its loans faster than the other banks.

Indeed, the only economic limit to credit creation by banks is the fact that the use of currency in hand-to-hand circulation rises as bank deposits and economic activity increase. Experience has shown that these ordinary needs for cash amount to about 2 percent of the total demand deposits in the economy. This sets a limit to the expansion of bank credit even if there were no legal or other restraints on bank lending. The limit is the amount of cash available: the banking system must have cash reserves of perhaps 2 percent of any increase in demand deposits to satisfy the demand of the general public for pocket cash.

Prudence may call for larger reserves, however. A bank may not be able to collect on all of its loans as they come due, but it must honor all the checks drawn against it if it wants to stay in business. Consequently, a reserve must be held against potential bad judgment on the part of the bank's lending officers and against the uncertainties of a changing economy. But these are not large items, and in normal good times a reserve of perhaps 5 to 10 percent is usually enough to take care of them. Even this reserve need not be held in cash. It can be invested in readily salable short-term government bonds, called Treasury "bills," that mature in 90 days or less.

In summary, then, no single bank can indiscriminately lend to its customers without limit. It must keep a sharp eye on its clearinghouse balances to make sure that its loan policies are not creating a continuous drain of cash. It must make sure it has enough cash on hand to meet its customers' needs for hand-to-hand currency. It must be careful to make safe loans that the borrowers can reasonably be expected to repay, and it must keep some highly liquid reserves on hand to compensate for mistakes.

But although each and every individual bank must follow a policy of caution and safety, the banking system as a whole can expand loans, and the money supply, to a point at which demand deposits are ten to twenty times the amount of reserves held by the banking system. Furthermore, if each bank seeks to maximize its profits, there will be a strong tendency for the system as a whole to expand demand deposits to the maximum level permitted by reserves and the rules of safety. Indeed, if there were no legal requirement that banks hold reserves, and no money was needed for hand-to-hand circulation, and all bank loans were perfectly safe, the banking system could expand loans and demand deposits *without limit.*

THE FUNCTION OF BANK RESERVES

Bank reserves do not make the banking system safe. Their function is to limit the amount of money created.

First, the problem of safety. Our private enterprise, profit-making banking system permits a very large expansion of loans and demand deposits, an expansion that can go far beyond the holdings of cash maintained by the banks. This multiple expansion of credit rests on public confidence in a bank's ability to honor checks drawn against it. In the absence of any arrangements to protect the system, unwise extension of credit by a single bank can result in failure to meet its obligations, and public confidence in the whole system might deteriorate. A "run" on all banks can start, bringing the whole system down. Similarly, economic events entirely outside the banking system, such as a stock market crash, might cause a similar "run." Since the system as a whole has cash reserves equal to only a fraction of total demand deposits, any continued effort on the part of depositors to get cash instead of holding bank deposits can cause the system to fail.

As long as demand deposits exceed the cash assets of the banks, the system is vulnerable. Reserves could prevent a breakdown only if they were equal in amount to the total of demand deposits.[1] Short of that requirement two devices have been used to preserve the system. One is the guarantee of bank deposits, up to $20,000, to assure the depositor that his money is safe. The second is the existence of a "lender of last resort," the Federal Reserve System, which stands ready to lend funds to any bank that has assets that can be used as security. Together, these arrangements keep depositors from panicking and can provide funds if a bank should have a temporary need. The only reasons for bank failures nowadays are bad management, thievery, or both, on the part of bank officers.

---

[1] A number of reputable economists, including the late Irving Fisher, advocated "100 percent reserves." Requiring banks to hold a dollar of reserves for every dollar of demand deposits would remove the power to create money from the banking system and lodge it in the monetary authority of government. Only as new cash was issued would the banks be able to make additional loans. Most businessmen and bankers consider this too high a price to pay, especially since safety can be achieved in other ways.

The problem of limiting the creation of credit is far more important. The flow of spending can be affected quite significantly by extension of credit. Yet a profit-oriented banking system has every reason to expand credit, whether or not expansion may be desirable at the time. Some mechanism to restrain the system is needed, and it is provided by the reserves banks are required to hold.

We turn now to the multiple expansion of bank credit, the mechanism by which it takes place and how it is limited by a required reserve.

MULTIPLE EXPANSION OF BANK CREDIT

In the United States, the reserves a bank must hold are set by the Board of Governors of the Federal Reserve System, within limits fixed by law. The reserves themselves are on deposit in the Federal Reserve banks,[2] which also operate the regional clearing houses for clearing of checks. This means that as checks are cleared through the banking system the reserves of individual banks rise or fall.

At the present time the Fed's reserve requirements average out at about 1 to 6. That is, banks must hold $1 in reserves for every $6 in demand deposits. The required reserve varies with the location of the bank, largely a vestige of bank practices from the pre-Fed days before 1914, but the average for the system as a whole is about 16 percent, or 1 to 6. As a result, the banking system is able to create and maintain demand deposits about six times as large as its reserves.

For example, in November 1967, the reserves of all banks that were members of the Federal Reserve System totaled $24.7 billion. Those reserves supported a total of $158.2 billion in demand deposits. The ratio of reserves to demand deposits was just a little more than 16 percent. The banking system as a whole was just about "loaned up" at the time; that is, almost all of the reserves were required to back up the existing level of demand deposits. "Excess reserves" totaled only $378 million and were more than balanced by $646 million that banks had borrowed from the Fed.

The process by which this six to one expansion takes place is not complicated. But a banker can't just write loans equal to six times his reserves. If he did, he'd quickly have adverse balances at the clearinghouse and would have to cut back. But even though one bank can make loans equal only to the "free" reserves[3] it has, the banking system as a whole will end up with loans and demand deposits equal to six times its reserves. Here is how it works.

---

[2] "Till money" (cash on hand) held by banks is also part of bank reserves, but amounts to only a small part of the total.

[3] "Free" reserves are those not needed as a reserve against the existing amount of demand deposits. That is, they are funds available for lending. "Free reserves" and "excess reserves" are phrases that mean the same thing.

The Starting Situation

We can begin our example with a reserve ratio of 20 percent. That is, all banks are required to keep a reserve of $1 for every $5 of demand deposits. This ratio is slightly different from the actual one, and was chosen solely for ease in calculating the changes. We propose to increase the *amount* of reserves available to the banking system and then show (1) the process by which multiple expansion takes place; and (2) the limit imposed by the reserve ratio.

All the banks in the system are assumed to be loaned up. That is, existing demand deposits are exactly five times the available reserves and there are no free reserves in excess of those required. The banks are eager to lend and are unwilling to hold excess reserves, so that any new funds they receive will be used for new loans to eager customers.

Step 1: The Creation of New Reserves

We now provide our banking system with $100,000 in new reserves. This is easily done. The usual method is for the Federal Reserve banks to buy government bonds. This purchase will automatically increase the reserves of the system. It happens like this:

The treasurer of a Federal Reserve bank writes a check for $100,000 to pay for the bonds. The check goes to a dealer in government securities, who deposits the check in his bank. His bank then sends the check through the clearing system. At the clearinghouse, located at the regional Federal Reserve Bank, the bank's account will be credited. That account at the clearinghouse is the bank's reserve, however, and is now $100,000 larger. The easiest way to understand how bank reserves are influenced by Federal Reserve purchases of government securities is to visualize the path taken by the check used to pay for the bonds, shown in Figure 16-1. The crucial step is the third one, in which

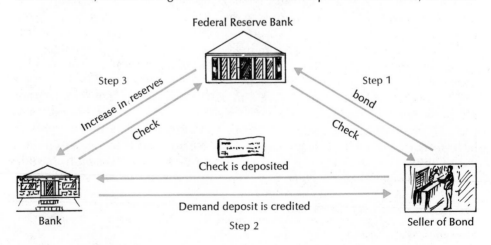

FIGURE 16-1
Purchase of Securities by a Federal Reserve Bank Increases
Member Bank Reserves

SOURCES OF BANK RESERVES

The banking system can obtain new reserves in a variety of ways. The foregoing example used the most important means, Federal Reserve purchases of government securities. The other chief influences on bank reserves are:

Changes in the amount of currency held by the public.

Treasury purchases and sales of gold.

Treasury receipts of tax payments and Treasury expenditures.

Changes in the volume of checks in the clearing system.

Bank borrowings from the Federal Reserve banks.

There are a few others as well, but they are usually quite insignificant: changes in the amount of cash held by the Treasury, changes in foreign-owned deposits in Federal Reserve banks, and purchase or sale of other assets by the Federal Reserve banks.

All of these sources of new reserves, even when added together, are less important than the purchase and sale of government securities by the Fed, which is the most flexible and fastest way of influencing the level of bank reserves. All of the other ways in which reserves are increased or decreased are the result of decisions made in the normal course of events by the public and government agencies. Only purchase or sale of government securities by the Fed is subject to direct control by the monetary authorities.

---

a commercial bank sends the Fed's original check back to the Fed for collection, and is paid by having its reserve account increased by the amount of the check.

What has happened as a result of the transaction? First, the person who formerly owned $100,000 of government bonds now has $100,000 more in his checking account. His total assets have not changed, but they are now held in a demand deposit instead of government securities. The bank has a new obligation, or liability, in the form of $100,000 in demand deposits, but it has additional assets in the form of $100,000 in reserves. Its balance sheet for the transaction will show the following:

Bank I

Assets		Liabilities	
Reserves	$100,000	Demand Deposits	$100,000

The Federal Reserve Bank has also had an increase in both its assets and its liabilities, with its balance sheet showing the following changes:

Federal Reserve Bank

Assets		Liabilities	
Government Securities	$100,000	Member bank reserves	$100,000

The net result for the banking system when the Federal Reserve Bank buys a new asset is a corresponding increase in demand deposits and reserves of the member banks.[4]

Step 2: The First Stage of Multiple Expansion

No bank likes to hold unused reserves that could be put to work earning income for its stockholders. In this case the bank that got the original increase in reserves will now find that its reserves are $80,000 greater than those required by a reserve ratio of 20 percent. These are "free" reserves, which the bank can use in any way it wishes. Its officers will want to lend that money to a customer, and when they do, its balance sheet will change:

A. Bank I. Initial position with excess reserves.

Assets		Liabilities	
Reserves		Demand deposits	$100,000
Required	$ 20,000		
Excess	80,000		
	$100,000		

B. Bank I. Intermediate position after making loans.

Assets		Liabilities	
Reserves	$100,000	Demand deposits	$100,000
Loans	80,000		80,000
	$180,000		$180,000

The customer who got the loan will quickly put his money to use, writing checks that will be deposited in other banks. As those checks pass through the clearing system, funds will be shifted from Bank I to a second *group* of banks. Both demand deposits *and* reserves will move as the transactions are cleared.

---

[4] Just the opposite occurs when the Federal Reserve System sells government securities. By reducing its assets it reduces the reserves of the banking system. Work out the exact process for yourself by following the transaction through from beginning to end.

This is what will happen:

C. Bank I. Newly created deposits are withdrawn.

Assets		Liabilities	
Reserves	$100,000	Demand deposits	$180,000
less	80,000	less	80,000
	20,000		$100,000
Loans	80,000		
	$100,000		

D. Second Group of Banks. Initial position.

Assets		Liabilities	
Reserves	$80,000	Demand deposits	$80,000

By the time the funds have been cleared to the second group of banks, Bank I will have arrived simultaneously at its final position.

E. Bank I. Final position.

Assets		Liabilities	
Reserves	$20,000	Demand deposits	$100,000
Loans	80,000		

This balance sheet of Bank I's final position contains in microcosm the multiple expansion of demand deposits. Compared with Bank I's initial position, the bank has succeeded in *reducing its reserves* to the minimum level required to cover its demand deposits. It does so by making loans to its customers. This action increases the demand deposits and reserves of *other* banks, which then are in a position to repeat the process.

This analysis also tells us why Bank I cannot lend five times the amount of its excess reserves. If it were to lend $400,000 to its customers ($80,000 $\times$ 5) it would lose $400,000 of reserves to other banks through the clearing system. This would bring its total reserve position down to $300,000 below where it started from, while its demand deposits would have gone up by $100,000. Since it started out all loaned up, it would now be $320,000 short in its required reserves. It is for this reason that no single bank can lend more than the free reserves it has.

Yet in our example so far, the total of demand deposits has risen by $180,000, even though new reserves in the system remain at $100,000, and the process of expansion is not ended.

Step 3: The Second Group of Banks Expands Its Loans

The second group of banks is now in a position of holding excess reserves. They need only $16,000 as a reserve against the new demand deposit of $80,000 that they have acquired. $64,000 is available in free reserves and can be lent to their customers, who will in turn write checks against their new deposits. After those checks have cleared, the balance sheet of the second group of banks will look like this:

Second Group of Banks. Final Position.

Assets		Liabilities	
Reserves	$16,000	Demand deposits	$80,000
Loans	64,000		
Total	$80,000		

Step 4: Effects on Other Banks

A third group of banks will receive new demand deposits and reserves of $64,000 when the checks from the second group of banks clear through the system. They in turn, will find themselves with excess reserves, will lend to their customers, and arrive at a new loaned-up balance sheet. Just to test your understanding of the process, see if you can fill out the blanks in the following balance sheets for the initial and final positions of the third group of banks.

A. Third Group of Banks. Initial Position.

Assets		Liabilities	
Reserves	—	Demand deposits	—
Loans	—		$64,000
Total	—		

B. Third Group of Banks. Final Position.

Assets		Liabilities	
Reserves	—	Demand deposits	—
Loans	—		$64,000
Total	—		

You should have been able to work it out correctly. Answers are given below.[5]

[5] A.	Reserves	$64,000	Demand deposits	$64,000
	Loans	0		
	Total	$64,000	Total	$64,000
B.	Reserves	$12,800	Demand deposits	$64,000
	Loans	51,200		
	Total	$64,000	Total	$64,000

Ultimately, the banking system as a whole will expand loans up to the point at which all of the new reserves will be required at the higher level of demand deposits and all free reserves have disappeared. The pattern of expansion is shown in Table 16–3.

TABLE 16–3
Multiple Expansion of Demand Deposits

	Demand Deposits	New Loans	Required Reserves
Bank I	$100,000	$ 80,000	$ 20,000
2nd Group of Banks	80,000	64,000	16,000
3rd Group of Banks	64,000	51,200	12,800
4th Group of Banks	51,200	40,960	10,240
Total for first 4 groups of banks	295,200	236,160	59,040
Total for remaining groups of banks	204,800	163,840	40,960
Final result	$500,00	$400,000	$100,000

The expansion has now come to an end. All the new reserves are being used as backing for the expanded level of demand deposits. The banking system has created an additional $400,000 of new money to supplement the original increase of $100,000, and a 5-to-1 expansion of the money supply has taken place.[6]

SOME QUALIFICATIONS

The process we have just described was broken down into its component parts in order to explain it systematically. In actual practice, all of the banks expand their loans together rather than in the strict sequence described here. An increase in reserves quickly spreads throughout the system and most banks start out with excess reserves. They all try to reduce their reserves to the

---

[6] The algebraic formulation for the multiple expansion of demand deposits is similar to the formula for the national income multiplier:

$$dD = dR \left(\frac{1}{r} \right),$$

where D = demand deposits,
R = reserves,
r = reserve ratio.

In the example used here the solution is

$$dD = \$100,000 \left(\frac{1}{0.2} \right) = \$100,000 \times 5 = \$500,000.$$

required level by increasing their loans, and as they all expand, the system as a whole reaches its upper limit of expansion.

A bank need not make loans for the multiple expansion to occur. It may buy securities or other investment assets, and this will have the same effect as a new loan. The bank will buy the assets by check and the check will be deposited in the seller's checking account. The result will be an increase in the system's demand deposits just as if a loan were made.

There are two factors that might prevent the full expansion to five times the new reserves (in our example). One is the leakage of cash into hand-to-hand circulation. Some of those who acquire larger demand deposits will want some of their assets in cash, and will withdraw some from the banking system. This leakage will have to come from the reserves of the banking system. The result will be a slightly smaller expansion.

Suppose, for example, that 2 percent of the new reserves were drawn out in cash as the system expanded. The new reserves available to the system would be only $98,000 and the new level of demand deposits would be

$$\$98{,}000 \left(\frac{1}{0.2}\right) = \$98{,}000 \times 5 = \$490{,}000,$$

or 2 percent less than if there had been no leakage.

The second factor that could keep expansion below the theoretical limits is the holding of excess reserves by the banking system. Suppose, for example, that each bank in the system decided to hold not just 20 percent reserves but an additional 5 percent of any new reserves it received. Bank officials may do this for a variety of reasons, say in preparation for large seasonal demands for loans a little later, perhaps at Christmas or Easter; in expectation of higher interest rates; or perhaps because of pessimism or prudence. Whatever the reason, they will be, in effect, imposing a greater reserve requirement upon themselves than is necessary, and the expansion of credit will be less than the maximum possible:

$$\$100{,}000 \left(\frac{1}{0.2 + 0.05}\right) = \$100{,}000 \times 4 = \$400{,}000.$$

Excess reserves can be very important. If businessmen are not eager to borrow and banks are not eager to lend, as during recessions or depressions, large amounts of excess reserves can pile up. This happened during the depression years of the 1930s, when the banking system at times had as much as $5 billion in excess reserves. This experience illustrates an important point:

Expansion of the money supply is not automatic. Although an upper limit is defined by the amount of reserves and the reserve ratio, the expansion of the system depends on the economic climate as seen by both businessmen and bankers.

THE NEED FOR CONTROL

Money and credit are the lifeblood of a private enterprise economy. Both the existing level of economic activity and economic growth require an appropriate level and expansion of the money supply. Yet that vital element is provided by profit-making business enterprises, namely banks, whose primary obligation is to their owners, not to the economy as a whole. An individual bank will maximize its profits when it has expanded its loans to the highest level consistent with safety. When all banks do this, a very large expansion can occur, which may or may not be consistent with the welfare of the economy as a whole. A stable economy may require constraint.

At other times the banking system may be loaned up, and unable to provide adequate amounts of credit. At these times the banks need additional reserves in order to expand loans.

It is for these reasons that all modern nations regulate the monetary system. In the United States loans are made by individual banks, who thereby ration the available credit among potential borrowers. But determination of the total amount of credit has been taken out of their hands. The following chapter explains how it is done.

Summary

Banks provide credit to business units and consumers, an operation vitally important to a modern economy. By making loans, banks create purchasing power in the form of demand deposits. If there were no legal limits placed on the process, this creation of money would be limited only by the need to keep a small reserve on the part of banks. This multiple expansion of credit is characteristic of modern banking. Indeed, if all banks expanded loans at the same rate and at the same time, there would be no limit to expansion.

Reserves do not provide safety. They serve to limit the expansion of credit.

The process of multiple expansion of credit occurs because profit seeking banks try to lend to their customers any funds not required for reserves. They reduce their reserves to the minimum level by loans that bring them a profit. The system as a whole ends up with a total of demand deposits larger than its reserves, even though no one bank has lent out any money it did not have.

Since this process obviously affects aggregate demand and the level of economic activity, all modern nations try to manage their monetary systems.

Key Concepts

Creation of credit. The process by which banks make loans to customers.

Clearing of checks. The process by which checks are debited and credited to the bank on which they are written. Balances at the clearinghouse result in increases or decreases in the reserves of individual banks and thereby influence bank lending policies.

Bank reserves. Funds that banks are required to hold on deposit at the Federal Reserve Banks (or in till money). The most important source of new reserves for the system as a whole is Federal Reserve purchases of government securities.

Free reserves. Reserves held by banks above the level required; sometimes called excess reserves. These are the funds available for expansion of credit. Banks are loaned up when they have no free reserves.

Reserve ratio. The required ratio of reserves to demand deposits.

Multiple expansion of bank credit. The process by which demand deposits in the banking system as a whole are increased to a multiple of the system's reserves.

From the *Wall Street Journal:*

"Federal Reserve steps toward a moderately restrictive credit policy continued in the week ended Wednesday. As a result, funds of major New York City banks available for lending and investing were the tightest in some weeks. Reflection of the more stringent conditions was found in a $93 million decline in the latest period in New York banks' loans to business."

Money and credit do not manage themselves. They respond to the needs of the economy and the desires of millions of borrowers and businessmen. The efforts of banks to make a profit influences the money supply and the flow of credit. The desire of the public to hold assets in the form of money, or its preferences for liquidity, influences the availability of credit and rates of interest. All of the millions of economic units make decisions about money and credit, and the decisions may or may not add up to a consensus that contributes to economic well-being.

FUNCTIONS OF A CENTRAL BANK

A guiding hand is needed to assure that the monetary system contributes to the general economic health of the community. The central bank performs this function. It seeks to guide the monetary and credit system into paths that are consistent with high levels of employment and economic growth and with stable levels of prices.

While the basic job of a central bank is to manage the monetary and credit system, it performs other functions as well. It acts as a lender of last resort, standing ready at all times to provide funds to the banking system as a whole or to individual banks in time of need. It also operates the central clearinghouses for the settlement of accounts between banks, including the clearing system for checks.

Finally, a central bank acts as the fiscal agent for the national government. The Treasury has its chief bank account there, out of which it makes payments and into which tax collections flow.[1] More important, the

The Federal Reserve System and Monetary Policy

17

---

[1] A qualification: In most countries, including the United States, the Treasury holds a portion of its bank balances in commercial banks.

central bank usually maintains a market for government securities and can provide an unlimited line of credit to the national government. This function of the central bank is of special importance today. As long as the central bank cooperates, there is no limit to the size of the national debt.

Nevertheless, the prime job of a central bank, the one it must deal with daily at the highest policy levels, is to manage money and credit in the public interest:

When the economy begins to falter, unemployment increases and output falls, the job of the central bank is to ease conditions in the money markets. This is done by increasing the amount of loanable funds and pushing interest rates down.

When the economy becomes overheated, with high levels of employment and output and prices starting to rise, the task is just the opposite. The central bank tries to tighten the money markets by decreasing the availability of credit and pushing interest rates up.

All this must be done within the framework of a growing economy. Economic growth requires increased debt and an increase of currency in circulation. As the central bank "leans against the wind" of recession or inflation, it must keep in mind the long-term need for expansion of both credit and money in order to facilitate economic growth.

A central bank will have two related tasks. Both are less important than looking after the monetary health of the economy.

The daily and weekly changes that take place in the money markets must be smoothed out, so that they do not interfere with the normal processes of production and distribution. Temporary shortages or surpluses of funds in the money markets can affect business activity, and should be counteracted.

The nation's balance of international payments influences and is influenced by the level of prices and interest rates. The central bank must continually keep in mind the effect of its actions on the balance of payments.

These are the great principles of central banking. Yet central banks do not order the commercial banks to lend more or lend less. They cannot specify interest rates. They cannot force banks to lend or businessmen to borrow. But they can encourage and cajole. They can create situations in the money markets that cause others to act in desirable ways. In essence, the job of the central banks is so to structure the money markets and credit system that bankers and businessmen voluntarily act in ways that further the general public interest.

THE FEDERAL RESERVE SYSTEM

The United States set up its central bank in 1914, after passage of the Federal Reserve Act in 1913. We were one of the last industrial nations to do so; Italy and Russia preceded us, and some countries, like Sweden and England, preceded us by more than 200 years. The American central bank is quite different in its structure from any other, with a complex relationship between banks, central bank, and government, and a system of twelve regional units instead of a single institution. Our Federal Reserve System is composed of three principal units:

1. The member banks
2. Twelve Federal Reserve Banks
3. A Board of Governors

Together they make up a structure within which the system of money and credit is managed.

First are the member banks. There are some 14,000 commercial banks in the United States. Of these, about 6,100 are members of the Federal Reserve System. There are a number of qualifications and requirements for membership, which are changed occasionally by Congress, but the membership comprises all of the banks of significant size. Although member banks include only 45 percent of all commercial banks, they hold 85 percent of all demand deposits. Member banks are required by law to keep their reserves on deposit in the Federal Reserve Bank for their region.[2] This automatically makes them part of the Fed's clearing system for checks, and insures that any changes in the money markets will affect the banks' reserve position.[3]

Second are the twelve regional Federal Reserve Banks, with their twenty-four branches. They are *not* owned by the federal government, but by the member banks in each region. Each member bank is required to buy stock in the regional Federal Reserve Bank equal to 3 percent of the member bank's capital plus surplus (with another 3 percent subject to subscription if called for). The member banks earn a dividend of 6 percent on this stock, with all profits above that going to the U.S. Treasury.

The officers and policies of the Federal Reserve Banks are not controlled by the member banks, however. Their top policy-making and operating officers are appointed by the Board of Governors of the Federal Reserve System. Each Federal Reserve Bank has nine directors, only six of whom are elected by the member banks. Three are appointed by the Board of Governors, including the Chairman and Vice-Chairman. In addition, the appointments of the president and first vice-president of the regional banks must be approved by the Board of Governors. These top officers can be removed by the Board of Governors, and this power gives the Governors ultimate control over policy. There have been disagreements over policy matters between the Board of Governors and presidents of the regional Federal Reserve Banks from time to time. But in each case the regional president has played the game, and has not tried to sabotage the Board's policy.

Third is the guiding force of the system, the Board of Governors, located in

---

[2] In addition, currency held in their vaults by member banks counts as part of their reserves.
[3] Banks that are not members of the Federal Reserve System keep their reserves with member banks. Some participate in the clearing of checks directly, by maintaining accounts at the regional Federal Reserve banks, and others indirectly through their reserve accounts with member banks.

Washington. Its seven members are appointed for staggered 14-year terms by the President, whose appointments must be confirmed by the Senate. The Board of Governors has certain administrative responsibilities and supervisory powers over the twelve regional banks and their branches, but its most important function is management of the monetary system. The Board controls the instruments of monetary management and determines the goals of monetary policy.[4] Thus, a privately owned system is controlled by public appointees whose chief responsibilities are the guidance of the money markets toward paths consistent with the general welfare.

The Board of Governors is not independent of the other federal agencies that deal with economic policy. It is expected to coordinate its money market management with the policies of the President and the executive branch of the government, including the Treasury, the Bureau of the Budget, and the President's Council of Economic Advisors. These agencies, together with the Board of Governors, make up the group responsible for development and implementation of national economic policy, within the framework of presidential and congressional responsibility.

There has been considerable debate over how independent the Board of Governors is or ought to be. The Fed's position is that it was established by act of Congress and is responsible to Congress for carrying out the purposes of the act and other congressional legislation. In practice, however, national economic policy is a seamless web, and those responsible for one sector cannot ride off in directions opposite to that taken by others. This means that the Fed must cooperate with other agencies if its legal responsibilities are to be fulfilled. On the other hand, the President cannot order the Fed to take action (although he appoints the members of the Board of Governors, he cannot remove them). This forces the executive branch (Treasury, Budget Bureau, Council of Economic Advisors) to reach agreement with the Fed on most major issues of economic policy. There·have been disagreements in recent years, but by and large the two groups have cooperated effectively. Nevertheless, there are some economists and members of Congress who feel that the Fed should not be independent and that all economic policy agencies should be directly coordinated by a single agency within the executive branch of the government.[5]

---

[4] A Federal Advisory Council of 12 members representing the Federal Reserve Banks advises the Board of Directors, but has no direct powers. The Federal Open Market Committee (12 members, 7 appointed by the Board of Governors and 5 named by the Federal Reserve Banks) determines policies for the entire system with respect to purchase and sale of government securities. These are the only two instruments the 12 regional banks can use to influence the policies of the Board of Governors except for informal channels.

[5] The chief deterrent to independent action by the Fed is the fact that Congress can always change the law. Independent action by the Fed may lead the President to ask Congress to subordinate the Board of Governors to the executive branch. A popular President with a significant majority in Congress could probably get such legislation through. So the Fed can maintain its independence only by not exercising it, except on relatively unimportant matters. It's a good example of the age-old proverb that power disappears if it is used.

WHOSE PUBLIC INTEREST?

It's easy enough to say that a central bank manages the money supply "in the public interest" or "with the goal of economic stability" in mind. But how are these phrases to be defined and who is to define them?

Policy conflicts can easily arise. For example, tight money may dampen inflationary pressures, but it can also slow down the achievement of full employment. Bankers may like the former, because it also brings higher interest rates and higher earnings for banks, but labor unions don't like the latter. Alternatively, easy money may promote higher levels of employment, but it can also ease the way toward higher prices.

The Board of Governors must decide these matters, and whichever way it decides, someone's interests are likely to be damaged.

The fact that the Board is at the apex of the banking system, many of its members are bankers, and it has close contact and communication with bankers, makes it easy for the Board to take on the attitudes of the banking community. Indeed, some have charged that the Federal Reserve Board is the bankers' lobbyist in the executive branch of the government, continually pressing for policies that tend to tighten the money markets, raise interest rates and dampen economic growth.

There is nothing automatic about monetary policy decisions. They require judgment as well as knowledge. The Board of Governors is composed of knowledgeable men, but their judgment may be colored, as everyone's is, by their associates, their backgrounds and their environment. This aspect of monetary policy is the great intangible factor in the situation, and makes almost any decision of the Board of Governors a controversial one.

MANAGING THE MONETARY SYSTEM

We have seen that the creation of demand deposits is limited by:

1. The amount of reserves held by commercial banks, and
2. The reserve ratio, that is, the proportion that must be maintained between reserves and demand deposits.

For example, with a reserve ratio of 20 percent and reserves of $1 million, a bank could maintain demand deposits totaling $5 million.

The chief instruments of monetary policy are designed to act on these two limiting factors. The money managers of the central bank can change either the amount of reserves or the reserve ratio. The resulting change in the reserve position of the banks will be felt in the money markets by changes in the availability of loans and the interest rates borrowers will have to pay.

Other actions can be taken, but they are much less important. The central bank can change the rate of interest it charges on loans to commercial banks. Or it can try to influence the money markets by exhortation, advice and public statements. Some direct regulation of interest rates or terms of loans in special areas of the money markets may be available. Any good central bank will use any or all of these instruments of money management if they are appropriate, but in the end the reserve position of the commercial banks is the key to effective action.

Open Market Operations

The Federal Reserve System can change the amount of reserves held by commercial banks by buying or selling government securities. The name, *open market operations,* comes from the fact that the transactions are carried out in the New York market for government securities, a market open to anyone, rather than directly with the Federal government. Just as you or I would do, the Fed will telephone a broker to make a purchase or sale and will pay by check,[6] an action that can create new reserves. This principle is important enough to merit careful review in greater detail, and is basically very simple.

Whenever the Fed acquires an asset the reserves of the member banks are increased.

The reverse is also true.

Whenever the Fed sells an asset the reserves of the member banks are decreased.

We already know why this happens. When the Open Market Account buys government securities it pays for them by a check written on a Federal Reserve Bank. The seller deposits the check in his bank, which sends the check through the clearing system. At the clearinghouse, which is the regional Federal Reserve Bank, the reserve account of the seller's bank is credited and the new reserves are now available.

It is useful to see what happens to the balance sheets of the participants. First, the seller of the government securities has exchanged one form of asset for another, for example, $100,000 of government securities for $100,000 in demand deposits.

---

[6] The purchase or sale is made by the Manager of the Fed's Open Market Account, under instructions from the Federal Open Market Committee (see p. 296, footnote 4), who operates out of the Federal Reserve Bank of New York. Purchases are made at the lowest available prices and sales at the highest, at the time of the transaction.

Balance Sheet of Seller

	Before			After	
	Assets	Liabilities		Assets	Liabilities
Bonds	$100,000		Demand Deposits	$100,000	

Meanwhile, the buyer of the securities, one of the Federal Reserve banks, has acquired both an asset and a liability:

Balance Sheet of Federal Reserve Bank
After Completion of Transaction

Assets			Liabilities
Government Securities	+$100,000	Member Bank Reserves	+$100,000

And the commercial bank has also increased both its assets and its liabilities:

Balance Sheet of Member Bank
After Completion of Transaction

Assets			Liabilities
Reserves	+$100,000	Demand Deposits	+$100,000

The member bank can then set in motion the chain of multiple expansion of credit by making loans and investments that reduce its new reserves to one-fifth of its new demand deposits, its excess reserves will move to other banks, and the process can go on until the system is once more loaned up.

The process works equally well in reverse. Sale of government securities will decrease the reserves of the banking system. When the Fed sells an asset, it is paid by a check from the buyer. The Fed collects by deducting the amount of the check from the reserve account of the member bank. By the time the transaction has been completed, the buyer's demand deposit has been reduced by the amount of his purchase of government securities. Instead of a demand deposit, he has government bonds. The commercial bank has lost reserves, but its demand deposits have been reduced by the same amount. The Federal Reserve Bank has reduced its assets by sale of the bond and this has led to a reduction in its liabilities, the reserves of the member banks.

Open market operations are controlled solely by the Fed. The member banks have no option whatsoever. Whenever the Fed wants to do so, it can raise the banking system's reserves by buying government securities, or lower the reserves by selling. Nor is there any limit to the amounts that can be bought: the system is kept solvent by the fact that increased reserve account liabilities are balanced by increased assets. There is a limit to the amount of government securities the Fed can sell, since it owns a finite quantity, but even that limit is flexible. The Fed can always "sell short" if it has to. That is, it can sell securities it does not have, borrowing them from a broker, and buying them later for delivery. But this is a theoretical rather than a practical limit to open market sales; in late 1967, for example, the Fed owned some $48 billion of U.S. government securities.

Furthermore, open market operations of any size can be carried out, and on very short notice. A small increase or decrease in reserves can be made very quickly, a large change very slowly, or vice versa. Open market operations are a highly flexible means by which the reserve position of the banking system as a whole can be quickly changed, to almost any extent that the Board of Governors feels is advisable.

Reserve Requirements

Ability of the banking system to expand credit can also be affected by changing the reserve ratio. This method of controlling the money supply is not used very often, however, because it has a large impact on the money markets. The Fed has found that a soft touch is usually better than a bludgeon.

The Board of Governors is empowered to vary the required reserve kept by member banks against their demand deposits, within certain limits. Member banks are divided into two classes for the purpose of this regulation, reserve city banks and other banks (usually called "country banks"). Reserve city banks are in the larger commercial centers of the country, and have over 60 percent of all member bank demand deposits. The country banks comprise all the other member banks. The distinction goes back to the pre-Fed days before 1914 and is related to the pattern by which banks used to deposit their reserves in other banks. Today the distinction is an anachronism, and there is no real need for it, but the Fed does have a long-range policy of maintaining differences in reserve requirements that are based on differences in the size of banks.

Changes in reserve requirements have a large effect on the reserve positions of the member banks. When reserve requirements were raised by only one-half of one percent in December 1967 (and even then on only demand deposits of over $5 million), the total increase in required reserves was about $550 million. At a 1 to 6 ratio, this amount of reserves could have been used as a basis for a $3.3-billion increase in demand deposits. The increase in the reserve requirements reduced the potential money supply by that amount. The objective, of course, was to tighten the money markets. In the words of the Board of Governors, "The action was taken in furtherance of the Federal Reserve's objectives of fostering financial conditions conducive to resistance of inflationary pressures and to progress toward equilibrium in the U.S. balance of payments position." [7] It was done shortly after Britain devalued

---

[7] *Federal Reserve Bulletin,* January 1968, p. 96.

TABLE 17–1
Member Bank Reserve Requirements, as of January, 1971
(Percent of Deposits)

	Reserve City Banks	Other Banks
Demand Deposits		
Legal limits	10 to 22	7 to 14
Present requirements (1/71)		
Up to $5 million	17	12½
Over $5 million	17½	13
Time Deposits		
Legal limits	3 to 6	3 to 6
Present requirements (1/71)		
Savings accounts	3	3
Other time deposits		
Up to $5 million	3	3
Over $5 million	5	5

Note: Why does the Fed have lower reserve requirements for the first $5 million of demand deposits and the first $5 million of time deposits other than savings accounts? In the case of demand deposits, it is apparently because small banks have less profitable opportunities for use of any excess reserves and tend to hold more than larger banks. The difference in reserve requirements tends to equalize the situation. As for time deposits, the difference is an adaptation to the appearance of large-denomination time *certificates of deposit,* which came into use on a large scale in the mid-1960s. Certificates of deposit are essentially transferable time deposits. They are used by large banks to attract deposits away from other financial institutions without having to provide the relatively large reserves required for demand deposits.

the pound, at a time when there was good reason to expect inflationary pressures because of spending for the war in Vietnam, and amid fear in the money markets that Congress would not take action to dampen the inflationary pressures adequately. Like most other instances in which reserve requirements were changed, it signaled a significant shift in the economic environment that justified fairly strong action.

Changes in reserve requirements are seldom used to force banks to reduce their loans. This may seem paradoxical, because it is such a good weapon to use for that purpose. The problem is that a forced reduction in lending can be very hard on business firms that just happen to be caught with a need to renew their old loans, and would discriminate against businesses that are short of working capital. This is true of small business most of the time, while big firms often have substantial reserves. The impact of changes in reserve requirements is not felt evenly throughout the business community. Instead, an increase in the reserve ratio is used most often to sop up the excess reserves of the system in order to make it more sensitive to open market purchases and sales, rather than to change the amount of loans outstanding.

Thus, when reserve requirements were raised late in 1967, the Fed knew that there would not be a forced reduction in bank lending. There were some $345 million of excess reserves in the banking system at the time, and commercial banks held some $62.5 billion in government securities that could be sold to accommodate their needy customers. The banks could shift some of their assets from government securities to business loans without changing the total of demand deposits against which reserves must be held.[8] Nevertheless, there was a noticeable tightening of credit as the banks adapted to the new reserve ratio.

If the Fed wanted to move in the other direction, toward easier money markets, changes in the reserve ratio could also be used. A *decrease* of 0.5 to 1 percent in the reserve ratio could immediately make available to the member banks something over $500 million of reserves. This would make possible an increase in loans and demand deposits of over $3 billion, assuming a 1 : 6 reserve ratio. The Fed could reasonably expect credit to be more easily available, on better terms to the borrower, after such action was taken.

The Federal Reserve Discount Rate

When a member bank borrows from its regional Federal Reserve Bank, it must pay interest on the loan, just as you or I or General Motors Corporation must pay interest when we borrow. The rate of interest charged is called the Federal Reserve discount rate, or sometimes the "rediscount rate." [9]

Borrowing from the Fed affects the reserve position of the borrowing bank. For example, if a bank suddenly finds itself without adequate reserves it can borrow the required amount, using government securities as collateral for the loan. The regional Federal Reserve Bank then credits the member bank's reserve account by the amount of the loan. Exactly the opposite occurs when the member bank pays off the loan. The Fed takes payment by reducing the member bank's reserve account.

Banks don't like to borrow from the Fed. They have to pay interest when they do, and this reduces the profits they can make from their loans and investments. In addition, a bank that is continually in debt to the Fed will sometimes receive an inquiry about why it is always in trouble, and perhaps a reprimand. So most banks borrow only on a temporary basis and only when they must bolster their reserve positions.

---

[8] A further discussion of this use of "secondary" reserves will follow later in this chapter.

[9] When a member bank borrows at the Fed it usually uses government securities as "collateral," or security for the loan. When the loan is repaid, the bank pays back the amount of the loan plus interest, say 4½ percent, for the time it held the money. This is called "discounting" and the interest rate is the "discount rate." In England it's called the "Bank rate," meaning the Bank of England.

A second procedure is available. The member bank may *sell* some of its commercial paper (promissory notes from business firms to whom the bank has made loans) to the Fed. The sale will be at a discount of 4½ percent. This is called rediscounting (because the bank has already charged interest on, or discounted, the original loan) and the interest rate is the rediscount rate. The Federal Reserve discount rate and rediscount rate are always identical. The rates will vary with the length of maturity of the loan and may differ from one Federal Reserve district to another.

The Fed encourages this attitude on the part of the member banks. It keeps the banks from borrowing more than they absolutely need, and thereby makes it easier for other instruments of credit control to operate more effectively. In fact, until recently the Fed assumed that no bank would borrow unless its reserve position made the loan absolutely necessary, and almost never turned down a bank's request for a loan.[10]

The Federal Reserve discount rate is not a very effective way of influencing credit conditions and the money markets. In the first place, the initiative for a loan must come from the member banks. The Fed takes a passive role, waiting for the bank to ask. Lowering the rate will not do much to encourage banks to borrow, however, because of the reluctance of member banks to be in debt to the Fed. Raising the rate won't have much impact either, because when banks have inadequate reserves they have little alternative but to borrow.[11]

Secondly, the Federal Reserve discount rate must remain very close to the rate of interest on short-term government securities. There is an interesting relationship here. If the Federal Reserve discount rate for a 90-day loan is 4½ percent while the rate of return on a 90-day Treasury bill is 5½ percent, a smart banker will borrow from the Fed rather than sell his Treasury bills in order to adjust his reserve position. Doing so will increase the system's reserves at a time when the Fed may not want greater ease in the money markets.

On the other hand, if the discount rate is well above the interest rate on Treasury bills, banks will sell their government securities before they come to the Fed to borrow. This puts the Fed out of touch with the money market climate and makes it more difficult to decide how to use the instruments of credit control.

As a result, the Federal Reserve discount rate tends to follow very closely the fluctuations that occur in the yield on Treasury bills. Yet that interest rate is the result of supply and demand conditions in the money market, *which in turn have been influenced by other instruments of credit control.* In order to avoid confusing the picture and to retain control of money market conditions, then, the Fed sets its discount rate so that it follows the fluctuations that occur in the yield on Treasury bills. The relationship between these two important interest rates in recent years is shown in Figure 17-1.

In spite of all this, the discount rate does have some uses as an instrument of credit control. It is watched by bankers and speculators as a confirmation

---

[10] Late in 1966, the presidents of the twelve Federal Reserve banks announced that the Fed's loan policies would be based on the general economic conditions of the country. Up to that time, loans to member banks had been based solely upon the bank's "credit worthiness" and upon the value of the collateral for the loan.

[11] A bank can always pay the penalty for inadequate reserves, which is one percent more than the discount rate on the amount of the inadequacy. It is cheaper to borrow from the Fed than to pay the penalty rate, however.

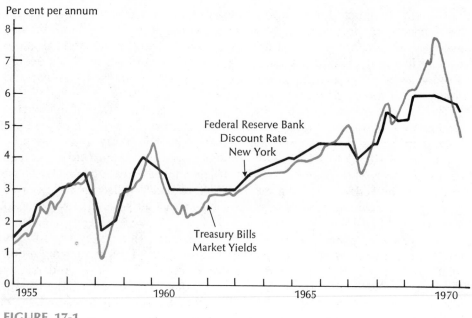

FIGURE 17-1
The Discount Rate and the Treasury Bill Rate, 1955–70

of the trends they have already observed in other market rates of interest. When the Fed raises the discount rate, the action is understood as confirming the fact that interest rates have risen and that money markets have become tighter. The psychological effect is to cause a little more tightening. When the Fed lowers its discount rate just the opposite occurs. Bankers and others in the money markets know that an easing of money market conditions has occurred, and there is a tendency toward a little greater ease as a result. Thus we have a most interesting paradox: one of the least effective of the instruments of monetary management is one of the most closely watched indicators of money market conditions.

Moral Suasion

It is sometimes possible for the Fed to influence credit conditions by public statements, by private discussions with bankers, and by developing "voluntary controls." For example, in 1966, when there was great concern over the nation's balance of international payments, the federal government, in co-operation with the Fed, developed a program to limit foreign loans by banks. There were no compulsory controls, just a set of guidelines that banks were asked to abide by. There was a very high degree of compliance. The circumstances were good: domestic money markets could absorb all the loans the banks could make and interest rates were rising so banks went along with the voluntary limitations on their foreign loans that the Fed asked for. Besides, there was always the threat of compulsion if the voluntary system didn't work. The episode indicated that "jawbone controls" could work under the proper conditions.

Most of the time, however, moral suasion is used only to set the stage for later action. A speech by a member of the Board of Governors may be a prelude to significant open market operations or use of some other credit control instruments, and may be part of a combined operation designed to achieve just the proper state of tension in the money markets. Standing alone, it may have little effect. But as part of a pattern that includes use of open market operations and changes in the discount rate, it could have a significant psychological effect on the money markets.

Special Credit Controls

The philosophy of the Federal Reserve System is to apply general tightness or ease in the money markets as a whole. It seeks to leave decisions about the use of the available funds to the forces of the money markets themselves. In the Fed's view, competition among lenders and borrowers should determine how the funds will be allocated among their alternative uses. This traditional policy is quite consistent with the development of modern economic theory: the level of economic activity must be managed in order to achieve economic health, but the allocation of resources should be left to market forces (if monopoly can be avoided) in order to achieve economic efficiency.

But from time to time even the Fed accepts some modification of this basic principle and uses special credit controls that affect only one segment of the money markets. One area of special concern is speculation on the stock market. If speculators borrow a large portion of the money they need to buy stocks, there will be considerably more speculation than if such borrowing were limited. For a variety of reasons, chiefly the stock market crash of 1929, Congress has given the Fed power to limit that type of borrowing by setting *margin requirements*. The proportion of the selling price of securities that the buyer is required to put up in cash is called the "margin." Thus, when margin requirements were set by the Fed at 70 in 1963, this meant that 70 percent of the purchase price had to be cash and only 30 percent could be borrowed. The Fed can set margin requirements at any level. In recent decades they have been fixed at between 50 and 90, depending on how the Fed has assessed the speculative pressures existing in the securities markets.

The Fed also has power to fix the ceilings on interest rates on time deposits, under "Regulation Q." These are the maximum rates that member banks can pay to depositors on savings accounts and other time deposits, including time certificates of deposit. At the present time, the ceilings range between 4 and 5½ percent, depending on the type of deposit.[12] These

---

[12] Don't confuse these maximum interest rates with the reserves member banks must keep against savings and time deposits (shown in Table 17–1).

ceilings are used to limit the amount of savings deposits that member banks can attract from outside the Federal Reserve System. By raising interest rates on savings deposits, member banks can cause the general public as well as large investors to shift their time deposits from savings and loan associations and savings banks to the member banks. Although this does not increase the amount of reserves in the banking system, it does cause a shift of funds from demand to time deposits. Funds move from the demand deposits of savings and loan associations in member banks to time deposits in member banks held by the public. Since time deposits have lower reserve requirements than demand deposits, excess reserves are created, which can then be used to expand credit still further. During periods of tight money, there is strong incentive for the member banks to get free reserves in this way. But the whole point of tight money is to prevent further expansion of credit. Imposing limits on the interest rates that member banks can offer closes this loophole and makes the other means of credit control more effective.

Other special credit controls have been available to the Fed in the past, but are no longer available. During World War II the Fed was given power to control the terms of installment contracts. Under "Regulation W" the down payment and the length of the loan (which determines the size of the monthly payments), as well as the interest charge, could be set by the Fed. The purpose was to dampen inflationary pressures created by wartime spending, particularly for articles in short supply, such as automobiles and furniture. Regulation W was effectively used by the Fed, but after the Korean War the enabling legislation was allowed to lapse. Constituents were complaining to their congressmen, inflationary pressures became much less of a problem, and the regulation was contrary to the Fed's philosophy.

The same was true of the Fed's power to control the terms of housing mortgages. This "Regulation X," also a product of the closely managed economy of World War II, was allowed to lapse in the 1950s. It operated in much the same way as the control over installment credit, and was designed to control the flow of funds into housing construction at a time of inflationary pressure and shortages of resources.[13]

Federal Reserve Credit

The basis of monetary expansion is the total reserve of the member banks. The Fed can make reserves available on its own initiative through open market operations. Member banks can also take the initiative by borrowing from the Fed. The total amount made available to the member banks is called Federal Reserve credit.

Federal Reserve credit is the chief stabilizing element in the money markets.

---

[13] The federal government continues to dabble in the market for housing funds. Mortgage loans are guaranteed by the Veterans Administration and the Federal Housing Authority. The Federal Home Loan Bank lends money to savings and loan associations, which do a great deal of mortgage lending. All of these government agencies seek to increase the flow of funds into housing, and unfortunately, their policies and those of the Fed are sometimes in conflict.

FEDERAL RESERVE CREDIT

The name given to the total amount of funds that the Fed has made available to create member bank reserves. It includes:

U.S. government securities owned by the Fed.

Loans and advances to member banks.

Federal Reserve "float" (uncollected checks that have already been credited to reserves).

It can be used to counteract some of the other factors that influence bank reserves. Bank reserves are affected not only by the operations of the Fed, but also by (1) the public's demand for currency, and (2) imports and exports of gold. An increase of currency in circulation draws reserves out of the banking system. So does loss of gold from the monetary gold stock.[14] The Fed must counteract these changes if it wishes to stabilize the money markets, and in recent years both have created problems.

In 1958 the lengthy drain of gold from the United States began in earnest. Monetary gold stocks fell from about $20.5 billion in 1958 to about $12.5

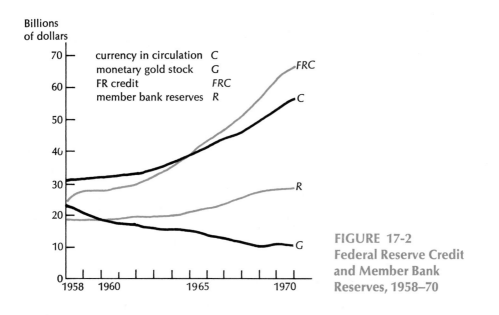

FIGURE 17-2
Federal Reserve Credit and Member Bank Reserves, 1958–70

---

[14] See the Appendix to Chapter 15 for an explanation of how bank reserves are affected by gold movements and changes in the amount of money in circulation.

billion at the end of 1967. This loss would have caused an equal loss of bank reserves if it had not been compensated for by creation of new reserves by the Fed.

During the same period, currency in circulation rose from about $31 billion in 1958 to over $46 billion at the end of 1967. This increase would also have caused a reduction in bank reserves unless the Fed had done something about it. When added to the loss of gold this would have meant a total reduction in bank reserves of about $23 billion.

The Fed acted to prevent a serious tightening of the money markets that could have had grave effects on business activity. Gradually over the ten-year period from 1958 to 1967 it increased the total of Federal Reserve credit by an amount just about equal to the increase of currency in circulation *plus* the loss of gold. It provided some $23 billion of new reserves to the banking system, chiefly through open market purchases of government securities. The total of Federal Reserve credit rose from some $28.4 billion to about $51.3 billion.

By neutralizing the effects of changes in the monetary gold stock and currency in circulation the Fed was able to avoid a serious deflation and shortage of funds. Since price levels were quite stable from 1958 through 1965 there was little concern that the increased money supply would feed inflationary price increases, although there is one school of thought among economists that argues that the monetary expansion of those years has contributed to the price increases of the post-1965 years. At the same time, the very low level of free reserves after 1958 kept the money markets closely related to changes in open market operations. The Fed was managing the money supply under a tight rein.

The Reserve Position of the Member Banks

The key to money market management is the reserve position of the member banks. The banks in the system, taken together, can have free reserves in excess of those required. Under these conditions the money markets will be relatively easy. Customers will find the banks ready to lend, and interest rates will be stable. Indeed, if the conditions of ease last long enough and the free reserves are large enough, interest rates will start to fall.

Just the opposite conditions prevail if bank reserves are inadequate and the member banks have to borrow from the Fed to meet their reserve requirements. This is the sign of tight money markets. Customers will find it more difficult to get new loans or renew old ones. Interest rates will tend to rise; and the tighter the money markets, the greater and faster the rise will be.

MONETARY POLICY SINCE 1946

Monetary policy since World War II has passed through four distinct phases. In 1945-1950, the Fed did not use its powers primarily to control the money markets, but to assist the Treasury in managing the war-induced increase

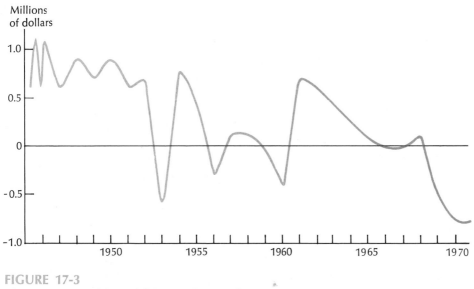

FIGURE 17-3
The Reserve Position of the Member Banks, 1945–70

in the national debt. Recovering its freedom of action in 1951, the Fed spent the decade of the 1950s largely fighting inflation. The resultant tight money policy seems to have done little to hold back price increases, but it did contribute to the abnormally slow economic growth of the fifties. A turnabout toward easy money came in 1960, coordinated with a shift in national economic policy toward economic expansion. Finally, monetary policy in the late sixties and early seventies has come to be dominated by concern for three chief problems: the level of economic activity, prices, and the balance of international payments.

Monetary policy during the first five years after World War II was dominated by the financial needs of the federal government. The chief task of the Federal Reserve System during the war was to make enough credit available to finance Treasury borrowings. The war was the chief problem, and the rising national debt had to be marketed. To this end, the Fed pledged itself to maintaining "stability" in the money markets—easy money markets that kept interest rates low and provided funds with which government securities could be purchased.

This policy continued into the postwar years. The Treasury continually had to refinance the national debt as securities came due, as well as issue new securities to finance the deficits of those years. Easy money and low interest rates simplified its task and kept carrying charges on the national debt at a relatively low level. The Fed continued its wartime policies of cooperating with the Treasury and provided substantial amounts of free reserves from 1945 through the early months of 1951.

These were years of strong inflationary pressures, for the most part, and the Fed became increasingly uneasy about its role in fostering inflation through easy money. Federal budget deficits, together with open market operations by the Fed, were adding additional fuel to the inflationary fires. Here is how it worked:

> The Fed was committed to maintaining the prices and yields of government securities at existing levels. This was done in order to keep down the cost of carrying the national debt: in officialese, "maintenance of orderly conditions in the money and securities markets." In order to "peg" prices and yields, the Fed used open market purchases to buy government securities when offerings exceeded the private demand for them. As a result, bank reserves were automatically expanded. The Fed had lost control of the money markets.

The problem came to a head when the war in Korea broke out in 1950, causing a surge in demand for credit and increased inflationary pressures. After much bitter debate within the government, the Fed was able to free itself from its obligation to maintain the price of government securities. In March of 1951, an "accord" was reached with the Treasury to that effect, which enabled the Fed to concentrate on more fundamental aspects of money market control.

The Fed then moved gradually to tighten the money markets. By mid-1952 the member banks had a negative position (loans at the Fed were larger than excess reserves). The recession of 1954 caused a turn toward easier money markets, only to be followed by a tight-money policy through 1955–1957. The recession of 1958 brought relative ease once more, but tight-money policies were again applied in the latter part of 1958 and lasted into early 1960. Except for the recessions of 1954 and 1958, this was a period of money market restraint as the Fed tried to fight the dragon of inflation.

In retrospect, this policy can be seen as a serious mistake. As we showed in Chapter 9, the fifties were a decade of inadequate economic growth in the United States. During the period of tight money, from the business cycle peak of 1953 to the peak of late 1960, GNP increased at an average annual rate of under 2.5 percent, compared with over 4 percent per year before 1953 and after 1960. Other factors were at work during this period to cause a relatively slow rate of economic growth, in particular, a slowdown in the expansion of federal government expenditures; but a major share of the blame must be placed squarely on the Fed's policy of tight money.

The policy did not have an immediate impact on price levels, either. Both consumer and wholesale prices rose through the 1950s, and the upward creep was not halted until the late 1950s (for wholesale prices), when substantial excess capacity began to be felt because of inadequate expansion of aggregate demand. Although monetary policy was revived, and the Fed used the full range of policy instruments at its disposal, the results were not good because the policy rather than the instruments were at fault.

A turnabout came in 1960. As part of the new administration's efforts to move the economy back to high levels of employment and output, the Fed adopted a policy of monetary ease. The reserve positions of the member banks showed a steady increase in free reserves throughout 1961. Credit was once more readily available to finance economic expansion.

A policy of easy money could not be single-mindedly followed, however. The problem was not the price level; it was relatively stable, and because of considerable slack in the economy, inflation was not an immediate threat. But a persistent deficit in the balance of international payments, which had become serious after 1958, was causing trouble.

If interest rates were allowed to fall below rates abroad, money held in the U.S. by foreign investors would be shifted from New York to other financial centers, such as London, Paris, or Zurich. These shifts of funds would worsen the balance of payments. Thus the extent to which the U.S. money markets could be eased was strictly limited, for monetary ease would soon bring interest rates down[15] and encourage transfer of funds abroad.

Because of these problems the Fed began to lower the total of free reserves in the banking system as early as 1962. The money markets were gradually tightened as the economy moved toward full employment, until by late 1966 a relatively tight market prevailed. The free reserves of the banking system had just about disappeared.

Then came the "credit crunch" of 1966. In an effort to escape from the limitations imposed on their lending policies as the Fed tightened the screws, banks began to attract deposits from savings and loan associations and savings banks by selling certificates of deposit at attractive rates. The resulting shift of savings into the banking system did two things: it reduced the effectiveness of the tight-money policy by creating excess reserves for the member banks, and it left the savings and loan associations strapped. They had to sell some of their assets to get the funds their customers were transferring, yet they couldn't raise their interest rates, partly because of regulations and partly because they had already lent the money on mortgages, sometimes at lower rates of interest than the banks were offering on certificates of deposit. The banks were able to pay such high interest rates, up to 5½ percent in some instances, because they were making *new* loans at the high rates that prevail when money is tight. This bidding for funds nearly brought on a financial disaster. Interest rates rose to the highest levels in half a century, yet bank loans were relatively easy to get if one was willing to pay the price. The trouble was that few were willing; there was a mad dash for liquidity as firms tried to reduce their inventories to get cash. The housing industry was particularly hard hit, since it is normally financed heavily through savings and loan associations. The downturn in housing and the

---

[15] The Fed actually tried to move long-term interest rates down (to encourage investment) while maintaining short-term interest rates (to prevent international transfers of funds). The technique was to buy long-term government securities while selling short-term Treasury bills. This "Operation Twist" had some success, but only in a limited way, because of the interrelatedness of the money markets.

reduction in inventories led the whole economy into a "minirecession" that escaped turning into a major downturn only because the Fed quickly eased the money markets. Three things became clear:

1. The money markets are a web of closely interrelated patterns.
2. Bankers can devise ingenious methods to provide funds to their customers even when money is tight.
3. Even small changes in the money markets can have a significant impact if the circumstances are just right.

The experience of 1966 showed that monetary policy cannot be effectively used when fiscal policy is moving in the opposite direction. This lesson was reiterated through the late 1960s. Government spending on the war in Vietnam created inflationary pressures that a policy of tight money could not eliminate. Efforts to eliminate these pressures by credit restraint only served to make the economy erratic. The old-fashioned "liquidity crisis" reappeared: business firms striving to increase their output in response to increased aggregate demand, unable to obtain the loans they need, bidding interest rates to high levels, causing cutbacks in output and the threat of bankruptcies unless credit is eased. This scenario, reminiscent of the days before the creation of the Federal Reserve System, forced monetary policy to adapt itself to the needs of a wartime economy and neutralized much of its anti-inflationary impact. As long as wartime spending was pushing aggregate demand upward, monetary policy could do little to hold it in check.

THE LIMITATIONS OF MONETARY POLICY

Experience with monetary policy in the last quarter century has brought to the fore a whole series of limitations on its use. Banks have developed a good deal of flexibility in their loan policies by juggling their asset portfolios. Substantial time lags between action by the Fed and effects in the money markets have become evident. Forecasting of economic conditions and the effects of monetary policy is often difficult. And the effects of action by the Fed are not always evenly spread through the economy. These limitations mean that monetary policy can be only one arm of national economic policy, and not the principal one. It must be strongly supplemented by other action if economic policy goals are to be achieved.

"Secondary" Reserves

Banks have developed a good deal of flexibility, making it difficult for the Fed to maintain the close control over money markets it would like to have. The chief source of flexibility is the so-called "secondary" reserves of the member banks. These are the federal government securities owned by banks. At the end of 1967 they amounted to about $47 billion. Here is how they can be used to foil the actions of the Fed, at least for a short period of time.

Suppose the Fed wishes to tighten the money markets. There is no need for quick action: the Fed manages its open market operations so that free reserves gradually fall as the GNP rises and bank loans increase. As more and more banks become loaned up they face the unhappy task of telling their customers that funds are not available. Rather than send them away to borrow elsewhere from a competitor, a bank will probably decide to sell some government securities out of its portfolio. This will provide the cash for loans to customers. The bank, in other words, shifts the composition of its earning assets from government securities to loans. It will do so for two reasons: It can earn more on the loans than on the securities, and it will keep its customers satisfied.

As a result of this action, however, the supply of funds for business loans keeps rising *even though bank reserves have not been increased*. The money markets have *not* been significantly tightened and the Fed's objectives have not been achieved.

When the banks sell government securities someone has to buy them. Since the Fed is not the buyer, it has to be someone in the private, nonbank sector of the money markets, probably an insurance company, investment fund, or some other large investor. These investors always hold some of their assets in cash, or are constantly receiving a flow of cash from the public. When they buy the securities their demand deposits, which were being held as an asset, are reduced. But the bank that sells the securities immediately lends the money *to someone who wants to spend it*. Bank deposits that were idle have now been activated. Money that had been held as an asset is now being spent.

Eventually the money markets will begin to tighten up, however. As sales of government securities mount, their prices will fall. This will happen partly because the supply offered in the market is increased, and partly because the holders of idle bank deposits must be given some incentive to shift the form in which they hold their assets. As the price of government securities falls, their yield will increase, which is equivalent to an increase in the rate of interest.[16] As the price falls, the banks will have to take increasing losses as they sell their government securities, and this is discouraging.

---

[16] This is a simple point, but it may require some explanation. Suppose a $1,000 bond carries an interest payment of 5 percent per year. The payment will be $50. Now let the price of the bond fall to $900. The $50 payment provides a yield (on the purchase price) of 5.55 percent:

$$\frac{\$50}{\$900} = 5.55 \text{ percent}$$

If this is a government bond, and the Treasury wants to sell more of them after the price has fallen, it will have to offer a payment of $55.55 on a $1,000 bond. The interest rate will have risen.

Alternatively, the Treasury could still market bonds with a face value of $1,000 and an annual "coupon" of $50, but it would get only $900 for them. The effective interest rate will still be the new and higher level established by the market.

For a time they can raise interest rates to compensate, but eventually this will start discouraging their customers. Sooner or later, the process of liquidating "secondary" reserves will start slowing down and come to an end. But it may take months, and in the meantime, funds for bank loans to their customers have not been significantly affected.

That isn't true of interest rates, however. The yield on Treasury bills will start rising quite soon after the banks start selling them. This will bring the Federal Reserve discount rate up, as the Fed keeps it in accord with the yield on Treasury bills. Other interest rates will also start moving upward, as investors and lenders start shifting their portfolios into higher-yielding Treasury bills. Tightness in the money markets will begin to show up in rising interest rates before bank lending starts to slow down.

Time Lags in Monetary Policy

The level of production and employment is not affected immediately by the Fed's efforts to tighten the money markets. Just how long the lags may be is not clearly known. And, of course, they will differ as circumstances change in the money markets and the economy as a whole. Just to give you an idea of the range of opinion among economists on this matter, some believe that about half of the effect of open market operations will be felt within about six months and the bulk of the effect within a year. At the other end of the scale are those who argue that significant effects are not felt for perhaps nine months to a year, while the full effects require two to three years before appearing. Most economists just throw up their hands and refuse to guess.

But there is agreement on one point: *There are serious time lags between action by the Fed and effects on the money markets,* and even longer lags in effects on GNP. These lags make it imperative that the Fed move carefully. It is quite possible that actions by the Fed, taken many months ago in the direction of tight money, will start to catch hold right in the middle of an economic downturn. In the intervening year the economy may have moved from overheating to slack, requiring easy money instead of tight. But the perverse effects of monetary policies may be contributing to the downturn instead of leaning against it.

Just the opposite may also be true. The Fed may try to stimulate recovery from a recession by easing the money markets, only to discover that when the ease occurs the economy is pushing on the full-employment ceiling, and the money markets need tightening.

Information and Forecasting Problems

Time lags in the effects of monetary policy put a great premium on economic forecasting and adequacy of information. In order to know what to do today, the Fed must have a good notion of what the condition of the economy is likely to be in six months or a year, when the effects of today's actions or inactions will be strongly felt. Yet the Board of Governors doesn't even know what is going on currently. All it has is information on the recent past, and the more recent its information the less accurate it is likely to be. Incomplete and inaccurate facts are the raw materials for decisions.

With that raw material, the Fed must forecast the direction in which the economy will be moving, together with the extent of economic slack, at the time today's policies affect the money markets and the level of GNP. We shall examine some of the problems of economic forecasting further on, and show that they are severe. All of the same difficulties and limitations apply to the forecasts made by central bankers. But the Fed has an additional problem: the Board of Governors must coordinate its forecast of the time lag built into its monetary policies with its forecast for the economy as a whole. Both sides of the equation can be in error. When that happens serious mistakes in monetary policy can be made.

The Board of Governors cannot avoid the problem by doing nothing. That also is a policy, for it implies that the economy is operating on an even keel and nothing needs to be done. There are three policy alternatives. The Board can lean toward tighter money to slow down economic expansion and reduce present or potential inflationary pressures. It can lean toward easier money to encourage an increase in economic activity or keep an expansion going. Or it can take a neutral position, which means that the economy doesn't need a nudge in either direction. But in all three cases accurate information and good forecasts are necessary for optimum results.

Portfolio Adjustments and Monetary Policy

Banks are not the only economic units to adjust their asset portfolios to changing money market conditions. People who make their living in the money markets adjust more quickly, perhaps, and to a greater extent than others, but changes in the availability of money and credit affect everyone. And just like the adjustments made by banks, this general accommodation made by the public may have results unforeseen by the monetary authorities.

Suppose, for example, that the public has become accustomed to a gradually expanding supply of money and near money, that is, currency, demand deposits, and time deposits, to meet its needs for liquid assets, and they feel comfortable about the amount they hold in relation to their other assets. As the economic theorist would explain the situation, portfolios are in equilibrium and there is no tendency to sell real assets and acquire money, or vice versa.

If, then, the money supply should decline or fail to grow as fast as it had been growing, people will find themselves squeezed. They will try to bring their holdings of money back into equilibrium with their other assets. To do so they will sell some of their other financial assets, such as securities. Businessmen caught in a financial squeeze of this sort will try to reduce their inventories in order to rebuild their cash positions. They reduce their output and lay off workers or slow down their investment in new plants and equipment.

These efforts to return to a new liquidity equilibrium will, in a chain effect, influence the incomes and assets of others. They, in turn, will try to reach a new adjustment in which they feel comfortable again with their holdings of cash and other assets.

The net result for the money markets may be greater ease rather than greater tightness. The drive for greater liquidity could end with a decline in the demand for credit, a fall in the rate of interest and *easier* money! This could happen if businessmen tried to reduce their debts and obtain cash by reducing their inventories. Bankers would then find that their loan portfolios were shrinking. No one can tell ahead of time just how these longer-range adjustments throughout the economy will work. If the initial tightness in the money markets is too great, it may set in motion a recession that dampens business activity so much that slack appears in both economic activity and the money markets. Something like this seems to have happened in 1966.

Just the opposite chain of events can occur if the money supply should grow more rapidly than people expect. If people already hold all the money they want, they will use the increased liquidity to bid up the prices of securities, other financial assets, and goods and services. Initially, yields and interest rates will fall. But incomes will rise, business will improve, demand for credit will increase, and it is quite possible that an artificially high rate of expansion will occur. When this happens the money markets will tighten up, interest rates will rise, and the markets will end up tighter rather than easier.

The Uneven Impact of Monetary Policy

Adjustments in the money markets often affect some sectors of the economy more heavily than others. This is particularly true as the markets tighten up. There is some evidence, for example, that large borrowers are among the last to feel the effects of tight money, and small borrowers are the first. For example, residential construction is done by relatively small firms; and home purchases by individuals are relatively small transactions. In both construction loans and mortgage loans the availability of credit seems to be very quickly affected by tighter monetary conditions. Similarly, sales of consumer durable goods are quickly affected. Knowing this, banks often make an effort to cut back their loans evenly across the board in order to avoid possible recriminations and charges of unfairness to the "little guy."

The main differences in impact arise from differences in the extent to which companies rely on loans for their operations. Most large corporations generate a large portion of their capital for investment and operations out of their earnings. These firms will be little affected by tight money because they borrow little. Most small firms, on the other hand, operate to a substantial extent on borrowed funds, and traditionally finance much of their expansion with loans; these firms will be influenced significantly by tight money. They will find that, relative to the larger firms, their operations are restricted by the rationing of credit by banks and their costs are higher because interest rates have risen. Thus, even though banks may make an effort to avoid favoring large borrowers, these differences of operation between large and small firms tend to work toward de facto discrimination against small businessmen.

THE USES OF MONETARY POLICY

This chapter has been a complex one. We started out by examining the functions of a central bank and the organization of the Federal Reserve System. We then looked at the mechanics of the various instruments of credit control—open market operations, changes in reserve requirements, the Federal Reserve discount rate, and others. Discussion of the reserve position of the member banks brought us to a review of central bank policy as it has actually worked in the United States since World War II. This review made it clear that monetary management is a highly complex job. It entails much more than simple manipulation of the instruments of monetary management to keep the economy on the right track. Secondary reserves give the member banks a good deal of flexibility in responding to changes in money market conditions. Serious time lags appear between Federal Reserve actions and effects in the money markets. These problems are compounded by difficulties in forecasting. Finally, portfolio changes may bring about entirely unlooked-for results.

The policy implications of these limitations are important. *Monetary policy alone cannot be relied upon to achieve the stability needed by a modern economy.* The best that it can do is to "lean against the wind." If the economy is operating at levels below full employment, the Fed can promote ease in the money markets. But monetary ease cannot assure that banks will lend and businessmen will borrow in just the amounts necessary to bring the economy to full employment. Indeed, too much ease in the money markets could lead to a speculative expansion of economic activity that could not be sustained, leading to later difficulties in both the money markets and in output and employment.

On the other hand, if the economy is overheating and a policy of tighter money markets is adopted and carried out, excessive tightness can bring about a downturn in economic activity. This may well have happened in 1966–67, when the "credit crunch" of the fall of 1966 was followed by a fall in industrial production in the winter and a leveling off of the growth in GNP. Yet if the money markets are not tightened enough in such a situation, an inflationary expansion could get out of hand and also lead to a downturn later on. There is a fine line monetary policy must follow, a golden mean of neither too much nor too little, yet the line is very difficult to find and adhere to.

Complicating the problem is the possibility that significant shifts in monetary policy may induce the very swings in economic activity that the policy seeks to avoid. Turning the flow of credit up and down shifts the economic environment within which decisions are made, first to expansion and then to contraction. Unless used very gingerly, monetary policy might itself provoke a pattern of boom and bust. Anything more than "leaning against the wind" could be dangerous.

These problems have led many economists to recommend a shift in the focus of monetary policy away from concern with short-run economic fluctuations. They feel it should, instead, emphasize the long-run growth pattern of the economy. According to this view, the money supply should grow at a rate consistent with the full-employment growth rate of the economy as a whole. Relationships should be worked out between the long-term potential growth of GNP, on the one hand, and the supply of money and credit on the other. Monetary policy should concentrate on maintaining those relationships. Emphasis should be placed on keeping interest rates as low as possible in order to stimulate investment, recognizing, of course, that inflationary pressures and problems in the balance of international payments may force modification of such a policy. But, according to this view, the whole emphasis in monetary policy should be placed on the environment of long-range economic growth.

If this is done, other means will have to be found to handle the problem of short-run fluctuations in economic activity. Monetary policy can lean in one direction or the other, but it can't do the whole job. *Monetary policy and fiscal policy must supplement each other.* When monetary policy leans toward ease, the tax and expenditure policies of the federal government should be expansionary. The two policies will complement and assist each other in achieving the necessary increase in GNP. On the other hand, when monetary policy leans toward tightness, federal fiscal policy should be moving toward reductions in total spending, either through tax increases or spending reductions or both. Monetary policy is an essential instrument of economic policy, but it can be used only for limited purposes and has limited effects. It must be coordinated with fiscal policies if it is to have any effectiveness.

Summary

The basic rationale for management of the monetary system by a central bank is that the private operations of individuals and banks can bring instability that is not in the best interests of the economy as a whole. The central bank seeks to ease the money markets when slack appears in the economy and to tighten them when expansion becomes too rapid or threatens inflation, while at the same time facilitating economic growth.

The Federal Reserve System is the central bank of the United States. It comprises some 6,000 privately owned member banks, 12 Federal Reserve Banks and a Board of Governors. The central banking functions are carried out by the Board of Governors and the Federal Reserve banks.

The instruments of credit control available to "the Fed" are open market operations, changes in member bank reserve requirements, changes in the Federal Reserve discount rate, "moral suasion," and some special credit controls. The lending power of the member banks is determined by their reserve position, which in turn is controlled by the Fed through the amount of Federal Reserve credit made available, largely through open market operations. Relative ease or tightness in the money markets is maintained through that relationship.

Monetary policy has important drawbacks that limit its usefulness, including the fact that banks usually hold secondary reserves, the time lags that exist between actions by the Fed and their actual impact, difficulties of forecasting, portfolio adjustments in the business world, and the uneven impact of tight money on different sectors of the economy. As a result of these difficulties monetary policy alone cannot be expected to stabilize the economy alone. It must be used together with fiscal policy.

Key Concepts

Federal Reserve System.   The U.S. central bank, together with the member banks that do the bulk of the commercial banking business.

Open market operations.   Purchase and sale of government securities by the Federal Reserve banks.

Required reserve ratio.   The proportion of reserves to demand deposits required of member banks.

Federal Reserve discount rate.   The rate of interest charged by the Federal Reserve banks when member banks borrow. Sometimes referred to as the *rediscount rate.*

Federal Reserve credit.   The total amount of reserves made available to the member banks by the Fed.

Secondary reserves.   Highly liquid assets owned by banks that can be sold to provide cash for loans to customers.

Portfolio adjustments.   Shifts in the holding of liquid assets throughout the private sector in response to changes in the money markets.

Changes taking place in the monetary system can influence the level of economic activity. The money supply, by its impact on economic decisions, affects the level of output and employment. In this chapter we will examine these connecting links in more detail in order to tie in more closely the analysis of national income equilibrium with the equilibrium that tends to be established in the monetary sector.

THE RATE OF INTEREST

When anyone borrows money he pays a price for it. That price is the rate of interest.[1] From the lender's point of view, money, which is a highly liquid asset, is given up in exchange for a less liquid asset, such as a promissory note, a government bond, or some other promise to pay. The payment received by the lender in exchange for the use of his money is, in effect, a payment for giving up liquidity.

Liquidity Preference, Money, and Interest Rates

The stock of money (currency plus demand deposits) in the economy at any time must be held by someone, either in their pockets or in their checking accounts. There is no other place for it. For example, if there is more money available than people desire to hold in their cash balances, those who have it will buy other assets. They will accumulate more of such near moneys as government bonds and other securities. Doing so will cause the prices of those securities to rise. As their prices go up, their yield, or rate of return will go down. This relationship is a simple one and is illustrated in the box on page 321.

When the yield from existing securities falls, new securities can be sold only at interest rates equivalent to the yield on old securities of a similar type. Any attempt to sell them for more will find no takers. For example, if a bond with a face value of $1,000 and an annual payment of $80 sells in the securities markets for $1,050 (yielding

Money and the Level of Economic Activity

18

---

[1] There are many rates of interest in the economy, depending on the type of loan, the borrower, the length of time of the loan, uncertainty, risk, and other factors. They are, however, systematically related to each other in a continuum. To simplify matters, the term "rate of interest" will be used as a proxy for the range of rates of interest that actually prevails.

> ## PRICES AND YIELDS OF SECURITIES
>
> *Take as an example a government bond with a face value of $1,000 and an annual interest payment of $80 (8 percent of face value). Let the price rise to $1,100. The payment of $80 now represents a yield of only 7.27+ percent. Just the opposite happens if the price of the security should fall. The yield would rise above 8 percent.*
>
> *Figure that one out yourself, assuming a price of $900 for the bond in the example above. What is the yield at that price?* [2]

a return of 7.6+ percent), any newly issued $1,000 bond could be sold for about $1,000 if it carried an annual payment of $76. This is equivalent to an interest rate of 7.6 percent, which is the same as the yield that could be obtained by buying an old bond on the open market. The basic idea is a simple one: the desire for liquidity (given the existing supply of money) determines the prices of securities *and* the rates of interest at which new loans can be made.

The desire for liquidity is given a special name by economists: *liquidity preference*. It can be defined as the amount of cash that economic units will be willing to hold at various rates of interest. If interest rates are high, investors will be willing to hold only relatively small amounts of money in cash. On the other hand, if interest rates are low they will have less desire to lend or buy securities and will hold more of their assets in cash. Shown on a diagram, the liquidity preference schedule will look like Figure 18-1.

The liquidity preference schedule is like a demand curve for money. The vertical axis shows the price of money and the horizontal axis shows the amount of money. The schedule itself shows how much money will be held at the various prices, just as a demand curve shows how much of a commodity consumers will be willing to buy at various prices. Just as a demand curve will shift its position as consumer tastes change, so the liquidity preference schedule will shift as the desire for liquidity changes. An increase in the willingness to hold cash shifts the schedule to the right (Figure 18-2), a decrease shifts it to the left (Figure 18-3).

The Monetary Equilibrium

The liquidity preferences of economic units interact with the supply of cash available to them to determine the rate of interest. This occurs in much the same way that demand and supply interact to determine the price of a com-

---

[2] About 8.9 percent. Did you get it right?

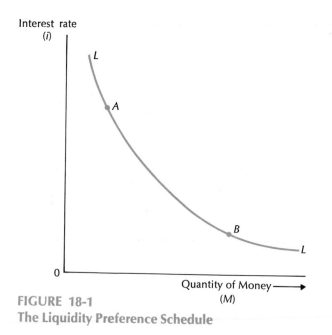

FIGURE 18-1
The Liquidity Preference Schedule

At high rates of interest (and high rates of return on security investments, economic
units will be willing to hold only small amounts of cash, *A*. When interest rates
are lower a larger amount of cash will be held, *B*.

Note how the liquidity preference schedule, *LL*, becomes parallel to the axes
at its extremities: at the upper level because of the need for some cash to carry on
normal economic activities, and at the lower level because yields on securities
are too low to cause holders of cash to shift their holdings. As more cash is acquired
it is merely held as money rather than being used to buy securities.

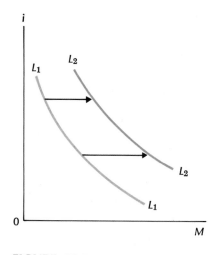

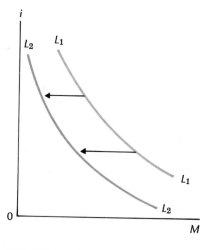

FIGURE 18-2
Liquidity Preference Increases

FIGURE 18-3
Liquidity Preference Decreases

modity. With a given liquidity preference schedule and a given supply of money, there is a unique rate of interest at which economic units will be willing to hold the existing amount of money. This condition defines the simple monetary equilibrium toward which the money markets will tend to gravitate. It is shown in Figure 18-4.

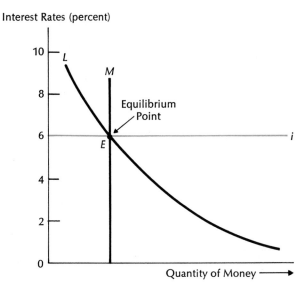

Interest Rates (percent)

FIGURE 18-4
Simple Monetary Equilibrium

E is the point at which the amount of money people wish to hold equals the amount available to be held. This equality determines the rate of interest.

If the rate of interest were higher, M would exceed L, people would buy securities, and their prices would rise and yields fall, bringing interest rates down toward i. Just the opposite would occur if interest rates were below the i shown in the diagram. L would exceed M, securities would be sold, their prices would fall and their yields would rise, and interest rates would go up.

Figure 18-5 shows what would happen if the quantity of money were to increase while the desire for liquidity remained the same. Interest rates would fall. On the other hand, interest rates would rise if the supply of money fell while liquidity preferences remained the same (Figure 18-6).

We can also show what would happen if the desire for liquidity were to change while the quantity of money remained the same. Figure 18-7 shows the effect of an increase in the desire for liquidity. Figure 18-8 shows what happens when the desire for liquidity decreases.

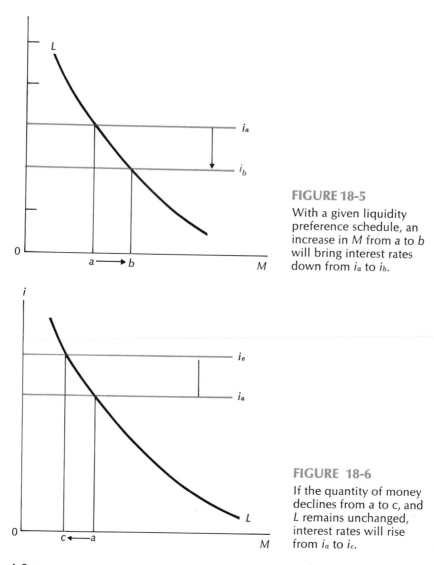

FIGURE 18-5

With a given liquidity preference schedule, an increase in M from a to b will bring interest rates down from i_a to i_b.

FIGURE 18-6

If the quantity of money declines from a to c, and L remains unchanged, interest rates will rise from i_a to i_c.

A Summary

The rate of interest is a price, determined in the money markets, that equates the demand for liquidity (liquidity preference) with the supply of liquidity (the quantity of money). In that sense it is no different from any other price. The money markets are like any other markets in that they tend toward an equilibrium in which the rate of interest serves to balance the quantity of money and the liquidity preferences of people who hold money and other assets. This monetary equilibrium does not stand alone, however. The rate of interest affects the level of investment and thereby the level of output and income. The level of output and income affects, in turn, attitudes of people toward business affairs and their desire for liquidity. There is a mutual interaction between the monetary equilibrium and the equilibrium level of national income.

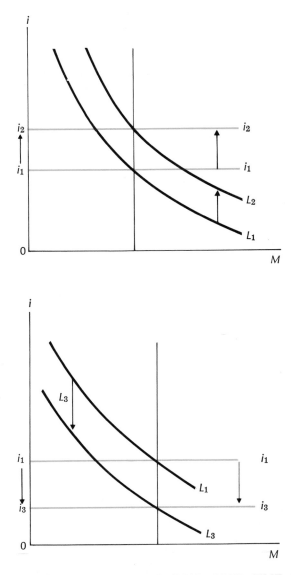

FIGURE 18-7

As the desire for liquidity rises from L_1 to L_2, assets are sold. The fall in their price brings yields and interest rates up from i_1 to i_2. At the new interest rates the owners of assets would just as soon hold on to them as sell them, and a new monetary equilibrium has been established.

FIGURE 18-8

As the desire for liquidity falls from L_1 to L_3, with no change in the quantity of money, interest rates fall from i_1 to i_3.

INVESTMENT DECISIONS AND THE RATE OF INTEREST

Businessmen are continually faced with a wide and large variety of investment opportunities. The owner of a grocery store, for example, may be able to expand his business and enlarge his profits by putting in a new line of prepared gourmet foods. Or he may add delivery services to extend the area he serves. Or he may attract new customers by adding to his advertising budget. In each case he will have to invest additional capital for which he will have to pay a price. And in each case he will expect the expansion to add to his revenues.

If the businessman is rational, he will make no investment unless the rate of return he expects from it is greater than the cost of capital (which is the interest rate on the money he borrows). Only if that is the case can he expect to add to his profits. He will not stop with one new idea, either. As long as he can find any investment for which the expected rate of return is greater than the cost of capital, he will try to borrow the money for it. This assumes, of course, that he has the capacity to manage it; otherwise it is not a feasible alternative for him. When the rate of interest is greater than the expected rate of return on new investment, however, it would be foolish to expand further.

The Marginal Efficiency of Investment

The marginal efficiency of investment is the name economists give to the expected rate of return on new investment.[3] It can be shown on a diagram, as in Figure 18-9.

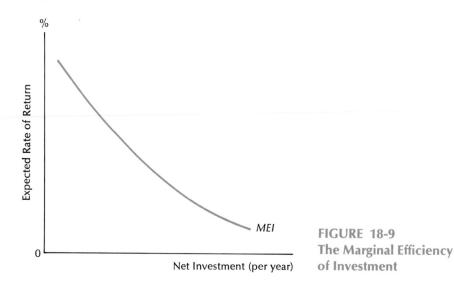

FIGURE 18-9
The Marginal Efficiency
of Investment

The schedule of the marginal efficiency of investment slopes downward and to the right, like a demand curve. The reason is that rational businessmen will first make the most profitable (expected) investments, saving the less profitable ones for later. As the total amount invested is increased, each succeeding investment has a slightly lower expected rate of return than the last, and so on. The rate of return on the last dollar invested declines in the pattern shown by the *MEI* schedule in Figure 18-9.

It is important to remember, however, that the *MEI* schedule shows *expected* rates of return on new investment. It is not a phenomenon that can be measured in the marketplace, like the quantity of money or the rate of interest. It is a psychological phenomenon that depends on the state of mind

---

[3] In this terminology "marginal" refers to the fact that we are dealing with increases to or decreases from a total, while "efficiency" refers to the expected rate of return. We could use the term "expected marginal rate of return on investment," but that phrase is just too big a mind-breaker.

of businessmen. It can fluctuate widely from time to time, depending on how businessmen view their prospects for the future. Nevertheless, that estimation of the course of future events is crucial in determining investment decisions.

The Rate of Interest and the Level of Investment

We are now able to connect changes in the rate of interest with changes in the level of investment. Businessmen can be expected to push the level of investment up to the amount at which the rate of interest is equal to the marginal efficiency of investment. Figure 18-10 shows the situation.

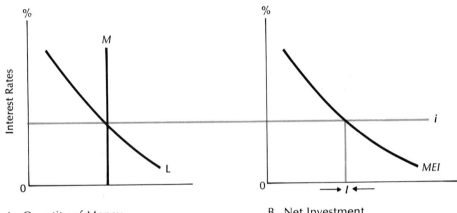

A. Quantity of Money   B. Net Investment

FIGURE 18-10
Investment and the Rate of Interest

Figure 18-10A shows how the level of interest rates is determined by the liquidity preference schedule and the quantity of money. Figure 18-10B shows how that rate of interest, together with the marginal efficiency of investment schedule, determines the amount of investment. As long as the *MEI* schedule lies above the rate of interest, an additional amount of investment is expected to add more to revenues than the money would cost. Investment will be increased up to the level at which $i = MEI$. Beyond the point at which $i = MEI$, the cost of the investment is greater than the returns that can be expected. This investment will not be made.

In this link between the monetary sector and the level of national income, the equilibrium in the money markets in which $M = L$, determining the rate of interest, is supplemented by another equilibrium in which $i = MEI$, determining the level of investment.

We can manipulate Figure 18-10B to become more familiar with the relationships it involves. For example, what happens if businessmen become more optimistic than they were earlier, that is, if their expectations about the future improve? The *MEI* curve would shift to the right; and we should expect them to increase their investment expenditures, as in Figure 18-11.

If such a change were to occur when the economy was already at full employment, the resultant multiplied increase in aggregate demand would set in motion inflationary price increases. The monetary authorities could then be expected to take action to raise interest rates. The effect would be to reduce the level of investment, as shown in Figure 18-12. Similar shifts would occur, but in the opposite direction, if businessmen became more pessimistic or if the monetary authorities brought interest rates down. You can work out these diagrams yourself.

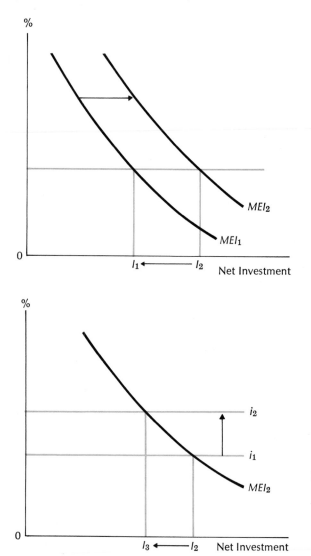

FIGURE 18-11

Optimism about the future shifts the *MEI* curve to the right. With no change in the rate of interest, investment will rise from I_1 to I_2.

FIGURE 18-12

An increase in interest rates from i_1 to i_2 causes the level of investment to fall from I_2 to I_3, assuming no further shift in the *MEI* schedule.

MONEY AND AGGREGATE DEMAND

We can now take the final step in linking the monetary sector to the level of aggregate demand. The equilibrium level of national income or net national product was shown in Chapter 11 to be the level at which desired savings equals desired investment as in Figure 18-13.

We have just finished showing how the level of net investment is determined, given the schedule of the marginal efficiency of investment, by the level of the rate of interest. Since the rate of interest is determined in the

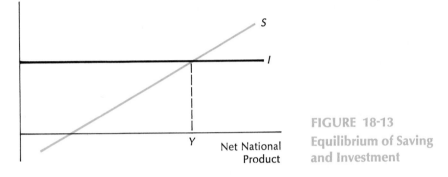

FIGURE 18-13
Equilibrium of Saving
and Investment

money markets, and in turn influences the level of investment, while investment affects the level of aggregate demand, there is a clear linkage between the monetary sector and the level of output and employment. Indeed, the vertical axis of Figure 18-13 is the same as the horizontal axis of Figure 18-10B. This enables us to show the linkage visually in Figure 18-14.

The rate of interest is determined by the intersection of the liquidity preference schedule and the quantity of money schedule in Figure 18-14A. The level of investment is determined by the intersection of the rate of interest with the marginal efficiency of investment schedule in Figure 18-14B. Finally, the investment schedule intersects with the propensity-to-save schedule to determine the level of net national product in Figure 18-14C. We have linked the monetary equilibrium ($L = M$) to the real equilibrium ($S = I$).

SOME QUALIFICATIONS

The synthesis of monetary and national income equilibria developed here has some limitations. In the first place, the rate of interest affects several important elements of the national income equilibrium in addition to business investment. The most important are consumer purchases of durable goods and housing construction. Expenditures for those purposes influence aggregate demand and the net national product, just as business investment does.

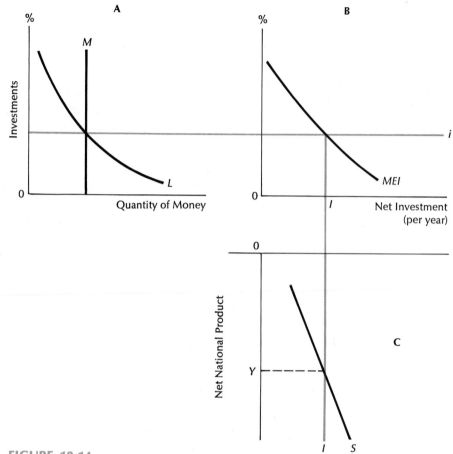

FIGURE 18-14
The Monetary Sector and the National Income Equilibrium

They might be included in the analysis at the same intermediate stage as business investment, perhaps in the following fashion:

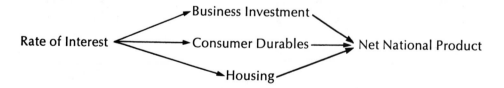

While there is no problem in postulating these relationships, the theoretical links to housing and consumer durables are lacking. Only for business investment is there a precise link, by way of the equality of savings and investment, to the equilibrium level of net national product.

A second difficulty lies in feedbacks from the level of NNP to the psychological variables of liquidity preference and the marginal efficiency of capital. We know that attitudes toward liquidity are influenced by the level of economic activity and the way it changes. The same is true of business expectations. Yet these feedbacks into the mechanism by which the two equilibria are maintained are not spelled out in the analysis.

A MORE GENERAL APPROACH

In recent years economists have come to analyze the impact of the monetary sector on the level of output and income in broader terms. This extension of the theory brings into the analysis the full range of assets held by people and economic units, from cash through securities to income-producing plant and equipment. It is based on the ability of people to shift their holdings of assets from one form to another, depending on the relative advantages expected to be derived from each. Since money is one form in which assets can be held, and the interest rate defines its earning power, a change in the monetary sector of the economy will permeate all other sectors by way of the asset holdings of economic units. The mechanisms by which those adjustments are transmitted from the monetary to the real sector are called *portfolio effects, wealth effects,* and *credit availability effects.*

Portfolio Effects

When the earnings (or expected earnings) from an asset change, the desire of investors to hold that asset will also change. An industrial enterprise, for example, may find its profitability rise by 10 percent. Its securities will become more attractive to investors and their prices will rise. To buy the more profitable asset, investors will sell other assets whose earnings have not risen, and their prices will sag. The price rise in one and the fall for the others will continue until an equilibrium is established in the prices of the various assets such that investors will no longer be willing to shift their holdings.

The same sort of adjustment occurs when the monetary authorities seek to ease or tighten credit. Let us start with an open market purchase of Treasury bills by the Federal Reserve System and trace its effects. The purchase will directly increase the reserves of member banks. The new free reserves can then be used to increase loans to business and consumers, thereby directly increasing total spending and aggregate demand. In addition, there are indirect results stemming from changes in the prices of securities and their yield.

The price of Treasury bills will rise somewhat, because of Federal Reserve buying. As we already know, this reduces their yield and is equivalent to a decline in the rate of interest. Banks, also, will use some of their free reserves to buy income-yielding securities, and the same thing will happen to their prices and yields.

Since nothing has happened to the earnings of industrial enterprises—the yield on investment in real capital has not changed—households and other economic units will be thrown out of equilibrium. They will tend to sell financial assets whose yields have fallen and buy real assets (or the securities that represent them) whose yields have not fallen. This is one important reason why the stock market averages rise when interest rates fall, and fall when interest rates rise. Fundamentally, what happens is that the desire to own real assets increases relative to the existing supply, and the price of real assets rises. Gradually, this increased demand will be met by increased output of capital goods: plant and equipment, inventories, housing and durable consumer goods. The whole real sector of the economy feels the stimulus, and output and employment rise.

Wealth Effects

Wealth effects depend on the value of assets held by households and business units. As the prices of securities go up because of Federal Reserve purchases of Treasury bills and the purchases made by banks with a portion of their free reserves, and as the demand for real assets increases their price, the value of assets throughout the economy is increased. Everyone's wealth is enlarged because the market price of both financial and real assets has been raised. This increase in wealth, even though it is only an increase in monetary value, will affect consumption and savings.

Every economic unit holds assets for a variety of purposes, and savings add to those assets. When price increases raise the value of asset holdings, there is less need to save. More funds become available for consumption or current spending. Of course, the flow of spending is directly increased by the loans to consumers and business firms that are made by banks out of newly created free reserves. But, in addition, there is the indirect effect on consumption spending of the rise in the value of wealth that is triggered by monetary ease and the consequent rise in the value of assets.

Credit Availability Effects

Portfolio and wealth effects are the chief means by which monetary policy affects economic activity. In addition, the ways in which some sectors of the economy are financed give monetary policy special leverage there. This is particularly true in housing construction and expenditures of local governments.

When tight money and high interest rates are generated by monetary policy, the flow of funds into mortgage financing is usually diminished. Savings that formerly flowed into savings and loan associations (which concentrate on mortgage lending) tend to shift to commercial banks, because banks can usually raise the rate of interest they pay on savings accounts more rapidly than savings and loan associations. Commercial banks tend to cut down on their mortgage loans when money is tight in order to accommodate their regular business customers. Finally, as interest rates rise, the yield on corporate bonds generally moves up more rapidly than yields on mortgages. The result of all of these forces, which can be exaggerated by low interest rates on government-sponsored FHA and VA mortgages and by regulation of interest rates charged by savings and loan associations, is to cut back the financing of housing construction more than other sectors of the economy.

Local government spending is affected by tight money in two ways. Legal restrictions often limit the interest rates local governments are permitted to pay when they sell bonds. And voters are less likely to approve new bond issues when interest rates are high and they feel other economic pressures. The result is that building of schools and other urban facilities tends to be affected more than economic activity in general when money is tight.

Credit availability also affects small business more than big business when money is tight. Big borrowers have more bargaining power in dealing with banks, and they generate more of their capital through retained earnings than small firms do. The smaller firm has a greater need for credit, as a general rule, and tends to be pushed toward the back of the line when credit availability tightens.

THE MONETARY AND REAL EQUILIBRIA

Monetary policy, operating through portfolio, wealth, and credit availability effects, influences levels of income, consumer spending, and business investment. The usual amplification of the initial impact through the multiplier, induced investment, and the acceleration principle then comes into play. As economic units seek to readjust their holdings of assets in response to changes in the yield and price of those assets, their spending decisions change and the level of output and income moves toward a new equilibrium. The process will continue until a new monetary equilibrium is achieved in which the existing supply of money is willingly held at the existing rate of interest. While this equilibrium is being achieved, the level of output and income is also moving to a new equilibrium in which desired investment is equal to desired savings. The mutual adjustment of the two equilibrium processes brings a general equilibrium that involves both the monetary and real sectors.

The adjustment process can also start in the real sector. For example, the expected rate of return on new investment can change in response to changing business attitudes about future events. Changes in the prices of investment assets will occur and their yields will change. This development will, in turn, affect attitudes toward the holding of cash assets, and the adjustment will be spread into the monetary sector. Wherever it starts, the movement toward a new equilibrium will involve both the level of economic activity and the monetary system.

At this stage economists have not been able to quantify the effects that we have traced here. But knowing the principal outlines has both greatly enriched and complicated the management of monetary policy. Above all, it has tended to make monetary policy much more cautious. If the actions of the monetary authorities have such a pervasive effect on the economy as a whole, it behooves the authorities to move slowly rather than quickly, making small changes rather than large and observing carefully all the while to evaluate the impact of their actions.

Summary

Changes in the monetary sector are reflected in changes in the level of economic activity as each sector seeks an equilibrium consistent with the other. The rate of interest is determined by the interaction of liquidity preference and the quantity of money. Interest rates, together with the marginal efficiency of investment, determine the amount of investment. Investment, together with the propensity to save, determines the level of economic activity.

This simple model can be elaborated to a more general set of relationships connecting the monetary and real equilibria, involving portfolio effects, wealth effects, and credit rationing effects of changes in the monetary sector. The economy tends toward a general equilibrium in which the existing supply of money is willingly held at the same time that desired savings equals desired investment.

The Appendix develops the concept of this general equilibrium in a more formal fashion.

Key Concepts

Liquidity preference.   The desire for liquidity. More formally: the amount of cash economic units will be willing to hold at various rates of interest. In this context, the rate of interest is the payment necessary to induce a lender to give up the liquidity embodied in cash.

Marginal efficiency of investment.   The expected rate of return on new investment.

Cost of capital.   The cost to the borrower of funds obtained for investment. In the context of this chapter it is taken as equal to the rate of interest.

Portfolio effects.   The impact of shifting asset holdings on the level of economic activity. Related to changes in the earnings of assets.

Wealth effects.   The impact of changes in the value of assets on the level of economic activity.

Credit rationing effects.   The impact of uneven availability of credit on the level of economic activity.

Monetary equilibrium.   That condition in the money markets in which the existing supply of money is willingly held by economic units.

Real equilibrium.   The level of economic activity at which desired savings equals desired investment.

Appendix 18

THE MONETARY EQUILIBRIUM AND THE
REAL EQUILIBRIUM FURTHER DEVELOPED

The linkages between the monetary equilibrium ($L = M$) and the real equilibrium ($I = S$) can be developed further into a more general set of relationships. We start with the proposition that any number of monetary equilibria are possible. Any rate of interest can be produced by a high demand for liquidity and a large quantity of money *or* by a low liquidity preference and a relatively small amount of money. In either case the $L = M$ equilibrium can be achieved.

The same is true of the real equilibrium. Any level of net national product can be produced by a high propensity to save and large amounts of investment *or* by a low propensity to save and small amounts of investment. Either one can bring about the $I = S$ equilibrium.

This situation inevitably raises the question: Is there a unique combination of net national product and rate of interest at which both the monetary sector and the real sector have found their individual equilibria? Intuitively one would argue that there must be such a combination. Can it be demonstrated?

THE LM CURVE

There are many combinations of net national product and interest rate at which the existing money supply will be willingly held by people and business firms, that is, at which $L = M$. A low net national product and low interest rate may do it at a time when the economy is depressed, and a high net national product and high interest rate will serve at times of greater prosperity. A graph can show all of the combinations of net national product and interest rate that will provide for an $L = M$ equilibrium, assuming no change in the quantity of money. Such a graph is Figure 18-15, with the resulting curve labeled *LM*, to indicate that at each point on the curve $L = M$.

The *LM* curve slopes upward to the right. The lower tail of the curve is horizontal. It indicates that at very low rates of interest there is no further reduction of interest rates that will get holders of cash to reduce their liquidity still further. This situation occurred during some of the worst years of the Great Depression of the 1930s, when increases in the quantity of money were ineffective in driving interest rates down any further from their already low levels. Holders of cash could not be persuaded to buy more assets, so the prices of those assets did not rise and bring interest rates down.

The upper tail of the *LM* curve is vertical. This shows the situation of full-employment inflation. Since net national product cannot rise, a continued growth in the money supply requires higher interest rates for maintenance of the monetary ($L = M$) equilibrium.

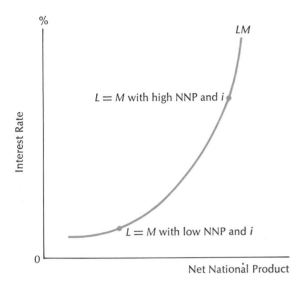

FIGURE 18-15
The LM Curve

In between the two tails of the *LM* curve, the monetary equilibrium is sustained partly by changes in the level of output and partly by changes in interest rates (which is, in itself, an important point to remember).

Moving Along the LM Curve

We can analyze what will happen if the net national product rises while the money supply remains constant. As economic activity rises, the need for money to carry on normal economic activity will increase. That is, the desire for liquidity will grow. To satisfy that desire, people and business firms will sell some of their other assets to get more cash. Prices of securities will decline, causing their yields to rise, which is equivalent to an increase in interest rates. In this fashion, a rise in net national product will bring an increase in L, which in turn will trigger higher interest rates until a new $L = M$ equilibrium is established. A higher level of net national product *and* higher interest rates are necessary to sustain the $L = M$ equilibrium as economic activity expands, so long as there is no change in the money supply.

Shifting the LM Curve

Now let us assume that for reasons of their own, the monetary authorities do not want interest rates to rise. They may wish, for example, to channel all of the stimulus for economic expansion into increases in output rather than partly into higher interest rates. If so, they will take steps to increase the money supply. With additional money available, the added demand for cash associated with an increase in economic activity could be satisfied without an increase in interest rates. This is equivalent to shifting the *LM* curve to the right, shown in Figure 18-16.

The *LM* curve can also shift because of changes in liquidity preference. Suppose businessmen become more optimistic about the future. They will reduce their cash balances to acquire assets, partly to be able to produce more in the future and partly because they expect profits and prices to rise. Purchase of assets will raise their prices, bringing yields and interest rates down. This will continue until interest rates

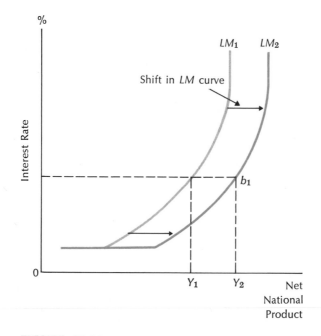

FIGURE 18-16
Shifting the LM Curve by Increasing the Money Supply

As NNP increases, the monetary authorities increase the money supply in order
to keep interest rates stable. The result is a shift of the LM curve to the right and an
increase in NNP from Y_1 to a new equilibrium at Y_2. What has happened is that
the increased demand for money has been fully satisfied through the enlarged
supply of money, and securities have not been sold to increase liquidity.

fall far enough (and prices of assets rise far enough) to halt any further efforts to
shift the composition of portfolios from cash to other assets. A new position for
the LM curve will have been established, as shown in Figure 18-17.

For purposes of policy formulation, however, shifts in the LM curve cannot be
induced by bringing about changes in the liquidity preference schedule. Policy makers
must rely on changes in the money supply if they wish to move the LM curve.

THE IS CURVE

In the real sector of the economy, there is a relationship similar to the LM curve of the
monetary sector. It is the IS curve, so called after the real equilibrium in which $I = S$.[4] Just as with the LM curve, there are a large number of possible $I = S$ equilibria
that are possible. Assuming a given propensity to save and a given marginal efficiency
of investment, a low interest rate and a high net national product could produce
an $I = S$ equilibrium. The low interest rate would be necessary to stimulate enough
investment to balance the large savings made when NNP is high. Conversely, a low

---

[4] Keep in mind in this chapter that an equilibrium $I = S$ situation means that desired investment
equals desired savings.

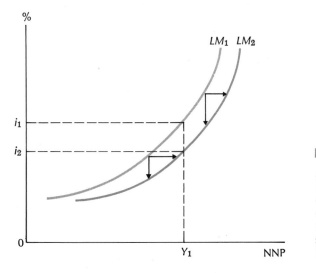

FIGURE 18-17

A decreased desire for liquidity, assuming no change in NNP and the stock of money, will bring interest rates down, indicating a shift to the right in the LM curve.

NNP and high interest rate could also result in $I = S$. Savings would be relatively small because of the low NNP, and the high interest rate would be needed to hold desired investment at that level. The series of possible $I = S$ equilibria can be drawn on a diagram with the same axes as the LM curve. It is shown in Figure 18-18.

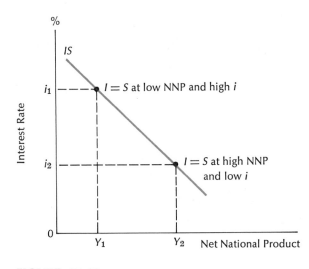

FIGURE 18-18
The IS Curve

At point $Y_1 i_1$ the savings that would result from NNP of Y_1 would be equal to the desired investment at interest rate i_1. If NNP were to increase to Y_2 the interest rate would have to fall to i_2 in order to increase I so that it would equal the S engendered by NNP at the higher level. This assumes, of course, no change in either the propensity to save or the expectations of businessmen.

Shifting the IS Curve

The *IS* curve can move around, but it does not shift in direct response to changes in the money supply. Rather, it moves if either the expectations of businessmen change or the propensity to save changes.

Suppose businessmen become more optimistic. The amount they are willing to invest at the existing rate of interest will be greater. With no change in the propensity to save, the increased desire to invest will trigger a growth in output. Net national product will rise until the increased savings generated by a higher NNP equals the higher level of desired investment. This is equivalent to a shift to the right of the *IS* curve, shown in Figure 18-19.

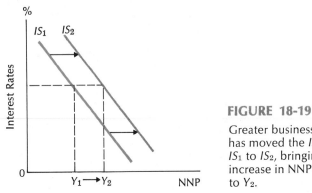

FIGURE 18-19

Greater business optimism
has moved the *IS* curve from
IS₁ to *IS₂*, bringing an
increase in NNP from Y_1
to Y_2.

The *IS* curve also responds to changes in the propensity to save. An increase in the propensity to save will shift the *IS* curve to the left, for example, assuming no change in business expectations as shown in Figure 18-20.

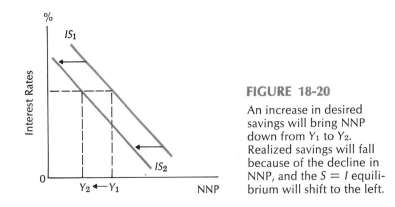

FIGURE 18-20

An increase in desired
savings will bring NNP
down from Y_1 to Y_2.
Realized savings will fall
because of the decline in
NNP, and the $S = I$ equilibrium will shift to the left.

Of course, all we have been doing here is manipulation of curves on a graph. Those manipulations are proxies for changes that go on in the real world, however. Remember that business expectations can change rapidly, making the marginal efficiency of capital highly volatile, while the propensity to save is much more stable (especially in the long run). Yet out of the continual shifts and changes that take place, a pervasive tendency to arrive at a' new equilibrium is operating, in which the level of NNP and the rate of interest are the variables that adjust as the new equilibrium is approached.

THE IS – LM EQUILIBRIUM

We can now put together the *IS* and *LM* curves to arrive at an equilibrium between the real sector of the economy (where $I = S$) and the monetary sector (where $L = M$). We shall assume that the following variables are held constant (in order to keep the curves from jumping around on the page):

1. The liquidity preference schedule.
2. The propensity-to-save schedule.
3. The marginal efficiency of investment schedule.

This is equivalent to saying that the economy's psychological environment does not change: the desire for cash, the desire to save, and business expectations are caught as if a motion picture has suddenly become a still photograph.

We shall also assume a given money supply as the fourth factor in the determination of the equilibrium. Under these conditions the *IS* curve and the *LM* curve are defined and held in place, as in Figure 18-21.

Figure 18-21 shows the unique equilibrium produced by the combination of interest rate and net national product at which both the national income equilibrium ($I = S$) and the monetary equilibrium ($L = M$) are achieved. To understand why only that point can be an equilibrium, and no other, we could compare the Y_1 level of net national product with any other, say Y_2.

If NNP is at Y_2, the interest rate that causes economic units to hold all of the money supply is i_2 (see Figure 18-22). But such a low interest rate will call forth a much larger amount of investment than is necessary to maintain NNP at the level of Y_2. The investment programs of businessmen will therefore set in motion an increase in NNP. As NNP moves up from Y_2 toward Y_1, the need for cash balances will rise. Assuming no increase in the money supply, interest rates will rise as assets are sold to get cash and the asset yields fall. That is, maintenance of the monetary equilibrium means that the adjustment from the Y_2 disequilibrium moves up the *LM* curve toward the point at which it is crossed by the *IS* curve (Figure 18-23). Once NNP has reached the level of Y_1, the desired level of investment at the existing interest rate just equals desired savings at Y_1, bringing about a national income equilibrium ($I = S$) consistent with the monetary equilibrium ($L = M$).

This example of the adjustment process is only one of several that could have been used to illustrate the movement toward equilibrium. Try to discover how the process would work if NNP were greater than Y_1, or if the interest rate were above the equilibrium level of i_1.

SHIFTS IN THE IS AND LM CURVES

A shift in either the *IS* curve or the *LM* curve will change the equilibrium point. A new combination of NNP and *i* will emerge to bring both the monetary and the real sectors into equilibrium.

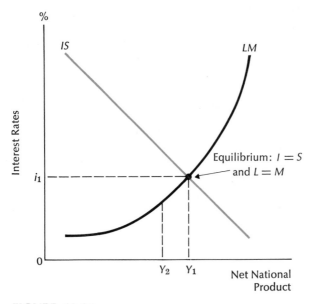

FIGURE 18-21

Equilibrium Between the Real and the Monetary Sectors of the Economy

In the money markets, interest rate i and a net national product of Y_1 will equate the demand for money with the supply available. All of the money available will be willingly held in cash balances.

The same combination of interest rate and NNP will equate the savings desired by income receivers with the investment businessmen wish to make.

The equilibrium point $(Y_1 i_1)$ is the only one which will bring about that double equilibrium. It is the only one consistent with both the propensity to save and marginal efficiency of investment schedules which determine the location of the IS curve, and the liquidity preference and money supply which place the LM curve.

The important point to remember is that both the IS and LM curves can be shifted by public policy measures. Changing the money supply through actions of the Federal Reserve System will affect the monetary equilibria and shift the LM curve. An increase in the money supply will shift it to the right, while a decrease will shift it to the left, if there are no other changes in the system.

On the other hand, changes in fiscal policy will affect the location of the IS curve. The tax and expenditure policies of the federal government affect the level of NNP. Net national product in turn will influence the amount saved and the desire to invest, causing a shift in the IS curve.

Perhaps the best way to keep in mind the way public policy affects the IS–LM equilibrium is to remember that monetary policy does not shift the IS curve, but can shift the LM curve, while fiscal policy does not shift the LM curve but does affect the location of the IS curve. We illustrate the different ways in which these two types of public policy affect the equilibrium in Figure 18-24.

Figure 18-24 helps us to understand better how monetary policy affects the level of investment and the level of net national product. Earlier in Chapter 18 we ex-

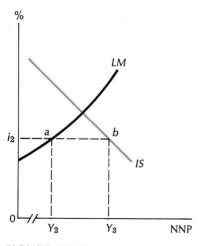

FIGURE 18-22

This portion of Figure 18-21 shows
the disequilibrium when NNP
$= Y_2$. The desired investment
called forth by interest rate i_2
would produce an equilibrium
NNP of Y_3 rather than Y_2. The
monetary equilibrium at a is not
consistent with the national income equilibrium at b.

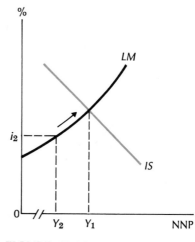

FIGURE 18-23

The path of adjustment from Y_2
moves up the LM curve until
the Y_1 level of NNP is reached.

plained a much simpler set of relationships in which the quantity of money, together
with the economy's liquidity preference schedule, determines the rate of interest.
The rate of interest, together with the marginal efficiency of investment, determines
the level of investment. Investment, in conjunction with the propensity to save,
then determines the equilibrium level of net national product. Although this set
of relationships is highly specific, it isn't general enough, as we can now see. The
relationships are far more complex, involving all units in the economy, not only
those who make investment decisions.

To recapitulate, the *IS–LM* analysis shows how the general adjustment of the entire
economy takes place. Let an increase in the money supply shift the *LM* curve. With
no change in the location of the *IS* curve, as in Figure 18-24A, a new equilibrium will
be established at a higher level of NNP, with a higher level of investment and lower
interest rates. A complex pattern of adjustment takes place in the move to the new
equilibrium, involving all economic units. Financial institutions use additional funds
to add to their portfolios, and as a result interest rates go down. Consumers buy
more, including durable goods and housing as well as nondurables. Businessmen
expand their output, requiring larger inventories and expansion of plant and equipment. The adjustment to the new equilibrium proceeds along the path of the *IS*
curve (still in Figure 18-24A) until a new monetary equilibrium is established at a
point at which both $L = M$ and $I = S$, where the new *LM* curve crosses the *IS* curve.

The *IS–LM* analysis has the advantage of generality. All of the effects of changes
in the monetary sector are embodied in the general principle of the $L = M$ equi-

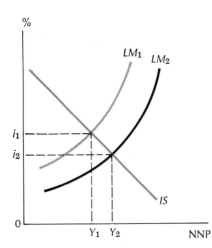

FIGURE 18-24
Public Policy and the
IS–LM Equilibrium

A. Monetary Policy Is Used to Raise NNP. An
increase in the money supply shifts the *LM*
equilibrium to the right, bringing an increase
in NNP from Y_1 to Y_2, and a decline in
interest rates from i_1 to i_2.

B. Fiscal Policy Is Used to Raise NNP. With
no change in the money supply, fiscal policy
(taxes and expenditures) moves the NNP
from Y_1 to Y_2, bringing with it a shift in the
IS curve to IS_2 and a consequent rise in
interest rates from i_1 to i_2.

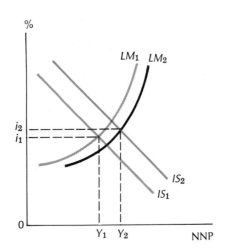

C. Fiscal and Monetary Policy Are Used
Together to Raise NNP. By using monetary
and fiscal policy together, the same
increase in NNP can be obtained, with a
smaller increase in interest rates. The
adjustments in both fiscal policy and
monetary policy will be smaller than if
either had to do the job alone.

librium and shifts in the *LM* curve. The same is true of the real sector, the $I = S$ equilibrium, and the *IS* curve. The analysis does not depend solely on reactions in the business community, but includes consumers as well, not to mention financial institutions.

But some of the gains of generality are lost when we get down to specifics. Exactly how are the various units of the economy likely to react, in specific situations, to policies such as in income tax surcharge, a decrease in federal expenditures, or a tightening of the money supply? Here is where economics becomes both an art and an empirical science, and public policy becomes a combination of theoretical analysis, empirical knowledge of economic behavior, and good (or bad) judgment. In the case of the *IS–LM* analysis, which is a relatively recent development in national income and monetary theory, a whole series of unanswered questions have been and are being raised about how behavior in the monetary and real sectors is related to the process of arriving at and sustaining a general economic equilibrium.

There is no doubt, however, about the reality of that equilibrium and the fact that the economy is continually seeking it.

Inflation

19

Every age has its demons, its great fears, its evil spirits. Salem had its witches; the medieval church, its heretics. To the economists who lived during the 1930s, the great fear was depression and unemployment. But after the exorcising of that devil from the body economic through the development of Keynesian macroeconomic theory and policy, a new threat has appeared. Inflation! This mysterious and misunderstood economic malady is the great bogey of our time. It is pictured as leading to economic collapse. It is feared as the destroyer of all that people have striven for and achieved. It is charged with eroding the inner fiber of the economy. It is seen as the golem that has taken up residence in the soul of the economic system.

Chapter 7 deflated the bogey of inflation somewhat. It showed that there has not been a consistent long-term trend toward higher prices in the U.S. economy, and that prices in the last quarter century have been remarkably stable, in spite of an upward creep. But the earlier discussion did raise a number of questions about price levels that deserve more extensive treatment.

First, some facts about recent trends. Figure 19-1 shows the movement of both consumer's and wholesale prices in the United States from 1946 through 1970. Three periods of relatively rapid increases are shown, separated by periods of relative stability. The first period of inflation was 1946–48, when the suppressed price increases of the war years could no longer be held in check. In two years consumer prices rose by 23 percent and wholesale prices by 33 percent. After two years of price stability (wholesale prices actually fell a little), the Korean War brought a second phase of mild inflation. From 1950 through 1953, consumer prices rose by 11 percent and wholesale prices by 7 percent, a considerably slower pace than in 1946–48.

Then followed a dozen years of relatively stable prices, in which the economy as a whole grew at a slow pace, particularly from 1953 through 1960. In spite of considerable economic slack, however, consumer prices crept steadily upward at a pace of about 1.5 percent annually. Wholesale prices were considerably more stable, increasing at a rate of only about 1 percent per year.

The third period of relative rapid increase in price levels came with the escalation of the war in Viet Nam, from 1965 onward. In five years, consumer prices rose by over 20 percent and wholesale prices by almost 10 percent.

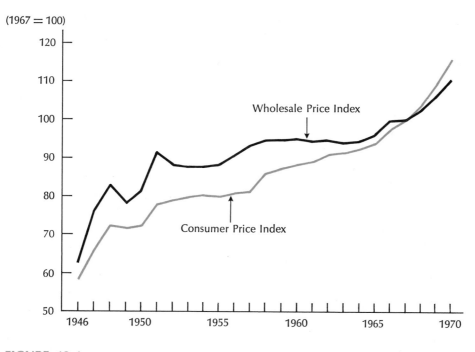

(1967 = 100)

FIGURE 19-1

Trends in Consumer and Wholesale Prices, 1946–70

Overall, the rise in prices from 1946 through 1970 was between 75 percent (wholesale prices) and 100 percent (consumer prices). But if the repressed inflation from World War II is eliminated, and the wartime inflation of 1965 to 1970, the increase from 1948 to 1965 was in the range of 17 percent for wholesale prices to 31 percent for consumer prices. It's not a very large increase for a period of 17 years.

An equally striking fact is that the bulk of the price increase has been associated with active warfare. During those times the productive capacity of the economy strains to produce for both civilian and military uses at the same time. Purchasing power is increased by wartime government spending, the competition for products and resources intensifies and prices are driven upward.

But the upward creep of prices in 1953–65, when there was substantial slack in the economy, tells us that inflation involves more than merely "too much purchasing power chasing too few goods." Even if the primary cause of inflation is excessive purchasing power, other factors have to be explored.

PRICES AND THE FLOW OF SPENDING

Increases in the general level of prices occur when the flow of spending grows faster than the economy's output. For prices to be pushed upward, aggregate demand must push ahead faster than aggregate supply, pressing on the economy's capacity to produce. This basic principle is sometimes subject to variations and exceptions, but it must always be borne in mind. It will help to correct some of the mistaken concepts about inflation that are widely current and often firmly believed.

For example, propaganda from labor unions sometimes charges that rising prices are caused by the excessive profits obtained by rapacious corporations that unconscionably gouge the unsuspecting public. Unions point to the rising profits that occur during inflation as evidence to support their position. But the cause of the price increases is an increase in purchasing power so that the goods are taken off the market at higher prices, and hence higher profits. Unless that increase in purchasing power occurred, business firms would sell less if they raised prices.

The shoe belongs on the other foot, too. Many otherwise rational people believe that higher wage rates cause inflation by increasing business costs and thereby forcing prices up. Here again, they ignore the fact that higher wages must be paid out of higher revenues or reduced profits. If they come from higher revenues, business firms can get those revenues only from an increase in purchasing power that has its source in an increase in aggregate demand.[1] If the higher wages come out of profits, there is, of course, no need for prices to rise.

The root of these misconceptions is a failure to distinguish between the causes of inflation, the process of inflation, and the institutional environment within which it occurs. No one today believes that the cause of malaria is the fever that accompanies the disease, or that malaria arises out of a swampy environment. We know that it is caused by a germ, that the fever is a symptom of the body's reaction to the germ, and that the germ is introduced into the body by a swamp-bred mosquito. Our knowledge of inflation has not progressed that far, at least in the minds of the general public. But to continue the analogy, inflation is a malaise of the body economic that is caused by demand outrunning supply; rising wages and profits are part of the symptoms; and an environment of big business and big labor increases the economy's susceptibility to the disease. It is important that these three aspects not be confused.

---

[1] A few economists have argued that the increased purchasing power can come from the higher wages themselves, thereby validating the original increase in wages and enabling business firms to raise their prices. Hence, a self-sustaining inflation. This argument implies, however, that important changes take place in the money market that involve either an increase in the money supply (itself a cause of increased aggregate demand) or an increase in the speed with which people spend their incomes. There is little or no evidence that these latter increases in the "velocity of circulation" of money occur at times when general increases in wage rates take place. As a result, this theory of self-generating inflation cannot be given much credence.

Sources of Increased Purchasing Power

Purchasing power can increase even after the capacity of the economy to produce has reached its peak. There are three sources from which the excessive spending can come:

1. Consumer savings. The stored-up purchasing power represented by savings can be drawn into the stream of spending. Savings were withdrawn from the flow of spending at some time in the past. If used to supplement current earnings, they can add to the flow of purchasing power an amount that was not created by current production. The additional purchasing power will bid up the prices charged for current output.

   Consumers, however, do not normally draw down their savings in this manner. The last time it happened on a large scale was in 1946–48, immediately after World War II. That was a special situation in which consumer savings had ballooned to a level some $80 billion above normal because of high wartime incomes, government bond drives, rationing, and price controls. When peace came, this large volume of excessive savings was quickly spent and contributed substantially to the 25 percent price rise of those years. In the absence of special situations like that, however, consumer savings usually remain in the form of savings. In normal times they do not feed the fires of inflation.

2. Credit expansion. Purchasing power can be expanded by continuing extension of credit. As long as banks have excess reserves, or if new reserves are created for them, the flow of spending can be increased by enlarged loans from banks to business firms and consumers. There is no reason why credit expansion need stop once the economy has reached full-employment levels of GNP, unless, of course, the monetary authorities take steps to halt it. Credit expansion can permit both consumer and business spending to rise even though the economy has reached its output capacity.

3. Government deficits. Budget deficits on the part of the federal government also promote increases in purchasing power. Budget deficits are financed by sale of government securities in financial markets, thereby drawing funds into the flow of spending. If this happens after full employment is reached, the resultant increase in aggregate demand must bring about price increases. Budget deficits are really just another form of credit expansion, and like credit expansion, this source of purchasing power is also subject to control by government policy makers.

None of these sources of additional spending are an inflationary threat so long as the economy has significant excess capacity for expansion of output. But when unemployment rates are low and output is pressing upon capacity, continued increases in aggregate demand will start to push prices up. Not much can be done to prevent consumers from dipping into past savings, but both credit expansion and government deficits can be controlled. Indeed, monetary and fiscal policies can even be used to counterbalance the effect of consumers' using their savings to buy now. As far as the economics of inflation is concerned, the malaise is controllable.

Aggregate Demand and Inflation

The relationship between increases in aggregate demand and prices can be shown diagrammatically by use of the analysis developed in Chapter 11. It is shown in Figure 19-2.

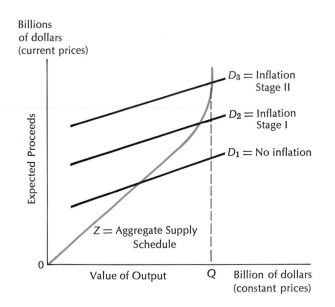

FIGURE 19-2

Aggregate Demand and Inflation

When aggregate demand (D_1) falls below the level needed to achieve full capacity ouput (Q), there is substantial unemployment and unused plant capacity. Prices do not rise. If this condition persists long enough, some prices may turn downward, particularly in competitive industries. When aggregate demand begins to approach full-employment levels (D_2), markets begin to tighten as shortages start to appear; unemployment diminishes; and industry begins to approach capacity levels of output. Business firms, particularly those in competitive industries, start to raise their prices to take advantage of the tight market conditions. Unemployment has not completely disappeared, however, and further increases in aggregate demand can bring reduced unemployment only at the price of further price increases. This stage of inflation is characterized by moderate rates of price increases (2.5 to 5 percent annually) and relatively low unemployment rates (3 to 5 percent of the labor force in recent U.S. experience).

A second stage of inflation would be reached if aggregate demand continued to increase until the economy's output capacity was reached. This situation would develop in the U.S. economy with manufacturing capacity utilization rates of 95 percent or more and unemployment rates of 1 to 1.5 percent of the labor force. These conditions prevailed in the heat of World War II (1944–45) and led to price, wage, and profit controls. Without these controls, an economy in Stage II could develop an inflationary spiral of rapidly rising prices, wages, and profits so long as aggregate demand remained high enough (D_3 in Figure 19-2). Even if aggregate demand were reduced, prices would probably continue to spiral upward for a time until the effects of the former excessive aggregate demand wore off.

THE INFLATIONARY SPIRAL

The process of inflation, like a malarial fever, is sometimes spectacular. The cause may be hidden, for increases in aggregate demand are not easy to spot. But rising prices are obvious to everyone, and so are rising profits and wages. This is the reason why the inflationary spiral itself is so often confused with the cause of inflation. What happens in the economy when aggregate demand continues to rise after the economy has approached its capacity to produce?

As markets begin to tighten, producers and sellers observe that shortages of both raw materials and finished products are starting to appear. Sellers realize that they can raise their prices without suffering a loss in sales; they do so and profits start to rise. With profits rising, producers begin to bid for the factors of production so that they may take advantage of greater profit possibilities. Prices of raw materials move upward. Interest rates go up as suppliers of capital take advantage of tighter money markets. Competition among employers for increasingly scarce labor causes wage rates to rise.

Rising costs—prices of materials, interest rates, wages—can start pressing profits downward, but increases in aggregate demand allow these higher costs to be passed on to consumers in the form of another round of price increases. This famous *cost-push* has been considered by some economists to be itself a cause of inflation, but in reality it is only one part of the inflationary process. Costs do rise during an inflation, and they do stimulate a desire to raise prices still further. But continuing increases in aggregate demand coming from credit expansion, government deficits, or (rarely) activation of past savings, are required to make the price increases possible.

If sellers tried to raise prices without a continued growth of aggregate demand, they would find that their sales would start to fall, and the other basic condition necessary for inflation—an economy at or near full-capacity output —would disappear. However, the upward spiral of prices, wages, profits, and interest rates can continue as long as aggregate demand rises faster than the economy's capacity to produce.

For example, take the case of an economy at full employment, with full use of existing output capacity. The labor force is growing at an annual rate of 1.5 percent, and productivity at 3.0 percent. Together they permit an annual growth in output of 4.5 percent. If aggregate demand were to rise at a faster rate, perhaps 8 percent per year, prices would be pushed upward. We can even calculate the expected increase in the general price level: 3.5 percent.[2]

The upward spiral of prices, wages, and profits goes on simultaneously, under the impact of excessive aggregate demand. All prices will rise, some more and some less, depending on the specific sectors of the economy into which the excessive demand flows most readily. This includes the prices of the factors of production—wages, profits, and interest rates—which are also pulled upward by the general tightness to be found in markets throughout the economy. Some of these prices, particularly wages and interest rates as well as prices of raw materials, are major components of the cost of production of other products. When these costs rise they exert pressure on businessmen to raise the prices of finished products and services if they can. This imparts the so-called "spiral" effect to an inflation, and may make it seem as if a self-generating process is at work. It isn't. Take away the excessive aggregate demand and the spiral will slow down and stop. The process by which an inflation slows down and stops may take some time, however. The inflationary spiral can continue for several years after the original increase in aggregate demand that started the spiral has disappeared. This lesson was brought home forcefully in 1969–71, when it became apparent that the inflationary pressures of large federal deficits in 1966–68 could not quickly be eliminated merely by reducing aggregate demand.

Factors Limiting an Inflationary Spiral

Even when an inflationary spiral is at work, the economy generates a number of anti-inflationary conditions that tend to slow down an inflation and bring it to a halt. Here are some of the most important:

1. Tight money. Bank credit expands as the GNP increases and prices rise. But there are limits. Sooner or later the banks will become loaned up, interest rates will move up and the expansion of bank credit will stop— unless, of course, the central bank feeds new reserves into the system.

---

[2] This calculation is not difficult to make. The shortcut is to take the difference between the rate of growth in aggregate demand and the rate of growth of potential output. The logic behind it is this: the increased output of the economy (104.5) must be priced at a level (x) that absorbs the total of aggregate demand (108), or

$$\frac{104.5\,(x)}{100} = 108.$$

Solving the equation yields x = 103.5.

2. Taxes. A progressive income tax will take a larger and larger bite out of rising incomes as people move into higher tax brackets. Taxes become a larger proportion of income, and a larger withdrawal from the flow of spending.

3. Government transfer payments. As incomes rise, some transfer payments decline, such as unemployment compensation. Others, like veterans' benefits and social security payments, remain the same, and become a smaller proportion of the growing flow of spending.

4. Holdings of cash and other liquid assets. As prices rise, consumers need more money for daily use. Withdrawal of money from bank reserves helps further to tighten the money markets. A related phenomenon is the need for larger cash balances by both business firms and consumers: as prices rise the purchasing power of liquid assets declines, and the value of those assets must be increased in order to maintain the same conditions of liquidity, so bank balances are increased. This effort to maintain liquidity is another reason why the money markets become tighter.

   However, during a *runaway* inflation attitudes toward liquidity change, as everyone tries to turn liquid assets into real assets. When that happens, the prevailing attitudes toward liquidity promote speculation and further inflation. Most inflations are not of this type, however, and attitudes toward liquidity are usually of the sort that tend to dampen inflationary pressures.

5. Imports and exports. As domestic prices rise, imported goods become better buys, and some of the increased aggregate demand is funneled out of the domestic flow of spending. Exports decline at the same time, because their prices rise and foreigners buy less. This decline reduces the domestic flow of spending.[3]

6. Stable incomes. Some groups in the economy have fixed or relatively stable incomes. For example, pensions will buy less (in real terms) as prices rise because their incomes do not rise as fast as prices. Dividend income from securities usually does not rise as fast as prices, either, and there are some other types of income that usually show the same pattern. The real purchasing power of recipients of income from these sources declines, and further price rises are thereby discouraged.

7. Increases in output. The output capacity of an economy rises even when prices are going up. To the extent that this happens, the inflationary pressures are reduced.

8. Increases in costs of production. Perhaps the most significant limiting factor in an inflation is the increase in cost of production that comes

---

[3] These effects on the net foreign balance assume no price level changes abroad. *Relative* prices are the key here: if a corresponding inflation is going on abroad the results would be quite different from those described here.

from rising wages, rising interest rates, and rising costs of raw materials. Unless aggregate demand continues to rise, these cost increases cannot be passed on to consumers, profit margins wither away, and business firms are forced to cut back production and employment. This development, which could easily lead to a recession and perhaps to a serious depression, is the chief reason for avoiding inflations. Unless an inflation is continued, allowing producers to pass on more price increases to consumers, an economic downturn can be produced by the effects of rising costs.

Even during an inflationary spiral, however, there are some firms and some industries whose costs rise faster than selling prices. Some of the steam is taken out of the inflationary spiral and the rise in prices is slowed.

The foregoing inventory of anti-inflationary forces generated by an inflation itself is not complete. But it should lay to rest the commonly held fears that, once started, an inflation must continue to cumulate until money is worthless, unless positive action is taken to halt the inflation. Just the opposite is true. Inflations normally tend to peter out unless they are continually fed by increases in aggregate demand.

Runaway Inflation

Some inflations have been known to get out of hand, in spite of the self-limiting changes in the economy that an inflation generates. Several famous examples come instantly to mind: China after World War II, Germany in 1922–23, Russia in 1920–21, France in 1794–97, and the American colonies in 1777–80. In these inflations prices rose so rapidly and to such heights that the money in use lost its value and had to be replaced by a new type.[4]

All of these runaway inflations occurred at times of political stress or turmoil. More important, all of the governments involved faced a very uncertain financial situation: demands on government expenditures were rising at a time when it was very difficult to levy and collect taxes. The governments turned to the printing press to obtain the funds they needed. Continuous large injections of purchasing power into the economy through government deficits, financed by newly printed currency, have been the causes of all the principal cases of runaway inflation.

Or, put negatively, we know of no case of runaway inflation that was not engendered by a deliberate overexpansion of the money supply, carried out as a conscious policy by the government. We know of no inflation that developed into a runaway inflation simply as the result of an upward spiral of prices, unaided by continuing increases in the money supply.

---

[4] The classic joke of every runaway inflation: the housewife takes her money to market in a bushel basket and brings her purchases home in her pocketbook.

WARTIME INFLATION

Wartime inflation is a special case of the general analysis of excessive aggregate demand. During wartime income is earned by workers and owners of other resources employed in producing military equipment. Just like any income, much of it is spent on consumption or investment (by business units). But the goods produced are not available for sale: they are shipped overseas and destroyed, for example, in the jungles of Southeast Asia, the locale of the Vietnam War. Since income is produced, but not supplies of goods available for sale, aggregate demand tends to outrun the available aggregate supply and prices are pushed upward.

Increased taxes to pay for the military goods are no answer, for as soon as payment is made by the government for the military goods the money is back in the hands of consumers and business units. Figure 19-3 illustrates the process quite simply.

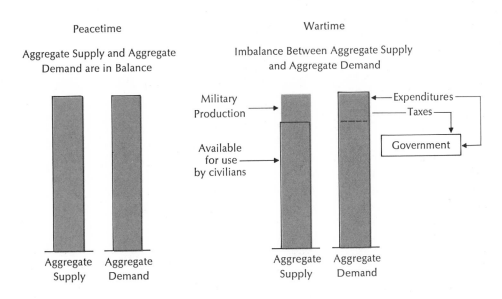

FIGURE 19-3
Wartime Inflation: Imbalance Between Aggregate Demand and Aggregate Supply

The goods available for use by civilians in wartime must rise in price in order to absorb the purchasing power created by production of both civilian and military goods. These price increases might be held in check by rationing and price controls, but the basic inflationary conditions will remain as long as part of the product is siphoned out of the nation's markets while full purchasing power is pumped in. Taxes only allow the government to buy the military production without running a budget deficit. They do not eliminate the excessive demand.

ENDING AN INFLATION

The medicine for inflation is reduction in aggregate demand. If the excess demand has come from increases in the money supply, that source can be eliminated by monetary policies aimed at tight money. All of the classic runaway inflations were ended by revisions in the monetary system and a halting of the printed presses.

If the source of inflation is government budget deficits, fiscal policies can be revised to eliminate them. For example, the U.S. inflation of 1967–69 was due in large part to federal deficits that reached $25 billion in the 1968 fiscal year (although monetary expansion in 1966–67 also was a factor). Reduction of that deficit and achievement of a balanced federal budget was the appropriate policy to follow in fighting the price increases.

The policies for coping with inflation are interchangeable to a substantial degree. A budget deficit can be partially offset by tighter money, and monetary expansion can be partially offset by a budget surplus. The important point to remember is that a proper mix of monetary and fiscal policies can keep the level of aggregate demand at levels that prevent inflationary increases in prices. Once an inflationary spiral has started, however, it takes time to run down. Increases in wages, interest rates, and prices of basic commodities do not rise equally and evenly, nor do the prices of finished products. It takes time for the rise in the cost of inputs to be reflected in the selling prices of outputs. It takes time for the economy to achieve a balance once again between its various sectors and industries. And during that time prices continue to rise and to adjust themselves, even after the cause of excessive purchasing power has been removed. The inflationary spiral will peter out and stop, but it may take as long as a year or two before it does.[5]

The temporary continuation of rising prices after the cause of inflation has been eliminated creates an important policy problem. Political demands to end rising prices may push the makers of economic policy to put on the brakes too hard. Aggregate demand may be reduced too far, bringing on unnecessarily high levels of unemployment. Meanwhile the post-inflation price adjustment continues to move prices upward. The result: rising unemployment *and* rising prices. The policy problem is indeed a difficult one. Not enough restraint will enable the inflation to continue, but at a slowed pace. Too much restraint will create unemployment. The best solution is probably to be found in the gradual imposition of restraints to avoid going too far, if political considerations permit it.

---

[5] In the next section of this chapter we shall point out that many prices go up easily but do not go down readily. This condition favors the continuation of an upward adjustment of prices as the aftermath of an inflation.

THE INFLATIONARY ENVIRONMENT

Price levels in the American economy have not shown large swings either upward or downward since the end of World War II. A relatively stable price level has prevailed, marked by an upward creep that has persisted from year to year with little pause. When a larger than usual slack appears in the economy, the upward creep slows and may temporarily halt. But when the GNP starts rising and unemployment rates fall, the upward creep begins once more and seems to move faster as the unemployment rate drops.

The behavior of the general price level was quite different in the hundred years prior to World War II. In that era it was characterized by large swings upward and downward, with the peaks and troughs of the long waves showing no consistent direction over the long run. Prices in the 1960s, for example, seem to have been at about the same level as they were just after the Civil War, in 1865. This earlier pattern was described in Chapter 6.

The difference between the two eras suggests that important changes have occurred in the economy. In particular, three structural elements in the economy seem to be important:

1. Government's commitment to high levels of employment and output.

2. Relationships between changes in productivity and changes in wage rates.

3. Administered prices.

High-Employment Policy

Government commitment to a policy of economic growth and high levels of employment provides a guarantee that markets will be relatively tight. Both fiscal and monetary policies are used to move aggregate demand upward at a rate approximately equal to the annual expansion of aggregate supply. Relatively low unemployment rates are permitted. In recent years, for example, a 4 percent rate of unemployment was thought to be only an "interim" target that could ultimately be improved upon. Indeed, in 1967–68 unemployment rates were pulled down below that level.

These two conditions, growing aggregate demand and relatively tight labor markets, provide the basic conditions for an upward creep in prices. In effect, government policies assure workers of jobs at prevailing wage rates and assure employers that their output will be sold at prevailing prices. If, for other reasons, wages and prices should be raised, the national government stands ready to provide the levels of aggregate demand needed to prevent unemployment or falling sales. This policy removes one of the chief deterrents to an upward creep in prices. It provides both labor and management with assurances that the agreements they reach about wages and prices will not serve to reduce either employment or sales.

Productivity, Prices, and Labor Unions

Strong unions and big business go together. Capital-intensive industries like steel, automobiles, chemicals, coal mining, and machinery manufacturing are characterized by large firms that deal with well-organized unions. There are some exceptions: textile manufacturing (where firms are generally not large) is mostly nonunion; and some strong unions operate in industries where small business predominates (trucking and clothing manufacture). The general rule, however, is that strong unions bargain with strong employers.

The result is usually a standoff, with neither side able to make significant gains at the expense of the other. This is an important point: collective bargaining between partners of equal strength usually limits the gains unions are able to obtain for their workers.

Opportunities for wage increases are created by two factors: (1) increases in output per man-hour; and (2) the ability of the employer to raise prices. Any wage increases that go beyond productivity gains will reduce the employers' profits, unless the higher costs can be passed on to consumers by way of higher prices. If prices can't be raised for fear of lost sales, the union will find strong management resistance to wage increases that exceed increases in productivity.

On the other hand, even an employer in a strong bargaining position finds it hard to hold wage increases below productivity gains, especially at times when aggregate demand is rising and unemployment rates are low. At those times the bargaining position of the union is strong, the employer is prosperous, and both parties expect wage increases to be forthcoming.

Usually, then, strong unions are able to obtain wage increases that match increases in output per man-hour, but they usually can't get wage increases that exceed the growth of output per man-hour. There are exceptions, and when they occur they raise costs of production, but the general rule is that productivity and wages rise at approximately the same rate.

For example, U.S. Department of Labor data show that for the 20 years from 1947 through 1966 the average annual increase in output per man-hour was 3.2 percent, exactly equal to the average annual increase in real compensation per man-hour.[6] These trends are not always the same in the short run, but they tend to even out. Thus from 1960 to 1965, real hourly compensation fell behind advances in productivity, and labor's share of the economy's total product fell from 63 percent in 1960 to 61 percent in 1965. But by 1969, rather large increases in hourly compensation brought labor's share back to the 1960 level. In the long run these disparities have tended to correct themselves, and compensation and productivity have moved up together.

It might appear on the surface that if hourly compensation (wages) does

---

[6] Real compensation per man-hour includes wages plus the estimated value of fringe benefits for *production* workers. It is corrected for changes in the price level to make it comparable with productivity measures, which are calculated on a real basis.

not exceed productivity gains, there is no need for employers to raise prices. Unfortunately, that is not the case.

Unions, for the most part, represent production workers rather than white-collar workers and are mostly found in the capital-intensive industries, where productivity tends to rise more rapidly than in other sectors of the economy. However, wage increases to production workers spread to white-collar workers in the same industry, and to workers in other industries, where productivity gains don't match those of the unionized production workers. When this *wage spread* occurs, costs of production rise and exert an upward pressure on prices.

For example, when the United Automobile Workers union negotiates increases in wages and fringe benefits for production employees, the auto firms will raise the wages and salaries of clerks, typists, and other white-collar workers, and even management personnel. The companies want to keep those workers happy (and not give them a reason to organize). The spreading effect does not stop there. When production workers at the Willow Run auto assembly plants get wage increases, the price of haircuts goes up in nearby Ann Arbor; the owners of barbershops raise the salaries of their barbers to keep them from quitting and taking jobs in the auto industry, and the increased costs (there has been no increase in productivity in barbering since the electrical clipper was introduced forty years ago) are passed on to consumers in higher prices. The effect of the wage increase has spread to other sectors of the economy.

WAGE SPREAD

The spread of wage increases from sectors of the economy with large productivity gains to sectors with low productivity gains. The result: rising costs of production in the latter.

The phenomenon of wage spread is one of the chief reasons for rising costs of production during periods of high prosperity. There are others as well: less efficient workers are hired as unemployment decreases, interest rates rise as money markets tighten, less efficient machinery is reactivated, and so on. Costs per unit of output do rise, on the average, for the economy as a whole. Labor costs are an important part of that upward push of costs, even when labor unions get no more for their members than productivity gains make possible. The wage spread sees to that.[7]

---

[7] Ewan Clague, former Commissioner of Labor Statistics in the U.S. Department of Labor, will find this discussion of wage spread quite familiar. Although he apparently did not originate the idea, he has been one of the few economists to give it the emphasis it deserves in explaining the inflationary environment of the modern economy. Clague's "Prices, Wages and Productivity in the Postwar Period" (mimeo, 1957) is a piece that unfortunately has never been published.

   Data on labor costs per unit of output in the private nonfarm sector of the
U.S. economy illustrate the upward push of costs from that source. Figure 19-4
shows that in the 1960–65 period, when considerable slack existed in the economy and prices were relatively stable, unit labor costs were quite stable. Wage
increases in the economy as a whole did not exceed gains in productivity.
But as the economy moved closer to full use of capacity and unemployment
rates began to fall to below 4 percent, costs per unit of output began to rise.
Wage increases outstripped productivity gains by a substantial margin in
1966–70.

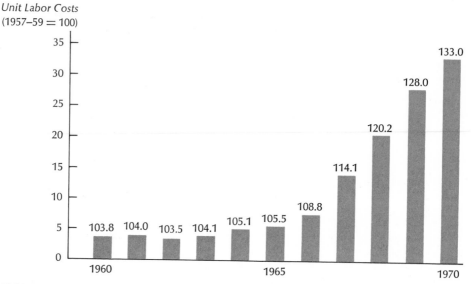

FIGURE 19-4
Unit Labor Costs in the Private Nonfarm Sector
of the U.S. Economy 1960–70
(Source: U.S. Department of Labor)

   We can summarize the way that large and strong labor unions contribute
to an inflationary environment. It is not that they are able to wrest from employers wage increases that exceed productivity gains. In most manufacturing industries, at least, their gains tend to be limited closely to those made
possible by increases in output per man-hour. But when wage increases spread
from there to other sectors of the economy, where productivity gains are
lower, increases in costs of production start to appear for the economy as a
whole, creating a cost-push, which puts upward pressure on the general level
of prices. When economic slack disappears, this cost-push is translated into
rising prices.
   This pattern does not differ significantly from that which would result from
the operation of market forces alone, in the absence of big unions, big busi-

ness, and collective bargaining. Under those conditions, when aggregate demand is at the high levels that produce tight markets, increases in productivity will be passed on to workers in the form of higher wages by employers who are competing to obtain and keep their workers. The same wage spread would be felt and the same cost-push would occur.

Another possible situation is one of big and strong employers with weak or nonexistent unions, as in the textile industry in the South. If this were the general situation, and productivity gains were *not* passed on to workers in higher wages, while prices were maintained, purchasing power would decline. Although the wage spread and cost-push could be eliminated in this case, it would be difficult to sustain high levels of aggregate demand. This very problem appears to have been one of the contributing causes of the Great Depression of the 1930s: productivity rose in the late 1920s while wage rates (and prices) remained stable. The slow erosion of purchasing power that took place helped to make the depression more serious.

The final possibility is one in which strong and well-organized unions bargain with relatively weak and dispersed employers. This situation characterizes the construction industry, and to some extent, local truck transportation. In this case there are few economic forces to check wage increases that exceed productivity gains in periods when aggregate demand is high and markets are tight. Costs rise, and sellers raise their prices in an effort to maintain profit margins, being able to do so because of high levels of aggregate demand. This result of union behavior is directly inflationary. Fortunately, it is the exception rather than the rule.

Administered Prices

The presence of big business and "administered prices" adds another dimension to the inflationary environment. The term "administered prices" refers to prices that are controlled to some degree by business firms, rather than solely by competitive market forces. We shall examine this phenomenon at some length later in this book. At this stage, however, we need only note that administered prices are common in many manufacturing industries, particularly those dominated by a single large firm or by a few firms. These are the same industries in which organized labor is strong and wage rates are determined through collective bargaining.

Where administered prices prevail, the price leader or leaders have some influence over prices. They are able to raise prices when costs rise. Their freedom to do so may be relatively large, or it may be limited, depending on the circumstances of the industry. But one thing is sure: the weakness of the forces of competition means that prices are seldom reduced. Occasionally problems will develop that force administered prices down. Excess capacity and foreign competition brought price reductions in steel in 1968, for example. But such incidents are the rare exception. Administered prices are often changed upward, but seldom downward.

The upward bias of administered prices creates an upward bias in the price system as a whole. it is one of the chief reasons for the failure of price levels to fall during recessions and for the ease with which they rise when the country is prosperous. Upward flexibility and downward rigidity characterize the price level of an economy in which administered prices are significant.

There is more than an upward bias, however. When aggregate demand is strong and markets are tight, it is relatively easy for price leaders in administered-price industries to raise prices without suffering a loss in sales. This ability to raise prices can make them less vigorous in resisting union demands for higher wages at the collective bargaining sessions. They have an added option open to them. They can agree to wage increases equal to productivity gains, and then add some more to be recaptured by price increases. Union leaders are as well aware of this possibility as business leaders, so the result, in administered-price industries, can be wage increases that exceed productivity gains. When that happens, the wage spread will be even greater and the increase in costs of production still larger.

WILL PRICES EVER STOP RISING?

Probably not. The modern economy is inflation-prone. Its institutional structure promotes inflation in at least three ways:

1. Government commitment to economic growth and prosperity can be counted on to provide levels of aggregate demand that keep markets tight.
2. Differing rates of productivity growth in various sectors of the economy mean that the wage increases obtained by strong unions in the most progressive sectors, by spreading to the more backward sectors, will raise costs of production there.
3. Large firms in administered-price industries are often able to pass on higher production costs to consumers by raising their prices.

As a result of this inflationary environment, prices can rise even when aggregate demand is not excessive. Economic growth brings technological change, which takes place unevenly throughout the economy. This unevenness leads to differing rates of increase of productivity in the various sectors of the economy. The spread of wage increases from the sectors with rapidly advancing technology causes a cost-push elsewhere, which is translated into rising prices by increases in aggregate demand. Strong unions accelerate this process by pushing for wage increases, while administered prices enable firms to settle for higher wages in collective bargaining negotiations. Behind it all stands the growth and high-employment policies of government, and the tendency of administered prices to resist downward pressures and respond to upward pressures. These conditions should lead us to expect a slow but steady increase in the general level of prices as a by-product of vigorous economic growth.

Meanwhile, the more spectacular sort of inflation, caused by excessive demand and usually associated with substantial increases in military expenditures, can be expected periodically as a by-product of the unsettled state of world affairs. At those times, too much purchasing power chases too little output, and the traditional inflationary spiral starts to work. These are the periods when prices rise rapidly, in contrast to the slower but persistent upward creep of prices that is inherent in the normal inflationary environment.

THE POLICY PROBLEM

Janus-like, inflation has two faces. One is its excessive aggregate demand face, sometimes called "demand-pull" inflation. Inflation of this type comes from growth in aggregate demand at a more rapid pace than the economy's ability to produce. Its sources in the past have been both public and private, primarily monetary expansion or government deficits and sometimes both. Our analysis indicated that this type of inflation sets in motion economic forces that tend to bring rising prices to a halt, that it is self-limiting rather than self-generating, unless continued expansion of aggregate demand from the public or monetary sectors continues to feed the inflationary fires.

The other face of inflation is the creeping "cost-push" that is rooted in economic growth and technological change. It is fostered by patterns of labor-management relations, administered prices, and government policy. This economic environment helps to explain why prices have been creeping upward over the last quarter of a century and why we ought to expect them to continue this trend. Even when aggregate demand is not high enough to reduce unemployment to only the frictional level (1.5 to 2.5 percent), even when some economic slack exists, we have to expect a slow upward movement in the general price level.

This inflationary economic environment creates a serious problem. There is a trade-off between economic slack and unemployment on the one hand, and rising prices on the other. For example, in 1965, when the unemployment rate averaged about 4.5 percent, consumer prices in the United States rose by just a little over 1.5 percent. But when unemployment rates were brought down in 1966 to about 4 percent, prices rose by 3 percent. The economy traded 0.5 percent reduction in unemployment (about 400,000 jobs) for a price increase of 1.5 percent.

The inflation-unemployment trade-off appears most clearly when markets are relatively tight but full employment has not yet been achieved. Figure 19-5 shows the relationship as it existed in the 1960s, with a trade-off curve roughly drawn in. It shows a tendency for prices to rise at a rate of about 1 percent annually, even with high unemployment rates. It also shows that prices can be expected to rise fairly rapidly, up to 4 percent annually, as unemployment rates fall toward 3 percent of the work force. The upper and lower tails of the curve are only estimated, however. The future is never certain: the locus of the curve probably varies from time to time as the eco-

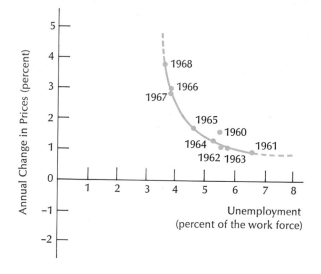

FIGURE 19-5
The Inflation-Unemployment Tradeoff

FIGURE 19-5
The Inflation-Unemployment Tradeoff

This inflation-unemployment tradeoff curve helps to explain why the aggregate
supply schedule in Figure 19-2 slopes upward as full employment is approached.
Figure 19-5 can be thought of as approximating a mirror image of the upper part of Z
in Figure 19-2. Although the two do not exactly correspond, the same economic
forces are at work.

nomic environment changes. The exact trade-off between inflation and unemployment is difficult to forecast accurately, even though recent experience
is clear enough.

Figure 19-5 shows that the American economy, as it is currently organized,
cannot bring unemployment down to frictional levels, say, 2.5 percent of the
work force, without generating price increases of over 4 percent annually.
Indeed, bearable rates of inflation of perhaps 1.5 percent per year would call
for moderately high rates of unemployment in the range of 4.5 to 5 percent
of the work force.

The dilemma is made even more uncomfortable when we examine the
groups in the economy who would most benefit from the two alternatives.
The greatest benefits from low unemployment rates go to the people most
frequently unemployed. This includes particularly such minority groups as
blacks, Puerto Ricans, and Mexican-Americans. Much of American poverty is
concentrated in those groups, and so is a large portion of unemployment.
Studies of income changes show that these groups have made progress relative
to the majority of Americans only when labor markets are tight and unemployment is pulled down close to frictional levels. If we wish to progress toward
a society of truly equal opportunities in which poverty is significantly reduced,

one way is to bring unemployment rates down to much lower levels than we have achieved in recent years.

On the other hand, unemployment rates of 3 percent, for example, can be expected to bring price increases of perhaps 4 percent annually. A rate of inflation that rapid poses a special threat to middle and lower-middle income groups. Families in those categories—with incomes of under $8,000 annually, to draw an arbitrary line—spend the bulk of their income on necessities and have little to spare. Price increases are a threat to their living standards and to their ability to maintain their way of life.

Other groups are also hurt by inflation. Older people especially, and others who receive fixed incomes, find their real purchasing power falling and their living standards squeezed. Unorganized workers, whose wage increases often lag behind price increases, are another. Union members, however, are generally able to get wage increases that keep up with prices. Creditors, or people such as bankers who lend to others, are said to lose as a result of price increases because they are repaid in dollars with lower purchasing power than those they lent. Few tears are shed for them, however, for they are usually able to avoid losses occurring from price increases.

The people hurt by inflation are also those who can least afford the tax increases the federal government would undoubtedly impose in an effort to hold back inflationary pressures. Higher taxes are a threat to the economic position of middle and lower-middle income families, just as higher prices are.

Finally, the rise of minority groups is seen as a threat to the family with under $8,000 in annual income. Fears of competition on the job and loss in property values if minority groups move into the neighborhood, however irrational, are nevertheless there. A policy that achieves high employment and brings with it benefits to submerged minorities, rising prices, and tax increases is likely to arouse substantial opposition among large numbers of people. All of these factors, some economic and some psychological, make it difficult for any administration to pursue a high-employment policy in the face of significant annual price increases.

At the other end of the policy continuum is the alternative of relatively high unemployment rates and relatively low rates of price increase. A combination of 5 percent unemployment and price inflation of 1.5 percent annually represents a possible position for an anti-inflation policy without excessively high unemployment. This position has the obvious disadvantages, however, of substantial waste of resources and slowed economic growth. Relatively stable prices would be purchased in exchange for substantial amounts of output and only by the sacrifice of considerable economic welfare.

There are some ways out of the dilemma, but each raises further problems. The costs of inflation can be reduced by providing for savings accounts and insurance policies that are tied to the cost of living. Old age benefits and other transfer payments can be escalated as prices rise. Such measures would ease the cost of inflation, but opponents claim that this action would only allow government policies to produce more inflationary pressures without arousing as much opposition. If that happened, the economy would become even more inflation-prone. The critics may be right.

On the other hand, the burden of unemployment could be reduced by assisting the lower segments of the labor force in other ways. Training and employment placement programs, special programs for education, housing and health, and broader income maintenance programs would reduce the need to follow high-employment policies. These programs are expensive, however, and face political difficulties of their own.

The problem of inflation is as much political as it is economic. We can do away with most of our creeping inflation with relatively high unemployment rates. Alternatively, we can eliminate most of our unemployment, but only at the cost of significant price increases: Other policies can reduce the costs of selecting one strategy or the other, but they also have their costs. Compromises will be made, and the political process will select the policy mix that is ultimately to emerge.

Wage and Price Guideposts

One way out of the dilemma is to try to keep prices in check by methods that are more direct than macroeconomic policies yet fall short of price controls. Such policies try to hold in check the inflationary pressures found in the wage spread and administered prices. If that can be done, other expansionary economic policies can bring the economy closer to full employment before price increases begin.

Wage and price guideposts in the U.S. were first developed in 1961 and 1962, although the need for them had been under discussion by economists and policy makers for a number of years before that. Emphasis was placed on wage behavior as the chief component of the inflationary push. The major proposition was that *wages in any industry should not be allowed to rise by more than the average increase in output per man-hour for the economy as a whole.* Price policies would reflect these wage increases. Prices should be reduced in those industries whose increases in productivity exceeded the national average, for in those industries costs of production would be falling; on the other hand, industries in which productivity gains were less than the national average would have rising costs of production, and they should be allowed to raise their prices. Exceptions could be made for special cases. The idea was that price declines would offset price increases and the average level of prices would remain stable.

The guideposts did not have a happy history. For a time they seemed to hold back some wage and price increases, but this was in 1963–65, when there was still considerable slack in the economy and price increases were small. As the economy moved closer to capacity and unemployment rates fell below 4 percent, inflationary pressures grew and the guideposts gradually gave way. In 1965, wage settlements in the steel and shipping industries were kept within the guideposts after some struggle, but early in 1966 a much-publicized breach was made in the construction trades in New Jersey. Later in 1966 the guide-post principle was completely defeated in settling a strike of airline machinists, and from 1967 onward less and less has been heard of them.

What was the trouble?

The chief source of difficulty was the process of inflation itself. By 1967 the economy had reached levels so close to full employment that further tightening of markets began to pull prices up. All of the inflationary pressures were beginning to appear and the inflationary spiral was beginning. Ex-hortations and political appeals could not keep them in check. While wage and price guideposts might help to retard the upward creep of prices growing out of the relationships between big business and big labor, they were no match for the strong pressures of an inflationary spiral fed by excessive aggre-gate demand. Guideposts were the wrong medicine for the disease.

A second difficulty was the failure of the guideposts to do anything about profits. Unions looked upon the guideposts as a limit placed on the gains available to workers. They were hardly enthusiastic to begin with, and became positively antagonistic when they saw profits rising substantially. For example, between 1963 and 1968 average weekly earnings in nonagricultural industries rose from $88.46 to $107.73, or 10.5 percent. During the same five-year period corporate profits after taxes rose from $33.1 billion to $51.0 billion, or 54.1 percent. Although comparisons of this sort are not very meaningful, the relatively large gains for business made workers feel that they were bearing the chief burdens imposed by the guideposts.

An important principle is involved. Government can ask economic interest groups to make sacrifices for achievement of national goals, price stability in this case, but unless the groups themselves perceive the sacrifices as being approximately equal they will eventually become disenchanted. This happened to the wage and price guideposts as soon as it became clear that they were helping hold back wage increases while profits were rising rapidly.

Nevertheless, the wage and price guideposts had some merit. Something like them is needed to provide a check to the upward creep of prices that can occur when the economy is below full-employment levels. But the experience of the 1960s shows that profits will have to be included too, and after that, probably other sources of income as well. The United States may move beyond wage and price guideposts toward a more comprehensive incomes policy, following the lead of some European countries.

Incomes Policy

An incomes policy seeks to restrain increases in the incomes of all of the factors of production in an effort to dampen or even halt the inflationary spiral. The policy includes restraints or controls on profits, wages, and other types of income, as well as administered prices. It won't work, of course, if inflationary increases in aggregate demand are continually pumped into the flow of spending. But if they are stopped and an inflationary spiral continues to work its cost-push way through the price system, as during the U.S. recession of 1970–71, an incomes policy may bring inflation to an end more quickly.

Alternatively, an effective incomes policy might delay the beginning of price increases as the economy moves out of the doldrums toward full employment. This would enable the economy to get closer to full employment before prices start rising.

The fundamental goal is to shift the inflation-unemployment tradeoff downward, so that price increases do not become significant until lower employment rates are achieved, as illustrated in Figure 19-6.

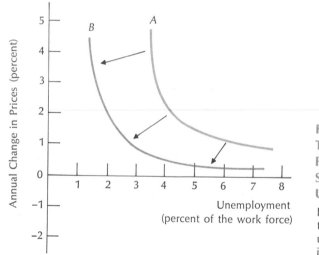

FIGURE 19-6
The Goal of Incomes Policy: A Downward Shift in the Inflation-Unemployment Tradeoff

Income policy tries to shift the tradeoff between unemployment and price increases from A to B.

Several elements of a possible incomes policy for the United States have already been proposed. First, it is necessary to have a set of guidelines against which any proposed increases in wages and prices can be judged. Even though our experience with the wage-price guideposts has not been favorable, something like them will have to be used to provide indicators of what might be allowable and what might be prohibited.

Second, a public review board independent of other economic policy making agencies (along the lines of the Federal Reserve's Board of Governors) could be established to enforce the guidelines. Several proposals along this line have been made, some as long ago as the mid-1950s. These proposals envisage that all wage agreements in a wide range of industries would be submitted to the board for its approval or disapproval when viewed within the framework of noninflationary guidelines. Price increases in administered price industries would also have to be submitted to the review board prior to being instituted.

In some proposals the public review board would hold hearings and publicize its findings that the proposed wage settlement or price increase is or is not consistent with the guidelines for price stability. If not, the increase could still go into effect, either immediately or after a waiting period. In those versions the objective is to alert and mobilize public opinion as the chief deterrent to inflationary pressures.

Other proposals have put forth a variety of enforcement procedures either to delay or to prohibit the institution of the wage settlement or price increase. The most imaginative would use a corporate income tax surcharge as the chief deterrent. If wages or prices or dividends or salaries of corporate officers were increased beyond the guidelines, the corporation would be subject to an increased profits tax, say 50 percent rather than the normal 48 percent. The surcharge could even be progressive, with the rate increasing the more the wage or price or dividend or salary increase exceeded the guidelines.

An intriguing concept lies behind this suggestion. It puts pressure where it belongs, on the decision makers in administered price industries. If businessmen know that reduced profits will be the inevitable result of wage settlements that increase their costs, unions will find that getting such settlements is increasingly difficult. Keeping profits down if prices are raised will help keep wage increases within the limits that are consistent with stable prices.

THE PRICE FREEZE OF 1971

In mid-August of 1971 President Nixon announced that all prices and wages (with a few exceptions) would be frozen for ninety days, in an effort to halt the inflation that had plagued the economy for a half-dozen years. He acted under authority provided by Congress under the Economic Stabilization Act of 1970. The President appointed a Cost of Living Council headed by the Secretary of the Treasury to administer the new price policies and placed enforcement in the hands of the Office of Emergency Preparedness (established in the early 1960s to cope with natural disasters or the aftermath of nuclear war), assisted temporarily by local offices of the Internal Revenue Service.

The price freeze was associated with other policies designed to deal with the nation's deficit in its international payments and an imminent international financial crisis. The value of the dollar was allowed to "float" relative to the price of gold. This move was expected to unleash additional inflationary pressures within the American economy unless action was taken, and the price freeze was the step selected. The international aspects of these measures are discussed in Chapter 45.

Prices and wages were fixed at their levels of August 15. Unprocessed agricultural products were excepted from the freeze. Profit, dividends, and interest rates were not included, chiefly because the enabling legislation did not provide authority to freeze them, although the President could have asked for authority to include them but did not. Many labor leaders were quick to express their dismay at these exceptions for to them they seemed to favor business firms and farmers, while wages were frozen. In retrospect, the exclusions were probably a mistake, for they reduced the acceptability of the new policies among one of the powerful economic interest groups whose support is essential if controls are to work.

The price freeze offered an umbrella under which the administration could seek to increase aggregate demand in an effort to reduce unemployment. To this end three changes in taxes were proposed.

1. Congress was asked to repeal the 7 percent excise tax on automobiles. This action was designed to increase automobile sales and expansion of employment in that industry.
2. An increase of $50 in personal income tax exemptions and an increase in the minimum standard deduction, scheduled for 1973, were to be moved up to 1972, in an effort to increase consumer spending.
3. A 10 percent tax credit for investment in new U.S.-built capital equipment was proposed, to promote business investment.

These tax reductions would bring a revenue loss estimated at about $6.3 billion. Part of that loss was offset by a 10 percent tax surcharge on imports and the remainder by a cut in federal employment. The net effect was a planned reduction in federal spending, on a balanced budget basis, of $4 billion to $5 billion. Although the administration publicized the tax reductions as stimulating the economy, the fact that a net reduction in federal spending was planned made the whole package somewhat deflationary.

Several other aspects of the tax package should be carefully noted:

The price increase of 1966–70 had reduced the real value of accumulated savings, causing consumers to raise their level of savings to about 8 percent of disposable income. This factor had contributed substantially to the 1969–70 recession, since it reduced consumer spending below normal levels. It could diminish significantly the stimulating effect of reductions in personal income taxes. Much of the reduced taxes could be expected to go into savings or debt reduction.

The tax credit for investment could not stimulate much additional investment spending, because of the large amount of excess capacity already present as a result of the recession. Even if it were successful, the results would be undesirable: the added investment would only increase the amount of excess capacity. On the other hand, the investment tax credit was strongly anti-inflationary. By widening profit margins it reduced cost pressures on business firms and eased the cost-push aspects of the inflationary spiral.

Under the circumstances in which it was adopted one would expect the price freeze to be fairly successful in slowing down or halting the inflationary price increases. The unemployment rate was about 6 percent and about 25 percent of manufacturing capacity was idle, indicating the existence of a significant amount of slack in the economy. The continuing inflationary spiral was not being fueled by excess demand in the current period, but was the result of wartime federal deficits from the past. If the price freeze could slow down or stop the inflationary spiral much of the force of inflation might be limited. But no policy makers or economists thought the inflationary pressures of the past could be eliminated entirely, and predictions were that the freeze would be followed after 90 days by a more comprehensive incomes policy designed to restrain increases in wages, profits and other incomes.

The psychological aspects of the price freeze were important. The business and financial community were encouraged by the administration's vigorous actions. After more than two years of relatively ineffectual economic policies that seemingly had little effect on inflation, the very fact that strong measures were taken gave renewed hope that the problem would be solved. This was an important reason for the surge in business confidence that brought an upward leap in stock prices even before any real economic results could be seen.

In one respect the 1971 price freeze was a fundamental departure from accepted economic doctrine. The post-Keynesian synthesis of economic theory and policy included the proposition that the private sector could allocate resources effectively and distribute incomes equitably if the federal government could assure stable economic growth. Experience in the second half of the 1960s implied that stable economic growth at close to full-employment levels was inflationary. Control of those inflationary pressures through accepted monetary and fiscal policies did not work. So even an administration ideologically disposed toward a minimum of government intervention in economic affairs moved into direct controls and intervention in matters pertaining to income distribution. As a portent of the future, the 1971 price freeze represented the next step beyond the unfortunate wage and price "guideposts" of the mid-1960s toward further economic planning.

Summary

Excessive aggregate demand is the fundamental cause of inflation. It can arise from use of past savings, government deficit spending, or excessive expansion of credit. The first cause seldom is a factor, and the latter two are under the control of government fiscal and monetary policy. An inflationary spiral of rising prices and costs can be set in motion, but it is normally self-limiting unless continually fueled by government deficits and/or expansion of credit. Wartime inflation is a variation: it can be brought about even without additional purchasing power by diversion of output from civilian to military uses.

Our economy is inflation-prone, and price levels start rising before full employment is reached. A combination of the government's commitment to maintain high levels of economic activity, the wage spread, and administered prices create a trade-off between unemployment rates and rising prices when the economy is close to full employment. This persistent problem is leading the United States toward an incomes policy that may comprise a combination of wage-price-profit guidelines and a public review board with sanctions to enforce its decisions.

Key Concepts

Inflation.   A persistent increase in the general level of prices.

Inflationary spiral.   The process of inflation, during which prices, costs, wages, and interest rates move upward in a sequence in which one increase sets others in motion.

Cost push.   That portion of the inflationary spiral in which rising costs create pressure on business firms to raise prices in order to maintain profits.

Runaway inflation.   Inflation that continues indefinitely until money loses its value. Past runaway inflations have always been caused by government fiscal or monetary policy, since an ordinary inflation tends to be self-limiting.

Wartime inflation.   Inflation caused or exaggerated by diversion of output to military uses.

Wage spread.   The spread of wage increases from sectors of the economy with large productivity gains to sectors with low productivity gains, causing the cost-push element to appear in the latter sectors.

Administered prices.   Prices whose level is controlled wholly or partially by large firms.

Inflation-unemployment trade-off.   The relationship between rising prices and falling unemployment at high levels of economic activity.

Wage-price guidelines.   Standards for wage and price changes designed to hold inflationary pressures in check.

Public review board.   A board whose function is to review wage and price changes for their possible inflationary effect.

Incomes policy.   A comprehensive policy limiting wage, price, and profit increases in order to diminish inflationary pressures.

The American economy can readily maintain itself on a full-employment growth path so long as the proper economic policies are maintained. Aggregate demand must be kept at levels high enough to provide the jobs needed by a growing work force whose productivity rises from year to year. The objective is to keep aggregate demand growing at a rate that continually presses upon the economy's ability to produce.

A national policy of maintaining full employment was formally stated in the Employment Act of 1946. Since then, a wide variety of fiscal and monetary policies have been tried in efforts to achieve the goal. The experience of the quarter century since 1946 has demonstrated that the goal can be achieved. A new policy instrument, the national economic budget, has been developed. This chapter will examine the strategic problems encountered by such policies and sketch the type of economic policies needed to achieve the goal of full employment and rapid growth.

An economy that continually presses upon its capacity to produce can be called a "high-pressure" economy. It avoids problems associated with large-scale unemployment and under-utilization of resources. But a high-pressure economy develops other problems, and we will give some attention to them:

1. It may bring steady increases in the national debt. This is an insignificant problem, but many people worry about it.
2. It may bring rising prices. This is a much more significant problem, and we have devoted Chapter 19 to it.
3. It may bring problems in the international balance of payments. This problem will be treated at some length in Chapter 45, but some attention will be given to it here.

Economists used to feel that maintenance of a full-employment growth path would solve most of our significant economic problems. The experience of the last quarter century has demonstrated the falsity of this hope. New problems have arisen to replace those that a high-pressure economy can eliminate. Some older problems have remained. So we will still have an agenda of unresolved economic problems even if we are wise enough to succeed in keeping the economy on its full-employment growth path.

The High-Pressure Economy

20

THE NATIONAL ECONOMIC BUDGET

The national economic budget is a device for analyzing the balance in the national economy between potential output and potential aggregate demand. On one side, it provides an estimate of how large the gross national product is likely to be, based on estimates of consumer spending, investment, and government purchases. On the other side, it provides an estimate of how large the GNP could be if it were to follow the economy's full-employment growth path. In other words, the national economic budget provides an estimate of the economy's potential growth in the coming year, a forecast of potential aggregate demand, and an estimate of any gap between the two. Economic policies to bridge the gap can then be devised. An example will clarify the concept.

Assume the following situation in the current year:

$$Y = C + I + G,$$

$$\text{where } Y = \$800 \text{ billion,}$$

$$C = \$600 \text{ billion,}$$

$$S = I = \$75 \text{ billion,}$$

$$G = \$125 \text{ billion (with a balanced budget).}$$

Let's also assume that there are 4 million persons unemployed, and that an increase in GNP of $25 billion would provide employment for just one million of the unemployed.

The first step in creating a national economic budget is to estimate the potential growth of the economy. Such an estimate requires forecasts of the growth of the work force and the increase in productivity. We can use the estimates made in Chapter 8.

1. Increase in the work force (corrected for changes in the length of the work year and other factors) = 1.5 percent.
2. Increase in output per man-hour = 3.5 percent.

Together, these factors provide an estimate of about 5 percent growth in GNP, from $800 billion to $840 billion.

We should add, however, enough spending to reduce significantly the total number of unemployed. Cutting it in half, from 4 to 2 million, would bring the total down to just about the frictional unemployment level (approximately full employment). This would require an additional increase of $50 billion in GNP, to a total of $890 billion. Such an increase would be very large, over 10 percent, and could cause difficulty if it triggered a growth so rapid that it could not be slowed down sufficiently in the following year. It would perhaps be wiser to aim for only half that reduction in unemployment, from 4 to 3 million, requiring only $25 billion more in total output.

We are now able to make an estimate, on the supply side, of the potential output of the economy for the coming year, shown below.

GNP in the initial year	$800 billion
Potential growth at 5% per year	40 billion
Additional output obtained by reducing unemployment by one million persons	25 billion
Goal for coming year	$865 billion
Required increase over previous year	$ 65 billion

The next step is to make an estimate of the expected aggregate demand during the coming year. Two methods have been widely used in recent years. One is the use of surveys in which a sample of consumers and businessmen are asked what they expect to spend during the coming year on such items as automobiles and housing (in the case of consumers) and on plant and equipment (in the case of businessmen). While there may be a gap between intentions and their realization, several of these surveys are widely available and remarkably accurate.

One type of spending is particularly easy to estimate. Government budgets are prepared and published well in advance, and actual spending usually differs little from the budgets. Information on government spending plans can be used to supplement surveys of consumer and business plans to provide insight into spending levels in the immediate future.

A second method for estimating aggregate demand that is increasingly coming into use is the computerized econometric model. The factors that influence aggregate demand are highly complex, but refined statistical estimating techniques are able to provide close estimates. Since all types of spending are related to each other systematically, by way of the circular flow of spending, the multiplier, and the acceleration principle, it is possible to bring all of them together in a system of simultaneous equations. The entire system, or model, can then be solved with the aid of high-speed computers. Several of these models are now available for research and forecasting purposes at the University of Michigan, the University of Pennsylvania, the Brookings Institution, and the Massachusetts Institute of Technology. They are all based on the fundamental Keynesian equation we are familiar with,

$$Y = C + I + G + X$$

All of the models break down C and I into their component parts: durable and nondurable consumer goods (for C); and housing, plant and equipment, and inventories (for I); and so on, each with a separate equation. Each model also has equations for estimating price changes, employment, and other variables, and the MIT model concentrates heavily on the monetary sector. The basic concept is the same for each: several equations are used to estimate the component parts of C, several for I, estimates of G are taken from budgets, and the model puts them all together to provide an estimate for Y, or gross national product.

Surveys, econometric models, and perhaps other techniques are used to provide estimates of expected spending for the forthcoming year. The methods are accurate enough so that an economist familiar with them can estimate the forthcoming year's GNP within 3 percent of the level subsequently achieved. These methods can be used to estimate the GNP and its components for the coming year. Continuing the example started above, suppose the forecast shows an expected increase in GNP from $800 billion to $820 billion, as follows:

$$C = \$610 \text{ billion,}$$
$$I = \$\ 80 \text{ billion,}$$
$$G = \$130 \text{ billion,}$$
$$GNP = \$820 \text{ billion.}$$

Note the interrelationships in this estimate. Investment is expected to increase by $5 billion from the initial year's $75 billion, and government spending by $5 billion. A multiplier of 2 will mean a GNP increase of $20 billion, implying a $10 billion increase in consumption.

Now we have problems. The expected increase in GNP is only half of that needed to provide jobs for a growing and more productive work force. If the estimate turns out to be accurate, unemployment will increase rather than decrease. Instead of falling by 1 million, unemployment will rise by about 800,000 persons. The national economic budget at this stage does not show a balance between the capacity to produce and the capacity to consume, but a growing deficit in aggregate demand that will continue to grow unless appropriate measures are taken to stimulate spending.

One way to fill the gap may be through increased government spending, without an increase in taxes, designed to bring GNP up to $865 billion from the expected $820 billion. With a multiplier of 2 that would mean, at first glance, a federal budget deficit of $22.5 billion:

Required GNP	$ 865 billion
Expected GNP	$ 820 billion
Gap	$ 45 billion
Additional spending needed ($k = 2$)	$22.5 billion

All of the additional spending may not have to come from the federal budget. A higher GNP may well induce higher levels of business investment than businessmen were planning. Going back to our econometric models or surveys may tell us that a GNP of $865 billion will bring investment spending of $85 billion instead of the planned $80 billion. The additional *I* will enable the government deficit spending program to be reduced by $5 billion.

A second revision will also have to be made. Taxes will rise as GNP goes up. In order to get a deficit of the necessary $17.5 billion ($22.5 billion minus $5 billion for induced investment), it will be necessary to reduce tax rates so as not to increase total taxes. Let's say that our econometric models predict that with existing tax rates and a GNP of $865 billion, tax revenues will rise by $7 billion, acting as a drag on the growth of aggregate demand. Tax rates will have to be reduced to eliminate that drag.

We can now restate the goals and policies of the national economic budget for the coming year. The goal is an increase in GNP large enough to provide for growth of 5 percent plus a reduction in unemployment of 1 million persons. A GNP of $865 billion will be needed. Achieving that growth would require the following spending:

$$C = \$632.5 \text{ billion,}$$
$$I = 85 \text{ billion,}$$
$$G = 147.5 \text{ billion,}$$
$$GNP = \$865 \text{ billion.}$$

The investment total comprises the $80 billion planned by business firms on the basis of their existing anticipations, plus $5 billion induced by the larger-than-expected growth in GNP. Government spending comprises $130 billion already planned for, plus a deficit of $17.5 billion. Tax revenues remain the same as expected ($130 billion) because of the planned reduction in tax rates to compensate for the growth in taxable income. The government deficit and induced investment provide the increase in spending of $22.5 billion needed to raise GNP by $45 billion ($k = 2$) above the expected level.

This is only one combination of policies that might be adopted. Tax rates could be reduced still further, providing a larger disposable personal income and higher *C*. Taxes on business firms could be adjusted to stimulate more *I*. Monetary policy could be eased to promote greater *I*. All of these policies would enable the increase in *G* (and the deficit) to be reduced. The policy mix that is finally selected may be extremely complex, and many alternatives are available. The example used here was highly simplified, but it shows the way in which the job can be done and how the national economic budget can be used.[1]

---

[1] The term "national economic budget" is a dirty word in Washington: it smacks too much of economic planning, which it is. Conservative congressmen and senators will have none of it. Nevertheless, the process we have explained above describes what the President's Council of Economic Advisers does and embodies in its annual report, but in a more complex fashion.

THE ECONOMIC POLICY MIX

A high-pressure economy is oriented toward full use of the economy's capacity to produce. Achievement of that goal in an economy in which most economic activity is carried on in privately owned business units, and in which spending by individual consumer units is the largest component of GNP, implies heavy reliance on the private sector of the economy. A socialist economy in which the growth pattern is controlled by government planning of the investment process may have a different emphasis. But for the United States in the second half of the twentieth century, one key to growth and high levels of GNP is the promoting of the dynamism inherent in the individual motivations of consumers and businessmen.

That does not mean laissez-faire. There are three ways in which the private sector can be made more dynamic. First, government spending and tax policies, like those in our example of the national economic budget, can keep aggregate demand at a high level. These are not "hands-off" policies, but imply a large role for government in planning the level of aggregate demand.

Second, the private sector requires large investment in social overhead capital, such as education, health, transportation facilities, and other services used by all. It also requires protection of resources from private misuse in order to preserve the human and natural environment of economic activity. These are areas in which positive government action can promote economic activity and expansion of the private sector.

Third, monetary policy can either hinder or help the private sector. Tight money policies tend to hold back private investment. When investment funds are hard to obtain, and costly when they are available, business investment is dampened. Tight money also holds back housing construction, because most housing is built with borrowed funds. Purchases of durable consumer goods, such as automobiles and electrical equipment, are also held back by tight money. Relatively easy money conditions, on the other hand, promote business investment, housing construction, and purchase of durable goods.

Monetary Policy

One key element, then, in a policy designed to promote a dynamic private sector is a long-range, persistent, and overriding policy of monetary ease. Whenever possible, business firms and consumers should have ready access to borrowed funds at low interest rates. This does not mean that monetary restraint should never be used as a stabilizing device. But it does mean that when alternatives are available emphasis should be given to fiscal rather than monetary restraint.

Monetary policy should also be consistent. Rapid changes in monetary policy, with easy money now and tight money next year, tend to create conditions of boom and bust in the private sector. They are not consistent with the stability required for long-range planning of investment expenditures and a stable pattern of production. To ensure growth in the private sector, then, a consistent policy of monetary ease is called for.

Automatic Stabilizers

The federal budget has several components that automatically produce a stabilizing effect on aggregate demand. The most important are the progressive personal income tax, unemployment compensation, and social security payments.

The progressive personal income tax is the most important of these. As GNP rises, personal incomes rise and some taxpayers move into higher tax brackets. They then pay a larger proportion of their incomes in taxes. Since this happens to many taxpayers across the country, the revenues of the federal government rise faster than GNP. Disposable personal income rises more slowly than GNP, thereby slowing down the pace of economic expansion.

Just the opposite effect occurs as the economy heads toward a recession. The proportion of income paid in taxes declines as incomes fall and families move into lower tax brackets. Disposable personal income falls more slowly than GNP, consumption spending tends to hold firm, and the decline in GNP is slowed.

Unemployment compensation programs have a dual effect. When the economy is on an upswing, unemployment falls, reducing government payments to the unemployed. At the same time, payroll deductions for payments into the unemployment insurance trust fund go up, because more workers are employed. Receipts rise, payments fall, and the net effect is to reduce the flow of spending. During a recession the flow is reversed. As unemployment rises, payments into the trust fund decline, because fewer people are employed. For the same reason, unemployment compensation payments rise. The net effect is to increase consumer incomes and bolster the flow of spending.

Social security payments act somewhat differently. In good times or bad they remain the same, thereby providing a certain amount of stable income for one group of consumers, even though other incomes may fluctuate. Contributions to social security fall during recessions, however, because fewer workers are employed.

There are similar automatic stabilizers in the private sector of the economy. Private pension systems have a stabilizing effect much like social security payments. Corporate dividend payments also promote stability: corporations tend toward regularity in their payments to shareholders even though their profits may rise significantly during prosperities and fall in recessions.

The automatic stabilizers help keep the economy on a relatively even keel. They can't do the whole job, however, because they do not affect all incomes in large amounts. Their most important function is to slow down the swings in the economy, thereby giving policy makers a little more time to assess the situation and determine the best course of action.

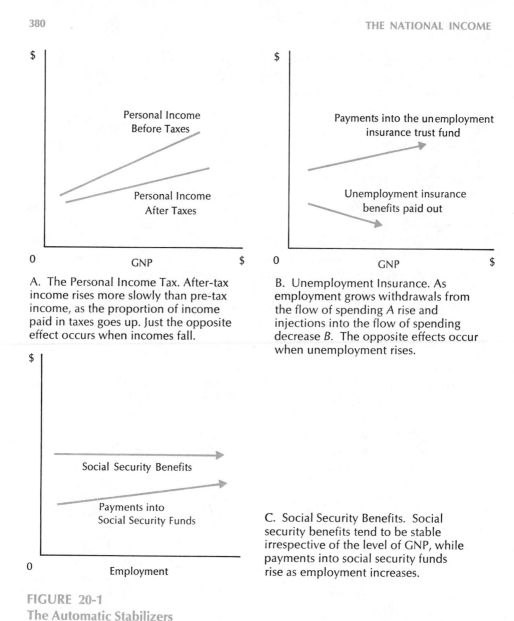

A. The Personal Income Tax. After-tax income rises more slowly than pre-tax income, as the proportion of income paid in taxes goes up. Just the opposite effect occurs when incomes fall.

B. Unemployment Insurance. As employment grows withdrawals from the flow of spending A rise and injections into the flow of spending decrease B. The opposite effects occur when unemployment rises.

C. Social Security Benefits. Social security benefits tend to be stable irrespective of the level of GNP, while payments into social security funds rise as employment increases.

FIGURE 20-1
The Automatic Stabilizers

Compensatory Fiscal Policy

An active fiscal policy, used as the chief means of stabilizing the economy and keeping it close to its potential growth path, must compensate for the ups and downs inherent in the private sector. When the private sector loses its dynamism and sinks below the full-employment growth path, government fiscal policy can be used to bring aggregate demand closer to the full-employment level. Taxes can be reduced, expenditures increased, and total spending thereby enlarged. When the private sector becomes overly dynamic and inflation threatens, just the opposite policies can be used to dampen the economy. Taxes can be raised and expenditures cut, and some of the excessive aggregate demand that is causing the trouble thereby eliminated. It is too much to expect that recessions or price increases can be eliminated altogether, but a proper compensatory fiscal policy can keep the economy very close to its full-employment growth path, as shown in Figure 20-2.

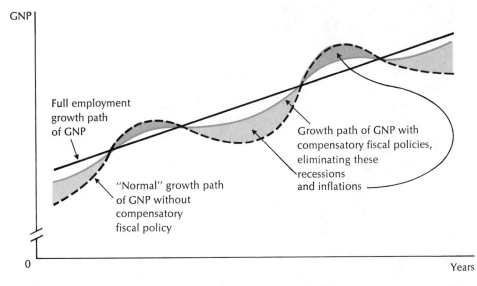

Compensatory fiscal policies add to aggregate demand recessions ▨▨▨ and reduce aggregate demand during inflations ▨▨▨ to keep the economy on a relatively stable growth path ——— .

FIGURE 20-2
Compensatory Fiscal Policy

The easiest way to increase aggregate demand during recession periods is to incur a budget deficit at the federal government level. With a multiplier of 2, the deficit will add to purchasing power an amount equal to twice the deficit. Such a deficit can be achieved by reducing tax rates, increasing spending, or both. If a deficit is not wanted, the same effects can be obtained by increasing both spending and tax revenues. In this case the added spending will have to be about twice the amount required if a deficit were achieved, since the balanced budget multiplier is approximately 1 instead of 2.

A budgetary surplus is the easiest way to reduce inflationary pressures, although again the same effect can be obtained through a balanced budget decrease in spending twice as large.

Budget deficits during recessions would probably not be balanced by budget surpluses during inflations. We have already noted that inflations tend to be self-limiting and self-reversing unless continually reinforced by further increases in aggregate demand from easy money or budget deficits.

This characteristic of inflations means that periods of exhilaration in the private sector of the economy should normally be relatively short and not particularly great. On the other hand, it is quite possible for the economy to reach and sustain an equilibrium level of GNP well below the full-employment level. If that is the case, a compensatory fiscal policy will require continual supplements to aggregate demand in order to keep it close to the full-employment growth path. In all probability that means persistent budget deficits. This situation is illustrated in Figure 20-3.

There may be periods of several years or more in which a compensatory fiscal policy requires persistent budget surpluses. These would be inflationary periods in which it would be necessary to reduce persistently the level of aggregate demand. If experience is any guide, these periods will be few and far between. On the other hand, periods of recession, depression, and even stagnation have been more common. During these periods a compensatory fiscal policy would undoubtedly lead to budget deficits. The net result will be a consistently rising national debt.

This is no reason to abandon the high-pressure policy. A large and rising national debt, properly managed, is no problem.

THE ECONOMICS OF THE NATIONAL DEBT

Everyone worries about the national debt—except economists. There is no other topic in economics that is more widely misunderstood, and none about which the average person has more misconceptions. Most people think that the national debt will have to be "repaid" at some time or other. It won't. Most people believe that the national debt is a burden on future generations. It isn't. Even if we tried we would find it almost impossible to shift the burden of the national debt to our children. Most people believe that the national debt can become so large as to bankrupt the federal government. Impossible! Most people think that a large national debt is a burden on the economy. It need not be, if it is managed properly, and that is not hard to do.

Quite the contrary. There is no economic limit to the size of the national debt, and a rising debt can bring important benefits. Any burdens that may arise appear only if the national debt is managed improperly or if it is increased or decreased at the wrong time for the wrong reasons.

The federal government, unlike you or me or General Motors Corporation or the State of Arkansas, has an unlimited line of credit. It can always borrow more, if it wishes, at existing rates of interest. Indeed, the federal government is the only economic unit in the national economy for which that is true. All other economic units can borrow only finite amounts, based on their income, wealth, and credit history. The reason is simple: the federal government controls the money supply, and can use the money supply to create its own line of credit.

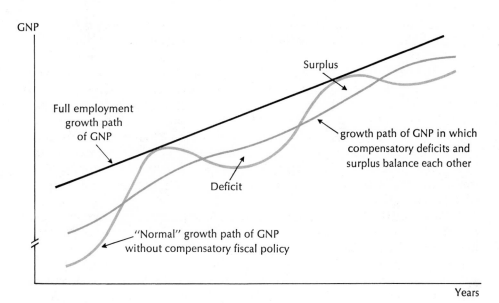

A. Balancing budget deficits with budget surpluses may keep the economy permanently below the full employment growth path.

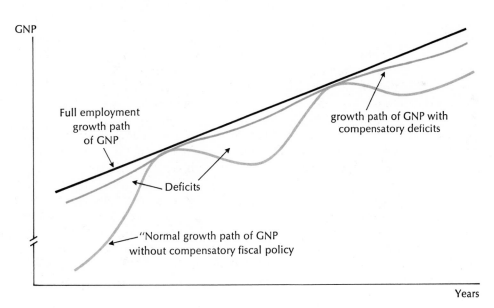

B. A true compensatory fiscal policy may bring a steady increase in the national debt.

FIGURE 20-3
Two Approaches to Compensatory Fiscal Policy

World War II provides an example. When the Treasury wished to borrow, say, $6 billion to pay for another batch of tanks, guns, ships and aircraft, and the banking system was loaned up so that it could not absorb any more government securities, the Federal Reserve System (our central bank) would step in and buy $1 billion of the new issue of Treasury bonds. Like any open market purchase, this created $1 billion of new reserves for the banking system. The banks were then able to buy the remaining $5 billion of Treasury bonds through the process of multiple expansion of bank credit. It almost seems too simple, yet that is exactly how most of the expenditures of World War II were financed. The process is known as monetizing the national debt, since it results in an increase in the money supply almost as great as the increase in debt.

There is one drawback to financing a war, or any other government expenditure, in this fashion. It adds to total spending without adding to output. If this is done when the economy is close to full employment, it can cause rising prices. If done at the wrong time, an increase in the national debt is inflationary. But if done at the right time, that is, when there are unemployed workers and unused plant capacity, the increase in debt can add to total output and to economic welfare. The increase in GNP is a net gain, because the resources and manpower would otherwise lie unused.

An important truth emerges: a rising national debt can benefit the economy if it occurs when there is economic slack. It can hurt the economy if it occurs when there is little or no economic slack.[2]

Whether the debt is a burden or not also depends on what the money is used for. If the debt is increased to pay for weapons of destruction that are shot up on the battlefield, the resources used are gone and have not contributed either to economic growth or economic welfare. On the other hand, if the debt is increased to provide jobs for the unemployed or assist the needy or build highways, it will increase welfare and promote growth. A second truth emerges: a rising national debt can hurt the economy if the funds are used wastefully. It can benefit the economy if the funds are used wisely.[3]

But what if the debt continues to grow and becomes very large—will it not then be a burden on the economy? A large debt can be a burden if it results in a redistribution of income. If interest payments on the debt are paid out of tax revenues, there will be a shift of income from those who pay taxes to those who own government securities. If the taxpayers are poor and the bondholders rich, the economy will be worse off.[4] Fortunately this is not a significant problem in the United States. Although government securi-

---

[2] The alert reader will note that it is not the debt itself that benefits or hurts the economy, but the deficit it finances.

[3] Here again, the debt is not the culprit or the hero, but the expenditures it finances, which are either wise or foolish.

[4] See Chapter 38 for an explanation of why total welfare is reduced by shifting income from the poor to the rich.

ties are largely owned by people with more than the average holding of wealth, the progressive federal income tax takes a larger than average share of tax revenue from them. While there may be a small income redistribution effect from paying interest on the national debt out of tax revenues, economists who have tried to measure it have been unable to find any significant shift. We conclude, therefore, that if a nation's tax system is based on ability to pay, there will be no problem of income redistribution arising from paying interest on the national debt.

Interest payments might be a burden for another reason, even if, as suggested above, they come out of one pocket and go right back into the other. Taxes to finance interest payments may have incentive effects on taxpayers. The folklore is that taxes reduce incentives, but they can also increase them. An increase in taxes will lower after-tax incomes, which may cause people in a success-oriented economy like ours to work harder in order to maintain their incomes and living standards. Economists who have studied the effects of taxes on incentives have been unable to decide which effect is stronger. We know that taxes can change the direction of economic activity, but there is no evidence to show that the present level and pattern of U.S. taxes affects the total amount of economic activity either favorably or unfavorably. Since interest payments on the national debt are so small relative to total Federal tax revenues (less than 10 percent) the incentive effects must be exceptionally small. Remember, too, that it is always possible to borrow to pay interest on the national debt, since there is no limit to the debt's size. That can be done if payment of interest out of taxes is ever felt to be a burden.

For the same reason, the national debt need never be repaid. Old debt matures, but it can always be replaced by new debt. If the banks are loaned up and can't take any more, the debt can always be "monetized" by Federal Reserve action. This happens almost every month, in fact. Old issues of federal securities mature, the Treasury sells new securities to replace them if it wishes, and the Fed sees to it that the money markets can absorb the new issue. No one in either the Treasury or the Fed expects anything else. The national debt is like a forest, in which each tree must eventually die but the forest goes on indefinitely.

If all of this applies to us, it also applies to our children. Future generations will be no more burdened by the national debt than we are. Even if they wished to repay the debt—and they don't ever have to do that—they will be repaying it to themselves. They will probably just replace old debt with new, just as we do. With proper attention to the tax system, there need be no significant incentive or income distribution effects, even if the debt is a great deal larger than it is now. And if changes in the size of the debt are managed with proper regard to timing and purpose, it can bring beneficial rather than harmful results.

One qualification is in order. If economic growth is slowed down, today's debt can burden future generations. For example, if we increase the national debt during a period of full employment, the deficit adds to inflationary pressures, and if the price increases draw resources away from investment and economic growth, future generations will have less. A better example is a wartime deficit, financed by increased debt, which draws resources into destruction rather than progress. But note this: Most of the losses from these misuses of the national debt are borne by the generation living at the time. Only a small portion of the burden can be shifted to future generations by way of investment and the rate of economic growth.

All that we have said about the national debt applies only to an internally owned debt. A national debt owned largely by foreigners, as the U.S. debt was up to the Civil War, can be a real burden. The payments of interest and principal, while made in U.S. dollars, are turned into foreign currencies by the recipients, who want to spend the money at home rather than here. For that to be done, U.S. goods must be sold abroad to make the foreign currencies available.[5] There will be less of our GNP left at home to meet domestic needs. Some of it will be exported and used by foreigners as we pay back what we borrowed from them. United States citizens will be that much poorer. This is no problem for the U.S. at the present time, however, for almost all of our national debt is owned by U.S. citizens or financial institutions.

The national debt should be thought of as an instrument of national economic policy, to be used along with other policy instruments to achieve and sustain a high-pressure economy. The deficits that are financed by the national debt can bring important real benefits in high levels of employment, output, and economic growth. Deficits should not be avoided with the thought that they result in a growth of debt, for the debt itself is no problem if it is properly managed. Proper management means, however, that deficits at times of full employment should be avoided. On the other hand, if the private sector grows slowly, government spending is needed to keep the economy on the full-employment path. When that happens the rise in the national debt should not be viewed as unfortunate, but as the inevitable accompaniment of the proper economic policies.

INFLATION AND THE
HIGH-PRESSURE ECONOMY

Any economy that continually presses upon its capacity to produce will be subject to rising prices. The high-pressure economy will avoid the losses due to unemployment and unused plant capacity, and it will achieve its growth potential. It will have other problems, however, and inflation is likely to be one of them. Alternatively, achievement of a reasonable degree of price stability acts as a constraint that limits the pursuit of full use of resources as the goal of economic policy.

---

[5] The reason for this, and the process involved, will be explained in Chapter 45.

Choices have to be made between these conflicting goals, and there are no clear economic criteria for determining which choice is best. Some will choose stable prices, even at the cost of substantial unemployment and slowed economic growth. Others will prefer rapid growth and reduction of unemployment to the minimal frictional level, even if this means annual price increases of 6 to 7 percent. Most economists are somewhere in the middle, but opinions differ widely among the professionals, too.

Two considerations should be borne in mind. First, some of the burdens of inflation can be reduced by relatively simple modifications of existing practices:

1. Transfer payments, such as veterans' benefits and social security payments, can be tied to the cost of living so that they rise as prices go up.

2. Similar provisions can be made for government securities, insurance policies, savings accounts, and other financial instruments held by savers. This will require changes in financial practices and in their regulation, which, however, are not impossible to accomplish.

Many adaptations of this sort will come about even without government action if the inflationary trend of the 1960s continues for any length of time. Some have already started in the insurance and banking fields.

Second, we should never forget that the losses due to unemployment and slow economic growth are real. They show up as lost output and lost opportunity. For example, a worker may find that prices go up faster than his wage or salary during an inflation. His economic position is worsened because his real income falls. But he is employed, his family is being fed, and the economy as a whole loses no output. But if inflation is halted at the cost of increased unemployment, someone loses his job, that family is considerably worse off, and output is reduced.

This example typifies the policy dilemma. Should many be made a little worse off in order to benefit a few a great deal, with the realization that the few are those at the very bottom of the economy? Which would you prefer —a little less inflation and more unemployment together with lost output, or less unemployment, greater production, and a little more inflation? Why?

THE BALANCE OF PAYMENTS AND THE HIGH-PRESSURE ECONOMY

The international balance of payments is a second constraint on the policies of a high-pressure economy. The balance of payments is simply the net amount of all payments by foreigners to Americans in a year, minus the payments by Americans to foreigners. A deficit means that we pay out more than we receive, building up debts to foreigners that are settled either in our sending them gold or in their acceptance of our promises to pay in the future. If deficits in the balance of payments keep building up, a nation will first lose gold and then the willingness of foreigners to hold more of its debts. Long before that happens the nation will have to change the policies that lead to the deficits in the first place, and that may include devaluing its currency for international trade purposes.[6]

One possible cause of a persistent deficit in the balance of international payments is rising prices. If prices in the United States rise faster than prices in the rest of the world, American exports will fall and imports will increase. Our payments from foreigners will decline and our payments to them will rise. If continued, these trends will cause a deficit in the international balance.

A high-pressure economy is likely to generate inflation. As long as aggregate demand presses upon the capacity to produce, competition among buyers will enable sellers to raise their prices. As long as a country's rate of price increase is no greater than in the other nations that compete with it in international trade, there will not be any serious problem. But if prices in the U.S., for example, start rising more rapidly than those in Western Europe, we are likely to find ourselves in growing difficulties in our financial relationships with the rest of the world. For this reason the domestic policies of a high-pressure economy are limited by the nation's balance of international payments. In the long run, domestic price levels have to be kept from rising more than prices in the rest of the world.[7]

PUBLIC POLICY IN A
GROWING ECONOMY

Modern economics has developed a theoretical framework and policy guidelines that tell us that serious depressions and unemployment can be avoided. Full achievement of the economy's growth potential is feasible. These goals cannot be achieved by a laissez-faire policy, however. They require positive policies whose major dimensions emerge from the analysis of economic growth and the national income.

A wide variety of policy combinations is possible. The strategy we have discussed may appeal to some and not to others. The fundamental concept is that in the long run a nation's wealth and welfare will be maximized if the economy continually presses upon its capacity to produce. A dynamic private sector helps achieve that goal, and policies leading to monetary ease

---

[6] Problems of the international balance of payments will be discussed in some detail in Chapter 45. The explanation in this paragraph is highly simplified, but it is enough to set the stage for an explanation of the connecting links between domestic policy and the international economy.
[7] Inflation has not been a prime cause of the U.S. balance-of-payments deficits over the last 15 years. Those deficits have been caused primarily by large overseas military expenditures. The situation might have been eased if U.S. prices had been lower relative to world prices, but this would only have made it possible to invest more resources in the jungles of Vietnam, to support democracy by greater military aid to the governments of Spain and South Africa, or to promote world peace by sending more arms to Israel and the Arab nations. The origins of our recent balance-of-payments problems have been more political than economic.

help make the private sector dynamic. There is need for a compensatory fiscal policy as well, in which both tax and expenditure policies are oriented toward promotion of investment, increased consumer demand, and provision of social overhead capital.

These high-pressure economic policies cannot be pursued without limit. They will tend to bring increases in the national debt (which is no problem as long as the debt is managed reasonably well) and inflation (which is a problem). If we really want a high-pressure economy, we will probably have to learn to live with a certain amount of steady inflation, although a good deal could be done to ease its impact.

The most serious problems of a high-pressure economy, however, concern the uses to which affluence will be put. One use will have to be greater investment in programs to solve the problems of conservation, and pollution and waste disposal, which are accentuated in a rapidly growing and affluent economy. A second problem area will center around the distribution of benefits from economic growth, both within the United States and in the international economy. None of these important problem areas—resources and the environment, income distribution, and the "third world" of underdeveloped countries—are ones in which the private enterprise sector functions well. Indeed, they are problems because the private sector accentuates rather than reduces them in many important respects.

There is a paradox here. The unrelenting pressure of individual wants and the desire for affluence creates a dynamism in the private sector of the economy that any policies designed to promote the growth of wealth and welfare would do well to nurture. Yet nurturing them brings problems the individual initiative of the private sector has great difficulty in solving, if it can solve them at all. The tensions between the private sector of the economy and the need for social programs are bound to create major issues of social engineering and political action. The high-pressure economy is not one in which all problems are solved.

Summary

Any modern nation can maintain a high-pressure economy that utilizes its output capacity fully and maintains full employment. Use of the national economic budget can show what is needed, and fiscal and monetary policies can assure the necessary level of aggregate demand. Automatic stabilizers built into the structure of the economy can make the job easier. A compensatory fiscal policy can lead to a consistently rising national debt, however, if continuing government deficits are needed.

The national debt is not a significant problem, since it has no economic limit, and need be a problem only if it is poorly managed.

Inflation is a more significant problem, and so is the balance of international payments. They limit the extent to which a nation can single-mindedly pursue the goals of a high-pressure economy. Perhaps the most important problem is the uses to which the output of a high-pressure economy are put, however.

Key Concepts

National economic budget.   An analysis of the balance in the national economy between potential output and potential aggregate demand, together with the policy proposals designed to bring the two together.

Automatic stabilizers.   Aspects of the flow of spending that tend to counterbalance increases or decreases in aggregate demand.

Compensatory fiscal policy.   The type of fiscal policy that seeks to compensate for insufficient aggregate demand.

Monetizing the national debt.   The process whereby increased national debt increases the reserves of the banking system, making possible a multiple expansion of bank credit. Occurs when part of a new issue of government securities is purchased by the Federal Reserve Banks.

THE
MARKET
ECONOMY
V

Part V of this book shows how a system of self-adjusting markets allocates resources in response to consumer demand. It builds on Chapter 5 in Part I, which introduced the basic principles by which resources are allocated in a market economy. In this part we stay strictly within the assumptions of a freely competitive system of markets—the purely competitive model, in the terminology of economic analysis—in order to focus on the essential elements.

Chapter 21 reviews the mechanics of the market mechanism in a form somewhat different from the earlier presentation in Chapter 5, and introduces the marginal analysis, the concept of the rational consumer, the nature of costs, and market equilibrium, four ideas that pervade all of microeconomics. The chapter emphasizes the important theme that freely competitive markets tend to maximize consumer welfare.

Chapter 22 starts to develop the theoretical model of pure competition by examining the relationship between prices and quantity demanded in the market for a good. An appendix explains the elasticity of demand, which is related to the shape of the demand curve. Chapter 23 looks behind the demand curve, introduces the concept of marginal utility, and indicates how the rational consumer can be expected to decide between work and leisure, and between spending and saving, and how he would allocate his expenditures among the various alternatives open to him.

Chapter 24 shifts the focus from the consumer to the producer. It examines the production costs that lie behind the supply curve for a good, particularly marginal costs, and goes on to show how the demand curve for a good is determined when profit-maximizing firms operate in markets in which they have no control over prices. Chapter 25 continues the analysis of the firm, broadens it to the industry as a whole, and shows the long-run triple equilibrium of market, firm, and industry that tends to develop under conditions of pure competition.

Chapter 26 then applies the analysis to U.S. agriculture to review the whole process of market adjustment and to indicate some of the complexities found in actual markets.

Throughout Part V there is strong emphasis on the tendency of the purely competitive economy to produce a welfare-maximizing pattern of production. That theme leads into Parts VI through IX which follow. Part VI indicates that market socialism can also achieve the goal of welfare maximization. Part VII shows why an economy featuring big business and monopolistic elements does not, at least in the terms developed in the analysis in Part V. Part VIII shows that the welfare-maximization principles developed in Part V assume as given the pattern of income distribution, and inquires into the sort of income distribution that will promote the greatest human welfare. Part IX looks at the public economy and how social choices made there fit into the market adjustment process of the private economy, and how they are related to human welfare. This brief look into the things that come after Part V indicates its extraordinary importance. The concepts developed in this part are essential for understanding a huge area in contemporary economics that deals in the most fundamental ways with the condition of man in the modern world.

Chapter 5 should be reviewed at this point for its picture of the functioning of a system of interrelated markets and as a prelude to the next fifteen chapters. In brief summary, three important tasks performed by a self-adjusting system of markets are:

1. Determining the pattern of production, in response to the purchases made by consumers and the costs incurred by producers.

2. Determining which resources are to be used and which are to be left idle, and the specific uses to which resources are put.

3. Determining the distribution of income to the owners of resources.

This chapter goes behind the allocative mechanics by which a system of freely adjusting markets makes these decisions to show that such a system of markets tends toward a maximization of benefits to individuals, assuming that the individuals act rationally and markets are free to respond to their decisions. The basic purpose of the chapter is to set forth the essential elements of the system as a whole prior to examination of its component parts.

The Basic Economics of Market Systems

21

FREEDOM, CONSTRAINTS, AND MARKET FORCES

The allocative mechanism of a market system involves many millions of independent decisions made by many individual consumers and producers. Advocates of the market economy as a way of organizing economic life emphasize the individual freedom implicit in a freely operating market economy and the individual benefits derived from it. But it must be remembered that freedom is never absolute. It always operates within constraints. In the case of the free market, those constraints are market forces, all-pervasive, impersonal and not amenable to control by individuals (except where monopoloid conditions exist). Those market forces determine prices for everything bought and sold in the market system. Values in exchange are determined by the market.

Relationships between prices provide individuals with the alternatives on which decisions are based. Decisions about what to buy, what to produce and sell, which resources to use for which purposes, and what to pay for

the use of resources, depend on prevailing prices. These prices are the constraints within which the individual functions. The market system itself, rather
than government, constrains individual behavior. The constraints of the market
are more rigid and intractable than those of any government. For example, if
you have a product you would like to produce and sell for support of yourself
and your family but can't find enough buyers or anyone to provide you with
capital—well, that's tough. You had better try something else, even if it requires
a style of life less attractive to you. Millions of farm families found this out the
hard way in recent decades. On the other hand, if government prohibits certain
types of economic activity, such as traffic in narcotics, the prohibition can be
overcome by engaging in them outside the law, or by bribery, or both. Thousands of members of the underworld have exploited these opportunities in
recent decades, to their great joy and profit.

Economic planners know about the limits imposed by the market. When
a government edict, or a government allocation of resources, or an attempt to
fix prices, collides with the forces of the market, the market usually wins. Black
markets during wartime rationing are an example. The way they arise can
be shown by using the simple supply-demand-price diagrams explained in
Chapter 4.

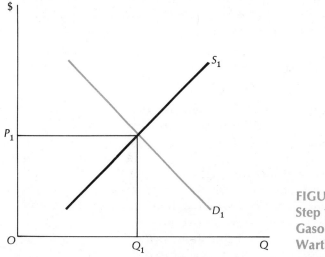

FIGURE 21-1
**Step 1: The Market for
Gasoline Prior to
Wartime Rationing**

In peacetime, the interactions of demand and supply determine the price
P_1 and the amount sold Q_1.

During wartime, allocation of gasoline resources away from civilian uses
causes the market supply schedule to shift from S_1 to S_2, leading to a higher
price P_2 if no controls are imposed.

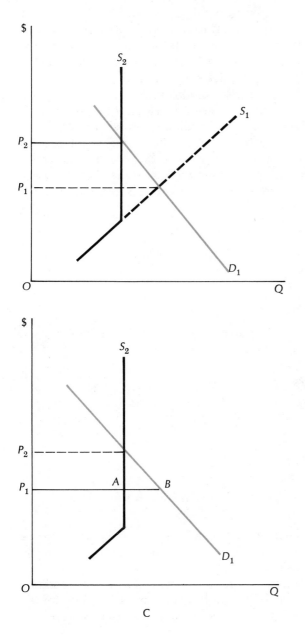

FIGURE 21-2
Step 2: Limited Civilian
Supplies of Gasoline in
Wartime Would Normally
Cause Its Price to Go Up

FIGURE 21-3
Step 3: Government
Imposes Price Controls
Designed to Keep the
Price of Gasoline at the
Pre-war Level

At the controlled price P_1, the quantity demanded exceeds the available
supply by amount AB. This excess demand will otherwise push the price up-

wards toward the market equilibrium P_2. The only way to prevent it is by rationing and police action against black markets. If the police action is weak and ineffective, the price will move up toward P_2, gasoline will be sold on the illegal market at the higher price, and supplies will tend to disappear from the legal channels of distribution. The black market will take over.

The only ways open to governments to prevent black markets are patriotic appeals and force. Both can be effective, depending on how strong the psychological appeals are, and how much force is applied. The result of their interaction with the market forces that push prices upward is indeterminate. That is, the prevailing price in the black market will fall somewhere between P_1 and P_2, depending on how vigorously the price controls and rationing are enforced.

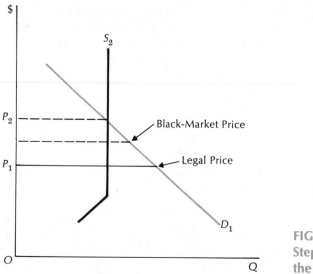

FIGURE 21-4
Step 4: The Legal Price and
the Black Market Price

The black market price will fluctuate between P_1 and P_2, depending on the amount of police power applied and the force of psychological appeals, always tending upward toward P_2 as a result of market forces.

The market mechanism is indeed powerful. Its effects can be modified somewhat, but the extent of that modification is limited and temporary for the most part. In the long run, the market forces that allocate resources and determine incomes tend to dominate efforts to control them.[1]

---

[1] Why should a government ration commodities? Why not let the market allocate them, even in wartime? The answer is that the market would allocate goods to those who can pay the higher price caused by restricted supply. Gasoline would go to the rich for their pleasure boats, for example, instead of to workers in munitions plants who need the gasoline to drive to work. Rationing and price controls are used to achieve social goals that would not be achieved through the market mechanism.

MARGINAL ANALYSIS

Market forces normally operate through small increases and decreases. This is particularly true of competitive markets composed of many buyers and sellers. It is less true of markets dominated by a few large sellers or buyers, but even there the decisions involve changes from one position to another.

Here is an example. You are the operator of an automobile service station, and have to determine how long you want to remain open. Should you close at 10:00 P.M., 11:00 P.M., or midnight, or should you stay open still longer? As a businessman, you want to make as much money as you can, and you don't care to operate when your costs exceed your revenues.

One part of the problem can be set aside immediately. No matter what your hours of operation, you have certain *fixed costs* that must be paid, such as rent, your own salary as owner or manager, accounting and other business services, and similar items. Since these bills must be met anyway, they have no relevance to a decision about whether to stay open an additional hour or to close an hour earlier.

Other costs will increase with the hours of operation. These *variable costs* include wages of the attendant, cost of gasoline and other items sold, cost of utilities for the added hours, and some other items. However, longer hours will bring in additional revenue. As long as the additional revenues exceed the costs incurred from longer operation, total profit from the enterprise will rise.

That relationship is the key: *when additional revenue exceeds additional costs, total profit rises.* A look at changes in revenues and costs will show the direction in which total profit is moving.

Now suppose that in experimenting with different closing times, you have accumulated the information shown in Table 21–1.

TABLE 21–1
Gasoline Station Operation

Hours of Operation	Receipts (Hourly)	Variable Costs (Hourly)	Change in Profits (Receipts minus Variable Costs)
10 P.M.–11 P.M.	$122	$86	+$36
11 P.M.–12 P.M.	84	72	+ 12
12 P.M.–1 A.M.	32	48	− 16
1 A.M.–2 A.M.	26	44	− 18

This information tells you that between 10:00 P.M. and 11:00 P.M. your receipts average $122 and your additional expenses are $86, with a net addition to profits of $36, and so on to 2:00 A.M. Up to midnight your profits rise, but decline thereafter. If you are interested in maximizing profits, you will keep the station open at least until midnight, but will certainly close it before 1:00 A.M.

Further experimentation may indicate a 12:30 A.M. closing time, if you wish to refine your decision still further. But at some time between midnight and 1:00 A.M. the additional costs will start to exceed the additional revenues, and you will be losing money that you need not lose.[2]

This way of thinking about decisions is called *marginal analysis*. Although applied here to a business decision, the method is applicable to any maximization problem. It is particularly relevant in the market economy because market prices can be used as measures of benefits and costs, at least as a first approximation.[3]

SOME DEFINITIONS

The marginal unit *is the last unit bought or sold. Economists call increases or decreases around that unit* the margin. *Benefits derived from the last unit are called* marginal utility *or* marginal satisfactions. *The costs associated with the last unit are* marginal costs. *The marginal analysis will be used extensively in the chapters that follow, so keep these definitions in mind.*

RATIONAL DECISIONS

Marginal analysis is the key to rational decision making in economic affairs. Indeed, it is a key to rational decisions in many fields. Take military strategy, for example. A commanding general has the goal of subduing an enemy. He has at his disposal a limited amount of resources in the form of men, guns,

---

[2] The figures used here are actual ones, somewhat simplified, taken from the operation of a service station operated by a nonprofit enterprise with which the author was associated and that employed the hard-core unemployed. We wanted to close at midnight, but the oil company that leased the station to us wanted it open all night. It was located at an expressway exit and they wanted to sell gas, whether we made money or not. So the lease was written to require 24-hour operation. It is of such material that the relationships between big enterprise and small are built.

[3] Economists have to be very careful here. Prices do not always measure full benefits and full costs. We have met this problem before and will keep coming back to it from time to time. For example, the cost of education is greater than the direct costs of the buildings, faculty, and other resources used in educating students. It also includes the value of the things students could be producing, but are not, because their time is spent in school. Likewise, the benefits are broader than those that accrue to the individual student and for which he might be expected to pay. They include the broader benefits others derive because educated people contribute more to society as a whole because of their education. As a result, the price charged for education (tuition) is less than the full cost to society, and also less than the full benefits. Subsidies are provided to educational institutions (even private ones), and indirectly to the students, because of these disparities.

ammunition, ships, airplanes, and other materiel. A good general will seek the strategy and tactics that will achieve his goal with the minimum expenditure of resources, so that he will have the maximum amount left to take care of the next enemy. At each step in his campaign he must weigh the potential gains against the potential losses. Only if the gains are greater than the losses will he be better off and the step worth taking.[4]

This formal type of economic analysis is characteristic of decision making in economic affairs. Businessmen in competitive markets can be expected to seek out that path of action which they believe maximizes their profits. Some may seek immediate profit and go for a quick killing. Others may take a longer-range view and develop a strategy to maximize profits in the long run. But one thing is clear: the business firm that does not try to make the largest profits will operate at a disadvantage when competing with those that do. It will generate less capital out of profits, and will have greater difficulty in obtaining capital from the capital markets. Investors certainly seek the greatest gains (taking risk and uncertainty into account), and their behavior gives the advantage to profit-maximizing firms. In a growing, competitive economy, the prosperous firms will be those that maximize profits, while those that do not will fall by the wayside.

With consumers the situation is less clear. An argument can be made, on logical grounds, that consumers seek to maximize the satisfactions they obtain from the use of their resources. They wouldn't be "rational" if they didn't. But that proposition is impossible to prove. Any pattern of behavior, no matter how odd or perverse it may appear to be, will fit the proposition that the person involved gets pleasure out of it. Masochists like to be whipped, and sadists like to whip them, according to the findings and theories of modern psychology.

Consumer behavior is influenced by the social system within which consumers function. People are educated in patterns of action that fit the standards and values of their family, community, work group, church, and the other groups within which their lives are carried on. Their choices are not "free," but are constrained by the social institutions within which they function. For example, a college professor does not act like a Mohawk war chief, even though he may give vent to some savage emotions when watching a football game or grading examinations.

Consumer behavior is influenced by social patterns, social environments, social attitudes, and habit. But within those constraints choices are still made, and it is here that comparisons of gains and costs can be made. The social

---

[4] This type of analysis has its limits. For example, this example from military strategy does not take into consideration the use of atomic weapons. Since both the U.S. and the USSR have such a large "overkill" ability, one cannot overcome the power of the other without being destroyed itself. While this situation doesn't make the two nations friendly toward each other, it does avert open warfare and channels their rivalry into other areas. As long as the leaders remain rational the world won't be destroyed.

environment may make available a relatively large area of decision making for individual choice. Or it can restrict those choices to a relatively narrow area. In either case, however, there will be opportunity for rational consumers to compare positions at the margin and to make welfare-maximizing decisions.

Reflect for a moment on the last time you ordered a dinner in a restaurant. How did you decide on steak, as compared with lobster or roast beef, or anything else on the menu. Consciously or unconsciously, there was a comparison of benefits to be derived from the alternatives, compared with the prices at which they were available. You made the selection you "liked" the most, given your tastes, the money you had at the time, and all of the other constraints that you may have felt. Within that framework, a welfare-maximizing decision was made.

All of these examples of rational action involve a comparison of benefits and costs at the margin, with the objective of maximizing net benefits. In all cases there is a choice among alternatives, and there are constraints imposed on the choice. That is the meaning of rational behavior as it is analyzed in economics.

THE NATURE OF COSTS

You win a free trip to Bermuda, with all of your expenses paid. Would you refuse to go? Some people would, strange as that may seem.

Why? Because they may feel that it would be better for them to spend the time doing other things. Example: The college professor who knows he is dying from an incurable cancer may want to finish the book he is writing that will finally get down on paper the unpublished results of his latest researches. He just can't afford the time a trip to Bermuda would take.

Another example: The businessman with a big deal on the fire, who stands to gain much more than the cost of a Bermuda vacation. If the deal goes through successfully, he could take ten vacations. In this case the vacation in Bermuda might be very expensive for him.

These two examples have one thing in common. The alternatives are worth more to the people involved than the free vacation. The costs are greater than the benefits. Even though there are no direct money costs, there are other costs involved in the choices. Those costs are the benefits that have to be given up because an alternative path of action is not taken. Everyone has a variety of ways to use his time and his resources. Some provide him with greater benefits than others. A rational choice will select the use that provides the maximum benefit. The cost of that choice is the benefit that could be obtained from the next most favorable use of time and resources.

All choices involve _opportunity costs_ of this type. Keep this principle in mind. It is one of the fundamental concepts of economics—indeed, of the logic of rational action in any sphere of life. No matter what choices we make, we must give up something in order to get what we want. Nothing in this world is free.

THE MARKET EQUILIBRIUM

The concept of equilibrium is fundamental to an understanding of how a market economy works. It is a very simple principle: any system reaches an equilibrium when the forces that operate within it are in balance. One force neutralizes another, leading to a stable relationship in which the existing pattern remains unchanged.

The solar system is a classic example of a physical equilibrium; in it, the gravitational forces and motions of sun, planets, and satellites have established a relationship that holds the system unchanged. There is motion within the system, and the system as a whole is moving, but the units within the system are so related to each other that their movements are repeated endlessly. Even Halley's comet returns periodically, following its odd but predictable track.

Two forces within the market economy lead to equilibrium: benefits and costs. Benefits are the force that causes people to take action. Costs provide the limits to that action. When an action is contemplated, the rational individual will balance the marginal benefits he expects to obtain against the marginal costs he expects to incur. When the marginal benefits exceed the marginal costs, he will take the contemplated action. When they don't, he will stay where he is.

The general principle can be stated in another fashion. If at the existing price charged for a commodity, the marginal benefits to consumers of increased output are greater than the marginal costs to producers, there will be strong economic forces set in motion to increase the output. Only when the marginal benefits from additional output fall to equality with the marginal costs (or marginal costs rise to equal marginal benefits) will there be no advantage to increased output. We should think of it in this way: as long as any consumer can increase his benefits by an amount more than the increased costs to any producer, the self-adjusting market is not at its equilibrium position.

Here is a hypothetical example. The price of milk is 35¢ per quart. But Joey Schlemiel is willing to buy an additional quart of milk at that price. That is, he judges that the benefits to himself that could be derived from another quart of milk are worth more than 35¢ worth of anything else, including savings. On the other hand, Billy Schlemazel would be willing to produce and sell one more quart of milk if he were paid 35¢ for it. His costs would be less than that amount. In a competitive market with a reasonably free system of information, Schlemiel and Schlemazel are brought together and make their transaction; indeed, that is exactly the function performed by competitive markets. Both will gain. Schlemiel will have acquired milk, which he values at more than 35¢, while Schlemazel will have acquired 35¢, which is worth more to him than the milk. The two will continue to trade until Schlemiel is no longer willing to pay more than 35¢ for a quart of milk, or until Schlemazel finds that producing and selling another quart costs him more than 35¢.

But why would Schlemiel stop buying milk at a price of 35¢ per quart? The fact that he does stop indicates that he would rather spend the next 35¢ on something else. At some point, Schlemiel decides that other opportunities for consumption (or saving) are more attractive to him. At that point the market price becomes a measure of both benefits and costs associated with the last quart purchased.[5]

❙Marginal benefits to buyer = Market price = Marginal costs to buyer. ❙

Now let's look at the seller. Suppose Schlemiel has all the milk he wants at a price of 35¢, but Schlemazel's cost of producing and selling another quart is only 33¢. It would clearly be to Schlemazel's advantage to lower the price, thereby inducing Schlemiel to buy more. And if he didn't lower his price, in a competitive market someone else would. So Schlemazel reduces his price as long as the price exceeds his additional costs. He will continue to do so until the price is just equal to the cost of producing and selling the last quart of milk, including whatever return will be large enough to make it worthwhile for Schlemazel to continue his operations.

Schlemazel, then, continues to produce additional milk until the revenues he obtains from selling one more quart are no greater than the cost of producing that quart. At that point he can no longer add to his profits. At that point the market price will measure both his revenues and his costs:

Marginal revenues to seller = Market price = Marginal costs to seller.

The essential element in reaching and preserving the market equilibrium is equality of marginal benefits and costs. As far as Schlemiel is concerned, the benefits from the last quart of milk he purchased are worth *to him* just what he paid for it, say 33.5¢, and neither more nor less. As for Schlemazel, the price of 33.5¢ provides gains just large enough to compensate him for the costs and effort of producing that last quart. Benefits and costs for both buyer and seller have been equalized at the margin.

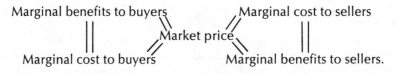

When that situation has been reached, neither buyer nor seller can improve his position, the price does not change, and the pattern of production and sales continues without change. The market is in equilibrium.

MAXIMIZATION OF BENEFITS

The market equilibrium that emerges from profit-maximizing behavior by sellers and welfare-maximizing behavior by buyers has one extremely important characteristic: *the total of benefits to both buyers and sellers is maximized.*

---

[5] The concept of cost used here is opportunity costs, discussed a few pages back.

The buyer, Schlemiel in our example, added to his total benefits with each quart of milk he purchased. But he finally stopped buying. If he were acting rationally, he must have decided that the added benefits were not equal to the added costs. For the last quart of milk he bought, however, Schlemiel must have decided that the additional benefits were at least equal to the additional costs. If he adds benefits every time he buys an additional quart, it must follow that when he stops buying he has maximized the total benefits he obtains. If he could add more net benefits, he wouldn't stop buying.

As for Schlemazel, the seller, his task was easier. He could calculate his revenues and his costs in dollars and cents. He could see that additional sales added to his net gains up to the last unit sold. But he stopped expanding his sales because another unit sold would add more to his costs than to his revenues. He also had arrived at a position that maximized his net gains.

The principle can be generalized for the economy as a whole. If each Schlemiel is at his best position, and each Schlemazel is also there, it is not possible for the group as a whole to move to anything better, at least for this set of transactions. Benefits to the group are maximized when each individual in the group maximizes his own individual benefits.[6]

SOME CONDITIONS

Maximization of benefits through the market mechanism, while a pervasive and continuing tendency wherever buyers and sellers exchange with each other, requires a number of conditions. Without them the maximization of benefits can only be approximated. The chief conditions are these:

1. Free markets. If markets are free of controls by both public and private sources of power, consumers and sellers are better able to select those paths of action that maximize their benefits. This is the most powerful argument against both private monopoly and public regulation. Constraints against freedom of action in the market limit the maximizing behavior of individuals.

2. Information. Both buyers and sellers must know about all the alternatives open to them. If they don't, they will not be able to maximize their benefits. For example, informative advertising helps, while deceptive advertising hinders the achievement of maximum benefits.

3. Full substitutability of the factors of production. Just as buyers and sellers must have full knowledge of all alternatives and access to them, so producers must be free to use resources for all purposes. Capital must be freely substitutable for labor, for example, in order that produc-

---

[6] The group as a whole can get together and decide that it is mutually beneficial to reduce individual benefits for each person in order to provide things that will be used jointly, such as parks or schools or nuclear weapons. This does not change the basic principle: the resources left in the hands of the members of the group will be allocated to achieve maximum benefits when each member of the group has achieved a position of maximum benefits.

ers may be able to minimize costs of production and produce what consumers want. If the technological relationships in production processes are rigid, the flexibility of adjustment of the entire economy is reduced, and the alternatives open to producers are limited.

In essence, a flexible economy with the greatest freedom of choice and the largest amount of information widely available to all is the one in which maximization of benefits can proceed the farthest. Anything that reduces flexibility of adjustment, knowledge, or freedom to choose will compromise the achievement of maximum benefits.

This proposition is the heart of the ideology of capitalism. The social philosophy that advocates laissez-faire as a policy rests on the economic analysis that connects individual decisions with maximum benefits by way of free markets. It is this philosophy, with its accompanying economic analysis, that Adam Smith systematically developed in the eighteenth century and that became the starting point for modern economic analysis.

Ideology is one thing; scientific analysis is something else. In the process of working out the *economics* of self-adjusting markets we learn a great deal about the world in which we live. However imperfect it may be, much of our economic activity takes place within the framework of a system of interrelated markets. Many markets are not free of private and public controls, knowledge is less than perfect, and resources are often immobile. Nevertheless, by starting with competitive markets, we can learn the essential elements of how market forces operate and develop a norm against which less competitive market situations can be judged. We can then move to consideration of monopoloid markets with various limitations on alternative choices, and look at how markets might function in a socialist economy. In doing so, we shall obtain a richer understanding of the larger alternatives facing the contemporary world. We embark, then, on an analysis of the theory of markets.

Summary

The interaction of supply and demand in self-adjusting markets indicates that market forces move powerfully toward their own equilibrium. They provide strong constraints within which economic activity is carried on and within which economic policy must function.

The market adjustment process involves small increases or decreases in moving from one position toward another. Although this process of adjustment is always going on and never comes to a halt, it can be analyzed as if it were moving from one equilibrium position to another through a series of small changes. This theoretical method is called the marginal analysis.

The market system is pushed toward equilibrium by the efforts of consumers and producers to maximize their individual net benefits. Individual comparisons are made of benefits and costs at the margin, and the costs of any choice are essentially the benefits from other choices that have to be foregone. The result of individual choices is a general equilibrium in which market prices play a key role. For any one good,

$$\text{Marginal benefits to buyers} = \text{Marginal cost to buyers} =$$

$$\text{Market price} =$$

$$\text{Marginal cost to sellers} = \text{Marginal benefits to sellers.}$$

This pattern of market equilibrium represents a welfare-maximizing position for both buyers and sellers.

This solution is subject to important conditions, all involving the flexibility of the market and complete freedom of choice by both buyers and sellers: markets must be free of public and private constraints, alternatives must be fully known, and factors of production must be fully substitutable for each other. Although these conditions are never fully present except in a theoretical analysis, the self-adjusting market can be expected to move toward a welfare-maximizing equilibrium to the extent that it does have the freedom and flexibility to adjust.

Key Concepts

Market equilibrium.   A stable relationship among market forces that leaves existing patterns unchanged. Occurs when all economic units have equated costs and benefits at the margin.

Opportunity cost.   The cost of anything is the benefit or satisfaction that could have been obtained by choosing something else.

Marginal unit.   The last unit bought or sold.

Marginal benefits.   Benefits obtained from the last unit, sometimes called **marginal utility**.

Marginal costs.   Costs associated with the last unit.

Marginal analysis.   The theoretical method that analyzes market forces in terms of marginal units, marginal benefits, and marginal costs. It assumes that rational decisions are made by an implicit or explicit use of marginal analysis by economic units.

This chapter is the first of two that deal with the demand side of the market for a product or service. They take up the shape and locus of the demand curve. The discussion starts with the law of demand in its simple and more general formulations. An appendix discusses the shape of the demand curve and the concept of elasticity of demand. The next chapter analyzes the welfare-maximizing behavior of consumers and the concept of marginal utility. Taken together these three units present the essential elements of the theory of consumer demand.

The Law of Demand

22

THE SIMPLE LAW OF DEMAND

Most of us, living as we do in the midst of a market-oriented society, are intuitively aware of the relationship between the price of a good and the amount buyers are willing to buy: the higher the price, the less bought in a given period of time. Conversely, if the price is lower, more will be bought. In other words, there is a general relationship between the price of a commodity and the amount demanded that can be expressed in a variety of ways:

1. Algebraically: $D_a = (f)P_a$. This is the general proposition that the demand for good a is systematically related to its price.

2. Geometrically: the demand curve, which pictures the relationship between price and the quantity demanded for good a, as in Figure 22-1.

3. Arithmetically: the demand schedule, as shown in Table 22–1, which gives the actual data used in constructing the demand curve for good a.

TABLE 22–1
Demand Schedule for Good a

P_a	Q_a (Units)
$10	10,000
11	9,000
12	8,000
13	7,000

direct Relationship

The relationship shown in the demand schedule, namely, a $1 increase in price associated with a 1,000-unit decline

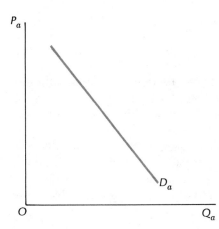

FIGURE 22-1
The demand curve shows that at higher prices relatively little will be purchased, while at lower prices more will be bought.

in purchases, can be expressed as an algebraic quantity; in that form it states the functional relationship between D_a and P_a, shown in the formula $D_a = (f)P_a$.

These three ways of stating the simple law of demand all say the same thing, merely moving from the more general to the more specific.

AN EXAMPLE FROM THE REAL WORLD

The normal relationship expressed by the simple law of demand can be readily illustrated. Figure 22-2 shows consumption and prices of apples in the United States between 1949 and 1960. For each year, the amount consumed and the

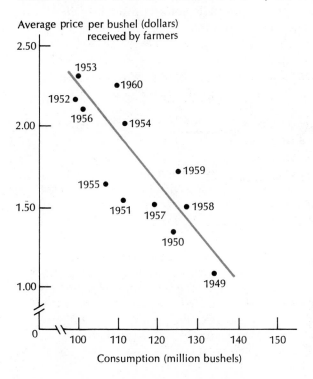

FIGURE 22-2
Prices and Consumption of Apples, 1949–1960
(*Source: U.S. Dept. of Agriculture*, Agricultural Statistics: 1963 *[Washington: U.S. Government Printing Office, 1963].*)

average price per bushel is plotted as a single point, with price measured horizontally and consumption measured vertically. A demand curve for apples has been drawn as a straight line that approximates the relationship between consumption and price shown by the scattered data for each year. The points on the chart fall in a rather narrow band around the demand curve, although none fall exactly on it. The demand curve for apples slopes downward to the right. This indicates that consumers buy more apples at lower prices and fewer apples at higher prices.

The fact that most of the points in Figure 22-2 are close to the demand curve tells us that price is an important element in determining consumer behavior in the market for apples. The fact that all the points lie off the demand curve itself and are scattered around it in a random pattern indicates that other factors also influence consumer purchases of apples.

THE GENERAL LAW OF DEMAND

Although there is a relationship between the price of a good and the quantity demanded, the large variation in the data suggests that other forces also influence the quantity of a good that consumers are willing to buy. Indeed, there are so many things other than price that affect consumer decisions to buy that a whole profession of market analysts has developed to advise businessmen about them. The more important additional forces are:

1. Prices of other goods. Purchases of one good will vary with the prices of other goods. If the price of chickens falls, some consumers will buy less beef and more chicken, substituting chicken for beef in their diet. If the price of shoes falls, and consumers buy more shoes, demand for shoelaces will probably increase. If rents rise substantially, creating a squeeze on consumer incomes, purchases of movie tickets, magazines, and more expensive cuts of meat may be reduced. The general rules are these:
   a. Where commodities are good substitutes for each other (chicken–beef), the effect of changes in the price of one on the sales of the other may be large.
   b. Where products are complementary to each other (shoes–shoelaces), a change in the price of one will affect its demand *and* the demand for the other.
   c. In some cases, where purchases of a good take up a substantial portion of consumer incomes (housing), a change in its price (rent) can affect the demand for everything else. *Income Effect*

2. Income. The level of family income is an important determinant of the amount of a good that is purchased. Generally speaking, the higher the family income, the greater the demand for goods of all kinds. For most goods, if family incomes rise while the price of the good does not change, total purchases will rise. Demand for the good is said

to increase, and the entire demand curve shifts upward and to the right. In some cases an increase in income may lead to a fall in demand for a good. For example, higher incomes may cause families to consume less bread and more meat. In this case bread would be called an *inferior good*: demand for it falls as incomes rise.

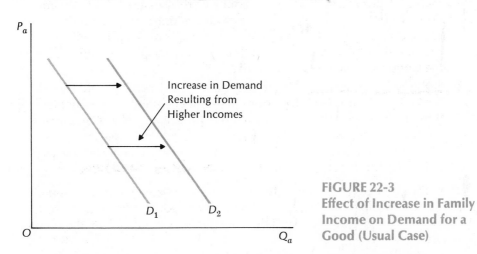

FIGURE 22-3
Effect of Increase in Family Income on Demand for a Good (Usual Case)

3. Distribution of income. Patterns of expenditure change as incomes rise. The very poor spend a very large proportion of their incomes on housing and food, save very little, and do not spend a great deal on books, travel, entertainment, education, and the like. The very rich, on the other hand, spend smaller proportions of their income on housing and food, and larger proportions go for savings, entertainment, travel, and so on. Since dollars represent votes in the marketplace, and turn up as demand for goods, a shift in the pattern of income distribution will shift the pattern of market demand.

4. Population and its characteristics. A large population means a potentially high demand for goods, and increases in population mean increases in demand for most goods. The characteristics of the population are also important. Better-educated people tend to buy more medical care and education. A population of small families will need more housing units than a population of large families, and the type of housing unit will differ as well. A young population consumes more food than an older population of equal numbers: food intake rises to a maximum during the teen-age years and then declines as people grow older.

5. Tastes and preferences. Many of our tastes and preferences are determined by the social institutions within which our lives are carried on, and the ways in which we are brought up. Catholics will eat substantial amounts of fish, and Jews little pork. Cornmeal and grits are popular in

the South, bagels and lox in the New York area, scrod in Boston, and pralines in New Orleans. Not very many North Americans eat breadfruit, which is popular in the South Pacific, but we do import large volumes of bananas and pineapple.

Within any society individual tastes will vary, and that, of course makes for diversity and wide availability of choices. Perhaps more important, tastes can change rapidly for many people simultaneously creating the fashions and fads that are especially prevalent in affluent economies with large amounts of discretionary income over and above the amounts required for necessaries.

6. <u>Stocks of durable good</u>s. An affluent society will also have built up substantial stocks of durable goods in use, such as houses, household furniture and appliances, electrical equipment, automobiles, and the like. Demand for new units will be heavily influenced by the age and condition of the existing stock. Once acquired, they need only be replaced as they wear out or become obsolete. **& other wealth**

The large number of factors that influence the demand for a commodity requires that we state the law of demand in more general form, to emphasize the fact that the price of a good is not the only determinant of the amount purchased:

$$D_a = f(P_a, P_b, \ldots, P_n, I, (S), t),$$

where D_a = demand for good a,
P_a = price of good a,
$P_b \ldots P_n$ = prices of other goods,
I = income,
S = stocks (in parentheses because it affects only durables or storable items),
t = time, a proxy for those factors that change relatively slowly, such as tastes, income distribution, and population.

This formulation tells us that demand for a good depends on its price, the prices of other goods, consumer incomes, stocks on hand (if the good is durable or storable), and a variety of other factors that change slowly over time. It is a a much more general statement than the simple law of demand, $D_a = f(P_a)$, which relates demand directly to price alone.

A Problem in Methodology and Its Solution

The general law of demand, while far closer to reality than the simple law of demand, is much less useful in analyzing the operation of a market economy. For a wide variety of analytical problems we should like to be able to take an established price as given, and then proceed to analyze how businessmen adjust their decisions to it. Yet many of the ways in which producers adjust to market prices affect incomes and their distribution, prices of other goods, and indeed, all of the components of the general law of demand. This creates difficulties in the analysis, because then the demand curve starts jumping around instead of standing still. This, in turn affects business decisions, which affect the factors that influence demand, which . . . well, to facilitate the analysis something has to be done to anchor the demand curve so that the rest of the market adjustment process can be carefully worked out.

The solution is to assume constancy of all but one factor in the general law of demand. We can *assume* that prices of other goods do not change, that incomes, stocks, income distribution, tastes and preferences, population and its characteristics, and all other influences except the price of the good itself, remain constant for purposes of the analysis. This is the famous *ceteris paribus* (other things being equal) assumption that is a feature of much economic analysis. Making this assumption reduces the law of demand to its simple form:

$$D_a = f(P_a),$$

and keeps the demand curve firmly anchored in one place on the page, as in Figure 22-4.

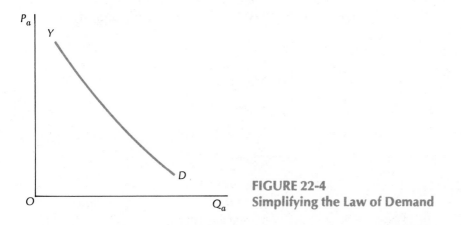

FIGURE 22-4
Simplifying the Law of Demand

This simplification is not made without cost, however. It is achieved only by restricting the scope and applicability of the analysis. First, only short periods of time can be covered. Since some factors that influence price undergo change slowly over time, their effect will not be felt if the time period under analysis is short enough. They will have such a small impact that their effect can legitimately be ignored.

Second, only small changes in prices and quantities can be analyzed. For example, a large change in the price of beef may cause consumers to change significantly their purchases of other goods. This will cause those prices to change, which in turn will affect the decisions of consumers about whether or not to buy beef. In short, a large change in the price of a good may so change the relationships between prices that a whole group of demand curves will shift position. To keep our analysis correct, after making the simplifying assumptions we must limit it to changes in price and quantity so small that their effect on markets for other goods is infinitesimally small.

At this point we can restate the simple law of demand:

The demand for a good is a function of its price:

$$D_a = f(P_a),$$

assuming instantaneous or very short time periods and very small changes in price and quantity.

Nothing is free even in theoretical inquiries. In order to make the analysis manageable, we have had to assume constancy in some important variables. Having done that, we must recognize that the ensuing analysis is correct only within some severe limits. Truth is a hard taskmaster.

Change in the Quantity Demanded

Our formulation of the simple law of demand implies that it exists only at one moment in time. Each point on the demand curve is an alternative to any other point on the curve at that moment in time. In Figure 22-5, if the price

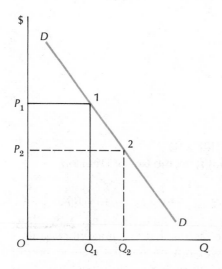

FIGURE 22-5
Change in Quantity Demanded
Given the demand curve DD, points 1 and 2 show different combinations of price and quantity. If the price were P_1, the quantity demanded would be less than if the price were P_2. A change in price brings a change in the price demanded.

were P_1, the quantity demanded would be Q_1. Alternatively, if the price were P_2, the quantity demanded would be Q_2. These are alternative positions on the same demand curve and in the same demand schedule.

Change in Demand

A change in demand means a shift in the entire demand schedule and the demand curve. You are familiar with that idea from Chapter 4, but it is important that it be repeated here to contrast it with the concept of the change in quantity demanded. A change in demand means that consumer tastes have changed, or one of the other factors in the general law of demand has changed, so that the whole curve shifts, as shown by Figures 22-6 and 22-7.

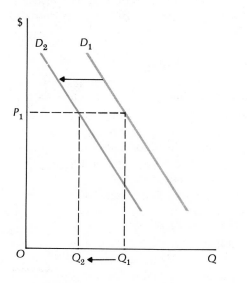

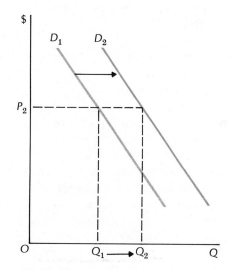

FIGURE 22-6
Decrease in Demand

A decrease in demand occurs when, without a change in price P_1, the quantity demanded falls $Q_1 \rightarrow Q_2$. The demand curve D_1 has shifted to the left D_2.

FIGURE 22-7
Increase in Demand

An increase in demand occurs when, without a change in price P_1, the quantity demand increases $Q_1 \rightarrow Q_2$. The demand curve D_1 has shifted to the right D_2.

**Distinguishing Between a Change in
Quantity Demanded and a Change in Demand**

Students of economics must always keep in mind the difference between a shift along the demand curve (change in quantity demanded) and a shift of the demand curve itself (change in demand). They each result from a different cause. A shift along the demand curve results from a change in price, with no change in the conditions that determine the demand schedule. A shift of the demand curve itself implies that the factors that determine the demand schedule have changed.

This distinction may seem inconsequential, but failure to grasp it can result in some ludicrous errors. For example, reasoning like the following has even crept into the *Congressional Record*, not to mention hundreds of examination papers written by college students:

> "A tax on automobiles will cause their price to rise. The increase in price, however, will cause consumers to buy fewer cars. This decrease in demand will bring the price back down to its former level."

You should be able to explain the fallacy in this line of argument. If you can't, reread the material on change in quantity demanded and change in demand and try again.

The Demand Curve at a Moment in Time

One other technical point about the demand curve must be emphasized. The demand curve as it emerges from the simple law of demand exists only at a single moment in time. That moment must be long enough to encompass changes in price and consequent shifts along the demand curve. But the moment in time must be short enough so that consumer tastes and incomes, the prices of other goods, stocks of durable goods, and other longer-range factors can't change enough to cause the demand curve to shift.

How long is this theoretical moment in time? Some economic theorists consider it to be instantaneous. Others call it a "day." Whatever its length, it is long enough to enable price to change but too short for any other changes to occur. The demand curve that exists during that moment in time is usually called the *market demand curve* and the time itself is usually called the *market period*. We shall use that terminology in the analysis that follows.

THE DEMAND FOR APPLES RECONSIDERED

Earlier in this chapter the demand for apples was used as an example of the relationship between price and quantity demanded. We used data from a twelve-year period, however, and then had the audacity to draw in a demand curve for apples for the entire time. Isn't that moment in time a little long? Won't incomes, tastes, and other factors have changed over such a long period of time? Of course, the answer is yes. The data shown in Figure 22-2 are subject to the influence of all the factors that are included in the general law of demand, which is why the individual points are scattered around the trend line. But the fact that a demand curve based on price and quantity alone emerges easily from inspection of the data shows that, in this case, the relationship between price and quantity overwhelms the effects of all other factors. It also tells us that in spite of the restrictions and qualifications necessary to state the law of demand correctly for purposes of economic analysis, there is a strong basis in reality for the proposition that

> for any commodity during a given period of time, the higher the price the smaller the quantity demanded, other things remaining the same.

Summary

The simple proposition that more of a commodity is sold at a lower price than at a higher price embodies a complex series of problems for economic analysis. The simple law of demand,

$$D_a = f(P)_a,$$

is a variant of the general law of demand,

$$D_a = f(P_a, P_b, \ldots, P_n, I, (S), t).$$

which is more accurate but less convenient for analyzing the functioning of markets. The simple law of demand is derived from the general law by assuming that all variables except P_a remain constant. This assumption fixes the locus of the demand curve, but at the cost of reduced generality.

The law of demand applies only to a single moment in time. Demand may shift from one moment in time to another, but this phenomenon must be carefully distinguished from alternative positions on the demand curve at a single moment in time.

Key Concepts

General law of demand. $D_a = f(P_a, P_b, \ldots, P_n, I, (S), t).$

Simple law of demand. $D_a = f(P_a).$

Quantity demanded. The amount of a good that will be sold at any given price.

Demand schedule. A schedule of quantity demanded at alternative prices for any good, based on the simple law of demand.

Demand curve. Graphic depiction of a demand schedule.

Change in demand. A change in the quantity demanded at alternative prices for any good. Shown by a shift in the position of the demand curve.

Appendix 22

ELASTICITY OF DEMAND

Chapter 22 explained why there is a functional relationship between quantity demanded and the price of a good. It did not attempt to discuss the quantitative relationship between Q and P, however. For example, if the price of automobiles is raised by 10 percent we would expect sales to decline, other things remaining the same, but will sales fall by more than 10 percent or less? Or, if the marketed wheat crop increases by 5 percent, prices should fall—but by more or less than 5 percent? These quantitative relationships between changes in P and changes in Q involve the *elasticity of demand*, a technical concept to which this appendix is devoted.

ELASTICITY OF DEMAND: CALIFORNIA GRAPES

When the United Farm Workers Union organized the grape pickers in California's San Joaquin Valley in the 1960s, the growers fought the union vigorously. Even after the wineries recognized the union and reached agreements on wages, the growers of table grapes (grapes sold as fresh fruit) refused to recognize the union and refused to bargain over wages, hours, conditions of work, or anything else. A strike of the grape pickers escalated into a national boycott of table grapes—California produces over 90 percent of the supply—and *la huelga* ("the strike") became *la causa* ("the cause") and something of a national issue. The dispute was not settled until 1970. Why were the growers of table grapes so adamant in their resistance to the union, when the growers of wine grapes were not?

One reason for the intransigence of the growers of table grapes is the relationship that prevails between the price of table grapes and the quantity sold. Table 22-2 shows some data for the years 1964 and 1965.

TABLE 22-2
California Grapes

	1964	1965	Percentage Change
Production (1000 tons)	3,145	3,975	+26.4
Average price per ton	$55.80	$41.00	−26.6

Between 1964 and 1965, production rose by a little over 26 percent; and prices fell by almost exactly the same proportion. As a result, total revenues to the producers were almost the same in the two years:

1964 production (1000 tons)	3,145
Average price per ton	$55.80
Total revenue	$175,491,000

1965 production (1000 tons)	3,975
Average price per ton	$41.00
Total revenue	$163,025,000

Even though the price of grapes in 1964 was $14.80 per ton more than in 1965, total revenues exceeded those of 1965 by only $12 million.

Under these circumstances, significant wage increases to the grape pickers would reduce the profits of the producers. Price increases would be associated with an equally proportionate decline in sales, leaving total revenue unchanged. Here is the sequence of events:

1. Wage increases lead to higher costs of production, which cause employers to. . .
2. Raise their prices, but. . .
3. Increased prices are accompanied by an approximately equal percent decline in sales, which means that. . .
4. Total revenues do not change significantly. Therefore. . .
5. Profits must decline, since costs of production have risen.

The dilemma is laid bare: what one party gains, the other loses.

This was not true of grapes used in the manufacture of wine. For a variety of reasons, the quantity of wine sold is little affected by changes in price. The wineries, then, could pass on to their customers any increases in costs of production. Total revenues would rise, enabling the wine producers to recapture the bulk of any increase in wages paid to field labor used in picking the grapes. Wage increases could be passed on to the retail customer, and would not come out of the producers' pockets. It was this characteristic of the market that enabled the Farm Workers' Union to obtain wage increases and union recognition from the wineries with relatively little difficulty. With table grapes, however, total revenues remain roughly stable even when prices rise or fall. Higher costs come out of the pockets of the producers and cannot be passed on to the final consumer.

The difference is a difference in *elasticity of demand*. Wine grapes have an *inelastic demand*: price changes have little impact on the quantity demanded. Table grapes have *unit elasticity*: price and quantity demanded change in the same proportion. Some other products may have an *elastic demand:* a small change in price is accompanied by a large change in the quantity demanded.

THE CONCEPT OF ELASTICITY

Elasticity is a technical term economists have borrowed from mathematicians. It is a measure of the relative changes in two related variables. For example, in the simple law of demand, a fall in price is associated with an increase in the quantity demanded. This relationship is more than merely an association, however. There are cause-and-effect relationships involved that enable us to conclude that, other things remaining the same, a fall in price causes an increase in the quantity demanded. In this instance, the increase in quantity demanded is a *dependent variable* (its change is caused by a change in another variable), while the fall in price is the *independent variable* (the cause of the change in the dependent variable).

We can now define *elasticity*, as the term is used in economics. Elasticity is the ratio between the relative change in a dependent variable and the relative change in an independent variable. The word *relative* in this definition is important. Changes in quantity demanded are measured in tons or bushels or gallons or some other unit. Changes in price are measured in dollars. The units are not comparable. To make them comparable, the changes can be transformed into percentages, that is into relative changes or ratios. Thus, an increase in sales of grapes of 100,000 tons, due to a fall in the price of grapes of five cents, is not very meaningful. But it is meaningful to say that a 2 percent decline in price brought about a 1 percent increase in sales.

PRICE ELASTICITY OF DEMAND

We can now define *price elasticity of demand*, in which price is the independent variable and quantity demanded is the dependent variable.

Price elasticity of demand: the ratio between relative change in quantity demanded and relative change in price,

or

$$E_d = \frac{\text{percentage change in quantity demanded}}{\text{percentage change in price}} . \qquad \frac{quantity}{price} \Big) change$$

ELASTICITY OF DEMAND AND TOTAL REVENUE

Elasticity of demand is important to economists primarily because of the information it gives about the impact of price changes on the total revenue of sellers. The relationship is worth some emphasis.

In the accompanying diagram, Figure 22-8, a relatively small drop in price is shown to bring a relatively large increase in the quantity purchased, so that a cut in price brings larger total revenues to the seller than the former higher price.

MEASURING ELASTICITY OF DEMAND

Price elasticity of demand measures the responsiveness of changes in the quantity demanded of a particular good to change in its price:

$$E_d = \frac{\text{relative change in quantity demanded}}{\text{relative change in price}} .$$

It would be computed as follows:

$$E_d = - \frac{dQ}{Q} \div \frac{dP}{P} ,$$

where Q = quantity demanded,
dQ = change in quantity demanded,
P = price, and
dP = change in price.

Note: The formula for elasticity of demand has a minus sign because the demand curve slopes downward. The relative change in quantity demanded would then be negative, so a minus sign is introduced to make the answer a positive number.

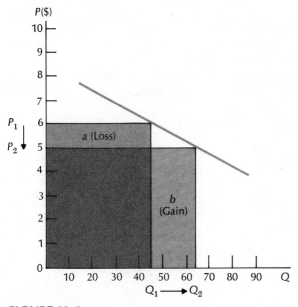

FIGURE 22-8

Measuring Elasticity of Demand

At a price of $6 per unit, 45 units are sold, for a total revenue of $270. In the diagram, total revenue is equal to the area of the quadrangle bounded by $6 on the vertical axis and 45 units on the horizontal axis.

When prices are reduced from $6 to $5 (16⅔ percent), the amount purchased goes up to 65 units (almost 45 percent), and total revenue goes up to $325. The new total revenue is equal to the area bounded by $5 on the vertical axis and 65 units on the horizontal axis.

The increase in total revenue is shown by inspection: rectangle b is larger than rectangle a, which means that the entire rectangle bounded by $P_2 Q_2$ is larger than the rectangle $P_1 Q_1$.

In the example given with Figure 22-8, price elasticity of demand equals 2.65. It is calculated as follows:

$$E_d = -\frac{dQ}{Q} \div \frac{dP}{P}$$

$$= -\frac{20}{45} \div \frac{-1}{6}$$

$$= \frac{0.444}{0.167}$$

$$= 2.65.[1]$$

---

[1] This answer is only an approximation that gives the rough dimensions of the answer. Why? Because the elasticity of a curve applies only to a single point, while in this case we are measuring it over an arc between two points. The calculation used here is based on a single point only, that comprising the $6 price and 45 units of sales. A closer approximation (but still an approximation only) could be obtained by computing an average elasticity over the whole arc. You will learn how to do that in your advanced courses in economic theory.

E > 1
elastic
demand

In this instance, the change in quantity demanded is greater than the change in price and E_d is greater than 1. This is characteristic of elastic demand.[2]

Demand can be elastic, inelastic, or have unit elasticity, depending on the responsiveness of changes in the amount demanded to changes in price:

Unit elasticity $(E = 1)$. A change in price causes an equally proportionate change in the amount demanded. When this happens there is no change in the total amount spent on the good.

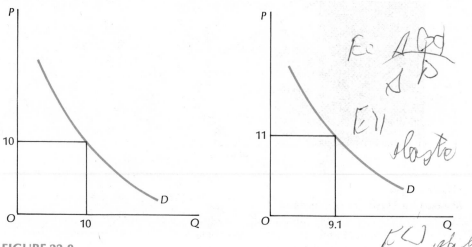

$E = \dfrac{\Delta Q}{\Delta P}$

$E \gtrless 1$
elastic

$E \lessgtr$ *inelastic*

FIGURE 22-9
Approximate Unit Elasticity
The price rises from $10 to $11, causing sales to fall from 10 to 9. Total revenue remains the same at approximately $100. The *PQ* rectangles in the two diagrams are about the same size.

Inelastic demand $(E < 1)$. A change in price causes a less-than-proportionate change in the amount purchased. In this case total revenue will rise if prices go up and fall if prices are reduced.

The limiting case for inelastic demand is $E = 0$. In that case the quantity purchased remains the same, irrespective of price, and the demand curve is vertical.

---

[2] These calculations assume that all other variables remain the same, while prices change. They don't in the real world. For example, at the beginning of this appendix we used the case of California grapes, and it all seemed very simple and straightforward. It isn't. Between 1964 and 1965, consumer incomes and other prices changed, along with *P* and *Q* for California grapes. Those other factors also affected *Q*. Statistical estimating techniques can be used to eliminate much of the influence of those other factors—you will learn how to do this if you study *econometrics*—but the raw data we used earlier still retain their influence. When all extraneous factors are eliminated, the price elasticity of demand for grapes turns out to be about 0.9, which is slightly inelastic. Since consumer incomes rise from year to year, however, the effect of rising incomes combined with consumer reactions to price brings the observed relationship in the marketplace to just about unit elasticity.

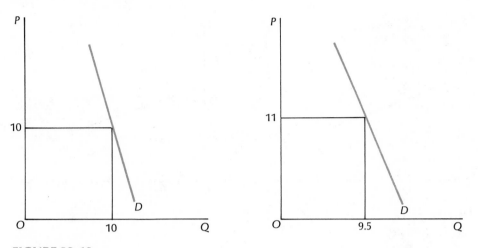

FIGURE 22-10
Inelastic Demand
A price increase from $10 to $11 is accompanied by a decline in purchases from 10 to 9.5. Total revenues from sale of the good have risen from $100 to $104.5. The second *PQ* rectangle is larger than the first. The elasticity of demand in this case is less than unity: it computes to -0.45.

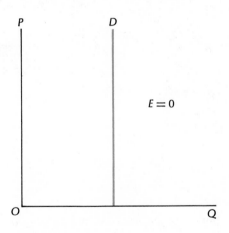

FIGURE 22-11
Perfectly Inelastic Demand

Elastic demand (*E* > 1). A change in price causes a more-than-proportionate change in the amount purchased. In this case total revenue will fall if prices go up and will rise if prices go down.

The limiting case for elastic demand is one in which a price increase reduces sales (and revenues) to zero, while a price decline raises sales (and revenues) to infinity. Where demand is perfectly elastic the demand curve is horizontal.

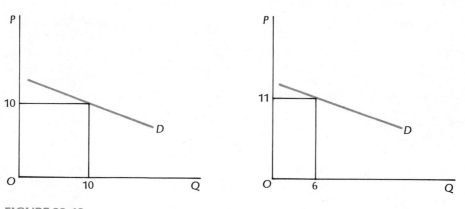

FIGURE 22-12
Elastic Demand

A price increase from $10 to $11 has brought total sales down from 10 to 6, and total revenues from $100 to $66. The computed elasticity of demand is 4.

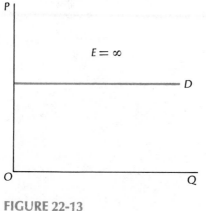

FIGURE 22-13
Perfectly Elastic Demand

Real-world examples of infinitely elastic or infinitely inelastic demand curves do not exist, but the limiting cases are helpful in clarifying the concepts.

FACTORS THAT INFLUENCE PRICE ELASTICITY OF DEMAND

The price elasticity of demand is influenced by the characteristics of the product or service. When there are lots of close substitutes for a good, price elasticity of demand is high. For example, a Ford is close substitute for a Chevrolet. If the price of Chevrolets goes up while the price of Fords is unchanged, the number of Chevrolets bought by customers should decline substantially. Customers will shift to Fords. The demand for Chevrolets, then, is elastic.

When the amount spent on a good represents a large percentage of the average consumer's income, a relatively small change in its price should have a relatively large impact on the quantity demanded. For example, a 20 percent increase in the price of candy bars will raise its price by only one cent (or reduce its size correspondingly) and should have little effect on the quantity bought. But a 20 percent increase in automobile prices would mean about $600 more. This is a substantial bite out of the average income, and could mean a significant reduction in automobile purchases. We should expect that demand for candy bars would be more inelastic than the demand for automobiles.

When the good is a necessity without close substitutes, such as bread, a rise in price will usually have little effect on sales. But if it is luxury, like truffles, then the demand will be more elastic under normal circumstances. The reason is that the necessity will have to be purchased even if the price is higher, while the luxury, by definition, need not be bought if the price rises.

There are other factors that influence the price elasticity of demand for any commodity, but those are probably the most important. Table 22–3 summarizes them in a list.

TABLE 22–3
Characteristics of Goods that Affect Elasticity of Demand

Elastic Demand	Inelastic Demand
Good substitutes	Few good substitutes
Large share of consumer incomes	Small share of consumer incomes
Luxuries	Necessities

Apply these characteristics to the market for grapes. The demand for wine grapes is relatively inelastic because the demand for wine is inelastic.[3] Wine takes only a small share of consumer incomes, and there are few good substitutes for it in the entertainment and other uses to which it is put. While it is a luxury, it is customarily used as an adjunct to various patterns of dining and entertainment, which largely determine how much is used, and price has little impact on how much is bought.

Table grapes, on the other hand, have numerous good substitutes (other fruit) and are a luxury food. Demand for them would be elastic except that they take up such a small share of consumer incomes, and after all, nothing else tastes quite like a fresh grape. The result is very close to unit elasticity of demand.

OTHER TYPES OF ELASTICITY

The sensitivity of quantity demanded to price is only one relationship that can be measured. The quantity of a good that consumers will buy is also influenced by incomes and by the prices of other goods. In addition, supplies coming into the market can be affected by selling prices to greater or lesser degrees. The concept of elasticity applies to all of these relationships and they will be introduced briefly.

---

[3] This is an example of derived demand: the demand for wine grapes is derived from the demand for wine. The concept is examined further in the next chapter.

Cross Elasticity of Demand

When commodities are good substitutes for each other, or if they are complements to each other, a change in the price of one will bring changes in the quantity purchased of the other. This relationship is called _cross elasticity of demand_. It is computed in a manner similar to the measurement of ordinary price elasticity:

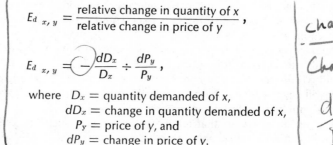

$$E_{d\ x,y} = \frac{\text{relative change in quantity of } x}{\text{relative change in price of } y},$$

or

$$E_{d\ x,y} = \left(-\right)\frac{dD_x}{D_x} \div \frac{dP_y}{P_y},$$

where D_x = quantity demanded of x,
dD_x = change in quantity demanded of x,
P_y = price of y, and
dP_y = change in price of y.

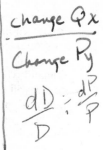

And cross elasticities can be unitary, elastic, or inelastic.

Cross elasticities of demand can indicate whether goods are good substitutes for each other. For example, if the price of Chevrolets goes up, the sale of Fords will rise. This will happen because some who would buy Chevrolets at a lower price switch to Fords when the price of Chevrolets goes up. The cross elasticity of demand between the two is negative, showing that they are good substitutes for each other in the eyes of buyers.

Complementary goods show just the opposite effects. If the price of bagels goes up the amount purchased will fall, and so will purchases of goods eaten with bagels, such as lox (and perhaps cream cheese). In this case, the cross elasticity of demand is positive, indicating a complementary relationship between the two products.

Income Elasticity of Demand

Changes in income also affect the demand for goods. This relationship is called the income elasticity of demand.

$$E_i = \frac{\text{relative change in quantity}}{\text{relative change in income}},$$

or

$$E_i = -\frac{dQ}{Q} \div \frac{dI}{I},$$

where Q = quantity purchased,
dQ = change in quantity purchased,
I = income, and
dI = change in income.

Like other measures of elasticity it can be unitary, elastic, or inelastic.

Income elasticity of demand can be a tricky phenomenon, and it has to be handled carefully. The reason is that incomes change over time, and so do such phenomena as population and price relationships. What looks like the effect of income changes may turn out to be the result of other forces. A good example of this is the often-repeated shibboleth that consumer demand for services has been rising faster than consumer demand for commodities in the years since World War II. Evidence for this trend has been adduced from facts that show an increased proportion of consumer incomes being spent on services and an increased proportion of employment in service industries. The evidence would appear to be conclusive.

But wait a moment. Prices of services have risen rapidly when compared with prices of commodities. If that is the case, the proportion of consumer incomes spent on services will rise even if consumer demand for services as compared with commodities *has not changed in real terms.* As for employment, productivity factors have been important. Output per man-hour has risen slowly in service industries but rapidly in commodity manufacturing. This would call for employment of a growing proportion of the labor force in service industries *even if the relative demand for services has not risen.*

Even if the market basket of goods and services bought by consumers had not changed its composition, these other trends in prices and productivity could cause the observed shifts in amounts spent and in employment.

Indeed, these doubts are borne out by empirical studies, which show that only a tiny fraction of the increase in consumer spending on services, and of the increase in service employment, has been due to increases in consumer incomes. Moral: Don't jump to conclusions about the effect of income changes on demand for goods.

THE IMPORTANCE OF ELASTICITY OF DEMAND

Elasticity of demand is not one of the most exciting of topics. Even by the standards of economics, a discipline that seems to have more than its share of unexciting ideas, elasticity of demand appears to be one of the least interesting. But before we leave it at that, reflect for a moment on what it can tell us about the nature of a self-adjusting market.

It tells us that the entire system is highly interrelated. If something happens over here, something else will happen over there. Nothing is independent. Everything affects everything else. Furthermore, elasticity of demand enables us to measure the extent of those interrelationships in some instances. Not all of the relationships, but some of them. And sometimes only the direction of the relationship can be shown and not the extent. Nevertheless, the concepts of elasticity of demand, cross elasticity, and income elasticity help develop a fuller understanding of the market economy as a system of interrelations and mutually determined variables.

The Rational Consumer

23

This chapter examines the behavior of consumers, and is based on the assumption that their decisions are directed toward maximizing the benefits derived from their market activities. The concept of utility and the principle of diminishing marginal utility are used to analyze the consumers' decision-making process. These concepts are then applied to consumer decisions about work and leisure, spending and saving, and the allocation of expenditures on different goods. There follows a brief discussion of whether, in fact, consumers act rationally—in the sense discussed in this chapter—and we conclude with some evaluations of how all this bears on the efficiency and effectiveness of the market adjustment process.

THE RATIONAL CONSUMER AND THE CONCEPT OF UTILITY

Behind the demand curve lie the decisions made by individual consumers. People decide whether to work more or less, to save and to spend, and what to spend their money on. These decisions have a profound effect on the economy as a whole, for these are the decisions that affect the actions of producers.

Consumers generally know what they want: food and shelter, a certain amount of ease and comfort, a little variety of experiences, the self-satisfaction that comes from doing something well, security against the uncertainties of the world, some approval from their fellows, and leisure. They also have a pretty good idea of how they value any one of these goals when compared with the others. Most consumers also know how much any one good will contribute to the achievement of these goals. And the market economy provides them with a set of prices at which any good can be purchased.

Consumers can use this information to maximize their satisfactions. Some may wish to maximize their wealth, measured by its money value. Others may have different goals: to be an outstanding creative writer or artist, to develop religious piety, to contribute to world peace, to gain power over other people. Whatever the goal, a rational person will use his resources so as to maximize the benefits he gets from the resources at his disposal.

Utility is the term most commonly applied by economists to the benefits or satisfactions obtained from a good or from a particular course of action. An individual will

428

save because the utility he obtains from saving a dollar is greater than the utility he could get from spending it. He works because the utility derived from his earnings is greater than the utility obtained from leisure. He buys an automobile because its utility is greater to him than the utility he could get by spending on other things. In each case, the crucial relationship is between the individual and the good, and is not inherent in the good itself. This is an important point: each individual values things differently from other individuals. A rare stamp may be valued highly by a stamp collector, but not by someone who collects old books. Utility is not a quality of the good itself, like its weight or color, but, like beauty, exists only in the eyes of the beholder.

We should be more specific. People make choices. If they do so after considering alternatives, there must be a basis for comparison. The alternatives must have something in common. This common characteristic is the utility they provide to the individual.

Utility and Freedom of Choice

Since individuals differ in the evaluations they place on things, it behooves us to recognize those differences. If we require all students to learn a foreign language as a condition of the granting of a college degree, for example, we may hit the preferences of some right on the nose. But not of others. Many would prefer taking other courses, which would provide them with more utility than the language courses. If we want to maximize utility, then, freedom of choice is necessary. This principle applies to the economy with particular force. Free choice among alternatives makes it possible for consumers to maximize the utility they obtain, and in so doing to maximize their welfare as they interpret it. If consumers are rational, they will proceed to do exactly that.

DIMINISHING MARGINAL UTILITY

The more we have of a good, the less we desire more of it. This widely observed characteristic of human behavior is fundamental to an understanding of the market economy. Economists have developed it into the principle of *diminishing marginal utility*. Here is an illustration:

Mr. X, who enjoys drinking beer, would derive considerable utility from having a bottle with dinner each Saturday night. If he could increase his consumption so that he could have beer with dinner some other evening too, he would increase his total utility, but probably not by the same amount as that obtained from just one bottle a week. A third bottle would bring still more utility, but a little less than the second bottle did. This process could go on, with additional consumption of beer bringing him more utility at a diminishing rate, until one more bottle would add nothing at all.

We might even set up a hypothetical utility schedule for Mr. X, as in Table 23–1, showing his consumption of beer per week, the total utility obtained from it, and the marginal (additional) utility derived from additional bottles of beer.

TABLE 23–1
Mr. X's Utility Schedule for Beer

Bottles Per Week	Total Utility	Marginal Utility
0	0	
1	9	9
2	17	8
3	24	7
4	30	6
5	35	5
6	39	4
7	42	3
8	44	2
9	45	1
10	45	0
11	44	−1
12	42	−2

Table 23–1 shows us that Mr. X's utility from beer consumption increases as he consumes more, up to 9 bottles per week. After 10 bottles, total utility begins to decline: maybe he starts to feel bad after that much drinking.[1] The right-hand column shows the marginal utility derived from each additional bottle of beer, falling slowly until it reaches zero with the tenth bottle and continuing into the negative range if consumption were to continue beyond that point.

The information given in Table 23–1 can be shown graphically in Figure 23-1. Total utility is shown to increase by an amount equal to the marginal utility derived from each additional unit, reaching its peak at 9–10 units and declining thereafter. Marginal utility shows its typical declining path.

Figure 23-1 has a steplike appearance because we are dealing with moderately large units of consumption. If beer could be stored and consumed in very small amounts the rectangles would become very narrow and the steps would become continuous lines, as shown by the curves in Figure 23-1.

One property of the marginal utility curve should be noted. The area under it at any level of consumption is equal to the height of the total utility curve at that level of consumption. This means that total utility can be measured

---

[1] One of Red Skelton's famous skits when he was just starting his career as a comic in the mid-1930s was a how-to-dunk-a-doughnut routine, which he did on the three-a-day vaudeville circuit. I was in the audience once when he stopped in the middle of the skit, threw away the half-eaten doughnut, and exclaimed, "I can't eat another one of these awful things. Three a day for six days a week is more than a man can stand."

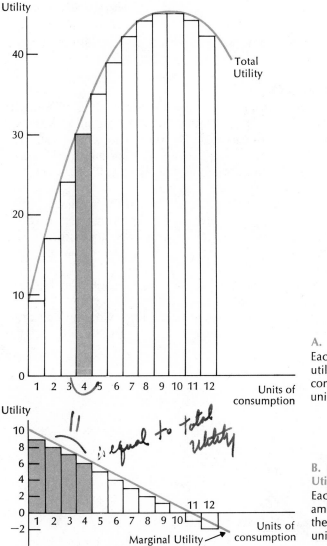

A. Total Utility
Each rectangle shows the utility obtained from consuming the indicated units of the good.

B. Diminishing Marginal Utility
Each rectangle shows the amount of utility added to the total by an additional unit of consumption.

is equal to total utility

FIGURE 23-1. Total and Marginal Utility
The shaded area in diagram A equals the shaded area in diagram B. The total utility from four units of consumption equals the sum of the marginal utilities derived from the first four units. In diagram B, the area under the marginal utility curve is equal to the total utility for that number of units, while utility derived from the marginal unit is equal to the height of the marginal utility curve:

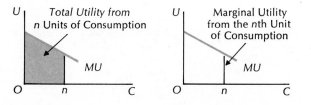

431

in two ways, and it will often be convenient to use the area under the marginal utility curve to do so.

THE DECISION TO WORK

Most consumer incomes come from work. The decision about whether to work or not must be made by everyone. Once made, there are other decisions about how much to work. A housewife may decide not to work at all. Her husband may take a job for 35 hours a week, instead of another for 40 hours. And he has the opportunity for "moonlighting" at a second job to increase his income.

Rational consumers will balance the gains and costs at the margin. On the one hand, money earned from work provides goods with utility. On the other hand, leisure has its uses too: it provides the time needed to enjoy income, for one thing. But more leisure means less income from work, while more work means less time to enjoy the income.

We show in Figure 23-2 how our rational man, Mr. X, would make a decision on this matter.

Figure 23-2 is constructed as a box diagram based on a working day of 18 hours (assuming six hours for sleep),[2] which Mr. X has to allocate between

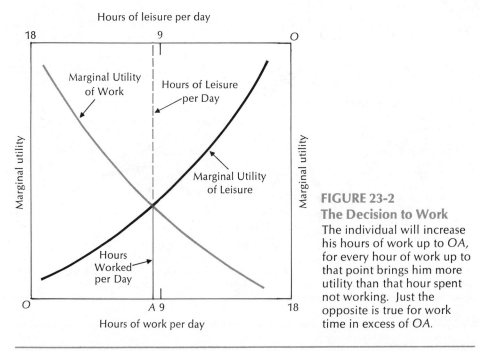

FIGURE 23-2
The Decision to Work
The individual will increase his hours of work up to OA, for every hour of work up to that point brings him more utility than that hour spent not working. Just the opposite is true for work time in excess of OA.

---

[2] We have simplified the problem by giving Mr. X six hours for sleep. He could restructure his problem by reducing that time and then reallocating the nonsleeping time between work and leisure. There is a story about a wandering Talmudic scholar, back in the old country, who had 24 pupils. He spent an hour a day with each one. So when he acquired a 25th pupil he decided to get up an hour earlier.

work and leisure. Marginal utility is measured vertically, hours of work per day from left to right on the bottom of the diagram, and hours of leisure per day from right to left at the top. The curve for the *MU* of work declines as hours of work increase, and so does the curve of the *MU* of leisure, but starting from the other side of the diagram. The curves cross at 8.5 hours of work and 9.5 hours of leisure. At this point Mr. *X* has reached an optimal situation. If he adds more work time he must reduce his leisure. In that case, the marginal utility of the work is less than the marginal utility of the leisure. He will be worse off if he trades leisure for work.

He will also be worse off if he trades work for leisure. The last hour of work brought him more utility than one more hour of leisure would have provided. If he doesn't work that hour he will be giving up more than he gets.

Mr. *X*, then, will maximize his total utility when

$$MU \text{ of work} = MU \text{ of leisure.}$$

OPPORTUNITY COST REVISITED

The decision between work and leisure is a good example of the principle of opportunity cost. The cost of an hour's earnings is the utility derived from an hour's leisure. And vice versa. The rational individual recognizes this fact. The cost of going to college includes the income the student could have earned as a producer, for example. And once in college the cost of studying for an economics examination is the benefit that could have been obtained from doing something else. Every choice we make involves these comparisons; and maximization of benefits (happiness?) requires that we equalize utilities at the margin.

THE DECISION TO SAVE

The decision to save or spend is much like the decision to work or not work. Some people are eager to consume immediately and do not want to postpone the gratification of their desires. They will save relatively little. Others are more concerned about the future and are willing to postpone some consumption until a later time. They will save more. In either case, the utility from future consumption must be balanced against the utility of present consumption.

There is another factor in saving, however. Money saved now can be lent to others who want to spend it now, enabling the saver to earn additional income. That income also has utility to its recipient.

Saving, then, has two different sources of utility to an individual. One is the utility of future consumption from the savings. The other is the utility of present consumption from the return earned by savings. Together they make up the utility derived from saving.

The rational consumer will make his decision about saving and spending so as to equate the marginal utilities involved. With a given amount of income, he will increase his spending, dollar by dollar, and reduce his savings correspondingly, until the utility derived from the last dollar spent just equals the utility obtained from the last dollar saved. Figure 23-3 illustrates the process.

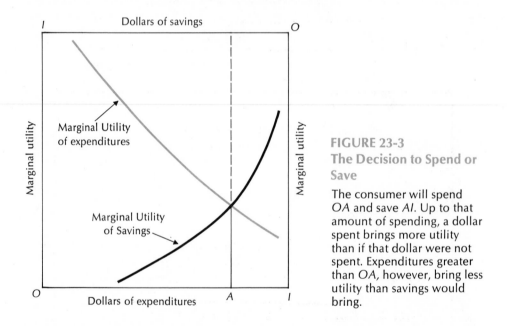

FIGURE 23-3
The Decision to Spend or Save

The consumer will spend *OA* and save *AI*. Up to that amount of spending, a dollar spent brings more utility than if that dollar were not spent. Expenditures greater than *OA*, however, bring less utility than savings would bring.

Figure 23-3 is much like Figure 23-2, except that it deals with a finite amount of income instead of a finite amount of time. Marginal utility is shown on the vertical scale, dollars of expenditure on the bottom horizontal scale, and dollars of savings on the top. The appropriate marginal utility scales for Mr. *X* are drawn. You will observe that in his scale of values spending brings greater utility than saving, for the marginal utility curve for expenditures lies higher on the diagram than the marginal utility curve for savings. As a result, he spends most of his income and saves relatively little, even after equating utilities at the margin. Another individual, with a different standard of values, will decide differently.

Rational Mr. *X* will increase his expenditures up to point *OA*, where the vertical line on the diagram is drawn. Up to that point each dollar spent brings him more utility than if he had saved that dollar. The portion of his income greater than *OA* (the *AI* segment of his total income) will be saved, for in that area of the chart a dollar saved provides greater utility than a dollar spent. At *OA* the marginal utilities are equal.

The rule of maximizing total utility from spending and saving is similar to the rule for other decisions:

$$MU \text{ of expenditures} = MU \text{ of savings.}$$

ALLOCATING EXPENDITURES

Rational decision making when there are only two alternatives is simple enough. The concept of opportunity costs tells us that the benefits from one must be compared with the benefits from the other. The concept of marginal utility leads to the maxim that the utilities derived from the last units of each must be equated if benefits are to be maximized.

The same maxim can be applied to decision making when there are many different alternatives. This type of problem arises when the consumer household decides how to spend its income among the many hundreds of products and services available to it in the market. It is a universal problem, and every household must solve it. The solution is to equate the marginal utilities derived from the last dollar spent on each alternative.

We start with Mr. *X*'s household, which has already decided what its trade-off between work and leisure will be. That decision determines its income. A decision about how much to save has also been made, which determines the income available for purchase of products and services. Now it must decide what to buy and the quantities of each that it desires. In making that decision it has a pretty good idea of its preferences (its marginal utility schedules), and the prices it will have to pay.

Following the rule that marginal utilities must be equated at the margin, the rational consumer household will equalize the utility derived from the last dollar spent on each item it buys. This rule can be written as:

$$\left\{ \begin{array}{c} \dfrac{MU_a}{P_a} = \dfrac{MU_b}{P_b} = \dfrac{MU_c}{P_c} = \cdots = \dfrac{MU_n}{P_n}, \\ \text{where } MU = \text{marginal utility,} \\ P = \text{price, and} \\ a, b, c, n = \text{products and services (goods).} \end{array} \right\}$$

You may wonder why we put the market price in this equation. That is done because units of different commodities are not comparable: one apple and one automobile mean different things. But dollars are comparable. A dollar spent on apples can be measured against a dollar spent on automobile transportation. So we use marginal utility per dollar (*MU/P*) as the unit for comparisons between goods.

This rule for maximization of utility is subject to one condition: the household must use up all of the income it has allocated for spending. If it has not done so, it could increase its consumption of all goods, keeping their marginal utility per dollar equal, and add to its total utility. This condition can also be expressed as

$$E = Q_a \cdot P_a + Q_b \cdot P_b + Q_c \cdot P_c + \cdots + Q_n \cdot P_n,$$

where E = total expenditures,
Q = quantities purchased,
P = prices of the various goods, and
a, b, c, n = goods.

This tells us that the sum of the amounts spent on all goods must equal total expenditures.

Figure 23-4 provides a diagrammatic illustration of the rule for rational expenditure allocation. The vertical axes show marginal utility per dollar for each good. The horizontal axes measure quantities of each good. The horizontal line I cutting across the four diagrams shows the income level that will use up the X family's income when allocated so that MU/P for each good are equal.
(A larger income would show I lower down, with more of everything being bought, while a smaller income would have I higher up and less being bought.)

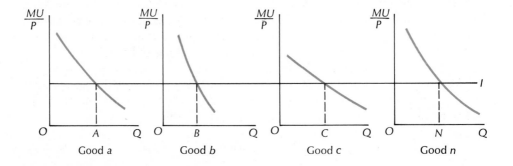

FIGURE 23-4
Rational Allocation of Expenditures by a Consuming Unit
The rational consumer will allocate his expenditures so that the marginal utility per dollar spent on each good is equal, subject to the condition that his entire income allocated for spending is used up. The equilibrium requires that

1) $\dfrac{MU_a}{P_a} = \dfrac{MU_b}{P_b} = \dfrac{MU_c}{P_c} = \cdots = \dfrac{MU_n}{P_n}.$

2) $E = Q_a \cdot P_a + Q_b \cdot P_b + Q_c \cdot P_c + \cdots + Q_n \cdot P_n.$

THE GENERAL EQUILIBRIUM
OF THE HOUSEHOLD

We can now summarize the conditions under which a rational household will maximize its utility. First, it will equalize the marginal utility of work and the marginal utility of leisure:

$$MU_W = MU_L. \tag{1}$$

Second, it will equalize the marginal utility of expenditures and the marginal utility of savings:

$$MU_E = MU_S. \tag{2}$$

Third, it will equalize the marginal utility per dollar spent on goods:

$$\frac{MU_a}{P_a} = \frac{MU_b}{P_b} = \frac{MU_c}{P_c} = \cdots = \frac{MU_n}{P_n}. \tag{3}$$

Finally, it will use up all of the income allocated to purchases of goods:

$$E = Q_a \cdot P_a + Q_b \cdot P_b + Q_c \cdot P_c + \cdots + Q_n \cdot P_n. \tag{4}$$

All of these decisions will influence each other. They are not made seriatim, but simultaneously. Indeed, many economists eliminate the first two conditions by lumping them into condition (3). That can be done if leisure and savings are included in the definition of goods. They have been kept separate here, to indicate that decisions on those matters are of a different order from decisions about purchases of goods and services.

These four conditions define the results of utility maximization by the rational household or rational consumer. We can presume that consumers will behave in this fashion in any situation involving choices. At the very least, lack of coercion will provide the opportunity for choices to be made in this fashion. Any consumer will be able to maximize his satisfactions and welfare, as he defines them, if he wishes to do so. If there is one fundamental argument for the market adjustment process as a way of making economic decisions, this is it.

However desirable such a pattern of free choice may be, the world is never perfect. Two considerations may effectively prevent the exercise of rational choices: consumers may not be rational, and social institutions may interfere with freedom of choice. In either case, welfare maximization will be short-circuited and a less-than-best solution emerge. These considerations create difficult problems of theory and policy for economists which have never been satisfactorily resolved. They will be discussed further in the latter part of this chapter and at various points throughout the book.

Exceptions

FROM INDIVIDUAL DEMAND
TO MARKET DEMAND

Having examined decision making by the rational consumer, we return to his demand for a single good, and use that as the basis for deriving a market demand curve for that good. First, we make the assumption that, for purposes of the analysis, everything is kept constant except the price and quantity of the good under consideration. Incomes, tastes, prices of all other goods, decisions to invest, along with anything else that might affect the outcome are not allowed to vary. This assumption enables us to isolate what happens in the market for a single good.

Second, we start with the individual consumer and his marginal utility schedule for the good under consideration which is shown in Figure 23-5. We should emphasize that the utility scale on the vertical axis is known only to the consumer himself. It is the basis for his comparisons of this good with all the other goods he could buy. But no one else knows what that scale looks like.

However, we do know something about one point on the scale and one point on the marginal utility curve. After the consumer allocates his expenditures, he buys, at the market price, a certain quantity of good a, shown in Figure 23-6 as OA on the horizontal axis. Since the consumer has purchased the marginal unit at price P_1, we conclude that the utility derived from that purchase was just worth it to him, and that therefore the price is a proxy for the marginal utility.

Third, we can vary the price, hypothetically at least, and derive other points on the marginal utility curve, as shown in Figure 23-7. In this way we can create a different vertical scale on the diagram by converting utility to price, *just as the*

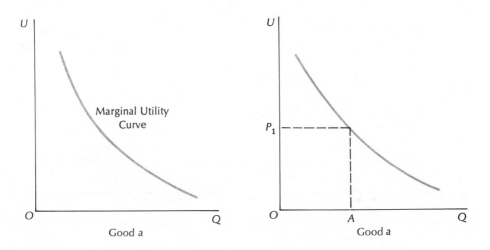

FIGURE 23-5
The Consumer's Marginal Utility
Schedule for Good a

FIGURE 23-6
The Consumer Buys at Price P_1

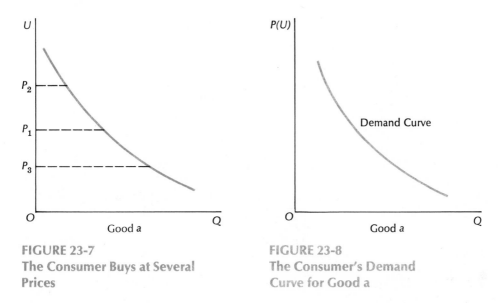

FIGURE 23-7
The Consumer Buys at Several
Prices

FIGURE 23-8
The Consumer's Demand
Curve for Good a

consumer himself would do it when faced with alternative prices in the actual market. We end up with the consumer's demand curve for good *a*, shown in Figure 23-8. This demand curve shows, like any demand curve for an individual, the quantities of the good that the consumer would buy at varying prices, within the range of price changes consistent with the *ceteris paribus* assumption.[3]

Finally, having derived the individual consumer's demand curve for good *a*, we can take the last step toward obtaining the market demand curve by adding up the demand curves (or schedules) for all consumers. At each possible market price for good *a*, each consumer will buy a given amount. Adding up these amounts for all consumers gives us one point on the market demand curve. Doing the same thing for each price will lead us to the entire market demand curve. Figure 23-9 illustrates the process.

The market demand curve for any good reflects the countless decisions made by millions of consumers. Those decisions, in turn, reflect the choices made by consumers on the basis of their individual preferences, which are rooted ultimately in their own values and goals. This is the first step in the argument that in a market economy free choice among alternatives by rational consumers offers the opportunity, at least, for society to maximize the welfare of those who participate in it.

---

[3] Some readers may object that this discussion merely belabors the obvious. In some respects they are right, for the transformation of *U* to *P* is a minor point. But it had to be explained. Many economists argue that utility cannot be measured, but can only be compared with other utilities. The point is well taken, so it is necessary to show how the consumer himself would react to alternative prices by buying different amounts of the good, and that this behavior is equivalent to substituting *P* for *U* on the vertical scale of our diagram.

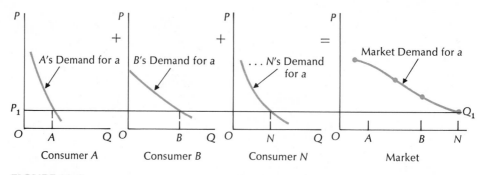

FIGURE 23-9

Adding Up Individual Demand Curves to Obtain a Market Demand Curve

At price P_1, consumers A, B, and N will buy quantities OA, OB, and ON, respectively, which are shown on the right-hand diagram as segments OA, AB, and BN, respectively, and designating point Q_1 on the market demand curve. Other points on the market demand curve can be similarly located and the entire curve will appear as shown.

DERIVED DEMAND

We have been able to show that the demand for goods by consumers rests ultimately on the welfare-maximizing choices made by consumers. We intend to go on to examine how the processes of production adjust themselves to these choices. If a perfect adjustment can be made, resources will be allocated in such a way as to maximize consumer welfare. If not, then only an approximately efficient allocation of resources can be achieved.

But what of those goods that are not part of the purchases of consumers, such as raw materials and semifinished goods bought by producers as inputs into the production process? Can they be brought into the system and be an integral part of a welfare-maximizing allocation of resources?

The answer is yes. Demand for raw materials and intermediate products is *derived* from demand for the finished products sold to final consumers, and ultimately related to the market adjustment process.

Here is an example. Consumer demand for shoes will determine how many shoes retailers order from manufacturers, both for current sales and for inventories. The orders from retailers will determine the production schedules of manufacturers, which in turn will determine the manufacturer's purchases of leather from the tanneries that produce it. They will pass the demand back one step further to the cattlemen who raise the cattle from which the hides are obtained. All the way down the line, even to the factors of production—labor, land, and capital—the demand for inputs into the production process is derived from the demand for the final products the inputs are transformed into.

The concept of derived demand cuts two ways, however. When the demand for final products is a rational decision made by informed consumers who thoughtfully pursue their best interests, the derived demand for inputs—factors of production, raw materials, and intermediate products—will reflect that pattern of consumer decisions if the market adjustment process functions effectively. On the other hand, when the demand for final products is the result of whim, or chance, or market power, or military aggression, the derived demand for inputs will mirror those patterns, and will be considerably less than ideal even if the market adjusts effectively to the pattern of demand.

ARE CONSUMERS RATIONAL?

There are three possible explanations for consumer behavior. Decisions can be thought of as purely haphazard or random, such as the "impulse buying" storekeepers try to encourage. Decisions can also be thought of as conforming to habit and custom, following accepted or learned modes of behavior. Or they can be thought of as acts of deliberate choice among alternatives.

We have emphasized the last interpretation, for a variety of reasons:
1. There is more consistency in consumer behavior than is implied by the "random" explanation.
2. There is more variety than the "habit" explanation would suggest.
3. Surveys of consumer behavior patterns indicate a high degree of thoughtful consideration of alternatives, especially for large purchases.

This is not to say that impulse and habit are unimportant determinants of consumer behavior. They undoubtedly are significant. But even impulse buying may satisfy some important psychological needs of the buyer, and habit is often only the ingrained rationality that comes from experience. The presence of impulse buying and habitual patterns of consumption may be evidence of rationality rather than irrationality!

Furthermore, all consumers don't have to be rational all of the time, in the sense described in this chapter, for the market adjustment process to work effectively. Only some need be rational at any time in order that the results may be desirable. If a businessman wants to maximize his profits, he must attract the largest possible number of customers to his product and his establishment. His offering must be an attractive alternative to the marginal buyer. The decisions made by the marginal buyer, based on a careful evaluation of alternatives, will determine the decisions of producers at the margin, and the market will adjust accordingly. If other consumers buy on impulse or in habitual ways, their behavior will also influence the market, but their decisions won't matter for those consumers who are trying to maximize their welfare. So we can accept the proposition that some buyers make many random decisions, and some are creatures primarily of habit. As long as some make rational decisions, and the market responds to them, the market adjustment process will move toward welfare maximization for those who care about it.

THE RATIONAL CONSUMER: IDEOLOGY AND POLICY

The theory of demand sketched in this chapter can be thought of in two ways. In a narrow sense, it tells us what to expect on the demand side of the market when we analyze the processes of price formation in a market economy. Normally, the amount of a good that consumers are willing to buy will be larger the lower the price. And vice versa: at higher prices, less will be bought. This general rule must be qualified, however, for changes in incomes, tastes, and prices of other goods can overwhelm the relationship between price and quantity in a single market for a single good.

More broadly, the theory of demand has important ideological and policy implications. It shows that in a market-oriented economy there is a tendency toward maximization of individual welfare that is deeply rooted in individual behavior. To the extent that consumers are rational and freedom of choice prevails, a market economy at least has the opportunity to achieve maximization of individual welfare. If the processes of production respond effectively to the patterns of consumer demand, the whole economy can be directed toward that goal by the market adjustment process.

Three qualifications must be entered at this point, all of which must have occurred to the reader. The first is that the pattern of consumer choices in the economy as a whole is strongly affected by the distribution of income and wealth. We can analyze the implications of consumer choice, given the existing pattern of income distribution, and argue that the market leads to an efficient outcome that tends to maximize consumer welfare subject to the constraint provided by the existing pattern of income distribution. That conclusion immediately raises the issue of what pattern of distribution of income and wealth is most likely to bring the highest degree of consumer welfare. We devote a whole section of this book (Part VIII) to that question.

The second qualification is that some choices are social choices rather than individual ones. They are made largely through government, and involve use of resources for such things as military purposes, public parks, sewage disposal and water supplies, and a whole range of other *public goods*, as they are called. Some very difficult issues of resource allocation and welfare maximization are involved here, and we devote another section of this book (Part IX) to them.

The third qualification is that the ability of the market mechanism to respond to consumer choices is limited by restrictions imposed upon it. Some of the most important of those restrictions are imposed by the structure of business enterprise itself, in the monopoloid character of many of our important industries. These problems are examined in Part VII.

These qualifications should not obscure the thrust of the theory of consumer choice, however. Without minimizing the problems of income distribution and social choice involved, the basic conclusion remains: subject to the constraints imposed by the existing patterns of income distribution, social choice and market restrictions, the market mechanism provides a powerful means for making welfare-maximizing decisions.

WIDENING THE AREA OF CHOICE

In order to achieve a pattern of welfare maximization, consumers must have freedom of choice and they must approach their decisions in a rational manner. Public policy designed to achieve these goals would address itself to promoting an adequate flow of information to consumers about qualities and quantities of the goods they buy, about the potential harmfulness of products, and about the terms on which purchases can be financed. In an economy such as ours, with a highly advanced technology and with many highly complex products, there is need for protection of consumers against the deception and irrational psychological appeals that can be used by sellers to shift consumer buying patterns into paths desired by producers and away from the paths consumers would otherwise follow. In recent years we have become increasingly aware of the effect of advertising and marketing strategies of business firms in shifting consumer preferences to patterns that fit the needs of producers. The extent of this shift is subject to debate and there is no agreement among economists about its significance. But certainly to the extent to which it occurs, there is a modification of the behavior described in this chapter and an added element of irrationality in the economic system as a whole.

Policies designed to promote greater freedom of choice among products are also important. In our economy they entail primarily the encouragement of competition among producers. For if producers compete with each other for the consumer's dollar, they will produce the things consumers want, and their profits will depend on how well they do so. The quest for profits will continually force producers to try out new products and to change old products in an effort to gain a greater share of the total market. This pervasive tendency in competitive markets provides a long-run, endless drive toward greater variety and extended choices. In contrast, one of the shortcomings of monopolistic practices and protected market positions among producers is the long-run tendency for consumer choices to be restricted. Probably the most pervasive barrier to the development of greater freedom of choice between products is the existence of monopolistic market control practices among producers.

Another vital area in which freedom of choice is restricted is in choice of occupation. Such a statement may seem strange in a country that prides itself on its openness and freedom of opportunity. But reflect for a moment on just a few of the things which restrict occupational choice in our society:

Tuition charges in institutions of higher learning, coupled with wholly inadequate scholarship and other aid programs.

Poor (sometimes abysmal) school systems in many central city and rural areas.

Discrimination in employment, which has effectively barred blacks, Spanish-speaking Americans, Indians, other minority groups, and women from many job opportunities.

Wide disparity in income, which tends to open opportunities for children of the wealthy and narrow them for children of the poor.

These and other restrictions on choice of occupation influence the choice between work and leisure and the income that can be earned by many individuals and families. If we wish to take advantage of the potential of a market economy for maximization of welfare, public policy will have to address itself to these problems.

When we move into the area of commodities and services, we find large opportunities for choice, but even here there are some formal restrictions. Narcotics, LSD, and marijuana are all banned. So is prostitution, and in many places, gambling. Sale of pornography is prohibited or limited. All of these restrictions are imposed by a society that, rightly or wrongly, wishes to preserve certain standards of morality and to eliminate a variety of behavior patterns considered to be antisocial and harmful.

Informal restrictions on choice can be far more significant than legal restrictions. Blacks know what this means. Patterns of housing segregation, and resulting segregation in schools and other aspects of life, are still a long way from being ended. Until very recently, housing segregation was supported by "restrictive covenants" in deeds to houses, which were enforceable in the courts. They no longer are, but the patterns persist, and for a variety of reasons, may even be increasing. Other informal restrictions on blacks developed in hotels, restaurants, public parks, and other public accommodations, and some of them are still to be found in spite of legislation and court orders. Nor are blacks the only group subject to these constraints. Indians and Mexican-Americans have felt similar discrimination, especially in the western and southwestern states.

Perhaps the most important restrictions are those related to the distribution of income. The poor have far fewer choices than the wealthy simply because they have fewer resources at their disposal. Choice between work or leisure is limited by the need for income. The needs of the family limit savings. There is little discretionary income above that needed for necessities. As incomes rise, choices in all of these areas expand, until the very wealthy have few restrictions. Many of the restrictions on choice we have noted here are eased as incomes rise.

We find then, that choices *are* restricted, and that the restrictions do not apply equally. Some serious minority group problems seem to persist interminably. Yet within the framework of restrictions, consumers have much freedom to make choices that will maximize their satisfactions. After all the qualifications, there is a substantial degree of rationality in consumer behavior. Most people seek to do the best they can for themselves in this sometimes trying, sometimes frustrating, sometimes idiotic world. One way to make it a little less trying, frustrating, and idiotic is to widen the choices and opportunities open to everyone.

discrimination

Summary

The rational consumer determines his choices in a fashion designed to maximize his total utility. He does that by equating utilities at the margin. The decision to work equates the marginal utility of work with the marginal utility of leisure:

$$MU_W = MU_L.$$

That decision determines his income, which he allocates between spending and saving by equating the marginal utility of expenditures with the marginal utility of savings:

$$MU_E = MU_S.$$

Expenditures are then allocated to maximize satisfactions by equating the marginal utility of a dollar spent on one good with the marginal utility of a dollar spent on any and all other goods:

$$\frac{MU_a}{P_a} = \frac{MU_b}{P_b} = \frac{MU_c}{P_c} = \cdots = \frac{MU_n}{P_n},$$

assuming that the total income is spent:

$$E = Q_a \cdot P_a + Q_b \cdot P_b + Q_c \cdot P_c + \cdots + Q_n \cdot P_n.$$

We are then able to derive the demand for any one commodity on the part of a single consumer, add them all up for all consumers, and arrive at the market demand for the commodity.

The demand for factors of production is derived from the market demand for the final product, bringing factors of production under the influence of rational consumer choices for final products.

This analysis assumes rational behavior, which is not an unreasonable assumption. The analysis is also subject to some important qualifications: consumer choices are restricted by the pattern of income distribution, only individual choices are included and not social choices, and the institutional framework is assumed to be one of freely adjusting markets.

Nevertheless, the fundamental import of the theory is tremendously important: subject to the constraints summarized in the last paragraph, the market mechanism is a powerful instrument for achieving maximum welfare for individual people.

Key Concepts

Utility.   The benefits derived by individuals from goods or from a particular action. Utility is not inherent in something, but is derived from the relationship between an object and a person.

Marginal utility.   Utility derived from a marginal unit.

Diminishing marginal utility.   Marginal utility decreases as the quantity of a good increases, within a given period of time.

Derived demand.   The demand for factors of production is derived from the demand for the final product.

Let us review for a moment. Chapter 5 showed that a system of freely operating markets tends to generate a pattern of production that matches the pattern of consumer wants. Building on that concept, Chapter 21 showed that the results tend to maximize welfare by equating benefits to consumers at the margin with costs to producers at the margin. Chapter 22 began a more detailed analysis of the process described in general terms in Chapter 21. Going back to the demand-supply-price analysis of markets sketched in Chapter 5, it focused on the demand side of the market and the factors that determine the locus and shape of the demand curve. The adjustment process responds to consumer demand so the analysis must start there also. Chapter 23 then went behind the demand curve to the concept of marginal utility as the basis of consumer wants to which the whole system responds.

Now the focus of the analysis shifts to the producer, to examine the ways in which he responds to the consumer demand whose foundations we laid out in the last two chapters. This portion of the analysis occupies the next three chapters. This chapter deals with two aspects of the decision-making process for the individual producers: the principle of profit maximization and the principle of least-cost combination of inputs. Chapter 25 examines the series of decisions regarding output, plant capacity, and production processes made by producers in competitive industries as they respond to the price for their product established by the interplay of market forces. The analysis is followed by an application to U.S. agriculture in Chapter 26 designed to show how the principles might be applied to a troublesome economic problem.

The analysis developed in these chapters will be used as a basis for examining socialism (Part VI) and the system of big business with monopoloid markets that actually prevails in the contemporary American economy (Part VII). It is not merely an academic exercise. The theory of competitive markets develops an understanding of how markets operate which can then be used both to analyze some of our economy's important problems and to judge how well it functions.

Behind the Supply Curve

24

THREE DECISIONS AND THREE TIME PERIODS

Although business firms make a wide variety of decisions, we are most directly concerned with the ways in which they respond to the demand for their products by consumers. The decisions involve:

1. How much to produce with the existing plant and equipment; *short run*
2. What size of new plant to build and what production processes to use; *long run*
3. How to respond to changing relative scarcities among the factors of production. *Very Long Run*

These three types of decisions imply three different time periods. Determining the level of output from existing plant and equipment can take effect almost immediately. Additional workers can be hired, or some of the present work force laid off. On the other hand, there are some inputs that can't be varied. The company's plant and equipment is there and either must be used or lie idle (unless it can be sold, rented, or leased to someone else). At least part of the management must be retained whatever the level of output. In other words, some inputs are fixed. The firm, in basing its decisions on the cost of its inputs and the price of its outputs, has the additional constraint of its existing plant. For purposes of economic analysis that time period is called *the short run*.

When the firm decides on the size of plant and selects from among a variety of available production processes, the implication is that all the factors of production can be varied within the existing state of the production arts. The firm has enough time to select the process it feels is best and to build the size of plant appropriate to that technology. For example, a steel firm can use several different technologies. It can use natural ore as a raw material, or beneficiated ore that has some of the impurities removed, or iron pellets that have a very high iron content, or steel scrap. Whatever the decision, a different type or style of reduction furnace and supporting facilities are required for each type of ore. Each source of iron requires different proportions of coal, limestone, and other inputs. Finally, whatever production process it chooses, the firm will have to select a preferred scale of operations. It can build a large plant or a small one for the processing of the ore and transforming it into steel. In planning for the future the firm must make a choice among the production processes available to it, and must select the size of operations it prefers. In terms of our time periods, this is the *long run*. All of the inputs can be varied, within the alternatives provided by existing technology and knowledge of production processes. The firm adjusts to the cost of its inputs and the price it can get for its product, but without the constraint imposed by an existing plant.

In the *very long run* even the techniques of production can be thought of as variable, so that even that fixed set of choices disappears. The inputs into the production process can be combined with complete flexibility, not subject to the constraints imposed by the existing technology. Firms are completely free to respond to the relative scarcity (and prices) of their inputs without any constraints imposed by plant size, existing production processes, or existing knowledge. In particular, as the economy grows, the relative abundance of labor, land, and capital can shift; their relative prices can change; and the firm will have to adapt to those changes.

These three time periods are theoretical constructs that help us analyze the three different types of decisions facing the business firm. They correspond to reality in that, in fact, firms make those decisions. They differ from reality in that the three sets of decisions often overlap each other, as do the actual time periods that are required in the business world to carry out the decisions made. Nevertheless, for the purpose of analyzing the response of firms to demand conditions, it is convenient to separate the three decisions into conceptually different time periods:

The short run: With a fixed plant and a given process of production, how much will the plant produce and what price will be charged for its output?

The long run: With existing technologies given, what size and type of plant will be built?

The very long run: When even technology can be varied and the relative prices of inputs change, how will the firm adapt?

PROFIT MAXIMIZATION: BASIC PRINCIPLES

Do you remember the example of the filling station operator who was trying to decide on his closing hours? It contains in microcosm the central elements of business decision making about how to use existing facilities to maximize profits. You will recall that the rule for profit maximization was that output should be increased as long as additional revenues (marginal revenue, MR) exceed additional costs (marginal costs, MC). Profits will be maximized at that level of output at which marginal revenues and marginal costs are equal, $MR = MC$.

That is half of the profit maximization problem. It concerns the way in which the firm adjusts output to the price it can get for it. The second part of the problem is internal to the firm, and concerns the way in which it organizes the production process to minimize the cost of production per unit of output. The internal problem is resolved by a process analogous to the way in which the rational consumer allocates his income, that is, by applying the equimarginal principle to the firm's inputs. Lower-cost factors are substituted for higher-cost ones at the margin, until costs at the margin are equalized.

Both of the criteria for profit maximization involve costs of production, and the next step in the analysis is to look at the cost structure of the firm.

A preliminary issue needs to be dealt with, however. Why should we assume that business firms maximize their profits? Aren't other goals important too, such as growth, market power, survival? Indeed they are, but one cardinal point stands out. When business firms compete strongly with each other, they are forced to stress profits as a primary goal: the firm that succeeds in maximizing profits not only makes money for its owners, but it also has better chances for survival than a firm that does not maximize profits. When competition is reduced or eliminated, however, there is less pressure on the individual firm to maximize its profits. A variety of other goals or motivations for business behavior may develop. But in a competitive economy the profit maximizing firm survives and flourishes, so we start our analysis with the simplifying assumption that the firm seeks to maximize its profits.

Normal Profits are Part of a Firm's Costs

The costs of production incurred by a business firm are the amounts that must be paid for all of the inputs required to keep the firm operating. Labor must be hired. Materials must be purchased. Management must be paid. Funds must be obtained with which to buy or lease productive equipment, and the owners must be paid for its use. All of these payments to owners of the factors of production are part of the firm's production costs.

A normal profit must be included in the costs of production. If a firm does not earn profits at least as large as those that could be earned by producing something else, the owners of the capital will take it out of the industry and put it to work elsewhere. This is the principle of opportunity costs at work, and it applies to business firms as well as to consumers. Just as a firm must pay wages as high as those its workers could earn elsewhere, so it must pay a return to capital just as high as the amount the capital could earn by being used to produce something else.

Normal profit, then, is defined as the return to capital just large enough to keep it employed in its current uses. It is as much a part of the costs of production as any other payment to a factor of production. In our analysis of the business firm, normal profits will always be included in the costs of production. All of the cost schedules developed and subsequently used in our analysis of markets have a normal profit figured into them.

TOTAL, FIXED, AND VARIABLE COSTS

Every businessman knows that to make a profit, total revenues must be larger than total costs. If they are not, he will be dipping into his working capital and ultimately will be unable to pay his bills. One portion of total costs is the operating costs directly associated with output, such as wages and salaries, materials, rent and utilities. They must be covered by revenues or the firm will quickly be forced to close down as its operating capital is used up. These operating costs vary with the level of output and are called *variable costs*.

In the short run, some costs are *fixed costs*. They are incurred no matter what the level of operations may be. Primary among them are those associated with the firm's plant and equipment: the cost of the capital that went into it and the administrative costs necessary to keep it running. They are present essentially because the plant and equipment are there and can't be changed; the cost of that fixed element in the firm's operations is also there and can't be changed.

In the long run, however, the size and nature of the firm's production plant are variable and the fixed costs become variable costs. In terms of the cost structure of the firm, this is the important distinction between the short-run and long-run periods and the decisions pertinent to each.

Total costs include both variable and fixed costs. A firm can't survive in the long run if its total costs exceed its total revenues. In the short run, however, in determining the level of output that maximizes profits or minimizes losses, only variable costs need be considered. Fixed costs can be ignored for that decision. Why? The reason is that no matter what the level of output, fixed costs remain fixed. In a comparison of one level of output with another to determine which is more desirable, the only difference is the variable cost. The fixed costs in the two comparisons cancel each other. We can see this relationship clearly in the hypothetical example given in Table 24–1.

TABLE 24–1
Total, Fixed, and Variable Costs

Quantity of Output	Total Cost TC	Fixed Cost FC	Variable Cost VC	Change in TC = Change in VC
14	$213	$100	$113	$13
15	226	100	126	14
16	240	100	140	15
17	255	100	155	16
18	271	100	171	17
19	288	100	188	18
20	306	100	206	

Total cost is the expense associated with production at each quantity of output, rising with the increase in output.

Fixed cost is the expense incurred irrespective of the quantity of output. It would be the same if output were zero or 100 units. It is not affected by changes in the quantity of output.

Variable cost includes all expenses not included in fixed costs, so that $TC = FC + VC$. It also increases as output increases, and the amount of the change is the same as the amount of the change in total costs. When put on a chart, as in Figure 24-1, the total cost curve rises, the fixed cost curve is horizontal, and variable costs are the difference between fixed and total costs.

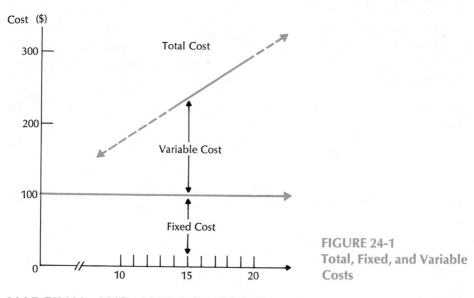

FIGURE 24-1
Total, Fixed, and Variable
Costs

MARGINAL AND AVERAGE COSTS

Two other cost concepts are important for an understanding of profit maximization: marginal costs and average costs. Marginal cost is the change in total cost that is associated with a change in output of one unit. Since total cost and variable cost rise by equal increments, marginal cost can be computed from either one. Average cost is the cost per unit of output. Like any average, it is obtained by dividing the total by the number of units. In any analysis of the market adjustment process, two different average costs are useful, average total cost and average variable cost:

$$\text{Average total cost} = \frac{\text{Total cost}}{\text{Output}},$$

$$\text{Average variable cost} = \frac{\text{Variable cost}}{\text{Output}}.$$

These cost concepts can be illustrated by taking the example given in Table 24–1 and extending it by several columns, as is done in Table 24–2.

TABLE 24–2
Marginal and Average Costs

Quantity of Output	Total Cost TC	Marginal Cost MC	Average Total Cost ATC	Average Variable Cost AVC
14	$213		$15.20	$ 8.07
15	226	$13	15.10	8.40
16	240	14	15.00	8.75
17	255	15	15.00	9.12
18	271	16	15.10	9.50
19	288	17	15.20	9.89
20	306	18	15.30	10.30

Marginal cost is the addition to total cost resulting from an increase in output of one unit. Average total cost is the total cost per unit of output. Average variable cost is the variable cost per unit of output. Average fixed cost, not shown here, is the difference between *ATC* and *AVC*.

The Shape of the Average Total Cost Curve

Table 24–2 shows the typical pattern followed by average total costs. They fall, reach a low point, and then start rising. Why? The reason is that the firm has fixed factors of production (hence fixed costs) to which other inputs are added in order to increase output. The *law of diminishing returns* comes into play. Initially, the increase in output attributable to a one-unit increase in the variable factors of production rises, then levels off, and falls. If the input is considered a cost, this is equivalent to saying that costs per unit of output fall, reach a minimum, and then start rising. The typical shape of the *ATC* curve is shown in Figure 24-2.

The Relationship Between Average and Marginal Costs

Table 24–2 also shows the typical relationship between marginal costs and average total costs. Indeed, it illustrates the relationship between any average

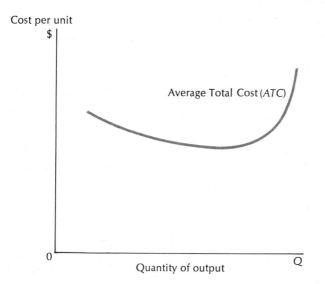

FIGURE 24-2
Typical Average Cost Curve
Note: The word "typical" is important. Average cost curves can show wide variations in their shape, within the "bowl" or "U" shape derived from the principle of diminishing returns. As drawn here, the AC curve is influenced very strongly at the right-hand side of the diagram by engineering capacity limits, and probably is close to the usual situation. In some cases, particularly in retailing, the bottoming out seems to be a horizontal section rather than only a point. Whatever the variations, however, the simple bowl shape is the typical case that we shall use in the analysis.

and marginal quantities. When average total costs are falling, marginal costs are below *ATC*. When average total costs are at their lowest point, marginal costs equal *ATC*. When average total costs are rising, marginal costs are higher than *ATC*. These relationships can be illustrated by data from Table 24–2:

1. When *ATC* is falling, *MC* < *ATC*.

Quantity of Output	Total Cost	Average Total Cost	Marginal Cost
14	$213	$15.20	
15	226	15.10	$13
16	240	15.00	14

2. When *ATC* is constant, *MC* = *ATC*.

Quantity of Output	Total Cost	Average Total Cost	Marginal Cost
16	$240	$15	
17	255	15	$15

3. When *ATC* is rising, *MC* > *ATC*.

Quantity of Output	Total Cost	Average Total Cost	Marginal Cost
17	$255	$15.00	
18	271	15.10	$16
19	288	15.20	17

A similar relationship exists between marginal costs and average variable costs. Here is an example, in which the data shown in Table 24–2 are extended to lower levels of output.

Quantity of Output	Total Cost*	Average Variable Cost	Marginal Cost
7	$150	$7.14	
8	156	7.00	$6
9	163	7.00	7
10	171	7.10	8

* Fixed cost = $100.

This example shows that when *AVC* is falling, *MC* < *AVC*; when *AVC* is constant, *MC* = *AVC*; and when *AVC* is rising, *MC* > *AVC*.

The Cost Structure of the Firm in the Short Run

The short-run cost structure of a typical firm can now be completed. The bowl-shaped average cost curve is associated with a marginal cost curve that cuts it from the bottom, crossing at the lowest point on the average cost curve, and lying above the average curve beyond that point. This cost structure is shown in Figure 24-3.

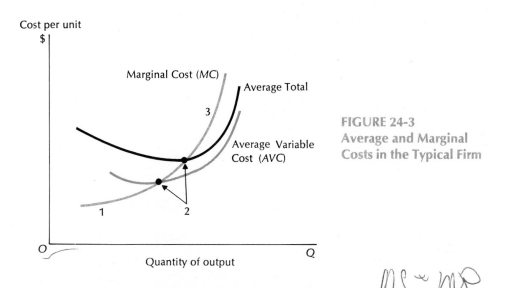

FIGURE 24-3
Average and Marginal
Costs in the Typical Firm

PROFIT MAXIMIZATION FOR THE FIRM

A firm will maximize its gains, or minimize its losses, at the level of output at which its marginal costs are equal to its marginal revenues, or where MC equals MR. This principle is so important for the analysis that follows in later chapters that it must be clearly understood at this stage of the argument.

The concepts of marginal cost and marginal revenue should be reviewed:

MC = additions to total cost resulting from additional unit of output.

MR = additions to total revenue resulting from additional sales of one unit.

The principle can be best understood for those cases in which the firm is a *price taker*. That is, the firm takes the price at which it sells each unit of output as given, set by the market in a competitive economy; by a planning agency in a socialist regime; or by a price control board in a wartime economy. Whenever the firm is a price taker, the price at which it sells its output becomes its marginal revenue as well. No matter how much it sells, one more unit of output can be sold at the existing price; and if one less unit is sold, total revenues are reduced by an amount equal to the existing price. The price is equal to marginal revenue, $P = MR$. In this case profits will be maximized where

$P(MR) = MC$. This proposition can be readily understood from Figure 24-4, which shows a firm's marginal cost curve, MC, and the price at which its products are sold. To simplify matters, we assume that the firm can sell all it wants at the market price, so that the price represents both its average revenue per unit sold and its marginal revenue, MR.

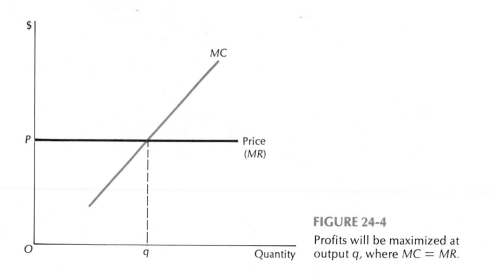

FIGURE 24-4

Profits will be maximized at output q, where $MC = MR$.

Suppose this firm were to produce and sell one more unit than q. In this case the added cost would exceed the added revenue and net profits would decline, as shown in Figure 24-5.

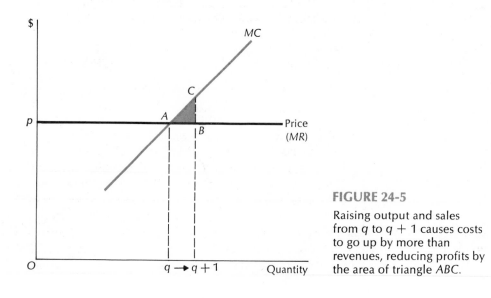

FIGURE 24-5

Raising output and sales from q to $q + 1$ causes costs to go up by more than revenues, reducing profits by the area of triangle ABC.

On the other hand, suppose the firm were to produce and sell one unit less than q. In this case the revenues it loses would be greater than its reduction in cost, and it would forego net gains it could earn, as shown in Figure 24-6.

The logic of this situation is clear. As long as the firm increases its output and sales up to the level of q it will be adding to its gains. In that range of output and sales, $MR > MC$. But increases in output beyond q will reduce its total profit, for at those levels of operation $MR < MC$. Profits can be maximized only at output and sales equal to q, where $MR = MC$.

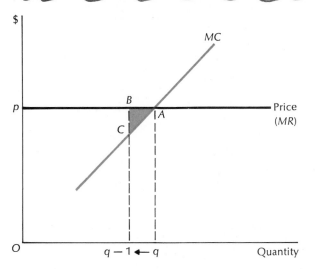

FIGURE 24-6

Reducing output and sales from q to $q - 1$ causes revenues to fall more than costs, reducing profits by the area of triangle ABC.

The Supply Schedule of the Firm

Its marginal cost curve becomes the supply schedule for a price-taking, profit-maximizing firm. It will produce and sell that quantity of output at which $MC = MR$, which represents a single point on its marginal cost curve. If the price were to change, profits would be maximized at a changed level of output, and again MC would be equal to MR but at a different point on the MC curve. This proposition is illustrated in Figure 24-7. Whatever the price, the output at which profits are maximized is determined by the MC curve, which indicates the quantities the firm would supply at various prices.

The Shutdown Point

Each firm has some level of output below which it will not find operating worth while. That shutdown point is defined by the intersection of the firm's MC curve with its average variable cost, $MC = AVC$. It is shown in Figure 24-8. Here is the logic behind that conclusion. When price is at P_1, the firm will minimize its losses with output q_1. It will be losing money, because revenue per unit is below total cost per unit, or $P < ATC$. At a price above p_1, something above average variable cost will be earned, and a contribution will be made

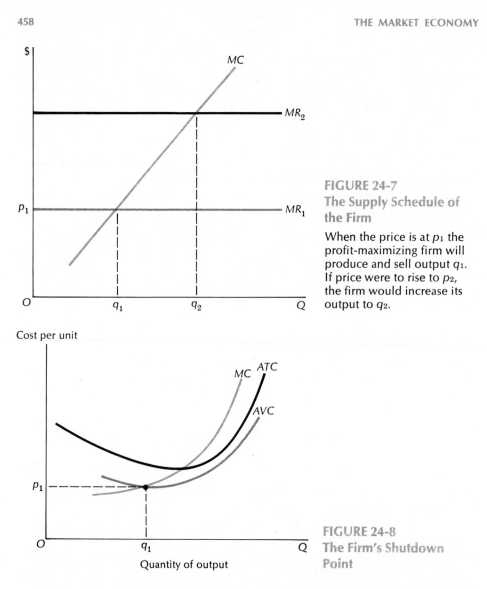

FIGURE 24-7
The Supply Schedule of the Firm

When the price is at p_1 the profit-maximizing firm will produce and sell output q_1. If price were to rise to p_2, the firm would increase its output to q_2.

FIGURE 24-8
The Firm's Shutdown Point

to paying some of the fixed costs and/or to normal profit. Below price p_1, however, $MR < AVC$. This means that the firm is not only failing to earn a normal profit and its fixed costs, but also failing even to earn its operating or variable costs. By closing down its operations, it can reduce its losses to only its fixed costs and normal profit. The firm will not operate in the output range between O and q_1. Output q_1 is its shutdown point.

The supply schedule of the price-taking firm, then, is its marginal cost curve for that range of output above the level at which $MC = AVC$.

THE SUPPLY CURVE FOR THE INDUSTRY

The industry's supply schedule can now be determined. It is obtained by adding up the amounts each firm would be willing to supply at various prices.

Those amounts are derived from the marginal cost schedules of the individual firms. Very simply, the supply schedule for the industry is the sum of the supply schedules, or marginal cost curves, of the individual firms. This relationship is shown in Figure 24-9.

MINIMIZING COSTS

At the same time that our firm is maximizing its profits, given its cost structure and the selling price for its product, it seeks to minimize its costs of production. Minimum costs per unit of output are as important for profit maximization as selection of the level of output at which $MR = MC$. There are strong incentives to move the entire cost structure of the firm downward, and we can expect that any firm competing strongly with others will continually seek ways to shift its internal operations toward lower costs of production. Competition is a great spur toward efficiency.

The key to reduced costs of production is substitution of lower cost inputs for higher cost ones at the margin. If the cost of labor falls, relative to the cost of other inputs, business firms can be expected to substitute labor for other factors of production. This basic principle applies throughout the production process.

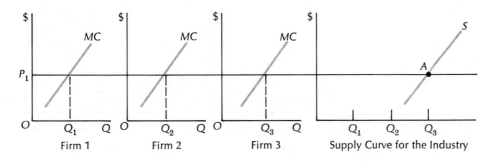

FIGURE 24-9

Adding Marginal Cost Curves of Individual Firms to Obtain Supply Curve for Industry

At price P_1, the three firms will produce and sell quantities Q_1, Q_2, and Q_3, which are summed to point A on the industry's supply curve. Other points on the industry's supply curve are obtained in the same way.

Here is an example. Large-scale immigration brought large numbers of relatively unskilled workers to the United States from Europe from about 1870 to 1910, during the period of our rapid industrialization. American industry used this type of labor to produce complex industrial products requiring intricate methods of production. Since skilled labor was relatively scarce (and relatively expensive), production methods that substituted capital equipment for labor skills were developed. One example is assembly-line production of automobiles that used relatively large amounts of capital, little skilled labor, and much unskilled and semiskilled labor. A contributing factor, of course, was the relative abundance of capital in a nation with large amounts of savings to make the capital available. In Europe, from which the unskilled labor came, skilled labor was more plentiful, relatively speaking, and consequently less expensive relative to capital. The result was the development of industrial processes that used proportionately more skilled labor than similar processes in the United States. These differences persist today, even though automobiles made in the United States and Europe compete with each other throughout the world. Different combinations of the factors of production produce essentially similar results.

In the short run, when the existing plant and production processes are fixed, the firm has some opportunities for substitution of factors of production for each other, but the opportunities are relatively limited. Production relationships have been largely determined by the prior decisions about which production processes to use and what size plant to build. Even then there is some flexibility in replacing untrained personnel with trained, in substituting a machine for workers (or workers for a machine, which doesn't seem to happen much these days), and in reorganizing little bits and pieces of the production process to reduce costs of production.

In the long run, however, processes and plant size become flexible, and the possibilities increase for substituting one input for another. The firm does not have much freedom to push its average and marginal cost curves downward very much in the short run, but in the long run it can push them down as far as the existing knowledge of technology and science will permit.

Here we see an important connecting link between economic growth and the allocation of resources. Advances in knowledge that come from education, and from research and development, can be used not only to increase the volume of output but also to lower costs of production and increase the efficiency of individual economic units.

We could go further at this point to discuss the theory of production in detail, but it isn't necessary. More will be said about that theory when we analyze the distribution of income, for the two are closely related. Both the distribution of income and the internal efficiency of the firm are affected by the prices that prevail in markets for the factors of production, and we defer further discussion.

MARGINAL COSTS
AND ECONOMIC WELFARE

Behind the supply curve for any commodity lie the costs incurred by producers. In this chapter we have treated those costs in monetary terms, because that is how they are seen by the firm and that is how they influence the firm's decisions. But we should never forget that behind those monetary costs to the firm are real costs to the economy as a whole. Units of labor and physical plant and equipment are used that could have other uses producing other things. The monetary costs to the firm are the way the market system expresses the opportunity cost to the economy as a whole. So when we say that costs at the margin determine the amounts that profit-maximizing producers are willing to supply to their customers, there is more to the matter than merely the principle of profit maximization.

Chapter 23 explained that the demand curve for a commodity is based on utility to the buyer at the margin. This chapter has added that the supply curve reflects costs to the producer at the margin. Since we know that at the market price, demand and supply are equal, with the S and D curves crossing at the prevailing price, it follows that the market-adjustment process creates an equilibrium at which marginal utility to the buyer equals marginal costs to the seller:

$$MU = MC.$$

Figure 24-10 illustrates this proposition, using a supply-demand-price diagram.

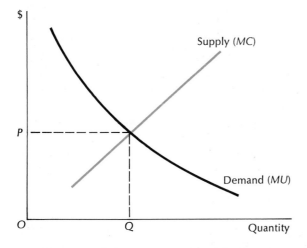

**FIGURE 24-10
Market Equilibrium
Revisited**

At the market price P, buyers will take quantity OQ, which is the same amount that producers are willing to supply. The money value to consumers of the last unit purchased, that is, the height of the demand curve at Q, is exactly equal to the additional costs incurred in producing that unit. Benefits at the margin are equal to costs at the margin. $MU = MC$.

The equality of marginal costs and marginal utility at the market price indicates that that net benefits are maximized. For example, referring to Figure 24-10, if output were one unit greater than Q, the additional costs to producers MC would be greater than the additional benefits to consumers MU. There would be a net loss of welfare. On the other hand, if output were one unit less than Q, consumers would be giving up marginal benefits greater than the cost savings to producers. Clearly, benefits to the society as a whole will be maximized at Q. We should remember, too, that these are real benefits and costs, with the monetary values merely reflecting the satisfactions obtained by consumers and the effort expended by producers.

A market equilibrium, then, tends to maximize net real benefits to the economy as a whole. The drive of consumers to maximize their satisfactions, together with the efforts of producers to maximize their gains, worked out in the environment of a freely adjusting market system, moves the society toward a welfare-maximizing result.

This conclusion is subject to a series of important qualifications that are already familiar. The existing distribution of income and wealth is taken for granted. Prices have to reflect all of the costs of production, social as well as private. There can be no restrictions on freedom of action in the market, either by private monopolists or government bureaucrats. "Public goods," or those that would not be provided by private enterprises motivated by profit, are excluded from the analysis. These are important limitations. Nevertheless, the basic concept is one of the most important ideas in the modern social sciences, for it suggests that properly structured markets can work effectively to promote human welfare. They don't solve all of our problems, but there are some for which they may work quite well.

Summary

Producers' efforts to maximize profits lie behind the supply of goods brought to market. Those efforts respond to two situations: the desire to maximize net revenues in the market, and the desire to minimize costs of production within the firm.

Maximization of net revenues in the market occurs when marginal revenues equal marginal costs. When the firm is a price taker, its *MC* curve above the shutdown point becomes its supply curve. The individual firms' supply curves can then be added to arrive at a market supply curve for the industry as a whole.

As for minimization of costs within the firm, that is brought about by substituting lower-cost factors of production for higher-cost ones at the margin, a process that is discussed more fully in Chapter 34.

When the market supply curve for a good is based on marginal costs, as it is for price takers, it also reflects real or opportunity costs to the economy as a whole. This enables the market-adjustment process to equate marginal benefits to buyers with marginal costs to producers and thereby maximize net benefits for the system as a whole.

Key Concepts

The short run.   Plant and equipment are fixed, the firm decides on its level of output and its price. In the case of the price-taking firm, only the level of output is at issue.

The long run. All inputs are variable. The firm selects the production process and size of plant it desires, given the existing technological choices available.

The very long run. All inputs are fully substitutable for each other: the technological constraint is removed. Firms respond to the relative scarcities (and prices) of the factors of production.

Normal profits. The return to capital that is just large enough to keep it in its current uses. Part of the costs of production.

Variable costs. Costs that vary with the level of output.

Fixed Costs. Costs incurred regardless of the level of output.

Total costs. Variable costs plus fixed costs.

Marginal cost. The change in total cost associated with a change in output.

Average cost. Cost per unit of output, either for total cost (average total cost), or for variable cost (average variable cost).

Shutdown point. The level of output below which a firm will not operate because it is not even earning its variable costs. At this point $MC = AVC$.

Key Diagram

The reader should be able to draw this diagram properly, label it correctly, state the meaning of the three curves, and show the relationship of MC to AVC and MC to ATC where they cross.

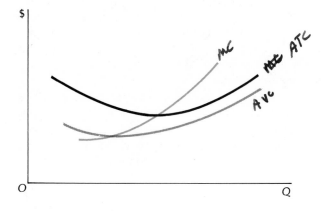

Market Adjustment Under Competitive Conditions

25

Our discussion of the general theory of markets up to this point has covered basic principles, the theory of demand, and the costs that lie behind the supply curve. We are now ready to go beyond the simple supply-demand-price relationships and examine the way in which producers adjust their output to the market prices for the goods they sell. Since we are now interested only in the reactions of producers, we do not consider any changes that may occur on the demand side of the market. We analyze producers' decisions: how much to produce, whether to enter or leave the industry, what size plant to build, and what production processes to use.

The simplest place to start is with competitive industries in which neither sellers nor buyers can influence prices in the market. That is, we assume that the number of sellers and buyers is so large, and each is so small relative to the size of the market as a whole, that all accept the market price as a factor in their environment over which they have no influence.

PURE COMPETITION

A purely competitive industry requires a number of sellers so large that the actions of any one firm has no appreciable effect on the fortunes of the other firms. Each firm can seek to maximize its profits without fear of retaliation from other firms. There are no "enemy" firms or rivals that have to be watched: the only factors that influence the firm's decisions are its internal cost structure and its external market conditions. In other words, the output of any one firm is so small when compared with the output of the industry as a whole that its actions do not influence market prices.

There are not many markets in which these conditions exist. The market for wheat or other basic farm products is one. Others come close. However, our purpose here is not to describe any single market accurately, but to get at the basic market-adjustment mechanism that works to a greater or lesser extent in many different markets.

Some additional assumptions will also help to simplify the analysis:

1. All firms in an industry produce a single homogeneous product. That is, the product of each firm is identical to the product of any other firm in the industry, in the eyes of the buyer.

2. There is full freedom of entry into the industry and exit from it for all potential sellers. Patent restrictions, long-term contracts, exclusive supplying agreements, and other restrictions on entry do not exist. Firms are also free to leave the industry if profits are too low.

These assumptions define the concept of _pure competition_ as economists usually use it—many firms; single, homogeneous products; free entry and exit.

PERFECT COMPETITION

Mobility of resources is closely allied to freedom of entry and exit. The factors of production must be free to move from place to place, from industry to industry, and from entrepreneur to entrepreneur. Of course, time must elapse while the factors are moving and being rearranged, and this has led to the distinction between the long run and the short run in economics. But whatever the time period, factors of production must be free to move anywhere in the economy in order that the market adjustment process may freely follow the desires of consumers and producers.

To complete the picture, each producer must have full knowledge of the market and the opportunities available there. It is obvious that this condition cannot be achieved, but it isn't too far wrong, either. Wrong decisions in the market lead to economic extinction if firms persist in them. We can assume that businessmen tend to make correct decisions, as if they had perfect knowledge, simply because those who make poor decisions are forced out of the market by their more successful colleagues.

A perfectly competitive industry cannot be found. It requires full mobility of resources and full knowledge, in addition to a large number of firms, a homogeneous product and free entry. Nevertheless, we make all these assumptions, in order to simplify the analysis of the market-adjustment process, knowing full well that the analysis will not describe reality. But it will help us understand the essential elements of the market-adjustment process.[1]

DEMAND FOR A FIRM'S PRODUCT

Our assumptions tell us that in a perfectly competitive industry the individual firm can sell any amount of its product at the existing market price. This conclusion follows from the requirement that the firm's output is so small, relative to the size of the market as a whole, that its actions will not affect price. As a result, the demand curve for the single firm is a horizontal line at the market price. This situation is shown in Figure 25-1.

---

[1] A general principle of scientific method is involved here. A methodology is selected with a definite purpose in mind, and may be quite inappropriate to another purpose. Here our purpose is analytical knowledge that will later be put to use in understanding reality. But we do not confuse the analytical model with reality any more than the engineer confuses the algebraic formulation of the stress factors in a steel bridge with the bridge itself.

In a competitive industry the individual firm must take the price of its product as a given element. If it is constrained in this way, it is freed in another: it can sell any quantity at that price. If the firm tried to charge a higher price, it would sell nothing; customers would go to other sellers of the identical product. Yet there is no incentive to sell at less than the going market price, since the firm can sell any amount it wishes at that price. Its demand curve is infinitely elastic at the existing price. Since the demand curve is horizontal, average revenue is constant. We already know that when average revenue is a constant, it equals marginal revenue, or AR = MR. The market price is therefore equal to the firm's average revenue and to its marginal revenue:

$$P = AR = MR.$$

The chief immediate problem facing the firm then becomes one of deciding which level of output will maximize its profits. This is the first step in the process of market adjustment.

PRICE TAKERS AND PRICE MAKERS

In the purely competitive model, the firm is a price taker. That is, it accepts the price determined in the market and adjusts its operations to the market price.

This condition distinguishes the purely competitive firm from those in monopoloid markets, where the individual firm has a greater or lesser degree of choice with regard to the price of its product. Firms in that situation can be termed price makers, although the degree of influence they have over the price of the product may vary widely.

THE FIRM IN THE SHORT RUN: CHOOSING THE LEVEL OF OUTPUT

We shall assume that the firm has plant and equipment already at hand. Its cost structure is like that described in the last chapter. That is, its average cost per unit of output falls for a time, and then starts to rise. The appropriate marginal cost curve follows from the shape of the average cost curve. The firm's demand curve, of course, is fixed at the market price, so that price equals marginal revenue and average revenue.

Putting these elements together enables the firm to determine the level of output at which profits are maximized. Remember that MR = MC is the profit-maximizing condition. An example is given in Figure 25-2.

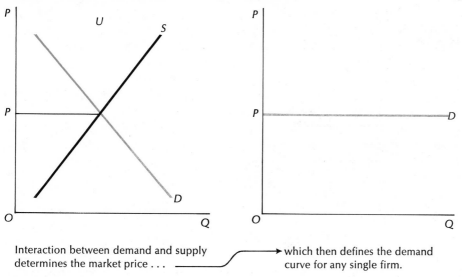

Interaction between demand and supply determines the market price . . . ——→ which then defines the demand curve for any single firm.

FIGURE 25-1
Demand Curve for a Single Firm

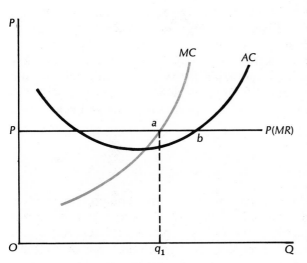

FIGURE 25-2
Competitive Firm Determines Level of Output at which Profits are Maximized

With the given cost structure and market price, output level q_1 will maximize profits. Up to that point additional revenues exceed additional costs as output increases. This adds to profits. Beyond that point additional costs exceed additional revenues as output goes up. Profits fall beyond q_1. Point a designates the profit maximizing output. Question: Why are profits *not* maximized at b?

Figure 25-2 was drawn in a special way. It was deliberately structured so that the firm would make extranormal profits. Normal profits (just large enough to keep the firm operating) are included in average costs. But at output level q_1, the selling price is greater than average costs. The difference is extranormal profits, shown in Figure 25-3.

When the typical firm is making profits greater than those necessary to sustain it, additional producers will be attracted into the industry. They will

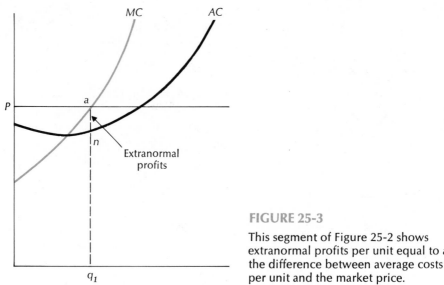

FIGURE 25-3

This segment of Figure 25-2 shows
extranormal profits per unit equal to *an*,
the difference between average costs
per unit and the market price.

move in from industries in which price-cost relationships do not enable
firms to make extranormal profits.

The entry of new firms will add to the supply of the product available on
the market. The additional supplies will bring prices down. As prices fall
the extranormal profits of individual firms will diminish and ultimately disappear. When that happens there will no longer be any incentive for new
firms to enter the industry, supplies available for sale will no longer rise, the
market price will stop falling, and the industry will have achieved an equilibrium. Figure 25-4 shows the equilibrium position of the individual firm
when that result occurs.

EQUILIBRIUM IN THE INDUSTRY AS A WHOLE

The process by which the industry as a whole reaches equilibrium involves
two distinct steps. First, each firm selects the level of output that maximizes
its own profits, given the market price for its product. This decision does
not affect prices in the market, for the firm is a price taker in a competitive
industry. Second, the number of producers is determined by the pattern of
entry into and exit from the industry. Decisions of many firms to enter or
not to enter affect the total supply in the market and, consequently, the
market price. When the market price reaches that level at which the number
of producers is stabilized, the industry will be in equilibrium. Each firm
remaining in the industry will have reached a profit-maximizing level of
output, and the number of firms will be established. There will be no
tendency for the market price or quantity sold to change. The two-stage
nature of the adjustment process is illustrated in Figure 25-5.

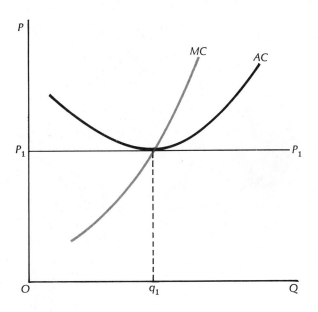

FIGURE 25-4
Equilibrium of Firm in Competitive Industry after Extranormal Profits Have Been Eliminated

The extranormal profits of Figure 25-2 have disappeared after entry of new firms into the industry has brought the market price down to P_1. This firm recovers all costs and earns a normal profit at output q_1.

Just as extranormal profits encourage firms to enter an industry, profits lower than normal will cause firms to leave. This will have just the opposite effects from those just explained. Supplies in the market will fall and prices will rise. This adjustment will continue until the market price equals average costs of production for the typical firm. At that point producers will be earning normal profits and the incentive to leave the industry will be gone. We can summarize the adjustment process as a whole, then, by looking at the position of the individual firm.

When the typical producer is making more than normal profits, the market adjustment process causes prices to fall (Figure 25-6).

When the typical producer is making less than normal profits, the market adjustment process causes prices to rise (Figure 25-7).

When the typical producer is making normal profits, and no more, the market adjustment process stops. Both firm and industry have reached an equilibrium position (Figure 25-8).

Is There a "Typical" Firm?

Our analysis of the market adjustment process under competitive conditions used the device of the "typical" firm. The concept simplified the analysis, but in doing so it enabled us to sweep under the rug several troubling analytical problems.

All producers are not alike. Some are more efficient than others. Some are more alert to the need for change and adjustment. Some have better management. As a result of these differences, the cost curves of individual firms will differ. Costs of production will be higher for some, lower for others. A market price that enables one firm to make normal profits will

FIGURE 25-5
Achievement of Equilibrium in a Competitive Industry

Stage I

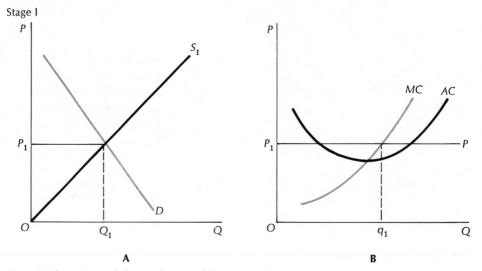

A   B

The initial position of the market equilibrium produces price P_1 and output (sales) Q_1 (diagram A). This position does not produce equilibrium in the industry because the typical firm makes extranormal profits (diagram B), attracting additional producers into the industry and leading to Stage II (diagrams C and D).

Stage II

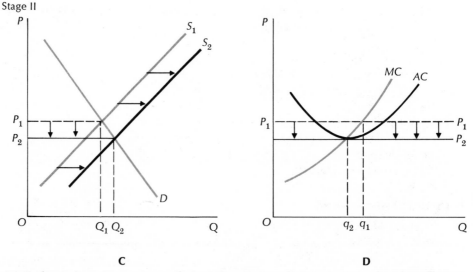

C   D

Entry of new firms increases supply in the market from S_1 toward S_2, causing the price to fall from P_1 to P_2 and the amount produced (sold) to increase from Q_1 toward Q_2 (diagram C).

The decline in market price causes the typical firm to reduce its output (sales) from q_1 to q_2 (diagram D), with a downward movement along its marginal cost curve. When the market falls to P_2, the extranormal profits of the firm are gone, entry into the industry stops, supply in the market stabilizes at S_2, and the industry has reached its equilibrium.

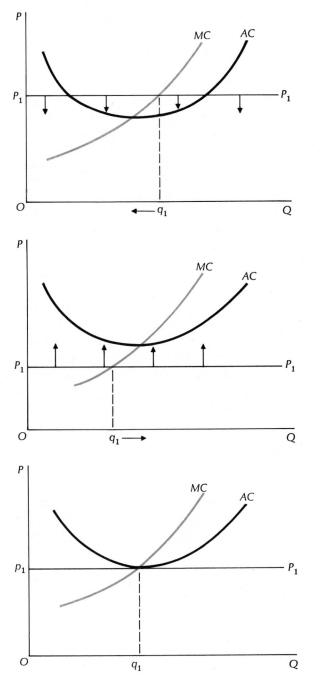

FIGURE 25-6
Extranormal profits cause new producers to enter the industry; supply increases, and the market price falls.

FIGURE 25-7
Profits below normal (or losses) cause some existing producers to leave the industry; supply decreases, and the market price rises.

FIGURE 25-8
When profits are at the normal level, producers have no incentive to either enter or leave the industry. Equilibrium.

leave another with losses, while a third may make profits substantially above the normal level. Under these circumstances, are we justified in resting the analysis of market adjustment on the actions of a "typical" firm?

Economic theorists have attempted to solve this problem in a variety of ways. One way out is to assume that all firms have exactly the same costs of production, and that the differences that actually occur are "rents" paid to the factors of production. For example, suppose a retail store to have a particularly favorable location, such as Broadway at 34th Street in New York. It would have to pay a high rent for that location, and the landowner, if he were a good bargainer, could extract rent payments that entirely eliminated the more-than-normal profits. Even if the store owned the land itself, a proper economic accounting of costs would charge off a portion of the "profits" to implicit rent. In this way, any special advantage that a firm might have over its competitors—location, patent rights, astute management, and so forth—could be allocated to rent or royalties. Likewise, any significant disadvantages of location or cost can be attributed to negative rents or royalties. The result is to bring costs of production of all firms to equality and make all of their cost curves identical.

A second way out is to assume that most firms are like the typical firm. This recognizes the possibility of differences in costs between firms. The luckier or more efficient ones will expand and grow. The less efficient will contract and tend to die off. The great majority will continue in business, adjusting as best they can to the competitive market environment. As for firms entering an industry for the first time, we can expect them to be in the middle range; they would not come in if they did not feel reasonably sure that they could meet the competition, but they would not have the experience to match the performance of the best.

Both of these ways of solving the problem of differences in cost curves end at about the same place. The first is closer to an analytically rigorous and "correct" analysis. But it gives up a good deal of reality. The second is more realistic and fits better our intuitive understanding of the situation. But it lacks the analytical rigor of the first approach. The important point is that both are consistent with the analysis of the market adjustment process as we have described it.

THE FIRM IN THE LONG RUN: CHOOSING THE SIZE OF PLANT TO BE BUILT

Up to this point in the analysis, we have assumed that the individual firm already has the plant and equipment it uses in production. Under those conditions its profit-maximizing decisions are limited to choosing the level of output. We also assumed that new firms entering the industry will build plants and acquire equipment identical to that of existing firms. These assumptions are equivalent to the assumption that each firm, old and new, has the same fixed costs. It is also equivalent to the assumption that there is a given technology to which all firms have access, and which all must use.

When these assumptions are relaxed we leave the world of the short run and move into the long run: all costs are variable. There are no fixed costs, the individual firm can choose the size of plant it wishes, and it can select the technology it wishes to employ. An illustration will help make the distinction clear. When a steel producer operates a blast furnace, the output of pig iron from the furnace can be varied with different types of inputs, but only within limits. Iron ore with a 50 percent iron content may allow an annual output of 200,000 tons. Using an enriched ore containing 65 percent iron may raise the annual output to 250,000 tons, partly because the input is richer and partly because it takes less time to burn out the impurities. The firm must then decide whether a shift to higher grades of ore, which also cost more, will bring greater profits or not. To the economist this is a short-run decision: the fixed costs of the blast furnace have been incurred and the only issue is the variable costs of the inputs.

A long-run decision concerns whether or not to build a blast furnace at all, and if so, the size at which it should be engineered. When these fixed costs can be varied, the firm can choose between blast furnaces or electric furnaces, or even direct reduction in oxygen furnaces, and all at a variety of capacity levels that in turn will vary with the quality of the inputs. The firm is in the position of having to choose the most efficient combination of all factors of production, and all of them can be varied in amount. There are, of course, technological limitations on the proportions in which the factors of production can be combined. But there are no fixed amounts of any one factor to limit the choices, as in the short-run case of existing plant and equipment.

In the long run, the firm can choose among a variety of sizes of plant, each one of which will have a different cost structure. A small plant may have relatively high costs, while costs in a larger plant may be lower. A still larger plant may run into higher costs because of technological problems, or management difficulties, or other organizational problems. The possible choices can be compared with each other, as in Figure 25-9.

In Figure 25-9, three alternative plants out of an almost infinite variety of plants with different output capacity are shown. Plant 1 is a small, relatively high-cost plant. Plant 3 is a large and also a relatively high-cost plant. Plant 2 is the one with the lowest possible cost structure. It is, of course, the one a competitive firm will seek to build. The long-run average cost curve, *LRAC*, is just tangent to each. It represents the choices the firm has. It is drawn in a dish-shaped form to indicate that cost structures change with plants of different size.

We have just noted that the competitive firm will select the plant that in the long run has the lowest cost of production.[2] The logic behind that

---

[2] The alert student will point out that this conclusion is obvious, and that we did not have to draw the long-run average cost curve to prove it. Correct! The *LRAC* curve was introduced at this point because it can move upward or downward as costs of inputs rise and fall or as technology changes, and firms have to adjust to those changes too, as we shall see in a moment.

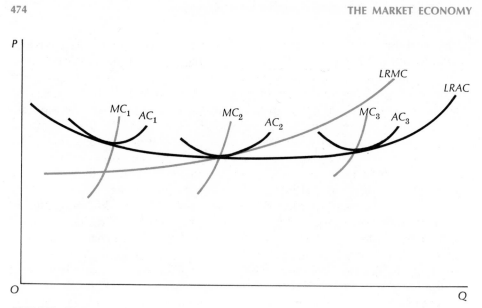

FIGURE 25-9
Long-Run Costs for Firm in Competitive Industry

Cost curves for three out of an infinite number of the possible plants that might be built
are shown. The long-run average cost curve *LRAC* is an "envelope" that is tangent to
the short-run average cost curves of each plant (AC_1, AC_2, AC_3, . . . , AC_n) at one point.
The long-run marginal cost curve, *LRMC*, shows the marginal cost associated with the
long-run average cost curve.

selection is that if it doesn't, other firms will, and it will be ultimately driven
out of business by more efficient producers. The result is that all surviving
firms will have selected plants close enough to the best size to enable them
to compete with the most efficient firms in the industry.

This lowest-cost plant is the only one that can maximize profits in both
the short run and the long run. Of all possible plant sizes, it is the only
one in which marginal costs equal average costs in both time periods. This
is shown in Figure 25-9: $MC_2 = AC_2$ at the same level of output at which *LRMC*
$= LRAC$. By contrast, $MC_1 = AC_1$ at a different level of output from that at
which *LRMC* $=$ *LRAC*.

We can show what happens in the long-run adjustment process in much
the same way that we demonstrated the short-run adjustment of the industry:

1. Supply and demand interact to determine prices in the market,
   and existing firms adapt to that price by selecting their profit-maximizing
   level of output. But let us now assume that they all have old-fashioned
   plants: a new technological discovery makes it possible to build
   plants with lower cost structures. This situation is shown in Figure
   25-10. The short-run equilibrium of the industry (Figure 25-10B)
   has been shattered by technological changes, which move long-run
   average costs downward from $LRAC_1$ to $LRAC_2$ (Figure 25-10C).

FIGURE 25-10

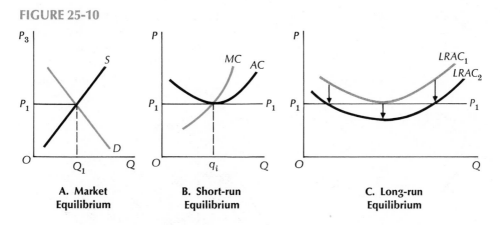

A. Market   B. Short-run   C. Long-run
Equilibrium   Equilibrium   Equilibrium

2. Firms both within and outside the industry discover that new plants
   will make extranormal profits by selling at the existing market price, P_1.
   Figure 25-11 shows the comparison.

FIGURE 25-11

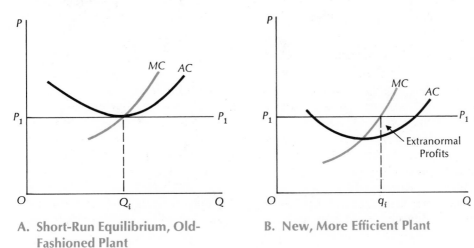

A. Short-Run Equilibrium, Old-   B. New, More Efficient Plant
   Fashioned Plant

3. As more new plants come into production, old ones are scrapped.
   Competition starts to pull the market price down as larger supplies come
   on the market. Ultimately a new long- and short-run equilibrium
   is established. Firms previously earning a normal profit begin to incur
   losses as the market price falls.
   The newer and lower long-run cost structure (Figure 25-12C) causes
   selection of the plant shown in Figure 25-12B. The lower costs enable
   the industry as a whole to reduce price and increase output
   (Figure 25-12A) until the price comes down to a level at which extranormal

profits have been eliminated (Figure 25-12B). This is the new
equilibrium of the industry, in the market (Figure 25-12A), the short
run (Figure 25-12B), and the long run (Figure 25-12C). Supply and
demand are equated in the market, and price equals marginal costs and
average costs for the individual firm in both the short run and the long run.

FIGURE 25-12

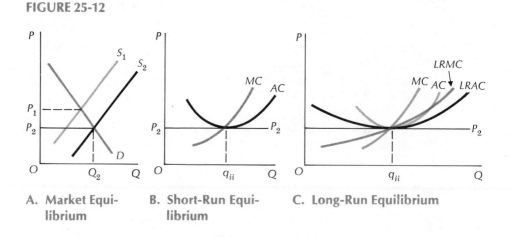

A. Market Equi-   B. Short-Run Equi-   C. Long-Run Equilibrium
   librium   **librium**

Economies of Large-Scale Production

One special attribute of the long-run cost curve was the starting point for
the modern theory of monopoly and monopoloid markets. Suppose demand
in the market is not large enough to support a large number of independent
producers, each with a lowest cost plant (Plant No. 2 in Figure 25-9). What if
only two or three such plants could be supported by the existing demand for
the product. In that case, the number of sellers would be too few for competition to prevail, for the decisions made by any one seller would affect the other
sellers.

In some cases only one seller might be able to supply the entire market
and monopoly would prevail. This situation would occur if a single plant
(such as Plant No. 1 in Figure 25-9) could supply the whole market. Even if
demand were to increase, a somewhat larger, lower-cost plant could be built
to supply the whole market at a somewhat lower price than before (if the
monopolist could be induced or forced to lower his price). Economies in
production can be achieved by increasing the scale of output in the declining
sector of the long-run average cost curve.

Although this aspect of the theory opened the way for theories of monopolistic industrial structures, it is not a common situation (except perhaps for
public utilities in local markets). We shall point out in a later chapter that
other factors besides "economies of scale" are chiefly responsible for monopoloid markets.

COST ADJUSTMENTS IN THE VERY LONG RUN

The analysis up to this point has assumed that market demand does not change: the demand curve stands still, and the profit-maximizing firm in a competitive industry adjusts to market demand on the basis of its cost structure. The result is the long-run triple equilibrium of the industry in the market, the short run and the long run.

But what happens if demand changes, if the demand curve shifts its position? In one sense, nothing happens to change the essential elements of the adjustment process. The firm and the industry merely adapt to the new environment and arrive at a new triple equilibrium based on the changed conditions of demand. That conclusion, while correct, ignores some of the things that can happen to the location of the long-run cost curve. We should analyze that problem in order to complete the picture of how the market-adjustment process takes place.

In a growing economy, the increases in wealth and income that accompany growth bring increases in the demand for a variety of goods. For example, more leisure time promotes the expansion of recreation industries, tourism, reading of books and magazines, and entertainment of all kinds. The market for a large range of products and services expands. In terms of our analysis, demand for those goods increases and the demand curve shifts upward and to the right in the usual supply-demand-price diagram, that is, from D_1 to D_2 in Figure 25-13. The increase in demand brings prices up from P_1 to

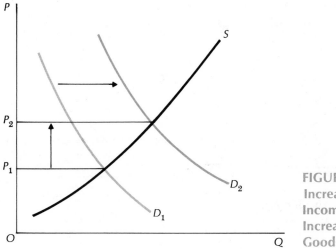

FIGURE 25-13
Increases in Wealth and Income Create Increases in Demand for Goods

P_2. We know from our earlier analysis that this price increase will raise profits for the typical firm above the normal level, drawing new producers into the industry. The resultant increase in supplies coming into the market will start bringing prices down until the extranormal profits are gone.

At this point the structure of long-run costs comes into the picture. If cost conditions do not change, the new plants will have the same short-run costs as those of the old producers, and extranormal profits will not be eliminated until prices have come down to the old level (see Figure 25-14).

FIGURE 25-14

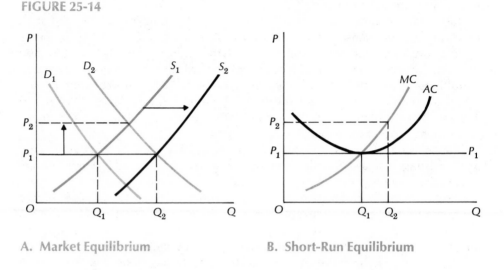

A. Market Equilibrium   **B. Short-Run Equilibrium**

The increase in *S* brings *P* back down to its old level (Diagram A) because cost structures have not changed.

As for the typical firm, the original increase in *D* that shifted prices upward from P_1 to P_2 caused it to increase its output from Q_1 to Q_2 (Diagram B). As new producers came into the industry and price fell back to P_1, it reduced its output back to Q_1 (Diagram B).

In the industry as a whole, however, the increase in supply to S_2 caused total output to rise to Q_3 (Diagram A).

The net result is enlarged output for the industry, no change in prices or costs, and reestablishment of the original equilibrium of the typical firm.

The situation we have just described may be called *constant costs in the very long run*. As growth of demand for the industry's product stimulates increased output, the cost of inputs, or materials, labor, capital, and so on, does not change. The long run adjustment of the industry can be made without higher costs of production or higher prices.

Another industry may have *increasing costs* in the very long run. In that case, the cost of one or more inputs rises as the industry expands in response to increases in demand. It is often an input from land or natural resources that figures in the cost increases. Firms in an industry using iron ore as an input, for example, will discover that their raw material costs go up as the richest and most readily available deposits of iron ore are used up, and as growth requires the opening up of new, higher-cost mines. We can analyze the process as shown in Figure 25-15.

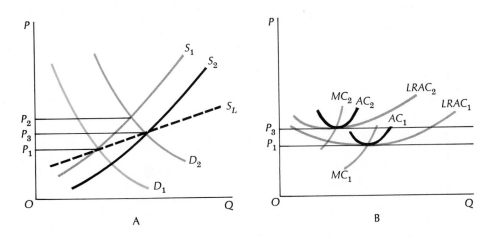

FIGURE 25-15

Demand increases from D_1 to D_2, pushing prices up immediately to P_2. The large extranormal profits bring in new producers and supply starts to increase from S_1 toward S_2. But the increased demand for inputs causes long-run costs to rise from $LRAC_1$ toward $LRAC_2$. Declining prices from increased supply and rising long-run costs meet at price P_3, at which point a new triple equilibrium has been established. The new price, P_3, is higher than the old, P_1.

In this instance, the supply curve for the industry rises in the very long run (shown by S_L in Figure 25-15A). That is, as demand increases with growth of the economy, the industry produces a growing output, but at steadily rising prices. In the long run more can be produced, but only along a path in which the triple equilibrium of the industry is achieved at rising prices.

This result contrasts with the industry that has constant costs in the very long run, where the supply curve in the very long run is horizontal at the price level consistent with the competitive triple equilibrium.

The final case is the industry with _decreasing costs_ in the very long run. This is just the opposite of the increasing cost industry: prices of some inputs fall when the industry expands in response to rising demand. There can be several reasons for declining costs of inputs. As an industry grows, some of the services it needs can be provided by outside firms. Maintenance services may have to be done by each firm, but if several firms are located near each other, an independent, specialized, and more efficient supplier of maintenance services may be organized to provide those services more cheaply than they can be carried out by the firms themselves. Another example: Growth of an industry may develop specialized labor skills in the labor market that may be hard to find if the industry is small and demand for the skills is correspondingly small. Again: Suppliers of materials may be able to reduce their costs (and prices) and the industry's demand for the materials goes up. In each of these instances the reduced costs of inputs

INCREASING-COST INDUSTRIES

Increasing-cost industries are no joke. They can cause serious economic problems for an entire nation. In an earlier chapter we noted that England's relative economic decline, which began in the late nineteenth century and continued past World War II, was partly caused by increasing costs of coal, as mines became deeper and mining more expensive. The United States has experienced something similar. Its resources of high-grade iron ore were very largely used up during World War II. New sources of ore were found after the war, but they were just as accessible to foreign producers as to American. As a result, part of the competitive advantage of U.S. steel producers was lost and the U.S. began to import more steel than it exported for the first time in over a hundred years. There were other reasons for the shift; bad management in an industry protected from competition by monopolistic practices was one, and high wage costs another. But the shift in the industry's raw materials base was one of the most important.

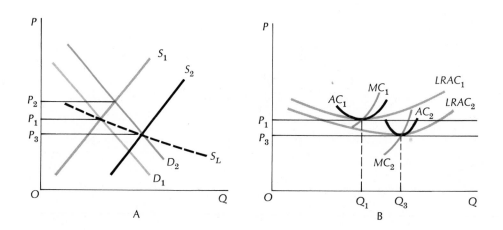

FIGURE 25-16

The increase in demand from D_1 to D_2 pushes prices up to P_2, drawing new firms into the industry. Expansion reduces long-run costs from $LRAC_1$ to $LRAC_2$, due to external economies, while at the same time supply rises from S_1 to S_2. The decreased long-run costs bring a new equilibrium at price P_3, which is lower than the original price. The supply curve slopes downward (S_L) in the very long run.

are due to growth of the industry as a whole. They are not due to the actions of any single firm. They are therefore called external economies, that is, savings external to the firm and not due to its internal decisions.

External economies are the chief source of decreasing costs in the very long run. As demand for the industry's product goes up and the industry expands, external economies bring long-run average costs down, and the industry's supply curve takes on a downward slope (see Figure 25-16).

Cost conditions, then, come in three variations in the very long run, depending on what happens to the costs of inputs:

Constant costs: Prices of inputs stay the same.
Increasing costs: Prices of inputs rise.
Decreasing costs: Prices of inputs fall.

All of these trends in the very long run are consistent with the triple equilibrium of a competitive industry. They show that this equilibrium can move up or down, or stay where it is, as far as costs are concerned, within the framework of a growing and expanding economy.

SUBSIDIES FOR DECREASING COST INDUSTRIES?

When an industry has long-run decreasing costs, it may be desirable to speed up its growth. As in the case of air transportation, the industry can be subsidized by direct payments to producers, or indirectly by public construction of facilities such as terminals. The object of such subsidies is to expand the industry faster than its normal growth pattern, enabling the entire economy to benefit from the industry's decreasing very-long-run costs.

A similar argument can be made for subsidies to new industries that initially operate on the declining portion of the long-run cost curve because the total market is not yet large enough to support a substantial number of low-cost producers. In either case, the subsidy would pay off as long as the lower production costs achieved by expansion more than offset the cost of the subsidy.

There are problems here, of course. The taxpayers who pay the subsidy may not be those who benefit from the expanded operation of the industry, and those who benefit may not be those who pay. Nevertheless, the economic principle stands, in spite of its political difficulties.

Isn't it curious? A theoretical analysis of the perfectly competitive private enterprise economy leads to an argument for government intervention.

REVIEW: FOUR ANALYTICALLY
DIFFERENT TIME PERIODS

Analysis of the market adujstment process is usually divided into four analytically distinct phases, as outlined in Figure 25-17. These time periods have been separated for purposes of analysis only. In practice, market prices and quantities sold are constantly changing, firms are deciding on their levels of output and capital expansion programs, and long-run cost relationships are shifting and causing adjustments in capital outlay programs of individual firms. All of the decisions and trends are related to and influence each other, and all are simultaneously adjusting to condition of price and cost.

THE MARKET-ADJUSTMENT
PROCESS IN PERSPECTIVE

The ideas developed in this chapter are some of the most important in all of economics. They are a distillation of the essential elements of Adam Smith's _Wealth of Nations_ (1776), David Ricardo's _Principles of Political Economy_ (1817), and Alfred Marshall's _Principles of Economics_ (1890) as amended and developed by a host of other economists up to the present day. In one form or another they comprise a central portion of the tool kit of all economists today. Everyone who wishes to have a working knowledge of economics must be thoroughly familiar with these principles.

Why are they so important? First, the method is a classic example of the use of logic in the analysis of economic processes. It starts with assumptions about behavior that reduce the problem to manageable proportions. Then the problem is divided into segments, "time periods" in this case, which allow one variable at a time to be studied while the other variables are held constant. Finally, by a series of successive approximations, the whole process under study is put together in such a way that any or all variables can change, yet the investigator has a sure understanding of what is happening to the system as a whole.

In the development of the method, a number of specific analytical techniques were used, especially geometric exposition. That style was used here because it lends itself well to the problem at hand. The explanation could have been done algebraically, and if you study advanced economic theory you will learn it that way. The important relationships to be grasped, however, are those that relate average and marginal costs to price and quantity variables. They are the ones that make the model go.

That point leads into the second reason for the importance of the market adjustment process. It tells us how markets function, in general and in the essential elements. There are no perfectly competitive markets. Yet whatever the imperfections and constraints, any market will adjust itself to the changes that are continually taking place in our world. The process of adjustment will have much in common with the competitive model, once the specific charac-

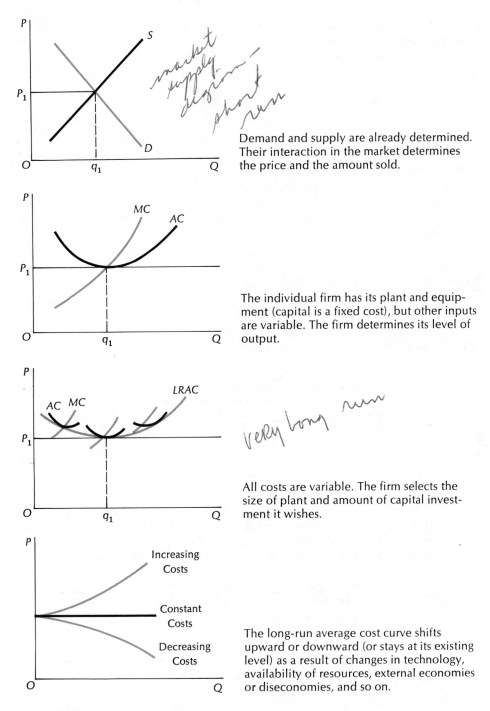

Demand and supply are already determined. Their interaction in the market determines the price and the amount sold.

The individual firm has its plant and equipment (capital is a fixed cost), but other inputs are variable. The firm determines its level of output.

All costs are variable. The firm selects the size of plant and amount of capital investment it wishes.

The long-run average cost curve shifts upward or downward (or stays at its existing level) as a result of changes in technology, availability of resources, external economies or diseconomies, and so on.

FIGURE 25-17
Four Analytically Different Time Periods of Market Adjustment

teristics of the market system in the real world are taken into account. One of our tasks later will be to analyze the market adjustment process as it exists under a variety of other conditions, including monopoly, a variety of monopoloid situations, and even a planned economy. In each case, the analysis of the specific situation will hark back to the fundamentals of market adjustment as they show up through analysis of the perfectly competitive market.

The theory of the competitive market system is important for a third reason. The role of the profit motive in a private economy becomes very clear. This motive is the driving force behind the adjustment process. The businessman's effort to maximize his profits causes him to make decisions about output levels, and whether to enter or leave the market, that bring the industry into equilibrium in the short run. He also selects the plant size that underlies the long run equilibrium. Even though only a few people earn profits, they are the ones who make the crucial decisions.

Finally, and the most important point, the market-adjustment process has important implications for welfare and efficiency. Earlier we concluded that rational consumers allocate their incomes to maximize utility, an action we equated with maximization of welfare. We also showed that in the market equilibrium, where supply and demand are equal at market price and the market is cleared, welfare is maximized because marginal utility to the buyer and marginal cost to the seller are equal. Now we were able to show that, as producers adjust their actions to consumer demand, they do so at the minimum possible real cost. The price that prevails in the long run in a competitive economy *cannot be any lower* for the existing level of output. The triple equilibrium of the firm and industry cannot produce prices any lower. Look at the diagrams again, in reverse order (Figures 25-18, 25-19, 25-20).

In other words, producers bring resources together in the least cost combinations, to produce at the lowest unit costs just that combination of goods that brings maximum welfare to consumers. When we understand this point, we realize why the idea of a competitive private enterprise economy has had such a hold on the minds of so many people.

Nevertheless, we must remember that this is a theoretical model only. Achievement of these welfare-maximizing results depends on the existence of four conditions, and they are not always found in a real-life economy:

1. Consumers must be free to choose among the goods available in the market. This means the absence of rationing, either in wartime or in a planned economy, and absence of legal restrictions imposed by government (such as prohibition of liquor or marijuana).

2. Markets must be free of controls over prices or quantity of sales, by either public authorities or private monopolies. It is in this respect, the existence of private monopolistic controls, that our economy shows its most serious deviation from the competitive model. Some types of planned economies are also subject to strong controls over produc-

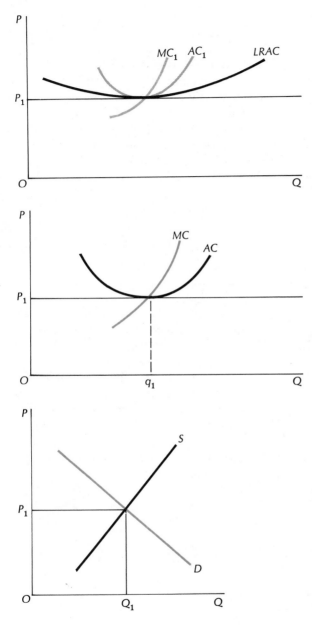

FIGURE 25-18

In the long run, price will be brought to the level at which it is tangent to the long-run cost curve. The profit-maximizing firm will select plant AC_1–MC_1, which is the lowest-cost plant possible.

FIGURE 25-19

With this plant the short-run equilibrium is one in which $P = AC$ at the lowest point on the average-cost curve. Prices can't be any lower while still keeping the necessary firms in the industry. Yet the existing producers are satisfied. Nor can prices be any higher, for then additional producers will appear.

FIGURE 25-20

Meanwhile, back in the market, supply and demand are equated and the market is cleared assuring welfare maximization by consumers.

ing units by government agencies, but, as we shall subsequently see, this deficiency is not necessarily present in all types of planned economies.

3. The entire price system must be organized in such a way that prices reflect real costs of production. If that does not happen, the resulting triple equilibrium will not have much meaning so far as maximization of welfare is concerned. Monopolistic practices in our economy can

prevent this condition from prevailing, and poor planning can have the same result in a planned economy.

4. <u>All outputs (and inputs)</u> must have prices attached to them. While this condition applies to all goods produced privately, it does not apply to all of those supplied by governments.

The world is different from the theory, but the theory enables us to make judgments about the world. We will use the theory for that purpose in the next two parts of this book, in discussions of economic planning and monopolistic practices. But first we will look at competition in practice in American agriculture.

Summary

In a purely competitive industry, the profit-maximizing firm adjusts its output to the level at which marginal cost equals marginal revenue. If the typical firm makes extranormal profits at that level of output, new firms will enter the industry. If less than normal profits are made, some firms will leave the industry. Those shifts will cause the market supply to change, which will cause the market price to change. At the same time all firms are building the size and type of plant at which production costs are minimized. These adjustments tend toward a triple equilibrium of market, firm, and industry in which demand and supply are equal at the market price, the typical firm is maximizing profits at a level of output that also minimizes average costs of production, and no firm makes either more or less than a normal profit. As production techniques change and as the relative scarcities of the factors of production change, the entire system will adjust as it continually seeks to reach a condition of simultaneous equilibria in market, firm, and industry.

Key Concepts

Pure competition.   A situation in which the number of sellers and buyers in the market is so large that no one unit has any influence over price. Prices are set solely by the interaction of the market forces of demand and supply. The product is homogeneous, and full freedom of entry and exit prevails.

Perfect competition.   A situation with all the characteristics of pure competition, plus full knowledge of all alternatives on the part of buyers and sellers, and unrestricted mobility of all resources.

Extranormal profits.   Profits above the normal profits that are included in the firm's costs.

Market equilibrium.   Supply and demand in the market are equal at the prevailing price.

Short-run equilibrium.   The individual firm is operating at the level of output that maximizes profits.

Long-run equilibrium.   Individual firms have built the lowest-cost plants, *and* entry or exit of firms has brought profits equal to normal profits to the typical firm.

Costs in the very long run.   Changes in the relative scarcities of the factors of production may bring increasing, decreasing, or constant costs, to which the firm and industry adjust.

Competitive Markets in Practice: The Case of U.S. Agriculture

26

The "farm problem" in the United States has been a continuing feature of the economic and political scene for over half a century. Farmers have not really been happy with their economic position for a hundred years, as the rural political movements that began during the post–Civil War decades indicate. Nevertheless, the ten years prior to World War I were a kind of golden age for American Agriculture that farm policy has sought to recapture ever since World War I disrupted it. In the past two-thirds of a century, American farmers have been subject to wide swings of great prosperity and great depression, and have been affected by the changes taking place in a highly dynamic economy. As businessmen in an industry with many of the characteristics of the textbook version of a competitive industry, they have had to adapt to these shifting circumstances as best they could. Agriculture has not been static. It has had to adapt to changing prices and costs, changes in demand, and changing technology. It has also been the subject of national economic policy and the political influences found in policy determination.

This chapter uses agriculture as a small laboratory to show the complexities of the market-adjustment process, the difficulties our agricultural policies have created, and what might happen if we should return to the market as the full determinant of agricultural prices and output.

AGRICULTURE IN A CHANGING WORLD

The prosperous era prior to 1914 led into a period of economic growth and technological change as well as the disruptions caused by war and depression. As the incomes of American consumers rose in the years after the First World War, their preferences with respect to farm products changed. The staple food crops such as wheat did not experience a large increase in demand. Instead, demand for the richer food products grew most rapidly: meat, dairy products, fruits and vegetables. This meant a shift in emphasis away from the extensive agriculture that used large amounts of land and relatively small amounts of capital and labor, toward a much more heavily capital-intensive agriculture using increasing amounts of capital and relatively small amounts of land and labor. These trends are shown in Figure 26-1.

Even meat production shows this shift. The vast ranches of the turn of the century that are celebrated in stories,

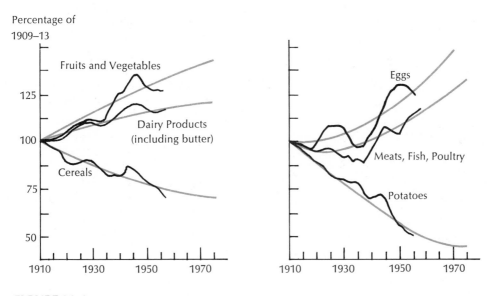

FIGURE 26-1
Trends in Eating Habits

The shift in demand for farm products from land-intensive to capital-intensive products has been going on for many years. If we continue to support and subsidize production of land-intensive crops, will farmers shift the use of their resources as they should? (Source: *Yearbook of Agriculture, 1958,* p. 469.)

songs, and movies have given way to the "feeder lot," where penned cattle are scientifically fed the amount and type of food that will produce the meatiest cattle in the least time.

This trend in American agriculture—the result of rising population and growing incomes—continues and will continue. It means that farms are becoming highly capitalized and are growing in size, and that they have long ago lost the "family farm" image of a farm family working the land itself and producing a very large part of its own consumption. The modern farm is a highly organized business enterprise.

Technological change has also helped to transform American agriculture. We usually think of it in terms of the substitution of tractors and other mechanical equipment for farm workers, and that transition has obviously been important. Employment of farm workers has declined in every decade since 1910, and has been substantially speeded up since World War II, while use of machinery and fertilizers has greatly increased.

Technological change has affected agriculture in other ways. The shift from horsepower to the internal-combustion engine (tractors, trucks, etc.) during the 1920s largely eliminated horses from the farm economy. Land that was formerly used to grow feed for horses was now freed to produce food for humans. The supply of food products could then be increased substantially.

TABLE 26–1
The Transformation of U.S. Agriculture, 1910–1968

Year	Employment (1000 persons)			Man-Hours of Labor Used (1957–59 = 100)	Value of Farm Implements and Machinery (Millions of dollars)	Farm Output (1957–59 = 100)	Work Stock (horses, etc.) (1000 head)	Index of Fertilizer Used (1957–59 = 100)	Units of Equipment Used on Farms	
	Total	Family Workers	Hired Workers						Tractors (Thousands)	Motor Trucks (Thousands)
1910	13,555	10,174	3,381	212	1,265	51		12		
1920	13,432	10,041	3,391	226	3,595	59	22,386	14	229	132
1930	12,494	9,307	3,190	216	3,302	61	17,612	20	851	845
1940	10,979	8,300	2,679	192	3,060	70	13,029	23	1,567	1,047
1950	9,926	7,597	2,329	150	11,216	86	7,415	55	3,394	2,207
1960	7,057	5,172	1,885	92	18,613	106	2,883	111	4,685	2,825
1968	5,610 (1965)	4,128 (1965)	1,482 (1965)	68		120	(series discontinued)	229	4,820	3,125

Sources: U.S. Department of Commerce, *Historical Statistics of the United States* (Washington: U.S. Gov't. Printing Office, 1960) and *Continuation to 1962* (Washington, 1965).

U.S. Department of Agriculture, *Agricultural Statistics, 1962, 1966* (Washington: U.S. Gov't. Printing Office, 1962, 1966).

U.S. Bureau of the Census, *Census of Agriculture, 1964* (Washington: U.S. Gov't. Printing Office, 1967).

U.S. Department of Agriculture, Economic Research Service, *Economic Tables, January, 1969* (Washington: U.S. Gov't Printing Office, 1969).

Unfortunately, this development occurred just after farm acreage had been expanded to meet the needs of the First World War, and continued through the fall in demand brought on by the depression of the 1930s. Almost simultaneously the production of synthetic fibers from wood and chemicals, such as rayon, nylon, and other synthetics, struck a blow at the market for cotton, wool, and other agricultural fibers.

These technological changes were imposed on the economic upheavals created by the First World War. During the war, U.S. agricultural production was substantially expanded in response to both high prices and patriotic appeals. For example, it was during 1915–19 that the western Great Plains were brought under the plow for the first time, creating the conditions that led to the great "dust bowl" tragedy of the mid-1930s. When the war ended and European agriculture recovered from wartime dislocations, the expanded capacity of U.S. agriculture hung over the market like a cloud, the problem compounded by similar developments in Canada, Argentina, and Australia. American agriculture never fully recovered, even during the otherwise general prosperity of the 1920s.

The depression years of the 1930s brought all of these problems to a head. Demand for farm products fell drastically as GNP declined and the world depression spread. Farm incomes followed. Economic disaster for rural and small-town America was averted only by the institution of large-scale price support and acreage restriction programs designed to sustain farm incomes.

One unlooked-for result of the farm policies of the thirties created additional problems of technological change. Acreage restrictions caused farmers to take their least productive lands out of production. This meant that the decline of acreage was proportionately greater than the decline of output. In addition, farmers used their remaining crop acreage more intensively. Plants were seeded closer together. Larger amounts of fertilizer were used. Newer and more productive types of seeds were developed (in large part by the agricultural research efforts of the federal government). The result was a sharp upswing in agricultural productivity that started in the mid-1930s and has continued to the present. It is shown in Figures 26-2 and 26-3. This change in the production relationships of the industry speeded up the transition from small-scale farming to agribusiness and greatly worsened the problem of surplus production.

World War II brought a respite. Like the First World War, it created a large increase in demand for farm products both as food and as industrial raw materials, and it caused a breakdown in European agriculture once more. The world market for farm products was booming in those years. But the farm prosperity of 1940–46, like that of 1915–19, could not last. The war ended, peacetime levels of demand returned, and European agriculture revived. Yet the rapid technological change begun before the war continued. There was a difference, however; we now had a series of agricultural support programs that protected farmers (but not farm workers or sharecroppers) from much of the strain of adjustment to changing conditions.

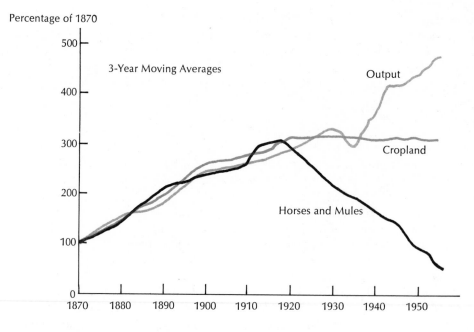

Percentage of 1870

FIGURE 26-2
Productivity in U.S. Agriculture
Up until the end of World War I, U.S. farm output rose just about as fast as cropland and animal power. Starting in the twenties, animal power was being replaced by the internal-combustion engine, but output did not grow much because cropland did not expand. The dip in output of the early 1930s caused by the depression was followed by rapid growth after 1935 in response to a drive toward more intense use of resources. (Source: *Yearbook of Agriculture,* 1958, p. 462).

TABLE 26-2
Productivity in U.S. Agriculture, 1940–65
(1940 = 100)

Year (1)	Farm Output (2)	Farm Labor Productivity (3)	Total Resources Used (4)	Resources Used per Unit of Output (5)
1940	100	100	100	100
1945	116	126	102	88
1950	123	166	104	85
1955	138	180	105	77
1960	151	219	104	69
1965	167	269	104	62

Source: Earl O. Heady, *A Primer on Food, Agriculture, and Public Policy* (New York: Random House, 1967). This little book provides an admirable review of agricultural problems and analysis of public policy alternatives.

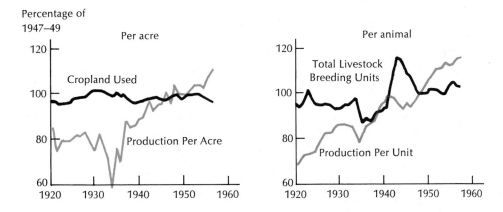

FIGURE 26-3
Farm Production

The remarkable growth in agricultural productivity after 1935 is shown dramatically by these two charts. Cropland in use has not expanded, but production per acre has shown a steady upward trend. Even animal products have shown the same trend, because of better feed, better stock, and better management. (Source: *Yearbook of Agriculture, 1958, p. 464.*)

As can be seen in Table 26–2, between 1940 and 1965, agricultural production in the U.S. grew by two-thirds (column 2), while resources used remained almost the same (column 4). Output per man-hour in agriculture more than doubled (column 3), while total resource productivity grew by almost 40 percent (column 5). These figures show a very high rate of change in the fundamental production relationships of the industry.

Agricultural price supports and acreage controls have attempted to bolster farm incomes by raising prices (or preventing them from falling). They have been successful, to a degree. But in another sense they have a perverse effect. By reducing economic pressures on farmers, they have reduced the need for agriculture to respond to the long-run changes in demand that economic growth brings. So we continue to subsidize the existing pattern of production while the structure of demand is slowly shifting. In addition, we continue to limit agricultural production while there is hunger at home and starvation abroad. These paradoxes make it clear that some basic maladjustments have developed in American agriculture.

THE FARMER AS BUSINESSMAN

Farming in the United States is not a simple occupation, and farmers are not poor peasants subsisting on their own produce. Most of our marketed agricultural production comes from commercial farms:

Eighty-one percent of agricultural production comes from about one million farms (30 percent of the total) with annual sales of $10,000 or more.

Ninety-two percent of agricultural production comes from the 45 percent of all farms with sales of over $5,000.

These figures mean that there are lots of farmers, but that the majority are quite small operators, many of whom work farms part-time, while a relatively small portion of all farms are the ones that count when considering the economics of agricultural markets.

This pattern shows up when we examine the benefits from government subsidy programs. Large farmers get the greatest benefits both in total payments and in proportion to their incomes. Table 26-3 shows the figures for 1964.

TABLE 26-3
Distribution of Government Payments to Farmers, by Size of Farm, 1964

Size of Farm (Annual Sales)	No. of Farms (Thousands)	Percentage of Farms	Percentage of Total Value of all Farm Sales	Government Payments per Farm	Percentage of Income from Government
$20,000 or more	401	12.7	62.5	$2,391	18.5
10,000–19,999	467	14.8	18.8	670	8.8
5,000– 9,999	504	16.0	10.4	350	6.4
2,500– 4,999	443	14.1	4.6	173	3.9
Under $2,500	1,338	42.4	3.7	51	1.2
All Farms	3,153	100.0	100.0	472	8.8

Source: U.S. Department of Agriculture, *Census of Agriculture*, 1964.

The reason that government payments to farmers go to the big farmers is that they are the ones that market the great bulk of farm products. Since the payments are keyed to market prices and supplies, they go to the commercial farmers who are the most active in agricultural markets.

Since the farm family is essentially a business unit, it typically has larger assets than nonfarm families, most of whom work for wages and salaries. On the average, farm families own about twice the wealth of nonfarm families; the data are shown in Table 26-4.

TABLE 26-4
Assets of U.S. Families, 1965

Type of Asset	Average Value of Assets	
	All Families	Farm Families
Home	$ 5,975	$ 5,501
Automobile	637	681
Business	3,913	25,767
Insurance, etc.	1,376	1,278
Cash, securities, etc.	11,170	11,233
Personal debt	483	486
Average net worth	22,588	43,973
Median net worth	7,550	26,250

Source: Earl O. Heady, *A Primer on Food, Agriculture and Public Policy* (New York: Random House, 1967), p. 15.

The most striking difference between farm families and others is in business assets, representing the value of the farm. This difference shows in the comparison of net worth at the bottom of Table 26–4. Half of all families in the U.S. had a net worth of less than $7,550, while half of all farm families had a net worth of over $26,250.

The fact that the farm is a business enterprise and that the farmer is a businessman does not mean that the "family farm" is disappearing or will disappear. It is true that commercial farms are becoming larger. The use of capital-intensive techniques means that large-scale production units are highly economical. But the consolidation of small farms into large ones, which has forced many farm families into the cities, has still left the typical farm to be operated by a single family. The majority of farms use only family labor, except for a few days of help at harvest time, and most of the capital comes from savings and borrowings based on family assets.

THE FAMILY FARM.   *Some striking statistics for the edification of city boys and girls:*

The average U.S. farm uses only 1.75 man-years of labor annually.

Only 6 percent of U.S. farms use more than 1.5 man-years of hired labor annually.

Although most farms are family-operated business enterprises, there are two other variations that should be noted. One is the giant farm enterprise, the elite of the industry. These are the 1,200 farms that sell over half a million dollars worth of farm products or more annually. They comprise only one-thirtieth of one percent of all farms, but they market as much as the smallest 40 percent of all farms (about $1.5 billion annually). Just behind these green giants is another group of lesser giants, the 21,000 farms with annual sales of $100,000 to $500,000 annually. These are the prosperous, productive farms that have taken advantage of the great advances in farm productivity made possible by technological change.

At the other extreme are some 350,000 farm families at the bottom of the industry that make up one of the most impoverished sectors of the economy. Their average annual return from sales of farm products was about $438 and their nonfarm earnings were $525 in 1961. And remember that these are averages: about half had lower incomes. This is the farm group that has been dispossessed by economic growth and technological change and has been unable to adjust to the new world. These families don't belong in agriculture. They can't make a go of farming without capital, and they can't get the capital.

They need relocation, retraining, and jobs in the nonagricultural sectors of the economy.

These are the units that comprise U.S. agriculture. A few very large, highly efficient, corporate or corporation-like enterprises, a large number of viable family-size business enterprises, and a group of farm families that have been unable to adapt to the new era of farming. These economic units have had to adapt themselves to wide fluctuations in demand, government programs designed to stabilize the industry, and rapidly rising productivity. It has not been a simple adjustment to existing conditions of demand as postulated by the analysis of the competitive market contained in the last chapter. Let's analyze it.

INELASTIC DEMAND
AND FLUCTUATING INCOMES

The demand for most basic farm products is inelastic. For example, an increase of one percent in the size of the marketed wheat crop can bring a five percent drop in price. The percentage change in quantity sold is much smaller than the percentage change in price. As a result, the incomes of producers can fluctuate widely with only small changes in the quantity sold.

Not all farm products have inelastic demand, but the large-volume, important ones do. Table 26–5 gives some examples.

TABLE 26–5
Elasticity of Demand, Selected Farm Products

Commodity	Elasticity	Commodity	Elasticity
Corn	0.1	Meat	0.5–0.6
Wheat	0.2	Milk	0.2–0.3
Cotton	0.5	All food	0.2–0.5

Source: Leonard W. Weiss, *Economics and American Industry* (New York: John Wiley and Sons, 1961), p. 74.

Let's see what happens when the weather and growing conditions are good, and a fine wheat crop comes in. Marketed supplies of wheat increase. As Figure 26-4 shows, this good luck for the farmer brings him a lower income.

The effect of changes in demand on farm incomes is also dramatic. A decline in demand will reduce the incomes of the producers of almost any product. But when demand falls for a product with inelastic demand, the decline in income can be catastrophic, as shown in Figure 26-5.

These two bits of economic analysis provide the basic rationale for income maintenance or crop control programs in agriculture. The inelastic demand for farm products brings large short-run swings in farm incomes when supplies increase or demand falls. Yet farmers have little control over either condition. The normal vagaries of weather and the usual fluctuations of economic activity can bring serious instability of income.

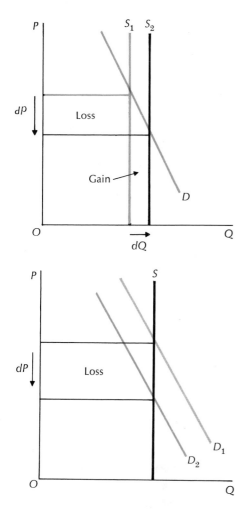

FIGURE 26-4

Inelastic Demand: Increased Output Results in Lower Incomes

Supply increases from S_1 to S_2 (dQ). Because demand is inelastic, a substantial fall in price (dP) results. The loss in income due to lower price exceeds the gain in income due to larger output.

FIGURE 26-5

Farm Income in a Depression

With S remaining the same. D falls from D_1 to D_2. The resulting fall in price causes a large loss in farm income. Note: What would happen to incomes if D were elastic? Figure it out by drawing the appropriate diagram on a separate sheet of paper.

LONG-RUN DISLOCATIONS IN AGRICULTURE

The previous section has shown that farm incomes are inherently unstable, that in some years farm incomes will fall. In other years they will rise, when demand increases from the year before or when supply falls. Won't the good income years balance the bad, leaving farmers with adequate average incomes?

Unfortunately, that has not happened, and the reason is the series of changes that have affected U.S. agriculture over the years. World wars, depression, and technological change, together with public policies for agriculture, have brought some serious dislocations. A long-run analysis that includes these factors is called for.

We can start by assuming that prior to World War II agriculture in the United States had achieved a long-run triple equilibrium analogous to that described in the previous chapter. It hadn't, but at some point during the upswing in farm prices early in the 1940s it came close. So this simplifying assumption is not too far from reality. Figure 26-6 shows such a situation.

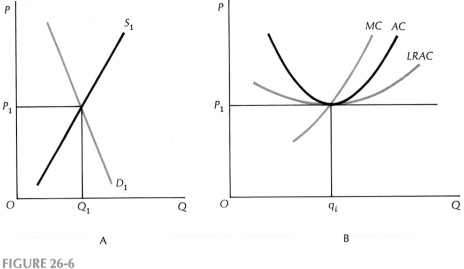

A   B

FIGURE 26-6
Agriculture in Long-Run Equilibrium

During World War II the demand for farm products rose substantially. Food supplies were needed by allies whose agricultural production had been disrupted or peacetime supply lines broken. The armed forces required large supplies. War industry needed more raw materials. Higher incomes caused civilian consumption to rise.

Farmers responded to the upward shift in demand by expanding output. Land set aside during the depression was brought back into production. New land, if available, was plowed up for crop production. Beef cattle herds were expanded. Within a relatively short time a new equilibrium was approached.

The new equilibrium had a higher cost structure, however. Use of less fertile land caused long-run costs to shift upward faster than productivity growth pulled them down (wartime shortages prevented substantial increases in capital equipment per farm). The new equilibrium based on wartime conditions is shown in Figure 26-7.

Fortunately, the war came to an end without complete destruction. But farmers found that in peacetime the demand for farm products fell back toward the prewar level. In the real world of 1946–47, demand didn't fall to such a level, but to keep the diagrams simple we can assume that it did. It won't alter the analysis significantly. At any rate, the decline in demand (back to D_1) would have created some almost insoluble problems of adjustment for farmers if government programs had not supported farm prices. The potential disequilibrium is shown in Figure 26-8.

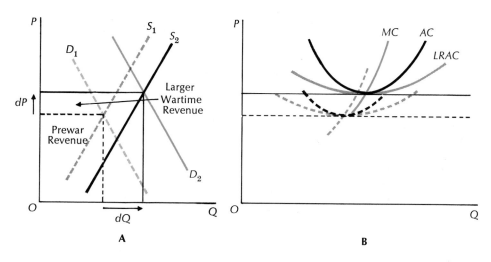

FIGURE 26-7

The Long-Run Equilibrium Under Wartime Conditions

The prewar equilibrium is shown in dotted lines, the wartime equilibrium in solid lines.
Demand has increased, price has risen, and cost structures have shifted upward.
Farmers did well as the industry moved to the new equilibrium: their total revenue rose.

The postwar disequilibrium would have left the farmer high and dry, with average costs considerably above market prices. If this had happened, we might expect the adjustment to continue if agriculture were an ordinary competitive industry. Some producers would leave the industry, supply would decrease and prices recover, and long-run costs would start coming down. Ultimately a new triple equilibrium very close to the prewar one would be reestablished. Unfortunately, agriculture is different. Output of farm products may expand readily in response to increases in demand, but it does not easily contract in response to decreases in demand.

There are many reasons for this "irreversibility" of supply in agriculture. Since farming is done by families, a reduction of output means changing the entire family life. It is harder to do that than merely give up a business enterprise. More important, much of the rise in costs during the war came about because of the increase in land values stimulated by wartime prosperity. A postwar readjustment would require that land values be reduced, and this would affect all farmers adversely. The adjustment in agriculture to a new postwar equilibrium would mean more than merely the elimination of marginal acreage and marginal farms. It would mean loss of part of the value of its assets by every farm unit.[1]

Under these conditions it is natural for farmers to organize for political ac-

---

[1] This matter will be discussed in detail a little later when we discuss the nature and growth of rent and its relationship to the farm problem.

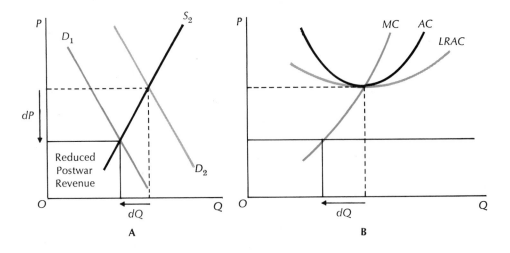

FIGURE 26-8
Postwar Equilibrium in Agriculture
The drop in demand to prewar levels (D_1) would have brought a sharp decline in price
(dP) and a more moderate decrease in output as the individual farmer moved down his
marginal cost curve. Total revenue would have been drastically reduced for both
the industry and the individual farmer.

tion. Under the slogan of "parity for agriculture" [2] farmers demanded maintenance of wartime levels of prices. This program of government price supports
then created the situation as shown in Figure 26-9.

In this situation, the government maintains the price of the farm product by
buying supplies produced so that the price stays at the level achieved in the
wartime equilibrium, enabling the individual farm enterprise to make normal
profits once more. This is equivalent to raising the price from the level
to which it would otherwise have fallen (dP). But this creates a disequilibrium. The industry and the enterprise maintain a higher output dQ_a at the
wartime equilibrium level, just as the higher price signals them to do. But
consumers reduce the quantity they purchase dQ_b, leaving a substantial surplus
in the hands of government agencies. The total income of farmers is back to
where it was, derived partly from sales to the public and partly from government purchases. But the costs are paid by the general public in the form of
high prices for food, and taxes to support government buying of surplus prod-

---

[2] *Parity* is a much abused term. Technically, it means a return to the relationships that prevailed
in 1914 between prices paid by farmers and prices received by farmers. A return to those good
old days is now so obviously impossible that the term has been applied in more recent years
to a number of other standards that relate farm incomes to incomes of city dwellers. Even these
economic meanings of the term have given way, however, in the face of the use of the term for
political purposes. No one knows what *parity* means any more, except some of the more vocif-
erous farm lobbyists and politicians.

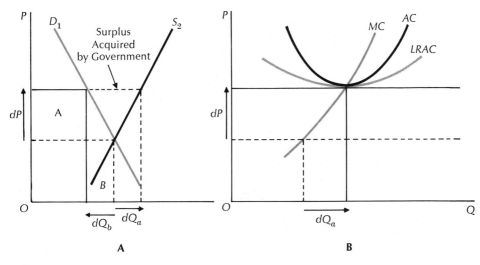

FIGURE 26-9
Government Price Support Programs

ucts. The total cost to the taxpayers is $dQ_a + dQ_b$ (the surplus crops) multiplied by the price of the commodity. The additional cost to consumers (for a reduced quantity bought) is rectangle A minus rectangle B.

One way to reduce the tax burden is to reduce the surplus. Special controls can be used for this purpose, such as soil banks, production allotments, acreage controls or marketing quotas. All of these devices have been tried, but their principal impact is to make farmers angry, because they reduce total farm income.

PRICE SUPPORTS AND SURPLUSES

Today's pattern of agricultural policies began in the Great Depression of the 1930s. The Commodity Credit Corporation was established to support the prices of selected farm products at predetermined levels. In addition to direct purchases, the CCC was authorized to make loans to farmers to hold commodities off the market. The farmer could pay off the loan by delivering the commodity, even though its market value was below the amount of the loan. In either case, the CCC would acquire commodities in the hope of maintaining prices close to the support level.

Two devices were used to control output. One was acreage allotments. Each farmer was allowed a given acreage on which to grow the crop. If he exceeded that acreage, he was denied price supports. The second device was marketing quotas. The farmer was allowed to sell only the amount grown on his acreage allotment. The two regulations duplicated each other, but the acreage allotment could be enforced by legal penalties.

The price support and acreage controls had two chief effects. First the CCC accumulated large stocks of agricultural commodities. This result was expected from a program that maintained prices at artificially high levels. Fortunately, however, the growth of demand in World War II enabled the CCC to dispose of its surpluses at a profit. The second effect was the start of the great increases in agricultural productivity. With prices maintained but acreage controlled, farmers had every incentive to increase output per acre by adding large doses of capital to their production inputs.

The prewar policies were continued after World War II. They had apparently paid off. Prices and farm incomes had been maintained and the whole program had turned out well because of the disposal of surpluses during the war. Under these circumstances any significant change was politically impossible.

But in the 1950s the avalanche began. Slowed national economic growth, together with rapidly rising agricultural productivity and good production years, brought the total surpluses held by the CCC to almost $8 billion by 1956. In an effort to hold back the growth of surplus stocks, marketing quotas were imposed in 1953 for the first time since the war. In addition, the use of surplus farm products in the foreign economic aid program was begun in 1954 and the soil bank was established in 1956. We will have more to say about these programs a little later in this chapter.

The basic change in the 1950s was a change in attitude, however. The long-term nature of the farm problem was generally recognized for the first time. Until then it had usually been analyzed as an essentially temporary phenomenon, but the huge surpluses of the mid-1950s brought a widespread understanding of the fundamental market disequilibrium that had developed.

LAND VALUES AND RENT

We have not yet touched upon that aspect of the maladjustment that concerns the value of land. Briefly, high prices for farm products mean that farm land produces greater value of output. The land is worth more, and the market reflects it with higher prices.

In agriculture there is always some land that earns just enough to warrant using it, but there is always additional land whose use cannot be justified on the basis of earnings. Consider Table 26–6, which shows a hypothetical schedule of output from different plots of land.

TABLE 26-6
Hypothetical Schedule of Output of Wheat from Four Plots of Land

Plot	Output per Acre (Bushels)
A	350
B	300
C	250
D	200

We can assume that costs of production are uniform at $400 per acre, that is, the same amount of input per acre is required for each plot but the output will vary because of differing fertility in the four plots.

Now let us provide our farmers with a market price of $1 per bushel. Will any of these plots be used? The answer, of course, is no. Plot A, the most productive, will produce 350 bushels that can be sold for a total of $350, but the cost of production is $400. Only a charitable institution would produce wheat on that land under the circumstances.

Suppose the price were to go up to $1.25 per bushel. A market-oriented farmer would calculate in the manner of Table 26-7.

TABLE 26-7
Producing Wheat on Four Plots, Price = $1.25 per Bushel

Plot	Output per Acre (Bushels)	Revenue	Cost	Profit or Loss (−)
A	350	$437.50	$400	$ 37.50
B	300	375.00	400	−25.00
C	250	312.50	400	−87.50
D	200	250.00	400	−150.00

It is clearly to the farmer's advantage to work Plot A (the cost includes an appropriate return for his own labor and use of capital).

At this point rent comes into the picture. The owner can either operate Plot A himself, or rent it to someone else for $37.50. The owner wouldn't care as long as he got the $37.50, while another farmer would be willing to pay that much since the $400 cost figure includes a normal return to labor and capital. The $37.50 is a rent earned by the land, which the owner receives whether he works the land himself or rents the land to someone else.[3]

Now let's raise the price of wheat to $1.50 per bushel, and see what happens. The calculation of potential returns now is shown in Table 26-8.

TABLE 26-8
Producing Wheat on Four Plots of Land, Price = $1.50 per Bushel

Plot	Output per Acre (Bushels)	Revenue	Cost	Profit or Loss (−)
A	350	$520	$400	$120
B	300	450	400	50
C	250	375	400	−25
D	200	300	400	−100

[3] This concept of rent is an economist's definition, and differs from that used by the accountant or the average man. In economics, rent is any return earned by a factor of production over and above the return necessary to bring it into production and keep it there. It is called a rent because the owner of the factor could (in theory, if not in fact) collect the rent by charging someone else who wants to use the factor.

The red ink has now disappeared for Plot B, which will be brought into production, earning a rent of $50, while the rent earned by Plot A will have risen to $120. When the price of wheat rises to $2 per bushel, all four plots will be brought into production,[4] with the following rents per acre:

$$A = \$300,$$
$$B = \$200,$$
$$C = \$100,$$
$$D = \text{no rent.}$$

The Value of Land

Differences in rents become differences in the value of land. The value of any asset depends on its earning power. Plot A is worth more than B because it earns more money; Plot B is more valuable than C; and C than D. The differences in their productivity are the reason, and those differences are reflected in both their rent and the price a buyer would be willing to pay for the plot.

This principle can be illustrated by taking the example of the four plots of land one step further. We start with Plot D, which is "no rent" land when the price of wheat is $2 per bushel, and assume that the price of wheat stays at that level.

Any producing asset will have a value, depending on how the marketplace evaluates its importance. Even if the asset is not producing, such as Plot D when the price of wheat was $1.50 per bushel, it will have a value based on estimates of its potential future earning power. To bypass all of the considerations that prevail among investors and speculators, let's assume that the market value of Plot D is $50 per acre when wheat sells for $2 per bushel. Let's also assume that an asset earning $100 per year is worth 10 times that amount —that investors are willing to pay $1,000 for a government bond on which they will earn an income of $100 annually. That is a convenient figure, for Plot C earns just $100 more per acre than Plot D, at a $2 per bushel price for wheat.

There is more *risk* in farming than in government bonds, however. Crops may fail or come in with low yields. *The price of wheat may fall.* All kinds of things could happen to bring the revenue from farming down. So the market will assign a higher risk to the revenue earned from Plot C, and its price will be correspondingly lower than government bonds with similar yields. Let's say that the market values agricultural land at only one-half the value it gives to no-risk investments like government bonds, or that the rent of $100 per acre for Plot C, when wheat sells for $2, is worth just $500 in the open market. This means that with Plot D worth $50 per acre, C would sell for $550 per acre, B for $1,050 per acre, and A for $1,550 per acre—as long as wheat sells for $2 per bushel.

But let the price of wheat go down, and stay down, and the value of farm

---

[4] Can you explain why Plot D will be used even though it earns a return no greater than the costs incurred in using it? (Here's a hint, if you're stuck: What is included in the costs?)

land will correspondingly decline. And if the price of wheat went up, and stayed up, the value of farm land would go up.

Price Supports and Land Values

Now we can understand the importance of agricultural price support programs to the farmer. Not only do they make his income larger and more stable than otherwise, but by maintaining relatively high prices, they add to the value of his assets. Compare, for example, the value per acre of the farm lands used in our hypothetical example when the price of wheat is $2 and $2.50 per bushel, based on the assumptions already made. Data for the comparison are provided in Table 26-9.

TABLE 26-9
Value of Farm Land per Acre

| | Price of Wheat per Bushel | |
Plot	$2	$2.50
A	$1,550	$2,425
B	1,050	1,800
C	550	1,175
D	50	550

Increases in agricultural productivity have the same effect on the value of farm land as increases in price. If the price of farm products can be stabilized, and if farmers invest in the more capital-intensive methods that raise output per acre, their costs of production fall relative to the income they earn. This, in turn, raises the rent earned by the land, which the market then "capitalizes" in the form of higher land values.

Changes in the value of U.S. farm land show these economic processes at work. Table 26-10 gives the relevant data.

TABLE 26-10
Wholesale Prices of Farm Products and Value of U.S. Farm Real Estate

| | Wholesale Prices of Farm Products | | Average Value per Acre | |
Year	(1926 = 100)	(1957–59 = 100)	Dollars	Index (1957–59 = 100)
1910	$ 74.3		$ 39.59	$ 36 (1912)
1920	150.7		69.37	64
1930	88.3	$ 54.0	48.52	42
1940	67.7	41.3	31.71	30
1950	170.4	106.4	64.96	65
1960		96.9	116.48	111
1968		102.2	177.67	170

The large increases in the value of farm land from 1910 to 1920 reflect the prosperity of World War I and its attendant increases in the market prices of farm products. The decline in land values to 1940 was the result of the farm troubles of those decades, compounded by the depression of the 1930s that kept the prices of agricultural products at low levels. Then came World War II and the postwar decades. The value of farm land went up to levels never reached before. First came the wartime prosperity, followed by price stabilization combined with large productivity gains. The result was a growth in economic rent that has been reflected in the prices people are willing to pay for farm acreage.

Now we can understand why farmers become so emotional when the subject of prices for farm products is discussed. It involves more than just their income. It also involves their wealth, the value of their net worth. Remember Table 26–4, which showed the average value of family assets for farmers at $25,767? That is a large chunk of assets. Much of it is in land, whose value depends on the market price at which its product can be sold. That price, in turn, is determined in part by the support programs paid for by the general taxpayer and consumer. The farmer, in one sense, is a speculator in land as well as a businessman producing a product for sale to consumers. Any solution to the farm problem and the basic disequilibrium that exists in American agriculture must take this aspect of agriculture into consideration.

FARM POLICY FOR THE FUTURE

The changing environment of American agriculture will influence the development of policy programs. Here is a brief summary of what we might expect over the next generation:

1. Demand for U.S. farm products will continue to grow as the national population increases and as incomes rise.
2. Higher consumer incomes will continue the relative shift away from basic crops toward a more highly diversified agriculture.
3. World population growth, called an explosion by some experts, will create a serious shortage of world food supplies. The problem here is that the poor abroad are unable to pay for the food they need. Poverty and population growth may be leading the world into a food crisis of significant size at some time in the 1970s.
4. U.S. agriculture will continue its large gains in productivity, probably at a rate faster than the growth of domestic demand, but probably not as fast as the growth of potential world demand.

These projected trends mean that the demand curves for most farm products will shift outward a little more slowly than the supply curves. Supplies will grow more rapidly than demand. If that occurs, the basic disequilibrium will become worse instead of better, unless land retirement plans have the opposite effect on supplies, or foreign aid programs add to the normal growth in demand. Indeed, these last two policies have been responsible for the fact that agricultural surpluses have been controlled and reduced in the last decade. The land retirement program of the Soil Bank, established in 1956, pays farmers for reducing their acreage and leaving the land idle. In some instances parts of farms were retired from production and in others whole farms have been retired. The program has run into some difficulties, but up to 30 million acres of a total U.S. cropland of some 400 million acres have been taken out of production.

The program designed to use U.S. farm surpluses to feed people in poor countries began with the Agricultural Trade and Development Act of 1954 (Public Law 480), which is usually abbreviated to P.L. 480. This legislation permits direct donations of farm products by the U.S. government for purposes of famine relief abroad. A number of these grants have been made. The largest part of the program has been made through sales to foreign governments, however. Payments are made in foreign currencies to the U.S. government. The foreign government then sells the farm products through its own trade channels at home. The U.S. government can use the payments to run our embassy or purchase military supplies if we have military units in the country. Most of the foreign currency has been, in practice, lent back to the foreign country for purposes of economic development, although some has been just accumulated and never used. In effect, most of these sales to foreign governments have been grants: we either have not used the funds obtained or have made loans we do not expect to be repaid.

The P.L. 480 program has a great deal of appeal. It feeds the hungry, and it disposes of U.S. surpluses. There are problems, however. It is costly—up to $2 billion annually in recent years. While the aid given is humanitarian in nature, it may not be the type most needed for economic development. Perhaps roads or schools or an agricultural training school would be more useful. Finally, large amounts of farm product aid may depress the existing agricultural markets of the receiving country. There are, then, a number of practical and political limits to the P.L. 480 program.

The soil bank and the P.L. 480 program represent steps toward a long-run solution, however. By reducing the disparity between demand and supply at existing levels of prices, they permit greater reliance on the market mechanism. It is not difficult for economists to go all the way and outline the essential elements of a return to the market equilibrium that adjusts output to consumer demand. The following section sketches one way in which such a return might be accomplished.

RETURNING AGRICULTURE TO THE FREE-MARKET EQUILIBRIUM

The best way to bring rationality back to the allocation of resources in agriculture is to start by eliminating price supports. By allowing farm prices to find their market level, the double burden on consumers of high prices for food and taxes to pay for price supports can be eliminated. This will dispose of one source of inefficiency in the economic system.

That step would bring a calamitous fall in farm incomes, however, along with large capital losses for farmers as the price of agricultural land plummets. Farm incomes can be maintained, however, by direct income payments to farmers designed to maintain their incomes. This proposal was made by former Secretary of Agriculture Charles Brannan back in the late 1940s, but nothing came of the proposal. There were two reasons: It would be expensive, and the farmers opposed it. It would also keep farmers from having to adjust to the changing pattern of market demand for farm products. But the idea has merit if it is modified in two ways:

1. It should be tied to a program of acreage and marketing controls designed to bring about a balance between demand and supply. Such a balance cannot be achieved overnight. It might well require a 10- to 20-year period of land-use planning for agriculture as a whole and for the individual farm. But the hard fact remains that some program of this sort is necessary if either farm prices or farm incomes are supported.

2. The program should be voluntary. Any farmer would be eligible for the income supports only if he agreed to abide by the land-use plan for his acreage. The plan itself could be worked out at the local level by agreement between the farmer and the county agricultural agent (a state employee supported by federal funds) within guidelines that fit the national program.

Of course, economic pressures to participate would be very strong. Any nonparticipating farmer would earn only the income obtained from sale of his output at the relatively low market price, since he would not receive the income support.

A gradual reduction of surpluses achieved by reducing market supplies will permit a gradual reduction in the income payments to farmers. Year by year, as the market equilibrium is approached, the burden of income payments can be reduced until they are eliminated altogether at the time the market equilibrium has been achieved. The process may take a generation, but by the end of the period the U.S. agricultural economy should be viable once more.

What would happen to the value of farm land? If the program is managed properly, its value should not fall. This can be accomplished by reducing the income supplement payments at an annual rate approximately equal to the growth in agricultural productivity, or about 5 to 7 percent annually, which fits well into the 15–20-year time schedule for the program. If this were done the cost reductions brought by increased productivity would offset the decline in income, thereby maintaining the value of the productive resources used.[5]

---

[5] Someone may object that this arrangement would eliminate incentives to raise agricultural productivity. Not at all! Farmers would have to raise productivity in order to *avoid losses* of both income and capital value. This incentive is just as great as the desire to increase profits.

The essential elements of a transition program of this sort can be shown with the same diagrams used to analyze the present disequilibrium situation. The process is shown in Figure 26-10.

A program of this sort should have several other features. Low-cost loans should be available to farmers who need added capital to enlarge their operations and increase the productivity of their land. Relocation and retraining assistance should be provided for those who have to give up farming during the transition. This aid will be particularly helpful to the very poor farm families.

Finally, a program designed to reduce large fluctuations in prices of farm products is needed in order to prevent future disequilibria. It should not be price supports, but rather a program that reduces the swings in farm prices that can occur from year to year. A federal agency could buy when prices sink and sell when prices rise, using its accumulated stocks as a reserve that rises or falls with market conditions. We already provide a somewhat similar service to the money markets through the Federal Reserve System. There is no reason why a roughly similar operation cannot be successful in agriculture.[6]

Solutions to the farm problem are not difficult to define. The one given here is a blend of planning and income supplements for a limited period of time that has as its goal a return to the free market without serious cost to the farmer. Although the early costs to the public would probably be larger than present programs, in the long run they would be eliminated entirely. Prices of agricultural products will be lower than if present price support programs are continued; and taxes to support these programs will be eliminated. A variety of administrative problems would almost surely appear, but they should not be so severe as to prevent achievement of the goals. The main drawback of a plan like this is political, and that is true of almost all of the other solutions that have been suggested. Farmers have adapted so well to the present policies that any erosion of the price support system arouses strong opposition.

Nevertheless, recent developments in farm policy have moved in the direction sketched here. Legislation has permitted price supports to be reduced and closer controls on production to be established. The result has been reduced surpluses and lower costs. Together with slowly rising demand and falling costs of production, these policies have helped the industry move closer to an equilibrium position. But the changes have been slow, and fluctuations in supplies from year to year have reversed the trend in several basic crops. If the problem is to be solved in our lifetime a more vigorous program is called for.

---

[6] Why not do the same for all industries? Answer: There are few in which prices fluctuate as much as they do in agriculture, and only in agriculture is there a danger of relatively permanent market disequilibrium. Only agriculture has the characteristic of ease in expanding output but difficulty in contracting.

FIGURE 26-10
Bringing U.S. Agriculture to a Viable Market Equilibrium

Step 1.
The Basic Disequilibrium

Step 2.
Market Prices plus Income Supplements

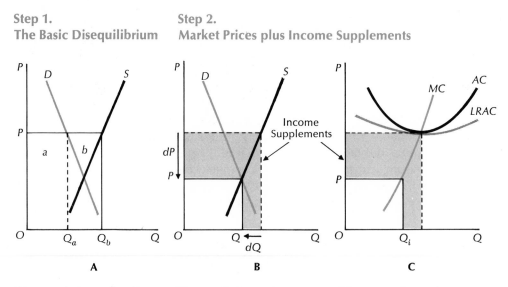

A

B

C

Diagram A shows the disequilibrium in the market for a farm product such as wheat. Price supports keep the price above the normal level, which would be found at the price level at which $D = S$. Rectangles $a + b$ equal total farm income from sale of wheat, with b coming from the price support program through purchase of the surplus.

Diagram B shows the start of the program. Price falls to P. The land use plan brings output down to Q. The income supplements paid to farmers are equal to the shaded area.

Diagram C shows the position of the individual farmer at the start of the program. The income supplements leave him with the same income, in spite of reduced prices and lower output.

FIGURE 26-10 (*Continued*)

Step 3. The Transition

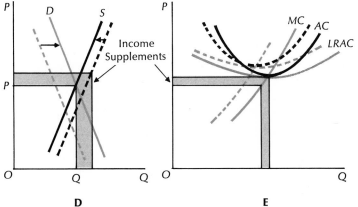

D

In the middle of the adjustment, demand *D* has increased (because of rising population and income) and land use planning has adjusted *S* downward somewhat even though productivity has increased. Some farmers will have been displaced from agriculture. These changes have reduced income supplements to the much smaller shaded area.

E

The individual farmer is much closer to his equilibrium, now that prices have moved up and his costs have been reduced (because of rising productivity). There aren't as many farmers still in business, however.

Step 4. The Goals

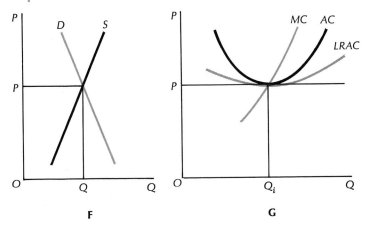

F

G

The program's goal is to achieve a new triple equilibrium. Demand has continued to grow slowly, and land-use planning has reduced the supply. Continued increases in productivity have brought costs down so that income supplements are no longer needed. The industry is viable; the burden on consumer and taxpayer has been lifted. Voila!

Summary

Competitive markets exist in a changing world. In the case of U.S. agriculture some of those changes have been so great that the market adjustment process has not been able to work smoothly. In particular, wars, the Great Depression, and very large changes in technology disrupted the industry. The impact of the disruptions was particularly strong because of inelastic demand for farm products and wide fluctuations in farmers' incomes. The results of these forces was the appearance of a long-run disequilibrium in U.S. agriculture. Agricultural policy has mitigated the effects of the disequilibrium on the farm enterprise, but has also hindered the normal course of adjustment that might have eliminated the disequilibrium.

By now there are strong economic and political forces that tend to preserve the status quo, as for example, the fact that price supports for agricultural products have now been capitalized into the value of the farm land.

It is possible to reconstruct the free-market equilibrium of U.S. agriculture, but that would probably require a transition period in which land-use planning, income supports for farmers, and other measures are used to substitute for the economic rigors of the market adjustment.

SOCIALISM
VI

The economic theory of competitive markets was developed in the framework of a private enterprise economy. In some respects the theory was an ideological rationale for capitalism. That is a narrow view, however, for a socialist society can use the market system to achieve an efficient allocation of resources within the framework of social ownership of the means of production. Part VI explores this concept.

Chapter 27 presents the distinguishing features of socialism and its ideology: social ownership of the means of production, equalitarianism, the brotherhood of man and cooperation. It examines the relationships between the individual and the state in several varieties of socialism, and distinguishes two types of economic planning that socialist economies might use, centralized administrative planning and market socialism. Chapter 28 examines the Soviet Union as a case study of planning by central administrative agencies, shows how and why central planning works, and indicates what it can accomplish as well as some of its problems. Chapter 29 shows how the principles of the self-adjusting market might be applied when the means of production are socially owned, to achieve a decentralized system responsive to the consumer and consistent with the preservation of individual freedoms.

The underlying theme of Part VI is that there are a variety of alternative ways to organize economic affairs successfully, each one of which produces different kinds of results. Private enterprise capitalism is not the only one that works, nor is it necessarily the one most consistent with the humanist ethic that is so strongly professed in our society.

Socialism differs from capitalism in two respects.[1] The first concerns property relations, while the second involves ideology. This chapter deals with the differences between the two systems, together with some of the forms they have taken in the contemporary world. The discussion seeks to indicate the varieties of forms that economic organization can take, laying out the chief alternatives available in the latter part of the twentieth century.

PROPERTY RELATIONSHIPS UNDER SOCIALISM

"Social ownership of the means of production" is the descriptive phrase that distinguishes socialist property relationships from the private property of capitalism.

A capitalist economy is founded on a wide recognition of the right of private ownership of the means of production. Ownership may take a variety of forms, such as individual proprietorships, partnerships, and corporations. The owners have unrestricted rights to buy, sell, or exchange their property. A pure capitalist economy would have no restrictions on these rights of ownership and purchase and sale of the means of production.

A socialist economy, however, substitutes ownership by society as a whole, or by workers as a group, for private ownership. Here again, the forms of ownership may vary widely, ranging from ownership of entire industries by the national government, to ownership of public utilities such as water systems by local governments, to ownership of a factory by those who work there, to complete communal living like that of the Israeli kibbutz. The fundamental idea, however, is that an individual participates in the ownership of the means of production because of his membership in a group rather than because of his legal ties to property itself.

Socialism and its Ideology

27

---

[1] The term *socialism* was invented by Pierre Leroux (1798–1871), a French reformer and journalist, who intended the word to be the antithesis of individualism and not the general name for an ideology and social movement that it became.

Karl Marx (1818–1883) was the first to apply the name *capitalism* to the private enterprise, market-oriented, industrial economy of the nineteenth century. He chose that word in order to emphasize the fact that owners of capital and workers were different people who performed different functions in the economy and therefore made up two distinct social classes of opposing interests. He called it capitalism to indicate the dominance of the capitalist class and the crucial importance of capital accumulation in the economy. One measure of the debt owed to Marx by modern social scientists is the fact that all use his descriptive term, although many define it differently.

This is a key concept of socialism, and the element that distinguishes it most clearly and most significantly from capitalism. Under capitalism, ownership of the means of production is a direct, legally defined relationship between people and things. The farmer, for instance, has the right to use tools and land because they are his. In a kibbutz, however, a farmer has those rights because he is a member of a commune that owns the tools and land. If he were to leave the commune he would give up his rights in it. The group rather than the individual is the significant producing unit of society and the economy.

Although basic concepts of property relationships are fundamentally different under socialism and capitalism, it would be hard to find a real-life economic system that is purely socialist or purely capitalist. The only known economies are mixtures, although a clear emphasis on one or the other may be found. Thus, private ownership of property clearly predominates in the United States and a capitalist emphasis is obvious. But there are socialist elements. The federal government owns and operates the Tennessee Valley Authority. Many local agencies own and operate public utility firms. Full freedom of the marketplace is restricted by regulation of the securities exchanges, antitrust laws, and regulation of industries "affected with the public interest," to give only a few examples. Capitalism in the United States is mixed with many elements of socialist property relationships.

Other mixed economies are found in other countries. In England a number of basic industries, such as banks, transportation, communications, coal mining, and the steel industry, are socially owned. Other sectors of the economy are privately owned. Even in the Soviet Union, the country in which social ownership has gone farthest, there are elements of private ownership of the means of production. Some of the livestock and implements on collective farms are private property, and handicraft manufacturing with employment of limited amounts of hired labor is permitted.

Many socialists used to think of their system primarily in terms of government ownership of the means of production. Karl Marx, for example, defined socialism as "nationalization of the means of production, distribution, and exchange," believing that ownership of the means of production determined the nature of society as a whole and the behavior of the people involved. He felt that man could be transformed by restructuring the economic environment, and that government ownership was the path to that goal.

Modern socialists are less rigid. Norman Thomas (1884–1968), the great American socialist leader of the first half of the twentieth century, believed that government should own natural resources, the banking and credit system, and giant monopoloid business firms, and that there should be a significant amount of economic planning. But he also believed that the remainder of the economy could stay in private hands and remain under the influence of competitive market forces. C. A. R. Crosland, a leading British socialist, goes even further. He sees the possibility of sharp conflict between nationalization of the means of production and the humanistic goals of socialism, as in the Soviet Union, and he advocates government ownership only when it can be shown to be more efficient than private ownership.

The emphasis, then, in modern socialism as it has developed in Western Europe and the United States has been shifting away from nationalization of industry toward other goals of socialism.

THE SOCIALIST IDEOLOGY

Socialism is based on a group of ethical principles that are rooted deeply in the traditions of Western culture. One of these ideals is equalitarianism— the belief that in basic human qualities all persons are the same and of equal value, and that artificial distinctions should not be made among them. Any socialist would agree that people differ in intelligence, ability, interests, and desires. Most would also agree that any society needs incentives to motivate people and help organize productive effort, and that any incentive system may lead to differences in earnings. But socialists also place heavy emphasis on equal treatment, equal opportunity, and elimination of artificial differences in income or privilege. They take a dim view of inheritance, dislike private schools that provide special educational opportunities for the wealthy, and protest any manifestations of rank and privilege.

This viewpoint runs deep in the heritage of Western culture. Judaic-Christian theology tells us that all men are the same in the eyes of God. This viewpoint has cropped out whenever men have protested against the organized inequality of their time. For example, the theme song of the peasants who marched on London in 1381 was

> When Adam delved and Eve span,
> Who was then the gentleman?

Similar sentiments motivated the American and French revolutions:

> We hold these Truths to be self-evident,
> That all Men are created equal . . . .

> Liberté, egalité, fraternité.

The socialist wishes to apply that ethical ideal to the economy, and also to political and social organization. The result is emphasis on equalitarian patterns of income distribution, distribution of great holdings of wealth, and elimination of economic privileges. Some would call it a "classless society."

A second ethical principle of socialism is belief in the brotherhood of man, manifested in concern for those who are in need. This ideal is closely related to the belief that the relationship of the individual to the social group is the most important social tie. Socialists believe that there is a collective responsibility for the alleviation of individual distress, for if the individual cannot function well, the effectiveness of the group as a whole is diminished. Socialists are eager to establish a welfare floor below which no individual is allowed to fall.

They look with favor on the social service and welfare philosophy that sides with the less fortunate and those in need. Social action against deprivation and poverty is high on the agenda of socialism.

A third socialist ideal is belief in the concept of cooperation. This aspect of socialism rejects competition, individualism, and rivalry in favor of group action, full participation by all in the decision-making process, and collective responsibility for the welfare of society. In its extreme form this ideal can be reduced to the normative proposition that people ought to work for the social good, and not for their own gain. In more moderate form, many socialists argue that people feel happier and work harder for goals that go beyond personal material benefits. At the very least, most socialists would like to organize the incentive system so that rewards go heavily to those who work for the social good.

This ethical principle of socialism presents several well-recognized difficulties. The first stems from the proposition that people are both individuals and social beings. Their motivations are also dual. The socialist would argue that a private-enterprise, capitalist society accentuates only one side of human nature while almost ignoring the other. The result is held to be distortion of the human psyche and development of the social evils of aggression, conflict, and materialism. Socialists argue that shifting the structure of society toward cooperative behavior patterns, with a different type of motivational pattern, would enlarge the values of human experience and lead the individual to a fuller and more rewarding life in which both personal and social goals can be more fully achieved.

The second difficulty arises from the nature of social groups. They may not express the cooperative ideal of brotherhood in their relationships with others. Their goals as groups may be selfish, restrictive, and harmful. Internally, they may be intolerant of dissent and demand excessive conformity. The human drive toward gregariousness and commonality may lead to narrowness rather than openness.

The cooperative ideal, then, is fraught with dangers on two sides. On the one hand, the socialist would bring it to birth out of an individualistic society. This involves a radical transformation of individual goals and motives and cannot be done merely by changing the ownership and top management of a giant firm from private to public. And on the other hand, the organizational structure of a socialist society must continually guard against the narrowness and special interests of groups themselves as it seeks a broad and far-reaching concept of brotherhood and cooperation.

SOCIALISM AND THE STATE

The socialist movement has taken three different views about the role of the state in a socialist society. They can be labeled the Marxist, the anarchist, and the democratic socialist positions.

The Marxist would use the state to create and manage a socialist society. This has, in fact, been done in the USSR. The Marxist view is that government is the arm of the social class that dominates the economy. In a capitalist economy the property-owning classes hold the reins of power. Their rule can be overthrown only when a revolutionary party representing the working class seizes power and uses the instruments of state control to dispossess the capitalists, nationalize the economy, and build a socialist society. The authority of the state would be used to remake the social order. This was the script followed by the Russian Revolution and the Soviet Communist Party. The ultimate goal is claimed to be an abundant economy and a classless society in which the coercive power of the state is allowed to wither away; but the slowness of that process in the USSR has caused may socialists to look for other paths to the good society.

The anarchist would do away with the state altogether. He sees the state as the chief source of oppression and the chief support of capitalism. He also sees a bureaucratic socialist state, like the USSR, as equally oppressive. An anarchist revolution would do away with both capitalism and the political apparatus of government. In its place the anarchist would substitute communes of workers who own and manage the enterprises in which they work. At one extreme there are anarchists who believe that this is all the public administration any society requires, but most see the need for governmental functions and economic planning through elected representatives of the communes.[2] All anarchists agree, however, on the need for control from below and full participatory democracy.

Democratic socialism is far more pragmatic. As it developed in England, Scandinavia, and other countries of Western Europe, it put its greatest stress on the welfare and equalitarian aspects of socialism, on cooperative enterprises, and on maintenance of traditional democratic practices in government. The result has been a mixture of policies and programs that vary widely from one country to another. England and the Scandinavian countries, for example, have tax systems that seek to prevent the accumulation of large fortunes and great agglomerations of economic power. In England some basic industries have been nationalized, while in Sweden emphasis is on cooperatives; yet in both countries an avowedly socialist regime has allowed 85–90 percent of economic activity to remain in private hands. Most Western European countries have very extensive welfare and social insurance programs that have largely succeeded in eliminating poverty. All except England have been successful in reducing unemployment rates to very low frictional levels

---

[2] Political organization based on worker representatives elected by economic units is called *syndicalism*. It has been represented in the United States by the IWW (Industrial Workers of the World), founded in 1905, and the Socialist Labor Party, which developed a Marxist version of a syndicalist workers' government under the leadership of Daniel de Leon (1852–1914).

and keeping them there most of the time. Ironically, France has made the greatest strides toward a planned economy in spite of having a nonsocialist political majority. Many variations on democratic socialism have emerged, with various mixtures of the welfare state, equalitarianism, public ownership, cooperatives, and economic planning. The one common element is the use of parliamentary democracy to move toward the goals of equalitarianism and social welfare. One result has been emphasis on security of the individual, with a consequent reduction in the role of competition and rivalry in everyday economic affairs. The state, in this development, is a democratic instrument through which the general public determines both goals and the speed of their attainment. The democratic socialist believes that public opinion must be changed to accept the socialist ideals and program, which can then be instituted by government action arrived at through democratic procedures. He rejects the "dictatorship of the proletariat" of the Marxist path to socialism in favor of a slower and less complete transformation of society that would preserve and use democratic procedures.

SOCIALISM AND ECONOMIC PLANNING

A socialist economy based on ideals of equality and cooperation, in which private enterprises either did not exist or did not dominate economic activity, would have to find its own methods of allocating resources, determining levels of output, and distributing the product. Rejecting the capitalist, market-oriented solution as based on individual and not social goals, the socialist moves toward economic planning.

Economic planning shows many faces, too. Even an economy based on private ownership of the means of production, like the capitalistic United States, has a government that seeks to plan the level of aggregate demand, the level of prices, and the rate of economic growth. We have shown, in the early parts of this book, how it is done and the economic analysis on which this type of planning is based. Socialist planning can be limited largely to similar efforts, if most enterprises are private, as they are in Britain and Sweden.

A far more interesting problem, however, is how an economy of publicly or socially owned enterprises will or can operate. What are the managerial and allocative alternatives? Briefly, they are two:

1. A socialist economy can be organized on the basis of a central authority that determines goals, draws up plans, creates incentives to promote their achievement, and supervises their accomplishment. This type of planning directed from the top is characteristic of large bureaucratic enterprises everywhere, from General Motors Corporation to the USSR.

2. A second style of planning is based on the market mechanism, and is sometimes called "market socialism." Here the central planners set prices, while managers of socialized enterprises react to them in an effort to maximize the returns to their enterprise. Based on the theory of the competitive market, this plan seeks to achieve a decentralized pattern of

decision making that cannot be achieved in either the centralized planned economy or the monopoloid capitalist economy. It is being developed in several eastern European countries.

The important point to note is that economic planning is an important feature of the policies of all advanced nations. The question is no longer whether planning can work, but what type of planning is most desirable. Aggregative economic planning is used extensively both in nonsocialist countries like the United States, France, and Germany and in socialist countries like England or Sweden, where the emphasis is on social welfare and equalitarianism rather than on social ownership of the economy. A socialist state based on a strong central government leading the transition to socialism, the USSR, uses a system of centralized, detailed planning. A third pattern is largely untried, although the beginnings of experiments are seen. This is the decentralized pattern of self-governing communities or economic units whose activities are coordinated through a market system. It may turn out that this will be the only effective alternative to the economy of large bureaucratic organizations characteristic of the United States and the Soviet Union.

Summary

Socialism differs from capitalism in both property relationships and ideology. It would substitute some form of social ownership of the means of production (or the most important ones) for the private ownership characteristic of capitalism. Property relationships under socialism are part of a larger ideology that emphasizes the role of the individual as a social being, as part of a functioning social group in which all participate. This concept of the place of the individual in society leads to the emphasis in socialism on equalitarianism, brotherhood, and cooperation.

The practical application of these ideals is difficult, for it entails a radical change from those characteristic of a capitalist economy as well as the dangers of narrow and selfish group behavior.

Socialists differ in their views about the role of the state and the importance of individual freedoms, particularly in the transition period from capitalism to socialism. Advocates of democratic socialism have tended to move slowly in socializing the means of production and have tended to emphasize equalitarianism and programs designed to promote social welfare in order to preserve individual freedoms.

Socialism implies economic planning and two chief types are possible. One is the centralized administrative planning of the USSR. The other is decentralized market socialism. They will be discussed in the two chapters that follow.

Key Concepts

Socialism. An economic system based on social ownership of the chief means of production in which the values of equalitarianism, brotherhood, and cooperation strongly influence social policy. These social goals imply the use of some form of economic planning.

The capitalist's definition of socialism: tyranny.

Capitalism. An economic system based on private ownership of the means of production, individualistic motivations and goals, and the market economy.

The socialist's definition of capitalism: tyranny.

Market socialism. A form of socialism that seeks to retain decentralized decision making and the welfare-maximizing results of the competitive market within the framework of democratic socialism.

The Soviet economy is only one variant of socialism. In the Soviet Union, industrial enterprises are owned by the government, together with most of the marketing system and all of the financial, transportation, and communications sectors. A system of production planning has been established to manage this vast network of enterprises. Control is largely from the center, requiring an elaborate network of administrative agencies. This chapter will examine the Soviet economy as a case study of central planning in a socialized economy based on state enterprise.

BASIC DECISIONS IN PLANNING

Before any plan for allocation and use of resources can be made, economic planners must make several fundamental decisions that will strongly limit, or in some instances determine, the way resources are to be used. These decisions include determination of:

1. The long-run goals.
2. The speed with which those goals can be achieved.
3. How resources can be mobilized to achieve the goals.

Only then can the planners turn their attention to the problems of planning how resources are actually to be used, the levels of output desired, and the techniques of administration.

Long-Run Goals in the USSR

In the Soviet Union there was a great debate over long-run goals and the speed of their attainment prior to the start of the first Five-Year Plan in 1928. The decisions made at that time have not been significantly altered, although in recent years some modifications have been made and discussion of long-run goals has occasionally occurred. In public, that is. We don't know much about the closed discussions taking place in the highest decision levels of Soviet planning and policy formulation.

The discussions of the late 1920s focused on the problem of economic growth. The Soviet economy by then had recovered to approximately the pre-World War I levels of output, after a sequence of war, revolution, and inflation that had seen a transformation from the old imperial, aristocratic government to the early stages of

Socialism and Economic Planning: The Case of the Soviet Union

28

socialism. The economy remained backward, however. Agriculture still dominated the economy, and its technology was preindustrial. Heavy industry was small and centered in only a few parts of the country. Much consumer goods production—shoes, for example—was still done by handicraft methods instead of in factories. Illiteracy was still strong. The country remained largely a rural, peasant society.

Yet the leadership was committed to an ideology, the Marxist variation of socialism, which looked to the industrial working class as the builder of a new social order on a worldwide scale. At the same time, the Soviet Union as the self-proclaimed bearer of world revolution faced a hostile world committed to a different ideology and to the preservation of a capitalist, private enterprise economy. Finally, the security of the regime at home was by no means certain: the proportion of the Soviet people strongly committed to the new ideology was probably a minority even as late as 1928. This was particularly true among the peasantry.

The policy discussions of the late 1920s emphasized the problem of backwardness in a hostile world, and embodied, in addition, a struggle for political power that saw the emergence of Joseph Stalin to predominance over his chief rival, Leon Trotsky. The policies that emerged from the debate and the struggle were these:

1. A socialist society based on an industrial working class had to be built by transforming a rural, agricultural nation to an urban, industrial one. This view was a fundamental policy inherited from the leader of the revolution, Nikolai Lenin.
2. The new society had to be protected against the expected counterattack of a hostile capitalist world. In 1930 Stalin predicted that the USSR had ten years to prepare—a prophetic vision.
3. The spread of socialism could best be achieved by demonstrating its superiority over capitalism to the workers of the world, especially in achieving economic growth and industrial expansion.

These considerations all pointed in the direction of rapid, large-scale industrialization. Economic growth became the primary goal of economic policy—to build a socialist society, to protect it from its enemies, and to promote its spread.[1]

The Speed of Attainment

Decisions about the rate of economic growth in the Soviet economy are made at the top levels of the government and the Communist Party. They

---

[1] Note how the Russian Revolution turned inward toward strengthening itself and fulfilling its goals internally. Active fostering of world revolution was given up, at least for a time, in spite of the rhetoric of the leaders. The dispute between Stalin and Trotsky focused on this issue in large part, and Stalin's political victory signalled the triumph of "socialism in one country" as a goal, instead of world revolution.

are expressed in the Five-Year Plans, which provide the economic goals the system seeks. For example, the Five-Year Plan for the 1966–1970 years called for percentage increases over the five years as shown in Table 28–1. The plan itself is much more detailed, but these figures illustrate the pattern of goal setting.

TABLE 28–1
Soviet Five-Year Plan, 1966–70

	Percentage Increase
National income	38–41
Total industrial output	47–50
Electric power	64–68
Coal	15–17
Steel	36–42
Motor vehicles	121–145
Refrigerators	212–229
Agricultural output	25
Productive fixed capital	50
Per capita real income	30
Retail trade	43.5

The goals of the Five-Year Plans are not selected without regard to the resources available to achieve them. Planning always starts from an existing position and the path projected into the future is constrained by the resources that can be mobilized and the effectiveness with which they can be used. Soviet planners have tended to select goals that strain the upper limits of the economy, "taut" planning as they call it, which does not allow for any slack. As a result, their goals are not always achieved.

Nor are the Five-Year Plans operational programs used to guide the decisions of individual enterprises. Annual plans perform that function. The annual plans provide specific targets that important sectors of the economy and principal industries are expected to achieve. They are then broken down into operating plans for each productive unit. They act as a bridge between the goals expressed in the Five-Year Plans and the daily operations of each economic unit. Later on in this chapter we shall have more to say about how the annual plans are drawn up and used.

At any rate, the Soviet economy has consistently sustained high rates of economic growth since the first Five-Year Plan started in 1928. With the exception of 1937–1950, when preparation for World War II, the war itself, and the aftermath of the war greatly slowed down economic growth, the economy of the Soviet Union has been able to sustain growth rates well above 5 percent annually.

TABLE 28-2
Average Annual Growth Rates of Soviet GNP, 1928–1965
(Percentages)

Period	Estimated Average Annual Percentage Increase
1928–1937	8.3
1937–1950	2.4
1950–1965	6.2

Note: All percentage rates of growth for the Soviet economy are approximations. The difficulties involved in the calculations are enormous. These estimates are simplified and adapted from calculations in Stanley H. Cohn, *Economic Development in the Soviet Union* (Lexington, Mass.: D. C. Heath and Co., 1969), Chap. 7.

This good track record, sustained over a long period of time, has not been maintained so well in recent years. There has been a tendency for the speed of Soviet growth to slow down, particularly since 1955.

TABLE 28-3
Average Annual Growth Rates of Soviet GNP, 1950-1965
(Percentages)

Period	Average Annual Percentage Increase
1950–1955	6.9
1955–1958	7.4
1958–1961	5.4
1961–1965	5.2

Source: Stanley H. Cohn, *Economic Development in the Soviet Union* (Lexington, Mass.: D. C. Heath and Co., 1969), Chap. 7.

In the USSR, economic growth no longer exceeds that of many other advanced nations, although it is still faster than in the United States. For example, during 1958 to 1965 the following countries all had more rapid growth in GNP than the Soviet Union: France (5.4 percent), West Germany (5.8 percent), Italy (6.1 percent), and Japan (12.0 percent).

The Soviet slowdown in growth, together with more rapid growth in some other industrial countries, has triggered within the USSR another important discussion of economic policy, together with the start of some economic reforms. We can understand why. There has been little change in the official doctrine that rapid economic growth is the cornerstone of Soviet economic policy.

Rapid economic growth has had its costs, however. Other goals have had to be compromised or sacrificed. Consumer goods, for example. Every ton of steel used to produce automobiles or refrigerators is one ton less for railroad rails or electrical generators. Each bushel of wheat used at home is one bushel less for sale abroad, the revenue then being available to buy foreign machinery.

Or working conditions. One hour cut from the working week is an hour not available for production. Every absentee worker means just that much less output. Every worker who moves from one job to another, requiring training or adaptation to the new job, means lost output.

Or distribution of income. Scarce skills, like those of engineers or plant managers, scientists and economic planners, have to be priced high in order to encourage people to acquire the skills and to push management into using them efficiently. Plentiful unskilled labor can correspondingly be priced cheaply. Considerations of economic efficiency call for substantial inequalities of earned incomes in a nation pushing rapidly toward industrialization.

Or labor discipline. A taut economy in which labor is fully utilized encourages workers to move from one job to another, seeking a better slot. In addition, restrictions on output of consumer goods reduce an important work incentive that can only be partially replaced by wage differentials. As a result of high labor turnover (moving from job to job), absenteeism, and shirking on the job, negative incentives to work began to appear in the late 1930s and were not eliminated until the 1950s.[2]

Mobilizing Economic Resources

The Soviet Union has used a variety of approaches to the problem of mobilizing resources to achieve its growth goals. First, it sought to use all of the available manpower resources. This meant elimination of the unemployment that still existed as the era of planning began, drawing women into the labor force on a large scale, and moving the increase in population from rural to urban locations and drawing it into industrial production. Or, put another way, the growth of the economy could be increased by adding to the manpower available for industrial production from those three sources. More labor inputs could bring greater industrial output.[3]

---

[2] The extremes of repression in the USSR, such as forced labor camps, were used primarily for political purposes and to eliminate real or fancied threats to the internal security of the regime. Negative incentives in the economy, which were introduced in the mid- and late 1930s and lasted until shortly before the death of Stalin in 1953, involved such devices as fines and reduced pay for absenteeism or failure to produce up to the assigned norms, restrictions on quitting a job to take another, and loss of housing or fringe benefits if a worker quit his job. Some still remain in mild forms. Many of these means of disciplining the labor force, as well as bodily punishment, were used by private business firms in the Western countries, including the United States, in the early stages of industrialization.

[3] This portion of the growth strategy resulted in some interesting changes in policy toward hours of work, retirement, and related matters. As long as substantial increases in total manpower could be obtained from the three sources given above, policy was directed toward shorter hours and improved retirement plans. Once the sources of additional manpower began to diminish significantly (by the mid- and late 1930s), and the pre–World War II arms race began, reductions in the work week stopped and pension plans were no longer improved. Even today the Soviet planners are reluctant to move toward those human goals in the face of the need for manpower to sustain the pattern of economic growth. And in recent years, when population growth has been slow (in large part because of 20–30 million deaths in World War II), shortages of manpower have been one reason for slowed economic growth.

Agricultural resources were also mobilized to achieve the growth goals. Farm products were needed to feed the growing industrial work force in the cities and its supporting services, to provide industrial raw materials, and for export to pay for imports of machinery. If agriculture were to do its part its output would have to be increased without using more manpower. This goal could only be achieved by large-scale mechanization of the still primitive Soviet peasant farming system. At the same time, the planners felt that it was necessary to draw any increases in farm output into the growth process, and not allow them to be used to raise farmers' standards of living.

These considerations led to the collectivization of Soviet agriculture during the early 1930s. By a combination of exhortation and force, peasant agriculture was ended. In its place a system of large-scale farming units was developed—the collective farms—which were, in theory, owned and run by the farmers themselves. In fact, they were managed by a combination of Communist Party and government officials and integrated into the system of national planning. The collective farms were supplemented by a network of government-owned machine-tractor stations that provided the agricultural equipment for mechanized production methods.

The Russian peasants largely opposed these measures and fought back with a combination of passive resistance and sabotage that was ruthlessly suppressed. The result was one of the great human tragedies of our time: several million Russian peasants literally starved to death during the winters of 1931–33. A side effect was the slaughter of millions of head of livestock, leaving the USSR with a deficiency of meat and dairy products that is still felt by the Soviet consumer.

Nevertheless, the government largely achieved its agricultural goals. Agricultural production was increased by perhaps as much as 50 percent (experts differ on this figure) with no increase in agricultural manpower. A system of payments for the services of the machine-tractor stations, plus a system of government procurement, succeeded in channeling the entire increase of output into government hands. Finally, the farm population remained stationary, freeing the population increase for the urban-industrial sector of the economy.[4]

Capital was also mobilized for economic growth. The chief device used for that purpose has been the turnover tax, which is deliberately used to reduce consumer purchasing power. The Soviet turnover tax is analogous to a sales tax, except that it is levied on producing units at the time an item enters the channels of trade, rather than being paid by consumers on retail purchases. For example, a steel mill will pay a turnover tax on each ton of steel sold to a

---

[4] Agriculture has remained a problem for the Soviet economy, however. There was little increase in output between the late 1930s and the late 1950s until a big effort to increase farm acreage was made by bringing lands in central Asia into production. A substantial increase was recorded, but by the early 1960s stagnation once more set in. The problem seems to be inadequate incentives and inadequate investment in agriculture, together with unwillingness on the part of planners to channel additional resources into farming instead of industry.

government procurement agency, or a sugar refinery on each pound of sugar sold to a wholesale distribution enterprise, and so forth.

The Soviet turnover tax is not uniform for all commodities, but varies considerably. On producers' goods, like steel, it is quite low or even nominal, and is used primarily for control purposes: the State Bank collects the turnover tax and audits the books of each enterprise for that purpose; in so doing it also checks up on how well the enterprise has fulfilled its production plans. The turnover tax on consumers' goods is often quite high, however, and performs a vital function for the economy. In its effect of raising prices to consumers, it limits the amount of goods they can buy, thereby freeing resources for investment purposes. At the same time, it provides large revenues to the government for investment (and other) purposes. In effect, the turnover tax forces consumers to save (in a real sense) while they continue to spend as much of their income as they wish. The function of the turnover tax in forcing consumers to save is illustrated in Figure 28-1.

FIGURE 28-1
The Soviet Turnover Tax as a Source of Savings

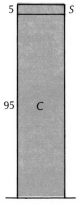

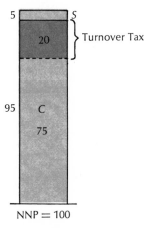

I. Hypothetical Soviet NNP Without the Turnover Tax. Money and real NNP = C + S, where C = 95 and S = 5. With consumers' sovereignty, only a small proportion of NNP would be available for investment S = I = 5. The resources available for investment equal 5, since 95 are used to produce consumers' goods.

II. Soviet NNP with the Turnover Tax. Money NNP = C + S, where C = 95 and S = 5, just as before. But production of C is reduced from 95 to 75 while its price is kept at 95 by a turnover tax of 20: real NNP = 75 + 25. The resources available for investment are raised from 5 to 25, and investment is financed out of savings (5) and the turnover tax (20).

In the early years of its rapid growth the Soviet Union was able to draw on additional resources that hitherto had been unused or only partially used. They included unused labor as well as the increase in agricultural production derived from the transition from peasant to collective farming. But the stimulus to growth from these sources was soon exhausted. At the present time they are not available on a large scale, and the Soviet Union now finds itself dependent primarily on capital accumulation and the normal growth of the work force to provide increased output. In this respect the USSR is in the same position as other industrial nations. The turnover tax and voluntary savings have become the chief means by which resources, now primarily capital, are mobilized to achieve the planners' growth goals.

THE PROCESS OF PLANNING

Once goals are defined, the speed of attainment decided, and methods available for mobilizing resources, the process of deciding what should be produced and in what quantities is a relatively simple but often arduous job. This is the task assigned to the annual production plans.

Soviet planning starts with "leading links." These are the important basic industries whose performance is essential for achievement of the year's goals, such as fuel, power, steel, grain production, and perhaps some other industries. A balance sheet will be drawn up for a leading link, steel, for example, that shows the resources expected to be available and the uses to which they will be put. In very simplified form, it would resemble Table 28–4.

TABLE 28–4
Simplified Materials Balance

Resources	Uses
1. Stocks on hand at the start of the year	1. Used in production
2. Production from existing plants	2. Used in other industries (These uses will be itemized here)
3. Production from new plants	3. Exports
4. Imports	4. Stocks on hand at the end of the year

In the final plan these estimates of resources and uses will have to balance each other, in total. One key element in the planning process is adjusting the various quantities to achieve a balance. Doing so will tell the planners where expansion can take place, or where it must take place in order to avoid bottlenecks. On the uses side of the balance sheet, the amounts used in other industries tie the leading-link industry to other sectors of the economy, defining the resources available to them. This enables the planning agencies to develop "balanced estimates," as they are called, for those industries as well.

On the resources side of the balance sheet for the leading-link industries, production estimates enable the planners to determine the inputs needed, including raw materials and semifinished products from supply industries. These estimates enable the planners to make "balanced estimates" for inputs as well as outputs.

A financial plan is also worked out, to provide the short- and long-term credit and payments necessary to carry out the production plans and their corollary input plans. A special plan is also developed for expansion and construction of new facilities. These four segments—production, input, expansion, and financial plans—make up the comprehensive annual plan.

The final plans, usually completed after two to three trials, result in a system of balanced estimates for each significant industry or product, all linked forward and backward to the others. This huge job requires a large planning bureaucracy, although in recent years the use of computers has greatly speeded up the process and reduced the manpower needed.

The balanced interindustry planning is done by a central agency, the GOSPLAN, or State Planning Commission, but does not become official until it is approved by the Council of Ministers, which is the top policy-making agency of government (analogous to our Cabinet).

Much of the inputs into the planning process are provided by the producing enterprises themselves and intermediate administrative agencies. Prior to the beginning of a year, the government announces the projected increase in output to be embodied in the economic plan for the coming year. Each enterprise is then expected to produce a plan for its operations that helps achieve those goals. Its draft plan is sent up to the next higher administrative unit, where the plans for a number of enterprises are coordinated and summarized and then sent further up the administrative hierarchy, until a ministry for an entire industry is able to submit a draft plan to the State Planning Commission. The draft plans are used as the basis for the complete set of balanced estimates for the economy as a whole drawn up by GOSPLAN.

Once the national plan is drawn up, with balances for each industry, it is then broken down by the ministries into plans for each industrial subdivision, which in turn develops plans for each plant or group of plants under its jurisdiction.

The plan, then, embodies the goals of national policy as determined by the Council of Ministers, the abilities and desires of local plant managers as developed in the draft plans, and the need for coordination and balance provided by GOSPLAN. In varying degrees, all of these elements influence the final plan.

The plan guides the operation of the individual unit. It can be specific in great detail, giving little leeway to the plant manager in deciding how the goals can be best achieved. This was the case until 1965, when a series of reforms were instituted to promote efficiency by giving greater responsibility to management at the local level. Under the reforms, which have not been fully

TABLE 28-5
Partial Input-Output Table for the USSR, 1959
(In Hundred Million Rubles)

	Ferrous ores and metals	Non-ferrous ores and metals	Metal products	Coal	Oil and other fuels	Electric power	Engineering	Chemicals and rubber	Wood and paper	Building materials	Textiles and clothing	Food processing	Other manufacturing
Ferrous ores and metals	11		4				29			2			
Non-ferrous ores		14					13	1					
Metal products							3						
Coal	13	2		18		8	3	2	1	3		2	
Oil and other fuels		1			11	5	2	1	3	2		2	
Electric power		2		2	2		4	2	1	2	2	1	
Engineering	2			2			43	1	3	6	2	4	3
Chemicals and rubber							13	23	2		6		4
Wood and paper				4			4	2	31	2	1	3	2
Building materials							1			13			
Textiles and clothing				1			4	5	4		154	2	
Food processing								4			6	134	8
Other manufacturing							2						
Construction													
Agriculture and forestry									2		45	165	2
Transport and communications	5	2		16	13		8	6	17	18	4	12	
Trade	2	2		1	7		4		5	4	14	37	7
Other material production													3
Total inter-industry purchases	46	26	7	47	36	15	133	51	72	54	237	365	33
Depreciation	4	2		4	4	5	9	2	3	3	2	4	1
Labour remuneration	13	10	2	31	6	4	70	10	32	20	23	25	7
Profits and taxes	6	3		-5	29	12	75	16	14	3	134	169	14
Imports	3	5		1	1		14	3	2		35	14	
Total outlays	70	47	10	77	75	36	302	82	123	82	432	578	55

Source: Michael Kaser, *Soviet Economics* (New York: McGraw-Hill, Inc: 1970), pp. 32–33.

TABLE 28-5 (*Continued*)

	Construction	Agriculture and forestry	Transport and communications	Trade	Other material production	Total inter-industry use	Private consumption	Public consumption	Gross investment	Exports	Total global output
Ferrous ores and metals	14					65			−2	7	70
Non-ferrous ores						35		3	6	2	47
Metal products	2					9					10
Coal			8			63	1	5	5	3	77
Oil and other fuels	4	11	10			56	2	5	7	6	75
Electric power	2		2			24	6	4	1		36
Engineering	23	18	6	2		117	32	6	135	12	302
Chemicals and rubber	3	5	4			64	4	6	6	2	82
Wood and paper	30	1	2	8	2	94	12	5	9	3	123
Building materials	57					74	5	3			82
Textiles and clothing	6	1	1	5		186	195	8	41	2	432
Food processing		16				170	356	12	31	9	578
Other manufacturing		1				5	48	6	−4		55
Construction									292		292
Agriculture and forestry		124				339	171	5	16	7	538
Transport and communications		8		1		113					113
Trade		29				114					114
Other material production	3					12	19	2	−3		30
Total inter-industry purchases	146	215	35	19	3	1540	852	70	541	53	3055
Depreciation	6	21	12	4	3	90	28	21			139
Labour remuneration	70	241	49	38	16	668					
Profits and taxes	70	48	17	52	8	666					
Imports		13				91					
Total outlays	292	538	113	114	30	3055					

adopted in all industries even now, the following items are included in the operating plan for the individual enterprise.

Total output

The main assortment of products

Total wages

Amount and rate of profit. This planned profit is used by the enterprise for bonuses and other incentives and workers' benefits, and as a source of capital for expansion.

Payments into and allocations from the state budget

Capital investment

Utilization of capacity

Introduction of new technology

Supplies of inputs

If this list seems highly detailed, it nevertheless represents a significant reduction in specifications from the earlier system. A number of Soviet economists have argued for even greater latitude for managerial decisions as a means of increasing efficiency and raising output. The present pattern represents a compromise between two styles of planning, one emphasizing central control and the other advocating decentralization.

TWO NEW TECHNIQUES OF PLANNING

The method of balanced estimates used in Soviet planning has been successful, but it is cumbersome and requires a substantial number of workers in the planning system. Its continued use becomes more difficult as the economy grows and becomes more complex. Two newer techniques permit a far more sophisticated approach to planning, and Soviet planners have been experimenting with them. One is *input-output analysis* and the other is *linear programming*. Using mathematical methods and high-speed computers, they may lead to greatly improved systems of planning in the relatively near future.

Input-Output Analysis

Input-output analysis is closely associated with Wassily Leontief, professor of economics at Harvard, originally a Russian citizen. It starts with construction of an input-output table that lists all of the main industries of an economy. The table shows where each industry's output is used and where its inputs come from. It is a tabular representation of all of the interindustry relationships in the economy, analogous to the balanced estimates of a Soviet plan. An idea of what a simple input-output table looks like can be obtained from the interindustry transaction matrix for 1959 drawn up by the USSR Central Statistical Administration. It is shown as Table 28-5.

The top row of the table, reading across, tells us which industries used the output of the ferrous ores and metals industry and how much each used. These data are summarized in Table 28-6.

TABLE 28-6
Excerpt from USSR Input-Output Table

Industry	Uses (In hundred million rubles)
Ferrous ores and metals	11
Metal products	4
Engineering	29
Building materials	2
Construction	14
Total interindustry use	65
Gross investment	−2
Exports	7
Total output	70

The first column of the input-output table, reading down, tells us the expenditures of the ferrous ores and metals industry for its inputs. These need not be listed here, but note that the totals for outputs and inputs are equal for all industries and that the economy is balanced.

The interrelationships shown by the table reflect the actual ones in the year for which the table is constructed, implying a fixed set of technological relationships in the economy. This assumption is an oversimplification, for technological relationships change over time, and factors of production can be substituted one for the other. But these shifts usually take place rather slowly, so the relationships shown by the table can be expected to stay much as they are in the immediate future.

Input-output tables can facilitate planners' decisions. Suppose, for example, the planners wish to increase the output of the steel industry by 10 percent. The relationships provided by the input-output table enables a calculation to be made that will indicate how much of the various inputs will be required and the uses to which the enlarged output would normally be put. But as the quantities in the input-output table for the steel industry are changed another group of industries is affected, and the changes there trigger adjustments in other industries. Like a pebble in a pond, the ripples are felt through the whole system via the relationships defined in the table. Fortunately, the entire input-output table can be computerized and the implications of almost any change or group of changes can be worked out in a relatively short span of time. The problem of sustaining a continued balance in the economy is soluble.

Linear Programming

The technique of linear programming attacks the problem of optimal combinations of inputs. Input-output analysis can't do that because of its implicit assumption of fixed technological relationships. Suppose the planners want to increase electric power production. That does not have to be done strictly in accord with the existing proportions of production in hydroelectric and thermal power plants. Indeed, there are more alternatives than just two: hydroelectric, thermal (coal, gas, oil), or nuclear. But instead of five, let's limit the choices to two for simplicity in the illustration, realizing that the solution can be generalized and solved mathematically for any number of alternatives.

The planners have to choose the optimal proportion of hydroelectric to thermal power plants for the production of electricity, trying to get the largest amount of output from the resources available. There are three constraints: amount of management available, amount of labor available, and amount of capital available. Each constraint limits the choices, and together they establish a transformation curve which shows the production possibilities for using the existing resources to produce various combinations of hydroelectric and thermal power. The planners can then select the point on the transformation curve that maximizes the output of electric power. A simplified solution can be shown geometrically.

Figure 28-2 shows the production possibilities for hydroelectric power (vertical axis) and thermal power (horizontal axis) with the given amount of capital, labor, and management available. The capital constraint line defines the production possibilities that the available amount of capital would permit: so much hydroelectric power if it were all used for that purpose; so much thermal power if it were all used for that; and the intermediate alternatives if it were divided between the two. The other limits are shown by the labor constraint line and the management constraint line. The practical choices beyond which the planners cannot go are shown by the production possibilities frontier ABCD.

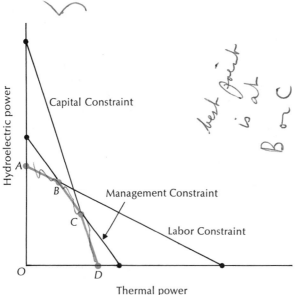

FIGURE 28-2
Linear Programming:
Choosing the Proper Mix
of Hydroelectric and
Thermal Power
Production

What point will the planners choose? The answer is complicated (and involves some mathematical theory) but it can be shown that the largest amount of electric power (or the largest revenues, if the problem is set up that way) will be produced at a "corner," like point B or point C, where two constraint lines cross. Furthermore, a computer can be programmed to examine the "corners" systematically and choose the one that provides the greatest output or revenue. It can select the combination of hydroelectric and thermal power that gets the best result from the limited resources available. With modern computers these calculations can be readily made with large numbers of alternatives and constraints.[5]

Linear programming, then, can supplement input-output analysis in the planning process. It can be used to select from among alternative production processes, to choose from among alternative locations for plants and distribution facilities, to select an appropriate product mix for a plant or an industry, and to solve a variety of other management problems. Indeed, it is so used by American business firms and is coming into increasing use by planners in the USSR. The procedure itself was invented by a Soviet mathematician, Leonid Kantorovich.

MAKING THE PLAN WORK

Devising a balanced plan is one problem. Keeping the economy operating along the lines of that balance is a larger problem. If one industry overproduces while another underproduces, stocks will pile up unused in one area while shortages, bottlenecks and unmet production quotas spread in other areas. A close watch must be kept, requiring rapid and accurate reporting of actual production levels from plants to higher administrative agencies. This information must then be used to identify imbalances immediately so that steps can be taken to eliminate them.

For this purpose the Soviet planners have devised "synthetic indices." A synthetic index indicates the relationship between planned production in two related industries. For example, coal is used in producing steel. Let us assume that the plan calls for production of 500 million tons of coal and 100 million tons of steel. The ratio between them is 5 to 1, a "synthetic index" representing the balance existing in the plan. Now let us suppose that in the first quarter of the year the index, based on actual production statistics, is 5.2 to 1. This can mean one or both of two things. Coal production may be running ahead of schedule, which means that more will be available to raise output in other industries using coal as a raw material. Or steel production may be falling behind, in which case it will have to be brought up to planned levels unless

---

[5] The procedure is called *linear programming* because the constraints are presumed to be straight lines. They need not be. The constraints may have a variety of shapes. The problem becomes more complex in that case, falling into the category of nonlinear programming, but these problems are soluble, too.

adjustments can be made in the industries that use steel as an input. The synthetic index gives early warning of these problems and tells the planners where to look for difficulties and where the adjustments will have to be made.

Plans have to be continually revised. Even the best balanced plan will develop imbalances as it is carried out. Changes in inventories give the planners time to identify the imbalances and correct them. They can change the plan while it is in operation, which is where balance is important, to maintain a balanced economy as well as a balanced plan.

INCENTIVES

The Soviet Union has established a system of varied incentives designed to promote achievement of its goals and fulfilment of plans. Plant managers, their subordinates, and rank-and-file workers receive bonuses for achieving or exceeding planned levels of output, paid for out of the enterprise's revenues. Promotions go to those who perform particularly well, while demotions are meted out to those who fail.

The wage and salary system provides incentives in the form of steeply progressive increases as an individual moves up the ladder from one job to another. Information on these matters is not easy to find for the USSR, since a socialist regime is naturally defensive about inequality, but Table 28–7 gives some monthly wage rates from the Soviet iron and steel industry obtained from a Soviet study of that industry published in 1950.

TABLE 28–7
Soviet Iron and Steel Industry Wage Rates, c. 1950*

Type of Employment	Monthly Earnings Exclusive of Bonuses (In Rubles)
Typist	410–525
Telephone operator	410–525
Stenographer	450–600
Truck driver	360–410
Bus driver	550–600
Bookkeeper	410–600
Economist	790–1000
Production foreman (Western area)	950–1200
Production foreman (Urals area)	1500–1920
Head, steel-making shop	2040–2520
Chief engineer, steel plant	2500–3000
Head, electric power station	2500–3000
Director, research institute	4800–6000

* Don't complain about the date. The figures show the general principle. If any reader can find equally authentic later data the author will be happy to use it in the next edition of this book.

These wage differentials tell us much. A high-salaried employee earns 10 to 12 times the income of a low-salaried employee, a differential substantially greater than those prevailing in similar U.S. industries. These differentials provide incentives for people to acquire the skills necessary to qualify for higher-paying jobs and to work hard to get into those jobs. The greater the differences, the greater this incentive effect. Notice, also, a variation on this theme. Higher salaries are provided in geographical areas where skills are in short supply: a production foreman in the Urals earns more than he would in a western area of the country. Wage differentials also provide incentives to management to use little of the high-cost skills, substituting lower-wage employees wherever possible. Here again, the greater the differential, the greater the incentive to economize.

Contrary to misconceptions held by many people, labor is not directed by the central planner in the USSR. Choice of occupation is freely made, and so is choice of job, based on a system of wage differentials. Soviet planners rely on market forces to obtain the necessary workers and give them incentives to acquire the needed skills. There are some minor modifications of the principle of freedom of choice of occupation, just as there are in the U.S. economy, but the market principle dominates the process by which labor is allocated among its various uses.

The Soviet Union also uses "socialist incentives." These are primarily psychological rather than material in nature, stressing patriotism, achievement of national goals, and the building of a socialist state. At times they have been quite effective, especially in the early years of the planned economy (1928–1935) and during World War II (1939–1945). Their effectiveness seems to have diminished considerably in recent years.

We have already mentioned negative incentives to work and labor direction, which began to appear in the late 1930s, were strongly developed during World War II, and lasted into the 1950s. They involved such labor legislation as the following:

The amount of social insurance benefits was tied to the length of time a worker was employed in one plant.

Permission of the employer had to be obtained if a worker wished to quit his job.

Workers trained in certain special skills had to work in jobs assigned to them by the government for a period of time.

These forms of labor direction are gone, for the most part—a result of the reaction against Stalinism. But some persist. Where industrial plants operate retail stores or housing developments, a worker's privileges in those units will cease if he quits his job. Recent legislation prevents a worker who quits his job several times during a year from using the government employment service to get another, an obvious effort to cut down on labor turnover. Workers must carry employment books that list their past employment and contain ratings by their employers. University and technical school graduates are subject to placement in government-assigned jobs for a period of time; however, their education was free and they received living allowances while in school. While these measures are not onerous, they do represent departures from full reliance on the market mechanism for allocation of labor and provision of incentives.

PRICES IN THE USSR

The Soviet Union has a complex system of prices. We shall concentrate on the pricing of consumers' goods, partly because this type of price in the USSR has some unique and interesting aspects, and partly because it is fitted closely into the system of planning.

All Soviet prices have three component parts, cost of production, planned profit, and turnover tax. Costs of production are self-explanatory. Planned profit provides for some capital accumulation, for bonuses, and for some fringe benefits to workers. The turnover tax, as part of its use in diverting resources to investment purposes, is used to raise the selling price to one that will clear the market at existing levels of output and demand; its revenues go to the government.

We have already discussed the role of the turnover tax in balancing the economy at the macroeconomic level. It also has a function in clearing the market for individual products. That function arises from the fact that cost of production plus planned profits do not equal the price that would clear the market in an economy in which output of consumers' goods is deliberately restricted in order to maximize production of investment goods. Figure 28-3 will make this point clear.

If the Soviet planners wished to adjust output levels to the wants of consumers, they could increase output and bring prices down to levels that just covered costs plus planned profit. Prices at those levels would be analogous to the long-run equilibrium price of the competitive market, just covering full costs of production (including a "normal" profit). But the larger output necessary to achieve them would reduce the resources available for investment and growth. Even the pricing system reflects the Soviet emphasis on economic growth.

THE EFFICIENCY OF SOVIET PLANNING

Soviet planning has a number of serious deficiencies. The emphasis on quantity of output from each production unit often causes plant managers to use inefficient methods of production, pile up inventories of materials, and sometimes produce unneeded goods. Costs of production are difficult to judge accurately in a system in which prices tend to remain fixed for long periods of time. Inadequate provision is made for the cost of capital, leading to a tendency toward overly capital-intensive methods of production.

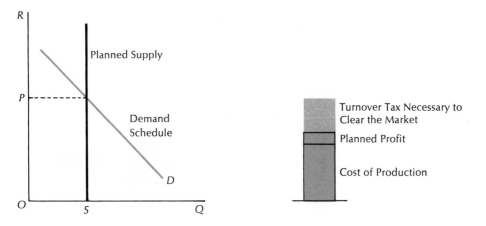

FIGURE 28-3

Soviet Prices: Use of the Turnover Tax to Clear the Market

Soviet planners restrict supply of consumers' goods in order to make resources available for investment. This requires price *P* to clear the market and avoid rationing and price controls, which would be awkward and difficult to enforce. Result: Imposition of a turnover tax just large enough to make up the difference between prices and costs plus planned profit.

Sometimes a strategic decision turns out to be wrong, such as a decision in the late 1920s to base the power supply primarily on coal rather than on oil and gas. A significant shift toward the more economical petroleum fuels has only been made in recent years. In the meantime, the economy has had to use more costly forms of power.

A particularly important drawback has been slowness in applying techno-logical advances that have been adopted in Western Europe and the United States at a much more rapid pace, particularly in electronics and computer sciences. The result has been relatively slow increases in productivity that have contributed significantly to the slowdown of economic growth in recent years.

From the point of view of the Soviet consumer, the chief deficiency of planning has been failure to give adequate attention to consumer preferences. The assortment of consumer goods, and their quality, made available in the stores was the end product of planners' decisions rather than consumers themselves. Inadequate supplies of some goods, shortages of others, frequent poor quality, and high prices have combined to bring a continuous barrage of criticism. The economic reforms of the late 1960s have attempted to ease the problem by giving enterprise managers greater flexibility and by putting greater stress on profitability as a criterion for judging the performance of manage-ment. These reforms are designed to make enterprises more responsive to consumer wants, and early indications are that some success has been achieved. A fundamental conflict is involved, however, between the "planner's sover-eignty" that would continue to push for rapid economic expansion and the "consumer's sovereignty" of a market-oriented economy.

Nevertheless, the Soviet planners have been highly successful in transforming a backward economy and society into an advanced one. They have also been successful in mobilizing the nation's resources to achieve very ambitious rates of economic growth. Perhaps their very successes have helped produce some of the problems the planning system now faces. Driving a relatively backward economy from the top, and driving it hard, may have been necessary to bring modernization and rapid growth. But a larger, more complex economy, and a far more sophisticated urban population probably requires another type of driving force, one stressing individual motivations more and central directives less. The Soviet Union has been grappling with that problem in recent years. Changes in planning have featured reforms toward decentralization, elimination of much of the repression of the Stalin years, and growing attention to production of consumers' goods. Indeed, some Soviet writers feel that easing of the driving force from the top is one reason for the slowdown in growth, and are reluctant to go further toward greater reforms.

In whatever way these issues may be resolved in the future, the Soviet Union has shown that economic planning can work. But the Soviet style of planning, run by a large and powerful bureaucracy and denying the basic tenets of consumer sovereignty, does not have a great deal of appeal in Western Europe or the United States. Socialists, in particular, have sought other approaches to economic management.

Summary

Any planned economy must determine its long-run goals, the speed of their attainment, and how resources are to be mobilized to attain them. The broad goal of the Soviet leaders was the building of a socialist society. In economic terms this goal was translated into a continuing drive for high rates of economic growth. The strategy decided on was use of centralized planning to push the economy forward as rapidly as possible. Rapid growth was achieved, but with several important costs: living standards were kept low, required work effort was kept at high levels, inequality of earned incomes was retained, and some forms of negative incentives to work and labor direction were introduced.

Resources of all kinds were mobilized for economic growth. Manpower resources were utilized more fully by eliminating unemployment, drawing women into the labor force, and drawing farmers into urban jobs. Collectivization and mechanization of agriculture raised the agricultural surplus, which was moved almost wholly into government hands to be used to promote industrialization. Capital was made available by holding consumption down via the turnover tax.

The process of planning operates through annual production plans supplemented by plans for inputs, expansion, and financing. The annual plans feature balanced estimates for all important industries, and these are tied together into a complex plan for the entire economy. The national plan is divided into operating plans for each economic unit. This cumbersome method has worked satisfactorily, but with enough difficulty to bring experiments with input-output analysis and linear programming. Implementation of the Soviet plans often requires modification and revision, but that should be expected of any plan.

The incentive system is tied to achievement of plans. Freedom of occupational choice is preserved by use of wage differentials designed to provide incentives to workers to select those occupations and localities where they are needed, and to provide signals to management to promote economy in the use of scarce skills.

Planning in the USSR has important flaws, and reforms are being made to provide plant managers with greater freedom of action. But planning has worked, and the goals given to the planners have been largely achieved.

Key Concepts

Balanced estimates.   The industry balances of resources and uses that make up the annual production plan in the USSR.

Five-Year Plan.   Production plan for a five-year period that states the goals the Soviet economy tries to achieve.

Turnover tax.   A Soviet tax on commodities at the time they first enter the channels of trade. It has two purposes: it raises prices so that markets are cleared (usually) and limits consumption to make resources available for investment uses.

Input-output analysis. A method of depicting and analyzing production relationships within the economy, based on the sources of industry inputs and the uses of industry outputs.

Linear programming.   A method of determining the optimum combination of the factors of production in a plant, enterprise, industry, or economy, based on the constraints provided by limited resources or inputs.

One of the most compelling arguments of the advocates of socialism is that a socialist economy can, if structured properly, orient itself toward consumer wants and avoid the heavy emphasis on central direction of the Soviet system, while still operating efficiently. This chapter will examine the theory underlying this argument and describe briefly some of the efforts now being made to achieve that goal in Eastern Europe.

PRICES AND WELFARE MAXIMIZATION

Our analysis in Chapters 21 through 25 showed that a competitive market economy tends to maximize the welfare derived from any given level of output, given the existing pattern of income distribution and assuming that prices reflect full costs of production. The argument also assumes that consumers seek to maximize their satisfactions and producers their gains. The market equilibrium that optimizes the use of resources has these characteristics:

Market Socialism

29

1. Prices clear the market, so that supply equals demand at the existing price ($S = D$).

2. Prices equal costs of production at the margin ($P = MC$).

3. Costs of production per unit are minimized ($P = AC$ at the lowest point on the AC curve).

When markets do not function effectively, however, serious inefficiencies and social costs can be incurred. This was illustrated by the example of American agriculture in Chapter 26. In later chapters the analysis will be extended to show what happens when competition is eliminated or seriously restricted. We shall also examine the determination of income distribution and how it affects the maximization of welfare.

At this point, however, we take up the question of whether the welfare-maximizing market equilibrium can be achieved only in a private economy. Is private enterprise a necessary condition for welfare maximization? Or can it also be achieved when the means of production are socially owned? Socialists say it can, and economic analysis supports their view.

MARKET SOCIALISM: BASIC CONCEPTS

Market socialism seeks to use self-adjusting markets to determine the pattern of production and the allocation of resources, while retaining other aspects of socialism such as social ownership of the means of production and an equalitarian pattern of income distribution. Use of the market mechanism would enable the economy to respond flexibly to consumer wants and provide for wide freedom of occupational choice. At the same time, the central government would retain control over macroeconomic policy to determine the level of investment and sustain full employment and the desired rate of economic growth. Social ownership of the means of production and distribution by the central government, cooperatives, or workers' organizations would eliminate private control of resources, enabling the pattern of income distribution to be based almost wholly on earned income. Yet even with social ownership of the means of production, consumer sovereignty would dominate the allocation of resources through the reliance of the economy on the market system for production decisions.

In short, market socialism seeks to retain the attractive aspects of the socialist ideology without resorting to planners' sovereignty and its inevitable compulsions, for which the Soviet Union has been so strongly criticized. The question is, Can it work?

THE ROLE OF PLANNING
IN MARKET SOCIALISM

Market socialism would retain a central planning commission for the nation as a whole. The function of central planning is restricted, however, to two major economic tasks:

1. Determination of the aggregate level of economic activity and the rate of growth of the economy. Fiscal and monetary policies similar to those used in any contemporary economy would be the chief policy instruments. Maintenance of a particular rate of economic growth, however, may require that the central government use its taxing powers to accumulate capital for that purpose. As we shall see in a moment, the uses to which that capital is put would be determined by the allocative forces of the market.

2. Determination of prices. Planners would have the job of setting prices for all inputs and outputs of the economy. This includes the products turned out by all economic units and also the raw material and semi-finished units they use as inputs. It would also include wage rates and salaries for labor inputs and interest rates charged for capital. Everything involved in the production and distribution of goods and services would have a price in a market socialist economy.

The Setting of Prices

The basic rule for the setting of prices by the central planners is simple but very important:

Prices must be set at levels that clear the market.

This means that the planners must set prices at which supply and demand are equal. Both shortages and surpluses are to be avoided by adjusting prices to eliminate them.

The logic behind this rule for price setting is the theory of competitive markets: When the market is cleared, both sellers and buyers are satisfied. The marginal benefits to the buyer derived from the last unit purchased are just equal to the marginal costs to the producer. This is the first condition for the system as a whole to reach a welfare optimum.

Prices that clear the market can readily be achieved by trial and error. Suppose, for example, the price of a product set by the central planning commission results in shortages in the market as in Figure 29-1. This situation will tell the planners that the first condition for optimum use of resources is not

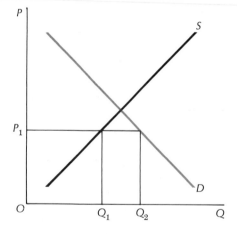

FIGURE 29-1

Shortages Under Market Socialism

At price P, the producing units are willing to supply quantity Q_1, but consumers wish to buy quantity Q_2. The result is bare shelves in the stores, inadequate inventories and customers lining up to buy when new shipments come in. The planners know from these signs that they should raise the price in order to clear the market.

being met, and that the price is too low. On the other hand, suppose that the planners find unsold goods piling up on the shelves and inventories rising, as in Figure 29-2. This is their signal to bring prices down. By a process of successive approximations, probably assisted by computers, input-output analysis, and economic forecasts, the central planning commission can arrive at a price that clears the market, leaving no unsold surplus and creating no shortages. Figure 29-3 shows what the adjustment process might be like.

There are striking similarities between price setting under market socialism and in the competitive model. The results are similar, the causes of the price movements are similar and the trial-and-error process of successive approximations are similar. In one case the mechanism works automatically—and is

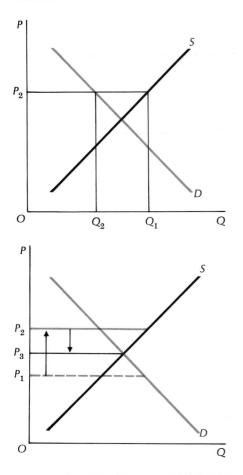

FIGURE 29-2

Surpluses Under Market Socialism

At price P_2, the producing units will supply quantity Q_1, while buyers will take only quantity Q_2. The difference represents unsold output, telling the planners that prices should be reduced.

FIGURE 29-3

Clearing the Market Under Market Socialism

Starting from a price set too low (P_1), the planners may overshoot the mark and raise the price too much, to P_2. Growing amounts of unsold output quickly cause them to move down again until they reach the equilibrium price at P_3.

perhaps subject to large shocks and wide fluctuations. In the other case the mechanism is managed, would probably avoid some of the price shifts of the competitive model, and may well function more smoothly.

Price setting in an economy based on market socialism is a massive job, however, requiring a managerial bureaucracy of some scope, particularly in a large and complex economy. But the planning system that limits itself to planning of prices will inevitably be smaller and more manageable than one that seeks to also plan production inputs and outputs. The results may well be worth the extra resources devoted to planning, since the practical alternatives in the modern world apparently are the planners' sovereignty of the Soviet Union or the quasi-monopolistic economy of the United States or Western Europe.[1]

---

[1] Some advocates of market socialism argue that the price planners under market socialism would probably be fewer in number than the people engaged in advertising and marketing in present-day America, whose services would no longer be needed under market socialism.

Adjustment of the Producing Unit

A market socialist economy cannot limit itself only to the setting of prices. It must also provide incentives to the management of socialist enterprises that lead to responses that maximize efficiency. The basic principle here is also simple but vitally important:

> *Management of enterprises must be motivated to maximize the profits of producing units.*

This means that rewards and incentive systems must be based on profit levels, and adequate indicators and measures of profit must be developed, just as in a private enterprise economy.

This operating rule is necessary to satisfy the second and third criteria of welfare maximization:

Prices must equal costs of production at the margin ($P = MC$).

Costs of production per unit must be minimized ($P = AC$ at the lowest point on the AC curve).

Incentive systems of this sort are not difficult to devise. Large corporations are quite able to do it, and the socialist systems of Eastern Europe have moved a long way in the same direction. Even the Soviet Union has taken some steps toward the same goal. The chief problem is not the incentives and rewards themselves, that is, high salaries, bonuses, and public recognition for success, but the devising of accurate measures of costs and accurate indicators of profit.

Under the assumption that these problems can be largely resolved, as many American corporations have already done, the enterprise managers must then be given a great deal of latitude in making decisions about which inputs to use, which outputs to schedule, and the best ways to combine inputs in the process of production. The better the reward system is and the freer the management, the closer the enterprise will come to maximizing profits, and the closer the enterprise and the industry will come to achieving the criteria of welfare maximization.

Any plant manager who seeks to maximize profits when his selling price is given will have a horizontal demand curve for his output, just as in the case of pure competition. As a price taker, he will try to move toward that level of output at which his selling price equals his marginal cost. His supply curve is his marginal cost curve. The enterprise in a market socialist economy will tend toward the same short-run equilibrium as the firm in the model of pure competition (Figure 29-4).

In the example given in Figure 29-4, the short-run, profit-maximizing solution is achieved. But not the long-run solution, which minimizes costs per unit of output. How is that brought about under market socialism?

In the first place, this enterprise could add to its profits by building another plant. Since its profits are above normal it will have every incentive to borrow the capital necessary to do so, subject to the price placed on loanable funds.

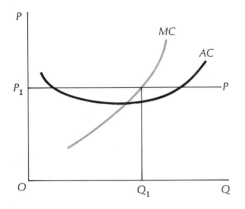

FIGURE 29-4
Short-Run Equilibrium of the
Enterprise in Market Socialism, I

With the price P_1 established by the central planning commission and not under the control of the enterprise manager, the level of output Q_1 at which profits are maximized, $P = MC$, is set.

Secondly, other enterprises will discover the profit opportunities available and will also have strong incentives to build additional plants or enter this type of production. Just as in a private competitive industry, the incentive of profits will bring additional capital and enterprise into this industry.

The result will be similar to that achieved by the competitive model. As output rises, supplies coming on the market are increased, surpluses start to appear, and the central planning commission brings the price down. This process can be expected to continue until the industry as a whole has reached its equilibrium size and expansion stops, shown in Figure 29-5.

This result may be slow in coming under market socialism if the producing enterprise is in a monopolistic position. For example, if it is a large automobile manufacturer in a relatively small nation, without significant foreign markets, the management may become lazy, allow inefficiencies to creep in, and permit the cost structure slowly to drift upward. It may still operate in the short run at the output that equates output with marginal costs, and appear to be maximizing profits, but it is not trying to push average costs downward.

For these reasons a market socialist economy may find it wise to provide incentives for management to bring average costs of production down. It may

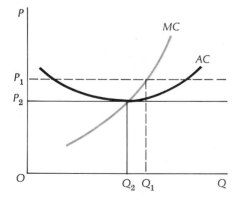

FIGURE 29-5
Short-Run Equilibrium of the Firm in
Market Socialism, II

As new plants are established in response to the high profits made at price P_1, the central planning commission brings the price down toward P_2 in order to keep the market cleared. Ultimately, the individual enterprises will be operating at price P_2 and output Q_2, at which point price equals marginal cost at the lowest point on the average cost curve.

encourage competition within enterprises for the managerial positions, or allow imports from other countries to discipline monopolistic industries. Even market socialism can have problems of monopoly if the size of the market, in combination with the best available technology, gives enterprises a monopolistic position. Indeed, this problem has already appeared in some of the Eastern European countries now moving toward market socialism.

In spite of these problems of application in practice, there is no theoretical or analytical reason why market socialism cannot achieve a close approximation to the optimal long-run adjustment of the competitive market economy. Its chief advantage is that firms are price takers, making it possible to achieve the cost-minimizing and optimal-output levels of the purely competitive model.

Wages and Salaries

Payments to workers under market socialism would also be designed to clear the market. Wages and salaries would be set by the central planning commission to equate the demand for labor with the available supply. For example, suppose a new shipyard is being established, which will need a substantial number of electricians in an area where they are in short supply. Wages would be set at levels high enough to draw electricians from other areas or to draw unskilled workers into appropriate training programs. Just like the trial-and-error process for product pricing, the pricing of labor services will seek to establish a market equilibrium.

Capital

The same is true of capital. Funds for investment can be made available from two sources. One is the earnings of the enterprise itself, which would be available for expansion. The more profitable enterprises would be the ones with the greatest resources for expansion, just as in the competitive market economy.

The second source of investment funds is the capital market, in the socialist economy dominated by state-owned banks. These banks would be reservoirs for the voluntary savings of individuals, and some would also dispense government-owned funds. Whatever the source, loans would be available to any enterprise at interest rates established by the central planning commission at levels designed to clear the money markets and assure a full-employment level of aggregate demand.

Just as in a private economy, the supply of funds available to enterprises and consumers could be managed with stable growth at full employment as the goal. Together with the demand for funds, this supply would establish the rate of interest that would balance demand and supply in the money markets. One task of the central planning commission would be continually to seek that level by trial-and-error adjustments of the interest rate.

This method of allocating capital would function effectively if the supply of funds were based solely on the voluntary savings of individuals and enterprises.

It would also function effectively if voluntary savings were supplemented by a political decision, presumably arrived at democratically, to add additional savings through taxes or borrowing by the central government designed to raise the level of capital accumulation and reduce aggregate consumption levels. The important point to remember is that the market mechanism would be used to ration investment funds among all those who would like them, with the amount available going only to those enterprises willing and able to pay the going price for it.

MARKET SOCIALISM
AND ECONOMIC EFFICIENCY

Advocates of market socialism are fond of pointing out that their system can come closest to approximating the welfare-maximizing equilibrium of the competitive market economy. Since prices are established by the central planning commission, they cannot be used by monopolistic firms to create more-than-normal profits and to gain special economic advantages. The individual enterprise must take the price as given and adjust its operations to that already established amount.

By contrast, they argue, the big enterprise in a capitalist economy can gain considerable influence over the market because of its size. To a greater or less extent, depending on circumstances, the big enterprise can set its own prices—to its own benefit and to the detriment of the public. These sources of private gain at the expense of the public would not exist under market social-ism. The result is a closer approximation to the economic efficiency of a competitive market system.

At the same time, much of the inefficiency of a private economy could be eliminated. A large amount of information would be available to the central planning commission. It could be made available to all interested enterprises to minimize overexpansion of a particular industry, for example. Similarly, control over the pricing process could dampen down erratic or excessive swings in prices caused in a private economy by the incorrect expectations or overenthusiasm of individuals or speculators. And the advocates of market socialism may be right. A well-managed pricing system may be more effective than a freely functioning one, particularly if it avoids monopolistic controls by producers.

MARKET SOCIALISM
AND EQUALITARIANISM

One of the chief advantages of market socialism is its ability to avoid the inequalities of income that arise in a capitalist economy through private ownership of the means of production and distribution. Almost all income would be earned income from wages and salaries. Differences in earned incomes may be large from one individual to the next, because of differences in productivity on the job. But the greater differences created in a private economy through accumulation of profits, interest, and rent, and by the unearned income resulting from ownership of great wealth, could be greatly reduced or eliminated entirely.

An economic system based on social ownership of the means of production need not provide payments to private individuals for use of resources. Instead, those payments could be retained by the community as a whole and used to achieve social rather than individual goals. Income from work would be the basis of the distribution of income. In a private enterprise economy, by contrast, the distribution of income is based on income from property as well as income from work. Since ownership of property is distributed in a relatively highly unequal fashion, it imparts a significant amount of inequality to the income distribution pattern. This factor could be largely eliminated in a socialist economy, enabling the economy as a whole to move toward a more equalitarian distribution of income. Such a move is likely to increase individual welfare.

DECENTRALIZATION OF DECISION MAKING
UNDER MARKET SOCIALISM

One of the great advantages of market socialism is a decentralized framework for decision making. Only prices and the level of aggregate demand would be determined by central planners. All other decisions would be made at the level of the producing enterprise. Consumers would be free to exercise their choices in spending their incomes. Workers would be free to choose their occupation and employment. All of this is possible because the market is used as the coordinating mechanism, enabling decisions to rest with the enterprise, the consumer, and the worker.

Decentralized decisions provide a sharp contrast with Soviet planning, with its heavy emphasis on control from the top and administrative allocation of resources. Although the recent trend in the USSR has been toward greater reliance on signals from the market, the basic principle of centralized administrative planning and resource allocation remains. A complex bureaucracy manages economic affairs for a powerful national state.

Market socialism could reverse the trend toward bureaucracy, which is also to be found in the large corporation of present-day capitalism, and provide a larger scope for individual action. If one of the problems of modern man is the conflict between individual goals and those of large organizations, market socialism offers one possible path toward a solution.

MARKET SOCIALISM
AND WORKERS' MANAGEMENT

Decentralization of economic decisions can open the way to effective patterns of workers' management. The full equalitarian promise of socialism cannot be achieved as long as workers do not have effective control over their own working lives. Yet in a large enterprise, whether privately or publicly owned, there has been little opportunity for grass-roots or "shop-floor" democracy. Representation of workers by unions has been only a partial answer.

Workers' self-management has been tried most extensively in Yugoslavia. It is based on the principle that the worker is sovereign insofar as decisions about his enterprise are concerned. In a firm with less than 30 employees all workers take part in making decisions. For a firm with 30 to 70 workers, the workers choose whether they will all participate or elect a representative group. Firms with more than 70 employees elect a workers' council. Half of the council is elected each year and no one can serve two consecutive terms; wide involvement is thereby assured. The council can have 15 to 120 members. The problem of remoteness in a large firm has been partially resolved by providing for separate councils for technically separate units.

The workers' council elects both a managerial board and the director of the enterprise. The director, who is elected for a four-year term, is the chief executive of the enterprise, analogous to the president of a U.S. corporation. The managerial board is elected annually from the members of the workers' council. It works with the director on proposing policies for approval by the council and assists in running the plant.

The workers' councils deal with matters of general policy. An official study gave this breakdown of the topics about which the councils decide:

Labor productivity, 22%

Expansion of the enterprise, 15%

Marketing, 14%

Distribution of income, 14%

Workers' living standards, 11%

Evaluation of the director and managerial board, 10%

Workers' education and training, 8%

Relations with other enterprises, 6%

The Yugoslav system of worker management is not perfect. Top management claims that the councils do not appreciate the complex, long-range problems of a large enterprise. Workers are often dissatisfied because they feel that they have no real say in day-to-day management. There has been a tendency to emphasize short-run gains through higher wages, with inadequate attention being given to research and improved technology, particularly where unemployment might be a threat. Automation has been resisted because of the threat of more intensive work. A tendency toward collusion between plants and the development of cartels has been observed, manifesting the age-old conflict between the producer and consumer.

These difficulties have not caused the government to move away from the principle of workers' control. But they have resulted in continuing revisions of the system in an effort to resolve problems while retaining and strengthening the concept of a self-management of the enterprise by the workers.

The Yugoslav pattern is beginning to spread. It was at the heart of the Czech economic reforms of the late 1960s and may well have been an important reason for the Soviet intervention. Sweden is also beginning to move in that direction.

The case of Sweden may be particularly important for other countries in Western Europe and North America. Sweden has had forty years of government by a party devoted to democratic socialism. The government provides a vast array of social services, the tax system has narrowed the range of incomes, and aggregative economic planning uses the government budget and monetary policy to maintain full employment. Wages and working conditions are settled by collective bargaining between national labor unions and associations of employers. "Works committees" elected by workers have been set up in many enterprises in the last quarter century to enable workers to advise management on a variety of matters, but these committees do not decide policy. Only about one-third of them work effectively, according to a recent estimate by a national union official.

The Swedish economy relies very heavily on production for export. Enterprises feel pressure, therefore, to keep costs and prices down to meet foreign competition. Increases in productivity are important to both business firms and the economy as a whole. The result is increased pressure on workers and a tendency toward greater intensity of work. In a situation like that, greater participation by workers in making decisions becomes vitally important. It can lead to increased productivity by itself, as well as to less opposition to improved technology. Considerable discussion of these issues has led to two proposals. The employer associations have suggested that union representatives be appointed to boards of directors of private firms. The unions, however, want "shop floor democracy," in which workers themselves participate in decisions about how the work will be organized. Both employers and unions recognize a need to reconcile increased productivity with increasing (or at least not decreasing) satisfaction on the job. The debate over how to achieve these goals is well on its way toward the pragmatic solutions characteristic of Swedish economic policy.

A similar discussion started even earlier in Norway. During the 1960s four experimental projects in workers' self-management were begun, in a sawmill, a cellulose plant, an electrical equipment plant, and a nationalized hydro-electric generating plant. They showed that a tremendous amount of talent and productivity can be released by establishment of self-managing working groups, and that present methods of management from the top stifle a great deal of human potential. These Scandinavian experiments are too new to show conclusively the conditions under which shop floor democracy and workers' self-management will work well. They are, however, an important development that will bear watching.

Shop floor democracy need not be limited to socialist enterprises. Several U.S. manufacturing plants have pioneered an "honor system" that does away with time clocks and gives workers substantial responsibility for decision making on the job. Not all have been successful, but those that work effectively report increased output per man-hour, reduced absenteeism, and significant increases in worker morale. Whether these forms of organization can develop further in a private enterprise economy remains to be seen, however. In Yugoslavia they are an integral part of a socialist system and have full support of the government and the prevailing political ideology. That is not true in the United States and only partially so in Scandinavia.

MARKET SOCIALISM
AND INDIVIDUAL FREEDOMS

Market socialism provides a mechanism by which economic freedoms can be reconciled with social ownership of the means of production. It retains the principles of consumer sovereignty and freedom of choice of occupation. It makes possible greater equality in income distribution than under private enterprise capitalism, together with wide participation in decision making by those most closely affected by the decisions. It enables rational and efficient decisions to emerge from a complex set of economic relationships without resort to the constraints and compulsion of centralized production planning. The contrast between the decentralized economy inherent in the theory of market socialism, and centralized planning as it developed in the Soviet Union is particularly striking. Finally, decentralized decision making permits a shift of authority from the top of bureaucratic organizations to the rank-and-file worker. It may be that some form of market socialism will be the key to a more humane and responsive economic and social order.

Summary

The theory of market socialism shows how an economy in which the means of production are socially owned can function through a decentralized system of decision making in which consumer sovereignty prevails and freedom of choice of occupation is retained. Central planning is restricted to maintenance of high levels of aggregate demand and planning of prices by a central agency.

The price-making rule is that prices must clear the market. This makes the individual enterprise a price taker in the same sense as the firm in the purely competitive model of self-adjusting markets. Plant managers respond to the price established by the central planning agency on the basis of a profit-maximizing rule supplemented by a system of incentives and rewards. Consumers are free to choose what they want to buy, and thereby signal producers about what to produce. Workers are free to take any job available. Capital is allocated through the price mechanism. The result should be a strong tendency to achieve the welfare-maximizing equilibrium of the purely competitive model.

The decentralized pattern of decision making in market socialism makes possible a variety of forms of workers' management, since production decisions are made at the plant level rather than by the central planners. Market socialism would avoid the difficulties engendered by centralized production planning in a Soviet-type economy and by an economy dominated by giant firms in the U.S. style.

BIG BUSINESS, MONOPOLOID MARKETS, AND PUBLIC POLICY

VII

The competitive model helps us to understand how market forces function, but we should be careful in applying it to the contemporary American economy. Few markets have the characteristics of pure competition and many are far from it. Large sectors of the American economy are dominated by large firms with a considerable degree of market power (which economists define as ability to influence prices). Even broader aspects of economic power are at work in the ability of these companies to exclude competitors, influence public policy, and affect the flow of capital.

On the other hand, pure monopoly is also rare. Economists have analyzed a wide variety of situations including monopoly (one seller), oligopoly (few sellers), and monopolistic competition (many sellers with differentiated products). These together make up a group of phenomena we have termed *monopoloid,* to indicate that they all have characteristics related to those of monopoly. One common characteristic of monopoloid markets is their inability to achieve the welfare-maximizing triple equilibrium of market, firm, and industry that is characteristic of pure competition.

Part VII deals with these issues. Chapter 30 sketches the place of big business in the American economy. Chapter 31 presents the economic theory of monopoloid markets by contrasting monopoly and monopolistic competition with pure competition. Chapter 32 looks at oligopoly, a highly varied situation much less amenable to generalization because of its variety, and stresses the tendency of large firms to create protected positions of power for themselves. Chapter 33 looks critically at public policy toward big business, including government support for big enterprise as well as government antitrust legislation and regulation of business enterprise.

The basic theme of Part VII is that one cause of the malaise afflicting modern America is the economic effects of big business and the impact of its economic and political power. One reason why contemporary economists are now searching for a new synthesis of economic theory and policy is the growing realization that new approaches are required in dealing with the malign effects of concentrated economic power.

The American economy is dominated by large corporations. Although there are some 11.5 million business enterprises in operation, the key sectors of the economy on which modern high standards of living are based, including manufacturing, transportation, communication, utilities, and finance, are the natural habitat of big business. Even in sectors dominated by small firms, such as services, wholesale and retail trade, and construction, some giants are to be found. And some supercorporations straddle several sectors of the economy as diversified "conglomerates."

BIG BUSINESS: THE PROBLEM IN PERSPECTIVE

The place of big business is increasing, although the trends are sometimes difficult to discern because of the constant flux and change going on in a modern economy. One way of getting a rough measure is to look at the share of GNP originating in those sectors of the economy dominated by oligopoly and large firms, as compared with sectors dominated by small firms. This is done for the years 1950 and 1967 in Table 30–1.

Big Business in the American Economy

30

TABLE 30–1
Big and Little Business, 1950 and 1967

Sector	Percent of GNP Originated	
	1950	1967
Small business	40.4	35.9
Big business	49.3	49.0 — stayed the same
Government and foreign	10.3	15.1
	100.0	100.0

Source: Adapted from William G. Shepherd, *Market Power and Economic Welfare* (New York: Random House, 1970), p. 70. The original data are from the *Statistical Abstract of the United States*, 1968.
Notes: The small-business sector includes agriculture, forestry and fisheries; construction; wholesale and retail trade; services. The big-business sector comprises manufacturing and mining; transportation; communication; utilities; finance, insurance, and real estate.

The striking feature of Table 30–1 is the increase in the role of government and the decline in the share of GNP from the small business sector of the economy. Big business managed to hold its own as far as proportionate share of GNP is concerned. But if we look only at the private portion of the economy, the proportion of GNP originating in the sectors dominated by big business is seen to have increased.

THE URGE TO MERGE

The predominance of big business is due more to mergers than to internal growth of firms. Compare, for example, the 200 largest manufacturing firms in 1947 and in 1968. Their share of all manufacturing assets rose from 42.4 percent to 60.9 percent. The total increase between the two dates was 18.5 percent. The increase due to mergers and acquisitions was 15.6 percent, while the effect of industry growth was only 5.2 percent. This means that without mergers and without growth of the industry the share of manufacturing assets controlled by the 200 largest industrials would actually have fallen somewhat, but partly because of growth and mostly because of mergers their share rose dramatically.

There have been three great periods of mergers and acquisitions during which the basic structure of the American economy was transformed into its present state. The first came around the turn of the century (1897–98 to 1902–3), and marked the culmination of the transition to a truly national economy and the development of capital markets capable of taking large securities offerings. Great combinations in many basic industries, as well as mining, railroads, and utilities, were organized. Where formerly some industries had many small and medium-sized firms, typically one giant corporation appeared that was either close to a monopoly or had such a large share of the market that it clearly dominated the others and was able to manage prices and other market conditions with considerable freedom. The classic case was formation of United States Steel Corporation. In this period the fundamental differences in structure between economic sectors dominated by big business and those dominated by small business were clearly defined for the first time, and they have persisted to the present time.

The first merger movement subsided after the securities market slump of 1903–4, which was followed by a period of slowed economic growth to the time of World War I. This intermediate period also saw the first significant enforcement of the antitrust laws against big business, the strengthening of railroad regulation, and passage of further antitrust legislation in 1914.

With the return of rapid economic growth and buoyant securities markets after World War I, a second merger movement began (1924–25 to 1930–31). There was a difference this time: lesser firms merged to challenge the industry leaders. In steel, for example, where in 1920 U.S. Steel was a goliath among pygmies, by the early 1930s Bethlehem and Republic and several other companies had been put together by merger and acquisition to create the present oligopolistic structure of the industry. This pattern was repeated in most of the manufacturing sector. Where single-firm monopoly or dominance had appeared in the first merger movement, it was replaced by dominance by groups of firms (oligopoly) in the second.

1st merger movement
1897-98 →
1902-03

US Steel Corporation

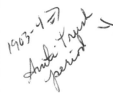

1903-4 →
Anti-Trust period →

2nd merger movement
1924-25 →
1930-31

There were exceptions to this pattern. The automobile industry in the 1920s began the process of attrition of small firms that has left the industry with progressively fewer producers as time has gone on. In public utilities, the second merger movement left the entire nation dominated by three giant firms, which were broken up during the 1930s partly by the collapse of their rickety financial structures in the Great Depression and partly by federal legislation and regulation.

The third merger movement began in 1944–45 and has continued unchecked up to the present. The number of mergers tended to grow from year to year through the postwar years, culminating in a great spurt in the late 1960s. Merger activity did not begin to fall until the extremely tight money and the queasy securities market of 1969–70 appeared. The industries most heavily affected were food and beverages, chemicals, metals, electrical and nonelectrical machinery, textiles and clothing, petroleum, aerospace, and transportation equipment. Other active fields included railroads, airlines, banks and insurance companies, hotels, and food retailing.

3rd merger movement 1944–45 → present

The quarter century of sustained merger activity after World War II was dominated by the largest companies—those with the most internal capital accumulation, the best access to capital markets, and the greatest public visibility. For example, 1,072 large manufacturing firms were merged into other companies; the 200 largest manufacturing companies gained 57 percent of their assets by participating in those mergers. Large firms not only dominate their industries, they also dominate merger activity.

Another feature of the period was the growth of conglomerates. These are large firms that have expanded into a wide variety of unrelated fields. A typical conglomerate will have divisions or subsidiaries in a variety of manufacturing industries, finance, service industries, transportation, wholesale and retail trade, and so on.

Finally, the large American corporation has begun to reach out internationally and expand overseas. United States business investment abroad has increased to about $3.5 billion annually and has been particularly strong in petroleum, electronics, and other "high-technology" industries. The growth of world trade, jet aircraft, and speedy communications have combined to pull U.S. industry increasingly into world markets. Manufacturing companies have opened branch plants or subsidiaries abroad, or have acquired foreign firms. To give some idea of the extent of U.S. penetration, about one in 14 workers in Scotland is employed by subsidiaries of U.S. firms, and over 20 percent of British exports are intrafirm transactions of U.S. subsidiaries with their parent firms. In 1970, the overseas portion of International Business Machines Corporation contributed more profit to the company than its domestic operations did. Large U.S. banks have followed manufacturers with branches and acquisitions. Some European and Japanese firms have taken the same path, and a group of truly international supercorporations is beginning to appear. This development is in its early stages, however, and most large corporations still rely primarily on the business they do at home.

U.S. MANUFACTURING INDUSTRIES

Manufacuring is the most important sector of the U.S. economy. It originates about 30 percent of GNP. The growing dominance of large firms in that sector is illustrated by data recently reported in a special study of corporate mergers prepared for the Federal Trade Commission.

> In 1968 the 200 largest industrial corporations controlled over 60 percent of the total assets held by all manufacturing corporations.

> The 100 largest manufacturing corporations in 1968 held a larger share of manufacturing assets than the 200 largest in 1950.

> The 200 largest in 1968 controlled a share of manufacturing assets equal to that held by the 1,000 largest in 1941.

A very large proportion of U.S. manufacturing industries are oligopolistic, with markets dominated by a relatively few large sellers. This unpleasant fact of economic life has become evident to even the most hardened advocate of private enterprise since the Bureau of the Census began publishing industrial "concentration ratios" in recent years.

A concentration ratio is the proportion of value added by the largest firms in an industry, usually calculated for the four largest firms. These ratios can be adjusted to reflect the fact that some markets are local rather than national, such as the markets for bricks, concrete, newspapers, milk, and bread. Thus, in the automobile industry about 95 percent of all new car sales are made by four firms, in steel about 55 percent, in drugs about 75 percent, and so on.

When adjusted to account for local and regional market patterns, about one-third of all value added in manufacturing is produced in industries with concentration ratios over 70 percent. Almost 80 percent of value added is from industries with concentration ratios over 40 percent. The average degree of concentration in American industry is about 60 percent. Only 12 percent of value added in U.S. manufacturing is from industries in which the top four firms hold less than 30 percent of the market.[1]

MONOPOLY AND OLIGOPOLY

There is very little complete monopoly in American industry. Several industries come close, however. Campbell Soup Company produces 90 percent of all canned soups and Western Electric 80 to 90 percent of all telephone equipment. This is about as close as we come to a single seller of any significant product.

Oligopoly (literally, a few sellers) is the rule in U.S. manufacturing. Table 30–2 is a listing of a few important industries showing the share of total sales made by the two, three, or four largest firms. Although the pattern varies

---

[1] These figures have been calculated from government data by William G. Shepherd and reported in *Market Power and Economic Welfare* (New York: Random House, 1970), pp. 104–8.

TABLE 30–2
Oligopoly in Some Important American Industries, 1968

Market and Leading Firms	Approximate Market Share
Motor vehicles (3 firms) General Motors, Ford, Chrysler	90–95
Petroleum refining (4 firms) Standard Oil (N.J.), Texaco, Gulf, Mobil	40–50
Iron and steel (4 firms) U.S. Steel, Bethlehem, Armco, Republic	50–60
Industrial chemicals (4 firms) Du Pont, Union Carbide, Dow, Monsanto	60–70
Aluminium (3 firms) Alcoa, Kaiser, Reynolds	80–90
Copper (3 firms) Anaconda, Kennecott, Phelps-Dodge	60–70
Metal containers (2 firms) American Can, Continental Can	80–90
Aircraft (3 firms) Boeing, McDonnell-Douglas, General Dynamics	80–90
Aircraft engines (2 firms) General Electric, United Aircraft	90–100
Drugs (4 firms) American Home Products, Merck, Pfizer, Lilly	70–80
Soaps and related products (3 firms) Proctor and Gamble, Colgate, Lever	60–70
Dairy products (3 firms) Borden, National Dairy, Carnation	60–70
Automobile tires and tubes (3 firms) Goodyear, Firestone, Uniroyal	70–80
Television broadcasting (3 firms) CBS, NBC, ABC	80–90

[handwritten annotation: concentration Ratio]

widely, most oligopolies in American industry are dominated by a single giant firm, with several other large ones trailing behind. This pattern of *unbalanced oligopoly* usually features strong price leadership (see Chapter 32) by the dominant firm. It often takes the form of an industry leader as large as the next two largest firms, the second largest as large as the third and fourth taken together, and so on down the line. Some typical examples are shown in Figure 30–1. *[handwritten: unbalanced oligopoly]*

Balanced oligopoly is not common, although it exists in a few industries. It is characterized by several firms of about the same size, strength, and market power. Industrial chemicals is one industry that might qualify as a balanced oligopoly, although each of the principal firms tends to dominate in particular product markets within the industry. (Figure 30–2). *[handwritten: balanced oligopoly]*

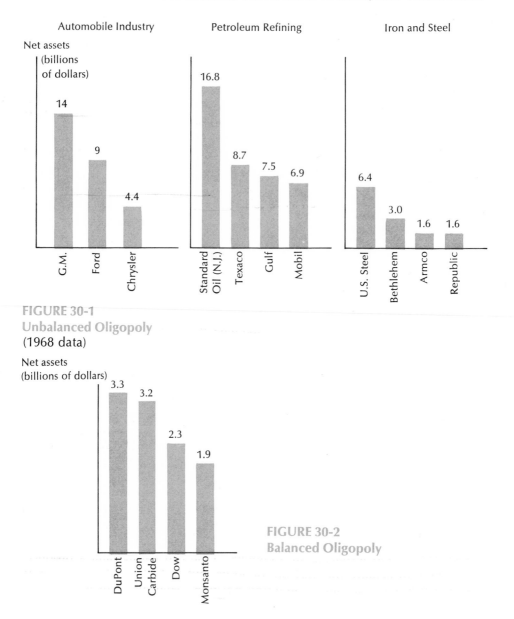

FIGURE 30-1
Unbalanced Oligopoly
(1968 data)

FIGURE 30-2
Balanced Oligopoly

BARRIERS TO NEW FIRMS

The patterns of economic concentration that have developed in the U.S. economy are supported and continued by barriers to entry of new firms. The chief barriers are product differentiation and their attendant selling costs, and large-scale production with its requirement of large investment in facilities. Other significant barriers include patents and trade secrets, control of raw materials by existing firms, and existing supplier-distributor relationships. To

barriers.

these should be added a variety of government restrictions. Counterbalancing these factors, however, are the continuous economic changes, particularly in consumer preferences and technology, that are at work in a dynamic economy.

I *Product differentiation* is a primary discouragement to new firms. In industries such as automobiles, whiskey, cigarettes, and gasoline, the existence of well-known brand names, continually publicized by large-scale advertising, contribute to serious disadvantages to new firms. Very large selling expenses may be necessary, forcing a new firm to incur higher costs per unit than established firms before it can achieve enough market penetration to hold its own against the established firms and the well-known brands. Indeed, the classic study of barriers to entry estimated that the cost disadvantage of new firms in such markets may be as high as 10 to 25 percent.[2]

II The *large amounts of capital required for entry* into the large-scale and mass-production industries are another important barrier to new firms. There have been no large new firms in the basic iron and steel industry since World War II, when government loans financed construction of the Kaiser Steel plant in California. No new firms have entered the automobile industry since mass-production assembly-line methods were widely adopted in the 1920s. Instead, there has been a steady attrition of smaller firms. When the need for large amounts of capital is associated with the cost disadvantages of product differentiation, as in the case of automobiles, the combined barriers become practically insurmountable.

III The other important limitations to entry are more subtle. Control over technology through *patents* can help build a large enterprise, while continued development of improvements, modifications, and extensions can prolong its predominance. Domination of the photoduplication industry by Xerox Corporation is a recent example, although its growth has been fostered also by shrewd and vigorous marketing programs. Patents, however, can also shelter a new firm from appropriation of its technology by already existing giant firms; Xerox itself operated in this shelter during its early growth years. Another example is the entry of Polaroid Company as an important participant in the photographic equipment industry.

IV *Control over raw materials* is significant in a number of industries. Most metals, sulfur, and fertilizers are examples. One can hardly fault a producer for seeking to acquire the best ore deposits, but restriction of those ores to his own use will give him a preferred position. However, ore deposits are

---

[2] Joe S. Bain, *Barriers to New Competition* (Cambridge, Mass.: Harvard University Press, 1956). It is possible that product differentiation can foster the entry of new firms producing specialized products for a sector of the market not well served by existing products. In the automobile industry, for example, American Motors was able to survive in the 1950s by doing that, and the growing popularity of small and sporty foreign cars in recent years was based on the same sort of situation. Note, however, that the giants of the industry have moved to occupy the new markets as soon as the venturesome newcomers were beyond the pioneering and exploratory stage.

used up in time, new ones are discovered, and in the long run these changes can erode an existing firm's position. This is one reason why producers in industries heavily dependent on supplies of raw materials move toward refining, fabricating, and distribution. The large capital requirements of these vertically integrated firms then become a significant deterrent to challengers. *Government barriers to entry* are seldom found in large-scale industry. They are found primarily in professional and semiskilled occupations that require relatively little capital and usually involve licensing or certification by a public body. A very wide variety of occupations is included—plumbers, dentists, doctors, lawyers, and beauticians are some common examples. Government licensing is used to restrict entry in some principal sectors of the economy however, including transportation (air, bus, intercity truck), banking, and public utilities, three economic sectors thoroughly dominated by big enterprises.

CAN COMPETITION SURVIVE?

The urge to merge rests upon some important characteristics of modern industrial technology, the financial system of modern capitalism, and the drive for profits. The technological imperative is strong. Much industrial technology requires the use of highly expensive equipment that can be used only for a single purpose or for very limited purposes. A steel rolling mill can cost up to $250 million, together with its supporting and auxiliary equipment, and it can be used only to produce steel strip and sheets. Its high cost requires either full and continuous use, or else prices high enough to cover interest on the capital investment and payment of the standby crew during the mill's down time. A number of industries have similar problems, including chemicals, petroleum refining, railroads, automobile production, much machinery manufacture, and more.

It is understandable that in an industry with those characteristics, existing firms may try to keep out newcomers (many of whom are already barred by high capital requirements), protect their markets from competitors, and maintain price levels. Division of markets and price fixing should be expected. Where those actions are legal, as in most European countries, formal market-sharing and price-fixing agreements are common, and the groups involved are called *cartels*. In this country such collusion is illegal, so American industry has turned to merger instead. At least up to 1950 there was little legal hindrance to mergers that brought significant market power, as long as it was not used in a predatory or "unreasonable" manner against other firms. As a result, American industry is characterized by a few large multiplant firms and oligopolies which, as we shall see, tend to follow policies that stabilize market shares and bring price structures that are flexible upward but are hard to move downward.

Generally speaking, the giant multiplant firms do not have cost advantages over smaller companies because of their large size, nor are they generally responsible for the significant advances in technology through research and development. Indeed, just the opposite appears to be the case: in most industries, moderate-sized firms are the ones with the lowest production costs and with often the lowest costs of distribution. One of the myths of our time is that modern mass production requires the giant enterprises we now have. Thus, in steelmaking, a plant with an annual production capacity of 1.5 million tons has approximately the same costs per ton as a plant with an annual capacity of 5 million or 10 million tons. The same is generally true of research, development, and technical innovation: the moderate-sized companies tend to be the leaders. The influence of technology on the size of firms is *not* the result of internal economies, but rests instead on the desire to reduce the market risks attendant on the use of expensive, single-purpose equipment, and to do so by gaining enough power to influence or control markets and prices.

A second factor in the urge to merge is the financial profit that can be obtained. This element in mergers has always been strong. If manipulated properly, a merger can provide large savings on taxes for the firm itself, resulting in larger after-tax profits per share and a higher price for the company's stock. This benefits both management and stockholders, while the higher profits and stock price can be used to finance another merger. This has, indeed, been the path followed by a number of conglomerates in recent years —until investors discovered that these financial manipulations really didn't affect the long-term profitability of the business operations themselves. In addition, there are profits to be made by financial institutions and law firms that manage the mergers. In some cases of large mergers, the fees for their services have ranged upwards to tens of millions of dollars.

Finally, we come to profits themselves. Large mergers of firms in the same industry can bring the market power that eliminates or dampens competition and brings extranormal, monopolistic profits. This temptation is always present, for one characteristic of monopoly positions is higher-than-normal profits.

Beyond these immediate causes of the merger movements, there is another and perhaps even more significant underlying cause: the need for economic planning. A modern industrial product is a highly complex item, whether it is an automobile, a jet aircraft, a computer, or a radio. Its complexity requires that a very large number of raw materials and semifinished products be brought together at exactly the right point in time and space to assemble the finished product. The automobile assembly line, for example, has a series of other assembly lines feeding into it such items as engines, transmissions, steering assemblies, wheels, and so on all the way back to the fabrication of steel sheets and castings in steel mills and foundries. The market system is a wonderful mechanism for coordinating the flow of all the inputs, for it enables the firm to buy what it needs at the going price to assure the availability of all the necessary components. But the market has its flaws. Delivery schedules may be missed and gaps may develop in the pipelines. If that were to happen, the huge assembly plant might have to close down (as it does nowadays if there is a strike in a small supplying plant), at considerable cost to the enterprise and its employees. These uncertainties could be overcome by holding substantial inventories of all the inputs, but the capital tied up there is also expensive. With proper coordination and a continuing, planned flow of inputs controlled by the enterprise itself, these higher costs of down time and large inventories can be cut or eliminated. The enterprise moves back to control its supplying plants and forward to control its distributors, creating a system of continuous flow from raw materials to retail sale under its own management. Planning replaces the market as the coordinating mechanism.

Note the importance of large capital investment in this relationship. Costly assembly facilities, like the automobile assembly plant, make down time expensive. Where that is not the case, as in home building, delays due to imperfect coordination are much less expensive and integration of operations much less necessary.

Once a firm is integrated back to its suppliers and forward to its distributors to keep a complex, expensive plant operating efficiently, it becomes strongly concerned about the stability of its markets and prices. The integrated system requires assured outlets for the product at prices stable enough to form the basis for production planning that may take years from product design to market. Add to that the large capital investment required, and all of the elements for a push to achieve market power are present. The economic risks associated with the use of a complex, expensive technology in a market system introduce the true technological imperative: an attempt to achieve coordination through planning rather than the market, which leads in turn to large size of firms and a drive to achieve control over markets and prices. This trend is not present to an equal extent in all sectors of the economy. It is found most strongly in the technologically advanced sectors, however, which helps to explain why they are the habitat of big enterprise.[3]

Well, can competition survive? Probably not, at least in the form implied by the economic theory of competitive markets. The economic costs of competition when expensive, single-purpose equipment is used; the profits to be made from mergers, the attraction of extranormal profits; the need for long-range planning—all of these factors point to a natural evolution of giant enterprise with significant market power. The history of the past hundred years confirms that analysis, and the analysis helps to explain the history. Nor does the growth of big enterprise seem to be halted or slowing down. There is probably more to come.

---

[3] The contribution to production planning made by economic stability helps us understand why big business needs big government—notwithstanding some vocal protests. Government policies designed to promote full employment and economic growth produce the lush natural environment in which the large modern corporation can flourish. Other types of firms can flourish, too, but the big enterprise requires it.

THE FINANCIAL SECTOR

Economic concentration in the economy's financial sector is difficult to estimate. It has been less studied than in the industrial sector, and the tendency of large financial institutions toward secrecy about their affairs has made systematic data difficult to obtain. Nevertheless, a considerable and mounting body of information indicates the existence of a high degree of concentration of control of the nation's financial assets.

Commercial banking shows approximately the same oligopolistic structure I as industry does. Although there are some 13,000 commercial banks in the United States, the 100 largest hold about 47 percent of all deposits and the 10 largest about 20 percent. Concentration on a national scale has declined somewhat in the last quarter century, however; in 1940 the 100 largest commercial banks held 57 percent of all deposits in commercial banks.

Most cities have high concentration ratios in banking. The average four-bank concentration ratio for the 17 metropolitan areas with deposits of over $1 billion was 68.5 percent in 1966. Smaller cities had even greater concentration. The 21 small metropolitan areas with deposits under $50 million had two-bank concentration ratios of 71.9 percent.

Insurance is the second most important sector of the financial markets, for II insurance companies draw a very large portion of the economy's savings and are a principal source of investment funds for housing and for industry. Their total assets amount to about $190 billion, and they generate some $11 billion of new funds annually.

The degree of concentration in insurance is even greater than in commercial banking, but has remained largely unchanged in the last twenty years. The twenty largest life insurance companies (by far the most important segment of the insurance business) hold about three-fourths of all U.S. life insurance company assets (which totaled over $188 billion in 1968). The fifty largest hold some 87 percent, although there are over 1,500 life insurance companies in all.

In the years since World War II, two other financial institutions have moved to positions of importance in financial markets. These are mutual funds and III pension funds. A mutual fund is an investment fund in which an individual buys shares. The money is then invested in securities or other assets, and dividends or other income of the fund are either reinvested or paid out to the owners. The mutual fund is usually managed by a separate, privately owned company that is paid a fee for its managerial services based on the amount of assets in the fund. Mutual funds have grown rapidly. Their ownership of securities reached $53 billion in 1969, rising from a little over $1 billion in 1949 and about 10 billion in 1959. The assets of all mutual funds are rising by about $5 billion annually.

Pension funds invest the assets of private retirement programs. Most of them IV are managed by the trust departments of commercial banks, thereby adding further to the economic clout of those institutions. In 1969, private pension funds in the U.S. owned some $80 billion of assets, including $40 billion of securities. Their holdings are rising at a rate of about $5 billion annually. The growth of pension funds is expected to accelerate sharply in the near future. They are expected to have total assets of about $200 billion by the early 1980s and will be generating an annual flow of $10 billion of new funds each year. These are only the private funds: public pension funds of federal, state, and local governments are equally as large.

Bank-managed trust departments are also an important element in financial markets. They manage assets held in trust for others, also for a fee. In 1969, the assets under their management, excluding pension funds and including only their private trust accounts, totaled about $125 billion.

The amount of capital controlled by these financial intermediaries is enormous. We sum it up in Table 30–3 by listing the assets at their disposal.

TABLE 30–3
Assets of Primary Financial Institutions, 1969
(Billions of Dollars)

Institution	Amount
Commercial banks	$ 600
Insurance companies	190
Mutual funds	53
Private pension funds	80
Bank trust funds	125
Total	$1,048

Although the concentration of control of these huge assets is difficult to measure exactly, these institutions make up a relatively cohesive financial community with many informal and sometimes formal ties binding them together. Commercial banks run the bank trust funds and manage most of the private pension funds. Many insurance companies are moving into the business of managing and selling mutual funds. Many banks, through their trust departments and the pension funds they manage, control large blocks of their own stock. Finally, there are many instances of interlocking directorates between large financial firms and between financial firms and other large business enterprises.

CORPORATE INTEREST GROUPS

The only comprehensive study of informal groupings of corporations in the U.S. economy was done for the year 1935. It was limited to the 250 largest corporations of that era, and showed that at least eight "more or less clearly defined interest groups," including 106 of the 250 with nearly two-thirds of the combined assets, could be identified through interlocking directorates alone.

Two clustered around large New York banking interests. By far the largest involved the greatest investment bank of that era, J. P. Morgan and Co., and the First National Bank of New York, together with 39 of the 250 largest corporations. The second largest was built around another investment bank, Kuhn, Loeb and Co., and included 15 major corporations.

banking

Three interest groups were constructed from the firms dominated by family interests, the Rockefellers (mainly in oil), the Mellons (companies headquartered primarily in Pittsburgh), and the Du Ponts (chemicals, GM, and related firms). The other three were loose groupings of companies related to each other through important banks in Boston, Cleveland, and Chicago.

family

Although the economy has changed quite sharply since the years of the Great Depression, and firms have grown, changed, and merged, and whole new industries have appeared, nevertheless the pattern of corporate interest groups continues. The membership and structure of any one group may shift, however. For example, when Richard K. Mellon died in 1970 his obituaries noted that the Mellon family still owned dominating interests in the following major corporations (assets in parentheses):

Gulf Oil Corp.	($8.1 billion)
Aluminum Corp. of America	($1.5 billion)
Mellon National Bank	($4.9 billion)
Koppers Co.	($0.5 billion)
Carborundum Co.	($0.3 billion)
General Reinsurance Co.	($0.3 billion)

The family also held, in addition to their interests in these firms with total assets of $15.6 billion, a substantial interest in the First Boston Corporation, an important investment bank associated with a number of large firms headquartered in New England, and Richard Mellon himself owned a $20 million investment in the stock of General Motors Corporation.

The interest groups centering around banking interests also remain. A 1968 investigation by a subcommittee of the House Committee on Banking and Currency showed that the Morgan banking group, much changed and transformed, is still strong. It is based now on the Morgan Guaranty Trust Co. of New York, whose commercial bank deposits of $7.3 billion make it one of the large New York banks, but by no means the largest. Its trust department, however, manages assets of some $17 billion. In these trust accounts it holds 5 percent or more of the common stock of 72 corporations. Its officers are on the boards of directors of more than 100 companies. Together these companies in which Morgan Guaranty has an important investment or managerial position have total assets of almost $30 billion. Repeat this pattern many times over on the same or smaller scale through the First National City Bank or Chase Manhattan Bank, the Bank of America, and the large banks in Chicago, Cleveland, Detroit, Pittsburgh, Boston, and Philadelphia, and we begin to see the way in which financial ties can bind corporations into informal groups through their financial affiliations.

INTERLOCKING DIRECTORATES

One of the most important ways in which large corporations are related to each other is through a common, or interlocking, body of directors. It is illegal for a member of the board of directors of one large firm to also sit as a board member of a competing firm. But it is not illegal for board members of two competing firms to be members of the board of a third noncompeting firm. Thus, it would be illegal if Mr. *A* were on the board of both General Electric Co. and Westinghouse Electric Corp. But it would not be illegal for Mr. *A* and Mr. *B* each to be on the board of the First National City Bank of New York, with Mr. *A* also on the General Electric board and Mr. *B* on the Westinghouse board. These indirect interlocking directorates are quite common, providing meeting places for common interests and serving to dampen rivalries by creating common interests among men who are supposed to manage competing interests.

It is difficult to estimate, or underestimate, the significance of these informal relationships. For example, in the electrical equipment industry a complicated system of interlocks tied the four chief firms together—General Electric, Westinghouse, Western Electric, RCA—through other industrial firms and financial institutions, and tied the large companies with smaller firms in the industry and with potential customers, suppliers, and competitors. This was the industry that, after a long history of incidents of price fixing, developed the greatest illegal price-fixing and market-sharing conspiracy in our history during the 1950s and early 1960s. The legal informal ties and the illegal conspiracies may have had no connection whatsoever, and interlocking directorates do not necessarily lead to violation of the law, but one is not surprised when the two occur in the same industry.

The Federal Trade Commission has documented the wide prevalence of interlocking directorates throughout American industry and the ties they create between industrial and financial firms.[4] Hardly any large-scale manufacturing industry is free of them, and almost all of the large firms are involved. According to the FTC, interlocking directorates

Tend to limit or eliminate competition.

May forestall the development of competition.

May give rise to communities of interest and create a united front against any who threaten habitual relationships or established preeminence.

Evoke preferential treatment in the distribution of materials in short supply.

May . . . create preferential access to market outlets.

May establish a vertical relation that assures adequate credit to favored companies and a withholding of credit and capital from their competitors.

Interlocking directorates are one of the main ways in which intimate ties between nominally independent firms are created and sustained. They help to formalize other ties based on customer-supplier relationships, credit and

---

[4] *Report of the Federal Trade Commission on Interlocking Directorates* (Washington: U.S. Government Printing Office, 1951).

other financial connections, and stock ownership that maintain a subtle web of relationships among the group of large firms that dominate much of the American economy.

TRADE ASSOCIATIONS

When firms are few, it is relatively easy to achieve cooperative behavior and community of interest. When they are numerous the task is more difficult. Some type of formal organization is necessary. In the American economy that need has been met by formation of trade associations.

> *"People of the same trade seldom meet together even for merriment and diversion, but the conversation ends in a conspiracy against the public, or in some contrivance to raise prices." (Adam Smith,* An Enquiry Into the Nature and Causes of the Wealth of Nations, 1776.)

A trade association is an organization through which firms in an industry or trade combine to further their common interests. The antitrust laws prohibit them from engaging in practices that restrict competition and most of them have never been charged with illegal activities. However, many of them do things that tend to create common patterns of behavior among their members. Among these activities are promotion of common cost-accounting methods (which tend to create a common cost basis for pricing); reporting of prices (which tends to identify and isolate price cutters); and reporting of sales and inventories (which can promote market sharing and restriction of output). The danger is that these relatively harmless activities will pass by imperceptible stages into illegal conspiracies. Over 200 legal actions have been brought against various associations for price fixing, division of markets, allocation of customers, and restriction of output.

The most important function of trade associations is their political activities. They are among the most important lobbyists with government administrators and legislatures at all levels of government. When firms in an industry wish to promote or hinder legislation, appropriations, and administrative rulings, the contacts with government are usually carried out by the industry's trade association.

ROLE OF THE STOCKHOLDER

The stockholders of large corporations have become little more than risk takers, delegating their functions as managers to corporation boards of directors. Although they remain the legal owners of the enterprise, they no longer control the making of policy.

This separation of ownership and control, first pointed out by Thorstein Veblen in his *Theory of Business Enterprise* (1902) and documented by Adolf Berle and Gardner Means in *The Modern Corporation and Private Property* (1932), rests upon very wide dispersal of stock ownership. A giant corporation like American Telephone and Telegraph has some 550 million shares of common stock outstanding, held by over 3.5 million shareholders, no one of which owns as much as 100,000 shares. Most shareholdings are under 1,000 shares. If a shareholder disagrees with the management's policies, he can protest or even vote his handful of shares against the management in the annual shareholder's meeting. But his only effective action is to sell his shares. He has a financial role to play, but he has no avenue to policy decisions. Risk taking, yes. Control, no. The effect of wide dispersal of ownership, the difficulties in making one's voice heard, plus the ease with which securities can be bought and sold, generally leaves management in command.

Management's independence is further strengthened by its ability to use profits and other internal flows of cash for investment purposes. Expansion can, and does, come largely from profits and depreciation allowances for large firms; some three-fourths of all investment spending by the 500 largest non-financial corporations comes from that source. This pattern may well benefit the stockholders in the long run if it raises the value of their shares enough to compensate them for reduced dividends. But whether they like it or not, they have nothing to say about the matter.

In spite of their large degree of independence of financial markets, corporate managements are nevertheless influenced by the financial sector. Large family stock holdings can be voted as a controlling bloc in some firms. The combined holdings of bank-managed trust and pension funds, mutual funds, and insurance companies, and their decisions about buying, holding or selling, affect the price of the company's stock and the financial community's evaluation of the company and its management. Continued bad performance may even attract a takeover effort by a conglomerate or outside financial group, which, if successful, may result in the ousting of the old management. Complete freedom of action is not held by any large corporation's management. But it is the financial markets and its banks, funds, and insurance companies, and not in most cases the nominal owners, that create the boundaries within which management must act.

THE BUSINESS ELITE

The business leaders of the rather small number of large firms that dominate the American economy (200, 250, 500, 750?) necessarily compose a small group. At the most it comprises a cadre of perhaps five thousand to ten thousand persons: top executives, members of the boards of directors, partners in big law and accounting firms, chief executives of important financial institutions. It is a tiny fraction of the total adult population.

As a group, the business elite comes predominantly from an urban, white, Protestant, upper or upper-middle income background. Recent studies of the social and economic characteristics of post–World War II business leaders by W. Lloyd Warner and C. Wright Mills, building on studies of earlier periods by Frank Taussig and William Miller show very few immigrants or sons of immigrants, small numbers from farm or worker or lower white-collar backgrounds, relatively few Catholics and Jews, and no blacks. About 10 percent of them inherited their top positions by moving into family-dominated companies. About 5 percent were entrepreneurs who built their own companies. Some 10-15 percent were professional men, mostly lawyers, who moved into top business positions after professional success. The majority of business leaders, however, some 70 percent, moved to top positions by working up through the business hierarchy. This is a much greater proportion than in the past. Seventy years ago the entrepreneurs and family-connected managers were far more important (68 percent), the career executive much less important (18 percent), and the proportion of lawyers and other professionals was about the same.

These data suggest that the business elite is a relatively open one. It brings in recruits from outside the already existing elite group, and this tendency appears to be increasing. The chief source of recruits is the system of higher education. The business elite has always had more education than the average, and today that is more true than ever. The educational system is a primary screening mechanism and this fact helps to explain why so many of the business elite are from upper and upper-middle income groups. They tend to be drawn heavily from the Ivy League colleges (from which most of the managers from "old wealth" families graduate) and from the large state universities (from which most of the career executives get their educations).

This first level of screening at the college level is supplemented by executive training programs and on-the-job training. There the aspiring top manager is indoctrinated with the business point of view and the ideology of management, there he learns to "fit in" with those already at the top, and there he develops the "good judgment" that top management requires. Since advancement depends on the judgment of those already at the top, a premium is placed on development of viewpoints and styles of life that already prevail. As Mills put it, "In personal manner and political view, in social ways and business style, he must be like those who are already in, and upon whose judgments his own success rests." The business elite is a self-perpetuating and self-selecting group which develops a common set of values, an accepted mode of behavior, and an unspoken but recognizable set of goals.

Its value system, in particular, stresses the desirability of wealth, both for the individual and the nation, and accepts as generally beneficent the institutions of private property and the national state. Indeed, strengthening and preservation of those institutions seems to be a fundamental point of agreement among the business elite, irrespective of individual political persuasion.

STRUCTURE OF ECONOMIC POWER

The American economy is dominated by giant corporations, particularly in those sectors to which we look for the sources of high and rising standards of living and technological progress. If there is any trend, it is toward increased concentration, primarily through mergers rather than internal growth of firms. The pattern of oligopoly that prevails is supplemented by the existence of informal ties that lead to community of interest between firms in the same industry and groupings of firms in unrelated industries. Throughout this system the principal financial intermediaries exert a growing influence. Control is not in the hands of ordinary stockholders, but rests instead with a business elite of executives, lawyers, financiers, and technical experts who share a common set of beliefs and attitudes.

This structure is a far cry from that envisaged by the pure theory of competitive markets. We should not expect it to function in the same fashion as the economy of the theoretical firm in a theoretically competitive environment. Nor does it, in fact. In the two succeeding chapters we shall analyze its performance, first by examining the general cases of monopoly and imperfect competition and then by taking a closer look at oligopolistic markets. The last chapter in this part of the book will then examine the relationships between government and business that have developed in an economy dominated by oligopolies. We shall be dealing throughout with the problem of economic power—how it is used, its effects, and how it might be brought under control.

Summary

Although they are relatively small in number, large corporations have a dominant and growing position in the U.S. economy. That position was attained largely by mergers rather than by internal growth of individual firms. The dominant pattern in industry is not monopoly, but oligopoly, with many important industries being characterized by a leading group of large firms in which a single firm is significantly larger than the other big ones. These positions of dominance are sustained by barriers to new firms, chiefly product differentiation with large selling costs, and large-scale production with large capital requirements. Other barriers can include patent control and control over raw materials.

The financial sector also shows a significant degree of concentration in banking, insurance, and control over trust and pension funds.

The big business community is bound together in several ways, chiefly through corporate interest groups, interlocking directorates, and trade associations, in addition to the financial ties that function through the relatively highly concentrated financial sector.

Stockholders have relatively little control over the policies of large corporations. Rather, control rests very heavily with business management itself. The business elite is a relatively open one, but it is a self-selecting and self-perpetuating group that passes on a business ideology from one generation to the next. The system as a whole is a far cry from the purely competitive model, with economic power and control over economic decisions managed by people rather than through the self-adjusting market.

Key Concepts

Monopoly. Literally, a single seller. Applied to an industry in which one firm supplies the entire output of a commodity.

Oligopoly. Literally, few sellers. Applied to an industry dominated by a small number of firms. In a balanced oligopoly, the leading firms are approximately the same size. An unbalanced oligopoly has a single firm that is considerably larger than the other leading firms.

Concentration ratio. The proportion of value added by the largest firms in an industry. Four-firm concentration ratios are the ones most commonly used.

Corporate interest group Several corporations allied with each other via stock ownership, interlocking directorates, or financial ties.

Interlocking directorates. A situation in which an individual is on the board of directors of several different firms. Interlocks can be direct (one person on the board of more than one firm) or indirect (two different directors of one firm are members of the board of a third firm).

Trade association. An organization of firms in the same line of business organized to further the common interests of its members.

Separation of ownership and control. The situation in many large corporations, in which management is largely independent of stockholder control, largely because of wide dispersal of stock ownership.

When the average person buys or sells common stock listed on the New York Stock Exchange, he trades at the market price prevailing at the time of his transaction. He has no control over the price. Rather, he decides only whether he will buy or sell, and if so, how much. This condition is characteristic of market competition.

The New York Stock Exchange is *not* an example of perfect competition, however. If a large mutual fund wishes to buy or sell stock in large quantities, say 400,000 shares of a stock in which normal trading is about 25,000 shares daily, that single transaction can have a decided impact on the prevailing price. A large purchase will pull the price up, while a large sale would push it down. This condition is characteristic of imperfect markets: the seller or buyer can influence the market price.

THE DEMAND CURVE FACED BY THE FIRM

These two conditions define the fundamental difference between perfectly and imperfectly competitive markets. In one case the seller can sell all he wishes to sell at the market price. In the other, the seller is able to sell more only if he reduces his price. If he wants a higher price he will have to accept a smaller quantity of sales.

The difference can be shown graphically by drawing typical demand curves as they are faced by sellers in the two circumstances, shown in Figures 31-1 and 31-2.

AVERAGE AND MARGINAL REVENUE UNDER IMPERFECT COMPETITION

When the demand curve for a firm's product slopes downward to the right, as in Figure 31-2, marginal revenues no longer coincide with average revenues. This condition can be illustrated (Table 31-1) with a hypothetical example in which the selling price falls as the quantity sold is increased.

When the firm sells 10 units the price per unit (average revenue) is $25. Total sales revenue is $250. But for the firm to sell 11 units instead of 10, the price would have to be reduced to $24 per unit for each of the 11 units sold. Total sales revenue would rise to $264, an increase (marginal revenue) of $14. Increasing the quantity sold to 12 would require a further price reduction to $23 per unit, generating total sales revenue of $276 and a marginal revenue of $12.

Monopoloid Markets: The Fundamentals

31

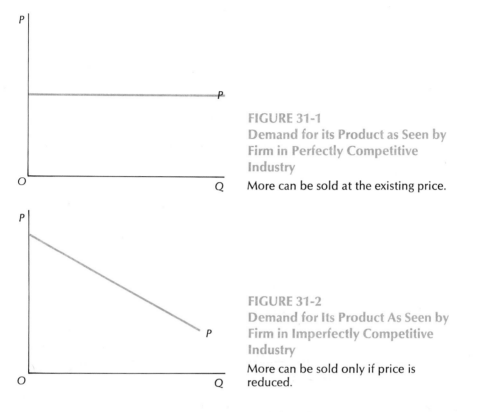

FIGURE 31-1
Demand for its Product as Seen by Firm in Perfectly Competitive Industry

More can be sold at the existing price.

FIGURE 31-2
Demand for Its Product As Seen by Firm in Imperfectly Competitive Industry

More can be sold only if price is reduced.

TABLE 31–1
Price and Marginal Revenue Under Imperfect Competition

Quantity Sold	Price (Average Revenue)	Total Revenue	Marginal Revenue
10	$25	$250	$14
11	24	264	12
12	23	276	10
13	22	286	8
14	21	294	6
15	20	300	

This example is only another illustration of the basic arithmetic relationship, explained in Chapter 24, that when an average quantity is falling, the corresponding marginal quantity lies below it. It is particularly applicable to the analysis of imperfect markets, however, for they are characterized by the phenomenon of falling average revenues for the individual firm. That characteristic relationship is a feature of all the analytical models of imperfect markets. We illustrate it in Figure 31-3, using the illustration shown in Table 31-1.

The implications of a downward sloping demand curve for the firm are im-

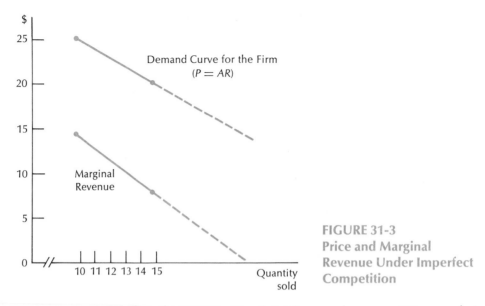

FIGURE 31-3
Price and Marginal
Revenue Under Imperfect
Competition

portant. It means that the results found in the purely competitive market *cannot* be achieved in an imperfectly competitive one. Why that is true will become evident when we examine two limiting cases: monopoly (a single seller of a product) and monopolistic competition (many sellers, but all face a downward sloping demand curve). For the present, it is sufficient to say that the downward-sloping demand curve makes it impossible to achieve the triple equilibrium of market, firm, and industry characterized by pure competition.

MONOPOLY

The simplest case of imperfect markets is that of a single seller. The demand curve he faces will be the same as the market demand curve for the product, and it will slope downward to the right (Figure 31-4). The monopolist is the industry, and the market demand curve is the firm's demand curve.

The monopolist will, of course, have cost conditions similar to those of any firm (except that he may not feel the same pressure toward highly efficient

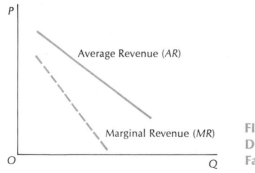

FIGURE 31-4
Demand Conditions
Faced by a Monopolist

operations that are felt by the competitive firm). In the short run, with his existing plant and equipment, average costs for the monopolist will fall, reach a low point, and then rise. Marginal costs will rise to cross the average cost curve at its lowest point, as in Figure 31-5.

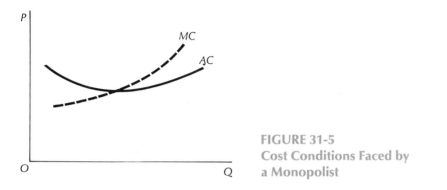

FIGURE 31-5
Cost Conditions Faced by
a Monopolist

What level of output and price will the monopolist choose? We can start with the assumption that he seeks to maximize his profits. He isn't worried about potential competitors because he controls all necessary patents, or owns some essential raw materials, or has colluded with potential competitors to exclude them from the market. These arrangements free him to concentrate single-mindedly on maximizing his gains.

Profit maximization requires that marginal cost MC equal marginal revenue MR. This is true for the monopolist, with his downward-sloping demand curves, just as it is true for the competitive firm with its horizontal demand curves. As long as marginal revenue MR is greater than marginal costs MC as output and sales increase, profits will rise. As soon as MC moves above MR, total profits will begin to fall. Profits will be greatest when MR = MC. When the profit-maximizing monopolist compares his cost and revenue conditions, he will be able to determine the unique level of output and price at which MC = MR and at which profit is greatest. That situation is illustrated in Figure 31-6. MC = MR at output Q_1 with price P_1 (remember that the demand curve AR tells the monopolist the price he can get for any level of output).

Pause for a moment to check your understanding of this analysis. Why does the monopolist select the output at which MC = MR? Why not where AR = AC, or where AR = MC? When he has selected output Q_1, why does he market it at a price equal to AR? Why not a lower price equal to AC? The answers are to be found in the explanations above, so be sure you know them before going on.

Monopoly Profits

The price and level of output fixed by the profit-maximizing monopolist in this example enables him to earn profits higher than normal profits. We have defined normal profits as those necessary to provide incentive for producers

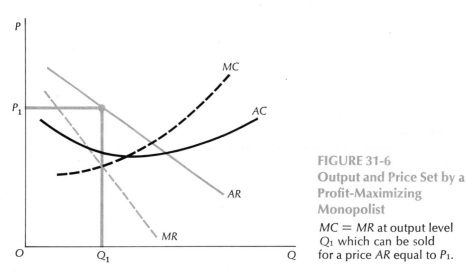

FIGURE 31-6
Output and Price Set by a Profit-Maximizing Monopolist

$MC = MR$ at output level Q_1 which can be sold for a price AR equal to P_1.

to continue producing. They are included in the average costs pictured in the diagrams. Whenever the price of a good exceeds its average costs of production, extranormal profits are being made (see Figure 31-7). This situation exists in the case of the profit-maximizing monopolist.

Extranormal profits

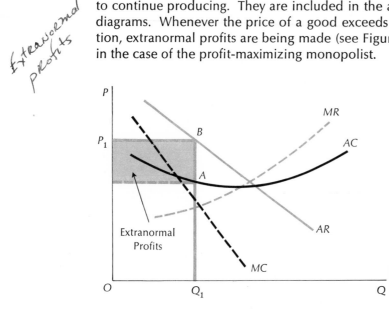

FIGURE 31-7
Extranormal Monopoly Profits

At output Q_1 and price P_1, cost per unit is Q_1A, which includes a normal profit. Revenue per unit is Q_1B. The difference AB is extranormal profit per unit. Since the number of units sold is equal to OQ_1, the total extranormal profit is $AB \times OQ_1$. It is shown by the shaded rectangle.

In a competitive industry the lure of extranormal profits would draw new firms into the industry, bringing prices down and reducing profits. The monopolist does not have to face this trauma, however. We have endowed him with the means of keeping competitors out, and where he has that power he is free to maximize his profits without interference. We shall shortly examine the situation in which the monopolist does have to worry about potential competition (or enforcement of antitrust laws) and show how he is likely to adapt to those horrors.

Monopoly and Competition Compared

If we compare the results of monopoly with those of competition, the evils of monopoly stand out quite clearly. Compare the equilibrium of the profit-maximizing monopolist (Figure 31-8) and a competitive industry made up of individual firms in equilibrium (Figure 31-9). To make the comparisons valid we assume the same levels of cost for both. The firm in the monopolized market charges a higher price than the price in the competitive market $(P_m > P_c)$. Its cost of production per unit of output is higher: in Figure 31-8, AC at output Q_m is higher than AC at output q_c in Figure 31-9. And the monopolist makes extranormal profits while the competitive firm does not. Furthermore, if we were to consider the capacity output of the firm to be that level of output at which AC is minimized, it is clear that the monopoly firm could increase its output beyond Q_m and produce at lower cost per unit.

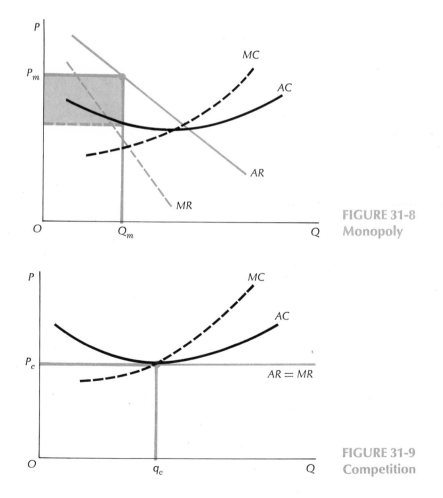

FIGURE 31-8
Monopoly

FIGURE 31-9
Competition

In this sense it has built wasted output capacity into its plant and equipment.[1]

Note that by shifting the relationships between costs and revenues for the monopolist a variety of special situations can be created in which extranormal profits are eliminated or wasted capacity removed. These curiosa are of technical interest to theoreticians, and should not obscure the general case pictured in Figure 31-8. The crucial point is that in the long run a monopolist can preserve extranormal profits and inefficient levels of production indefinitely, while they are soon eliminated in a competitive industry.

Monopoly, furthermore, results in a price that differs from costs at the margin ($P > MC$). It is impossible for benefits to consumers at the margin to equal costs to producers at the margin. The key requirement for maximization of welfare cannot be achieved.

The Monopolist and Potential Competition

Few monopolists are ever in a position that enables them to forget completely about potential competition. Even the owner of an exclusive patent must fear the development of a new technology that achieves the same results as his. The firm that controls its sources of raw materials has to consider the possibility of newly discovered resources.

These considerations can lead a monopolist to depart from the simple profit-maximizing strategy and move to one designed to limit potential competition. He will increase output and reduce price in an effort to meet a larger portion of the market demand while accepting lower profits. It is even possible that, at one limit, he will reduce his price and increase his sales so as to earn no more than a normal profit. To the extent that a monopolist is willing to accept lower profits, he will reduce the threat of potential competition. He can also reduce the possibility of prosecution under the antitrust laws with the same strategy.

How far will he go? The logic of the situation tells us that, in extremis and under the imminent threat of a new producer entering the industry, a monopolist may move to prices that eliminate extranormal profits entirely. In that case his position would be that shown in the Figure 31-10.

Monopoly Prices: The Limits

We can now review the limits within which we can expect monopoly prices and output to be established. At one extreme is the high price and low output of the monopolist who single-mindedly pursues the goal of profit maximization. At the other extreme is the lower price and higher output of the monopolist who insures against the threat of potential competition by eliminating any profits above the normal level.

---

[1] A special definition of plant capacity is involved here. The *economic capacity* of a plant is the output level at which AC is at its lowest point. The physical or technological capacity is greater than that output level. Excess capacity exists when the output level is below the one at which AC is minimized. In the discussion that follows, we shall use the word *capacity* to mean economic capacity as defined here.

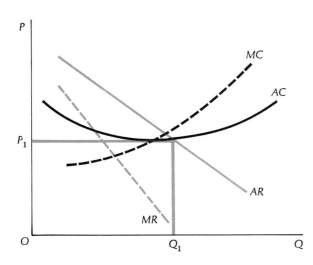

FIGURE 31-10
**Monopoly Pricing
Designed to Forestall
Potential Competition**
Price P_1 and sales of Q_1
eliminate extranormal
profits, for $AR = AC$. At
this price the firm is taking
a loss on its marginal
units $(MC > P)$ and would
probably do so only
under the greatest pressure.
It would be hard to con-
vince management to
increase output beyond the
point where $P = MC$ and
they at least are able to
break even at the margin.

In practice, both considerations—profits and potential competition—are in
the minds of most monopolists. As a result, the price and output selected will
fall between the two limits, the exact locus depending on the relative strength
of the two motives in influencing the monopolist's actions. The economic
analysis cannot provide a specific answer, but only a range within which the
solution will fall.

Nevertheless, one conclusion is evident. The monopoly price will be above
the competitive price, and the level of output will be different.[2] This means
that the optimal welfare results of the competitive case cannot be achieved.
The extent of the departure from that norm is not accurately determinable,
however, because the monopoly solution is indefinite within upper and lower
limits.

We should note, too, that even potential competition can discipline a monopolist to sell more at lower prices than he would if he were fully free to
maximize profits. He probably would not go all the way to the price and output at which $AR = AC$, but he can be expected to move partially in that
direction from the higher price and lower output at which $MR = MC$ and
profits are maximized. The moral is interesting: the threat of competition can
have some influence even when competition itself is absent.

MONOPOLISTIC COMPETITION

Competition between sellers does not necessarily bring about the conditions
needed for perfect competition. Far more common is the case of monopolistic competition, in which there is a substantial number of sellers with each

---

[2] There is one possible case in which the monopoly solution and the competitive solution
coincide: if the monopolist seeks to forestall all potential competition by eliminating extranormal profits, *and* his *AR* curve crosses his *AC* curve at its lowest point. This concurrence
would be accidental, however.

one facing a downward sloping demand curve. It combines some of the features of the competitive model with some of the monopoly model.

The distinguishing feature of monopolistic competition is that each seller would do less business at a higher price, but would not lose all his customers to sellers charging lower prices. Conversely, at a lower price he could increase his sales, but would not take away all the trade from competitors charging more.

Here are some examples of monopolistic competition:

1. Retail gasoline sales. There is considerable competition among retailers, but buyer loyalty to brand names and other intangibles retain customers against lower prices charged by some dealers.
2. Ladies ready-to-wear clothing. Sales competition with large advertising expenditures creates partially protected markets for individual sellers.
3. Retail drugstores. Customary price markups maintain relatively high prices, but entry of new stores pulls profits down to the normal level and maintains considerable excess capacity. Lower prices would mean larger sales per store, and fewer stores.

These three examples taken from many possible ones indicate some of the chief features of monopolistic competition. It can be found almost anywhere, but is especially prevalent in retail trades. One of its characteristics is sales competition through advertising. Sales competition is often associated with the development of brand names designed to obtain consumer loyalty to the product of a specific firm, even though the product may be the same as the product of another firm or insignificantly different. Another important feature is relatively easy entry into the business. This is particularly true of retailing. Ease of entry often leads to many stores in the same line, no one of which makes more than a minimal normal profit and all of which have considerable excess capacity. Finally, much monopolistic competition is characterized by markup pricing, in which a fixed percentage is added to direct costs in order to determine the final selling price to the customer. One effect of markup pricing is to shift competitive practices away from the use of lower prices and toward advertising and other types of sales competition. When that happens the consumer pays higher prices rather than lower ones.

All of these examples of monopolistic competition have one characteristic in common: the firm faces a downward sloping demand curve. If it wished to sell more, prices would have to be reduced. In order to avoid this type of competition, alternatives are sought that will maintain sales in the face of higher prices (brand names, advertising) or that will mute price competition in the whole trade (markup pricing).

Monopolistic competition is a complex phenomenon. In analyzing it we will first take the simple case of a few firms without sales competition or collusion, in which firms seek to maximize profits. Next, we will show what happens when entry into the industry or trade is unrestricted. This second step is the essential part of the theory. We then move to two refinements: selling costs and markup pricing.

Monopolistic Competition with Restricted Entry

When there is a single seller of a product, the firm's demand curve is the same as the market demand curve. If several additional firms enter the market, each will get a share. Total demand will be divided among them. Furthermore, the demand curve facing any one of the sellers will be more elastic than that in the market as a whole. This is true because a higher price will lose customers to other sellers in the same market as well as to other products entirely. And a lower price will draw trade from other sellers as well as money that otherwise would be spent on other products. As additional firms enter a monopolized market, therefore, the firm's demand curve will shift in two ways. First, it will move to the left as its sales fall. Second, the slope will diminish. Figure 31-11 shows what happens.

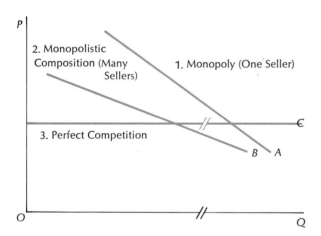

FIGURE 31-11
The Firm's Demand Curve as New Firms Enter a Formerly Monopolized Market
The monopolist's demand curve is shown at A. As additional sellers enter the market, the demand curve for any one will move into the intermediate area B. If enough firms enter, the industry can become perfectly competitive, with each firm having a horizontal demand curve C.

In the case of monopolistic competition, if we assume that each firm seeks maximum profits, the results are analogous to those of the profit-maximizing monopolist, with the exception that the firm's demand curve is almost sure to lie in a position that entails excess production capacity.

Monopolistic Competition with Free Entry

The extranormal profits earned by the firm in the restricted entry case, illustrated in Figure 31-12, will continue to attract additional firms into the industry or trade. If that should happen, the individual firm's demand curve will continue to shift downward and become flatter, approaching more closely the horizontal demand curve of the perfectly competitive industry. The individual firms may differentiate their products by using brand names, advertising, and

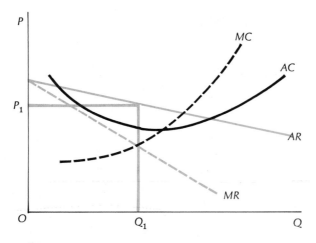

FIGURE 31-12
Monopolistic Competition with Restricted Entry
The firm's demand curve has shifted downward and become flatter than the monopolist's demand curve. But there are still extranormal profits; prices are higher than the perfectly competitive level and output is below the firm's capacity (defined as the output at which $MC = AC$).

creating customer loyalty. As more firms enter, however, the shifting locus of the firm's demand curve will ultimately eliminate extranormal profits. This will occur when the AR curve moves to a position tangent to the AC curve. At this stage the profit maximizing firm's position will be as in Figure 31-13.

This analysis shows that "competition," as it is usually understood, is not sufficient to bring about maximization of welfare. Wherever market imperfections exist, whether because there are not enough sellers or because sellers

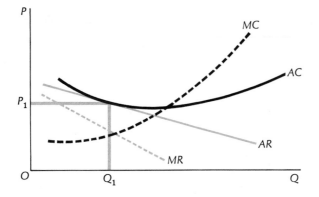

FIGURE 31-13
Monopolistic Competition with Free Entry
Extranormal profits are gone $AR = AC$, profits are maximized $MR = MC$, but because $MC = AC$ the firm has excess capacity and the price is higher than it would be if the industry were perfectly competitive. Note: Why does $MC = MR$ at the same sales level at which $AR = AC$? The answer is derived from the mathematics involved. The AR curve is tangent to the AC curve at quantity Q. The mathematics of marginal, total, and average quantities is such that at the point of tangency of two average curves, the marginal quantities are the same. Always remember to draw this diagram in that way. The MC and MR curves intersect directly below the point of tangency of AR and AC.

high prices
excess capacity

differentiate themselves from each other through brands, trademarks, advertising, or similar devices, there is a persistent tendency for excess capacity and
relatively higher prices than necessary to prevail. Prices remain above marginal
costs, and it is impossible to equate benefits and costs at the margin. This is
true even if there are no barriers to entry, sellers act completely independently,
and firms try to maximize their profits.

Selling Costs

The analysis of monopolistic competition is not changed significantly by the
use of advertising to create product differentiation and customer loyalty. The
same results will prevail, except that the firm's cost curves will be shifted upward by the amount of the selling costs, as shown in Figure 31-14. Shifting the

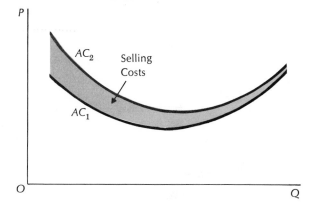

advertising - other selling costs

FIGURE 31-14
Selling Costs Shift Cost
Curves Upward

Selling costs shift the AC
curve upward from AC_1
to AC_2, drawn here to show
reduced selling costs per
unit as Q increases.

average cost curve upward merely results in a different locus of the price and
quantity sold by the firm, whether it is the restricted entry or free entry case.
Since costs have risen, the ultimate cost to the buyer will be increased.[3]

MARKUP PRICING

Markup pricing (sometimes called "full cost" pricing) is an interesting variant
of monopolistic competition, in which sellers emphasize survival rather than
profit maximization. It is by far the most widespread trade practice in retailing. It reduces price competition among sellers to the "loss leader" type and
emphasizes "ethical" business practices and "rules of the game" that help

---

[3] Propaganda from the advertising industry contends that advertising can enlarge the market
for a product, making possible economies of large-scale production and bringing lower prices
to the consumer. Unfortunately, there are no known cases in which that has occurred. It is
possible for advertising to increase the sales of one firm's output (Ford cars, Salem cigarettes,
for example) but all of the voluminous research devoted to the effects of advertising cannot
document a single case in which the market for a product (automobiles, cigarettes) has been
enlarged, except very temporarily. Moral: Don't believe the wolves when they tell you how
pleasant it is to be devoured.

discount houses arise out of markup pricing

small business firms survive in what otherwise might be a cost-cutting jungle. However, in the long run it leads to the appearance of the "discount house" type of large retailer that drives the small retail store to the wall anyway.

A retailer usually adds a percentage of the wholesale price to the cost of an item in order to arrive at his selling price. For example, an economics text-book may cost the bookstore $6.00 when the store buys it from the publisher. The usual markup is 25 percent for textbooks. The store will therefore add $1.50 (25 percent of $6) to its cost, arriving at a selling price to the student of $7.50. The added $1.50 is expected to cover all other costs plus a normal profit.[4]

The objective of markup pricing is to achieve a price satisfactory to the sellers. This inevitably means one that is above the lowest point on the typical firm's average cost curve. Any lower price would not provide the higher-cost seller with the normal profits minimally satisfactory to him. The initial situation, then, would be that shown in Figure 31-15.

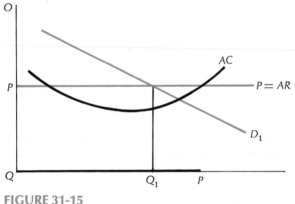

FIGURE 31-15
Markup Pricing: Stage I

The price, established by the markup over the wholesale price, is at *P*. The firm's sloping demand curve D_1 then determines how much the firm will sell at that price Q_1. In this case the extranormal profit per unit is the difference between *P* and *AC* at output Q_1. The *MC* and *MR* curves are not drawn because firms using markup pricing are not profit maximizers in the sense that the perfectly competitive firm is. Those curves are not relevant to its decisions.

[4] Markups are often quoted in terms of the price to the customer. Thus the textbook markup is usually stated as 20 percent, meaning 20 percent of the retail price, which is equal to 25 percent of the wholesale price. Some other customary markups are listed below:

Item	Percentage of Retail Price	Percentage of Wholesale Price
Paperback books	10	11.1
Other nontextbooks	40	66⅔
Men's clothing	50	100
New automobiles	20–25	25–33⅓
Jewelry	50–90	100–900

The extranormal profits earned in Stage I will attract additional sellers, all of them following the customary markup price because it is the easiest course to follow and it provides extranormal profits as well. There is no reason to rock the boat and get other sellers mad. As new firms enter, the demand curve for any one firm will shift to the right and become more elastic, until the extranormal profits are gone and there is no longer any incentive for new sellers to appear. This temporary equilibrium is shown as Stage II in Figure 31-16.

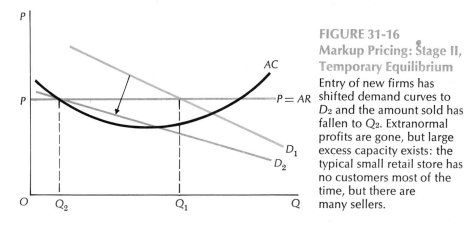

FIGURE 31-16
Markup Pricing: Stage II, Temporary Equilibrium
Entry of new firms has shifted demand curves to D_2 and the amount sold has fallen to Q_2. Extranormal profits are gone, but large excess capacity exists: the typical small retail store has no customers most of the time, but there are many sellers.

Stage II is only temporary, however. A smart operator will realize that if he reduces his price below the customary price he will increase his sales and make extranormal profits, even if he doesn't reduce costs below those of other sellers. This development, shown as Stage III in Figure 31-17, changes the whole situation by bringing in the discount seller. Now another round of entry into the trade starts, this time by discount houses, and the same process

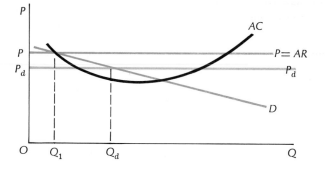

FIGURE 31-17
Markup Pricing: Stage III, The Discount House Appears
The discount seller establishes price P_d, while his "ethical" competitors maintain the old markup price. His sales increase to Q_d while the other sellers who survive make do at sales of Q_1. The discounter is able to make extranormal profits, since his price exceeds his average costs.

of attrition of extranormal profits occurs. But this time it is accompanied by dis-appearance of the older firms that stick to the traditional markups. Ultimately, the results of monopolistic competition with free entry will develop, but not until after several rounds of erosion of markup through successive discount house cuts. The final stage is shown in Figure 31-18.

FIGURE 31-18
Markup Pricing: Final Stage, Long-Run Equilibrium

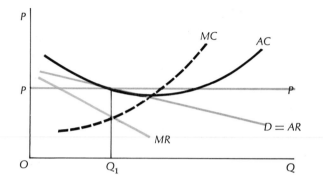

Extranormal profits are gone when the firm's de-mand curve is tangent to the AC curve. We can now show the MC and MR curves, because in that situation MC = MR and profits are maximized. This has oc-curred as a result of the economic processes at work, even though no seller sought that result.

We now know why "fair trade" laws are so popular among retailers. Fair trade laws make it mandatory that sellers adopt the suggested retail price established by a manufacturer of a brand-name article. Those suggested prices embody customary markups and prevent discounting and similar "unethical" practices. Their effect is to protect the higher prices that enable many sellers to survive with just normal profits in the Stage II temporary equilibrium in our analysis of markup pricing.

Most fair trade laws are unenforceable now, because of some key U.S. Supreme Court decisions. Franchising has taken their place, however, in an effort to create both brand-name distinctiveness for the seller rather than the product, and to enforce a fixed markup price on the retail outlets by means of the franchise contract. In the long run, however, the results will be no differ-ent: discount franchisers and independent operators will appear, the older ones will either disappear or meet the competition, and the results of monop-olistic competition with free entry will prevail. Only when the manufacturer can control the retailer's access to the product, as in automobile retailing, do the rounds of discounting fail to appear. In that and similar instances the solution does not go beyond the Stage II temporary equilibrium.

THE EFFECTS OF COMPETITION

The analysis of monopolistic competition and its variants must be a sobering experience for those who uncritically assume that "competition" answers all economic problems. It doesn't. Even in retailing, the sector of the economy in which competition is most prevalent, elements of monopoly are ubiquitous. Almost all retailers face downward sloping demand curves. The result is that the long-run monopolistic competition solution tends to prevail very widely.

Furthermore, the retailer's downward sloping demand curve is largely his own creation, aided and abetted by the manufacturer who seeks to distinguish his product by brand names, trademarks, and advertising. Efforts on the part of manufacturers and retailers to gain more than a normal profit bring about a situation in which it is impossible for the economy as a whole to maximize its welfare. Prices end up higher and output lower than those at which maximum benefits are obtained. Prices diverge from marginal costs. The irony of it all is that the extranormal profits whose quest started the process prove to be ephemeral. In the long run they disappear. Selling costs make the situation even worse: their chief effect is to raise prices to the final buyer even further.

These results are most clearly seen in the analysis of markup pricing. Most retail products are priced that way. Yet it is one of the best examples of how results differ from the intentions of individuals. Sellers who start out by seeking extranormal profits and the shelter that customary prices give to existing firms end up fighting for their very existence. If they survive, they find themselves acting as profit maximizers but making no more than normal profits. Yet the effect on the economy as a whole is far from ideal. Maximum economic efficiency, or getting the greatest net welfare from the available resources, is not achieved.

Summary

Imperfect markets are characterized by a downward sloping demand curve for the firm, which causes marginal revenue to diverge from average revenue. In the case of pure monopoly, even if the monopolist is a profit maximizer, the normal result is a higher price and lower output than in the case of pure competition. In addition, the monopolist gains extranormal profits.

If the monopolist is concerned about forestalling potential competition he will reduce or eliminate his extranormal profits, increasing his output and lowering his price toward the level at which $P = AC$. The price and output will still be different from the purely competitive price in the usual case.

Monopolistic competition with restricted entry brings results similar to those of the pure monopoly case: extranormal profits, high price, and reduced output when compared with pure competition. Even free entry in the monopolistic competition case, which can eliminate extranormal profits, leaves the price and output different from the competitive norm.

Selling costs do not change the basic nature of the result, except that they add to the costs of the firm and shift the resultant price and output.

Markup pricing, which is very common where monopolistic competition is found, is an interesting variation on the same theme, and again illustrates the point that the downward sloping demand curve prevents the achievement of a welfare-maximizing equilibrium. In all of these cases $P > MC$, and it is impossible for marginal benefits to equal marginal costs.

Key Concepts

Monopolistic competition.   A situation of numerous sellers, each one of which faces a downward sloping demand curve.

Markup pricing.   A method of pricing in which a seller adds a fixed percentage of cost to the cost of an item to arrive at a selling price.

Key Diagrams

The reader should be able to label properly and explain the two diagrams below.

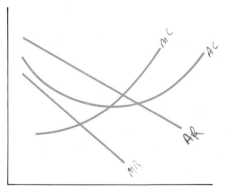
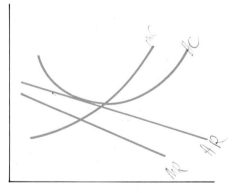

Although economic analysis can provide a theory of competitive markets that provides definite results with respect to prices and levels of output, the determinateness disappears when we analyze monopoloid markets. Large firms may have objectives quite different from the simple assumptions of theoretical models, and the means for achieving those goals are broader than decisions about prices and quantities. In addition, decisions are interrelated: what one firm does affects other firms and influences their behavior. This chapter will examine the larger issues of market strategy within which big business decisions are made, concentrating on the monopoloid firm and its policies as the characteristic situation in the American economy. Focusing on price and market strategy, we are inevitably drawn into consideration of market power, entrenched economic positions and their implications.

Oligopoly: Market Strategy and Pricing Policies

32

PRICES AND MARKET STRATEGIES

Pricing policies are part of the market strategies adopted by business firms. In competitive markets, prices are determined outside the firm by forces beyond its control: the company's market strategies must take the price of its product as given. But in monopoloid markets the firm has some discretion in setting its prices: price is one variable to be coordinated with sales expenditures, marketing policies, and other aspects of market strategies.

The goals and objectives of market strategies also influence pricing policies. It is a little too simple to assume that all firms seek to maximize their profits, for profits are only one goal that can be sought. One firm may be willing to sacrifice immediate profits in order to grow more rapidly. Another firm may seek to maximize the shareholder's equity per share and sacrifice some growth as well as immediate profits. A third may seek a high degree of stability of output and earnings. All of these strategies may be thought of as "maximizing profits in the long run," but each will result in a different pricing policy to fit into a different market strategy.

Several commonly observed pricing policies and accompanying market strategies are characteristic of large oligopolistic firms in American industry.[1] The price leader

---

[1] The following discussion of price and market strategies draws heavily on A. D. H. Kaplan, J. B. Dirlam, and R. F Lanzilotti, *Pricing in Big Business: A Case Approach* (Washington: Brookings Institution, 1958).

in the automobile industry, General Motors Corporation, seeks to achieve a *target return on investment,* after taxes, of 20 percent. The pricing policy works this way:

1. A standard operating level is selected as the level of output the company prefers.
2. Cost of production per unit, including both direct and indirect costs, is calculated for that standard output.
3. An amount sufficient to achieve after tax profits on investment of 20 percent is added to that standard cost. This determines the price.
4. The company then seeks to sell the standard output at the determined price, staying within the selling and other overhead costs per unit already included.

This policy has been highly successful in recent years. The target level profits have been achieved in most recent years, along with a market share of a little over half of domestic new car sales.

The steel industry's price leader, United States Steel Corporation, has built its pricing policy around the goals of *price stability* and *stability of profit margins*. Price stability is important in an industry with very large investment in costly, single-purpose equipment. A steel rolling mill costs close to $100 million, and it can't be used to do anything but produce rolled steel sheets or strip. If price cutting should start, the selling price could be driven down to levels just equal to the mill's operating costs (labor plus materials inputs) with nothing left over to pay for the large capital investment. No company could survive in such a situation. Hence the need in the industry for a leader devoted to keeping prices stable at profitable levels.

Steel mills also last almost indefinitely with proper maintenance, yet technological change goes on. Unless pricing policies protect the profit margins of the older mills, the investment in them will be lost. Newer mills will make larger profits, of course, but it is only natural for the largest firm in the industry to protect itself by setting prices that keep up the value of its older mills. Since most other firms in the industry have similar problems they usually find little to criticize in the leader's actions.[2]

---

[2] One of the underlying problems of the famous 1962 "rollback" of steel prices involved the issue of profit margins. In the previous decade, U.S. Steel had made a major miscalculation and invested heavily in equipment to make heavy steel products (such as structural beams) and had given too little attention to investment in light steel products (such as sheets and strip). The result was significant excess capacity that could be carried only if prices were raised. This problem was not faced by other large steel firms, whose investment policies had been more in line with market developments. United States Steel was really attempting to set a price that would validate its own mistakes, and the economy as a whole would have had to pay for it. So when the federal government forced U.S. Steel to rescind its price increases, the other firms in the industry were quite willing to accept that action, just as they were willing to accept the original price increase.

When companies *follow the leader* in their pricing policies, there is little to say. They may bask in the shelter of a price umbrella held by the price leader, protecting them from the rigors of competition. Or they may use the umbrella to expand vigorously in a few selected portions of the market, thereby earning better profits than the leader (who protects his leadership position by blanketing all parts of the market). Or they may try to cut costs while accepting the leader's price. Or they may try to develop their own brands within the larger market to obtain an even more protected position. Whatever they do, however, the fact that they accept the leader's price prevents cost benefits from seeping down to the final customer.

A third objective of market strategy and price policy may be to *maintain or improve the company's market position*. Sears, Roebuck and Co. follows such a policy. Its pricing structure seeks to achieve a return on its investment of 15 percent, with a lower limit of 10 percent considered acceptable in relatively poor years. However, it also seeks a growing share of the retail markets in which it participates. The chief technique used to achieve that goal is consistently low prices compared with those of other retailers. The low prices are achieved primarily at the manufacturing level, by either company-owned (or partially owned) plants or contractual buying arrangements with independent companies. By eliminating seasonal swings in output and by operating close to capacity, these "tied" producers are able to cut costs per unit of output below those of most other producers. Elimination of selling costs by the manufacturer (Sears is the customer) also helps cut costs. As a result, Sears is usually able to achieve its target level of profits *and* enlarge its relative share of total sales volume.[3]

Finally, we come to *pricing to meet competition*. General Foods Corporation is a good example. General Foods has emphasized specialty or novelty food products, such as Jell-O, Postum, and Sanka. Its general pricing rule is "one-third to make, one-third to sell, and one-third for profit." But that type of margin is impossible to maintain over the long haul as imitators and competitors appear, except for a few products whose imitation is difficult. After an initial period of high profits on a new product, prices are cut to meet the competition attracted by the high profits, and prices drift down to more normal levels. The company's policy, however, has been to introduce new specialty food products in a continuous stream, with high initial profit margins and relatively high noncompetitive prices that it expects to reduce slowly as competitors appear.

It should be clear from this brief discussion of prices and market strategies that big enterprises have considerable leeway in setting prices and adjusting

---

[3] Note the anomaly here. Why enlarge your sales volume while maintaining the rate of profit at a given level? Why doesn't Sears take its cost advantages in rising profit rates and slower growth? No one knows the answer, but apparently the company does not seek maximum profits because management wants a larger share of the market.

THE TOP DOG NEVER STOPS IMPROVING THE BREED.

First Greyhound got to be the world's biggest bus line. Next we successfully diversified. Now we're ploughing those diversified profits right back into new super-facilities. All built with our own funds, not the government's. And you know why we do it? We like being top dog.

THE GREYHOUND CORPORATION
WE'VE GOT MORE GOING FOR YOU

FIGURE 32-1
Big Enterprise: What
Makes Sammy Run?
(Reprinted by courtesy of
The Greyhound Corporation)

them to fit into larger market strategies. These are all "administered prices," freed in some degree, sometimes quite significantly, from the market forces of demand and supply.

ADMINISTERED PRICES

Administered prices of the sort described above can be distinguished from prices determined by market forces by two characteristics. They are established by administrative decision by officials of corporations as matters of operating policy or business planning. In addition, the price administrators have the power to implement or validate their price decisions within wide limits. Administered prices are a characteristic feature of oligopoly, defined and illustrated in Chapter 30 as an industry with a few dominant firms, as well as monopoly.

Establishment of price by the administrative decisions of corporate officials determines much of the market strategy of the firm. Such a decision determines in advance the terms on which the firm will participate in the economy; and the market response to the price and sales expenditures determines the amount sold and the company's operations. Price policy and sales strategy become dominant from the time an enterprise or product is conceived. For example, when planning a new product a corporation may first determine what customers feel the "appropriate price" should be, and then, with price determined, direct its engineers to design a product to sell at that price while yielding the necessary markups to cover selling costs and corporate profits.

Pricing in this fashion becomes a serious problem when monopoly or oligopoly is present. In a competitive situation like that of the model of pure competition of economic theory, the firm must either meet the prevailing market price or devise an improved or lower-cost product. It takes corporate planning to do that, but the key to the situation is that under competitive conditions the price is established by the market and the firm responds to it.

When monopoly or oligopoly prevail, however, the firm has considerable latitude within which it can establish the price that it seeks so that the firm can achieve its corporate profit or other goals. High rates of profit, maintenance of a large share of the market, or growth of the enterprise itself become more significant in making corporate decisions, and response to changes in costs or consumer demand less significant. The function of prices in causing producers to respond to the desires and needs of consumers is reduced. Instead of adapting their prices to the market and their production decisions to the relative profits that appear, firms tend to adapt to changes through their selling efforts and by using their market power to dampen competition from other firms. For example, in the 1950s when the few producers of heavy electrical equipment found that large reductions in demand for their output were threatening the prevailing administered price structure, they began to collude to fix prices and divide the market. The result was one of the most spectacular antitrust cases in our history, and the public discovered that profits, not progress, was the industry's most important product.

Administered prices, taken together with an industrial structure containing significant monopoloid elements, have three effects. They contribute to an unsatisfactory response of firms to the changing wants of consumers. They lead to efforts to manage consumer wants through advertising and similar sales expenses that raise costs and waste resources. And they promote additional efforts to diminish competition.

Administered prices also react differently from competitive prices to changes in aggregate demand. They tend to be stable and unchanging not only under normal conditions, but also when aggregate demand falls. Oligopolistic firms using administered prices hold their prices steady when sales decline, reducing their output and employment instead of prices. This action puts the main burden of adjustment on workers and their families. It also affects long-run planning of plant capacity and costs by the firms themselves; they plan for plants that can "break even" at relatively low levels of output. Thus, in the steel industry for example, most steel mills do not start losing money on current operations unless output falls below 40–50 percent of plant capacity. The results of this pattern are two: profits are high when output is close to capacity levels, and the industry does not have strong barriers to development of excess capacity. The typical administered-price industry features price stability, substantial layoffs during recessions and depressions, and large unused capacity in normal times.

Administered prices also contribute significantly to inflation. They are part of the inflationary environment of the economy, along with big labor unions and government policy toward growth and employment, that lead the modern economy into slow but steady price increases. The stability of administered prices keeps them from going down during periods of economic slack, but it is easy for them to rise during inflations. The result is that the economy has a significant sector in which prices tend to rise in the long run.[4]

THE KINKED DEMAND CURVE

The tendency of administered prices to remain stable over long periods of time is supported by a theoretical analysis of the situation faced by the oligopolistic firm. The normal situation faced by such a firm is one in which it can expect other firms in the industry to match any price reductions it may make in order to protect their sales and share of the market. It can also expect other firms to not match an increase in price because of their desire to increase their sales at its expense. These expectations rest on the normal situation of substantial excess production capacity available in the industry. The oligopolistic firm, therefore, has every incentive to hold prices where they are. Reductions would be matched quickly, so no one firm could gain. But increases would not be matched and the firm trying to raise its prices would lose. These expectations are equivalent to the existence of a kink or bend in the firm's demand curve at the prevailing price, shown in Figure 32-2.

The situation changes, however, if the economy is expanding and firms in the industry are operating close to their production capacity. In that situation, no firm has any incentive to cut prices: it would expect other firms not to match its cuts because they would know the price cutting firm could not sell much more anyway. It would be unable to satisfy the new customers it could attract. On the other hand, there is considerable incentive to increase prices. Since sales are large and growing and capacity operations are the rule, any firm would match price increases in order to get its share of higher profits. In this situation the kink has reversed itself, as in Figure 32-3.

The oligopolistic industry, then, normally tends to sustain the existing prices for its product. But when aggregate demand is rising and begins to push on the capacity to produce in industry after industry, the oligopolistic industry will

---

[4] For other and conflicting views on administered prices see *Administered Prices: A Compendium on Public Policy* (Washington: U.S. Senate Subcommittee on Antitrust and Monopoly, 1963).

FIGURE 32-2
The Oligopolist's Kinked Demand Curve
(With Unused Plant Capacity in the Industry)

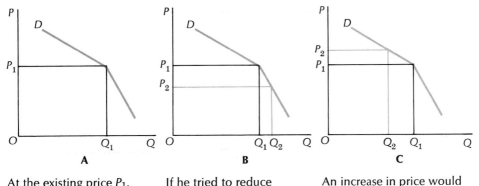

A	B	C
At the existing price P_1, the oligopolist sells output Q_1.	If he tried to reduce price in order to sell more, other firms would match his reductions, so that sales would increase only slightly.	An increase in price would bring a large loss in sales, however. Wisdom, therefore dictates price stability as long as the existing price brings reasonable profits.

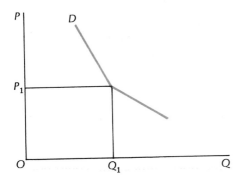

FIGURE 32-3
The Oligopolist's Kinked Demand Curve
(At Capacity Operations)
At price P_1 and output Q_1, reduction in price could bring greatly enlarged sales because other firms would not be expected to match the price cut. But why do it, since Q_1 is the firm's capacity output. On the other hand, an increase in price would be eagerly followed by other firms because they know they won't lose many sales. The result: Prices go up as everyone follows the leader.

see its selling prices move up. This situation builds a permanent ratchet type of price increase into the economy; administered prices tend to go up when demand is strong, but do not go down when demand is slack.

This tendency is reinforced by patterns of collective bargaining between big businesses and big unions. It is difficult for management bargainers to hold the line against large demands by strong unions when both sides know that when demand is strong all the firms are very likely to follow a price increase necessitated by rising labor costs. This is exactly the situation described in Chapter 19 to explain why dynamic growth policies plus administered prices plus strong unions equal creeping inflation.

The kinked demand curve of an oligopolist has another interesting property that is of interest to economists: the marginal revenue curve associated with it has a gap, so that the firm would not change its output level even if its marginal costs or demand were to shift substantially. Assume an oligopolistic firm that perceives a kink in its demand curve at the existing price. The mathematical relationship of marginal to average quantities is such that its marginal cost curve will appear with a gap, as in Figure 32-4.

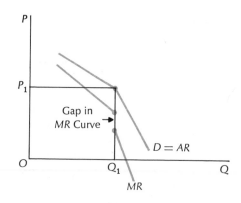

FIGURE 32-4

The kink in the oligopolistic demand curve creates a gap in the MR curve at the existing quantity of output. Why? Because change in the slope of AR is associated mathematically with discontinuity in MR.

Now draw the oligopolist's marginal cost curve so that it passes through the gap in his marginal revenue curve (Figure 32-5). In this case, even if the oligopolist were trying to maximize his profits, his price and output would not be changed in response to changes in either marginal costs or demand unless they were large enough to shift the MC curve out of the gap in the MR curve. This situation is added reason to believe that prices will remain stable while costs or demand conditions change.

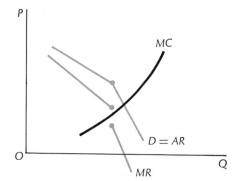

FIGURE 32-5

When the oligopolist's MC curve passes through the gap in his MR curve (which may or may not be the case, but it is highly possible) he will have no reason to change its price even if D or MC change.

PRICE LEADERSHIP

No sector of the economy is static and unchanging. New products appear to challenge the old. New technologies bring changes in production costs. Consumer preferences shift. Sometimes these changes occur rapidly and simultaneously. But however it may appear, change requires adjustment on the part of business firms even in those industries dominated by large and powerful enterprises. Indeed, some changes in products, processes, or marketing techniques are initiated by large firms in efforts to enlarge or maintain their position.

Change is potentially unsettling in an oligopoly, for the action of one firm will affect others and their reaction will in turn affect the first. A price reduction, for example, could set off a chain reaction of retaliation, leading to a price war in which all are injured. The sensitivity of oligopoly to such changes is one reason for the tendency toward stable prices, as shown by the kinked demand curve analysis. It also leads to *price leadership,* in which pricing policy for the entire industry is determined by one firm. The leader is usually the largest firm, which has the largest coercive power to bring to bear upon lesser firms if they should step out of line.

Price leadership is widespread in the U.S. economy, as one would expect in an economy with many industries dominated by a relatively few firms in each. General Electric dominates pricing for such important household equipment as refrigerators and washing machines. International Harvester calls the tune for farm tractors and other farm machinery. General Motors makes the price levels and price differences in the automobile industry. United States Steel dominates the market for iron ore and basic steel (although in recent years some smaller firms have been taking the lead in pricing some of the lighter steel products). Aluminum Corporation of America administers prices for aluminum and its products. The list could go on almost indefinitely and would include most of the industries dominated by a few firms, together with the basic products and many of the lesser products in those industries.

The price leader looks after its own interests, of course. Its leadership is used to help attain its profit goal at levels of production at or close to what the firm regards as a normal percentage of capacity. It is also used to help sustain its share of the market and consequently preserve its position of leadership.

Leadership, however, also provides some constraints on the dominant firm that prevent single-minded concentration on its own interests. If a price change is contemplated, the leader must assess the situation to determine whether the other large firms are willing to go along. If they do not, the change may have to be revoked. On the other hand, if the firm is big enough it can impose its will on the others.

Price leaders are not completely isolated from market forces. Changes in costs may enable small firms to cut prices; if this pattern becomes widespread it may be impossible to hold price levels up. A shrinking market or a growing one can make all firms restless. Imports may indicate that domestic prices are too high. When these and other changes occur, however, it is the price leader's task to assess their strength and probable duration, and then to lead the industry to a new level of prices consistent with the changed conditions and profit goals.

PRICE LEADERSHIP

Price leadership sometimes prevails against the interests of all firms except the price leader. In the mid-1950s, for example, the Venezuelan government was pressuring U.S. Steel for higher royalties from the USS iron ore concessions there, claiming that the world price was high enough for USS to pay more for its mining rights. As part of its counterattack, USS began selling iron ore once more in the U.S. Great Lakes region, which it had not done in over fifteen years, in order to impose a reduced price on Lake Erie iron ore. It was able to do so because it was, and remains, the largest iron ore producer in the region. It was then able to show the Venezuelan government that, with the new market price that prevailed, its iron ore profits were not high enough to allow for higher royalties on the ore it mined in Venezuela. The other U.S. iron ore producers howled in rage, but all they could do was retire to their dens and lick their wounded profits.

Price leadership is designed to preserve order and stability. Under normal conditions, it prevents the price competition that could undermine the profits of all the leading firms in an industry. When economic conditions change, leadership enables the industry to adapt in an orderly fashion that does not threaten anyone's position or profits, and does not open the way to price competition.

DIFFERENTIATED PRODUCTS

Although the oligopolistic firm has strong reasons to support and sustain the existing relationships within its industry, primarily for fear of the reaction of other firms to unsettled conditions, it also has strong reasons to build a defensive position for itself as a protection against possible changes. Product differentiation achieved by use of brand names, advertising, or styling is the easiest path to follow. If consumers can be induced to buy a firm's product because the name is familiar, because it has certain features that are slightly different from other products, or because of the product's reputation, the firm will be more secure against any attacks on its sales from other companies and may even be able to charge higher prices than other firms charge for similar products.

The classic example is aspirin. All aspirin is chemically the same, and is produced in bulk by only two U.S. manufacturers. It is packed into pills with a variety of components to hold it in the pellet form (hence the claims of "speed" of dissolving; but by the time the aspirin gets to the portions of the digestive tract where the body absorbs it, any pill will be dissolved). Yet in spite of the homogeneity of all aspirin, a variety of trade names are publicized. One, Bayer Aspirin, is more expensive than others, largely because of extensive advertising. Bayer also induces retailers to give its product more prominent display by enabling the retailer to earn a higher markup, made possible by the higher price.

Its advertising and other sales efforts enable Bayer to achieve a relatively inelastic demand curve for its brand. This is the fundamental reason for product differentiation of all kinds. It enables the seller of the branded product to raise his price above the others without losing enough customers to reduce his profits. Indeed, he may well enlarge his profits. Figures 32-6 and 32-7 show the relationship between elasticity of demand and product differentiation.

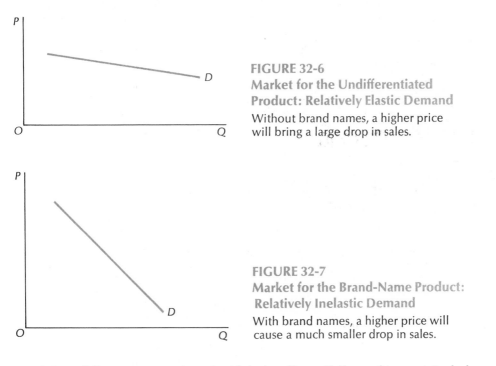

FIGURE 32-6
Market for the Undifferentiated
Product: Relatively Elastic Demand
Without brand names, a higher price will bring a large drop in sales.

FIGURE 32-7
Market for the Brand-Name Product:
Relatively Inelastic Demand
With brand names, a higher price will cause a much smaller drop in sales.

Product differentiation is found widely in oligopolistic markets, particularly those producing goods sold directly to final consumers. It introduces an element of rivalry into markets that lack significant price competition. When the differentiation goes beyond mere brand names and introduces qualitative differences, it brings a larger variety of products for consumers to choose among. On the other hand, it can bring a great proliferation of seemingly different brands, all of which are similar in their essential characteristics, and requiring large advertising expenses to keep them continually before the public.

NONPRICE COMPETITION: SELLING COSTS, MODEL CHANGES, AND KEEPING UP WITH THE JONESES

Product differentiation opens the door to several varieties of nonprice competition. One is advertising and other sales efforts. Where differentiation is largely by brand name rather than in the product itself, oligopolistic firms can spend large amounts on advertising. The soap industry spends over 10 percent of its total revenues on advertising, while the cigarette and whiskey industries spend close to 15 percent of revenues (after excise taxes). The automobile industry spends only 1–2 percent of its revenues on advertising, however, because there is more real difference in the product than in the other industries cited.

The auto industry uses model changes instead. It is such a tight oligopoly that the principal source of competition is last year's models available as used cars. General Motors' chief competitor this year is General Motors Corporation last year. To forestall as much of that competition as possible, each year's model is restyled, or has added options, or a former option becomes standard equipment. The auto firms try to keep a steady stream of changes coming every year.

Closely related to model and styling changes is the much criticized "planned obsolescence" of some durable consumers' goods. If enough changes occur in models and styling over a period of, say, three years, there may be little demand for well-made products that have a useful life of five to ten years. There is little reason, then, to design products to last. A circular chain of cause and effect is set up:

1. Oligopolistic pricing policies eliminate or greatly diminish price competition, leading to . . .
2. Product differentiation, which in turn triggers . . .
3. Frequent model and styling changes and large selling expenses. The result is . . .
4. Rapid *market* obsolescence of durable goods, causing manufacturers to produce . . .
5. Shlock.[5]

Yet shlock may be exactly what the public wants. Consumers who spend to keep up with or outpace the Joneses want the latest and fanciest products. Model and styling changes help them use their income to validate claims to social status.[6]

---

[5] A Yiddish word meaning shoddy goods. Rhymes with flock. Sometimes spelled schlok. A store that sells shoddy is a shlock-house.

[6] An auto executive friend of the author's put it this way: "We don't make shlock. Besides, that's what the public wants."

COERCION

The market strategy and price policy of large firms can also include coercion of smaller firms. The objective may be to strengthen the larger company's market, or to protect its share against a too vigorous pygmy that wants to grow. Or a firm may seek to become the only seller in the market, attempting to drive other firms into bankruptcy or mergers.

Example from real life; only the names have been changed to conceal the guilty: Two firms supplied crackers to grocers in Metropolia. One was a nationally known giant whose well-advertised brand sold for 30¢ per pound. One was a local firm whose product was priced at 28¢. The price differential resulted in a division of the market highly favorable to the giant. The local firm decided to increase its share by lowering its price to 27¢. The giant immediately imposed a "penalty price," in that one local market of 26¢. The local firm tried to recreate the 2¢ price differential by reducing its price to 24¢. The giant reimposed the "penalty" by pricing its crackers at 23¢. Within a week enthusiastic shoppers were buying crackers at 14¢ a pound, the local firm's management was frantic, and terms of surrender were arranged: prices were established once more at 28¢ for the local firm and 30¢ for the giant. The local firm's president sighed with relief, "Boy, we'll never try *that* again." They didn't. The cracker market in Metropolia has been "orderly" and market shares have gone largely unchanged for the last twenty years.

This type of price warfare was used by the old Standard Oil Co. back in the 1880s to build the most famous "trust" of that period, leading directly to passage of the Sherman Antitrust Act of 1890 and the outlawing of predatory price-cutting. To give the devil his due, however, Standard Oil always offered to buy out smaller firms at a good price and only drove them to the wall if they refused to sell. In the cracker case cited above, the "penalty price" was clearly an illegal move on the part of the giant. The small firm *could* have sued for triple damages under provisions of the Sherman Act: the case would have been in the courts for years, and the firm bankrupt in three months.

Almost all forms of coercion of other firms, particularly the use of prices for that purpose, have been outlawed by the various antitrust laws. Although these practices are illegal, they are occasionally found. One reason for their scarcity in recent years has been the continuing expansion and growth of the economy. It has not been necessary for one firm to challenge another in order to grow. Nevertheless, there are still instances in which price leadership is ineffective and product differentiation and advertising do not suffice, and a firm steps out to challenge others. At those times coercive action is likely to occur.

Another common predatory practice is known as "the squeeze." It occurs in integrated industries like metals manufacturing. The large dominant firm may produce the basic metal as well as finished products made from the metal. It also sells the metal to nonintegrated fabricators. In this situation the dominant firm will sometimes use its market power to hold down the prices of finished products while it raises the price of the basic metal that it sells to other fabricators. All firms will find their profits on fabricated products going down, but the integrated giant will make it up on sales of the basic metal to the other manufacturers, who are caught in a squeeze between high materials prices and low prices for finished products. The squeeze can be employed in such industries as copper, steel, and aluminum to provide high profits for large integrated firms, to keep small firms from growing, or even to drive fabricators into mergers with the large firms on favorable terms.

COLLUSION

Collusion among large firms to restrict or eliminate competition is also illegal. Yet it occurs, in spite of the antitrust laws. The benefits are often so attractive that oligopolistic firms tend naturally to be drawn into schemes for fixing prices, dividing markets, and sharing customers. But collusion is illegal, and vigorous enforcement of the antitrust laws is the only safeguard against it.

The most widely publicized example of price fixing and market sharing in recent years, and probably the largest of all time in terms of money losses to the general public, was the electrical equipment conspiracy of 1955–60.[7] This case concerned the pricing of electrical apparatus and supplies used by large electrical generating plants, products that had an annual sales volume of over $1.75 billion. The conspiracy involved some very large firms (such as General Electric and Westinghouse) as well as the medium-sized and small companies that make up a series of interlocking oligopolies in the heavy electrical equipment industry.

The industry had a long history of price and market-sharing conspiracies dating back to before World War I. Sixteen conspiracy cases had been brought by the Department of Justice against various groupings of electrical equipment manufacturers between 1911 and 1949, with either General Electric or Westinghouse or both being involved in every case. Trade associations have always been important in the industry, and GE was often a leader in their activities.[8] The industry was dominated by GE ($4 billion of annual sales, one quarter in electrical apparatus) and Westinghouse ($2 billion of annual sales, half in electrical apparatus), with other large companies like Allis-Chalmers ($500 million annual sales) trailing behind.

---

[7] The electrical equipment case has been written up several times. See John Fuller, *The Gentlemen Conspirators* (New York: Grove Press, 1962); John Herling, *The Great Price Conspiracy* (Washington: Robert B. Luce, Inc., 1962); Richard A. Smith, *Corporations in Crisis* (Garden City, N.Y.: Doubleday & Co. Anchor Books, 1966), Chaps. 5–6; and Clarence C. Walton and Frederick W. Cleveland, Jr., *Corporations on Trial: The Electric Cases* (Belmont, Cal.: Wadsworth Publishing Co., 1964). All are fascinating reading.

[8] Gerard Swope, president of General Electric, proposed in 1932 that industry trade associations take the lead in stabilizing prices and production during the depression. This proposal for "self-government of industry" was later developed into the ill-fated National Recovery Administration (NRA) of the New Deal years. Crucial to NRA were "codes of fair practice" for various industries, the great majority including provision for minimum prices or costs.

This particular price-fixing conspiracy was a direct result of the slowdown in national economic growth that occurred in the 1950s. The industry was equipped for the highest levels of production in its history when demand for electrical apparatus fell drastically. The chief suppliers began cutting prices in order to keep their plants busy, only to discover that profits disappeared. This situation triggered a series of secret meetings among executives of the important firms. Decisions taken at these meetings included schemes for selection of the firms that would be low bidders on sales to the federal government, electric utility companies, contractors, and industrial corporations; guidelines to determine the prices each firm would quote; and the share of sales each company would get. For example, sales of power switchgear assemblies to the federal government were divided as in Table 32–1.

TABLE 32–1
Sales of Power Switchgear Assemblies

Company	Percentage of Sales
General Electric Co.	39
Westinghouse Electric Co.	35
I-T-E Circuit Breaker Co.	11
Allis-Chalmers Mfg. Co.	8
Federal Pacific Electric Co.	7

Contact between the firms included elaborate codes and secrecy to avoid detection. Meetings were held at fashionable hotels, resorts, and clubs, but never at the same location twice. Expense accounts were doctored to conceal the location of meetings. But in spite of the hugger-mugger, the whole affair was uncovered.

The conspiracy was broken by the glare of publicity. The Tennessee Valley Authority, tired of receiving identical bids on electrical equipment, began including information about them in its news releases. Picked up by a Knoxville newspaper, the information set in motion an investigation by the U.S. Senate Subcommittee on Antitrust and Monopoly. Public hearings at Knoxville uncovered more evidence of collusion in bidding, and the Department of Justice began a grand jury investigation in Philadelphia. Just when it seemed that only circumstantial evidence could be developed, one of the conspirators, an executive of one of the smaller companies, confessed everything. He gave names, dates, and full details of the whole sordid business. Brought to trial, there was little the companies could do but confess their guilt. Twenty-nine firms were fined, from $7,500 each for some of the smaller ones up to $437,500 for General Electric. A number of individuals were fined and several were briefly jailed.

One feature of the case was the morality expressed by the principals. Most of the individuals involved seemed to feel that their behavior was only natural in the circumstances, that "everybody did it." Or that they had little choice:

the business system led inevitably to such things. The top management of big firms, like GE, professed abhorrence of the conspiracy and ignorance of the price fixing, and put all of the blame on the lower-rank executives who were actually caught. Even more revealing was the behavior of GE stockholders at the next annual meeting after the trial: "They hooted down the few management critics who called for an impartial investigation and they assailed a complaining union leader with cries of 'Shut up' and 'Throw him out,' " according to the *New York Times*.

Yet Federal Judge J. Cullen Gainey, in his formal statement prior to sentencing said, "One would be most naive indeed to believe that these violations of the law, so long persisted in, affecting so large a segment of the industry, and finally, involving so many millions upon millions of dollars, were facts unknown to those responsible for the corporation and its conduct." And one of the lawyers defending a GE vice-president explained that "what he did was something that he inherited as a young man as a way of life that had been established within the General Electric Company even before he came."

EFFECTIVE COMPETITION?

This chapter's analysis of prices and market strategy in oligopolistic industries has shown that markets are typically restricted and managed. Markets are only partially free. Competition is highly imperfect. The particular degree of market restriction and limitation of competition will differ from industry to industry and from one sector of the economy to another.

It is also clear that the results of oligopoly are widely different from those ideal outcomes derived from the theory of competitive markets. To the extent that stable administered prices and shares of the market protect firms from the gales of competition, we can expect their internal efficiency to be diminished. To the extent that lack of competition brings prices above and output below the competitive norm, we can expect a diminution of economic welfare.

But are those the only economic goals one asks of an economy? John M. Clark, one of America's great economists, argued persuasively that efficient production in the sense described by the theory of competitive markets is only one objective of many. Others are innovation and the diffusion of its benefits very widely through society; the maintenance of high and stable employment; and economic and political freedoms. He gives U.S. industry high grades on those aspects of its performance, particularly in the areas of innovation and its diffusion.[9]

Clark's views supplement those of Joseph Schumpeter. Schumpeter argued that a private enterprise economy generates a process of "creative destruction" in which innovations continually appear and threaten the established position of dominant firms. Where market control exists and either monopoly profits

---

[9] See John M. Clark, *Competition as a Dynamic Process* (Washington: Brookings Institution, 1961) for the best statement of Clark's position.

or economic sluggishness persists, the protected economic position becomes a target for innovators of all kinds. The monopolistic position falls to the attack of new firms and new men, upgrading the whole economic performance of that sector of the economy.[10]

The challenge to entrenched position envisaged by Schumpeter can come from a variety of sources. Technological innovation is one. New products, new processes, and new raw materials that promise reduced costs or expanded markets are a direct result of the continuing attack on the economic status quo. When established firms seek to gain control over the innovation process they become part of it themselves, using new products and processes to continually stake out growth positions for themselves. Examples of this behavior are found in the chemical and petroleum industries, where *some* of the leading firms have been important innovators. Indeed, the financial resources and long-range planning of large firms may be needed in order to mount an effective program of research, development, and innovation. On the other hand, it is quite possible that the process of innovation itself may be administered for purposes of stability while new firms are kept out by various barriers to entry. The automobile industry is a good example; since the late 1920s, when the industry took on its present tight oligopoly form, every significant technological advance was introduced first on foreign cars, whether developed initially by a U.S. company or not. We should also recall from Chapter 31 that the bulk of U.S. research and development spending is related to the military and is financed by the federal government, and that the most innovative firms tend to be medium-sized rather than either the giants or the small ones. While the general propositions advanced by Clark and Schumpeter may be valid and lead to the conclusion that some degree of business size and oligopolistic structure may be most conducive to technological advance and its diffusion, it is difficult to justify the position of a single firm in a specific industry—say, General Motors Corp. in automobiles or Parke, Davis and Co. in pharmaceuticals—without an evaluation of their specific performance.

One source of challenge to entrenched positions is the market for business enterprises themselves. A firm doing poorly will find the value of its securities falling. Enterprising business executives, spotting the poor performance, can use the financial resources of their own firms to buy control of the laggard, inject new capital and imaginative management, and revive the backward firm. One spectacular historical example is the Union Pacific Railroad: Edward H. Harriman used the resources of the Illinois Central Railroad to gain control of the badly run and dilapidated UP in 1897 and turn it into one of the nation's most profitable lines. A more recent example is the case of Norton Simon, Inc., a recently built conglomerate based on a middle-sized food-manufacturing firm whose resources were used to gain control of and revive a number of

---

[10] See Joseph A. Schumpeter, *Capitalism, Socialism and Democracy* (New York: Harper and Bros., 1942).

troubled firms in a variety of industries. The "corporate takeover" is one way in which the financial markets provide for the entry of new capital and new management even in industries with strong barriers to new firms.

The public can also benefit from competition between giant firms. The "countervailing power" of a giant buyer such as Sears, Roebuck or A & P can balance the market power of a giant seller like General Electric or General Foods. The bargaining power of U.S. Steel can mitigate that of the steelworkers' union. A large department store can sell its own line of private brands of manufactured goods. To some extent power will beget power and one center of power will neutralize another, although the danger of collusion between centers of power may require a very watchful economic policeman with strong punitive powers.[11]

Some of the most sophisticated observers of the American economy argue that these elements have made an oligopolistic system a workable one. The nature and sources of its inefficiencies are different from those of the Soviet economy noted in Chapter 29, but like the Soviet system, it works. It works, they argue, because consumers are free to buy what they like; because ambitious people continually seek to gain a share of the advantages held by those established and vested interests that prevail throughout big business; because the elite of big business is a circulating one in which entry of newcomers depends to a large extent on innovative and managerial ability; and because government attacks monopoly through the antitrust laws and regulates firms "affected with the public interest."

This resolution of the problem may not be adequate, however. A system of supercorporations *may* be effective in contributing to rising living standards and accommodating to economic change, but if advertising adjusts consumer preferences to the sales needs of big enterprise, rather than the other way around, the rationality of the system as a whole may be seriously deficient. If one result is heavy reliance on military spending that is in part fostered by a mutuality of interest between big business and big government, then the system as a whole may be destructive rather than constructive. There are larger issues related to the place of big enterprise and a managerial elite in a democratic society. Economic power has political implications, and a self-selecting business elite, even an open one, can exert influences throughout the social system that go far beyond such economic issues as price, quantity of output, profits, and the nature and speed of innovation. This issue, which has not been a strong theme in this book so far, will become increasingly important as we examine public policy toward business in the next chapter and the public economy in Part VIII.

---

[11] See J. Kenneth Galbraith, *The American Economy: The Theory of Countervailing Power* (Boston: Houghton Mifflin, 1952) for a fuller development of the theme of countervailing power.

Summary

The pricing and market strategies found in oligopolistic industries are widely varied. Some of the more prominent ones are:

Pricing to achieve a target return on investment.

Price stability and stability of profit margins.

Following prices established by a leader.

Maintaining or improving market position.

Pricing to meet competition.

All of these strategies involve administered prices that are established by company policy with significant freedom from market forces.

Administered prices mean that firms do not readily respond to consumer wants, they lead to efforts to manage consumer wants, and they promote lessening of competition. They are, in addition, one of the reasons for the existence of an inflationary environment in the economy.

The kinked demand curve faced by oligopolistic firms, based on expectations of rivals' behavior, is an additional explanation for the relative stability of administered prices. It also helps to explain why administered prices are flexible upward but not downward when they do move.

When changes come to oligopolistic markets they do not trigger widespread competitive behavior. The adjustment is instead usually "orderly" and under the leadership of a principal or dominant firm.

Oligopoly does not mean a complete absence of rivalry. Firms compete for sales by means of differentiated products, selling efforts, and model and style changes. The result is rapid obsolescence of many durable goods and high selling costs that must be absorbed in the prices of goods sold.

Rivalry can also lead to efforts on the part of large firms to preserve the status quo. Large firms may coerce small firms, and groups of firms may collude to gain advantage or preserve existing relationships. These practices are illegal, but the economics of oligopoly provide strong incentives to break the law.

Many economists have argued that the existing structure of the American economy works effectively to produce the things consumers want and to facilitate an improving standard of living. To a considerable degree there is much sense in that point of view. But at the very least it ignores the problem of the larger place of a big business system in a democratic society and its implications for the locus and structure of power.

Key Concepts

Administered prices.   Prices established by business firms as part of the firm's operating policy, independent of market forces to a greater or lesser degree. These are the prices established by firms that are *price makers.* Distinguished from prices determined wholly by market forces, which are competitive prices, and are accepted by price takers.

Kinked demand curve.   The demand curve for the individual firm in many oligopolistic markets. It has a "kink" at the existing price that is caused by the expectations the firm has of the actions its rivals are likely to take if the firm changes its price.

Price leadership.   The pattern of price setting in many oligopolistic markets in which a single firm sets the price and other firms follow. It is designed to promote "orderly" transition from one price to another and eliminate competitive pricing practices.

Product differentiation.   A form of rivalry among oligopolistic firms in which essentially similar products are provided with relatively small differences. Often associated with large selling costs.

Nonprice competition.   Competition via selling efforts, model changes, and product differentiation characteristic of oligopolistic industries in the absence of significant price competition.

The existence of a high degree of oligopoly and significant amounts of market power create major problems of public policy. Is the economic power of the large corporation a danger in a democratic society? If it is, what remedies are there? In a more restricted sense, what should be done about the purely economic effects of market power? Should monopoly be tolerated? Should it be eliminated wherever possible and prevented from arising elsewhere? If it can't be eliminated or prevented, should it be regulated, and if so by whom, to what ends, and with what instruments? Or is government ownership the only answer where monopoly or great market power exists?

In the United States, public policy toward big business has concentrated almost wholly on the economic effects of business behavior. Policy has sought to do two things:

1. Preserve competition and prevent monopoly through antitrust legislation.
2. Regulate monopolies when it is impractical to eliminate them.

Economic Organization and Public Policy

33

There have been some important exceptions, however, and in some instances the federal government has fostered and supported monopoloid practices and market control.

Public policy in the United States has given little attention to the significant problems that arise when important sectors of the economy are dominated by large firms whose actions are not sanctioned or controlled by the public. The growth of big business has gone largely unchecked, except where a clear impact on markets and prices is evident.

This chapter will examine these issues: first, antitrust legislation to promote competition, public utility regulation, and government support of private market control. It will then look at some of the principal issues of economic power and the problems and dilemmas of nonpolicy in that area.

MAINTAINING COMPETITION

Prevention of monopoly and promotion of competition are the chief function of the antitrust laws. There are three significant pieces of legislation: the Sherman Act (1890), the Clayton Act (1914), and the Federal Trade Commission

Act (1914). Two important amendments to the Clayton Act should also be included: the Robinson-Patman Act (1936), which is actually a law that restricts competition in retailing; and the Celler-Kefauver Act (1950), which forbids mergers that tend to diminish competition.

The Sherman Antitrust Act

The Sherman Antitrust Act of 1890 came as a reaction against the many business efforts to control markets, fix prices, and eliminate competition of the early decades of large-scale industrialization in the United States. The spread of a national network of railroads created large regional and national markets in place of the former local markets protected from competition by high transport costs. Concurrently, technological changes were creating industries with high capital costs and expensive, single-purpose equipment. The simultaneous opening of markets to more sellers and the growth of industries requiring sales and price stability, together with the great instability added by recurring business cycles, led to a great movement in industry to control the economic environment. The trust, from which the Sherman Act takes its name, was one such device: competing firms in the same industry would deposit their voting stock with a single board of trustees, which would then have voting control (but not ownership) of the formerly independent firms. A simpler device was the holding company, formed to buy stock control over formerly independent firms. Less effective than either of these devices were varieties of cartels, that is, voluntary agreements among firms to divide markets, fix prices, pool sales revenues for division on a prearranged basis, or limit output. The cartels tended to break down under the stress of depressions and financial crisis, leading to more formal arrangements like trusts and holding companies. These, in turn, led to the great public outcry against monopoly that produced the Sherman Act.

The wording of the Sherman Act is simple and inclusive, and broad enough to require considerable interpretation by the courts:

> Every contract, combination . . . or conspiracy, in restraint of trade or commerce among the several states, or with foreign nations, is declared to be illegal.

And

> Every person who shall monopolize, or attempt to monopolize, or combine or conspire . . . to monopolize any part of the trade or commerce among the several states, or with foreign nations, shall be deemed guilty of a misdemeanor.

Enforcement of the Sherman Act (and the Clayton Act, to be described shortly) is the responsibility of the Antitrust Division of the U.S. Department of Justice, by way of legal prosecution of violators of the law. Injured private parties can also sue violators for triple damages, under the Sherman Act.

This broad law, which could have been used to prevent the rise of giant corporations to their present positions of dominance, received its first setback because of failure to enforce it. Enforcement requires a lawsuit brought by the Attorney General of the United States against persons or firms accused of violations. Yet from the beginning the attorneys general failed to act, and Richard Olney, a former corporation lawyer who served in the position from 1893 to 1895, thought the law should be repealed and refused to enforce it. When a case was finally brought to the Supreme Court in 1895, involving a sugar industry trust that had about 98 percent of the nation's sugar refining capacity, the court decided that this indeed was a monopoly, but in manufacturing, not commerce, and the Sherman Act did not apply. This interpretation of the law was not reversed until 1899. But by then the gates had been opened to the merger movement of 1895–1901 through which many industries were organized in giant, quasi-monopolistic form.

This reluctance to challenge size and market control as antithetical to the intent of the law continued as a basic attitude until after World War II. In 1911, two great cases involving Standard Oil and American Tobacco came before the Court, which ordered the dissolution of those firms not because of their monopoly positions (which were indisputable), but because they used their power unreasonably to harass other firms. This famous "rule of reason" was applied in the next decades to such firms as Eastman Kodak, United Shoe Machinery Corp., International Harvester, and U.S. Steel, each of which held a near monopoly or overwhelming market dominance in its industry. In each case the courts held that no offense had been committed because the firms had not attacked or attempted to coerce their few rivals. They didn't have to; since they achieved dominance during the first merger movement because of the benign neglect of the Department of Justice and the courts, their size alone was enough to cause rivals to accept their leadership. "Mere size" was not an offense according to the earlier Supreme Court interpretations of the antitrust laws.

This famous "rule of reason" was not overturned until 1945. In that year, an antitrust suit against Aluminum Co. of America could not be heard by the Supreme Court because too many of its members had participated in the case as attorneys general to obtain a quorum. The case was heard instead by the federal court in New York under Judge Learned Hand. Hand overturned the rule of reason on the ground that large size in relation to the industry as a whole brought market dominance and the evils of monopoly even if the firm did not consciously exercise its power. Hand held that such monopoly power was prohibited. His rule of thumb was that control of 90 percent of aluminum production "is enough to constitute a monopoly; it is doubtful whether sixty or sixty-four percent would be enough; and certainly thirty-three percent is not." This landmark decision at last accepted the contention that the word "monopolizing" included high degrees of concentration and the tacit cooperation that accompanies them.

While this long sequence of changing judicial interpretation of "monopoly" has been going on, the courts have consistently outlawed restraint of trade in its many forms. This has included rate agreements between railroads, market sharing, price fixing, collusive bidding on supply contracts, exclusive selling arrangements of several types, restrictions of output, among many others; the list of prohibited collusive actions is a very long one.

The Clayton Antitrust Act

The Clayton Antitrust Act (1914) exhibits some of the same limitations as the Sherman Act, and probably for the same reasons. Its prohibitions of predatory action were clear and effectively enforced, but where it sought restrictions on corporate power and size the results were ineffectual.

The act itself was in large part a reaction against the revelations of the 1911 antitrust suits against Standard Oil and American Tobacco, which had shown how a giant corporation could ruthlessly suppress or gobble up its rivals. There was demand for legislation that would outlaw the specific tactics used, and in the 1912 national election campaign the topic of big business and monopolistic practices was one of the main issues. The new President, Woodrow Wilson (trained as an economist, incidentally, although his academic career was spent mainly as a historian and political scientist), immediately sought legislation to prevent repetition of the evils found in petroleum refining and tobacco manufacturing. The Clayton Act was one result.

The specific practices outlawed by the Clayton Act were only four in number. Two related to market practices. Price discrimination was forbidden except when it was the result of real differences in cost or when it was used "in good faith to meet competition." Thus, the practice by Standard Oil of cutting prices in a local market to drive a rival to the wall, while maintaining them at higher levels in other areas, was henceforth illegal. The act also forbade agreements between supplier and distributors in which the supplier offers one line of goods only if the distributor agrees to also take another (tying contracts), and in which the distributor agrees not to handle the goods of other suppliers (exclusive dealing contracts). These were devices used extensively by American Tobacco. These prohibitions of the Clayton Act have been effectively enforced in the subsequent years.

Two other provisions of the Clayton Act tried to deal with the structure of big enterprise, and they proved to be ineffective. One forbade acquisition of competing firms by stock ownership. The other forbade direct interlocking directorates among competing firms.

It was useless to forbid a firm from buying stock control of a competitor if the assets themselves could be bought. Instead of holding companies (like Standard Oil) owning a controlling interest in rival firms, the competitors could merely merge, or the large firm could buy the assets of the smaller. This is exactly what happened in the merger movement of the 1920s.

The loophole in the law was not closed until 1950, when the Celler-Kefauver Act amended this portion of the Clayton Act to forbid any corporate acquisitions whose effect "may be substantially to lessen competition or tend to create a monopoly." This broad language has enabled the Department of

Justice to challenge and prevent a number of large mergers. But it still permits the conglomerate mergers across industry lines that have enabled concentration in the economy as a whole to continue to grow.

As for interlocking directories, prohibition of direct interlocks has merely caused a shift to indirect interlocks as the basis for corporate community of interest groupings. The distinction between the two is shown in Figure 33-1. Up to the present time no effort has been made to close this loophole in the Clayton Act.

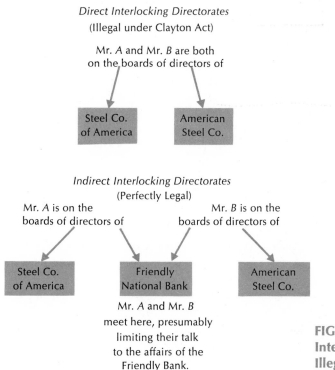

Direct Interlocking Directorates
(Illegal under Clayton Act)

Mr. *A* and Mr. *B* are both
on the boards of directors of

Steel Co. of America   American Steel Co.

Indirect Interlocking Directorates
(Perfectly Legal)

Mr. *A* is on the   Mr. *B* is on the
boards of directors of   boards of directors of

Steel Co. of America   Friendly National Bank   American Steel Co.

Mr. *A* and Mr. *B*
meet here, presumably
limiting their talk
to the affairs of the
Friendly Bank.

FIGURE 33-1
Interlocking Directorates:
Illegal and Legal

The Federal Trade Commission

When the Clayton Act was passed in 1914, President Wilson had wanted a long list of predatory monopolistic practices outlawed and a commission established to enforce the law. Congress balked, however, and only a few specific practices were named in the Clayton Act. The special commission was established by the Federal Trade Commission Act (1914), which also outlawed "unfair methods of competition." The FTC has five members appointed by the President. It is authorized to investigate unfair methods of competition, deceptive practices, monopolistic devices, and practices in restraint of trade, and to prosecute violators of the law. It can issue cease-and-desist orders to halt illegal practices, which the accused can appeal to the courts.

The FTC has never been a strong and vigorous watchdog over the economy, however. Most of its activity has been in the areas of retail trade and small business, protecting consumers against small businessmen and small business-men from each other. Few of its activities have involved big business and the use of market power (except for a campaign in the 1930s against pricing practices in steel and chemicals). Intended as a body with powers to initiate action against violators of the law, it has instead taken a largely passive role, waiting for complaints to be brought to it.

One interesting case was brought by the FTC against a firm using deceptive advertising in the sale of patent medicines. The company was convicted, but the conviction was reversed by the Supreme Court in 1931 on the ground that while the advertising was clearly deceptive it hurt only the customer and not competitors, who used the same kind of deception in their advertising. This decision led ultimately to passage of the Wheeler-Lea Act (1938), which out-lawed "unfair or deceptive acts or practices" and provided for enforcement by the FTC. The FTC also enforces a variety of legislation requiring proper labeling of textiles and furs and seeking to protect the public against misrepresentation. Needless to say, action by the FTC in this area has also been less than vigorous, although potentially it has tremendous weapons available for a large-scale program of consumer protection.

The Robinson-Patman Act

The conflicting attitudes toward big business and competition that prevail in the United States, and that have affected both the administration and legal interpretation of the antitrust laws, are exemplified in the way retail trade has been treated. When chain stores began spreading in the 1920s, their impact on independent retailers was blunted by national prosperity. But during the Great Depression of the 1930s, when competitive pressures really began to squeeze, independent retailers sought legislative help. In particular, they objected to the large discounts chain stores were able to get when they bought in large quantities from manufacturers and other suppliers, claiming that in many instances the cuts were not justified by savings in costs. The result was passage of the Robinson-Patman Act (1936), which tightened the Clayton Act's prohibition on price discrimination that served to lessen or injure competition and specifically outlawed certain business practices that evaded the Clayton Act.

This legislation has been highly controversial. It was designed to reduce the buying advantage of big firms, but as it has been administered the law has sometimes prevented price reductions that could be shown to be based on real savings in cost. This discrimination in favor of small buyers has promoted the survival of higher-cost systems of retail distribution. The law also tends to inhibit price cutting when markets turn soft, and has helped to promote that downward rigidity of prices, which is one facet of the slow and persistent rise in the consumer price index of recent decades. As one scholar put it:

> "By requiring that discounts be justified by actual rather than potential differences in cost, it has discouraged price reductions that might profitably have been made. By outlawing the practice of setting lower prices, in some part of a market, to test the possibility of increasing sales, it may have prevented reductions that would soon have been generalized."[1]

ANTITRUST: WHERE DO WE GO FROM HERE?

The dilemma of antitrust is that it has permitted the development of an economy dominated in large part by big business and has allowed that economy to structure itself in oligopolistic form. At the same time it has outlawed a large variety of specific business practices that are the natural mode of behavior of giant firms and oligopolies. The drive toward market control, price stability, and a live-and-let-live attitude is the natural outcome of the oligopolistic structure that antitrust has failed to attack.

Counter forces are at work, however, that keep the development inherent in that natural outcome from overwhelming the economy. Competition, in a broad and pervasive sense, keeps breaking through. It operates in ways quite different from those described in the traditional, and static, theory of competitive markets. Here are some of those ways:

Internal Competition.   Every large corporation is composed of discrete units in competition with each other for the capital and other resources available to the corporation. The more successful, efficient, and profitable divisions will get more of those resources. This constant competition within the firm itself promotes the efficient use of resources. The large corporation can be an effective organization for the management of large amounts of productive resources.[2]

Technological Change.   New products challenge the old. New production processes offer alternative ways to produce existing products. The advance of science brings synthetic materials and chemicals that do the same job as existing materials. As these changes occur, the protected market positions of existing firms are challenged.

Large firms seek to gain control over the process of technological change by doing as much of it themselves as they can. This control is aided by their access to large capital resources for research and development, and by their

---

[1] Clair Wilcox, *Public Policies Toward Business* (Homewood, Ill.: Richard D. Irwin, Inc., 3rd ed., 1966), pp. 219–20.

[2] This point is a two-edged sword for apologists of the large corporation. It implies that managerial units smaller than the giant corporation as a whole are the more efficient. If that is true, why not break up the giants and let their more efficient subunits compete in the larger market?

ability to buy into smaller firms that may develop newer technology. Those who have studied the economics of technical change tell us that the giant firms do not originate innovations to the extent that their market dominance would suggest, but that their market position and sources of capital enable them to develop new products, processes, and materials on a large scale.

Technological change, then, does not normally challenge the market position of giant firms. But it does force them to be progressive rather than conservative in their attitude toward it.

Economic Growth. A rapidly growing economy offers wide opportunities for business firms. A giant corporation that does not grab its share will see its position deteriorate as other firms fill the gap. This situation pushes the giants into policies that emphasize growth if only to protect their status, not to mention the added advantages of aggressive growth policies.

Economic growth also widens opportunities for technological change and development of new products, reinforcing the tendencies just described. Economic growth, furthermore, offers new firms an opportunity to gain a foothold in even tightly controlled industries and enables small firms to become larger. Growth provides more rivals for the giants and widens opportunities for these rivals, as well as giving incentives to the giants themselves to adopt progressive growth-oriented policies.

The pervasive long-run effects of technological change and economic growth enable the American economy to work relatively satisfactorily in spite of industrial structures that tend to be restrictive in nature. The immediate economic effect of oligopoly may be excessive selling costs, profits higher than normal (in the sense implied by the theory of market competition), and output levels that differ from the most desirable ones. But these short-run effects have been unable to swamp the longer-range impact of economic growth and technological change.

What has been said here means that the government policies designed to promote economic growth, investment in human capital, and support for research perform a far broader function than is usually attributed to them. Without such policies, the nation's industrial structure would be much less bearable than it now is.

Seen in this context, the antitrust laws seem less important. But that may be only an illusion. One reason for corporation concern for growth and technological change stems from the fact that corporate positions cannot be sustained in the long run by monopolistic controls. That path is outlawed. The only other way is through adaptation to growth and change, and most large American corporations have learned that fact. Even if the antitrust laws are not used to attack the power structure of the economy, their vigorous enforcement helps an economy dominated by giant firms to operate more acceptably than it otherwise would. The ghost of Senator John Sherman sits at the head of the table at every meeting of every corporate board of directors.

REGULATING MONOPOLY

In some industries, government has accepted monopoly as unavoidable or competition as impractical, particularly in public utility services and transportation. Without a competitive market to protect the consumer and to force firms to provide adequate services at reasonable prices, administrative regulation has been used as a means of control. An institutionalized form of conflict has been established, the results of which are seldom fully satisfactory to anyone. The regulated sector of the economy seems always to be in a state of crisis. The reasons for that condition illuminate many of the basic economic realities of a big-business–high-technology economy.

The legal basis for public utility regulation is the concept of business firms "affected with the public interest." This means a firm or firms that provide an essential service to the community as a whole, yet being so small in number, could exact a large toll from the community for those services. The legal principle was first defined in the famous case of *Munn* v. *Illinois* in 1877.

The Illinois legislature passed a law in 1871 for the regulation of grain elevators and warehouses in Chicago, including establishment of maximum rates. One company refused to comply, on the grounds that the law deprived it of property without due process and was an unwarranted interference with interstate commerce. In the trial it was shown that nine companies controlled the business, that they met periodically to establish grain storage rates, and that the potential sites for grain elevators were strictly limited; that is, a monopoly prevailed. The trial also showed that grain storage in Chicago was vitally important to both the city's economy and to midwestern farmers. The U.S. Supreme Court upheld the law on the argument that the state's police power could be used to regulate an industry "affected with the public interest," namely, one that has a monopoly of an essential public service and is therefore in a position from which "a tribute can be exacted from the community," to quote a later case.

Thus public utility regulation was born. For almost sixty years after *Munn* v. *Illinois,* the courts wrestled with the problem of which industries came under the category of those "affected with the public interest." Finally the problem was given up; in 1934, the U.S. Supreme Court held that the definition was up to the state legislature or Congress.[3] Thereafter it was up to the people, speaking through their elected representatives, to determine the industries to be regulated. The result has been a large expansion of government regulation.

The federal government is very largely responsible for regulation of the transportation industries, including railroads, intercity motor transport, airlines, and pipelines; the natural gas industry; and the various communications industries. The federal and state governments share responsibilities for regulation of electric power production, with the greater part of the job being done by

---

[3] The case was *Nebbia* v. *New York*, involving state regulations of milk production and distribution.

state agencies. State and local governments share the regulation of a wide variety of other types of enterprises, mostly small, such as barbershops and beauty parlors, restaurants, liquor stores, nursing homes (the list is almost endless), primarily with health purposes in mind but sometimes including prices and other aspects of the business.

The economic basis of regulation, at least in theory, is that competition cannot prevail because one firm could supply the market at lower costs per unit of output than two or more firms. If the market were left unregulated, the forces of competition would lead to the survival of only one seller, which as a monopoly would then be able to extract large profits from the community dependent on its services. The situation is sometimes called a "natural" monopoly, since it would result from the normal operation of economic forces. The general theoretical analysis is shown in Figure 33-2.

Once regulation of prices begins, however, the regulatory process must be extended very deeply into many aspects of the industry. Methods of accounting must be controlled in order to prevent escalation of costs due to inefficiency, dishonesty, or efforts to evade the intent of regulation. The value

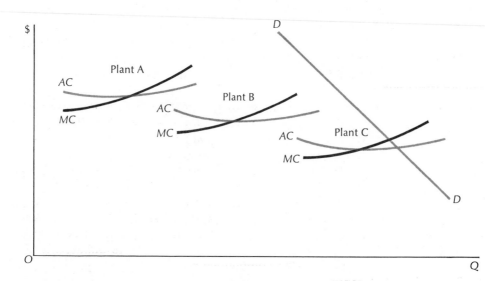

FIGURE 33-2

Natural Monopoly

Economies of large-scale production give Plant C a cost advantage over smaller producers. Competition could prevail for a time, but mergers and bankruptcies would soon leave but one firm. Alternatively, firms A and B could agree to share the market and fix prices, but this would mean higher costs of production and economic waste. With only one producer, however, lower costs need not be passed on to the public, calling forth regulation.

The line DD shows the market demand curve for the product, and the three AC curves show average costs for plants of three different sizes. As plant size is increased average costs of production are reduced. Since the size of the market is limited relative to the size of the lowest-cost producer, a single supplier would emerge.

of the utility's business assets must be determined in order to set a fair base on which the utility's rate of return on its investment can be estimated. That rate of return, together with the base, will help determine the rates. Furthermore, the rate structure must be set, because any utility has several types of customers —families, business firms, and so on—each with varying needs and ability to pay. Finally, the quality of service, safety, and efficiency must all be considered. By this time there is not much a utility does that is not under the jurisdiction of the regulatory agency.

The fact of regulation, however close and detailed, is not the underlying cause of the permanent crisis in public-utility regulation. Most of the differences between utility and regulatory body can be resolved satisfactorily, particularly since the utility always has resource to legal action if it can show that its rates are kept so low as to constitute deprivation of property. A utility is entitled to "a fair return on a fair value" and both utility and regulatory commission know it, while the courts are there to enforce the rule.

Nor is the problem necessarily that the regulatory commissions tend to be "captured" by the industries they are supposed to regulate, although that has always been an issue. Utility regulation is a complex job, requiring detailed knowledge of both the industry and the law. Appointments to commissions generally go to knowledgeable people, yet where can they be found outside the ranks of lawyers employed by the utilities themselves? Such people tend to have the attitudes and viewpoints of the companies and see issues through the industry's eyes. It is hard to get both knowledge and the consumer's point of view in the same person. The choice is often between lack of competence combined with a consumer viewpoint versus high competence combined with an industry viewpoint. The result is often predominance of the industry viewpoint on the regulatory commissions themselves.

Yet the fundamental difficulty lies elsewhere. Efforts to hold the returns to utilities down to the level that would prevail in a competitive market are doomed to failure in an economy in which many, and perhaps most, industries are oligopolistic or monopoloid in nature. The stable prices and substantial profits of industries like automobiles, petroleum refining, chemicals, and electrical equipment make it extremely difficult to attract capital to utilities whose rates of profit are kept close to the competitive norm by regulatory bodies. If profits on invested capital in most industrial oligopolies run upwards from 15 percent per year, how can even a sheltered and regulated monopoly get the capital it needs for expansion if its earnings are held to a "mere" 10 percent annually. Indeed, in recent years many regulated firms have tried to use the capital available from profits and depreciation charges to diversify into other and unregulated types of enterprise. The result has been significant deterioration of services and failure to expand rapidly enough to meet the needs of an expanding economy.

This economic reality can be stated as a very simple proposition. In an economy in which the chief alternative for the use of capital is investment in growing and monopoloid sectors of the economy, efforts to hold profits in regulated industries to competitive levels bring deterioration of service. Only if something close to oligopolistic profits is allowed can deterioration of service be prevented. If the rest of the economy were strongly competitive, this dilemma could be avoided. It isn't, however, so the regulatory agencies are in the unenviable position of either allowing high rates of return and correspondingly high charges or forcing an increasingly poor quality of service on the public. Again, no one is hurt except the consumer.

The next stage in the drama of public utility regulation is almost upon us. The alternatives to the present impasse are basically only three in number. They are:

1. Deregulation and reliance on competition. Let gas compete with electric power, telephone lines with microwave radio, and railroads with trucks, buses, and airlines; and let companies within each industry compete more strongly with each other. Modern technology may make possible a solution along these lines to a much greater extent than appears on the surface.

2. Subsidies to maintain better services. This solution merely passes on the burden to the general taxpayer and shifts it from the direct user of the service, however.

3. Government ownership. This solution may be nearer than we think for the nation's railroads. It has already occurred for railroad passenger service.

A fourth alternative is the present system, in which the quality of an essential service is held as a hostage for monopoloid profits.

GOVERNMENT SUPPORT OF MARKET CONTROL

The petroleum industry is the second largest industry in the United States, exceeded only in total sales by the automobile industry. Its fuel products are essential for the modern economy. One might expect government policy to promote competition in such a large and important segment of the economy. That is not the case. Instead, the federal and state governments cooperate with the eighteen large integrated oil companies in maintaining a system of market control. No one is hurt except the consumer.

First, the domestic market is protected from competition from abroad by federal legislation that restricts and licenses imports of crude oil. Import restrictions help maintain the domestic price of oil and its refined products above the level of a free market.

Second, production of crude oil within the U.S. is limited so as to maintain existing prices. The process operates as follows:

a. Each producing state (except California) has a regulatory commission empowered to set production quotas for that state's oil wells. An Interstate Oil Compact Commission, established by federal law and having the oil producing states as members, reaches agreement on each state's share of current output.

Until recently the U.S. Bureau of Mines made monthly estimates of consumer demand for gasoline and other petroleum products (based, of course, on existing prices), which were used to establish state production quotas. California does not participate because all of its oil is used in the state and more imported, so it does not need production quotas.

b. The quotas are enforced by the federal government. The Connally "Hot Oil" Act (1935) prohibits the transportation in interstate commerce of any oil produced above the quotas set by the state commissions.

Third, control of pipelines from oil fields to refineries by the industry giants gives them a strategic advantage over independent companies. A "consent decree"[4] by which independents have access to the pipelines on equal terms confirmed this position legally. It enables the pipeline owner to earn a profit from transporting his competitor's raw materials.

The effect of these practices is to stabilize prices and protect the existing large firms from challenges to their market position. The oil industry is able to charge prices for its products that not only give it a normal profit, but enough more to provide almost all the capital needed for investment in expanded capacity. The rest comes from the tax subsidy provided by large depletion allowances, which also provides incentives for the companies to expand their output in the U.S. Few large oil companies ever have to get new capital by borrowing or issuing new stock.[5] This enables the existing stockholders to monopolize the full gains from economic growth rather than share those gains with suppliers of new capital. Capital for expansion comes from the consumer of gasoline and fuel oil, and from the taxpayer, but the gains go to oil company stockholders.

There is a dual justification for this system: it is supposed to promote conservation of oil supplies and maintain large domestic production as an aid for national defense. But just to state these twin goals is to point out a basic contradiction. Conservation of domestic supplies is antithetical to maintenance of large domestic production. If we really wanted to conserve supplies at home, we would use imported oil to a far greater extent.

As for national defense, it is argued that the U.S. needs a large domestic oil production in case foreign supplies were to be cut off in times of war. If this argument ever made sense, it no longer does. War with the only nation able to cut off foreign oil supplies would last perhaps six minutes. The U.S. has oil supplies enough for that. Besides, there wouldn't be much oil refining

---

[4] A consent decree is a court order under which a firm or firms accused of violating the antitrust laws agree to a settlement agreeable also to the Department of Justice, without admitting that they were guilty of anything for which they were charged.

[5] The inflation of the late 1960s forced the large oil companies to go to the capital markets for new capital on a significant scale for the first time since the 1920s.

capacity left. At best it might be argued that the U.S. bargaining position in international politics may be strengthened if the domestic oil market is supplied from domestic sources. But this is a tenuous argument: Bargaining with whom? For what? And how will the U.S. position be strengthened?

The general principle illustrated by the example of the oil industry is not widely understood or appreciated. *When a community or a nation becomes dependent on a single company or group of companies for a vitally important product or service, the company or companies can exact a large and sometimes increasing toll from the community as a condition of continuing to provide the product or service.* The oil industry has national security as its hostage, and its toll is prices high enough to provide all of the capital needed for replacement, for expansion, and for diversification (into chemicals, for example).

Political power is often added to economic power. The oil industry is supported by the votes of congressmen and senators from states and localities heavily dependent on the oil industry for jobs and prosperity. Now that the industry has become dependent on artificially high prices to sustain relatively high levels of domestic output, any large change in the system that controls production will encounter very strong political opposition.

The petroleum industry is not the only one supported by government programs that help fix levels of output and prices. Agriculture is the most obvious example (see Chapter 26). In that case the subsidies come directly out of government appropriations and are obvious to all. The chief beneficiaries are the large agricultural enterprises. The oil industry has been more subtle: its subsidies come from tax exemptions, which are not obvious, and from artificially high prices, which are *really* hidden.

Another recent example is the textile industry. Plagued by rising imports of cheap fabrics and clothing imported from Asia, it was able in 1970 to get import restrictions imposed against its competition and continues to push for more. The existing firms and employees are benefited, of course, but the buyer of textile products pays prices higher than he would otherwise have to pay. Since imported textiles and clothing are primarily in the lower-price lines, it is the poor consumer who bears the largest share of the burden. The chief beneficiaries in this case are workers as well as business firms.

These patterns of market control have their source in the federal government. For agricultural industries, the federal government operates a production and import quota system that effectively controls the output and price of sugar; milk production and marketing is controlled in the "milk sheds" of big cities; and a system of agreements among growers of commodities produced within limited geographical areas, such as fruits, nuts, and some vegetables, is administered by the Department of Agriculture. All of this is in addition to the price controls–subsidy system applied to important crops.

For many years, the federal government sought to control output and prices of bituminous coal, but several attempts failed, the latest being price controls during World War II, which were allowed to lapse in 1943. The union succeeded where government failed, however. Now output is managed by the United Mine Workers of America in cooperation with the principal producers. The union contract stipulates that the miners will work only when they are "willing and able." At times when output appears to be too great to maintain existing prices, the workers are not "willing and able" to work more than, for example, a three-day week. At times the length of the work week is managed by the large firms, and at times by the union, but both have similar interests in stabilizing prices. The benefits to the companies are obvious. The union is able to get high wages for its members because of the "stabilized" prices. This system of output management was the outgrowth of earlier efforts of the federal government to achieve stable (read "profitable") prices in the industry. It continues under union-management auspices partly through lack of knowledge on the part of the public and partly through tacit acceptance by the federal government. Without it, prices and wages in the industry would be lower and the cost of electric power would be reduced. Again, only the consuming public is hurt.

The federal government has supported and promoted big enterprise and market control in other ways. Its research program in atomic energy developed an entirely new source of power, and then turned it over for development to the existing regulated monopolies in electric power. Procurement for defense and the military has strongly tended to favor large firms. So did the strategic materials stockpile program, which is now largely phased out. Tax policies providing for rapid amortization of new investment have been of special help to large firms. Indeed, the two economists who have studied the situation most fully have written: "The Federal government—although by tradition, popular regard, and legal mandate the defender of competition—has by a process of functional perversion become one of the principal bulwarks of concentration and monopoly."[6]

PUBLIC OWNERSHIP

One alternative to an economy based on large corporations grouped informally with each other is public ownership. This "socialistic" alternative has been given little consideration and not much trial in the United States, although one of the most successful publicly owned enterprises in all the world, the Tennessee Valley Authority, is run by the federal government. The TVA precedent is worth exploring further.

First, we should note that public ownership of utilities is quite common at the level of local government. This includes a wide variety of enterprises

---

[6] Walter Adams and Horace M. Gray, *Monopoly in America: The Government as Promoter* (New York: Macmillan, 1955). Although old and partly out of date, this book is still the best general statement of how the federal government promotes market control in the economy. See also Clair Wilcox, *Public Policies Toward Business* (Homewood, Ill.: Richard D. Irwin, 3rd ed., 1966), Chaps. 27–32.

such as water systems, sewer systems, garbage and trash collection, swimming pools, golf courses, and tennis courts. Most port facilities in large cities like New York or San Francisco are publicly owned. Even some electric power and telephone services are publicly owned, either by governments or by the families that use the service. None need be public; in almost all parts of the country there are private enterprises that operate all of the business activities named above.

Second, there is no reason to believe that a large bureaucratic private corporation need be any more or less efficient than a large bureaucratic public enterprise. Business firms seem to be more efficient than government agencies, most of the time, because their performance can be measured in dollars of cost and profit. Most government services are not subject to such simple criteria for purposes of evaluation because their goals are usually more diverse than those of private firms. But where the behavior of government agencies can also be measured with the yardstick of the market, as in the case of TVA or the Port of New York Authority, some highly efficient operations are found. Who would be so brave as to argue that the Penn Central Railroad is more efficient than the Pennsylvania Turnpike Authority or the New York Through-way Authority?

Third, the great drawback to public enterprise is lack of freedom from political interference. Special and often narrow interests are allowed to impinge upon the decision-making process, drawing it away from efficiency considerations and toward political expediency. This was the underlying problem of the Post Office, which may have been even less efficient an organization than the Penn Central Railroad.

Fourth, the government-owned enterprise has a striking advantage that the private corporation does not share; its long-term goals are to further the public welfare rather than to further private interests. This pervasive theme influences all of the activities of government-owned enterprises, from selection of management through labor relations to determination of the level and type of services it will provide. Profits are not there to be piled up or distributed to the owners, but are inherently limited and are to be used for the benefit of the public. No private corporation can do that.

These remarks would imply that, ideological considerations aside, public ownership of business enterprises, properly structured to eliminate political interference and to provide market tests of efficiency and effectiveness, may be a highly useful alternative to the giant private corporation.

Public ownership need not encompass all of an industry in order for it to be useful. One significant firm in an industry, owned by the public, can provide a working "yardstick" against which privately owned firms may be judged. It can also prevent the tight control of a market leader from being effective. Indeed, an industry in which only one firm is publicly owned, competing with several private enterprises, may provide the best environment for good performance for the industry as a whole. Desire on the part of the public firm's management to show that they can do a better job than private enterprise, countered by the private firm's efforts to do well so as not to be nationalized, can provide a healthy discipline for both. This situation has certainly prevailed in the electric power industry ever since the establishment of TVA.[7] Public-private competition has also worked well in railroad transportation in Canada, where half the railway network is publicly owned and half is owned by a single private firm. The private firm is thriving, the public firm is subsidized (its lines run through less densely populated areas) and Canada has noticeably better rail transport services than the U.S., with its private but regulated system.

This "yardstick" approach to improved performance in monopoloid industries, via public-private competition, might well be applied to industrial oligopolies as well as to public utilities and transportation. Why should not the federal government own and operate one of the large integrated steel companies, one of the large automobile manufacturers, one of the large pharmaceutical firms, one of the chief electrical equipment manufacturers, one of the large oil companies? At the very least, there would be less tacit and overt collusion, for one of the large firms, the public one, would refrain from playing that game. At best, those industries would get a larger dose of competition than any of them have experienced for decades. It would do everyone a lot of good. Even the consumer would benefit.

ECONOMIC POWER AND THE LARGE CORPORATION

The large corporation is more than an organization that produces and distributes goods and services. Its decisions affect the lives of many people: employees, customers, and the general public. The choices available to customers are the result of administrative decisions within corporate organizations. Wage decisions affect the distribution of income. Decisions about levels of output influence the prosperity of many communities. Decisions about location of plants influence the growth or stagnation of local areas. Market strategies affect the prices paid by consumers and influence the sharing of economic gains by stockholders, workers, and customers. In all of these ways, corporate decisions govern various aspects of individual lives and the way of life of communities and the nation. In this broad sense, the large corporation takes on some aspects of government: its decisions affect the way people live and the alternatives open to them.

This aspect of the large corporation is well recognized by corporate executives. A conscious effort is made to be "good corporate citizens." A good deal of the advertising and public relations efforts of large corporations is

---

[7] Competition between public and private firms in the same industry should be on an equal basis, especially with respect to the cost of capital. This has not been true of TVA, which is able to borrow with U.S. Treasury guarantees, thereby obtaining capital at lower cost than private firms. This special advantage should not be continued since it represents a national subsidy for users of electric power in the TVA service area.

devoted to the theme that the corporation seeks to do things that benefit the community. "Progress is our most important product" was the advertising theme of one of the giant conspirators in the electrical equipment price fixing case. But when community welfare or equity or other public goals become objectives of corporate policy, one of the long-standing distinctions between the public and private sectors becomes obscured. The private corporation takes on a public aspect.

Corporate power is characterized by the independence of corporate management from any well-defined responsibility to anyone. The stockholder typically offers few restraints. Government gives a generally free hand to corporate decisions within a broad legal framework. The chief restraints are the corporate rewards and promotion system, the financial community, and the network of intercorporate relationships. Corporate power is exercised by men who are largely responsible to themselves alone. The essence of the problem, then, is that corporate power is unilaterally used in ways that increasingly affect the public, yet the public has little influence over that power.

The power of the large corporation manifests itself in many ways. Perhaps its most pervasive influence is exerted through the mass media by way of advertising. A philosophy emphasizing the virtues of materialism, of consuming more, of buying the latest style runs continually through advertising appeals. One reason for its use is its success: it taps some deep and persistent attitudes on the part of the general public. But it also contributes to the persistence of those values.

Politically the large corporation has its greatest leverage at the local and state level. Plant location, expansion, or contraction are powerful levers with which tax concessions, zoning laws, roads and related matters become items for negotiation between sovereign powers rather than merely the results of the will of the people. In this contest the corporation has some major advantages: great scope of choice, strong financial resources, knowledgeable management and the best legal talent, while governments at the local and state level are often weak and change frequently.

Finally, the large corporation affects the larger society in subtle ways. Business leadership tends to become society's leadership. Business leaders become government administrators, particularly in such federal departments as State, Defense, Commerce, and Interior, and in agencies like the Atomic Energy Commission and the Central Intelligence Agency. Most of the "national security managers" of the last thirty years have been businessmen (or lawyers from firms specializing in corporate law). Business leaders take a leading role in big charitable organizations and on the boards of trustees of big foundations and universities. Indeed, business leadership is usually a necessary prerequisite for leading positions in such organizations. The result: the value system and attitudes necessary for promotion within the large corporation are transferred to many other aspects of American life.

We can sum these points by saying that the economic position of the large corporation enables its leaders to shape political action, attitudes, and a whole way of life into its own image. Along the way, some special economic advantages may be obtained for particular corporations. But even if that were not the case, and antitrust laws and utility regulation are attempts to minimize the toll, the significant import of the giant corporation is its tendency to become the dominant force throughout the entire social and economic order.

THE ALTERNATIVES BEFORE US

The significance of big business for present-day America goes beyond the issues of market power, narrowly defined to mean influence over prices. As the characteristic economic organization of our time, big business influences our value system, our public policy, and our goals. Its presence and growing influence require a rethinking of some of our most widely accepted social policies.

The choices of policy, when reduced to the essentials, come down to three large alternatives.

1. The present policies that have led to a large and growing presence and influence for big enterprise can be continued. They promise more of the same gradual accretion of big-business influence. Radicals claim that down that path lies fascism.

2. Big business can be socialized and brought under government owner-ship and management. There are two variations of the socialist solution.
   a. One is the centralized and perhaps authoritarian variety that involves detailed administrative planning. Conservatives argue that this solution leads directly to 1984.
   b. The second variant is a decentralized system of market social-ism as described in Chapter 29. The problem here is that it is largely untried.

3. The third choice is to retain private enterprise but without the giant corporation. Make little ones out of big ones, even at the cost of some inefficiency. Nationalize the few giants that can't be effectively broken up. But get back to more competitive markets.

The first solution is the easiest, for it essentially retains the status quo and keeps up on our present path of development. All of the others are radical solutions, for each represents a substantial break from the existing pattern. Which do we want?

Summary

Public policy toward big business has been a curious mixture. The antitrust laws were a reaction against the rise of big business, but they have not been effective in curbing its growth. The "rule of reason" interpretation of the Sherman Act allowed large firms to continue as long as they did not harass other firms: it gave tacit approval to the live-and-let-live policies that naturally develop in oligopolistic industries. The Clayton Act's provisions that were directed against bigness were ineffective. The Federal Trade Commission has not taken vigorous action against big business. The Robinson-Patman Act has had the unintended effect of holding back price competition. On the other hand, all of this legislation has permitted strong action against business firms that restrict or eliminate competition by collusion, coercion, or other means.

Regulation of monopoly was developed simultaneously with antitrust policy to cover those sectors of the economy in which competition was thought to be impractical. It has not been an unqualified success either. Quality of service tends to deteriorate unless returns to the regulated industry are equal to those that can be earned elsewhere, and that includes the oligopolistic and high-profit industries. At the present time there is widespread agreement that current regulatory practices are unsatisfactory. The alternatives are deregulation and return to competition, public subsidies, or public ownership.

While government policy has been ostensibly one of controlling the growth of big business and regulating monopoly, the federal government has done many things to promote big enterprise. The petroleum industry is perhaps the best example, but there are others as well.

Finally, public ownership is another approach to the problem, especially since publicly owned enterprises seem to be potentially as efficient as large-scale private enterprises. One form of public ownership might be particularly effective: "yardstick" operation of a small portion of an industry that is designed to force the remaining privately owned portion to operate more effectively.

Public policy toward big business is confused. Antitrust policy and regulation are ostensibly intended to protect the public interest, while other government policies foster and succor big enterprise. Public ownership has been used only on a small scale. Meanwhile the economic and political power of big business has become a serious problem that few are willing to face.

Key Concepts

Antitrust laws.   Laws designed to prevent monopoly and promote competition, chiefly the Sherman Act (1890), Clayton Act (1914), Federal Trade Commission Act (1914), and Robinson-Patman Act (1936).

"Rule of reason."   The legal rule that only "unreasonable" restraint of trade was prohibited by the Sherman Act.

Public utility regulation.   Government regulation of "natural monopolies," later broadened to industries "affected with the public interest," when preservation of competition was felt to be impractical.

"Yardstick" firm.   A government-owned and -operated firm in an otherwise private industry.

THE DISTRIBUTION OF INCOME AND WEALTH

VIII

The five chapters of Part VIII examine the distribution of income in the contemporary economy. We start in Chapter 34 by showing that the pricing of the factors of production rests to a very large degree on their productivity. In an economy in which there are significant deviations from the purely competitive model, as in ours, analysis of income distribution must go beyond the market forces of supply and demand and the productivity of the factors of production to analyze the impact of market power as it is exercised by big business and big unions. That is done in Chapter 35, which examines unions and collective bargaining and the role they play in the distribution of income. In Chapter 36 we take a further look at the facts about the distribution of income in the United States, going beyond the material provided in Chapter 7, to inquire into the persistence of poverty in an affluent society. We find that some of the causes of poverty are built into the structure of our economy and tend to preserve and perpetuate low incomes. Chapter 37 looks at the other end of the scale, at the distribution of wealth. It pinpoints the ownership of property as another factor that determines the pattern of income distribution. Finally, we ask the crucial question in Chapter 38: What sort of income distribution is most likely to maximize human welfare? The conclusion favors redistribution of income along more equalitarian lines, which many economists would dispute as a value-laden, unscientific answer.

At any rate, the five chapters expound five elements important in determining the distribution of income:

Market forces, especially the productivity of the factors of production.

The locus and structure of economic power.

Structural or institutional elements in the economy that tend to perpetuate poverty.

The distribution of wealth and income from property.

Government policies.

The theory of marginal productivity is the cornerstone of the analysis of the distribution of income in the modern economy. The return to any factor of production is determined by the interaction in the market between demand for the factor and its supply. Behind the demand curve, however, is the usefulness of the factor of production to its users. That usefulness is derived from the productivity of the factor in generating income for the firm that uses it. These fundamental propositions are worked out in this chapter through the marginal analysis under the assumption of profit-maximizing behavior on the part of business firms. The theory, however, has serious limitations as an explanation for the pattern of income distribution, and the chapter closes with a discussion of the most significant difficulties.

The Theory of Marginal Productivity

34

DEMAND AND SUPPLY IN FACTOR MARKETS

In a competitive market economy the price of any factor of production is determined by the interaction of demand and supply in the market. Figure 34-1 shows the situation. The earnings of the factor will rise if the demand for it goes up. Both the price and the amount used will rise. Even though the supply of the factor may increase, as long as the demand for it outpaces the growth in supply, the price it earns in the market will go up. Real wages for example, have risen in the United States well above the level of fifty years ago, even though population has grown and immigration has brought additions to the labor force. The underlying reason has been an increase in the demand for labor that overcame the effects of the increase in supply. Figures 34-2 and 34-3 show these relationships of demand and supply in the labor market.

DEMAND FOR A FACTOR OF PRODUCTION

The demand for a factor of production is determined by its productivity at the margin. Just as the demand for a consumer's good is based on its utility at the margin, so the demand for a producer's good (any input into the production process) is based on its usefulness at the margin to the user.

Here is an example. A manufacturer of electronic circuits can add another worker to his assembly line at an hourly rate of $3.00. Doing so will increase his total

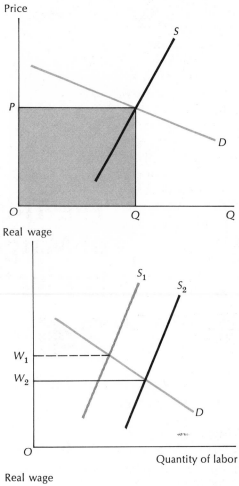

FIGURE 34-1

Determination of Income of a Factor of Production in a Competitive Market

The price per unit of the factor is OP, the number of units used or employed is OQ, and the total income earned by the factor is equal to $P \times Q$ (the shaded area).

FIGURE 34-2

If there had been no change in the demand for labor, the increase in the size of the work force that shifted the supply from S_1 to S_2 would have brought real wages down from W_1 to W_2.

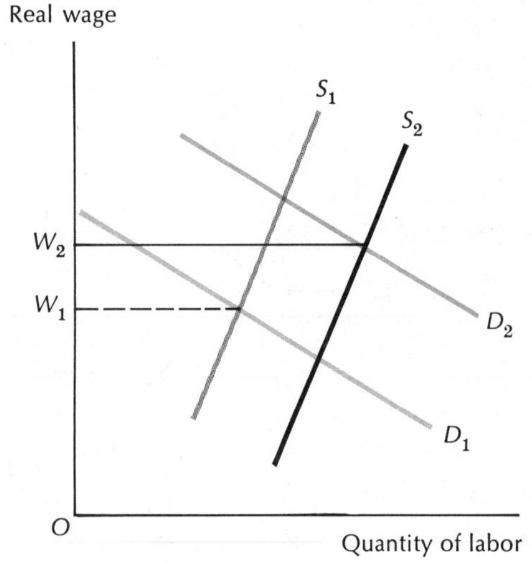

FIGURE 34-3

Instead, while the supply of labor increased from S_1 to S_2, the demand for it increased from D_1 to D_2, bringing real wages up from W_1 to W_2.

output per hour by 10 units, which are sold for 50¢ each. The manufacturer's revenues will increase by $5 per hour (10 units × 50¢), but his costs will rise only $3 (we assume that there are no other additional costs aside from the added worker). Hiring the additional worker will add $2 to net revenues, and the employer will do so. This is exactly parallel to the decision of a consumer on whether he should or should not buy another unit of a good. In that case the consumer (the buyer) compared costs with utility at the margin. In this case the employer (the buyer) compares costs with revenue at the margin.

Marginal Revenue Product

Economists have given the name *marginal revenue product* to the increase in revenue resulting from an increase in employment of a factor of production. In our last example it was the $5 per hour increase in revenue derived from hiring an additional worker.

As an employer adds units of any factor of production to his existing operations he will increase his output, but at a diminishing rate. This is because of the law of diminishing returns: As a variable factor of production is added to a fixed factor, or to a fixed combination of other factors, increases in output will be obtained; the increases will start diminishing in size at some point, however. This proposition was explained and illustrated in Chapter 3.

In competitive markets, each unit of output is sold at the market price, irrespective of the amount sold by a single firm. The marginal revenue product is equal to the marginal physical product multiplied by the price of the product:

$$MRP = MPP \times P.$$

It follows that the marginal revenue product will decline in exactly the same pattern as the quantity of the marginal product, as in Table 34-1.

TABLE 34-1
Marginal Productivity in Competitive Firm

Number of Units of Factor A	Number of Units of Output	Marginal Physical Product	Price of Output per Unit	Value MPP × P	Marginal Revenue Product
100	1000				
101	1010	10	$10	$100	$100
102	1019	9	10	90	90
103	1027	8	10	80	80
104	1034	7	10	70	70
105	1040	6	10	60	60

The case of the firm in a monopoloid industry is different. It cannot sell increases in output unless it reduces its price. Its marginal revenue product will reflect not only a declining physical product due to diminishing returns, but also the price reductions required to sell increased output. This means that its marginal revenue product will be below that of an identical competitive firm and will fall more rapidly. Table 34-2 gives an example of those relationships for a monopoloid firm identical with the competitive firm of the previous table.

TABLE 34-2
Marginal Productivity in Monopoloid Firm

Number of Units of Factor A	Number of Units of Output	Marginal Physical Product	Price of Output per Unit	$MPP \times P$	Marginal Revenue Product
100	1000		$10.00		
101	1010	10	9.95	$99.50	$49.50
102	1019	9	9.90	89.10	38.60
103	1027	8	9.85	78.80	27.85
104	1034	7	9.80	68.60	17.25
105	1040	6	9.75	59.50	7.80

The differences in the two cases can be shown graphically, in Figure 34-4 and Figure 34-5.

The difference between the two occurs because for the monopoloid firm MR is below the selling price for its product, while for the competitive firm $MR = P$. As the tables show, $MRP = MPP \times P$ for the competitive firm but not for the monopoloid firm. For the latter, $MRP = MPP \times MR$ to provide a different MRP even though MPP is the same.

This distinction is important, for the demand for a factor of production is determined by its marginal revenue product. A firm may be willing to hire

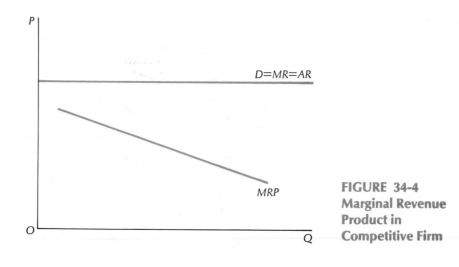

FIGURE 34-4
Marginal Revenue
Product in
Competitive Firm

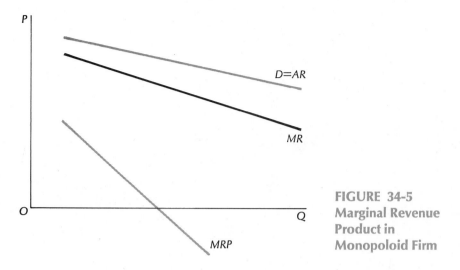

FIGURE 34-5
Marginal Revenue
Product in
Monopoloid Firm

an additional worker for a wage that equals the additional revenue derived from hiring the worker. But it won't hire the added worker if the wage is greater than the additional revenue obtained.

EQUILIBRIUM OF THE INDIVIDUAL FIRM

We have shown that the individual firm is faced with a declining MRP curve as it adds additional units of a factor of production to its existing operations, whether its industry is competitive or monopoloid. The next step is to analyze its decision to hire. How much of the factor will the firm use? How many units will it hire?

Here the competitive and the oligopolistic firm must part company. We can assume that the competitive firm seeks to maximize its profits, for if it didn't it couldn't survive in the long run. The oligopolistic firm, as we have already seen, may or may not seek to maximize its profits either in the long run or the short run. Knowing the behavioral rules for firms that maximize profits, we can start with that case.

First, we specify the situation. The firm uses only two factors of production, labor and capital. The prices of both factors are determined by the inter-action of demand and supply in competitive markets. Finally, the firm's goal is profit maximization, which is achieved by equalizing costs and revenues at the margin. We shall start with the decision to employ labor, but the analysis will apply to capital as well.

With a fixed amount of capital, the firm will increase its employment of labor until labor's marginal revenue product equals the wage rate. As long as MRP is greater than the wage rate, an additional worker can be hired and profits can be increased. A competitive firm will do just that, up to the point at which MRP falls to equal the wage rate. This profit-maximizing situation is shown in Figure 34-6.

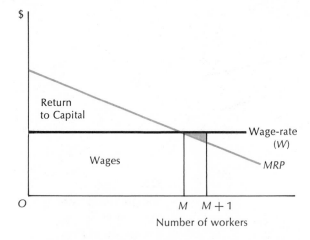

FIGURE 34-6
Marginal Productivity and
Profit Maximization
(Labor the Variable Factor)

Exactly the same analysis can be applied to capital and the return paid to it. The firm will increase its use of capital up to the point at which capital's marginal value product is just equal to the payment that must be made for its use. Holding the number of workers constant but adding capital to the enterprise merely reverses the position of the diagram, as shown in Figure 34-7.

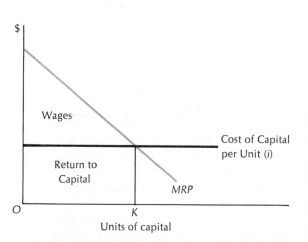

FIGURE 34-7
Marginal Productivity and
Profit Maximization
(Capital the Variable Factor)
Increasing the amount of capital with a fixed amount of labor, the firm employs K units of capital. At that point capital's *MRP* equals its cost (given by the rate of interest in the money markets) and a profit-maximizing position has been reached. The areas marked "Return to capital" in this figure and Figure 34-6 are equal, and so are the areas marked "Wages."

Factors of production are not used independently of each other, however. A more expensive factor can be replaced by a less expensive one, to a limited extent in the short run but very widely in the long run. In the short run, with the size of the plant and its process of production fixed, not much substitution of factors can take place. In the long run, a wide variety of plant sizes can be chosen, along with one of the several production processes that are usually known. Substitution of factors can be very wide in the long run. Whatever the time period, the search for the least-cost combination of factors goes on simultaneously with the effort to push the use of each factor to the point at which $MRP = P$ for the factor.

The least-cost combination of the factors of production is achieved when the MRP derived from a dollar's worth of one is equal to the MRP derived from a dollar's worth of any other. If we designate the factors as $a, b, c, \ldots, n$, then

$$\frac{MRP_a}{P_a} = \frac{MRP_b}{P_b} = \frac{MRP_c}{P_c} = \cdots = \frac{MRP_n}{P_n}.$$

This formulation is analogous to the consumer's utility-maximizing allocation of his income. In this case, a similar principle is involved, except that it is a producer allocating his limited resources to maximize profit instead of a consumer allocating limited income to maximize satisfactions.

Suppose that a firm does not achieve this least-cost combination of the factors of production, that is, that

$$\frac{MRP_a}{P_a} > \frac{MRP_b}{P_b}.$$

In this case, the last dollar spent on hiring Factor a brings in greater revenue than the last dollar spent on hiring Factor b. The firm could raise its profits by using less of Factor b and more of Factor a. By substituting a for b, it will eventually move to the least-cost combination of the factors.

There are two basic conditions for profit maximization in the internal operations of a firm that must be simultaneously achieved:

Strong 1. $MRP = P$ for each factor of production. *PRofit maximization*

Weak 2. $\frac{MRP_a}{P_a} = \frac{MRP_b}{P_b}$ for all factors of production used in combination. *Cost minimization*

2 is implied in 1

The first condition is subsumed under the second; that is, if the second is achieved the first will automatically be achieved. We have separated them here for purposes of analysis, however. The first adds strength to the analysis that showed the welfare-maximizing relationship between marginal utility and marginal cost in the market-adjustment process. It shows that each factor's use within the individual firm reflects that same adjustment. The second condition is the basic principle of cost minimization that was briefly alluded to in Chapter 25. It shows how substitution of lower for higher cost factors of production enables the firm to minimize average costs and provides the basis for its decision about which process of production to use and which size plant to build. Both of those decisions involve cost minimization, based on the second condition cited here.

THE DEMAND CURVE FOR A
FACTOR OF PRODUCTION

We can now move from the individual firm's demand for a factor of production to the market demand curve for the factor. For any factor of production, the MRP curve defines the firm's demand for the factor of production. The industry's demand for the factor will be the sum of the demands of the individual firms. The total demand for the factor in the economy as a whole will be the sum of all the industry demand curves for the factor. This, of course, brings us back to the original demand curve for the factor, which, together with the supply curve, determines its price and the total income paid to the factor.

Underneath the market demand curve is the productivity of the factor at the margin. In the case of pure competition, the price that firms are willing to pay for the factor reflects the factor's marginal physical product, and through it the influence of diminishing returns. In the case of monopoloid firms a second element is at work, however. That element is the firm's market position, which results in a marginal revenue product curve influenced both by diminishing returns and by the structure of the industry.

RETURNS TO THE FACTORS OF PRODUCTION

When we apply the theory of marginal productivity to the distribution of income in the economy as a whole, the analysis seems initially to be a simple extension of the theory, at least as long as we stick to the case of pure competition. It tells us that the total revenue (and total output) of the economy is distributed to the factors of production according to their productivity at the margin.

We are given inputs 1, 2, . . ., n, each one of which has a price determined by the interaction of demand and supply in the market. Since the demand curve for the factor is its marginal revenue product, $P = MRP$ for each factor. We should then be able to multiply each factor's MRP by the number of units employed, add those sums together, and obtain the total income earned:

$$MRP_1 \times N_1 + MRP_2 \times N_2 + \cdots + MRP_n \times N_n = TRP,$$

where marginal revenue product of Factor 1 times the number of units of Factor 1 *plus* the marginal revenue product of each other factor times its number of units *equals* the total revenue product.

This proposition embodies a distribution of income among the factors of production in which each factor's share of the total is determined by its marginal revenue product and the number of units of the factor. Since the units of any factor are homogeneous, no one unit can be distinguished from any other and each will get its proportionate share of that factor's portion of the whole; that is, each unit of any factor will receive a return equal to the MRP of that factor. Thus, all units of a particular type and skill level of labor will receive a wage equal to the MRP of that type of labor.

MARGINAL PRODUCTIVITY AND ECONOMIC JUSTICE

The theory of marginal productivity is the cornerstone of the argument that economic justice is one of the products of a competitive private enterprise economy. The market mechanism assures any factor of production a return (wage, profit, rent) equal to its contribution to total output at the margin. If a worker, for example, is offered a wage lower than his marginal revenue product, he can go somewhere else, to an employer who will be willing to pay him a wage equal to his *MRP*, if we assume competitive conditions in the labor market. The employer, on the other hand, motivated by his desire to maximize profits, pushes added employment until *MRP* = *W*. Both market opportunity and business motivations assure that the wage will equal *MRP* in a competitive market. Since the same is true of capital and any other factors of production, whatever their quality, no one can exploit anyone else and everyone gets what he deserves. At least, according to the theory.

The economic justice that emerges from the market is a special sort, however. It means inequality rather than equality. Individuals are born different, with different combinations of skills and abilities. These inherited differences will be reflected in differences in productivity and hence in incomes. Individuals also have different experiences in their youth and education that create differences in attitudes, motivations, and skills. These differences will also be reflected in differences in productivity and in income. Even if we leave out of consideration such factors as inherited wealth (and position) and unearned incomes, the concept of economic justice embodied in the theory of marginal productivity is one that is rooted in the values of the marketplace. An individual's income is determined solely by the value placed upon his efforts by the marketplace. A human being is, indeed, worth only as much as he is valued in the market. The competitive market economy first defines what is meant by economic justice and then proceeds to achieve it.

IS THERE A SURPLUS?

One point needs to be cleared up before we go any further. Is all of the value of the economy's output accounted for when each factor of production earns a return equal to its *MRP*? If it is, the theory of marginal productivity is a satisfactory explanation. If it isn't, something is wrong: there may be a surplus or a deficit to fight over.

Karl Marx argued that a private enterprise economy produced *surplus value* represented by the profit paid to capital. He argued that all production is the result of human effort, and that a return to labor was the only justifiable one. Capital was thought of as the result of past labor effort which had been appropriated by capitalists (owners of capital) who had no right to its earnings since they did not labor for that reward. The attempt of capitalists to enlarge this surplus and appropriate more was seen by Marx as the root of the conflict between labor and capital that would ultimately destroy capitalism.

Even if Marx's analysis were wrong, however, a disparity between the total output of an economy and the earnings postulated by the theory of marginal productivity would open the door to conflict over how a surplus or a deficit would be shared.

We can visualize the problem by returning to the analysis of the individual competitive firm and its decisions to hire the various factors of production. In Figure 34-8 (the same as Figure 34-6) the firm equalizes the wage rate

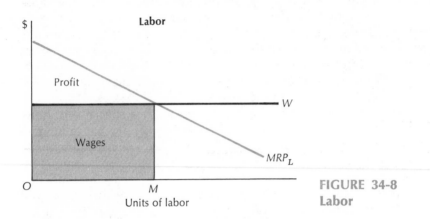

FIGURE 34-8
Labor

with labor's *MRP* and employs *M* workers. The shaded rectangle is the amount of the total output paid to labor, while the upper triangle is the profit paid to capital (assuming only two factors of production).

Now turn to Figure 34-9 (the same as Figure 34-7), where the shaded rectangle is the profit earned by capital as a result of the firm's decision to employ *N* units of capital, based on a cost of capital set by *I* and an *MRP* schedule for capital as shown. The wages in Figure 34-8 plus the profit in Figure 34-9 must add up to the total area under the *MRP* curve in Figure 34-8 if the theory is to be an adequate explanation of the division of income

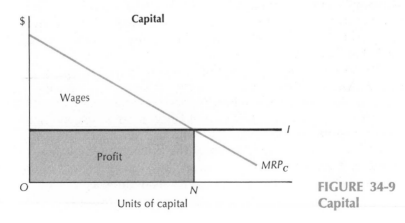

FIGURE 34-9
Capital

between the two factors. The rectangle of one diagram must equal in area the triangle of the other diagram. If it does not, there will be either an unexplained surplus or an unexplained deficit and conflict between the two factors of production.

This may seem like a trivial problem, but its resolution involves some of the fundamental issues of modern society. Is there an inherent conflict within capitalism between labor and capital? Or is it possible to achieve a just division between the two? In the ideological debates engendered by Marxism, this issue has been quite important, and for a time it appeared as if the economists had an answer.

There is a mathematical proof for the proposition that the entire product will be used up in paying each factor of production a return equal to its productivity at the margin. The proof, however, requires two highly restrictive assumptions. One is that total output can be increased indefinitely without causing an increase in the cost per unit of output. The other is that pure competition prevails. Yet the former is contradicted by the limitations of technology (except, *perhaps,* with exceptionally long time horizons) and the latter by the organizational facts of the economy, (except, again *perhaps,* in the very long run). As a result, the theory of marginal productivity satisfactorily explains the pattern of income distribution only in the long run and only if both restrictive assumptions prevail.

The inability of economic analysis to show conclusively that the economy's total product will be exhausted if each factor is paid a return equal to its marginal revenue product makes it impossible to accept the theory as a general explanation for the distribution of income.

THE VALIDITY OF THE THEORY

The problems we have with the theory of marginal productivity seem to leave any theory of income distribution a complete wreck. A theory that tells us how a profit-maximizing firm will determine its use of the factors of production, when the price of the factor is determined in the market, cannot be generalized into a consistent theory of income distribution.

But it cannot be ignored altogether. For it tells us that under competitive conditions there is a tendency for each factor of production to earn a return equal to its productivity at the margin. Clearly there are pure market forces that tend to equalize rewards with the marginal contribution made to total output.

Even the failure of the theory to provide an adequate explanation of the total pattern of income distribution is helpful. The difficulties of the theory lead us to expect conflict over income distribution. It even tells us where to look for its sources: in technological factors, or in the gains and losses created by monopoloid elements in economy. We have already seen that monopoloid characteristics pervade the American economy, just as many competitive characteristics do, and that the mixture varies from one sector of the economy to another. We also know that labor and management bargain, and sometimes fight, with each other over the division of revenues. Neither would behave that way if market forces were the sole determinant of rewards.

We can also observe that people invest large sums and important parts of their lives in education and training that increases the value of their work and brings higher incomes. If rewards did not depend on productivity, at least in part, we should not expect to find such behavior.

Although the theory of marginal productivity helps us to understand some of the market forces that affect the distribution of income, it is at best a partial explanation. To understand income distribution in the modern economy, we must go beyond the pure economics of the market to examine the bargaining power that economic interest groups bring to bear on each other, the structural causes of poverty, the effect of large holdings of property, and the impact of government. In the next chapter we will begin those inquiries by looking at labor unions and their impact on the distribution of income and the locus of economic power.

Summary

The price of a factor of production is determined in the market for that factor, and depends on the conditions of supply and demand that prevail.

The demand for any input by the individual firm, when the price of the input is given, depends on the input's marginal revenue product. The profit-maximizing firm will use any input in the quantity at which its price is equal to its marginal revenue product. The profit-maximizing firm will also substitute less expensive factors for more expensive factors until the marginal revenue products per dollar for each are equal to each other. The firm will achieve an internal profit-maximizing equilibrium when

$$MRP = P \quad \text{for each input,}$$

$$\frac{MRP_a}{P_a} = \frac{MRP_b}{P_b} = \frac{MRP_c}{P_c} = \cdots = \frac{MRP_n}{P_n},$$

where $a, b, c, \ldots, n$ are its inputs.

When the theory of marginal productivity is generalized to a theory of income distribution, it must be limited to the purely competitive model in the long run. It is only under those conditions that payments to inputs on the basis of their productivity at the margin can be shown to result in full exhaustion of the product. Nevertheless, the theory explains market forces that are always at work; one of the elements in any general analysis of the distribution of income must be the productivity of factor inputs at the margin.

Key Concepts

Theory of marginal productivity.   The economic analysis that shows that under conditions of pure competition in the long run, the return to a factor of production is determined by its productivity at the margin.

The student should be able to draw, label, and explain the following key diagram in discussing the theory of marginal productivity.

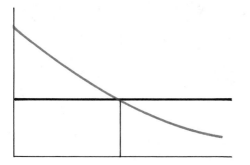

Least-cost combination of the factors of production.   Within the enterprise, the combination of inputs that minimizes the cost of the production for any level of output, such that

$$\frac{MRP_a}{P_a} = \frac{MRP_b}{P_b} = \frac{MRP_c}{P_c} = \cdots = \frac{MRP_n}{P_n},$$

where $a, b, c, \ldots, n$ are the inputs.

Marginal revenue product.   The change in total revenue associated with a change in the quantity of a variable input into the firm's production process.

Labor Unions and Collective Bargaining

35

Chapter 34 examined the market forces that influence the distribution of income. It stressed the point that in a competitive economy the productivity of the factors of production is an important force in determining their incomes. But departures from pure competition may leave a potential residual whose distribution cannot be explained by productivity alone.

Another factor must be considered: the economic power of the participants. On the business side, that power is embodied in the oligopolistic structure of big business. On the workers' side, it is found in their unions. In some occupations, workers are able to restrict the labor supply to bring higher wages. But the far more important case is the labor market in which big enterprise faces big union to bargain over a division of wages and profits between limits imposed by economic forces. A blend of power relationships and market forces determines wage rates, profits, and the distribution of income. This chapter explains how it happens. It starts with an analysis of imperfect labor markets to show why there is a conflict between capital and labor that is not settled by the market-adjustment process, briefly describes the pattern of union organization in the United States, shows why labor-management conflict led to our present labor legislation that requires collective bargaining, analyzes the process of bargaining, and ends with an evaluation of the current pattern of labor-management-government relationships in terms of the public interest.

IMPERFECT LABOR MARKETS: THE SUPPLY SIDE

In a perfectly competitive economy there would be no union organization. Wages would be determined solely by the market forces of demand and supply. Competition among sellers would eliminate extranormal profits in the long run. Any increase in wage rates above the normal level would bring reduced employment, since costs of production would be raised and profits reduced below normal. As long as there is free entry to and exit from the market on the part of both employers and workers, and no restrictions on their market behavior, the competitive solution should prevail. Wage rates will seek their competitive level, involuntary unemployment would disappear, and excess profits would be eliminated.

Labor markets are shot through with imperfections, however. Some workers, particularly those with significant skills, have been able to organize all workers with those skills, restrict entry into their occupations, and gain higher incomes by restricting the market supply of their skills. The simple economic analysis of that situation is shown in Figure 35-1.

Wage rate

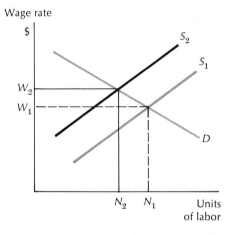

FIGURE 35-1
Labor Market with Workers'
Monopolistic Position

The demand for labor in a particular occupation is shown by D. The competitive market supply is shown by S_1. Union organization of workers may bring a restriction of entry into the occupation, shifting the supply curve to S_2. Instead of N_1 number of workers employed at wage W_1, the wage goes up to W_2 and employment falls to N_2.

The situation shown in Figure 35-1 is far more common in the American economy than most people appreciate. The classic examples usually given are the craft unions in the construction industry. Entry is restricted in two ways. Unions control the apprenticeship programs that qualify new entrants for union membership (although many present members have bypassed apprenticeships to take skill examinations after learning on the job). Unions in local areas are also able to deny membership to qualified union members from other areas, thereby holding back migration. These restrictions have been used in the past to give favored consideration to relatives and friends of existing members, and to prevent blacks and other minorities from moving into the higher skilled crafts, thereby helping to create a social as well as an economic problem. Now that pressures are being brought on the building-trades unions to provide greater opportunities to minority groups, the members see this development—correctly—as reducing their control over entry and their ability to restrict the supply of workers, and as a threat to their economic position.

Workers in the building trades are not the only ones who restrict the supply of labor in their occupations, and labor unions are not the only device for doing so. Workers in a number of public service occupations, such as beauticians and barbers, benefit from similar restrictions on supply through state laws requiring completion of educational programs and passing of tests before people are allowed to practice those occupations. Perhaps the most notorious example is to be found in the medical professions, in which state and national organizations of doctors, supported by state legislation, set standards for admission to the profession. Members of those associations largely manage and staff the medical schools and determine the numbers of new students admitted. One result of the limited number of doctors this system admits to the profession is a high standard of individual competence. Another result is high incomes for those admitted. The plumber who fixes your kitchen sink and the surgeon who removes your appendix are brothers under the skin; both are beneficiaries of a systematic restriction of entry into their occupations. The plumber does it through his union, the surgeon through his professional organizations.

IMPERFECT LABOR MARKETS: THE DEMAND SIDE

Many large business firms are dominant buyers of labor in the markets from which their labor is drawn. Some typical examples are:

1. The textile mill in a small Southern town.
2. The branch manufacturing plant of a giant corporation located in a small Midwestern city.
3. Groups of plants of a large manufacturer located in a small city. General Motors Corporation in Flint, Michigan, for example.

Let's examine these cases of domination of the labor market by a large firm. Firms in these situations know that the supply curve of labor in their locality slopes upward. That is, more labor could be drawn from the local labor market only by raising wage rates. The higher wage would have to be paid to all workers, however, not just the last ones hired. The increase in costs to the employer will equal the wage necessary to hire the marginal worker plus the increase in wages paid to everyone else. Put in terms of economic analysis, the rising supply curve for labor in the market as a whole is accompanied by a marginal supply curve that lies above it.[1] These supply conditions are shown in Figure 35-2, along with the demand curve for labor based on labor's marginal product.

The employer who finds himself in the situation shown in Figure 35-2 will maximize his profits by employing N workers. At that level of employment the marginal cost of labor, shown by the MS curve, equals the marginal revenue product of labor, shown by the demand curve D. However, N units of labor can be hired at wage W, which will be the wage offered by the profit-maximizing dominant employer.

---

[1] A simple example will show the relationship between the average and marginal supply curves for labor. Suppose a firm hires 100 workers at $3 per hour. The firm's wage bill is $300 per hour. It then increases employment to 101 workers, but has to pay $3.01 to attract the marginal worker. The firm raises wages for everyone to that level. The wage bill is now $304.01 (101 X $3.01). The increase of the average wage to $3.01 brought a marginal increase in wage costs of $4.01. The marginal quantities are greater than the average quantities when the average rises.

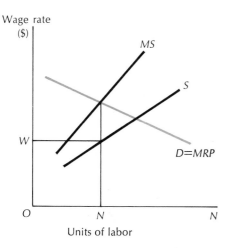

Wage rate
($)

Units of labor

FIGURE 35-2
The Labor Market with a
Dominant Employer

MS is the marginal supply curve for labor as it is seen by the dominant employer. It shows the marginal cost to him of employing additional amounts of labor. *S* is the market supply curve of labor, showing the average wage needed to draw forth any given amount of labor. His demand curve for labor is *D*, which is derived from the marginal product of labor.

Two further points can be made. First, the wage rate in this employer-dominated labor market will be lower than if market forces alone determined the outcome, as shown in Figure 35-3. Second, the worker's wage is below labor's marginal revenue product. The employer pockets revenues that would go to the worker if wages equaled labor's marginal revenue product, as shown in Figure 35-4.

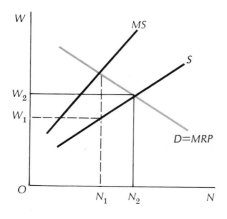

FIGURE 35-3

The employer-dominated labor market will have wages equal to W_1 and employment equal to N_1. If it were a competitive market, the wages would be W_2 and employment N_2.

We now can get a better understanding of the role of labor unions and why they are organized. In an economy of big business units with high degrees of market power in the hands of employers, it is possible for large firms to press wage rates below the level that would otherwise be set in competitive labor markets. Furthermore, those wage rates are "exploitive" in the sense that labor earns less than its marginal revenue product in this situation.

It is not surprising to find labor unions emerging in those sectors of the economy in which large firms developed market power in labor markets. The

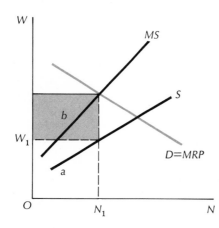

FIGURE 35-4

If the dominant employer paid a wage equal to labor's marginal revenue product, the total wage bill would be $a + b$. By paying wage W_1, the employer retains b and pays only a.

growth of big business brought a preponderance of market power to the buyer of labor in many important sectors of the economy. The reaction on the part of workers was to organize unions to match that power. The sentiments of the song "Solidarity Forever," almost the anthem of the union movement, express the idea in terms any worker can understand:

> When the union's inspiration through the
>   workers' blood shall run,
> There can be no power greater anywhere
>   beneath the sun,
> For what force on earth is weaker than
>   the feeble strength of one,
> But the union makes us strong.
>
> Solidarity forever!
> Solidarity forever!
>
> For the union makes us strong.

The same idea was stated somewhat more prosaically by Senator Barry Goldwater:

"As America turned increasingly, in the latter half of the nineteenth century, from an agricultural nation into an industrial one, and as the size of business enterprises expanded, individual wage earners found themselves at a distinct disadvantage in dealing with their employers over terms of employment. The economic power of the large enterprises, as compared with that of the individual employee, was such that wages and conditions of employment were pretty much what the employer decided they would be. Under these conditions, as a means of increasing their economic power, many employees chose to band together and create a common agent for negotiating with their employers."[2]

---

[2] Barry Goldwater, *The Conscience of a Conservative* (New York: Hillman Books, 1960), pp. 47–48.

UNION OBJECTIVES AND THE CONFLICT WITH MANAGEMENT

When unions organize in sectors of the economy populated by giant firms, oligopolistic industries like steel, automobiles, petroleum refining, chemicals, and rubber, they can make large gains for their members. The profits that result from wage rates below labor's marginal revenue product can be captured for labor, in whole or in part. Just as the firm may seek to keep the wage at a level that maximizes the firm's profit, the union seeks to raise the wage to a level at which the firm is making only a normal profit. The difference between the two wage levels gives both sides plenty to fight over. Figure 35-5 illustrates this source of the conflict between union and management.

Wage rate

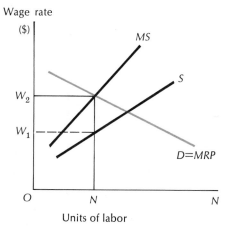

FIGURE 35-5
Conflict Between Union and Management

Management seeks to employ N workers at wage W_1 in order to maximize its profits. The union knows, however, that wage W_2 will leave the firm with normal profits when N workers are employed, and seeks to push the wage up to that level. The result is a conflict between the two parties.

Back in the old days, prior to passage of the National Labor Relations Act, many employers used a wide variety of tactics, including violence, to prevent organizations of unions among their employees. If unions were organized, some employers tried to gain control over them. Their purpose was to maintain the powerful market position that enabled them to keep wages down at or near the level of W_1. Unions, on the other hand, sought to organize workers and use the strength of the union organization to force employers to pay higher wages, pushing wage rates up toward the level of W_2.

The struggle between labor and management is a real one. In an economy of large firms, market forces do not bring a wage rate that is fully determined by supply and demand. There is an area of indeterminacy (in Figure 35-5 it is the difference between W_1 and W_2) within which the economic power and bargaining skill of labor and management determine the outcome.

LABOR UNIONS IN THE UNITED STATES

The numerical strength of labor unions in the United States is often exaggerated. In 1970, there were about 18 million union members in a civilian work force of about 80 million, or about 22.5 percent. Compared with 1960 the number

FEATHERBEDDING

A union that uses its market power to restrict entry and thereby raise wage rates faces the possibility of technological changes that reduce the demand for labor. Unions in that position sometimes try to prevent employers from adopting the new techniques, as the building trades unions have done, often through local building code legislation restricting the use of new materials that save on labor costs. Another example: the railroad unions supported so-called "full crew laws" in many states, to require train crews of a size appropriate to steam engines and visual signals even though diesel locomotives and radio communications are now widely used.

The general principle can be shown by economic analysis. In Figure 35-6, the union has restricted the labor supply to S_2, leading to the relatively high wage rate of W_1, with employment of N_1 workers. Technological changes are introduced that reduce demand for labor to D_2. The new market conditions would normally bring wage rates down to W_2 and employment to N_2. How can we expect the union to react?

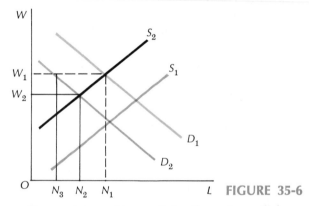

FIGURE 35-6

The most favorable result for the union will be maintenance of wage rates at W_1. But this result would bring employment down to N_3, unless the union is able to get the employers to maintain employment at N_1 either by provisions of the union contract or by legislation. The amount of unnecessary labor, or featherbedding, would be the difference between N_3 and N_1. Sometimes a union contract will not allow layoffs because of technological change, but will permit gradual attrition due to retirements to bring the labor force down to N_3. This change implies a further reduction in the supply curve of labor in the occupation, however, if wage rate W_1 were to be maintained in the long run.

is a little larger and the percent a little smaller. Union membership tends to be heavily concentrated in a few sectors of the economy. There are some 94 unions with over 25 thousand members each, but large unions dominate the picture. The seven unions with more than 500 thousand members have a total membership of about 6½ million, or some 35 percent of all union membership. Table 35–1 is a list of the largest ones, and their approximate membership.

TABLE 35–1
Seven Largest Labor Unions in the U.S.

Union	Number of Members
Teamsters	1,666,000
Automobile workers	1,339,000
Steelworkers	943,000
Machinists	800,000
Electrical workers	724,000
Carpenters	700,000
Retail clerks	510,000
Total (7 unions)	6,482,000

If we were to add the next seven largest unions, their total membership would reach about 9 million; half of all union members are accounted for by the fourteen largest unions.

Union membership is geographically concentrated as well. Over 35 percent of all nonagricultural workers are union members in the great industrial states of the northeast, ranging from New York west to Missouri and Minnesota and south to the Ohio and Potomac Rivers. The percentage in the Pacific Coast states is only slightly less. On the other hand the southern, southwestern, mountain, and Great Plains states average less than 20 percent union membership.[3]

TYPES OF UNIONS

Labor unions are typically divided into *craft* and *industrial* unions, although the distinctions have become blurred over the years.

The carpenters' union (United Brotherhood of Carpenters and Joiners of America) is as close to the concept of the old craft union as any large present-day union. Its members have particular skills in construction and woodworking that distinguish them from other workers in the same industry (plumbers, sheet-metal workers, roofers, and so on). Only those workers who show proficiency in those skills through union-run tests are eligible for membership. The union represents only those workers in dealing with employers.

---

[3] For collectors of trivia, West Virginia is the most heavily unionized state (44 percent of the nonagricultural work force) and South Carolina the least unionized (under 7 percent).

Craft unions are found in industries in which the various skilled trades make up a large portion of the work force. Construction is the classic example. Railroads also had a group of craft unions until recently, when a number of them combined to form a single union in a declining industry. In some industries the craft and the work force are practically identical, as in the case of teachers, barbers, and musicians, and the craft union represents the entire work force.

In many of the principal industries of the United States, the work force is composed primarily of semiskilled or unskilled workers, up to 80 and 90 percent in some instances. These are the industries in which industrial unions have been formed: steel, automobiles, mining, electrical equipment, machinery, chemicals, petroleum refining, men's and women's clothing, and others. Unions in these industries are open to all workers regardless of skills, whether they are unskilled laborers, semiskilled assembly-line workers, or skilled craftsmen. The automobile workers' union (United Automobile, Aerospace, and Agricultural Implement Workers of America) is a typical industrial union. The bulk of its membership is made up of workers on the industry's assembly lines, but it also includes lowly sweepers and highly paid tool and die makers. Just like the craft unions, however, the UAW has the fundamental purpose of bringing together into one organization those workers who have close common interests in order to deal more effectively with employers.

UNION ORGANIZATION

A large national union with hundreds of thousands of members requires a working structure, just as any large organization does. At the bottom stands the local union, which represents workers in dealing with their direct employer. The local union negotiates with the employer on issues that pertain specifically to the local plant and local workers. It also participates in settling grievances that may arise under the terms of a contract.

At the top is the national union, of which the locals are a part. It often negotiates the basic terms of union contracts that apply to all employers across the nation, or to all workers employed by the same company, as in steel or automobiles. It also assists the local in disputes that the local may get involved with, promotes extension of union organization, and operates union retirement or other welfare programs. In between there may be regional administrative units, depending on whether the activities of the union require it.

Finally, most national unions are affiliated with one of the two labor federations. The largest is the AFL–CIO (American Federation of Labor–Congress of Industrial Organizations), and most of the country's unions are affiliated with it. The other is the ALA (Alliance for Labor Action), which is little more than an agreement between the Teamsters and the United Automobile Workers to cooperate with each other. The functions of the federations are primarily political action and general support for the activities of the national unions that compose the federations. The important functioning units are the national unions and the locals rather than the federations. They do the bargaining, participate in grievance procedures and the establishment of work rules, and collect the dues.

THE HERITAGE OF VIOLENCE

The United States is the only large industrial nation in which violence, on both sides, was a continued and characteristic aspect of labor-management relations. Other nations have had occasional or sporadic outbreaks of violence during strikes, and have experienced riots of employees that were directed against employers rather than the government. These events did not occur continuously, however, as they did in the United States in the days before passage in the mid-1930s of federal legislation that set up a framework for collective bargaining. In the United States, private armies were used by both labor and management in some industries. There were corporations whose chief business was supplying strikebreakers and "industrial munitions" to firms intent on stopping the organization of unions, including machine guns and other weapons as well as the personnel to man and command them.

Table 35–2 lists some of the leading incidents in the continuing warfare between labor and capital from the Civil War to the Great Depression.

TABLE 35–2
The Continuing Conflict Between Capital and Labor, 1860–1940

Date	Activity
1862–75	Guerrilla warfare in the anthracite coal area of Pennsylvania between the "Molly Maguires" and the mining companies.
1874	Tompkins Square Riot in New York City.
1877	Railroad strike with particularly heavy violence at Martinsburg, West Virginia, and Pittsburgh, Pennsylvania.
1886	General strike in Chicago, culminating in a riot at the McCormick Harvester Co. plant and the "Haymarket massacre."
1892	"Homestead massacre" near Pittsburgh during a strike of workers at the Carnegie Steel Co. Attempted assassination of Henry C. Frick, the company's general manager.
1894	Pullman strike with widespread violence centered in Chicago.
1892–99	Continuous violence in mining areas of northern Idaho, starting with a strike at Coeur d'Alene in 1892 and culminating in martial law and federal troops in 1899. Former Governor Steunenberg was murdered later, in 1905, and a spectacular trial of union leaders followed.
1901–3	Strikes and violence in mining areas of Colorado.
1902	Anthracite coal strike in Pennsylvania; sporadic violence and mobilization of the National Guard.
1906	Strike against the Pressed Steel Car Co. at McKees Rocks, Pennsylvania, with pitched battles between strikers and state police.

TABLE 35–2 (*Continued*)

Date	Activity
1905–10	Series of dynamitings of buildings erected with nonunion labor, by leaders of the Iron Workers' Union, culminating in the bombing of the *Los Angeles Times* in 1913.
1909–15	"Free speech" violence in Fresno and San Diego, California and Everett, Washington over the right of the Industrial Workers of the World (IWW) to hold public meetings.
1912	Textile workers' strike in Lawrence, Massachusetts, with riots and mass police attacks on women and children.
1913–14	Coal mine strike in southern Colorado with guerrilla warfare between workers and strikebreakers, culminating in the "Ludlow massacre" by the Colorado National Guard. Over 50 dead, many more injured.
1915	Strike at Bayonne, New Jersey, against Standard Oil Company. Eight dead; 17 severely wounded.
1919	National steelworkers' strike, featuring large-scale use of private armies by the steel companies and retaliatory violence by workers, particularly in Pennsylvania; Federal troops and martial law in Gary, Indiana; National Guard sent to East Chicago and Indiana Harbor.
1918–19	Centralia, Washington: campaign by war veterans to drive the IWW out, culminating in the shooting of four American Legionnaires on Armistice Day, 1919, and lynching of an IWW leader.
1920–22	Strikes and open warfare in bituminous coal mining areas of West Virginia, Pennsylvania and Illinois.
1922	Textile mill strikes throughout New England, with sporadic violence.
1929	Wave of strikes in the southern textile industry with deaths from violence in Gastonia and Marion, North Carolina, and Elizabethton, Tennessee. General mob violence directed against union activity.
1928–34	Guerrilla warfare in bituminous coal mining areas of West Virginia, Pennsylvania, and Kentucky, most spectacularly in "bloody Harlan" County, Kentucky, in 1931.
1934	"Battle of Rincon Hill" during longshoremen's strike in San Francisco. One hundred eighteen casualties, including 3 dead. National Guard sent to Toledo, Ohio, to stop strike-connected violence.
1937	"Memorial Day massacre" during strike against Republic Steel Corporation. Eighty-eight casualties, including 4 dead.

The underlying reasons for this dismal sequence of events are obscure, and few American social scientists have studied labor violence in detail. Radicals attribute it to the class warfare characteristic of industrial capitalism. Most historians of the American labor movement have concentrated on the rise of unions as their central concern and have not analyzed the causes of violence. Our earlier economic analysis pinpointed the source of the conflict in labor markets that spawned labor unions in response to the presence of big business, but that only explained the existence of conflict, not why it led to violence. Whatever the cause, violence in labor relations brought a polarization of communities into warring camps increasingly antagonistic to each other. It was the class conflict that Marx claimed was characteristic of capitalist society, and seemed to be tearing the social fabric apart. As one of the songs which came out of "bloody Harlan" in the early 1930s put it:

> Down in Harlan County there are no
> neutrals there;
> You either be a union man or a
> thug for J.H. Blair.
> Which side are you on?
> Which side are you on?

NATIONAL LABOR LEGISLATION

Strikes and violence ultimately brought a national policy designed to promote peaceful settlement of disputes between labor and management. Collective bargaining between the two parties was to replace conflict. Such an arrangement implied that workers had to be represented by unions if bargaining was to succeed; and that implied a willingness on the part of employers to accept unions as the workers' representatives and to bargain with them. These were the principles underlying the National Labor Relations Act of 1935 (the Wagner Act).

The National Labor Relations Act was designed to protect the workers' right to organize and prevent employer opposition to union organization. It also required employers to bargain "in good faith" with the legitimate representatives of employees. A National Labor Relations Board (NLRB) was established to enforce the act. Its chief role has been to manage elections among employees to determine whether a majority wish to be represented by a labor union that would then be certified as the representative of all the employees, and to prevent "unfair labor practices" on the part of employers that were either efforts to prevent organization of unions or refusals to bargain. Under this protective umbrella, and influenced by the tight labor markets of World War II, union membership rose from about 4 million in 1934 to over 15 million in 1948.

The new national labor policies were not fully accepted. In particular, distrust of collective action remained and was inflamed by nationwide strikes in basic industries after World War II as the economy moved to a new pattern of wages and hours of work during the conversion from a wartime to a peacetime economy. A reaction set in that brought passage of the Labor-Management Act of 1947 (the Taft-Hartley Act). This legislation moved toward protection of employers, individual workers, and the general public. It restrained certain types of actions by unions as well as employers. It provided individual workers with protections against arbitrary action by unions and set up procedures by which unions could be decertified as bargaining agents when workers no longer wanted them. It protected employers caught in the crossfire of jurisdictional disputes between unions.

The most important part of the Taft-Hartley Act dealt with "national emergency" disputes, or those that imperil the national economy because of their breadth or the essential nature of the service provided. It provided for a "cooling-off period" of 80 days during which efforts to resolve the dispute could be made, and for a vote among employees on whether to accept management's last offer. If that failed, the President could refer the dispute to Congress with recommendations for resolving it.

Even after passage of the Taft-Hartley Act, complaints about unions continued. In particular, corruption in some unions, especially in New York and Chicago, and infiltration of unions by underworld elements brought passage of the Labor-Management Reporting and Disclosure Act of 1959 (Landrum-Griffin Act). It provided a "bill of rights" for individual union members, established a series of provisions dealing with the financial responsibility of unions, and gave enforcement teeth to protection of the rights of members. It took twenty-five years, but a national system for peaceful settlement of labor disputes was ultimately forged. It doesn't work perfectly—few social policies ever do—but it has eliminated a large portion of the violence and conflict that formerly characterized American labor-management relations.

COLLECTIVE BARGAINING

Collective bargaining is the name given to the process of negotiation that takes place between unions and management. Its goal is a contract between the two parties that embodies an agreement between them with respect to a wide variety of issues. Among the principal topics that most collective bargaining contracts cover are the following:

Definition of the bargaining unit to which the agreement applies.

Wages, including such items as overtime pay and paid holidays or vacations.

Hours of work.

Grievance procedures that provide ways to settle disputes that might arise under the contract.

Rules for suspension and discharge, and other disciplinary measures.

Rules for seniority.

Payment of union dues if they are to be deducted from workers' paychecks by the employer and paid directly to the union (the "checkoff").

Effective date and termination of the contract.

Looking down this list, one sees most of the topics that define relations between employees and employers. Indeed, the purpose of collective bargaining is to reach agreement on these matters so that productive work can continue without interruption under conditions that are acceptable to both parties.

Wages are usually the chief bone of contention, but there are times when other issues loom large, such as retirement and pension plans, safety conditions within the plant, and hours of work. Most of these other issues are reducible to the money equivalent of wages, however. Their dollar cost to the employer can be estimated, and the employer is usually more concerned about the total cost of wages plus other provisions of the contract than he is about the individual items. As a result, most disagreements in collective bargaining can be resolved once the total "cost of the package" is agreed on.

Bargaining Space and Bargaining Limits

Our earlier analysis of the economics of the situation in which a large union faces a large employer or group of employers showed that there were economic limits beyond which neither side could be pushed.

> The employers' profits can't be pushed below normal profits. If they are, the employer can be expected to move his capital elsewhere in the long run.
>
> Wages can't be pushed below those that draw forth the necessary labor. If they are pushed below that level workers will find jobs elsewhere or remain idle.

These two positions define the *bargaining space* within which unions and management contest with each other for advantage. Within that space agreement is possible. Management tries to keep wages plus the value of other benefits as close as possible to the level just necessary to get adequate supplies of labor. Unions try to raise wages plus the value of other benefits as high as they can without pushing the firm out of business. There are *bargaining limits*, which are defined by the economic alternatives open to labor and capital. See Figure 35-7.

The practical limits to the bargaining space are narrower than the limits enforced by economic alternatives. Before those limits are reached, one party can be expected to refuse to compromise any further, negotiations will break down, and a strike will occur. The reason is that pushing either party to the economic limit of the bargaining space implies its destruction. See Figure 35-8.

If the union allows the wage rate to fall to the lower limit and stay there, the union would have little economic reason for its existence. Workers would do just as well by getting jobs elsewhere. Any self-respecting union would go out on strike before it accepted any such settlement. The minimum it would settle for without a strike would have to be enough above the lower limit of the bargaining space to give the membership a reason to remain members.

Likewise, the upper limit is seldom achieved. At that limit the employer would do just as well by moving his capital elsewhere. As it is approached, his willingness to have his workers strike increases and further concessions are harder and harder to get. The union finds that if it wants to settle without a

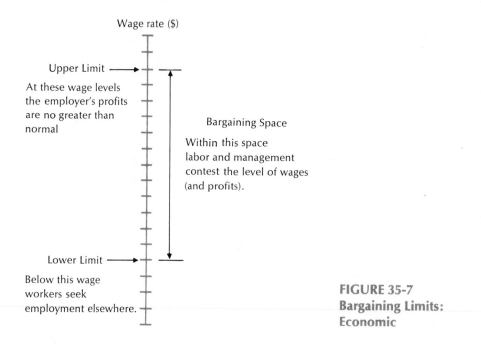

FIGURE 35-7
Bargaining Limits:
Economic

strike, it can't push the employer's profits all the way down to the normal profit level.

These considerations are particularly important when both parties consider their relationship to be a relatively permanent one. If both sides anticipate bargaining with each other in another year, they will have to maintain workable relationships, and that means not pushing the other party to the wall.

The Bargaining Process

We are now ready to examine the bargaining process itself. We want to determine why some disputes are settled peacefully, and why some lead to strikes; what kind of division of the bargaining space between labor and capital occurs; and what the relative importance of market influences and economic power is in effecting that division.

The first point to keep in mind is that neither party in the bargaining process knows the other's position. Management does not know the minimum for which the union will settle. Nor does the union know the maximum wage increase that management would willingly give.[4] Uncertainty prevails on both sides.

---

[4] Don't get hung up on the fact that most labor-management bargaining involves a variety of fringe benefits as well as wages. Fringe benefits can always be reduced to monetary costs and equated with a wage increase. In this discussion, where we use the term "wages" we include the monetary equivalent of fringe benefits such as paid vacations, retirement plans, and so forth.

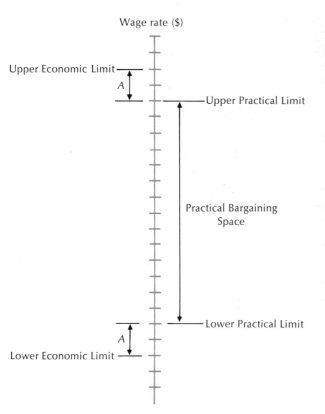

**FIGURE 35-8
Bargaining Limits:
Practical**

The practical bargaining limits on the right side of the diagram define the area of nonantagonistic conflict: in that area the right of the other party to continue to exist is accepted by both parties. The economic limits to bargaining shown on the left define two additional areas of antagonistic conflict (marked *A* on the diagram): in the upper area, management might just as well go out of business and move to some other line of endeavor; in the lower area, workers could do just as well without the union. The longest and most bitter strikes occur when one of the two parties pushes the dispute into these areas or beyond, implying that it wishes the destruction of the other party.

Uncertainty about the other party's position leads each one to take extreme positions, which are known to be unrealistic. The purpose is to try to discover how far the other party will give in or compromise while giving up as little as possible yourself. Yet these initial positions can't be so extreme as to forfeit all credibility.

The union, for example, will make an initial demand that it knows to be greater than the maximum that management can be expected to grant without a strike. Anything less than that maximum means that the union would be gratuitously giving up some of its bargaining space and its potential gains. Having made such a demand, the union's strategy will be to compromise gradually, while trying to learn from management's reactions exactly where its point of maximum concessions is located.

Management, likewise, will make an initial offer that it knows is so low that it lies below the minimum the union would accept without calling a strike. It, too, will then seek to compromise its offer upwards until it can determine where the union's minimum is located.

During the bargaining process each party may try to bluff the other party,[5] compromises will be made on one issue in order to gain advantage on another, and in the most important part of the whole process, each party will try to learn what the other party's true position is while trying to conceal its own. This is the essential element of bargaining skill. Another important aspect of the process is public opinion, particularly in important and highly visible negotiations, for the ultimate results are often colored by the attitude of the public and government.

In the typical bargaining situation an agreement is possible if two conditions are met:

1. The maximum the employer is willing to grant is equal to or greater than the minimum the union is willing to accept.

2. The process of bargaining does not create so much hostility that the parties fail to recognize that there is an area of potential agreement.

We show this overlapping area of potential agreement graphically in Figure 35-9.

Once the two parties sense that they have compromised into the area of potential agreement, the bargaining is likely to become intense and difficult.

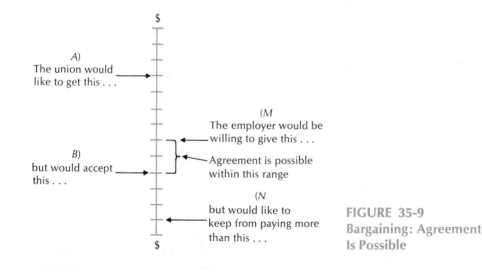

FIGURE 35-9
Bargaining: Agreement
Is Possible

---

[5] The bargainer's prayer: "Lord, make me conciliatory but unyielding." A bluff won't work unless it has credibility, which a negotiator may even seek to achieve by putting himself in a position from which he can't retreat. For example, the union may whip up such rank-and-file enthusiasm for a particular point that management knows there can't be much compromise by the union leadership. The management negotiators must then decide whether to give in so that they can continue to deal with that leadership, or fight on that issue and risk getting a tougher union leadership in the future. Complicated, isn't it?

Each side can then gain by being stubborn and trying to get the other side to make the largest compromises. Negotiations can become protracted even though there is little difference between the positions taken by the two parties. This is one reason why many disputes are not settled until the last moment.

On the other hand, it is quite possible that there will be no overlap of union minimum and employer maximum, and no area of potential agreement. This can develop because of rigidities on either side. Either the union leadership or the union membership may feel that it can't compromise any further. Perhaps other unions have obtained large gains, or the cost of living has risen substantially, or there is an internal struggle for power within the union, or bitter feelings have developed between management and its work force. On the other hand, management may feel that its stockholders (or financial backers) will vote it out if larger concessions are given, or that the federal government may step in to try to keep prices down, or other internal management problems may intervene. In any event, pressures on one or both of the parties to the bargaining process may keep them from compromising enough to enable an agreement to be reached. Under these circumstances a strike is almost sure to occur. This situation is diagramed in Figure 35-10.

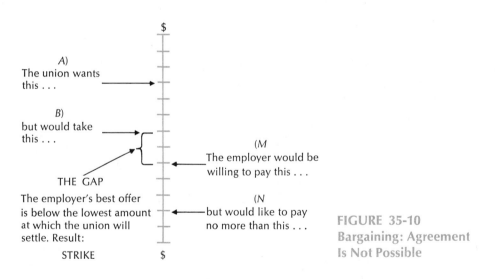

FIGURE 35-10
Bargaining: Agreement
Is Not Possible

Most union-management negotiations result in agreement and a contract acceptable to both parties. Strikes are not particularly frequent. The average union member in the U.S. participates in a strike about once every seven years. When strikes occur, they usually are short: the average union member loses about 2 to 2.5 days of work annually because of strikes.

The economic loss due to strikes is usually negligible. This is true even of the spectacular, long strikes in basic industries. In steel or automobiles, for example, firms build up backlogs of output prior to strikes and work overtime afterwards to catch up. Workers may even come out ahead because of time-and-a-half overtime pay before and after a strike. As for output, little is usually lost, because customers are able to postpone their purchases until after the struck industry is back at work. In a durable-goods industry like steel or automobiles, these factors combine to create a situation in which real economic losses, and financial losses to either workers or firms, do not start building up until after a strike has been going on for about eight weeks.

The case is different for industries producing perishables or services. In that case the economic losses start almost immediately. For example, a strike of truckers or railroad workers slows down economic activity generally, affecting equally those industries producing durables, nondurables and services. While output in the durable-goods industries would otherwise be made up later (if the transportation strike is relatively short), other industries can't make up the lost output. Generation of income will fall (the multiplier works itself out here), and the entire economy is affected. That is why government usually intervenes to halt widespread strikes in transportation, but usually does not intervene in other industries.

When a strike occurs, who is responsible? The common response is to blame the union. It is, after all, the unit that decides it will not continue under the existing situation, or will not accept management's last offer. But this is only the way things appear on the surface. Why not blame management because it didn't accept the union's last offer? When looked at as a problem in bargaining, it quickly becomes apparent that both sides are equally to blame, or equally blameless. Negotiations break down because the bargaining positions of the *two* sides do not overlap and enable an agreement to emerge.[6]

The strike is a test of economic strength. The employer's fixed costs continue even though his operations may not. As financial reserves are used up, the costs of continuing the strike mount and a settlement looks more attractive. The maximum wage increase the employer would be willing to give starts to move upward. Similar pressures are felt by the union. Some members can get other jobs temporarily, but they usually don't pay as well; other members can't get other work. Family savings start to disappear, and the union's strike fund declines. Financial stress begins to appear among the rank-and-file union membership and this puts pressure on the union leadership. The minimum wage increase for which it will settle moves downward. As the strike continues, then, the gap between the two parties shrinks until a point is reached at which settlement is possible. The function of the strike is to cause the bargaining positions of the two parties to shift to ones that include an area of potential agreement that did not previously exist.

---

[6] It is also possible that there was an overlap but the two parties could not find it. We will return to this problem a little further on in this chapter.

Mediation, Conciliation, and Arbitration

Third parties can often intervene in disputes between labor and management with good results. Sometimes an agreement is possible during the bargaining stage, but the two parties do not realize it. Perhaps the negotiations themselves have created anger and bitterness that prevents agreement on the economic issues. Under these conditions a third party can help both labor and management understand that an area of potential agreement exists when neither party has recognized it.

If a strike should occur, it can continue on its own momentum, with the two parties unaware of the growing willingness to settle that economic pressures create. Unless they can be brought together by a third party, the strike may continue long after a settlement is possible.

There are three types of third-party intervention in labor-management disputes:

Mediation occurs when a third party endeavors to assist the disputants in reaching an agreement on their own. The mediator acts as a middleman who tries to bring the parties together.

Conciliation occurs when a third party tries actively to work out terms of a settlement with the disputants. The conciliator goes beyond acting merely as a stimulus to negotiation and participates in the effort to find a common ground for agreement.

Arbitration occurs when a third party makes the decision for the disputants. There are two types of arbitration:
1. Under the terms of an existing contract, its meaning or applicability may be disputed. Many contracts provide for an arbitrator to decide on interpretation of the meaning or applicability of the contract if the disputants cannot settle the matter among themselves.
2. In negotiating a new contract the two parties may agree to have an arbitrator decide on some of the issues rather than fail to agree on a new contract. In some countries, *compulsory arbitration* is provided for some or all disputes.

In the United States third party intervention in labor-management disputes is quite common. The federal government and some state governments have mediation and conciliation services that try to bring disputes to settlement and avoid strikes. A large number of union contracts provide for arbitration of disputes that arise under the contract. The emphasis, however, is on voluntary agreement between labor and management. Public policy has consistently emphasized that the best interests of labor and management are most effectively furthered if they can agree rather than have a decision imposed upon them from the outside. That is the reason why compulsory arbitration has never been widely used in the United States.

ARBITRATION: AN EXAMPLE

Disputes that arise under collective bargaining agreements are often resolved by referring them to arbitration by a third party. Here is an actual case, taken from the records of the American Arbitration Association, the case of the

Handicapped Papermaker

Despite a glass eye, and limited vision in the other eye (which was corrected by glasses), Richard J. did very satisfactory work as a machine operator in a paper mill for six years, and he had never suffered an accident in that time. Richard's job was such that if an accident had occurred, it might have been serious, for his machine had sharp knives for cutting cardboard, and they could very easily cut through a careless finger.

In October, 1962, Richard suffered a slight cold, or infection, in his natural eye, and saw the company doctor, and eventually an ophthalmologist, about it. The latter found no occupational disability and recommended that Richard seek private treatment. A report of this examination was given to the insurance company that handled the paper mill's workmen's compensation coverage. This was the background of a grievance that eventually arose.

It seems that the insurance company sent a safety engineer to the plant who, after an inspection, advised management to transfer Richard to a less hazardous job. Fearful that if he did not comply with this request, he might be held liable for "negligence", the employer transferred Richard to a job management regarded as safer. Unfortunately, it was a job that paid less than Richard had been earning.

On hearing the union's protest, management examined the collective bargaining agreement very closely and relied on a clause that gave the employer the right to demote employees for "good cause." This alone justified the action the company took, the industrial relations director argued.

The union answered that Richard had done his job reasonably well and that an insurance company's recommendations were not binding in an area where only labor and management jointly had decisive power.

This case ultimately went to arbitration by a third party. If you were the arbitrator, what would your decision be? Why?

MARKET FORCES AND ECONOMIC POWER

In an economy populated by big firms and big unions the economic power of those units affects the wage bargain and indirectly the level of profits. Their market power is not unlimited, however. Even in the short run, market influences are important. Alternative employment opportunities or leisure provide a limit below which even a relatively large employer is unable to push the level of wages he pays. On the other hand, if wages are pushed to levels that make it impossible for the firm to earn a normal profit, the capital will move elsewhere to take advantage of other alternatives. Between these upper and lower limits, there is a substantial space for conflict between labor and capital. In this country we have tried to substitute collective bargaining for more violent methods of resolving the conflict, with a rather high degree of success.

But economic power has not been excluded from the process. The bargaining positions of the two parties are based, in the end, on their willingness and ability to withstand a strike. Although in some sectors of the economy a strike must be relatively long before significant losses start for either party, it will ultimately start to hurt. The party hurt the most and soonest will usually shift its position the furthest, of course. Its reserves and resources diminishing more rapidly than those of the other party, it will compromise its position to gain a settlement and end the strike. Financial resources and reserves become the ultimate determinant of the "winner" and the "loser."

The distribution of income, then, is determined in part by the productivity of the factors of production and in part by the organization of economic power. Power becomes the arbiter of justice.

MUTUALITY OF INTERESTS

So far in this chapter we have stressed the conflict of interest between labor and management, and collective bargaining as a means of resolving the conflict. We should not lose sight of the fact that unions and management have common interests as well.

Some writers stress the fact that both labor and capital require each other in order to produce the goods that are needed both by workers and owners of capital. This argument has been made for generations by advocates of a private enterprise system, and it is true, of course. Labor can't produce much without using capital, and capital must be combined with labor in any production scheme. But physical combination of the two factors in the processes of production does not necessarily require preservation of any one social organization of production, be it socialist or capitalist. Capital and labor can be combined if capital is either privately or publicly owned, and there are many examples to illustrate the point; the Canadian railroad system, TVA, and the privately owned electric power companies, or municipal and private water supply systems come immediately to mind.

A more subtle mutuality of interest has grown up between big business and big unions in the contemporary American economy in spite of the contest between the two that is continually played out in collective bargaining. The current pattern of labor-management relations has helped to preserve and stabilize the positions of big business and big unions. Long-term contracts, industrywide bargaining, grievance procedures, and arbitration, even the process of collective bargaining itself, contribute to the security of both sides.

Corporations gain uniform wage rates throughout the industry. The uniformity eliminates one source of cost differences between firms and facilitates maintenance of common prices in oligopolistic industries. It is easier to prevent price competition if all firms have a similar cost base. Long-term contracts assure large corporations of known wage costs over a period of one to three years, facilitating the planning that gives large firms an advantage over small. Firms are protected against unauthorized strikes and work stoppages that could disrupt production lines. As long as collective bargaining agreements are reached, the industry is protected against government intervention in determining wages and working conditions.

Unions as organizations also benefit from the current pattern. Exclusive bargaining agreements protect the union from having its membership raided by other unions. Grievance procedures and arbitration offer a means by which members' discontent is channeled into agreed upon settlement procedures, thereby reducing the pressures of internal discontent that might arise within the union. Even union dues are often collected by the firm and paid directly to the union. Finally, a wise business management will protect a "reasonable" union leadership by seeing to it that the membership of the union obtains economic gains large enough to keep them contented with the union leadership as well as with their jobs.

In recent years this growing mutuality of interest between big union and big business has been disturbed by the process of inflation. As long as the economy expands at a rate fast enough to maintain reasonably full employment, and government fiscal and monetary policies provide the necessary level of total spending, it is tempting for both unions and management to seek gains that promote inflationary price increases. We examined this problem in Chapter 19 and concluded that the structure of the economy made the whole system inflation-prone. As long as wage increases plus fringe benefits do not exceed productivity gains, there is no internal cost pressure on the business firm. But it is tempting for unions to try to push for greater gains, particularly in oligopolistic industries in which administered prices can be moved upward so that profits are not damaged. As long as government stands ready to maintain aggregate demand at full-employment levels, the burden is shifted to the general public, for the mutual benefit of workers and business firms. Inflation can be a safety valve that eases the conflict between unions and management.

On the other hand, when inflation is caused by excessive aggregate demand as it was during the escalation of the Vietnam war, and government imposes fiscal and monetary policies designed to halt the rising prices, the conflict between unions and management is intensified. Union members press for wage increases to compensate them for the rapid rise in prices, while management is faced with both rising costs and government pressures to keep prices from going up. These conflicting pressures make it more difficult to find areas of potential agreement in collective bargaining, and the mutuality of interest between the two parties tends to diminish.

THE BLUE-COLLAR BLUES

With all of these elements in the larger picture working themselves out through the market and collective bargaining and the grand strategy of big business–big labor–big government relationships, what is happening to the ordinary Joe on the assembly line? He has the blues. He may be living well, but affluence bypasses him and his life doesn't get any easier. The job is not very rewarding. And his total life pattern leaves much to be desired.

An American working man can look forward to doing the same job for his entire working life. Only a limited few move up to supervisory positions. Jobs of higher skill and higher pay are available, and significant numbers of workers move into them by reason of their seniority in lower-ranking jobs. But progress is slow and even the higher-rated jobs are usually routine, unchanging ones.

One result of that pattern is a growing economic squeeze as the worker becomes older. Aside from an occasional or erratic jump to a higher-level job, the production worker can expect wage increases approximately equal to the growth of productivity, say 3 to 4 percent annually. But his living expenses rise by 6 percent each year, on the average, according to the U.S. Bureau of Labor Statistics. He marries, has children, buys a home, raises his children and sends them to school, buys insurance—these costs rise at about twice the rate of his increase in base pay. By the time he reaches 45 years of age his budget may be tighter than it was twenty years before. Unless he has been able to move up in the pay scale at his plant he may well be worse off economically than he was when he started his working life. In the next twenty years of his working life the pressures may ease as his immediate family obligations are reduced, but other things become important; typically the middle-aged worker feels that his retirement pension, life insurance, and health benefits are inadequate.

Lack of satisfactions on the job are also felt by large numbers of workers. Many production jobs are repetitious, boring, and mind-deadening. They do not stimulate the imagination, use the full range of skills people are capable of developing, or promote the development of the individual as a person. Production jobs contain fewer of the elements that make for personal satisfaction than white-collar jobs at the same income level. They are also more dangerous, and injury and disability more common.

Away from the job, the worker's environment brings him into intimate contact with some of the more severe environmental problems of our time. He is likely to live in an urban neighborhood beginning to show signs of decay, located closer to the urban sources of air pollution than others. Crime is likely to be more prevalent in his home neighborhood, along with greater fear of crime. Black workers in the central cities, where almost all of them live, feel this problem more than others.

The effects of the blue collar blues are felt in a number of ways. Absenteeism from the job is increasing. In the automobile industry it doubled between 1960 and 1970, to reach a daily average of 5.3 percent. On days before and after weekends absenteeism is so strong that the automobile manufacturers now employ a "Friday–Monday" work force that works only on those two days, replacing absent production workers. Closely related to absenteeism are alcoholism and drug addiction, seen by some authorities as means by which workers escape both boredom and the realization that they are caught on a treadmill. Lack of pride in the job leads to sloppy work and defective products. Resentment produces deliberate sabotage of the finished product. Both poor quality of production and sabotage have become problems of increasing concern to production managers in a number of American manufacturing industries.

None of these problems is new. They have been with working people in industrial societies for a hundred years or more. But the point is that they are still with us and have become more significant in recent years. Economic growth has brought higher standards of living, and most working people are far better off today in many material aspects of their lives than their counterparts of fifty or a hundred years ago. Labor unions have helped bring that about. But what of the psychic aspects of life: the desire to move oneself forward and lead a richer life as one grows older, the urge to do meaningful and self-satisfying things, the desire for a favorable environment? More and more Americans are coming to feel that the next step forward will have to be some better answers to those human problems that lie behind the forces of the market, bargaining, and the organization of power.

Summary

When labor markets are imperfect the structure of economic power influences the returns to the factors of production. In some markets, unions are able to restrict the supply of labor to raise wages. In labor markets with a dominant buyer, the firm maximizes its profits at a wage rate below labor's marginal revenue product, thereby creating a range within which unions could push wages up. Together these two market situations help explain why unions have been organized in individual crafts and in industries dominated by oligopolies. They also define the nature of the economic conflict between unions and management.

A little over one in five persons in the work force are union members. But unions are highly concentrated in the principal industries of the industrial sector of the economy, whether they are craft or industrial unions.

Labor-management relations in the U.S. were characterized by a high degree of violence prior to the passage of national labor legislation in the mid-1930s. That legislation and its more recent amendments established collective bargaining between unions and management as the framework within which the conflict between the two must be worked out.

The bargaining process is complex. It takes place within economic limits imposed by the market system: a maximum defined by the employer's normal profit and a minimum defined by employment opportunities elsewhere for the workers. Both limits are essentially the opportunity costs of capital and labor. The practical limits of bargaining lie somewhat within the economic limits, for there is a zone close to the upper and lower economic limits that implies intent to destroy the other party. Within these limits each party tries to reach a settlement most satisfactory to itself by gaining the maximum possible concession from the other side.

Agreement is not always possible, however. In those cases a strike brings pressure on both parties to make greater concessions in order to avoid further costs of the strike.

Finally, third parties can sometimes intervene effectively to promote agreement. Mediation and conciliation can help the parties find the area of agreement that they may not have been able to discern themselves. Arbitration can provide a solution when voluntary agreement is not possible.

The bargained solution is based ultimately on the economic power of the two parties. However, the system as a whole has brought a growing mutuality of interest between unions and management that creates stability in their relationships and tends to diminish the conflict between them. Meanwhile, the industrial worker has become disenchanted in many ways and finds that he is not leading the kind of life he desires.

Key Concepts

Dominant buyer of labor.   A firm large enough so that its demand for labor affects the wage rate, leading to an upward sloping supply curve for its labor supply.

The student should be able to draw, label correctly, and explain the following diagram, which illustrates the analysis of a dominant buyer of labor dealing with a labor union.

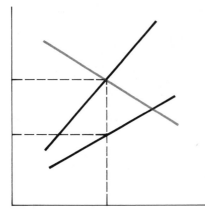

Marginal supply curve for labor.   Shows the marginal cost of additional units of labor for a dominant buyer of labor.

Craft union.   A union whose membership is restricted to workers in a particular occupation.

Industrial union.   A union whose membership is open to all workers in an industry, regardless of the workers' occupations.

Labor federation.   An organization whose membership comprises two or more labor unions.

National Labor Relations Act.   The legislation that established collective bargaining as the method for settling disputes between labor and management as a matter of national policy.   Passed in 1935, the Wagner Act was amended by the Taft-Hartley Act in 1947 and the Landrum-Griffin Act of 1959.

Bargaining space.   The area of disagreement between union and management within which an agreement is possible.

Bargaining limits.   The economic limits of bargaining are defined by the opportunity costs of the two parties.   These are normal profits for the employer and other employment opportunities for the workers.   The practical limits lie within the economic limits, since pushing either party to the economic limit implies its destruction.

Mediation.   In labor disputes, a third party attempt to assist the disputants in reaching agreement.

Conciliation.   In labor disputes, a third party attempt actively to work out an agreement in cooperation with the disputants.

Arbitration.   Settlement of a dispute by a third party.

The distribution of income in the United States is partly determined by the market forces embodied in the theory of marginal productivity. They set the upper and lower limits within which the organized bargaining power of labor and capital determine the terms on which the factors of production will be rewarded. These two sets of forces, markets and bargaining power, operate within a framework that also influences income distribution patterns, especially for those persons at the bottom. In two respects, that framework creates a persistent problem of poverty. It keeps some people from earning adequate incomes, and it tends to keep them poor once they are in that state. On the other hand, other structural elements tend to preserve the position of the wealthy.

This chapter and Chapter 37 examine these aspects of the distribution of income. Here we look at the pattern of income distribution and the fact of its stability over the years. Then we turn to the condition of poverty and its persistence, and inquire into the ways it might be reduced or eliminated. Chapter 37 looks at how the other half lives, the distribution of wealth and its implications.

TRENDS AND PATTERNS IN THE DISTRIBUTION OF INCOME

In the United States there was a noticeable shift toward greater equality in income distribution between 1929 and 1944. Since 1944 there has been practically no change in the pattern. Unfortunately, data for the years before 1929 are so poor and so sparse that no firm statements can be made about the earlier period.

Table 36-1 shows the data on which these conclusions rest. The distribution of incomes by families and unrelated individuals is broken down by quintiles. Each quintile contains 20 percent of the income recipients. Thus, the lowest 20 percent of all consumer units received 3.5 percent of personal income in 1929, 4.1 percent in 1935–36, and 4.9 percent in 1944. By 1962, their share had fallen (not significantly) to 4.6 percent. Meanwhile, the share of the highest 20 percent had fallen from 54.4 percent in 1929 to 51.7 percent in 1935–36 and 45.8 percent in 1944. Again, there was little change to 1962. The share of the top 5 percent fell even more dramatically, from 30 percent in 1929 to 19.6 percent in 1962.[1]

The
Distribution
of Income
and the
Problem
of Poverty

36

---

[1] All of these data on income distribution are subject to the limitations of national income accounting, noted earlier in this chapter, and must be treated only as an approximation. Not all income is reported, and no adjustment is made for changes in the pattern of home production.

The data in Table 36-1 show income distribution before federal income taxes are paid. Correction can be made for that factor, shown in Table 36–2 for 1929 and 1962 to indicate how much it would change the situation. Note that it made little difference in 1929, but that the more steeply progressive federal income tax made a significant difference in 1962.

TABLE 36-1
Percentage Distribution of Family Personal Income, Selected Years, 1929–1962

Quintiles	1929	1935–1936	1944	1962
Lowest	3.5	4.1	4.9	4.6
Second	9.0	9.2	10.9	10.9
Third	13.8	14.1	16.2	16.3
Fourth	19.3	20.9	22.2	22.7
Highest	54.4	51.7	45.8	45.5
Total	100	100	100	100
Top 5 percent*	30.0	26.5	20.7	19.6
Concentration ratio	0.49	0.47	0.39	0.40

Sources: For 1944 and 1962: *Survey of Current Business,* March 1955, p. 20; April 1958, p. 17; and April 1964, p. 8. For 1935–36: Selma F. Goldsmith et al., "Size Distribution of Income Since the Mid-Thirties," *Review of Economics and Statistics,* Vol. 36 (February 1954), p. 9. For 1929: Selma F. Goldsmith, "The Relation of Census Income Distribution Statistics to Other Income Data," in Conference Research in Income and Wealth, *An Appraisal of the 1950 Census Income Data,* Studies in Income and Wealth, Vol. 23 (New York: Princeton University Press, 1958), p. 92. For 1929 Mrs. Goldsmith gives a figure (12.5 percent) for only the two lowest quintiles combined; this percentage was allocated between two percentiles by Alan MacFayden and published in Edward C. Budd (ed.), *Inequality and Poverty,* (New York: W. W. Norton and Co., 1967) p. xii.
Note: Family personal income includes wage and salary receipts (net of social insurance contributions), other labor income, proprietors' and rental income, dividends, personal interest income, and transfer payments. In addition to monetary income flows, it includes certain nonmonetary or imputed income such as wages in kind, the value of food and fuel produced and consumed on farms, imputed net rental value of owner-occupied homes, and imputed interest. Personal income differs from national income in that it excludes corporate profits taxes, corporate saving (inclusive of inventory valuation adjustment), and social security contributions of employers and employees, and includes transfer payments (mostly governmental) and interest on consumer and government debt.
* Consumer units include farm operator and nonfarm families and unattached individuals. A family is defined as a group of two or more persons related by blood, marriage, or adoption, and residing together.

The shift toward greater equality of income can be shown graphically by a clever device called the "Lorenz curve," named after Max Lorenz, the statistician who invented it. It is based on a calculation of the cumulative share of income received. For example, from Table 36-1 we can see that the lowest 20 percent received 3.5 percent of personal income in 1929, the lowest 40 percent received 12.5 percent, the lowest 60 percent received 26.3

TABLE 36-2
Percentage Distribution of Family Personal Income after Federal Individual Income
Tax Liability, 1929 and 1962

Quintiles	1929	1962
Lowest		4.9
Second	12.6	11.5
Third	13.9	16.8
Fourth	19.5	23.1
Highest	54.0	43.7
Total	100	100
Top 5 Percent	29.5	17.7

Sources: Figures for 1962 from *Survey of Current Business*, April 1964, p. 8. Estimates for 1929
from Selma F. Goldsmith, "Impact of the Income Tax on Socio-Economic Groups of Families in
the U.S.," in Colin Clark and Geer Stuvel (eds.), *Income Redistribution and the Statistical Foundations of Economic Policy*, Income and Wealth Series X (London: Bowes and Bowes 1964),
p. 268.

percent, and so on, until the lowest 100 percent received 100 percent of all
income. These points can be plotted on a chart to show the Lorenz curve
of income distribution. This has been done in Figure 36-1 for three of the
distributions in Table 36–1, those for 1929, 1935–36, and 1962.

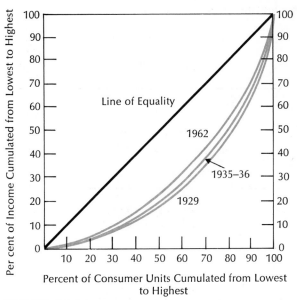

FIGURE 36-1
Lorenz Curves for the Distribution
of Family Personal Income

The straight line drawn diagonally across the chart shows perfect equality of income: one percent of the income recipients receives one percent of the income, two percent receives two percent of the income, and so forth. Any deviation downward shows some inequality. Perfect inequality would be shown by a curve following the lower and right borders of the chart, a distribution in which 99 percent gets nothing while the richest one percent gets all of the income. The degree of inequality can be measured by the area between the line of equality and the actual distribution: the ratio of that area to the total area under the line of equality is called the *concentration ratio,* and is shown on the bottom of Table 36–1.

Note how the U.S. concentration ratio fell from 0.49 in 1929 to 0.39 in 1944, and remained almost exactly the same (0.40) in 1962. A Lorenz curve for 1944 would be almost identical to the one for 1962 shown on Figure 36-1.

International comparisons indicate that patterns of income distribution in the more advanced industrial nations are much the same, even though Great Britain, for example, has a somewhat more equalitarian pattern than the United States. Less developed nations typically show considerably greater *inequality*, however. There tend to be more of the very poor and the very wealthy, with a smaller "middle class." Table 36-3 illustrates these patterns for Great Britain in 1952 and India in 1950.

TABLE 36-3
Distribution of Household Personal Income, Selected Nations

	1952	1950
	Great Britain After Taxes	India Before Taxes
Quintile	(Percentage)	(Percentage)
Lowest	6	7.8
Second	12	9.2
Third	18	11.4
Fourth	22	16.0
Highest	40	55.4
Total	100	99.8

Sources: Harold Lydall and J. B. Lansing, "A Comparison of the Distribution of Personal Income and Wealth in the United States and Great Britain," *The American Economic Review*, March, 1959, p. 48. Simon Kuznets, "Quantitative Aspects of the Economic Growth of Nations," No. 8, "Distribution of Income by Size," *Economic Development and Cultural Change*, January, 1963, p. 13.

The relatively stable pattern of income distribution in the United States suggests that we should take a closer look at the upper and lower ends of the Lorenz curve. Who are the poor and why do they remain poor? Who are the wealthy and what are the sources of their wealth? We turn now to the first of these questions.

HOW DO YOU RANK?

Where do you rank in income? Table 36–4 gives the percent of all U.S. families whose income was below each indicated figure. For example, if your family income in 1969 was $10,000, your family had more income than 52.1 percent of all families.

TABLE 36–4
Income Rank

Income	Percentage with Less	Income	Percentage with Less
$1,000	1.4	$ 6,000	24.7
1,500	2.7	7,000	30.8
2,000	4.5	8,000	37.8
2,500	6.8	9,000	45.1
3,000	9.0	10,000	52.1
3,500	11.5	12,000	65.3
4,000	14.1	15,000	79.5
5,000	19.2	25,000	96.1

Source: U.S. Bureau of the Census, Income in 1969 of Families and Persons in the United States, Current Population Reports, Series P-60, No. 75, December 14, 1970.

THE PERSISTENCE OF POVERTY

When Jacob Riis wrote *How the Other Half Lives* in 1890 he proposed an antipoverty program that has a curiously modern ring. Included were parks, settlement houses, better schools, improved law enforcement, enforcement of housing laws, building of low cost housing, and employment programs. He demanded that affluent Americans take a hand in solving the problems of the slums through private charity. With the substitution of public programs for private charity, this outline of action could substitute for the antipoverty programs of 1970. Yet Riis wrote *eighty years ago*. In the intervening decades the average standard of living in the United States has risen dramatically. Yet the conditions pictured so vividly by Riis were reiterated by Michael Harrington's *The Other America*[2] and by more recent studies. While the face of poverty may change, the fact of poverty remains.

---

[2] Michael Harrington, *The Other America* (New York: Macmillan Company, 1962).

Earlier in this book (Chapters 3 and 7) some of the facts about the persistence of poverty were given. They can be briefly reviewed:

1. The average American has had a relatively steady and substantial growth in his standard of living.

2. Since the end of World War II, the proportion of households with incomes below "minimum subsistence" has fallen slowly to about 12 percent of all households. The *number of persons* in those households has remained around 20 million, however.

3. Much less progress has been made in reducing the proportion of households that are below a "minimum adequacy" income, and the number of persons in households with incomes below that level has risen.

The data on which these conclusions are based carried the trends through 1960. Later information shows that there has been little change in the picture over the last ten years. By 1968, the percentage of the U.S. population below the minimum subsistence level was still 12 percent and the number remained around 22 million, according to studies done by the Departments of Commerce and Health, Education and Welfare for the President's Council of Economic Advisors.[3]

WHO ARE THE POOR?

The poor are widely distributed throughout the United States. They are found in all regions of the country, in rural and urban areas, among all races and nationality groups, in all types and sizes of family units. Poverty does tend to be concentrated, however. The incidence of poverty is greater in the southeastern states than elsewhere. Some regions, like Appalachia, have a great deal of poverty. In urban regions poverty tends to center in the inner city, although there is some evidence that it, too, is becoming suburbanized. Families headed by women have a very high incidence of poverty. People with less education and people with poor health or physical disabilities tend to be poor. There is a great deal of poverty among the aged. And race matters a great deal: a far larger proportion of blacks (and some other racial minorities) are poor, as compared with whites. When several of these characteristics are combined the chances of a family's being poor are greatly increased.

---

[3] The minimum subsistence level used to determine the "poverty line" in these studies is calculated by the Social Security Administration. It is based on a minimal food plan designed by the Department of Agriculture. The cost of this food budget is then multiplied by three to obtain the necessary minimum subsistence income.

This estimate has been strongly criticized on two grounds. First, the poor do not have the information, expertise, or opportunity to buy such a minimum, nutritionally sound market basket of food. Second, the poor family's budget is closer to four times its expenditure on food (the standard of three times was based on 1958 budget studies). At the very least, the poverty line calculated in this fashion is an absolute minimum, and it tends to understate the amount of poverty. Perhaps that is why it is so widely used in government reports.

A Bureau of the Census study of conditions in 1966 gives a good picture of the poor in America today. Their definition of poverty included 30 million poor persons (as compared with the 22 million below the poverty line in the 1968 studies just mentioned). About 20 million were white and 10 million non-white. This proportion indicates the high incidence of poverty among non-whites: they make up about one-twelfth of the population and one-third of the poor. Even these figures understate the extent of poverty among minority groups, for many Spanish-speaking Americans (Puerto Rican and Mexican-American) are in the white category.

The position of minority group children was even worse. Families too poor to afford a minimum budget had 12.5 million children under 18 years of age, of whom 5 million (about 42 percent) were nonwhite. *More than half of all nonwhite children were growing up in poverty.*

Lack of adequate employment was probably the chief direct cause of poverty. More than two-thirds of the heads of poor families did not work at all or worked only part time during 1966. The remaining one-third worked full time but did not earn enough to raise the family income to adequate levels. Table 36-5 shows these appalling figures.

TABLE 36-5
Employment Status of Heads of Poor Families, 1966

State of Employment	Percent
Unemployed	40
Employed part time	27
Employed full time	32
Unreported	1
Total	100

Source: U.S. Bureau of the Census, *The Extent of Poverty in the United States, 1959 to 1966,* Current Population Reports Series P-20, No. 54, May, 1968.

SOCIETY'S REJECTS

These racial and employment characteristics of the poor can be supplemented by data from other sources. There are about 4.5 million disabled persons in the U.S., of whom about one-third will be rehabilitated and will rejoin the work force as self-supporting workers. Another one-third could be rehabilitated but are not—a huge waste and a great human tragedy. Another third are permanent charges on society.

The disabled category does not include persons in mental institutions, some 380,000 in 1969. A preliminary survey of mental hospitals in the vicinity of Ann Arbor, Michigan, by the author indicated that up to one-third of the inmates have no significant mental illness and are of working age (18–64). They are not released, however, because

1. Many have problems of dependency resulting from long years in the mental hospital.

2. They have no outside means of support; that is, they lack the skills
   or education necessary for employment.

These conditions appear to be similar to those present in mental hospitals throughout the nation. Apparently one function of our mental hospitals is to act as huge poorhouses for the hard-core unemployed! This category of people is not included in our estimates of the numbers of the poor, however.

The disabled are only an extreme example of persons whose earning power is reduced because of poor health. A survey of working people in the 30–44 age group in 1967, made by the U.S. Department of Labor, showed that those whose health was excellent or good worked for wages about 20 percent higher than those whose health was fair or poor. Many of the latter were employed in low-wage occupations, about which we shall have more to say shortly.

The aged are another and larger group among the poor. The decline of death rates and increased longevity, together with inability to compete with younger workers for jobs, has brought an increasingly serious problem of poverty among the aging. Only one-third of those over sixty-five are in the work force, as compared with two-thirds in 1900. About one-third of all poor families are headed by someone over 65 years of age, while the proportion of aged in the population as a whole is only about one in seven. The proportion of aged poor among single individuals is even higher.

Old-age insurance, the medical care program for the aged, and private pensions keep the aged from starving, and a substantial portion of the aged are above the poverty line. But a large number of older Americans must supplement their income from these sources with additional funds from welfare agencies. One of the tragedies of an industrial society is the way in which many older people are shunted aside after a lifetime of work and allowed to end their lives in poverty, poor health, and idleness, subsisting on totally inadequate old-age assistance programs.

Perhaps the largest group among the poor are families headed by women. Desertion has always been the poor man's substitute for divorce, and the tensions of a life of poverty create additional strains that tend to break up families. It is these broken families, most of them headed by women, that make up the bulk of the 12.5 million persons receiving welfare payments totaling some $8.5 billion (in 1970). This represents 6 percent of all Americans, and in some cities the percentages are spectacularly large: 15 percent in New York City; 25 percent in Newark, N. J.

The proportion of families headed by women is one of the best single indicators of poverty. About 8 percent of white families and 27 percent of black families had incomes below the poverty line in 1967. The percentage of families headed by women was: white, 9 percent; black 27 percent. The correlation between these two figures has been very close over the last thirty years. It is troubling to note, then, that while the percentage of white families headed by women has remained almost constant at around 9 percent in the last three censuses, the percentage of black families headed by women has risen from 17 percent (1950) to 22 percent (1960) to 27 percent (1970). This rise indicates a worsening and deepening of black poverty over the years.

All of these groups of people—the disabled, people with poor health, the aged, and broken families, have two characteristics in common. They are poor for reasons beyond their own control. And, for a variety of reasons, they are rejected by the economic system from jobs with adequate earnings. When they come up against the test of the marketplace they either produce too little to make their employment worthwhile to employers, or have family responsibilities that take them out of the marketplace. They become wards of society, subsisting on transfer payments derived from the productive effort of others.

A DIGRESSION: WELFARE PAYMENTS TO THE POOR

The rapid rise in the number of persons receiving welfare payments (technically, aid to families with dependent children, or AFDC), from 7.1 million in 1960 to 12.5 million in 1970 has made welfare a national issue. A great deal of hostility has developed toward the welfare recipient, who is sometimes typically pictured as a southern black woman moving to a northern city that pays relatively high benefits, getting rid of her husband to become eligible for welfare and having illegitimate children to qualify for higher benefits. The husband, meanwhile, is pictured as lazy, a cheater living illegally on his wife's benefits, while the soft-hearted welfare worker looks the other way.

Most of this stereotype has been shown to be wrong. Studies indicate that there is probably less cheating among welfare recipients than for example, among the affluent on their income tax returns. Most welfare families do not have illegitimate children, although illegitimacy is high among the poor (they can't afford abortions; and forced marriages, which are an important reason for less illegitimacy among low-middle income families, is not considered to be a workable solution). The typical welfare family does not stay on welfare indefinitely: the average period is 2 to 3 years. About half of all welfare families are white. In the broken family, the husband usually left long before the mother went on welfare. Finally, unemployment is by far the chief reason for a family going on welfare.

Criticism of the welfare system from the social work profession and sociological studies takes a different tack. This line of thought emphasizes the self-perpetuating nature of poverty and the way in which the welfare system worsens the problem. It perpetuates dependency. It keeps family incomes too low to permit children to grow up like others, or to allow normal family efforts to help itself. Administration of the system "shows little regard for them [recipients] as human beings, defeats their attempts to regain self-esteem and self-direction, and tends to prolong the duration of dependency," according to one study of the system in New York.[4] Another expert, Daniel Moynihan, argued that the welfare system "maintains the poverty groups in society in a position of impotent fury. Impotent because the system destroys the potential of individuals to improve themselves. Fury because it claims to be otherwise."[5] The system as a whole institutionalizes poverty. Although no one family may receive welfare payments forever, the system as a whole continues indefinitely, sustaining a group of poor families whose membership may change but that persists as a group.

If these views are correct, the welfare system in the United States must be seen in a new light. While preventing starvation and the extremes of human degradation, it preserves poverty and continues its causes from one generation to the next. Indeed, if we were serious about ending poverty, and welfare payments to families now on welfare were increased to levels high enough to move them above the poverty line, the total cost would be approximately doubled. Calculations made by the author for the year 1968 indicate that the $3.5 billion spent for AFDC in that year would have had to have been raised to $7 billion, just for those families then on welfare. Such a doubling of welfare payments would have to overcome strong political and ideological barriers.

On the other hand, welfare payments are a main source of income for society's rejects. Significant reductions in welfare payments could well lead to serious social unrest, and that is not politically tolerable either. The resultant equilibrium leads to what might be called "Fusfeld's rule":

> Welfare payments to the poor are set at that level at which the resultant unrest can be held in check by the existing instruments of law and order.

THE LOW-WAGE WORKER

The working poor are full-time employees whose wages do not enable them to earn enough to get above the poverty line. There are more of them than one would suspect. About 7 percent of all employed heads of families earn less than a poverty-line income even though they are employed full time throughout the year. About 30 percent of all employed single individuals (not members of a family) are in the same situation. Roughly 8.5 million working people are in this category of the working poor.

The reason, of course, is low wages. In February 1968, over ten million employed persons (19.5 percent of all production and nonsupervisory employees) earned wages less than $1.60 per hour. Almost 3.5 million of them earned less than $1 per hour. A quick calculation illustrates their economic position:

---

[4] Greenleigh Associates, Inc., *Report to the Moorland Commission on Welfare of the Findings of the Study of the Public Assistance Programs and Operations of the State of New York* (1964), p. 3.

[5] Daniel Moynihan, "The Crisis in Welfare," *The Public Interest, No. 10* (Winter 1968), pp. 3–29.

Full-time employment at 40 hours per week for 50 weeks per year
= 2000 hours.
Wage per hour = $1.60.
Annual income (2000 × $1.60) = $3200.

Compared with a poverty-line income for a family of four in 1968 of $3,500–
$3,800 (depending on location), this leaves a gap of $300–$600.

Some families with these low incomes are able to supplement these earnings
with overtime or second jobs. Others are not, and not all are able to hold jobs
employing them for a full forty hours each week. The hard fact is that the
large number of low-wage jobs in our presumably affluent society causes many
workers to spend their lives working for seriously inadequate wages.

A very large portion of the low-wage jobs are in service industries rather
than production jobs, and there are many entire industries in which the bulk
of the workers earn wages that keep them in poverty. Table 36-6 shows some
of those industries in urban areas, with recent data on employment, average
hourly earnings, and the proportion of workers earning less than $1.60 per
hour. Read it and weep.

Table 36-6
Selected Low-Wage Industries Employing Urban Poor

Industry	Year	Total Employment	Average Hourly Earnings	Percentage Earning Less Than $1.60/Hr
Nursing homes and related facilities	1965	172,637	1.19	86.3
Laundries and cleaning services	1966	397,715	1.44	72.5
Hospitals (federal excluded)	1966	1,781,300	1.86	41.2
Work clothing	1964	57,669	1.43	72.8
Men's and boy's shirts	1964	96,935	1.45	70.4
Candy and other confectionery	1965	49,736	1.87	34.2
Limited-price variety stores	1965	277,100	1.31	87.9
Eating and drinking places	1963	1,286,708	1.14	79.4
Hotels and motels	1963	416,289	1.17	76.1
Department stores	1965	1,019,300	1.75	59.6
Miscellaneous retail stores	1965	968,200	1.75	58.0
Retail food stores	1965	1,366,800	1.91	47.6

Source: Barry Bluestone, "Low Wage Industries and the Working Poor," *Poverty and Human Resources Abstracts*, Vol. III, No. 2 (March-April, 1968), pp. 1–13.

The fact that so much low-wage employment is in service industries means that those who earn higher incomes and buy the services benefit in the form of low living costs. If the service industries paid decent wages, everyone else who bought food services, health and hospital services, laundry and dry-cleaning services, and all the others would have to pay more. Their real incomes would be reduced. This basic economic relationship helps to explain the strong political opposition to adequate welfare payments. If families on welfare received incomes above the poverty line there would be little incentive for others to work in low-wage, dead-end jobs. Higher wages would have to be paid in order to draw enough workers into service industries. That would mean not only higher taxes to pay for the larger welfare payments, but also lower real incomes for the taxpayers because they would be paying more for the services they use.

The existence of low wages in service industries also helps to explain why local governments are reluctant to support antipoverty programs on a large scale, why token programs are all that have been developed. Elimination of poverty will require turning the low-wage industries into high-wage industries. This, in turn, would raise the price of services, unless significant technological advances in the service industries could be achieved. Raising the price of services would then raise costs of production in the high-wage industries that are the base of the local economy; wages in those industries would have to go up to compensate workers for the decrease in their real incomes, and the services used directly by firms in the high-wage industries would cost more. These higher costs would create a competitive disadvantage with other localities and local economic growth would tend to slow down, to the disadvantage of many local economic interests. Just as local economic growth is hampered by high taxes, so it would be hampered by higher wages in the service industries when compared with other localities.

For example, in the Detroit area any significant increase in wages in the low-wage service industries there would have both a direct and indirect effect in raising costs of production in the automobile industry there. The auto companies would gradually shift production to plants elsewhere. The effect would be felt in reduced economic growth and more unemployment in southeastern Michigan.

These economic relationships help to explain why it is to the advantage of local economic interests to have their city's poverty program come last with the least. They also help explain the strong drive to force welfare recipients to work in order to be eligible for welfare payments. Additional workers in the low-wage service industries help keep wage rates down. Finally, we must note the close relationship between the low-wage industries and the continuance of poverty. Low-wage employment builds poverty into the basic structure of the present-day American economy and this poverty will not be eradicated by simple programs that skirt the fundamental causes.

THE DYNAMICS OF POVERTY

Poverty begets poverty. The conditions the poor live in perpetuate their low incomes. This proposition is true even though some individuals may move out of poverty. While that is happening others remain poor and additional people fall into poverty.

Who are the recruits? They come from a wide variety of sources. The technology of an industrial society creates some: those injured or disabled by the hazards of modern life and industrial technology; workers whose skills become obsolete because of technological change; farmers and farm workers displaced by our changing agriculture. The economics of an industrial society creates others: the aged and the young whose level of productivity is low and who are therefore not hired until labor markets become very tight. The educational system creates more: those who drop out of school or are pushed out before they have acquired the skills or credentials necessary for high-wage jobs. Racial attitudes add to the numbers of poor: minority groups are systematically excluded from high-wage jobs and crowded into low-wage employment, pushing earnings there down still more. All of these aspects of the economy tend to create the economic rejects who make up the army of the poor.

Once a family is poor the conditions under which it lives helps to keep it poor. Low incomes mean poor diets and poor housing, which lead to poor health, low productivity, and low incomes. Low incomes lead to poor education and limited educational opportunities, which lead to low skills, poor earnings, and low incomes. Low incomes limit mobility, which in turn limits opportunities and brings reduced earnings. The frustrations and buffetings of poverty lead to discouragement and apathy in some of the poor.

Poverty is characterized by a system of *circular causation with cumulative effects*. The conditions that lead to poverty tend to be perpetuated by poverty itself, creating a vicious circle in which the effects of poverty cumulate to make it extremely difficult for individuals to fight their way out. The circle of causation can be visualized in Figure 36-2, which shows a highly simplified version of the complex social and economic relationships that prevail in the world of the poor.

This systematic nature of poverty and the reinforcement of the conditions of poverty help to explain why poverty persists in an affluent society. When the case is seen in this fashion, the surprising element is that many individuals are able to escape from poverty and move into higher income levels. It is a tribute to the resiliency and initiative of the human being, just as the way in which poverty becomes systematic and self-preserving is an indictment of what might otherwise be an affluent society.

POVERTY AND MINORITY GROUPS

We have already noted the high proportion of blacks among the American poor; about one-third of the poor are nonwhite, but nonwhites make up a

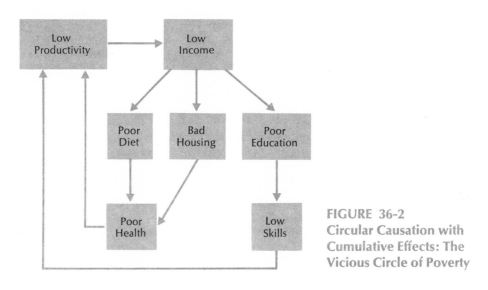

FIGURE 36-2
Circular Causation with
Cumulative Effects: The
Vicious Circle of Poverty

little less than 12 percent of the total population. Although a little less than
1 in 10 whites are poor, about 40 percent of blacks are poor.

Racial discrimination is usually given as the chief cause of the high incidence
of poverty among racial minorities, and in a general sense that is correct. But
discrimination of a voluntary, individualistic nature is less important than the
systematic and institutionalized discrimination that is built into the structure
of labor markets and job opportunities. Relatively few employers are consciously "racist" in their employment policies, but many who seemingly act
without prejudice participate in a systematic exclusion of blacks and other
minorities from a wide variety of jobs. Minority groups, among which we
number women, are crowded into a relatively small number of occupations for
which the excessively large supply of workers serves to keep wage rates down.
In other occupations, the supply of workers is correspondingly reduced, bringing higher wages to the white male workers employed in those jobs.

We illustrate the effects of "crowding" of minorities into a few occupations
in Figure 36-3. Start with two occupations requiring identical skills, but blacks
are crowded into one. The wage rate in that occupation will be reduced by the
large number of workers seeking employment, and according to the theory of
marginal productivity, more will be hired in each establishment. Meanwhile, in
the other occupations reserved for whites, the elimination of workers from the
minority group reduces the supply of workers, raises wage rates, and results in
higher productivity at the margin, shown in Figure 36-4.

This analysis clearly shows who benefits. It is the white worker. He earns
more. It makes little or no difference to the employer, who goes about the
readjustment of his work force in response to the wage levels he finds in the
market. Meanwhile the black worker, or any other minority worker, bears
the burden in the form of lower earnings. Nor is the level of total employment

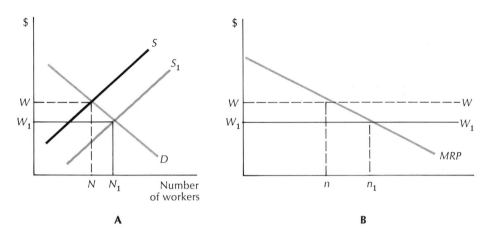

FIGURE 36-3
"Crowding": Effects on Occupation into Which Minority Group Is Concentrated

Crowding of minority groups into this occupation increases the supply of workers from S to S_1, bringing the wage down from W to W_1 and creating a low wage occupation. The individual employer pushes his employment up from n to n_1 as a result of the reduced wage, and productivity at the margin is reduced.

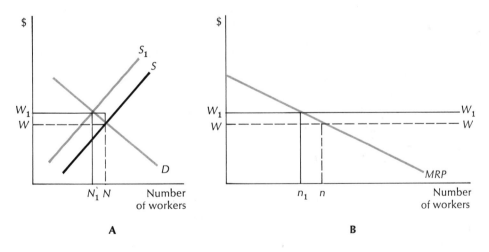

FIGURE 36-4
"Crowding": Effects on Occupation From Which Minority Group Is Excluded

In the uncrowded occupation the reduced supply of labor brings higher wages ($W \rightarrow W_1$) and less employment ($N \rightarrow N_1$) while the individual employer reduces the number he employs at the higher wage ($n \rightarrow n_1$).

likely to be affected significantly. Wages in both occupational groups can be expected to move to the levels that will clear the market and provide employment to all willing workers, assuming that the level of aggregate demand is high enough.

There is a social cost, however. It would be possible to move workers from the crowded occupation, where their marginal productivity is low, to the uncrowded occupations, where their marginal productivity would be higher. This would bring a net gain of output to the economy as a whole. Doing so would also eliminate the prevailing wage differentials and bring down the earnings of white workers in those occupations. It is exactly this elimination of differences in marginal productivities for workers with similar skills that would occur in a competitive color-blind economy, but which does not occur here because of the institutionalized pattern of keeping the minority group in a relatively few menial occupations.[6]

There are additional indirect effects on the economy. Not only are the low-wage occupations and industries overexpanded, but there are other labor market effects:

1. Low wages for minority groups reduce incentives to work, resulting in lower labor market participation.
2. Minority groups tend to move into criminal occupations, where rewards are correspondingly greater.
3. The few minority group members who are able to get jobs outside the crowded occupations are willing to take lower pay than the majority, because their alternatives are so much poorer.

No individual employer, nor individual worker, need have any personal feelings of animosity toward minority groups, or any "taste for discrimination," as one theory of labor market discrimination phrases it,[7] for the system as a whole to crowd minorities into low-paid jobs. The necessary conditions are accepted patterns of behavior or rules of the game that systematically channel minority groups into a relatively small number of occupations and exclude them from opportunities in other occupations.

---

[6] The thoughtful reader will note that the effects of crowding are not limited to racial minorities. It applies to women as well. The analysis was first developed in an effort to explain the low wages paid to women.

[7] See Gary S. Becker, *The Economics of Discrimination* (Chicago: University of Chicago Press, 1957). Becker argues that employers and employees have a "taste for discrimination" that increases the satisfactions they receive from the job or the enterprise to balance the social losses created by discrimination. Becker's theory rescues the theory of utility from a tight corner. It also shifts the blame from the social and economic system to individuals, implying that if people can be changed, the economic system can remain untouched; this perhaps explains its popularity. The more realistic crowding hypothesis was developed by Francis Y. Edgeworth, "Equal Pay to Men and Women for Equal Work," *Economic Journal*, Vol. 32 (December 1922), pp. 431–57. The author is heavily indebted to Barbara Bergman of the University of Maryland, who has produced an important series of papers on the crowding hypothesis.

As far as blacks are concerned, crowding into menial occupations is only the most recent form of coerced labor to which they have been subjected. Slavery was the first. The sharecropping and debt tenure systems in Southern agriculture after the Civil War was the second. When that pattern broke up under the combined impact of black migration to the north after 1910 and the technological revolution in agriculture, blacks moved into the system of crowding into menial occupations in both Southern and Northern cities. As a form of coerced labor, it does not have the legal sanctions that preserved slavery, or the combination of legal sanctions and social controls that preserved sharecropping and debt tenure in the South for almost a hundred years. But it is based on strong pressures from within the labor market, as the recent efforts to provide equal opportunities for blacks and other minority groups indicate. It is an important reason for the continued existence of poverty in modern America.

PROGRAMS TO ELIMINATE POVERTY

Public policy toward poverty has passed through several stages of development. In the days of the laissez-faire state, poverty was seen as the responsibility of private charity and local government. As a more positive attitude toward public responsibilities developed during the 1930s, opinion shifted and the federal government began to develop programs to alleviate poverty. Chief among these efforts was the social security legislation of the mid- and late 1930s that provided help for the aged and the blind and was later extended to widows and orphans (the origins of AFDC). But whether public or private, these efforts focused on income for the poor rather than on attacking the causes of poverty.

That approach was continued after World War II, supplemented by the Keynesian proposition that full employment and economic growth would gradually move the poor upward to affluence. As the 1950s ran on into the 1960s, the limited gains from that approach became evident at about the same time that the cities exploded into violence in the mid-1960s. New approaches were made necessary by the force of events.

One of the new approaches fitted neatly into the Keynesian policies that were directed toward full employment and growth. It was _investment in human capital._ Just as economists were discovering the importance of education, health, and productive skills for economic growth, they simultaneously realized that the poor were badly educated, in poor health, and had limited productive skills. In addition, they realized that the inflationary trade-off between prices and unemployment might be reduced if the effective labor force could be increased through manpower development programs and elimination of discrimination in employment.

The antipoverty programs of the 1960s were born out of these considerations. If only the poor could be changed enough, they could earn their way to affluence by themselves. The changes were to be brought about by enlarged expenditures for special programs for the poor: manpower training, education, health, housing, and related needs. The existing poor were to be upgraded and the next generation was to be provided with an environment in which poverty could not flourish. And while the poor were being changed, the elimination of racial discrimination in employment, together with full employment, would provide opportunities for the deserving poor to rise. As for regions of the country in which low incomes were common, their special problems could be met by regional development programs.

This philosophy was expressed in a series of important federal legislation: the Area Redevelopment Act (1961), the Manpower Development and Training Act (1962), the Economic Opportunity Act (1964), and the Appalachian Regional Development Act (1965). These laws were supplemented by other programs in the already established education, health and welfare agencies of the federal government, as the framework for a great antipoverty drive was put together.

The results have not been encouraging. The first flaw was inadequate funding. The war in Vietnam and the military-space expenditures of the federal government took funds and resources that could have gone into a large-scale antipoverty program. The second flaw was the ineffectiveness of the programs themselves. Programs designed to upgrade the poor did not always have that effect, or they were successful in only a portion of the cases. Some of that result was expected, but public officials were unprepared for the large proportion of instances in which investment in human capital seemed to have little impact. Even if a great deal more money had been poured into the antipoverty program, it may not have been much more successful. The third flaw was failure to strike at the roots of poverty. Even if individuals could be rehabilitated, there would be little impact on the problem as a whole if others were falling into poverty. Poverty might be reduced if more people moved up and out of poverty than fell into it, but as long as the low-wage industries remained and as long as measured unemployment rates remained above the approximately 2 percent level of frictional unemployment there would be a hard core of poverty that could not be eliminated.[8]

INCOME FOR THE POOR

The limitations of the "human capitalist" approach to poverty has focused attention on several proposals for income supplements as a means of eliminating poverty. The two most widely discussed have been the *guaranteed annual income* and *children's allowances*. Both are based on the assumptions that the

---

[8] These thumbnail criticisms are controversial. However, it is hard to find praise for the various antipoverty programs outside of official government reports and even those are full of discussions of deficiencies and limitations. Three short paperback books can give a much fuller appraisal: Oscar Ornati, *Poverty Amid Affluence* (New York: Twentieth Century Fund, 1966); David Hamilton, *A Primer on the Economics of Poverty* (New York: Random House, 1968); and Ben B. Seligman, *Permanent Poverty: An American Syndrome* (Chicago: Quadrangle Books, 1970).

causes of poverty cannot be eliminated but that low incomes can. The obvious solution is to provide the poor with higher incomes.[9] This remedy has the advantage of not requiring any changes in the basic structure of the economy, while at the same time it can reduce very substantially the other programs and personnel required to administer welfare and antipoverty programs. It has the disadvantage of costing the taxpayers a substantial sum to provide for non-earners.

The Guaranteed Annual Income

The simplest form of the guaranteed annual income is a direct payment to the poor whose other income leaves them in poverty. The government would provide additional funds to bring their income up to some minimally acceptable level. Proposals along these lines were made in the early 1960s by Robert Theobald.[10] He was concerned that automation would eliminate jobs and incomes, leaving the economy with inadequate aggregate demand to maintain full employment. The obvious solution was to reorganize the system of income distribution away from earned income to a government-guaranteed income based on the growth of an affluent, high-technology economy. Although not directly oriented to the elimination of poverty, such a program would have that effect.

From the other side of the political spectrum came the idea of the negative income tax, proposed by Milton Friedman.[11] He proposed to replace welfare payments and other aid to the poor by direct payments through the income tax system. For families and individuals below the poverty line, their obligation to pay income taxes to the government would be replaced by a government obligation to pay them. The lower their income the larger the government's payment would be. For example, a break-even income for a family of four might be set at $5,000, at which point the family's income tax liability would be zero and its payment from the government would be zero. If its income were above $5,000, it would pay the regular tax. If its income were below $5,000, the family would receive a payment from the government on a pre-arranged schedule, perhaps half the difference: a $4,000 income would entitle the family to a $500 payment. It would be feasible to fill the gap entirely, or the schedule of payments (the negative tax) could be even smaller, depending on government policy goals. A possible schedule of payments is shown in Table 36-7.

---

[9] When asked during a television interview "What do the poor need most?" economist Milton Friedman of the University of Chicago responded, "Money."

[10] Robert Theobald, *Free Men and Free Markets* (New York: Clarkson N. Potter, 1963), Ch. 7. The idea is an old one. It was proposed in the 1790s in England and by John Stuart Mill in the mid-nineteenth century.

[11] Milton Friedman, *Capitalism and Freedom* (Chicago: University of Chicago Press, 1962), Ch. 12.

TABLE 36–7
A Negative Income Tax

Family Income Before Taxes or Supplement	Tax Payments (+) or Income Supplement (−)	Family Income After Taxes or Supplement
$8,000	+$ 500	$7,500
7,000	+ 250	6,750
6,000	+ 100	5,900
5,000	0	5,000
4,000	− 500	4,500
3,000	− 1,000	4,000
2,000	− 1,500	3,500

At incomes above $5,000 the family pays an income tax to the government, at a progressive rate. At incomes below $5,000 the family receives an income supplement equal to half the difference between its income and $5,000. These rates and the break-even income could be changed, and are only illustrative.

How much would all this cost? It all depends on where the break-even income is fixed and the rate at which the negative tax is set. Roughly, a negative income tax with the break-even income set at $1,000 per family member, and a negative tax equal to half the difference between that amount and actual income, would cost about $25 billion annually at the family income levels of the late 1960s. Reducing the break-even level to $750 per family member ($3,000 for a family of four) would reduce the cost to about $6 billion.

Aside from its cost, the negative income tax has two other potential liabilities. It represents a high tax on additional earned income for the poor. For example, look at a family earning $3,000 in the example given in Table 36–7. Its income after supplements would be $4,000. Now suppose that its earnings go up by $1,000, to a total of $4,000. Its income after supplements would go up to only $4,500. It was able to raise its after-tax income by only $500 even though its earnings rose by $1,000. This is equivalent to a marginal income tax rate of 50 percent, a rate now paid only by the very rich.

A second difficulty is more important. A negative income tax that supplements earned income gives employers incentives to reduce the wages they pay and thereby shift part of their costs to the general taxpayer. This is the so-called "Speenhamland effect," named for a system of welfare payments to the working poor in England in the late eighteenth and early nineteenth centuries, which caused deterioration of wage rates for the working poor. It brought intensification of poverty and was partly responsible for the degraded position of working people during the early years of industrialization. Similar effects could be felt today with any system that supplements the wage income of the poor in order to keep families out of poverty.

Children's Allowances

Children's allowances do not have these limitations. Since they are tied to the size of the family rather than to income, they do not tend to reduce the incentive to work or exert downward pressure on wage rates.

A children's allowance is a direct payment to families and is based on the number of children. It would be paid to all families, regardless of their income, just as the present system of tax deductions for dependents (a form of children's allowance) is available to everyone—except the poor, who do not pay income taxes and therefore do not get the benefit of the deduction. The size of the allowance can be high enough to keep a family above the poverty line, say, $1,000 per child.

This simple idea has some drawbacks. It might encourage large families and excessive population growth, although that has not been the experience of other countries. To guard against that possibility the allowance could be reduced as the number of children increased, say, $1,400 for the first, $900 for the second, $600 for the third, and so on. Children's allowances would also provide payments to affluent families who do not need the money. But a recapture tax based on incomes could compensate for that and reduce the net cost as well.[12] Finally, a system of children's allowances would not reach poverty among those who are not in families with children; but it would at least reach families now receiving AFDC and many of the working poor.

EMPLOYMENT AS THE CURE FOR POVERTY

The chief difficulty with income supplements as the cure for poverty is that the American political system has never been willing to sanction transfer payments high enough to solve the problem. The history of old-age benefits and AFDC provides ample illustration of that proposition. Apparently we shall always have the poor with us because we won't pay enough to bring them out of poverty.

At the same time, income payments alone do not touch either the low productivity of the poor or the structural elements in the social and economic order that continue a portion of our people in poverty. Although investment in human capital can raise the potential earning power of individuals, our experience with that approach showed that it has severe limitations.

A third possibility is maintenance of such high levels of aggregate demand that the unemployment rate is cut to about 2 percent and kept there. If that is done, lack of employment will ultimately be removed as a primary cause of poverty. The hard-core unemployed and the discouraged worker will be drawn back into the labor force. Second jobs will be available, as well as jobs for more than one earner in the family. Employment opportunities will be

---

[12] An imaginative proposal along those lines has been made by Harvey E. Brazer, "The Federal Income Tax and the Poor," *California Law Review*, Vol. 57 (April, 1969), pp. 442–49.

widened for blacks and other minority groups, for evidence from the past shows that earnings differences between whites and blacks are significantly diminished only during periods of seriously tight labor markets.[13]

True full employment would not solve the problem of low-wage employment, however. That will have to be tackled directly, with minimum-wage legislation that forces minimum-wage rates up to levels that will support a family at a standard of health and decency. For the early 1970s, this means an income of about $7,000 for an urban family of four. Translated into a minimum wage for full-time employment, that would mean $3.50 per hour, compared with the present $1.65, and without the present exceptions that leave significant portions of the low-wage work force uncovered. We could hardly expect such a change to be made overnight, for the repercussions would be very great. But it certainly could be accomplished over perhaps a five-year period with 40-cent increases in the minimum each year.

Increases in the minimum wage of that scope would leave some of the present low-wage workers unemployed because their productivity would make it unprofitable for the private sector to continue to employ them. There may be as many as 4 million workers in that situation. Three things could be done to take care of that problem.

1. The maintenance of high levels of aggregate demand would assure that some would find jobs.
2. A large-scale program of training and retraining could upgrade the skills of many. Much investment in human capital would be needed.
3. Governments could seriously accept responsibility as "employers of last resort" to employ the remainder in public service jobs.

Although displacement of workers resulting from a significantly higher minimum wage may seem initially to be an insurmountable problem, it would appear on further examination to be surmountable.

We should recognize, however, that many things would cost more, including some widely used services. A redistribution of real income in favor of the low-wage worker would occur, to the detriment of higher income groups. But that is the whole point; there is no way to get rid of poverty in America without providing the poor with a larger share of the pie, even if we make the pie as a whole somewhat larger.

All of these comments about the labor market assume equality of opportunity. Since that is not a proper assumption to make, the final point in an employment program to end poverty would have to be strong equal-opportunity legislation with vigorous enforcement procedures and sanctions with teeth in them. Discrimination on the basis of race and sex will have to be eliminated.

---

[13] See Dale L. Hiestand, *Economic Growth and Employment Opportunities for Minorities* (New York: Columbia University Press, 1964).

A final comment. True full employment, elimination of low-wage jobs and full equality of opportunity would still leave untouched all those who are out of the labor market or only intermittently in it: the aged, for example, or the disabled, or the family headed by a woman. There would still be a need for guaranteed incomes and transfer payments for those groups and others. Any attack on poverty will have to have many aspects in addition to the employment, wage, and equal opportunity programs suggested here. It will require substantial income transfers also. Perhaps even more important: it will require national policies that give the ending of poverty a higher priority than world power.

Summary

Income distribution patterns in the United States have remained largely unchanged since the end of the Second World War. Although average incomes have risen, the pattern of distribution as shown by a Lorenz curve has not changed.

Poverty has remained, in spite of a reduction in the proportion of poor households to about 12 percent of all households. The poor are characterized by high unemployment rates, disabilities, or poor health, old age, broken families, and racial minority status. Welfare payments have tended to preserve poverty while making it more bearable for the poor who receive them. Finally, a very large portion of the poor hold full time jobs in low-wage industries from which they earn less than the income needed to put them above the poverty classification.

The economic system creates conditions that serve to preserve and perpetuate poverty, in a pattern of circular causation with cumulative effects. Blacks and other minorities are particularly afflicted with poverty because of a job market that crowds them into menial occupations where their productivity and their incomes are low.

Programs to eliminate poverty have been unsuccessful in part because they have not recognized the systematic nature of the problem. Particularly, programs for investment in human capital may enable some individuals to escape poverty while the causes that lie within the economic system are untouched. Income payments to the poor in the form of a guaranteed annual income or children's allowances have the drawback of high cost and unwillingness of the American political system to make available adequate funds for that purpose. A thoroughgoing employment policy to end poverty may be the best alternative, but it also would be very hard to implement. The prospect is that poverty will remain a feature of the American economy for a long time to come.

Key Concepts

Lorenz curve.   Graphic depiction of the income distribution pattern. A straight line from the origin at a 45° angle shows an equal distribution, with the degree of inequality increasing as the actual distribution diverges from it.

Vicious circle of poverty.   The interrelated conditions of the poor that serve to reinforce and preserve poverty in a system of circular causation.

"Crowding."   The tendency of workers from minority groups to be excluded from many occupations, forcing them to take jobs in a relatively few menial or low-paying occupations.

Guaranteed annual income.   Provision of a minimum income to people. One version is the *negative income tax* in which the federal government would make payments to those whose incomes were below a specified figure.

Children's allowance.   A government payment to a family, based on the number of children in the family.

Americans are fascinated by the wealthy, but we study the poor. There are few decent studies of the distribution of wealth, and there is no government agency that regularly publishes data on that topic. Good information on holdings of wealth in the United States is almost as hard to find as the facts about income distribution in the USSR. There may be a moral here. This chapter tries to remedy the situation somewhat. After examining the limited facts about the distribution of wealth in the United States it inquires into the economic functions of wealth, the problem of unearned income, and the relationship between wealth and power. Just as we looked at the many at the bottom of the economy in the last chapter, here we look at the few at the top.

SOME BASIC FACTS

The most comprehensive recent study of wealth ownership in the U.S. was done by Robert Lampman of the University of Wisconsin.[1] It brings the data up to 1956. Sponsored by the National Bureau of Economic Research, if found that the distribution of wealth was considerably more unequal than the distribution of income. Lampman compared the Lorenz curves of gross income of spending units in 1952 with the net worth of spending units in 1953. The striking difference is shown in Figure 37-1.

The personal wealth (net worth) of U.S. adults in 1953 was estimated at $1,120 billion. Its distribution was highly skewed in favor of the wealthy, as follows:

> Half of the adult population at the poorer end of
> the distribution owned just over 8 percent of the
> wealth, and two-thirds owned about 18.5 percent.
> At the other extreme, 1.6 percent of the adult population, at the wealthy end of the scale, owned
> 27.6 percent of the nation's personal wealth.

Table 37–1, as taken from Lampman's book, summarizes the facts as he found them.

Our first conclusion is that the ownership of wealth is distributed in a highly unequal pattern. A relatively small number of people hold a relatively large proportion of the fruits of economic activity.

[1] Robert J. Lampman, *The Share of Top Wealth-Holders in National Wealth: 1922–1956* (Princeton, New Jersey: Princeton University Press, 1962).

The
Distribution
of Wealth

37

Per cent of gross
income or net worth

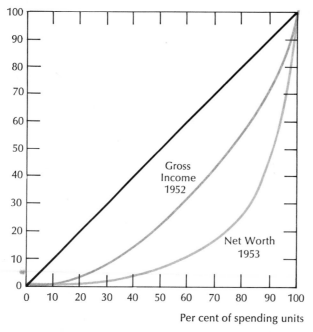

FIGURE 37-1
Lorenz Curves of Total
Money Income and Net
Worth Among
Spending Units Ranked
by Income and
Net Worth

*(Source: 1953 Survey of
Consumer Finances,
reprinted from Federal
Reserve Bulletin, 1953.
Supplementary Table
5, p. 11.)*

TABLE 37–1
Estimated Distribution of Total Adult Population by Gross Estate Size,
United States, 1953

Gross Estate Size (dollars)	Number of Persons Aged 20 and over (millions)	Percent	Average Estate Size (dollars)	Total Gross Estate — Billion dollars	Percent
0 to 3,500	51.70	50.0	1,800	93.1	8.3
3,500 to 10,000	19.00	18.4	6,000	114.0	10.2
10,000 to 20,000	21.89	21.2	15,000	328.4	29.3
20,000 to 30,000	6.00	5.8	25,000	150.0	13.4
30,000 to 40,000	2.00	1.9	35,000	70.0	6.3
40,000 to 50,000	0.80	0.8	45,000	36.0	3.2
50,000 to 60,000	0.35	0.3	55,000	19.3	1.7
Total under 60,000	101.74	98.4	7,900	810.8	72.4
60,000 to 70,000	0.18	0.1	61,000	10.5	0.9
60,000 and over	1.66	1.6	186,265	309.2	27.6
All estate sizes	103.40	100.0	10,800	1,120.0	100.0
Median estate size			3,500		

Source: Lampman, *Share of Top Wealth-Holders*, p. 213.

IS OWNERSHIP OF WEALTH BECOMING
MORE CONCENTRATED?

According to Karl Marx, who wrote over a century ago, one of the inherent weaknesses of capitalism was a trend toward greater concentration of wealth. Ultimately, Marx predicted, a capitalist economy would face a revolution brought about, in part, by the polarization of society into two warring camps. According to Marx, these groups would be:

1. A small number of very wealthy capitalist-financiers who gathered into their hands a growing share of the productive resources of the economy. At the same time, competition, the attrition of business cycles, and the results of technological change would make this top group smaller and smaller. Both centralization and concentration of wealth would increase over the years.

2. At the other extreme was a growing mass of workers whose incomes and wealth were held down by the presence of unemployment because of business cycles and technological change. Although Marx was willing to concede that the level of life of the working class might be raised, he insisted that, *relative to the wealthy,* the economic position of the worker must worsen.

The growing conflict between the dispossessed and the possessors, Marx argued, would ultimately bring on a social revolution in which the tables were turned, the majority seized power, and a new social order was constructed.

Crucial to this analysis is the proposition that growing concentration of wealth in the hands of a few was an inherent characteristic of a private enterprise economy. Is it? The answer is not obvious, although ideologies of left and right continually claim the truth.

Lampman's study found that inequality in ownership of wealth decreased between 1922 and 1956. In 1922, the top 1 percent of all wealth holders owned 32 percent of all personal wealth. In 1953, the proportion had fallen to 25 percent.

The change was not the result of a steady decline, however. In the prosperous, low-income-tax twenties (1922–1929), the share of the very rich in total personal wealth rose to 38 percent. The early depression years pulled their share down drastically to 30 percent by 1933, but by 1939 their share recovered to 33 percent. World War II, with its changed tax structure and artificial economic environment, brought the share of the very rich down to 26 percent in 1945 and 22 percent in 1949. Then a moderate but steady rise began to the 25 percent level in 1953. Other data cited by Lampman indicate a continuing rise to 1956. These trends are shown graphically in Figure 37-2.

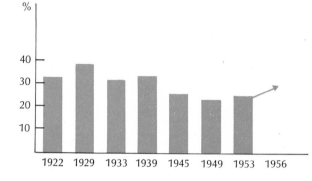

FIGURE 37-2
Share of Top 1 Percent
of Holders of Wealth in
Total Personal Wealth,
U.S., 1922–1956

(Source: Lampman,
Share of Top Wealth-
Holders, *p. 202.)*

No one knows what the trend has been since 1956.[2] But we can make some informed guesses. Periods of consistent peacetime growth in GNP have been associated with a rising share of wealth for the very wealthy. This was true of 1922–29, 1933–38, and 1949–56. If the 1949–56 trend is projected beyond 1956, the U.S. would have gotten back to the 1922 figure of 32 percent of personal wealth in the hands of the top 1 percent of wealth holders sometime in the mid-1960s.

These speculations about recent trends in ownership of wealth are partially supported by a study made by the Board of Governors of the Federal Reserve System, which reported that at the end of 1962, 22 percent of personal wealth was held by 200 thousand households owning assets worth more than $500,000 each. This is less than four-tenths of 1 percent of all households. This compares with Lampman's figures for 1953 showing that 1 percent of families held 25 percent of personal wealth. While Lampman and Federal Reserve studies are not strictly comparable, together they suggest that the trend toward greater concentration of wealth has continued in recent years, but at a rather slow pace.

The *1962 Survey of Consumer Finances* showed somewhat similar results.[3] The proportion of consumer units reporting net worth of less than $1,000 remained just about the same (30–31 percent) between 1953 and 1962, while the proportion reporting $10,000 or more rose from 29 to 34 percent. At the level of the very wealthy, however, the survey reported "no great shift toward greater concentration" between 1953 and 1962.

---

[2] A critique of Lampman's findings found his estimates a little low and confirmed the post–World War II increase in concentration of wealth through 1958. See James D. Smith and Staunton K. Calvert, "Estimating the Wealth of Top Wealth-Holders from Estate Tax Returns," in American Statistical Association, *Proceedings of the Business and Economic Statistics Section* (Washington, D.C.: American Statistical Association, 1965), pp. 248–265.

[3] George Katona, Charles A. Lininger and Richard F. Kosebud, *1962 Survey of Consumer Finances* (Ann Arbor, Mich.: Institute for Social Research, The University of Michigan, 1963), pp. 177–242.

Economic factors affecting the concentration of wealth seem to work both toward and against an increased share for the very wealthy. Most of their assets, such as bonds, common stock, and real estate, produce income. As the economy grows, the earning power of these assets also grows, creating capital gains for their owners. The rest of us hold assets primarily in the form of durable consumers' goods: automobiles, houses and their furnishings, and the like. These assets often are used up over the lifetime of the family and require replacement or maintenance instead of producing income. The assets of the rich usually add to their wealth, while the assets of the middle class family usually do not. As a result, the rich tend to become richer as their wealth begets greater wealth.

On the other hand, middle-income families add to their wealth by saving from their incomes to a greater extent than the wealthy do. This pattern counters the tendency for the growing wealth of an affluent society to concentrate itself in the hands of those who are already rich. While the wealthy add to their assets primarily through capital gains, the merely affluent add to theirs primarily through savings. As the total amount of wealth in the economy increases, both groups seem to move ahead at somewhat similar rates. The only ones left behind appear to be the poor, who have neither earning assets nor incomes large enough to generate significant amounts of savings. The net result seems to be a relatively stable pattern of ownership of wealth, but with the poor unable to keep up with the rest.

INCOME FROM PROPERTY

In a market economy wealth is measured by its value in money. The marketplace gives wealth a value by placing a price on it. In the case of consumer goods, such as a Rolls Royce automobile or a mansion, the price reflects the uses or utility of the goods and their cost of production. Most wealth, however, is in the form of the means of production, or capital, and its price reflects its earning power.

Having made these simple, almost self-evident points, we now enter an area of confusion in contemporary economics. There is no agreement on the determinants of the earning power of capital. Conflicting theories abound, and there has been no successful integration of the macroeconomic theories of the rate of interest described in the earlier parts of this book and the productivity theories that arise from microeconomic analysis. There is even a group of astute economists centered in Cambridge, England who argue that the very concept of capital is misleading.

The problem goes back a long way. The distinction between rent, interest, profit, and wages became a major issue in economics in England in the early nineteenth century. The social changes of the early period of industrialization featured the emergence of a working class and a business-financial-industrial class out of a social order that had formerly been dominated by a landed aristocracy. Political issues in the English Parliament were dominated by the clash of interests of businessmen and aristocrats, while the conflict between labor and capital developed in the factories and the new industrial cities. In those circumstances the economists of the period turned to the problem of determining the sources of income of the contesting parties and the distinctive features of the return to land, capital and labor.

In the second half of the nineteenth century, and particularly after 1875, the focus shifted as a result of the rise of Marxism. Marx had argued that all the earnings of the factors of production were the result of human effort and at bottom a product of labor. Even land had no value in and of itself, but became valuable only after human labor improved it and brought it into production. As for capital, it was obviously the result of past productive effort —the present embodiment of past labor. The ideological implications of the Marxian position are obvious. If all of the means of production are the result of collective human effort they should be owned collectively by the group that made the effort, the workers. In the Marxist view, private ownership of the means of production enabled the owners to obtain income that they did not produce and were therefore not entitled to receive. In the words of the nine-teenth-century socialist Pierre Joseph Proudhon, "Poverty is theft"—or of novelist Honore de Balzac, "Behind every fortune is a crime."

One response of economics to the Marxist challenge was the emergence of the theory of marginal productivity. This theory performed the social function of justifying the earnings of property and opposing the Marxist theory of ex-ploitation.

The theory of marginal productivity has some serious defects, however. It is rigorously correct only for the purely competitive model in the long run. It does not adequately account for monopoly gains. It is essentially a static theory and does not give proper consideration to the time period of the life of capital, or to innovation and economic change, or to the uncertainties of the business world in an ever-changing market environment. It does not explain why capital accumulation takes place. In short, it does not explain why land and capital are different from labor and why, therefore, a payment to their owners is justified.

TOWARD A NEW SYNTHESIS

Economists now realize that the factors of production are so closely inter-twined that distinguishing separate returns to capital, labor, and land is almost impossible. Wages and salaries embody a return to investment in human capital as well as a return to labor itself. The productivity of land is the result of natural fertility, the improvements that have been made to it, and the intelligence and education of the person who manages it as part of a producing unit. Capital is not a disembodied phenomenon independent of the develop-ment of technology and the process of economic growth. Yet much of the current economic analysis of the returns to the means of production remains within the framework of a separation of labor, land, and capital into distinct elements in the production process. In some respects, this part of economic theory seeks to distinguish "pure" or "economic" rent, interest, and profit in an effort to salvage the very concepts themselves.

If we try to cut through the extraneous ideological matters that the theory of income distribution has inherited from the past we find a hard core of meaningful propositions that might serve as building blocks for a new synthesis. We start with the concept of capital.

CAPITAL

Capital was defined earlier in this book as the tangible and intangible tools of production that the economy has accumulated as a result of its productive efforts. It includes both capital goods (things used to produce other things) and knowledge of how to organize and run the productive system.

Capital is distinguished from labor, which can be defined as the human effort used in the production system. Capital can also be distinguished from land and other natural resources because capital is itself a product of the economic system while land and natural resources are not. Land and natural resources are limited in amount and are not increased by economic activity. In one respect capital and land are similar, however. Both produce a stream of income that has a market value and that gives value to the capital or land.

In the case of land, we have already examined the basis of rent in the differing levels of productivity of different qualities of land: rent on highly productive land will be greater than rent on less productive land. This concept of differential rent is applicable to resources other than land. Take baseball players, for example. Willy Mays drives baseballs out of Candlestick Park and paying customers in. His high productivity enables him to demand and obtain a high salary, a small portion of which is labor income earned for playing baseball (a major-league centerfielder of ordinary skills will earn perhaps $15,000 annually). A large portion of Mr. Mays' salary is rent that is paid for his high productivity, in terms of revenues for the San Francisco Giants.

Despite the differences between capital and land, they are both property and both are part of the privately owned wealth in a private enterprise economy. They are productive wealth used in the economic system. Both produce streams of future income. In this chapter we move, therefore, to a more general concept of capital that includes all elements in the factors of production that produce a stream of income extending into the future.

The Return to Capital

Capital earns a return by producing more goods and services than were used to produce the capital itself. A stream of output is created over the lifetime of the capital that is larger than the stream of output that would be available if the capital were not used. The difference is the addition to output that can be attributed to capital. It has a value in the market that people are willing to pay for, that in turn endows the capital itself with a market value.

A simple example will illustrate the return to capital. A farmer may be able to grow two bushels of wheat on an acre of land using the simple techniques of plowing the land and then sowing the seed by hand. However, if he were to develop and build a simple planter that would enable him to plant the seed in rows, he could keep out weeds more easily and increase his output to, say, six bushels per acre. The planter is an addition to the farmer's capital which may last for 20 years before it needs to be replaced. The planter creates a stream of continuing real income equal to four bushels of wheat per acre for that period of time. Building the planter, of course, requires time and other inputs, so the net addition to output due to its use will equal the total increase in output minus the inputs that were used to produce the capital. But the value of the planter to the farmer depends on the net addition to output attributable to its use, and not upon the value of the resources used to build it.

This is the first important point about capital. Capital itself has no intrinsic value. It is the stream of ouput that flows from capital that has a value, defines the productivity of capital and determines the market price that the capital will have.

The return to capital can be measured in terms of money. For example, assume that a piece of capital equipment costs $10,000, and that the annual net increase in output from its use is worth $1,000 at present prices. Assume, further, that the equipment has a life of twenty years and will be worth $2,000 as scrap at the end of that period of time. The stream of income from the capital equipment can then be calculated:

$1,000	annual increase in income resulting from use of the capital equipment.
$\times$ 20	number of years of life of the capital equipment
$20,000	
+ 2,000	scrap value of the capital equipment
$22,000	return to the capital equipment over its life.
−10,000	original cost of the capital equipment
$12,000	total net return to capital.

To summarize the example, an expenditure of $10,000 at the present time would enable the purchaser to earn $22,000 over a period of 20 years, with the stream of income comprising 20 annual amounts of $1,000 and a final payment of $2,000 at the end of the period. This works out to an annual interest rate of about 5 percent.

The monetary return is similar to a real rate of return on capital. All of the dollar amounts in the previous example could have been expressed in terms of units of land-labor-capital or their equivalent. If done that way, the example would have yielded a real rate of return also equal to about 5 percent.

The rate of return yielded by capital, expressed in either real or monetary terms, depends on the size of the stream of output that is produced by the capital. Expressed as a percentage, it enables us to translate the future stream of income into a present value, or a present value into a future stream of income.

Expectations and the Rate of Return

Up to this point the theory of capital has been explained in terms of certainty. The stream of output produced by capital was treated as if it were a concrete and real phenomenon. Although that approach is useful as a starting point, it has to be modified to account for uncertainties and risk. The flow of output in the future is not yet realized. It may not materialize, or it may be less than anticipated, or its price may fall. The capital equipment itself may not last its full expected life. These considerations mean that the whole analysis must be expressed in terms of expectations. Whatever the rate of return on capital may turn out to have been when looking backward in time, decisions about the use of capital always involve a future stream of output. It is the expected rate of return on capital that must be dealt with.

When business opinion is optimistic, the evaluation of a future stream of income will be higher than when business opinion is pessimistic. For example, when the economy is prosperous and growing well, common stocks will sell for perhaps 18 times earnings. The common stock of a firm whose profits were $1 for each share will sell for $18. In less prosperous times with less optimism, the same stock with the same earnings will sell for perhaps $14 per share. Although nothing may have happened to reduce the earnings, expectations will have changed and the future stream of earnings has reduced value. The value of the stock, which represents ownership of physical capital, has fallen because the expected rate of return is lower.

Capital in Alternative Uses

Capital is not merely an undifferentiated glob of something. It is embodied in concrete types of capital equipment, like blast furnaces, or motor trucks, or machines. It can also take the form of skill and knowledge. In each of these forms capital will earn a rate of return, producing a stream of income greater than the original capital itself.

In a market economy, particularly one in which competition prevails, we can expect a long-run tendency for the rates of return on each type or form of capital to be equalized. There may be differences due to greater or lesser risk, but if we correct for those differences, we can expect the profit-maximizing behavior of economic units to push toward equal rates of return. If the expected rate of return on capital in one use were greater than the expected rate of return in another, we would find capital moving from the second to the first use, in the long run, until the returns were equalized.

Marginal Productivity and the Demand for Capital

Capital, like any factor of production, is subject to the principle of diminishing marginal productivity. As the amount of capital is increased, given the other factors of production, its rate of return at the margin diminishes. This is the reason why, in the long run, the rate of return in alternative uses tends to be equalized: shifting capital away from one use raises productivity at the margin in that use, while the use to which it is shifted shows a declining productivity at the margin. These changes go on until the rates of return are equalized.

Economic growth, which may involve increased amounts of all factors of production, may overcome the falling tendency of the rate of return on capital. But if capital becomes more abundant relative to other factors of production, even though all factors are increasing in amount, the tendency for its rate of return to fall will still be present.

It is convenient, however, to abstract from the growth situation when analyzing the return to capital. The presence of diminishing marginal productivity leads to a demand curve for capital much like the demand curve for any factor of production, as shown in Figure 37-3.

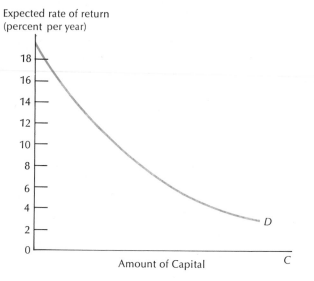

FIGURE 37-3
The Demand for Capital

The vertical axis measures the expected rate of return on capital in percent per year. Small quantities of capital are associated with high rates of return, while larger amounts of capital produce lower rates of return. Productivity at the margin declines as more capital is applied, causing the expected rate of return to fall.

We can summarize the factors that determine the demand for capital. The real rate of return on capital is the key factor: capital produces a stream of future output greater than its own cost (in either real or monetary terms). Decisions are made about the future only in terms of expectations, however, so the real rate of return is meaningful only as an expected rate of return. Finally, the expected rate of return on capital is subject to the principle of diminishing marginal productivity, which provides us with a downward sloping demand curve for capital.

Abstinence, Time Preference, and the Supply of Capital

We now turn to the supply side of the capital market. Capital is produced from inputs that are not used to produce consumer goods or other things. If we assume a full employment economy, the supply of capital can come from only one source: the abstinence of consumers. Consumers must abstain from consuming now in order to make inputs available for the production of capital goods.

If consumers place a high value upon present consumption they will make relatively few inputs available for capital accumulation. If they place a high value on future consumption they will make relatively large amounts of inputs available for that purpose. Economists call this element in capital theory the *time preference* of consumers.

Whatever the attitudes of consumers, a high rate of return from capital will bring forth more capital than a low rate of return. This relationship enables us to postulate a supply curve for capital. It is shown in Figure 37-4.

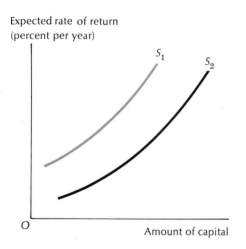

Expected rate of return (percent per year)

S_1

S_2

O

Amount of capital

FIGURE 37-4

The Supply of Capital

S_1 shows the amount of capital that would be made available at various rates of return in an economy with a high time preference for present consumption — an economy of grasshoppers. S_2 shows the amount of capital that would be made available at the same rates of return in an economy with a high time preference for future consumption — an economy of ants. In both cases a high rate of return brings forth more capital than a low rate of return.

Determining the Rate of Return on Capital

We can now put together the demand and supply sides of the market for capital and determine the rate of return that capital will earn, together with the amount that will be provided. The market solution is shown in Figure 37-5.

Figure 37-5 tells us that there is a real rate of return on capital that the economy will tend to produce, based on the time preferences of consumers, the real productivity of capital, and the expectations of investors. If time preferences shift, the supply of capital will change and the real rate of return will change. If the expectations of investors change, or if the flow of output from the use of capital changes, the demand curve will shift and the real rate of return will change.

This market adjustment process has a vitally important quality. Underlying the demand for capital is the flow of output that is produced by capital. Underlying the supply of capital is the sacrifice of current consumption made by consumers. The two elements, real benefits and real costs, are equated at the margin.

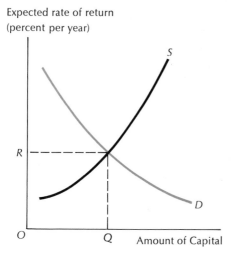

Expected rate of return
(percent per year)

FIGURE 37-5
**Market Determination of the Rate
of Return on Capital**
With a given demand for capital (based
on the expected rate of return) and a
given supply of capital (based on the
time preferences of consumers), the
rate of return on capital R and the quantity made available Q will be determined.

BACK TO THE REAL WORLD

We emerge from the theory of capital with one point firmly established. Capital is productive. A second point follows from the first. In the long run, capital earns a rate of return based upon its productivity and upon the abstinence of consumers. This means that the owners of capital will obtain an income from the capital they own. Those who abstain from consuming, who save part of their incomes, will benefit from their savings by obtaining the earnings that accrue to capital. Indeed, the market adjustment process will tend to maximize welfare by equating benefits and costs at the margin, so that the cost of abstinence to savers will equal the benefits from the productivity of capital at the margin.

Does this justify private ownership of capital? Only superficially. The owners of capital do not have to be private economic units in order for savers to be paid a rate of return equal to the productivity of capital at the margin, or for capital to earn its market-determined rate of return. All that is necessary is that the market mechanism operate to bring about a market-determined equilibrium of the demand for capital and its supply. We have already seen that this sort of market adjustment can readily be achieved in a socialist economy if the principles of market socialism are followed.

Our argument, however, does justify a return to savings on the grounds of welfare maximization. Even in a market socialist economy, earned income would include both income from work and income from savings. Inheritance of capital is another matter. The owner of inherited wealth did not work to earn it, nor did he save to acquire it. The income from inherited wealth is, in that sense, pure unearned income. On what grounds can it be justified?

INHERITED WEALTH AND UNEARNED INCOME

Very little is known about the significance of inheritance as the basis for large incomes and great wealth. Surveys of people with high *incomes* indicate that only about 20 percent of their wealth can be attributed to inheritances and their appreciation in value. When people with large *assets* are surveyed, however, the importance of inheritance turns out to be much greater.[4] Where sociologists have studied the sources of large accumulations of wealth in the United States they have found that

> "Nearly all the current large incomes . . . are derived in fact from *old* property accumulations by inheritors."[5]

One study of the very rich found that inheritance was an increasingly important source of wealth. Of the very rich in 1950, 68 percent came from upper-income families and 62 percent had relatives among the very rich of earlier generations. A quarter of a century earlier (1925), 56 percent of the very rich came from upper-income families and only 33 percent had very rich relatives from the previous generation. As for the very rich in 1900, only 39 percent were children of upper-income parents, and 88 percent of that select group were known to have inherited fortunes of at least half a million dollars.[6] Apparently it is becoming easier, not more difficult, to transfer wealth from one generation to the next.

The income provided by inherited wealth is the clearest example of unearned income that there is. The individual who receives it does so only because of the accident of birth. Even if he devotes his energies to the management of his assets, and busies himself with increasing his wealth, any income above a manager's salary is unearned. A paid manager could do the job equally well and perhaps better. The salary of the manager is earned income, but anything above a manager's salary is unearned. Where assets of the wealthy are managed by others all of the net income is unearned.

We could put it another way. Even if we were to assume that a bloc of wealth should be held together as an investment, and managed to maximize its earning power after the death of its owner, the *maximum* amount of resources society needs to pay for that task is the salary of the manager. Any payment

---

[4] Robin Barlow, Harvey E. Brazer and James N. Morgan, *Economic Behavior of the Affluent* (Washington, D. C.: The Brookings Institution, 1966), pp. 87–91.

[5] Ferdinand Lundberg, *The Rich and the Super-Rich,* (New York: Lyle Stuart, Inc., 1968), p. 132. Lundberg states his case in a florid, muckraking style, but it is hard to argue with his facts. Other more scholarly studies bear out Lundberg's conclusion. See E. Digby Baltzell, *An American Business Aristocracy* (Glencoe, Ill.: The Free Press, 1958), and *The Protestant Establishment: Aristocracy and Caste in America* (New York: Random House, 1964); and G. William Domhoff, *Who Rules America?* (Englewood Cliffs, N. J.: Prentice-Hall, 1967).

[6] C. Wright Mills, *The Power Elite* (New York: Oxford University Press, 1956), p. 107.

above that amount is unearned income for the owner. The benefit derived by the economy as a whole from the use of the capital would be there in any case, whether or not payment is made to the inheritor.

The organization and management of American business enterprise shows a massive dissociation of wealth from active management. We have already noted the large-scale separation of ownership and control in the large corporation that leaves management decisions in the hands of a well-paid bureaucracy. It is the top levels of that business hierarchy that make the decisions determining the growth patterns, production, and marketing strategies, and immediate business tactics pursued by large firms. Stockholders have little direct impact on those decisions.

Business decisions are influenced, however, by what happens in financial markets. If poor decisions are made, profits and growth will be poor, the price of the company's stock will reflect the poor showing, and it will be difficult for the firm to attract capital and other resources. In these circumstances the financial managers who make decisions for holders of large wealth will direct their funds toward the more successful firms and away from the less successful, which is exactly what happens in the money markets anyway.

Perhaps an illustration of what we might do, but don't, will make the point clear. Let us suppose that the United States had death taxes which prevented the inheritance of more than $50,000. Mrs. Gotrocks, a wealthy widow, dies and leaves an estate of $50 million, of which all but $50,000 must be paid to the government in taxes. Such an estate will have been invested in a wide variety of assets, such as stocks and bonds, real estate, and so on, which will have to be sold in order to pay the taxes. Sale on the open market will put those assets into the hands of investors of all kinds, individuals as well as corporations, who will continue to manage their investments just as well or as badly as they did before. The real assets whose ownership has been sold continue producing as before, since only their ownership has shifted. Output in the economy has not changed one bit. The market couldn't care less about the locus of ownership. Even though the fortune was broken up and dispersed there was no change in the production of goods. The real cost to the economy of dispersing the Gotrocks fortune was zero.

In this sense the income from inherited wealth is essentially passive. It does not contribute in any significant way to the overall growth of the economy, nor do those who own it significantly influence the decision-making process. It is unearned.

The economic analysis of inheritance does not stop here, however. Would these capital assets have been accumulated in the first place if there was no way to pass on the benefits to an heir? Does not the desire to leave a legacy provide incentives for saving that help to promote economic growth? Beyond that, are there not other beneficial economic functions performed by inheritance of wealth?

The Economic Functions of Inheritance

Inheritance of privately owned wealth antedates the development of the modern market economy by thousands of years. Our present patterns of inheritance were taken over from a feudal society dominated by a landed nobility, in which peasant households within manorial villages were the basic economic units. Inheritance performed two very important functions in that type of economic organization:

1. It assured the continuity of a decision-making, governing elite from one generation to the next.
2. It provided for the continuity of viable manors and household units from one generation to the next.

When urban-centered trade and handicraft production developed in the later medieval and early modern period, inheritance played a similar role. It enabled merchant enterprises and handicraft shops to survive as producing and managerial units even though the individual owners might retire or die. In the political sphere it provided for continuity of the national state through succession of rulers by means of family inheritance.

It was in this environment that our present law of inheritance was developed. Although much of the detail has changed, the basic legal concepts have remained. Yet the economic (and political) environment has changed. The modern corporation has developed as the chief instrument for preserving the continuity of enterprises over time. Although the ownership may change as stock changes hands, and although the management may change through retirements and promotions, the corporation continues as an economic unit. Merit and personnel development programs have in large part replaced inheritance as the chief source of continuity of management. Securities markets have largely replaced inheritance in creating continuity by providing for a continuous organization in spite of the continuous changing of owners. Where those developments have been held back in some family-controlled corporations, the dominant owners have usually been replaced by professional corporate executives in the making of business decisions. Something similar has happened in the political structure. Political constitutions, both formal and informal, provide for continuity of political units, selection of leadership and administrative cadres, and transfer of power from one generation to the next. It is hard to escape from the conclusion that many of the functions of inheritance are now performed better and more democratically by other economic and social institutions.

Inheritance, however, could perform other functions in a market-oriented economy. It could provide significant incentives for individuals to save and accumulate wealth to pass on to their children, thereby promoting economic growth and expansion. Inherited wealth may also be an important source of savings that promote further economic growth. These are familiar arguments; but we find them emanating primarily from those who have wealth to pass on, from those who have received it recently, or from their spokesmen. Such arguments must necessarily be examined for empirical content.

The evidence on these points is scanty, at best. But it tends to show that the motive to pass wealth on to future generations accounts for an insignificant amount of the economy's savings, and that those who hold inherited wealth tend to save less than their share of wealth would imply. The second point can be disposed of first. We have already cited the fact that the very wealthy save proportionately less of their income than middle income groups do. Lampman found that the top one percent of holders of wealth, with some 22–25 percent of all personal wealth in the mid-1950s, were responsible for about 15 percent of personal savings. These figures suggest that a redistribution of wealth *away* from the top 1 percent of wealth holders would tend to *increase* total savings.

The argument is as follows: If 75 percent of the wealth (99 percent of all families) does 25 percent of the savings, while 25 percent of the wealth (1 percent of all families) does 15 percent of the saving, and *if holding of wealth is functionally related to savings*, then a shift of wealth to the top 1 percent will reduce total savings and a shift away from that group will increase total savings. This is, of course, a logical proposition that could be verified only by trying it out and measuring the results. But the logical deduction from Lampman's data is that concentration of ownership of wealth, as it now exists in the United States, does not contribute significantly to total savings.

But what about the desire to leave a legacy? Is that an important motive for saving? To answer that question we can turn to the so-called "life cycle" analysis of savings.

Savings and the Family Life Cycle

The pattern of savings in a family changes as changes take place in the age and size of the family, and the economic situation in which it finds itself. A young family will tend to live beyond its current income in the early years, partly because its income is relatively low, partly because it must invest in housing and other durable goods at an initially large cost, and partly because the size of the family and its expenses increase as children are born. Debts appear and increase at this stage, or parents may provide financial assistance. As family income grows and equipment expenditures diminish, income moves up relative to spending, and savings start to reduce the family's debts. As debts disappear, positive net savings start to accumulate. At the next stage, children complete their schooling, become economically independent, and move out on their own. The family's expenses fall and net savings grow as the parents start to prepare for retirement. Finally, after retirement the family's earned income usually drops precipitately and savings are drawn upon quite heavily to sustain the level of living the couple would like to maintain. Ideally, the savings would provide maximum utility if they fell to zero at the moment the last of the family unit died, leaving nothing for inheritance. According to this analysis, the life cycle of family savings would resemble Figure 37–6.

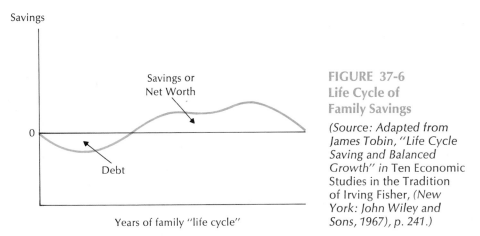

Savings

0

Debt

Years of family "life cycle"

FIGURE 37-6
Life Cycle of
Family Savings

(Source: Adapted from James Tobin, "Life Cycle Saving and Balanced Growth" in Ten Economic Studies in the Tradition of Irving Fisher, *(New York: John Wiley and Sons, 1967), p. 241.)*

There is not much room in the family's life cycle for saving to build up a legacy. By the time children are educated and on their own the parents are looking ahead to retirement. When retirement comes, there is not enough income to make much saving possible, particularly since patterns of spending and the style of life have been established for some time.

For these reasons, the life-cycle analysis of savings deliberately omits the desire to leave an estate to heirs as a significant element in savings behavior. Instead, it stresses such factors as age, family income, size of family, current spending needs, and provision for old age. Empirical studies based on this approach are highly consistent with the theory. That point is important: if significant factors influencing saving were not included in the theoretical analysis, the observed behavior would differ from the behavior predicted by the theory. The absence of divergence indicates that the desire to leave a legacy is not an important motive for saving.

Other evidence supports that conclusion. The Brookings Institution study of affluent Americans, cited earlier in this chapter, found the following reasons for saving among people with incomes over $10,000 per year in 1963:

1. Half said that they saved to accumulate funds for retirement years.
2. One-third saved "for a rainy day," to meet emergencies.
3. Some saved without any ultimate purpose in mind, which might be called the "pack-rat syndrome."
4. A few said they were unable to save at all.

5. A significant group said that they saved in order to leave a bequest.
This motive was weakest among the lower range of incomes
but grew stronger as incomes rose, presumably because the other,
more important motives for saving could be readily satisfied
by past savings or out of current income.[7]

Other survey data support these findings: people save, or try to save, primarily to meet emergencies such as illness or unemployment, for retirement or burial expenses, and for education of their children.[8]

It is difficult to escape the conclusion that the desire to leave a legacy to one's children is the least important motive for saving and the one least likely to be missed. On the other hand, some saving is done for that reason. It is done, however, primarily by those with high incomes (over $100,000 annually), and represents a relatively small proportion of total savings. We have already seen that, proportional to their wealth, the very rich save less than the rest of us. The savings on which we must rely for economic growth and expansion come instead from the voluntary and contractual savings of the far more numerous middle-income groups and business firms, and from the two together through the taxes they pay. Although we do not usually consider the latter to be savings, a part of government revenues is directed toward investment in human capital (education, health, and so on) and in an economic sense represents part of society's savings.

ESTATE AND GIFT TAXES

Most industrial nations impose taxes on the transfer of wealth from one generation to the next.[9] The United States is no exception. The federal estate tax was introduced in 1916, during World War I, and gift taxes appeared in 1924–25 to prevent evasion of estate taxes. All states except Nevada also

---

[7] Barlow et al., *Economic Behavior of the Affluent,* pp. 31–33. Some of the very, very wealthy must save because it is impossible to spend their income as fast as it is generated. There is a perhaps apocryphal story about John Paul Getty, the oil multimillionaire, to the effect that he once attempted to give a very lavish party that cost more than the income his assets earned while the party was in progress—and failed!

[8] George Katona, Charles Lininger and Eva Mueller, *1964 Survey of Consumer Finances* (Ann Arbor, Mich.: Institute for Social Research, The University of Michigan, 1965), pp. 111–112.

[9] The popular term "inheritance taxes" is used by most people in referring to taxes on wealth transfers between generations. The more general term is "taxes on intergenerational transfers of wealth"; the category has several subdivisions:

   Estate taxes: taxes levied on the estate of someone who dies.

   Gift taxes: taxes levied on gifts, when both the giver and recipient are still living.

   Inheritance taxes: taxes paid by an heir on that portion of an estate he receives.

The U.S. tax system includes only estate and gift taxes. They are the ones people refer to when they use the popular term "inheritance taxes."

levy death duties of some kind.[10] The present U.S. transfer taxes have been largely unchanged since 1948.

The federal estate tax applies to all estates above $60,000. The rates range from 3 percent on the smaller estates up to 77 percent on estates of $10 million or more. The gift tax rates are somewhat smaller, ranging upward from 2¼ percent to 57¾ percent. These, then, are progressive taxes designed to bear more heavily on larger accumulations of wealth than on smaller.

Surprisingly, there has been no decent study of the impact of estate and gift taxes on the distribution of wealth in the United States.[11] The consensus among economists is that they have little impact on incentives to work and save, and that they check the tendency of economic inequality to increase. They also induce splitting of fortunes within families and promote the establishment of trusts that tie up property for long periods of time. They also induce the wealthy to put property into tax-exempt foundations and trust funds.

The most obvious characteristic of our inheritance laws is their complexity. The possibilities of reducing estate and gift taxes are so many and varied that armies of lawyers and accountants are kept busy minimizing the effect of estate taxes on the estates of the wealthy. It is safe to say that no area of the tax system offers more ways of legally avoiding tax liability than the federal estate and gift tax. They could have a far greater impact on the concentration of wealth than they now have.[12]

A DIGRESSION: OTHER TYPES
OF UNEARNED INCOME

The income from inherited wealth is not the only form of unearned income in the American economy. Here are some other types of income that are received without the performance of some economically useful function:

---

[10] A few states had death duties even before the federal tax. Others started levying estate taxes in the 1920s. Some states sought to become tax havens for the wealthy by providing immunity against estate and gift taxes. This favored treatment was halted by amending the federal estate tax law to allow estates a credit against the federal estate tax equal to 80 percent of state estate taxes. Since the states would now sacrifice to the federal treasury some tax revenues they could obtain, without increasing significantly the liability of their residents, they passed death duties of various kinds, and the interstate competition for wealthy residents suddenly ceased.

[11] One study of British experience concluded that the much heavier transfer taxes there have helped promote a leveling of income and wealth in Britain, showing that they can be used to reduce unearned income if the public wishes to use them for that purpose.

[12] The student may wish some references to further reading on transfer taxes. Start with C. Lowell Harris, "Public Finance" in Bernard F. Haley (ed.), *A Survey of Contemporary Economics*. Vol. 2 (Homewood, Ill.: Richard D. Irwin, 1952), pp. 287–290. A good text on public finance will have a chapter on transfer taxes. Try John F. Due, *Government Finance* (Homewood, Ill.: Richard D. Irwin, 1963), Chap. 19. The most exhaustive recent study is Carl S. Shoup, *Federal Estate and Gift Taxes* (Washington, D.C.: The Brookings Institution, 1966).

1. Capital gains of some types. The value of many assets goes up because of economic growth in the economy as a whole or in an individual industry. Is this increase earned? For example, the owner of well-located real estate in a growing city discovers that the value of his property rises because of rising population and more intensive use of land. His growing wealth is the result of other people's effort rather than his own.

   On the other hand, an increase in the value of common stocks represents growth in the earning power and productivity of the real assets of business firms. They represent profits that have been left in the business to accumulate there. Having raised its worth, these capital gains are earned income just as much as profits that have been actually paid out to the owners.

2. Income from speculation. Prices of securities and commodities can fluctuate widely, enabling speculators to profit by buying at the low point and selling at the high. When this is done an economic function is performed; prices tend to be stabilized.

   But what about the speculative manipulator or the man with inside information? The first tries to manipulate prices up or down. Our securities laws make these practices illegal, and *some* of the more flagrant abuses have actually been found out and the perpetrators punished. The insider problem is more insidious. A corporation director may know that his firm is negotiating a large contract with a supplier that will greatly strengthen the supplier's business position. A strategic purchase of the supplier's stock can bring large and rapid "capital gains." Who earned them?

3. "Windfall" gains. These are unanticipated gains that result from chance or luck. For example: you are a farmer in West Virginia on whose land a horticulturist discovers a tree bearing a new kind of apple that turns out to be the Golden Delicious. *That* actually happened.

4. Monopolistic profits. Gains derived from monopoly are dysfunctional: they harm the economy rather than help. Yet in many sectors of the economy they are widely prevalent. Since monopoly has already been discussed at length, we only mention monopoly profits here.

All of these sources of income have the same basic character. They are over and above the payments that need to be made for useful products and services. No necessary function is performed by the recipients of these payments, in contrast to earned incomes paid in the form of wages and salaries, profits, and rent.

Unearned income has another characteristic: it can be very large. Many large American fortunes have had their origins in capital gains from land values, speculative manipulation of securities markets, and monopoly. Our present laws, regulations, and tax structure were not always present, and in earlier periods of greater latitude in business behavior a good case could be made for the proposition that the largest rewards went to those whose behavior was most antisocial. Many of these large accumulations of wealth are still with us, institutionalized in the form of family holdings, trusts, and foundations, and help to explain the present pattern of the distribution of wealth.

WEALTH AND ECONOMIC POWER

Wealth brings power. As the motto of the Medici family of Renaissance Florence put it, "money to get power; power to protect the money." Those among us who have large economic resources are able to maintain a larger control over events and the actions of others than people who have fewer resources. This enlarged control over the environment can be achieved in a variety of ways:

1. Since consumer spending helps to determine the allocation of resources, wealth becomes votes in the marketplace to direct resources toward uses desired by the wealthy.
2. Political campaigns are costly. Contributions from the wealthy can be and are used to influence selection of candidates for office and the issues that candidates develop.
3. Use of the media of communication is costly. Wealth can be and is used to influence newspapers, television, and other media through ownership, which provides direct control of editorial policy, or through advertising and purchase of broadcast time.
4. Gifts by wealthy persons to educational institutions, charities and community funds, and other organizations can be and are used to influence the policies of those institutions.
5. Foundations established and controlled by the wealthy can be and are used to influence the policies followed by recipients of grants.

These are some of the more obvious ways in which wealth can be used to achieve power. Almost everyone can add other ways, or give specific examples, from his own experience.

Unfortunately, empirical studies of just how much power is derived from wealth, and in what kinds of situations, are largely lacking. These are not issues on which statistics are easily collected, or even on which good case studies can readily be developed.[13]

---

[13] In recent years political scientists have studied the locus of political power, especially at the local level. Two contrary theories have emerged. One, called "pluralism," is that power in American society tends to be widely dispersed among a variety of interest groups, both organized and unorganized. The classic statements of this position are Robert Dahl, *Who Governs?* (New Haven: Yale University Press, 1961) and *Pluralist Democracy in the United States* (Chicago: Rand McNally, 1967). The countertheory argues that power in American society is concentrated in the hands of a small group of business, government, military, educational, and labor leaders. The key statement of this position is C. Wright Mills, *The Power Elite* (New York: Oxford University Press, 1956), although two earlier works are better documented: Robert S. and Helen M. Lynd, *Middletown* (New York: Harcourt, Brace, 1929) and *Middletown in Transition* (New York: Harcourt, Brace, 1937).

Nevertheless, the status of inherited wealth is clear. It performs little or no function in the economy as a whole, whether it be promoting economic growth or maintaining prosperity or improving the efficiency of the economy. Yet to the extent that inherited wealth brings power to those who hold it, it runs counter to the basic precepts of a society that places high values on dispersal of power and equality of treatment among individuals. Those goals are hard enough to achieve without the additional impediment provided by inherited wealth.

In a broader context, the relationship between wealth and power is the strongest argument for greater dispersal of wealth through more effective transfer (inheritance) taxes. To the extent that wealth begets power, and power is used to strengthen and increase holdings of wealth, a nonfunctional and noneconomic relationship affects the way in which the rewards of economic activity are divided in the long run. A society that places high value on economic justice, even if justice is defined in marginal productivity terms of rewards commensurate with contribution to society, should not tolerate the patterns of distribution of wealth characteristic of contemporary America.

We must recognize, however, that these judgments about holdings of wealth are not based solely on an *economic* analysis of wealth and its impact. They are based in part on the political economy of wealth, that is, on the relationship between wealth and the locus of power in society. They are also based, in part, on *value judgments* about what is just and what is unjust, although the definition of justice used here is rooted in economic analysis. The whole topic is a wonderful illustration of the proposition that science (economics in this instance) can help us analyze a problem, but that answers to the large and important questions force us to go beyond science if the answers are to be meaningful.

Summary

Wealth is more unequally distributed than income. There is some indication that the distribution of wealth is becoming more unequal, although the trend is by no means clear. A few very wealthy people have a great deal of wealth, however; middle income groups maintain their proportionate share through savings, while many at the bottom have very little.

Income from property is based on the stream of income produced by capital. The value of capital depends on its rate of return, which is derived from the productivity of capital and the time preferences of consumers. Although the market may determine the rate of return, and thereby the value of capital, it is not necessary that capital be privately owned. The return to capital is determined by market forces, irrespective of ownership.

Most of the great holdings of wealth were largely inherited by their present owners, and the income obtained is largely unearned. Inheritance performs little useful function in the modern economy, since the continuity of economic units and their management is assured by other social institutions. The desire to leave an inheritance is one of the least important motives for saving. Income from inheritance performs no economic function and there would be little if any economic loss if inheritance of large amounts of wealth were ended.

Key Concepts

Capital.   Defined earlier as the tangible and intangible tools of production that the economy has accumulated as a result of productive effort, the concept was broadened in this chapter to include all assets that produce a stream of future income, including land.

Rate of return to capital.   The percentage that relates the size of the stream of future income produced by capital to the present, enabling a present value to be placed on the capital.

Time preference.   The attitude of consumers toward future income. Consumers can be expected to prefer present income to future income, creating a need to pay them a return for savings.

Earned income.   Income paid to a recipient who performs some sort of work or other service that would not be performed if the income were not received.

Unearned income.   Income paid to a recipient who does not perform a service. Total output would not be changed if the unearned income were eliminated.

Transfer taxes.   Taxes upon the transfer of wealth from one person to another, such as taxes on gifts or inheritances.

Life cycle analysis of savings.   The analysis that postulates a shifting pattern of family savings and net worth, starting and ending with zero net worth.

The Redistribution of Income

38

A CAUTIONARY FOLKTALE

Two maggots riding on a WPA worker's shovel one day in 1935 were dislodged when the worker put the shovel down to lean on it. One maggot fell into a pile of manure, the other into a crack in the sidewalk. The fortunate maggot waxed fat and sleek in his rich environment, so well off that even his parasites developed parasites. One day he waddled away from his manure pile toward the crack in the sidewalk, and peering down, he found himself staring into the emaciated face of his former fellow-traveler, who had subsisted on a few crumbs that occasionally fell into the crack. The thin, starving maggot, amazed at his brother's prosperity, asked in a weak voice from the lower depths: "How is it, my friend, that you're so prosperous and fat, while I am at the last extremity?" The disdainful reply came booming back: "Ha! Brains and hard work!"

The facts about distribution of income can tell us only what the existing pattern is, not what it ought to be. The latter is a question that every society must decide. Even a policy of laissez-faire is such a decision, for it accepts the distribution that results from the existing mixture of market forces, institutional structure, organization of power, and distribution of wealth. Yet many of the factors that affect income distribution are amenable to social control and are affected by the actions of men. Indeed, much existing social policy has an impact on the distribution of income, yet the basic goals involved are seldom discussed. It is as if such discussions are taboo. This chapter seeks to remedy that situation: it raises the issue of the relationship between income distribution and human welfare and the policy position on that issue appropriate to a modern economy.

SOCIAL POLICY AND THE DISTRIBUTION OF INCOME

Income distribution in an economy organized in a system of markets is not wholly determined by market forces alone. As the last three chapters have indicated, in present-day America such other factors as the structure and organization of power, institutional patterns, and the distribution of wealth also have an impact. So does luck, as the tale of the two maggots suggests. We have no way of measuring the relative importance of any of these factors, but one point can be made: many of them can be affected by social policy.

Some examples will illustrate the point. The pattern of income distribution in France as it existed prior to the French Revolution, or in Russia before the Russian Revolution, was sharply changed after those revolutions. In France the locus of power shifted, in large part, from a landed, hereditary aristocracy to a business-oriented middle class. The distribution of income and wealth soon reflected the shift in economic and political power. In Russia, power shifted into the hands of a militant political revolutionary group with a Marxist ideology, and the new structure of power quickly influenced the distribution of economic assets and benefits.

Closer to home, the oil depletion allowance in U.S. tax laws helps to structure the pattern of income distribution, and so do such other tax provisions as those concerning rapid depreciation of real estate and tax exemptions for income from state and local government bonds. Although any individual can legally take advantage of them, only some are in a position to do so. They help to create a pattern of income distribution that affects the whole economy. And these tax provisions are clearly the result of a political process that rests on the existing structure of political and economic power. In a differently organized economy, they might be entirely absent, and as the economic order changes, these tax provisions will change also.

These considerations lead inevitably into questions of social policy. What would be the economic effects of income *redistribution*? Would the economy as a whole be better or worse off if income were distributed more equally or less equally? How would redistribution of income effect economic welfare? economic growth? Suppose we were to move from our present pattern, by one means or another, in which direction should we move, toward greater equality or greater inequality?

INCOME DISTRIBUTION AND ECONOMIC WELFARE

A more equalitarian distribution of income will probably increase economic welfare. This basic proposition has emerged from the long and sometimes acrimonious debate on this issue that has gone on among economists over the last half century. Like all general principles, it must be hedged by some important qualifications, and standing by itself it does not carry the argument for the advocates of equalitarianism, but it is nevertheless an important starting point in any discussion of the economics of income distribution.

A technically correct statement of the proposition would have to be put this way:

> If we can assume that the satisfactions derived from income are similar between individuals, an equal distribution is most likely to maximize the welfare derived from any given level of income.

To put it in more homely language, if a dollar is taken from a rich man and given to a poor man it is more likely that total welfare will be increased than decreased.

This proposition rests heavily on the principle of diminishing marginal utility, which can be applied to income just as well as it can be applied to products and services. When an individual obtains a greater income his utility is increased, but the increases in utility diminish in size as incomes go up. This follows from the proposition that an individual will satisfy his most urgent wants first, leaving his less urgent wants for satisfaction later.[1]

Apply the rule to the division of income between two individuals, each of whom has different schedules of the marginal utility of income, with 100 percent of total income to be distributed between them. The analysis is illustrated in Figure 38-1. Curve *AA* shows the marginal utility (measured vertically) of different amounts of income (measured from the left axis) for Mr. *A*. Curve *BB* is a similar curve for Mr. *B*, but is measured from the right axis. The proportions in which the income can be divided are shown on the horizontal axis. The curves have been drawn so that Mr. *B*'s curve is higher than Mr. *A*'s. If income were distributed in such a way as to maximize welfare, it

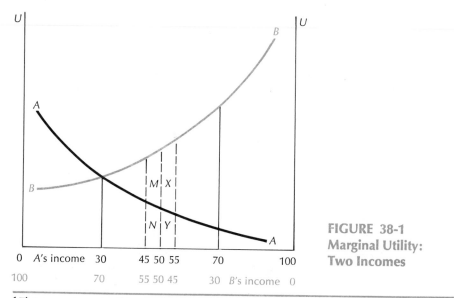

FIGURE 38-1
Marginal Utility:
Two Incomes

[1] There are two possible exceptions to the rule of diminishing marginal utility of income. First, experience with large incomes may educate one in the enjoyment of luxuries. Taking a dollar from an experienced wealthy spender and giving it to a *nouveau riche* may not increase total welfare. Second, expenditures may be complementary and the utilities more than additive. For example, a successful man may buy a convertible and then get himself a mistress, which he might not be able to do without the convertible, and the combined utilities may be greater than if the two were separable. These exceptions, however, mean only that a shift to greater equality of income should be accomplished gradually so that the poor can learn how to spend money effectively, and that it should be substantial and widespread so that the general benefits overcome the relatively few special cases.

would be at those levels at which the marginal utilities were equal, or 30 for A and 70 for B. (You should review the reason for that statement.) But no one knows the location of AA and BB. For all we know, they might be just the opposite. If that were the case, and B got 30 while A got 70 the result would be the 70/30 line on the other side of the diagram, where the marginal utility for one would be much greater than for the other.

Now consider an equal, or 50/50, income distribution between the two. Marginal utility will still differ between A and B. If we move to greater inequality, say 45 for A and 55 for B, total utility will be increased. B will gain M + N, while A will lose only N. The net gain is equal to M.

But hold on. We don't know where those curves are located. Suppose the move were in the opposite direction, to 55 for A and 45 for B. Then there would be a net loss of utility. B would lose X + Y and A would gain only Y, for a net loss of X.

Since the likelihood of a net gain is the same as the likelihood of a net loss (we have no way of knowing where an individual's utility curve is located), it would appear that the losses would balance the gains. That is true of numbers, but not for utility. For each pair that balance—loss against gain and gain against loss—the net loss is greater than the net gain. That is shown in Figure 38-1 where X (the net loss) is larger than M (the net gain). Even though the probability of a gain is equal to the probability of a loss, the size of the probable loss is greater than the size of the probable gain.

The conclusion is inescapable. If we wish to achieve the income distribution most likely to maximize the utility derived from a society's current income (or output), the income (or output) should be divided on an equalitarian basis. This proposition is subject to two qualifications, one theoretical and one practical.

First, it assumes that satisfactions are comparable between individuals, that is, that the benefits or utility derived by Mr. White from the uses to which he puts his income are qualitatively similar to those obtained by Mr. Black from the use of his income. Utility is utility, irrespective of the person who obtains it. This is clearly an assumption, for there is no way of proving scientifically that it is true. But this common-sense assumption is one that most people would be willing to make.

Consider the counterassumption, that A's utility is qualitatively different from B's. This is also a proposition that cannot be proven. More important, it implies that the psychological makeup of each person is qualitatively different from that of all other individuals. While there may be some who are willing to support such an extreme view of human individuality, it is not consistent with the regularities in human behavior documented by the findings of modern sociology and psychology. Faced by comparable stimuli, any group of people (from the same cultural background) tend to respond in similar ways. Indeed, this tendency is the basis of order rather than chaos in the social system, and is one of the foundations of the institutions and rules on which any organized social system is based.[2]

The second qualification is much more important as a practical matter. An equalitarian distribution of income implies a lower rate of savings than a more unequal distribution does. The affluent save a larger proportion of their income than the poor do. Taking a dollar from a rich man and giving it to a poor man will have the effect of reducing savings in the economy and thereby reducing the potential rate of economic growth. Since economic growth is one way of bringing greater affluence, the goal of maximizing welfare derived from the existing level of income and output clashes with the goal of raising the level of income and output.

INCOME DISTRIBUTION AND ECONOMIC GROWTH

The distribution of income can affect economic growth patterns in two different ways, through savings patterns and through incentives. The way income is distributed does not determine either, but is *one* factor that influences both.

First, patterns of saving. We already know that an economy in which savings are a large portion of current income will have a higher growth *potential* than an economy that saves less. Savings represents resources and output not used for consumption, making them available for investment, or other uses. An economy that saves 25 percent of its income will have a potentially more rapid rate of growth than a similar economy that saves only 20 percent of its income.

We also know that savings come largely from the upper and upper-middle income families. Data on income and savings show that in recent decades in the U.S.:

1. The upper 10 percent of income-receiving units accounted for about 75 percent of total personal savings.
2. One hundred percent of savings is accounted for by the top 40 percent of income recipients.
3. The bottom 60 percent of income recipients dissaved as much as it saved.

This information suggests that even though the very wealthy save proportionately less than the merely affluent, a larger volume of savings would be made available for economic growth if income were shifted into the hands of upper-income groups.

These empirical findings are theoretically sound. We should expect to find an increasing marginal propensity to save as incomes rise. Current and urgent

---

[2] This digression was necessary because some economists feel that the assumption of comparable utility is not proper in a scientific analysis, and that economists, *as economists*, should therefore be silent on the question of the desirability of income equality. But as a practical matter, most economists who take that position agree that in the real world the assumption of comparability can be made.

needs are cared for and it becomes possible to set funds aside to meet less urgent future needs. The hypothesis of a declining marginal utility of income brings us to the conclusion that inequality leads to higher savings and more rapid economic growth, while equality diminishes the growth potential by diminishing the ability to save.

This basic principle is subject to several serious qualifications. The most important is empirical: most underdeveloped areas of the world have considerably more unequal income distribution patterns than the advanced nations. We illustrated this phenomenon in Chapter 7. It can bear reemphasis. Latin American countries, for example, have a larger proportion of their incomes going to families at the upper income levels, and a smaller proportion going to the poor, when compared with the United States. Yet those countries have not been noted for the speed of their growth. Indeed, some economists argue that the highly skewed pattern of income distribution in Latin America is an important retarding factor on economic growth.

One reason may be the importance of consumer spending in providing incentives for investment. We have already seen that the growth of discretionary income in the hands of consumers has been one of the great stimuli for growth of the American economy in the last half century. A balance is needed between consumption and savings in order to develop and sustain a viable growth path for the economy.

A more important consideration is the role played by government monetary and fiscal policy. Full use of resources and adequate rates of economic growth can be maintained with any pattern of income distribution. The essential requirement is maintenance of a full-employment level of aggregate demand. Any modern economy can sustain whatever growth rate its social policy determines to be desirable. If private savings are inadequate to achieve it, the needed resources can be made available through public policy.

INCOME DISTRIBUTION AND INCENTIVES

The relationship between economic incentives and income distribution is not well understood. Evidence is very scanty on the relationship between monetary rewards and the length and intensity of work.

The folklore of our society is clear on these matters. It emphasizes the incentive effects of income distribution; an equalitarian distribution of income is said to destroy incentives. Why should one work hard when his rewards will be only as large as those going to someone who is lazy? This question implies its own answer: the hard work and striving for success that lead to economic growth require unequal rewards. Income inequality is necessary to achieve the growth that society wants, according to the conventional wisdom.

Facts and folklore are sometimes inconsistent, and that may be true in this case. Incentives are clearly necessary in order to motivate people. But it is by no means clear that monetary incentives are as important in motivating people as our folklore would have it. For example, Fortune asked, "What Makes the

Boss Work?" and came up with the answer that patterns of behavior among executives cannot be adequately explained by income incentives. Rather, the boss seemed to be motivated by a large number of things connected with his status, prestige, and power. A series of studies undertaken at the Harvard University Graduate School of Business, on the effects of taxation, has indicated that taxes may influence the uses to which investment funds are put, but they do not seem to have much impact on the total amount of investment. Finally, a recent study, *Economic Behavior of the Affluent*, published by the Brookings Institution, found that

> "The picture of the high-income individual emerging from our study is that of a hard-working executive or professional, whose decisions about how much to work are dictated by the demands of his job and by his health, rather than by taxes or other pecuniary considerations."[3]

These conclusions apply to the average American also. A study of *Productive Americans* published by the University of Michigan's Institute for Social Research concluded that

> "The United States is affluent today because its people are hardworking, ambitious and progressive. Many of them do economically productive work for purposes other than monetary rewards; we estimate that such unpaid work in 1964, if it could be measured, would be found to have increased the country's estimated Gross National Product by 38%."[4]

This study found, for example, that people with low hourly earnings worked longer hours than those with higher earnings. Limited rewards apparently stimulated *greater* effort in a drive to achieve acceptable living standards.

We all know of specific instances in which reward systems or taxes inhibit the incentive to work and earn. The most widely cited example is the system of high marginal income tax rates at the upper income levels. The evidence is far from clear on the effect of those tax rates on work effort. Two counterbalancing tendencies are at work. One is the inhibiting effect of taxes. If 50 percent of the additional income earned from work effort must be paid out in taxes, an individual may decide it is not worth the candle, and go fishing. Countering that effect is the tendency of someone seeking specific high income goals to work more if difficulties are placed in his path. An individual may work even harder if half of his marginal increases in income are taken in taxes. The important point is that *both* effects are felt, and the present state of knowledge cannot indicate which one is the stronger, at present rates and levels of taxation.

Perhaps the firmest conclusion we could reach is that the shift toward greater equality in income distribution that occurred in the United States between 1935

---

[3] Robin Barlow, Harvey E. Brazer and James N. Morgan, *Economic Behavior of the Affluent* (Washington, D.C.: The Brookings Institution, 1966), p. 2.

[4] James N. Morgan, Ismael A. Sirageldin and Nancy Beerwaldt, *Productive Americans* (Ann Arbor, Mich.: Institute for Social Research, The University of Michigan, 1966), p. 5.

and 1945 seems not to have had an inhibiting effect on either incentives or economic growth. In all fairness, we must recognize that no one knows, on the basis of either fact or theory, whether a similar shift in the future would either promote or diminish work incentives.

INCOME DIFFERENTIALS AS A RATIONING DEVICE

Most people think of income differences as incentives only for the recipients. Thus, if we want someone to work hard, we feel that he has to be rewarded for his past efforts and have opportunities to earn more in the future. A structure of rewards and opportunities is necessary to promote attitudes leading to hard work and maximum effort.

The theory of marginal productivity is itself a reflection of the economic forces underlying such a system of rewards and incentives. It shows that a competitive market economy will produce, by itself, a system of differential rewards based on differences in productivity for the various classes and types of labor effort. A doctor will earn more than a sailor, and a professor more than a janitor, because the market values his product more at the margin.

These income differentials also serve a rationing function. A businessman, for instance, will not put a physicist to work sweeping floors when research scientists must be paid $18,000 a year and janitors $5,000. The physicist will be put to work in the laboratory, where he will produce at least $18,000 worth of research. Scarce skills, with high levels of marginal productivity, will have high earnings (and high cost). They will be used where their high costs will pay off, and that will be in their most efficient uses.

This is one reason for wide differences in earned incomes in the Soviet Union. Scarcity of skilled scientists and engineers requires that they be used where they are the most productive. Placing high costs on their use by paying them high salaries is one way that economic planners get administrators to economize on the use of these skilled people. A more equalitarian pattern of wages and salaries would lead to waste of those scarce resources on less productive activities that could be carried out with less skilled and more plentiful types of labor.

Income differentials are an important source of economic efficiency, not necessarily because of the incentives they give to workers, but because of the incentives they give to managers. Executives are constantly striving to substitute less costly for more costly factors of production. A wage and salary schedule in which differences are based on marginal productivities enables them to do so. The result is greater efficiency in resource allocation.

In contrast, by removing some of the penalties for inefficiency, an equalitarian system of rewards offers less incentive to managers to operate efficiently.

This is an important point. Even if a nation should decide that, as a matter of social policy, income after taxes should be equalized, it would still be desirable to have incomes before taxes accord with marginal productivities.

INCOME REDISTRIBUTION AND SOCIAL POLICY

This chapter has come to some important conclusions that are quite different from the conventional wisdom. We found some compelling reasons to favor more equalitarian patterns of income distribution than those that now prevail. We found no strong reason to feel that greater equality would significantly affect either the rate of economic growth or work incentives. We did find, however, that income differentials for earned incomes were a desirable prod toward efficient allocation of resources.

We are led to an interesting social policy. Wherever possible, market forces should be allowed to determine income differentials for earned income, provided that economic power and monopoloid positions can be avoided, prevented, or neutralized. Inherited wealth and large accumulations of property should be avoided and the present patterns terminated. Beyond that, further moves toward equalitarianism, which may well be desirable on welfare-maximizing grounds, should be achieved by income transfers through government, in order not to disturb the rationing effect of differential earned incomes.

Summary

The distribution of income in a complex modern economy is the product of a number of variables, including market forces, economic power, the economic institutions that perpetuate poverty, the ownership of property, and government policy. Within that framework, it is possible to analyze the welfare aspects of income distribution to determine if a more equal or a less equal distribution is desirable.

If we wish to maximize the likelihood that welfare will be maximized, more equal distribution rather than less should be sought. Higher incomes should be reduced and lower income increased. Doing so would probably have little impact on economic growth or work incentives, contrary to the generally accepted view.

Income differentials from earned incomes are an important incentive for management of enterprises to economize on expensive inputs, however. This consideration means that income redistribution by transfer payments after earned income is received is a more desirable method of redistributing income than a policy of equalizing earnings.

THE
PUBLIC
ECONOMY
IX

The growth of government has brought to the fore a range of economic activities that are partially or wholly carried on outside the system of markets that allocates resources in the private sector. Different types of goods and services are involved. These are public goods that, for several reasons, cannot be priced in the way privately produced goods are priced. They are paid for out of tax revenues that must be obtained from the public. Social choices rather than individual choices are involved. These considerations give rise to a public economy that exists side by side and entwined with the private sector.

Part IX expands the discussion of resource allocation to the public economy. Chapter 39 shows the extent and unique characteristics of the public sector, and the political nature of social choices. Chapter 40 examines public revenues and the impact of taxation on the economy. Chapter 41 presents a systematic statement of the economics of war and defense. Chapter 42 examines the crisis of the cities, and Chapter 43 the crisis of the environment.

The theme of Part IX is the pervasive nature of political influences in the public sector's decision-making process. Here the power structure whose base is in the economy makes itself felt by strongly influencing the economic activities of the public sector. Politics and the uses of power are keys to the economics of the public sector. We have moved a long way from the self-adjusting market in which market forces rule, through the monopoloid sectors of the economy in which markets are managed to a greater or lesser extent, to a public sector in which political economy dominates the scene.

The role of government in twentieth-century American economy is large and expanding. We have already examined some of the important functions of the federal government in establishing a framework within which the modern economy can flourish. Some of the more important are promotion of economic growth; maintenance of high levels of aggregate demand, including management of the monetary system; maintenance of competition and regulation of monopoly; resolution of labor-management conflicts; socialization of the risks of a private enterprise market economy; and promotion of equity in distribution of income. In discussing these aspects of government policy, it became clear that goals were often not achieved, and that policy compromises and confusions have been numerous. Nevertheless, we must recognize that the private sector of the economy would present a vastly different aspect if these types of government action were not present. Government has served to stabilize the economy, promote its growth, resolve some of its most difficult conflicts, reduce the risks faced by individuals and business firms, and influence distribution of the economy's fruits.

The political economy that has emerged from these policies has made for a fruitful economy, in which living standards have risen and economic security has been provided for most people. At the same time, the economic environment enables big business enterprises to flourish and great wealth and power is available to some.

In addition to these functions, governments continue to perform their essential and traditional functions. They carry out the daily housekeeping tasks necessary in any community, such as fire and police protection, sanitary and sewer services, and others. Government is also responsible for national defense and international relations, essential functions in a political system of national states.

In carrying out their many activities, governments spend varying amounts of money. For example, military and international affairs account for some 30 to 40 percent of the expenditures of all governments in the United States. The resolution of conflicts, however, which may be an even more important function, costs very little. Maintenance of a legal and operational framework for collective bargaining is a very minor budget item, and consumer protection (related to the customer-seller conflict) is only a little more costly. The importance of a government function is not always measurable by its cost.

The Public Sector

39

Nevertheless, governments must raise money to carry on their operations and they must allocate their revenues to particular purposes. In doing so, the economy feels an impact in three different ways:

1. The amount of government expenditures affects the level of economic activity.
2. Taxation and expenditures affect the distribution of income. It is impossible to devise a tax system that falls with equal impact upon all. It is also impossible to spend government funds in a manner that affects everyone equally.
3. Governments provide services and products that would not normally be provided by the private sector of a market and profit-oriented economy.

THE GROWTH OF GOVERNMENT EXPENDITURES

Government spending in the United States has grown considerably more rapidly than the economy as a whole. From the beginning of the twentieth century to the late 1960s, spending by all governments in the United States—federal, state, and local—rose from under $2 billion (in 1902) to about $134 billion (in 1968), corrected for changes in the price level. This is a multiplication of 67 times. Over the same period, GNP increased about 20 times, or only about one-third as fast.[1]

Government employment has risen significantly faster than employment in the private sector. Civilian employment by all governments rose from a little over one million persons in 1900 to over 12 million in 1967, a twelvefold increase. In the same period total employment outside the public sector rose from 27 million to 62 million, an increase of a little under 2.5 times.

This trend of growth in government spending does not seem to be affected by political ideologies. It has gone on equally under Republican and Democratic national administrations at the federal level. On the other hand, federal spending has been affected by major wars. Large wartime increases in spending are not balanced by equally large postwar reductions. Instead, a new plateau is reached, which is moved upward by the next war to a still higher level.[2]

---

[1] Some notes on this comparison: the figures are corrected for changes in prices. See Table 39–1, Note, for the way in which the correction was made.

The GNP figure for 1902 is only a rough estimate, since data back that far are not highly accurate.

The government spending figures include transfer payments; GNP does not. This is the most serious difficulty with the comparison; but is there any other convenient way to make such comparisons?

[2] The two authoritative studies of these phenomena are Solomon Fabricant, *The Trend of Government Activity in the United States since 1900* (New York: National Bureau of Economic Research, 1952); and M. Slade Kendrick, *A Century and a Half of Federal Expenditures* (New York: National Bureau of Economic Research, Occasional Paper No. 48, 1955).

The growth has taken place at all levels of government. Federal spending has grown most rapidly, state spending next, and local government least of all. Yet even local government spending grew from about $900 million in 1902 to over $60 billion in 1968. The shift in the locus of government spending is shown by the fact that prior to World War I local governments spent more than the state and federal governments combined. By the mid-1930s, the upswing in federal spending had reversed the picture: Washington was spending as much as all other governments together. During World War II, federal spending rose to about ten times the spending of all state and local governments, and it is now about double. That is, the federal government spends close to two out of three dollars spent by all governments in the U.S. Table 39-1 gives the figures that illustrate these changes.

TABLE 39-1
Federal, State, and Local Spending, Selected Fiscal Years, 1902–1970
(Billions of Dollars)

Year	Total	Federal	State	Local	Percentage Federal
1902	1.7	0.6	0.2	0.9	35
1913	3.2	1.0	0.4	1.9	31
1936	16.8	9.2	3.1	4.4	55
1944	109.9	100.5	4.1	5.4	91
1970	334.5	210.6	63.5	60.4	63

Notes: Figures for each year may not add to total because of rounding.

A rough estimate of how these figures would be affected by correcting for changes in the price level can be made by using the old consumer price index based on 1937–39 = 100. On that basis, the 1909 dollar was worth $1.62 and the 1970 dollar 40 cents, or about one-fourth the pre-World War I level. The corrected increase in total government spending, 1902–1968, would be from about $2 billion to about $134 billion. The federal proportion of the total would not be changed, of course.

TYPES OF PUBLIC SPENDING

Government spending has focused on services that normally are not provided by the private sector. A breakdown of government expenditures for any recent year makes that situation evident. Table 39–2 shows the pattern for 1967. The largest portion of government spending is for national defense and international affairs. Table 39–2 minimizes the spending for that purpose. Much of all government debts are incurred by the federal government in fighting recent wars. Significant sums spent on the military are hidden in some of the other items, such as social insurance (veterans benefits), general administration, and part of the spending on development of the economy. If all military and military-related spending were included in the national defense and international relations category, the total would be about $100 billion to $105 billion rather than $75 billion, and the proportion of all government spending going for those purposes would amount to 38–40 percent.

TABLE 39-2
Government Expenditures, 1967
(All governments: federal, state, and local)

Service		Amount (Billions of Dollars)	Percentage
Community services (post office, utilities, prisons, sanitation, fire and police, libraries, etc.)		$ 41.6	16
National defense and international relations		74.6	29
Expenditures on human capital		52.4	20
Education	40.5		
Health	9.4		
Housing and urban development	2.5		
Social insurance and public welfare		44.4	17
Development of the economy		27.4	11
Transportation	17.3		
Natural resources	10.1		
Interest on debt		13.4	5
General administration		4.5	2
Total		$258.3	100

The proportion of these expenditures made by federal, state, and local governments is quite irregular. The federal government has exclusive responsibility for military and international affairs. It also spends substantial amounts on social insurance and secondarily on community services (primarily the postal services). The functions of state governments center on highways, hospitals, and schools. Local governments concentrate on education and community services. These emphases show up clearly in government budgets and are shown in Table 39-3.

TABLE 39-3
Government Spending, Fiscal Year 1967
(Billions of Dollars)

Function	Federal	State	Local
Community services	$18.9	$ 4.2	$18.5
National defense and international relations	74.4		
Expenditures on human capital	6.0	12.8	33.6
Social insurance and public welfare	30.4	9.1	5.0
Development of the economy	10.4	11.4	5.6
Interest on debt	10.4	1.0	2.0
General administration	1.2	1.2	2.1

One last point: the proportion of government expenditures on general administration is only 2 percent. This does not include administration of programs in the various functional categories, but covers only general governmental costs. We should also note that the federal government's general administrative costs of $1.2 billion are used to manage a $188.5 billion operation, while local governments spend $2.1 billion to manage expenditures totaling $49.8 billion. Yet there are some who say that local governments are more efficient than the federal government.

THE THEORY OF PUBLIC SERVICES

Whatever level of government provides the services, government services differ in some important ways from goods produced in the private sector. Two principles are involved: the nonexclusion principle and the zero marginal cost principle. Together they help to explain why some facilities and services are provided publicly while others remain in the private sector.

The *nonexclusion principle* is the simplest. There are some services that are enjoyed by everyone. No one can be excluded from the benefits. Since no one can be excluded it is impossible to charge a price for their use. The classic example is a lighthouse on a dangerous and rocky shore. Once established and sending out its beacon of light, its signal can be seen by all ships. No ship can be excluded from its benefits. If all can use the light, no one would be willing to pay for it voluntarily, and no ship can be charged a fee. Since a price cannot be charged, no private enterprise could be induced to establish a lighthouse, and if it is to be built at all, public auspices are necessary. In contrast, an ordinary product like bread, or circuses, can be provided by the private sector because those who don't pay can be excluded from enjoying the product.

Many public services involve the nonexclusion principle. National defense is one. Although everyone benefits from protection against the Green Meanies, no one can be excluded, no fee can be charged only to the users, and all must pay. So if you are wondering why you have to pay taxes to support the House Committee on Un-American Activities, or the National Guard, or the FBI, or the CIA, credit it to the nonexclusion principle.

Education is only partially subject to the nonexclusion principle. Individuals can certainly be excluded from its direct benefits, a fee could be charged, and it would be possible for the private sector to provide educational services. The nonexclusion principle enters because of the secondary effects of education: the entire society benefits from increased education and all participants in the social order share in the benefits. We find, as a result, that even public colleges charge tuition, but students are also subsidized by public funds. At the elementary and secondary level, however, the secondary effects are so important to a democratic society that education is free.[3]

---

[3] The secondary effects of education are so significant that most states require young people to have formal education through 16 years of age, even though some individuals feel that the benefits to them are so small that even free education is not worthwhile. They would like to drop out but can't.

There are many public services with a mixed private-public character, like education. Here are some examples:

Port facilities in a large city.

Recreation facilities for the poor.

Sanitation and sewage facilities.

These services are usually provided through public agencies and sometimes by a combination of public and private efforts. The public activity arises because the private sector will provide a level of services based only on charging for the immediate benefits. Since secondary benefits accrue to all, a public interest in a higher level of service develops and public services are provided.[4]

The second basis for public services is the *zero marginal cost principle*. There are some services for which the cost of one more user is nil. If welfare is to be maximized, no charge should be made, and if no charge is made the service won't be provided by the private sector. The classic example is a highway bridge. Users could be excluded and a toll charged that would pay for all costs plus a normal profit. Private enterprise would be quite feasible. But the marginal cost of one more person crossing the bridge is zero or very close to it. If net benefits from use of the bridge are to be maximized, then the usual rule of $P = MC$ should be applied. This would mean no charge and would require public subsidies or public enterprise.

A specific example is the great Mackinac Bridge connecting the upper and lower peninsulas of Michigan. This $100 million monument to the annual slaughter of the upper peninsula deer charges a toll of $3.50 per car for a crossing. The toll is intended to cover costs of operation, maintenance, and retirement of the bonds issued to finance construction. The only subsidy involved is low interest rates on the bonds because of a state guarantee.[5] Otherwise, the bridge might as well be operated privately. But there is public pressure for a free bridge, and rightly so. The marginal cost of bridge crossings is nil, and if benefits are maximized the toll would be reduced to zero so that it equals marginal costs. At any toll some people would not pay, even though the benefit to them is greater than marginal costs. Figure 39–1 shows the principle in graphic form.

---

[4] Economists today sometimes distinguish between pure *social wants* (those fully subject to the exclusion principle) and *merit wants* (those for which the public desires a higher level of output than that provided privately). Richard Musgrave makes that distinction in *The Theory of Public Finance* (New York: McGraw-Hill, 1959), pp. 9–14. The economist who originally developed these ideas, John Stuart Mill, in *Principles of Political Economy* (1849), recognized that "merit wants" were like other social wants, but based on secondary rather than direct benefits.

[5] The toll is not high enough; the bridge loses money and must be subsidized directly. Incidentally, part of the maintenance cost is paint, which shows up as blue and gold (University of Michigan colors) in the daytime but appears as green and white (Michigan State University colors) under artificial light at night. Such is the politics of public services, about which more shortly.

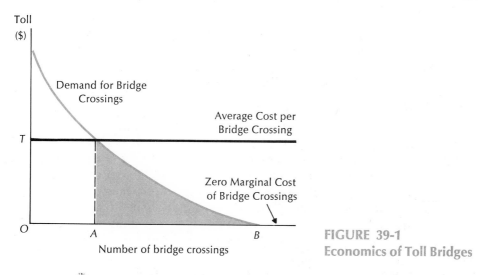

FIGURE 39-1
Economics of Toll Bridges

To summarize, public services in a private enterprise economy tend to be based on the old folklore maxim that government should do those things private enterprise cannot do (the nonexclusion principle) or cannot do so well (the zero marginal cost principle). In one way or another, the great bulk of government expenditures shown in Table 39–2 involve those principles with respect to either direct effects or their secondary effects.

PUBLIC SERVICES AND THE POLITICAL PROCESS

The nature of public services is such that a price cannot easily be justified for them. Either the nonexclusion principle prevails for direct or indirect benefits, or the zero marginal cost principle is present. This being the case, the market mechanism cannot readily be used to organize production and allocate output. Instead, political processes are used to determine the level of output, the extent of service, and the price (or tax), if any, that will be charged.

This aspect of public services creates difficulties that are not present in the private sector. The chief problem is lack of measurability of the benefits and costs involved. In the private sector both can be reduced to dollars and cents. As we have seen, in competitive markets both the real costs of production and the real benefits to consumers are reflected in supply and demand schedules in the market. Prices reflect an adjustment process that tends to maximize net benefits.

The public sector does not function within this neat framework. Costs can be calculated, just as in the private sector, and voters are often very sensitive to their level. But benefits are not measurable, particularly at the margin, because price signals are not given to the decision makers. With no prices attached to public services, it is impossible to obtain an accurate measure of the benefits obtained by those who use public services.

For example, a city provides recreational services for young people that are paid for from taxes levied on taxpayers who generally do not use the services. An accurate decision on the extent of recreational services to be provided would involve equating the marginal benefits to users with the marginal costs to taxpayers. The users' marginal benefits cannot be measured because no price is charged (in this example). The taxpayers' marginal costs cannot be measured because he normally does not pay a recreation services tax but a general property or sales tax out of which recreational facilities are paid for. Furthermore, an individual taxpayer may not use the services at all. When that happens, a transfer of real income is made from him to the user of the services.

One apparent way out of this dilemma is to charge a fee for the services to be paid by the actual user. The direct marginal benefits could then be equated at the margin with marginal costs. This is only an apparent solution, however. The indirect benefits of recreation programs for youth accrue to the community as a whole, like education, and all participate in the benefits. No one can be excluded. It is a public good. In addition, a fee may exclude exactly those young people for whom recreation services provide the greatest benefits to the community as a whole. No, a fee does not solve the problem. The result is that benefits cannot be measured, nor can those individuals who benefit the most be identified.

Lack of measurability of the benefits throws the decision-making process into the political arena. Once there it is subject to such political processes as

1. Logrolling, or "you vote for my project and I'll vote for yours." (A variant is "you support mine or I'll vote against yours").

2. Consensus, that is compromising until majority support can be obtained.

3. Lobbying, or political pressure from organized interests to achieve their goals.

4. Bribery, or payment to the politician because it is the cheapest way to get what you want.

Whether a rational decision emerges from these processes is difficult to determine. It may or may not. Since marginal benefits cannot be measured there is no way to tell.

A second basic problem with public services is the fact, already briefly noted, that their costs are borne generally by all taxpayers while their benefits may accrue more to some than to others. In the private sector this problem is avoided by the price system: if you want something you pay for it, if you don't want it, you don't pay. In the public sector the problem is different: you pay for the service whether you want it or not. This element in the situation has important political repercussions. It leads to logrolling. It leads to compromises in which programs are modified so as to provide benefits to enough people to get the measure adopted. It brings efforts to shift costs to the general taxpayer while benefits go to a few via subsidy or subsidy-type programs.

Again, all of these processes may or may not bring desirable results. Since we have no good way of measuring benefits at the margin, we cannot tell.

All of this uncertainty and difficulty leads to a third important problem in the political process. The absence of firm quantitative guidelines leads to use of emotional appeals and ideological criteria for programs of public services that can often obscure the economic reality beneath them. The emotions aroused by such recent issues as comprehensive medical insurance, guaranteed annual incomes, and large military expenditures illustrate the problem.

These factors bring the public economy inevitably into the political arena. There is no escape. Especially in the modern world, in which public wants have been expanding over the last seventy years and have become important elements in the level of production and the flow of income, and strongly affect the uses to which resources are put, the functioning of the political economy is an integral part of the economy as a whole. The nature of public wants makes it so.

NON-MARKET DECISION MAKING

In recent years some important advances in public-sector decision making have been achieved. They seek to introduce a higher degree of rationality into problems of social choice by identifying goals, specifying alternatives, and analyzing benefits and costs. These non-market decision-making techniques are still in the early stages of development, but they offer the promise of more efficiency and less politics. The most important are program budgeting, cost-benefit analysis, and systems analysis.

Program Budgeting

Program budgeting is a new method for organizing the decision-making process. The first step is to specify the *goals* that a particular agency or department of government seeks to achieve, together with a *target date* for their achievement and *criteria* by which their achievement can be judged. In the ideal case all the goals should be quantified, that is, stated in measurable terms: so many hydrogen bombs produced, a given percent reduction in air pollution in a specified area, a given reduction in the unemployment rate, or others. The second step is to list the various *programs* that could achieve the goals. The programs could be quite different from each other and involve rather widely different alternatives. Some programs may bring results rapidly and others slowly, and this may require some flexibility in the target date set in the original goals. Some may achieve the goals more fully than other programs, and this will introduce flexibility into the goals themselves. The third step is to calculate or estimate the costs of the alternative programs, and their benefits, in order to determine which program is best. There are several ways in which this step can be accomplished. One is by use of cost-benefit analysis, which will be explained presently. Another is linear programming, which was described in Chapter 28. Finally, a budget is constructed which expresses the chosen program in terms of monetary appropriations and the uses that will be made of them.

Program budgeting is essentially a logical approach to planning by rational people. Goals are selected, alternatives are enumerated, costs and benefits are calculated, and an operating plan is constructed. Its essential element and the characteristic that is new is the application of economic analysis to complex problems, achieved by comparing the costs and benefits associated with the various alternatives.

An Example of Cost-Benefit Analysis

Program budgeting implies use of analytical techniques like cost-benefit analysis. A simple example of cost-benefit analysis shows its essential elements. A flood control project is planned for a small valley. Four alternative programs are possible, each with different costs and effects. Which one should be chosen, if any? A cost-benefit analysis compares the estimated damages in an average year with no flood protection and with the four proposed flood protection schemes.[6] For each alternative the annual cost (mostly the cost of the capital) and the estimated reduction in flood damage are calculated. The figures are shown below in Table 39-4.

TABLE 39-4
Cost-Benefit Analysis: Alternative Projects

Plan	Annual Cost	Average Annual Damage	Benefit (Reduction of Damage)
No protection	0	$38,000	
A — Levees	$ 3,000	32,000	$ 6,000
B — Small reservoir	10,000	22,000	16,000
C — Medium reservoir	18,000	13,000	25,000
D — Large reservoir	30,000	6,000	32,000

In each case the annual benefit exceeds the annual cost. But plan C is best. Its superiority can be seen if we examine the incremental costs and benefits involved in moving from the less to the more costly plans,[7] as shown in Table 39-5.

Plan C costs $8,000 more than Plan B, but its benefits are $9,000 greater. The increase in benefits from moving from Plan B to Plan C are greater than

---

[6] The example is taken from Otto Eckstein, *Public Finance* (Englewood Cliffs, N. J.: Prentice-Hall, 1964).

[7] We use the term "incremental" rather than "marginal" for a technical reason. The term "marginal" applies to increases in benefits per dollar of increase in annual costs. That calculation can't be made because the alternatives involve large jumps or increments. The same principles are involved, however.

TABLE 39-5
Cost-Benefit Analysis: Incremental Costs and Incremental Benefits

Plan	Incremental Cost	Incremental Benefit
No protection		
A — Levees	$ 3,000	$ 6,000
B — Small reservoir	5,000	10,000
C — Medium reservoir	8,000	9,000
D — Large reservoir	12,000	7,000

the increase in costs by $1,000. But moving from Plan C to Plan D brings a $12,000 increase in costs in exchange for only a $7,000 increase in benefits. It's not worth it.

Some Limitations of Cost-Benefit Analysis

One of the difficult parts of any cost-benefit analysis is determining what to include in the costs and the benefits, particularly when there is no simple market price that can be attached to them.

Whose costs and whose benefits are to be included in a cost-benefit analysis? The money cost of constructing a reservoir for a flood control project can be readily estimated. The reservoir may have a variety of side effects, however. For example, during flood periods it may be full, but much of the time it may be largely empty, leaving mudflats or swampy areas that are either unsightly or harmful to the nearby residents. None of these costs will be borne by the down-river townspeople who are protected from the floods and get the benefits, but they may be heavily felt by upriver farm families.

One problem is that some costs, such as those borne by the upriver farmers, are not readily measurable. That being the case, such costs are likely to be ignored in a simple cost-benefit analysis. They shouldn't be, but they often are. An example was the case of the supersonic transport plane (SST). The cost of the project did not include a possible increase in skin cancer caused by greater radiation triggered by disturbance of the ozone layer in the atmosphere, for example. One way out of this dilemma is to include a sophisticated list of all costs and benefits, unmeasurable as well as measurable. "Shadow prices" based on reasonable and informed estimates of what the prices might be if they were determined in the market can then be given to the unmeasurable costs and benefits. That, of course, is better than nothing, but it sometimes involves heroic assumptions about relative values that may differ widely between individuals.

A second problem is that most government projects or programs involve a redistribution of income between economic interests. Pure cost-benefit analysis ignores that problem and leaves the decision to the political process. That is not a full solution. We have already seen that, on welfare grounds, a more equal distribution of income is more desirable than a less equal distribution. A project that can be justified on the basis of a cost-benefit analysis may move the real distribution of income (after costs and benefits) toward greater inequality. Yet the income distribution effects of a program or project are seldom included in cost-benefit estimates.

The difficulties of cost-benefit analysis limits its usefulness. It can be used to evaluate specific programs when decisions have already been made about goals and about the desirability of a general objective. But cost-benefit analysis is of limited use in making those prior decisions. In flood control schemes, for example, the side effects, income distribution effects, and other largely unmeasurable effects must be considered in determining that a flood control policy is desirable. Cost-benefit analysis can help in making the decision by showing that the direct and measurable benefits exceed the direct and measurable costs, and it can help identify the other considerations that enter into the decision. Once the decision to develop flood control programs is made it can also help determine which ones are economically sound (direct benefits exceed direct costs), and which ones among various alternatives are the best. But even in those more restricted decisions, cost-benefit analysis does not resolve all of the problems that arise because it is itself limited in scope.

Systems Analysis

Systems analysis goes beyond cost-benefit analysis to examine all of the component parts of policy formulation, including the intangible elements that enter into the decision-making process. Systems analysis provides a method of identifying the essential features of highly complex problems. It can generate "models" of the system under analysis that can be used for "simulation" of the actual operation of the system in order to determine the expected results of alternative programs. The simulation is a substitute for actual trials and can turn up defects in proposed programs that lead to improvements while projects are still in the planning stage. As an approach to problem solving and decision making, systems analysis has been used in a variety of military, engineering, and business applications, and is beginning to be used to analyze problems of social choice in the governmental process.

Any system comprises a flow of inputs through a process to produce outputs, with information flowing to a control mechanism and directions flowing from the control mechanism to the process. Depending on the complexity of the system, there are a variety of information feedbacks that influence the way the system operates. In addition, any system functions under constraints that limit its operation, and almost all systems include in their outputs some wastes that are not usable. A simplified schema of a system, showing the general conceptional framework, is diagramed in Figure 39–2.

The heart of any system is the sequence of input→process→output which operates under constraints imposed by technology, natural environment,

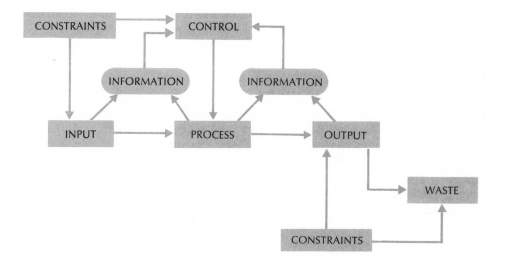

FIGURE 39-2
Generalized Concept of a System

and social organization. Most systems involving people require a set of controls and information flows as well, while in natural systems the controls are usually part of the process itself. When the process does not include its own controls, information feedback to the controls is necessary.

Some systems are "closed," in that output becomes input into the same system. The ecological system of plant and animal life is a closed system. Even the wastes of some of its subsystems become part of the inputs for other subsystems that make up part of the whole. Other systems are "open," in the sense that the inputs come from outside the system itself and the outputs are used outside the system. Most production processes in the economy involve open systems—a fundamental reason why we face problems of pollution and environmental incompatibility, as we shall see in Chapter 43.

Systems analysis can be applied to a wide variety of complex social choices. In the public economy it has been most extensively used in planning military spending and space exploration. It has been much less widely adopted in planning social programs, but there is no reason why it could not be adapted to fighting poverty, improving the delivery system for medical care, or analyzing the problems of urban growth. The essential elements are similar: specifying the end products or outputs, analyzing the process by which they can be obtained, and identifying the necessary inputs. When those tasks are completed, evaluation of alternatives by cost-benefit analysis can lead to selection of the best method of achieving the goals. Systems analysis is the general method that identifies the ways in which goals can be achieved;

cost-benefit analysis compares them in order to select the one with the greatest net benefits; a program budget expresses the decision in operational terms.

Planning in the Public Economy

The methods of non-market decision making that have been sketched here are all parts of a comprehensive system of planning. They are substitutes for the automatic decision making system embodied in market relationships that work effectively when costs and benefits accrue to individual economic units and price tags can be applied to them. When public goods are involved, however, the market system does not work effectively and other methods have to be used. The political process has been the predominant one used in the past and it is still very widely used in making social choices. Its great defect is very heavy reliance on power and influence rather than rational analysis of all of the alternatives. As the role of government has expanded, more rational methods of planning have emerged, such as systems analysis, cost-benefit analysis, and program budgeting. Sophisticated economic planning based on those techniques is the next stage in the development of the public economy whose growth over the last half century or more has been so spectacular.

THE PROBLEMS AHEAD

When the newer methods of non-market decision making are seen as sophisticated methods of planning, they raise further problems at a higher level of complexity. They imply a centralization of decision making in the hands of expert analysts whose skills and access to information place them in a strategic position to control events affecting the lives of millions. Even if the experts themselves do not occupy the seats of power they will serve those who do. Better methods for making non-market decisions enable a center of administrative power to operate more efficiently, which is exactly their purpose. They suggest an economy and society with greater central control rather than less. One has visions of *Dr. Strangelove* and the system losing control over itself; of Karel Capek's play, *R. U. R.,* in which the robots advance downstage to attack the audience; of the final incident in *1984* when the protagonist, just released from a re-education camp, feels an uncontrollable surge of love upon seeing Big Brother's picture thrown upon the screen; of *Catch 22* and the essential irrationality of rational systems.

Yet there is another aspect of non-market decision making with exactly the opposite implications. Systems analysis not only identifies goals, it also identifies the constraints within which the system must function. If those constraints entail a given distribution of income or structure of power or ownership of productive resources, the systems analysis of alternatives will identify the constraints and analyze the way in which they limit the possible choices.

The results may then be used to raise questions about whether the constraints themselves should not be changed in order to move toward a more desirable set of alternatives. These considerations suggest that once the rational analysis of alternatives is started it can become revolutionary in nature. The systems approach to management, which starts as an effort to increase efficiency, can lead to recognition of the need for fundamental changes in organizational structure.

Non-market methods of decision making cannot avoid the political problems associated with social choice. Goals must be selected before alternative methods of achieving them can be analyzed. In a market system the goals emerge out of the many interrelated decisions made by individuals pursuing their own best interests. But non-market decisions involving social choices require a selection of goals by political processes involving the organization and use of power. It is only after the goals are selected that the rationality of systems analysis, cost-benefit analysis, and program budgeting can be applied.

Summary

Governments perform a wide variety of functions in the present economy that create the environment within which economic activity is carried on. Beyond those functions, government expenditures affect the level of economic activity; taxes and government spending affect the distribution of income; and governments produce goods and services in substantial amounts.

Spending by all levels of government has increased more rapidly than the economy as a whole has expanded in this century, but has concentrated on services that are not normally provided by the private sector, such as national defense and education.

Two elements characterize production of goods and services by governments. One is that prices cannot be attached to some goods because no one can be excluded from consuming them; they must be produced by government or not at all. The other is that some goods have no marginal costs; if welfare is to be maximized they will be supplied free by a public agency.

These principles do not take politics out of the public economy. Government actions are heavily influenced by the economic and political power of special interest groups of all kinds. Efforts have been made in recent years to apply several new types of nonmarket decision-making methods to the decisions made within governments. Some of them are promising steps toward more rational management, but we are a long way from solving the intricate problems of rational social choice.

Key Concepts

Nonexclusion principle.   The principle that some goods have to be supplied by a public agency because no price can be charged for them since no one can be excluded from using them.

Zero marginal cost principle.   The principle that public agencies should supply some goods free in order to maximize consumer welfare, since the goods in question have no marginal cost.

Program budgeting.   A method for determining government budgets in which goals, programs, and benefit-cost comparisons are related to each other and expressed in terms of expenditures.

Cost-benefit analysis.   A technique for comparing alternative programs that makes possible selection of the program that provides the greatest net benefits.

Systems analysis.   A technique used to identify the essential elements of complex problems and to determine alternative methods for their solution.

Like the weather, everyone complains about taxes but no one does anything about them. One reason, perhaps, is that our tax system is terribly complicated and difficult to understand. A cynic could point out that one reason for the complications might be to keep the average voter from understanding the system so he won't know what to do about it. Any tax system is a reflection of the political and economic power structure of the social order. Taxes have to be paid by someone, and others can avoid them. The result is a continuous struggle for advantage by individuals and groups to get the benefit of government services while others pay the costs. Taxes affect economic growth, the distribution of income and the allocation of resources. They involve our concepts of equity and justice. Yet these larger issues are often lost sight of in the continuous struggle for advantage that goes on behind the scenes.

TAXES AND THE CONFLICT OF INTERESTS

There is continuous conflict and tension within any system of taxation. First, there is tension between the government that levies the tax and the taxpayer who pays it. Governments need money, and the first requirement is to get it. But not many people like to pay taxes, so the second requirement is to get it as painlessly as possible. This leads to the two laws of taxation as seen by the bureaucrat:

1. A good tax is one that raises money.
2. The best tax does it without the taxpayer knowing he is paying it.

It follows from these principles that any tax system will be full of hidden taxes, taxes that can be shifted from the person who pays to others who don't realize they are bearing the real burden, and taxes that are levied because they yield revenues now even though the long-run effects may be bad.

Nevertheless, most governments that rely heavily on tax revenues, as practically all do, are continually starved for revenues. Taxpayers are reluctant to vote for new or higher taxes, they seek to evade payment wherever possible, and try to shift the burden of the tax to others.

This leads into the second fundamental conflict, that between interest groups. Farmers try to have taxes paid by businessmen. Businessmen want taxes that are paid by consumers. The rich want to tax the poor and the poor the rich. Polluters want the general public to bear the cost of antipollution devices. Shipping companies want the public to bear the cost of harbor development. And so on, ad infinitum. Innumerable pressure groups want to get the benefits from government expenditures while others pay the cost.

A variation on this theme is exemption from taxes. Interest groups seek to pay less than their share of the cost of government through special tax privileges. One notorious example is the larger-than-normal depletion allowance granted to oil producers.

These considerations lead to the two laws of taxation as seen by the taxpayer:

1. A lower tax is better than a higher tax.
2. If we have to have taxes, it is best if someone else pays them.

Finally, trying to stand above this hurly-burly is the economist, who analyzes taxes in terms of their effects on economic welfare via the allocation of resources, on the distribution of income and the equity of the tax burden, and on economic growth and incentives. Most of the time no one listens.

ILLEGALITY AND TAX COLLECTORS

Perhaps the most intriguing aspect of tax systems is illegality on the part of tax collectors. We usually think of such behavior as characteristic of oriental despotisms, but consider:

Item: The U.S. Internal Revenue Service often continues to enforce tax collection procedures designed to maximize the taxpayer's liability even though federal courts have held those procedures to be improper or illegal. The excuse given by the IRS for this behavior is that the legal ruling applied to a specific case only.

Item: In most localities the local property tax laws require uniform assessment of property for tax purposes. Yet assessment officials usually assess business property at higher rates than residential property and undeveloped or farm acreage at the lowest rates of all. Oil and coal lands are often assessed far below their true value. In most places this is done knowingly, in spite of specific legal prohibition of such practices.

When tax administrators act illegally, how can taxpayers be expected to act?

Yet our tax system, federal, state, and local, is the outcome of all of these conflicting forces, and the political power that special interests are able to mobilize. The wonder is that it makes as much sense as it does. This situation creates an understandable feedback. If taxpayers view the tax system as full of favored or sheltered positions for some and undue burdens for others, their opposition is increased, which reinforces the tax bureaucrat's attitude, and the whole system moves further from the economist's goals of equity and rationality.

TYPES OF TAXES

Now that we have paid our respects to the basic irrationality of the tax system, we should examine its size and structure. In 1967 total tax receipts and other charges collected by the federal, state, and local governments were $201.4 billion, or $1,072.50 per capita. Naturally it was the largest amount collected in any one year up to that time. The total is larger now, and so is the amount per person. Around the turn of the century the total was about $1.6 billion (about $17 per capita). As late as 1940 the total was only $16.5 billion and the per capita amount was $102.77. Price levels have risen, of course, but we still buy a lot more government than we used to.

The chief federal taxes are the personal and corporate income taxes. Together they are responsible for about 72 percent of all federal tax receipts. The bulk of the remaining federal tax revenues come from employment taxes and taxes on commodities (excise taxes). States and local governments also use income taxes, but their chief revenues (76 percent of their total revenue) come from sales taxes and taxes on property. Table 40-1 breaks down the totals by chief types of tax.

TABLE 40-1
Tax Revenues by Type of Tax, 1969
(Billions of Dollars)

	Federal	State and Local	Total
Individual income tax	$ 87.2	$ 8.9	$ 96.1
Corporate income tax	36.7	3.2	39.9
Excise and sales taxes	15.2	26.5	41.7
Property taxes		30.7	30.7
Employment taxes *	39.9	9.8	49.7
Other taxes	5.8	7.4	13.2
Total	184.8	86.5	271.3

Source: Tax Foundation, Inc., *Facts and Figures on Government Finance, 1971.*
* Chiefly social security and retirement program taxes.

Our next step is to take a closer look at the major taxes that provide the great bulk of government revenues in the United States. In doing so, we shall examine a number of features of the tax system associated particularly with each type of tax:

The individual income tax and the concepts of progressive, proportional and regressive taxes.

Excise and sales taxes and the question of who actually pays a tax and bears its burden.

Property taxes and the relationship of taxes to urban development and special economic interests.

The corporate income tax and problems of determining the full economic effects of a tax.

In the discussions that follow one point will become clear: the tax system raises revenues, but it also has important effects on the relative economic positions of rich and poor, businessman and consumer, and special interests and the general public. At times it is hard to tell whether the good guys are winning or losing.

THE PERSONAL INCOME TAX

All taxes are controversial, and the personal income tax is perhaps the most controversial of all. At the very least, it is the one under the most constant attack. The attack comes mostly from the conservative (that is, wealthier) side of the political spectrum, for the key fact about the personal income tax is that at the federal level it is moderately "progressive," and even state or local income taxes either are also progressive or could be made progressive.

A *progressive tax* is one that takes a larger proportion of income in taxes, the higher the income. Table 40-2 is an example. The key to whether a tax is progressive or not lies in the increasing percentage of income paid in taxes, not in the amount paid.

TABLE 40-2
Progressive Tax

Income	Percentage of Income Paid in Taxes	Amount of Tax
$ 5,000	10	$ 500
10,000	15	1,500
15,000	20	3,000

For example, the tax rates in Table 40-3 are an example of a *proportional tax,* in which the percent of income paid in taxes remains the same irrespective of income. In this case the amount of the tax rises as income increases, but the ratio of tax to income remains constant at 10 percent.

TABLE 40-3
Proportional Tax

Income	Percentage of Income Paid in Taxes	Amount of Tax
$ 5,000	10	$ 500
10,000	10	1,000
15,000	10	1,500

A *regressive tax* is the opposite of the progressive tax. In this case the percentage of income paid in taxes declines as income rises, as in Table 40-4.

TABLE 40-4
Regressive Tax

Income	Percentage of Income Paid in Taxes	Amount of Tax
$ 5,000	10	$500
10,000	8	800
15,000	6	900

Note that in this particular illustration the amount of tax still rises as income rises, but not very much. The distinguishing feature of the regressive tax is the declining proportion of taxes to income in the middle column, however. If the tax is steeply regressive it is even possible that the amounts shown in the last column could also decline.

Many state or local income taxes are designed as proportional taxes. For example, a local income tax may require payments equal to 2 percent of total income.[1] The federal income tax is designed to be progressive, however. This design is modified by a huge number of exemptions and modifications that enable the few people with very high incomes to pay smaller proportions of their income in taxes than many people with lower incomes. Let's look at this very highly controversial situation.

The progressiveness of the federal income tax is built into the basic rates charged. These rates are modified by deductions and exemptions open to all taxpayers, which depend upon the number of persons in the household.

---

[1] Most state and local income taxes allow some exemptions, and people with higher incomes are usually better able to avoid paying taxes on part of their income than people with lower incomes. In practice, this makes most state and local income taxes somewhat regressive.

Table 40-5 is an example of the progressiveness of the system as illustrated by the tax paid by a married person with two dependents.

TABLE 40-5
Federal Income Tax for Married Person with Two Dependents

Income	Tax *	Tax Rate (Percentage of income paid)	Income After Tax
$ 1,000			$ 1,000
2,000			2,000
3,000	$ 4		2,996
4,000	144	3.6	3,856
5,000	308	6.2	4,692
6,000	474	7.9	5,526
7,500	737	9.8	6,763
10,000	1,198	12.0	8,802
15,000	2,217	14.8	12,783
20,000	3,397	17.0	16,603
25,000	4,743	19.0	20,257
50,000	14,392	28.8	45,608
100,000	40,579	40.6	59,421
250,000	136,310	54.5	113,690
500,000	305,623	61.1	194,379
1,000,000	644,248	64.4	355,752

* For incomes of $5,000 or less, the optional standard deduction was used; above that, deductions were assumed to be 10% of income.

The progressiveness of the basic system has been strongly modified by provisions that enable persons with higher incomes to avoid some of the tax liabilities they would otherwise incur. Some of the more important are:

1. Certain types of income do not have to be reported for tax purposes or can be offset by "losses" or "costs." This includes
   a. Income earned as interest on state and local bonds.
   b. Losses on business activities.
   c. Depletion allowances on natural resources (such as oil) and large depreciation charges on income producing real estate can be deducted from earned income for income tax purposes.
   While many of these provisions make sense for ordinary business activities they provide large loopholes for tax avoidance.
2. "Capital gains" are taxed at a flat rate of 25 percent, irrespective of an individual's income. This allows for substantially reduced taxes on income from increased values of securities and other assets. It also enables corporation executives to be paid in part by capital gains rather than salaries, through stock option plans. The greatest benefits accrue to families with incomes over $75,000 annually.

3. "Income splitting" (filing of separate returns by husband and wife) enables families to move downward to lower tax brackets. The major benefits accrue to families in the $15,000–$20,000 income ranges.

There are many similar loopholes in the tax system, some created originally in order to provide tax privileges for special economic interests and now all but impossible to remove from the system. They are all regressive in nature, because they usually apply to income other than earned salaries or wages. The rationale for most of them is that they are designed to encourage capital investment, increase initiative, or subsidize activities important to the national interest. As such, they embody the "trickle down" theory of economic benefits: that encouraging capital and promoting the interests of the wealthy stimulates economic growth and thereby benefits everyone. The cost, however is a distortion of the tax system that fosters a particular pattern of income distribution that may well be far from the best.

One regressive aspect of the federal personal income tax is the individual exemption. At the present time a taxpayer is allowed to reduce his taxable income by $1,200 for each dependent. On the surface it seems as if this affects everyone equally, but it doesn't. It allows the richer person in a higher tax bracket to reduce his tax payments by more than the poorer person in a lower tax bracket. For example, if you have a taxable income of $25,000, one personal exemption reduces your tax by $600. But if your taxable income is $9,000, the personal exemption saves you only $120. That happens because the tax rate on income in the $22,000–$26,000 range is 50 percent, while the rate is only 10 percent on income in the $8,000–$10,000 bracket. The basic principle is that when the tax rates are progressive with each increase in income, as ours are, any flat exemption that applies to everyone makes the system less progressive. Thus, an income tax exemption for families with children in college, a widely supported proposal, would benefit Mrs. Gotrocks more than Mr. Steelworker or Mr. Blackman. Perhaps it would make more sense to abolish the present personal exemptions and use the additional revenue for a federal scholarship program based on need.

The net result of these and other provisions of the federal income tax law is to make the whole system far less progressive than the nominal rates would suggest. Average tax rates at all income levels are below 30 percent and no one pays a tax above 50 percent of his income, however large that income might be. Indeed, effective tax rates tend to decline somewhat for incomes above $150,000 annually. Figure 40–1 shows the situation as it prevailed in 1962, giving the nominal rates and actual rates.

The Pros and Cons of Progressive Taxation

Supporters of progressive taxation start with an underlying bias against income inequality on ethical grounds. It can be argued that every participant in the economic life of a society makes his contribution to that society. All should,

Tax rates (percent)

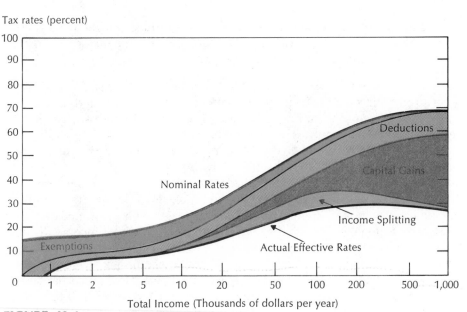

Total Income (Thousands of dollars per year)

FIGURE 40-1

Nominal and Actual Federal Income Tax Rates, 1962

The horizontal scale is a logarithmic or ratio scale, so that a straight line on the
chart represents a constant rate of change. The total income shown on the horizontal
scale does not include income unreported for tax purposes—such as interest on state
and local bonds.
(Source: Joseph A. Pechman, Federal Tax Policy *(Washington: Brookings Institution,
1966), p. 66.)*

therefore, be treated equally. Contributions may be unequal because individual abilities differ, but the differences in abilities may rest on factors over which the individual has little control, such as heredity, the influence of the socialization process in the early ages, and access to the educational system. Since differences in contribution to society are usually not the result of individual choices, in this view, there is no ethical basis for differences in reward.

The ethical argument is supplemented by the point, explained in Chapter 38, that the marginal utility of income diminishes as income rises. Applied in a simplistic fashion to the tax system, this principle leads to the argument that the wealthy can afford to pay a larger percentage of their income than the poor because their welfare will be less strongly affected.

Finally, there is the political argument. Large inequalities of income (and wealth) put greater political power in the hands of the rich. This power can be used to change the rules of the game and direct more wealth and power to the wealthy until the whole social fabric becomes dominated by an oligarchy of the wealthy few. A progressive tax system is one way in which this sort of development can be held in check.

The opponents of progressive taxation have had difficulty in answering these arguments, although the debate goes on. The chief response has been on economic grounds, stressing the incentive effects of progressive taxes. It seems to many a matter of common sense that if the government takes away a sizable percentage of increases in income, people will work less. This effect will reduce the production potential of the economy by making leisure more attractive relative to work. On the other hand, it is equally sensible to argue that a modest reduction in incomes will stimulate more work in order to maintain incomes at the former level. As we noted in Chapter 38, attempts to measure these conflicting effects of taxes on work effort have been inconclusive: some work harder, others work less, and the net effect seems to be very small—at present tax rates.

Opponents also argue that in the long run progressive taxation will reduce the supply of capital by reducing saving. They argue that people with high incomes save a larger proportion of their incomes than people with lower incomes, causing a progressive personal income tax to reduce the flow of savings available for investment and economic growth. On the other hand, much government spending is for investment in human capital, which is now more important for economic growth than private investment in plant and equipment (refer to Chapter 10 for the data). If that is true, economic growth will benefit from a tax system that assures an adequate flow of revenues into governmental hands, instead of one that leaves the income in the hands of private individuals.

The heart of the debate remains on the plane of ethics, however. If one views the social order as composed of discrete individuals who exercise free choice among alternatives, the arguments for progressive taxation do not make much sense. People should be rewarded for their efforts because they choose to make those efforts. They could choose not to, and society as a whole would suffer. Social justice, in this view, is that an individual *ought* to get what he earns. On the other hand, if one views the social order as a cooperative effort in which individual actions are determined by one's heredity, background, and place in the world, there is a strong presumption that rewards *ought* to be more or less equal. In this view, earnings are the result less of individual choice and more of forces beyond individual control, and reducing those earnings will not affect the size of the pie.

Arguments such as these can only be settled in the political arena. There the argument that the rich can afford to pay at a higher rate than the poor has carried the day. This implies acceptance of the argument that a more equalitarian distribution of income tends to increase aggregate welfare, as long as total output does not seem to be affected.

Two Conflicting Principles of Equity

The argument over progressive income taxes involves a fundamental disagreement over the question of how to achieve equity in taxation. One side would apply the ability-to-pay principle. The other side emphasizes the benefit principle.

The *benefit principle* is the older one. Taxes are levied to pay for public goods and services that benefit those who use them. One principle of equity is that the users should pay the cost of the services. This principle might be applied easily when those who benefit from a public service can be readily identified, such as the users of water from a publicly owned water supply system. But it is extremely difficult or impossible to apply to true public goods characterized by the nonexclusion principle, as explained in the last chapter. The problem is that water can be priced and supplied by a private firm perhaps as well as by a public agency, and market principles of pricing can be applied to it; but what does one do about the costs of operating the lighthouse on a rocky shore whose services can't be priced?

The same sort of problem arises for the other type of public good, the one whose marginal costs are nil and welfare maximization dictates that it be supplied free. If it isn't priced, the users can't be required to pay for it.

Advocates of the benefit principle are forced to fall back on the assumption that for most public goods the benefits are about the same for each person, so the tax burden should be borne equally. Or that benefits are proportional to income, so that taxes should be proportional rather than progressive or regressive. Or that benefits are linked to property ownership and taxes should be based on the value of property. At the very least, what started out as an apparently simple rule ends up in a maze of uncertainty.

The *ability-to-pay principle* is more widely accepted today, but its rationale has also been widely questioned. It is based on the principle of diminishing marginal utility, and is related to the idea that a more equalitarian distribution of income produces greater social welfare than a less equalitarian one. In its simplest form, it holds that the rich should pay proportionately more taxes than the poor because they are richer and can afford it. A dollar taken in taxes from the rich man reduces his satisfactions less than a dollar taken from a poor man. In that sense the rich man can afford to give up the tax dollar more readily than the poor man.

We have already examined the logic behind this argument in Chapter 38 and found that it has a great deal of validity, but is correct only in terms of probabilities and requires the assumption that the utilities or satisfactions of the poor and the rich be comparable. Many economists argue that this assumption cannot be proven and is highly unscientific.

The ability-to-pay principle has a broad plausibility, however, when applied to the two extremes of the distribution of income. Dollars can be used to provide a vacation in Acapulco for Mrs. Gotrocks' daughter, or food for the children of a poor rural family in Appalachia. Whatever the comparability of utilities, one's first reaction is to feed the kids.

The ability-to-pay principle also has some administrative justification: you can collect taxes only from people with the income to pay. Tax officials from time immemorial have tried to apply that simple rule. It means that those with higher incomes must bear the larger burden because they are the only ones who have the money.

Even if the ability-to-pay principle is accepted—because of its logic, or its common sense plausibility or its administrative feasibility—the problem of equity is not resolved. How much progressivity should be introduced into the tax system? Isn't a proportional tax enough, since the rich pay a larger dollar amount than the poor? Indeed, that is true even for some regressive taxes. These kinds of questions are not answered by the general principle.

The search for concrete standards of equity in taxation is doomed to failure. Neither the benefit principle nor the ability-to-pay principle provide definitive answers. The solution to the problem is inevitably thrown into the political arena, where the resolution of the problem depends in large part on the relative strength and power of contesting interests.

EXCISE AND SALES TAXES

An excise tax is a tax on the production or sale of an individual commodity, such as alcoholic beverages or tobacco products. A sales tax differs in that it is a tax on sales of all commodities (unless some are specifically exempted). Excise taxes have an ancient history. They include such classic taxes as those on salt or matches that have been famous throughout history. The famous tax on tea levied in the American colonies by the British government, which led to the Boston Tea Party of 1773, was essentially an excise tax levied in the form of a tax on importation of tea.

Governments love excise taxes because they bring in large revenues and are usually concealed from the purchaser. Most commodities on which excises are levied have an inelastic demand, which means that a large tax will have little effect on the amount purchased. This in turn means that the tax can be high without a significant loss in revenues. On the other hand, if demand for the commodity were elastic, the price plus tax would bring substantially reduced sales, and the tax yield would not be high. Figures 40-2 and 40-3 show the distinction.

These diagrams help to explain why excise taxes are levied only on certain commodities: on necessities that people must buy, on luxuries for which price is an insignificant element in the decision to buy, or on "big ticket" items like automobiles, for which the tax is a small percentage of the selling price. These are the items for which demand is inelastic.

Excise taxes are shifted largely to the final buyer of the taxed commodity, even though the manufacturer may be the one who pays the tax directly to the government. The tax is embodied in the sale price to the consumer, raising the price he pays by the amount of the tax. Even where the tax is made known through revenue stamps as on cigarettes or alcoholic beverages,

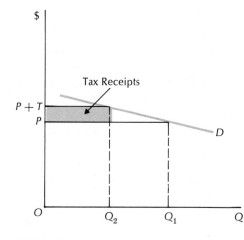

FIGURE 40-2
Excise Taxes on Commodities with
Elastic Demand

The excise tax raises price from P to
$P + T$, but the quantity purchased falls
from Q_1 to Q_2. Tax receipts are small.

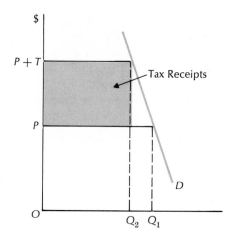

FIGURE 40-3
Excise Taxes on Commodities with
Inelastic Demand

A large excise tax raises the price to
the consumer from P to $P + T$,
but causes only a small decline in the
quantity sold, from Q_1 to Q_2. The
result is large receipts from the tax,
to the delight of Treasury officials.

or on gasoline pumps, few buyers pay any attention to the amount of the
levy.[2]

Sales taxes differ somewhat from excise taxes in that they are collected from
the consumer at the point of sale. They are usually levied as a fixed percentage
of the sale price, and usually apply to all commodities. Most sales taxes in
the United States are levied by state and local governments. Since they apply
to all commodities and are borne by consumers, sales taxes have the great
political advantage of not arousing the opposition of important business
interests. They also are borne most heavily by lower income groups and do
not arouse the opposition of the wealthy. This also has political advantages.

---

[2] The basic rule that an excise tax is shifted to the consumer is strictly and wholly true only for
products of competitive industries. Where monopolistic elements are present, a part of the tax
cannot be shifted, and reduced profits to the monopoloid firms result. In addition, the proposition that the price of the commodity is increased by the amount of the tax is strictly correct
only for industries with constant costs in the long run. With long-run increasing costs, the price
will rise a little less than the tax; with decreasing costs the price will go up by a little more
than the tax. These are minor qualifications, however, the details of which can be looked up
in any good textbook on public finance or taxation. The basic rules remain: excise taxes raise
the price of the taxed commodity by an amount close or equal to the amount of the tax, and
the tax (or almost the whole amount) is paid by those who buy the commodity.

Sales taxes are one of the most regressive elements in the U.S. tax system. The reason for their regressiveness is that people with lower incomes spend a larger proportion of their income and save less than people with higher incomes. A larger proportion of their income is therefore subject to the tax. For example, a study in Illinois showed that poor families with income of $1,000–$2,000 annually spent 80 percent of their income on taxed commodities, while families with incomes above $10,000 spent only 45 percent on goods subject to the sales tax. This regressive feature of the sales tax is sometimes modified by exempting food and medicine from the tax, but while popular with the poor this exemption is not admired by financial officials because it reduces revenues very substantially.

THE PROPERTY TAX

Property taxes are the mainstay of public revenues for local governments, including school districts and a wide variety of other local government units. They are under greater local control than any other tax, yet they are more poorly administered, more unfairly levied, and have the most serious evil effects of any tax.

Why, then, are they so widely used? Briefly, because they bring in revenue, and local governments need revenue. Land and buildings can't run away and hide, so they are there when the tax assessor comes around and can always be seized if the tax isn't paid. Furthermore, it is very difficult to shift property taxes to someone else. The homeowner, of course, bears the burden himself. Owners of rental property are able to shift the tax to renters in the long run but not in the short run. In the short run, housing rents are determined by the supply of and demand for rental housing and property taxes must be paid out of the landlord's revenues. In the long run, reduced returns from higher taxes influence the supply of property available for rent and the burden shifts to the renter while the landlord's profits return to normal. Thus the renter is affected in the same way as the homeowner. How this happens is shown in Figures 40-4 through 40-6. As for farmers and owners of business and commercial property, they are unable to shift the property tax to others. It adds to their costs, but selling prices are determined by supply and demand in the market. It is only because costs affect supply in the long run that property taxes can shift the allocation of resources somewhat if they bear more heavily on one industry than another. In short, property taxes are a good source of revenue; they cannot be avoided, and usually cannot be shifted to others.

Nevertheless, property taxes have had a very serious impact on urban development and are an important reason why slums and deteriorating housing are a feature of the urban scene. By being taxed for improvements to housing, owners and landlords are discouraged from maintaining their property adequately. If we wanted to encourage good housing, we should tax land but not its improvements.

Confusion

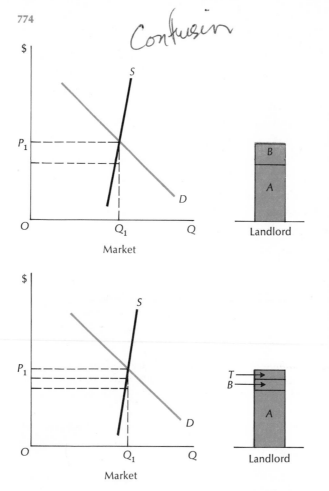

FIGURE 40-4
Who Pays the Property Tax on Rental Property? Before the Tax
The rental payment P_1 is determined by supply and demand in the market. The owner's profit B is the difference between total revenues $A + B$ and the owner's costs A.

FIGURE 40-5
Who Pays the Property Tax on Rental Property? After the Tax: The Short Run
The imposition of a property tax does not change demand and supply in the market, so the price and total revenue are unchanged. The owner's profits B are reduced by the amount of the tax, T.

Perhaps an even more harmful aspect of property taxes is the almost universal practice of taxing undeveloped land at very low rates while developed property is taxed at much higher rates. In most localities this practice is forbidden by law, but it is nevertheless achieved by setting a taxable value on undeveloped land at levels much below its market value while assessing developed property at levels much closer to its market value. This practice enables speculators to buy and hold land for future gains at very little cost to themselves. Builders then find that the price of land is higher and home buyers have to pay more for their houses. Because prices are higher, there is less building, contributing to our persistent housing shortage. Builders move further out beyond developed areas to build, leaping over the speculative tracts and leaving them as irregular weed-filled areas of urban sprawl. As a result, streets are extended and cost more, sewer and other utility lines are longer and more expensive, and the fiscal strain on local governments is increased. The fiscal strain is compounded, of course, by low tax yields on the underassessed and undertaxed open lands.

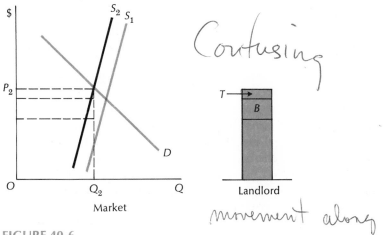

FIGURE 40-6

Who Pays the Property Tax on Rental Property? After the Tax: The Long Run

In the long run, reduced profits relative to earnings on other investments reduce the supply of rental housing from S_1 to S_2, rents go up to P_2 and the owner's profits B return to normal. Because there are fewer rental units, total profits of all owners are reduced even though profits per unit recover to where they were before. The full impact of the tax is now felt by the renter, while the individual owner is just as well off as he was before. (B in this figure is just as large as B in Figure 40-4.)

By contrast, if undeveloped land were properly taxed, speculative land could not be held so easily for long periods, the demand for land would be reduced by cutting down the practice of holding it for increased prices, and the price of land would be lower. The cost of housing would thereby be reduced. There would be less urban sprawl, and costs of urban services would be reduced. One side effect would be to bring about a more centralized urban development and hence more open space in the long run. Government revenues would be greater, both from higher taxes on undeveloped land and greater revenues from improvements, and more funds would be available for urban planning and other city services.

All of this has been known in detail for a hundred years, ever since the radical American economist Henry George (1839–1897) published his pamphlet *Our Land and Land Policy* in 1871. Yet perverse property tax policies persist. Why? The reason, apparently, has been the important role or dominance of real estate interests in local governments, and farmers in state legislatures. Low taxes on land bring an increased demand for land and thereby raise its price, benefiting all those whose assets are held in land at the expense of everyone else. While few economists today would accept George's view that a single tax on land alone would solve most of our economic problems, there are few who would not agree that the inequitable (and sometimes corrupt) administration of the property tax exaggerates our already difficult urban problems.

THE CORPORATE INCOME TAX

The corporation income tax is levied by the federal government on the earnings of corporations. It appears simple. The first $25,000 of corporate profits is taxed at a rate of 22 percent. Everything over that pays 48 percent. The reason for the difference is to aid small firms as compared with larger ones.

But now everything becomes *very* complicated. In order to determine profits, a firm must deduct costs from revenues, with the difference being the amount taxed. This gives firms every incentive to overstate costs and understate revenues. Since most firms pay the 48 percent rate, they can provide expense accounts and bonuses for executives, raising costs and having about half of the actual expense offset by reduced taxes. Advertising, in effect, costs only 52 percent of the total bill, with Uncle Sam paying the remainder. Depreciation charges can be set at very high figures, reducing corporate taxes in the short run: a machine that lasts ten years can be depreciated in five, reducing taxes now at the expense of higher taxes later (this is equivalent to a short-term loan from the federal government). In these and other ways the allocation of resources is distorted.

The corporate income tax brings about a form of double taxation. The corporation's profits are taxed. It then pays dividends out of its after-tax income. Those dividends become part of the taxable income of individuals who pay the personal income tax. Two taxes are paid on the same income. In addition to the inequities involved, this situation provides incentives for the corporation to spend more for expansion instead of paying larger dividends. The expansion creates capital gains for the stockholders, who can then sell their stock and be taxed at a rate of only 25 percent on the gains instead of 48 percent on the corporate profits and perhaps 20–35 percent on the dividends. This process encourages the growth of big business, not for economic reasons, but as a device for tax avoidance.

Even the question of who pays the corporate income tax is not clear. The easy answer is the corporation itself. Since an income tax is on profit, which is calculated after costs are accounted for, it does not affect prices charged to consumers. The firm maximizes its profit on the basis of market conditions and the tax then comes off the top. This analysis does not take administered prices into account, however. When firms have some control over the prices they charge, they can anticipate the corporate income tax and try to gain profits after taxes that are as large as profits before taxes. In the setting of prices, the tax on profits becomes an implicit cost, is embodied in selling prices, and is thereby passed on to the consumer. There is some indirect evidence that this is what happens: rates of profit are lower today than they were in the days before the corporate income tax, but they aren't 48 percent lower. If the corporation bore the entire burden of the tax, they would be. Apparently a combination of adjustments has occurred. Costs are probably overstated somewhat, firms are using more of their earnings to finance expansion, and some of the corporate income tax has probably been shifted to consumers in the form of higher prices.

These considerations indicate that the corporate income tax has had a variety of influences on resource allocation, the distribution of income, the structure of industry, and the burden of taxation. Yet no one knows exactly how or to what extent. It is this last point that is most important: here is an important tax whose impact is largely unknown and subject to wide speculation. Since it brings in large revenues and can't be shown to be significantly harmful (although it may be; we just don't know), it answers the Treasury officials' need for a productive tax whose burdens are largely hidden.

SHIFTING AND INCIDENCE OF TAXES

Economists use the terms shifting *and* incidence *in discussing where the burden of a tax comes to rest.*

Incidence of a tax is the location of the unit that bears the economic burden of the tax. In the short run, the incidence of a tax on rental property is on the owner. In the long run, it is on the renter. Shifting of taxes *refers to the process by which the incidence changes. The burden of an excise tax is shifted from the business firm that actually makes the payment to the customer who pays a higher price for the product.*

Shifting and incidence problems can be very complex, as we saw with the corporate income tax, and widely spread, as we saw with the property tax.

NEUTRALITY IN TAXATION

Most economists would agree that taxes should influence the pattern of production as little as possible. This view is consistent with the proposition that the private sector tends to adapt to consumer demand in a welfare-maximizing pattern. Taxes, it is argued, should distort the pattern as little as possible.

For example, a general sales tax that is levied equally on all commodities is superior to an excise tax, which is levied only on a few commodities. The excise tax increases the price of the goods on which it is levied and consumers tend to buy less of those goods than they otherwise would. This distortion of consumer behavior is greater than would be created by a sales tax of equal amount that does not discriminate against some commodities.

Even a sales tax would distort the choice between spending and saving to some extent, so it is not completely neutral. Neither is an income tax, which may have some impact on the choice between work and leisure. For some taxes, like the corporate income tax, so little is definitely known about its incidence that its neutrality is very hard to assess.

Indeed, no tax is completely neutral with respect to the allocation of resources, and some distortion is inevitable. We must think in terms of degrees of neutrality. The broader the base of the tax and the fewer the possibilities for shifting its incidence the more neutral it will be.

DOES THE UNITED STATES HAVE A PROGRESSIVE TAX SYSTEM?

When all aspects of the whole tax system in the United States are taken into account and their incidence estimated according to the best current knowledge, the U.S. tax system shows up as highly *regressive* up to incomes of $10,000 annually. It becomes progressive after that level, but even then, the tax burden on the poor is significantly greater than that borne by the affluent. The progressivity of the federal income tax is more than overcome by the regressiveness of the bulk of other taxes. State and local taxes show a distinctly regressive character throughout. Table 40-6 shows the pattern as of 1960, according to the most recent professional estimates.

TABLE 40-6
Taxes as a Percentage of Income, 1960

Family Income	Federal Taxes	State and Local Taxes	Total	Percentage of Families	Percentage of Income
Under $2,000	37.8	26.2	64.1	14	2
$2,000–2,999	42.0	25.1	67.2	9	4
3,000–3,999	33.6	18.0	51.6	9	5
4,000–4,999	28.1	17.4	45.5	11	8
5,000–7,499	20.8	12.4	33.2	28	28
7,500–9,999	15.7	7.1	22.8	15	20
10,000 and over	26.6	5.3	31.9	14	33
Total	23.9	9.8	33.7	100	100

Table 40-6 shows some interesting facts. About one-third of all family income is paid in taxes to all levels of government combined. Families with incomes above $5,000 pay a somewhat smaller proportion, but the 45 percent of all families with incomes below $5,000 pay a considerably higher tax rate. About 70 percent of the total burden is federal taxes and the remainder is state and local.

State and local taxes are consistently regressive. Their regressiveness is greater than federal taxes, primarily because they fall so lightly on incomes of the more affluent. Federal taxes are also regressive (although the very poor get a little break because of income tax exemptions). The only significant element of progressiveness in the system is the federal tax burden of the affluent, which is strong enough to affect the overall pattern.

It is indeed shocking to discover that the poor pay over half their income in taxes as compared with slightly under one-third for the affluent.

THE NET DISTRIBUTION OF BURDENS AND BENEFITS

Government budgets not only take away income in the form of taxes, they also provide benefits in the form of expenditures. It is possible to estimate the net effects of government budgets by supplementing tax burdens with expenditure benefits. The task is not an easy one and some heroic assumptions have to be made. For example, how should the benefits from general government expenditures such as police protection and national defense be allocated? Should they be distributed to each family equally, or according to income? As for taxes, how shall the burdens of the corporate income tax be allocated, to the stockholder or the customers, and in what proportions? These and other problems make any estimates of redistribution of income through government budgets both a difficult task and subject to controversy.

Nevertheless, two worthwhile estimates of this sort have been made, and their results are summarized in Table 40-7, which shows the redistribution of incomes after taxes and benefits from government spending. Both were based on sophisticated (but somewhat different) assumptions about the burdens of the various sorts of taxes and the distribution of benefits from government spending. The results show a strikingly similar pattern existing in the late 1930s, the mid-1940s, and 1960. There is a net redistribution in favor of the poor and against the upper-middle and upper income groups, while there is little change in the net incomes of lower-middle income families. As of 1960, the poorer one-third of all families had higher incomes, while the affluent upper 15 percent had lower incomes. The majority in the middle showed little impact from government budgets. When allowance is made for changing price levels and for the somewhat different methodologies of the two estimates, there has been remarkably little change over the years.

TABLE 40-7
Redistribution of Incomes Through Government Budgets

Income of Consumer Unit	Redistributed Income as a Percentage of Original Income		
	1938–39	1946–47	1960
Under $1,000	123.2	173.4	155.1
$1,000–1,999	100.9	122.4	
2,000–2,999	96.5	111.1	144.4
3,000–3,999	96.7	106.6	118.5
4,000–4,999	98.0	98.5	98.7
5,000–7,499	100.9	92.6	97.1
7,500–9,999	80.8	78.6	101.7
$10,000 and over			86.8

Source: Data for 1938–39 and 1946–47 is from John H. Adler, "The Fiscal System, the Distribution of Income and Public Welfare", in Kenyon E. Poole (ed.), *Fiscal Policies and the American Economy* (New York: Prentice-Hall, 1951), p. 396. Data for 1960 is from W. Irwin Gillespie, "Effect of Public Expenditures on the Distribution of Income," in Richard A. Musgrave (ed.), *Essays in Fiscal Federalism* (Washington: Brookings Institution, 1965), p. 162.

Two further points should be made about Table 40-7. The redistribution of income toward the poor, which it shows, would be changed if general government expenditures were allocated differently. Table 40-7 is based on the assumption that those expenditures are equally beneficial to each person. One could argue, however, that the protection aspects of government, particularly police and fire protection and national defense, are more valuable to the rich than the poor. The benefits from those expenditures could be allocated according to income, and this would reduce the redistribution of income from the affluent to the poor, leaving the middle income groups largely unaffected. If the allocation of these benefits were done according to holdings of wealth the picture would be even more different.[3] If one wished to argue the best possible case for the welfare-maximizing effects of government budgets, one would use the data in Table 40-7. A critical view would start from different assumptions and bring different results.

CONCLUSIONS: THE OVERALL PICTURE

Taxes and budgets reflect the prevailing ideology and the structure of economic power. The economist can do little more than analyze their impact in terms of burdens and benefits. The analysis involves the theory of tax incidence (who pays the tax and in what form) and the shifting of tax burdens (whether the real effects are felt by the person who actually pays the money or by someone else). This chapter has shown how the analysis can be done and some of the results. Perhaps the single most important conclusion is that the tax system of the United States is far from being an ideal one. It hurts the poor and benefits the rich. This pattern is modified by the distribution of benefits from expenditures, but whether the system as a whole tends to redistribute incomes from the rich to the poor remains largely an open question. If we take seriously the proposition that a poor family will gain more welfare from an additional dollar than an affluent family will lose by giving up a dollar, then we must be highly critical of the U.S. tax system and skeptical about the net benefits from government budgets as a whole.

The tax system is equally deficient with respect to problems of economic stability and growth. Little consideration is given to the effects of taxes on these important questions. An important tax, the corporate income tax, is maintained even though its macroeconomic effects are largely unknown and its effect on the corporate structure may well be to strengthen giant enterprise. The property tax as it is now structured and administered has clearly detrimental effects on patterns of urban development, yet it continues as is because it is such a good producer of revenues. The loopholes and exemptions present in the federal income tax are there largely because of pressures from special

---

[3] We have no idea of how different it would be. This type of estimate has never been made—illustrating some of the ideological preconceptions of contemporary economics.

economic interests rather than because of careful consideration of their impact on the economy as a whole. And so on, almost ad infinitum.

Yet it would be possible to devise a tax system to promote equity in income distribution, sustain prosperity and promote economic growth. A tax system of that sort would be quite different from the present one.

Summary

Any tax system involves the interplay of widely divergent economic interests, and the outcome is normally a hodgepodge of compromises arising out of conflict between government, taxpayers, and organized economic interest groups.

In the United States the most important taxes are the individual and corporate income taxes, excise and sales taxes, property taxes, and employment taxes.

The federal individual income tax has progressive base rates, but income splitting, deductions, exemptions, and special treatment for capital gains make it much less progressive, and even somewhat regressive at very high incomes. Arguments for and against progressive taxation rest ultimately on value judgments. Although the ability-to-pay principle argues that the rich are better able to pay taxes than the poor, it does not provide any guidelines to the degree of progressiveness that is desirable. The benefit principle holds, by contrast, that taxes should be paid by those who benefit from public services, but it is extremely difficult to apply in practice.

Excise and sales taxes are strong revenue producers. Excises are generally levied only on commodities with inelastic demand, which limits their usefulness. They are generally shifted to the final buyer of the taxed commodity and no pretense to fairness is made. Sales taxes are widely used by state and local governments, imparting a strong trend toward regressiveness to the tax system as a whole.

Property taxes, used widely by local governments, are usually not shiftable, except that in the case of rental property they are shifted to the renter in the long run. The administration of property taxes is almost uniformly poor, and they have been one reason for our present urban problems.

As for the corporate income tax, little is definitely known about its incidence and shifting, except that, as a double tax, it tends to promote the growth of big business by encouraging investment of retained earnings by business firms rather than payment of higher dividends to stockholders.

Taking all taxes together, the U.S. has a generally regressive tax structure, modified by rather limited progressivity in the upper middle and upper incomes. When government benefits are allocated to recipients, the combination of taxes and benefits redistributes real income in a progressive fashion; but there are doubts about that conclusion because of the way the studies allocated benefits.

Key Concepts

Progressive tax.   Takes an increasing percent of income in taxes as incomes rise.

Proportional tax.   Takes the same percent of income in taxes as incomes rise.

Regressive tax.   Takes a declining percent of income in taxes as incomes rise.

Tax incidence.   The incidence of a tax is the locus of the ultimate tax burden. *Shifting* of the incidence occurs when one economic unit is able to compensate for its tax payment at the expense of another.

Tax neutrality.   Occurs when taxes do not affect any decisions in the private sector. Complete neutrality is impossible.

Ability-to-pay principle.   The principle that taxes should be based on ability to pay because a marginal tax dollar is allegedly less useful to a richer person than to a poorer one.

Benefit principle.   The principle that taxes should be based on the amount of benefits that individuals receive from government services.

When a nation goes to war, a group of economic issues appear that are quite different from those of peacetime. Resources must be shifted from civilian to military uses. This must be done with minimum damage to production incentives. The strains imposed on the economy are almost sure to bring problems of inflation. Under these conditions a modern nation will move to economic planning and production allocations and a variety of other administrative economic controls.

A limited war brings similar problems but on a smaller scale. Solutions to the economic problem are more difficult, however, largely because the psychological environment does not permit full use of wartime mobilization methods.

The economy devoted heavily to military production but not actively at war is another phenomenon entirely. It provides jobs and security for many people and develops a psychological and political environment conducive to its continuation, even though much of its productive effort produces no economic benefits.

THE BASIC ECONOMIC PROBLEM IN WARTIME

When a nation goes to war, its basic economic problem is one of shifting the use of resources from civilian or peacetime uses to military or wartime uses. All other problems, like financing the war and keeping prices under control, for example, are secondary and derive from the problem of how to shift resources into producing swords and out of production of plowshares.

The problem can be visualized in the simple terms of the production possibilities frontier. When an economy at full employment wishes to produce more military goods it can do so only by reducing production of civilian goods, as shown in Figure 41-1. Only when a country has significant amounts of unused capacity can it have more of both military and civilian goods. This was the position of the United States entering World War II. The high levels of unemployment of the Great Depression still prevailed, the economy was operating inside its production possibilities frontier, and for almost two years the enlarged wartime spending pushed up both civilian and military output. By the end of 1943, the classic wartime problem prevailed, as illustrated in Figure 41-2.

The
Economics
of War
and Defense

41

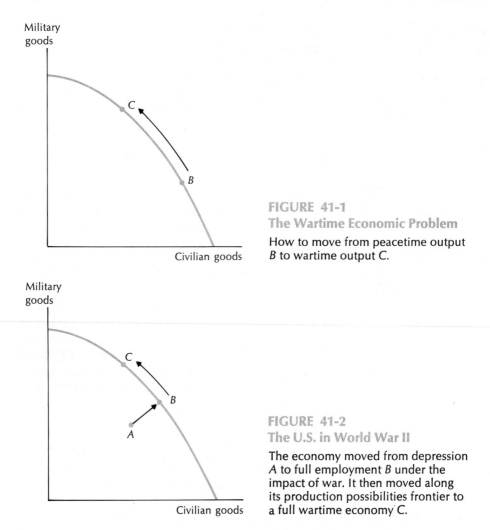

FIGURE 41-1
The Wartime Economic Problem

How to move from peacetime output *B* to wartime output *C*.

FIGURE 41-2
The U.S. in World War II

The economy moved from depression *A* to full employment *B* under the impact of war. It then moved along its production possibilities frontier to a full wartime economy *C*.

When a war lasts a long time, investment is also channeled into military production. This distorts the production possibilities of the economy by increasing military production capacity by larger amounts than civilian goods capacity. Figure 41-3 shows the distortion.

WARTIME MOBILIZATION

The mobilization of manpower and resources for the armed forces and military production is usually accomplished by use of nonmarket means. Men are drafted. Materials for production are controlled by administrative allocations. Manpower and materials for civilian production are restricted. A system of allocative planning run by a war production bureaucracy is evolved. This was the pattern that started in World War I and was developed on a large scale in

Military
goods

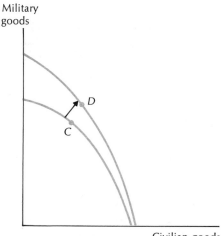

Civilian goods

FIGURE 41-3
Investment in Wartime

Planning of investment in wartime
enlarges production capacity for military
goods more rapidly than for civilian
goods. The economy can then move
from C to D (or some other point on
the outer curve).

World War II. It was not used during the limited wars in Asia (1953–55 and
1962 to date), largely because the economic conversion to war was limited.

This need not be the pattern of wartime mobilization. It would be theoretically possible to rely fully on the market mechanism. The government could
enter the market and bid away from the private sector all of the resources and
manpower needed for war production. The added spending would be inflationary, however, unless taxes are raised by more than the increased government spending.

A DIGRESSION

Why must taxes be increased by more than the increase in
government spending if inflation is to be avoided? Answer:
The balanced budget multiplier. An increase in G accompa-
nied by an equal increase in T will raise GNP by an amount
equal to G. For GNP to be held constant, T must exceed G.

Why, then, does a modern nation move to planning, allocations, and manpower controls when under the stress of war? The answer, apparently, lies in
the area of incentives. If people were taxed heavily, even in wartime, public
support of the war would be damaged. Every war creates a variety of reactions,
from enthusiastic support, to lukewarm acceptance, to doubts, to unspoken
opposition, to overt opposition. The costlier the war, the more people can be
expected to oppose it, and the shorter the period of enthusiasm on the part of

supporters. One of the largely unrecorded chapters of history is the opposition that has prevailed in all nations to all wars, even when the patriotic response has seemed to be overwhelming. It is important then that wartime planners minimize the sacrifices required in wartime. This means that taxes cannot be raised high enough to reduce demand for civilian goods so as to free all of the resources required for the desired production of military goods.

In addition, higher incomes act as an incentive to draw additional workers into the work force and to get all workers to work harder. Patriotic appeals are used for these purposes, but patriotism plus cash works better. If prices were allowed to rise, wiping out workers' income gains, these incentive effects would be reduced.

Reliance on monetary incentives has its limitations, however. It can't very well be applied to the armed forces. The wage necessary to get soldiers to give up their lives may be very high, running the expenses of the war up to astronomical levels. These costs can be shifted away from taxpayers to non-voting youths by drafting them into the armed forces, providing them with patriotic appeals supported by the threat of death for desertion, and marching them off to war. The absence of effective incentives, however, requires that military operations based on manpower acquired in this fashion be organized on the basis of discipline, threat, and command.

If the major costs of the war are borne by drafted youths, it seems unfair for the civilian sector to be allowed to profit excessively. Burdens must be partially equalized, at the very least, or opposition to the war will escalate. Taxes, wage controls, and profit limitations become inevitable. But since those devices reduce incentives, they also reduce the ability of the government to obtain the necessary shift in use of resources through the market mechanism. Planning is used instead.

In this fashion the policy compromise inherent in a war economy is evolved. Economic burdens on the civilian population must be held in check in order to avoid an early appearance of "war weariness." The effort to keep the cost of the war from being fully apparent leads to use of a military draft. This creates equity problems, so the civilian sector is asked to do its share by paying higher taxes and making other voluntary sacrifices. But this policy conflicts with the "war weariness" constraint. Incomes are therefore allowed to rise, taxes are inadequate to finance the war fully, and production planning and controls are used to mobilize resources. In the process, a problem of inflation is created, which must be held in check by further economic controls.[1]

---

[1] The wartime economic problem is never presented to the public in these terms. War is not a time for rationality, but for emotion. A rational analysis would lay bare all of the irrationality involved. Wartime policy-makers don't seem to think in these terms, either. They are pragmatic men with problems to solve. They find their way to solutions for the economic problems of war based on their perception of the current situation, as they balance incentives and attitudes against the need for mobilization of resources in ways that fit everyday events. In this way, wartime management of our economy develops in somewhat different fashion with each war, even though the basic economic issues and problems are similar.

WAR AND INFLATION

Inflation accompanies wars. In theory this need not be so, but the pragmatic compromises inherent in a wartime economy make it inevitable. An economy straining to produce beyond its capacity requires a safety valve. Inflation provides it.

Wartime inflation, like any inflation, is caused by excessive aggregate demand. And, like any inflation, it can start even before full employment is reached. The situation is complicated, however, by the fact that products are diverted from civilian markets into the military sector. Even if demand were held down by taxes, the diversion of goods would be enough to cause inflationary price increases. This point is not obvious, and it requires some further explanation.

Imagine a peacetime economy at full-employment equilibrium with stable prices. Now send that economy to war, adding more government spending. But have the government raise taxes to pay the entire costs of the war. Production allocations shift production out of civilian goods and into military, while payment is made out of the increased taxes. One might suppose that the inflation problem would be solved, since both incomes and civilian production are reduced by equal amounts. That is not so. Figure 41–4 shows what happens.

The essence of the problem is that purchasing power remains as before but is still excessive because the amount of goods available for sale is reduced. That happens even if we assume that taxes are raised to cover all war expenses, and we have already seen why that cannot be done. Indeed, wartime inflation can be avoided only if the government runs a budgetary surplus whose multiplied effect is equal in amount to the diversion of resources from the civilian to the military sectors. The surplus is needed to reduce consumer incomes below their peacetime levels in order to match the reduction in goods available for sale. But who ever heard of a wartime budget in surplus? Any government that tried it would be accused of failing to pursue the war fully.

Another alternative is to reduce the propensity to consume with war bond sales drives. This has the psychological advantage of seeming to help supply the armies, but its true purpose is to reduce inflationary pressures. War bond sales performed this function in both the First and Second World Wars.

A third alternative is price controls and rationing. If they are effective, they will leave excess purchasing power in the hands of consumers because the limited supply of goods available at fixed prices will not absorb all of the wartime purchasing power. Savings will pile up in banks and the bond drives will sop up some more. It also helps if some sectors of the economy are left unregulated to help take the pressure off the more important regulated sectors. Nightclubs, gambling, and prostitution are the usual areas left uncontrolled, as long as their prosperity and rising prices do not absorb too much manpower.

In spite of all the remedies and safety valves, prices are almost sure to rise

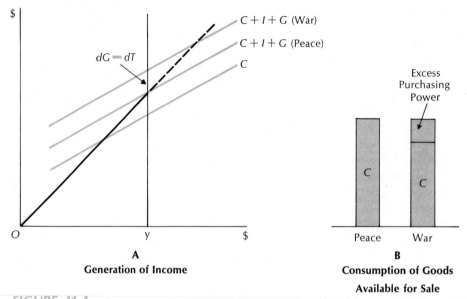

FIGURE 41-4
Wartime Inflation

With production levels fixed at Y, government spending and taxes rise by equal
amounts. Since real output cannot go beyond the full-employment level of peacetime,
the spending of that money takes resources away from the civilian sector, as shown
in the right-hand bar chart (B). Yet incomes available for spending are not reduced (A)
because taxes are immediately replaced in the consumers' pockets by government
spending. The excess purchasing power shown in B is exactly equal to the increase
in government spending (in this simplified version).

anyway. The fundamental economic imbalance, that is, too much money
chasing too few goods, remains. At best, wartime price controls and rationing
can only postpone the inflationary pressures until after the war is over by
preventing consumers from spending, and forcing them to save during the
war.

TOTAL WARS AND LIMITED WARS

The wartime economy described to this point is based on the experiences of
World Wars I and II. We shall not see their like again. World War III will be
different: it might last minutes instead of years. The economic problems of
World War III are to be found instead in the arms race and limited wars that
are leading up to it and the reconstruction (if any) that will follow. Nevertheless, the fundamental economic problems remain, albeit on a reduced scale.
Resources must be allocated to the military and away from civilian uses, and
inflationary pressures must be accommodated.

The example of the war in Southeast Asia is instructive. As the war began
to escalate in 1965, the economy was approaching the level just below full

employment at which prices could be expected to start rising. A larger number of young men began to be drafted into the armed forces and military spending rose. Mobilization of increased resources for military use was starting, but a basic policy decision was made to avoid as much as possible such devices as tax increases, production allocations, and price controls. The national administration tried to act as if the economy could have more swords without reducing the number of plowshares. The economic strategy was to use the market economy to bid away resources from the private sector by increased government spending. But since tax increases were to be minor at best, the result was a $26 billion deficit in the federal budget in the 1968 fiscal year.

The inflation of the late 1960s followed. Not only was GNP increased by the multiplied effect of the deficit, but the resources available for civilian uses had been diminished.

A new administration in 1968 tried to adapt, but went only part way. The avowed strategy was to end the war (or reduce its intensity) so that military expenditures might be leveled off (no one seriously contemplated a large reduction), thereby eliminating the main cause of inflation. In the meantime the administration sought to restructure the federal budget by reducing spending on nonmilitary items. The reallocation of resources was to take place within the federal sector. Like the previous administration, the basic policy decision was to leave the private sector untouched by production allocations and price controls.

The new administration also had to deal with the problem of inflation it had inherited from the economic policies of the previous administration. Rather than use price, wage, and profit controls, it used a tight monetary policy administered through the Federal Reserve System. But that policy had come too late. The inflation of 1969–70 was caused primarily by the federal deficits of 1966–68, and tight money in 1969–70 could have little effect on the spread of its effects through the price system. But tight money in 1969–70 could—and did—affect production in 1970. The result was the 1970 recession, at a time when price increases were continuing at a rate of some 6–7 percent annually. The recession had the effect of reducing incomes in the civilian sector of the economy, something that should have been done three years earlier if the inflation were to have been avoided. Finally, the administration resolved its dilemma by using the price freeze of 1971 to hold back further inflation, hoping to reduce unemployment through easier monetary policies and other economic stimulants.

The economic strategy of the limited war contains all of the essential elements of the economics of the old-fashioned total war, but at a reduced degree of intensity. Pioneered in the Korean War and worked out in greater detail in the Southeast Asia war, it now adds up to the following propositions:

1. Wars limited in scope and length require mobilization of additional resources for the military.

2. This can be accomplished through the market economy by increasing government expenditures for military purposes.

3. Inflation does not become a serious problem until the economy approaches full employment.

4. When inflation becomes a threat, the shift to increased military spending requires a reduction in government spending on nonmilitary budget items.

5. If that does not work because of the size of the resource shifts required by the war, tight money can be used to reduce production in the private sector.

6. If the war continues to escalate, the full panoply of war mobilization policies will have to be used, including production allocations, wage and price controls, profit limits, and war bond drives.

7. Any significant delay in application of Propositions 4–6 opens the way to inflation.

THE MILITARIZED ECONOMY

Most American are unaware of the extent to which the American economy has become militarized. Professor Seymour Melman of Columbia University estimated that in 1969 about 20 percent of the U.S. civilian labor force was directly or indirectly employed as a result of military spending. This included 1.1 million civilians employed by the Department of Defense, 3.4 million persons serving in the armed forces, and 3.4 million workers directly employed on war contracts. In addition, there were about 10 million persons employed as a result of the purchasing power created by the primary employment listed above. This makes a total of about 18 million jobs out of a total employment of about 80.5 million (including the armed forces).[2]

A more normal picture might be obtained by looking at the economy prior to the escalation of the Southeast Asia war. Going back to 1966, and using data published by the U.S. Department of Commerce and Department of Labor, we find that:

1. Almost 7 percent of all employed persons were employed in defense industries. These are industries in which a significant portion of total employment is on defense production.

2. About 8 percent of all *manufacturing* employment was directly on defense contracts, and about 22 percent was in defense industries.

Manufacturing employment is particularly important, for it is the economic base on which the economies of most large cities rest. Other sectors of the economy, such as wholesale and retail trade, construction, financial services,

---

[2] Seymour Melman, "U.S. Industrial Economy Unprepared for Peace," *The New York Times*, June 7, 1970.

and so on, depend for their prosperity on the "export" industries of an area, such as automobiles in Detroit and southeastern Michigan, steel in Pittsburgh and western Pennsylvania, shipbuilding in southern Mississippi, and military contracts in Los Angeles, San Diego, Dallas, and even smaller cities like Wichita, Kansas.

There is a high degree of concentration of military production. More than half is accounted for by a few states: Massachusetts, Connecticut, New York, New Jersey, Texas, California, and Washington. Some are highly dependent on defense contracts for their prosperity. Table 41-1 shows the proportion of all manufacturing employment on defense contracts and in defense industries for the seven states that had over half of all military production in 1966.

TABLE 41-1
Manufacturing Employment in Defense, 1966

Selected States	Percentage in Defense Industries	Percentage on Defense Contracts
Massachusetts	27	10
Connecticut	44	19
New York	21	8
New Jersey	23	8
Texas	26	11
California	38	24
Washington	37	13
National average	22	8

Source: Computations by the author from data published by U.S. Department of Commerce and U.S. Department of Labor.

Military production is also highly concentrated in a relatively few large corporations. The hundred largest defense contractors supply about two-thirds of the approximately $40 billion-worth (1969) of military supplies contracted for by the Department of Defense, and only ten firms accounted for 30 percent of the total. This is out of a total of fifteen thousand to twenty thousand prime contractors. Much of the actual production is subcontracted to other firms, and by subcontractors to still more firms. But this serves to draw large numbers of firms into the web of military production while it eases the administrative problem for the Department of Defense by reducing significantly the number of firms it must deal with directly.

Close connections are maintained between the large military contractors and the Department of Defense. Some are informal: many retired military officers of high rank are hired by large defense contractors, and some of the chief procurement officers of the Department of Defense are recruited from defense contractors. At more formal levels, the Department of Defense has established an Industrial Advisory Council, whose chief function is to help plan future defense-systems technology. Its membership is composed of representatives of the federal government and the large military contractors. Thus the contractors help to plan the very system on which they will be bidding (competitively) in the near future; their advantage over newcomers should be obvious.

A significant portion of the capital equipment used by military contractors is supplied by the federal government, almost $12 billion-worth in 1967. The private firms are allowed to make a profit on this capital, just as if it belonged to them. Some have illegally used it in producing for civilian markets, according to congressional investigations, but the firms still manage to get more contracts. Indeed, the symbiotic relationship between the Department of Defense and its primary contractors has caused such a proliferation of rules, procedures, and regulations that the big defense contractors take on increasingly the aspect of government arsenals and the procurement arm of the Department becomes more and more like a giant producing enterprise.

Finally, a high concentration of technically skilled persons are dependent on military production. According to Melman, "More than half of the nation's research and development budgets and manpower work for the military." [3] One out of five of all U.S. engineers work for the military or on military contracts, including 59 percent of the aeronautical engineers, and 22 percent of the mechanical and metallurgical engineers.

This concentration of military production locally, industrially and occupationally makes conversion from military to civilian production quite difficult. If government spending were shifted strongly from military needs to social, for example, education, health, and housing, different workers would be employed, in different localities. Fewer highly technical skills would be required, production would shift to less highly capital-intensive industries, and the locus of output would shift. All of these conversions would create significant structural changes in the economy, the work force, and the educational system. Although the level of aggregate demand could be maintained at high employment levels the transitional problems would still be great.

Realization of this fact has created a widespread pattern of support for military spending and sharp competition for military production contracts, not only by corporations but also by public officials and union leaders. There is competition for new contracts both to promote expansion and to maintain existing jobs and the other economic interests dependent upon them.

A political feedback is established. When jobs in military production become important, votes in Congress tend to support military appropriations. Thus, in 1966 to 1968, "normal" times before the large upsurge in antiwar sentiment, U.S. senators from states strongly dependent on military contracts were substantially more hawkish than senators from states with relatively

---

[3] Melman, *The New York Times*, June 7, 1970.

little defense employment.[4] These economic interests are fostered by the Department of Defense and by military contractors themselves. The Department maintains a corps of "political liaison" employees larger in number than the U.S. Senate and House Representatives combined. This lobbying effort is supplemented by that of the large military contractors and their trade associations. Labor union officials have also helped bring pressure on congressmen and senators when large contracts or installations were at stake.

When military production becomes important to an economy to the extent that has happened in the United States, with perhaps one in five employed persons dependent on that sector of the economy for his job and his status in society, a group of strong special economic interests develop around continuation of the policies that require large military expenditures. Wide general support for policies that require large military production can be expected to develop, which in turn makes possible the continuation of that heavy emphasis in the economy. Even though it may be quite feasible to organize the economy around a different emphasis, such a transition can become increasingly difficult. The great danger of militarization of the economy is that it can expand beyond the real need for it and continue longer than necessary.

THE MILITARY-INDUSTRIAL-ACADEMIC COMPLEX

Close relationships between the public and private sectors of the economy centering in the area of military production and foreign affairs have led to concern about the influence of a "military-industrial complex." President Dwight D. Eisenhower, in a speech to the nation on January 17, 1961, first used the term to describe the "conjunction of an immense military establishment and a large arms industry" whose influence is felt throughout the entire nation. "Our toil, resources, and livelihood are all involved, so is the very structure of our society," he said, cautioning that the nation must be on guard against unwarranted influence in the councils of government exercised by

---

[4] This is the result of a study made by the author. The states were divided into three groups. "Hawk" states were those whose work force had significantly greater employment in defense industries, on defense contracts, and in defense installations than the national average. "Neutral" states were not significantly different from the national average. "Dove" states were significantly below the national average in defense employment. Here is how their senators voted on issues involving support for or opposition to military programs.

Type of State	Percentage of U.S. Senate Votes Against Military Programs
Hawk	6
Neutral	28
Dove	21

the military-industrial complex. But Eisenhower went on to draw in the universities, calling attention to "the prospect of domination of the nation's scholars by federal employment, project allocations and the power of money." [5]

This military-industrial-academic complex can be best defined as "a natural coalition of interest groups with an economic, political, and professional stake in defense and space." [6] It includes the military officers whose responsibility is to assure preponderance of U.S. military power over any actual or potential enemies. It includes the large business firm with defense contracts. It includes the union whose members depend heavily on jobs in military production. It includes the local businessmen in areas where military production is an important support for the local economy. It includes the congressman concerned about the prosperity of his district, and about campaign contributions from local business and labor. It includes the university that does scientific research related to weapons, participates in overseas assistance programs, and receives funds for support of graduate students in a variety of fields associated with military, space, and international programs of the federal government.

Two important economic issues are involved. One concerns the problem of economic efficiency. A continuing series of congressional investigations and reports over the last fifteen years has uncovered serious inefficiency and waste in the procurement process. Profits on military production have traditionally been higher than in the civilian economy.[7] Significant errors in procurement programs have been made, on the side of both the Department of Defense and private contractors, which resulted in excessive costs and poor performance of the finished products.

The second issue concerns the influence of the military-industrial-academic complex over national policy in both international and domestic affairs. This is far more important, for it involves the social preferences that determine the mix of military and civilian production in the economy as a whole. Even if the military procurement system were highly efficient, producing high-quality weapons systems at minimum costs, the problem of national goals and their translation into economic terms would remain.

There are three chief positions on the question of the influence of the military-industrial complex on national policy. Military officers and corporate

[5] Address by President Dwight D. Eisenhower to the nation by television and radio, Jan. 17, 1961. Published in U.S. Department of State, *Bulletin*, Vol. 44, Feb. 6, 1961.

[6] Walter Adams, "The Military-Industrial Complex and the New Industrial State," *American Economic Review*, Vol. 58, No. 2 (May 1968), p. 655.

[7] This is a highly controversial statement that has been vigorously denied by the leading military production contractors, who present figures to show that their profits are lower than in the civilian sector. However, they include in the computations the value of the capital provided by the federal government. If that is excluded (as it should be), the profits made on military production, per dollar of private capital invested, are generally higher than in the civilian sector. This has been less true in the last few years, however, because of reforms in the procurement process triggered by congressional investigation.

officials generally argue that the civilian leaders determine policy and they merely carry it out. The radical (Marxist) position is that the military and industrial leaders use their position to make large economic gains at the expense of oppressed workers both at home and abroad. A third position rejects both of the others, arguing that the influence of the militarized sector of the economy has become so pervasive that it now influences, and perhaps dominates, all aspects of public economic policy. Let us examine each position.

Military leaders are undoubtedly correct when they argue that ultimate responsibility for public policy decisions rests with the President and Congress. The military may be very persuasive, and may be supported by lobbyists from big defense contractors, but the final decisions about budgets and programs are made by the national security managers, those political figures, administrators, and civil servants who hold top positions in the Department of Defense, State Department, Atomic Energy Commission, Central Intelligence Agency, and related agencies of government. They are the men who devise the strategies and defense systems Congress is subsequently asked to fund.

The national security managers, however, are drawn very heavily from the ranks of big business, large financial institutions, and the law firms that serve the business and financial community. A study sponsored by the Brookings Institution showed that 86 percent of the civilian heads of the military departments of the federal government were either businessmen or lawyers with a business practice. A more recent study by Gabriel Kolko showed that 60 percent of top foreign policy decision makers came from big business, the investment sector, and law. Another study by Richard Barnet showed that 70 out of 91 civilians in top national defense positions had backgrounds in big business or high finance. Perhaps this situation is only natural, for administrators with experience in handling large organizations are needed in the national defense portion of the public sector, and they can be found more readily in big business than elsewhere. But the result is that the national security managers are drawn largely from the business elite and have the viewpoints that dominate that group. Few have ever held elected political positions, which means that their views have never been tested against those of the general electorate. Finally, the general policies and viewpoints that the national security managers bring to their jobs undoubtedly are similar to those of the military leadership and the large defense contractors. No. It is not enough to argue that civilians make the final decisions. The U.S. political economy has evolved in such a way that those chosen to make strategic decisions about military and international affairs share the values that lead to large expenditures on military and military-related programs.

This last point would seem to lend support to the exploitation theory advanced by some leftists. That theory sees the military-industrial complex as the portion of the domestic economy that most obviously gains from an imperialist foreign policy. At home, it is argued, the costs of militarism are borne by young men drafted into the armed forces, by workers generally who find their apparent economic gains eaten up by wartime inflation, and by low-income workers (especially blacks). Those who gain are the wealthy owners of big corporations and giant financial institutions. This argument maintains that a restricted few benefit while the costs are paid by the many.

This position has a certain plausibility. There are important economic interests that profit from military production. It is undeniable that the aerospace industry, the petroleum industry, the electronics industry, and much of the nation's research and development effort are directly or indirectly supported by military spending. These industries must also be financed, and a variety of financial institutions have become involved with their continued prosperity.

The point should not be pushed too far, however. It would be hard to identify large economic gains from the wars in Korea and Southeast Asia to firms other than direct military contractors. For the rest of the economy, including big business, the examples of Japan and Germany show that a private enterprise economy dominated by big business does not require large military expenditures for sustained prosperity and economic growth. Private economic interests could gain just as much from an economy devoted to peaceful productive effort.

The third view of the U.S. political economy seems much more plausible. A militarized economy affects all Americans. The jobs and economic security of some are directly created by military spending, and for others indirectly. The economic payoff is widespread. Only when that payoff stopped after 1965 or 1966, with escalation of the Southeast Asia war and its attendant manpower draft, higher taxes, and inflation, did public opposition to the war become important. As long as the economic costs could be held to low levels while jobs and prosperity continued, there was not a great deal of antiwar sentiment. Viewed in this fashion, the military-industrial-academic complex is seen only as that sector of the economy that has the most obvious interest in continuance of military production. Economic benefits to many others flow from the same source. Government decisions in the national security area reflect these interests.

This discussion of the militarized economy must close on a note of paradox. The economic interests of the ordinary American lead him to support continuation of the existing division of economic effort and resources between military and civilian production. This is in part because of the benefits derived from high levels of employment, and in part because of the threat to his security that a large economic change might bring. On the other hand, he doesn't want large-scale war because he (and his sons) must bear the cost. A militarized economy is fine, but not active war.

The economist might argue that the ordinary American could have just as much economic security and greater welfare if only the nation were seriously to explore alternative methods of sustaining world order that did not require great armaments expenditures. But that would require a rather large wrench in thinking and in values that is not likely to come when people are relatively well satisfied by the existing economic system; in Germany and Japan it required a great military disaster to cause such a shift.

SOME CONCLUSIONS

This chapter has ended on a pessimistic note, implying that for the foreseeable future the American economy will retain its strong emphasis on military and military-related spending, not because a few special interests benefit but because much of the economy has come to depend on it. There is sure to be sharp disagreement about that judgment.

But beyond that immediate point there is a far more significant one. An economy in which government plays an important role develops feedbacks from public policy to the economy and back again to public policy. These relationships may be mutually supportive, such as, for example, those between big business and big government explored in Chapter 33 and those described in this chapter's discussion of the military-industrial-academic complex. Public and private interests may also be in conflict, which is the usual interpretation of the relationship between government and business. Whatever the relationship, in today's mixed economy the policies of government affect the economy and the economy affects government policies. In this sense, contemporary economics shades gradually into the study of a new type of political economy in which the sharp dividing lines between economics and politics become blurred. The economics of war and defense is only one example of that trend.

A related point should also be noted. Whether the discussion in this chapter centered on the economics of full wartime mobilization, or limited wars, or large military spending, an underlying theme was the way in which psychological factors influenced choices among the alternatives open to policy makers. A complex set of changing relationships exists among public policy, economy, and public opinion. The social psychology of emotion-laden topics like war and national security creates another range of effects and feedbacks that influence economic policy.

Summary

A wartime economy must shift resources from civilian to military uses while creating as little opposition to the war as possible. A long war also channels investment into the military sector at the expense of the civilian sector.

Wartime mobilization is usually accomplished by centrally directed production planning. Primary reliance on the market system to reallocate resources is avoided because it would be inflationary: taxes cannot be used to reduce civilian demand enough to avoid inflation because they reduce public support for the war and diminish work incentives. A military draft is used to keep down costs, thereby shifting a significant portion of the real costs of the war from taxpayers to youths.

Inflation is the inevitable result of the wartime political economy. It can be held in check by bond drives, rationing, and price control; and some unregulated sectors of the economy can absorb a portion of the excess purchasing power, but at best the bulk of the inflationary pressures can only be postponed and not eliminated.

The problem of limited wars is similar, but on a reduced scale. The United States government has tried to mobilize resources for limited wars very largely by reallocating federal expenditures and incurring large deficits. Tight money has also been used to reduce civilian production. But reluctance to use production allocations, rationing, and price control brought strong inflationary pressures.

In the modern economy, preparation for war and sustenance of large military and military-related programs develop a strong dependence on the military sector. The militarized economy tends to develop vested interests in continuing the military emphasis, interests that have been termed the military-industrial-academic complex. A broad base of support for continued large military spending is created that makes a shift away from the militarized economy difficult to accomplish.

Problems in the public economy focus very heavily on the crisis in urban areas. America is becoming more heavily urbanized, which indicates that cities are a vital and important element in an economy growing toward greater affluence. Yet at the same time our cities are sick. The paradox of urban growth and urban pathology rests on the conflicts and economic disparities of the economic forces that generate cities. When we view cities and their relationship to the economy as a whole, we can analyze the economic factors that create urban growth and its spread. When we view cities as social organizations, we can analyze the sources of their problems. The pathology lies in the latter area, the dynamism in the former.

THE NATURE OF CITIES

In 1299 a Venetian fleet made the first successful commercial voyage between the Mediterranean Sea and Northern Europe. Using the compass, a device imported from China only shortly before, the fleet was able to sail far out into the Atlantic and avoid the storms that heretofore had shattered the frail sailing ships of that day against the rocky shores of Spain and France. This great breakthrough in transportation enabled merchants to ship by sea instead of over land. They settled in their home cities instead of traveling in groups to places of trade and commerce, and the era of the merchant house began to supersede the age of traveling traders. These changes marked the beginning of cities as the economic centers we know in Western civilization.

The first urban crisis came quickly. A phenomenal growth of urban populations occurred in the first half of the fourteenth century, particularly in the cities of northern Italy and those portions of Europe adjacent to the North Sea. In an era when little was understood about sanitation, when urban governments were rudimentary, and when cities were restricted to the narrow confines of walled towns, the growth of urban populations created the conditions conducive to disease and plague. In 1347, hardly a half century after the urban population explosion began, the first wave of plague struck. The Black Death swept through Europe, first decimating the urban population and then spreading to the countryside as people fled the cities, carrying the disease with them. In the next half

The
Economics
of Cities

42

century successive epidemics wiped out one-third to one-half of Europe's population.

Perhaps the Black Death would have come anyway. But its virulence and spread was fostered by the intimate symbiosis of rats and humans in the early cities. Rats multiplied in the filthy cities, became infected with the plague from rats apparently arriving in trading vessels from Asia, and were bitten by lice that then bit people, and the plague was transferred to the human. The disease was conquered only when improved sewage and sanitation systems were developed, together with immunity that arose among the survivors. London, for example, installed its first underground sewers shortly after the Black Death plague.

The medieval cities were small, having 5,000 to 50,000 population in the fifteenth century, for the most part; but they already illustrated in microcosm the essential characteristics of modern cities. They were centers of commerce and administration for surrounding areas. The larger ones manufactured products for export to other regions. Urban growth created suburbs beyond the city walls. And the typical urban social structure appeared: wealthy families who dominated the economic life of the cities and controlled their government, workers who were employed for wages in the business and commercial establishments, and a population of criminals and near-criminals who made up the urban underworld. Extremes of poverty and wealth were just as prevalent then as now, and medieval cities periodically erupted in violence emerging from social strife. Cities five hundred years ago were smaller than today, but they exhibited all of the basic economic and social characteristics of the modern metropolis. The chief difference is that today the problems affect far more people and a much greater proportion of the population.

URBAN GROWTH TODAY

The United States is becoming increasingly urbanized. Over the years, a larger proportion of a growing population is found in cities. Almost 75 percent of the U.S. population lives in places characterized as urban by the Bureau of the Census, according to 1970 figures. The proportion was just over 50 percent only a half century ago, in 1920 (see Table 42-1). During that 50 years the nation's population more than doubled from about 92 million to about 205 million. All but about 6 million of the increase was in urban areas.

TABLE 42-1
The Shifting U.S. Population
(Millions of Persons)

Type	1920	1970	Increase
Urban	47	154	107
Rural	45	51	6
Total	92	205	113

Cities in the United States have been growing not only in size of population, but also in area. Every year some 400 thousand to 500 thousand acres of land are converted to urban uses. In fact, the urbanized area has been growing more rapidly than the urbanized population, indicating that the density of population in our cities has been decreasing. Two trends have been at work simultaneously. Urban areas are growing and they are becoming more decentralized.

Urban growth is apparently the result of greater economic advantages within large metropolitan areas. A large city is more self-contained than a small city. When a city has a large and diverse population, a furniture factory, for example, can market its output nearby. If it were located in a smaller city, it would have to market a large portion of its output elsewhere, thereby incurring transportation costs that a big city producer would not incur. Multiply this example many times for a wide variety of products and services, and it is apparent that the larger the city, the greater the possibilities for such economies.

These advantages have a qualitative dimension as well. A small city may not generate enough consumer demand for symphony concerts or ballet to support an orchestra or dance company. But a large city will be able to support these and other activities simply because there are enough people around to provide adequate support for them. The diversity of products, services, and activities generated in a large city provide a larger number of alternatives to the individual consumer than are available in a smaller city. As we have already pointed out, a larger number of alternatives for the consumer is generally associated with greater opportunities for him to maximize his welfare.

From the point of view of both the producer and the consumer, then, the larger the city, the greater the economic advantages. For this reason we can expect the trend toward increased urbanization to continue. Even if the nation's population were to remain constant, the economies attendant on urban growth would draw people into urban areas.

Are There Limits?

The economic advantages due to urban growth do not appear to diminish as metropolitan areas become larger, although the evidence on this point is not conclusive. On the other hand, the disadvantages of larger cities become more important as their size increases. Some are physical problems, such as air pollution, refuse disposal, traffic congestion, water supply, and other public facility difficulties. Although the economic relationships of urban life may push toward greater size, existing technology may limit the optimum size for a water supply system or a refuse disposal system. Pushed beyond those limits by urban growth, the public facilities may be forced to operate on a scale that is highly inefficient.

Huge metropolitan areas may also create disadvantages from the standpoint of human values. Anonymity and impersonality are characteristic qualities of urban life that seem to become greater as the size of cities grows. Cities are hotter than the countryside during the summer months, because buildings and pavements absorb heat during the day and radiate it after sundown. These psychological and physical discomforts tend to counterbalance the economic advantages in larger cities.

Whatever the reasons, the large metropolitan areas like New York, Chicago, and Los Angeles tend to grow less rapidly than the smaller and medium-sized metropolitan areas. In the smaller cities the economic advantages have not yet pushed the population and the area to the size at which the psychological and social disadvantages are significant influences in holding back further growth.

DECENTRALIZATION WITHIN URBAN AREAS

As our urban areas have grown, the importance of the center has declined. Suburbs have expanded and satellite cities have emerged around central cities. Inside the central cities, blighted areas around the core have developed and downtown business areas have declined. What sometimes appear to be rings of growth around a decaying center is a characteristic pattern of many urban regions.

Decentralization within cities is hard to measure, but there are several indications of a persistent trend away from the center. For example, in the 1960 census there were 59.4 million persons in the central cities of our metropolitan areas. That number increased to 62.2 million in 1970, a growth of less than 5 percent. The metropolitan area suburbs grew by over 25 percent in the same period, however, from 59.6 million to 74.9 million. The proportion of metropolitan area populations in the central cities fell from 49.9 percent to 46.1 percent.

Jobs have migrated to the outskirts along with people. At this writing data for comparison are not available from the 1970 census, but Table 42–2 shows some earlier comparisons of the proportion of jobs in metropolitan areas that were located in central cities rather than suburbs.

TABLE 42–2
Proportion of Employment in Central Cities, 18 U.S. Metropolitan Areas, 1948–58
(Percentage)

Type	1948	1958
Manufacturing production workers	70 *	60
Wholesale trade employees	89	82
Retail trade employees	79	72
Service employees	86	80

Source: Edward L. Ullman, "The Nature of Cities Reconsidered," in William H. Leahy et al. (ed.), *Urban Economics: Theory, Development and Planning* (New York: The Free Press, 1970), p. 9.
* Data for 1947

Changes in the technology of production, transportation, and communication lie behind the decentralization within cities. During the railroad era a premium was placed on central city locations. Railroad passenger stations brought people into the central downtown area. Freight terminals brought raw materials in and made a central location for manufacturing plants economical, particularly since finished products could be shipped nationwide from a single plant.

With the development of mass-production assembly-line technology, the situation began to change. Large single-level plants laid out to encompass continuous-flow processes required extensive acreage that was available only in the suburbs. Some early illustrations of that trend were the manufacture of railroad cars at Pullman, Illinois (1880), the establishment of the huge United States Steel Corp. plant at Gary, Indiana (1906), and the moves of Ford Motor Co. from Detroit, first to Highland Park (1909) and then to Dearborn, Michigan (1917–20).

Early moves to the suburbs were facilitated by the introduction of streetcars and interurban electric trains in the 1880s and 1890s, a mode of transportation that tended to create radial corridors of suburbs extending out from the central city. Motor transportation was the most important technological change, however. It opened up all areas within short motor trips for both residences and industrial locations. Transportation was freed from the rigid constraints of rail or streetcar lines. Parking lots for employees' cars became necessary, putting even greater stress on large acreage and suburban locations. Hilly and wooded sites became available for residences. The automobile and motor truck made possible both a greater geographical spread and a wider number of alternatives for residential and industrial development.

Other technological changes facilitated urban decentralization. The telephone made possible a communication network suited to wide decentralization. The motion picture enabled recreation to be dispersed into outlying neighborhoods. Television brought the dispersal of entertainment still further, right into the individual household.

All of these technological changes have promoted low-density development as well as geographic dispersal. Single-story factories rather than multiple-story ones are the rule, usually surrounded by open areas for parking and truck pickup and delivery. One- and two-story residences are the rule rather than high-rise apartments, although high-rise buildings do prevail in areas where land is limited by natural features, as on Manhattan Island in New York.

We find, then, two types of economic forces at work in creating the modern city. On the one hand, economic advantages draw people and economic activities into urban areas. On the other hand, the technologies of production, transportation, and communication promote decentralization within urban areas.

Decline of the Central Business District

As urban areas become decentralized, the central business districts of central cities lose their functions and tend to deteriorate. This process has been particularly noticeable in the quarter century since World War II. The movement of people to the suburbs brought a shift outward in retail trade to shopping centers and large branch department stores. As downtown shopping lessened, a variety of supporting services such as eating places and movie theaters closed or moved outward also. These trends were promoted in most large cities by the geographical fact that central business districts were no longer the city's geographical center. Most U.S cities developed on water and growth was more in one direction than another. In Chicago, for example, the lake location made it impossible for growth to take place eastward. In St. Louis, the Mississippi River acted as a similar barrier. Lopsided growth took away the central aspect from central business districts.

Contributing to the decline of central business districts was the growth of a deteriorating ring of slums and blighted areas around them. In some instances, these were industrial areas built up a century or more in the past in what was then the suburban countryside. They became obsolete, however, as the economy and technology changed; the Chicago stockyards are a classic example. In part the blighted areas were the outcome of speculation and land taxation practices. As central business districts grew and land values rose, speculators bought land in the path of development and held it for appreciation; they were often abetted by low property taxes that enabled them to buy and hold for substantial periods of time. When further development of the central business district was required, the land held by speculators was too expensive, so builders jumped over that area to buy less expensive land further out, leaving a permanent ring around the business center that ultimately became slums and blighted areas. On Manhattan Island in New York, for example, the intensively developed financial district at the southern end of Manhattan is separated by several miles of relatively low-density development from the central commercial district that starts at about 42nd Street, which was developed later. In Detroit, the first stage of growth of the downtown business district stopped at Grand Circus Plaza, to begin again several miles further north in the area now occupied by the Fisher and General Motors buildings. Almost every big city shows the effect of this pattern of development.

When the move to the suburbs came on a large scale after World War II, the central business districts themselves began to deteriorate, leaving a central core of commercial areas whose principal functions were being lost, and an already deteriorated and blighted ring of slums.

Central business districts have not lost all of their functions, however, and many of them retain a strong vitality. They are changing to emphasize increasingly the administrative and financial services required by the areas they serve. New York is a national and international center for those services. Washington is a national governmental services center. Chicago performs a similar function for the entire Midwest, and Los Angeles for the Pacific Coast. Regional administrative-financial-governmental centers are emerging in Boston, Atlanta, Dallas, Detroit, St. Louis, Kansas City, Minneapolis–St. Paul, Seattle, San Francisco, Denver and other metropolitan areas. In all of these cities, a shift away from retail trade and related activities in the central business districts is being countered by growth of the downtown as an administrative and financial center. Old functions decline, to be replaced in part by newer ones.

CITIES AS CENTRAL PLACES

A characteristic feature of cities has always been the performance of a variety of functions for a surrounding territory. Some of these central place functions serve only a small population, such as a general store in a small village of several hundred people. Other central place functions serve a larger group, such as the legal and administrative work of a county seat, where an economical size requires a served population of perhaps 25,000. We can carry the analysis of central place functions to still larger units. For example, the Midwestern United States could be expected to generate a large urban center providing administrative, financial, governmental, and other services for the entire region between the Allegheny Mountains and the Rocky Mountains. Chicago performs those functions. It is located on the lower tip of Lake Michigan because of transportation advantages; but even without those special considerations there would have been a large urban center somewhere near the center of that great region anyway. Lesser central places serving subareas of the region have also grown up, and still smaller cities in sectors of the subareas, right down to county seats and market hamlets. In each case, central functions are performed for a surrounding area, and the size of the city is determined very heavily by the type of central functions performed and the size of the population in the complementary area.

Transportation routes and costs help to determine the area for which a city performs central functions. A good example is the port of Baltimore during the heyday of the railroad era, say 1880 to 1940. Its trade "hinterland" from which goods were exported and to which imports came from abroad was defined by relative costs of transportation to and from inland areas, compared with other ports on the east coast of the United States. That area was served by the lines of the Baltimore and Ohio Railroad, developed by Baltimore business and financial interests. The economics of transport costs served to channel the development of a railroad enterprise along lines that enabled the port's central place function to be performed.

The concept of central places helps to explain the location of cities and the pattern of a hierarchy of cities arranged over the area of a nation or region. It also helps to explain why the system of cities changes, for the types of central functions change, the population of the complementary areas grows and shifts, and transportation technology and costs change. Central place functions give cities the qualities of both stability and change.

CITIES AS EXPORT CENTERS

Many cities grew up originally around manufacturing industries whose products were exported from the city to other parts of the national or world economies. Many examples come immediately to mind: steel from Pittsburgh, automobiles from Detroit, whiskey from Peoria, movies from Los Angeles, cameras from Rochester, aircraft from Seattle, ships from Pascagoula, insurance services from Hartford, clothing from New York. Almost every substantial city has one or more important export products it provides to other areas. Together with central place functions, the export industries of cities define a large portion of their activities.

The export base generates complementary industries that either provide inputs into the export sector or process the output still further. For example, the automobile industry in and around Detroit has stimulated the growth of steel manufacturing in plants that produce the steel used in cars. It has brought to the area rubber tire factories, plants manufacturing machine tools and automobile parts, and firms that haul the finished automobiles to market. These complementary industries have diversified further, becoming export industries themselves, in part. Rubber products, machine tools, machinery, foundry products, and plastics are shipped elsewhere as well as to the auto plants within the region.

These export industries and their complements require a large supporting base of other industries that supply both products and services to workers and business firms. These are the industries that provide food, clothing, shelter, and services to the city itself and enable it to function as a viable unit. Many of these products and services are imported from other areas, but many are produced locally.

As cities grow in size, the market provided by the local population tends to absorb more and more of the output of its export industries and their complements. Some industries that may have exported substantial amounts of output to other areas now find that they can sell all of their product within their own metropolitan area. To supply other markets they can establish branch plants. Indeed, the larger the urban area the greater is the tendency for self-sufficiency. A small city is usually far more dependent on its exports than a large city, while the large city carries on more of its business within itself. As cities grow, they tend to become less dependent on their export base and rely more on their own internal markets.

A city of 10,000 population typically has about one-third of its employment in jobs related to supplying and servicing its own population, with two-thirds employed in the export and related industries. These proportions gradually shift as the city becomes larger. A city of 500,000 is about evenly divided between the two types of activities, while a city of 10 million persons will have about two-thirds of its employment in industries depending on sales within itself and only one-third in the export sector. Table 42–3 shows the general relationship, based on data from the 1940 and 1950 censuses.

TABLE 42–3
Proportion of Total Employment Dependent on Demand Internal to the Metropolitan Area

Population	Percentage of "Internal" Employment
10,000	32
100,000	43
500,000	50
1,000,000	54
10,000,000	65

Source: Edward L. Ullman and Michael F. Dacey, "The Minimum Requirements Approach to the Urban Economic Base," *Papers and Proceedings of the Regional Science Association,* 1960, pp. 175–94.

The tendency of large cities to become self-contained has been strengthened by the growth of motor transportation. In the railroad era, raw materials were brought to a city's export industries through the low-cost bulk transport facilities of railroads. The finished products were then distributed nationally by rail. This technology fostered the growth of single centers of production, like steel in Pittsburgh and whiskey in Peoria.

The advent of the motor truck and good highways changed the relative locational advantages of manufacturing industries, however. Assembly of bulky inputs by rail remains feasible almost anywhere. But finished products distributed by truck can be handled most economically within a 450-mile radius of the factory. The result has been the dispersal of production in industry after industry into regional branch plants located away from the central plant that at one time may have shipped to the entire country. To this change in transport costs can be added the growth of population, which has increased the size of the market in the various regions of the country to make large branch factories economically feasible. Thus, in the largest cities there has been a relative decline in the importance of export industries because of both dispersal of production and the greater self-sufficiency characteristic of growing metropolitan areas. Other cities, meanwhile, have been taking on more of the function of export centers to complement their role as central places for their areas.

CITIES AS SOCIAL ORGANIZATIONS

Although cities are formed by economic forces, they are made up of people. Cities are social organizations within which people interact with other people, earn their livings, and work out their individual destinies. As social organizations, cities not only reflect the activities of people, but also channel those activities. Urban life is carried on within the framework offered by the city, within the opportunities and constraints of the economic life of the city, and under the influence of the city as a functioning social unit. If the urban economy offers opportunities, it offers them to people; if it has problems, it creates

CITIES AS EXPORT CENTERS: SOME EXAMPLES

We can understand the location of steel production in the Pittsburgh region. The costs of assembling nearby coal, local limestone, and iron ore from the upper Lake Superior region were minimized there. But why did automobile production center in Detroit and the movie industry in Hollywood?

The early automobiles were essentially buggies equipped with internal combustion engines. Both technologies were brought together in Detroit. Buggy-making was located in Michigan because there were nearby supplies of hardwood lumber. Machine shops, essential in making engines, were located in Detroit to serve the lake shipping industry, and had excess capacity because of the seasonal nature of the industry. Much capital came from the declining lumber industry, seeking new investment opportunities. Local entrepreneurs brought all of these elements together.

Hollywood provides a more interesting story. Movie making began in New York, at the nation's theatrical center. But the early cameras were patented and royalties had to be paid for their use. To escape these costs, some producers went to New Jersey, but that proved to be too close to New York lawyers and legal proceedings: injunctions could be obtained before the shooting of the film was completed. Cuba was tried next, but it proved to be inconvenient as well as too near New York. Finally, the Los Angeles area was selected. It was 3,000 miles from New York courts, and injunctions could be avoided by skipping quickly across the border into Mexico. Dry sunny weather for outdoor film-making was a minor factor. By the time the camera patents were invalidated the industry had found a home there. The financial center of the industry remained in New York, however.

problems for people. We sometimes lose sight of this aspect of the urban economy, for cities are often impersonal and cold, and people can function within them with a high degree of anonymity. Indeed, this is perhaps the greatest paradox of urban life: the city as a social unit brings vast numbers of people together to achieve goals requiring a high degree of coordination of individual activities, yet individual relationships are generally the impersonal ones of an exchange economy. Privacy within crowds is the characteristic attribute of the city.

The Three Nations

The population of any large metropolitan area can be divided into three distinct groups, based on average family income. At the top are the relatively affluent, with annual family incomes of $15,000 or more. Relatively few in number, they make up perhaps 5 to 10 percent of the urban population in the typical metropolis. At the bottom are the poor, those families with annual incomes below $7,500. In a large metropolitan area, they compose about 20 percent of the population. In the middle are the neither affluent nor poor, those families whose annual incomes are between $7,500 and $15,000. They are the bulk of the urban population, about 70 to 75 percent of the total.

In the economic geography of cities, these three income groups generally live apart from each other. The homes of the affluent tend to cluster together in the more desirable areas: in wooded or hilly terrain, near lakes or the shore, or in "gold coast" or "blue stocking" apartment house areas adjacent to the downtown area. The poor, on the other hand tend to crowd into the slums and blighted areas that ring the downtown, often immediately adjacent to industrial areas. The great majority in the middle income range fill out the rest of the metropolitan area.

The boundaries of the areas occupied by the affluent and the poor are clearly defined, although they may shift as changes in population and income occur. This does not mean that there are no affluent or poor families living in areas that are largely occupied by the middle-income majority. There are. But it does mean that there are areas that are occupied almost exclusively by the poor, others almost exclusively by the rich, and others dominated by middle-income families. It is as if the city were made up of three nations, one affluent, one poor, and one in between the extremes, each with clearly defined boundaries.

To illustrate this phenomenon, Figure 42-1 shows a simplified map of the Chicago metropolitan area. It shows the approximate built-up area (almost 7 million population) as well as the limits of the city (about 3⅓ million population). It also shows the industrial districts and downtown business district that support the economic life of the whole metropolitan area. Finally, it also shows the boundaries of the three nations. The affluent live primarily along the north shore suburban lakefront, with a secondary concentration in the high-rise apartment section just to the north of the downtown area on the lake shore; there are also several scattered affluent communities in the western and southern suburbs. The poor live in large areas of old housing around the downtown area, very often close to industrial areas, and in some scattered regions to the south of the city that are also near industrial development. The middle-income majority occupy the bulk of the area and dominate the suburbs spreading to the west, north, and south of the city.

The three income groups of today's cities seldom associate with each other outside of their economic relationships. They may come into contact with each other at work, or when shopping downtown, or at places of entertainment, or while traveling, but at home persons in each group associate with

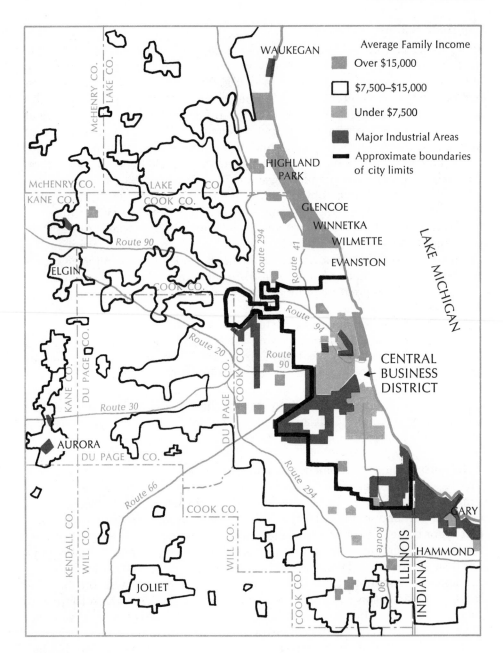

FIGURE 42-1
Chicago: The Three Nations

others who are relatively similar in income and status. With all of the diversity and the extremes of income of a modern city, the place of residence is a refuge among others largely of one's own kind.

Five Cultures

Economic disparities are complicated by cultural differences in American cities. We used to think of cities as great melting pots, in which people of many different nationalities and cultural backgrounds were "Americanized," becoming essentially similar to other Americans in their basic attitudes and values. The city was seen, in this view, as part of a socializing process that tended to produce a homogeneous population that could live in harmony together because almost everyone shared the same culture.

Recent sociological studies and surveys of attitudes and beliefs have changed that view. Even the historians and sociologists who most strongly advocated the "melting pot" theory of urban life now recognize that the typical American city is the home of at least four and perhaps five cultural patterns, each distinguished by different attitudes and value systems. Rather than being characterized by cultural harmony, the American city is characterized by cultural differences and potential cultural antagonisms and strife.

The five cultures are distinguished primarily by racial and religious differences, and each came to the United States at a different time during the various waves of immigration and migration affecting the United States. They are:

1. White–Protestant.
2. White–Catholic.
3. White–Jewish.
4. Black–Protestant.
5. Latin–Catholic.

The five cultures are distinguished by different patterns of attitudes and values concerning such topics as the family, religion, the role of the state and political authority, wealth and affluence as a goal, social mobility, and education. Social psychologists not only find consistent patterns of attitudes and values, they find that an individual's racial and religious background is strongly associated with those patterns. Just as income status helps to define one's behavior, so a person's background of race and religion strongly influence his values.

Before the era of large-scale immigration that began after 1830, the predominant values and attitudes were those of the white–Protestant culture, which characterized the great bulk of the earlier immigrants to the North American colonies and the early United States. The roots of the black–Protestant culture were present, however, among the slaves of the South and the few free blacks of the North. The era of large-scale immigration from 1830 to 1910 brought a wide variety of newer national groups, a large influx of Catholics, and a smaller immigration of Jews, particularly from eastern and southern Europe after the Civil War. The immigrants were segregated to a greater or lesser degree in the urban ghettos of our great cities. Here their cultural, racial, and national cohesiveness was strengthened rather than weakened by the fact of segregation. These loyalties were maintained as many of them rose up and out of the ghettos to form homogeneous subcommunities within the larger city. Even today many nationality-religious neighborhoods remain as distinctive enclaves. Dispersal, of course, has followed, but a large portion of the cultural differences remain as white Protestants, Catholics, and Jews intermingle in the vast areas occupied by the middle-income majority.

More recently, the urban ghettos have been occupied by blacks and Latins, and a similar process of strengthening their distinctive cultural patterns through segregation has occurred. The migration of blacks from the South began on a large scale only after immigration was slowed by legislation after 1910 and after the decline of cotton culture forced them out of Southern agriculture. Latin migration has been more recent, occurring after World War II from the southwestern states, Puerto Rico and Caribbean and Central American areas. These are the groups that now make up the majority of the poor in the urban ghettos.

Conflict in the Cities

When American cities are analyzed in terms of income levels and cultural patterns, the current problems of conflict and antagonism can be more clearly understood. The affluent are predominantly white Protestant, with a sprinkling of white Catholics and white Jews. The great middle-income majority is a mixture of all three of those groups, but each has a tendency toward keeping itself separate from the others and each tends to retain a somewhat different set of attitudes and values. Conflict among those groups can often be acrimonious, as, for example, in the current conflicts over state aid for parochial schools and the liberalization of abortion laws. Finally, there is the American under class, distinguished by poverty, by race, and by cultural differences in attitudes, values, and way of life. Conflict, not harmony, is inherent in the economic and cultural differences. The American city is not made up of a homogeneous population with common economic interests and cultural values.

THE ECONOMICS OF THE GHETTO

Urban poverty areas are set apart from the rest of the city by the ways in which the ghetto relates to the economy, as well as by their location. The ghetto economy is, in some ways, a world apart from the relatively affluent, progressive economy that surrounds the ghetto. It is a permanently depressed area, with inadequate sources of income, that does not participate significantly in the economic growth of the rest of the nation. There is a steady drain of income and resources from the ghetto, sustained only by continuing injections of welfare payments and other income transfers from government. The poverty of the ghetto tends to reinforce itself by creating conditions that perpetuate poverty. And although some individuals are able to move up the economic ladder out of the ghetto, others drop down into it, and the system continues even though the individuals may change. Racial attitudes have helped to create and sustain the urban ghettos, but economic relationships perpetuate it.

Permanent Depression

The urban ghettos are permanently depressed. Unemployment rates average two to three times those of the rest of the economy. When national unemployment rates are 5 percent, the rate in the urban ghettos ranges upward from 10 and 15 percent. A very large portion of the hard-core unemployed are ghetto residents: they are the ones most easily discouraged, who don't seek work because little is to be found. Many ghetto workers are employed only part time, further adding to the unemployment problem.

When they are employed, ghetto workers generally work for low wages and often in menial occupations. If we take the U.S. Department of Labor's minimum health and decency income for a family of four as a standard, about two-thirds to three-quarters of all employed persons in the central city ghettos earn wages that would not provide that income even if they were employed full time during the year. The percentage will vary from city to city, but the fact remains that the ghetto is the home of the working poor.

The low wages of the working poor are kept low in two ways. First, the high unemployment rates of the ghetto provide a group of surplus workers whose presence in the market keeps wages from rising. Second, crowding of blacks, Latins, and other minority groups into the low-wage, menial occupations keeps down productivity at the margin for those who are employed.

The low-wage occupations are primarily in the service industries on which the other parts of the urban economy rest. They include hospital services, food services, retail trade, laundries and cleaning services, hotels and motels, and related activities. Low wages in those occupations enable the great middle-income majority to pay less for those services than they would have to pay if the urban ghettos and their poverty could be eliminated. The chief economic function of the urban ghetto is to provide a low-wage labor force for the rest of the city.

The Drain of Resources

One of the things that keeps the ghetto economy poor is a continuous drain of resources and income out of the ghetto and into the more affluent economy outside. Largely unmeasured and perhaps unmeasurable, the outflow includes savings, physical capital, human resources, and income.

The savings of ghetto residents, however small they may be, flow into banks and other financial institutions, which then lend the money primarily to borrowers outside the ghetto. The income of ghetto residents is used to buy goods produced outside the ghetto, in stores usually owned by persons who live outside the ghetto, whose employees are often residents of other areas. Physical capital flows outward largely through housing. The ghetto landlord lets his property deteriorate, taking in cash the funds that otherwise would be used to maintain the property. A similar pattern often prevails with public facilities, inadequate maintenance being one way that physical resources are shifted out of poor areas by city governments. Finally, human capital is drained out by the movement of some of the better-educated young people into the more progressive sectors of the economy.

In most communities the drain of resources and income is compensated by a counterflow of resources based on the export sector of the community's economy. That sector is largely absent in the ghetto. Its chief export is low-wage labor, and much of that is unemployed or partially employed. The drain of resources and income from the ghetto is countered by continuous injections of transfer payments from the rest of the economy. The welfare system, unemployment compensation, old age benefits, medical assistance payments and other income transfers provide about $10 billion annually to sustain the urban ghettos. Without those transfers the level of life in the poor areas of our cities would be considerably lower and the poverty considerably worse.

The Permanent Ghetto

The population of the ghettos is not static. Migration brings in a continual stream of people from rural areas. This was particularly true in the 1950s, as a result of the mechanization of Southern agriculture. This migration continues, with the stream varying in size, from such sources as Puerto Rico, the rural and small-town South, and the Spanish-speaking Southwest.

Technological change is also a source of the ghetto population. Displacement of workers through automation is felt particularly by blacks and other minority groups. Displaced white workers are often able to move into other jobs lower down in the wage scale, with those finally displaced being those at the bottom of the work force. They are usually black or Latin or from other minorities, and many of them are young men and women who have the least work experience.

On the other hand, many ghettoites work their way out through the educational system and the high-wage sectors of the economy. Since many ghettoites are from racial minority groups, however, the barriers to outward movement are strong.

Whether the ghettos expand or contract is the result of these conflicting forces. During the 1950s, when technological change was rapid and unemployment rates were rising, the population and area of our urban ghettos expanded rapidly in numbers and a little less rapidly in area. The accumulating economic and social tensions that developed were in large part responsible for the urban revolts and riots that began in 1964 and have continued sporadically since then. In recent years, however, the growth of the ghettos has slowed down, and in some of our large cities the population density of the ghettos seems to have declined. The ghetto area has expanded more rapidly than the ghetto population in those cities.

The Ghetto as an Economic Subsystem

The urban ghetto should be thought of as a subsystem within the larger economy. It has functional ties to the rest of the economy, but the ghetto is set apart from the mainstream by its characteristic income flows and population movements. We can summarize this combination of separateness and functional relationship to the larger economy in the form of a simplified systems analysis of the urban ghetto, as diagramed in Figure 42-2.

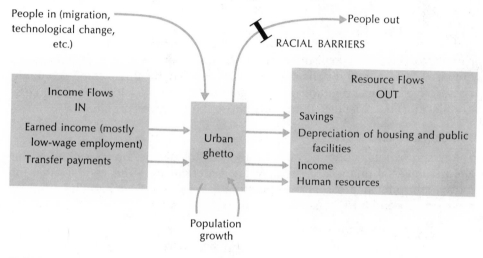

FIGURE 42-2
The Urban Ghetto as an Economic Subsystem

The size of the urban ghetto is determined by the following flows: population growth within the ghetto; the flow of people inward as a result of migration, technological change, and other causes; and the flow of people outward who can overcome racial barriers. The relative poverty of the ghetto is determined by the relationship between the flow of resources outward to the affluent sectors of the economy, on the one hand, and the inward income flows, mostly from low-wage employment and transfer payments, on the other hand.

The ghetto, then, is a quasi-enclave within the larger economy. It is exploited in two ways. First, it provides the economy with a permanent supply of low-wage labor. Second, the outflow of resources benefits economic interests outside the ghetto. Together with the racial attitudes characteristic of the white Protestant-Catholic-Jewish cultures outside the ghetto, these economic relationships explain the special characteristics of the depressed areas of the central cities.

SICK CITIES

America's urban areas are plagued by problems. To some, the problems appear to be specific ones: traffic congestion, air pollution, inadequate water supplies, insufficient parks and recreational facilities, overburdened police and fire protection services, inadequate refuse disposal services, poor school systems, deteriorated housing, and the like. Each of these problems has a specific solution, which usually takes the form of enlarged public expenditures for expanded public services or facilities. Almost any expert in urban affairs could work out solutions for any city's problems in any of these areas and come up with a rather accurate estimate of the costs.

The costs are the barriers to effective action. Cities do not have the tax revenues to meet their problems, and we shall examine their fiscal crisis presently.

The sickness, however, is more than financial. It is rooted in the social and economic structure of the city, on the one hand, and the motivational patterns of the individualistic society, on the other. A city is essentially an exercise in cooperative behavior. Yet it is divided by three chief economic classes, five cultural traditions, and a ghetto of exploited low-wage workers. Conflict must be expected, along with a host of unresolved problems.

The Urban Financial Crisis

The most obvious economic manifestation of the sickness of our cities is the almost universal financial crisis they are experiencing. The central cities of most metropolitan areas are desperate for revenues to meet their rapidly mounting expenditures. The causes of the crisis are numerous.

1. Inflation has increased the costs of providing urban services. Wage and salary increases have been particularly significant in raising costs, because most city services are labor-intensive rather than capital-intensive and increases in productivity have been hard to achieve.

2. Growing unionization and militancy among city employees contributes to the upward push in costs. Relatively low salaries and wages have been traditional for policemen, firemen, sanitation workers, teachers, and clerical workers in city governments. These employees are now pushing for higher incomes, and city budgets have to be adjusted upward.

3. The low-income ghettos of the central cities are high-cost areas, requiring larger public expenditures per person for general city services, education, and welfare than middle- or high-income areas. As central cities become increasingly ghettoized, the financial strain is increased. Simultaneously, the tax base of the central cities diminishes because of the deterioration of property values and the movement of business and industry to the suburbs.

4. Migration of middle- and upper-income groups to the politically separate suburbs removes from the central cities the higher-income families who might be able to pay for the higher costs of central city

government. At the same time, those suburbanites who continue to work in the central city use city services without contributing directly to paying for them.

5. Political fragmentation of most metropolitan areas into hundreds of separate jurisdictions creates competition to keep tax rates down. Tax increases in the hard-pressed central cities can increase the exodus of both people and business enterprise to the suburbs, where tax rates are often lower. City officials are quite aware of the fact that tax increases now may help solve their short-run problems, only to worsen their problems in the long run.

The urban financial crisis reflects the division of metropolitan areas into rich, middle-income, and poor areas. The central cities are increasingly the home of low-income minorities, with an anemic tax base and mounting expenditures. The suburbs, on the other hand, are largely white and sufficiently affluent to support relatively high levels of public services with relatively low tax rates. The fiscal disparities are the result of an economic imbalance created by the way in which the economic system as a whole distributes the fruits of economic activity, together with the desire of suburbanites to avoid the costs that the income disparities create.

A TALE OF TWO CITIES

Newark is the largest city in New Jersey. Its real estate tax equaled 7.9 percent of the average value of residences in 1966, and local taxes took 15 percent of gross family income. Yet the city government is in the midst of a continuing financial crisis.

Honolulu is the largest city in Hawaii. Its real estate tax equaled only 0.8 percent of the average value of residences in 1966, and local taxes took only 1.5 percent of gross family income. The city government has no serious fiscal problems.

Why the difference? Newark is part of a politically fragmented metropolitan area in which the central city is over 50 percent black and poor, the city must meet the bulk of the costs of public education, and the city bears a substantial portion of its welfare costs. Honolulu, on the other hand, includes almost all of the higher-income suburbs in its boundaries, and the state government pays almost all the cost of public education and welfare. Underlying these differences are vicious racial hostilities in New Jersey and basic racial harmony in Honolulu.

Solving the Financial Crisis

A program for solving the urban financial crisis has been proposed by the Advisory Commission on Intergovernmental Relations, which was established in 1959 to advise the federal government on problems arising from relationships between governments.[1] The commission proposed a four-point program for relieving the financial pressures on cities.

1. Establishment of metropolitan governments that would blanket both central cities and suburbs.

2. Assumption of the costs of public education by state governments.

3. Assumption of the full costs of the welfare system by the federal government.

4. No-strings revenue sharing of federal tax revenues with state and local governments.

The Commission also recommended a number of reforms in the tax system that would bring greater balance to the system as a whole, but the four items listed above were the most important.

The immediate financial problems of urban areas would undoubtedly be alleviated by these measures—if they could be implemented. The basic difficulties would largely remain, however. Metropolitan governments would clearly be dominated by the great middle-income majority that fled the central cities to avoid taxes and racial minorities and poor people and their problems. It is difficult to understand how the problems of the latter will be resolved by placing political power in the hands of the former. A metropolitan area government will have a better tax base as a result of broader boundaries, but power to use it will be in the hands of those who have the lesser need.

State support for public education is subject to similar limitations, but to a lesser extent. Poor children need larger appropriations per pupil to achieve educational parity with children of more affluent parents, partly because they must overcome the effects of poverty and partly because poor families spend less on informal family investments in human capital. At the present time the suburbs spend more per pupil than the central cities do ($574 compared with $449, in 1965), and that disparity could certainly be reduced. But state governments dominated politically by the more affluent suburban voter could hardly be expected to reverse the situation by spending twice as much to educate ghetto children as suburban children, which is a ratio that might come close to rectifying the present educational disparities. Racial animosities are also involved: one might expect Hawaii to perform better than Mississippi, or any of the northeastern industrial states.

---

[1] See *Urban America and the Federal System* (Washington, D.C.: U.S. Government Printing Office, 1969).

Federal revenue sharing with state and local governments has the same deficiencies. As long as political decisions are dominated by the middle-income suburbs, we cannot expect adequate programs to meet the needs of the central cities. Immediate financial pressures on local governments can be alleviated by shifting the tax burden to the state and federal governments, but if the suburbanite doesn't want to pay taxes to solve the problems of the poor he won't vote for them at the state or federal levels any more than he will at the local level.

THE PERMANENT URBAN CRISIS

If we follow the foregoing line of analysis, it becomes apparent that there are no solutions to the sickness of our cities within the framework of the current economic status quo. The immediate fiscal crisis can be alleviated by adopting the proposals of the Advisory Commission on Intergovernmental Relations. But our cities are sick because our economy and society are fragmented. The urban poor are largely excluded from the benefits that the great majority obtain from a growing and affluent economy. Poverty, reinforced by racial attitudes and cultural differences, is preserved by the ghettoization process operating in the central cities and is supported by exploitive patterns of low-wage employment and a poverty-preserving welfare system. As long as these conditions remain, our cities will be sick. Solutions are to be found in programs that eliminate poverty, reduce disparities in the distribution of income, and create the economic base for a unified society. Measures that merely provide for improved transportation, or low-cost housing, or improved city revenues may reduce the intensity of our urban problems, but will not eliminate them.

Summary

Economic activity tends to become more highly centralized in urban areas because of economic advantages generated by urban growth. At the same time, forces of decentralization promote a shift of population and economic activity outward from the central portions of metropolitan areas. Central cities are declining while the suburbs grow. The forces of urban growth are to be found primarily in the economic functions cities perform for their surrounding areas, together with the export of goods to the rest of the economy. As metropolitan areas increase in size, their export role becomes less important as an economic base and their function as an integrated central place becomes more important.

As a social unit, the city reflects the structure of the larger economy of which it is a part. American cities are divided by income disparities and by varied cultural patterns and value systems. They are the home of the ghetto, an economic subsystem characterized by permanent depression, low-wage labor, and a system of income flows that perpetuate its condition. These characteristics of the city are behind today's urban problems, which show up most clearly in a financial crisis that could probably be alleviated. The underlying causes of the urban problem will not be eliminated by a resolution of financial problems, however, for they lie deep within the economic relationships that create inequality and preserve racial animosities.

THE RIVER RHINE

In Köln, a town of monks and bones
And pavements fanged with murderous stones
And rags, and bags, and hideous wenches;
I counted two and seventy stenches,
All well defined, and several stinks!

Ye Nymphs that reign o'er sewers and sinks,
The river Rhine, it is well known,
Doth wash your city of Köln;
But tell me, Nymphs! what power divine
Shall henceforth wash the river Rhine?

Samuel Taylor Coleridge (1772–1834)

The Economics of the Natural Environment

43

One of the pressing current problems of the public economy is that of preserving the environmental framework within which economic activity is carried on. The problem arises because air, water, and land are essential to the maintenance of life, yet are also used as parts of the economic system. In particular, they are used as reservoirs for the disposal of wastes from the economy. This use can spoil their use in the ecological system. In this chapter we examine the growing incompatibility of the economic and ecological systems, together with the efforts now being made to bring the two systems into greater compatibility.

OPEN SYSTEMS AND CLOSED SYSTEMS

As the industrial economy has spread to all parts of the world over the past two hundred years, pulling all the peoples of the continents and all of the world's resources into its orbit, we have gradually become aware of the limited resources available for human use. Until the last half of the twentieth century men were always able to move into relatively unoccupied territories and find new resources as inputs for the industrial economy. Indeed, that can still be done, for all of the mineral resources have not been opened up, all of the oil has not been discovered, virgin forests are still to be found, and unused agricultural land is still available. As we pointed out earlier in discussing the relationship between resources and economic growth, when natural resources are used up in one area, there are always less productive resources that can be tapped, and an advancing technology continually finds substitutes. Exhaustible resources may mean diminishing returns or higher costs, but they don't bring disaster.

⌐ We are coming to realize, however, that the outputs of man's production system are never used up, but only change their form. Matter cannot be destroyed. It is only transformed. Except for the energy that continuously enters the earth's atmosphere from the sun, mankind must live with only those resources that are now available on the earth. The economic system may continue to transform inputs into outputs and waste products, but in the long run the ouputs and wastes must become part of the inputs. The natural world is a closed system, in which there is a continuous processing of inputs to become outputs that must be recycled as inputs once more.

By contrast, an open system continually draws inputs from sources other than the system's outputs. The outputs are then distributed independently of the inputs. An open system emphasizes the throughput, the level of production, the amount of the output. A closed system emphasizes the continuation of the process as an end in itself. The fundamental differences between the two are shown in Figure 43-1.

A. Simple Open System

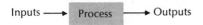

An open system requires continual supplies of new inputs to continue functioning

B. Simple Closed System

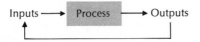

A closed system uses its own output to continue functioning.

FIGURE 43-1
Open and Closed Systems

In the production and consumption activities carried on in the modern economy none of the natural resources used as inputs are destroyed. All must eventually return to the natural environment. Our economic institutions are well organized to develop natural resources and channel them into productive uses. But after those resources become residuals, or unusable or waste products, and are no longer of value to people, they must be returned to the natural environment. At the present time the most common method of return is dispersal into air, water, and land.

Wastes are usually disposed of by diluting the reservoirs of air, water, and land. Those reservoirs are beginning to fill up, however. The natural regenerative forces that break down wastes and recycle waste materials are unable to function as rapidly as new wastes are dumped into the reservoirs. Some of the wastes are harmful products that do not exist in nature or are produced in such large quantities that the natural environment may never be able to absorb them fully. In other instances, natural substances are concentrated in amount so that they become local problems: mercury is a problem not because it is produced by man, but because it is concentrated by man out of a natural environment in which mercury is highly dispersed.

The dispersal of residuals from the system of production and distribution back into the natural environment does not close the economic system. Production and distribution continue to draw inputs of natural resources and labor from the human and ecological systems in which the economy is embedded. And wastes continue to be deposited back in the natural environment. The ecological system is closed, however, for natural resources can only be changed in form and not destroyed. As the production system of modern society has grown in size and spread more widely, the damaging effects of its waste disposal processes have escalated. We now realize that production of goods and services is only a subsystem within a larger general system of relationships that encompasses both man and his environment. We live in a closed system in which there is no choice, in the long run, but to recycle all outputs back through the system as a whole.

TYPES AND SOURCES OF POLLUTION

Pollution of the natural environment is usually classified into three types: air, water, and land pollution. The last is sometimes called solid waste pollution, since it usually involves disposal of solids like paper, garbage, or glass.

The basic sources of pollution, however, are to be found in people and production. With any given level of technology, the larger the population the greater the potential pollution from sewage, garbage, and trash. With a given number of people and level of technology, the greater the production of goods and services, the greater the production of waste and the potential pollution. The great variable is technology. It can be developed in ways that are compatible with life, or antagonistic to life. Indeed, as population grows and production increases, we shall have to give far greater attention to the development of technologies that have reusable wastes that are not harmful to plant and animal life, including human beings.

Air Pollution

Air pollution has five chief sources. As of 1965, automobiles were responsible for about 60 percent of all air pollution, by weight of total pollutants. Industrial production accounted for about 17 percent of all air pollution in

1965, chiefly sulfur oxides and particulate matter. Electric power plants were not far behind, with 14 percent, the bulk of whose air pollution was sulfur oxides. The remaining air pollution was created by space heating, mostly in homes (6 percent) and incineration of refuse (3 percent). About half of all air pollution was in the form of carbon monoxide; sulfur oxide contributed about 15 percent; and the other chief pollutants were hydrocarbons, nitrogen oxides, and particulate matter.

The data on air pollution are deceptive, however. Some pollutants may be extremely harmful to health even though there are only tiny traces of them in the air. Lead from automobile exhausts is one example. Mercury from industrial smoke is another: only about 1,500 tons are emitted annually, but the emissions are concentrated in only a few places and can be extremely harmful to nearby plant and animal life.

Water Pollution

Water pollution comes from a number of sources. One type has already been eliminated, the disease-bearing infections such as typhoid. The most important continuing source of water pollution, organic sewage, is also the most amenable to treatment. The only real barrier to elimination of sewage pollution is unwillingness on the part of taxpayers to incur the costs. Other sources of water pollution are more difficult to eliminate: plant nutrients from sewage and fertilizer washoff promote growth of algae in bodies of water; organic chemicals such as pesticides, insecticides, and detergents are difficult to break down, and they tend to accumulate; inorganic chemicals like sludges and residues from industrial waste are more easily eliminated, but the cost of doing so may be high; radioactive substances are now only a small problem, but will probably become more significant as greater use is made of atomic energy. Land sediment from soil erosion is also a significant cause of water pollution in some areas, particularly in metropolitan suburbs where a large amount of construction activity takes place. Finally, there is waste heat from industry and electric power plants.

Although these eight sources of water pollution can be identified, there has never been a comprehensive study of the total amount of pollutants deposited in our water supplies. We just do not know how great the problem is nor what it would take to restore our water supplies to full usability and prevent further deterioration.

Solid Waste

The United States produces about 3.5 billion tons of solid waste each year. Almost nine-tenths of that amount is agricultural and animal waste as a byproduct of food production. Only about 360 million tons is urban waste. The urban waste is the larger problem, because disposing of it creates other forms of pollution: air pollution if the waste is burned (almost 40 percent of all urban waste is paper) and land pollution if it is dumped. Garbage is a good example. It accounts for about 12 percent of all urban waste. Some

73 percent is dumped openly on land, about 15 percent is burned, 8 percent is used in sanitary landfills, and only 4 percent is reused or used for composting. Most garbage ends up polluting either the land or the air.

THE TECHNOLOGY OF POLLUTION

Pollution of the air from automobiles typifies the incompatibility of some forms of technology with the natural environment. About 90 percent of automobile pollution comes from carbon monoxide (75 percent) and hydrocarbons (14 percent). Both of these waste substances are harmful to animal life when breathed. The wastes of the technological system are harmful inputs into the biological system.

This situation stands in sharp contrast to the symbiosis that exists in nature between animal and plant life. Animals use oxygen as a fuel and produce carbon dioxide as a waste material that is breathed out. Plants, however, use carbon dioxide and produce oxygen as a waste. The two forms of life, taken together, recycle each other's waste products in a closed system. Clearly, the great technological task of the future will be the restructuring of technology itself to make it more compatible with the natural environment.

An advanced technology need not be incompatible with a life-sustaining environment. The development of hydroelectric power changes the nature of river valleys by creating lakes that were not there before. The lakes often remove agricultural land from production. But they also create new recreational facilities and produce electricity in a far cleaner way than thermal power plants that use coal, oil, or gas. Built as part of a multipurpose watershed development program, hydroelectric power plants can contribute to improved uses of natural resources that make possible higher standards of living for more people.

Unfortunately, we know relatively little about the compatibility of technological processes with the natural environment. For example, scientists dispute about prospective changes in the weather. Some have argued that the growing amount of carbon dioxide and heat discharged into the air will cause the polar ice caps to melt and drown coastal cities.[1] Others say that the earth's temperature has been falling in recent years because discharge of particulates into the atmosphere reflects heat from the sun. Still another view is that the increase in particulate matter was caused primarily by volcanic activity and only marginally by man. The moral is that it is easy to become alarmed, but harder to become informed. Far greater information about the natural world is needed if we are to make sensible decisions about resource use and waste disposal.

---

[1] Melting of the north polar ice cap will make little difference in water levels, because the ice is already floating and is not very thick. The south polar ice cap is the problem. It is on land and is miles high in places. Furthermore, at the right temperature it is likely to slide off the land in vast units almost overnight to create instant and large changes in the level of the oceans. Was something like that the cause of the Biblical flood?

IS THERE AN ENERGY CEILING?

Economic growth requires increased production of energy for use in the production process. Energy production in the U.S. increases at an annual rate of about 3.5 percent, doubling about every twenty years. More rapid economic growth would speed up the increase, while slower growth will retard it. Energy production releases heat into the atmosphere, and according to some scientists could cause a rise in the temperature of the earth's atmosphere unacceptable to man. Major climatic changes would occur, with corresponding shifts in the ecological basis of life. Air-conditioned environments would become necessary for human survival within one to two hundred years, according to this scenario of events.

Some scientists question these forecasts, and future research may show that there are no practical energy ceilings, but contemporary scientific analyses suggest that there are. If correct, these analyses indicate that limits will have to be placed on population growth and living standards in order to preserve the ecological foundations of modern society. They also imply that the structure of the economy will have to shift to a "steady state" and a closed rather than an open production system. These ecological problems created by an expanding economy may unleash the most revolutionary of social and economic changes.

EXTERNALITIES

Pollution is an example of an economic phenomenon that economists have labeled "externalities". Externalities are costs (or benefits) that do not accrue to the economic unit that creates them.

We have met externalities before in discussions of the public economy. One aspect of some public goods is that part of their benefits is obtained by economic units other than those who acquire the goods. For example, students obtain an education in publicly supported colleges and universities and get economic benefits from it. The community as a whole also benefits in a variety of ways from having a larger number of educated citizens. These latter benefits are externalities, sometimes also called "spillover effects" or "neighborhood effects." They accrue to people other than those who are the direct consumers of the goods.

Pollution creates external costs rather than external benefits. Goods are produced and sold to consumers, but if the producer does not have to pay for use of air, water, or land to dispose of the wastes from production, none of the costs of waste disposal are included in the price of the goods. Yet inconvenience or losses may be created for other people by the process of waste disposal if it pollutes resources that the other people wish to use.

For example, a papermill may deposit effluent into a river far upstream from any other user of the river's water. The natural cleansing action of water flow brings the purity of the water back to its original state before any communities downstream take water out for human consumption. In this case there are no external costs, except perhaps for those fishermen who no longer find fish in the stream just below the mill. However, let a second papermill be established on the river, or perhaps a third and fourth. By the time the water gets downstream to the towns below it no longer is usable in its natural state and must be purified before being used by people. Now there are external costs which must be borne by others than those who use the paper.

The external costs involved in this illustration are the costs of purifying the water downstream so that it will be fit to use. Resources that could be used to produce other things must be devoted to water purification. These costs should properly be included in accounting for the total costs of producing paper in the mills upstream. The total costs, therefore, include two separate items:

1. *Internal costs* incurred by the papermills themselves, including the value of those raw materials and productive services used by the producing companies.
2. *External costs* incurred by the downstream communities, including the value of the resources used to restore the purity of the water.

External costs result in a misallocation of resources. Where external costs exist, the costs of production of the economic unit that decides on levels of output and prices are lower than they would be if all costs were internal. Competition will then tend in the long run to push selling prices down to levels that just cover average internal costs. The competitive price will be below average total costs by an amount equal to average external costs. The lower costs will tend to bring forth larger output of the good in question. When competition prevails, any good whose production involves external costs will tend to be overproduced and underpriced in comparison with goods whose production does not involve external costs.

When monopoloid conditions prevail, the results of external costs for price and output are less clear. However, they offer an opportunity for higher monopolistic profits and/or a larger share of the market that business firms can be expected to exploit.

External costs have a further important characteristic: they involve involuntary exchange transactions. External costs are imposed on people by others and are not incurred voluntarily. Internal costs, on the other hand, are incurred willingly by economic units that seek to gain from the transactions they engage in. But when an asphalt plant, for example, fills the air with smoke, it imposes costs that others have to bear whether they like it or not.

We can understand now why pollution of the environment is such a prominent feature of the modern economy. Any individual economic unit can benefit from pollution created by disposal of its wastes. Its costs are reduced. Its price can be lowered and either its sales can be greater (in the competitive case) or its profits can be enlarged (in the monopoloid case). Furthermore, the external costs created by its actions must be involuntarily accepted by other economic units. External costs, by reducing costs to the producing unit, enable it to obtain economic gains at the expense of others. Exploitation of the natural environment really means exploitation of other people.

EXTERNAL COSTS AND COMMON PROPERTY

It is relatively easy for producers to create external costs through the natural environment because the use of air and water is normally free of charge. We do not pay to breathe the air nor use the water of lakes, rivers, and oceans. Those resources are not owned by any individual, in the normal state of things, but are available for common use, much like a public park. They are a "commons" available to the entire community.

The fact that vital portions of the natural environment are available for common use without charge makes them particularly subject to congestion. At low levels of use an additional user may impose virtually no cost on others. As the number of users mounts, however, an additional user can cause others to incur costs or discomforts. It is then that externalities start. Perhaps the classic example is automobile exhaust emissions. No one automobile emits enough exhaust to bother anyone, except perhaps some very old cars that function inefficiently. Yet many automobiles together can create highly uncomfortable and even dangerous amounts of exhaust-laden smog. The cost of pollution attributable to any single automobile owner is nil, but the cost attributable to all taken together may be great.

Common use of the natural environment also means that no one is responsible for maintaining the commons and no one has a strong economic incentive to do so. Since any single economic unit makes a very small use of air or water, any costs it incurs in preserving those resources will produce benefits primarily for other economic units. As one observer commented, if General Motors Corporation owned the Mississippi River, the company would jolly well charge for its use and preserve the river as an income-producing property. But since no one owns the air and the water, no one has a direct economic interest in preserving them. River water is free and our streams become polluted. This is one reason why public parks are littered while private backyards are spotless, and why publicly owned housing deteriorates rapidly while most privately owned homes are relatively well maintained.

As the economy grows and output expands, we can expect the burden placed upon the environmental commons to increase. There is some evidence that production of residuals increases faster than total output. In a private enterprise economy that trend should be expected, for individual units can gain to the extent that they can force others to bear external costs. At the very least, we should expect a growing problem of residuals, even if the ratio of waste production to output remains the same, for total output is growing. Yet the size of the environmental commons remains the same.

CAN WE SOLVE THE PROBLEM OF POLLUTION?

Three solutions to the problem of the environment have been widely discussed. All three have been tried, and all have been found to be only partial solutions with severe defects. The three methods are subsidies, regulation, and effluent charges. The defects common to all three are first, the attractiveness to individual economic units of shifting economic burdens to others, and second, the political difficulties involved in getting them to act differently.

Subsidies

One current strategy for achieving water pollution control is to subsidize construction of municipal water treatment plants. The federal government will provide up to 55 percent of the cost of construction (but not operation) of local waste treatment plants. Lesser subsidies are available to industrial plants. Some plants are connected to municipal sewer systems and can benefit from subsidies to the local government. Special tax amortization provisions are also available for pollution control facilities. The subsidies have to be supplemented with enforcement by means of establishment of standards, court orders, and fines, for even with a subsidy it is cheaper just to dump untreated wastes into a lake or stream.

The consensus among experts is that the subsidy system has not worked effectively. Federal appropriations have lagged, and local governments have held up their expenditures until federal funds become available. Enforcement proceedings are costly and time-consuming, and the political power of large firms has effectively hindered enforcement. A number of waste-treatment plants constructed under the program have not operated efficiently and have failed to accomplish the tasks for which they were presumably designed. All of these deficiencies were detailed in a recent report to the U.S. Congress that evaluated the program.[2]

---

[2] In case you want to look it up: U.S. General Accounting Office, *Examination into the Effectiveness of the Construction Grant Program for Abating, Controlling, and Preventing Water Pollution*, Report to the Congress by the Comptroller General of the United States, No. B-166506, November, 1969.

In recent years the environment protection strategy has shifted to regulation. Under the Environmental Policy Act (1969) a Council on Environmental Quality modeled after the Council of Economic Advisors was established. In 1970 a federal government reorganization established the Environmental Protection Agency (EPA) as part of the executive branch of the government. The EPA combines all of the pollution control and related research activities of the federal government that were formerly scattered and isolated in various federal agencies. These administrative changes were supplemented by legislation in 1970 to require maintenance of air quality standards and their enforcement by the federal government. Proposals were placed before Congress to extend and strengthen the Refuse Act of 1899, which was until recently an unenforced law requiring industries to obtain licenses to discharge wastes into navigable streams and their tributaries.

These actions indicate that a new era in pollution control has begun. The strategy appears to be regulation, but without significant economic incentives. Government enforcement of regulations designed to achieve administratively determined quality standards is the technique to be used. For example, the clean air legislation of 1970 requires the federal government to establish air quality standards to be enforced by state governments with federal assistance. Stringent emission standards for automobiles and aircraft are to be achieved by 1976 at the latest, with federal enforcement.

The management of the pollution control program is being led by the federal government, while enforcement is divided between federal and state governments. Mobile sources of air pollution will be regulated federally, while stationary sources will be regulated by the states. Water quality standards will be regulated primarily by federal agencies, with some assistance from the states.

Perhaps the most encouraging aspect of this turn in national policy is the evidence it provides of a public commitment to manage the ecological commons of air and water with a view to maintaining acceptable quality standards. Many economists, however, are skeptical of the results of regulation when strong economic interests are at stake. The history of regulation in other areas of the economy is not good: regulation tends to be more expensive than economic incentives; it creates a regulatory bureaucracy; the bureaucracy tends to be captured by those whom it regulates; legal challenges lead to protection of property rights rather than the public interest. All of these dangers are present in regulation of environmental standards. The problem is compounded by the fact that our knowledge of environmental relationships and our technological capabilities are limited. Economists might be pardoned if they yearn longingly for the use of economic incentives, for we know that they can work.

Economic Incentives

The most commonly proposed economic incentives are effluent charges. An effluent charge is essentially a tax on a producer of waste requiring him to pay a fee for every unit of harmful waste that he dumps into the water or air. For example, a municipality that discharges untreated sewage into Lake Erie may have to pay a charge of $10 for each 1,000 gallons of discharge. If the sewage is treated to remove 90 percent of the pollutants the charge may be reduced to $1. If all of the pollutants are removed, the charge might be eliminated altogether. By varying the amount of the charge, any desired level of water purity might be achieved. If absolutely no discharge of pollutants is desired, the authorities could enact an outright ban, just as governments prohibit use of certain drugs. But short of complete prohibition, reduction of pollution to any desired level can be achieved by establishing the proper charge.

The idea behind effluent charges is to internalize costs that heretofore were external. Imposing additional costs on users of the environmental commons will cause them to economize on the use of that resource by diminishing their wastes. In doing so, actual costs of production are raised to levels closer to real costs and in the long run the misallocation of resources we discussed earlier will be reduced.

The Level of Effluent Charges   The success of effluent charges in reducing pollution would depend on the standards set by the administrative agency charged with managing them. The simplest technique is a variation of cost-benefit analysis that compares the marginal cost of pollution abatement to the polluter with the marginal cost of pollution to the community.

Figure 43-2 shows the fundamentals of the concept. Curve A is essentially a demand curve for pollution abatement. It shows the costs to the community,

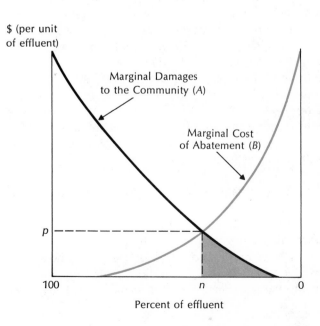

FIGURE 43-2
Effluent Charges to Reduce Pollution

Curve A shows the marginal damages to the community of the pollution caused by an industrial plant. Very high when no effort is made to reduce pollution, the costs to the community fall to zero before all of the effluent is eliminated. Curve B shows the marginal cost of eliminating the pollution at the source by reducing the effluent. Note that total elimination is very costly and may not be possible, but (as in the typical case) some effluent can be eliminated without cost if the firm's engineers would only put their minds to it.

at the margin, of any given level of pollution from the effluent of an industrial plant. It indicates the price per unit of effluent a rational community would be willing to pay for pollution abatement for any given discharge of effluent. Curve B shows the marginal cost to the industrial firm of reducing pollution.

In this simple case the optimal level of pollution abatement would occur as a result of levying an effluent charge equal to p. With a charge at that level, it would pay the firm to reduce its effluent to level n. At lower levels of effluent discharge, the firm's marginal cost of pollution abatement would exceed the effluent fee and clearly would be unprofitable. At abatement levels greater than n the firm could save money by reducing its effluent, since its marginal abatement costs would be less than the effluent fee.

The solution shown in Figure 43-2 would not eliminate all losses due to pollution. Those losses that remain are shown by the shaded area, but they are relatively small compared to the losses that have been eliminated (shown by the unshaded area under Curve A). Note, however, that all damages due to pollution could be eliminated if the effluent charge p were set high enough. Such action would raise the marginal costs of abatement to levels well above marginal benefits to the community. Although a charge that high might satisfy the conservation purist, it goes beyond economic rationality to a different set of values. If the polluter were a public agency, such as the community's sewage treatment plant, the community would be wise to set the effluent charge at p, thereby equalizing its benefits and costs at the margin.

Some Extensions and Qualifications   Advances in pollution abatement can be made, with reduced effluent charges, if technological advances reduce the cost of abatement. On the other hand, if community attitudes change toward a demand for less pollution—that is equivalent to shifting the curve of marginal damages upward—a higher level of effluent charges will be required. These extensions of the analysis are shown in Figures 43-3 and 43-4.

All of this analysis of effluent charges must be qualified, however, by the very great difficulties encountered in estimating the damages to the community caused by pollution. Everything said earlier about similar problems with cost-benefit analysis applies here as well, with the added problem that the polluter is probably bringing to bear upon the pollution control agency all the pressure he can to get them to minimize their estimate of damages. When this is added to the difficulty of estimating dollar amounts when prices are not available, it should not surprise us that the estimates of damage probably will tend toward the low side.

Effluent charges have several advantages, however. They provide a strong economic incentive to voluntary action by private economic interests to move in the direction of the public interest in protecting the environmental commons. They achieve that goal with a minimum amount of regulation and legal action for enforcement. If effluent charges are administered properly, business firms are encouraged to find lower-cost methods of pollution abatement that can then be followed by reduced charges. Finally, by internalizing at least some

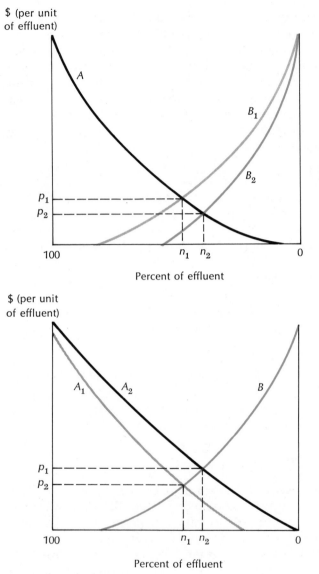

$ (per unit
of effluent)

100

Percent of effluent

**FIGURE 43-3
Reducing Effluent
Charges**

Reduced costs of pollution abatement permit lower effluent charges to eliminate more pollution. Reduction of marginal abatement costs from B_1 to B_2 enables the effluent charge to be lowered from p_1 to p_2, while reducing the effluent from n_1 to n_2.

$ (per unit
of effluent)

100

Percent of effluent

**FIGURE 43-4
Raising Effluent Charges**

Increased demand for pollution abatement requires higher effluent fees to achieve the new goals. Greater demand for pollution abatement means that the marginal costs of pollution to the community have risen, in the opinion of its citizens, from A_1 to A_2. An optimal abatement program would raise the effluent charge from p_1 to p_2 in order to reduce the effluent from n_1 to n_2.

external costs, effluent charges make possible a more efficient allocation of resources in the long run.

If effluent charges have such great advantages, why were they considered and rejected when the recent environmental legislation was passed? The congressional hearings have the answer. Businessmen opposed effluent charges because they would add another cost to their operations. Apparently they felt that regulation would be less costly to them. Representatives of municipal governments opposed effluent charges because local governments would have

to pay for discharging untreated sewage. On the other hand, the federal program to subsidize local sewage treatment plants adds to their revenues. Conservationists appeared not to understand how effluent charges would work,
calling them "a license to pollute"—as if regulation is not!—and did not realize
the incentive they would provide to business firms and municipalities voluntarily to reduce their emission of pollutants. Perhaps underneath the conservationists' position was the realization that effluent charges would bring use
of the environmental commons more fully into the price system, moving away
from the principle of free public use.[3]

THE QUESTION OF EQUITY

The poor and the near-poor bear more of the burden of pollution than do
the rich. They are not able to avoid air pollution or noise pollution by moving
to the suburbs, as readily as middle or upper income families. This problem
is particularly intense for racial minorities. The urban poor show a high incidence of chronic respiratory conditions such as asthma and emphysema. The
air they usually breathe is contaminated by automobile exhaust emissions.
Industrial workers are often subject to high degrees of pollution on the job,
including high temperatures, toxic gases and fumes, noise, dust and high humid-
ity. In addition, they often live near the factories that belch smoke and fumes
into the atmosphere they and their families breathe.

Meanwhile, the plant manager works in an air-conditioned office, lives in
an air-conditioned home in the suburbs, and travels between the two in an
air-conditioned car. His company's public relations man is very likely to point
out that elimination of pollution can raise costs and threaten the employment
of the company's workers. And the company's profits, which add to the income of stockholders, are derived, in part, from production methods that
involve environmental pollution.

The benefits of pollution control are likely to accrue chiefly to low-income
families and to production workers. Those groups, however, are also likely
to bear the larger burden of the costs of pollution abatement. Effluent charges
are analogous to an excise tax. They are levied on the production of products
and services. Like any excise tax, they add to costs of production and in the
long run are embodied in the sales price of the product or service. And, like
any excise tax, effluent charges are regressive. The poor spend a larger proportion of their income than the rich, pay the same prices for the same goods
as the rich, and would end up paying a larger proportion of their income in
the form of higher prices caused by effluent charges. The same is true of any

---

[3] Effluent charges may become part of national anti-pollution policies, after all. In July, 1971,
the Nixon administration decided to push for a tax on sulfur emissions. Conservationists supported it, and the executive director of the Sierra Club announced that his organization now
favors taxation as a means of controlling pollution. Coal, oil, and mining companies opposed
the idea.

costs of pollution abatement incurred by business firms under regulatory restrictions. The costs will be passed on to consumers by price increases, which
will be most burdensome to low income families.

Fiscal measures other than effluent charges may be still more uneven in
their effects. A survey of chief executives of large corporations published by
Fortune in February, 1970 showed that business leaders favor a program of
accelerated depreciation for pollution abatement investments, investment tax
credits and federal matching grants as incentives for antipollution measures.
That path would provide subsidies and tax cuts for corporations in exchange
for pollution controls, with the general taxpayer paying the bill. The general
public would bear the costs of environmental protection, whereas now it bears
the costs of pollution.

These equity problems illustrate once again the fundamental issues of
economic justice that are found in a private enterprise economy, and the way
in which they affect the public economy.

1. Individual economic units can make gains by shifting part of their
   costs to either the environmental commons or to the general public.
2. Influence over government policies can have a significant economic
   payoff, tending to bring economic units into the political arena in
   pursuit of economic gains.
3. The existing patterns of distribution of income and wealth tend to
   perpetuate themselves in the operation of the market adjustment process.

These considerations suggest two broad conclusions. There are strong incentives for economic units to seek and use political power. The slogan, "Money
to get power; power to protect the money," has real significance. And one
way to protect the status quo is to keep solutions to problems within the
framework of the market mechanism, for it is out of that mechanism that the
existing structure of wealth and power has emerged.

Seen in this light, the economics of the natural environment and pollution
control has a significance far greater than its application to the solution of an
immediate problem. It lays bare some of the most fundamental relationships
between economics and politics in a market economy, and raises in still
another context the basic equity problems of such a society.

THE LONG RUN

Even problems of equity recede into relative insignificance when we consider
the longer range relationships between economy and environment. None of
the policies with respect to protection of the environment that have emerged
in the last few years provides anything more than a temporary solution at best.
Subsidies, regulation, and even effluent fees remain largely within the framework of an open production system. Inputs remain independent of outputs
and wastes are still to be disposed of outside the system of production itself.
The technological framework remains largely the same.

Yet if pollution is to be reduced and the environmental commons preserved, the material substances now called pollutants will have to be transformed into either benign or useful substances. They can't be made to just disappear. They must be recycled back into the production processes of the economy or into the ecological system. Instead of being destructive or harmful, they must be changed to useful and life-supporting substances.

Closed production systems imply goals and priorities different from those associated with open production systems. One high-priority goal in a closed system is the maintenance of the system itself. Continuation of production rather than expansion of production becomes the keynote of the system. Preservation of the capital stock becomes more important than increasing the capital stock. Maintenance of a steady state becomes more important than growth. In such a system, waste is recycled rather than disposed of, because it is necessary for the viability of the system as a whole.

We are a long way from a closed production system. The implications of such a system for economic motivations, the property system, population policy, and governmental institutions are enormous. It should be clear that our current environmental problems are pushing us in that direction. We move reluctantly, however, as indicated by the move toward regulation as national policy, instead of a set of incentives built into the system. Nevertheless, in the long run there is no way to bring the production system into harmony with the ecological system without recycling wastes and turning outputs into inputs. We have to move toward a closed production system.

Summary

The modern economy has an open production system in which inputs are transformed into outputs. Part of the output is waste that is disposed of by dumping it into the environmental commons of air, water, and land. The resultant pollution threatens to overwhelm the ecological system that supports life.

In economic analysis pollution is an externality: a cost not borne by the producer. Using the environmental commons as a reservoir for waste disposal, economic units are able to shift some of their production costs to others. These external costs are forced upon others against their wishes, and result in misallocation of resources. Yet there are strong incentives in our economy impelling producers to use the environmental commons in this fashion.

Subsidies to municipalities and, to a lesser extent, to producers have been used to alleviate the problem but have not had much success. Recently we have turned to regulation of polluters by federal and state governments as the problem worsened. The economic path to a solution—use of effluent charges to provide incentives to reduce discharge of wastes—has been largely rejected at this stage, although it is probably the most promising in the short run. Effluent charges do not adequately deal with problems of equity, however, and in the long run more fundamental solutions will have to be found that move toward a closed rather than an open production system.

Key Concepts

Open system. A system in which inputs are drawn from outside the system itself and outputs are disposed of outside the system.

Closed system. A system that uses its own outputs as its inputs, and does not rely on anything outside the system itself either as a source of inputs or as a means of using outputs.

Residuals. The unusable outputs of a system. Wastes.

Externalities. Costs or benefits that do not accrue to the economic unit that creates them.

Internal costs. Costs of production that are directly paid by an economic unit.

External costs. Costs of production that are shifted by an economic unit to others. The costs of pollution are a typical external cost.

Effluent charge. A fee levied by a public agency on a producer of waste for each unit of harmful waste discharged.

THE
INTERNATIONAL
ECONOMY

X

We now return to the economics of market adjustments, a topic we strayed from in discussing the public economy. International economic relations can be understood best in terms of long-run adjustments in competitive markets. Fundamental exchange and cost relationships dominate the analysis.

Chapter 44 explains the basic economics of international trade and introduces the concept of *comparative advantage* to show that specialization and trade leave all nations better off than self-sufficiency and no trade. The international economy operates in a world with many different currencies, leading to complex financial relationships. The international financial system is dealt with in Chapter 45, along with the U.S. balance of payments, the relationship between currencies and the current problems of the system. Chapter 46 examines barriers to trade, finds them detrimental to human welfare and strongly supports free trade between nations. Finally, Chapter 47 takes up the problems of the underdeveloped third world. It sketches the reasons for the continued poverty of those countries and indicates the methods some have been able to use to set in motion a continuing process of economic growth.

The theme of Part X is the presence of a group of unresolved problems that plague the nations of the world: a rickety international financial system, the persistence of trade restrictions, the poverty of the underdeveloped countries and the possibility of economic conflict with the advanced nations. The family of nations has not been able to cope with these problems very effectively, and they act as a constant irritant throughout the world economy.

Upon learning that you have progressed this far in your studies of economics without becoming overly discouraged, your rich and eccentric uncle, whom you have not seen since Christmas of the year you were eight years old and who has been engaged in trading milk and whiskey with the Indians of the upper Amazon, endows you with exactly $1 million, provided that you use it in international trade between England and the United States, dealing in milk and whiskey, of which he is very fond. Puzzled, you inquire into the situation and discover that prices and shipping costs prevail as shown in Table 44-1.

TABLE 44-1
Prices of Milk and Whiskey in England and U.S.

	In England	In U.S.
Price of milk	1s/ gal	$1/ gal
Price of whiskey	£1/ gal (= 10s)	$5/ gal

Note: Shipping costs between the U.S. and England for both milk and whiskey are 1¢ per gallon.

Your uncle glances at these figures and remarks gleefully, "Aha! You'll make a fortune!"

"How?" you respond. "Don't I have to know the exchange rate between English and American currency?"

"What an idiot," responds your uncle. "You have no more intelligence than an eight-year-old. Didn't they teach you *anything* in your economics course? I think I'll take my million and visit Las Vegas."

"Wait," you respond in an agonized voice. "I'll figure it out."

The first thing you notice is that milk is cheap in England, compared with the United States. You can buy ten gallons of milk there for what one gallon of whiskey would cost. In the United States milk is more expensive: it is equivalent to one-fifth gallon of whiskey rather than one-tenth.

Just the opposite is true of whiskey. It is relatively cheap in the United States and relatively expensive in England. In the U.S. you would have to give up only five gallons of milk to get one gallon of whiskey, while in England the exchange would be ten for one.

These relative prices can be easily compared, as shown in Table 44-2. This was the relationship your uncle saw at a glance: whiskey is cheap in the U.S. while milk is cheap in England *relative to the prices of other things*.

Put another way, English milk is relatively cheap and English whiskey relatively expensive *compared with their prices in the U.S.* Correspondingly, U.S. milk is expensive and whiskey cheap *compared with their prices in England.*

TABLE 44–2
Relative Prices of Milk and Whiskey

	In England	In U.S.
Price of milk (in gallons of whiskey)	0.1	0.2
Price of whiskey (in gallons of milk)	10.0	5.0

This information is all one needs. "Buy cheap and sell dear," you murmur as you reach for the telephone to set the following transactions in motion:

1. *Buy* 200,000 gallons of whiskey in the U.S., at $5/gal for $1,000,000
2. Ship it to England, where you *sell* it for 10s/gal, a total of £200,000
   Shipping costs, to be settled later, are $2,000.
3. *Buy* 2,000,000 gallons of milk in England at 1s/gal, for £200,000
4. Ship it to the U.S. by refrigerated tankship, where you *sell* it for $1/gal.
   You receive $2,000,000
   Shipping costs at this stage are $20,000.

Settling your accounts, you end up by almost doubling your original $1 million:

Cash on hand when transactions end	$2,000,000
Cash on hand at start	1,000,000
Shipping costs	22,000
Telephone calls	0.40
Net gain	$ 977,000.60

At this point you call in your eight-year-old brother, explain the simple transactions to him, and leave him in charge of the original $1 million. Reaching for the telephone you call your uncle, "About that trip to Las Vegas. . . ."

THE FLOW OF TRADE AND FACTORS OF PRODUCTION

These transactions have set in motion a flow of trade between the two nations. The U.S. exports whiskey and imports milk, while England exports milk and imports whiskey. At the root of this trade are international differences in price relationships. These price relationships are, in turn, based on differences in costs of production within the individual countries. The 1 to 5 ratio between the prices of milk and whiskey in the U.S., that is, the relatively costly milk and cheap whiskey, is the outcome of all of the economic forces within the country that bring prices to approximate the long-run average costs of production for each commodity, modified by whatever monopoloid industrial structures that may prevail. The same is true of the 1 to 10 ratio in England.

This is a key point in the analysis. As we shall see in a moment, the flow of trade causes adjustments in relative prices within trading countries, and these in turn set in motion the long-run market-adjustment process that brings prices into accord with long-run costs of production. Relative prices within any nation will then reflect the real economic relationships that exist within that nation—real costs, real benefits, and net welfare.

Much depends on the availability (and the price) of the factors of production. In the United States land is relatively plentiful, labor is scarce, and capital is abundant. This makes land and capital relatively inexpensive and labor relatively costly. Capital-intensive products that use relatively large amounts of capital and little labor will be relatively inexpensive in the U.S. and will be the sort of item exported, like automobiles, machinery, electrical equipment, and so on. On the other hand, labor-intensive products will be relatively expensive in the U.S. and these items will be high on our list of imports.

A tropical country, on the other hand, which has much labor and land but little capital, will tend to export labor- and land-intensive products such as rubber, cocoa, or bananas while it imports capital-intensive products from countries like the U.S. and the industrial nations of Europe.

The scarcity relationships between the factors of production vary from region to region and from country to country. No two are exactly the same. Four main divisions of the world economy can be distinguished, based on the relative scarcity or abundance of the factors of production within the divisions. They are shown below in Table 44-3.

TABLE 44-3
Relative Scarcity of Factors of Production

Main International Trade Areas of the World	Labor	Capital	Land
Western Europe	Scarce	Plentiful	Scarce
Great Plains areas			
Mature (U.S.)	Scarce	Plentiful	Plentiful
Developing (Australia,			
Canada, . . .)	Scarce	Scarce	Plentiful
Tropics	Plentiful	Scarce	Plentiful
Japan	Plentiful	Plentiful	Scarce

Each area exports characteristic products based on its particular endowment of the factors of production. Hong Kong, for example, which like Japan has very plentiful labor, much capital, and very little land, exports highly labor-intensive products of industry, such as textiles and clothing. Malaysia, however, with plentiful land and labor and little capital, exports land- and labor-intensive plantation products such as rubber. The list could go on indefinitely.

These relationships among the factors of production change with time.

Although the natural resources of an area remain the same, except as technology enables their utilization to change, population growth and capital accumulation change the pattern of relative scarcities. For example, a hundred years ago the United States was a typical developing Great Plains nation, with an abundance of land relative to labor and capital. Its principal exports were land-intensive commodities such as wheat and cotton. With growth of population and a very high rate of capital accumulation, the relative scarcities have changed. Now an industrial nation in which capital is relatively abundant and labor the scarcest factor of production, the principal exports are capital-intensive industrial products. These kinds of changes proceed at varying rates of speed everywhere. The pattern of world trade continues to change, subtly and slowly, in response to them.

EQUALIZATION OF RELATIVE PRICES

The relative price ratios used in our little tale about trade in whiskey and milk are only the beginning. They cannot be maintained. The flow of trade itself will cause them to change and ultimately be brought into equality with each other. The process is simply another example of how a system of self-adjusting markets functions under the impact of buyers and sellers who seek to maximize their gains.

Return to the example. Prior to the flow of trade between the two countries, the price of milk in the U.S. was $1 per gallon and whiskey $5 per gallon. Trade brought exports of whiskey and imports of milk. The additional supply of milk coming into domestic markets will drive its price down below $1, while the export demand for whiskey will push its price above $5. The 1/5 ratio of their prices will start going down toward the 1/10 ratio prevailing in England.

Just the opposite events occur in England. The original price of whiskey (10 shillings per gallon) will fall because imports raise the supply available, while the price of milk (1 shilling per gallon) will rise because of the export demand. The original 1/10 ratio of their prices will rise toward the 1/5 ratio prevailing in the U.S.

Somewhere in between the two original ratios the two will meet, pushed toward that point by milk exports from England and whiskey exports from the U.S. Trade between the two nations will continue to increase until the equality of relative prices is established, and the equality will be maintained by one specific level of trade. Any deviation from equality will set in motion a change in the level of trade that will bring the system back to its equilibrium.

This is brought out forcefully to you upon your return from Las Vegas, where you lost all your gains at the gaming tables. Your brother meets you at the door furiously, claiming that you deceived him; he followed your directions and ended up with no profit at all. He didn't even cover his shipping costs. Mystified, you look at the prices prevailing when he bought and sold and discover that they were as in Table 44–4.

TABLE 44-4
Prices of Milk and Whiskey after Trade

	In England	In U.S.
Price of milk	1s 1d/ gal	90¢/ gal
Price of whiskey	8s 8d/ gal	$7.20/ gal

You realize then that the trading you did the day before you turned over the business to your brother was just enough to bring the price ratios in *both* countries to just 1/8.

"You haven't done anything since?" you ask him carefully.

"No," he replies.

At this point you make a few discrete telephone calls, discover that prices have gone back to their original levels, and once more set the original transactions in motion. Only this time you plan to pass up Las Vegas.

THE LONG-RUN ADJUSTMENT

Changes in domestic prices set in motion by the flow of trade between countries have the same effects on output as any change in prices. For industries in which prices rise, profits are increased and resources are attracted to them. Where prices fall, however, profits decline and resources move out. Output rises in the former and declines in the latter until profits in the two are equalized and the long-run equilibrium is reached. Monopoloid influences and other market imperfections or restrictions may set limits beyond which the adjustments cannot go, but the tendency is always there.

In our whiskey-milk illustration, for example, international trade reduces the price of milk in the U.S. and increases the price of whiskey. Production of milk in the U.S. will decline and production of whiskey will rise until the producers in both industries are once more earning just a normal profit. The opposite trend will take place in England, where the price movements are in the opposite direction, but a new long-run equilibrium also will be established there.

These changes can be visualized as shifts along the production possibilities frontier in both countries, as shown in Figure 44-1.

THE GAINS FROM TRADE

International trade enables both parties to gain from the exchange, in the sense that each country can have more goods than without trade. Without trade a nation will have to use large amounts of resources to produce high-cost items. With trade it can specialize in the things it does efficiently while trading with other countries to obtain its other needs. In the process, it can have more of everything.

Look at the whiskey-milk example we have been using. Before the trading operations began, the price of milk in the U.S. was $1 per gallon and whiskey .

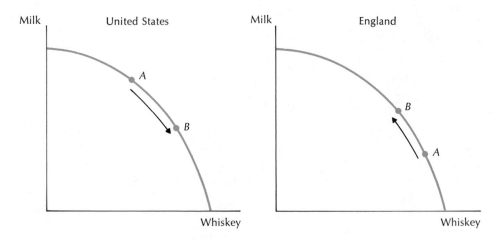

FIGURE 44-1
International Trade Brings Shift Along Production Possibilities Frontier
As a result of the long-run adjustment to international trade the U.S. produces more whiskey and less milk, while England produces more milk and less whiskey.

$5 per gallon. For another 5 gallons of milk to be obtained, resources would have to be shifted from whiskey production, requiring a 1 gallon reduction in whiskey output. But if that gallon of whiskey were exported and sold in England, the proceeds would buy 10 gallons of milk. The net gain is exactly 5 gallons of milk, with no change in the amount of whiskey available for domestic use.

The same is true for England. For another gallon of whiskey to be obtained from domestic production, output of milk would have to be cut by 10 gallons. But with trade that added gallon of whiskey could be obtained by the exporting of only 5 gallons of milk to the U.S. Here also there is a net gain of 5 gallons of milk.

At the end of the process of long-run adjustment, the gains at the margin are smaller, because the relative price ratios have been equalized at 1/8. At that ratio, one gallon of whiskey exported from the U.S. will bring 8 gallons of milk in England. This is a net gain of 3 gallons of milk when compared with producing it domestically, without trade, at a 1/5 ratio.

Correspondingly, in England 8 gallons of domestic milk can be traded for 1 gallon of imported whiskey. This is a net gain of 2 gallons of milk, for without trade an additional gallon of whiskey could be obtained only by reducing output of milk by 10 gallons.

For the world economy as a whole there has been a net gain of 5 gallons of milk as a result of that last marginal trade. The gain was divided, with 3 gallons going to U.S. consumers and 2 gallons to English consumers. There is nothing magic about the source of those gains; they come from the specialization of each nation in the production it does most efficiently.

The gains from trade can be graphically shown in relation to the production possibilities frontier. They enable both parties to trade to move *beyond* the production possibilities frontier and have more than they would be able to produce on their own. This is shown in Figure 44-2.

In our specific whiskey-milk example the gains from trade accruing to the U.S. are pictured in Figure 44-3 to show the move beyond the domestic production possibilities frontier in detail.

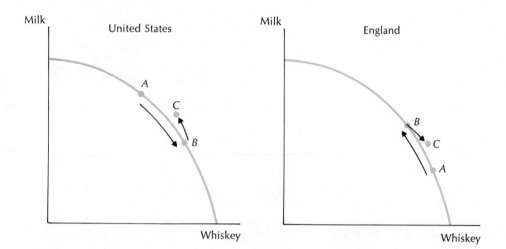

FIGURE 44-2
International Trade Enables Nations to Move Beyond Production Possibilities Frontier

Specialization induced by international trade enables each nation to move from *A* to *B*. It trades part of its increased output of the specialized product for other goods that it can get on favorable terms in the international economy, ending up outside its domestic production possibilities frontier.

THE TERMS OF TRADE

The division of the gains from international trade depends on the equilibrium price relationships established by the flow of trade. Those relationships are called the *terms of trade*. They may be favorable to countries specializing in capital-intensive exports if there is a general shortage of capital in the world economy. They may be favorable to land-extensive exports if there is a general lack of food or other products of agriculture, as there usually is during big wars. Furthermore, the terms of trade may shift as the world economy develops and changes; the introduction of synthetic rubber worsened the trading position of nations specializing in rubber exports, for example.

To pin this idea down, note in our whiskey-milk example that the 1/8 equilibrium price ratio between milk and whiskey established by trade between

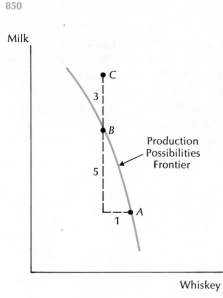

FIGURE 44-3
U.S. Gains from Whiskey-Milk Trade with England

By producing more milk at home, the U.S. could get 5 gallons of milk by reducing whiskey production by 1 gallon. Alternatively, it can trade 1 gallon of whiskey and get 8 gallons of imported milk, for a net gain of 3 gallons of milk. Instead of moving from A to B on the production possibilities frontier, it can move from A to C. At C it will have as much whiskey as at B, plus 3 gallons of milk more than it would have at B.

England and the U.S. left 60 percent of the gains with the U.S. and 40 percent with England. If the ratio had ended up less favorably to the whiskey exporter, say 1/7, the proportions would have been reversed. See if you can work out the arithmetic.

THE INTERNATIONAL ECONOMY

We have just sketched in nontechnical terms the basic propositions on which international economic relationships are based. A brief summary is in order, because the matter is somewhat complex and was treated in highly compact fashion.

1. International trade is based on relative scarcities of the various factors of production, which vary from region to region and from country to country.
2. These relative scarcities would lead to different relative prices within countries if there were no trade.
3. Those different relative prices offer opportunities for private gain if trade is allowed, however, leading to a flow of trade between areas and nations.
4. The flow of trade sets in motion a long-run adjustment within the domestic economies of the trading nations that brings about greater specialization on export commodities.
5. Specialization is the source of real gains from trade that are divided among the trading nations according to the terms of trade that develop out of the national-international economic equilibrium.

These basic propositions lead to a fundamental policy proposition: international trade leads to increased output. As long as the trade is free and unrestricted, following the profit-maximizing pattern of a competitive economy, it brings gains to both parties to the exchange. Under those conditions more trade is better than less. Any restrictions such as tariffs, quotas, exclusive trading rights, and other barriers to imports and exports reduce the amount of trade, reduce the gains, and leave everyone worse off. This policy of free trade will be examined more fully in the next chapter. Before we get to it, however, some possible points of confusion and some terminology need to be examined.

THE PRINCIPLE OF COMPARATIVE ADVANTAGE

The theoretical analysis of the basis for international trade is called the principle of *comparative advantage*. A nation has a comparative advantage in production of a commodity if its opportunity cost of producing the commodity is lower than that of a second nation. A corollary of that principle applies specifically to the case of two nations and two commodities: if a nation has a comparative advantage in one commodity the other nation *must* have a comparative advantage in the other.

Our whiskey-milk example was an illustration of the principle. The opportunity cost of producing a gallon of whiskey in the U.S. was 5 gallons of milk. In England the opportunity cost was 10 gallons of milk. We say, then, that the U.S. has a comparative advantage in whiskey production.

Looking at England, we see that the opportunity cost of producing milk is 0.1 gallon of whiskey. In the U.S. it is 0.2 gallons of whiskey. England has a comparative advantage in milk production.

All of this merely repeats the basic principle, but it is important for the reader to know the terminology used by economists and to have a careful statement of the theoretical principle.

ABSOLUTE ADVANTAGE

At this point the student must be warned against one of the most common misconceptions about international trade, one very widely held. It is this: a nation exports those things that it produces more cheaply than other nations, and imports those things produced more cheaply elsewhere. The example usually given is something like bananas in Guatemala. It takes little land, labor, and capital to produce bananas in Guatemala, while if they were produced in hothouses in the U.S., it would require much more land, labor, and capital. *Therefore*, the argument runs, the U.S. imports bananas from Guatemala. The argument sounds plausible, and we are all familiar with it; indeed, we were all taught it by the teachers and geography books we had in elementary school.

Well, there's no help for it: you'll just have to unlearn it, because it's wrong.

In this chapter the principle was never stated that way. If we were to translate the case of Guatemalan bananas properly into the principle of comparative advantage, it might turn out this way: the cost of producing bananas in Guatemala is less, *relative to the cost of producing other things*, than it is in the U.S. The direct comparison of physical costs of production between the two nations must never be made.

A little reflection and some specific examples will show why this is so. Example: It takes less land, labor, and capital to grow wheat in the Mohawk Valley of New York, or in tidewater Virginia, than it does in North Dakota or Kansas. In fact, tidewater Virginia is known for some of the highest wheat yields per acre in the world, much higher than for the wheat-growing areas of the Midwest. Why, then, is no wheat grown there? Because other crops are *more* profitable. The opportunity costs of producing wheat are too high. The area produces peanuts instead, and Smithfield hams from hogs fed on peanuts.

Another example: Your rich uncle may be a better typist than his secretary, but it would be foolish for him to do his own typing. He can earn perhaps $500 per day as a businessman, while he can hire a typist for $40 per day. He won't give up $500 in order to save $40, even though he could do more typing than the secretary in one day.

When lower real costs of production exist, an *absolute advantage* prevails. This is true of wheat production in tidewater Virginia or your uncle's typing skills. A nation has an absolute advantage in production of a commodity if for a given amount of effort, it can produce more of the commodity than another nation.

Yet it is quite possible for a nation with an absolute advantage in a commodity to specialize in other things while the nation with an absolute disadvantage in that commodity specializes in producing it and exporting it. Like Kansas wheat or your uncle's typist.

Take our whiskey-milk example, for instance. Suppose the U.S. had an absolute advantage over England in production of both whiskey and milk. That is, suppose it could produce both commodities at lower cost in units of land-labor-capital than England, as indicated in Table 44–5. We have agreed now that the U.S. can produce both milk and whiskey at lower real cost (units of land, labor, and capital) than England. *Yet this makes no difference to the flow of trade.* The original price ratios on which your profit-making series of trades was based have not changed, and the profit-making behavior of businessmen will not have changed. The original flow of trade set in motion by the price relationships will develop. Indeed, turn the situation around and give England an absolute advantage in both commodities. The flow of trade will continue just as before.

TABLE 44–5
U.S. Has an Absolute Advantage in Production of Both Milk and Whiskey

	U.S.		England	
	Price	Units of Cost	Price	Units of Cost
Milk	$1/gal	5	1s/gal	10
Whiskey	$5/gal	25	£1/gal	100

International trade is based on comparative advantages, not absolute advantages. It may appear at times that absolute advantages are important, for a nation with an absolute advantage in a product may also have a comparative advantage in it. But it is the comparative advantage that is significant.

Don't be trapped by the following question, a favorite on economics examinations:

> True or false: A nation will specialize in production of goods that it can produce at lower cost than other nations.

That statement is false. It would be true only if the phrase "relative to other products" is inserted after "at lower cost." Or if the phrase "opportunity cost" were to replace the word "cost."

SOME QUALIFICATIONS

The astute reader of this chapter will already have identified several assumptions made in the analysis which should be made explicit. First is the assumption of full employment. The illustrations of the production possibilities frontier were all based on the proposition that without trade a nation would produce along the frontier and not within it. Trade would not bring unemployment.

This assumption may not be correct in the real world. A nation may export capital-intensive products and import labor-intensive ones, making it more difficult to maintain full employment at home. A shift in relative costs may create difficult employment problems in some areas or industries if international markets are suddenly lost. The resulting unemployment may more than offset the gains from trade.

Two points can be made in defense of the full-employment assumption. First, macroeconomic policies can keep any economy at or close to full employment with any pattern of world trade that may prevail. Second, special employment and manpower development programs can ease the transition of labor from an industry with declining exports. In the long run, the gains from trade can be expected to prevail.

There is a second important assumption in the theory: market prices within individual countries reflect the real relative scarcities that prevail. This assumption may also be untrue:

1. Monopolies and market control may distort scarcity relationships in favor of the owners of monopolized resources or firms.
2. In planned economies relative prices may be deliberately distorted for noneconomic purposes.
3. Producers may not bear the full costs of production (pollution, social insurance, and so on), enabling them to exploit one of the factors of production.

All of these potential distortions are serious. By preventing relative prices from fully reflecting relative scarcities, they prevent the welfare-maximizing level of trade (and sometimes direction of trade) from developing. Their most significant effect, however, is in distorting the distribution of the gains from trade *within* a nation, in favor of monopolists, or the political goals of planners, or producers in general.

From the point of view of other trading nations, these internal distribution effects should not interfere with a general policy of maximizing trade. For example, if a nation follows a policy of keeping wages down in its export industries in order to gain an advantage over other trading nations, the other countries can buy just that much more cheaply in international markets. They will reap the advantages of low wages in the exporting country and their consumers will pay lower prices, provided, of course, that their macroeconomic and manpower policies are able to sustain full employment at home. It is foolish, then, for a country like the United States to keep out low-cost Asian textiles and clothing by imposing import quotas and high tariffs in order to protect the jobs of U.S. workers. We can protect the workers (rather than their jobs) by proper domestic economic policies, while we allow U.S. consumers to buy low-priced imports and raise their standard of living.

Summary

Relative scarcities of the factors of production vary from country to country. They are the basis of international trade. Without trade they lead to differences in relative prices of final goods which, in turn, would bring traders into operation to take advantage of the different relative prices and make a profit through trade.

The flow of trade starts a process of adjustment in the trading nations that leads to increased specialization in production of goods for export. The adjustment involves both relative prices and resource shifts into the export industries. One result of the flow of trade is a tendency toward a worldwide general equilibrium in which relative prices are equalized between nations.

Specialization provides gains from trade which are divided among the trading nations according to the terms of trade that develop out of the national-international equilibrium.

The fundamental policy proposition derived from the analysis of international trade is that free and unrestricted trade brings gains to both parties. As long as a nation is able to maintain full employment, more trade is better than less.

Key Concepts

Comparative advantage.   A nation has a comparative advantage in production of a good if its opportunity cost of producing it is less than another country's opportunity cost of producing the same good.

Absolute advantage.   A nation has an absolute advantage in producing a good if its cost in terms of units of land, labor, and capital is less than another country's cost in units of land, labor, and capital.

When Congress was debating government support for construction of a supersonic transport airplane (SST) in 1970, one argument made in favor of the program was that it would help solve the U.S. balance of payments problem. The argument ran as follows:

> The supersonic transport would be built by other nations. If Americans were to travel on those foreign-owned planes, they would pay in U.S. dollars, increasing the deficit in the U.S. balance of payments. On the other hand, if foreigners were to travel on U.S.-owned planes, they would pay in foreign currencies, thereby easing U.S. balance of payments problems. Similar problems would arise with U.S. airlines paying dollars to buy the foreign aircraft, instead of foreign airlines buying U.S. aircraft.

Most economists recognized this argument as fallacious, although a few very highly respected ones actually expressed this view in print. They won't be named here out of professional courtesy, for it's equivalent to an astronomer stating that the sun revolves around the earth.

Why is that argument a fallacy? After all, it does seem to have a certain logical plausibility. The fallacy arises from failure to consider what happens to the U.S. dollars that foreigners receive when Americans buy their products or services. Let's take up the case of U.S. purchases from foreigners and see what happens.

An American airline buys a foreign SST for, say, $20 million. The seller probably doesn't want dollars. He needs his own currency, in order to pay his suppliers, workers, and other creditors. So he sells the dollars to a business firm that wants dollars for one of three purposes:

1. To buy American products or services.

2. To invest in the U.S. economy.

3. To build up its bank account in its New York bank.

It is possible for a variety of intermediate transactions to take place. For example, a bank may acquire the dollars and lend them to a firm that buys American goods. But in the end there are only three uses to which the U.S. dollars can be put, buying U.S. goods, or building up investments, or increasing dollars cash balances.

In any case, the dollars are used to make payments to

Americans. When the payment is for American exports, by far the largest purpose for which these funds are normally used, it is clear that a reciprocal exchange of products and services has occurred. A U.S. firm got an SST while a foreign buyer got an equal amount of U.S. exports. When the payment is for the purpose of increasing balances in U.S. banks, the foreign firm has obtained a larger U.S. bank account while Americans have obtained an SST. When the payment is for investment purposes, the foreigner has obtained an income-producing asset while Americans have obtained an SST. As for the payments themselves, one group of Americans paid out $20 million while another group received $20 million. A reciprocal exchange of assets occurred, with a reciprocal set of payments moving in the opposite direction. Figure 45-1 shows the flow of payments involved in these transactions.

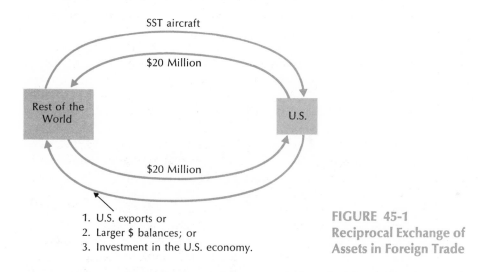

1. U.S. exports or
2. Larger $ balances; or
3. Investment in the U.S. economy.

FIGURE 45-1
Reciprocal Exchange of
Assets in Foreign Trade

The basic point, and it is fundamental to an understanding of international economic relationships, is *that trade and payments must always balance*. If a nation sells to foreigners, it *must* buy; if a nation buys, it *must* sell. As in the examples given above, it is impossible for Americans to buy foreign goods and services without foreigners also buying U.S. goods and services. At times the transactions may include either real or financial investments, but the fundamental balance will always be there.

One qualification of the general principle must be noted, however. As foreign-owned U.S. bank balances increase, their owners may not wish to enlarge them further and may desire payment in other forms, such as gold. Gold isn't very useful, for it doesn't earn income as an investment does, or provide satisfactions in the way commodities or services do. But if foreigners don't want to hold larger amounts of dollars (perhaps because of inflation in the U.S.) and don't want either U.S. goods or U.S. investments (perhaps also because of inflation in the U.S.) gold may be their best bet. As we all have learned in recent years, this situation can lead to a variety of sticky problems in the balance of payments, some of which will be discussed later in this chapter. The problems arise, however, not because the U.S. airline bought the SST, but because of other economic policies or nonpolicies that are behind the inflation that causes foreigners to want gold instead of U.S. dollars.

TRADE AND INVESTMENT

Any nation that sells more abroad than it buys will build up its holdings of financial assets abroad. In a private enterprise economy these assets will be owned by its citizens rather than by the government. Since it is more profitable to own an income-producing investment than a bank account, these funds normally gravitate into foreign investments. Conversely, a nation that buys more abroad than it sells will become an object of investment by foreigners.

This basic relationship has led economists to postulate a hypothetical pattern of development and change in its trade relations for any nation engaged in international trade. Initially, a relatively undeveloped nation will buy more abroad than it sells, owing to the fact that its productive capacities are poorly developed. Lack of capital will also make it an attractive object of investment to foreigners, who will have investment funds available because of their large exports to the relatively undeveloped nation. In this first stage the new nation will have an "unfavorable" balance of trade—imports are greater than exports—and it will import capital from abroad. The capital of course, will be owned by foreigners, and payments of interest and principal on the debt will grow. In this stage it is a *young debtor nation*. The United States was in this stage of development up to about the Civil War.

As the nation's economy grows through internal savings and import of capital, its exports can be expected to increase more rapidly than its imports, until exports exceed imports and it has a "favorable" balance of trade. When that happens, its foreign investments will grow and its citizens will begin to buy out the investments by foreigners that were made in years past. Nevertheless, it will be a net debtor in its foreign economic relations because the interest and principle it pays annually to foreigners is greater in amount than similar payments coming in from foreigners. At this second stage it is a *mature debtor nation*. The United States was in this stage of development during the second half of the nineteenth century, roughly.

Continuation of the trends of the mature debtor stage will ultimately bring large foreign investments while the domestic investments owned by foreigners are gradually bought back. This is made possible by a continuing "favorable" balance of trade. Gradually payments of interest and principal paid by foreigners will grow until they exceed the amounts paid to foreigners. During this·stage the nation becomes a net creditor rather than debtor, since its foreign investments are larger than the total it owes to foreigners. This third stage is that of the *young creditor nation*. The United States has been in this stage during most of the twentieth century.

Ultimately, the building up of foreign investments will bring in such large payments of interest and principal each year that these funds can be used to pay for imports on a larger scale. A nation's citizens can live off of the fat of the land by consuming not only from domestic production but also through imports. The former "favorable" balance of trade is now "unfavorable," with the excess of imports over exports being paid for with the returns from foreign investments. This fourth stage is that of a *mature creditor nation*. Great Britain had reached this enviable position before 1914, but lost it by the close of World War II because it had to sell very large portions of its foreign investments to pay for imports of food and war material in the First and Second World Wars.

The pattern can be summarized as follows:

Stage   I: Young Debtor Nation. Imports exceed exports and capital is being imported from abroad.

Stage   II: Mature Debtor Nation. Exports exceed imports and foreign investments are growing. Nevertheless, net payments on debt and investments move to foreigners.

Stage III: Young Creditor Nation. Exports exceed imports, and foreign investments have expanded so that net payments on debt and investments are inward.

Stage IV: Mature Creditor Nation. Imports exceed exports once again, paid for by earnings on foreign investment and debt owed by foreigners.

This scenario is not a universal one. However, it has been followed in broad outline by the major industrial nations of western Europe and North America, and by other countries with similar backgrounds and economic organization. The United States has resisted moving into the mature creditor stage, and this policy has helped create some important problems for the world economy. United States policy has been reluctant to allow imports to grow to levels larger than exports, partly because of the effects of imports on domestic employment and partly because of difficulties with the U.S. balance of payments. This policy has brought a continuing buildup in U.S. foreign investments, which has added to foreign resentment of the U.S. economic presence. It has probably also contributed to expropriation of U.S.-owned investments abroad, since the normal course of repatriation of foreign investments is aborted by a continued exports surplus on the part of the owning country. At the same time, still higher U.S. standards of living have been foregone by the retention of a variety of import quotas and tariffs. In the normal course of events, U.S. citizens would gradually be disposing of foreign investments to help pay for enlarged imports. This would provide some satisfaction of the nationalist impulse in less developed countries while improving economic welfare at home. Instead, we resist the growth of imports, thereby penalizing our own citizens and increasing political tensions.

We should note, however, that the process by which a nation's citizens build up their foreign investments is rooted in the normal flows of trade and capital movements of the international economic system. The process would take place even in the absence of government assistance to its citizens, tariffs, colonialism, or spheres of influence. This does not mean that a conscious policy of economic aggrandizement by a nation, on behalf of its businessmen, has no impact on the world economy. Of course it has. But economic analysis tells us that the international spread of capital, motivated by a desire for gain, is a characteristic feature of the international economy. The result, in the long run, can be greater economic development in the country receiving capital imports as well as higher living standards in the capital-exporting nation. But it can also lead to a position of economic dominance by the capital-exporting nation, a position it may seek to maintain beyond its time, as may well be the case today with respect to the United States.

THE BALANCE OF INTERNATIONAL PAYMENTS

The balanced flows of any nation's participation in the world economy consist of several different kinds. One is merchandise exports and imports, supplemented by services such as shipping and insurance. A second is capital movements or investments, in which the citizens of one nation acquire owner-ship of income-producing assets in another nation. A third consists of a variety of government transactions. Finally, there are short-term financial transactions and gold movements that serve to achieve a balance in which payments in one direction equal payments in the other direction.

All of this can be summarized for any country in a formal statement of its *balance of international payments*. It is not mysterious or difficult to under-stand once you realize that it is only an accounting of all the receipts and expenditures in international trade of a nation's citizens during a year.

The balance of international payments has the following components:

Section I shows private trading in goods and services. It is sometimes called the "current account" for the private sector, because it shows all of the private transactions other than capital movements. It includes merchandise imports and exports and "invisible" imports and exports. The latter are payments for transportation, travel, and other services; interest and dividends on investments and royalty payments; private gifts and public pensions.

Section II shows U.S. government transactions, including sales of military goods, other military expenditures, and government grants and loans.

Section III is the capital account. It includes private investment by Americans abroad and foreigners in the U.S. It also includes short-term capital movements, that is, changes in U.S.-owned bank balances abroad and foreign-owned bank balances in the U.S.

Section IV shows the official settlement transaction, including gold movements in and out and changes in "official reserves." [1]

The U.S. balance of payments for 1970, which is summarized in Table 45–1, illustrates how all the figures are put together. Table 45–1 tells an interesting story. Section I shows that so far as regular day-to-day transactions in the private sector were concerned, the U.S. had a favorable balance of $6.0 billion. Foreigners owed us that much more than we owed them in these private transactions. The federal government reversed the coin, however, as shown in Section II. It paid out $6.9 billion more than it received, leaving a net deficit after Sections I and II of some $0.9 billion.

Section III shows the flow of capital. There was a net outflow of capital from the U.S. of $9.0 billion, bringing the total deficit to $9.9 billion. The bulk of the outflow ($6.4 billion) was "hot money" fleeing from the dollar in expectation of the dollar crisis that came in 1971. Without those transfers of private liquid assets the deficit would have been $3.5 billion.

Section IV of the account shows how the deficit was settled. Official reserve transactions with foreign governments and the International Monetary Fund, including gold sales of $0.8 billion, brought net credits of $3.2 billion, almost enough to achieve a balance in ordinary times. But 1970 was not an ordinary year. A crisis in the international financial system was building up, and a run on the dollar was starting, featured by the flight of "hot money" already noted. That flow was counterbalanced by short-term credits from foreign central banks and other international organizations of $7.8 billion, which postponed the crisis until the summer of 1971. At this point the entire account should balance, just as your personal checkbook is balanced. But it doesn't (like my checkbook), so the unexplained difference is chalked up to errors and omission, which are shown on the next to last line.[2]

---

[1] A nation's official reserves are held in three forms. One is gold. A second is foreign currencies convertible into gold, usually the "key currencies"—dollar, pound, or mark. A variation of the second type is foreign currencies borrowed from other governments under so-called "swap" arrangements. The third is reserve assets at the International Monetary Fund. The latter were originally created by a nation's contribution to the IMF when it was established in 1945 (or by later contributions) in the form of gold or currencies convertible into gold. A recent variant of reserve assets at the IMF is "special drawing rights," which will be explained later in this chapter. Any member of the fund (nations are members) therefore has a reserve position at the IMF, together with gold and key currencies, out of which it can settle obligations owed to other trading nations. In times of emergency it may also borrow from the IMF if special conditions are met.

[2] I used to spend hours trying to reconcile my checkbook with my monthly bank statement, and never found an error on the part of the bank. Then I studied the balance of international payments. Now all I do is reconcile the two sums by an "errors and omissions" entry, saving untold hours. Who says it doesn't pay to study economics?

TABLE 45-1
U.S. Balance of Payments, 1970
(Billions of Dollars)

	Debits	Credits	Balance
I. Goods and Services, Private Sector			
Imports and exports	$39.9	$42.0	
Services	9.5	9.8	
Private remittances	0.9		
Investment income	5.1	9.6	
	55.4	61.4	+$6.0
II. U.S. Government			
Military expenditures and sales	4.8	1.5	
Grants and loans, etc.	5.4	1.8	
	10.2	3.3	−6.9
III. Capital Account			
Long-term	5.3	3.1	
Short-term	1.1	0.7	
Net change in private liquid assets	6.4		
	12.8	3.8	9.0
Net deficit (−) or surplus (+) to be financed			−9.9
IV. Settlement and Balancing Items			
Official reserve transactions (including gold flow)	0.9	4.3	
Net change in official liquid assets		7.8	
Errors and omissions	1.3		
	2.2	12.1	+9.9

Note: The balance sheet shown here has been rearranged somewhat from the official balance sheet in order to simplify the presentation. Figures may not add to totals because of rounding.

THE PLACE OF THE UNITED STATES IN WORLD TRADE

The United States is the most important single participant in world trade. It accounts for about 15.5 percent of the world's exports of goods and usually just a slightly smaller fraction of the world's imports.

The U.S. is one of nine nations (excluding the USSR and other "Soviet bloc" countries) with exports and imports in excess of $10 billion in 1969. These nine countries accounted for two-thirds of the world's exports and almost that large a share of imports. Scan Table 45-2 to note the major trading nations and their shares of world trade.

TABLE 45-2
Merchandise Exports and Imports of Major Trading Nations, 1969

	Imports	Percentage of World Imports	Exports	Percentage of World Exports
United States	$ 38.5	15.1	$ 38.0	15.6
West Germany	25.0	9.8	29.0	11.9
United Kingdom	20.0	7.8	17.5	7.2
France	17.4	6.8	15.0	6.2
Japan	15.0	5.9	16.0	6.6
Canada	14.4	5.7	14.4	5.9
Italy	12.5	4.9	11.0	4.9
Netherlands	11.0	4.3	10.0	4.1
Belgium-Luxembourg	10.0	3.9	10.0	4.1
Total, 9 major trading nations	163.8	64.2	160.9	66.5
Total, world	254.4	100.0	243.0	100.0

Note: The value of imports includes insurance and shipping costs, while the value of exports does not. This accounts for the difference between world exports and imports. None of these figures include data for the USSR, mainland China, Cuba, or the Soviet sphere countries of Eastern Europe.

Although the U.S. is the most important single participant in the international economy, world trade is not particularly significant to the U.S. domestic economy. United States exports were only four percent of the U.S. gross national product in 1969. A very small segment of the U.S. economy is very important in world economic affairs.

Other major trading countries are in a quite different position. Exports are far more important to them than they are to the U.S., tying them much more closely to the world economy, as shown in Table 45-3.

TABLE 45-3
Exports as Percentage of GNP: U.S. and Eight Other Major Trading Nations, 1968

Country	Exports as a Percentage of GNP
United States	4
West Germany	23
United Kingdom	18
France	14
Japan	10
Canada	24
Italy	18
Netherlands	43
Belgium-Luxembourg	38–76

The United States is also the largest supplier of capital to the international economy. United States foreign investments in 1963 were estimated by the Department of Commerce at about $104 billion. By 1970 they were probably in the neighborhood of $130 billion bringing a net income to their owners of almost $7.9 billion. We do not have comparable figures for other major nations, but an idea of the relative magnitude of foreign investments can be obtained from balance-of-payments data on net income earned on foreign investments, shown in Table 45–4. Switzerland is added to this table because a significant portion of European foreign investment income is probably reported through Swiss banks and corporations.

As Table 45–4 indicates, U.S. earnings on foreign investments dwarf all the others, amounting to 91 percent of the net earnings for the nine major trading nations plus Switzerland. It's hard to imagine a more dominant position in world capital markets.

TABLE 45–4
Net Income Earned on Foreign Investments, U.S. and Eight Other Major Trading Nations (and Switzerland), 1968
(Millions of Dollars)

Country	Net Investment Income
United States	$6,420
West Germany	(—) 226
United Kingdom	1,005
France	346
Japan	(—) 254
Canada	(—) 970
Italy	34
Netherlands	200
Belgium-Luxembourg	34
Switzerland	441

The dominant position of the United States in today's world economy has come about primarily because of U.S. economic growth and the large annual savings created by a hard-working, thrifty, acquisitive, and success-oriented people. The very size of the U.S. national income means that its imports will be large. Its advanced technology assures large exports. Large amounts of savings create a spillover into international investment. All of this adds up to a position of dominance in the international economy with respect to both trade and investment. Contributing to the strong U.S. position has been the historical fact of two great world wars, in which the trade and investment positions of the major Western European nations were seriously eroded: Britain, France, and Germany lost ground during the wars while the U.S. forged ahead in technology, capacity to produce, and international investments. But those changes merely hastened a development that would have come anyway.

The U.S. position in world trade has been complicated by a persistent deficit in international payments, beginning in 1950. These deficits have not been due to domestic inflation, for price increases in other parts of the world have tended to be greater than in the U.S. Nor have they been due to the inability of U.S. industry to compete in world markets. United States exports have consistently exceeded U.S. imports (through 1970), to bring a "favorable" balance of trade in the balance of payments. The chief villain in the drama has been large government military expenditures abroad throughout the 1950s and 1960s, along with foreign military and economic aid programs.

The argument might be made that if the U.S. government spent less abroad foreigners would have fewer U.S. dollars to buy our exports and therefore our excess of exports over imports would decline and possibly disappear. There is some truth to that argument. But under those circumstances, our imports would fall also (because of lack of foreign currencies with which to buy them), and a new relationship with less total trade would be established in which the ratio of exports to imports would probably be close to the present one. It is hard to escape the conclusion that the U.S. balance-of-payments deficit is due to the military posture the U.S. has taken in the years since World War II.

The deficits have not been exceptionally large, averaging $1.2 billion annually over the last decade. They would be larger (averaging $2.7 billion annually) if short-term foreign investments in the U.S. were added to the deficit, as they are in some calculations.[3] Table 45-5 shows the deficits for the years 1960–1969, to give you an idea of how they have fluctuated.

TABLE 45-5
U.S. Balance-of-Payments Deficits (−) and Surpluses (+), 1960–1969 (Billions of Dollars)

Year	Official Transactions Only	Short-Term Foreign Investment Included in the Deficit
1960	−$ 3.4	−$ 3.9
1961	− 1.3	− 2.4
1962	− 2.7	− 2.2
1963	− 2.0	− 2.7
1964	− 1.6	− 2.8
1965	− 1.3	− 1.3
1966	+ 0.3	− 1.4
1967	− 3.4	− 3.5
1968	+ 1.6	+ 0.2
1969	+ 1.9	− 7.1
Total, 1960–69	− 11.9	− 27.1
Annual Average	− 1.2	− 2.7

[3] The logic of adding them into the deficit is that these are holdings of dollars for which their owners could demand foreign currency or gold at any time, creating a "run" on U.S. reserves. On the other hand, some of those dollars are held for purposes of carrying on international trade, since the dollar is much used as an international monetary unit. Why argue? Let's say that the average U.S. balance-of-payments deficit during the 1960s was between $1.1 billion (on an "official transactions" basis) and $2.7 billion (on a "liquidity" basis).

THE INTERNATIONAL FINANCIAL SYSTEM

Any nation whose trade and capital exports dominate the world economy will take on added importance in the international financial system. This is true of the United States at the present time. Since U.S. exports and imports are the largest in the world, foreign business firms, banks, and central banks find it highly convenient to hold bank accounts in New York banks. Their dollar accounts can be readily used to carry out the many and varied types of transactions required in international trade; and other firms and banks are always willing to accept dollars because they know that the dollars can always be used when they have to make payments. In this fashion the dollar has become a sort of international money, generally acceptable in making payments in many international transactions.

The British pound was in a similar position in the years before 1914, for largely the same reason, and it still retains some of its importance as a form of international money because trade among the former nations of the British Empire remains important. The West German mark is becoming more significant as an international money, too, also for the same reasons; West German trade and capital exports are important elements in the world economy.

The dollar is the most important of these "key currencies," however. It is so important that dollar balances held by foreigners have formed the basis of the so-called Eurodollar. These are dollars held in bank accounts in European banks (and European branches of U.S. banks) that are borrowed and lent, and used for business transactions of all kinds, while circulating outside the U.S. entirely. No paper money is involved; it is solely a money of account circulating by check. But a German businessman may borrow dollars from a Swiss bank to make a payment to an Italian businessman, with the dollars circulating from account to account in perfect freedom and fully acceptable to all who receive them. At least, this was true prior to August 1971, when the dollar's tie to the price of gold was ended.

The use of dollars for these purposes reflects the need for some kind of international monetary system in which all of the varied currencies of the world find a common denominator that reduces them to comparable terms, in which an exporter or importer can obtain the currencies he needs in order to carry out international transactions, and that provides a means of making payments in a form that all participants are willing to accept. Gold and silver performed those functions for many years, and in the nineteenth century the gold standard was the basis of the international monetary system. Over the last half century, however, the world economy has been moving toward newer forms of international money and toward a managed system.

THE GOLD STANDARD

In the second half of the nineteenth century and prior to the First World War the major nations of the world defined their monetary units in terms of gold, and national governments stood ready to redeem their paper money or coin with gold. This meant that anyone, including importers and exporters, could take dollars to the U.S. Treasury, for example, trade the dollars for gold, export the gold to England, take it to the British Treasury, and there exchange the gold for pounds. In this form the system was called the *gold bullion* standard.

The gold bullion standard had important implications for the domestic economy of nations. Since the currency could be exchanged for gold by anyone, either the banking system or the central bank had to keep a reserve of gold with which to redeem the promise to exchange currency for gold. Gold became the ultimate reserve of the domestic banking system, upon which expansion of bank credit was based. If gold flowed into the country, monetary reserves grew and bank credit expanded, bringing general expansion of the economy with it. If gold flowed out, however, monetary reserves fell and bank credit contracted, resulting in a slowdown of economic activity.

It is easy to understand why, in those days, a nation desired a payments surplus. It brought gold imports, monetary expansion, and economic prosperity. Conversely, a payments deficit would bring a drain of gold, monetary contraction, and economic slowdown. These domestic impacts of the gold standard very often brought intervention by central banks designed to mitigate the internal economic effects of foreign transactions, and the system was never fully automatic for that reason.

This system was substantially modified during the period between the two world wars, as nations sought to gain greater control over their internal economic affairs. Programs designed to stabilize the economy and counteract inflation and depression created a desire to cut the ties between conditions within a nation's economy and other countries. Besides, there wasn't enough gold available to provide reserves large enough to satisfy the needs of world trade. Gold came to be held solely by the central banks and used only in settling international accounts. Currencies continued to be defined in terms of gold but were no longer redeemable in gold. Currencies still had a common denominator and central banks were able to clear their transactions with each other by transferring gold among themselves, but importers and exporters were restricted to use of the world's currencies in their transactions. The system has been named the *gold exchange standard*. Gold remains the basis of the ratios at which currencies exchange for each other, and accounts between central banks can be settled by exchange of gold.

The gold exchange standard has led to much greater use of "key currencies." With national currencies extensively used to settle private international accounts, the currencies of the important trading nations are widely acceptable in making payments, the dollar, pound, and mark in particular. Central banks are continually called upon to supply them. So they naturally hold reserves of them. Thus a dual system has arisen: part of the reserves held by central banks is in the form of gold (or claims to gold) and part is in the form of the "key currencies," namely, dollars, pounds, and marks.

THE VALUE OF A NATION'S CURRENCY

The use of key currencies in international trade implies that the value of a currency does not fluctuate widely. If values did vary widely, importers and exporters would have difficulty in estimating profits from their future transactions, and investors would be uncertain about their long-run returns. Increased uncertainties would tend to hamper both trade and movements of capital, and thereby interfere with the growth of the international economy.

What determines the value of a nation's currency? As we have already noted, the value of money depends on what it will buy, that is, on price levels. Thus, if U.S. prices rise, the value of the dollar will fall. But if British prices, for example, rise just as fast, the relative value of the two currencies will not change. Changes in the relative value of currencies depend on price levels in the various countries. If U.S. prices rise faster than British prices, the value of the dollar will fall relative to the value of the pound and more dollars will have to be exchanged for a British pound. And if British prices rise faster than U.S. prices, the opposite occurs.

These basic relationships are translated into short-run supply and demand changes in the market for foreign currencies. If U.S. prices rise relative to prices abroad, foreigners will buy fewer U.S. exports and need fewer U.S. dollars. The demand for U.S. dollars will fall. United States citizens, on the other hand, will tend to buy more foreign goods, enlarging the supply of dollars held by foreigners. With an increased supply of dollars and a reduced demand, the price of dollars will fall; foreigners will have to give up less of their currency to obtain any given amount of dollars. In its fundamentals, the international value of a nation's money depends on the relationship of the domestic price level to price levels abroad. But in the short run, currency values move with demand and supply conditions in the foreign exchange markets of the world.

STABILIZING CURRENCY VALUES

Under the old gold bullion standard there were limits within which the values of currencies could fluctuate. The limits were based on the cost of shipping gold, and were called "gold points." For example, prior to 1914 the dollar and pound were each defined in terms of gold so that $4.86 was equal to £1. Further, the cost of shipping $4.86 in gold between New York and London was approximately 3 cents. Under those circumstances, if the value of the dollar on the foreign exchange market rose to, say, $4.82 = £1, it would pay an Englishman to turn in his pounds to the British treasury for gold, ship the gold to the U.S. for 3 cents, and turn it in to the U.S. treasury for dollars at the official value of $4.86. For each £1 so transferred he would make a profit of one cent; not much, but it adds up to a respectable total when millions of pounds or dollars are involved. Indeed, even a fraction-of-a-cent's difference would be enough to start the gold moving. In this fashion speculators kept the value of the world's currencies within a range above and below the gold value of currencies that was determined by the cost of shipping gold. In the case of the dollar, those "gold points" were about $4.83 and $4.89.

Of course, gold transfers affected monetary reserves and domestic economic activity, as we have already noted. These changes in the level of economic activity would presumably counteract the domestic economic events that were originally responsible for the rise or fall of the value of the nation's currency. Inflation would bring a fall in the value of currency, loss of gold, a decline in bank reserves, less bank credit, and a slowdown in economic activity that would end the inflation, for example. The system was thought to be self-adjusting, assisted, of course, by monetary policy designed to smooth the adjustments that might otherwise be seriously disruptive.

The system of international financial relationships that prevailed until 1971, based on the gold exchange standard and key currencies, functioned differently. Under the Bretton Woods agreement each nation was responsible for keeping the value of its currency within 1 percent of its "par" value. Its "par" resulted from the definition of the currency in terms of gold. For example, the gold content of the dollar, as defined by U.S. law, is four times the gold content of the franc, as defined by French law. This made one dollar equal to four francs, or one franc equal to 25 cents. The French government, through its central bank, had to keep the value of the franc, as it was bought and sold on the foreign exchange market, within a range of 24¾ cents and 25¼ cents. To do so, it would buy francs whenever the price fell toward 24¾ cents and sell francs when the price rose toward 25¼ cents. This was an open-market operation just like any open-market purchase or sale, except that it entailed purchase or sale of the nation's currency on the foreign exchanges rather than the usual operations in the government securities market. Under normal conditions these stabilizing operations were sufficient to contain short-run fluctuations in a currency's price within the required bounds of 1 percent of par value and maintain a system of *fixed exchange rates*.

The Bretton Woods system broke down under the impact of the dollar crisis of 1971, which will be discussed more fully later in this chapter. The system had depended upon the fact that at least one currency, the dollar, had a firm value in terms of gold that was sustained by the willingness of the U.S. Treasury to buy gold from foreign central banks at $35 an ounce—and to redeem dollars from them at the same price. When the dollar crisis came, the Treasury could no longer continue to redeem dollars for gold, and stopped doing so. This cut the direct tie between dollars and gold, and the value of the dollar began to "float" relative to other currencies. This action also ended the obligation of central banks to keep to the fixed exchange rates of the Bretton Woods system. A whole new set of relationships between the chief currencies of the world began to emerge, based on their supply and demand in world markets and the underlying trade flows and domestic price levels that in turn influence the markets for foreign exchange.

The dollar crisis itself had its immediate cause in a huge U.S. balance of payments deficit that could have caused the loss of the entire U.S. gold reserve. It was in order to prevent that from happening that the U.S. allowed the dollar to "float."

LONG-RUN ADJUSTMENTS

A nation faced with a continuous drain of payments to foreigners will have to take steps to stop the drain. A variety of actions can be taken, all of which affect the domestic economy and its relationships with the rest of the world.

Inflation can be halted by forcing a reduction in total spending at home through fiscal restraint and tight money. Reduced aggregate demand will automatically bring a decline in spending for imports, and after a time it should slow down and end the domestic inflation. New price relationships will bring less imports and more exports. The revised flow of trade will bring reduced demand for foreign currencies and increase the nation's currency available to foreigners, until the value of nation's currency in foreign exchange markets moves back to its normal or "par" value. This is the course of events that might be aimed at, at least. One reason for the dollar crisis of 1971 was the failure of such domestic policies to work properly.

Sometimes the problem is more fundamental than a period of domestic inflation. The basic terms of trade can turn against a nation, making it harder to sell its products in world markets. For example, Brazil in the nineteenth century was the world's chief supplier of rubber, which was collected from trees growing naturally in jungle forests. A comparatively lower-cost method of production, plantation agriculture in southeast Asia, was developed, and Brazilian rubber could no longer compete in world markets. Similar problems were created for Southeast Asia fifty years later when comparatively low-cost production of synthetic rubber was achieved.

Sometimes the difficulties are very fundamental. England, for example, with an economy based on low-cost supplies of coal, found its position in world trade steadily worsening as the costs of coal production rose (relative to other areas of the world). The relative prices of English exports increased causing the value of exports to rise much more slowly than the value of imports. These changes were so gradual as to go almost unnoticed, but so persistent as to mount significantly in the long run. This trend was coupled with the sale of foreign investments needed to finance two world wars, which reduced the ability to pay for imports. As a result, England has been faced with a very serious and continuing international financial problem. Indeed, the problem is even more complex than described here, although the basic difficulties are clear enough.

In these situations a nation has little choice but to devalue its currency. *Devaluation* means simply a change in the definition of the currency in terms of gold. The price of gold is raised, making the nation's currency worth less. This action changes the relationship between the domestic currency and foreign currencies, and thereby influences the flow of imports and exports. By influencing the flow of foreign trade, devaluation affects a nation's balance of payments and also its domestic economy, hopefully to a large enough degree to correct the imbalances that created the problem in the first place.

Here is how the scenario would be expected to work itself out in the case of a country facing a persistent deficit in its international payments, having exhausted its supplies of foreign exchange, unable to borrow more and approaching the end of its gold reserves. It decides to devalue its currency by, say, 20 percent. It does so by paying 20 percent more for gold at its treasury or central bank. In the case of the United States, this would mean that instead of paying $35 per ounce for gold the Treasury would pay $42.

This action will not initially have any effect on the domestic economy, but it will affect the nation's terms of trade with the rest of the world. Where formerly the ratio of exchange between the dollar and the franc was $1 = 4 francs and the franc could buy 25¢ worth of U.S. goods, after devaluation the ratio would be $1.20 = 4 francs, and the franc could buy 30¢-worth of U.S. goods. This change will affect imports and exports. More U.S. dollars will be needed to buy foreign goods. French merchandise that formerly cost 25¢ will now cost 30¢. Americans will therefore buy less abroad, and imports will decline. Just the opposite effect occurs with respect to exports. The Frenchman who formerly paid one franc to get 25¢-worth of U.S. exports now finds that his franc buys 30¢-worth. He gets more for his money than before and buys more. In effect, the prices paid by Americans for imported goods will rise, while the prices paid by foreigners for U.S. exports will fall. The result is an increase in exports and a decrease in imports. Fewer payments are owing to foreigners while larger payments come in from them. If the devaluation is large enough, the imbalance in the flow of international payments will be corrected and the value of the nation's currency can be stabilized at the new and lower level.

Any nation, then, has a choice between two basic policies when faced by a persistent imbalance in its international payments. It can reduce domestic prices by inducing a recession. Tight money and budgetary restraint can cause enough unemployment to reduce domestic prices to levels that encourage exports and diminish imports far enough to balance the international accounts. This policy may work, but at substantial cost to the domestic economy.

Alternatively, the currency can be devalued. This policy will not normally cause unemployment at home. Indeed, by stimulating exports, it can promote greater domestic production and employment. Nevertheless, some economic interests will be damaged, including business firms and banks who have large international dealings and hold dollar assets overseas. Their assets will be worth less and the amount of business they can do will decline. From the point of view of the economy as a whole, however, devaluation is preferable to depression as a means of correcting fundamental imbalances in a nation's international payments.[4]

Revaluation is the opposite of devaluation, and occurs when a nation lowers the price of gold by paying less for it at the treasury. The German mark has been revalued several times in recent years. The reason for revaluation is a persistent payments surplus. After foreign bank balances are built up and gold stocks pile up, why should a nation keep on exporting goods and services in exchange for merely monetary assets? Even King Midas had too much gold. In that situation it is better to raise the value of your currency, reduce your exports, and have more output to raise living standards at home.

RESTRUCTURING THE SYSTEM

By the late 1960s several problems in the international financial system became important enough to cause moves to devise some better approaches. One problem is that of inadequate reserves. International trade is growing, requiring that central banks hold more gold and key currencies to handle their needs. Reserves are needed to settle accounts among countries and to take care of temporary imbalances in settlements. There is far from enough gold in the world's monetary systems to handle these needs. The use of key currencies, especially the dollar, as international monetary reserves has helped fill the gap. But as the U.S. payments deficit persisted without a significant effort on our part to correct it, worry about an eventual devaluation of the dollar (or its equivalent) made foreign holders of dollars more reluctant to add to their reserves in the form of dollars. Something in addition to gold and key currencies is needed.

The first step toward providing enlarged international reserves was the establishment of special drawing rights at the International Monetary Fund on January 1, 1970. These are called SDRs, and are reserve assets created by the Fund for its members, in proportion to their initial allocation of contributions to the Fund. They are available for any nation to use in settling international balances with another member of the Fund. The purpose is to enlarge the total of reserve assets, supplementing gold, key currencies, and IMF reserve positions (which originally came from gold and convertible currencies), thereby

---

[4] This whole discussion must be qualified by the fact that circumstances in individual cases can complicate the simplicity implied by an explanation of the basic principle. For example, devaluation hasn't helped England a great deal, because higher-cost imports mean higher prices of food and raw materials (these are the bulk of English imports) and thereby push up English costs of production. This quickly eats up most of the gains made possible by lower export prices created by devaluation. England really has had little choice but depression, and for understandable reasons the government has been unwilling to push that policy very far. The result: recurring international payments problems and periodic devaluations that provide only temporary relief.

allowing world trade to expand without fear that the international monetary system will prove inadequate.[5]

The second problem revolves around long-run adjustments to payments deficits, particularly on the part of the U.S. We have a large impact on the world economy, yet because foreign trade is of so little importance to our economy as a whole we have been reluctant to use domestic deflation as a remedy because of its high cost internally. Devaluation is undesirable to us, too, because it would damage the dollar as the predominant key currency and thereby diminish the importance of the New York financial market as a center of world finance. It would also raise the cost of U.S. military and military-related expenditures abroad. National prestige and power help to restrict the alternatives policy-makers are willing to consider. It was the inability of the system as a whole to resolve the problem of U.S. payments deficits that brought the crisis of 1971 to a head and forced the nations of the world to move toward more changes in the international financial system.

THE DOLLAR CRISIS OF 1971

The dollar crisis had been building up for many years. It came to a head in 1971 because our favorable balance of trade disappeared. In that situation it was no longer possible to finance the large military expenditures abroad that the U.S. government customarily makes, a run on the dollar began, and the U.S. was forced to "float" the dollar.

Data from Table 45-1, the balance of payments for 1970, will illustrate the problem. A favorable balance on trade, services, remittances, and investments of $6 billion (Section I) was partially balanced by net foreign investments of $2.6 billion (from Section III), leaving a net surplus from the private sector of $3.4 billion. But U.S. government transactions (Section II), mostly military, had a deficit of $6.9 billion, turning the private surplus to a net deficit of $3.5 billion. This is the normal deficit that does not include the special problem of "hot money." Deficits of that size could be handled within the framework of the Bretton Woods system as long as foreign central banks were willing to accumulate dollars and foreign business firms were willing to hold substantial assets in dollars. Those conditions depended, however, on the basic favorable balance from trade, services, and investment income.

---

[5] The 1970 allocation of SDRs created new international reserves equal to $3.4 billion. Two more allocations of about $3 billion each took place on January 1, 1971 and January 1, 1972, for a total of about $9.5 billion in the first round. This represents an increase in world monetary reserves of about 13 percent over the 1969 level. The U.S. allocation from the first $3.4 billion was $867 million, or 25.5 percent of the total. SDRs can be created only at intervals of about 5 years, and upon an affirmative vote of a majority of Fund members. These restrictions mean that creation of SDRs will be an orderly process responding to a generally accepted need for a larger amount of world monetary reserves. Although not designed to solve the problems of nations with persistent payments deficits, they do provide a little more leeway.

As long as the favorable balance remained, the deficit could potentially be turned into a surplus and the value of the dollar sustained.

The crushing event was the disappearance of the U.S. trade surplus early in 1971. The inflation that had been triggered by the Vietnam War, and which was not held in check by the economic policies of 1969–70, brought reduced exports and increased imports. For the first time in this century the U.S. balance of trade was unfavorable, in the first six months of 1971. Knowledge-

---

THE GROWING CRISIS OF THE U.S. DOLLAR, 1944–71

1944. A fixed exchange rate system based on the U.S. dollar is established at the Bretton Woods Conference. The value of the dollar is fixed by a gold price of $35 per ounce. Other nations in the system agree to maintain the value of their currencies within one percent of par value.

1949. Peak of the dollar shortage: The U.S. stock of gold reaches $24.6 billion. The British pound is devalued.

1950. First deficit in the U.S. balance of payments. Except for three years (1957–58, 1968), there has been a deficit in every year since 1950, if short-term transfers of "hot money" are included. By 1970 the cumulative deficit reaches $50 billion.

1960. Speculators push the price of gold to $40 per ounce, forcing central banks to intervene in the London gold market to keep the price down.

1961. The German mark is revalued upward, representing a devaluation of the dollar relative to the mark.

1962. The French government tries to pressure the U.S. into action to halt the U.S. balance of payments deficits, by turning in dollars for U.S. gold. The policy continues through 1966 and brings a $3 billion reduction in the U.S. stock of gold.

1963. The U.S. government levies an interest equalization tax on foreign borrowing in the U.S. The action is equivalent to a slight devaluation of the dollar, since it makes dollars borrowed by foreigners in the U.S. worth a little less.

1965. The U.S. government establishes "voluntary" controls on dollar investments abroad, which is also equivalent to a slight devaluation of the dollar, since it reduces the usability of U.S.-owned dollars held abroad.

able investors knew that it was only a matter of time before the dollar would have to be devalued, and began shifting their assets out of dollars and into other currencies.

The unfavorable trade balance brought the flow of "hot money" to a flood, reaching a level of over $1 billion *each month* for the first half of 1971. Together with the shift in the trade balance and continued high levels of military spending abroad, this brought the U.S. payments deficit up to almost

THE GROWING CRISIS OF THE U.S. DOLLAR *(Continued)*

1967. British pound is devalued for the second time in ten years, setting off a world monetary crisis lasting into 1968.

1968. Mandatory controls over the export of dollars are established by the U.S. government. In March another run on gold leads to a two-price gold market: one is a free market price for private transactions and the other is the official fixed exchange rate price. The price in the private market moves above $35 an ounce and stays there, indicating that the official exchange rate for the dollar is too high.

1969. France devalues the franc. The German mark is "floated" in the foreign exchange markets and then revalued upward for a second time.

1970. Special drawing rights are introduced as a supplement to gold, dollars, and other key currencies as part of the system of international monetary reserves. The U.S. balance of payments deficit for the year is $10 billion, the highest annual deficit up to that time.

1971. The U.S. balance of payments deficit for the first six months alone reaches $12 billion (an annual rate of $24 billion); the U.S. balance of trade shows a deficit for the first time in the century. Massive international capital movements force Germany to float the mark in early May, and Switzerland to revalue its franc upward. The U.S. gold stock falls below $10 billion for the first time since World War II, and U.S. borrowing power at the International Monetary Fund is almost exhausted. The price of gold in the free market reaches $42 an ounce, indicating that the dollar is overvalued (at par) by at least 15 percent and maybe more. The U.S. dollar is floated on August 15, to halt a worldwide flight from the dollar.

$12 billion for the first half of the year alone. For the most part, foreign central banks continued to absorb this deficit by accumulating dollars, but by August, 1971, it was obvious that they would not continue to do so much longer. The U.S. government was finally forced to take action.

The action was the "new economic policy" of August 15, 1971. It included the following actions:

1. The U.S. Treasury stopped redeeming in gold the dollars held by foreign central banks. We had only about $10 billion in gold left, and that wouldn't have covered the new obligations of the first half of 1971 alone. This action left the dollar to "float" on the international financial markets, where it could be expected to move to a new value relative to other currencies some 15 percent below its old par. To minimize the extent of this devaluation, step 2 was taken.

2. A 10 percent surcharge on existing U.S. tariffs was decreed. This was equivalent to increasing the price level of foreign goods by 10 percent for American buyers. A devaluation of the dollar by 15 percent would have reduced U.S. prices to foreign buyers by 15 percent, but foreign price levels would rise 10 percent for Americans. The net change was 5 percent, and that was the approximate fall in the value of the dollar in foreign exchange markets that initially occurred.

3. The next step sought to halt U.S. domestic inflation, for that was the immediate cause of the unfavorable trade balance. Prices and wages were frozen to break the inflationary spiral and provide time to work out more effective long-run policies.

4. Finally, something could now be done about U.S. unemployment if price increases were brought under control. Expansionary monetary and fiscal policies were instituted. These steps, and the price-wage freeze, were discussed in Chapter 19.

These measures made a logical and coherent package, and were a sensible response to the immediate situation as it existed in the summer of 1971. They had some long run-implications, however. First, they shattered the Bretton Woods system of international financial arrangements that had lasted for a quarter of a century. A new system would have to be built, but it would evolve in a framework of crisis in which each nation was scrambling to protect its domestic economy from the effects of the U.S. action and simultaneously trying to further its own interests. International cooperation would have to emerge, if it could, from a situation in which national self interest was given heightened importance.

This was by far the most significant aspect of the problem. U.S. foreign policy in the years following World War II, culminating in the Vietnam War, had succeeded in shattering the international financial arrangements that the policy makers of 1945 had hoped would provide a framework for world economic cooperation. Instead we may well be entering an era of worldwide economic nationalism, rivalry, and conflict.

Finally, the underlying cause of the 1971 crisis remains. As long as the United States continues to maintain a foreign policy and military presence that creates a continuous payments deficit, the world's financial malaise will continue. Even if the international financial system were restructured, it would have to provide a means for financing those deficits. The only other alternative is a basic shift in U.S. foreign policy.

WHERE DO WE GO FROM HERE?

Two proposals have come to the fore in recent years in an effort to break the impasse in the international financial system. One is *flexible exchange rates.* Supported primarily by economists, this proposal would free nations from their responsibilities for maintaining the foreign exchange value of their currencies within one percent of par value. Instead, supply and demand would rule the foreign exchange markets, freed from counterspeculation by central banks, and currencies would exchange for each other largely on terms related to purchasing power and price levels within each country.

And why not? There would be no need for gold movements under such a system. If a nation's balance of payments were in deficit, its excessive payments abroad would cause the foreign exchange value of its currency to fall until a balance was achieved. Freed from concern about meeting the deficit, each nation's domestic economic policies could concentrate on maintaining full-employment growth.

Here the international financial experts disagree. They argue that rising and falling exchange rates will make speculators out of foreign trade businessmen and international investors. Not knowing what will happen to the value of currencies while they are in the midst of trade or investment transactions, they will become more cautious and the level of trade and international investment will fall. This view is undoubtedly correct, but no one can tell how large the effect is likely to be.

While this issue is debated, along with a number of ingenious proposals to allow for flexible exchange rates without too much flexibility, another proposal has come to the fore. Why not turn the International Monetary Fund into *an international central bank?* That has already been partially done by creation of SDRs. Perhaps the major trading nations should go all the way and establish a central bank for central banks, with power to lend and borrow and create international reserves through open market operations in the foreign exchange market. This idea has already been broached. It would enable fixed exchange rates to be reestablished (or rates fixed within wider limits than in the past), and might even make possible systematic adjustments to take care of long run shifts in international trade relations.

Summary

A nation's balance of international payments is closely related to its international trade. The two must balance, since the payments are essentially a flow in the opposite direction from trade: a nation must pay for what it buys.

During the process of economic growth and development a nation will normally pass through a series of stages with respect to its trade and payments, moving through the following conditions: young debtor nation to mature debtor nation to young creditor nation to mature creditor nation. Each stage involves a different combination in the balance of trade and payments.

The balance of international payments accounts for all payments between a nation and the rest of the world, with a deficit or surplus being settled by official transactions between central banks and between a country's central bank and the International Monetary Fund.

The United States has had a persistent deficit in its international payments for the past two decades, with the exception of an occasional year in which special circumstances prevailed. The U.S. is the world's largest trading nation and the largest source of investment funds for the world economy. Because of that, its currency is used as a principal reserve currency by the central banks of many other countries.

Gold (as well as the English pound) was formerly the basis for world monetary reserves. Today the world monetary system is based on a multiple system of reserves, the U.S. dollar primarily (supplemented by the English pound and German mark as additional key currencies), accounts at the International Monetary Fund, and gold. Under the Bretton Woods agreements, each central bank had the obligation to keep the value of its currency within 1 percent of its par value, which is the value of the currency in terms of gold. Short-run fluctuations in the values of currencies were contained under this rule, but persistent imbalances were not. Long-run adjustments require devaluation or revaluation of some nations' currencies from time to time.

The international monetary system had some serious problems, created in large part by U.S. payments deficits, and changes have been improvised to meet them. Probably the most serious problem is the fact that the U.S. economy has a great impact on the system as a whole, but the system as a whole has little impact on the U.S. economy. The economic policies adopted by the U.S. to meet its own needs can therefore cause serious problems for the world economy. This basic problem led to the dollar crisis of 1971, the breakdown of the Bretton Woods system, and the uncertainties that followed. Although several methods can be devised to meet immediate problems, the fundamental issue is the direction of U.S. foreign policy. Military spending abroad creates U.S. payments deficits which must then be financed. The alternative is a change in U.S. policy that scales down military spending abroad.

Key Concepts

Debtor nation.   A nation that makes net payments of principal and interest on investments to foreign nations.

Creditor nation.   A nation that receives net payments of principal and interest on investments from foreign nations.

Balance of international payments.   A formal accounting statement of all of the payments made between a nation and the rest of the world.

Balance of trade.   That portion of a nation's balance of international payments that reflects trade in goods and services only. Does not include governmental transactions or capital inflow or outflow.

Key currency.   A currency in which many nations hold a portion of their international monetary reserves. Includes the dollar, pound, and mark at the present time.

International monetary reserves.   Reserves held by central banks to settle international payments among them. Includes gold, key currencies, and accounts at the International Monetary Fund.

Currency devaluation.   A change in the definition of a currency in terms of gold in which the price of gold is raised.

Fixed exchange rates.   An agreed-on ratio of exchange between currencies maintained by central banks.

Flexible exchange rates.   The ratio of exchange between currencies is allowed to fluctuate in response to supply and demand in the foreign exchange market.

Benjamin Disraeli, later British prime minister, in a speech in Parliament on April 25, 1843:
  "Free trade is not a principle, it is an expedient."
The same speaker, same place, on March 17, 1845:
  "Protection is not a principle, but an expedient."

Barriers to Trade

46

Ever since the mid-1930s the United States has led a worldwide movement to reduce tariffs and other barriers to world trade. In recent years, however, the trade liberalization movement has slowed down both here and abroad. In the late 1960s the United States began to swing away from its policy commitment to freer trade and started a move toward greater protection for domestic industry.

In this chapter we examine foreign trade policy. We shall evaluate the arguments that have been presented in favor of protectionism to find them largely invalid. The economic interests that benefit from protection are strong, and further progress toward free trade, or even efforts to halt the protectionist drive, will depend on solutions to some difficult international economic problems whose presence gives credence to the pleadings of special interests.

THE MOVEMENT TOWARD FREE TRADE

The heyday of U.S. tariff protection was the 1920s. Back in the days when a President could say "The business of America is business," the tariff acts of 1921 and 1922 and the Smoot-Hawley Act of 1930 moved tariffs to their highest levels in the nation's history. The New Deal turned this policy around. The Trade Agreements Act of 1934 enabled the President to negotiate tariff reductions with other countries, with the same benefits to be made available to other trading nations. Some progress was made prior to World War II, but this was a period of economic nationalism throughout the world and the U.S. policy ran against the tide.

The world situation changed after World War II. Problems of reconstruction were so great that twenty-two important trading nations set aside their special national interests to sign the General Agreement on Tariffs and Trade (GATT). This agreement established a general code for commercial policy: all nations were to be treated alike, and discriminatory treatment was barred. In addition, quantitative restrictions such as import quotas were prohibited (except under special circumstances). The most important result of GATT's establishment, however, was a series of general tariff reductions in 1945, 1949, 1950–51, 1956, 1960–61, and 1967. By this time fifty-three nations were parties to the agreement.

The net effect of the drive to liberalize world trade is perhaps best indicated by the lowering of U.S. tariffs. In 1934 the average tariff duty was 48 percent of the value of the imported item. By 1970 it was about 8 percent. Similar patterns prevail among the other GATT nations.

Now, however, the superfluous tariffs have been eliminated and the GATT nations are down to those whose reduction would trigger shifts in the allocation of resources within nations. This would mean unemployment and economic stress in individual industries and regions within countries. Further tariff reductions are going to be difficult.

ECONOMIC BLOCS

Concurrently with the move toward freer world trade, regional economic groups of nations have formed. The chief "blocs" are:

1. The Soviet–East European group.

2. The European "Common Market."

3. The European Free Trade Association.

There are other economic groupings as well. The Latin American countries have taken some faltering steps toward common international trade policies, and the nations formerly part of the empires belonging to France and Great Britain maintain special economic ties with those countries.

Economic integration proceeded in Europe along with the GATT tariff reductions. In 1957 the Treaty of Rome brought to fruition more than a decade of work toward economic cooperation in Europe. It established the European Economic Community (EEC) of six nations—France, West Germany, Italy, Belgium, Netherlands, and Luxembourg. These countries agreed to remove tariffs and other trade barriers among themselves; to allow free movement of labor, capital and business enterprise within the community; to establish common policies toward agriculture, transport, and business practices; to harmonize their monetary and fiscal policies; and to adopt a uniform external tariff on trade with the outside world. Despite problems of transition, the move toward a single Western European economy has been successful. Talks designed to lead to a common monetary system have even begun. A European *common market*, the name given to the emerging European economy, is in the process of appearing.

Seven European nations that for a variety of reasons did not join in the Treaty of Rome formed a looser economic federation in 1960 called the European Free Trade Association (EFTA). This "outer seven," as they are called, includes Great Britain, Norway, Sweden, Denmark, Austria, Switzerland, and Portugal. The members of this group have also reduced tariffs among themselves, but have not moved toward a common external tariff. The main purpose of EFTA is to protect its members from adverse economic effects of the common market set up by the "inner six" EEC countries.

The Soviet–East European bloc was far more political in its origins. It was formed in 1949 as a response to the recovery of Western Europe under the U.S. sponsored Marshall Plan for economic assistance, and to the increasing conflicts between east and west during the Cold War. It is called the Council of Economic Mutual Assistance (CEMA) or COMECON. Initially it stressed trade agreements between the USSR and the Eastern European countries (which were highly favorable to the USSR); but during the 1950s emphasis shifted toward investment and economic development designed to create complementary production, enlarged trade, and closer economic cooperation. For example, the USSR and four East European nations have joined to develop Soviet phosphate deposits, which will provide fertilizers to be exported to Eastern Europe. Also, Czechoslovakia has provided financing for electric power stations that will feed power into a six-nation electric power grid.

Growth of these and other economic blocs are a paradox. Internally they provide for reduced tariffs and elimination of other barriers to trade. But if they sustain barriers to trade with other countries, even at reduced tariffs, they can become a threat by diverting trade to internal producers and away from those outside the bloc. If firms within the European Common Market supply a larger share of Common Market needs, producers in England or Scandinavia will supply a smaller share because of the Common Market tariffs against outsiders. This can cause a shift in resource allocation away from lower cost producers outside the Common Market to higher-cost producers inside. It was fear of this "trade diversion effect" that led to formation of the European Free Trade Association among the "outer seven" countries that did not join the Common Market.

THE SHIFT TOWARD ECONOMIC NATIONALISM

The existence of strong economic blocs and the slowing down of the movement toward free trade combined with increased world tensions in the late 1960s to start a move toward greater trade restrictions. The worldwide inflation that attended escalation of the war in Vietnam made many nations concerned about their openness to unfavorable economic developments imported from abroad. Worries about stability of the international financial system, that are related to the long-continuing U.S. balance-of-payments deficit, contributed to feelings that nations should protect their own interests. The threat of rapid technological change and the spread of international corporations added to the uneasiness.

THE THEORY OF THE SECOND BEST

This problem of trade diversion resulting from customs and tariff unions has led to an important development in policy theory. It would seem logical that welfare could be increased if one or several units in a system moved from a less preferred to a more preferred position, like the countries of the European Common Market moving to a system of freer trade among themselves. But if the units are part of a larger system of interrelated parts, the system as a whole may be worse off; in this case, if trade is diverted to higher-cost producers. Few would argue against the proposition that freer trade is better than more restricted trade for the world economy as a whole. But attempts to get there through steps that benefit one portion only may be a "second best" alternative that actually leaves the system as a whole worse off. This "theory of the second best," as it has come to be called, has wide applicability throughout the social sciences and public policy. Watch for similar situations in other contexts. They are far more common than one would suspect.

In the United States, for example, inflation raised costs of production for several products subject to sharp competition from foreign producers. Shoes, textiles, clothing, and certain types of electrical equipment, all with relatively labor-intensive production patterns, were faced with rising imports from the Far East. Steel produced in Europe and Japan began to penetrate U.S. markets. Oil import quotas were established in the mid-1960s. Meanwhile, the European Common Market worked out a program of agricultural subsidies combined with tariffs and import restrictions designed to protect its farmers. West Germany had developed a system of subsidies for domestic producers to promote sales abroad. Japan has long had a network of legislation intended to limit foreign penetration of its home market. It was clear by 1970 that a battle was forming between the advocates of free trade and the concept of one big international economy and the proponents of special economic interests and economic nationalism.

The decision by the United States in the summer of 1971 to let the dollar "float" and to impose a 10 percent tariff surcharge on imports was widely interpreted around the world as a major step toward economic nationalism by the U.S., and is sure to trigger protective measures by other countries. Perhaps even more significant for the long run were the simultaneous efforts by the U.S. government to get foreign steel firms to voluntarily reduce their exports to the U.S.: this action was a move toward reconsituting the nefarious worldwide steel cartel of the 1930s.

THE PHILOSOPHY OF ECONOMIC NATIONALISM

Restrictions on foreign trade are rooted in attitudes of patriotism and nationalism that put national or local interests at very high levels of priority, and that look on foreigners with fear and suspicion. In a world of sovereign national states it is commonly assumed that benefits to one mean less for the others—that there is a limited amount of employment or trade available in the world and that one nation's advantage is another's disadvantage. This belief flies in the face of the theory of comparative advantage, which shows that economic cooperation through trade leads to more for all.

There is nevertheless, a modicum of validity to the ideas of the economic nationalists. *At any given level of world trade*, the division of the gains from trade depends on the terms of trade. It may be possible for a nation to make gains at the expense of others by so manipulating prices and the flow of trade as to move the terms of trade in its favor. A large portion of the bargaining and jockeying among nations involves this principle. The difficulty is that two or more can play the same game. The long-run result is a series of restrictions on trade that move all the participants to lower levels of real welfare. Temporary advantages are destroyed by retaliation that leaves everyone worse off.

What a nation can do to improve its position in world trade is to promote lower costs of production at home by investing in transportation facilities, promoting capital accumulation and technological advances, and improving the health, education, and efficiency of its work force. Achieving those goals will enable it to cut costs of production in the long run. Its exports will be more attractive to foreign buyers and its position in world trade will be strengthened. To achieve the maximum benefits, however, it will have to trade freely with others and take advantage of international specialization. Such action will shift some of the benefits of the nation's improved efficiency to others and the gains will be worldwide.

The economic nationalist, on the other hand, will argue that imports take jobs away from domestic workers. They also reduce profits made by domestic producers and thereby slow down capital accumulation. Exports, on the other hand, provide employment and promote profits, leading to a stronger domestic economy. Furthermore, new industries may be hampered by having to compete with imports from firmly established foreign producers. Finally, some industries are essential to national defense and should be sheltered from foreign competition. These arguments, however plausible they may seem, are *all* fallacious. Even the last two, which have some validity, cannot justify barriers against trade.

KEEPING OUT IMPORTS: THE METHODS

There are seven methods generally used to keep imports from entering domestic markets. Taxes on imports are the most common. These *tariffs*, as they are called, are usually a specified percentage of the market value of the item. By raising the selling price to the ultimate consumer, tariffs reduce the quantity consumers are willing to buy and leave a larger share of the market to domestic producers. They also enable domestic producers to sell their output at higher prices. If the domestic industry is competitive, it will have a larger number of producers, after the long-run adjustment. If there are significant monopoloid elements in the domestic industry, the profits of producing firms will also be higher.

Quotas are a second way to reduce imports. These restrictions on the amount of an item that may be imported limit directly the supply available for sale in domestic markets. The United States has import quotas on sugar, for example, in order to preserve uneconomic production within the country.

Internal excise taxes are another method. For example, the U.S. excise tax on diamonds raises their sale price, reduces the quantity purchased, and results in smaller imports. The purpose of this tax is to raise revenues, not to protect domestic producers, but its effect is to reduce imports when there is little or no domestic production.

Administrative and public health *rules* are used to keep out contagious diseases and insects harmful to agriculture. They are sometimes enforced as a means of protecting domestic producers. *Government purchasing* is very often used to favor domestic industry over foreign, as when the U.S. government pursues "Buy American" policies.

Systems of *import permits* are often used by developing countries to limit imports generally, and to channel them to necessary products. A country like Brazil, for example, may not have enough foreign currency plus gold to pay for all that its citizens wish to import. It uses import permits to limit the total amount its citizens can spend abroad and particularly to cut down on buying of luxuries. Finally, a nation may require that foreign trade be carried on by *government agencies*. This is the practice of the Soviet Union, the East European countries and China, but some non-Communist countries (Egypt, Burma) use the same method.

KEEPING OUT IMPORTS: THE RATIONALE

Most of the pleas for import restrictions make little sense—except to the special interests of workers and business firms in the industries affected. Here are the chief arguments.

Protection defends a high standard of living. This general statement is usually made as a self-evident proposition without further elaboration. Yet there is hardly anything better for a nation's standard of living than cheap imports. Light from the sun is free: should we close up all our windows and expand our electric bulb production? Will this raise living standards? Domestic living standards will be raised by low-cost imports in exactly the same way that they would be raised by a new and lower-cost method of production at home.

A variation on that theme is the argument that *protection defends high-wage workers against low-wage foreign competition.* This issue is more complex.

First, we know that low-cost imports raise real incomes for everyone, including high-wage workers. Second, we know that the dollars earned by foreign producers from their sales in the U.S. must be spent here on U.S. goods. This means that U.S. workers will be employed in making the goods foreigners buy. As long as the U.S. exports capital-intensive goods using little labor, where we have a comparative advantage in international trade, U.S. wage rates will remain high. Third, if we shift to labor-intensive industries paying low wages, keeping out these imports, our high-wage pattern will be modified and lower living standards will prevail. Fourth, high wages for American workers are the result of high productivity. To sum it up, the logic of the argument that protection defends a high-wage pattern reduces itself to the following patently ridiculous proposition: A high-wage economy is preserved by paying low wages to its workers.

This whole argument depends, however, on our ability to maintain full employment at home. For example, when low-cost imports of textiles and clothing start coming into the U.S., domestic production and employment in those industries may well fall. It would be nice if the effect were gradual, if workers were retrained for higher-skilled jobs, and if those jobs were available because aggregate demand is kept at full-employment levels. Those three conditions may not be met, however, even though the latter two could be achieved with very little cost. Under those circumstances an import tariff or quota might be justified as a temporary measure to ease the transition and give workers, firms, and the national government time to adapt to the new conditions. The problem here is that the tariff may not be temporary and the adaptation might never occur.

It is also possible that imports may influence the distribution of income within a nation, although there is little or no empirical evidence that it does. The argument is as follows: imports produced by low-wage foreign labor reduce the scarcity of labor relative to land and capital within the importing nation. This will shift the distribution of income in favor of other factors of production and reduce labor's share. However, if full employment is maintained, the shift in relative scarcities of the factors of production may well not occur (which is probably why empirical studies show no such effect). And even if these distribution effects did occur, they could be countered by domestic measures such as taxation. The national government can influence the distribution of income internally while the nation as a whole gains the advantages of international trade and specialization.

Another argument of the economic nationalists is that *protection is justified as a means of equalizing the competitive position of domestic producers.* Foreign manufacturers may have "unfair" advantages if their workers are not unionized, if their workers get pensions through public rather than private social insurance programs, and so on and on. These advantages should be neutralized by tariffs, runs the argument, so that competition can then be carried on fairly and evenly. This seemingly valid argument, which appeals to our feelings of sportsmanship and fair play, has little to recommend it. If foreigners wish to subsidize their exports, our standards of living are raised. Why should we hurt ourselves by applying a tax that merely serves to raise the prices of what we buy? The assumption is, of course, that we are smart enough to maintain full employment at home by use of proper domestic economic policies. Under those conditions, the "fair competition" argument makes no sense.

It begins to carry weight during depressions. When unemployment is high, any nation may be tempted to export some of its unemployment by encouraging its producers to "dump" exports abroad at unprofitable prices, while sustaining prices at home. This can be done by export subsidies and import tariffs and quotas, and was quite common during the depression of the 1930s. Once started, however, these policies bring retaliation by other countries, who are also affected by the depression. They raise tariffs and impose quotas as well. The result is fewer jobs and higher unemployment in both countries. "Beggar thy neighbor" policies would work if the neighbor would only stand still for them. He doesn't, however, and everyone is worse off.

A variation on this theme may occur if a single industry in one country has overproduced and dumps surplus output in other countries, to the detriment of employment and profits in that industry in the importing countries. Macroeconomic policies designed to keep aggregate demand at full-employment levels are not flexible enough to handle that problem, and counterpolicies may be called for. The problem here is that domestic special interests may try to keep out low-cost goods that reflect long-run comparative advantages by arguing that the low prices represent unfair "dumping" at prices below costs of production.

Another form of unfair competition may occur if a monopoly or cartel deliberately sets out to destroy producers in other countries by selling at prices below costs of production. After the local producers are gone the price of the product is then raised to monopolistic levels. In cases like that, retaliatory quotas or tariffs may well be justified.

These exceptions to the general rule against trade restrictions have to be carefully applied. It is very easy to use tariffs to eliminate comparative advantages under the theory that competitive conditions are being equalized. It is not enough to show that foreign producers have lower costs. Those lower costs are reflections of comparative advantage in most cases. Where they are artificially created by public policy, and are relatively permanent, we should take full advantage of the subsidy by buying as great a quantity of the subsidized products as we can. Only if there is *temporary* selling below cost to accommodate business errors or to generate a monopoly position are countermeasures justified.

We now come to two arguments for protection of domestic industry that have partial validity, the *national defense* and *infant industries* arguments. In both cases, however, protection by tariffs, quotas, or other trade restrictions is the most expensive method of achieving the desired goals. Direct subsidies are the cheaper way.

The national defense argument is that *protection is required for the survival of industries for national defense.* During time of war it may be necessary to produce highly complex instruments, like watches or computers, requiring skills that cannot be developed overnight. A permanent supply of labor and scientific skills must be maintained, and the only way to do it is by sustaining domestic producers during times of peace. This point is well taken, but it does not follow that trade restrictions are the best way to achieve the goal.

The problem is that tariffs and other trade restrictions raise the price of a product irrespective of whether it is imported or produced at home. While the consumer pays a higher price for both, the domestic manufacturers get the benefit only from the higher price of the latter. A direct subsidy, on the other hand, would have to pay only the equivalent of the benefit to the domestic producers, and would therefore be less costly than a tariff.

One might wonder why subsidies are not used instead of tariffs. There are two reasons. Tariffs are a hidden tax, while subsidies are obvious. It is easier for special interests to get away with a hidden tax than to be continually in the public gaze while slurping at the trough of public revenues. Furthermore, a tariff bears most heavily on consumers (which means low-income families more than high-income families), while taxes to pay for a subsidy would come primarily from the progressive federal income tax. A tariff is a means by which the poor can be made to bear more of the burden than the rich.

The infant industries argument is related to the much larger problem of economic development. It holds that protection is needed to enable new industries to survive against the competition of established producers abroad. The protection need only be temporary, however, until the domestic industry is mature enough to withstand foreign competition. Comparative advantages are derived from more than the natural endowments of different nations. They change as the labor force grows, capital is accumulated, and income levels change. The development of commerce and industry involves a learning process in which labor and business enterprise develop skills that reduce costs. And expansion of industry may bring long-run cost reductions because of the development of peripheral services in other sectors of the economy. Yet if an industry is fully exposed to foreign competition it may never be able to grow enough to take advantage of the learning process and external economies, and the whole process of economic development may be aborted. Tariffs or import quotas may not only protect the domestic producers, they may also encourage foreign firms to leap over the barriers by establishing manufacturing plants within the tariff walls, thereby attracting foreign capital for economic development.

This argument has great appeal in developing countries. Indeed, its greatest supporters have been found in Germany and the United States during the nineteenth century, and in many of today's developing nations. One must note, however, that vigilance is required to assure that the tariffs really are temporary. The danger is a political one: a truly infant industry doesn't have the political clout to get tariff protection, yet by the time it has grown enough to be politically strong it probably doesn't need the tariff. Furthermore, the argument does not apply to new enterprises in an already developed economy, since its validity depends on the relationships between industry and general economic development. Finally, just as in the case of the national defense argument for protection, direct subsidies are a cheaper method of achieving the same goals. In the case of a truly underdeveloped country, however, the fastest path to economic growth may be through squeezing the living standards of the poor a little further in order to free resources for development. If the nation is sure that the benefits do not go to the wealthy but are channeled into economic growth, a tariff that protects infant industries may well be an effective device to stimulate economic development.

THE INTERNATIONALIST OUTLOOK

Knowledge of the basic economics of international trade inevitably pushes one toward the view that the world economy is a seamless web in which the advantages of one nation both contribute to and depend on the welfare of other nations. A peaceful world in which trade between nations results in greater welfare for all is one of the great visions that is opened up. Furthermore, the ties between nations that are created by trade can promote world peace; if it can be shown that the material interests of people depend on peaceful continuation of international economic relations, a strong force for world peace is created.

Free world trade is a fragile thing, however. Exclusive control over key raw materials may give the business enterprises of one nation an advantage over those of another. Special interests may demand special privileges in domestic markets, and may be politically strong enough to obtain them. Working people may fear loss of jobs. Militarism and nationalism may create the ideological base that makes possible a move toward economic nationalism. Unsettled political conditions in the world, such as a continuing crisis in the Middle East, or long-standing international antagonisms, may encourage nationalist economic policies. These uncertainties and hostilities can open the way to economic policies that exacerbate existing difficulties, with subsequent retaliation and a heightening of world tensions, suspicions, and hostilities. International economic policies can add to the threat system that makes the condition of man in the modern world poorer than it might be.

On the other hand, man's condition can be significantly improved, in a material sense by the economic welfare created by international trade, and in far broader ways by promotion of a more reasonable and peaceful world.

Summary

The movement toward free trade that dominated world trade policy for twenty years after World War II is beginning to give way to moves toward economic nationalism, particularly in the United States.

Barriers to trade such as tariffs, quotas, and various impediments to imports diminish trade and reduce the benefits from trade. They are usually justified by arguments that the entire economy of a nation will benefit from trade restrictions, but all of those rationales fly in the face of the analysis that free trade benefits a nation. They are all arguments for special advantages for private economic interests that must ultimately be paid for by the general public. Indeed, outright subsidies are generally less costly than trade restrictions.

Protectionist arguments make some sense only in the case of underdeveloped countries trying to develop industry. Industrial development may lead to comparative advantages in strong export industries, but the development may not occur unless those industries are protected initially. Even that protectionist argument would lead only to relatively temporary trade barriers, however. In the long run, a free trade policy is the most beneficial one.

Whatever the trade and financial problems of the international economy may be, its greatest human and economic problem is the poverty of the "third world." These are the poor countries, more concerned with their own problems of poverty, backwardness, and underdevelopment than they are with the rivalries of the great powers and the conflict between the United States and the Soviet Union. This chapter examines their economic status and the reasons for it, the policies they have adopted to promote economic development, and the progress they have made or their lack of it. The objective is to gain a better understanding of why the world is divided into rich and poor nations and what some of the consequences of that division are.

THE THIRD WORLD

The third world is poor. Two *billion* people live in countries with a GNP per person of less than $200. Another 600 million live in countries with a per capita GNP between $200 and $1,000. Only 900 million live in the richer countries with a GNP per capita of over $1,000.[1]

Let's examine the differences. There are 22 relatively rich countries with a GNP per capita above $1,000. Topping the list is the United States ($3,980), Sweden ($2,620), and Switzerland ($2,490). At the lower end of this group are Japan ($1,190), the Soviet Union ($1,110) and Libya ($1,020), the last being an oil-rich newcomer. Aside from Japan, Libya and Israel ($1,360), all are in Europe or North America. Only if Puerto Rico ($1,340) is included as a separate entity is there a representative from Latin America in that group. All of these countries showed rising living standards in the 1960s. Between 1961 and 1968 every one except New Zealand had an average annual increase in GNP per capita of over 2 percent and almost all were well above that figure. These are the rich nations and they are becoming richer at a relatively rapid pace.

The poor nations can be divided into two groups. One can be called the developing nations. Although poor (GNP per capita below $1,000 in 1968), they have rising living standards (average annual increase in GNP per capita above 2 percent in 1961–68). There are 46 coun-

Economic Development and the Third World

47

---

[1] The data are for 1968 and are from *World Bank Atlas* (Washington: International Bank for Reconstruction and Development, 1970), pp. 2–3.

tries in this category, with a total population in 1968 of about 1.5 billion. These countries, as a group, are keeping up with the rich nations and some individual countries are catching up. Included are the communist countries of Eastern Europe (Hungary, Poland, Romania, Bulgaria, Albania, and Yugoslavia), where the economies are dominated by government enterprise and economic planning. Also included in this group are most of the noncommunist countries of Southern Europe, Turkey, and the Near East. Outside of those areas, the only major developing countries (populations of 20 million or more) are Mexico, Ethiopia, Pakistan, Thailand, North Vietnam and South Korea.

The second group are those that are falling behind both the rich countries and the developing nations. They are poor, and they are staying poor: their average annual increase in GNP per capita was less than 2 percent between 1961 and 1968. There are 53 countries in this category, with almost 2 billion people. Some of the world's most heavily populated countries are in this second group, including China (730 million), India (525 million), and Indonesia (115 million). Other large ones are Brazil (88 million), Nigeria (63 million), Philippines (36 million), Egypt (32 million), Burma (26 million), Argentina (24 million), and Colombia (20 million). In many of these countries the problem is not that economic development is not taking place. Strong programs of industrialization are under way in most of them, but growth of living standards is hampered by rising populations. If population growth can be slowed, a large number of these countries would move into the first category of developing nations.

Unfortunately, there are some countries that not only are losing ground relative to the rich and the developing countries, but whose living standards are actually falling. They had a declining GNP per capita in 1961–68. Sixteen countries are in that unfortunate position, with a population in 1968 of 173 million. The largest is Nigeria (63 million people) which was torn by civil war through much of the 1960s, and 10 of the 16 are in tropical Africa. If anything encouraging can be derived from their poor performance, it is that they represent a very small proportion of the world's population. In most of the world, living standards are rising and much more could be achieved with effective population control measures.

HOW IS IT POSSIBLE TO PRODUCE SO LITTLE?

It's easy. For example, in East Pakistan half of the farmers have less than 3 acres of land. The average yield is about 1,000 pounds of rice per acre and the farmer gets about 5¢ per pound for his crop. There you are:

3 acres × 1,000 lb/acre × $0.05/lb = $150.

And no allowance is made for costs in this example.

Characteristics of Poor Countries

Although poor countries differ markedly from each other, and any generalizations about them must be qualified by the great variety they exhibit, they differ as a group from the advanced countries in several important respects. The "typical" poor or underdeveloped country

1. Has a relatively large portion of its resources devoted to primary production—agriculture, mining, fishing—and a relatively small proportion devoted to manufacturing.
2. Has a rapidly growing population.
3. Has substantial amounts of unused or underused resources.
4. Has an economically backward population, with high illiteracy rates and relatively low average levels of educational attainment.
5. Lacks adequate capital for the development of its human and natural resources.
6. Has an export orientation in those sectors of the economy that have been developed.

Food and raw materials dominate the economies of poor countries. In the third world of Asia, Africa, and Latin America two-thirds to four-fifths of the population work in agriculture. Two forms of organization dominate. In some areas, plantations of large size concentrate on cash for export: rubber, cotton, tea, coffee, sugar, bananas, cocoa, sisal, and others. In other areas peasant cultivation on small plots is devoted primarily to subsistence agriculture, although some peasant farming is heavily oriented toward cash crops for the market. In both patterns there is a high density of population relative to land, productivity is low, and methods of production are backward when compared with the highly capital-intensive agriculture of the more advanced nations. Agriculture need not lead to low incomes and backwardness; the high incomes prevailing in the advanced agricultural areas of New Zealand and Australia attest to that fact. It is the backward technology, small amounts of land per person, and large populations of the poor countries that help keep them poor.

Some poor countries are heavy producers of minerals. The third world accounts for a high proportion of world production of aluminum, copper, tin, manganese, chromium, tungsten, nitrates, and petroleum. The bulk of large mining enterprises are not locally owned, but are owned by foreign companies. Capital must come from abroad, along with managerial and technical skills, while the mineral products are exported. Labor is drawn from the local population at the low wages established by market forces in a poor country.

Population pressures are related directly to the conditions in agriculture and labor markets. Birth rates are high and death rates have been cut by importation of modern medical and public health measures. With low productivity in agriculture and a relatively small amount of land per farmer, the amount of food production per person is low. These relationships create the ideal conditions for the population trap discussed earlier in this book. Improved agricultural productivity triggered by improved technology or land reform can set in motion a more rapid increase in population than in output, keeping incomes low and preserving the backwardness of the population and the economy indefinitely. The result is a population with a large proportion of young people who have to be supported by a relatively small proportion of people of working age who are underemployed because the amount of land per worker is so small.

Despite population pressures, most poor countries have large amounts of unused resources. This may seem to be a paradox, but it is nevertheless true. Large reserves of minerals, petroleum, and natural gas are available, along with underdeveloped forest resources and hydroelectric power sites. "Cultivable wasteland" is found in large amounts throughout Asia, Africa, and Latin America. Irrigation could provide for large increases in the area of arable land through many parts of Asia and North Africa. These opportunities remain untapped, partly because of lack of capital and partly because market demand is weak in poor parts of the world.

Population pressures on the land set in motion large migration to cities. Some of the largest and most rapidly growing urban areas of the world are in poor countries, where cities of almost endless slums develop. Lack of industrial employment—because purchasing power is low—makes for high unemployment rates as well as political unrest. The political unrest, in turn, inhibits economic development by creating higher risks for capital.

Shortages of capital keep the economy undeveloped. Although estimates on these matters are subject to wide error, the amount of capital per person in advanced countries is probably about 10 times the level in poor countries. Furthermore, in poor countries capital accumulation through savings is low, because incomes are low and the great majority of people must spend all or almost all of their incomes for consumption. In a consideration of the third world as a whole, savings are probably in the range of 5 to 10 percent of national income. This low proportion of savings is, in many countries, hardly enough to maintain a constant amount of capital per person, particularly where there are high rates of population growth. A significant portion of the savings is made by the wealthy, income distribution being even more unequal than in the more affluent countries, and much of those savings is invested in real estate or in the advanced countries rather than in domestic industry. The limited savings are not used as effectively as they might be.

Where economic development does take place in poor countries, it tends to be heavily oriented toward foreign trade. The typical pattern is for exports to be dominated by a few primary products, like coffee in Colombia, bananas in Guatemala, rubber and tin in Malaya, tea in Ceylon, or copper and other minerals in the Congo. Foreign capital is invested in those industries, the transportation system is oriented toward exporting them, financial institutions are heavily involved in financing of imports. Imports, on the other hand, are often heavily dominated by luxuries, like automobiles, which are imported by the relatively few rich, and manufactured goods which might be produced domestically if the economy were more highly developed.

HOW IS IT POSSIBLE TO LIVE ON $200 A YEAR, OR LESS?

It's hard. A family of four in Nigeria (GNP per capita: $70 in 1968) eats six pounds of yams or cereal per day—day after day. It is filling, but less nutritious than many other foods. This basic food is supplemented by a few ounces of beef or fish, some beans, okra, pepper, and milk. The family spends money on only a few items, such as salt, oil, soap, firewood, kerosene, and matches. Occasionally there will be a large purchase: a lantern, some clothes. And that's all. There isn't any money for anything else.

THE DYNAMICS OF UNDERDEVELOPMENT

The characteristics of poor countries are closely related to each other in a system of *circular causation with cumulative effects*. Each element in the syndrome of underdevelopment helps to create and reinforce the other elements. The effect is an accumulation of forces that are strong enough to keep the economy poor and underdeveloped. Just as there is a vicious circle of poverty in an affluent society like the United States, there are *vicious circles of underdevelopment* in the third world.

Consider the situation in a poor country. An underdeveloped country with a backward population has low output per person. This low productivity causes low incomes, which in turn lead to low levels of purchasing power and small savings. Inadequate purchasing power provides little economic incentive to expand investment, and investment funds are inadequate anyway, because of low savings. Low levels of investment continue the pattern of underdevelopment and economic backwardness, completing the circle of causation and continuing the process by which the country remains poor. We show the pattern schematically in Figure 47-1.

Within this broad framework other relationships provide additional reinforcement to the pattern of underdevelopment. Low incomes have the same effects on productivity that they have in advanced countries. They lead to poor diets, poor health, and inadequate education, which reinforce low productivity and pass it on to the succeeding generation. An economically backward

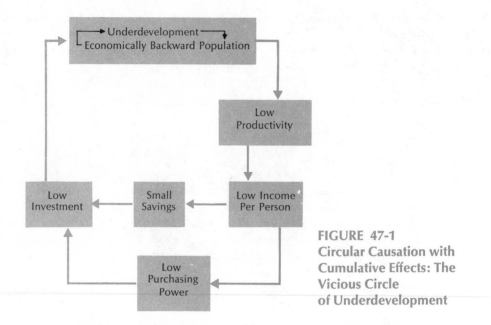

FIGURE 47-1
Circular Causation with
Cumulative Effects: The
Vicious Circle
of Underdevelopment

population is unable to develop and fully use the natural resources available, and much of them lie idle. Lack of education and low rates of literacy mitigate against population control programs, so that the population tends to rise rapidly if there are gains in output, thereby keeping the population poor and backward. And through it all runs the larger social and economic problem of the nation as a whole: a low rate of savings means that the resources available to change things are meager, even if there were the will to do so.

Colonialism and Economic Development

The heritage of colonialism is part of the reason for underdevelopment in poor countries. Although political colonialism was largely ended for the third world in the ten years following World War II, the economic effects of dependency have not been fully eradicated. And, in some respects, the present economic relationships of the poor countries with the affluent nations continue patterns from the colonial era that inhibit development.

The colonial era before World War II often brought *enclaves* of modernized economic sectors within a traditional economy. In the modernized sector, the population was literate, worked for wages or engaged in commerce, and had learned to use some forms of modern technology, such as railroads, automobiles, electric power, clocks, and simple machinery. In the traditional sector, the population was largely illiterate and engaged in subsistence agriculture; they were unused to wage labor and accustomed to a preindustrial technology. The contrast was usually between urban and rural economies, but the underlying difference was between the beginnings of an industrial society and an existing preindustrial one.

The enclave of modernization, however, was generally oriented toward production for export. It was dominated by foreign capital attracted by the economic opportunities found in international trade. Important markets were abroad rather than at home and a large local demand was not the source of development. Typical examples were the sugar of Cuba, coffee of Brazil, oil of the middle east, rubber of Malaya, and many others. Tied into the metropolitan economy of North America and Western Europe, modernized enclaves in the poor countries were essentially extensions of the advanced economies rather than independent centers of economic development.

The existence of enclaves of economic development hindered the development of other parts of the colonial country's development. Profits went to the owners of the capital, and they were largely foreigners. Resources of all kinds were attracted by the commercial activities of the enclave, including the human talents and savings (however large or small they might be) from the underdeveloped hinterland, making it even poorer than before and further reducing the possibilities of growth. Capital and entrepreneurship were drawn into the export-producing enclave, and products, profits, and talent were drawn from there into the modernized world economy of which the enclave was a part. A schematic diagram (Figure 47-2) showing the resources, capital, and talent drained from the underdeveloped hinterland and pulled into the metropolitan economy indicates the dynamic elements of the relationship.

FIGURE 47-2
Enclaves of Development in Underdeveloped Countries
Within the underdeveloped country the economic enclave draws resources, savings, and talented people out of the hinterland, leaving it less able to improve its economic base.

Although the economic enclave was highly characteristic of the colonial period, it has not disappeared with the ending of political colonialism. The economic relationships remain wherever large cash crop or mineral production for export dominate a poor country's economy and are controlled by foreign capital. Economic aspects of colonialism have persisted and remain part of the problem.

"Dualism" in Underdeveloped Countries

Outside the modernized enclave, a different sort of dualism appeared. The hinterland not only had a preindustrial technology and peasant agriculture, it also had a different social and economic structure. The pattern was feudal, in the general sense of a landowning aristocracy with a dependent peasantry.

The form this feudal relationship took was highly varied, and it was seldom as formally organized with tight legal sanctions as the classic feudalism of medieval Europe. There were, however, some common economic relationships that were very widely found:

1. A large portion of the land was owned by a small number of elite landowning families.
2. A wide variety of economic relationships enabled the landowners to appropriate the surplus above subsistence levels produced by the very much larger number of peasant farmers.
3. The peasantry was tied to the land by a combination of legal requirements, debt, force, and lack of opportunity elsewhere.
4. Population pressures served to keep the peasantry tied to the land by assuring a surplus labor supply.
5. The agricultural surplus appropriated by the landowning elite was turned into cash by sale of exports on world markets.
6. The resultant income helped support a commercial, urbanized sector in the poor country that was devoted largely to meeting the needs of the landowning aristocracy together with the limited middle class and government structure the system required.

Those readers familiar with the feudal economy of medieval Europe will immediately recognize similarities. Indeed, the system of sharecropping and debt tenure developed in the southeastern United States in the period between the Civil War and World War II was a variant of the general type. The essential pattern is of a landowning elite that gains control of the surplus produced by a peasant population, with the surplus as the base for a commercial sector that acts as a link with the world economy.

The result is the dualism seen within the underdeveloped hinterland itself: a poor, and backward rural peasantry existing side by side with the luxury of the landed families, while the commercial cities are "capitalist islands in a noncapitalist world." The basic economic relationships are diagrammed in Figure 47-3.

The feudal or quasi-feudal structure of the colonial pattern enabled some economic development to take place, but there were sharp limits to it. To the extent that export production could be developed for world markets, the underdeveloped country could appear to be well off. To the extent that the agricultural surplus could be increased, the commercial and urban sector could grow. But without the stimulus of a large domestic demand for mass consumed goods the type of broadly based economic growth of the countries of North America and Western Europe could not be achieved.

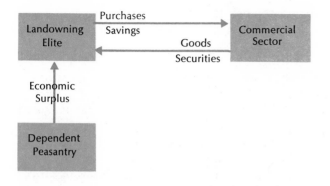

FIGURE 47-3   "Dualism" in Underdeveloped Countries

A backward peasant sector produces an economic surplus appropriated by the landowning elite, whose expenditures and savings move into the highly developed commercial sector in the cities, where they become part of the world economy. The rural sector, drained of its surplus, remains backward. The commercial sector, based on a relatively small market, has limited prospects for growth.

There was a natural political alliance based on the economic interests of the advanced countries and the domestic aristocracy. Both benefited from continuation of the existing system. The business and financial interests of the advanced countries benefited from the export trade that they controlled and the profits obtained from it. The landowning elite of the poor countries benefited from the exploitive position they held in relation to the peasantry. In much of Asia, particularly India, southeast Asia and Indonesia they became the partners in government of the British, French, and Dutch. In Latin America they gained political independence in the nineteenth century but then became the allies of North American enterprise in a mutually satisfactory pattern of political and economic dominance. When the anticolonial revolts came after World War II in the third world, the upheaval was as much a domestic economic and political revolt as a nationalistic independence movement. Yet in many poor countries, particularly in parts of Latin America, Asia, and the Middle East, the older colonial pattern of elite landowners and dependent peasants still remains a force to be reckoned with.

Exports and the Terms of Trade

Colonial economic relationships between the poor and the affluent nations have been reinforced by the emphasis on exports of primary products and imports of manufactured goods in the foreign trade of the third world. A nation that exports raw materials and foodstuffs sells commodities whose prices fluctuate widely, and whose output can be a glut on the market for extended periods of time. When a country's exports are dominated by one or two such commodities, its whole economy will feel the repercussions of wide price swings and prolonged depression. Neither condition is good for economic development.

The "terms of trade" between commodities and manufactured goods become important to the poor countries. If the prices of their exports fall, relative
to the prices of their imports, their position in world trade is worsened. The
ability of exports to pay for imports of capital as well as needed manufactured
goods diminishes. This is apparently just what happened during the era of the
great colonial empires from about 1875 to the start of World War II. Prices of
primary products fell by about one-third, relative to prices of manufactured
goods, between 1876–80 and 1938, according to a United Nations study published in 1949. This shift in the terms of trade was beneficial to nations exporting manufactured goods, since those goods could be traded for increasing
amounts of food and raw materials. It was harmful to the countries exporting
primary products, since it took increasing amounts of their exports to obtain
a given amount of manufactured goods.

There has been some disagreement among economists as to whether the
terms of trade have continued to move against the poor countries as a long-
term trend in the years since World War II. Several influential Latin American
economists claim that they have, but a 1958 panel of experts set up to investigate the problem denied that there was necessarily such a trend. The problem is that prices of primary products fluctuate much more than prices of
manufactures, and this makes the measurement of a long-term trend very
difficult until after it has been under way for quite a while.

Two prominent U.N. economists, Paul Prebisch and Hans Singer, argue that
basic differences between the poor and the rich nations tend to bring about
a worsening of the terms of trade for poor nations. Here are the comparisons
they make:

In the advanced countries

1. Manufactured goods are produced in oligopolistic industries where prices
   are flexible upward but not downward.

2. Labor is organized and tends to keep wage rates up.

On the other hand, in the poor countries

1. Primary products are produced in competitive industries in which expending
   output keeps prices from rising.

2. Population pressure and underemployed labor keep wages down, and workers
   are generally not organized in strong unions.

3. As incomes rise in the advanced countries, the demand for primary products,
   especially food, rises less rapidly, leaving the exports of the poor countries
   with a smaller share of the market.

These differences, according to Prebisch and Singer, cause prices of manufactured goods to remain stable or rise, while the prices of primary products
tend to fall. Even during inflationary periods the long-run trend will be for
primary products to rise in price less than prices of manufactures.

The Heritage of Colonialism

These economic relationships of the colonial era, which have persisted in varying degrees to the present, were supplemented by political dominance on the part of the advanced countries. The citizens of colonial powers usually had special tax and legal privileges in the colonies and could acquire land and mineral rights on favored terms. Banks and shipping companies had special privileges and often a monopolistic position. Tax systems and debt payments drained revenues to the colonial powers, while efforts were made to have colonies pay the costs of their own administration. Tariff protection for industry in the colonies was usually denied, and the sort of economic development that would compete with home industry was hindered by colonial powers. Finally, little was done to promote the development of human resources, and the top administrative positions were reserved for citizens of the colonial powers.

In spite of all this there is considerable doubt that a colonial nation like England or France made a net gain from its colonies. Large military forces and

---

RICHES AND POVERTY IN THE THIRD WORLD

Buenaventura, a city of 130,000 people, is the largest port on the Pacific coast of Colombia. Oil tankers and freighters take the enormous riches of its hinterland into the commerce of the world—oil, coffee, sugar, cotton, even frozen shrimp. Near the wharves are busy offices of private firms and government agencies. The government is spending money on improving the port. Between 1960 and 1970, U.S. economic aid to Colombia amounted to over $1 billion, and private U.S. interests invested another $1 billion. Yet the city is poverty-ridden. The paved streets end a few blocks behind the Catholic Church, which faces a row of bars, cafés, and brothels. The slums begin, a wilderness of wooden and sheet-metal shacks, ragged children, and skinny dogs, receding into swamp and jungle. Some say that 80 percent of the population is unemployed (that's right: 80 percent) and that the chief occupations are theft and prostitution. Those who work earn the low wages found in areas with very high unemployment rates. Ninety percent of the population is black, descendants of slaves brought in many years ago. Students at Del Valle University in Cali, a hundred miles inland from Buenaventura, agitate against "gringo imperialism" and wear images of Che Guevara.

navies, subsidies to merchant marines, and costs of administration were large and had to be borne by the general taxpayer. Important economic interests in trade, finance, shipping, and industry within the colonial power seem to have gained clear advantages, however, while the average citizen paid his taxes, sent his sons into the army, and basked in the glory of national power.[2]

The underdeveloped and poor nations of the third world entered the second half of the twentieth century with this background of colonialism. In the ten years after World War II most of them moved to political independence. But economic development was harder to achieve. The economics of colonialism dominated their situation: economic enclaves oriented toward exports that tended to drain the country of resources for growth; a quasi-feudal agricultural economy that left the mass of peasant farmers impoverished; and an emphasis on primary production that may well have brought long-term disadvantages in world trade. Built into the economic structure, these elements of the institutional environment served to reinforce the vicious circle of poverty and underdevelopment in which those nations were caught.

THE STAGES OF ECONOMIC GROWTH

Most theories of economic development have little use if we want to understand the third world. There is one that students should be familiar with, however—not because it is useful, but because of the influence it has had on the policies of the rich countries. It is the theory of the stages of economic growth put forth by W. W. Rostow.[3]

At the beginning is the *traditional society*, heavily agricultural, with a preindustrial technology, a hierarchal society with little opportunity for upward social mobility, and having low productivity.

In the second stage the *preconditions for economic growth* are established. Using the example of western Europe in the late seventeenth and early eighteenth century, Rostow emphasized an interrelated group of social and political changes within the traditional society that free the economic sector for later rapid growth. In Western Europe ". . . all that lies behind the break-up of the Middle Ages" helped create the preconditions for growth, in addition to the application of science to industry and agriculture and the appearance of entrepreneurs who applied the scientific advances to cost-cutting methods of production. "Leading sectors" of the economy are stimulated by the new processes of production and their expansionary effect is spread to other parts of the economy. An essential precondition is increased productivity in agriculture in order that food output may rise more rapidly than population.

[2] There is a large literature on whether colonialism paid off, and to whom. The standard works, which show that it did not, are by Grover Clark, *A Place in the Sun* (New York: Macmillan, 1936) and *The Balance Sheets of Imperialism* (New York: Columbia University Press, 1936).

[3] Walt W. Rostow, *The Stages of Economic Growth: A Non-Communist Manifesto* (Cambridge, Mass.: Harvard University Press, 1961).

The *takeoff into sustained growth* follows. A critical point is reached at which the forces that hold the economy in its existing mold are broken by the forces of economic progress. The chief feature of this turning point is an increase in savings from about 5 percent of national income to about 10 percent or more. In this period a manufacturing sector with high growth rates emerges. Finally, these changes stimulate political and social changes, which together with the economic changes constitute an "industrial revolution." This stage lasts about 25 years according to Rostow: 1783–1802 for England, 1830–1860 for France, 1843–1860 for the United States, 1878–1900 for Japan, and after 1952 for India.

The takeoff is followed by a *drive to maturity*. A steady rate of savings equal to 10 to 20 percent of national income enables output to continue growing faster than population, bringing with it steady increases in output per person. New sectors of the economy are stimulated to rapid growth as the older ones mature, keeping the process going. Initially based very heavily on expansion of heavy industry and transportation, the initiative for further growth gradually shifts to those sectors of the economy producing for high-income consumers. This period, of about 60 to 100 years, leads to the final stage.

The final stage is that of *high mass consumption*, typified by the U.S. economy of the post–World War II era.

Rostow's scenario for economic growth is obviously derived from the historical experience of the industrial revolution and its aftermath in Western Europe and the United States. It embodies two key points. First, a self-sustaining process of growth can be established if the rate of savings rises above 10 percent of national income. Second, a set of social and political changes like those that occurred in the developed countries is necessary to create an institutional framework within which economic growth can develop. What Rostow is saying to the underdeveloped countries is that they should be like the non-communist advanced countries if they want to be affluent.

The concept of "the takeoff" has special meaning for the policies of the advanced nations. If self-sustained growth can be achieved by driving to get beyond a critical point of resistance, the advanced countries could help by a program of economic and technical aid that would perhaps be initially large but would last for only a limited time. It might be possible to gain acceptance for aid programs if that analysis were accepted.

Rostow's paradigm fitted very neatly into the politics of the era of the cold war, and helps to explain why it has been so influential. At a time when the United States and the Soviet Union were in sharp competition for the political allegiance of the third world, Rostow's analysis told the poor countries that their interests lay in allying with the West at the same time that it told the West that its investment in aid to the poor countries need not be unlimited in either amount or length of commitment.

In spite of its obvious political implications, Rostow's analysis brought two concepts into the analysis of economic development that have had a lasting impact on economic thought and policy. One is the concept of "takeoff." Much economic development policy in the poor countries is devoted to raising the rate of savings, and the level of 10 percent of national income is often thought of as the critical level necessary to break out of the circular causation of underdevelopment. The second is the concept of "self-sustained growth." While economists are by no means sure of exactly what the underlying causes are (Part III of this book has some answers), it is clear that the pattern of growth in Western Europe and North America in the last two hundred years was quite different from the previous two hundred years and from the experience of most of the rest of the world until very recently. Self-sustained growth is characterized by high rates of capital accumulation, expanding markets and rising purchasing power, innovation, and technological changes. This is what the rich nations have been able to achieve and what the poor nations seek.

JAPAN: MAKING IT

Japan is now the third industrial nation in the world, behind only the U.S. and the USSR, and catching up fast. In 1870 it was one of the poor, backward nations. What happened? A feudal regime was overthrown, a land reform program was instituted, and a heavy land tax provided revenues for establishment of government enterprises in banking, insurance, shipping, and manufacturing. Private enterprise was subsidized. Advanced technology was imported for both agriculture and industry. The silk industry was developed as a leading sector, and manufactured exports to the large Asian market were encouraged. Education received large expenditures and was completely modernized, and the proportion of GNP going to research and development was as large as in Germany or France. Running as a continuous theme through the years was a low wage rate, brought about by a growing population and a shift of labor from farm to city, which gave Japanese industry a strong position in world trade. But the most important factor in Japan's success was a strong government commitment to economic expansion that self-consciously directed national policy toward that goal.

THE DEVELOPING COUNTRIES

At the beginning of this chapter we noted that there is a group of developing countries whose growth in living standards is as good, on the average, as the rich countries. There is a second group with rising living standards, but whose population is growing so rapidly that the gap between them and the rich countries is widening. Both of these groups of countries share a common concern for economic growth and in most of them expansion of industrial production, improvement of agriculture, and growing commerce attest to a strong process of development toward a modern, industrial economic base.

How have they managed it?

First of all, political independence has freed the old colonies from the hindrances to development inherent in their former status. They have been free to adopt policies suited to their own needs and goals.

Secondly, modern health, nutrition, and sanitation have improved productive efficiency. They have also opened the way to rapid population growth in some countries, but in others the most important aspect of this modernization has been its contribution to higher productivity through improved health.

Third, education has been heavily stressed. Illiteracy has been reduced and in the developing countries that are catching up to the rich ones the populations are predominantly literate.

Finally, policies designed to promote economic development have been successfully applied, with great stress on expansion of industry. In all of this, the lead has been taken by governments, and the spread of pragmatic, growth-oriented policies is probably the most important single reason for the improved living standards of the developing countries.

Economic Development Policies

The successes of the developing nations have been largely due to government policies designed to promote industrialization. Expansion of manufacturing, with its attendant transportation and commercial and financial facilities, has been the primary emphasis. Most of the developing countries have also sought agricultural expansion—with a few notable exceptions such as India and Pakistan, where it was most needed—but the chief developmental thrust has been in industry. In some countries, such as Egypt, Mexico, Yugoslavia, Taiwan, and South Korea, land reform that favored small proprietors and broke up large estates was accomplished, but not much was done in that direction in the other developing countries. For the most part, the governments of the developing countries have not tried to remake the social structure as a precondition of economic development; that was characteristic of the communist countries. They have instead taken the politically less risky path of developing industrial expansion on top of the existing social and economic structure. Industrialization would become the predominant aspect of the economy as it grew relative to the rest.

Industrialization requires capital. Economic development requires that capital be mobilized along with labor and other resources for the expansion of industry. In the developing countries, this mobilization of capital and other resources is done partly by government, partly by encouraging private industry, and partly by importing capital from abroad.

Government as a Source of Capital

Government revenues as a proportion of GNP have risen substantially in the developing countries, from about 15 percent in 1950 to almost 20 percent in 1965. The figure is still well below the 33 percent characteristic of advanced countries, but the developing nations do not have the large social insurance programs (or military spending, usually) of the rich countries.

Governments have also been able to mobilize resources through inflation. Tax increases have their limits in poor countries, but resources for development can still be obtained by government borrowing of funds and expansion of the money supply. If excessive aggregate demand pushes up prices, the citizen's incomes may buy less but the government will have the funds to pay for industrial expansion. The underdeveloped nations have used inflation to get resources for industrialization just as the United States government used it to free resources for use in the Vietnam war. Resources can also be obtained by expropriation of private property, but only Yugoslavia and Egypt did that on a large scale.

Private Domestic Sources of Capital

The developing countries promote private industry and channel private savings into industrial expansion. A variety of methods are used to create opportunities for profit. Market demand expands because of inflationary pressures, but foreign products are kept out by high tariffs. Imported capital goods are let in with low tariffs, however. Capital gains taxes are almost nonexistent and business taxes are light. Tax exemptions are available for new enterprises, and high depreciation allowances are available. Even where government-owned industrial enterprises have been established, there has been little opposition from private industry because the public projects have generally been too big for private capital to take on, or have been in low-profit sectors. Some of the developing countries are hostile to foreign capital, but that has been to the advantage of local businessmen.

Low wage rates that are the result of population pressures have also promoted industrialization. Few developing countries have strong unions, and few have effective social insurance programs or minimum wage legislation. As a result of these factors, labor's share of the value added in industrial production is considerably lower than in the advanced countries. This situation helps to explain why the distribution of income is more unequal in the poor countries than in the rich, but it also helps promote private investment in industrial expansion.

FOREIGN CAPITAL FOR ECONOMIC DEVELOPMENT

The flow of capital to the third world in the years from 1950 to 1970 from all of the advanced nations together totaled about $150 billion. About $80 billion to $90 billion of that was development assistance from governments and the remainder private capital investment. Military aid totaled another $25 billion, approximately.

We can get a more accurate idea of the scope of the flow of foreign capital from the advanced countries to the third world from data recently made available by the Organization for Economic Cooperation and Development (OECD), which was established in 1960 by 20 European nations together with Canada and the United States to promote their own and world economic development. In the nine-year period of 1960–68, the OECD nations provided $96.5 billion of development assistance and private capital to the less developed countries, of which 55 percent was from public sources and 45 percent was private capital investment. The total has been rising, from $7.9 billion in 1960 to $12.3 billion in 1968 (but the figures are not corrected for changes in the price level). Development aid from governments leveled off at about $6 billion to $6.5 billion annually in the second half of the period. Private investment has continued to grow, but in a somewhat erratic fashion.[4]

The Politics of Foreign Aid

The motives for foreign aid on the part of the advanced countries have been heavily political. In the 1950s, there were only two main donors, the United States and the Soviet Union. The U.S. was trying to "contain" the USSR, and concentrated its economic aid on countries bordering the Soviet Union (and China), particularly Taiwan, South Korea, Turkey, and Greece. The Soviet Union countered these moves, starting in the mid-1950s, in an effort to gain greater influence in the countries along its borders, and has extended substantial aid to Cuba since the Castro regime came to power. France and England began in the 1950s to extend economic aid to their former colonial areas, in large part to preserve and strengthen economic ties with those areas. United States aid broadened out to cover the whole of the third world during the 1960s, but in recent years the emphasis on aid associated with U.S. political and military commitments has returned. The obviously political goals of economic aid programs have begun to be supplemented in the 1960s by more disinterested motives, but to a small degree; and smaller nations like Sweden, Norway, Switzerland, and Canada have begun to help. The chief motives on their part are a feeling of moral obligation to help the poor countries and a desire to counterbalance the motives of *realpolitik* that dominate the aid programs of the great powers and principal trading nations.

About three-fourths of all economic aid is "tied" to purchases in the lending or granting country. The country receiving the aid is required to spend the

---

[4] *Resources for the Developing World* (Paris: Organization for Economic Corporation and Development, 1970). In addition to the OECD countries there has been a flow of capital from Japan and from the USSR, so the figures given here show the bulk of capital movements to the developing countries but they do not show the total. The other sources would not change the totals greatly. For example, in the fifteen-year period of 1954–68, aid to underdeveloped countries from the USSR, Eastern Europe, and China amounted to just under $10 billion.

money on additional exports of the aid-giving country or on technical assistance that it supplies. This usually means higher costs than if the goods or
assistance were bought freely in the open market. Recent estimates indicate
that tied aid reduces the real benefits to the underdeveloped countries by about
10 to 15 percent. It also benefits the economy of the country giving the aid
by widening its markets. More important, tied technical assistance links the
technologies of the two countries and leads to additional exports, as well as
private capital flows from the advanced to the poor country to the exclusion
of other potential suppliers.

These aspects of foreign aid to underdeveloped countries, both the political motives and the predominance of tied aid, lend credence to the charge
of "neocolonialism" made against the economic aid programs. They are
oriented toward political and economic benefits to the aid-giving country and
the industrial, commercial, and financial enterprises located there. Without
those benefits, the amount of the aid would undoubtedly be much reduced
and the terms on which it is offered would be stiffer. The United States, as
the largest supplier of economic aid and technical assistance, is the nation
most vulnerable to this charge, although all of the important aid-giving countries, including the USSR, are guilty of the same practices. From the point of
view of the developing countries, they have little choice in the matter, but
we should not be surprised that they don't like it.

The World Bank and the International Development Association

The International Bank for Reconstruction and Development (IBRD), usually
called the World Bank, was established in 1945 by the famous conference at
Bretton Woods, New Hampshire, which also set up the International Monetary
Fund. The two new international financial institutions were designed to ease
the financial problems of the readjustment period following World War II
and to promote greater stability in international financial affairs.

Early in its history the World Bank concentrated on European economic
reconstruction, but in the late 1950s it shifted its major activities to development loans to the poor countries. The Bank operates by selling its securities
in the advanced countries to obtain capital, and then lending to the governments of the underdeveloped countries at a somewhat higher rate of interest.
It has been very conservative in its lending policies, meaning that it takes few
risks on projects that may not earn enough to pay back the principal and
interest; and its interest rates have been high. By the end of 1967 the World
Bank had made a total of only $10.8 billion in loans, and not all of them were
to the third-world countries.

The limited effectiveness of the World Bank as a source of development
funds brought strong criticism from the poor countries. Pressure from them
led to formation in 1960 of the International Development Association (IDA).
Funds are contributed to the IDA from advanced nations, and loans are made
at low interest rates to underdeveloped countries for projects that may not

be financially self-liquidating. By the late 1960s its outstanding loans were still under $2 billion.

Both the World Bank and the IDA avoid the political and economic ties that are inherent in unilateral aid programs (although both have a strong U.S. influence in their management). The magnitude of the flow of capital through them into the poor countries is relatively small, however. Where the costs of the loans are low (through IDA), the magnitude of the effort is small. Where the effort is greater (through the World Bank), the costs are considerably higher. The situation reinforces the conclusion of our earlier discussion of the politics of foreign aid: significant amounts of foreign aid on liberal terms are usually available only when the country providing the aid gets political or economic benefits.[5]

Private Foreign Investment

In recent decades the flow of private capital into the developing countries has averaged about 40 percent of the total. It has been motivated by the desire for profit and has followed the lead of patterns of trade. About half has gone into the petroleum industry and has concentrated on a few countries in the Near East, North Africa, and Latin America. Another large portion went into development of mineral resources, and most of the remainder into manufacturing. In total it has averaged about $3 billion to $3.5 billion annually over the last 20 years, fluctuating in the range of $2.5 billion to $6 billion.[6]

About three-fourths of all foreign private capital invested in the third world is in direct ownership of physical assets. That is, a foreign company will build and own a manufacturing plant, for example. Only about one-fourth is investment in securities (stocks and bonds) of independent companies operating in the third-world countries.

This situation is the reverse of the pattern prevailing before World War I, during the period in which the United States was moving from a debtor to a creditor nation. In those days the great bulk of foreign investments in the U.S. were in the form of securities rather than productive facilities directly owned by foreign firms. As the U.S. position in the world economy changed through economic development, Americans were able to acquire ownership of the foreign-owned assets by purchasing securities in the open market. As U.S.

---

[5] There are some other international financial institutions whose purpose is to assist the underdeveloped countries with capital funds. The International Financial Corporation (IFC), a subsidiary of the World Bank, makes loans to private enterprise in less developed countries. Established in 1956, it made loans totaling only $137 million annually. The Inter-American Development Bank (IDB) is about as large as the IDA, and operates in Latin America. Neither of these institutions has made much of an impact.

[6] There has been a flow in the other direction of about $1 billion to $1.5 billion annually, as capital owned in the third world moves into investments in the advanced countries, largely to find security against political and economic uncertainties. Much of this flow is from oil-producing countries into investments in government securities of the advanced nations.

exports increased and a favorable balance of trade appeared, the foreign exchange acquired was used, in part, to repatriate the securities of American firms held by foreigners.

Today the situation is different. The U.S. is now the largest supplier of private capital to the world economy, including the third world. But in the third world most of that capital goes into direct investment rather than securities, making repatriation extremely difficult to accomplish without political intervention. This helps to explain why many developing countries require that majority ownership of enterprises using foreign capital be held by their own citizens, why expropriation of foreign enterprises occurs with a fairly high degree of regularity, and why an atmosphere of hostility to foreign capital sometimes prevails.

THE POPULATION PROBLEM

Population growth in the third world is much more rapid than in the developed countries. In the last twenty years population grew in the poor countries at about 2.5 percent annually and the rate has been increasing. In the developed countries the rate of population growth has averaged about 1 percent and is falling. This is the chief reason why there is a growing gap between the living standards of the rich and the poor nations. Unless population growth can be brought under control, the gap will increase and huge numbers of people will remain poor.

This general proposition must be qualified by the fact that in most poor countries output has been growing more rapidly than population. Measured by that criterion, most of the third world has made progress toward higher standards of living, although in many parts of countries like India and Pakistan a significant portion of the population is living at bare subsistence levels and a little less food would bring much higher death rates. The general picture, however, is one of the standards of living well above bare subsistence levels and slowly rising in most of Latin America, Africa, and many parts of Asia. Indeed, that is probably the reason why governments in the third world have given so little attention to population problems until recently.

Patterns of Population Growth

The population of the world has not always grown rapidly. Until about two hundred years ago it grew only slowly to a level of about 750 million to 800 million people. Technology changed little and living standards remained low for the vast majority in a world devoted primarily to agriculture. Population grew only when the cultivated area devoted to agriculture expanded or in areas where improved agricultural techniques were developed, such as Western Europe.

In the second half of the ninteenth century, the world's population began to grow far more rapidly than ever before. New lands were opened up to agriculture in great areas like the United States, Canada, Argentina, and Australia. New and highly productive food crops came into wide use, like potatoes and sweet potatoes, corn, cassava, and peanuts. More scientific techniques stressing seed selection and fertilizers spread widely. New methods of transportation, the railroad and steamship, reduced costs of shipping food into population centers. These factors enabled the populations of Europe and North America to grow rapidly, until the spread of birth control techniques slowed down the growth after the 1870s.

Meanwhile, the populations af Africa and Asia began to increase, slowly at first and then more rapidly as the technology developed in Europe and North America began to spread to those areas. Particularly after World War II, modern public health measures were widely introduced. Food supplies continued to increase and better standards of nutrition were more widely maintained. The result was a rapid fall in death rates while birth rates continued high in almost all parts of the third world. Today the world's population is about 3.5 billion, or four to five times its size two hundred years ago, and it is rising rapidly. Population experts say that it could double in the next fifty years, with the great bulk of the increase coming in the poor nations.

Policies of Population Control

Population control has not been high on the agenda for action in the third world until the last ten years. Prior to World War II, the explosive population growth of recent decades had not yet appeared and in much of the colonial areas there was not much incentive for colonial powers to take action. Then, in the years up to 1960 most of the third world was preoccupied with gaining independence and trying to start down the path toward industrial growth. It was only in the 1960s that it became evident that significant increases in living standards could be achieved only if population control was developed along with industrial expansion.

Recognition of a problem and development of policies to solve it do not necessarily coincide, and this has been true of population control. Methods that work in the advanced countries, such as contraceptive pills and intrauterine devices, have had much less success in poorer countries. Widespread use of abortions, successful in Japan, has not been readily adaptable to other countries. Experts recognize many reasons for the difficulties encountered in spreading family-planning techniques widely in poor countries, but two fundamental ones stand out:

1. Diffusion of information is difficult in populations with low literacy rates.

2. Large families, meaning numerous children, are advantageous in peasant agriculture because they provide more manpower and productive effort.

These factors seem to indicate that the process of industrialization will have to proceed much further before the family-planning programs that are now beginning to take hold in many poor countries will have much effect.

The next great step in economic development policy, which has already begun, will be greatly expanded population control and family-planning programs. They will embody much greater research and development of better methods, experimentation with diverse public information and educational programs, and considerably expanded allocation of funds to them. As in industrialization programs, some nations will be more successful than others. The successful ones are very likely to be those that have already promoted strong industrial growth, and, just as in the case of industrialization, they will serve as models for others.

THE FUTURE OF THE THIRD WORLD

It is easy to be overly pessimistic about prospects for the third world. The countries are poor, and a limited few are getting poorer. Population growth remains a great threat to further advances and continues to be an unsolved problem.

But much of the third world has set in motion a process of economic development, with government policies designed to stimulate industrial expansion taking the lead. This is not "self-sustained growth" in the sense of Rostow's theory, for there is little evidence that it would continue unabated in many countries without the persistent help of government policies (and foreign aid, in some cases). In another sense it is self-sustained growth, however, in that most governments are strongly committed to their growth-stimulating policies.

Furthermore, those governments are only beginning to realize now the nature of the population trap they are exposed to and are just beginning to explore possible population policies. Twenty years ago the same could be said for economic growth policies, yet two decades have seen the emergence of successful growth strategies. It can be hoped that something similar will happen in the sphere of population control.

Many of the developing countries may be heading for political problems. Industrial development based on a favored group of industrial leaders and firms, superimposed upon the dualism of a quasi-feudal agriculture and cities full of underemployed poor, may be the first stage that leads to domestic turmoil rather than self-sustained growth. Already some dividends of that sort are beginning to develop.

Another and perhaps more significant problem is appearing—the scarcity of resources. Continued economic growth in the rich countries will draw more and more of the world's resources to them. Will there be enough to meet their needs as well as those of the developing nations? Or will the developing nations seek to keep those resources for their own use? Already there are forecasts that show that there won't be enough minerals, coal, food, and fiber to meet the needs of both unless population growth is immediately slowed down and technological change speeded up. Beyond the population problem is the prospect of worldwide competition and conflict between the poor and the rich nations, replacing the East-West confrontation of the past quarter century. Having achieved independence and moved into an era of industrialization and modernization, the developing nations now must face their internal population problems, and as a group, their relationships with the rich nations.

Summary

The third world is poor. It is poor because it is primarily agricultural, has unused resources, its population tends to rise rapidly, most of the population in economically backward, capital is inadequate, and a large portion of the economic development is export-oriented. Enclaves of development tend to draw resources out of the hinterland into the international economy, while in the hinterland a dual economy of dependent peasants and landowning elite hinders economic growth in many countries. Vicious circles of underdevelopment tend to preserve low levels of economic development in a pattern of circular causation with cumulative effects. The heritage of colonialism is one reason for the third world's difficulties, especially the colonial emphasis on encouragement of exports rather than internal economic development.

Theories of economic development have not been very useful in resolving the problem. The Rostow model of stages of economic growth has been widely discussed, but it is derived primarily from the historical experience of the advanced countries and was most significant as a justification for economic aid programs by the advanced countries.

Nevertheless, a number of third-world countries have started strong industrial development, led by government policies to encourage economic growth. Political independence and public health and education programs have contributed, but pragmatic industrialization policies are the heart of the progress that has been made. Capital accumulation in the private sector is fostered, supported by government programs to mobilize capital and import of capital from private and public sources abroad. Foreign aid, however, usually has had political strings attached. Where it hasn't, foreign aid has been meager. Private foreign investment has its problems, too, for it can bring dominance of the domestic economy by large international corporations.

Population growth remains a great problem for the developing countries, and it has not been solved. Many of them are beginning now to attack that problem seriously, however.

Another problem is the unevenness of the gains from economic growth that imposes an industrial sector on countries with a poor peasantry and huge amounts of low-wage labor.

Development of the third world also raises the issue of the adequacy of world resources and whether resources will be used to raise living standards primarily in the third world or in the already relatively affluent countries. The world may be on the verge of a great and continuing conflict over that issue.

Key Concepts

Economic development. The process of self-sustaining economic growth that leads to higher standards of living and increases in GNP per person.

Circular causation with cumulative effects. A system of cause-and-effect relationships in which the composite result is reinforcement of existing conditions. An effect reinforces a cause in a circular relationship that preserves the system as a whole.

Enclaves of modernization. Areas or economic sectors within underdeveloped countries that have close economic ties to the world economy. They tend to draw resources out of the hinterland, making economic development more difficult there.

Dualism in underdeveloped countries. The situation in which a dependent peasantry produces an economic surplus appropriated by a landowning elite, keeping the peasantry poor and the elite prosperous. This socio-economic dualism should be distinguished from the technoeconomic dualism that characterizes the relatively capital-intensive economy of the developed enclave and the labor-intensive economy of its hinterland.

EPILOGUE

Where Do We Go From Here?

The Keynesian macroeconomics that developed out of the Great Depression was at the cutting edge of social reform. It was associated with the New Deal and its effort to revive the American economy and remake it into a more humane system responsive to the needs of people. Achievement of full employment was only one aspect of a group of policies that also included support of labor unions as an instrument of self-help for the working man; socialization of many of the risks of a private enterprise economy through unemployment insurance, social security, and related measures; opposition to big business and monopoly (after 1936); assistance to farmers; and regional planning through TVA. To the reformers of the 1930s, all of these measures were part of a grand movement toward a freer, more equalitarian society.

A third of a century later the New Deal reforms have been extended and have become part of the institutional framework of economic life. The economy has changed, but has it become freer and more equalitarian?

It is certainly highly troubled. Inflation prevails in the midst of serious unemployment. The international economy moves from one financial crisis to another. Cities are torn by conflict, and the natural environment is endangered. Young people, blacks and other minorities, and many intellectuals are variously alienated, frustrated, or hostile. Many working people are dissatisfied with their lives. Instead of weil-being, economic growth brought a crisis of confidence. What went wrong?

One thing that went wrong was a shift in the locus of governmental power to the federal government, and within the federal government to the executive branch. As the only political unit able to deal with problems on a national scale, the federal government took on larger functions. Control over the spending of large government funds placed increased power in the hands of the executive branch, which managed those funds. Economic stability and full employment policy became the responsibility of the president. Large military and military-related expenditures moved the national security managers to positions of greater prominence. All of these changes shifted the locus of governmental power from state and local governments to Washington, and within Washington to the executive.

Another thing that went wrong was the continued and perhaps increasing concentration of economic power in the big business community. Giant industrial and financial corporations have become increasingly important in the nation's economic life. Their price, production, and market strategies govern the behavior of many important sectors of the economy. If they are not prosperous the economy is not prosperous, and they depend on national prosperity for their own growth. This is what Charles Wilson, Secretary of Defense in the Eisenhower administration and former president of General Motors Corporation, meant when he made the famous comment, "What's good for the United States is good for General Motors, and vice versa."

Big business and big government have been coming together in an increasingly symbiotic relationship. Big government needs big business because the giant corporation has become the key to effective functioning of the economy. In addition, big enterprises are the source of the weaponry the national government requires. Government, in return, provides the environment of economic growth within which large enterprises function best. Government also educates the managers and technical experts that big enterprises need, maintains the framework within which labor disputes are settled, and seeks to maintain a system of world order conducive to the growth of international corporations. The economic power of the large corporation and the political power of the federal government are allies.

The post-Keynesian-neoclassical synthesis in economics reflected these underlying economic and political realities. The economic policy consensus through the 1950s and into the 1960s stressed the idea that full employment and strong economic expansion would create a healthy economy in which the private sector could allocate resources effectively and distribute the national income equitably. In particular, the dividends from economic growth would provide satisfactory increases in real income for all, or almost all. The remaining poverty could be alleviated by special programs, and the backward nations could move onto the development path with economic assistance. Strong economic growth could achieve all of these goals without significant changes in the patterns of income distribution and ownership of wealth, or in the structure of power. Economic growth would validate the status quo. In this fashion the liberal economics of the thirties became the conservative economics of the sixties.

Sustained full employment and economic growth were the twin keystones of a political and economic understanding between those who held and exercised power and those who did not. The levers of power remained in the hands of those persons who managed big business and big government. In exchange for allowing them a relatively free rein, the great middle income majority obtained the material benefits that accrued from a quarter-century of economic expansion. When it became clear in the 1960s that a significant number of poor people were not gaining from the growth of affluence, a policy of income maintenance and guarantees was developed to stabilize their economic position. An accommodation was reached in which a relatively few hold power and wealth, the great majority are well off, and a minority are poor. Economic growth and full-employment policies provide a material payoff to the majority, who are expected not to question seriously the leadership that manages the system, while the poor are managed through a system of income transfers. The leadership itself is relatively open, and the children of the middle income majority are able to qualify for leadership positions through education, ability, and acceptance of the goals and attitudes of the existing leadership.

The American war in southeast Asia broke up the tacit agreement between the haves and the have nots. The war laid bare the fact that the locus of power had shifted to a relatively small economic and political elite whose control over the decision-making process was supplemented by careful manipulation of public opinion and the political process. The gains from economic growth stopped as the costs of the war escalated, taking the form of the military draft, taxation, and inflation. Real incomes of many people stopped rising in the late 1960s, and even began to fall for a large portion of the families whose incomes were below $15,000 annually. Many young people saw, perhaps more clearly than their elders, the essential polity compromise that traded affluence for power, and refused to accept it. Blacks and other minority groups, segregated in their urban ghettos and developing a racial and political consciousness, refused to accept their continued status as second-class citizens. The whole system of polity broke down.

Nevertheless, the economics of government policy-making continues to stress macroeconomic stability, concentrating on the problem of inflation. The political economy of that emphasis should be clear, and almost obvious. Inflation has been gobbling up the gains from economic growth that would normally go to the great majority of middle income Americans. If that can be stopped the policy compromise could be reestablished and any upheaval in social and economic relationships avoided. If, in addition, the poor can be satisfied by a guaranteed minimum income, the whole post-World War II polity compromise might gain a new lease on life. This was the direction of economic policy in the early 1970s.

There are alternative strategies that might be developed, however. We do not have to reconstruct the world in the image of the past. And in thinking about these matters it is well to bear in mind the great lessons that can be learned from modern economics.

1. It is possible to maintain steady prosperity. The great depressions and cycles of economic activity that cursed the economic system before 1940 can be prevented.

2. Any reasonable rate of economic growth can be sustained, as long as the growth rate is one that the great majority of people are satisfied with.

There are costs associated with economic growth, however, and one of the costs of rapid growth may be inflation. But if people are willing to bear the costs, the economic policies are there that can bring about the desired growth.

3. The market mechanism, in spite of the difficulties it sometimes encounters, is a highly effective framework for decision-making. In particular, it permits freedom of action and a high degree of freedom of choice. The trick is to keep it functioning effectively and without the constraints imposed by private or public controls.

4. There are some aspects of economic life that require non-market methods of decision-making. We are only in the beginning stages of an effort to understand the best ways of handling those problems.

These four propositions deal only with mechanisms and not with goals, however. The conventional wisdom tends to use these instruments of policy with the objective of preserving the existing social and economic order and the present structure of power. But if we are concerned primarily with human welfare and want to build a more humane economy, a new set of priorities begins to appear.

First, a more equalitarian distribution of income would make possible affluence for all. A trillion-dollar GNP for 200 million people means an average annual income for a family of four of about $20,000. If we assume that one-quarter of that amount must go to government, there remains about $15,000. The elimination of poverty clearly is possible, and should have very high priority. It will require a drastic shift in the distribution of income, wealth, and power, however.

Equality means more than leveling. It can become real only with increased freedom for the individual to choose his life work and pursue it without hindrance. Only part of the gains from work are to be found in income and wealth; another part is derived from the satisfactions one obtains from knowing that a job was well done and in feeling that one's inner needs were met. Those satisfactions can come only when an individual is free of constraints imposed by others. True equality requires freedom.

The expansion of individual freedom is no simple task in an economy of giant corporations and huge government programs. The breakup of large corporations into smaller units and the decentralization of government would have to be high on the list of priorities. Greater reliance will have to be placed on the market mechanism as a means of coordination if we are to move significantly away from an economy managed from the top. Expansion of individual freedom demands greater use of the self-adjusting market, but without the inequalities that it has meant in the past.

A society of equals in which people are free requires more than mere abolition of monopolies and arbitrary powers. People must be protected from "the tyranny of the majority" as well, and this requires an atmosphere of tolerance of dissent and individuality. It also assumes tolerance of conflict, a consensus that no one is to be destroyed no matter what his position or views may be, and faith that conflicts can be resolved by reason. A society made up of free and equal individuals can be expected to generate conflict, and it must be prepared to face that fact with equanimity. One requirement is that in the decision-making process each person must count for one and nobody for more than one. Another requirement is that decisions of the majority respect the rights and privileges of the minority. These principles are fundamentals of democracy, but they are often more respected in the breach than in the observance.

A humane society requires, in addition, a better accommodation between man, technology, and the natural environment. Very high priority will have to be given to preserving the ecological basis of life. At several points in this book we stressed the necessity of moving toward a closed economic-ecological system in which outputs become inputs, in which maintenance of the stock of capital takes precedence over additions to the stock of capital, and in which the continuous functioning of the system is more important than growth. These changes will require shifts in the attitudes and motivations that determine the economy's goals; they will not come easily or rapidly. But they must come eventually if continuous degradation of the environment is to be avoided.

Finally, modern dynamic psychology tells us that people need a sense of community, a feeling of fraternity with other people. This objective may be the most difficult of all to achieve, for in some respects it stands in conflict with the goals of freedom and individuality. The market mechanism can be highly impersonal in its operation, and complex modern technologies can have the effect of separating rather than joining people. Nor should we forget that one way to achieve the brotherhood of man is to exclude all those who are different, and there is a brutal, authoritarian version of the fraternity ideal that produced *Ein Reich! Ein Volk! Ein Fuehrer!* Nevertheless, a humane society will have to seek ways of building cities that bring people together, and developing technologies that create human interactions. High priority must go to economic relationships that build human relationships.

None of these goals can be achieved within a single nation. The world is too much a unit for that, although a start can be made within the United States alone. In the long run, however, the less fortunate, underdeveloped countries will have to be brought into the modern world as full economic and political partners, however difficult that task may be.

A humane economy requires more than prosperity and economic growth, more than efficient allocation of resources. It demands changes in the framework of economic institutions to achieve greater equality and freedom. It requires dispersal of the economic power and governmental authority that support the present disposition of income, wealth and power. It requires a social environment that brings a sense of community and a feeling of fellowship into human relationships. It demands compatibility between technology and the natural environment. And all of these things must be done on a worldwide scale. These are the economic goals of the future, to which our present affluence as well as the gains from economic growth can be applied.

INDEX